Weiss Ratings' Guide to Banks

Weiss Ratings' Guide to Banks

A Quarterly Compilation of Financial Institutions Ratings and Analyses

Spring 2020

GREY HOUSE PUBLISHING

Weiss Ratings
4400 Northcorp Parkway
Palm Beach Gardens, FL 33410
561-627-3300

WeissRatings
Independent. Unbiased. Accurate. Trusted.

Published by Grey House Publishing, Inc., located at 4919 Route 22, Amenia, NY 12501; telephone 518-789-8700. Grey House Publishing neither guarantees the accuracy of the data contained herein nor assumes any responsibility for errors, omissions or discrepancies. Grey House Publishing accepts no payment for listing; inclusion in the publication of any organization, agency, institution, publication, service or individual does not imply endorsement of the publisher.

Grey House Publishing
4919 Route 22
PO Box 56
Amenia, NY 12501-0056

Edition No. 117, Spring 2020

ISBN: 978-1-64265-548-3
ISSN: 2158-5962

Contents

Terms and Conditions

This document is prepared strictly for the confidential use of our customer(s). It has been provided to you at your specific request. It is not directed to, or intended for distribution to or use by, any person or entity who is a citizen or resident of or located in any locality, state, country or other jurisdiction where such distribution, publication, availability or use would be contrary to law or regulation or which would subject Weiss Ratings or its affiliates to any registration or licensing requirement within such jurisdiction.

No part of the analysts' compensation was, is, or will be, directly or indirectly, related to the specific recommendations or views expressed in this research report.

This document is not intended for the direct or indirect solicitation of business. Weiss Ratings, LLC and its affiliates disclaims any and all liability to any person or entity for any loss or damage caused, in whole or in part, by any error (negligent or otherwise) or other circumstances involved in, resulting from or relating to the procurement, compilation, analysis, interpretation, editing, transcribing, publishing and/or dissemination or transmittal of any information contained herein.

Weiss Ratings has not taken any steps to ensure that the securities or investment vehicle referred to in this report are suitable for any particular investor. The investment or services contained or referred to in this report may not be suitable for you and it is recommended that you consult an independent investment advisor if you are in doubt about such investments or investment services. Nothing in this report constitutes investment, legal, accounting or tax advice or a representation that any investment or strategy is suitable or appropriate to your individual circumstances or otherwise constitutes a personal recommendation to you.

The ratings and other opinions contained in this document must be construed solely as statements of opinion from Weiss Ratings, LLC., and not statements of fact. Each rating or opinion must be weighed solely as a factor in your choice of an institution and should not be construed as a recommendation to buy, sell or otherwise act with respect to the particular product or company involved.

Past performance should not be taken as an indication or guarantee of future performance, and no representation or warranty, expressed or implied, is made regarding future performance. Information, opinions and estimates contained in this report reflect a judgment at its original date of publication and are subject to change without notice. Weiss Ratings offers a notification service for rating changes on companies you specify. For more information visit WeissRatings.com or call 1-877-934-7778. The price, value and income from any of the securities or financial instruments mentioned in this report can fall as well as rise.

Date of Data Analyzed: September 30, 2019

Data Source: Call Report data provided by SNL Financial.

Welcome to Weiss Ratings'
Guide to Banks

Most people automatically assume their bank will survive, year after year. However, prudent consumers and professionals realize that in this world of shifting risks, the solvency of financial institutions can't be taken for granted. After all, your bank's failure could have a heavy impact on you in terms of lost time, lost money (in cases of deposits exceeding the federal insurance limit), tied-up deposits, lost credit lines, and the possibility of being shifted to another institution under not-so-friendly terms.

If you are looking for accurate, unbiased ratings and data to help you choose a commercial bank, savings bank, or savings and loan for yourself, your family, your company or your clients, Weiss Ratings' Guide to Banks gives you precisely what you need.

Weiss Ratings' Mission Statement

Weiss Ratings' mission is to empower consumers, professionals, and institutions with high quality advisory information for selecting or monitoring a financial services company or financial investment.

In doing so, Weiss Ratings will adhere to the highest ethical standards by maintaining our independent, unbiased outlook and approach to advising our customers.

Why rely on Weiss Ratings?

Weiss Ratings provides fair, objective ratings to help professionals and consumers alike make educated financial decisions.

At Weiss Ratings, integrity is number one. Weiss Ratings never takes a penny from rated companies for issuing its ratings. And, we publish Weiss Safety Ratings without regard for institutions' preferences. Our analysts review and update Weiss ratings each and every quarter, so you can be sure that the information you receive is accurate and current – providing you with advance warning of financial vulnerability early enough to do something about it.

Other rating agencies focus primarily on a company's current financial solvency and consider only mild economic adversity. Weiss Ratings also considers these issues, but in addition, our analysis covers a company's ability to deal with severe economic adversity in terms of a sharp decline in the value of its investments and a drop in the collectability of its loans.

Our use of more rigorous standards stems from the viewpoint that a financial institution's obligations to its customers should not depend on favorable business conditions. A bank must be able to honor its loan and deposit commitments in bad times as well as good.

Weiss's rating scale, from A to F, is easy to understand. Only a few outstanding companies receive an A (Excellent) rating, although there are many to choose from within the B (Good) category. A large group falls into the broad average range which receives C (Fair) ratings. Companies that demonstrate marked vulnerabilities receive either D (Weak) or E (Very Weak) ratings. So, there's no numbering system, star counting, or color-coding to keep track of.

How to Use This Guide

The purpose of the *Guide to Banks* is to provide consumers, businesses, financial institutions, and municipalities with a reliable source of banking industry ratings and analysis on a timely basis. We realize that the financial safety of a bank is an important factor to consider when establishing a relationship. The ratings and analysis in this Guide can make that evaluation easier when you are considering:

- A checking, merchant banking, or other transaction account
- An investment in a certificate of deposit or savings account
- A line of credit or commercial loan
- Counterparty risk

The rating for a particular company indicates our opinion regarding that company's ability to meet its obligations – not only under current economic conditions, but also during a declining economy or in an environment of increased liquidity demands.

To use this Guide most effectively, we recommend you follow the steps outlined below:

Step 1 To ensure you evaluate the correct company, verify the company's exact name as it was given to you. It is also helpful to ascertain the city and state of the company's main office or headquarters since no two banks with the same name can be headquartered in the same city. Many companies have similar names but are not related to one another, so you will want to make sure the company you look up is really the one you are interested in evaluating.

Step 2 Turn to Section I, the Index of Banks, and locate the company you are evaluating. This section contains all federally-insured commercial banks and savings banks. It is sorted alphabetically by the name of the company and shows the main office city and state following the name for additional verification.
If you have trouble finding a particular institution or determining which is the right one, consider these possible reasons:

- You may have an incorrect or incomplete institution name. There are often several institutions with the same or very similar names. So, make sure you have the exact name and proper spelling, as well as the city in which it is headquartered.
- You may be looking for a *bank holding company*. If so, try to find the exact name of the main bank in the group and look it up under that name.

Step 3 Once you have located your specific company, the first column after the state shows its current Weiss Safety Rating. Turn to *About Weiss Safety Ratings* for information about what this rating means. If the rating has changed since the last edition of this Guide, a downgrade will be indicated with a down triangle ▼ to the left of the company name; an upgrade will be indicated with an up triangle ▲.

Step 4 Following the current Weiss Safety Rating are two prior ratings for the company based on year-end data from the two previous years. Use this to discern the longer-term direction of the company's overall financial condition.

Step 5 The remainder of Section I; provides insight into the areas our analysts reviewed as the basis for assigning the company's rating. These areas include size, capital adequacy, asset quality, profitability, liquidity, and stability. An index within each of these categories represents a composite evaluation of that particular facet of the company's financial condition. Refer to the Critical Ranges In Our Indexes table for an interpretation of which index values are considered strong, good, fair, or weak. In most cases, lower-rated companies will have a low index value in one or more of the indexes shown. Bear in mind, however, that Weiss Safety Rating is the result of a complex qualitative and quantitative analysis which cannot be reproduced using only the data provided here.

Step 6 If the company you are evaluating is not highly rated and you want to find a bank with a higher rating, turn to the page in Section II that has your state's name at the top. This section contains Weiss Recommended Banks by State (rating of A+, A, A- or B+) that have a branch office in your state. If the main office telephone number provided is not a local telephone call or to determine if a branch of the bank is near you, consult your local telephone Yellow Pages Directory under "Banks," "Savings Banks," or "Savings and Loan Associations." Here you will find a complete list of the institution's branch locations along with their telephone numbers.

Step 7 Once you've identified a Weiss Recommended Company in your local area, you can then refer back to Section I to analyze it.

Step 8 In order to use Weiss Safety Ratings most effectively, we strongly recommend you consult the *Important Warnings and Cautions* listed. These are more than just "standard disclaimers." They are very important factors you should be aware of before using this Guide. If you have any questions regarding the precise meaning of specific terms used in the Guide, refer to the Glossary.

Step 9 Make sure you stay up to date with the latest information available since the publication of this Guide. For information on how to set up a rating change notification service, acquire follow-up reports, check ratings online or receive a more in-depth analysis of an individual company, call 1-877-934-7778 or visit www.weissratings.com.

About Weiss Safety Ratings

The Weiss Ratings are calculated based on a complex analysis of hundreds of factors that are synthesized into five indexes: capitalization, asset quality, profitability, liquidity and stability. Each index is then used to arrive at a letter grade rating. A weak score on any one index can result in a low rating, as financial problems can be caused by any one of a number of factors, such as inadequate capital, non-performing loans and poor asset quality, operating losses, poor liquidity, or the failure of an affiliated company.

Our **Capitalization Index** gauges the institution's capital adequacy in terms of its cushion to absorb future operating losses under adverse business and economic scenarios that may impact the company's net interest margin, securities' values, and the collectability of its loans.

Our **Asset Quality Index** measures the quality of the company's past underwriting and investment practices based on the estimated liquidation value of the company's loan and securities portfolios.

Our **Profitability Index** measures the soundness of the company's operations and the contribution of profits to the company's financial strength. The index is a composite of five sub-factors: 1) gain or loss on operations; 2) rates of return on assets and equity; 3) management of net interest margin; 4) generation of noninterest-based revenues; and 5) overhead expense management.

Our **Liquidity Index** evaluates a company's ability to raise the necessary cash to satisfy creditors and honor depositor withdrawals.

Finally, our **Stability Index** integrates a number of sub-factors that affect consistency (or lack thereof) in maintaining financial strength over time. These include 1) risk diversification in terms of company size and loan diversification; 2) deterioration of operations as reported in critical asset, liability, income and expense items, such as an increase in loan delinquency rates or a sharp increase in loan originations; 3) years in operation; 4) former problem areas where, despite recent improvement, the company has yet to establish a record of stable performance over a suitable period of time; and 5) relationships with holding companies and affiliates.

In order to help guarantee our objectivity, we reserve the right to publish ratings expressing our opinion of a company's financial stability based exclusively on publicly available data and our own proprietary standards for safety.

Each of these indexes is measured according to the following range of values.

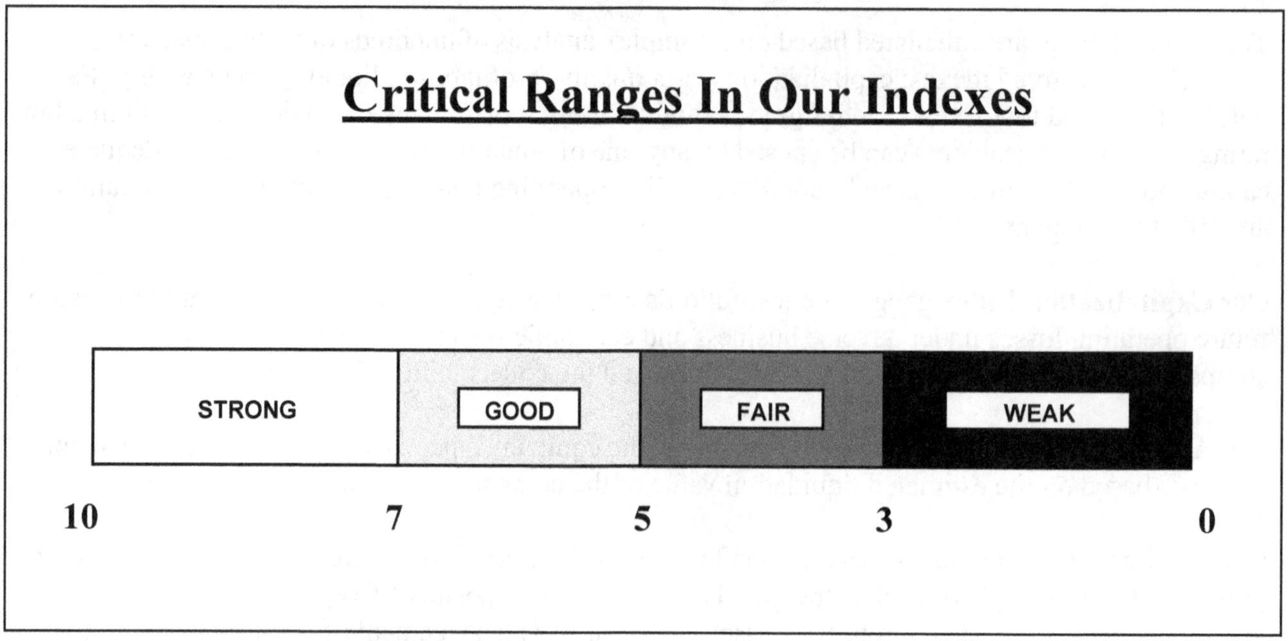

Finally, the indexes are combined to form a composite company rating which is then verified by one of our analysts. The resulting distribution of ratings assigned to all banks looks like this:

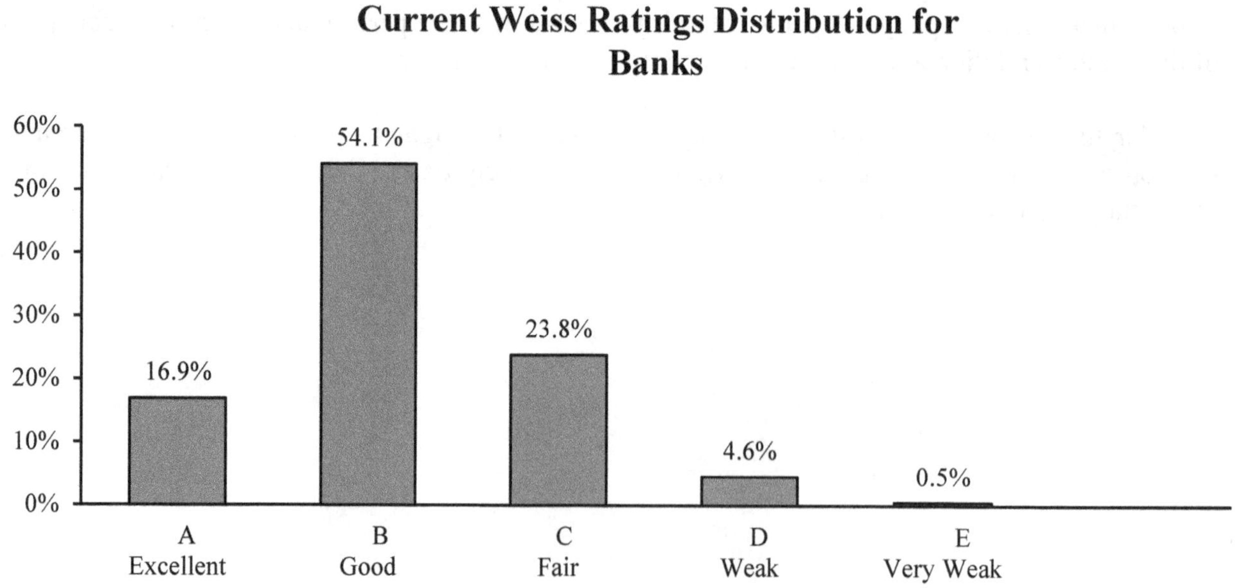

What Our Ratings Mean

A **Excellent.** The institution offers excellent financial security. It has maintained a conservative stance in its business operations and underwriting practices as evidenced by its strong equity base, high asset quality, steady earnings, and high liquidity. While the financial position of any company is subject to change, we believe that this institution has the resources necessary to deal with severe economic conditions.

B **Good.** The institution offers good financial security and has the resources to deal with a variety of adverse economic conditions. It comfortably exceeds the minimum levels for all of our rating criteria, and is likely to remain healthy for the near future. Nevertheless, in the event of a severe recession or major financial crisis, we feel that this assessment should be reviewed to make sure that the company is still maintaining adequate financial strength.

C **Fair.** The institution offers fair financial security, is currently stable, and will likely remain relatively healthy as long as the economic environment remains relatively stable. In the event of a severe recession or major financial crisis, however, we feel this company may encounter difficulties in maintaining its financial stability.

D **Weak.** The institution currently demonstrates what, in our opinion, we consider to be significant weaknesses which could negatively impact depositors or creditors. In the event of a severe recession or major financial crisis, these weaknesses could be magnified.

E **Very Weak.** The institution currently demonstrates what we consider to be significant weaknesses and has also failed some of the basic tests that we use to identify fiscal stability. Therefore, even in a favorable economic environment, it is our opinion that depositors or creditors could incur significant risks.

F **Failed.** The institution has been placed under the custodianship of regulatory authorities. This implies that it will be either liquidated or taken over by another financial institution.

\+ The **plus sign** is an indication that the institution is in the upper third of the letter grade.

\- The **minus sign** is an indication that the institution is in the lower third of the letter grade.

U **Unrated.** The institution is unrated due to the absence of sufficient data for our ratings.

Peer Comparison of Bank Safety Ratings

Weiss Ratings	Veribanc	Bauer Financial	IDC Financial	Bankrate.com	Lace Financial
A+, A, A-	Green, Three Stars w/ Blue Ribbon recognition	5 stars, 4 stars	201-300	1, Five stars	A+, A
B+, B, B-	Green, Three Stars w/out Blue Ribbon recognition	3 ½ stars	166-200	2, Four stars	B+
C+, C, C-	Green Two Stars, Yellow Two Stars	3 stars	126-165	3, Three stars	B, C+
D+, D, D-	Green one star, Yellow one star, Green no stars	2 stars	76-125	4, Two stars	C, D
E+, E, E-	Yellow no stars, Red no stars	1 star	1-75	5, One star	E

Important Warnings and Cautions

1. **A rating alone cannot tell the whole story.** Please read the explanatory information contained here, in the section introductions and in the appendix. It is provided in order to give you an understanding of our rating philosophy as well as to paint a more complete picture of how we arrive at our opinion of a company's strengths and weaknesses. In addition, please remember that our safety rating is not an end-all measure of an institution's safety. Rather, it should be used as a "flag" of possible troubles, suggesting a need for further research.

2. **Safety ratings shown in this directory were current as of the publication date.** In the meantime, the rating may have been updated based on more recent data. Weiss Ratings offers a notification service for ratings changes on companies that you specifiy. For more information call 1-877-934-7778 or visit www.weissratings.com.

3. **When deciding to do business with a financial institution, your decision should be based on a wide variety of factors in addition to Weiss Safety Rating.** These include the institution's pricing of its deposit instruments and loans, the fees you will be charged, the degree to which it can help you meet your long-term planning needs, how these costs/benefits may change over the years, and what other choices are available to you given your current location and financial circumstances.

4. **Weiss Safety Ratings represent our opinion of a company's insolvency risk.** As such, a high rating means we feel that the company has less chance of running into financial difficulties. A high rating is not a guarantee of solvency nor is a low rating a prediction of insolvency. Weiss Safety Ratings are not deemed to be a recommendation concerning the purchase or sale of the securities of any bank that is publicly owned.

5. **All firms that have the same Weiss Safety Rating should be considered to be essentially equal in safety.** This is true regardless of any differences in the underlying numbers which might appear to indicate greater strengths. Weiss Safety Rating already takes into account a number of lesser factors which, due to space limitations, cannot be included in this publication.

6. **A good rating requires consistency.** If a company is excellent on four indicators and fair on one, the company may receive a fair rating. This requirement is necessary due to the fact that fiscal problems can arise from any *one* of several causes including poor underwriting, inadequate capital resources, or operating losses.

7. **Our rating standards are more conservative than those used by other agencies.** We believe that no one can predict with certainty the economic environment of the near or long-term future. Rather, we assume that various scenarios – from the extremes of double-digit inflation to a severe recession – are within the range of reasonable possibilities over the next one or two decades. To achieve a top rating according to our standards, a company must be adequately prepared for the worst-case reasonable scenario, without impairing its current operations.

8. **We are an independent rating agency and do not depend on the cooperation of the companies we rate.** Our data are derived, from quarterly financial statements filed with federal regulators. Although we seek to maintain an open line of communication with the companies being rated, we do not grant them the right to influence the ratings or stop their publication. This policy stems from the fact that this Guide is designed for the protection of our customers.

9. **Inaccuracies in the data issued by the federal regulators could negatively impact the quality of a company's Safety Rating.** While we attempt to find and correct as many data errors as possible, some data errors inevitably slip through. We have no method of intercepting fraudulent or falsified data and must take for granted that all information is reported honestly to the federal regulatory agencies.

10. **Institutions that operate exclusively or primarily as a trust company may have skewed financial information.** Due to the nature of their business, these companies often record high profit levels compared to other more "traditional" banks. Trust companies can usually be recognized by the initials "TC" or "& TC" in their names.

11. **This Guide does not cover nonbank affiliates of banking companies.** Although some nonbank companies may be affiliated with the banks cited in this Guide, the firms are separate corporations whose financial strength is only partially dependent on the strength of their affiliates.

12. **There are many companies with the same or similar sounding names, despite no affiliation whatsoever.** Therefore, it is important that you have the exact name, city, and state of the institution's headquarters before you begin to research the company in this Guide.

13. **Affiliated companies do not automatically receive the same rating.** We recognize that a troubled institution may expect financial support from its parent or affiliates. Weiss Safety Ratings reflect our opinion of the measure of support that may become available to a subsidiary bank, if the subsidiary were to experience serious financial difficulties. In the case of a strong parent and a weaker subsidiary, the affiliate relationship will generally result in a higher rating for the subsidiary than it would have on a stand-alone basis. Seldom, however, would the rating be brought up to the level of the parent.

    This treatment is appropriate because we do not assume the parent would have either the resources or the will to "bail out" a troubled subsidiary during a severe economic crisis. Even when there is a binding legal obligation for a parent corporation to honor the obligations of its subsidiary banks, the possibility exists that the subsidiary could be sold and lose its parental support. Therefore, it is quite common for one affiliate to have a higher rating than another. This is another reason why it is especially important that you have the precise name of the company you are evaluating.

14. **This publication does not include foreign banking companies, or their U.S. branches.** Therefore, our evaluation of foreign banking companies is limited to those U.S. chartered domestic banks owned by foreign banking companies. In most cases, the U.S. operations of a foreign banking company are relatively small in relation to the overall size of the company, so you may want to consult other sources as well. In any case, do not be confused by a domestic bank with a name which is the same as – or similar to – that of a foreign banking company. Even if there is an affiliation between the two, we have evaluated the U.S. institution based on its own merits.

Section I

Index of Banks

An analysis of all rated

U.S. Commercial Banks and Savings Banks

Institutions are listed in alphabetical order.

Section I Contents

This section contains Weiss Safety Ratings, key rating factors, and summary financial data for all U.S. federally-insured commercial banks and savings banks. Companies are sorted in alphabetical order, first by company name, then by city and state.

<u>*Left Pages*</u>

1. Institution Name — The name under which the institution was chartered. If you cannot find the institution you are interested in, or if you have any doubts regarding the precise name, verify the information with the bank itself before proceeding. Also, determine the city and state in which the institution is headquartered for confirmation. (See columns 2 and 3.)

2. City — The city in which the institution's headquarters or main office is located. With the adoption of intrastate and interstate branching laws, many institutions operating in your area may actually be headquartered elsewhere. So, don't be surprised if the location cited is not in your particular city.

Also use this column to confirm that you have located the correct institution. It is possible for two unrelated companies to have the same name if they are headquartered in different cities.

3. State — The state in which the institution's headquarters or main office is located. With the adoption of interstate branching laws, some institutions operating in your area may actually be headquartered in another state.

4. Safety Rating — Weiss rating assigned to the institution at the time of publication. Our ratings are designed to distinguish levels of insolvency risk and are measured on a scale from A to F based upon a wide range of factors. See *About Weiss Safety Ratings* for specific descriptions of each letter grade.

Highly rated companies are, in our opinion, less likely to experience financial difficulties than lower rated firms. See *About Weiss Safety Ratings* for more information. Also, please be sure to consider the warnings regarding the ratings' limitations and the underlying assumptions.

5. Prior Year Safety Rating — Weiss rating assigned to the institution based on data from December 31 of the previous year. Compare this rating to the company's current rating to identify any recent changes.

6. Safety Rating Two Years Prior — Weiss rating assigned to the institution based on data from December 31 two years ago. Compare this rating to the ratings in the prior columns to identify longer term trends in the company's financial condition.

7. Total Assets

The total of all assets listed on the institution's balance sheet, in millions of dollars. This figure primarily consists of loans, investments (such as municipal and treasury bonds), and fixed assets (such as buildings and other real estate).

Overall size is an important factor which affects the company's ability to diversify risk and avoid vulnerability to a single borrower, industry, or geographic area. Larger institutions are usually, although not always, more diversified and thus less susceptible to a downturn in a particular area. Nevertheless, do not be misled by the general public perception that "bigger is better." Larger institutions are known for their inability to quickly adapt to changes in the marketplace and typically underperform their smaller brethren.

8. One Year Asset Growth

The percentage change in total assets over the previous 12 months. Moderate growth is generally a positive since it can reflect the maintenance or expansion of the company's market share, leading to the generation of additional revenues. Excessive growth, however, is generally a sign of trouble as it can indicate a loosening of underwriting practices in order to attract new business.

9. Commercial Loans/ Total Assets

The percentage of the institution's asset base invested in loans to businesses. Commercial loans are the traditional bread and butter of commercial banks, although many have increased their business lending in recent years.

10. Consumer Loans/ Total Assets

The percentage of the institution's asset base invested in loans to consumers, primarily credit cards. Consumer lending has grown rapidly in recent years due to the high interest rates and fees institutions are able to charge. On the down side, consumer loans usually experience higher delinquency and default rates than other loans, negatively impacting earnings down the road.

11. Home Mortgage Loans/ Total Assets

The percentage of the institution's asset base invested in residential mortgage loans to consumers, excluding home equity loans. Savings banks have traditionally dominated mortgage lending.

This type of loan typically experiences lower default rates. However, the length of the loan's term can be a subject for concern during periods of rising interest rates.

12. Securities/ Total Assets

The percentage of the institution's asset base invested in securities, including U.S. Treasury securities, mortgage-backed securities, and municipal bonds. This does not include securities the institution may be holding on behalf of individual customers.

Although securities are similar to loans in that they represent obligations to pay a debt at some point in the future, they are a more liquid investment than loans and usually present less risk of default. In addition, mortgage-backed securities can present less credit risk than holding mortgage loans themselves due to the diversification of the underlying mortgages.

13. Capitalization Index

An index that measures the adequacy of the institution's capital resources to deal with potentially adverse business and economic situations that could arise. It is based on an evaluation of the company's degree of leverage compared to total assets as well as risk-adjusted assets. See the Critical Ranges In Our Indexes for a description of the different critical levels presented in this index.

14. Leverage Ratio

A regulatory ratio defined by the federal banking regulators as core (tier 1) capital divided by tangible assets. This ratio answers the question: How much does the institution have in stockholders' equity for every dollar of assets? Thus, the Leverage Ratio represents the amount of actual "capital cushion" the institution has to fall back on in times of trouble. We feel that this is the single most important ratio in determining financial strength because it provides the best measure of an institution's ability to withstand losses.

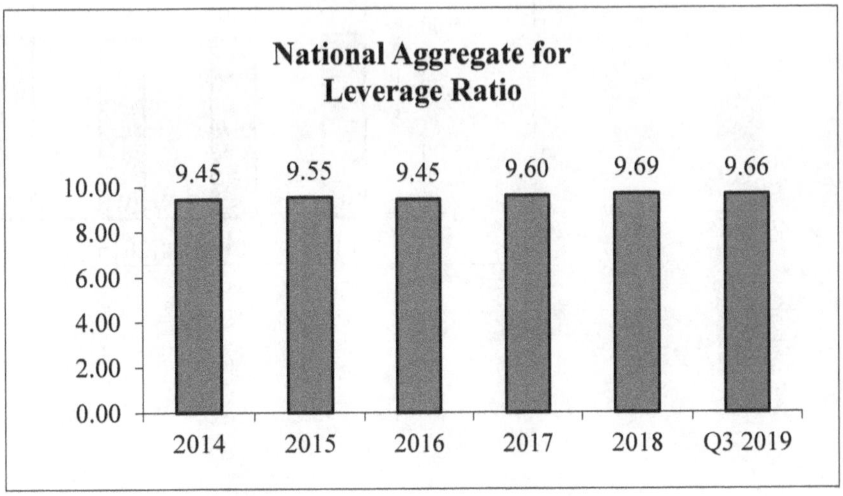

15. Risk-Based Capital Ratio

A regulatory ratio defined by the federal banking regulators as total (tier 1 + tier 2) capital divided by risk-weighted assets. This ratio addresses the issue that not all assets present the same level of credit risk to an institution. As such, all assets and certain off-balance sheet commitments are assigned to risk categories based on the level of credit risk they pose and then weighted accordingly to arrive at risk-weighted assets.

For instance, assets with virtually no risk, such as cash and U.S. Treasury securities, are risk-weighted at 0% and therefore, not included in the calculation. Assets with low risk, for example, high quality mortgage-backed securities and state and municipal bonds, are partially weighted at 20%.

Those assets possessing moderate risk, such as residential mortgages and state and local revenue bonds are partially weighted at 50%. And finally, assets considered to possess "normal" or "high" risk, including certain off-balance sheet commitments such as unfunded loans, are risk-weighted at 100%. The summation of these categories of risk-weighted assets results in the figure used in the denominator of this ratio.

Please be aware that not all banks and savings banks are required to report risk-weighted assets as defined by the federal regulators. Consequently, we have estimated this figure when necessary based on estimates used by the regulators themselves.

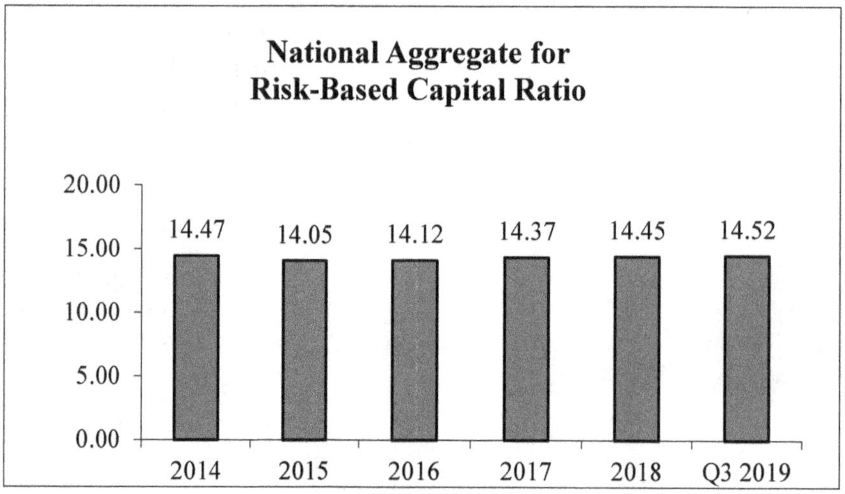

Right Pages

1. Asset Quality Index

An index that measures the quality of the institution's past underwriting and investment practices, as well as its loss reserve coverage. See the Critical Ranges In Our Indexes for a description of the different critical levels presented in this index.

2. Adjusted Nonperforming Loans/ Total Loans

The percentage of the institution's loan portfolio which is either past due on its payments by 90 days or more, or no longer accruing interest due to doubtful collectability plus a portion of all restructured loans, less government guaranteed GNMA loans and those loans protected by the FDIC. This ratio is affected primarily by the quality of the institution's underwriting practices and the prosperity of the local economies where it is doing business. While only a portion of these loans will actually end up in default, a high ratio here will have several negative consequences including increased loan loss provisions, increased loan collection expenses, and decreased interest revenues.

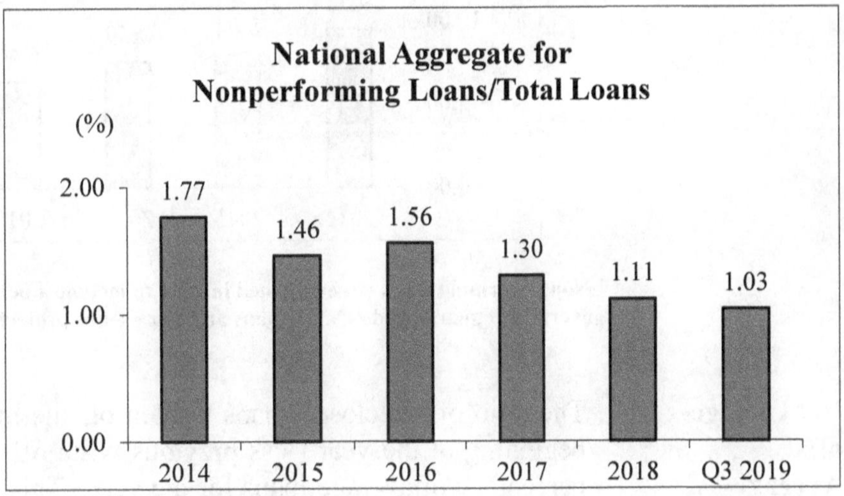

[1]**Nonperforming loans were adjusted in 2011 to include a portion of all restructured loans, less government guaranteed GNMA loans and those loans protected by the FDIC.**

3. Adjusted Nonperforming Loans/ Capital

The percentage of past due 90 days and nonaccruing loans plus a portion of all restructured loans, less government guaranteed GNMA loans and those loans protected by the FDIC to the company's core (tier 1) capital plus reserve for loan losses. This ratio answers the question: If all of the bank's significantly past due and nonaccruing loans were to go into default, how much would that eat into capital? A large percentage of nonperforming loans signal imprudent lending practices which are a direct threat to the equity of the institution.

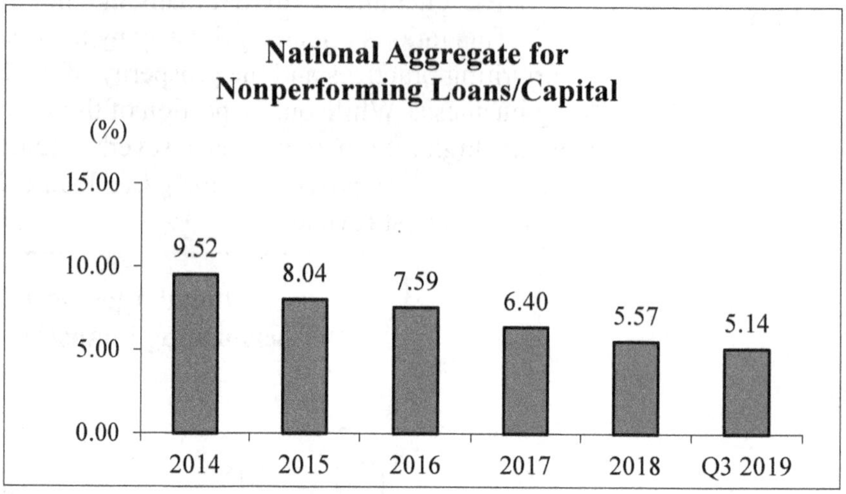

[1] **Nonperforming loans were adjusted in 2011 to include a portion of all restructured loans, less government guaranteed GNMA loans and those loans protected by the FDIC.**

4. Net Charge-offs/ Average Loans

The ratio of foreclosed loans written off the institution's books since the beginning of the year (less previous write-offs that were recovered) as a percentage of average loans for the year. This ratio answers the question: What percentage of the bank's past loans have actually become uncollectible? Past loan charge-off experience is often a very good indication of what can be expected in the future, and high loan charge-off levels are usually an indication of poor underwriting practices.

5. Profitability Index

An index that measures the soundness of the institution's operations and the contribution of profits to the company's financial strength. It is based on five sub-factors: 1) gain or loss on operations; 2) rates of return on assets and equity; 3) management of net interest margin; 4) generation of noninterest-based revenues; and 5) overhead expense management. See the Critical Ranges In Our Indexes for a description of the different critical levels presented in this index.

6. Net Income

The year-to-date net profit or loss recorded by the institution, in millions of dollars. This figure includes the company's operating profit (income from lending, investing, and fees less interest and overhead expenses) as well as nonoperating items such as capital gains on the sale of securities, income taxes, and extraordinary items.

7. Return on Assets The ratio of net income for the year (year-to-date quarterly figures are converted to a 12-month equivalent) as a percentage of average assets for the year. This ratio, known as ROA, is the most commonly used benchmark for bank profitability since it measures the company's return on investment in a format that is easily comparable with other companies.

Historically speaking, a ratio of 1.0% or greater has been considered good performance. However, this ratio will fluctuate with the prevailing economic times. Also, larger banks tend to have a lower ratio.

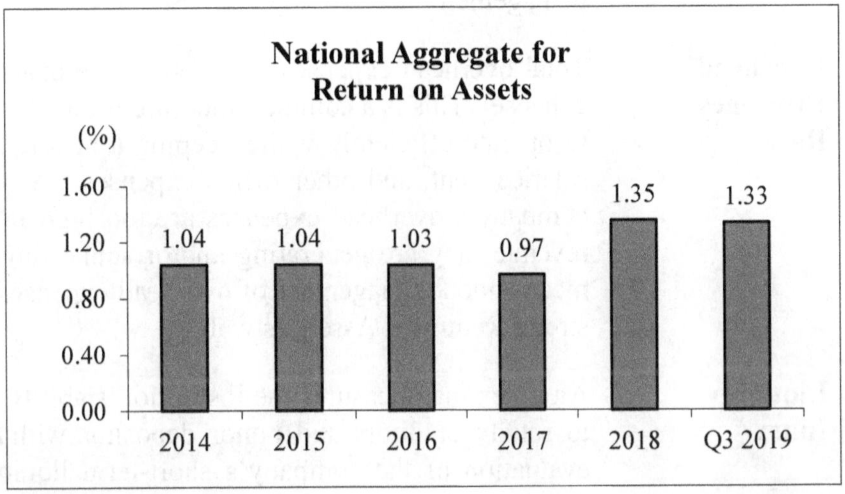

8. Return on Equity The ratio of net income for the year (year-to-date quarterly figures are converted to a 12-month equivalent) as a percentage of average equity for the year. This ratio, known as ROE, is commonly used by a company's shareholders as a measure of their return on investment. It is not always a good measure of profitability, however, because inadequate equity levels at some institutions can result in unjustly high ROE's.

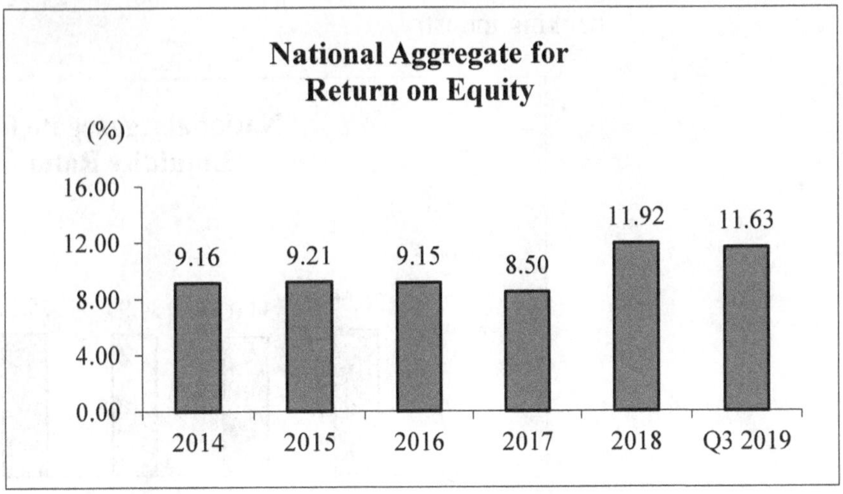

9. Net Interest Spread

The difference between the institution's interest income and interest expense for the year (year-to-date quarterly figures are converted to a 12-month equivalent) as a percentage of its average revenue-generating assets. Since the margin between interest earned and interest paid is generally where the company generates the majority of its income, this figure provides insight into the company's ability to effectively manage interest spreads.

A low Net Interest Spread can be the result of poor loan and deposit pricing, high levels of non-accruing loans, or poor asset/liability management.

10. Overhead Efficiency Ratio

Total overhead expenses as a percentage of total revenues net of interest expense. This is a common measure for evaluating an institution's ability to operate efficiently while keeping a handle on overhead expenses like salaries, rent, and other office expenses. A high ratio suggests that the company's overhead expenses are too high in relation to the amount of revenue they are generating and/or supporting. Conversely, a low ratio means good management of overhead expenses which usually results in a strong Return on Assets as well.

11. Liquidity Index

An index that measures the institution's ability to raise the necessary cash to satisfy creditors and honor depositor withdrawals. It is based on an evaluation of the company's short-term liquidity position, including its existing reliance on less stable deposit sources. See the Critical Ranges In Our Indexes for a description of the different critical levels presented in this index.

12. Liquidity Ratio

The ratio of short-term liquid assets to deposits and short-term borrowings. This ratio answers the question: How many cents can the institution easily raise in cash to cover each dollar on deposit plus pay off its short-term debts? Due to the nature of the business, it is rare (and not expected) for an established bank to achieve 100% on this ratio. Nevertheless, it serves as a good measure of an institution's liquidity in relation to the rest of the banking industry.

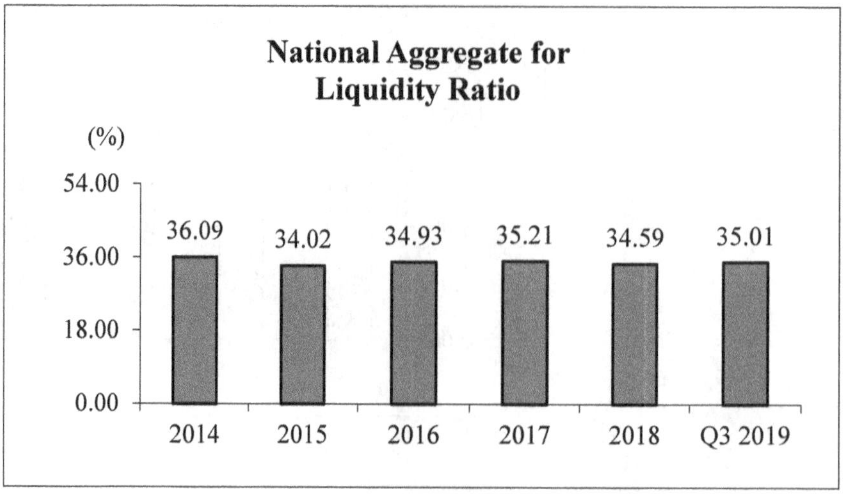

13. Hot Money Ratio

The percentage of the institution's deposit base that is being funded by jumbo CDs and brokered deposits. Jumbo CDs (high-yield certificates of deposit with principal amounts of at least $100,000) and brokered deposits (pooled funds sold by brokers seeking the highest interest rate available) are generally considered less stable (and more costly) and thus less desirable as a source of funds.

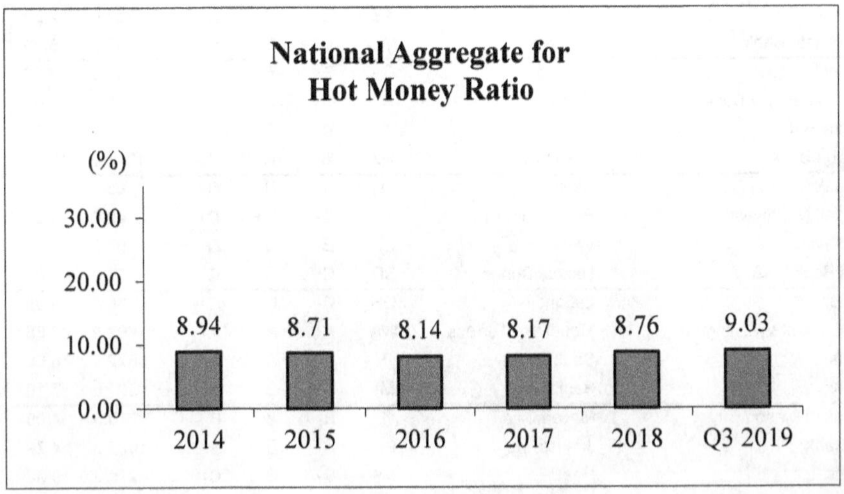

14. Stability Index

An index that integrates a number of factors such as 1) risk diversification in terms of company size and loan diversification; 2) deterioration of operations as reported in critical asset, liability, income and expense items, such as an increase in loan delinquency rates or a sharp increase in loan originations; 3) years in operation; 4) former problem areas where, despite recent improvement, the company has yet to establish a record of stable performance over a suitable period of time; and 5) relationships with holding companies and affiliates. See the Critical Ranges In Our Indexes for a description of the different critical levels presented in this index.

Name	City	State	Rating	2018 Rating	2017 Rating	Total Assets ($Mil)	One Year Asset Growth	Asset Mix (As a % of Total Assets) Comm-ercial Loans	Cons-umer Loans	Mort-gage Loans	Secur-ities	Capital-ization Index	Lever-age Ratio	Risk-Based Capital Ratio
▲ 1880 Bank	Cambridge	MD	**B+**	B	B	377.1	6.47	5.1	0.4	24.1	11.7	**10.0**	13.7	21.0
1st Advantage Bank	Saint Peters	MO	**C**	C	D+	109.4	2.85	14.6	0.1	10.6	2.2	**8.1**	10.4	13.4
1st Bank	Broadus	MT	**A-**	A-	B+	47.4	0.44	5.3	1.4	0.6	0.0	**10.0**	15.4	32.5
▲ 1st Bank & Trust	Broken Bow	OK	**A-**	B+	A-	156.9	2.63	4.2	15.7	20.0	23.8	**10.0**	11.5	22.9
1st Bank in Hominy	Hominy	OK	**C-**	D+	D	40.3	2.83	14.9	7.9	9.7	22.5	**7.1**	9.1	23.4
1st Bank of Sea Isle City	Sea Isle City	NJ	**C**	C	C	245.3	-5.68	0.1	0.2	47.8	8.8	**9.4**	10.6	19.6
▲ 1st Bank Yuma	Yuma	AZ	**B**	B	B-	355.0	12.34	8.9	0.4	2.8	4.8	**8.3**	9.8	13.7
1st Cameron State Bank	Cameron	MO	**C**	C-	C	57.3	-8.70	1.2	1.6	27.7	21.8	**8.1**	9.8	27.2
1st Capital Bank	Salinas	CA	**B+**	B-	C+	637.5	5.08	6.1	0.0	22.3	10.7	**9.5**	10.7	15.3
1st Colonial Community Bank	Cherry Hill	NJ	**C+**	C+	C	545.0	1.09	4.0	0.9	38.9	17.2	**6.5**	8.5	14.4
1st Community Bank	Sherrard	IL	**C**	C	C	64.4	3.89	3.5	2.0	15.0	11.9	**8.6**	10.4	13.8
1st Constitution Bank	Cranbury	NJ	**B**	B	B	1342.0	12.59	24.0	0.1	6.8	15.8	**7.4**	11.4	12.8
▲ 1st Equity Bank	Skokie	IL	**C-**	D	D	95.2	-3.99	14.3	0.1	17.3	0.2	**10.0**	15.2	21.9
1st Equity Bank Northwest	Buffalo Grove	IL	**B-**	C+	C+	40.9	-4.20	6.5	0.2	20.2	0.0	**10.0**	22.2	29.8
▲ 1st Federal Savings Bank of SC, Inc.	Walterboro	SC	**B-**	C+	D+	97.7	7.00	0.1	1.6	64.2	7.5	**7.5**	9.4	17.4
1st Financial Bank USA	Dakota Dunes	SD	**C**	C	C	657.9	-1.02	0.2	68.8	0.1	7.8	**10.0**	25.2	29.9
1st National Bank	Lebanon	OH	**C-**	C	C+	195.6	5.33	2.7	0.6	29.7	12.8	**5.6**	7.6	13.0
1st Security Bank of Washington	Mountlake Terrace	WA	**A**	A	A-	1693.9	42.35	6.5	18.8	20.5	6.3	**9.5**	11.6	14.5
1st Source Bank	South Bend	IN	**A-**	A-	A-	6672.9	6.09	48.1	2.1	6.0	15.5	**8.0**	11.0	13.4
1st State Bank	Saginaw	MI	**C+**	C+	B-	291.6	7.10	33.1	0.2	5.3	0.9	**6.5**	10.0	12.1
1st State Bank of Mason City	Mason City	IL	**B-**	B-	B	25.3	-4.08	1.2	7.1	15.0	42.3	**10.0**	15.2	35.4
1st Summit Bank	Johnstown	PA	**B**	B	B	1098.3	4.79	8.6	2.8	24.4	44.4	**8.3**	9.9	19.2
▼ 1st Trust Bank, Inc.	Hazard	KY	**C-**	C	C-	271.2	9.33	20.9	2.0	18.6	4.0	**6.8**	8.8	12.4
▲ 1st United Bank	Faribault	MN	**A-**	B	B	143.2	-1.57	11.5	1.8	7.7	31.2	**10.0**	11.3	17.4
21st Century Bank	Loretto	MN	**B**	B+	B+	509.1	13.48	18.7	0.1	9.4	10.7	**10.0**	12.1	17.2
▼ 22nd State Bank	Louisville	AL	**D-**	C-	C	135.0	0.21	7.9	1.9	25.2	14.9	**9.5**	10.7	17.1
5Star Bank	Colorado Springs	CO	**A-**	A-	A-	250.7	15.86	7.0	0.2	12.9	0.8	**10.0**	16.4	18.3
▲ AB&T	Albany	GA	**B**	B-	B-	191.6	9.61	18.3	2.1	18.2	0.7	**5.6**	8.9	11.5
Abacus Federal Savings Bank	New York	NY	**B-**	B-	B	335.3	-0.38	0.0	0.0	61.3	0.0	**10.0**	12.3	23.3
Abbeville Building & Loan	Abbeville	LA	**B-**	B-	B-	53.6	-2.62	0.0	0.0	41.8	1.8	**10.0**	27.9	38.0
▲ Abbeville First Bank	Abbeville	SC	**C**	C	B	78.7	2.94	3.0	0.8	42.7	27.5	**10.0**	11.0	21.6
AbbyBank	Abbotsford	WI	**B-**	B-	B-	527.0	5.88	3.3	0.5	15.2	14.1	**6.3**	8.9	12.0
▲ Abington Bank	Abington	MA	**B-**	C+	C+	577.4	117.30	1.7	0.1	43.1	8.3	**10.0**	11.2	16.6
Academy Bank, N.A.	Kansas City	MO	**A-**	A-	A-	1619.1	21.05	21.3	1.0	13.1	9.9	**10.0**	14.8	18.0
▼ ACB Bank	Cherokee	OK	**D+**	C	C+	130.0	-1.89	7.2	2.1	9.6	15.0	**8.2**	10.8	13.5
Access Bank	Omaha	NE	**B**	B	B-	637.9	20.96	15.0	0.3	10.9	10.0	**6.7**	11.0	12.3
AccessBank Texas	Denton	TX	**B-**	B-	B-	424.2	14.21	11.0	2.2	11.9	12.0	**7.3**	9.3	12.7
ACNB Bank	Gettysburg	PA	**A-**	B+	B	1722.0	5.25	4.6	0.8	24.0	12.0	**8.5**	10.0	14.9
▲ Adams Bank & Trust	Ogallala	NE	**B+**	B	B+	825.3	4.94	9.8	2.0	13.5	2.5	**8.0**	11.2	13.3
Adams Community Bank	Adams	MA	**C**	C	C	618.2	8.25	1.5	1.4	67.7	6.9	**6.5**	8.5	14.8
▲ Adams County Bank	Kenesaw	NE	**B**	C+	B-	179.8	5.05	3.7	0.8	3.6	30.8	**8.3**	9.8	14.0
Adams State Bank	Adams	NE	**B+**	B+	B+	51.2	1.88	5.5	4.2	15.5	21.0	**10.0**	19.4	22.9
Adirondack Bank	Utica	NY	**C**	C	C	901.7	7.84	10.9	1.2	24.2	31.0	**5.8**	7.8	16.4
Adirondack Trust Co.	Saratoga Springs	NY	**B**	B	B-	1204.4	1.32	7.2	3.3	14.5	22.0	**8.4**	9.9	15.5
▲ Adrian Bank	Adrian	MO	**B+**	B-	B-	142.5	2.00	6.7	5.1	10.0	22.4	**10.0**	12.0	18.1
▲ Adrian State Bank	Adrian	MN	**C+**	C	C+	50.5	4.39	6.6	1.2	3.2	3.8	**7.2**	9.8	12.6
Advantage Community Bank	Dorchester	WI	**A-**	A-	B+	148.8	2.58	9.3	2.1	14.2	17.3	**10.0**	12.8	19.6
Affiliated Bank, N.A.	Arlington	TX	**B-**	B	B-	950.6	32.52	12.4	0.5	25.8	0.0	**7.6**	11.9	13.0
Affinity Bank	Atlanta	GA	**D+**	D	D-	328.1	12.34	42.6	0.2	0.1	5.3	**6.0**	9.8	11.7
AIG Federal Savings Bank	Wilmington	DE	**U**	U	U	37.7	9.32	0.0	0.0	0.0	84.2	**10.0**	97.7	555.4
AimBank	Littlefield	TX	**A-**	B	B	1546.0	13.24	13.7	0.9	12.1	27.0	**7.9**	9.6	14.5
Alamerica Bank	Birmingham	AL	**D**	D+	C-	20.7	-23.54	10.0	0.7	7.4	2.9	**10.0**	17.2	22.9
Alamosa State Bank	Alamosa	CO	**A-**	A-	A-	265.3	6.48	4.0	3.9	6.8	26.2	**9.0**	10.3	20.3
Albany Bank and Trust Co., N.A.	Chicago	IL	**B+**	B+	B+	610.3	4.27	6.5	0.1	3.3	9.3	**10.0**	16.0	22.0
▲ Alden State Bank	Sterling	KS	**C**	C-	C-	20.0	-4.15	12.5	8.9	19.1	17.5	**10.0**	12.4	21.7
Alden State Bank	Alden	MI	**B+**	B+	A-	217.9	6.50	4.1	2.4	19.6	6.4	**9.6**	12.5	14.7
Alden State Bank	Alden	NY	**B-**	B-	B	346.5	3.61	8.5	1.3	52.2	11.2	**10.0**	12.8	19.2
Alerus Financial, N.A.	Grand Forks	ND	**A-**	A-	B+	2225.8	2.52	19.6	4.2	25.4	12.5	**7.7**	10.5	13.1
▲ Algonquin State Bank	Algonquin	IL	**C**	D+	D-	133.9	-10.50	2.7	13.0	12.2	21.0	**10.0**	11.2	15.5
▲ All America Bank	Oklahoma City	OK	**C+**	C+	B	453.0	7.28	5.6	2.4	17.5	9.5	**6.6**	9.4	12.2

Asset Quality Index	Adjusted Non-Performing Loans as a % of Total Loans	Adjusted Non-Performing Loans as a % of Capital	Net Charge-Offs Avg Loans	Profitability Index	Net Income ($Mil)	Return on Assets (R.O.A.)	Return on Equity (R.O.E.)	Net Interest Spread	Overhead Efficiency Ratio	Liquidity Index	Liquidity Ratio	Hot Money Ratio	Stability Index
5.8	2.24	na	0.00	**5.7**	3.1	1.08	7.63	3.75	63.8	**3.3**	26.2	13.7	**8.1**
7.3	0.03	0.2	0.10	**3.3**	0.5	0.62	6.02	3.58	78.2	**0.8**	13.8	32.2	**5.3**
8.8	0.00	na	-0.33	**9.0**	0.9	2.49	16.82	4.21	44.1	**5.6**	57.3	9.9	**8.0**
7.9	0.00	na	0.08	**10.0**	3.6	2.99	26.99	4.81	44.1	**4.4**	32.3	10.3	**8.5**
5.7	1.13	na	-0.02	**4.1**	0.3	0.89	10.08	3.81	74.6	**3.1**	42.6	20.2	**3.5**
6.3	1.01	na	0.00	**3.3**	1.0	0.52	4.90	3.98	81.9	**4.0**	20.2	9.3	**5.2**
6.6	0.42	na	0.07	**7.6**	4.0	1.51	14.85	4.98	64.2	**4.4**	26.3	7.9	**6.8**
7.4	0.85	na	-0.01	**2.9**	0.2	0.49	5.06	3.10	80.6	**5.8**	50.0	7.1	**4.1**
7.6	0.00	na	-0.01	**5.8**	5.4	1.16	11.36	4.06	63.3	**4.9**	16.7	2.8	**6.7**
5.4	1.44	na	0.63	**4.1**	2.8	0.67	8.22	3.55	66.1	**1.1**	9.7	23.7	**4.9**
3.9	0.63	na	0.00	**3.3**	0.4	0.76	7.41	3.61	82.9	**1.5**	17.2	25.8	**5.0**
6.5	1.11	na	0.07	**6.0**	10.9	1.19	9.58	4.04	61.0	**1.9**	13.8	19.7	**8.9**
1.7	7.21	na	0.00	**5.2**	0.9	1.20	8.15	3.18	62.5	**0.9**	24.4	40.1	**8.6**
6.9	1.13	na	0.00	**4.1**	0.2	0.69	3.10	2.95	79.1	**0.8**	24.8	63.1	**7.3**
9.2	0.04	na	0.01	**4.0**	0.4	0.51	5.55	4.07	84.9	**2.7**	15.4	15.3	**4.9**
2.1	3.81	11.5	4.77	**8.0**	6.5	1.31	5.34	18.02	70.9	**0.4**	18.0	22.7	**8.1**
4.3	0.38	11.7	0.03	**2.8**	0.7	0.51	5.95	3.22	89.3	**1.2**	10.4	27.9	**4.3**
6.9	0.16	1.0	0.18	**8.6**	17.3	1.40	12.05	4.64	64.4	**1.2**	12.4	18.7	**10.0**
7.2	0.44	1.7	0.12	**7.7**	73.4	1.51	12.74	3.80	56.6	**1.8**	15.2	13.4	**10.0**
3.2	2.37	na	0.21	**5.7**	2.5	1.15	11.92	4.35	63.7	**4.8**	24.8	4.8	**6.0**
6.2	2.80	na	0.12	**3.9**	0.2	0.95	6.63	3.02	71.0	**5.7**	72.8	11.9	**6.5**
8.3	0.45	3.0	0.16	**4.6**	8.3	1.03	10.57	2.89	62.8	**3.3**	32.0	19.2	**8.3**
2.7	2.42	na	0.03	**2.8**	0.8	0.40	4.50	2.91	81.1	**0.7**	15.9	43.1	**4.1**
7.0	0.43	1.3	0.00	**6.0**	1.6	1.51	11.32	3.87	65.3	**6.4**	44.2	2.2	**7.8**
7.3	0.59	na	0.05	**6.4**	5.1	1.35	11.77	3.39	52.2	**0.8**	12.2	3.2	**7.2**
3.0	3.90	na	0.52	**0.2**	-1.2	-1.11	-11.31	3.37	108.9	**0.7**	15.9	45.8	**5.2**
7.2	0.71	1.9	0.00	**6.5**	2.0	1.15	6.76	4.78	61.7	**1.4**	12.1	25.6	**8.0**
8.3	0.19	na	0.05	**5.0**	1.5	1.05	10.67	3.87	66.7	**4.1**	11.4	7.5	**7.4**
9.1	0.36	na	0.00	**3.1**	1.2	0.48	3.63	3.30	81.6	**0.6**	12.3	34.9	**7.7**
4.4	1.09	na	0.00	**3.1**	0.1	0.26	0.89	4.67	93.4	**2.4**	4.3	16.1	**8.0**
8.2	2.89	na	0.11	**2.7**	0.3	0.54	4.60	3.21	84.4	**2.6**	36.2	22.5	**6.0**
5.2	0.84	na	0.03	**3.9**	2.5	0.64	7.24	3.33	67.5	**1.2**	18.0	22.3	**6.6**
7.0	1.70	na	0.00	**3.0**	1.4	0.48	3.25	3.25	75.2	**1.4**	13.6	23.9	**6.7**
7.3	0.59	3.0	0.44	**6.5**	14.0	1.19	8.05	3.39	69.9	**0.9**	8.3	31.3	**8.5**
1.0	3.68	na	0.42	**6.7**	1.7	1.68	17.56	4.04	44.2	**0.7**	14.3	48.2	**5.6**
7.8	0.12	0.6	-0.11	**5.5**	5.0	1.21	9.44	4.30	67.3	**3.3**	22.0	13.0	**7.4**
5.9	1.22	na	-0.03	**3.9**	1.9	0.64	6.74	3.75	76.9	**1.6**	23.0	25.3	**5.3**
7.3	0.54	na	0.05	**6.9**	18.4	1.48	14.85	3.93	56.6	**3.1**	9.8	13.4	**8.7**
7.7	0.28	na	0.05	**6.8**	7.9	1.32	11.88	4.69	66.1	**2.0**	7.8	18.3	**8.4**
5.9	0.74	na	0.12	**3.1**	3.1	0.68	7.40	3.14	80.2	**2.6**	10.9	11.4	**5.9**
6.5	0.00	na	0.00	**6.3**	2.0	1.59	16.55	3.07	44.9	**0.8**	7.5	25.5	**5.9**
8.3	0.00	na	-0.02	**5.9**	0.5	1.43	7.37	3.68	60.5	**2.3**	25.3	17.3	**8.5**
3.6	2.08	17.0	0.10	**3.5**	5.1	0.79	10.19	3.33	80.1	**1.5**	9.5	18.5	**4.7**
7.9	0.25	1.1	-0.02	**5.3**	10.0	1.13	10.47	3.47	69.7	**4.2**	21.5	9.6	**9.1**
6.1	0.94	na	0.04	**8.6**	2.8	2.63	22.94	4.32	43.5	**3.9**	25.5	10.6	**7.7**
4.1	0.02	na	-0.02	**8.3**	0.8	2.09	21.99	4.44	50.7	**1.8**	12.5	19.9	**6.6**
8.6	0.00	0.0	0.00	**6.4**	1.4	1.29	9.87	3.66	55.5	**5.1**	37.0	6.8	**7.5**
7.2	0.12	0.4	0.00	**5.3**	5.2	0.82	5.95	4.51	76.1	**0.7**	12.8	45.2	**7.7**
8.0	0.03	0.2	0.06	**4.0**	1.8	0.75	7.21	3.28	68.2	**1.4**	16.5	26.2	**5.4**
10.0	na	na	na	**10.0**	2.4	8.87	9.18	2.59	30.4	**4.0**	na	100.0	**7.0**
8.2	0.10	na	0.08	**7.2**	15.9	1.44	13.33	4.10	56.1	**2.0**	22.9	24.7	**8.8**
3.0	1.18	19.3	1.84	**0.2**	-0.7	-4.53	-23.10	3.71	287.0	**1.0**	31.9	46.5	**3.9**
8.6	0.32	na	0.10	**8.7**	4.2	2.20	21.77	3.91	43.7	**4.3**	35.0	11.8	**8.0**
7.4	0.38	na	-0.01	**5.3**	4.3	0.94	5.88	3.39	59.6	**1.4**	25.8	27.9	**8.4**
8.3	0.00	na	-0.05	**2.7**	0.1	0.43	3.51	3.63	87.2	**1.7**	29.5	24.1	**5.3**
6.8	1.98	na	0.03	**6.9**	2.0	1.32	10.29	4.51	56.9	**4.5**	31.9	9.5	**7.0**
3.2	3.80	na	0.57	**7.0**	3.7	1.43	11.47	4.28	50.9	**3.4**	11.9	11.6	**7.7**
7.1	0.35	1.9	0.35	**8.0**	25.4	1.55	12.89	3.84	72.9	**4.4**	10.3	5.5	**9.8**
7.8	0.38	na	0.00	**2.5**	0.6	0.52	4.85	3.57	88.3	**4.9**	19.9	3.5	**4.5**
4.3	0.96	na	0.25	**7.3**	5.5	1.66	16.32	4.53	58.4	**3.1**	10.8	12.9	**6.7**

Name	City	State	Rating	2018 Rating	2017 Rating	Total Assets ($Mil)	One Year Asset Growth	Asset Mix (As a % of Total Assets) Commercial Loans	Consumer Loans	Mortgage Loans	Securities	Capitalization Index	Leverage Ratio	Risk-Based Capital Ratio
Allegiance Bank	Houston	TX	**C+**	B-	B-	4902.2	61.57	13.0	0.9	12.9	7.2	**8.8**	10.7	14.0
▲ Alliance Bank	Francesville	IN	**A-**	B+	A-	310.0	5.36	7.6	0.4	5.3	31.2	**10.0**	12.5	18.7
▲ Alliance Bank	Topeka	KS	**B+**	B	B	110.7	17.07	17.3	2.4	18.8	2.9	**10.0**	11.8	17.0
Alliance Bank	Saint Paul	MN	**B**	B	B-	637.4	8.01	18.5	1.1	4.6	10.5	**7.6**	11.3	13.0
Alliance Bank	Cape Girardeau	MO	**B+**	B+	B+	273.0	15.30	5.6	2.3	16.1	4.1	**10.0**	12.4	15.1
Alliance Bank	Sulphur Springs	TX	**B-**	B-	B-	972.0	31.34	5.4	1.3	13.3	35.7	**7.5**	9.4	16.1
Alliance Bank	Mondovi	WI	**B**	B-	B-	187.9	11.13	3.3	3.6	17.1	13.1	**7.7**	9.5	14.1
▲ Alliance Bank & Trust Co.	Gastonia	NC	**C**	D+	D	150.5	-0.32	9.4	0.5	8.8	16.4	**6.6**	8.7	12.2
Alliance Bank Central Texas	Waco	TX	**C+**	C+	C+	318.5	4.26	8.8	2.4	28.7	15.7	**5.6**	7.6	12.9
Alliance Community Bank	Petersburg	IL	**C+**	B-	B	272.4	107.52	3.4	5.1	18.1	33.0	**8.9**	10.2	17.4
Alliant Bank	Madison	MO	**B+**	B+	B+	161.8	0.36	4.5	1.1	26.9	4.7	**9.0**	10.3	15.1
Allied First Bank,sb	Oswego	IL	**C**	C-	C	103.6	23.02	4.0	0.8	42.4	7.9	**10.0**	12.0	24.0
▼ AllNations Bank	Calumet	OK	**D**	D	D	45.0	-12.50	11.2	2.3	3.1	23.7	**9.8**	10.9	19.8
Ally Bank	Sandy	UT	**B+**	A-	A-	167073.0	10.59	24.4	35.9	10.4	16.6	**8.0**	10.2	13.3
Alma Bank	Astoria	NY	**D-**	D-	D-	1190.4	2.62	13.5	0.0	2.5	3.1	**7.7**	10.2	13.1
▼ Almena State Bank	Almena	KS	**D-**	D+	C+	86.2	-31.67	17.6	3.5	4.6	14.7	**0.4**	4.5	6.8
Alpine Bank	Glenwood Springs	CO	**A-**	A-	B+	3841.2	4.83	3.6	1.0	18.4	18.8	**8.1**	9.8	13.6
▲ Alpine Capital Bank	New York	NY	**A**	A-	A-	258.0	-0.73	1.2	2.5	1.9	28.6	**10.0**	20.3	38.8
Altabank	American Fork	UT	**A**	A	A	2443.8	10.52	9.2	0.6	3.7	13.1	**10.0**	12.5	17.6
▲ Altamaha Bank and Trust Co.	Vidalia	GA	**B**	B-	B+	170.4	7.40	11.0	4.0	15.4	22.2	**10.0**	11.9	18.1
Alton Bank	Alton	MO	**B+**	B+	B+	64.8	-1.30	4.3	9.0	14.6	24.7	**10.0**	15.6	17.5
Altoona First Savings Bank	Altoona	PA	**B**	B	B-	232.1	6.35	5.1	4.7	30.4	1.0	**10.0**	14.4	20.9
Alva State Bank & Trust Co.	Alva	OK	**C+**	C+	B+	405.6	5.84	7.8	2.0	2.8	17.1	**10.0**	13.3	17.4
▲ Amalgamated Bank	New York	NY	**B**	B-	C-	5030.9	8.47	8.3	3.4	26.8	24.8	**7.1**	9.0	14.6
Amalgamated Bank of Chicago	Chicago	IL	**B**	C+	B-	891.1	2.50	2.2	4.3	3.8	18.5	**9.9**	10.9	17.3
Amarillo National Bank	Amarillo	TX	**B+**	A-	A-	5389.7	34.37	26.6	15.4	5.3	5.4	**5.5**	9.9	11.3
Ambler Savings Bank	Ambler	PA	**B**	B	B	414.7	4.23	0.7	0.0	46.8	24.2	**10.0**	12.8	26.2
Amboy Bank	Old Bridge	NJ	**B-**	B-	B	2332.4	-0.72	1.4	0.0	14.0	19.2	**10.0**	16.4	20.2
Amerant Bank, N.A.	Coral Gables	FL	**C+**	C+	C+	7854.9	-6.76	14.4	1.2	3.5	19.9	**9.2**	10.8	14.4
Amerant Trust, N.A.	Coral Gables	FL	**U**	U	U	9.0	3.49	0.0	0.0	0.0	60.6	**10.0**	94.8	202.8
Amerasia Bank	Flushing	NY	**B+**	A	A-	680.9	11.83	2.1	0.2	18.6	0.1	**10.0**	12.4	16.6
America's Community Bank	Blue Springs	MO	**C**	C+	B-	31.2	11.95	4.0	2.0	27.6	0.8	**9.3**	11.6	14.4
▲ American B&T of the Cumberlands	Livingston	TN	**B**	B-	B	254.5	10.95	10.8	4.9	30.2	4.2	**7.2**	9.1	12.6
American Bank	Bozeman	MT	**A-**	A-	A-	454.5	4.50	12.5	0.2	10.0	7.0	**9.1**	10.4	14.8
▲ American Bank	Wagoner	OK	**C+**	C	C-	29.0	0.53	1.2	5.6	2.6	50.0	**10.0**	22.8	75.8
American Bank	Allentown	PA	**B+**	B	B	649.8	2.12	7.5	0.2	11.6	9.2	**7.6**	10.3	13.0
American Bank	Beaver Dam	WI	**B-**	C+	C+	149.9	-2.24	2.7	1.4	20.4	11.3	**9.4**	10.6	16.5
American Bank & Trust	Huron	SD	**B**	B	B+	928.4	5.46	12.6	1.2	2.8	16.4	**6.1**	9.4	11.8
American Bank & Trust Co.	Opelousas	LA	**A-**	A-	B+	187.7	4.87	9.4	3.7	29.2	16.9	**10.0**	12.4	19.1
American Bank & Trust Co., Inc.	Bowling Green	KY	**B**	B	B+	426.1	12.58	7.7	1.2	24.3	7.9	**5.3**	8.6	11.2
American Bank & Trust Co., Inc.	Covington	LA	**C**	C	C	179.6	6.34	5.4	1.4	25.7	1.7	**6.6**	8.6	12.8
▲ American Bank and Trust Co.	Tulsa	OK	**A-**	B+	B+	228.1	1.95	14.8	0.2	2.5	38.3	**10.0**	11.7	17.9
American Bank and Trust Co., N.A.	Davenport	IA	**B-**	C+	C-	368.4	8.64	8.5	0.9	21.8	10.5	**10.0**	11.7	16.3
American Bank Center	Dickinson	ND	**B-**	B-	B-	1514.8	9.56	6.9	16.0	3.7	28.1	**7.2**	9.1	12.8
American Bank of Baxter Springs	Baxter Springs	KS	**B**	B	B-	102.0	2.68	5.2	1.3	6.7	45.3	**10.0**	12.0	35.3
American Bank of Commerce	Wolfforth	TX	**B**	B	B-	971.0	2.68	9.1	0.5	10.9	29.6	**7.7**	9.5	14.0
American Bank of Missouri	Wellsville	MO	**B**	B	B-	394.9	21.32	9.4	0.1	23.9	5.5	**6.7**	9.3	12.2
American Bank of Oklahoma	Collinsville	OK	**C**	C+	C	316.4	13.77	21.5	9.2	14.2	2.0	**4.1**	8.7	10.6
American Bank of the North	Nashwauk	MN	**C+**	C-	D+	526.6	-3.66	11.8	1.6	15.5	16.7	**9.0**	10.3	15.1
American Bank, N.A.	Le Mars	IA	**C+**	C+	C+	327.4	9.24	7.4	1.4	5.4	1.5	**8.5**	11.3	13.8
American Bank, N.A.	Corpus Christi	TX	**B-**	B	B	1516.1	10.13	19.7	0.5	6.8	33.8	**7.5**	9.4	15.4
▲ American Bank, N.A.	Dallas	TX	**B**	C+	C+	83.3	51.18	0.3	34.6	0.5	31.6	**10.0**	13.0	24.6
American Bank, N.A.	Waco	TX	**B**	B	B	446.9	0.57	10.9	1.6	24.1	14.4	**9.5**	10.7	16.5
American Business Bank	Los Angeles	CA	**B**	B-	B-	2331.6	11.23	16.2	0.7	0.6	31.2	**6.9**	8.9	13.8
▲ American Commerce Bank, N.A.	Bremen	GA	**C+**	C+	B-	339.4	15.04	4.2	1.2	15.4	1.5	**10.0**	11.9	16.4
American Community Bank	Glen Cove	NY	**B**	B	B+	225.1	7.88	1.4	0.0	15.6	8.8	**10.0**	12.6	17.6
American Community Bank & Trust	Woodstock	IL	**B+**	B+	B	580.9	4.34	14.4	0.1	8.7	16.2	**10.0**	12.9	18.8
American Community Bank of Indiana	Saint John	IN	**B-**	B-	B	226.6	3.96	5.5	0.4	27.0	3.5	**7.4**	9.3	13.1
▲ American Continental Bank	City of Industry	CA	**A-**	B+	A-	268.3	22.25	4.5	0.0	25.4	4.3	**10.0**	13.5	17.5
American Eagle Bank	South Elgin	IL	**D+**	C-	C+	274.3	9.97	1.4	47.7	7.9	5.2	**4.8**	7.9	10.9

Asset Quality Index	Adjusted Non-Performing Loans as a % of Total Loans	Adjusted Non-Performing Loans as a % of Capital	Net Charge-Offs Avg Loans	Profitability Index	Net Income ($Mil)	Return on Assets (R.O.A.)	Return on Equity (R.O.E.)	Net Interest Spread	Overhead Efficiency Ratio	Liquidity Index	Liquidity Ratio	Hot Money Ratio	Stability Index
3.5	1.46	na	0.05	**5.5**	40.6	1.13	7.48	4.29	61.8	**1.4**	15.1	20.9	**9.6**
7.7	1.53	na	-0.04	**7.0**	3.8	1.71	13.07	4.08	60.6	**4.2**	37.6	11.9	**8.7**
7.2	1.23	na	0.07	**5.6**	0.8	1.08	9.11	4.47	62.6	**2.1**	29.0	22.5	**5.8**
4.2	1.58	8.9	-1.09	**6.1**	7.2	1.59	13.98	4.15	66.4	**2.2**	15.0	15.9	**9.1**
6.9	0.56	na	0.01	**4.5**	1.6	0.86	6.62	3.71	68.2	**2.6**	13.1	15.6	**7.7**
8.0	0.47	1.1	0.04	**4.1**	7.0	0.96	9.49	3.33	74.5	**4.4**	29.3	9.5	**6.8**
5.0	1.00	5.4	0.02	**5.3**	1.6	1.20	12.24	3.67	67.8	**3.4**	25.8	13.2	**6.5**
2.9	2.09	na	0.47	**4.0**	0.8	0.77	8.58	4.47	75.4	**4.2**	29.6	10.4	**4.3**
8.5	0.58	na	0.00	**3.3**	1.4	0.60	7.53	3.29	76.0	**0.9**	20.3	38.8	**4.4**
3.2	2.43	na	0.00	**4.8**	2.6	1.24	9.48	3.55	68.9	**4.8**	38.1	10.2	**6.8**
6.5	0.50	3.6	0.00	**5.2**	1.5	1.24	12.14	4.27	75.5	**1.2**	13.1	26.7	**7.0**
6.0	2.69	na	0.02	**6.6**	2.5	3.71	31.83	3.67	91.8	**2.0**	28.7	15.4	**4.3**
0.3	22.28	na	1.23	**0.0**	-0.8	-2.17	-17.44	3.51	112.0	**5.0**	21.1	2.7	**4.0**
4.7	0.90	5.2	0.66	**6.9**	1634.0	1.34	13.08	3.32	45.0	**1.0**	18.3	20.4	**9.5**
0.4	6.94	33.5	0.07	**3.0**	4.0	0.46	4.49	3.13	78.4	**0.6**	9.5	39.4	**8.0**
0.1	20.62	140.4	6.75	**1.3**	-6.0	-6.94	-119.14	3.84	86.7	**0.3**	10.9	67.1	**4.6**
7.8	0.83	3.3	0.08	**8.5**	46.3	1.66	16.73	4.77	62.6	**5.3**	21.1	2.4	**9.5**
7.1	4.30	na	0.00	**8.3**	3.7	1.94	9.94	3.71	40.0	**4.5**	87.3	17.2	**9.0**
7.1	1.60	na	0.04	**9.9**	33.1	1.95	14.54	5.10	48.3	**4.8**	20.1	4.9	**10.0**
5.2	2.53	na	0.58	**5.3**	1.4	1.13	9.59	4.65	74.6	**2.5**	21.5	17.3	**7.7**
5.6	0.99	na	0.24	**8.4**	0.9	1.83	12.49	4.43	60.1	**1.9**	19.4	20.1	**7.9**
8.4	0.52	na	0.06	**4.7**	1.6	0.95	6.62	4.16	66.7	**1.8**	22.4	22.5	**7.6**
2.1	5.32	na	2.04	**4.6**	1.9	0.63	4.80	4.01	39.1	**1.4**	24.5	28.1	**7.7**
5.4	1.98	8.4	0.29	**4.7**	35.2	0.96	10.11	3.58	64.6	**4.3**	13.2	6.6	**7.6**
5.3	1.08	na	0.26	**4.4**	5.1	0.86	8.24	4.07	76.9	**4.8**	30.6	6.2	**5.1**
5.0	0.73	4.6	0.23	**8.3**	71.3	1.80	16.39	4.03	55.4	**2.3**	12.9	17.6	**9.7**
8.7	0.99	na	0.00	**4.0**	2.5	0.82	6.43	2.92	64.6	**2.3**	16.9	17.9	**7.2**
3.6	6.62	14.5	-0.07	**8.7**	45.3	2.62	16.28	3.37	42.1	**2.7**	20.3	16.8	**10.0**
6.7	0.57	3.3	0.12	**3.9**	47.4	0.79	7.37	2.98	73.0	**1.4**	22.9	24.2	**7.8**
10.0	na	na	na	**9.5**	0.3	3.58	3.81	2.41	82.8	**4.0**	na	0.0	**5.7**
7.5	0.00	na	-0.01	**10.0**	11.3	2.34	19.43	4.72	34.4	**0.7**	13.0	46.6	**9.2**
4.5	0.00	na	0.16	**3.2**	0.1	0.50	4.24	3.90	83.0	**0.7**	8.9	38.0	**6.0**
7.3	0.21	na	-0.20	**5.8**	2.4	1.33	14.88	3.81	67.8	**0.8**	18.7	38.9	**6.2**
7.3	0.30	na	0.07	**7.2**	5.2	1.63	15.78	4.52	58.9	**5.7**	33.3	2.4	**8.0**
9.8	0.00	na	0.07	**2.8**	0.1	0.55	2.47	3.34	83.8	**6.9**	95.8	8.4	**6.5**
7.3	0.24	1.1	0.00	**6.4**	6.4	1.34	12.87	3.15	46.1	**1.7**	9.4	19.9	**7.6**
6.2	0.83	na	0.08	**4.6**	1.0	0.88	8.42	4.11	73.3	**4.4**	22.4	6.7	**5.7**
7.9	0.09	na	0.04	**7.4**	11.8	1.72	17.22	3.97	55.7	**2.7**	19.1	15.1	**7.9**
8.7	0.06	0.5	0.05	**7.1**	2.4	1.77	14.40	4.19	59.9	**4.1**	13.8	8.1	**7.4**
6.7	0.42	2.9	0.13	**5.6**	3.4	1.11	13.13	3.59	59.6	**1.1**	16.1	27.2	**6.4**
4.1	0.96	na	0.02	**3.4**	0.8	0.58	6.74	4.44	83.3	**1.4**	18.0	22.3	**4.5**
8.9	0.16	na	0.00	**5.7**	2.0	1.12	10.08	3.65	58.6	**1.5**	26.0	28.9	**6.7**
7.6	0.88	na	-0.01	**3.9**	1.9	0.70	6.00	3.65	84.2	**3.5**	9.7	9.9	**6.8**
3.5	2.32	13.7	0.14	**6.7**	15.5	1.40	15.13	3.65	60.2	**2.5**	4.8	14.6	**7.9**
8.9	2.75	na	0.01	**3.7**	0.7	0.88	7.64	2.95	83.1	**2.9**	37.8	19.9	**6.7**
8.0	0.64	2.2	0.10	**5.1**	7.7	1.06	11.23	3.84	66.5	**3.4**	23.9	13.0	**6.7**
8.3	0.15	0.8	0.09	**4.4**	2.2	0.81	7.76	3.47	69.9	**1.1**	11.3	29.9	**5.8**
3.9	1.22	7.7	0.08	**4.6**	2.1	0.90	10.38	4.60	78.6	**0.7**	12.3	37.6	**4.6**
2.6	3.55	na	-0.33	**7.1**	5.8	1.47	13.57	3.98	66.9	**4.8**	15.8	3.3	**6.2**
3.6	0.95	6.8	0.01	**6.7**	3.6	1.53	13.56	3.20	53.2	**1.7**	12.9	17.4	**7.7**
6.5	1.32	na	0.02	**4.4**	10.7	1.00	11.48	3.95	77.2	**5.9**	36.6	6.5	**8.2**
6.7	0.13	na	2.21	**4.4**	0.5	1.06	6.55	6.09	58.8	**3.4**	62.8	25.9	**4.7**
7.0	0.19	na	0.02	**4.7**	3.4	1.06	9.98	3.85	72.8	**2.4**	24.6	18.2	**6.8**
8.6	0.12	0.7	0.00	**5.1**	16.1	0.96	11.72	3.68	60.8	**6.3**	32.8	2.0	**6.8**
5.1	1.32	na	0.02	**7.1**	3.3	1.36	12.31	4.07	53.4	**0.7**	13.3	34.2	**8.1**
7.7	0.03	na	-0.01	**3.5**	0.9	0.58	4.60	3.62	80.9	**1.9**	22.8	20.1	**8.0**
8.7	0.17	na	-0.01	**3.7**	2.7	0.64	4.78	3.21	72.2	**2.8**	35.1	19.1	**8.2**
4.4	1.84	na	0.05	**4.0**	1.0	0.62	6.76	3.52	76.9	**2.1**	14.8	18.7	**6.0**
8.7	0.04	na	-0.05	**7.5**	2.4	1.34	9.64	3.75	55.7	**0.9**	27.0	60.9	**8.1**
5.5	0.24	na	0.34	**5.0**	1.8	0.89	11.36	3.24	57.1	**0.8**	21.7	46.5	**4.3**

Name	City	State	Rating	2018 Rating	2017 Rating	Total Assets ($Mil)	One Year Asset Growth	Asset Mix (As a % of Total Assets) Commercial Loans	Consumer Loans	Mortgage Loans	Securities	Capitalization Index	Leverage Ratio	Risk-Based Capital Ratio
American Eagle Bank of Chicago	Chicago	IL	**C-**	C-	C+	97.2	-8.03	3.9	28.0	13.5	8.4	**8.4**	9.9	14.7
▲ American Equity Bank	Minnetonka	MN	**D+**	D	D+	51.4	22.28	20.1	0.7	32.7	0.0	**10.0**	11.8	16.8
American Exchange Bank	Elmwood	NE	**B**	B-	B-	46.2	-4.90	18.3	2.3	8.0	20.8	**10.0**	12.4	18.2
American Exchange Bank	Henryetta	OK	**B-**	B-	B-	67.9	3.73	6.3	9.5	37.5	8.2	**10.0**	12.0	18.2
American Exchange Bank	Lindsay	OK	**B+**	B+	B	74.6	9.89	5.7	4.0	6.3	59.3	**9.6**	10.8	20.7
▼ American Express National Bank	Salt Lake City	UT	**B-**	B+	B+	120171.3	3.12	23.8	56.2	0.0	4.3	**8.7**	10.1	14.5
American Federal Bank	Fargo	ND	**B**	B+	B+	634.1	7.12	4.0	0.9	13.7	8.1	**6.7**	8.7	12.8
American First National Bank	Houston	TX	**A-**	B+	B+	1870.5	18.63	6.6	0.3	3.6	6.2	**8.0**	11.2	13.4
▲ American Heritage Bank	Clovis	NM	**B+**	B	B	95.2	6.24	12.4	0.4	9.4	27.3	**10.0**	11.7	15.9
American Heritage Bank	Sapulpa	OK	**B-**	B-	B-	1124.0	3.04	5.5	2.9	14.6	52.0	**6.9**	8.9	20.5
American Heritage National Bank	Long Prairie	MN	**A-**	A-	A-	361.1	3.05	7.9	0.5	10.0	9.8	**10.0**	11.4	16.8
American Interstate Bank	Elkhorn	NE	**A**	A	A	109.9	1.11	12.0	0.9	24.8	0.0	**10.0**	19.6	21.8
American Investors Bank and Mortgage	Eden Prairie	MN	**B-**	B-	B-	72.6	3.24	0.5	0.2	25.5	22.6	**10.0**	12.6	18.1
American Metro Bank	Chicago	IL	**C**	C	C	81.4	8.99	1.1	0.0	25.4	0.0	**9.6**	10.7	16.5
American Momentum Bank	College Station	TX	**B+**	A-	A-	1658.9	53.72	12.3	0.3	12.9	9.9	**10.0**	12.9	15.3
American Nation Bank	Ardmore	OK	**B**	B	B	441.3	6.53	3.2	4.3	19.3	33.6	**8.9**	10.3	15.9
American National Bank	Oakland Park	FL	**B+**	A-	A-	300.8	-3.27	7.0	0.0	3.0	4.7	**10.0**	14.1	19.4
American National Bank	Omaha	NE	**B**	B	B	3961.6	7.02	14.7	18.4	5.8	16.9	**6.3**	9.5	12.0
American National Bank & Trust	Wichita Falls	TX	**B**	B+	A-	819.4	22.60	4.7	3.3	9.9	11.7	**8.9**	11.1	14.1
American National Bank and Trust Co.	Danville	VA	**B+**	A-	A-	2441.6	35.89	10.7	0.5	13.3	12.3	**7.7**	10.3	13.0
American National Bank of Minnesota	Brainerd	MN	**B-**	B	B-	300.7	6.23	2.7	2.5	33.8	2.7	**10.0**	11.0	15.9
▲ American National Bank of Mount Pleasant	Mount Pleasant	TX	**A-**	B+	B+	103.7	3.20	7.3	8.3	15.8	35.2	**10.0**	13.4	26.5
American National Bank of Texas	Terrell	TX	**B+**	B	B	3251.6	7.01	6.3	0.9	13.2	31.3	**6.8**	8.8	13.1
▲ American National Bank-Fox Cities	Appleton	WI	**A-**	B+	A-	300.6	3.85	20.8	0.2	5.2	17.8	**10.0**	13.4	16.2
▲ American Plus Bank, N.A.	Arcadia	CA	**A-**	B+	A-	565.9	12.18	13.9	1.8	14.5	4.0	**10.0**	13.9	16.2
▲ American Pride Bank	Macon	GA	**A-**	B+	A-	195.1	4.78	4.8	0.2	4.8	6.1	**10.0**	14.6	17.8
American River Bank	Rancho Cordova	CA	**B**	B	B	721.7	7.70	3.2	3.4	4.1	38.3	**7.5**	9.3	16.8
American Riviera Bank	Santa Barbara	CA	**B**	B	B+	697.3	18.37	11.0	0.1	13.5	6.0	**7.1**	10.3	12.6
American Savings Bank	Tripoli	IA	**B+**	B+	A-	50.4	7.45	6.1	1.9	8.6	39.5	**10.0**	20.7	29.1
American Savings Bank, F.S.B.	Honolulu	HI	**B+**	B+	B+	7135.3	2.97	8.2	3.8	34.4	18.9	**6.8**	8.8	14.0
American State Bank	Osceola	IA	**B**	B+	B+	220.2	3.95	15.2	4.4	11.9	17.1	**7.5**	9.3	13.5
American State Bank	Sioux Center	IA	**C**	C	C+	948.6	6.32	16.5	2.0	3.6	1.2	**8.5**	11.7	13.8
American State Bank	Arp	TX	**C+**	C+	C+	440.2	61.59	13.9	3.3	21.4	3.3	**5.2**	8.6	11.1
American State Bank & Trust Co	Williston	ND	**B+**	B+	A-	623.6	5.58	5.5	4.0	5.5	43.9	**10.0**	11.8	20.5
American State Bank & Trust Co.	Wichita	KS	**B-**	B	B	648.1	-3.07	8.7	2.1	4.5	24.8	**9.6**	11.6	14.7
▲ American State Bank of Grygla	Grygla	MN	**B-**	C+	B-	58.9	15.80	7.3	6.4	11.2	12.8	**10.0**	11.0	17.9
American Trust and Savings Bank	Lowden	IA	**B-**	B-	C+	32.5	-3.50	2.9	1.9	0.6	29.6	**10.0**	19.5	51.7
▲ Americana Community Bank	Sleepy Eye	MN	**C**	C	D+	127.7	7.74	12.0	0.5	7.7	13.0	**6.0**	8.1	11.8
AmeriFirst Bank	Montgomery	AL	**C+**	C	C	185.3	3.64	15.3	2.6	16.4	11.7	**9.2**	10.4	14.4
Ameriprise Bank, FSB	Minneapolis	MN	**U**	U	U	2808.8	10955.	0.0	3.3	0.0	86.3	**6.2**	8.2	18.7
Ameris Bank	Atlanta	GA	**B+**	B+	B	17675.2	55.85	8.1	9.1	21.0	8.4	**6.6**	10.0	12.2
AmeriServ Financial Bank	Johnstown	PA	**C+**	C+	C+	1157.6	0.16	13.3	1.6	13.7	15.3	**6.5**	9.5	12.1
AmeriState Bank	Atoka	OK	**C+**	C+	B	277.6	3.02	7.2	8.1	18.2	3.1	**7.4**	9.2	13.5
AMG National Trust Bank	Greenwood Village	CO	**A-**	A-	A-	471.3	12.86	2.5	4.5	2.5	52.9	**7.6**	10.4	13.0
▲ Amistad Bank	Del Rio	TX	**A-**	B+	B+	28.8	-2.11	2.4	1.1	5.5	0.0	**10.0**	15.5	22.1
Amory Federal S&L Assn.	Amory	MS	**C-**	C-	C+	81.3	0.38	0.0	0.7	68.1	5.9	**10.0**	13.0	29.1
Anahuac National Bank	Anahuac	TX	**B+**	B+	A-	179.2	46.87	4.3	4.6	11.8	35.3	**8.0**	9.7	20.5
ANB Bank	Denver	CO	**B+**	B+	B+	2607.7	1.66	6.5	0.3	15.5	27.6	**6.3**	8.3	13.3
Anchor Bank	Juno Beach	FL	**C**	C	C	143.2	14.64	10.2	1.8	13.2	9.3	**7.1**	9.6	12.6
Anchor D Bank	Texhoma	OK	**B+**	B+	A-	230.1	37.95	7.7	4.3	4.6	26.8	**8.6**	10.1	15.7
Anchor State Bank	Anchor	IL	**C+**	C+	C+	16.3	9.90	7.4	1.7	1.6	14.5	**10.0**	12.3	17.9
Anderson Brothers Bank	Mullins	SC	**C+**	C+	C	846.9	12.80	6.3	29.4	16.0	3.1	**7.1**	9.6	12.5
▲ Anderson State Bank	Oneida	IL	**B**	B-	C+	89.6	4.66	2.4	2.1	4.4	31.2	**10.0**	15.7	35.9
▼ Andes State Bank	Lake Andes	SD	**D+**	D+	C-	22.3	-15.02	5.4	6.0	5.9	10.7	**10.0**	12.3	22.5
Andover Bank	Andover	OH	**B-**	B	B	427.9	7.58	0.4	1.0	29.4	40.4	**7.4**	9.2	20.4
Andover State Bank	Andover	KS	**C+**	C+	C+	112.0	16.35	10.0	1.0	18.2	4.5	**5.4**	8.0	11.3
Andrew Johnson Bank	Greeneville	TN	**A-**	B+	B+	382.8	2.97	5.0	1.1	30.7	8.0	**9.7**	10.8	15.7
Androscoggin Savings Bank	Lewiston	ME	**C+**	C+	C+	1098.8	7.16	10.7	0.2	27.0	8.4	**8.1**	10.5	13.4
Angelina Savings Bank, SSB	Lufkin	TX	**C+**	C+	C+	66.2	-2.27	12.1	18.8	20.1	0.0	**6.9**	8.9	18.6
Ann Arbor State Bank	Ann Arbor	MI	**A-**	A-	A-	333.1	7.54	17.1	1.3	7.8	15.4	**10.0**	12.3	15.4

Asset Quality Index	Adjusted Non-Performing Loans as a % of Total Loans	Adjusted Non-Performing Loans as a % of Capital	Net Charge-Offs Avg Loans	Profitability Index	Net Income ($Mil)	Return on Assets (R.O.A.)	Return on Equity (R.O.E.)	Net Interest Spread	Overhead Efficiency Ratio	Liquidity Index	Liquidity Ratio	Hot Money Ratio	Stability Index
3.0	1.06	na	0.32	**1.8**	0.1	0.12	1.22	2.74	88.9	**0.7**	23.9	51.7	**4.6**
4.5	0.88	na	1.02	**1.0**	0.0	-0.02	-0.14	4.67	98.7	**0.7**	12.2	28.4	**4.9**
8.3	0.00	na	-0.46	**7.4**	0.7	1.88	16.70	4.09	55.1	**3.2**	20.3	13.7	**6.8**
5.1	1.55	na	0.41	**4.8**	0.5	1.01	8.75	4.87	74.1	**3.2**	18.5	10.2	**6.5**
9.2	0.00	na	0.03	**6.5**	0.9	1.59	15.04	3.88	56.8	**6.3**	73.6	8.9	**6.8**
3.0	1.18	8.0	2.61	**10.0**	4302.8	4.75	48.81	7.24	59.6	**1.1**	21.3	1.7	**10.0**
6.2	0.40	na	0.20	**5.1**	5.1	1.12	13.08	4.24	67.8	**1.6**	5.5	13.5	**7.5**
7.0	0.12	1.0	0.05	**8.1**	21.5	1.62	14.49	4.20	44.0	**0.8**	17.1	53.9	**10.0**
6.2	1.36	na	0.08	**7.5**	1.3	1.86	15.47	4.77	61.7	**2.6**	35.5	21.1	**7.5**
8.9	0.39	na	0.06	**4.4**	9.3	1.09	11.98	3.20	68.4	**3.7**	27.7	15.3	**7.8**
7.1	0.27	0.9	0.00	**7.1**	3.5	1.29	10.44	3.82	54.8	**4.7**	21.3	4.9	**8.0**
7.5	0.00	0.0	-0.02	**10.0**	2.6	3.18	17.46	4.87	33.8	**4.1**	11.3	7.4	**10.0**
9.8	0.02	na	-0.05	**3.6**	0.3	0.57	4.78	3.44	76.3	**1.1**	23.1	32.2	**6.4**
4.7	2.41	na	-0.04	**3.0**	0.3	0.41	3.95	3.80	88.2	**0.7**	18.9	56.2	**5.6**
5.1	1.07	4.6	0.06	**8.5**	20.5	1.63	11.55	4.79	55.8	**2.8**	17.4	15.6	**9.9**
7.2	0.44	na	-0.02	**4.9**	3.9	1.19	11.61	3.34	64.3	**1.4**	33.2	43.5	**6.8**
7.5	0.07	na	0.00	**7.0**	3.1	1.28	9.29	4.23	53.4	**4.2**	26.1	9.0	**8.7**
6.2	0.61	2.7	0.08	**6.6**	45.4	1.59	15.89	3.63	56.4	**2.8**	17.0	8.1	**9.4**
4.3	0.58	3.5	0.05	**5.7**	7.2	1.23	11.36	3.63	67.5	**1.6**	10.7	12.3	**8.0**
7.6	0.13	0.8	0.00	**5.0**	15.8	0.94	7.28	3.79	71.6	**2.5**	15.0	16.8	**10.0**
6.4	1.19	6.1	0.00	**3.7**	1.5	0.68	6.29	4.17	83.4	**0.7**	15.2	31.5	**7.3**
8.3	0.01	na	0.10	**6.3**	1.1	1.50	11.41	4.06	65.1	**2.3**	36.6	27.1	**8.4**
7.4	0.45	1.7	0.13	**5.8**	28.4	1.22	12.78	3.85	65.3	**4.1**	11.1	7.8	**8.7**
6.6	0.39	na	-0.30	**9.3**	5.5	2.50	18.11	3.60	48.4	**0.8**	21.2	23.9	**9.6**
7.2	0.00	na	0.00	**9.7**	7.2	1.76	12.72	3.62	34.5	**0.6**	13.7	57.2	**9.8**
7.0	1.15	na	0.00	**6.8**	2.2	1.55	10.69	4.29	67.1	**0.9**	20.9	40.1	**9.0**
6.7	1.60	na	-0.03	**4.5**	4.4	0.85	7.39	3.59	65.2	**3.7**	26.1	11.8	**8.3**
7.2	0.05	na	0.00	**5.6**	4.8	0.99	9.12	4.35	66.8	**3.1**	18.8	12.9	**7.4**
8.0	0.00	na	0.00	**6.6**	0.6	1.52	7.28	3.48	52.6	**4.8**	56.8	13.7	**9.3**
6.1	1.16	6.3	0.46	**5.9**	60.7	1.14	12.40	3.86	59.7	**4.2**	13.3	7.4	**8.2**
5.1	0.69	na	0.31	**8.2**	3.0	1.81	19.15	4.07	56.4	**1.2**	13.2	29.0	**7.5**
3.0	1.15	na	0.09	**6.8**	11.3	1.61	13.56	3.38	49.0	**1.4**	7.9	20.2	**8.4**
5.5	0.45	na	0.33	**3.7**	2.3	0.74	7.40	5.00	79.0	**1.0**	11.3	30.8	**5.1**
5.4	3.29	na	0.11	**9.6**	10.6	2.35	19.67	3.52	44.4	**5.8**	41.3	4.9	**9.4**
5.4	2.12	na	0.00	**4.6**	4.3	0.89	6.57	3.93	69.3	**3.4**	17.2	12.1	**8.2**
4.1	1.56	na	0.06	**5.9**	0.6	1.48	13.43	4.12	66.7	**5.2**	32.9	5.4	**5.0**
9.3	0.18	na	-0.57	**2.7**	0.1	0.35	1.87	3.09	84.2	**6.2**	79.6	10.1	**6.5**
5.3	2.03	na	-0.02	**4.2**	0.6	0.63	7.73	4.02	79.7	**3.2**	16.5	9.3	**3.4**
5.1	1.46	4.9	0.15	**3.8**	1.0	0.72	6.52	4.11	75.3	**1.7**	18.4	23.0	**5.8**
9.9	0.00	na	2.20	**6.6**	9.1	1.08	11.55	2.34	59.1	**8.7**	104.1	0.0	**7.0**
4.8	0.93	4.1	0.10	**6.4**	119.5	1.19	8.83	4.02	66.3	**2.6**	9.7	12.7	**9.9**
8.2	0.22	na	0.02	**3.8**	6.2	0.71	7.76	3.43	76.4	**2.8**	7.4	14.4	**7.3**
3.0	2.27	na	0.07	**5.8**	2.7	1.29	14.75	4.33	72.3	**0.8**	18.5	33.8	**6.4**
9.0	0.00	na	0.00	**9.5**	6.8	1.91	19.84	2.20	68.1	**6.8**	46.4	0.3	**7.4**
7.5	0.06	na	0.01	**7.8**	0.3	1.54	10.02	5.27	72.2	**4.5**	23.1	6.6	**7.7**
7.9	0.00	na	0.00	**0.8**	-0.1	-0.22	-1.67	1.97	114.1	**1.4**	33.9	56.4	**5.3**
8.1	0.00	na	-0.05	**5.0**	1.3	1.14	10.83	4.28	73.0	**1.7**	21.5	23.4	**7.0**
8.9	0.22	1.5	-0.01	**6.0**	28.7	1.48	18.01	3.90	65.0	**5.0**	19.8	3.1	**7.7**
4.8	0.07	na	-0.17	**2.7**	0.2	0.15	1.50	3.29	101.3	**1.0**	16.2	30.3	**5.8**
8.2	0.00	na	0.01	**5.7**	2.2	1.38	12.94	3.64	65.3	**0.6**	15.2	48.0	**7.2**
8.6	0.00	na	0.00	**4.0**	0.1	0.75	6.10	3.81	72.9	**3.4**	36.4	14.8	**5.6**
3.2	1.11	8.4	1.25	**8.2**	9.3	1.51	15.93	7.37	60.9	**1.3**	11.4	26.3	**6.6**
9.3	0.00	na	0.05	**4.2**	0.7	1.09	6.96	2.91	57.9	**5.9**	69.7	10.4	**7.7**
2.0	6.41	na	0.03	**3.2**	0.1	0.66	5.66	3.39	76.7	**1.7**	41.7	32.8	**3.8**
7.8	0.66	na	0.03	**4.1**	2.9	0.94	9.32	3.12	75.4	**4.5**	33.3	10.5	**6.4**
4.1	0.62	na	0.00	**3.9**	0.6	0.75	9.83	3.95	74.1	**3.0**	13.2	13.8	**4.4**
7.8	0.43	2.1	0.02	**6.5**	3.5	1.24	11.67	4.50	63.9	**3.3**	18.6	12.8	**7.0**
4.4	2.56	na	0.00	**3.5**	5.2	0.66	6.21	3.32	76.1	**0.8**	12.4	13.3	**8.5**
5.5	1.58	na	0.03	**5.0**	0.5	1.06	11.53	4.49	73.0	**5.4**	43.0	8.0	**4.8**
8.3	0.50	2.3	0.06	**6.4**	3.0	1.27	10.54	3.67	60.4	**1.6**	21.9	22.8	**7.8**

Name	City	State	Rating	2018 Rating	2017 Rating	Total Assets ($Mil)	One Year Asset Growth	Asset Mix (As a % of Total Assets) Comm-ercial Loans	Cons-umer Loans	Mort-gage Loans	Secur-ities	Capital-ization Index	Lever-age Ratio	Risk-Based Capital Ratio
Anna State Bank	Anna	IL	**B+**	B+	B+	83.7	6.27	1.2	2.5	20.7	42.0	**10.0**	16.2	36.5
▲ Anna-Jonesboro National Bank	Anna	IL	**B+**	B	B-	219.7	-3.51	2.9	4.8	26.5	35.5	**10.0**	14.4	29.1
Anstaff Bank	Green Forest	AR	**B**	B	B	698.7	7.81	7.5	3.9	17.5	13.3	**6.7**	9.2	12.3
Anthem Bank & Trust	Plaquemine	LA	**C**	C-	C-	157.2	8.16	23.0	1.1	21.3	16.5	**8.8**	10.2	15.3
Antwerp Exchange Bank Co.	Antwerp	OH	**B-**	B	B-	116.7	11.99	7.3	3.6	25.2	11.7	**8.5**	10.5	13.7
ANZ Guam, Inc.	Hagatna	GU	**B-**	C+	C	322.8	0.75	8.3	0.3	8.0	0.0	**10.0**	15.5	42.9
▲ Apex Bank	Camden	TN	**B-**	C-	C+	591.5	5.63	3.7	1.9	53.0	0.3	**10.0**	13.1	20.1
▲ Apollo Bank	Miami	FL	**B-**	C	B-	746.8	9.17	8.8	2.5	15.7	15.9	**8.0**	9.7	13.9
Apollo Trust Co.	Apollo	PA	**B**	B	B-	158.8	-2.00	4.9	1.8	44.0	21.0	**9.9**	10.9	20.5
Apple Bank for Savings	New York	NY	**B-**	C+	C+	15107.7	10.89	34.3	0.1	0.7	22.8	**5.3**	7.3	14.3
Apple Creek Banking Co.	Apple Creek	OH	**B-**	C+	C+	143.4	6.58	6.8	0.3	24.6	12.2	**6.3**	8.3	12.6
▲ Apple River State Bank	Apple River	IL	**B+**	B	B	360.5	11.95	8.2	3.0	11.1	27.0	**9.2**	10.5	16.9
Applied Bank	Wilmington	DE	**A**	A	A-	194.9	11.73	0.2	0.0	3.1	0.0	**10.0**	23.6	60.9
Aquesta Bank	Cornelius	NC	**B**	B-	B-	504.8	10.50	9.2	0.0	7.8	12.1	**9.4**	10.9	14.5
▲ Arbor Bank	Nebraska City	NE	**C**	C-	C	352.2	8.17	16.8	1.4	10.7	7.8	**4.3**	8.4	10.6
Arcola First Bank	Arcola	IL	**B-**	B-	B-	111.0	2.69	1.0	0.3	3.1	77.8	**10.0**	11.4	29.2
Argentine Federal Savings	Kansas City	KS	**C**	C	C	55.6	5.91	0.0	0.4	54.0	25.6	**10.0**	13.5	29.5
Arizona Bank & Trust	Phoenix	AZ	**B+**	B+	B	695.2	6.95	19.3	1.3	10.8	18.3	**6.6**	9.9	12.2
Arkansas County Bank	De Witt	AR	**B**	B-	C+	181.0	3.13	4.5	2.3	16.8	29.3	**10.0**	11.3	19.2
▲ Arlington State Bank	Arlington	MN	**B**	C+	B-	50.6	-4.65	4.4	1.7	3.6	33.1	**10.0**	11.5	24.7
Armed Forces Bank, N.A.	Fort Leavenworth	KS	**A-**	B+	A-	1122.9	4.14	12.3	0.5	10.5	14.4	**10.0**	18.4	25.6
Armor Bank	Forrest City	AR	**C**	C	D+	95.0	11.24	5.6	1.4	12.6	19.2	**8.1**	9.8	16.1
Armstrong Bank	Muskogee	OK	**B-**	B-	B-	1025.4	10.74	5.8	5.6	20.0	15.0	**9.0**	10.4	15.3
Armstrong County Building and Loan Assn.	Ford City	PA	**C**	C	C	86.9	0.19	0.0	0.6	53.5	31.4	**10.0**	14.9	35.0
▼ Aroostook County Federal S&L Assn.	Caribou	ME	**C+**	B-	B-	134.3	8.35	12.3	11.2	53.3	12.2	**9.9**	11.0	17.9
Arrowhead Bank	Llano	TX	**A-**	B	B-	192.9	9.17	5.0	4.0	21.2	15.0	**9.2**	10.5	17.9
Arthur State Bank	Union	SC	**B+**	B	B-	511.5	2.25	5.4	1.5	29.1	17.5	**8.1**	9.7	15.2
Artisans' Bank	Wilmington	DE	**C**	C	C	542.4	1.62	6.3	0.2	17.3	19.2	**6.6**	9.1	12.2
Arundel Federal Savings Bank	Glen Burnie	MD	**C+**	C+	C+	431.3	-0.61	0.0	0.1	66.3	13.0	**10.0**	15.2	32.1
Arvest Bank	Fayetteville	AR	**B-**	B-	B-	19331.6	4.73	11.0	8.3	17.8	19.9	**6.4**	8.4	12.2
Ashton State Bank	Ashton	IA	**B**	B+	B+	49.6	2.24	8.0	2.4	9.2	27.4	**10.0**	13.2	16.8
Ashton State Bank	Ashton	NE	**D-**	D-	D-	20.6	-4.21	3.1	1.6	0.2	4.4	**8.0**	11.0	13.3
Asian Bank	Philadelphia	PA	**C+**	C+	C+	228.9	11.46	0.8	0.0	15.7	3.1	**6.7**	8.7	13.0
▼ Asian Pacific National Bank	San Gabriel	CA	**C**	C+	B-	55.9	-1.91	0.2	0.0	5.2	33.9	**10.0**	17.7	32.6
▼ Aspire Financial	Fargo	ND	**D+**	C	C	40.7	46.62	16.1	1.1	1.9	0.3	**5.9**	9.3	11.6
▲ Associated Bank, N.A.	Green Bay	WI	**B**	B-	B-	32553.2	-2.66	16.5	1.1	25.0	17.6	**6.4**	8.4	12.1
Associated Trust Co., N.A.	Milwaukee	WI	**U**	U	U	63.9	-11.12	0.0	0.0	0.0	1.6	**10.0**	85.8	153.2
Astra Bank	Scandia	KS	**B-**	C+	C	286.8	-10.30	9.1	1.2	12.6	22.7	**7.5**	9.7	12.9
Atascosa Bank	Pleasanton	TX	**B**	B-	C	89.1	-4.23	3.2	2.4	2.8	44.1	**8.2**	9.8	34.9
▲ Athol Savings Bank	Athol	MA	**B-**	C+	C+	448.5	1.74	1.6	3.0	46.1	20.7	**10.0**	13.6	22.2
Atkins Savings Bank & Trust	Atkins	IA	**B+**	B+	A-	96.9	9.45	8.5	4.0	11.9	26.6	**10.0**	13.4	19.1
Atlanta National Bank	Atlanta	IL	**C+**	C+	C+	59.4	2.64	3.1	3.2	11.3	55.9	**10.0**	13.9	32.1
▲ Atlantic Capital Bank, N.A.	Atlanta	GA	**B+**	B	C+	2411.2	-16.35	29.0	0.9	1.3	13.7	**10.0**	13.6	15.1
Atlantic Community Bankers Bank	Camp Hill	PA	**B**	B	B	820.9	12.52	1.8	0.0	2.5	16.3	**10.0**	12.7	22.6
Atlantic Union Bank	Richmond	VA	**B+**	B+	B+	17395.8	30.37	11.8	4.1	9.8	14.5	**7.3**	10.6	12.8
▲ Auburn Banking Co.	Auburn	KY	**B-**	C+	B-	81.0	3.66	5.7	4.6	24.8	16.8	**7.7**	9.5	13.0
Auburn Savings Bank, FSB	Auburn	ME	**C**	C	C	80.7	4.52	5.1	0.7	59.0	6.2	**7.2**	9.1	14.7
▲ Auburn State Bank	Auburn	NE	**A-**	A-	A-	176.2	3.25	2.2	1.3	9.2	36.8	**10.0**	18.3	29.3
▲ AuburnBank	Auburn	AL	**A-**	B+	B+	825.7	1.97	4.6	1.1	11.1	30.4	**10.0**	11.2	18.0
▲ Audubon State Bank	Audubon	IA	**B**	B	B	119.0	7.35	5.4	3.0	12.2	7.0	**7.9**	9.6	13.3
Austin Bank, Texas N.A.	Jacksonville	TX	**A**	A-	B+	1842.8	4.32	8.1	6.1	23.2	13.8	**10.0**	14.1	19.8
Austin Capital Bank SSB	Austin	TX	**B+**	B+	A-	127.6	24.29	3.3	3.1	56.5	1.6	**9.4**	10.6	20.8
Austin County State Bank	Bellville	TX	**B+**	B+	B+	184.8	10.45	18.7	1.3	22.8	14.7	**8.7**	10.1	14.8
Auto Club Trust, FSB	Dearborn	MI	**D-**	D	D	559.8	10.85	0.0	18.5	25.9	39.4	**8.9**	10.2	17.1
Availa Bank	Carroll	IA	**B+**	B+	B+	1068.0	57.07	8.1	0.6	9.6	16.8	**7.1**	9.2	12.6
AVB Bank	Broken Arrow	OK	**B**	B	B	384.7	7.02	14.6	0.5	24.3	8.3	**8.5**	10.5	13.8
Avidbank	San Jose	CA	**B+**	B	B-	1112.4	19.19	32.1	0.1	0.5	4.8	**5.7**	11.2	11.5
Avidia Bank	Hudson	MA	**B**	B	B-	1659.9	4.67	24.0	0.7	22.1	14.2	**8.1**	9.7	13.6
Axiom Bank, N.A.	Maitland	FL	**C+**	B-	B-	684.9	5.04	9.7	15.4	23.6	8.0	**10.0**	13.0	18.0
Axos Bank	San Diego	CA	**A-**	A-	A-	10877.7	11.33	7.7	3.2	43.8	1.7	**6.9**	9.1	12.5

Asset Quality Index	Adjusted Non-Performing Loans as a % of Total Loans	Adjusted Non-Performing Loans as a % of Capital	Net Charge-Offs Avg Loans	Profitability Index	Net Income ($Mil)	Return on Assets (R.O.A.)	Return on Equity (R.O.E.)	Net Interest Spread	Overhead Efficiency Ratio	Liquidity Index	Liquidity Ratio	Hot Money Ratio	Stability Index
9.4	0.67	na	0.00	**4.8**	0.7	1.07	6.75	3.24	59.5	**3.2**	47.8	20.5	**7.9**
5.6	2.08	na	0.27	**5.2**	1.7	1.04	7.36	3.92	60.9	**2.7**	30.3	18.4	**6.6**
6.5	0.44	na	0.05	**5.8**	7.2	1.45	14.61	3.92	63.1	**1.5**	11.4	23.9	**7.3**
5.1	1.73	na	0.00	**3.3**	0.7	0.59	5.74	3.97	86.2	**0.9**	17.3	33.7	**5.8**
4.3	1.33	na	0.00	**3.7**	0.5	0.65	6.05	3.90	80.2	**3.8**	12.7	9.6	**6.2**
6.1	5.81	na	-0.01	**3.6**	1.3	0.57	3.66	3.58	82.0	**7.0**	88.3	7.9	**7.5**
3.8	0.99	15.8	0.06	**10.0**	16.8	3.86	28.47	7.57	41.6	**0.6**	14.9	41.2	**9.8**
4.4	0.88	na	0.00	**5.3**	5.5	1.02	10.43	3.52	61.4	**2.4**	22.4	13.5	**6.8**
8.7	0.14	na	0.02	**4.8**	1.3	1.06	10.22	4.06	72.2	**3.5**	14.4	6.8	**6.8**
7.7	0.02	0.1	0.00	**4.2**	97.3	0.89	10.27	2.49	52.0	**1.8**	20.9	23.7	**6.4**
8.8	0.11	0.9	0.00	**5.6**	1.2	1.11	13.72	4.53	67.8	**4.8**	17.6	3.9	**4.4**
8.2	0.38	na	0.01	**5.9**	3.6	1.42	13.64	3.33	61.3	**2.5**	26.1	17.6	**6.7**
9.5	0.00	na	0.01	**8.7**	2.7	2.05	8.54	4.00	68.0	**8.2**	87.1	0.1	**9.0**
5.9	0.33	2.2	-0.01	**4.8**	3.3	0.93	9.29	3.62	67.5	**4.0**	12.8	8.3	**5.0**
5.4	1.79	na	0.21	**5.0**	3.1	1.22	14.70	4.06	72.5	**1.4**	8.8	20.1	**5.5**
10.0	0.00	na	0.00	**2.8**	0.4	0.50	4.33	2.27	81.8	**6.1**	63.5	10.0	**6.7**
8.9	0.41	na	0.00	**2.3**	0.1	0.22	1.64	3.02	87.9	**1.6**	33.9	37.5	**7.2**
6.7	0.80	2.2	0.06	**8.7**	9.1	1.77	16.97	4.44	56.0	**5.0**	25.4	3.2	**8.0**
4.9	1.92	na	0.15	**6.3**	2.0	1.55	13.70	4.32	62.3	**1.8**	23.3	22.9	**7.1**
8.3	0.79	na	-0.44	**6.3**	0.6	1.65	15.35	3.61	59.9	**5.6**	57.3	9.7	**6.0**
5.3	1.94	na	-0.25	**9.6**	15.2	1.89	10.12	3.69	68.0	**5.2**	27.7	6.9	**9.0**
5.6	1.82	na	0.30	**1.4**	0.0	0.06	0.34	3.19	87.8	**1.9**	24.7	20.8	**4.7**
4.3	1.89	10.2	0.26	**7.6**	10.8	1.43	12.44	4.52	64.5	**2.4**	26.6	23.6	**8.5**
9.4	0.36	na	0.00	**2.1**	0.1	0.20	1.34	1.55	80.5	**2.1**	43.4	40.4	**6.8**
5.1	0.89	na	0.10	**2.9**	0.4	0.43	3.87	3.21	77.4	**1.7**	21.2	23.9	**6.2**
8.6	0.02	0.8	0.04	**6.6**	2.4	1.70	16.54	4.43	60.3	**5.9**	36.1	2.0	**5.9**
5.7	1.50	5.5	0.05	**6.0**	4.4	1.17	12.26	4.27	68.7	**4.9**	23.9	3.9	**6.2**
4.8	1.44	na	-0.02	**3.2**	2.1	0.52	5.53	3.42	81.8	**2.7**	25.1	16.3	**6.0**
5.9	2.48	na	0.02	**2.3**	0.7	0.20	1.33	2.31	88.0	**1.6**	25.5	26.8	**7.3**
4.1	1.35	5.8	0.28	**4.4**	110.8	0.77	6.76	3.77	79.3	**5.1**	21.5	3.9	**9.0**
4.9	2.00	10.0	0.04	**5.8**	0.5	1.34	10.19	3.18	54.5	**2.2**	29.5	21.3	**7.6**
0.0	1.93	na	0.82	**2.7**	0.1	0.34	3.16	4.31	83.9	**2.1**	24.2	18.0	**3.3**
4.6	0.94	na	-0.01	**5.2**	1.8	1.09	12.73	3.44	57.1	**0.9**	22.0	42.4	**5.6**
9.5	0.00	na	0.00	**1.9**	0.1	0.11	0.66	2.78	95.5	**1.4**	32.9	53.4	**7.8**
6.0	0.05	na	0.38	**2.8**	0.1	0.40	3.56	3.98	88.1	**2.6**	33.8	19.7	**4.7**
5.6	0.67	3.6	0.24	**5.0**	262.9	1.05	9.59	2.86	63.7	**3.2**	12.3	6.5	**9.9**
7.2	na	0.0	na	**9.5**	10.8	22.53	26.08	2.62	76.6	**4.0**	292.9	0.0	**6.3**
5.3	0.44	na	0.01	**4.1**	2.1	0.94	9.34	4.03	73.7	**4.0**	8.9	7.8	**5.9**
9.9	0.00	na	0.21	**5.4**	0.9	1.26	13.05	3.09	48.8	**6.7**	94.5	9.4	**4.8**
9.1	0.67	2.6	0.04	**3.2**	1.9	0.58	4.35	2.85	83.0	**2.4**	32.6	16.6	**7.2**
5.5	0.00	na	0.00	**7.3**	1.1	1.58	11.97	3.35	39.8	**2.4**	37.4	25.6	**8.2**
9.2	0.50	na	-0.04	**3.3**	0.3	0.63	4.54	3.08	75.3	**5.6**	58.9	10.0	**6.7**
7.1	1.03	3.2	0.12	**5.5**	45.2	1.13	8.03	3.54	58.9	**4.8**	18.0	0.8	**8.7**
9.0	0.31	0.6	-0.16	**3.4**	3.1	0.55	4.11	2.33	85.5	**2.4**	42.6	27.8	**7.7**
5.8	0.33	2.0	0.18	**5.9**	152.8	1.23	7.68	3.83	61.7	**2.7**	14.4	13.5	**9.8**
5.9	1.05	na	0.00	**7.9**	1.1	1.91	21.02	4.47	60.1	**1.7**	15.8	21.9	**6.7**
5.2	2.76	na	-0.04	**3.1**	0.2	0.33	3.58	3.58	88.0	**1.0**	9.0	30.5	**4.4**
8.9	0.49	na	0.03	**6.0**	2.0	1.54	8.54	3.55	53.7	**2.4**	22.7	18.0	**8.3**
8.8	0.04	na	0.00	**5.3**	7.1	1.14	10.36	3.48	61.7	**3.0**	24.2	14.9	**7.8**
6.1	0.49	na	0.09	**7.7**	1.6	1.87	15.71	4.04	50.6	**1.2**	13.3	23.6	**8.6**
6.4	0.96	4.2	0.15	**8.9**	22.8	1.67	11.79	4.62	60.0	**3.8**	14.6	10.5	**10.0**
9.2	0.07	na	0.00	**5.7**	1.0	1.16	9.93	3.66	91.9	**0.8**	18.0	44.9	**6.2**
7.5	0.03	na	-0.02	**5.4**	1.6	1.22	12.18	4.31	68.7	**0.8**	19.5	39.5	**7.3**
6.8	0.58	2.6	0.09	**0.0**	-3.9	-0.95	-9.06	1.43	133.7	**0.9**	28.9	42.1	**6.6**
7.3	0.31	2.3	-0.02	**5.3**	7.6	1.06	9.22	3.58	61.9	**2.3**	21.1	16.9	**9.4**
5.4	0.74	na	-0.01	**4.1**	2.0	0.69	6.51	4.22	72.6	**1.6**	9.6	21.9	**7.3**
6.7	0.42	3.0	-0.01	**7.7**	10.3	1.36	12.42	4.76	56.7	**2.0**	16.9	19.8	**9.2**
5.7	1.09	6.4	0.24	**4.1**	8.4	0.69	6.71	3.91	79.9	**1.2**	20.4	8.4	**8.1**
4.4	2.07	na	0.22	**2.8**	1.4	0.29	1.88	4.32	90.6	**0.8**	20.7	35.6	**7.8**
6.3	0.57	5.1	0.27	**9.8**	143.5	1.84	19.23	4.32	40.2	**1.2**	7.6	15.7	**9.0**

Name	City	State	Rating	2018 Rating	2017 Rating	Total Assets ($Mil)	One Year Asset Growth	Asset Mix (As a % of Total Assets): Commercial Loans	Consumer Loans	Mortgage Loans	Securities	Capitalization Index	Leverage Ratio	Risk-Based Capital Ratio
BAC Community Bank	Stockton	CA	**B-**	B	B-	645.0	-3.45	4.5	1.4	6.6	21.4	**9.0**	10.3	14.7
BAC Florida Bank	Coral Gables	FL	**B+**	B	B-	2270.8	4.45	3.1	0.4	52.9	6.7	**8.5**	10.0	18.6
▲ Badger Bank	Fort Atkinson	WI	**A-**	B+	B+	136.7	-1.64	5.6	1.2	34.1	13.6	**10.0**	13.2	20.9
▲ Baker-Boyer National Bank	Walla Walla	WA	**B+**	B	B	606.2	2.03	9.5	0.7	11.5	18.3	**7.9**	9.6	18.4
▲ Balboa Thrift and Loan Assn.	Chula Vista	CA	**B-**	B-	B+	325.0	9.17	0.0	75.1	0.7	0.0	**9.3**	12.5	14.5
Baldwin State Bank	Baldwin City	KS	**C+**	B-	B-	78.1	3.62	4.8	3.0	25.1	31.9	**9.8**	10.9	28.1
Ballston Spa National Bank	Ballston Spa	NY	**B-**	C+	C+	577.2	11.33	6.7	4.8	34.2	12.7	**7.8**	9.6	13.6
▼ Baltic State Bank	Baltic	OH	**C+**	B+	B+	71.7	20.11	6.6	3.4	38.1	4.0	**5.9**	8.6	11.7
▼ Banc of California, N.A.	Santa Ana	CA	**C**	B-	B+	8598.8	-16.13	6.4	0.1	20.6	9.0	**9.6**	10.8	15.7
BancCentral, N.A.	Alva	OK	**C**	C	C	524.8	2.77	12.4	1.8	3.4	35.5	**5.7**	7.9	11.5
BancFirst	Oklahoma City	OK	**A-**	A-	B+	7553.8	-0.40	15.9	4.7	12.3	6.8	**8.6**	10.1	14.1
Banco Do Brasil Americas	Miami	FL	**C+**	C+	B-	653.9	-1.74	1.5	0.9	47.1	4.4	**7.6**	9.4	19.4
▲ Banco Popular de Puerto Rico	San Juan	PR	**C-**	D+	D+	41933.0	9.76	5.5	12.7	14.9	36.3	**7.7**	9.5	19.7
Banco Santander Puerto Rico	San Juan	PR	**C+**	C	C	6184.4	18.21	2.8	5.5	15.9	35.9	**10.0**	16.9	38.2
Bancorp Bank	Wilmington	DE	**B**	B-	D+	4947.1	13.36	5.7	17.0	1.4	29.6	**7.6**	9.4	25.1
BancorpSouth Bank	Tupelo	MS	**B+**	B+	B+	19863.0	15.09	8.6	1.3	18.9	13.9	**5.4**	9.1	11.3
▲ Bandera Bank	Bandera	TX	**B+**	B	B	70.4	-6.20	3.3	4.2	31.9	10.0	**9.6**	10.7	26.7
Banesco USA	Coral Gables	FL	**B**	B-	C	1835.5	47.25	10.8	0.0	19.0	16.7	**5.6**	7.6	12.0
Bangor Savings Bank	Bangor	ME	**B-**	B-	B-	4597.2	5.88	6.1	0.5	23.4	22.7	**7.1**	9.1	13.7
BANK	Wapello	IA	**C+**	C+	C-	92.7	4.21	9.1	6.5	19.4	0.0	**10.0**	12.7	15.9
Bank & Trust Co.	Litchfield	IL	**B**	B-	B-	341.3	11.31	9.1	5.5	16.0	24.4	**9.3**	10.5	15.5
Bank 1st	West Union	IA	**A-**	A-	A-	121.0	0.29	5.0	2.6	16.7	19.2	**10.0**	15.1	21.2
Bank 21	Carrollton	MO	**C+**	B-	B	147.8	-0.19	6.8	0.7	33.6	3.8	**5.7**	7.7	12.4
▲ BANK 34	Alamogordo	NM	**C+**	C+	C+	384.8	3.21	4.3	0.1	11.1	10.5	**9.1**	10.4	14.4
▲ Bank and Trust of Bryan/College Station	Bryan	TX	**A**	A-	A-	629.8	4.46	3.2	0.5	21.1	17.0	**10.0**	11.7	18.1
Bank and Trust, SSB	Del Rio	TX	**B+**	B+	B+	426.8	3.94	5.0	3.4	38.5	20.1	**7.4**	9.3	17.1
Bank First, N.A.	Manitowoc	WI	**B**	B	B+	2157.4	24.48	13.1	1.5	18.2	8.4	**5.1**	9.8	11.1
Bank Forward	Hannaford	ND	**B**	B	B-	654.8	9.87	9.2	3.0	9.7	4.5	**7.2**	10.0	12.7
Bank Independent	Sheffield	AL	**B**	B	B	1706.6	8.16	19.8	1.5	13.5	2.2	**6.8**	9.4	12.3
Bank Iowa	West Des Moines	IA	**B**	B	B	1354.6	5.61	6.2	1.0	8.6	19.1	**7.3**	9.3	12.7
Bank Leumi USA	New York	NY	**B**	B	B-	6808.5	-4.79	26.5	0.0	0.4	19.6	**9.7**	12.0	14.8
▲ Bank Michigan	Brooklyn	MI	**C-**	D	D-	103.5	3.94	9.5	0.1	16.3	10.0	**7.8**	9.5	13.6
Bank Midwest	Spirit Lake	IA	**B-**	B-	B	939.2	3.05	21.9	0.7	5.7	11.0	**5.8**	9.2	11.6
Bank Northwest	Hamilton	MO	**A-**	A-	B+	159.9	0.08	8.5	2.5	12.2	12.1	**8.4**	10.0	14.6
Bank of Abbeville & Trust Co.	Abbeville	LA	**B-**	B-	C+	173.5	-1.71	7.8	2.1	14.7	34.6	**10.0**	17.2	30.6
▲ Bank of Advance	Advance	MO	**A-**	B+	A-	328.8	-0.04	6.9	6.3	30.5	14.8	**10.0**	14.2	19.6
▲ Bank of Akron	Akron	NY	**B-**	C	C	388.9	14.73	9.7	0.4	23.7	9.8	**7.8**	9.7	13.2
Bank of Alapaha	Alapaha	GA	**B+**	B+	A-	176.9	10.87	25.1	8.5	18.7	12.5	**10.0**	11.3	16.2
▲ Bank of Alma	Alma	WI	**A**	A-	A	243.9	7.46	4.7	0.8	6.3	29.0	**10.0**	47.1	63.3
Bank of America California, N.A.	San Francisco	CA	**A-**	A-	B+	13363.0	-13.24	0.0	0.0	76.6	0.0	**10.0**	14.8	34.5
▲ Bank of America, N.A.	Charlotte	NC	**B+**	B	B-	1812976.0	0.84	16.4	9.3	12.1	23.4	**6.8**	8.9	13.5
Bank of Anguilla	Anguilla	MS	**C-**	C-	C+	150.7	-1.20	5.8	5.5	7.8	19.6	**9.5**	10.7	14.9
Bank of Ann Arbor	Ann Arbor	MI	**A-**	A-	B+	1713.9	3.59	16.2	0.8	6.8	4.7	**7.7**	10.6	13.1
▲ Bank of Austin	Austin	TX	**D+**	D		163.7	42.73	26.3	0.0	2.0	10.1	**10.0**	20.0	26.1
Bank of Baker	Baker	MT	**C+**	C	C-	141.1	5.05	13.2	0.9	2.8	14.2	**10.0**	12.1	16.4
Bank of Bartlett	Bartlett	TN	**C+**	C	C	351.8	-2.73	5.7	3.1	22.7	20.2	**6.4**	8.4	14.1
Bank of Bearden	Bearden	AR	**B**	B	B	54.4	-2.68	7.9	5.7	10.2	20.8	**8.7**	12.4	13.9
Bank of Beaver City	Beaver	OK	**B**	B	B	128.5	-10.43	11.8	2.8	15.1	30.6	**10.0**	11.2	17.8
Bank of Belle Glade	Belle Glade	FL	**B-**	C+	C	99.3	-1.35	5.3	0.4	13.1	33.1	**8.1**	9.7	27.5
Bank of Belleville	Belleville	IL	**C+**	C+	C+	226.0	17.55	14.1	0.8	12.4	13.3	**6.1**	8.2	12.2
▲ Bank of Bennington	Bennington	NE	**B-**	C	C+	145.9	16.42	19.1	2.7	14.1	11.2	**9.5**	12.4	14.6
Bank of Bennington	Bennington	VT	**B**	B	B-	423.7	3.01	2.4	0.2	57.3	11.6	**10.0**	11.3	21.1
▲ Bank of Benoit	Benoit	MS	**C-**	C-	C-	17.4	15.42	2.9	8.7	0.6	38.0	**10.0**	11.5	26.7
▲ Bank of Billings	Billings	MO	**B-**	C+	C+	58.5	1.95	12.1	3.9	31.6	0.0	**8.7**	10.1	14.2
Bank of Bird-in-Hand	Bird in Hand	PA	**B**	B	C+	452.5	39.07	6.6	0.0	21.6	0.0	**10.0**	12.5	15.6
Bank of Blue Valley	Overland Park	KS	**B+**	B	B	1346.3	127.12	14.8	2.0	3.8	26.9	**9.6**	11.2	14.6
Bank of Bluffs	Bluffs	IL	**B-**	B-	C+	54.4	-2.47	3.7	5.9	17.2	23.9	**10.0**	14.4	23.4
▲ Bank of Bolivar	Bolivar	MO	**B-**	C+	C+	305.6	6.27	5.4	3.3	26.5	9.1	**6.7**	8.7	12.5
Bank of Botetourt	Buchanan	VA	**B-**	C+	C+	484.6	14.04	5.2	4.5	28.5	3.0	**8.6**	10.8	13.8
Bank of Bourbonnais	Bourbonnais	IL	**B+**	B+	A-	68.1	7.07	1.5	4.6	11.7	0.7	**10.0**	13.2	18.9

Asset Quality Index	Adjusted Non-Performing Loans as a % of Total Loans	Adjusted Non-Performing Loans as a % of Capital	Net Charge-Offs Avg Loans	Profitability Index	Net Income ($Mil)	Return on Assets (R.O.A.)	Return on Equity (R.O.E.)	Net Interest Spread	Overhead Efficiency Ratio	Liquidity Index	Liquidity Ratio	Hot Money Ratio	Stability Index
4.8	0.66	na	0.00	**5.8**	6.7	1.39	13.62	4.08	65.3	**5.1**	28.1	3.8	**7.6**
6.4	1.82	7.8	-0.01	**7.0**	24.0	1.42	14.71	3.16	50.0	**1.5**	26.3	42.1	**8.5**
7.1	0.58	na	-0.01	**8.2**	2.5	2.51	19.11	4.16	50.8	**4.4**	19.6	6.8	**7.3**
7.7	0.80	na	-0.01	**5.8**	5.3	1.19	12.48	3.97	75.2	**6.5**	46.9	2.2	**6.7**
4.5	0.46	na	1.40	**4.1**	1.3	0.56	4.41	5.91	59.9	**0.4**	8.8	76.4	**6.3**
5.9	1.67	na	1.44	**3.0**	0.3	0.51	4.82	2.81	71.5	**5.1**	39.0	9.2	**6.3**
6.3	0.36	na	0.05	**4.2**	3.1	0.75	8.34	3.65	74.0	**4.3**	5.3	5.6	**5.8**
8.6	0.03	na	0.01	**3.7**	0.3	0.50	5.71	4.58	87.7	**1.6**	6.6	20.1	**4.2**
7.4	0.94	4.6	0.70	**2.5**	16.7	0.23	2.09	2.94	68.7	**1.8**	15.9	19.1	**7.2**
3.9	1.33	7.9	0.04	**2.8**	2.3	0.56	6.37	3.25	82.8	**0.9**	22.8	33.4	**5.4**
6.7	0.70	3.6	0.06	**8.7**	96.7	1.69	15.49	3.87	55.1	**5.0**	23.0	5.0	**9.2**
8.7	0.00	na	0.22	**3.6**	3.2	0.64	6.06	3.45	79.7	**1.9**	28.5	24.6	**7.9**
1.7	8.26	28.5	1.03	**7.2**	453.0	1.52	15.23	4.38	57.4	**4.2**	20.1	8.4	**7.6**
3.1	9.93	19.2	0.96	**6.2**	61.7	1.42	8.27	4.08	60.7	**4.8**	28.0	9.3	**7.2**
5.0	1.72	5.9	0.06	**8.3**	55.5	1.56	16.53	3.96	65.2	**2.6**	44.7	0.0	**5.4**
5.4	0.63	3.3	0.05	**6.2**	168.4	1.21	9.76	3.86	68.2	**3.5**	8.0	10.4	**9.7**
6.9	0.22	na	-0.05	**7.0**	0.9	1.78	16.79	4.24	61.4	**5.6**	47.4	7.9	**6.5**
8.5	0.76	2.7	-0.12	**6.4**	19.9	1.79	21.35	3.23	65.9	**1.8**	28.3	36.8	**6.5**
8.2	0.41	2.1	0.01	**3.8**	24.7	0.73	7.37	3.02	78.6	**3.7**	13.7	5.4	**8.2**
3.8	2.80	na	0.08	**2.8**	0.3	0.43	3.29	4.08	86.3	**1.6**	9.6	20.6	**7.4**
6.0	0.77	3.2	0.05	**5.1**	2.5	1.02	9.69	3.56	64.2	**1.6**	18.7	23.4	**6.5**
8.4	0.15	na	-0.01	**7.4**	1.5	1.69	11.63	4.05	57.0	**4.0**	28.0	11.1	**8.9**
5.7	1.33	na	0.05	**4.6**	1.2	1.04	13.48	3.41	71.7	**1.9**	18.8	19.8	**5.8**
5.6	1.20	na	0.00	**3.5**	0.2	0.49	4.78	3.86	82.0	**1.9**	15.4	13.0	**6.1**
8.7	0.04	na	0.00	**9.2**	8.5	1.83	16.42	4.10	46.5	**4.2**	21.3	8.1	**8.7**
8.4	0.17	na	0.01	**5.6**	4.2	1.33	13.79	4.10	73.0	**3.1**	10.1	12.8	**6.2**
5.8	0.42	2.5	0.55	**7.4**	20.0	1.42	13.37	4.01	50.9	**3.6**	10.6	10.0	**9.2**
5.2	0.38	3.7	0.04	**7.9**	9.1	1.92	18.40	4.49	67.7	**1.4**	7.3	15.0	**8.9**
5.1	1.13	8.1	0.64	**7.5**	18.1	1.46	14.91	5.57	65.4	**1.8**	17.1	18.9	**8.7**
7.5	0.61	3.3	0.00	**4.4**	9.8	0.99	10.76	3.38	71.1	**1.6**	13.4	24.1	**8.6**
4.7	1.55	10.3	0.52	**5.0**	56.4	1.07	9.02	3.53	59.3	**1.4**	23.8	26.8	**8.5**
3.6	1.42	na	0.07	**2.2**	0.7	0.89	9.42	3.80	96.4	**0.8**	18.0	35.0	**3.8**
4.2	0.88	na	0.16	**5.7**	7.5	1.09	11.27	3.95	68.3	**1.6**	14.4	16.2	**7.2**
7.5	0.29	1.8	0.03	**9.6**	3.0	2.34	25.28	4.44	46.3	**3.9**	15.1	9.4	**7.6**
8.7	3.52	na	0.01	**3.5**	0.9	0.67	3.98	3.34	76.4	**3.1**	36.0	18.1	**7.9**
7.1	0.89	na	0.07	**10.0**	5.8	2.34	17.37	4.75	53.2	**1.6**	8.3	20.8	**9.5**
4.8	1.55	na	-0.02	**5.7**	3.9	1.39	13.92	3.96	66.1	**1.5**	9.2	16.0	**6.2**
5.1	0.90	na	0.10	**5.3**	1.2	0.94	8.47	3.77	61.9	**0.9**	17.1	33.5	**6.4**
8.6	2.53	na	0.00	**10.0**	5.5	3.09	6.62	4.64	14.5	**7.0**	72.1	5.2	**10.0**
6.3	3.29	11.3	0.02	**9.5**	223.0	2.08	15.11	2.99	15.6	**5.7**	26.5	0.0	**8.7**
5.4	0.94	3.5	0.38	**7.9**	20464.0	1.53	12.94	3.14	47.1	**6.2**	40.5	2.7	**10.0**
2.4	2.51	na	-0.26	**4.4**	1.0	0.93	9.46	4.64	72.8	**1.0**	12.0	30.9	**5.2**
8.1	0.11	0.7	0.08	**9.7**	25.2	1.99	17.74	4.38	48.5	**3.5**	16.6	6.1	**9.8**
8.3	0.00	na	0.00	**0.8**	0.1	0.08	0.39	3.60	89.9	**5.2**	36.8	7.1	**2.3**
3.2	2.37	na	0.33	**9.5**	2.1	2.06	16.77	4.75	50.6	**4.6**	17.1	5.0	**8.5**
2.9	2.84	na	0.06	**4.3**	2.2	0.82	9.45	4.05	79.0	**4.5**	19.4	6.0	**4.3**
7.6	0.38	na	0.00	**6.8**	0.6	1.63	13.55	3.88	54.8	**4.3**	42.9	14.2	**7.6**
8.0	0.77	na	0.64	**4.2**	0.9	0.86	7.93	3.74	76.3	**1.7**	21.2	23.4	**6.9**
8.2	2.98	na	0.00	**4.1**	0.7	0.87	9.49	3.05	64.0	**5.2**	55.7	11.4	**5.0**
8.6	0.00	0.1	0.00	**3.0**	0.8	0.51	6.45	2.80	78.2	**1.1**	18.5	27.6	**4.5**
7.5	0.04	na	0.43	**4.2**	0.9	0.83	6.51	4.51	69.1	**4.6**	17.0	4.8	**5.3**
7.3	1.01	4.9	0.15	**4.0**	2.4	0.76	6.92	3.12	70.7	**3.0**	15.3	13.0	**6.5**
5.0	0.82	na	0.31	**3.6**	0.1	0.80	7.36	4.19	74.5	**3.2**	70.5	28.0	**3.7**
2.8	1.35	7.4	-0.03	**5.0**	0.4	0.92	6.47	5.47	73.8	**3.7**	8.8	10.1	**6.7**
8.8	0.04	na	0.00	**4.6**	2.8	0.93	6.91	2.95	56.3	**1.7**	20.2	22.8	**6.6**
6.3	0.40	1.7	0.04	**5.0**	8.2	1.13	8.12	3.87	70.7	**5.8**	35.0	6.4	**7.4**
6.3	1.25	na	0.55	**3.3**	0.3	0.63	4.26	3.96	77.5	**2.5**	27.2	13.3	**6.9**
6.0	0.42	na	0.01	**4.2**	1.9	0.85	10.04	3.80	74.2	**1.4**	10.3	21.8	**5.4**
5.7	0.37	na	0.08	**5.1**	3.7	1.09	10.44	3.88	64.8	**1.2**	10.6	28.1	**5.9**
7.2	0.00	na	0.02	**3.3**	0.2	0.46	3.31	3.28	81.5	**1.5**	25.9	28.4	**6.8**

Name	City	State	Rating	2018 Rating	2017 Rating	Total Assets ($Mil)	One Year Asset Growth	Asset Mix (As a % of Total Assets) Commercial Loans	Consumer Loans	Mortgage Loans	Securities	Capitalization Index	Leverage Ratio	Risk-Based Capital Ratio
Bank of Bozeman	Bozeman	MT	**C+**	C+	C+	77.4	3.57	14.7	0.6	21.7	2.1	**7.2**	10.0	12.7
▼ Bank of Brenham, N.A.	Brenham	TX	**B**	B+	B+	455.2	20.60	2.5	1.0	7.3	78.5	**9.3**	10.5	29.1
Bank of Brewton	Brewton	AL	**C+**	B	C+	47.3	-7.18	6.4	10.8	5.8	45.1	**10.0**	22.7	43.0
Bank of Bridger, N.A.	Bridger	MT	**B**	B	B	530.5	6.56	4.9	2.2	8.5	43.6	**6.8**	8.8	17.1
Bank of Brodhead	Brodhead	WI	**B+**	B+	A-	157.4	5.04	8.7	1.2	9.4	31.7	**10.0**	15.3	23.4
Bank of Brookfield-Purdin, N.A.	Brookfield	MO	**B-**	B-	B-	88.4	-3.34	1.1	1.3	5.9	50.2	**10.0**	12.6	36.2
Bank of Brookhaven	Brookhaven	MS	**B+**	B+	B	166.0	9.33	7.6	2.4	15.2	27.6	**10.0**	12.1	19.8
Bank of Buffalo	Buffalo	KY	**B**	B	B	73.5	0.80	1.5	5.6	28.0	38.8	**10.0**	11.1	18.5
▲ Bank of Burlington	Burlington	CO	**B+**	B	B	65.1	13.12	9.3	1.0	0.0	12.0	**10.0**	14.2	21.6
Bank of Cadiz and Trust Co.	Cadiz	KY	**B-**	B-	C+	117.6	10.50	3.1	2.8	23.7	27.0	**7.0**	9.0	16.8
▲ Bank of Calhoun County	Hardin	IL	**C+**	C	C	66.8	0.65	1.2	2.5	31.0	12.5	**7.8**	9.5	18.8
Bank of Camilla	Camilla	GA	**B+**	B+	B+	104.5	4.99	10.9	1.2	14.5	31.7	**10.0**	16.4	16.6
Bank of Canton	Canton	MA	**B**	B	B+	644.0	-1.71	1.3	0.3	30.9	8.8	**10.0**	11.7	16.3
Bank of Carbondale	Carbondale	IL	**B+**	B+	B+	246.2	12.65	9.4	2.2	17.6	21.5	**10.0**	13.6	22.6
Bank of Cashton	Cashton	WI	**A-**	A-	A-	96.4	9.18	18.0	2.2	14.0	15.8	**10.0**	11.0	15.1
Bank of Castile	Castile	NY	**B**	B	B	1483.1	-1.12	13.0	0.6	16.4	17.3	**6.2**	8.9	11.9
Bank of Cattaraugus	Cattaraugus	NY	**D+**	D+	D+	23.9	3.13	7.8	7.2	17.8	33.9	**7.0**	9.0	20.0
▲ Bank of Cave City	Cave City	AR	**B-**	C+	B-	122.0	10.66	6.7	4.3	19.3	11.9	**7.8**	9.6	16.4
▲ Bank of Central Florida	Lakeland	FL	**B+**	B	B	511.9	4.04	13.6	2.7	14.3	18.5	**7.1**	9.1	13.8
Bank of Charles Town	Charles Town	WV	**B-**	B-	B-	504.9	6.23	3.9	1.6	36.1	8.5	**9.3**	10.6	15.4
Bank of Charlotte County	Phenix	VA	**A-**	A-	A-	139.8	3.83	7.3	3.7	38.6	14.2	**10.0**	15.4	23.0
Bank of Cherokee County	Hulbert	OK	**C+**	C+	C+	116.6	15.06	4.0	9.6	25.1	2.8	**6.3**	8.3	12.6
Bank of Chestnut	Chestnut	IL	**D**	D	D-	18.1	-0.84	3.2	9.8	34.1	12.4	**8.6**	10.1	15.8
▲ Bank of Clarendon	Manning	SC	**A**	A-	A-	277.5	6.83	5.6	2.9	12.4	29.0	**10.0**	14.9	24.2
▲ Bank of Clarke County	Berryville	VA	**B+**	B	B+	844.5	8.47	5.3	1.0	22.5	16.3	**9.0**	10.7	14.2
Bank of Clarks	Clarks	NE	**C+**	C+	C+	39.1	9.11	4.9	13.4	3.9	3.7	**8.3**	11.4	13.6
Bank of Clarkson	Clarkson	KY	**B+**	B+	A-	120.6	2.98	1.7	5.9	26.4	21.2	**10.0**	13.9	18.0
▲ Bank of Cleveland	Cleveland	TN	**B+**	C+	B	278.7	4.48	4.4	0.6	18.9	1.4	**10.0**	15.3	20.4
▲ Bank of Clovis	Clovis	NM	**A-**	B+	B	207.7	4.63	12.1	3.2	13.2	31.8	**10.0**	13.1	27.4
Bank of Colorado	Fort Collins	CO	**A-**	A-	A-	4427.8	14.91	3.7	0.9	11.8	31.4	**7.2**	9.2	14.9
▲ Bank of Columbia	Columbia	KY	**B-**	C+	B-	143.8	4.52	11.0	5.8	20.3	14.6	**8.5**	10.3	13.8
Bank of Commerce	Ammon	ID	**A**	A	A	1254.9	6.44	14.8	0.8	2.1	9.9	**10.0**	16.6	18.5
Bank of Commerce	Chanute	KS	**B-**	B-	B-	181.0	6.79	10.4	2.9	14.2	29.0	**7.6**	9.4	18.6
Bank of Commerce	White Castle	LA	**B-**	B-	B	59.5	1.69	13.9	3.0	11.2	27.6	**10.0**	12.7	19.3
▲ Bank of Commerce	Greenwood	MS	**B+**	B	B+	545.6	12.99	7.4	2.9	18.5	31.5	**9.2**	10.5	17.7
▲ Bank of Commerce	Chelsea	OK	**B+**	B	B-	148.3	2.51	8.9	7.7	15.0	12.0	**10.0**	12.8	18.3
▲ Bank of Commerce	Chouteau	OK	**C+**	C	C	38.2	-3.16	6.7	3.5	14.9	37.4	**7.2**	9.1	20.1
▲ Bank of Commerce	Duncan	OK	**C-**	D+	C-	309.6	1.30	17.3	1.8	5.1	5.4	**8.7**	11.9	13.9
Bank of Commerce	Stilwell	OK	**B**	B+	A-	81.3	0.89	16.8	3.3	5.7	21.3	**10.0**	12.8	17.7
Bank of Commerce	Rawlins	WY	**A-**	A-	A-	140.1	10.82	7.5	1.9	18.8	33.8	**10.0**	12.0	22.3
Bank of Commerce & Trust Co.	Crowley	LA	**B-**	B-	B-	303.1	0.51	4.5	2.2	5.8	65.6	**10.0**	13.3	30.7
Bank of Commerce and Trust Co.	Wellington	KS	**B-**	B-	B-	79.7	4.06	6.2	5.1	17.3	35.8	**6.3**	8.3	15.8
▲ Bank of Cordell	Cordell	OK	**B**	B-	B-	37.4	-5.50	15.5	1.1	40.8	0.8	**10.0**	11.1	16.6
Bank of Coushatta	Coushatta	LA	**B-**	B	B	224.0	5.99	2.6	1.8	16.1	52.4	**8.7**	10.1	15.9
Bank of Crocker	Waynesville	MO	**C+**	B-	C-	124.9	0.51	2.5	1.8	15.0	35.3	**10.0**	11.6	26.5
Bank of Crockett	Bells	TN	**B+**	B+	A-	177.5	11.75	7.0	2.6	4.9	51.9	**9.6**	10.7	19.4
Bank of Cushing	Cushing	OK	**B+**	A-	A-	116.0	11.28	10.8	3.2	1.2	51.3	**10.0**	14.5	26.2
▲ Bank of Dade	Trenton	GA	**A-**	B+	A-	108.3	3.48	1.6	4.9	26.1	44.6	**10.0**	11.5	25.7
Bank of Dawson	Dawson	GA	**B+**	B+	A-	123.8	7.23	4.4	3.2	18.1	15.8	**10.0**	19.4	27.7
▲ Bank of Deerfield	Deerfield	WI	**A-**	B+	A	155.0	8.85	6.0	1.1	29.4	6.6	**10.0**	12.7	16.2
Bank of Delight	Delight	AR	**A-**	B+	A-	133.3	9.42	8.3	2.5	16.3	6.7	**10.0**	14.0	18.1
▲ Bank of Delmarva	Salisbury	MD	**C-**	C-	C	792.3	7.39	7.9	0.2	15.5	7.1	**6.8**	9.0	12.4
Bank of Denton	Denton	KS	**C**	C	C+	18.3	-1.21	4.5	10.9	29.7	22.6	**10.0**	18.9	30.9
Bank of Denver	Denver	CO	**C+**	B-	C-	232.0	4.74	0.5	7.4	11.1	18.8	**9.1**	10.4	16.2
▲ Bank of DeSoto, N.A.	Desoto	TX	**B+**	B	B-	180.9	-0.47	8.2	14.8	19.7	1.3	**10.0**	11.5	18.7
Bank of Dickson	Dickson	TN	**B**	B	B	238.2	6.49	3.4	2.3	37.7	33.5	**10.0**	13.2	26.7
Bank of Dixon County	Ponca	NE	**B**	B-	B	90.7	-0.53	10.4	6.0	15.8	15.2	**10.0**	12.6	18.7
Bank of Doniphan	Doniphan	NE	**B**	B-	B-	114.3	1.48	10.4	3.1	10.2	21.4	**5.5**	9.8	11.4
▲ Bank of Dudley	Dublin	GA	**B+**	B	B	217.6	0.37	9.5	4.4	15.6	12.2	**10.0**	13.0	19.6
▼ Bank of Eastern Oregon	Heppner	OR	**D+**	C	C-	482.8	20.27	10.0	0.9	4.5	4.9	**4.3**	9.4	10.6

Arrows denote recent upgrades ▲ or downgrades ▼

Asset Quality Index	Adjusted Non-Performing Loans as a % of Total Loans	Adjusted Non-Performing Loans as a % of Capital	Net Charge-Offs Avg Loans	Profitability Index	Net Income ($Mil)	Return on Assets (R.O.A.)	Return on Equity (R.O.E.)	Net Interest Spread	Overhead Efficiency Ratio	Liquidity Index	Liquidity Ratio	Hot Money Ratio	Stability Index
4.4	1.39	9.1	-0.01	5.1	1.9	3.25	28.67	4.67	81.5	1.0	7.9	30.5	6.8
7.3	3.52	3.8	0.01	4.1	3.1	0.94	7.26	2.32	52.1	2.6	53.6	47.3	7.6
2.1	17.52	22.1	0.33	3.3	0.2	0.58	2.62	3.99	81.9	5.7	47.7	7.1	6.6
6.7	1.50	na	0.02	5.1	3.8	0.96	9.36	3.51	62.2	4.1	31.4	11.6	6.9
8.8	1.27	na	0.00	4.8	1.1	0.99	6.51	3.39	63.8	2.5	42.6	28.9	7.5
9.6	0.00	na	-0.01	3.9	0.7	0.95	7.80	2.86	66.7	6.0	61.5	7.8	7.0
8.8	0.00	na	0.07	4.6	1.2	0.97	8.05	3.56	70.3	2.5	35.6	23.7	7.0
6.5	0.60	na	0.23	6.3	0.8	1.49	13.04	3.16	52.7	2.0	42.5	28.8	7.7
8.8	0.00	na	0.00	6.1	0.6	1.46	10.16	3.73	59.8	3.1	46.4	21.6	7.2
6.0	0.71	4.6	0.23	4.1	0.7	0.90	9.61	3.70	76.3	2.9	39.2	21.2	4.5
6.0	1.60	na	0.06	3.2	0.3	0.57	5.69	3.24	76.0	4.3	34.1	11.6	4.7
6.7	2.70	na	-0.03	5.4	0.9	1.17	7.43	4.15	69.4	1.8	25.6	23.8	7.8
7.8	0.08	na	-0.05	4.7	4.1	0.84	7.65	4.03	73.8	4.6	12.9	4.3	7.1
4.4	5.28	na	0.10	5.2	1.6	0.96	7.19	3.65	55.1	4.9	25.0	3.9	6.6
7.8	0.13	na	0.19	7.3	1.2	1.73	15.48	3.72	54.8	3.3	30.9	14.4	8.0
8.5	0.19	1.6	0.02	7.3	16.4	1.45	17.24	3.68	53.3	3.8	3.3	7.4	7.4
5.2	2.19	na	0.03	3.3	0.1	0.61	7.55	4.44	84.9	5.3	25.0	1.1	3.0
4.5	1.28	na	0.13	5.0	0.9	1.07	11.69	4.32	72.9	1.1	9.0	24.2	5.7
8.5	0.04	na	0.08	6.0	5.2	1.33	15.53	3.41	56.2	4.5	29.5	8.7	6.5
7.1	0.79	na	0.00	4.0	2.5	0.66	6.54	3.40	78.2	1.8	13.9	19.3	6.0
7.4	0.99	4.6	0.06	6.0	1.2	1.16	7.56	4.67	70.5	3.4	17.7	12.0	8.7
4.8	1.07	na	0.07	3.1	0.4	0.48	5.60	4.36	87.8	1.9	20.1	20.1	4.5
2.2	2.62	16.5	0.17	2.5	0.1	0.34	3.45	3.93	77.6	4.5	18.4	3.9	4.0
8.8	0.47	1.1	0.01	6.9	2.9	1.40	9.78	3.75	58.3	4.5	29.9	9.1	8.5
6.8	0.74	na	0.24	5.7	7.2	1.17	10.87	4.03	68.5	3.6	23.2	11.7	8.1
3.2	0.49	5.2	-0.12	5.3	0.3	0.99	8.68	4.98	72.9	3.8	13.9	10.1	6.3
8.5	0.00	0.7	0.01	8.1	1.5	1.68	12.47	4.35	58.0	2.7	21.3	16.3	7.0
5.9	0.69	na	-0.15	8.9	3.3	1.59	10.60	4.42	57.3	3.8	13.7	9.9	9.3
8.6	1.02	na	0.10	6.3	2.0	1.31	10.26	4.33	63.4	2.2	28.2	20.7	7.4
6.5	0.59	4.4	0.01	7.5	47.0	1.50	15.36	3.39	53.8	4.6	28.5	11.2	8.8
4.9	0.89	na	0.05	8.8	2.1	1.99	19.51	4.48	58.8	1.7	12.8	20.9	8.2
8.2	0.31	1.4	0.11	10.0	20.9	2.34	14.50	5.12	36.0	4.1	28.5	13.5	10.0
8.8	0.03	na	0.00	3.8	1.2	0.86	9.22	3.15	72.9	4.0	25.6	10.1	5.7
5.9	2.38	10.8	0.00	3.9	0.4	0.85	7.01	3.94	78.3	2.7	8.4	14.9	6.6
6.1	0.46	na	0.03	7.9	6.1	1.62	15.13	3.30	45.6	1.8	23.6	22.2	7.4
7.7	0.50	na	0.07	5.5	1.4	1.25	9.48	5.25	74.6	2.9	20.4	15.1	6.5
8.6	0.00	na	0.18	4.3	0.3	0.92	10.56	4.14	77.6	4.5	27.3	7.8	4.9
2.4	2.37	na	0.77	6.0	3.3	1.41	11.76	4.47	60.6	1.5	16.3	24.3	7.4
5.7	0.97	na	0.10	8.0	1.3	2.20	16.73	5.15	58.9	1.8	15.0	20.4	7.4
9.0	0.09	0.4	-0.02	6.2	1.4	1.34	10.55	4.00	60.3	1.5	17.5	25.4	7.4
6.8	3.22	na	0.08	3.4	1.5	0.62	5.21	2.65	70.9	4.5	34.2	10.7	6.1
6.9	0.27	na	0.09	3.9	0.5	0.84	9.26	3.79	78.1	2.8	26.9	16.7	5.8
8.6	0.00	na	-0.08	9.3	0.8	2.54	24.08	5.30	54.4	0.6	3.1	35.6	6.8
4.9	3.73	na	0.13	5.5	2.4	1.41	14.38	3.38	58.0	2.6	35.0	21.5	6.5
6.6	2.83	9.3	0.24	2.4	0.4	0.41	3.56	3.30	86.8	3.2	42.1	19.6	6.3
8.9	0.10	na	0.01	6.8	1.8	1.42	12.73	3.52	49.7	1.6	30.0	31.2	7.0
7.1	0.60	na	0.91	5.7	1.2	1.44	6.36	4.13	54.1	5.4	62.2	13.3	6.4
6.4	1.70	na	-0.60	7.2	1.4	1.68	15.93	4.16	62.3	5.0	34.5	7.3	8.3
5.4	2.24	na	0.03	8.4	1.9	2.07	11.05	4.74	54.4	1.2	15.3	29.3	8.5
8.5	0.65	na	0.00	9.0	2.1	1.94	15.33	4.01	53.6	0.6	11.2	50.3	9.6
8.0	0.38	na	0.05	7.6	1.9	1.88	13.71	3.76	50.8	0.8	14.4	34.9	9.2
2.3	1.80	9.9	0.19	5.5	5.8	1.02	10.48	4.16	63.5	1.5	17.8	19.4	5.6
6.6	1.05	na	0.07	4.2	0.1	0.93	4.94	3.33	69.0	4.8	27.3	4.5	6.6
7.1	0.04	na	0.20	6.7	2.3	1.32	13.27	4.89	61.9	3.7	13.2	10.1	6.1
6.8	0.76	na	0.26	9.2	2.7	2.09	17.74	6.97	62.0	2.7	37.5	22.6	7.9
5.7	3.28	na	0.00	4.2	1.5	0.90	6.74	3.49	69.7	3.7	34.2	14.5	7.3
6.3	1.73	na	-0.12	6.8	0.9	1.32	11.05	4.07	55.0	2.0	7.3	18.1	6.9
7.8	0.00	na	0.08	4.8	0.8	0.94	8.56	4.51	73.9	3.4	17.4	12.1	6.8
6.2	1.57	na	0.17	6.7	2.2	1.33	10.63	4.75	64.7	3.7	15.0	10.6	7.7
1.2	3.09	na	0.14	5.4	3.3	0.95	9.75	5.44	73.5	4.4	12.1	5.5	5.5

Name	City	State	Rating	2018 Rating	2017 Rating	Total Assets ($Mil)	One Year Asset Growth	Asset Mix (As a % of Total Assets) Comm-ercial Loans	Cons-umer Loans	Mort-gage Loans	Secur-ities	Capital-ization Index	Lever-age Ratio	Risk-Based Capital Ratio
▲ Bank of Eastman	Eastman	GA	**C-**	D+	D+	163.9	-9.23	8.7	6.1	25.3	6.0	**10.0**	11.2	17.7
Bank of Easton	North Easton	MA	**B-**	B-	B-	154.2	11.21	0.0	0.4	43.4	20.0	**10.0**	11.8	26.7
Bank of Edison	Edison	GA	**C**	C	C	50.1	6.12	4.5	5.8	9.1	42.9	**7.8**	9.6	19.2
Bank of Edmonson County	Brownsville	KY	**B-**	B-	B+	217.9	2.67	2.7	3.0	28.8	17.6	**10.0**	12.2	19.1
Bank of Elgin	Elgin	NE	**B**	B+	B+	56.6	-8.65	3.4	1.1	0.6	4.4	**10.0**	15.2	20.1
▲ Bank of Elk River	Elk River	MN	**B+**	B	B	448.7	3.04	16.4	2.4	9.9	28.6	**7.9**	9.6	14.9
▲ Bank of England	England	AR	**B+**	B	B+	471.1	46.68	4.3	0.7	58.7	7.7	**7.3**	13.1	12.7
Bank of Erath	Erath	LA	**B**	B	B	99.4	-2.07	11.5	2.6	18.7	13.1	**10.0**	13.9	21.3
▲ Bank of Estes Park	Estes Park	CO	**A-**	B+	B-	139.6	7.18	1.5	0.1	14.2	21.7	**8.6**	10.0	20.3
Bank of Eufaula	Eufaula	OK	**B-**	B-	C+	94.6	-1.07	3.0	7.3	14.6	49.3	**10.0**	14.1	34.1
▲ Bank of Evergreen	Evergreen	AL	**B-**	C+	B-	60.4	0.09	10.3	3.7	22.8	23.7	**10.0**	13.7	25.2
Bank of Farmington	Farmington	IL	**B-**	B-	B+	180.4	3.58	11.4	3.4	14.9	21.0	**10.0**	11.6	17.8
▲ Bank of Fayette County	Piperton	TN	**B-**	B-	B-	659.6	7.27	5.7	7.1	31.7	6.7	**7.1**	9.2	12.6
Bank of Feather River	Yuba City	CA	**B+**	B+	B+	135.7	16.36	8.5	0.0	4.1	0.0	**7.8**	11.4	13.2
Bank of Fincastle	Fincastle	VA	**D**	D-	E	222.2	9.62	9.9	0.7	15.1	9.4	**10.0**	11.6	16.1
Bank of Forest	Forest	MS	**B+**	B+	B	203.3	2.94	5.8	4.7	10.0	26.6	**10.0**	13.6	21.3
Bank of Frankewing	Frankewing	TN	**B**	B+	B+	303.0	14.73	9.6	4.3	19.1	3.4	**10.0**	11.4	16.3
▲ Bank of Franklin	Meadville	MS	**A-**	B+	B-	146.1	10.33	7.6	4.6	22.0	24.6	**10.0**	11.6	18.1
Bank of Franklin County	Washington	MO	**C+**	C	C-	273.1	10.81	11.2	2.3	18.5	11.1	**5.2**	9.0	11.2
▲ Bank of George	Las Vegas	NV	**A-**	B+	A	312.9	36.53	3.8	0.0	1.6	1.1	**10.0**	12.2	20.0
▲ Bank of Gibson City	Gibson City	IL	**C+**	C	B-	86.3	6.04	6.1	4.9	12.6	16.6	**6.4**	8.4	13.2
Bank of Gleason	Gleason	TN	**B+**	B+	A-	112.6	1.54	2.8	7.3	12.3	52.3	**10.0**	23.5	47.4
Bank of Glen Burnie	Glen Burnie	MD	**C-**	C	C-	383.4	-6.78	3.7	28.3	20.6	16.9	**7.4**	9.3	13.2
▲ Bank of Glen Ullin	Glen Ullin	ND	**C**	D+	D-	62.1	14.83	5.7	1.2	2.5	8.3	**5.4**	10.2	11.3
Bank of Grain Valley	Kansas City	MO	**A-**	A-	A-	93.8	0.68	13.2	0.7	15.5	15.0	**10.0**	22.6	40.5
Bank of Grand Lake	Grove	OK	**B-**	B-	B-	183.1	10.17	5.2	2.6	26.4	11.5	**5.7**	7.7	11.9
Bank of Grandin	Grandin	MO	**C+**	B-	B	168.9	8.59	11.4	6.7	13.1	31.0	**10.0**	15.7	21.9
▲ Bank of Gravette	Gravette	AR	**C+**	C+	B-	135.9	4.74	3.8	2.6	16.4	20.2	**6.7**	8.7	14.8
Bank of Greeley	Greeley	KS	**B**	B	B	38.3	2.62	5.0	4.2	17.2	11.9	**10.0**	13.5	26.3
▲ Bank of Greeleyville	Greeleyville	SC	**B**	C+	B-	88.4	0.77	13.1	9.0	14.3	20.4	**10.0**	12.3	19.5
Bank of Greene County	Catskill	NY	**B+**	B+	B+	1406.8	18.67	5.9	0.4	23.9	33.7	**6.7**	8.7	15.8
Bank of Guam	Hagatna	GU	**C+**	C+	C+	1944.2	0.65	10.7	11.9	7.9	21.1	**6.6**	8.6	14.1
▲ Bank of Gueydan	Gueydan	LA	**B**	B-	B-	74.8	-3.70	4.8	6.9	1.0	60.0	**10.0**	21.2	52.3
Bank of Halls	Halls	TN	**B**	B	B+	85.8	3.08	11.6	2.5	7.1	34.9	**10.0**	11.0	15.9
▲ Bank of Hamilton	Hamilton	ND	**C+**	C-	C-	18.9	-8.13	2.8	2.8	0.0	5.9	**10.0**	14.4	43.4
Bank of Hancock County	Sparta	GA	**B+**	B+	B+	73.2	-1.78	5.0	5.7	15.3	59.8	**10.0**	21.0	40.4
▲ Bank of Hartington	Hartington	NE	**B-**	C+	B-	94.3	2.55	11.7	1.7	6.8	12.3	**7.9**	9.9	13.2
Bank of Hawaii	Honolulu	HI	**B**	B	B	17643.5	4.01	4.9	6.2	25.7	31.5	**5.0**	7.0	13.0
Bank of Hays	Hays	KS	**B-**	B-	B-	254.1	1.93	11.3	2.2	8.9	26.7	**9.4**	10.6	16.6
▲ Bank of Hazelton	Hazelton	ND	**B**	B-	C+	54.8	4.24	1.5	0.6	0.8	21.2	**10.0**	11.2	19.2
Bank of Hazlehurst	Hazlehurst	GA	**D+**	D	D-	118.8	-5.86	11.0	2.8	7.1	25.0	**10.0**	12.7	22.0
▲ Bank of Hemet	Riverside	CA	**B+**	B+	A	722.3	-0.62	1.4	0.1	0.2	8.3	**9.2**	10.9	14.4
▲ Bank of Herrin	Herrin	IL	**B-**	B-	B	250.4	-0.28	9.9	1.8	14.1	20.8	**9.9**	10.9	15.2
Bank of Hillsboro, N.A.	Hillsboro	IL	**B**	B-	B	360.7	8.37	7.3	0.8	9.0	19.3	**10.0**	11.2	15.0
▲ Bank of Hindman	Hindman	KY	**C+**	C	C	211.4	7.18	6.3	1.7	15.6	35.5	**8.4**	9.9	16.3
Bank of Holland	Holland	NY	**B-**	B-	B-	144.0	7.25	2.8	2.0	42.2	23.6	**5.9**	7.9	13.6
▲ Bank of Holly Springs	Holly Springs	MS	**B**	B-	B	244.2	12.62	10.8	7.8	21.6	10.9	**10.0**	14.3	20.9
Bank of Holyrood	Holyrood	KS	**B+**	B+	B+	63.4	1.38	18.9	6.9	24.1	8.4	**10.0**	14.6	22.6
Bank of Hope	Los Angeles	CA	**B**	B	B-	15380.2	0.99	14.1	0.2	5.7	11.5	**9.7**	12.4	14.7
Bank of Houston	Houston	MO	**D-**	D-	E+	31.6	-9.17	2.2	0.5	6.4	27.4	**8.5**	10.0	18.8
▼ Bank of Houston, N.A.	Houston	TX	**D+**	C	B-	120.0	96.21	14.2	2.4	8.5	3.6	**10.0**	34.1	40.7
▲ Bank of Hydro	Hydro	OK	**A-**	B+	A-	121.0	-2.66	4.8	2.1	34.3	0.0	**10.0**	11.8	16.0
▲ Bank of Iberia	Iberia	MO	**C**	D+	D+	55.6	-1.25	3.0	6.3	26.4	19.2	**7.4**	9.2	17.6
Bank of Idaho	Idaho Falls	ID	**B-**	B-	B+	466.5	41.08	7.0	1.9	6.3	17.3	**10.0**	13.1	17.8
Bank of Jackson	Jackson	TN	**B-**	B-	B-	191.4	4.25	6.0	1.5	8.1	62.4	**8.6**	10.1	18.5
▲ Bank of Jackson Hole	Jackson	WY	**B-**	C+	B+	912.6	10.12	5.2	0.2	17.9	2.0	**8.6**	10.0	14.2
Bank of Jamestown	Jamestown	KY	**B-**	B-	B-	205.6	5.55	4.5	1.1	9.9	28.6	**9.1**	11.4	14.3
Bank of Kampsville	Kampsville	IL	**B**	B	B	109.0	2.12	3.2	6.7	18.6	34.8	**10.0**	17.9	30.4
▲ Bank of Kaukauna	Kaukauna	WI	**C**	D+	D+	97.6	-0.33	17.1	1.9	9.4	3.5	**8.2**	9.8	13.8
Bank of Kilmichael	Kilmichael	MS	**B+**	B+	B	175.5	-0.55	12.3	6.0	14.0	24.3	**8.5**	10.0	16.2

Asset Quality Index	Adjusted Non-Performing Loans as a % of Total Loans	Adjusted Non-Performing Loans as a % of Capital	Net Charge-Offs Avg Loans	Profitability Index	Net Income ($Mil)	Return on Assets (R.O.A.)	Return on Equity (R.O.E.)	Net Interest Spread	Overhead Efficiency Ratio	Liquidity Index	Liquidity Ratio	Hot Money Ratio	Stability Index
2.9	3.03	na	0.27	4.6	1.2	0.93	8.60	5.16	81.1	2.5	20.8	17.1	4.4
9.7	0.45	na	0.01	3.8	0.8	0.73	6.24	2.57	64.5	3.0	43.4	22.0	6.3
5.7	1.19	4.4	0.10	4.0	0.4	1.01	11.11	3.84	78.0	2.3	32.0	21.9	4.7
3.6	4.48	na	-0.02	6.5	2.4	1.51	12.54	3.84	61.1	1.1	18.3	31.9	8.6
6.8	0.00	na	0.00	9.2	1.0	2.35	15.66	4.06	47.6	4.5	15.2	5.7	8.9
8.0	0.00	na	0.01	7.3	5.1	1.57	16.66	4.06	65.4	4.4	33.4	10.8	6.6
6.7	0.92	na	0.01	9.4	8.2	2.87	20.68	3.40	90.9	0.6	8.5	39.8	9.1
5.2	2.32	11.4	-0.02	4.1	0.6	0.77	5.73	4.55	78.5	1.8	15.6	20.0	6.9
9.3	0.00	0.0	0.00	6.1	1.5	1.53	14.77	3.94	63.3	6.9	56.1	2.7	6.9
8.9	0.23	na	0.04	3.6	0.6	0.77	5.72	3.56	72.5	3.2	40.6	19.3	5.7
4.4	4.64	na	0.34	4.5	0.3	0.75	5.57	4.27	67.2	2.1	33.9	27.0	5.8
7.1	2.23	na	0.15	3.6	0.9	0.68	5.88	3.47	71.3	1.9	22.8	20.8	6.6
4.9	0.91	na	0.09	6.1	5.7	1.19	13.37	3.95	59.8	0.5	5.4	38.9	6.1
8.3	0.00	na	0.01	7.8	1.3	1.38	12.38	5.05	60.1	1.5	12.8	23.1	7.4
5.1	2.35	na	0.11	2.6	0.7	0.45	3.75	3.86	86.2	3.2	21.4	13.5	4.6
5.5	2.06	9.4	0.07	5.8	2.2	1.45	10.83	4.11	66.3	2.4	33.3	22.0	8.2
6.6	1.63	na	0.03	6.5	2.6	1.20	10.71	4.12	63.9	0.8	20.4	36.9	7.5
6.9	0.58	na	0.12	6.8	1.5	1.37	12.21	4.56	65.6	2.9	22.9	15.4	6.4
4.3	2.25	10.5	0.20	3.9	1.4	0.73	8.09	3.54	71.0	3.2	13.8	12.9	4.4
7.0	0.00	na	0.45	10.0	4.2	2.10	16.02	5.44	54.3	3.4	31.8	15.1	9.3
5.1	1.36	na	0.18	5.7	0.7	1.15	9.33	3.62	53.4	3.4	22.0	12.9	5.0
8.8	0.36	na	0.25	4.7	1.0	1.17	4.98	3.45	68.2	4.4	76.0	19.9	8.1
2.6	1.56	11.6	0.14	2.8	1.2	0.41	4.61	3.39	84.5	3.8	24.0	11.0	4.0
2.8	0.38	na	-0.04	10.0	1.0	2.35	19.74	4.55	44.5	0.6	11.5	46.2	8.0
8.9	0.00	na	0.00	7.7	1.3	1.84	8.34	4.18	55.1	5.5	44.5	7.5	9.1
4.8	1.53	na	0.05	5.2	1.5	1.16	15.04	3.64	68.3	0.9	20.7	21.7	4.7
5.3	7.61	na	0.63	5.3	1.5	1.24	7.77	3.66	62.1	1.4	20.9	27.5	8.5
4.4	0.57	na	0.07	3.2	0.4	0.38	2.81	3.91	81.4	1.6	25.5	26.4	7.3
8.7	0.15	na	0.02	5.3	0.4	1.33	10.31	3.27	60.2	4.5	44.5	13.2	7.5
6.3	1.78	na	0.15	6.8	1.0	1.54	12.70	4.64	68.1	3.0	28.0	16.1	7.0
8.4	0.58	3.3	0.12	6.3	12.6	1.33	15.73	3.49	55.7	5.1	9.2	1.0	7.5
3.4	3.31	18.1	0.40	4.7	12.4	0.85	10.86	4.99	76.5	2.3	15.1	17.8	6.3
6.5	4.47	5.4	0.53	3.9	0.5	0.81	3.99	3.02	64.9	4.1	80.6	23.2	6.0
4.0	4.01	na	0.01	6.0	0.7	1.20	11.08	3.65	59.4	1.3	21.4	28.9	7.1
9.7	0.00	na	-0.10	3.0	0.1	0.57	4.13	2.70	72.9	7.5	95.7	2.8	5.4
9.0	0.23	na	0.03	3.9	0.5	0.90	4.25	4.28	80.9	4.8	39.8	11.1	7.7
7.1	0.00	na	0.00	5.4	0.9	1.29	13.40	4.41	69.1	3.5	13.8	11.3	6.2
8.0	0.54	3.4	0.11	6.3	168.7	1.29	18.54	3.07	55.5	4.0	20.5	10.0	6.7
3.6	6.11	13.6	0.05	5.5	2.1	1.09	10.37	3.35	55.1	1.7	21.4	23.4	6.7
8.9	0.00	na	0.00	6.5	0.6	1.63	15.12	3.50	54.7	4.9	58.4	13.6	5.5
0.6	10.99	na	1.26	2.7	0.5	0.54	4.02	3.99	62.5	5.2	30.4	4.8	6.0
7.4	0.00	na	0.00	9.8	14.9	2.75	25.49	4.37	39.3	4.9	13.5	2.5	9.4
4.7	1.61	na	0.26	5.8	2.7	1.46	13.98	4.16	61.9	4.6	13.1	4.4	6.4
6.4	3.03	na	-0.03	5.0	2.6	0.96	8.59	3.39	62.9	2.5	12.7	16.1	6.7
3.9	3.41	na	0.00	3.8	1.3	0.84	6.83	2.97	64.2	1.8	31.5	30.1	7.0
5.9	0.87	na	0.02	4.4	1.0	0.98	12.85	3.72	69.6	2.9	15.6	14.6	4.9
4.3	3.24	na	0.41	6.6	2.5	1.43	9.87	4.65	67.5	1.3	14.6	27.9	9.2
4.6	2.25	10.5	1.49	5.8	0.6	1.32	9.00	3.80	48.1	0.9	24.3	28.7	7.7
5.1	0.94	2.7	0.04	6.5	139.1	1.22	8.26	3.42	52.3	0.8	15.7	30.6	10.0
9.3	0.00	na	-0.01	0.3	-0.1	-0.22	-2.85	3.58	133.5	6.2	58.1	6.2	2.5
8.4	0.00	na	-0.01	0.7	-0.3	-0.43	-1.60	5.04	100.0	4.4	43.5	14.0	6.0
7.7	0.08	na	0.13	10.0	2.5	2.71	23.80	5.06	47.4	1.1	2.4	27.2	8.7
4.8	2.11	na	0.06	3.4	0.2	0.49	5.37	4.29	86.5	3.4	41.1	18.0	3.7
5.5	1.82	na	0.21	4.0	2.4	0.93	8.73	4.91	87.4	6.4	42.7	1.3	6.8
9.2	0.88	na	0.00	4.1	1.2	0.87	8.28	2.89	68.8	2.8	50.0	30.4	6.0
6.5	1.19	na	0.00	7.3	8.8	1.37	12.96	4.00	54.8	4.2	23.8	8.6	7.3
8.5	0.78	na	0.01	4.4	1.5	1.03	9.18	3.41	63.8	1.6	10.7	22.3	6.2
7.4	2.22	na	-0.07	4.1	0.7	0.84	4.74	3.15	67.2	4.6	49.4	14.3	8.1
3.8	4.37	na	0.00	5.2	0.7	1.23	12.47	3.34	80.3	1.8	23.8	6.8	6.2
4.9	1.28	na	0.36	6.7	2.1	1.56	15.83	4.39	59.0	1.8	23.1	21.8	7.2

Name	City	State	Rating	2018 Rating	2017 Rating	Total Assets ($Mil)	One Year Asset Growth	Asset Mix (As a % of Total Assets) Commercial Loans	Consumer Loans	Mortgage Loans	Securities	Capitalization Index	Leverage Ratio	Risk-Based Capital Ratio
▲ Bank of Kirksville	Kirksville	MO	**B+**	B	B	430.7	-4.90	3.7	0.6	15.0	37.8	**10.0**	12.0	38.6
Bank of Kremlin	Kremlin	OK	**C+**	C+	C-	298.3	3.72	9.6	2.2	7.3	10.7	**10.0**	11.4	16.4
Bank of Labor	Kansas City	KS	**C**	C	C-	622.5	3.43	21.4	0.1	3.3	41.0	**7.2**	9.1	16.1
Bank of LaFayette, Georgia	Lafayette	GA	**B**	B	B	258.2	5.91	1.2	6.5	21.9	56.4	**10.0**	13.3	43.8
▲ Bank of Lake Mills	Lake Mills	WI	**A-**	B+	B	228.1	8.59	1.7	9.2	34.3	8.7	**10.0**	12.6	17.1
Bank of Lake Village	Lake Village	AR	**B+**	B+	B+	66.3	-7.63	2.8	1.8	4.5	24.2	**10.0**	12.6	21.8
Bank of Landisburg	Landisburg	PA	**B+**	B+	A-	300.2	1.65	1.9	1.8	45.0	13.9	**10.0**	18.7	33.0
Bank of Laverne	Laverne	OK	**B**	B	B	57.1	-2.11	6.6	5.9	0.9	28.7	**10.0**	17.1	27.7
Bank of Lewellen	Lewellen	NE	**C+**	B-	B	22.6	-3.61	4.5	1.4	0.0	25.3	**10.0**	27.2	49.2
Bank of Lexington, Inc.	Lexington	KY	**B**	B	B	249.1	-3.67	1.4	0.1	42.2	3.6	**10.0**	11.1	19.1
▲ Bank of Lincoln County	Fayetteville	TN	**A-**	B	B+	146.0	4.77	7.5	1.8	14.3	8.9	**10.0**	13.4	16.7
Bank of Lindsay	Lindsay	NE	**C+**	C+	C+	72.7	6.01	5.7	1.7	0.1	2.9	**8.5**	11.9	13.7
▲ Bank of Little Rock	Little Rock	AR	**C+**	C-	C+	197.2	-1.97	14.3	2.4	22.1	29.6	**10.0**	11.2	18.2
Bank of Locust Grove	Locust Grove	OK	**B**	B	B	40.1	24.89	27.3	35.3	2.9	9.4	**10.0**	12.5	16.3
▲ Bank of Louisiana	New Orleans	LA	**C-**	D-	D-	77.4	-1.29	2.2	5.1	35.1	1.9	**8.0**	9.8	13.3
▲ Bank of Louisiana	Louisiana	MO	**B-**	C+	C+	53.8	4.62	9.1	1.6	16.2	24.1	**8.8**	10.2	15.6
Bank of Lumber City	Lumber City	GA	**C**	C	C	23.5	-6.22	8.1	11.8	14.4	12.7	**10.0**	16.0	25.0
Bank of Luxemburg	Luxemburg	WI	**C+**	B-	B-	386.8	10.17	14.5	1.6	15.3	13.6	**6.2**	9.4	11.9
Bank of Madison	Madison	GA	**B+**	B+	B+	224.2	0.14	4.9	0.8	14.1	19.9	**10.0**	14.1	17.5
Bank of Magnolia Co.	Magnolia	OH	**B**	B-	C+	81.6	-3.79	4.0	4.8	25.8	26.7	**10.0**	11.7	25.5
Bank of Maple Plain	Maple Plain	MN	**B+**	B+	A-	86.9	-2.02	11.5	1.2	19.8	37.2	**10.0**	13.8	24.8
Bank of Marin	Novato	CA	**A-**	A-	A-	2592.1	1.83	6.1	1.1	6.3	19.4	**9.5**	11.3	14.6
▲ Bank of Marion	Marion	VA	**A-**	B	B	385.9	0.49	2.4	3.7	32.9	27.8	**10.0**	11.9	21.0
Bank of Mauston	Mauston	WI	**A-**	A	A-	300.3	3.88	4.8	2.0	9.8	30.5	**10.0**	12.9	19.4
Bank of Maysville	Maysville	KY	**B+**	B+	B	127.0	0.46	0.5	1.0	31.4	30.5	**10.0**	18.2	30.5
▲ Bank of Mead	Mead	NE	**B**	B-	B-	27.3	-4.26	10.5	5.4	17.0	30.7	**10.0**	11.9	21.7
Bank of Milan	Milan	TN	**B-**	B-	B	79.1	20.15	8.0	1.2	19.4	24.9	**8.5**	10.0	15.6
▲ Bank of Millbrook	Millbrook	NY	**B**		B-	229.4	-0.37	1.9	1.7	21.7	38.5	**10.0**	11.4	26.0
Bank of Milton	Milton	WI	**B**	B	B	125.0	7.98	5.9	2.2	22.5	16.2	**6.3**	8.9	12.0
Bank of Mingo	Williamson	WV	**C-**	C-	D-	84.4	6.71	13.5	11.5	35.3	12.9	**8.9**	10.2	15.5
Bank of Missouri	Perryville	MO	**B+**	B+	B	1800.5	3.01	8.8	3.9	17.7	17.8	**8.8**	11.5	14.0
Bank of Monroe	Union	WV	**A-**	A-	B+	145.0	1.64	6.5	3.3	26.0	22.9	**10.0**	15.6	25.5
▲ Bank of Montana	Missoula	MT	**A-**	B+	A-	94.0	8.72	26.8	3.6	9.3	0.0	**10.0**	12.5	17.2
Bank of Montgomery	Montgomery	IL	**D**	C-	C-	40.9	-4.62	12.4	1.8	13.1	27.5	**6.6**	8.7	22.3
Bank of Monticello	Monticello	GA	**B**	B	C+	109.1	-2.71	6.2	7.1	27.7	15.7	**10.0**	11.1	18.1
▲ Bank of Monticello	Monticello	MO	**A-**	B+	B+	111.9	3.22	6.5	4.4	12.9	18.6	**10.0**	12.5	17.2
Bank of Morton	Morton	MS	**B+**	B+	A-	68.8	3.01	5.2	9.6	41.1	12.0	**10.0**	15.0	22.6
Bank of Moundville	Moundville	AL	**C**	C	C-	93.5	1.34	6.3	2.6	4.6	64.8	**8.8**	10.2	22.4
▲ Bank of New Cambria	New Cambria	MO	**B**	B-	B-	30.8	-0.94	2.7	0.7	6.7	21.2	**10.0**	14.0	23.0
Bank of New Castle	New Castle	DE	**D+**	C-	C-	18.0	1.64	0.0	0.0	0.0	0.9	**10.0**	97.2	484.4
Bank of New England	Salem	NH	**B-**	C+	B	1029.1	10.99	5.2	0.0	0.2	0.2	**10.0**	14.5	15.7
Bank of New Glarus	New Glarus	WI	**B-**	B-	B	309.7	8.94	17.4	1.8	14.4	10.0	**9.2**	11.9	14.4
Bank of New Hampshire	Laconia	NH	**B-**	B-	C+	1739.1	4.60	4.8	2.8	30.7	11.7	**6.4**	9.1	12.0
Bank of New Jersey	Fort Lee	NJ	**C**	C-	D+	961.7	7.86	2.5	0.0	5.7	2.8	**6.8**	10.0	12.3
Bank of New Madrid	New Madrid	MO	**A-**	A-	A-	98.6	3.25	2.2	3.0	19.2	37.1	**10.0**	12.2	15.0
Bank of New York Mellon	New York	NY	**B**	B	B-	304096.0	11.35	0.5	0.0	0.3	39.7	**5.0**	7.0	14.5
Bank of New York Mellon Trust Co., N.A.	Los Angeles	CA	**U**	U	U	1360.5	-34.54	0.0	0.0	0.0	12.6	**10.0**	64.4	299.5
▲ Bank of Newington	Newington	GA	**C**	C	C-	145.5	9.89	4.8	2.2	23.8	0.7	**6.6**	8.6	12.2
Bank of Newman Grove	Newman Grove	NE	**C**	C-	C	34.7	2.89	0.3	1.6	0.0	16.8	**7.4**	11.6	12.8
Bank of O'Fallon	O'Fallon	IL	**A-**	A-	B+	311.7	-3.74	4.6	5.4	42.6	5.6	**10.0**	14.4	24.1
Bank of Oak Ridge	Oak Ridge	LA	**B-**	C+	C+	52.7	6.87	19.7	1.1	10.2	14.9	**10.0**	11.9	17.0
Bank of Oak Ridge	Oak Ridge	NC	**B-**	B-	B-	466.8	6.60	11.6	0.9	18.7	9.3	**7.7**	10.3	13.1
Bank of Ocean City	Ocean City	MD	**A-**	A-	B+	382.9	4.75	3.5	0.5	17.4	13.2	**8.7**	10.1	15.0
Bank of Odessa	Odessa	MO	**B+**	B+	B+	268.3	8.80	9.7	3.9	39.5	16.1	**10.0**	19.2	31.6
Bank of Okolona	Okolona	MS	**D+**	C	B-	200.9	4.27	19.5	5.9	16.0	14.5	**8.5**	10.0	15.4
Bank of Old Monroe	Old Monroe	MO	**A**	A	A	391.8	10.20	9.5	0.4	10.5	22.1	**10.0**	15.1	19.9
▲ Bank of Ontario	Ontario	WI	**B-**	C+	B-	50.3	1.98	7.3	3.4	27.5	10.2	**10.0**	12.0	24.7
▲ Bank of Orchard	Orchard	NE	**B-**	B-	B-	24.6	-3.09	9.0	4.7	0.2	17.7	**10.0**	14.7	33.3
Bank of Orrick	Orrick	MO	**C-**	C-	C-	33.8	2.27	1.3	2.2	19.5	38.9	**7.9**	9.6	20.6
Bank of Palmer	Palmer	KS	**C+**	C+	C+	45.3	5.60	2.0	3.9	7.4	38.1	**9.8**	10.8	18.9

Asset Quality Index	Adjusted Non-Performing Loans as a % of Total Loans	Adjusted Non-Performing Loans as a % of Capital	Net Charge-Offs Avg Loans	Profitability Index	Net Income ($Mil)	Return on Assets (R.O.A.)	Return on Equity (R.O.E.)	Net Interest Spread	Overhead Efficiency Ratio	Liquidity Index	Liquidity Ratio	Hot Money Ratio	Stability Index
7.1	2.99	na	0.00	**5.1**	4.5	1.35	11.80	2.39	48.4	**4.2**	41.8	14.4	**7.4**
5.6	1.17	na	0.04	**7.9**	4.6	1.99	18.55	4.03	52.8	**0.7**	15.8	34.7	**8.0**
5.6	2.52	6.9	0.17	**3.0**	1.8	0.42	4.83	3.91	89.4	**5.7**	44.6	7.1	**5.2**
6.2	2.73	na	0.24	**4.2**	1.6	0.79	6.60	3.08	68.9	**3.4**	22.0	12.9	**6.8**
5.8	1.44	6.5	0.00	**7.8**	3.1	1.87	15.14	4.02	60.2	**2.5**	8.0	12.5	**8.1**
7.1	2.63	na	0.15	**5.8**	0.6	1.27	10.17	4.17	62.8	**2.2**	18.0	10.9	**6.7**
6.3	3.96	na	0.03	**6.2**	2.7	1.26	6.86	3.59	57.7	**1.9**	16.9	19.5	**8.4**
6.0	1.99	na	0.01	**5.7**	0.6	1.32	7.98	4.34	64.8	**3.3**	41.8	18.9	**7.1**
8.8	0.00	na	0.00	**4.3**	0.2	0.85	3.20	3.75	73.0	**3.9**	53.6	16.0	**5.7**
9.1	0.00	na	0.00	**3.8**	1.6	0.81	7.34	3.48	72.5	**0.8**	17.0	24.4	**6.9**
8.2	1.05	na	-0.03	**9.0**	1.7	1.54	11.57	4.97	59.9	**1.0**	13.6	31.5	**8.0**
6.9	0.04	0.3	0.00	**3.2**	0.3	0.53	4.47	3.33	81.9	**0.6**	9.2	40.0	**5.8**
3.4	4.32	na	0.90	**3.5**	1.1	0.75	6.90	3.75	89.7	**4.8**	30.5	6.1	**4.7**
4.7	0.93	na	-0.10	**9.3**	0.5	1.61	12.48	5.92	60.2	**1.7**	16.1	21.9	**6.6**
2.3	2.24	na	0.49	**6.0**	2.0	3.32	32.10	4.87	121.7	**4.7**	26.3	6.0	**5.2**
5.5	1.51	na	2.47	**1.7**	-0.3	-0.71	-6.79	3.97	87.6	**1.8**	21.1	21.4	**6.9**
7.3	2.59	na	-0.01	**3.6**	0.1	0.77	5.00	5.41	87.6	**2.6**	40.4	19.8	**4.6**
3.1	2.41	16.5	0.06	**4.9**	2.6	0.96	10.29	3.86	70.8	**3.1**	19.2	13.7	**5.4**
6.3	1.54	na	-0.06	**5.4**	1.8	1.09	8.09	4.29	68.2	**3.8**	10.6	9.5	**7.9**
8.9	0.58	2.1	0.00	**4.5**	0.6	0.94	8.12	3.69	69.9	**5.7**	40.1	5.3	**6.5**
6.7	1.02	na	-0.01	**5.8**	1.0	1.47	10.95	3.34	57.5	**5.1**	40.9	9.3	**7.6**
6.9	0.69	1.9	0.00	**7.1**	26.1	1.38	11.22	4.08	55.3	**5.7**	26.3	3.0	**10.0**
7.5	0.00	2.9	0.37	**5.6**	3.4	1.20	9.94	4.45	67.8	**4.3**	22.6	7.7	**6.8**
7.8	1.05	na	0.09	**9.8**	6.1	2.74	21.36	3.88	39.9	**2.5**	25.2	17.5	**9.0**
8.5	0.56	na	-0.01	**4.8**	0.9	0.92	4.78	3.60	67.5	**3.6**	24.3	12.1	**8.2**
8.4	0.00	na	-0.15	**5.0**	0.2	0.94	8.21	3.56	63.1	**5.1**	28.9	4.6	**6.4**
9.2	0.00	na	-0.02	**4.5**	0.5	0.98	10.00	3.79	73.7	**4.5**	44.0	13.2	**4.9**
8.8	0.22	na	0.03	**4.6**	1.7	1.04	9.38	3.36	67.7	**6.2**	43.5	2.8	**6.3**
7.4	0.18	na	0.00	**6.3**	1.2	1.25	13.64	4.06	59.1	**2.0**	25.2	20.1	**6.9**
5.1	1.11	na	0.81	**2.6**	0.2	0.39	3.75	4.28	92.1	**1.2**	13.4	28.7	**2.6**
5.7	1.56	5.1	0.30	**6.4**	19.0	1.44	11.36	3.88	64.1	**3.9**	9.3	8.7	**9.2**
8.7	0.81	2.1	0.03	**6.3**	1.4	1.34	9.62	4.10	64.7	**3.2**	29.3	15.3	**8.6**
8.2	0.00	na	0.00	**10.0**	1.8	2.75	21.81	4.85	51.5	**2.0**	19.3	16.5	**8.4**
8.0	0.00	na	2.79	**0.8**	-0.2	-0.64	-6.98	2.85	80.5	**4.6**	57.3	15.1	**4.6**
4.9	1.59	11.0	-0.07	**7.2**	1.4	1.77	16.79	4.50	60.7	**3.6**	18.5	11.5	**6.2**
6.2	0.89	na	0.15	**7.7**	1.6	1.96	16.36	4.17	52.7	**2.7**	18.2	13.7	**7.5**
5.0	1.91	na	0.07	**9.3**	0.9	1.75	11.67	5.49	67.0	**1.1**	12.4	29.1	**9.3**
9.4	0.25	na	0.01	**2.8**	0.4	0.61	6.71	2.61	83.6	**3.0**	47.4	24.1	**4.6**
9.1	0.00	na	-0.01	**4.0**	0.2	0.75	5.62	3.90	75.6	**6.2**	49.1	3.9	**6.8**
7.5	0.00	0.0	0.00	**7.7**	0.2	1.63	1.68	2.43	5.7	**2.3**	75.0	100.0	**3.0**
5.6	1.11	na	0.01	**9.6**	11.8	1.65	11.29	4.12	39.0	**0.7**	16.0	21.2	**10.0**
5.0	2.22	na	0.02	**9.0**	3.9	1.76	14.32	4.50	53.6	**3.5**	15.3	11.7	**7.8**
6.8	0.51	na	0.01	**4.1**	9.9	0.78	7.68	3.57	71.7	**3.1**	10.0	7.0	**8.2**
3.1	1.69	11.6	0.01	**3.3**	3.5	0.50	4.95	2.88	74.5	**0.7**	14.8	41.5	**6.3**
8.0	0.00	na	0.00	**7.3**	1.3	1.77	14.65	4.32	56.0	**1.6**	11.1	21.7	**7.7**
9.0	0.40	0.3	0.07	**4.7**	1995.0	0.99	10.38	1.23	68.8	**3.6**	56.0	23.8	**7.2**
6.5	na	0.0	na	**10.0**	131.1	12.81	15.63	2.30	49.9	**9.3**	151.9	0.0	**7.0**
3.5	2.60	na	0.17	**6.2**	1.2	1.15	13.07	5.12	63.8	**1.1**	12.3	30.1	**5.6**
4.0	0.18	na	0.00	**3.6**	0.2	0.76	6.87	3.86	80.9	**2.9**	7.8	13.9	**5.4**
8.7	0.13	1.5	0.01	**5.7**	3.5	1.50	10.56	2.91	47.5	**1.4**	19.5	28.0	**8.5**
8.6	0.04	na	0.01	**3.6**	0.3	0.66	5.66	3.72	78.1	**0.9**	16.9	34.6	**6.3**
4.0	1.06	7.5	0.13	**5.1**	3.7	1.05	10.22	3.97	69.5	**0.7**	12.9	29.0	**6.5**
8.8	0.00	na	-0.12	**8.5**	4.2	1.61	15.22	4.02	46.3	**4.4**	30.5	9.5	**7.0**
6.1	0.77	6.9	0.00	**6.8**	2.6	1.31	6.85	3.34	45.0	**1.8**	8.1	19.5	**7.9**
1.9	4.80	na	0.50	**6.8**	2.4	1.61	16.34	4.17	65.6	**0.9**	21.8	38.6	**8.1**
8.7	0.87	na	-0.21	**9.4**	6.4	2.29	14.99	4.24	50.1	**3.2**	22.9	9.6	**9.6**
4.4	1.92	na	-0.02	**8.9**	1.0	2.57	22.24	4.84	53.4	**1.1**	5.3	27.4	**7.8**
8.7	0.00	na	0.00	**3.8**	0.1	0.76	5.30	2.98	71.4	**4.7**	75.0	15.8	**6.8**
5.1	2.58	na	0.38	**2.2**	0.0	0.11	1.05	3.97	93.8	**5.9**	40.7	3.9	**4.9**
5.5	0.16	na	0.00	**4.4**	0.4	1.03	9.69	3.45	70.0	**5.6**	48.9	7.8	**5.2**

Name	City	State	Rating	2018 Rating	2017 Rating	Total Assets ($Mil)	One Year Asset Growth	Asset Mix (As a % of Total Assets) Commercial Loans	Consumer Loans	Mortgage Loans	Securities	Capitalization Index	Leverage Ratio	Risk-Based Capital Ratio
Bank of Pensacola	Pensacola	FL	**C**	C-	D+	86.7	2.38	2.9	1.5	22.8	31.7	**10.0**	13.9	29.3
Bank of Perry County	Lobelville	TN	**C**	C+	B	172.3	3.61	7.8	16.0	41.6	4.1	**7.5**	9.4	13.8
Bank of Pontiac	Pontiac	IL	**B+**	B+	A-	559.6	0.19	11.1	4.6	23.6	14.0	**10.0**	13.6	20.0
▲ Bank of Prague	Prague	NE	**B+**	B	B	29.4	6.15	13.0	10.7	1.6	17.1	**10.0**	14.7	19.7
Bank of Prairie Du Sac	Prairie Du Sac	WI	**A+**	A+	A+	442.7	5.54	11.0	0.5	5.6	28.3	**10.0**	16.1	22.3
Bank of Prairie Village	Prairie Village	KS	**A-**	B+	B+	102.9	4.80	9.2	0.9	24.0	25.5	**10.0**	11.8	21.9
Bank of Princeton	Princeton	NJ	**B+**	A-	B	1379.6	11.72	2.2	0.0	11.0	7.9	**10.0**	13.3	15.4
Bank of Protection	Protection	KS	**B**	B	B	66.0	-2.07	5.4	3.9	6.4	14.4	**10.0**	14.8	19.9
▲ Bank of Putnam County	Cookeville	TN	**B**	B-	B-	869.4	8.10	4.6	2.8	21.2	26.3	**5.7**	7.7	13.9
Bank of Rantoul	Rantoul	IL	**B-**	B-	B+	231.0	2.63	14.2	0.8	1.9	45.1	**9.2**	10.5	17.1
Bank of Richmondville	Cobleskill	NY	**B-**	B-	B-	152.9	7.78	2.6	3.2	33.7	25.2	**10.0**	11.8	25.2
Bank of Ripley	Ripley	TN	**B**	B	B-	218.0	-0.78	1.4	8.2	7.6	52.9	**10.0**	15.5	28.5
▲ Bank of Romney	Romney	WV	**B**	B-	B-	306.4	7.42	2.2	6.8	44.2	18.1	**10.0**	12.0	20.8
Bank of Salem	Salem	AR	**B+**	B	B-	143.5	6.92	12.5	5.8	23.9	2.0	**10.0**	11.4	15.7
Bank of Salem	Salem	MO	**B-**	C+	C+	102.8	1.66	2.0	3.7	32.2	33.2	**8.2**	9.8	19.2
Bank of San Antonio	San Antonio	TX	**B**	B	B	813.6	6.55	24.6	0.9	7.6	7.9	**5.2**	9.8	11.2
Bank of San Francisco	San Francisco	CA	**A-**	B+	B	361.1	12.38	22.6	0.0	34.3	0.0	**9.8**	10.9	16.4
Bank of San Jacinto County	Coldspring	TX	**B**	B	B	40.5	2.22	4.0	2.4	32.8	19.3	**10.0**	14.6	42.3
▲ Bank of Santa Clarita	Santa Clarita	CA	**B+**	B	C+	316.6	5.11	5.5	1.4	2.7	3.3	**10.0**	11.7	15.5
Bank of South Carolina	Charleston	SC	**A**	A-	B+	452.8	5.46	11.3	1.2	12.7	21.7	**10.0**	11.1	16.5
▲ Bank of South Texas	Pharr	TX	**B-**	C+	B-	138.0	1.22	4.8	1.1	23.3	6.0	**8.9**	10.2	15.4
▲ Bank of Southern California, N.A.	San Diego	CA	**B-**	C+	B	839.1	14.17	12.8	0.3	9.1	2.0	**8.9**	11.7	14.1
▲ Bank of Southside Virginia	Carson	VA	**A-**	B+	A	564.3	2.67	2.2	18.5	5.4	25.0	**10.0**	19.0	31.3
Bank of Springfield	Springfield	IL	**C-**	C-	C	1055.0	2.55	20.7	0.9	10.3	5.9	**5.8**	9.2	11.6
▲ Bank of St. Elizabeth	Saint Elizabeth	MO	**A-**	B+	A	152.7	10.16	1.8	7.1	50.9	0.0	**9.3**	10.6	17.5
▲ Bank of St. Francisville	Saint Francisville	LA	**B**	B-	B	144.2	10.00	4.6	2.6	18.1	10.6	**9.5**	10.7	14.8
▲ Bank of Star Valley	Afton	WY	**B+**	B	B+	228.2	8.55	7.4	7.7	9.6	34.5	**9.5**	10.7	17.0
▲ Bank of Steinauer	Steinauer	NE	**C**	D+	C-	11.7	-1.59	6.6	8.3	40.9	3.4	**9.5**	10.6	16.9
Bank of Stockton	Stockton	CA	**A**	A-	A-	3312.5	9.06	6.7	11.1	5.7	13.9	**10.0**	17.2	15.5
Bank of Stronghurst	Stronghurst	IL	**C+**	C+	C+	74.2	4.33	2.3	1.7	6.5	55.8	**10.0**	17.3	36.6
Bank of Sullivan	Sullivan	MO	**B-**	B-	B-	527.1	8.69	10.0	2.2	31.6	6.8	**7.8**	9.5	13.8
Bank of Sun Prairie	Sun Prairie	WI	**B+**	B+	A-	434.7	7.18	7.4	1.0	8.0	7.9	**9.6**	12.3	14.6
▲ Bank of Sunset and Trust Co.	Sunset	LA	**B+**	B	B	148.5	8.84	13.6	0.6	25.1	12.3	**8.1**	9.7	14.5
Bank of Tampa	Tampa	FL	**B+**	B+	B	1874.1	10.94	14.6	3.4	3.8	27.0	**7.1**	9.5	12.6
Bank of Tennessee	Kingsport	TN	**B**	B	B	1436.8	9.16	10.3	0.5	21.6	13.3	**5.5**	8.9	11.3
▲ Bank of Tescott	Tescott	KS	**A-**	B	B+	387.3	-0.92	2.2	1.7	23.1	20.8	**10.0**	14.0	19.7
Bank of Texas	Midland	TX	**A-**	A-	B+	380.0	1.94	31.1	0.1	1.6	1.3	**8.4**	13.5	13.7
▲ Bank of the Bluegrass & Trust Co.	Lexington	KY	**A-**	B+	A-	265.6	2.46	3.2	0.7	22.1	21.3	**10.0**	11.7	17.4
▲ Bank of the Federated States of Micronesi	Pohnpei	FM	**A-**	B+	A-	177.5	3.58	7.7	9.0	1.0	34.0	**10.0**	13.8	30.6
▲ Bank of the Flint Hills	Wamego	KS	**B-**	C+	B	303.3	5.68	13.9	1.9	17.9	9.3	**6.7**	10.2	12.3
Bank of the James	Lynchburg	VA	**B-**	B-	B-	708.5	6.15	11.0	1.3	17.7	8.2	**6.1**	9.3	11.8
▲ Bank of the Lowcountry	Walterboro	SC	**B**	B-	B-	233.1	11.69	4.8	1.4	17.4	26.9	**9.3**	10.5	19.0
▲ Bank of the Mountains, Inc.	West Liberty	KY	**C-**	C-	B-	72.3	3.74	4.2	18.2	28.0	6.5	**9.8**	10.8	15.6
▼ Bank of the Orient	San Francisco	CA	**B**	B+	B-	927.3	10.86	8.1	0.0	17.2	5.1	**9.4**	10.6	14.5
Bank of the Pacific	Aberdeen	WA	**A-**	B+	B	944.1	0.90	10.6	6.6	9.1	10.5	**9.0**	11.0	14.1
▲ Bank of the Panhandle	Guymon	OK	**A-**	A-	A	163.9	3.73	10.7	1.1	8.9	28.0	**10.0**	13.0	17.7
▲ Bank of the Prairie	Olathe	KS	**B-**	B-	B	138.5	-2.09	16.0	0.6	17.2	19.7	**8.6**	10.1	14.5
▼ Bank of the Rockies	White Sulphur Spring	MT	**C-**	C	C	152.3	5.73	11.8	1.7	8.7	15.3	**9.5**	10.8	14.6
Bank of the Sierra	Porterville	CA	**A-**	A-	A-	2635.7	7.02	4.4	0.3	8.0	22.8	**9.9**	11.4	14.9
Bank of the South	Pensacola	FL	**C**	C-	D+	79.8	5.19	0.0	0.1	5.3	47.6	**10.0**	18.3	58.3
Bank of the Southwest	Roswell	NM	**B**	B	B	156.2	2.90	24.6	6.9	15.8	0.1	**7.5**	9.4	13.6
▲ Bank of the Valley	Bellwood	NE	**C**	C-	C+	305.1	22.64	6.7	1.8	3.9	13.0	**5.1**	8.0	11.1
Bank of the West	San Francisco	CA	**B**	B	B	91025.8	3.88	15.2	17.0	10.3	18.2	**7.8**	10.2	13.2
▲ Bank of the West	Thomas	OK	**A**	A-	B+	144.8	-6.20	10.1	0.4	6.3	0.0	**10.0**	13.1	15.6
Bank of the West	Grapevine	TX	**B**	B	B	493.4	-0.77	7.1	0.5	7.9	8.0	**7.7**	9.4	13.5
Bank of Tioga	Tioga	ND	**C+**	B-	B	333.6	-4.30	2.5	0.7	3.1	65.9	**8.0**	9.7	19.7
▲ Bank of Travelers Rest	Travelers Rest	SC	**B+**	B	B	795.8	9.65	5.9	4.5	13.8	24.2	**8.4**	9.9	15.5
▲ Bank of Turtle Lake	Turtle Lake	ND	**B-**	C-	C+	54.5	3.12	9.5	1.5	0.5	8.6	**9.6**	12.0	14.6
Bank of Utah	Ogden	UT	**A**	B+	A	1440.1	10.64	5.6	0.3	2.4	8.5	**10.0**	13.0	16.4
Bank of Utica	Utica	NY	**B+**	B+	A-	1135.1	6.76	2.8	0.4	0.2	83.6	**10.0**	20.7	20.0

Asset Quality Index	Adjusted Non-Performing Loans as a % of Total Loans	Adjusted Non-Performing Loans as a % of Capital	Net Charge-Offs Avg Loans	Profitability Index	Net Income ($Mil)	Return on Assets (R.O.A.)	Return on Equity (R.O.E.)	Net Interest Spread	Overhead Efficiency Ratio	Liquidity Index	Liquidity Ratio	Hot Money Ratio	Stability Index
9.1	0.00	na	0.00	**2.1**	0.2	0.27	2.01	2.65	84.2	**4.5**	51.5	14.5	**5.7**
5.1	0.62	na	0.06	**8.2**	2.2	1.74	18.47	4.52	57.1	**1.2**	5.4	21.7	**7.4**
6.6	1.14	na	0.22	**6.5**	5.0	1.22	9.18	3.86	55.0	**1.7**	13.3	14.8	**8.2**
7.5	0.00	na	0.06	**10.0**	0.6	2.63	18.06	4.77	56.4	**4.1**	31.1	11.4	**9.0**
8.7	0.19	0.4	0.00	**9.8**	6.0	1.83	11.45	3.75	40.8	**5.5**	41.2	7.5	**9.7**
9.1	0.00	na	0.00	**6.5**	1.1	1.46	12.67	3.67	56.8	**2.4**	28.3	19.2	**7.7**
6.2	1.07	3.6	0.49	**3.9**	6.8	0.68	4.79	3.41	62.0	**1.1**	12.5	26.1	**9.9**
7.2	0.02	na	0.18	**5.3**	0.6	1.15	8.04	4.18	60.6	**1.4**	11.0	25.2	**7.2**
8.9	0.00	na	0.06	**5.0**	7.2	1.12	14.82	3.14	65.6	**3.2**	33.2	16.9	**5.9**
2.6	6.44	na	0.41	**7.6**	3.2	1.86	16.20	3.80	45.1	**1.8**	15.1	18.7	**8.5**
6.8	1.32	6.8	0.32	**3.6**	0.7	0.63	5.64	3.77	77.6	**4.1**	26.1	9.6	**6.3**
5.8	4.24	9.6	0.22	**4.2**	1.5	0.87	5.67	3.95	72.6	**3.0**	38.2	19.4	**7.5**
4.9	2.87	na	0.03	**5.2**	2.4	1.11	10.69	3.72	64.1	**1.3**	19.2	14.1	**6.1**
5.2	1.43	9.1	0.06	**8.8**	1.6	1.50	12.76	4.56	58.2	**1.2**	17.4	25.9	**7.6**
6.3	0.88	na	0.03	**4.1**	0.8	1.01	10.98	3.07	68.6	**2.8**	22.4	15.5	**5.3**
7.0	0.01	0.1	0.03	**6.5**	7.7	1.31	12.98	3.78	62.5	**4.8**	17.2	4.0	**7.0**
8.6	0.00	0.0	0.00	**5.9**	2.9	1.12	10.04	4.23	61.0	**1.8**	14.8	20.3	**6.3**
9.7	0.00	na	0.00	**4.5**	0.3	1.01	7.06	4.77	80.8	**4.8**	61.5	14.8	**6.7**
7.2	0.36	1.1	0.00	**5.4**	2.6	1.10	9.88	3.22	54.1	**1.1**	20.0	19.3	**6.7**
8.3	0.61	3.4	0.11	**9.3**	5.7	1.77	15.93	4.55	52.0	**5.2**	29.5	4.0	**7.9**
5.4	0.68	na	0.17	**6.6**	1.4	1.36	10.99	6.15	71.8	**0.8**	23.7	39.2	**7.2**
5.5	0.32	na	0.00	**5.1**	5.1	0.89	6.55	4.30	67.6	**1.2**	14.1	18.8	**7.7**
7.7	0.41	na	0.04	**7.4**	7.0	1.65	9.09	4.04	58.4	**6.7**	62.7	5.5	**9.3**
0.7	4.15	32.2	0.00	**4.2**	5.5	0.72	7.69	3.90	72.4	**4.3**	12.3	6.8	**6.8**
8.0	0.10	na	0.02	**8.9**	2.2	2.00	16.75	4.49	60.0	**1.8**	15.5	20.2	**8.7**
5.5	1.61	na	0.07	**5.3**	1.3	1.28	11.97	4.46	72.8	**2.4**	15.7	17.3	**6.7**
7.0	1.07	na	0.00	**8.4**	3.5	2.10	20.51	4.15	47.2	**3.1**	33.2	17.4	**8.2**
8.2	0.00	na	0.00	**4.6**	0.1	0.98	9.80	4.52	78.0	**4.3**	9.4	5.5	**3.9**
7.6	0.63	1.3	0.11	**9.2**	103.5	4.34	25.88	4.02	46.5	**6.1**	43.2	7.4	**10.0**
9.3	0.21	0.3	0.03	**3.0**	0.3	0.55	3.33	2.76	80.7	**4.9**	56.8	13.5	**7.1**
3.8	2.15	na	0.24	**5.6**	4.8	1.23	12.86	3.80	60.0	**1.5**	9.9	23.1	**6.9**
4.3	1.53	na	0.14	**4.4**	2.7	0.85	6.98	3.48	67.7	**1.7**	11.9	17.0	**8.2**
8.6	0.09	na	0.05	**5.6**	1.3	1.20	12.52	4.05	63.0	**1.1**	10.8	27.7	**6.4**
7.2	0.76	4.7	0.17	**6.2**	17.1	1.32	13.95	4.08	61.5	**6.6**	34.3	1.0	**7.9**
7.9	0.44	3.1	0.01	**5.8**	14.7	1.39	15.90	3.83	65.9	**3.5**	11.8	7.4	**8.6**
5.8	1.46	7.4	0.19	**6.1**	4.0	1.35	10.00	3.61	53.0	**1.1**	17.7	31.5	**9.4**
8.2	0.00	na	0.00	**9.8**	7.6	2.77	21.64	4.03	31.1	**0.8**	21.4	54.4	**9.4**
7.4	0.01	na	-0.03	**6.9**	2.6	1.33	11.08	3.73	66.9	**3.6**	27.9	11.2	**8.4**
7.4	5.01	na	0.52	**6.6**	2.0	1.56	10.98	4.30	61.0	**6.6**	82.6	9.6	**8.2**
4.9	0.75	na	0.12	**4.3**	2.1	0.93	9.18	3.88	72.1	**1.6**	12.8	20.8	**6.5**
6.5	0.39	2.8	0.06	**4.4**	4.4	0.85	9.30	3.89	75.8	**2.1**	13.5	16.7	**6.1**
6.1	1.96	na	-0.06	**4.7**	1.7	1.01	9.68	3.66	67.3	**1.9**	22.8	21.0	**6.0**
3.5	1.34	na	0.47	**4.3**	0.4	0.73	6.79	5.84	80.4	**1.6**	15.8	23.4	**5.4**
4.1	1.58	12.5	1.01	**4.4**	5.0	0.76	6.89	3.94	63.8	**1.2**	18.5	30.6	**7.8**
7.5	0.19	1.0	0.01	**7.8**	10.8	1.59	12.98	4.82	66.3	**4.4**	13.6	4.1	**8.2**
7.5	0.96	na	0.15	**6.9**	2.0	1.68	13.11	4.09	60.3	**1.6**	19.9	24.0	**9.1**
6.1	0.00	na	0.68	**4.7**	1.0	0.91	9.13	3.73	67.2	**1.0**	25.0	34.4	**6.5**
2.3	3.04	na	0.00	**5.8**	1.6	1.39	12.04	5.67	74.6	**4.4**	19.6	6.8	**7.7**
7.2	0.88	3.1	0.05	**7.8**	28.3	1.48	11.76	4.26	56.3	**1.9**	19.4	18.8	**9.8**
9.5	0.00	na	0.00	**1.6**	0.1	0.20	1.11	2.55	90.3	**7.2**	80.4	4.0	**5.9**
7.4	0.02	na	0.21	**6.0**	1.6	1.37	14.52	6.73	76.3	**4.8**	12.8	2.9	**5.6**
3.8	0.21	na	0.03	**3.9**	1.7	0.79	9.37	3.47	67.9	**0.6**	11.8	34.3	**4.8**
5.4	0.75	3.0	0.19	**4.0**	514.5	0.77	5.49	2.88	64.0	**2.8**	23.8	11.4	**9.8**
7.1	0.00	na	0.01	**10.0**	2.7	2.42	18.75	5.10	52.0	**1.0**	10.4	30.0	**9.3**
4.7	0.49	2.8	0.10	**5.4**	5.1	1.36	14.47	4.48	69.2	**3.9**	22.9	10.3	**7.0**
7.1	3.52	na	0.02	**3.8**	4.8	1.85	19.29	2.85	87.1	**3.1**	70.7	31.5	**5.6**
7.2	0.53	na	0.14	**6.0**	8.1	1.41	14.28	3.60	63.6	**3.6**	33.3	14.9	**7.5**
4.9	0.17	na	-0.01	**6.8**	0.5	1.33	10.82	4.49	58.2	**1.4**	12.8	25.2	**6.3**
7.2	0.04	na	0.08	**10.0**	23.0	2.24	17.18	4.82	52.2	**4.6**	18.2	5.1	**10.0**
9.9	3.58	na	0.89	**5.2**	13.6	1.61	7.80	1.71	50.1	**4.7**	88.2	23.9	**8.7**

Name	City	State	Rating	2018 Rating	2017 Rating	Total Assets ($Mil)	One Year Asset Growth	Asset Mix (As a % of Total Assets): Commercial Loans	Consumer Loans	Mortgage Loans	Securities	Capitalization Index	Leverage Ratio	Risk-Based Capital Ratio
Bank of Vernon	Vernon	AL	**A-**	B+	B+	162.9	10.29	15.5	1.9	15.4	14.3	**10.0**	16.0	23.3
Bank of Versailles	Versailles	MO	**B**	B	B	262.8	2.86	1.1	0.9	61.9	0.5	**10.0**	13.3	23.8
▲ Bank of Vici	Vici	OK	**C+**	C-	C+	34.9	-7.24	23.4	14.3	2.6	19.3	**10.0**	13.5	21.2
Bank of Walker County	Jasper	AL	**C**	C+	B-	71.9	2.37	13.6	3.3	23.3	12.9	**10.0**	11.1	15.9
Bank of Washington	Washington	MO	**D**	D	D	721.3	6.66	24.8	0.7	8.7	6.3	**9.5**	13.1	14.6
▲ Bank of Waynesboro	Waynesboro	TN	**A-**	B+	A-	173.1	4.24	7.0	6.2	19.3	14.4	**10.0**	13.5	19.7
Bank of Western Oklahoma	Elk City	OK	**B-**	B-	B-	312.1	15.01	7.6	0.8	13.6	7.5	**4.7**	7.7	10.8
▲ Bank of Weston	Weston	MO	**B**	B-	C+	147.7	0.31	6.9	0.9	17.5	12.8	**6.6**	8.6	12.2
Bank of Whittier, N.A.	Whittier	CA	**C+**	B-	B-	72.0	26.47	0.1	0.5	18.0	0.0	**10.0**	15.3	23.8
Bank of Wiggins	Wiggins	MS	**B+**	B+	B+	167.9	-8.84	8.1	5.4	17.3	31.2	**10.0**	18.0	32.3
Bank of Winnfield & Trust Co.	Winnfield	LA	**B-**	B	B	137.6	-0.17	11.0	3.8	17.1	32.5	**10.0**	13.8	27.4
▲ Bank of Winona	Winona	MS	**B**	B	B-	122.9	7.10	1.8	3.4	20.9	41.5	**10.0**	11.1	21.6
▲ Bank of Wisconsin Dells	Wisconsin Dells	WI	**B+**	B	B-	589.3	1.66	5.7	0.4	7.6	12.8	**9.0**	11.7	14.2
▲ Bank of Wolcott	Wolcott	IN	**B+**	B	B+	170.2	6.90	6.1	1.1	12.5	25.0	**10.0**	11.2	17.1
Bank of Wrightsville	Wrightsville	GA	**C+**	C	C	57.2	2.25	9.1	2.8	14.2	26.7	**9.1**	10.4	15.9
▲ Bank of Wyandotte	Wyandotte	OK	**C-**	C-	C-	12.8	4.39	9.3	11.1	14.1	23.6	**7.8**	9.5	17.0
Bank of Yates City	Yates City	IL	**C-**	C-	D+	70.7	8.35	9.1	7.9	23.4	22.4	**7.7**	9.5	15.3
Bank of Yazoo City	Yazoo City	MS	**B**	B	B-	240.9	-3.93	5.0	2.0	18.1	33.9	**10.0**	12.2	20.4
▲ Bank of York	York	SC	**B+**	B-	B-	228.8	1.72	4.1	3.0	10.2	20.7	**10.0**	12.5	30.6
Bank of Zachary	Zachary	LA	**B-**	B-	B-	239.6	-1.45	2.5	2.0	36.4	21.6	**8.3**	9.9	18.1
Bank of Zumbrota	Zumbrota	MN	**B+**	B	B	165.3	3.59	14.1	2.7	13.8	16.4	**8.4**	13.2	13.7
▲ Bank OZK	Little Rock	AR	**A-**	B+	B+	23402.7	5.96	3.0	12.5	3.7	10.3	**10.0**	15.2	15.1
▲ Bank Plus	Estherville	IA	**C+**	C	C-	129.3	-4.54	2.1	1.9	7.1	11.5	**6.1**	9.1	11.8
Bank Rhode Island	Providence	RI	**B**	B	B	2474.8	7.08	17.7	0.0	9.8	10.2	**6.6**	9.8	12.2
▲ Bank Star	Pacific	MO	**B**	B-	C+	135.3	-3.21	4.4	2.7	32.4	4.9	**8.4**	9.9	15.5
▲ Bank, N.A.	McAlester	OK	**A-**	B+	B+	377.4	4.89	4.5	3.1	17.0	30.6	**10.0**	11.3	19.6
▲ Bank3	Memphis	TN	**D+**	D-	D	230.7	29.16	28.4	0.6	6.4	11.6	**10.0**	13.4	15.7
Bank7	Oklahoma City	OK	**A**	A	A-	825.8	10.05	30.6	0.2	4.6	0.0	**10.0**	12.3	16.3
▲ bankcda	Coeur d'Alene	ID	**A-**	B-	C	137.6	11.17	14.4	0.9	6.3	29.8	**10.0**	12.9	17.9
▲ BankChampaign, N.A.	Champaign	IL	**B+**	B	B	224.7	-0.56	12.3	0.3	19.7	13.7	**8.8**	10.2	14.9
BankCherokee	Saint Paul	MN	**B-**	B-	C+	275.1	1.64	17.5	0.8	10.3	17.6	**6.9**	8.9	13.9
▲ Bankers Trust Co.	Des Moines	IA	**B**	B-	C+	4919.5	9.97	18.9	0.4	9.2	11.4	**6.3**	9.7	12.0
Bankers' Bank	Madison	WI	**B**	B	B	747.8	10.62	2.1	0.8	6.4	11.6	**9.7**	10.8	15.6
Bankers' Bank of Kansas	Wichita	KS	**B+**	B+	B+	170.8	0.47	12.7	12.0	3.0	3.0	**10.0**	16.0	20.4
Bankers' Bank of Kentucky, Inc.	Frankfort	KY	**C+**	C+	C+	134.6	19.74	1.7	0.0	1.6	0.7	**9.5**	10.7	34.8
▲ Bankers' Bank of the West	Denver	CO	**A-**	B+	B+	382.9	7.26	8.5	0.1	0.4	7.2	**10.0**	13.6	18.4
BankFinancial, N.A.	Olympia Fields	IL	**B+**	A-	B	1489.4	-2.65	29.5	0.1	3.2	0.8	**9.9**	10.9	15.5
▲ BankFirst	Norfolk	NE	**B+**	B+	A-	754.1	57.29	7.9	1.0	8.0	15.9	**6.2**	9.4	11.9
BankFirst Financial Services	Macon	MS	**B**	B	B-	1273.3	30.72	8.5	1.0	15.1	15.7	**8.2**	9.8	13.8
BankFlorida	Jupiter	FL	**D-**	D	C	90.9	-1.89	6.0	0.4	32.1	10.6	**6.6**	8.6	12.6
BankGloucester	Gloucester	MA	**C**	C	C	278.5	5.20	3.4	0.2	45.8	8.3	**6.5**	8.5	12.9
BankIowa of Cedar Rapids	Cedar Rapids	IA	**B**	B	B+	682.6	3.04	9.6	2.1	17.7	14.9	**8.1**	10.9	13.4
BankLiberty	Kansas City	MO	**B+**	A-	A-	581.5	3.70	10.1	0.4	9.8	1.8	**8.3**	11.2	13.6
BankNewport	Middletown	RI	**B+**	B	B	1753.4	8.40	8.0	4.3	27.8	13.8	**8.2**	10.6	13.5
BankNorth	Arthur	ND	**C**	C+	B+	411.3	1.62	7.5	1.4	3.7	2.1	**5.9**	10.4	11.7
BankORION	Orion	IL	**B**	B-	B-	477.7	4.90	7.5	2.6	17.9	29.2	**10.0**	11.2	19.1
BankPacific, Ltd	Hagatna	GU	**B-**	B-	B-	145.2	5.13	8.9	27.2	39.3	0.8	**10.0**	11.9	17.3
BankPlus	Belzoni	MS	**B+**	B+	B	2965.6	9.56	11.4	2.0	16.4	11.7	**7.7**	9.6	13.1
BankSouth	Dothan	AL	**A-**	A-	A-	182.2	7.22	9.6	1.6	34.5	20.6	**10.0**	20.3	33.6
BankSouth	Greensboro	GA	**A-**	A-	A-	715.6	14.34	3.0	0.7	38.8	3.8	**7.5**	9.4	13.4
BankStar Financial	Elkton	SD	**B-**	B-	B	201.5	12.86	6.8	2.4	16.6	14.5	**6.5**	8.5	13.1
▲ BankTennessee	Collierville	TN	**B-**	C+	B-	311.4	6.27	12.0	3.3	22.4	4.8	**7.6**	10.0	13.0
BankUnited, N.A.	Miami Lakes	FL	**B+**	B+	B+	32873.8	4.50	12.5	0.0	17.0	24.1	**7.2**	9.1	13.4
▲ BankVista	Sartell	MN	**C**	C-	C+	336.4	18.86	17.6	1.8	13.4	4.0	**5.0**	8.7	11.0
Bankwell Bank	New Canaan	CT	**B**	B	B	1855.9	-1.32	11.8	0.0	8.8	5.7	**8.2**	10.9	13.5
BANKWEST	Rockford	MN	**B+**	B+	B	153.7	7.82	11.6	1.8	13.4	18.3	**8.9**	10.3	16.5
▲ Bankwest of Kansas	Goodland	KS	**B+**	B	B	110.6	0.67	3.1	1.8	2.5	12.7	**10.0**	12.4	15.6
▲ BankWest, Inc.	Pierre	SD	**C**	C	C	1099.7	6.11	6.0	9.0	4.4	14.7	**8.2**	10.3	13.5
Banner Bank	Walla Walla	WA	**B+**	B+	B+	11794.6	15.52	10.9	1.3	9.0	14.6	**7.1**	10.2	12.6
Banner Banks	Birnamwood	WI	**B-**	B-	B-	99.1	4.58	2.2	0.4	5.4	36.4	**10.0**	12.1	27.7

Asset Quality Index	Adjusted Non-Performing Loans as a % of Total Loans	Adjusted Non-Performing Loans as a % of Capital	Net Charge-Offs Avg Loans	Profitability Index	Net Income ($Mil)	Return on Assets (R.O.A.)	Return on Equity (R.O.E.)	Net Interest Spread	Overhead Efficiency Ratio	Liquidity Index	Liquidity Ratio	Hot Money Ratio	Stability Index
7.6	0.50	na	-0.01	**7.1**	1.6	1.40	8.57	3.97	59.7	**2.0**	26.0	21.1	**7.5**
6.6	2.64	na	0.07	**4.9**	2.0	1.02	7.85	3.30	59.4	**2.8**	14.9	15.0	**8.3**
3.0	4.97	na	0.05	**4.8**	0.3	1.13	8.96	4.59	78.1	**2.6**	37.4	23.3	**6.2**
4.0	2.75	na	-0.01	**4.2**	0.5	0.94	8.95	4.39	75.6	**0.8**	16.6	37.0	**6.5**
1.0	5.40	na	0.05	**7.1**	9.5	1.78	14.05	4.11	57.2	**1.8**	15.0	16.8	**8.0**
6.9	1.31	na	0.10	**8.7**	2.1	1.64	12.47	4.85	56.7	**2.1**	26.5	20.5	**8.3**
6.0	0.02	2.2	0.05	**8.3**	4.5	1.97	23.56	4.89	57.7	**0.7**	11.9	36.2	**6.7**
6.8	0.55	2.2	0.00	**6.5**	1.9	1.67	20.18	4.41	64.6	**3.0**	14.4	14.2	**5.6**
8.4	0.00	na	-0.13	**2.6**	0.2	0.31	1.86	2.29	87.3	**2.7**	65.1	50.7	**6.9**
8.1	0.43	na	0.06	**4.6**	1.2	0.90	5.25	3.78	73.9	**3.2**	47.8	23.4	**7.5**
5.0	3.18	na	1.65	**3.0**	0.6	0.55	4.54	3.41	77.3	**4.0**	39.7	14.8	**7.3**
5.8	2.68	na	0.05	**5.4**	1.2	1.30	11.49	3.87	65.0	**4.2**	41.6	14.6	**6.7**
6.5	0.16	na	-0.07	**8.3**	6.6	1.52	12.97	3.79	48.5	**2.4**	14.2	11.5	**8.7**
5.8	2.43	na	0.07	**7.1**	2.0	1.61	14.18	3.89	56.2	**2.3**	34.7	20.9	**8.4**
6.0	0.56	na	0.01	**5.2**	0.6	1.32	14.64	4.13	67.3	**3.2**	23.4	13.8	**4.9**
7.6	0.00	na	0.13	**4.5**	0.1	0.51	5.78	5.31	79.3	**4.4**	35.0	6.7	**4.0**
2.1	3.00	20.1	-0.01	**2.7**	0.2	0.40	4.39	3.62	81.7	**3.1**	24.4	14.3	**4.3**
6.7	0.00	na	0.23	**4.4**	1.8	0.93	8.59	3.40	70.3	**2.8**	27.1	16.6	**6.8**
6.7	3.03	na	0.09	**5.5**	2.0	1.16	9.56	3.55	60.8	**5.9**	54.7	9.1	**6.9**
6.9	0.92	na	0.17	**3.5**	1.0	0.56	5.85	3.92	80.8	**3.0**	21.9	14.5	**6.0**
5.6	0.94	na	-0.08	**6.2**	1.8	1.44	11.04	3.87	63.7	**1.8**	10.1	17.2	**8.2**
5.8	0.37	1.4	0.11	**9.8**	325.1	1.91	11.02	4.40	39.8	**1.0**	14.7	20.4	**10.0**
6.3	0.08	na	-0.02	**4.4**	1.0	0.99	9.27	3.85	67.4	**1.2**	6.0	19.7	**6.6**
4.5	0.66	5.5	0.06	**5.0**	18.5	1.03	7.90	3.42	61.5	**2.2**	4.3	13.7	**8.3**
7.5	0.04	na	0.00	**4.7**	0.9	0.91	7.88	4.42	65.5	**4.1**	14.2	7.7	**6.3**
7.1	1.10	na	0.29	**7.5**	4.9	1.72	16.03	3.88	57.2	**4.8**	43.9	12.2	**8.1**
8.3	0.00	na	0.00	**1.2**	0.8	0.53	4.68	3.07	86.7	**1.0**	24.3	21.9	**4.8**
7.7	0.81	3.2	0.00	**6.9**	3.6	0.61	5.03	5.70	73.9	**1.2**	19.6	27.0	**8.8**
8.0	1.22	na	-0.05	**5.5**	1.1	1.11	9.94	4.50	67.9	**6.1**	40.6	2.7	**6.3**
7.6	0.24	na	-0.01	**5.4**	2.2	1.31	13.06	3.90	70.6	**0.7**	12.2	22.8	**6.7**
8.1	0.21	na	-0.13	**4.5**	1.6	0.80	9.37	4.05	74.0	**5.6**	33.2	3.2	**4.9**
5.6	1.52	7.4	0.19	**6.8**	48.7	1.39	14.32	3.42	55.1	**2.4**	15.2	17.4	**8.8**
8.6	0.00	na	0.04	**4.6**	5.6	0.98	9.39	2.33	71.8	**1.7**	35.8	7.5	**6.8**
7.2	1.10	na	0.34	**6.2**	1.5	1.12	7.49	3.80	78.9	**0.8**	24.7	12.2	**7.7**
9.6	0.00	na	0.00	**3.4**	0.6	0.58	5.54	1.38	69.7	**7.9**	77.7	0.0	**6.9**
8.5	0.15	na	-0.01	**6.0**	3.3	1.18	8.79	3.55	76.7	**1.7**	38.3	34.5	**7.8**
7.1	0.12	na	0.48	**4.8**	9.2	0.80	7.39	3.64	63.3	**2.2**	15.4	17.2	**10.0**
6.7	0.35	na	0.01	**9.2**	9.9	1.78	16.06	3.86	43.1	**3.5**	15.4	11.6	**9.1**
5.1	1.26	na	0.01	**5.5**	9.9	1.10	10.82	3.61	66.5	**2.8**	12.0	14.9	**8.4**
4.8	1.20	na	0.12	**0.0**	-0.6	-0.84	-8.53	3.30	146.0	**1.3**	17.8	24.8	**4.7**
4.2	2.23	na	0.00	**3.9**	1.3	0.62	7.43	3.68	76.4	**1.5**	13.3	24.2	**4.9**
6.9	0.69	na	0.00	**4.6**	5.5	1.10	9.74	3.17	68.0	**1.3**	7.8	21.2	**7.9**
6.8	0.35	na	-0.01	**8.5**	6.1	1.49	10.87	4.59	58.9	**4.5**	20.3	5.4	**6.3**
5.7	1.59	na	0.22	**5.5**	14.0	1.10	10.17	3.72	65.0	**2.5**	19.2	14.5	**9.0**
2.8	1.37	na	0.13	**8.2**	6.0	1.95	16.00	5.10	58.8	**2.9**	4.0	13.6	**9.0**
6.8	1.85	na	0.00	**4.8**	3.6	1.03	8.54	3.32	60.4	**2.8**	19.9	15.4	**6.8**
2.6	3.17	19.0	0.15	**3.6**	0.6	0.55	4.65	5.44	87.1	**4.9**	10.6	2.4	**6.3**
6.3	0.70	5.2	0.19	**6.4**	30.1	1.38	14.65	3.97	68.7	**4.1**	16.0	8.6	**7.4**
9.0	0.00	na	-0.10	**5.5**	1.6	1.21	5.97	3.50	62.0	**2.6**	30.5	18.6	**8.8**
6.4	0.64	4.9	-0.02	**8.0**	9.7	1.98	21.04	4.19	82.0	**2.0**	12.5	18.8	**8.3**
5.3	0.45	na	0.19	**5.5**	1.7	1.25	12.80	3.77	62.9	**0.8**	10.1	26.1	**6.2**
5.2	0.62	na	-0.04	**6.3**	3.3	1.44	13.25	4.42	66.1	**1.6**	10.8	22.1	**7.2**
6.6	0.79	5.4	0.06	**5.0**	239.1	0.98	10.36	2.55	52.9	**1.5**	20.1	13.8	**8.4**
4.1	0.71	na	0.05	**5.0**	2.2	0.92	10.76	3.81	68.5	**0.8**	15.1	29.6	**5.0**
4.8	0.83	5.5	0.20	**5.8**	17.4	1.24	11.83	3.16	52.1	**0.8**	11.4	35.2	**8.6**
5.7	1.72	6.6	0.00	**7.1**	1.9	1.72	17.02	4.45	64.4	**5.5**	33.1	3.4	**6.8**
7.4	0.00	na	0.00	**6.1**	1.3	1.43	11.83	4.88	62.8	**1.2**	18.1	14.6	**7.9**
3.2	2.22	14.1	0.04	**5.7**	9.4	1.17	11.03	4.03	73.0	**2.1**	15.3	6.9	**10.0**
7.5	0.21	1.0	0.07	**6.6**	115.4	1.33	10.01	4.42	63.1	**4.2**	17.0	5.1	**9.9**
6.1	3.04	na	0.00	**3.7**	0.6	0.82	6.76	2.90	71.0	**6.2**	65.1	7.4	**7.3**

Name	City	State	Rating	2018 Rating	2017 Rating	Total Assets ($Mil)	One Year Asset Growth	Asset Mix (As a % of Total Assets) Comm-ercial Loans	Cons-umer Loans	Mort-gage Loans	Secur-ities	Capital-ization Index	Lever-age Ratio	Risk-Based Capital Ratio
Banner Capital Bank	Harrisburg	NE	**C+**	B-	B-	189.1	16.48	12.4	2.6	2.6	6.6	**6.0**	10.3	11.8
Banterra Bank	Eldorado	IL	**B-**	B-	B-	1865.5	8.12	23.3	21.7	5.6	18.6	**5.4**	8.3	11.3
Bar Harbor Bank & Trust	Bar Harbor	ME	**B**	B	B	3610.0	1.50	6.7	0.3	33.3	18.7	**6.7**	8.7	13.5
Bar Harbor S&L Assn.	Bar Harbor	ME	**B-**	B	B	103.4	-0.93	0.0	0.5	64.1	5.6	**10.0**	11.2	22.9
Baraboo State Bank	Baraboo	WI	**B**	B	B	386.4	-0.19	8.5	1.3	8.3	14.5	**9.6**	11.3	14.7
Barclays Bank Delaware	Wilmington	DE	**C**	C	C	34445.0	4.48	0.6	76.4	0.0	0.3	**10.0**	14.1	19.5
Barrington Bank & Trust Co., N.A.	Barrington	IL	**B**	B	B-	2604.1	20.55	28.4	16.9	26.4	4.3	**5.7**	13.3	11.5
Barwick Banking Co.	Barwick	GA	**D**	D	D-	12.1	12.62	1.1	1.3	0.7	47.7	**5.6**	7.6	76.2
▲ Basile State Bank	Basile	LA	**C+**	C+	C	56.6	3.26	9.9	9.6	40.5	1.6	**10.0**	11.6	18.6
Bath Savings Institution	Bath	ME	**A-**	A-	A-	972.1	5.66	5.4	1.1	30.6	19.0	**10.0**	14.8	22.5
Bath State Bank	Bath	IN	**B-**	B-	B+	163.8	2.71	3.7	1.8	19.0	8.0	**8.5**	10.0	14.8
Battle Creek State Bank	Battle Creek	NE	**B-**	B-	B-	33.9	7.13	53.7	1.6	2.7	8.1	**10.0**	13.9	17.6
Baxter State Bank	Baxter Springs	KS	**C+**	C+	C+	25.5	-6.26	1.9	8.8	34.2	20.5	**10.0**	21.2	36.2
Bay Bank	Green Bay	WI	**B+**	B	B	103.5	7.76	11.7	4.7	14.4	14.8	**10.0**	14.8	23.2
▲ Bay Port State Bank	Bay Port	MI	**C+**	C-	C-	109.5	10.45	10.9	2.6	20.0	0.1	**5.5**	7.7	11.4
Bay State Savings Bank	Worcester	MA	**C**	C	C+	425.0	0.68	2.1	0.9	51.4	3.6	**7.3**	9.2	12.9
Baybank	Gladstone	MI	**C**	C	C+	106.6	10.54	18.6	11.1	21.0	16.2	**6.9**	9.1	12.5
▲ BayCoast Bank	Swansea	MA	**C+**	C	C	1858.8	13.78	11.3	3.7	22.3	7.3	**4.7**	8.8	10.9
▲ BayVanguard Bank	Sparrows Point	MD	**B**	C+	C+	297.4	83.37	0.9	4.5	47.3	5.1	**10.0**	20.5	33.2
BBVA USA	Birmingham	AL	**C+**	C+	C+	91975.3	3.21	18.1	7.8	15.2	15.1	**7.2**	9.1	14.1
BCB Community Bank	Bayonne	NJ	**B-**	C+	C+	2823.9	7.13	3.5	0.0	19.1	3.5	**7.2**	9.2	13.0
BCBank, Inc.	Philippi	WV	**C+**	C+	C+	142.2	5.27	5.5	4.3	15.8	16.1	**8.4**	9.9	14.8
Beach Community Bank	Fort Walton Beach	FL	**E**	E	E-	491.3	5.07	6.0	0.2	16.5	13.7	**10.0**	11.3	17.0
▲ Beacon Business Bank, N.A.	San Francisco	CA	**B-**	C+	B	140.6	0.47	8.7	0.0	6.8	7.4	**10.0**	13.0	20.6
Beacon Community Bank	Charleston	SC	**D**	D		105.0	112.43	5.4	0.2	27.8	6.4	**10.0**	27.7	33.6
▲ Beal Bank USA	Las Vegas	NV	**C**	C-	C	4840.1	-14.67	48.2	0.0	3.4	14.2	**10.0**	41.0	47.6
▲ Beal Bank, SSB	Plano	TX	**C+**	C-	C	1593.6	-30.82	16.3	0.6	38.7	13.5	**10.0**	24.8	39.8
Beardstown Savings s.b.	Beardstown	IL	**C+**	C	C	52.1	2.72	0.2	11.8	49.2	18.2	**9.7**	10.8	19.8
Beartooth Bank	Billings	MT	**B-**	B-	B-	48.5	5.61	14.3	0.6	15.4	0.1	**10.0**	16.0	20.2
Beauregard Federal Savings Bank	DeRidder	LA	**B+**	B+	B+	66.4	1.06	7.1	7.6	45.4	14.3	**10.0**	17.6	33.3
Bedford Federal Savings Bank	Bedford	IN	**B**	B	B	132.6	6.58	3.5	2.6	47.1	0.0	**10.0**	12.1	19.5
Bedford Loan & Deposit Bank	Bedford	KY	**B**	B-	B-	94.0	1.66	0.6	9.2	33.0	31.3	**10.0**	14.3	24.8
▲ Belgrade State Bank	Belgrade	MO	**B**	B-	C+	275.1	6.28	8.1	4.2	30.0	7.3	**8.0**	9.7	15.3
Bell Bank	Fargo	ND	**B+**	B+	B+	6266.2	22.25	16.2	2.6	15.6	1.4	**5.1**	9.5	11.1
▲ Bellevue State Bank	Bellevue	IA	**A-**	B+	B+	120.5	7.69	11.8	5.4	20.7	7.7	**10.0**	15.2	16.3
Belmont Bank & Trust Co.	Chicago	IL	**C**	B-	B-	533.6	21.46	14.1	1.2	9.0	19.0	**8.4**	9.9	15.3
Belmont Savings Bank	Bellaire	OH	**B**	B	B	376.6	-1.96	1.3	2.2	13.7	66.5	**10.0**	18.4	63.4
Belmont Savings Bank, SSB	Belmont	NC	**C+**	B-	B-	92.2	-1.21	0.0	0.0	67.2	5.6	**10.0**	20.5	40.0
Belt Valley Bank	Belt	MT	**B**	B	B+	64.7	2.95	3.4	3.5	29.0	7.3	**10.0**	15.7	19.1
Ben Franklin Bank of Illinois	Arlington Heights	IL	**D-**	D	D-	100.0	6.04	1.5	0.0	31.6	5.6	**8.4**	9.9	15.6
Benchmark Bank	Plano	TX	**B+**	B+	B+	713.2	22.59	8.4	2.4	17.4	0.2	**7.1**	9.1	13.1
▲ Benchmark Community Bank	Kenbridge	VA	**A-**	A-	A	700.4	13.28	5.4	2.3	39.8	5.7	**9.4**	10.6	16.3
Bendena State Bank	Bendena	KS	**B-**	B-	B-	67.2	5.32	4.7	3.0	12.5	17.1	**8.2**	9.8	13.9
Beneficial State Bank	Oakland	CA	**C-**	C-	C-	1056.2	5.25	12.7	8.3	3.7	4.0	**9.1**	10.4	15.8
▲ Bennington State Bank	Salina	KS	**B-**	C+	B+	706.0	3.45	6.6	1.5	16.1	24.5	**10.0**	11.8	18.3
Benton County State Bank	Blairstown	IA	**B**	B	B+	45.0	4.87	3.0	0.1	6.3	17.2	**10.0**	14.3	18.8
▲ Benton State Bank	Benton	WI	**C-**	D+	D+	65.5	0.37	6.3	4.5	34.7	4.3	**7.0**	9.0	12.8
Berkshire Bank	Boston	MA	**B-**	B-	C+	13504.8	12.50	14.4	3.4	24.4	13.0	**6.6**	9.1	12.2
Berkshire Bank	New York	NY	**B**	B	B-	642.9	-5.78	1.2	0.1	6.4	27.1	**10.0**	18.3	30.2
▲ Bessemer Trust Co.	New York	NY	**A-**	B+	A-	867.3	32.44	9.7	24.5	0.0	31.5	**8.7**	10.1	21.8
Bessemer Trust Co. of California, N.A.	San Francisco	CA	**U**	U	U	11.3	11.48	0.0	0.0	0.0	75.6	**10.0**	99.9	794.2
Bessemer Trust Co. of Delaware, N.A.	Wilmington	DE	**U**	U	U	23.0	11.84	0.0	0.0	0.0	68.6	**10.0**	96.2	347.9
▲ Bessemer Trust Co., N.A.	New York	NY	**A**	A-	A-	1841.1	-20.03	11.1	16.0	0.0	45.1	**10.0**	11.0	28.1
▲ Best Hometown Bank	Collinsville	IL	**D**	D-	D	115.6	4.71	3.5	0.5	41.0	9.7	**9.0**	10.3	16.5
▲ Better Banks	Peoria	IL	**B-**	C+	C+	290.3	-3.64	3.2	30.7	18.8	21.9	**6.8**	8.8	13.5
Beverly Bank & Trust Co., N.A.	Chicago	IL	**B**	B	B	1585.4	19.77	35.1	13.0	2.9	6.9	**5.5**	10.7	11.4
Biddeford Savings Bank	Biddeford	ME	**B**	B-	B-	504.7	1.77	4.6	0.5	43.9	5.7	**10.0**	11.1	15.0
Big Bend Banks, N.A.	Marfa	TX	**A-**	A-	A-	136.5	9.40	1.6	3.3	2.7	62.7	**10.0**	14.8	53.3
Big Horn Federal Savings Bank	Greybull	WY	**C+**	C+	C+	259.9	2.93	10.0	2.6	10.6	29.2	**9.3**	10.5	21.4
Bippus State Bank	Huntington	IN	**B-**	B-	B	183.4	3.83	13.4	3.0	13.1	13.9	**10.0**	11.4	15.1

Asset Quality Index	Adjusted Non-Performing Loans as a % of Total Loans	Adjusted Non-Performing Loans as a % of Capital	Net Charge-Offs Avg Loans	Profitability Index	Net Income ($Mil)	Return on Assets (R.O.A.)	Return on Equity (R.O.E.)	Net Interest Spread	Overhead Efficiency Ratio	Liquidity Index	Liquidity Ratio	Hot Money Ratio	Stability Index
3.8	1.66	8.0	0.00	**4.2**	1.1	0.83	7.41	4.07	76.4	**0.7**	10.6	32.9	**6.6**
5.5	0.56	na	0.09	**6.0**	19.4	1.42	15.48	3.49	59.8	**1.7**	16.4	18.0	**9.3**
5.7	0.82	4.4	0.02	**4.2**	21.4	0.79	6.94	2.78	68.6	**1.1**	12.7	9.7	**8.7**
6.9	1.81	na	0.00	**3.2**	0.4	0.48	4.39	2.34	75.9	**1.0**	26.2	41.0	**6.6**
5.2	2.00	na	-0.16	**6.2**	3.4	1.21	10.73	3.91	63.8	**4.2**	24.0	8.9	**7.7**
2.6	1.07	7.5	4.05	**6.6**	300.0	1.16	7.71	8.33	53.6	**1.6**	24.3	9.9	**9.3**
5.8	0.61	3.3	0.06	**8.6**	23.3	1.43	9.29	3.71	80.5	**3.0**	7.6	9.7	**8.5**
10.0	0.00	0.0	0.00	**0.9**	0.0	0.03	0.42	2.09	101.4	**6.9**	91.2	6.1	**1.3**
3.9	2.83	na	0.15	**8.8**	0.9	2.07	18.22	5.56	62.5	**1.7**	20.1	23.6	**8.0**
9.0	0.37	1.6	0.00	**7.3**	11.3	1.62	11.51	3.41	67.2	**1.7**	13.2	16.3	**8.8**
4.0	1.28	na	0.07	**4.3**	1.2	0.97	9.92	3.49	74.9	**1.4**	13.7	25.0	**7.6**
7.8	0.41	2.2	0.00	**3.5**	0.2	0.62	4.47	3.35	78.5	**0.8**	16.4	35.2	**6.9**
3.2	6.31	17.4	0.01	**3.5**	0.1	0.71	3.10	5.30	83.2	**6.1**	36.8	1.6	**6.0**
5.9	2.38	6.0	0.07	**5.7**	0.8	1.04	7.09	4.49	75.9	**2.6**	30.9	18.3	**7.9**
5.4	0.94	na	0.28	**5.1**	0.8	1.03	13.67	4.30	68.7	**1.5**	9.8	22.3	**4.1**
5.4	1.25	na	0.00	**2.6**	1.4	0.44	4.74	3.08	84.2	**1.3**	7.8	17.7	**5.5**
3.4	2.23	na	0.21	**5.4**	0.9	1.12	12.35	4.36	66.2	**2.4**	20.8	17.4	**5.1**
6.3	0.59	3.6	0.11	**3.5**	9.7	0.75	8.08	3.26	85.4	**0.8**	12.9	25.8	**6.7**
5.6	2.33	5.3	0.28	**4.3**	1.9	0.83	4.39	3.76	67.2	**4.9**	18.0	2.9	**6.2**
3.8	1.17	5.4	0.87	**3.4**	442.6	0.65	4.64	3.25	61.7	**2.6**	22.3	10.8	**10.0**
4.5	1.22	7.1	0.01	**4.4**	17.5	0.85	9.26	3.25	60.2	**0.9**	16.5	38.6	**6.8**
5.0	1.42	6.4	0.03	**3.4**	0.5	0.52	5.60	3.84	82.7	**3.3**	16.4	12.8	**5.3**
6.0	1.51	na	-0.01	**0.6**	0.8	0.21	1.82	3.20	96.8	**1.3**	26.1	31.5	**0.0**
4.5	0.76	na	-0.14	**5.0**	1.2	1.12	8.41	5.05	80.0	**2.4**	34.8	24.2	**8.4**
9.0	0.15	na	0.00	**0.0**	-2.1	-3.13	-9.64	3.38	178.9	**0.8**	20.1	37.9	**1.5**
3.0	5.03	7.9	0.66	**6.3**	22.5	0.58	1.37	8.04	74.8	**1.2**	25.3	27.1	**8.8**
2.8	8.59	18.6	0.36	**3.7**	-3.7	-0.25	-0.91	5.34	122.3	**1.7**	30.5	11.1	**8.0**
2.8	2.06	na	0.26	**3.4**	0.2	0.59	5.40	3.79	77.1	**2.6**	25.1	17.0	**5.6**
7.5	1.44	3.0	0.00	**5.6**	0.4	1.06	6.29	4.54	66.6	**1.3**	22.8	30.3	**7.5**
5.2	2.35	10.1	0.02	**9.3**	1.0	1.98	11.55	4.95	59.0	**2.4**	20.4	17.5	**9.5**
7.0	0.79	na	0.14	**4.2**	0.7	0.76	6.34	4.04	75.6	**1.8**	20.5	20.9	**6.5**
6.7	1.98	na	0.13	**4.6**	0.7	0.98	6.88	4.00	73.0	**3.5**	26.6	13.3	**7.6**
6.9	0.13	na	0.21	**6.3**	2.4	1.20	12.90	4.57	68.0	**1.6**	17.2	24.4	**5.0**
7.8	0.24	1.8	0.04	**6.9**	53.7	1.21	12.92	4.04	67.8	**4.4**	2.2	4.1	**8.3**
6.9	0.51	na	-0.03	**9.8**	2.0	2.28	15.53	3.77	40.1	**3.2**	20.1	13.4	**10.0**
5.4	0.80	na	0.10	**8.0**	5.2	1.37	13.49	3.82	46.2	**1.1**	27.8	38.7	**7.2**
9.4	1.92	na	-0.16	**3.7**	2.1	0.72	4.01	3.21	69.4	**3.7**	68.3	28.2	**7.1**
9.9	0.65	na	0.00	**2.6**	0.2	0.33	1.62	3.06	84.9	**0.9**	25.1	46.9	**7.3**
3.7	2.12	na	0.02	**9.5**	0.8	1.74	11.41	4.85	52.9	**2.5**	11.2	16.2	**7.9**
8.5	0.64	na	-0.16	**0.0**	-0.6	-0.78	-7.38	3.56	125.2	**0.8**	19.2	27.9	**4.4**
7.9	0.27	na	-0.09	**8.6**	9.3	1.92	20.39	4.37	75.2	**4.6**	26.1	5.3	**6.5**
7.1	0.63	na	0.07	**7.4**	7.1	1.38	13.10	4.53	65.0	**3.8**	16.2	9.9	**8.3**
3.7	1.12	7.8	0.02	**8.4**	1.0	2.07	21.25	4.09	54.4	**3.8**	8.6	9.0	**6.3**
5.4	1.10	5.8	0.39	**2.1**	2.1	0.27	2.37	4.19	89.8	**2.3**	27.9	26.7	**7.5**
4.2	5.21	na	0.11	**8.0**	10.2	1.92	16.68	3.34	42.3	**3.2**	21.0	13.4	**9.0**
7.6	0.00	na	0.00	**5.8**	0.4	1.19	8.35	3.61	62.8	**1.9**	30.0	26.2	**7.7**
2.1	3.57	24.7	0.01	**3.1**	0.2	0.43	4.75	4.19	89.7	**0.9**	14.4	30.8	**4.6**
5.1	0.44	3.7	0.40	**3.8**	74.9	0.75	5.78	3.20	64.2	**0.8**	15.8	28.6	**8.9**
7.9	0.80	na	0.04	**4.0**	3.5	0.69	3.98	3.31	69.7	**4.1**	51.1	17.4	**7.9**
7.5	0.00	na	0.00	**10.0**	20.6	3.23	34.12	1.83	71.7	**6.2**	36.1	0.0	**8.2**
10.0	na	na	na	**10.0**	0.9	10.86	11.01	2.08	60.0	**4.0**	na	0.0	**7.0**
10.0	na	na	na	**9.5**	7.1	43.12	48.83	1.94	66.8	**4.0**	na	0.0	**7.0**
7.3	0.00	0.0	0.00	**9.5**	58.2	3.91	30.03	1.61	84.9	**5.8**	22.9	0.0	**8.6**
7.7	0.56	na	0.05	**0.7**	0.0	0.03	0.31	2.34	111.3	**0.8**	18.3	44.1	**4.0**
6.6	0.15	na	0.07	**3.7**	1.9	0.87	9.31	3.48	77.9	**3.9**	25.6	10.8	**6.0**
7.0	0.39	1.7	0.03	**6.1**	12.6	1.16	10.34	3.51	64.5	**1.6**	10.8	14.1	**8.2**
8.4	0.31	na	0.00	**4.9**	3.9	1.03	9.82	3.28	74.0	**1.6**	10.6	13.3	**6.7**
9.7	0.00	na	0.92	**5.3**	1.3	1.33	8.59	3.47	64.8	**7.0**	81.7	7.2	**8.8**
4.6	3.31	na	0.26	**3.2**	1.1	0.55	5.14	3.43	77.0	**4.3**	38.4	12.8	**6.4**
6.7	0.92	na	0.08	**8.1**	2.7	1.99	18.27	4.33	58.5	**3.7**	16.5	9.1	**8.7**

Name	City	State	Rating	2018 Rating	2017 Rating	Total Assets ($Mil)	One Year Asset Growth	Asset Mix (As a % of Total Assets) Commercial Loans	Consumer Loans	Mortgage Loans	Securities	Capitalization Index	Leverage Ratio	Risk-Based Capital Ratio
Bison State Bank	Bison	KS	**D**	D	D-	14.2	43.39	13.7	7.0	23.2	9.8	**8.9**	10.2	19.4
Black Hills Community Bank, N.A.	Rapid City	SD	**B-**	B-	B	319.5	14.31	11.6	0.2	9.5	3.4	**6.9**	10.2	12.5
Black Mountain Savings Bank, SSB	Black Mountain	NC	**C+**	C+	C+	41.1	1.78	0.0	0.6	64.5	0.0	**10.0**	12.5	31.8
▲ Black River Country Bank	Black River Falls	WI	**B+**	B+	B+	78.9	1.27	4.4	4.7	38.3	7.5	**10.0**	11.6	17.4
▲ Blackhawk Bank	Beloit	WI	**B**	B-	B-	972.9	26.44	25.2	0.7	10.0	23.6	**7.7**	9.7	13.1
▲ Blackhawk Bank & Trust	Milan	IL	**A-**	B+	B	1381.1	3.75	11.6	0.8	7.5	44.4	**10.0**	11.8	19.6
BlackRidgeBANK	Fargo	ND	**D+**	D+	C-	490.1	5.03	9.6	3.0	23.7	6.4	**5.0**	7.8	11.0
Blackrock Institutional Trust Co., N.A.	San Francisco	CA	**U**	U	U	4182.1	-6.68	0.0	0.0	0.0	6.7	**10.0**	68.1	143.3
BLC Community Bank	Little Chute	WI	**A-**	A-	A-	300.2	26.17	10.3	0.3	12.1	14.6	**10.0**	11.5	15.3
Blissfield State Bank	Blissfield	MI	**B-**	C+	C+	98.6	0.98	7.0	3.1	17.2	36.0	**10.0**	11.4	20.1
Bloomsdale Bank	Bloomsdale	MO	**B**	B+	A-	228.0	2.10	7.6	2.0	19.6	22.1	**7.6**	9.4	13.6
Blue Foundry Bank	Rutherford	NJ	**B-**	C+	C+	1775.6	5.27	0.0	0.0	45.1	8.5	**10.0**	12.8	21.9
Blue Grass Federal S&L Assn.	Paris	KY	**C+**	C	D+	35.6	7.17	7.1	3.2	46.9	14.0	**10.0**	23.7	44.0
Blue Grass Savings Bank	Blue Grass	IA	**B**	B	B+	199.0	3.34	10.1	0.7	18.0	35.5	**10.0**	16.2	28.4
▲ Blue Grass Valley Bank	Blue Grass	VA	**C**	D+	D+	43.4	-3.94	7.0	4.8	32.9	7.7	**10.0**	11.7	21.9
Blue Ridge Bank	Walhalla	SC	**C+**	C+	B-	131.0	-7.27	1.4	2.0	32.8	27.6	**8.8**	10.2	19.7
Blue Ridge Bank and Trust Co.	Independence	MO	**C-**	C	B-	562.5	-0.25	13.1	13.3	6.0	15.4	**8.7**	10.2	13.9
Blue Ridge Bank, N.A.	Martinsville	VA	**C+**	C+	B-	735.3	49.24	6.0	5.1	31.2	18.4	**6.4**	8.4	12.9
Blue Sky Bank	Pawhuska	OK	**B**	B+	A-	234.8	6.62	25.4	0.8	7.0	3.5	**8.1**	11.5	13.4
▲ BlueHarbor Bank	Mooresville	NC	**A-**	B+	B+	239.8	15.03	9.1	0.2	15.2	6.8	**10.0**	13.4	15.9
Bluff View Bank	Galesville	WI	**B+**	A-	B+	105.4	5.43	6.0	2.5	17.8	13.0	**10.0**	18.9	20.7
▲ BMO Harris Bank, N.A.	Chicago	IL	**B**	B-	C+	138843.9	16.59	27.7	4.6	6.9	13.9	**6.8**	10.3	12.4
BMO Harris Central N.A.	Roselle	IL	**U**	U	U	7.9	0.33	0.0	0.0	0.0	0.0	**10.0**	86.6	443.7
BMW Bank of North America	Salt Lake City	UT	**A-**	A-	A-	10515.0	4.01	0.8	71.6	0.0	24.9	**10.0**	15.8	17.0
BNA Bank	New Albany	MS	**A-**	A-	A-	525.0	3.61	2.3	4.6	26.1	29.9	**10.0**	12.5	19.7
BNB Bank	Bridgehampton	NY	**B+**	B+	B+	4735.8	6.50	13.0	0.5	10.8	15.9	**8.0**	10.0	13.3
▲ BNC National Bank	Glendale	AZ	**B**	B-	B	1083.1	9.44	7.8	4.1	16.1	35.7	**9.3**	10.5	17.1
BNY Mellon Trust of Delaware	Wilmington	DE	**B**	B	B-	124.1	12.67	0.0	0.0	16.8	0.0	**10.0**	52.6	113.6
BNY Mellon, N.A.	Pittsburgh	PA	**B**	B	B-	27823.0	19.13	0.3	7.9	29.7	4.8	**6.3**	8.3	12.8
BOC Bank	Amarillo	TX	**A-**	B+	B+	62.0	26.76	26.2	0.1	9.8	11.8	**10.0**	16.5	27.5
Bodcaw Bank	Stamps	AR	**B-**	B	B+	112.6	32.79	17.0	5.0	24.7	27.2	**8.1**	9.8	14.7
Boelus State Bank	Boelus	NE	**C+**	C+	C+	16.3	3.18	1.6	5.9	0.6	2.3	**10.0**	13.5	32.6
Bogota Savings Bank	Teaneck	NJ	**B-**	B	B	665.8	3.33	0.4	0.1	58.6	9.8	**10.0**	11.3	18.5
BOKF, N.A.	Tulsa	OK	**B**	B	B	43031.9	30.78	20.8	1.0	4.9	26.4	**5.6**	8.0	11.5
▲ BOM Bank	Natchitoches	LA	**B**	B	B+	477.0	13.14	7.2	3.3	24.6	3.7	**6.9**	9.7	12.4
▲ Bonanza Valley State Bank	Brooten	MN	**C**	C	C	65.6	2.84	10.4	2.9	35.4	6.6	**5.3**	8.6	11.2
Bonduel State Bank	Bonduel	WI	**B+**	B+	B+	60.8	4.10	7.5	4.1	11.9	39.3	**10.0**	22.1	41.8
Boone Bank & Trust Co.	Boone	IA	**A-**	A-	A-	150.3	5.84	3.8	0.4	3.2	38.1	**10.0**	11.1	16.2
Boonville Federal Savings Bank	Boonville	IN	**D+**	D	D+	54.1	8.91	7.3	8.8	44.1	11.6	**7.1**	9.0	15.7
Border State Bank	Greenbush	MN	**B-**	B-	C+	632.6	17.07	12.0	6.6	9.9	14.5	**6.9**	9.3	12.4
Boston Private Bank & Trust Co.	Boston	MA	**B**	B	B	8654.4	4.44	6.5	1.5	35.9	11.4	**7.2**	9.1	13.1
Boston Trust Walden Co.	Boston	MA	**A-**	A-	A-	51.5	-0.55	0.1	0.0	0.0	4.7	**10.0**	49.9	83.7
Boundary Waters Bank	Ely	MN	**C**	C	C	111.2	-0.81	1.7	1.1	13.4	3.1	**8.2**	12.6	13.5
▲ Bradford National Bank of Greenville	Greenville	IL	**B+**	B	B	318.3	7.71	3.3	1.3	13.3	49.9	**10.0**	11.2	18.1
▲ Brady National Bank	Brady	TX	**B-**	B-	B-	120.6	1.79	11.0	1.9	9.8	38.8	**7.8**	9.5	17.4
Brainerd S&L Assn., A Federal Assn.	Brainerd	MN	**D**	D	D	66.8	-2.67	0.3	1.5	60.1	8.4	**5.5**	7.5	13.5
Branch Banking and Trust Co.	Winston-Salem	NC	**B+**	B+	B	229886.0	6.37	14.1	7.7	13.3	23.9	**8.1**	9.7	14.0
Brannen Bank	Inverness	FL	**B-**	C+	C+	540.0	3.16	0.2	1.1	41.3	23.5	**4.5**	6.5	16.3
Branson Bank	Branson	MO	**B**	B	B	235.7	13.51	7.2	2.1	24.9	4.7	**8.0**	9.6	13.5
Brantley Bank and Trust Co.	Brantley	AL	**B+**	B+	B+	69.2	-2.70	10.6	3.7	7.0	46.9	**10.0**	15.5	27.1
Brattleboro S&L Assn.	Brattleboro	VT	**C**	C	C	219.2	9.94	4.1	0.7	42.5	0.1	**6.0**	8.0	12.2
Brazos National Bank	Richwood	TX	**B+**	B+	A-	32.7	28.79	0.5	1.4	75.0	0.0	**10.0**	27.9	48.7
▲ Breda Savings Bank	Breda	IA	**A-**	A-	A	64.2	4.79	5.3	0.8	13.9	33.7	**10.0**	11.8	17.7
Bremer Bank, N.A.	Saint Paul	MN	**B+**	B+	B+	13057.6	8.35	10.1	1.3	7.1	25.5	**7.4**	9.3	13.0
Brenham National Bank	Brenham	TX	**B+**	B	B	379.2	12.92	3.0	1.2	8.3	46.8	**9.0**	10.4	18.4
Brentwood Bank	Bethel Park	PA	**B**	B	B-	695.0	11.08	3.2	0.0	33.1	16.0	**10.0**	12.1	17.3
▲ Brickyard Bank	Lincolnwood	IL	**C-**	D+	D+	122.3	11.47	12.9	0.7	11.8	3.8	**10.0**	11.8	18.8
Bridge City State Bank	Bridge City	TX	**B**	B	B	210.2	0.58	4.5	0.9	8.9	53.0	**8.9**	10.2	23.5
Bridge Community Bank	Mount Vernon	IA	**B+**	B+	B+	98.9	11.46	11.4	4.1	23.4	12.9	**10.0**	11.7	16.1
Bridgewater Bank	Bloomington	MN	**A-**	A-	B+	2227.3	18.32	12.5	0.2	9.7	11.8	**6.9**	10.9	12.4

Asset Quality Index	Adjusted Non-Performing Loans as a % of Total Loans	Adjusted Non-Performing Loans as a % of Capital	Net Charge-Offs Avg Loans	Profitability Index	Net Income ($Mil)	Return on Assets (R.O.A.)	Return on Equity (R.O.E.)	Net Interest Spread	Overhead Efficiency Ratio	Liquidity Index	Liquidity Ratio	Hot Money Ratio	Stability Index
6.8	0.78	na	0.14	**5.6**	0.2	1.62	15.16	5.86	83.9	**4.5**	34.9	8.4	**3.9**
7.2	0.13	na	-0.01	**5.5**	2.9	1.31	13.42	3.74	64.6	**0.8**	16.8	38.0	**7.3**
10.0	0.00	na	0.00	**2.3**	0.1	0.24	1.88	2.82	89.2	**1.5**	34.2	45.1	**6.0**
7.2	1.07	na	0.00	**5.7**	0.8	1.29	11.36	3.91	65.2	**1.5**	11.4	23.8	**8.0**
4.9	1.31	6.0	0.01	**5.2**	7.2	1.10	11.11	4.17	73.5	**4.1**	13.5	7.8	**6.7**
7.9	1.24	na	-0.16	**5.5**	14.1	1.39	11.20	2.94	50.9	**3.0**	14.7	14.3	**9.5**
2.7	3.20	na	0.20	**2.9**	1.0	0.26	2.39	3.99	92.5	**1.6**	14.9	18.5	**6.4**
6.5	na	0.0	na	**9.5**	365.3	11.39	13.90	2.82	55.7	**4.0**	52.7	0.0	**7.0**
7.6	0.00	0.0	0.01	**6.2**	3.0	1.47	12.52	3.02	50.9	**1.5**	29.7	16.4	**9.5**
5.2	3.81	na	0.01	**3.6**	0.7	0.89	8.07	3.55	79.0	**5.5**	53.1	9.7	**6.6**
6.6	0.44	na	-0.01	**9.5**	4.1	2.42	25.50	4.02	45.1	**1.6**	18.4	19.7	**8.1**
8.9	0.40	2.3	0.00	**3.1**	5.5	0.43	3.29	2.72	77.3	**1.2**	17.4	30.5	**8.9**
9.2	0.51	na	0.00	**2.2**	0.1	0.27	1.04	3.79	100.4	**2.1**	38.7	32.5	**5.4**
5.8	2.05	na	-0.01	**4.8**	1.5	1.02	6.40	2.74	52.2	**2.7**	45.9	25.6	**7.8**
3.1	3.09	na	0.56	**3.9**	0.2	0.62	5.49	3.80	74.9	**3.9**	32.4	13.1	**5.9**
5.8	2.45	na	0.25	**3.7**	0.7	0.67	6.69	3.74	81.4	**4.8**	46.6	12.8	**5.9**
3.5	2.11	na	0.06	**5.7**	4.5	1.08	10.87	3.81	66.5	**3.9**	17.2	9.9	**7.0**
3.9	0.95	na	0.17	**5.6**	5.2	1.09	12.36	3.50	74.2	**0.6**	9.0	33.0	**5.9**
3.3	1.43	na	-0.12	**7.3**	2.8	1.70	15.11	5.10	66.0	**1.1**	24.0	31.3	**7.4**
8.0	0.06	na	-0.03	**6.1**	2.2	1.27	9.70	3.95	59.1	**1.4**	13.2	16.7	**8.0**
7.0	1.22	na	0.14	**8.0**	1.5	1.95	10.23	4.32	64.1	**3.0**	12.6	10.7	**10.0**
4.7	1.35	6.1	0.08	**4.7**	980.1	1.03	7.95	2.91	59.8	**3.5**	26.3	9.4	**9.8**
10.0	na	0.0	na	**3.5**	0.0	0.27	0.31	8.29	-100.0	**4.0**	na	0.0	**7.0**
5.6	0.11	0.5	0.20	**8.5**	136.4	1.45	9.36	2.04	27.3	**1.8**	33.7	2.2	**10.0**
6.3	1.44	5.3	-0.01	**6.5**	5.4	1.39	11.48	3.42	54.4	**3.2**	27.9	14.8	**8.6**
5.6	1.14	4.9	0.17	**5.2**	40.2	1.14	9.80	3.40	55.8	**4.4**	14.1	5.6	**8.7**
8.5	0.63	na	0.06	**5.4**	10.0	1.32	13.14	3.09	73.2	**2.8**	29.7	12.1	**8.7**
3.9	15.67	na	-0.01	**9.5**	4.2	4.72	6.87	2.80	37.0	**8.7**	112.9	0.0	**8.4**
6.8	0.07	0.3	0.00	**5.6**	222.0	1.07	7.68	1.06	63.6	**1.9**	34.0	61.9	**8.4**
8.5	0.00	na	0.14	**9.1**	0.9	2.36	14.11	4.46	60.2	**4.6**	49.8	13.5	**8.0**
4.9	0.82	na	0.03	**5.3**	1.0	1.24	12.98	3.86	56.2	**1.0**	26.1	48.1	**5.3**
8.4	0.12	0.3	0.00	**4.1**	0.1	0.73	5.09	3.17	62.4	**3.8**	68.2	19.0	**6.7**
9.5	0.24	na	-0.01	**2.6**	1.6	0.33	2.99	1.76	74.9	**0.6**	13.2	49.6	**7.2**
5.8	0.94	3.8	0.17	**6.2**	393.3	1.27	12.30	3.16	59.3	**3.6**	17.8	6.4	**9.1**
5.4	0.36	na	0.20	**9.1**	7.5	2.27	23.40	5.03	60.6	**3.3**	12.2	12.2	**6.7**
5.8	0.54	na	-0.06	**4.7**	0.5	1.05	11.68	4.28	72.5	**3.2**	5.8	11.4	**4.3**
8.8	0.34	na	0.05	**4.8**	0.5	1.15	5.27	3.42	57.5	**5.7**	61.0	9.9	**8.0**
9.1	0.10	0.4	0.02	**5.7**	1.1	1.14	10.17	3.12	59.2	**2.9**	38.6	18.8	**7.8**
6.7	0.16	na	0.11	**1.7**	0.1	0.14	1.53	3.21	88.2	**1.8**	32.3	30.6	**4.0**
4.2	1.36	7.8	-0.08	**4.4**	4.3	0.94	9.55	3.80	73.3	**1.3**	15.1	15.7	**6.6**
8.3	0.34	2.3	0.00	**4.3**	56.8	0.89	9.36	2.98	67.2	**3.4**	11.9	7.8	**8.4**
6.5	0.00	0.0	0.00	**10.0**	15.9	45.17	52.73	13.82	56.3	**3.1**	93.7	100.0	**10.0**
1.4	2.98	na	-0.03	**5.1**	0.7	0.88	6.83	4.56	73.4	**1.3**	11.1	27.0	**6.2**
5.8	3.11	na	0.03	**5.8**	3.2	1.43	11.11	3.71	61.2	**4.3**	41.7	11.8	**8.1**
5.7	1.11	na	0.01	**4.1**	0.9	1.01	11.06	2.97	71.9	**3.4**	22.4	12.5	**5.8**
5.0	2.16	na	-0.01	**0.2**	-0.2	-0.32	-4.36	3.32	114.4	**1.5**	17.6	15.6	**2.9**
5.9	0.58	2.2	0.21	**7.4**	2589.0	1.56	11.90	3.32	57.9	**4.9**	23.5	5.2	**10.0**
6.0	1.43	na	-0.01	**8.2**	8.1	2.04	31.39	3.91	53.3	**5.5**	42.5	7.7	**5.8**
6.4	0.39	na	0.00	**5.3**	1.6	0.96	9.72	4.07	71.9	**2.5**	13.8	15.4	**6.0**
8.7	0.03	na	0.30	**6.0**	0.7	1.32	8.56	4.96	64.7	**4.9**	52.1	12.4	**6.8**
5.4	0.66	na	0.03	**3.3**	0.7	0.47	5.28	3.61	86.4	**3.5**	12.6	11.2	**4.9**
8.1	0.05	na	0.00	**10.0**	0.6	2.77	9.27	5.36	88.1	**1.0**	14.4	31.5	**8.0**
8.8	0.00	na	0.00	**6.8**	0.7	1.55	13.83	3.59	55.8	**3.9**	38.9	15.2	**8.5**
6.0	0.95	5.0	0.05	**6.0**	121.8	1.29	13.57	3.41	58.8	**2.3**	19.0	8.6	**8.9**
6.6	2.09	na	0.00	**6.1**	4.2	1.55	15.11	3.81	59.6	**4.6**	53.0	15.5	**6.8**
8.8	0.35	na	0.00	**3.8**	3.7	0.71	6.05	2.90	72.1	**2.7**	13.8	14.2	**7.7**
5.3	2.91	na	-0.01	**4.0**	0.8	0.96	8.00	3.81	75.9	**1.1**	27.9	42.9	**4.6**
6.8	1.74	na	0.14	**4.8**	1.7	1.06	10.88	3.27	61.8	**6.8**	62.5	5.2	**5.8**
8.4	0.00	na	0.04	**5.4**	0.8	1.10	9.68	3.81	65.5	**1.7**	15.0	17.5	**6.1**
7.3	0.06	0.4	0.00	**7.8**	23.3	1.49	13.59	3.67	46.4	**0.9**	17.8	28.7	**9.5**

Name	City	State	Rating	2018 Rating	2017 Rating	Total Assets ($Mil)	One Year Asset Growth	Asset Mix (As a % of Total Assets) Comm-ercial Loans	Cons-umer Loans	Mort-gage Loans	Secur-ities	Capital-ization Index	Lever-age Ratio	Risk-Based Capital Ratio
Bridgewater Savings Bank	Raynham	MA	**C+**	C+	C+	622.9	3.41	6.5	2.9	32.3	19.0	**7.5**	9.4	15.0
▼ Brighton Bank	Brighton	TN	**E**	E	E-	41.0	-27.24	10.0	1.3	33.9	13.7	**4.9**	6.9	13.2
▲ Brighton Bank	Salt Lake City	UT	**A-**	B+	A	208.7	-2.62	3.9	0.3	5.3	18.4	**10.0**	12.9	17.9
Bristol County Savings Bank	Taunton	MA	**B-**	C+	C+	2279.7	4.52	6.5	14.3	31.5	16.0	**8.4**	12.0	13.7
Bristol Morgan Bank	Oakfield	WI	**C**	C+	B	102.2	1.06	11.2	1.4	18.3	13.8	**9.9**	10.9	15.7
▼ Broadway Federal Bank, F.S.B.	Los Angeles	CA	**C**	C+	B-	412.2	-1.24	0.1	0.0	19.0	3.3	**10.0**	11.7	20.6
▲ Broadway National Bank	San Antonio	TX	**B+**	B	B	3820.1	3.20	7.5	3.7	11.6	29.6	**9.9**	10.9	15.9
Brookline Bank	Brookline	MA	**B**	B	B	4979.0	8.29	25.5	0.8	10.9	5.1	**6.8**	10.5	12.3
▲ Brookville Building and Savings Assn.	Brookville	OH	**B**	B-	B-	45.0	-0.23	3.5	0.8	50.8	14.4	**10.0**	18.9	36.0
Brown Brothers Harriman Trust Co.	Wilmington	DE	**U**	U	U	10.5	13.40	0.0	0.0	0.0	64.5	**10.0**	75.0	154.1
Brown Brothers Harriman Trust Co., N.A.	New York	NY	**U**	U	U	13.8	1.45	0.0	0.0	0.0	61.0	**10.0**	69.5	135.0
Bruning Bank	Bruning	NE	**B-**	B-	B-	352.4	-1.06	7.9	0.8	1.7	21.3	**9.1**	12.5	14.3
Brunswick Bank and Trust Co.	New Brunswick	NJ	**B-**	B-	C+	226.9	23.08	1.4	0.0	16.2	5.0	**10.0**	14.8	16.8
Brunswick State Bank	Brunswick	NE	**C**	C+	B	130.1	4.55	15.0	5.2	0.0	6.1	**5.6**	9.9	11.5
Bryant Bank	Tuscaloosa	AL	**A-**	A-	B	1733.5	9.04	11.7	1.0	8.6	22.1	**8.9**	10.2	15.0
▲ Bryant State Bank	Bryant	SD	**B+**	B	B	35.1	-2.03	15.2	6.1	1.2	8.2	**10.0**	11.7	17.7
Bryn Mawr Trust Co.	Bryn Mawr	PA	**B+**	B	B	4813.7	10.09	8.7	1.0	15.5	12.8	**7.3**	9.8	12.8
▲ BTC Bank	Bethany	MO	**B**	B	A-	554.8	15.38	9.1	1.9	11.4	13.4	**10.0**	13.7	16.3
BTH Bank, N.A.	Quitman	TX	**A-**	B+	B	1807.0	-4.57	31.0	0.7	18.2	17.6	**10.0**	14.7	18.8
Buckeye Community Bank	Lorain	OH	**B+**	B+	B+	174.1	4.15	26.5	0.1	8.0	12.1	**10.0**	13.2	18.0
▼ Buckeye State Bank	Powell	OH	**D-**	D-	D-	110.5	15.01	6.8	27.3	7.0	16.3	**9.2**	10.8	14.3
Buckholts State Bank	Buckholts	TX	**A-**	A-	A-	79.1	4.28	18.5	2.5	15.8	32.2	**10.0**	18.1	34.0
▲ Buckley State Bank	Buckley	IL	**B-**	C+	C+	41.7	-0.75	6.3	0.6	0.3	26.9	**10.0**	12.8	19.3
▲ Buena Vista National Bank	Chester	IL	**A-**	B+	A-	207.6	4.44	5.8	6.8	21.8	27.9	**10.0**	12.7	18.0
Buffalo Federal Bank	Buffalo	WY	**B**	B	B	124.2	5.94	9.3	4.6	16.3	19.2	**9.9**	10.9	16.1
Burke & Herbert Bank & Trust Co.	Alexandria	VA	**B+**	B+	B+	2915.7	-3.96	1.3	0.1	14.3	24.9	**10.0**	12.3	17.4
▲ Burling Bank	Chicago	IL	**A-**	B	B-	132.3	-0.55	8.8	0.9	29.9	21.0	**9.8**	10.9	19.3
▲ Burton State Bank	Burton	TX	**B**	B-	B-	68.9	11.11	2.1	3.9	11.4	10.7	**9.5**	10.7	29.7
Busey Bank	Champaign	IL	**A-**	A-	A-	7803.7	-0.55	14.0	0.4	15.3	14.8	**8.7**	11.1	13.9
Business Bank of Texas, N.A.	Austin	TX	**B-**	C	C+	100.0	-7.90	15.0	0.0	2.6	23.9	**10.0**	14.5	21.9
Business First Bank	Baton Rouge	LA	**B**	B-	C+	2222.7	32.26	16.8	1.0	9.9	13.0	**7.4**	11.2	12.8
Butte State Bank	Butte	NE	**B-**	C+	B-	41.3	3.01	9.7	3.2	1.5	23.3	**10.0**	12.5	18.5
Byline Bank	Chicago	IL	**B**	B-	C+	5433.0	10.53	22.4	0.2	6.4	19.1	**8.5**	10.7	13.7
▲ Byron Bank	Byron	IL	**B-**	C+	B	275.8	2.05	8.4	2.6	11.5	29.5	**9.1**	10.4	17.1
C3bank, N.A.	Encinitas	CA	**B+**	B+	A-	326.8	7.33	1.5	0.0	4.6	1.7	**10.0**	12.8	16.0
▲ Cache Bank & Trust	Greeley	CO	**C**	C-	D+	114.6	-5.34	7.7	3.6	8.0	20.1	**10.0**	11.9	23.1
Cache Valley Bank	Logan	UT	**B**	B-	B	1440.5	16.31	10.3	0.5	6.4	1.8	**9.6**	11.5	14.6
Cadence Bank, N.A.	Atlanta	GA	**B+**	B+	B-	17849.3	51.89	32.8	0.6	13.5	9.6	**7.6**	11.3	13.0
▲ Caldwell Bank & Trust Co.	Columbia	LA	**C+**	D+	D+	158.1	-1.51	6.2	4.7	28.6	5.5	**10.0**	11.5	15.1
▲ Calhoun County Bank, Inc.	Grantsville	WV	**B-**	B-	B+	154.5	12.38	3.5	15.1	50.2	5.7	**8.8**	10.2	17.0
▲ California Bank of Commerce	Lafayette	CA	**C+**	C+	B-	1094.9	14.74	37.5	0.0	0.4	3.3	**6.5**	11.2	12.1
California Business Bank	Irvine	CA	**D**	D	D	82.7	-13.66	10.8	12.5	1.3	0.0	**10.0**	15.2	23.4
California First National Bank	Irvine	CA	**A**	A	A-	145.4	-48.59	12.5	0.0	0.0	3.5	**10.0**	43.4	54.6
California International Bank, N.A.	Westminster	CA	**D**	D	D	45.4	-5.03	17.4	0.0	3.5	1.4	**10.0**	30.0	44.1
California Pacific Bank	San Francisco	CA	**A**	A	A	74.6	6.21	4.6	0.0	4.3	0.0	**10.0**	43.6	50.3
Callaway Bank	Fulton	MO	**B-**	B-	B-	387.7	2.02	9.5	1.2	21.6	12.4	**7.2**	9.8	12.7
▼ CalPrivate Bank	La Jolla	CA	**B-**	B+	A-	999.6	33.29	20.4	0.6	5.3	7.3	**7.4**	10.9	12.8
▲ Calvin B. Taylor Banking Co.	Berlin	MD	**A**	A-	A-	554.8	-0.69	2.8	0.2	20.2	11.6	**10.0**	15.7	25.6
▲ Calwest Bank	Irvine	CA	**B**	B-	B-	226.5	16.93	14.1	0.5	10.9	6.4	**6.4**	9.2	12.1
Cambridge Savings Bank	Cambridge	MA	**B-**	B-	B-	4125.5	8.13	9.4	0.2	20.3	14.6	**8.3**	10.1	13.6
▲ Cambridge State Bank	Cambridge	MN	**B-**	C	B	79.2	1.01	14.1	0.9	13.5	18.2	**10.0**	12.1	20.9
Cambridge Trust Co.	Cambridge	MA	**B+**	B+	B+	2841.9	42.88	4.6	1.1	32.5	14.9	**5.5**	7.5	11.4
Camden National Bank	Camden	ME	**B+**	B+	B	4500.5	7.87	7.4	0.5	26.8	20.3	**7.0**	9.0	13.0
Camp Grove State Bank	Camp Grove	IL	**D**	D+	D+	19.5	9.07	3.5	2.5	3.0	12.4	**10.0**	12.2	25.7
Campbell & Fetter Bank	Kendallville	IN	**B-**	B-	B-	311.6	-1.76	3.7	6.3	43.2	27.1	**9.3**	10.6	24.5
Campbell County Bank, Inc.	Herreid	SD	**B+**	B+	A	139.6	44.32	5.8	1.1	0.1	19.4	**10.0**	14.3	17.1
Campus State Bank	Campus	IL	**C**	C-	C-	21.8	4.82	0.0	13.6	15.6	9.2	**10.0**	11.9	19.0
Canandaigua National Bank and Trust Co.	Canandaigua	NY	**B+**	B	B	2978.2	5.62	9.2	19.6	20.3	13.0	**7.7**	9.6	13.1
Canandaigua National Trust Co. of Florida	Sarasota	FL	**U**	U	U	3.7	-0.27	0.0	0.0	0.0	13.6	**10.0**	100.	538.2
Canton Co-operative Bank	Canton	MA	**B-**	C+	C+	122.8	9.26	0.0	0.0	37.6	18.6	**10.0**	15.6	27.6

Asset Quality Index	Adjusted Non-Performing Loans as a % of Total Loans	Adjusted Non-Performing Loans as a % of Capital	Net Charge-Offs Avg Loans	Profitability Index	Net Income ($Mil)	Return on Assets (R.O.A.)	Return on Equity (R.O.E.)	Net Interest Spread	Overhead Efficiency Ratio	Liquidity Index	Liquidity Ratio	Hot Money Ratio	Stability Index
8.5	0.00	na	0.00	**3.2**	2.5	0.54	5.75	3.16	83.3	**3.0**	21.1	14.6	**6.4**
1.7	3.85	36.7	-0.48	**1.6**	0.0	-0.05	-0.82	4.63	100.7	**3.4**	15.6	12.1	**0.0**
7.2	2.65	na	0.00	**9.8**	4.1	2.65	20.85	5.45	51.3	**5.8**	30.6	0.8	**9.4**
6.8	0.60	2.2	0.01	**4.4**	19.8	1.30	9.77	3.21	74.9	**3.2**	19.9	12.0	**10.0**
5.8	3.37	na	0.07	**2.4**	0.1	0.10	0.89	3.59	94.6	**2.2**	32.9	21.8	**5.9**
6.3	1.38	na	-0.07	**2.0**	0.4	0.12	0.95	2.56	99.8	**0.5**	9.8	53.2	**7.1**
7.5	0.55	1.7	-0.03	**5.4**	36.6	1.33	11.98	3.59	67.1	**5.1**	26.3	6.7	**9.5**
5.6	0.68	4.1	0.12	**7.3**	48.6	1.36	12.20	3.63	49.4	**1.0**	5.8	22.7	**8.5**
9.6	0.21	na	0.00	**4.2**	0.3	0.82	4.37	3.83	72.8	**3.1**	35.9	18.0	**7.3**
10.0	na	na	na	**10.0**	1.6	21.38	30.57	2.19	80.1	**4.0**	263.5	0.0	**5.5**
10.0	na	na	na	**9.5**	1.8	18.42	29.07	2.24	85.9	**4.0**	212.8	0.0	**6.7**
8.4	0.00	na	0.00	**4.4**	2.5	0.95	7.82	3.47	68.9	**2.4**	10.7	14.7	**7.4**
6.1	1.08	na	0.03	**3.5**	0.9	0.56	3.86	4.05	82.6	**1.7**	13.0	21.1	**7.0**
3.0	1.76	na	0.11	**9.0**	2.0	2.07	21.82	4.11	41.6	**0.6**	8.3	40.9	**8.2**
8.7	0.31	1.7	0.02	**6.5**	19.2	1.54	14.95	3.67	59.1	**2.9**	22.2	16.5	**9.2**
8.0	0.21	na	1.72	**5.8**	0.4	1.32	11.58	5.59	56.4	**4.7**	33.6	9.4	**6.9**
6.2	0.53	2.5	0.19	**6.0**	39.7	1.14	8.57	3.78	66.0	**2.7**	14.3	7.4	**9.6**
5.0	1.10	na	0.01	**6.5**	5.2	1.33	9.45	4.05	58.1	**0.7**	4.8	28.7	**9.0**
5.8	2.23	10.9	0.31	**7.1**	21.7	1.61	12.00	3.47	37.1	**0.9**	18.2	39.2	**9.6**
7.8	0.38	na	-0.04	**6.1**	1.5	1.22	9.49	4.25	65.9	**1.4**	14.3	16.6	**7.5**
5.4	0.19	na	0.68	**0.0**	-1.1	-1.42	-10.88	2.97	137.4	**0.8**	12.1	34.4	**4.9**
6.3	0.63	na	0.02	**9.5**	1.4	2.43	13.91	4.18	45.1	**4.7**	44.3	12.5	**9.8**
7.5	0.00	na	-0.01	**4.9**	0.4	1.26	10.52	3.34	56.8	**5.5**	40.9	6.7	**5.4**
6.3	1.40	na	0.08	**6.2**	1.9	1.22	8.80	4.31	65.3	**4.3**	27.2	9.2	**7.8**
8.4	0.10	na	0.01	**4.7**	0.9	0.92	8.87	4.07	75.9	**3.2**	21.2	13.6	**6.7**
6.5	0.84	3.3	-0.01	**3.8**	18.4	0.83	6.89	3.33	76.1	**3.6**	14.7	11.1	**9.9**
9.0	0.00	na	0.00	**6.5**	1.7	1.65	16.05	4.30	59.7	**2.7**	25.2	16.4	**6.3**
9.3	0.03	na	0.00	**6.0**	0.8	1.56	13.06	2.82	42.5	**3.9**	71.4	21.4	**6.5**
5.9	0.65	2.9	0.13	**7.7**	78.1	1.35	9.25	3.53	55.9	**3.4**	15.0	11.3	**10.0**
6.2	2.37	na	-0.26	**3.0**	0.3	0.40	3.12	3.11	84.7	**1.5**	34.4	40.4	**5.7**
5.5	0.70	3.9	0.13	**5.8**	20.3	1.28	9.60	4.22	60.4	**1.2**	14.3	29.1	**9.0**
6.4	0.24	na	-0.09	**7.4**	0.9	2.90	22.81	4.21	50.6	**1.2**	28.6	18.5	**6.3**
4.3	1.09	7.4	0.36	**6.0**	44.3	1.12	8.28	4.59	62.9	**2.1**	18.3	16.9	**8.9**
5.0	2.45	na	0.00	**5.5**	2.7	1.40	13.09	3.27	63.8	**1.6**	20.4	24.0	**6.9**
7.4	0.00	na	1.51	**4.6**	1.0	0.40	2.95	4.03	59.7	**3.1**	13.8	6.0	**8.4**
8.8	1.35	na	0.00	**2.6**	0.3	0.34	3.20	3.28	84.1	**3.3**	44.1	19.5	**5.3**
4.6	1.98	7.5	0.31	**10.0**	20.8	2.12	18.57	5.14	45.8	**4.0**	27.0	13.3	**10.0**
5.0	0.86	5.0	0.49	**7.1**	169.7	1.28	9.44	4.12	49.7	**2.9**	14.3	11.4	**9.6**
3.7	1.78	na	0.60	**4.1**	1.0	0.86	7.49	4.83	74.4	**0.6**	12.5	51.3	**5.3**
4.5	0.77	na	0.07	**4.1**	0.8	0.75	7.57	4.27	77.8	**1.6**	13.4	21.7	**5.9**
5.6	0.65	na	0.26	**4.8**	6.7	0.86	7.23	4.18	69.0	**3.0**	7.0	13.4	**9.1**
6.5	0.00	na	0.00	**0.0**	-0.7	-1.12	-7.29	3.60	127.8	**3.6**	26.1	12.5	**5.4**
8.9	0.00	0.0	0.29	**9.8**	4.0	2.86	7.09	4.89	45.1	**1.8**	34.7	32.1	**9.3**
7.7	0.00	na	-0.05	**0.0**	-0.7	-2.10	-6.96	4.94	131.7	**2.6**	45.9	29.3	**5.4**
7.6	0.00	0.1	0.00	**10.0**	1.6	2.77	6.53	6.15	44.8	**3.0**	40.2	16.9	**8.9**
6.5	1.02	na	0.02	**4.1**	2.2	0.77	7.93	3.82	76.3	**2.9**	3.2	11.7	**5.4**
7.2	0.00	0.0	1.67	**2.2**	-1.7	-0.25	-2.21	4.81	74.1	**1.4**	13.7	13.5	**7.4**
8.3	1.22	na	0.02	**8.7**	6.7	1.69	10.48	4.06	47.1	**5.8**	36.1	2.8	**9.4**
7.4	0.00	na	-0.05	**4.9**	6.6	4.08	42.41	4.03	82.8	**4.6**	15.7	2.5	**6.7**
5.6	0.70	4.7	0.01	**4.5**	28.9	0.97	9.66	3.28	62.1	**2.2**	12.9	12.4	**8.5**
8.9	0.45	1.1	-0.01	**3.9**	0.5	0.92	7.98	3.79	74.5	**6.2**	46.6	3.3	**5.3**
8.6	0.16	na	0.10	**5.1**	18.2	0.97	12.17	3.25	67.7	**4.4**	18.7	6.8	**7.0**
7.6	0.43	2.2	0.07	**6.5**	44.1	1.34	11.99	3.23	54.8	**3.4**	9.1	8.8	**9.2**
5.8	2.54	4.7	2.37	**0.0**	-0.3	-2.04	-15.86	3.08	125.2	**1.6**	47.0	33.9	**3.7**
9.0	0.00	0.2	0.01	**3.9**	1.8	0.75	7.93	3.02	70.1	**4.4**	26.2	7.6	**5.6**
2.4	1.44	na	0.04	**10.0**	2.0	2.33	13.28	4.89	49.8	**1.4**	16.0	13.0	**9.5**
6.9	0.50	2.7	0.00	**4.8**	0.2	1.15	10.01	3.77	72.1	**3.6**	38.4	14.2	**4.9**
6.7	0.30	na	0.26	**7.5**	32.9	1.51	15.63	3.66	57.9	**2.9**	5.3	13.7	**8.4**
10.0	na	na	na	**3.3**	0.0	1.07	1.08	0.62	96.8	**4.0**	na	0.0	**7.0**
8.0	3.02	na	0.00	**3.3**	0.6	0.60	3.90	3.26	75.5	**4.1**	44.3	15.7	**7.6**

Name	City	State	Rating	2018 Rating	2017 Rating	Total Assets ($Mil)	One Year Asset Growth	Asset Mix (As a % of Total Assets): Comm-ercial Loans	Cons-umer Loans	Mort-gage Loans	Secur-ities	Capital-ization Index	Lever-age Ratio	Risk-Based Capital Ratio
Canton State Bank	Canton	MO	**C-**	C-	D+	35.4	8.10	3.8	1.9	30.5	26.5	**7.0**	9.0	16.5
Canyon Community Bank, N.A.	Tucson	AZ	**D**	D	D+	96.4	2.76	19.1	0.0	1.1	13.2	**10.0**	12.1	35.7
Cape Ann Savings Bank	Gloucester	MA	**A-**	B+	B	676.5	8.10	2.0	0.2	42.0	16.6	**10.0**	24.2	40.4
Cape Cod Five Cents Savings Bank	Orleans	MA	**B-**	B-	B-	3617.8	5.78	2.8	0.6	55.0	10.2	**8.1**	9.7	15.3
Capital Bank	Houston	TX	**B-**	B-	B-	468.4	10.78	6.0	1.5	8.7	9.1	**7.1**	9.2	12.6
Capital Bank and Trust Co.	Irvine	CA	**U**	U	U	205.1	14.53	0.0	0.0	0.0	63.2	**10.0**	73.9	165.5
Capital Bank of Texas	Carrizo Springs	TX	**B+**	B	B	87.0	28.57	0.5	0.6	5.5	16.9	**10.0**	13.2	49.8
Capital Bank, N.A.	Rockville	MD	**B**	B	B	1274.1	19.68	10.4	3.4	26.9	2.9	**5.6**	8.6	11.5
Capital City Bank	Tallahassee	FL	**B**	B	C+	2911.8	3.89	6.4	9.6	12.2	21.0	**9.3**	10.5	16.7
▲ Capital Community Bank	Provo	UT	**C+**	C+	B	468.7	24.35	14.6	29.2	0.9	2.6	**8.5**	10.0	14.0
Capital One Bank (USA), N.A.	Glen Allen	VA	**B-**	B-	C+	120248.2	1.95	7.4	76.6	0.0	12.5	**10.0**	14.2	17.8
Capital One, N.A.	McLean	VA	**B-**	B-	C+	318177.5	9.55	8.9	22.6	0.1	20.7	**7.6**	9.4	15.2
▲ Capitol Bank	Madison	WI	**A-**	B+	B-	379.5	5.43	15.3	0.1	9.1	14.7	**9.0**	12.1	14.2
Capitol Federal Savings Bank	Topeka	KS	**B**	B	B	9358.5	-1.10	0.7	0.1	70.1	12.9	**10.0**	12.1	24.3
Capitol National Bank	Lansing	MI	**B-**	C	D+	116.5	-1.70	11.1	0.2	4.0	0.9	**10.0**	12.7	18.4
Capon Valley Bank	Wardensville	WV	**B-**	B-	B	160.7	5.36	8.5	9.2	39.6	4.5	**10.0**	11.1	15.8
CapStar Bank	Nashville	TN	**B**	B-	C	2033.3	43.58	18.8	1.4	8.7	10.2	**7.2**	10.6	12.7
Captex Bank, N.A.	Trenton	TX	**D**	D	D+	185.6	5.25	3.5	8.7	15.5	16.4	**10.0**	12.2	18.3
Carmine State Bank	Carmine	TX	**B**	B	B	82.9	3.85	2.4	6.8	12.1	30.7	**10.0**	12.6	44.0
▲ Carolina Bank & Trust Co.	Florence	SC	**B+**	B+	B+	481.0	3.41	7.6	1.6	19.6	7.2	**10.0**	13.1	20.1
▲ Carolina Trust Bank	Lincolnton	NC	**C+**	C	C+	622.6	33.94	8.8	0.8	11.2	10.2	**8.6**	11.2	13.9
Carroll Bank and Trust	Huntingdon	TN	**B-**	B-	B-	291.8	5.95	6.5	6.6	30.4	7.1	**8.9**	10.3	14.7
Carroll Community Bank	Eldersburg	MD	**D+**	C-	C-	185.7	-5.66	3.1	0.1	25.2	7.1	**7.6**	9.5	13.0
Carroll County Trust Co.	Carrollton	MO	**C**	C	C+	156.5	-0.57	3.5	2.0	5.6	42.9	**6.9**	10.9	12.4
Carrollton Bank	Carrollton	IL	**B-**	B-	C+	1919.8	16.47	25.2	0.4	13.5	8.0	**5.3**	8.2	11.2
Carrollton Federal Bank	Carrollton	KY	**C+**	C+	B-	32.1	0.17	0.2	4.0	49.4	5.9	**10.0**	16.3	29.1
Carson Bank	Mulvane	KS	**C+**	C+	C-	122.4	-0.83	8.7	1.7	16.7	17.3	**6.0**	8.0	12.4
▲ Carter Bank & Trust	Martinsville	VA	**C**	D+	D	4020.1	-0.20	6.3	1.8	11.6	18.3	**8.9**	10.3	14.7
Carthage Federal S&L Assn.	Carthage	NY	**B**	B	B	251.1	7.79	0.0	2.2	53.6	7.0	**10.0**	11.8	28.3
Carver Federal Savings Bank	New York	NY	**D**	D	D-	589.8	-4.34	1.7	0.6	22.0	14.6	**10.0**	11.5	16.9
Carver State Bank	Savannah	GA	**C-**	C-	D+	41.3	3.95	17.2	3.2	22.6	6.2	**9.3**	10.6	17.1
▲ Casey County Bank, Inc.	Liberty	KY	**B**	B-	B	196.0	7.16	5.9	6.6	24.1	18.1	**10.0**	12.3	19.2
Casey State Bank	Casey	IL	**B-**	B	B+	327.9	9.34	15.8	6.1	10.2	17.0	**9.2**	10.5	14.5
▲ Cashmere Valley Bank	Cashmere	WA	**A**	A-	A-	1655.3	9.22	4.1	12.6	7.6	30.1	**10.0**	12.2	20.2
▲ Cass Commercial Bank	Saint Louis	MO	**A-**	B+	A	862.1	1.71	32.6	0.0	0.1	0.0	**10.0**	17.0	19.1
▼ Cass County Bank, Inc.	Plattsmouth	NE	**C**	B-	B-	73.4	5.36	12.1	0.8	18.8	5.9	**9.0**	10.6	14.2
▲ Castle Rock Bank	Castle Rock	MN	**A-**	B+	B+	202.5	0.60	10.4	4.1	12.1	44.5	**10.0**	15.5	29.3
▲ Castroville State Bank	Castroville	TX	**B**	B-	B	174.9	11.80	4.9	5.2	27.4	25.7	**7.8**	9.5	16.7
▲ Catahoula-LaSalle Bank	Jonesville	LA	**C**	C	C	178.7	-0.56	19.7	5.3	8.5	25.2	**10.0**	11.5	16.6
Cathay Bank	Los Angeles	CA	**A-**	A-	B+	17971.2	9.32	14.2	0.0	27.1	7.9	**8.8**	11.4	14.0
▲ Catlin Bank	Catlin	IL	**B-**	C+	C+	63.2	6.95	8.8	1.5	29.7	20.4	**8.4**	10.0	17.2
Catskill Hudson Bank	Kingston	NY	**C**	C	C-	525.2	12.34	6.2	0.3	3.9	26.0	**6.0**	8.0	12.2
▲ Cattaraugus County Bank	Little Valley	NY	**B-**	C+	C+	251.4	6.78	11.5	0.9	17.8	10.6	**6.8**	8.9	12.7
▲ Cattle Bank & Trust	Seward	NE	**A-**	B+	A-	281.7	2.45	4.1	0.6	22.3	16.1	**10.0**	13.1	17.9
Cayuga Lake National Bank	Union Springs	NY	**B**	B	B	153.8	4.66	5.6	2.9	32.3	38.1	**7.8**	9.5	21.2
CB&S Bank, Inc.	Russellville	AL	**B**	B	B-	1915.5	17.33	6.6	1.7	10.1	34.8	**9.0**	10.3	16.1
CBank	Cincinnati	OH	**B**	B-	B	188.5	12.33	19.5	1.6	9.0	5.9	**8.9**	11.4	14.1
CBBC Bank	Maryville	TN	**B**	B	B	357.9	1.43	3.2	0.6	7.1	31.2	**10.0**	15.6	24.4
▲ CBC Bank	Bowling Green	MO	**C**	C-	D+	37.3	4.61	4.0	1.1	9.8	41.8	**7.0**	9.0	29.5
▲ CBI Bank & Trust	Muscatine	IA	**B+**	B-	B+	576.2	8.12	9.3	1.8	13.5	18.4	**10.0**	11.7	17.4
▲ CBW Bank	Weir	KS	**A**	A-	A-	65.0	52.81	2.7	2.8	0.8	6.2	**10.0**	19.8	218.6
CCB Community Bank	Andalusia	AL	**B+**	A-	B+	510.5	2.74	7.8	1.4	16.4	6.2	**9.8**	11.2	14.8
Cecil Bank	Elkton	MD	**E-**	E-	E-	174.2	-18.05	14.8	0.1	14.7	16.2	**4.2**	6.2	14.5
▲ Cecilian Bank	Cecilia	KY	**B+**	B-	B-	921.3	4.83	4.9	4.4	19.2	23.9	**9.5**	10.7	15.7
Cedar Hill National Bank	Charlotte	NC	**U**	U	U	12.9	7.49	0.0	0.0	0.0	81.3	**10.0**	84.2	129.8
Cedar Rapids Bank and Trust Co.	Cedar Rapids	IA	**B+**	B+	B+	1595.1	17.65	27.2	0.6	5.8	11.9	**5.9**	10.0	11.6
Cedar Rapids State Bank	Cedar Rapids	NE	**D+**	C-	C-	51.4	2.07	12.6	2.5	7.5	8.7	**4.5**	8.3	10.8
▲ Cedar Security Bank	Fordyce	NE	**B-**	C+	D+	48.6	0.57	9.6	2.6	12.3	5.6	**10.0**	15.2	18.4
Cedar Valley Bank & Trust	La Porte City	IA	**C**	C	C+	74.5	14.16	7.5	4.2	22.3	17.0	**6.4**	8.6	12.0
CedarStone Bank	Lebanon	TN	**B**	B	B	207.5	3.60	6.5	3.2	30.6	17.2	**9.2**	10.5	15.4

Asset Quality Index	Adjusted Non-Performing Loans as a % of Total Loans	Adjusted Non-Performing Loans as a % of Capital	Net Charge-Offs Avg Loans	Profitability Index	Net Income ($Mil)	Return on Assets (R.O.A.)	Return on Equity (R.O.E.)	Net Interest Spread	Overhead Efficiency Ratio	Liquidity Index	Liquidity Ratio	Hot Money Ratio	Stability Index
6.4	0.33	na	-0.11	**2.8**	0.1	0.46	4.39	3.68	88.2	**4.9**	29.0	6.1	**5.0**
9.1	0.00	na	0.00	**0.3**	-0.2	-0.30	-2.50	2.88	114.2	**6.4**	44.6	1.9	**6.0**
8.1	1.39	3.5	0.00	**7.5**	8.7	1.81	7.58	2.82	66.6	**2.4**	41.8	30.7	**9.2**
7.7	0.55	4.2	-0.02	**3.9**	19.5	0.74	7.75	3.14	74.3	**2.4**	10.7	16.8	**7.4**
5.8	0.53	4.2	0.05	**5.9**	3.8	1.13	12.44	4.34	65.8	**1.4**	22.0	28.1	**5.7**
10.0	na	na	na	**9.5**	33.9	24.02	36.93	2.53	77.3	**9.9**	196.3	0.0	**6.7**
9.4	0.00	na	0.00	**5.2**	0.7	1.16	8.73	3.11	60.8	**6.7**	64.6	4.4	**6.6**
5.4	0.52	5.5	0.05	**7.2**	11.4	1.33	15.29	5.77	73.8	**1.2**	7.7	21.8	**7.4**
5.5	1.25	3.8	0.15	**5.4**	23.8	1.07	9.11	3.92	71.3	**5.6**	22.9	1.2	**9.0**
5.9	0.15	na	1.61	**6.7**	4.4	1.29	12.92	5.84	40.4	**0.8**	23.6	59.8	**6.4**
2.4	0.61	9.3	4.80	**10.0**	2475.2	2.79	19.36	11.29	47.9	**0.5**	17.1	76.1	**8.3**
4.9	0.99	3.3	0.95	**4.8**	2162.1	0.93	6.92	3.73	70.8	**5.9**	45.7	6.4	**8.1**
7.5	0.03	na	-0.05	**6.7**	3.7	1.31	11.05	3.66	54.5	**1.7**	16.4	19.2	**7.9**
9.7	0.10	0.6	0.00	**4.6**	69.6	0.98	7.77	2.26	47.5	**1.5**	11.6	24.9	**9.8**
3.7	3.79	10.4	-0.14	**5.4**	0.9	1.05	8.03	4.94	72.7	**4.5**	19.8	4.4	**7.4**
5.7	2.33	na	0.53	**3.8**	0.6	0.52	4.66	4.62	82.0	**1.8**	10.4	19.4	**6.2**
7.7	0.30	na	0.00	**5.4**	17.6	1.18	9.62	3.69	65.7	**2.5**	15.8	13.3	**7.3**
7.0	0.40	na	-0.01	**0.1**	-0.9	-0.68	-4.62	4.15	106.4	**2.7**	16.8	15.7	**5.5**
9.1	0.03	na	0.01	**3.9**	0.5	0.90	7.09	2.86	66.1	**3.2**	81.0	42.1	**7.1**
6.0	1.53	na	0.13	**6.3**	4.3	1.20	9.51	3.90	57.9	**4.1**	22.7	8.7	**7.6**
5.1	0.72	na	0.03	**5.0**	4.9	1.06	9.17	4.23	68.7	**1.4**	18.5	23.7	**7.3**
5.7	0.72	na	0.04	**4.7**	1.7	0.79	7.63	4.52	75.4	**1.4**	9.1	24.0	**5.8**
3.7	1.37	na	0.03	**1.9**	0.2	0.17	1.88	3.18	95.1	**0.7**	9.5	25.0	**4.6**
3.1	3.37	na	0.00	**3.1**	0.8	0.63	6.03	2.97	77.9	**2.7**	36.0	13.8	**5.8**
8.3	0.16	1.0	0.06	**4.4**	14.1	1.06	12.83	3.20	69.3	**2.8**	19.1	15.9	**7.9**
5.9	5.09	na	-0.02	**3.5**	0.1	0.57	3.56	4.22	82.2	**2.8**	17.9	15.2	**6.7**
7.4	0.11	0.8	0.30	**4.3**	0.9	0.97	12.26	3.86	77.2	**1.6**	13.5	21.9	**4.2**
4.0	1.61	9.2	0.15	**3.2**	23.0	0.75	6.71	3.02	71.2	**2.0**	21.7	23.1	**7.4**
9.7	0.39	na	0.05	**4.0**	1.4	0.80	7.05	2.91	67.1	**1.2**	23.9	31.0	**6.8**
2.8	2.34	12.9	0.06	**0.4**	-3.0	-0.69	-6.16	3.16	118.1	**0.8**	20.0	27.7	**6.2**
2.5	5.54	na	1.17	**3.4**	0.1	0.42	3.95	5.24	83.1	**1.2**	28.8	21.6	**4.2**
5.5	1.93	na	0.11	**6.7**	2.1	1.41	11.45	4.42	59.7	**2.9**	14.3	14.4	**7.1**
2.6	2.55	16.5	0.09	**5.9**	3.3	1.40	13.32	3.87	58.2	**1.6**	17.0	22.9	**6.9**
7.5	1.35	na	0.10	**6.5**	17.4	1.50	11.55	3.34	58.0	**5.6**	40.5	9.8	**10.0**
7.1	0.00	na	-0.01	**9.8**	12.2	1.95	12.13	3.88	41.9	**1.5**	18.9	9.8	**10.0**
1.5	4.86	25.3	0.05	**3.3**	0.4	0.67	6.18	4.11	78.5	**1.2**	15.5	18.7	**5.2**
8.0	1.39	na	0.09	**5.7**	2.2	1.46	9.54	3.07	43.5	**3.6**	53.1	20.7	**8.1**
6.6	0.62	na	0.09	**5.5**	1.3	1.06	11.28	3.54	57.9	**1.2**	18.7	30.2	**5.9**
3.5	2.88	17.2	0.09	**5.1**	1.6	1.22	10.92	4.08	69.1	**3.2**	20.1	13.5	**6.2**
7.0	0.60	2.8	-0.05	**9.0**	213.9	1.66	12.28	3.65	43.3	**0.8**	14.1	37.2	**10.0**
6.8	0.75	na	0.63	**5.2**	0.5	1.05	10.43	4.23	69.6	**2.9**	13.3	14.2	**5.1**
5.7	1.10	na	0.10	**3.2**	1.8	0.50	6.53	3.27	82.3	**2.0**	14.9	19.2	**2.5**
5.6	0.99	na	0.41	**4.2**	1.5	0.78	8.97	4.17	75.3	**3.8**	5.8	8.0	**5.9**
7.0	0.99	na	-0.08	**6.6**	3.1	1.49	11.60	3.67	60.1	**1.4**	9.8	24.6	**8.8**
9.5	0.00	na	0.01	**3.9**	0.9	0.83	9.59	3.26	72.2	**3.3**	31.7	15.7	**5.0**
5.7	1.89	6.8	0.18	**4.4**	12.0	0.92	7.37	3.63	71.0	**4.4**	33.0	13.7	**8.7**
8.2	0.00	na	0.00	**5.0**	1.6	1.18	9.90	3.65	68.9	**0.8**	14.0	34.3	**7.3**
8.9	0.74	na	0.02	**4.6**	2.6	0.97	6.28	3.47	65.8	**3.0**	42.2	21.1	**7.7**
9.9	0.00	na	0.00	**2.7**	0.1	0.50	5.84	2.75	83.5	**6.8**	59.9	2.3	**3.8**
6.1	1.35	na	0.10	**5.3**	4.3	1.06	8.63	3.40	66.2	**2.9**	34.5	18.4	**7.8**
9.9	0.32	na	-0.03	**9.5**	3.1	6.04	31.64	3.38	52.2	**8.4**	115.2	0.7	**8.5**
6.1	0.56	na	0.13	**7.6**	6.3	1.67	15.07	4.30	57.7	**1.4**	15.3	24.0	**9.0**
6.0	1.53	5.6	-0.04	**0.0**	-2.1	-1.46	-23.15	2.42	151.3	**3.5**	35.3	15.7	**0.0**
7.0	0.55	na	-0.09	**6.2**	9.5	1.40	13.04	3.64	60.8	**2.9**	14.4	14.7	**7.5**
10.0	na	na	na	**9.8**	0.5	5.14	6.27	2.43	72.1	**10.0**	424.5	0.0	**7.0**
8.0	0.07	0.4	-0.02	**9.0**	20.5	1.84	16.84	3.29	53.3	**1.7**	21.6	12.8	**8.3**
4.0	1.49	na	0.00	**3.5**	0.2	0.63	7.73	3.76	77.5	**0.6**	8.3	35.0	**3.0**
6.1	2.07	na	0.22	**5.0**	0.3	0.93	6.31	4.10	70.5	**3.3**	33.0	15.6	**6.4**
7.5	0.00	na	0.10	**5.2**	0.6	1.16	14.23	4.01	64.7	**3.6**	9.8	10.6	**3.3**
8.8	0.31	na	0.09	**4.5**	1.4	0.87	8.57	3.66	68.8	**1.3**	16.5	27.2	**6.2**

Name	City	State	Rating	2018 Rating	2017 Rating	Total Assets ($Mil)	One Year Asset Growth	Asset Mix (As a % of Total Assets) Commercial Loans	Consumer Loans	Mortgage Loans	Securities	Capitalization Index	Leverage Ratio	Risk-Based Capital Ratio
▲ Celtic Bank	Salt Lake City	UT	**B**	B-	B	947.1	18.28	44.4	2.6	0.3	0.6	**10.0**	19.9	21.4
▲ CenBank	Buffalo Lake	MN	**B**	B-	B	66.3	-3.41	6.5	5.0	2.0	24.7	**5.8**	8.0	11.6
▲ Cendera Bank, N.A.	Bells	TX	**B+**	B	B-	105.6	7.25	7.5	1.3	39.5	3.0	**10.0**	12.9	17.8
Cenlar FSB	Ewing	NJ	**A-**	A-	A	1191.6	5.38	0.0	0.0	39.2	46.5	**7.2**	9.1	22.8
Centennial Bank	Conway	AR	**B+**	B+	B	14884.5	-0.09	9.9	3.2	10.6	14.0	**10.0**	12.3	15.3
▲ Centennial Bank	Trezevant	TN	**B-**	C+	B-	584.2	27.70	10.8	5.3	16.9	9.5	**8.3**	10.4	13.6
Centennial Bank	Lubbock	TX	**B**	B+	A-	782.6	1.95	6.8	0.9	13.5	16.1	**7.9**	10.2	13.3
Center National Bank	Litchfield	MN	**A-**	A-	A-	196.9	2.05	9.5	6.3	7.7	34.8	**10.0**	11.7	16.4
Center Point Bank and Trust Co.	Center Point	IA	**B**	B-	B-	34.1	-0.82	5.2	3.1	25.3	28.1	**6.1**	8.1	12.9
Centera Bank	Sublette	KS	**B-**	B	B	262.6	1.30	5.2	1.1	6.7	43.3	**7.1**	9.0	16.9
▲ CenterBank	Milford	OH	**B**	B-	B	218.6	27.59	19.5	0.1	18.7	4.6	**7.3**	9.9	12.8
CenterState Bank, N.A.	Winter Haven	FL	**B+**	B+	B	17409.1	41.98	7.1	1.5	11.3	11.5	**6.4**	10.0	12.0
Centier Bank	Merrillville	IN	**B+**	B+	A-	4811.3	13.56	4.8	7.7	12.4	9.0	**6.7**	9.7	12.3
▲ Centinel Bank of Taos	Taos	NM	**A-**	B+	A-	276.3	11.50	3.0	1.0	16.4	45.8	**6.8**	8.8	23.6
Central Bank	Little Rock	AR	**B**	B+	B+	242.2	16.42	9.4	0.2	21.7	18.5	**8.3**	10.7	13.6
Central Bank	Tampa	FL	**C+**	B-	B+	189.0	13.16	9.0	0.1	19.2	4.5	**7.2**	9.4	12.6
▲ Central Bank	Storm Lake	IA	**B-**	C+	C+	913.6	6.16	21.0	2.1	12.1	7.5	**5.6**	10.1	11.4
▲ Central Bank	Savannah	TN	**B**	C+	C-	98.6	7.00	3.9	4.8	41.7	13.0	**10.0**	12.1	23.0
Central Bank	Houston	TX	**B+**	B+	B+	748.5	5.26	13.0	0.5	30.8	14.5	**8.4**	9.9	13.7
▲ Central Bank	Provo	UT	**A-**	B+	A	1194.9	8.16	5.3	1.2	5.3	24.5	**10.0**	16.5	23.4
Central Bank & Trust Co.	Lexington	KY	**B+**	B	B-	2701.2	6.15	8.9	4.1	16.1	9.3	**9.5**	11.4	14.6
▲ Central Bank and Trust	Lander	WY	**B**	B-	B	153.3	6.31	9.1	1.9	17.2	29.5	**8.6**	10.1	17.5
▲ Central Bank Illinois	Geneseo	IL	**B**	B	A-	919.9	5.13	5.7	0.8	7.6	33.3	**8.5**	10.0	14.2
Central Bank of Audrain County	Mexico	MO	**B**	B	B	178.9	7.58	6.2	3.9	11.2	33.6	**5.4**	7.4	14.2
Central Bank of Boone County	Columbia	MO	**B+**	B+	B+	2169.1	14.42	5.6	5.4	11.2	27.8	**6.6**	8.6	13.1
Central Bank of Branson	Branson	MO	**B+**	B	B-	336.3	-2.72	9.2	6.7	15.4	25.1	**8.9**	10.2	14.9
Central Bank of Kansas City	Kansas City	MO	**A**	A	A-	216.2	30.77	21.4	0.0	1.1	0.0	**10.0**	16.4	18.8
Central Bank of Lake of the Ozarks	Osage Beach	MO	**B+**	B+	B	820.5	9.12	4.1	4.7	16.5	34.9	**7.2**	9.1	14.8
Central Bank of Moberly	Moberly	MO	**B**	B	B-	184.9	-1.69	5.6	13.8	6.0	33.0	**7.0**	9.0	14.5
Central Bank of Oklahoma	Tulsa	OK	**B**	B	B-	692.6	-0.49	11.2	0.3	14.5	1.2	**7.6**	11.8	13.0
Central Bank of Sedalia	Sedalia	MO	**B+**	B+	B	424.1	5.59	7.3	16.6	7.8	23.6	**6.7**	8.7	12.8
Central Bank of St. Louis	Clayton	MO	**B+**	B+	B	1904.9	4.41	13.1	1.0	10.7	11.2	**7.7**	10.9	13.1
Central Bank of the Midwest	Lee's Summit	MO	**B+**	B+	B	1770.9	-0.13	12.0	10.7	3.7	17.6	**6.5**	9.3	12.1
Central Bank of the Ozarks	Springfield	MO	**B+**	B+	B	1411.7	8.40	10.0	12.3	11.4	18.2	**7.5**	9.8	12.9
Central Bank of Warrensburg	Warrensburg	MO	**B**	B	B	252.9	1.37	4.4	2.3	7.8	31.4	**8.4**	9.9	17.6
Central Federal S&L Assn.	Cicero	IL	**C-**	C	C-	187.9	6.05	0.0	0.0	60.2	10.5	**9.6**	10.7	20.4
Central Federal S&L Assn. of Rolla	Rolla	MO	**C**	C	C-	69.3	-1.14	2.1	1.1	39.6	6.8	**10.0**	30.3	44.3
Central National Bank	Junction City	KS	**B**	B	B-	973.4	9.20	6.2	2.0	5.9	28.0	**10.0**	11.0	17.9
▲ Central National Bank	Waco	TX	**A-**	B+	B+	928.9	5.94	15.3	1.0	33.5	7.3	**7.3**	9.2	13.1
Central National Bank of Poteau	Poteau	OK	**B**	B+	A-	248.2	5.95	12.1	3.4	15.5	29.2	**10.0**	11.1	19.1
Central Pacific Bank	Honolulu	HI	**A-**	A-	A-	5967.9	4.36	9.4	8.8	26.2	19.9	**7.5**	9.4	13.5
Central Savings Bank	Sault Sainte Marie	MI	**B**	B-	C+	271.2	5.70	7.6	5.4	19.0	23.1	**10.0**	13.3	21.7
▲ Central Savings, F.S.B.	Chicago	IL	**B**	B-	B+	103.6	-9.61	0.0	0.1	30.4	3.7	**10.0**	25.0	34.9
Central State Bank	Calera	AL	**A-**	A-	A-	328.3	8.87	5.5	2.0	16.3	14.6	**9.8**	10.9	17.2
Central State Bank	Elkader	IA	**B**	B	B	323.8	21.91	11.6	2.2	16.3	12.9	**6.5**	8.7	12.1
Central State Bank	State Center	IA	**C**	C+	B-	307.5	9.20	17.3	1.2	4.2	23.0	**7.9**	12.2	13.2
Central State Bank	Clayton	IL	**C+**	C+	B-	144.2	6.96	11.4	8.3	25.9	2.1	**10.0**	15.3	20.3
Central Trust Bank	Jefferson City	MO	**B+**	B+	B	2645.3	5.64	6.4	7.8	9.3	46.9	**5.6**	7.6	13.7
Central Valley Community Bank	Fresno	CA	**A**	A	A-	1584.0	4.29	6.0	2.8	2.6	29.7	**10.0**	11.4	16.0
CentreBank	Veedersburg	IN	**B+**	A-	B	79.3	1.25	12.3	3.1	23.5	0.3	**10.0**	13.0	21.5
Centreville Bank	West Warwick	RI	**C**	D+	C	1257.3	1.84	0.6	0.1	33.7	24.1	**10.0**	24.3	28.4
Centric Bank	Harrisburg	PA	**B+**	B+	B-	790.3	10.50	24.8	0.1	9.2	5.0	**8.6**	11.0	13.8
▲ CenTrust Bank, N.A.	Northbrook	IL	**C+**	C-	D+	125.8	1.91	27.6	0.3	8.9	10.2	**7.5**	9.5	12.9
▲ Century Bank	Shenandoah	IA	**B**	B	B+	102.8	13.20	2.7	1.0	2.8	24.1	**8.4**	9.9	15.3
Century Bank	Lucedale	MS	**C+**	B-	B+	330.7	4.46	7.0	11.6	12.3	21.7	**9.7**	10.8	16.0
▲ Century Bank	Santa Fe	NM	**B+**	B	B	875.6	3.61	16.5	2.7	4.0	28.8	**7.7**	10.1	13.0
Century Bank and Trust	Milledgeville	GA	**B-**	B-	B+	257.5	0.69	4.2	1.2	12.8	25.7	**10.0**	11.3	16.6
Century Bank and Trust	Coldwater	MI	**B**	B	B	328.4	7.59	9.3	2.3	16.7	17.9	**10.0**	12.8	17.7
Century Bank and Trust Co.	Medford	MA	**C+**	C+	C+	5282.2	8.84	3.9	0.1	7.4	46.4	**5.0**	7.0	13.7
▲ Century Bank of Florida	Tampa	FL	**C+**	C	C-	82.0	1.73	11.5	2.0	24.5	7.4	**6.8**	8.9	14.5

Asset Quality Index	Adjusted Non-Performing Loans as a % of Total Loans	Adjusted Non-Performing Loans as a % of Capital	Net Charge-Offs Avg Loans	Profitability Index	Net Income ($Mil)	Return on Assets (R.O.A.)	Return on Equity (R.O.E.)	Net Interest Spread	Overhead Efficiency Ratio	Liquidity Index	Liquidity Ratio	Hot Money Ratio	Stability Index
5.4	1.56	na	0.52	**10.0**	30.2	4.61	24.00	6.75	51.4	**0.4**	9.7	0.9	**8.8**
6.5	0.64	na	-0.01	**4.3**	0.5	0.98	12.55	3.85	72.4	**2.5**	11.6	16.0	**5.1**
8.5	0.15	na	0.00	**5.1**	0.9	1.20	9.50	5.17	75.6	**0.8**	8.4	18.5	**7.1**
9.8	0.27	1.0	0.00	**8.6**	26.2	2.95	32.67	2.76	92.1	**7.6**	52.4	0.0	**8.8**
4.7	0.59	2.3	0.07	**9.8**	236.0	2.09	11.70	4.44	37.7	**2.0**	13.3	13.9	**10.0**
4.4	1.41	na	0.66	**6.5**	4.2	1.11	9.92	4.87	59.7	**1.3**	16.5	23.5	**6.2**
6.9	0.81	na	0.00	**4.8**	6.7	1.12	11.29	4.21	74.7	**2.5**	5.7	15.7	**7.8**
8.4	0.19	na	0.05	**5.8**	2.0	1.38	11.80	3.62	63.7	**2.7**	11.4	15.3	**7.9**
6.7	0.00	na	0.14	**4.4**	0.2	0.85	10.52	3.52	72.3	**2.6**	28.7	18.4	**4.8**
7.9	0.54	na	0.98	**4.4**	2.0	0.96	10.24	3.49	65.4	**2.2**	25.6	19.4	**6.0**
6.4	0.01	na	-0.03	**7.2**	2.1	1.40	13.61	4.41	62.2	**0.7**	9.4	31.3	**6.3**
6.1	0.34	1.5	0.07	**7.3**	157.9	1.38	8.53	4.34	60.6	**3.3**	14.9	10.3	**9.9**
6.5	0.13	0.9	0.07	**7.5**	49.8	1.45	14.86	3.71	55.4	**2.0**	11.2	13.0	**9.2**
8.7	0.28	na	0.00	**8.4**	4.1	2.08	23.25	3.63	49.1	**5.8**	54.8	9.5	**6.6**
7.4	1.46	na	0.00	**4.8**	1.4	0.82	7.64	2.92	61.4	**0.6**	17.5	61.6	**6.6**
4.2	0.53	na	0.00	**4.7**	0.8	0.61	6.80	3.64	78.2	**0.8**	18.5	45.5	**5.6**
7.8	0.09	na	-0.02	**6.9**	8.9	1.35	13.88	4.02	61.1	**1.3**	11.4	23.6	**7.5**
6.7	4.80	na	-0.04	**4.1**	0.6	0.84	6.58	4.45	81.4	**2.3**	25.7	18.6	**6.4**
7.1	0.28	2.1	0.05	**6.0**	7.9	1.41	14.82	5.61	71.3	**1.1**	10.9	27.7	**6.8**
7.6	0.08	na	0.01	**10.0**	17.5	2.06	12.54	5.50	51.9	**4.3**	28.3	12.8	**10.0**
7.0	0.47	2.6	0.21	**5.6**	23.9	1.22	10.48	4.07	71.3	**2.4**	14.6	17.4	**9.3**
6.3	0.31	na	0.07	**6.1**	1.9	1.68	17.26	4.33	63.7	**4.4**	13.2	5.8	**5.5**
5.9	0.57	na	0.04	**7.5**	10.2	1.50	13.00	3.92	53.9	**5.4**	43.8	8.5	**8.3**
5.6	0.87	4.7	0.03	**6.7**	1.8	1.35	16.74	3.13	53.0	**4.9**	25.5	3.7	**6.6**
8.3	0.29	1.3	0.09	**8.2**	24.0	1.58	18.02	3.22	50.8	**5.7**	32.4	6.4	**7.7**
3.7	2.56	13.3	0.20	**7.2**	3.8	1.46	14.50	4.00	57.5	**3.8**	11.1	8.3	**7.3**
6.9	0.00	0.0	-0.49	**10.0**	7.7	5.39	32.06	4.81	53.0	**1.3**	21.7	12.2	**9.5**
6.6	0.68	2.9	0.08	**9.2**	9.8	1.71	18.82	3.91	54.7	**4.1**	31.8	11.4	**7.5**
7.2	0.23	1.3	0.10	**5.6**	1.7	1.19	13.55	3.17	53.8	**4.7**	14.2	3.3	**6.6**
3.4	0.72	2.7	0.04	**8.2**	7.9	1.50	7.97	4.20	47.8	**0.6**	2.7	23.3	**8.5**
5.8	0.32	2.5	0.15	**9.6**	5.8	1.87	20.01	4.02	50.0	**3.6**	8.3	9.3	**7.7**
7.8	0.21	1.3	0.00	**7.7**	22.7	1.55	13.14	3.52	53.0	**4.0**	5.6	6.6	**7.0**
5.2	1.14	3.6	0.25	**6.9**	19.1	1.43	10.10	4.30	58.9	**4.9**	14.2	3.2	**8.6**
7.5	0.07	0.5	0.11	**6.8**	13.7	1.33	13.31	3.60	60.5	**4.3**	16.7	7.0	**8.0**
2.5	2.74	8.8	0.08	**5.7**	2.3	1.22	8.52	3.34	60.0	**4.1**	27.8	9.7	**8.2**
6.6	3.54	na	-0.05	**1.7**	0.1	0.09	0.86	2.76	96.7	**2.2**	31.3	22.9	**6.0**
8.9	0.15	na	0.00	**2.5**	0.1	0.25	0.83	3.51	90.6	**3.1**	29.8	15.4	**6.8**
8.1	0.53	0.9	0.13	**4.3**	7.1	0.98	8.63	3.38	78.1	**4.2**	18.8	7.5	**7.8**
8.7	0.01	na	0.00	**8.5**	14.0	2.09	22.97	3.87	45.4	**1.4**	15.3	16.1	**8.1**
7.4	0.75	na	0.07	**8.3**	3.5	1.86	17.47	4.27	60.9	**2.8**	17.7	15.5	**8.2**
8.2	0.18	0.8	0.13	**5.5**	46.8	1.07	11.55	3.37	61.1	**2.3**	11.5	17.5	**8.3**
4.2	4.88	15.7	0.14	**6.1**	2.5	1.27	9.64	4.02	64.1	**3.5**	36.6	16.2	**7.2**
5.6	0.91	na	-0.01	**5.0**	0.6	0.70	2.80	3.89	74.1	**0.7**	14.9	38.9	**7.5**
8.6	0.18	na	0.24	**7.1**	3.9	1.60	14.85	4.14	60.4	**1.6**	19.5	24.9	**7.9**
6.1	0.35	2.6	0.05	**4.2**	2.4	1.00	9.87	3.43	64.4	**1.6**	19.6	15.1	**6.9**
4.1	3.46	na	0.33	**5.5**	3.6	1.55	12.85	2.74	50.9	**1.3**	31.1	52.0	**8.9**
1.7	4.93	na	-0.04	**10.0**	2.8	2.63	17.04	4.56	48.6	**1.1**	8.2	29.1	**9.2**
7.1	0.88	3.5	0.06	**4.2**	30.0	1.56	19.33	2.73	67.6	**4.7**	14.0	4.5	**7.1**
7.3	0.44	1.3	0.02	**7.1**	17.5	1.49	10.04	4.55	63.7	**5.9**	31.9	5.0	**10.0**
6.3	0.54	na	0.00	**8.2**	0.9	1.50	12.04	5.09	63.0	**4.2**	27.9	10.2	**7.0**
9.6	0.22	0.4	0.00	**5.9**	17.4	1.87	7.95	2.84	73.5	**4.3**	49.3	18.3	**9.5**
4.8	1.26	6.1	0.12	**5.5**	6.0	1.05	9.29	3.89	63.0	**0.9**	10.2	30.7	**7.2**
4.6	1.12	na	0.05	**4.5**	1.0	1.03	11.21	4.18	70.5	**0.6**	15.0	60.2	**3.8**
8.1	0.00	na	0.15	**5.3**	0.8	1.12	11.37	3.40	55.3	**5.0**	36.0	8.3	**5.6**
5.7	1.62	na	0.13	**5.6**	2.7	1.08	10.15	4.34	70.6	**3.4**	19.9	12.6	**6.9**
8.1	0.39	na	0.11	**6.1**	8.9	1.37	13.55	4.83	69.3	**4.3**	26.2	8.8	**7.6**
6.9	2.22	na	0.00	**7.3**	2.9	1.49	14.81	4.15	59.3	**2.1**	20.4	14.2	**7.2**
6.7	1.19	na	0.17	**6.2**	3.4	1.42	11.38	4.08	64.9	**5.7**	34.1	3.0	**7.2**
9.1	0.15	0.6	0.01	**3.6**	30.0	0.77	11.91	2.11	63.1	**3.5**	8.9	10.1	**4.5**
5.3	1.03	na	-0.02	**3.4**	0.4	0.63	7.26	3.94	83.2	**2.4**	27.0	18.6	**4.4**

Name	City	State	Rating	2018 Rating	2017 Rating	Total Assets ($Mil)	One Year Asset Growth	Asset Mix (As a % of Total Assets) Commercial Loans	Consumer Loans	Mortgage Loans	Securities	Capitalization Index	Leverage Ratio	Risk-Based Capital Ratio
Century Bank of Georgia	Cartersville	GA	A-	A-	A-	198.5	1.63	6.6	1.6	9.2	21.0	8.4	9.9	18.8
▲ Century Bank of Kentucky, Inc.	Lawrenceburg	KY	C+	C	C+	141.9	2.44	4.6	1.3	37.0	11.3	9.9	10.9	15.8
▲ Century Bank of the Ozarks	Gainesville	MO	B+	B	B	176.0	1.08	9.0	3.1	19.1	2.2	6.9	9.8	12.4
Century Next Bank	Ruston	LA	B	B	B	489.3	59.54	10.3	3.4	30.1	0.2	8.7	10.1	14.4
Century S&L Assn.	Trinidad	CO	C+	C	C	90.3	-5.72	0.0	0.5	18.0	56.8	10.0	15.2	41.8
Century Savings Bank	Vineland	NJ	C+	C+	C+	443.2	-0.08	1.0	0.0	23.0	38.4	10.0	15.5	28.1
CerescoBank	Ceresco	NE	B	B	B+	49.6	0.90	10.3	4.8	13.9	19.4	10.0	16.7	21.4
▲ CFBank, N.A.	Worthington	OH	B-	C+	C+	785.0	29.59	18.7	0.0	23.8	1.2	6.5	10.0	12.1
▲ CFG Community Bank	Baltimore	MD	C	C-	C+	1098.1	39.67	26.5	0.1	1.8	4.4	10.0	14.9	17.3
cfsbank	Charleroi	PA	C+	C	C+	484.8	-1.41	1.2	1.3	50.5	21.9	10.0	15.1	29.9
Chain Bridge Bank, N.A.	McLean	VA	C+	C+	C+	711.3	-2.58	1.7	0.5	23.2	53.8	6.0	8.0	20.0
▲ Chambers Bank	Danville	AR	B-	C+	B	845.2	3.70	9.3	0.7	13.1	4.1	7.1	9.8	12.6
Chambers State Bank	Chambers	NE	B+	B+	B+	60.8	2.07	11.7	3.9	1.9	0.3	10.0	29.9	36.7
▲ Champion Bank	Parker	CO	A-	B-	C+	73.2	28.73	1.4	0.0	5.6	0.0	10.0	19.5	61.4
▲ Champlain National Bank	Willsboro	NY	B-	C+	C+	380.0	10.15	6.0	8.9	18.5	22.2	7.1	9.0	14.6
▲ Chappell Hill Bank	Chappell Hill	TX	C+	C	C	33.4	16.36	5.3	3.2	30.7	0.0	7.7	9.4	15.7
▼ Charis Bank	Justin	TX	C+	B	A-	93.6	6.38	9.3	0.3	12.4	0.0	10.0	21.3	38.2
Charles River Bank	Medway	MA	C-	C-	C-	251.8	8.19	3.1	2.5	37.7	12.1	6.1	8.2	13.7
Charles Schwab Bank	Henderson	NV	B+	B+	B+	207757.0	-4.26	0.6	1.5	5.4	85.3	5.4	7.4	22.9
Charles Schwab Premier Bank	Henderson	NV	U	U	U	13527.0	3.46	0.0	0.0	0.0	95.6	5.4	7.4	35.0
▲ Charlevoix State Bank	Charlevoix	MI	B+	B	B	205.3	2.37	6.0	2.6	17.7	19.3	7.2	9.1	15.8
Charlotte State Bank & Trust	Port Charlotte	FL	A-	A-	B+	379.3	4.71	0.3	0.2	21.3	30.4	8.9	10.3	19.7
Charter Bank	Johnston	IA	B+	B+	B+	163.3	4.56	6.2	2.8	20.2	27.2	10.0	11.5	18.9
▲ Charter Bank	Corpus Christi	TX	B	B	A-	299.4	7.14	16.8	0.2	4.7	38.1	7.4	9.3	14.7
Charter Bank	Eau Claire	WI	A	A	A	949.7	6.29	12.3	0.6	14.3	17.1	10.0	12.9	16.8
Charter West Bank	West Point	NE	B-	B	B+	298.0	18.73	11.0	2.3	15.6	8.6	8.0	9.7	13.7
▼ Chasewood Bank	Houston	TX	C-	C	D	88.9	-23.76	5.6	0.2	8.7	26.5	9.9	10.9	17.4
Cheaha Bank	Oxford	AL	A	A	A	206.7	1.98	7.3	4.2	20.0	34.9	10.0	13.0	22.2
▲ Chelsea Groton Bank	Norwich	CT	A-	B	B-	1159.7	2.51	5.5	0.5	47.2	11.7	10.0	16.2	21.8
▲ Chelsea Savings Bank	Belle Plaine	IA	A-	A-	A	118.4	-0.81	12.7	1.5	12.5	44.8	10.0	14.9	28.2
▲ Chelsea State Bank	Chelsea	MI	A	A-	A-	292.2	-2.55	12.3	0.4	5.5	21.1	10.0	12.4	20.9
Chemung Canal Trust Co.	Elmira	NY	B-	B-	C+	1789.4	2.25	11.9	8.3	13.9	15.0	6.9	8.9	13.1
Cherokee State Bank	Cherokee	IA	B	B+	A	228.7	1.22	4.2	0.8	6.1	29.0	10.0	11.9	17.2
Chesapeake Bank	Kilmarnock	VA	B+	A-	B	940.7	14.83	13.8	1.2	11.0	30.3	9.4	10.6	15.3
▲ Chesapeake Bank & Trust Co.	Chestertown	MD	B+	B	B	109.0	-0.21	2.8	1.4	38.2	19.7	8.9	10.3	16.6
Chesapeake Bank of Maryland	Baltimore	MD	B-	B-	C+	217.6	0.05	3.1	0.2	31.7	19.2	10.0	18.9	31.2
Chester National Bank	Chester	IL	B-	B-	C+	61.4	-23.26	2.3	2.4	56.7	15.0	10.0	13.8	25.2
▲ Chesterfield State Bank	Chesterfield	IL	C-	D+	D+	17.2	-2.59	13.2	6.2	30.1	0.0	10.0	11.4	20.1
Chetopa State Bank & Trust Co.	Chetopa	KS	B-	B-	B-	37.6	7.21	8.3	4.7	20.2	18.9	9.2	10.5	17.0
▲ Cheyenne State Bank	Cheyenne	WY	B-	C+	B-	40.3	-4.63	3.6	0.8	24.8	3.2	10.0	16.7	23.6
Chicago Trust Co., N.A.	Lake Forest	IL	U	U	U	111.4	0.72	0.0	0.0	0.0	1.7	10.0	99.0	468.2
▼ Chickasaw Community Bank	Oklahoma City	OK	B	B+	A-	202.1	8.22	14.5	2.1	28.8	8.9	6.6	8.6	13.4
Chillicothe State Bank	Chillicothe	MO	B	B	B	119.7	-3.38	3.1	5.3	26.1	27.5	6.6	8.6	16.6
▲ Chino Commercial Bank, N.A.	Chino	CA	B+	B	B	235.3	16.45	2.3	0.1	7.2	17.8	10.0	11.0	17.9
▲ Chippewa Valley Bank	Hayward	WI	B-	B-	B-	446.8	4.58	8.8	0.4	19.4	9.4	6.3	8.4	12.6
Chisholm Trail State Bank	Park City	KS	C-	C	C	91.4	19.93	5.8	2.2	19.2	21.6	8.7	10.1	14.2
Choice Financial Group	Fargo	ND	B+	B+	A-	2215.8	7.76	22.5	0.7	6.1	4.0	5.1	10.0	11.1
ChoiceOne Bank	Sparta	MI	B	B	B	661.0	2.28	12.2	3.7	12.4	23.3	7.7	9.8	13.0
CIBC Bank USA	Chicago	IL	B	B+	B+	31742.8	17.17	26.5	0.6	3.9	15.1	6.6	11.1	12.2
CIBC National Trust Co.	Atlanta	GA	U	U	U	272.2	14.20	0.0	0.0	0.0	0.0	10.0	76.3	189.3
CIBM Bank	Champaign	IL	C+	C+	C+	692.4	-3.68	7.2	0.1	27.3	17.1	9.3	10.5	14.7
Ciera Bank	Graham	TX	C+	B	B+	633.0	11.03	12.6	0.6	9.5	9.6	8.5	11.3	13.8
▼ Cincinnati Federal	Cincinnati	OH	C+	B-	B-	221.5	25.19	0.2	0.4	52.7	1.1	10.0	11.0	15.5
Cincinnatus S&L Co.	Cincinnati	OH	B-	B-	B-	95.9	7.33	0.6	0.8	44.1	0.0	10.0	22.9	36.3
CIT Bank, N.A.	Pasadena	CA	B+	B+	B+	45380.9	11.14	23.5	0.0	13.2	12.9	8.8	10.8	14.0
Citibank, N.A.	Sioux Falls	SD	B+	B	B	1472915.0	4.09	11.6	12.2	5.4	21.9	7.2	9.1	14.9
Citicorp Trust Delaware, N.A.	Greenville	DE	U	U	U	21.8	-9.98	0.0	0.0	0.0	1.0	10.0	83.3	493.2
Citizens & Northern Bank	Wellsboro	PA	A-	A-	A-	1626.9	27.98	7.1	1.3	31.9	21.5	10.0	12.3	18.8
Citizens 1st Bank	Tyler	TX	A+	A+	A+	704.8	-2.00	1.8	0.8	8.9	55.3	10.0	20.6	52.6
Citizens Alliance Bank	Clara City	MN	B-	B-	B-	829.4	14.28	11.1	1.4	7.9	18.1	4.7	8.0	10.9

Asset Quality Index	Adjusted Non-Performing Loans as a % of Total Loans	Adjusted Non-Performing Loans as a % of Capital	Net Charge-Offs Avg Loans	Profitability Index	Net Income ($Mil)	Return on Assets (R.O.A.)	Return on Equity (R.O.E.)	Net Interest Spread	Overhead Efficiency Ratio	Liquidity Index	Liquidity Ratio	Hot Money Ratio	Stability Index
8.9	0.29	na	-0.03	**7.0**	2.1	1.42	12.69	4.16	60.4	**4.9**	35.2	8.6	**7.5**
3.9	3.50	na	0.02	**7.0**	1.7	1.61	15.56	3.71	60.2	**1.2**	8.1	21.8	**8.1**
8.1	0.17	na	0.04	**9.9**	2.8	2.12	21.31	5.09	54.9	**3.6**	6.1	9.9	**8.1**
6.6	0.36	na	0.08	**6.1**	4.5	1.26	11.65	4.50	64.3	**1.3**	13.5	11.1	**6.2**
7.6	3.64	na	0.34	**2.4**	0.3	0.37	2.51	2.92	83.6	**2.6**	58.0	40.9	**6.4**
7.6	1.85	na	0.17	**2.8**	1.3	0.39	2.78	3.25	85.3	**5.8**	43.2	5.8	**6.9**
8.3	0.29	na	0.23	**5.9**	0.5	1.31	8.18	3.54	56.1	**3.0**	22.0	14.7	**7.3**
6.5	0.75	na	-0.01	**6.5**	7.8	1.46	15.44	3.21	59.8	**0.5**	5.5	29.9	**6.3**
3.6	1.07	na	0.07	**9.3**	13.7	1.90	10.95	4.99	61.2	**0.9**	18.5	43.7	**10.0**
6.4	2.03	na	0.37	**1.8**	1.1	0.30	2.03	2.79	84.5	**2.4**	32.3	21.5	**6.6**
9.8	0.00	0.0	0.00	**3.7**	3.4	0.71	8.58	2.73	68.4	**6.8**	64.8	5.5	**5.1**
5.8	0.82	na	0.12	**5.6**	8.1	1.28	10.98	3.90	68.6	**0.8**	12.9	34.8	**8.6**
6.8	0.15	na	0.00	**9.4**	0.9	2.06	6.96	4.25	41.1	**0.9**	22.4	26.9	**8.4**
9.5	0.86	1.2	0.00	**9.5**	1.1	2.14	10.27	2.97	66.5	**4.1**	82.2	22.9	**9.0**
6.9	0.28	na	0.01	**5.0**	2.7	1.00	12.76	3.95	68.9	**1.1**	12.9	22.4	**4.5**
8.7	0.00	na	0.00	**5.2**	0.3	1.26	13.74	4.63	70.6	**1.8**	23.9	22.1	**5.0**
3.9	0.00	na	0.00	**1.3**	-0.2	-0.33	-1.30	5.44	105.8	**6.0**	56.3	6.7	**8.3**
7.1	0.39	na	0.01	**2.4**	0.6	0.32	4.02	3.11	87.4	**2.0**	25.1	19.9	**4.3**
9.9	0.13	0.1	-0.02	**8.2**	2675.0	1.65	22.66	2.37	10.1	**7.5**	81.8	0.0	**6.6**
10.0	na	0.0	na	**8.1**	198.0	1.88	24.60	2.65	7.2	**8.3**	83.6	0.0	**8.3**
6.1	1.53	na	0.00	**8.0**	2.7	1.92	20.59	4.21	62.2	**6.4**	45.6	2.6	**7.0**
7.8	1.07	2.6	-0.50	**9.5**	6.9	2.49	25.33	3.93	57.1	**6.6**	46.5	1.5	**8.3**
8.8	0.03	na	0.06	**4.8**	1.4	1.13	9.93	3.17	62.8	**3.6**	43.1	17.6	**7.1**
5.8	0.49	na	0.01	**10.0**	7.4	3.49	32.47	6.69	50.0	**4.2**	45.7	15.6	**8.2**
7.5	1.12	4.9	0.02	**8.6**	13.8	2.01	15.34	3.67	45.7	**1.8**	23.3	15.8	**9.9**
6.7	0.66	na	0.03	**8.0**	4.3	2.11	22.54	3.67	71.9	**1.0**	16.3	26.8	**6.6**
7.9	0.00	na	0.00	**2.0**	0.1	0.17	1.80	3.60	93.4	**1.6**	35.1	42.8	**4.3**
8.8	0.55	na	0.24	**7.6**	2.3	1.46	10.89	4.37	61.2	**1.3**	30.1	35.8	**9.1**
7.2	1.83	6.3	0.00	**7.0**	14.6	1.72	10.90	3.71	69.8	**4.7**	23.4	7.7	**9.9**
7.0	1.78	na	-0.02	**7.5**	1.6	1.76	11.91	3.85	50.4	**5.8**	56.6	10.0	**8.9**
8.5	1.42	na	-0.29	**7.2**	3.8	1.67	13.99	3.98	58.3	**6.1**	41.8	3.4	**9.0**
3.6	1.86	12.1	0.07	**4.3**	10.8	0.83	8.67	3.67	68.3	**4.6**	13.6	5.1	**8.0**
4.7	2.42	na	-0.01	**6.6**	2.3	1.33	11.56	3.37	53.6	**1.7**	23.8	14.8	**8.1**
6.7	0.28	1.4	0.09	**6.6**	10.0	1.49	13.35	4.12	75.0	**2.3**	21.9	16.0	**7.8**
7.1	0.48	na	0.01	**7.0**	1.3	1.67	16.27	3.91	59.2	**3.4**	11.9	11.9	**6.9**
8.8	0.33	na	-0.02	**3.0**	0.7	0.43	2.29	3.62	82.0	**1.7**	34.5	34.0	**7.0**
9.5	0.00	na	0.01	**2.8**	0.2	0.39	3.07	3.20	86.1	**2.0**	17.6	19.5	**5.8**
5.6	0.40	na	-0.02	**3.1**	0.1	0.45	4.06	3.59	87.8	**2.0**	27.3	19.5	**3.9**
8.3	0.00	na	0.00	**7.5**	0.5	1.66	16.25	3.77	55.7	**1.2**	8.8	26.4	**6.3**
8.8	0.05	na	0.00	**4.7**	0.3	0.85	5.17	5.48	86.4	**3.0**	20.2	14.5	**6.6**
8.9	na	0.0	na	**9.5**	2.0	2.42	2.44	2.98	74.4	**4.0**	na	0.0	**7.0**
5.7	0.84	4.7	0.16	**5.6**	1.4	0.98	9.55	4.98	81.2	**0.6**	9.5	22.1	**6.8**
5.1	1.45	na	0.11	**5.1**	1.2	1.27	14.40	3.47	65.1	**5.4**	35.7	5.6	**6.0**
7.2	1.05	na	-0.07	**7.2**	2.2	1.37	12.17	4.25	61.1	**4.8**	33.2	5.6	**7.0**
4.7	1.06	na	-0.03	**6.4**	5.2	1.54	18.31	3.92	59.7	**3.1**	13.0	8.4	**6.4**
6.2	0.70	4.5	0.02	**2.7**	0.3	0.41	4.03	4.20	87.3	**4.7**	23.1	5.1	**4.6**
4.7	0.95	5.6	0.05	**9.0**	24.7	1.53	12.12	4.64	53.2	**2.5**	8.0	11.9	**10.0**
4.9	1.29	5.4	0.18	**5.2**	5.3	1.06	8.95	3.73	73.6	**2.9**	29.5	13.3	**7.5**
4.3	1.34	3.9	0.19	**5.0**	243.3	1.08	5.42	3.44	45.8	**3.0**	21.1	8.0	**10.0**
6.5	na	0.0	na	**9.5**	19.9	10.73	13.58	2.57	75.0	**5.0**	226.0	100.0	**6.3**
5.0	1.36	7.1	0.13	**3.1**	2.6	0.50	4.11	2.90	85.2	**1.2**	14.5	20.3	**7.9**
5.6	0.81	na	0.01	**8.7**	9.8	2.22	17.86	4.61	58.6	**1.8**	21.1	22.1	**8.7**
6.4	0.72	2.9	0.02	**2.9**	0.6	0.39	3.54	2.95	87.7	**1.4**	8.5	24.6	**5.8**
7.2	2.98	na	-0.02	**3.4**	0.4	0.54	2.35	3.78	83.4	**1.9**	23.3	20.5	**7.1**
5.8	1.19	7.3	0.41	**5.0**	324.9	0.98	8.47	3.15	65.4	**1.8**	23.8	20.0	**9.6**
6.5	0.96	4.2	1.02	**5.7**	13044.0	1.21	11.67	3.16	50.9	**3.7**	44.1	9.7	**8.2**
10.0	na	0.0	na	**10.0**	1.3	6.64	7.19	2.84	78.4	**4.0**	na	0.0	**7.0**
5.9	0.85	na	0.03	**6.7**	14.5	1.30	9.75	3.91	67.3	**2.6**	10.3	15.5	**10.0**
9.5	0.38	na	0.00	**7.2**	9.2	1.76	8.41	2.91	37.6	**3.3**	51.7	25.0	**10.0**
4.9	1.02	5.4	0.04	**5.9**	7.7	1.28	14.66	3.76	57.3	**0.8**	17.9	22.8	**7.2**

Name	City	State	Rating	2018 Rating	2017 Rating	Total Assets ($Mil)	One Year Asset Growth	Asset Mix (As a % of Total Assets) Commercial Loans	Consumer Loans	Mortgage Loans	Securities	Capitalization Index	Leverage Ratio	Risk-Based Capital Ratio
Citizens and Farmers Bank	Toano	VA	A-	A-	B+	1605.7	7.42	3.7	20.1	20.2	11.9	9.7	11.1	14.7
Citizens B&T Co. of Grainger County	Rutledge	TN	B+	B+	B+	205.7	-0.31	3.1	1.8	11.0	61.2	10.0	17.4	36.5
▲ Citizens Bank	Enterprise	AL	B-	C+	B-	147.3	2.60	10.0	1.2	19.7	11.3	8.9	10.3	15.0
Citizens Bank	Greensboro	AL	A-	A-	A-	96.4	1.01	5.6	4.8	6.6	43.9	10.0	14.8	28.1
Citizens Bank	Batesville	AR	B-	B-	B-	917.3	8.02	8.1	2.7	18.8	11.9	5.6	8.7	11.5
▲ Citizens Bank	Nashville	GA	B	B-	B	245.9	-1.00	7.6	4.4	30.7	14.7	10.0	14.4	24.7
Citizens Bank	Sac City	IA	C	C	C	55.1	4.07	11.5	2.5	10.8	28.6	7.9	9.6	15.7
▲ Citizens Bank	Mooresville	IN	B-	C+	B-	488.4	1.30	2.5	40.8	5.4	20.7	9.1	10.7	14.3
▲ Citizens Bank	Hartford	KY	B-	C+	C-	116.3	22.69	6.6	5.6	30.2	9.0	4.5	7.9	10.8
Citizens Bank	Hickman	KY	B	B+	B+	138.8	8.80	6.0	3.0	14.6	19.6	10.0	12.6	19.1
Citizens Bank	Morehead	KY	B-	B-	B-	142.9	5.88	1.4	5.2	36.8	9.7	6.4	8.5	14.2
▲ Citizens Bank	Mount Vernon	KY	C+	C-	C+	145.3	3.49	3.6	4.7	41.0	7.7	9.4	10.6	15.9
▲ Citizens Bank	Butler	MO	B-	C+	C+	151.6	25.60	9.8	2.4	26.9	1.4	5.3	8.3	11.2
Citizens Bank	New Haven	MO	C+	B-	B	229.9	9.35	6.3	1.6	19.0	8.6	7.4	11.9	12.9
▲ Citizens Bank	Byhalia	MS	B+	B	B	75.5	2.72	3.3	7.7	19.9	25.5	10.0	12.8	26.4
Citizens Bank	Columbia	MS	B-	B-	B-	425.4	1.54	9.0	4.5	23.0	9.7	9.4	10.6	16.2
▲ Citizens Bank	Farmington	NM	A-	B+	A-	680.8	-1.33	9.2	0.8	12.0	55.9	9.2	10.4	22.7
▲ Citizens Bank	Corvallis	OR	A	A-	B	805.3	2.23	6.9	0.5	4.8	35.5	10.0	11.4	18.4
▲ Citizens Bank	Olanta	SC	B	B-	B	573.2	33.52	7.7	4.1	21.9	12.4	8.2	9.8	15.2
Citizens Bank	Carthage	TN	A	A	A+	618.0	5.84	4.3	3.2	11.5	49.9	10.0	18.1	28.2
Citizens Bank	Elizabethton	TN	A	A-	A-	865.5	4.03	11.5	2.3	6.8	24.1	10.0	12.4	16.1
▲ Citizens Bank	Hartsville	TN	B+	B	B	239.9	13.85	5.4	3.1	21.6	11.4	9.4	10.9	14.5
▲ Citizens Bank	Amarillo	TX	B+	B	B+	170.3	5.83	3.7	0.2	2.8	6.0	8.2	10.7	13.5
Citizens Bank	Kilgore	TX	B	B	B	418.5	10.16	19.5	0.9	8.5	10.0	10.0	13.6	19.0
Citizens Bank	Mukwonago	WI	B	B	B	768.8	4.04	8.9	0.2	8.4	19.1	10.0	13.2	17.9
▲ Citizens Bank & Trust	Guntersville	AL	B	B-	B-	541.8	8.12	9.9	2.2	12.2	24.1	8.5	10.0	15.2
Citizens Bank & Trust	Rock Port	MO	B	B	B	99.1	16.35	10.4	2.6	6.5	33.1	10.0	12.2	24.1
Citizens Bank & Trust Co.	Van Buren	AR	A-	A	A-	401.1	1.58	6.7	5.2	15.4	31.9	10.0	13.2	20.5
▲ Citizens Bank & Trust Co.	Eastman	GA	B-	C	C-	155.5	20.34	12.7	2.1	20.6	13.0	9.0	10.4	16.5
Citizens Bank & Trust Co.	Campbellsville	KY	B	B	B	227.0	12.41	14.2	3.1	18.6	37.0	10.0	16.6	28.1
▲ Citizens Bank & Trust Co.	Covington	LA	B-	C	C+	124.2	4.93	6.0	0.6	20.0	7.5	9.6	10.7	16.5
Citizens Bank & Trust Co.	Plaquemine	LA	B-	B-	B	313.7	3.57	5.5	0.9	18.2	8.8	10.0	12.0	16.1
Citizens Bank & Trust Co.	Vivian	LA	B-	B-	B-	142.3	4.51	4.4	2.7	23.0	30.7	10.0	12.6	21.9
▲ Citizens Bank & Trust Co.	Hutchinson	MN	C+	C+	B	215.9	4.27	15.6	1.3	19.4	24.4	7.0	9.0	13.7
Citizens Bank & Trust Co.	Marks	MS	D	D+	C	141.9	3.19	6.8	3.1	13.0	10.7	5.0	8.0	11.0
▲ Citizens Bank & Trust Co.	Big Timber	MT	C+	C+	B-	111.7	0.53	4.7	1.8	7.4	11.8	9.6	10.8	18.0
▼ Citizens Bank & Trust Co.	Saint Paul	NE	D+	C	B-	210.7	2.53	10.7	2.1	6.2	15.7	8.0	11.7	13.4
Citizens Bank & Trust Co.	Atwood	TN	C	C-	D+	24.7	-2.54	1.1	12.9	21.0	45.1	8.7	10.1	26.4
Citizens Bank & Trust Co. of Ardmore	Ardmore	OK	B	B	B	219.3	1.05	6.5	2.6	33.0	21.5	8.3	9.9	16.5
▲ Citizens Bank & Trust Co. of Jackson	Jackson	KY	C	D+	D	139.5	-2.56	8.7	6.9	31.8	7.2	7.0	9.0	12.6
▲ Citizens Bank & Trust, Inc.	Trenton	GA	A-	B+	B+	106.0	7.31	4.2	8.2	35.1	24.6	10.0	12.0	21.7
▲ Citizens Bank and Trust	Lake Wales	FL	B-	C+	C+	665.7	4.31	6.6	7.3	11.1	33.4	5.7	7.7	13.0
Citizens Bank and Trust Co.	Kansas City	MO	B	B-	B-	907.7	11.54	12.0	1.1	15.3	15.9	9.1	11.0	14.3
Citizens Bank and Trust Co.	Blackstone	VA	A-	A-	A-	401.4	4.93	4.1	2.8	24.9	29.5	10.0	13.8	24.5
Citizens Bank Co.	Beverly	OH	A-	A-	A-	228.0	6.10	7.3	2.0	32.0	19.9	10.0	12.9	19.5
Citizens Bank Minnesota	New Ulm	MN	B	B	B	421.2	7.24	6.8	1.0	21.7	16.5	6.5	10.2	12.2
▲ Citizens Bank of Ada	Ada	OK	B	B-	B-	188.6	-4.45	12.9	3.1	21.1	22.8	10.0	11.0	17.5
▲ Citizens Bank of Americus	Americus	GA	B+	B	B	330.8	6.83	11.5	1.8	9.0	19.5	8.1	9.7	17.2
▲ Citizens Bank of Cape Vincent	Cape Vincent	NY	C+	C+	C+	69.9	0.08	0.6	2.3	40.2	39.0	8.3	9.9	25.5
▲ Citizens Bank of Charleston	Charleston	MO	A-	B+	A-	139.4	10.19	7.7	5.0	8.1	7.3	10.0	18.0	27.2
Citizens Bank of Chatsworth	Chatsworth	IL	D	E+	E-	31.2	-1.16	11.4	1.7	3.1	19.7	10.0	12.4	16.5
▲ Citizens Bank of Clovis	Clovis	NM	A-	B+	A-	347.0	-2.26	4.3	0.6	3.3	29.2	10.0	12.8	20.7
Citizens Bank of Cochran	Cochran	GA	B-	B-	B-	105.2	17.83	10.5	4.5	25.0	8.8	9.1	10.4	15.7
▲ Citizens Bank of Cumberland County	Burkesville	KY	B	B-	B	76.0	2.24	4.2	11.8	25.8	9.7	10.0	14.1	21.0
Citizens Bank of Edina	Edina	MO	B	B+	A-	73.1	5.06	8.3	3.1	5.9	5.4	10.0	12.4	16.1
▲ Citizens Bank of Edinburg	Edinburg	IL	C	C-	C-	26.1	4.40	1.8	2.0	11.2	18.3	8.3	9.9	19.0
Citizens Bank of Edmond	Edmond	OK	B-	C+	B	298.9	11.93	5.9	0.6	20.5	7.0	8.9	10.3	14.3
Citizens Bank of Eldon	Eldon	MO	A-	A-	A-	155.1	5.64	7.3	9.5	24.0	6.2	10.0	13.5	19.0
Citizens Bank of Fayette	Fayette	AL	B+	B+	B	190.1	2.50	5.8	3.8	3.4	68.7	10.0	20.9	45.8
▲ Citizens Bank of Florida	Oviedo	FL	C+	C	C+	354.4	16.76	4.3	0.5	9.4	16.9	6.5	8.5	12.7

Asset Quality Index	Adjusted Non-Performing Loans as a % of Total Loans	Adjusted Non-Performing Loans as a % of Capital	Net Charge-Offs Avg Loans	Profitability Index	Net Income ($Mil)	Return on Assets (R.O.A.)	Return on Equity (R.O.E.)	Net Interest Spread	Overhead Efficiency Ratio	Liquidity Index	Liquidity Ratio	Hot Money Ratio	Stability Index
6.9	0.49	2.0	0.80	**7.0**	16.1	1.39	12.10	5.70	68.7	**2.4**	17.1	17.7	**8.8**
6.2	6.36	na	0.00	**5.3**	1.8	1.18	6.81	3.60	64.9	**5.4**	57.5	12.2	**8.1**
6.0	2.48	na	0.56	**5.0**	1.2	1.04	10.82	4.14	69.4	**2.5**	18.9	13.2	**6.1**
8.6	0.39	1.6	-0.05	**6.6**	1.0	1.40	9.74	3.41	46.7	**3.2**	51.7	23.1	**7.8**
4.9	0.82	5.0	0.04	**4.3**	5.2	0.79	7.95	3.83	72.3	**1.4**	13.8	19.4	**7.0**
5.8	2.57	na	0.13	**4.4**	1.8	0.97	6.97	3.76	73.1	**1.3**	17.1	28.7	**7.6**
6.0	0.15	na	0.00	**5.4**	0.5	1.30	14.62	3.52	65.0	**2.3**	27.7	19.4	**4.6**
6.1	0.20	na	0.00	**5.1**	3.8	1.06	9.99	3.48	67.3	**3.9**	8.0	8.4	**6.6**
8.2	0.03	na	0.01	**6.0**	1.1	1.26	15.19	3.96	64.4	**0.8**	8.8	33.6	**5.7**
6.7	0.33	na	0.39	**4.4**	1.1	1.09	8.81	3.79	68.3	**1.3**	9.7	25.2	**6.0**
4.5	1.32	na	0.03	**4.4**	1.0	0.95	9.78	4.63	79.7	**3.9**	15.6	9.5	**5.5**
3.8	1.28	na	0.25	**4.2**	1.0	0.89	8.21	4.31	77.1	**1.3**	11.8	26.1	**6.4**
4.5	1.15	na	0.15	**8.8**	2.1	2.14	25.95	6.10	62.8	**2.6**	10.8	15.3	**5.3**
3.1	1.64	10.3	-0.02	**4.9**	1.7	0.99	8.64	3.92	62.9	**1.6**	6.2	11.7	**7.9**
7.5	0.63	na	0.07	**5.1**	0.6	1.12	8.91	4.68	72.8	**5.1**	48.0	11.0	**6.4**
4.4	1.55	na	0.16	**6.7**	5.3	1.66	18.01	4.17	65.1	**1.5**	13.3	23.3	**7.2**
7.7	0.65	na	0.07	**7.4**	9.2	1.77	17.17	3.52	53.1	**5.5**	49.8	10.0	**8.2**
8.9	0.03	na	-0.03	**7.0**	8.1	1.38	12.50	4.23	55.1	**6.5**	45.3	1.6	**7.2**
5.2	1.00	na	0.06	**5.5**	4.6	1.09	10.56	4.04	69.0	**3.9**	26.5	11.2	**6.6**
9.0	0.00	na	0.05	**9.8**	10.0	2.21	12.19	3.82	30.9	**3.0**	58.9	33.8	**10.0**
5.8	0.88	na	0.13	**9.5**	13.2	2.26	17.71	4.22	59.1	**2.3**	10.6	16.9	**9.8**
7.1	0.37	na	0.03	**7.8**	2.3	1.36	12.43	4.51	58.1	**0.8**	16.4	37.4	**7.3**
7.3	0.00	na	0.00	**9.7**	3.0	2.44	22.74	4.55	47.7	**1.9**	22.3	20.3	**8.0**
5.7	2.17	na	0.15	**4.5**	2.9	0.94	7.08	4.25	68.3	**4.4**	34.7	11.2	**6.4**
4.9	1.55	6.6	0.08	**6.0**	6.8	1.20	9.44	3.60	60.5	**3.7**	10.8	10.0	**7.6**
7.6	0.53	na	0.05	**4.7**	4.4	1.12	11.49	3.81	68.8	**2.0**	18.3	19.4	**5.9**
8.7	0.55	na	0.04	**4.4**	0.7	1.01	8.36	3.41	72.2	**2.2**	34.7	26.1	**6.8**
5.7	1.87	7.3	0.13	**9.3**	5.2	1.71	13.15	3.93	50.3	**1.7**	10.0	20.7	**9.3**
8.8	0.10	na	-0.02	**4.3**	1.2	1.13	10.74	4.77	74.6	**3.1**	22.5	14.0	**4.5**
7.7	1.60	na	-0.01	**4.9**	1.8	1.11	6.64	3.40	65.7	**4.5**	37.0	11.7	**7.2**
5.2	0.49	na	0.01	**5.4**	1.1	1.15	10.93	4.36	73.2	**1.8**	20.2	21.0	**6.2**
4.1	2.17	na	0.04	**5.2**	2.5	1.06	9.75	4.03	63.6	**1.7**	12.0	20.7	**7.2**
5.2	2.65	na	0.10	**3.7**	1.0	0.91	7.10	4.02	83.5	**4.1**	40.3	14.5	**6.6**
6.4	2.67	na	0.03	**6.9**	2.6	1.61	18.77	4.03	55.9	**4.4**	18.3	6.8	**6.9**
1.8	2.33	na	5.11	**1.0**	-3.3	-3.18	-35.67	3.99	75.0	**1.3**	18.7	27.9	**4.3**
4.0	3.69	na	-0.16	**6.9**	1.2	1.38	11.63	4.08	53.6	**3.1**	29.5	16.2	**7.3**
1.1	0.00	na	-0.01	**7.4**	2.3	1.53	13.28	4.22	55.6	**1.1**	11.4	20.6	**7.7**
6.2	0.19	3.0	0.15	**3.5**	0.1	0.68	7.07	3.17	76.2	**1.1**	25.3	32.9	**4.4**
8.9	0.01	na	-0.01	**4.9**	2.0	1.17	12.34	3.82	72.0	**3.2**	19.7	13.5	**6.5**
3.1	1.84	na	0.16	**3.9**	1.1	0.99	10.01	4.43	77.0	**0.8**	9.5	31.0	**4.7**
7.5	1.15	na	0.14	**6.6**	0.9	1.20	10.46	4.88	68.8	**3.5**	28.4	13.7	**7.1**
6.6	0.53	na	0.04	**4.9**	6.0	1.22	14.93	3.82	72.7	**5.6**	31.5	2.5	**6.1**
5.5	1.81	6.2	0.08	**4.3**	5.5	0.86	7.54	3.61	75.2	**2.4**	17.3	15.8	**6.8**
8.6	1.02	2.9	-0.01	**7.1**	4.3	1.46	11.06	4.00	60.1	**3.8**	34.3	14.0	**8.1**
8.8	0.09	na	0.04	**6.1**	2.0	1.21	9.11	4.37	60.3	**3.7**	8.5	9.6	**8.5**
7.8	0.13	0.4	0.00	**4.2**	2.5	0.79	7.65	3.13	69.4	**2.8**	18.0	15.1	**6.4**
7.5	0.76	na	-0.03	**4.8**	1.6	1.06	10.21	4.61	76.8	**4.2**	18.0	8.0	**5.1**
7.5	0.94	na	0.03	**7.4**	3.5	1.43	15.23	3.78	53.6	**4.3**	29.5	9.8	**7.0**
7.0	0.66	na	0.07	**3.3**	0.3	0.59	6.42	3.48	75.1	**4.9**	25.6	4.3	**5.1**
7.4	0.95	na	0.01	**9.6**	1.9	1.82	10.33	4.12	45.8	**3.1**	32.0	17.0	**8.7**
3.0	4.58	na	0.43	**0.0**	-0.2	-1.02	-7.34	4.43	112.0	**4.5**	17.6	5.4	**2.4**
7.6	0.01	na	-0.09	**8.0**	5.0	1.95	16.08	3.78	47.6	**1.9**	30.4	24.1	**8.1**
7.6	0.12	na	0.01	**3.3**	0.4	0.53	4.95	4.39	83.5	**1.0**	21.8	33.5	**5.2**
5.0	2.44	na	0.24	**8.7**	1.1	2.01	15.02	5.40	60.3	**2.2**	27.4	19.6	**8.8**
6.9	0.09	na	0.25	**10.0**	1.1	2.15	17.66	4.69	37.0	**2.5**	9.3	16.1	**8.3**
6.4	0.00	na	0.01	**5.5**	0.2	1.10	11.33	3.89	58.2	**5.9**	37.9	2.8	**4.3**
5.0	0.73	na	0.02	**4.6**	2.5	1.14	13.26	4.26	74.0	**2.6**	15.2	15.9	**5.8**
5.3	1.39	7.7	0.34	**6.3**	1.5	1.28	9.45	4.39	59.8	**3.3**	18.4	12.8	**7.7**
8.4	4.43	na	0.93	**4.5**	1.4	0.99	4.76	3.06	57.9	**4.0**	78.4	27.6	**8.4**
5.5	1.80	na	0.00	**4.0**	1.8	0.75	8.67	3.84	73.6	**3.3**	30.3	15.1	**5.0**

Name	City	State	Rating	2018 Rating	2017 Rating	Total Assets ($Mil)	One Year Asset Growth	Asset Mix (As a % of Total Assets) Commercial Loans	Consumer Loans	Mortgage Loans	Securities	Capitalization Index	Leverage Ratio	Risk-Based Capital Ratio
Citizens Bank of Georgia	Cumming	GA	**B**	B	B	329.4	7.75	5.6	1.4	9.1	30.4	**9.8**	10.9	16.7
Citizens Bank of Kansas	Kingman	KS	**B-**	B-	B-	378.6	62.35	5.3	1.4	17.5	24.4	**8.8**	10.2	14.4
Citizens Bank of Kentucky	Paintsville	KY	**B**	B	B	645.9	10.20	8.2	3.0	17.7	20.8	**10.0**	11.2	16.9
▼ Citizens Bank of Lafayette	Lafayette	TN	**B+**	B+	B	929.6	1.60	4.9	5.4	14.5	25.2	**10.0**	11.7	17.8
▲ Citizens Bank of Las Cruces	Las Cruces	NM	**B+**	B+	A-	612.1	10.83	10.3	0.6	7.9	19.6	**8.9**	10.5	14.1
Citizens Bank of Morgantown, Inc.	Morgantown	WV	**B-**	B-	B	38.4	4.48	1.6	1.7	45.9	29.6	**10.0**	18.9	35.2
▲ Citizens Bank of Newburg	Rolla	MO	**B-**	C	C	148.7	-1.87	11.5	1.8	25.1	10.7	**10.0**	11.4	15.1
Citizens Bank of Philadelphia, Mississippi	Philadelphia	MS	**B-**	B-	B-	1049.4	9.00	5.5	1.2	6.6	41.4	**7.1**	9.1	16.4
Citizens Bank of Rogersville	Rogersville	MO	**B-**	B-	B-	92.3	-0.18	13.9	5.2	26.7	8.6	**8.2**	10.3	13.5
▲ Citizens Bank of Swainsboro	Swainsboro	GA	**B**	B	B	214.2	4.43	14.1	6.0	24.8	8.5	**9.7**	10.8	16.8
Citizens Bank of The South	Sandersville	GA	**B+**	B	B	253.2	1.88	9.5	3.9	31.1	10.7	**10.0**	11.8	17.9
▲ Citizens Bank of West Virginia, Inc.	Elkins	WV	**B-**	C+	B	282.6	6.41	5.2	18.8	37.6	5.6	**10.0**	11.1	16.7
▲ Citizens Bank of Weston, Inc.	Weston	WV	**B+**	B-	B	204.6	0.07	19.5	3.6	20.0	21.0	**10.0**	11.8	19.3
Citizens Bank of Winfield	Winfield	AL	**A**	A	A	249.1	5.97	2.7	7.2	5.0	69.7	**10.0**	22.8	45.8
Citizens Bank, N.A.	Providence	RI	**B-**	B-	B-	164652.4	29.76	21.7	16.0	13.6	15.1	**7.2**	9.9	12.7
▲ Citizens Bank, N.A.	Abilene	TX	**B+**	B	A-	106.9	1.07	10.7	6.6	17.3	17.8	**8.0**	9.6	13.3
Citizens Building and Loan, SSB	Greer	SC	**B+**	A-	B+	139.4	7.07	0.0	0.2	55.0	14.8	**10.0**	21.0	41.9
Citizens Business Bank	Ontario	CA	**A-**	A	A	11330.3	-1.23	7.3	0.1	3.7	20.1	**10.0**	12.1	15.7
Citizens Commerce Bank	Versailles	KY	**C-**	C-	D	266.8	12.95	4.5	0.9	27.0	14.1	**8.1**	9.8	14.6
Citizens Community Bank	Hahira	GA	**B+**	B+	A-	136.4	2.10	5.5	4.1	22.5	25.0	**10.0**	12.9	20.7
Citizens Community Bank	Mascoutah	IL	**B+**	B+	B+	399.4	2.37	5.4	1.1	10.7	31.8	**10.0**	11.8	17.8
▲ Citizens Community Bank	Pilot Grove	MO	**B**	B-	B	104.3	1.76	5.0	2.6	16.6	9.9	**10.0**	12.4	16.3
▲ Citizens Community Bank	Winchester	TN	**B**	B-	B	236.0	7.01	12.8	3.3	18.1	15.6	**10.0**	13.2	19.3
Citizens Community Federal N.A.	Altoona	WI	**B-**	B-	C+	1475.3	51.26	7.5	4.2	16.1	12.7	**8.2**	10.2	13.5
Citizens Deposit Bank & Trust	Vanceburg	KY	**B**	B-	B-	475.5	8.75	2.4	2.1	17.9	31.4	**7.3**	9.2	15.8
▲ Citizens Deposit Bank of Arlington, Inc.	Arlington	KY	**A-**	B+	A	233.1	10.41	14.9	5.3	14.6	25.5	**10.0**	15.9	24.2
Citizens Federal S&L Assn.	Covington	KY	**B**	B+	B+	39.5	3.32	0.0	0.0	47.6	19.4	**10.0**	28.0	65.1
Citizens Federal S&L Assn.	Bellefontaine	OH	**C**	C	C	135.3	0.14	0.0	0.1	60.1	15.2	**10.0**	13.2	27.6
Citizens First Bank	The Villages	FL	**A**	A	A-	2345.1	11.14	9.2	0.1	7.2	63.2	**10.0**	11.5	17.8
▲ Citizens First Bank	Clinton	IA	**B-**	C+	B-	204.9	0.73	26.6	2.9	13.3	2.7	**7.2**	10.1	12.7
▲ Citizens First Bank	Viroqua	WI	**B-**	C+	C	221.0	7.91	5.4	2.6	9.2	14.5	**9.7**	10.8	15.1
▲ Citizens First National Bank	Storm Lake	IA	**A**	A-	A	201.1	0.86	11.0	4.2	4.4	33.3	**10.0**	11.5	18.1
▲ Citizens First State Bank of Walnut	Walnut	IL	**C**	D+	D	47.3	4.12	6.2	4.7	24.7	23.5	**7.4**	9.3	16.9
Citizens Guaranty Bank	Irvine	KY	**D+**	C-	C-	200.0	23.25	10.9	7.8	35.2	10.9	**3.2**	6.5	10.1
Citizens Independent Bank	Saint Louis Park	MN	**B-**	C+	C+	295.7	9.17	10.7	7.0	11.6	24.4	**10.0**	11.8	18.7
Citizens National Bank	Greenleaf	KS	**B-**	B-	B-	169.8	0.22	3.4	2.6	10.7	55.1	**9.8**	10.9	23.9
Citizens National Bank	Sevierville	TN	**A**	A	B+	1101.2	4.74	5.9	0.4	13.7	12.0	**10.0**	11.6	15.2
Citizens National Bank	Cameron	TX	**B**	B	B-	414.3	0.63	4.6	0.6	6.5	29.7	**10.0**	11.5	16.5
Citizens National Bank	Crockett	TX	**B**	B-	C	88.9	0.70	8.8	6.7	7.2	14.2	**10.0**	11.9	25.9
▲ Citizens National Bank at Brownwood	Brownwood	TX	**A-**	B+	A-	215.5	6.70	9.1	6.5	12.7	36.8	**10.0**	12.8	23.9
Citizens National Bank of Albion	Albion	IL	**B**	B+	A-	318.8	-1.50	8.8	3.9	14.9	24.2	**10.0**	17.1	25.2
▲ Citizens National Bank of Bluffton	Bluffton	OH	**C+**	C	B	868.7	5.06	8.5	0.4	8.1	14.8	**7.7**	9.9	13.1
Citizens National Bank of Cheboygan	Cheboygan	MI	**C+**	C	C+	329.0	8.25	3.5	2.1	18.2	27.9	**6.2**	8.2	16.2
▲ Citizens National Bank of Crosbyton	Crosbyton	TX	**B+**	B	B	49.0	-1.80	2.1	2.5	2.6	5.1	**10.0**	18.0	46.6
Citizens National Bank of Greater St. Louis	Maplewood	MO	**C+**	C+	B-	505.3	4.85	16.1	0.7	13.8	16.7	**8.5**	10.5	13.8
▲ Citizens National Bank of Hammond	Hammond	NY	**D+**	D	D	25.2	7.21	4.6	10.5	43.1	22.3	**7.7**	9.4	20.7
▲ Citizens National Bank of Hillsboro	Hillsboro	TX	**B+**	B	B	165.0	-3.21	7.7	3.5	8.0	61.2	**10.0**	14.7	34.4
Citizens National Bank of Lebanon	Lebanon	KY	**B**	B	B	124.0	0.32	2.3	3.6	12.7	51.0	**10.0**	11.9	28.1
Citizens National Bank of McConnelsville	McConnelsville	OH	**B**	B	B-	95.6	2.60	1.8	6.2	45.8	19.7	**10.0**	12.1	23.6
Citizens National Bank of Meridian	Meridian	MS	**A-**	B+	B+	1432.5	4.99	9.8	1.8	16.3	21.8	**8.5**	10.8	13.8
▲ Citizens National Bank of Park Rapids	Park Rapids	MN	**B+**	B-	B	264.7	-0.47	7.2	9.2	25.8	10.4	**10.0**	11.2	16.0
▲ Citizens National Bank of Quitman	Quitman	GA	**B+**	B	B	99.0	-0.20	2.2	14.3	14.8	12.3	**10.0**	13.8	19.9
Citizens National Bank of Somerset	Somerset	KY	**B**	B+	B+	431.3	12.89	3.0	4.5	23.3	36.7	**9.4**	10.6	17.9
▲ Citizens National Bank of Texas	Waxahachie	TX	**B-**	C+	B	1162.0	5.78	7.3	0.7	11.1	0.9	**8.1**	10.8	13.4
Citizens National Bank of Woodsfield	Woodsfield	OH	**C+**	C	C	141.2	13.40	3.5	1.3	26.2	43.2	**4.8**	6.8	19.9
Citizens National Bank, N.A.	Bossier City	LA	**B+**	B	B-	1003.0	8.13	8.3	0.7	13.6	17.2	**9.6**	10.8	15.4
▲ Citizens Progressive Bank	Winnsboro	LA	**C**	D+	D	163.1	2.01	9.0	3.9	20.9	6.7	**8.1**	9.8	13.4
Citizens S&L Assn., FSB	Leavenworth	KS	**C**	C	C	174.7	-1.48	0.4	0.4	47.5	39.9	**10.0**	21.6	61.8
Citizens Savings Bank	Anamosa	IA	**B+**	B+	B+	124.7	1.08	5.4	1.1	8.6	32.8	**9.5**	10.7	16.0
▲ Citizens Savings Bank	Hawkeye	IA	**A-**	B+	B+	27.8	-6.46	1.4	1.7	9.9	54.8	**10.0**	15.2	25.9

Asset Quality Index	Adjusted Non-Performing Loans as a % of Total Loans	Adjusted Non-Performing Loans as a % of Capital	Net Charge-Offs Avg Loans	Profitability Index	Net Income ($Mil)	Return on Assets (R.O.A.)	Return on Equity (R.O.E.)	Net Interest Spread	Overhead Efficiency Ratio	Liquidity Index	Liquidity Ratio	Hot Money Ratio	Stability Index
8.1	0.63	na	0.02	**7.1**	3.2	1.34	12.91	3.90	54.4	**3.7**	38.4	16.1	**7.2**
5.9	0.82	na	0.16	**4.0**	2.5	0.86	6.68	4.32	79.4	**4.5**	18.7	5.5	**7.6**
5.5	1.50	na	0.02	**4.4**	4.2	0.91	6.55	3.79	69.8	**1.6**	19.7	23.7	**8.0**
4.5	2.49	11.9	0.00	**6.5**	8.7	1.26	10.54	3.98	61.5	**1.4**	24.4	28.1	**8.3**
7.6	0.31	na	0.00	**9.6**	10.0	2.31	22.02	4.49	55.4	**4.5**	17.7	5.4	**8.8**
6.0	2.46	na	0.02	**4.0**	0.2	0.60	3.28	4.82	82.5	**3.3**	36.4	17.1	**7.4**
6.4	0.91	na	0.04	**3.9**	1.0	0.90	7.88	3.63	71.0	**1.3**	4.4	23.9	**5.5**
5.2	2.61	na	0.01	**3.3**	4.2	0.54	6.12	2.60	78.7	**2.6**	14.7	16.2	**6.8**
5.6	0.52	na	0.01	**5.0**	0.8	1.17	10.74	4.09	69.1	**1.7**	12.5	20.2	**7.4**
6.8	0.39	na	0.16	**6.8**	2.0	1.30	12.32	4.65	64.2	**2.1**	17.4	18.6	**6.7**
7.7	0.67	na	0.05	**5.4**	1.9	1.04	8.92	4.78	68.7	**1.9**	14.7	19.7	**6.4**
3.9	1.65	na	0.26	**5.8**	2.4	1.14	11.37	4.28	62.5	**1.9**	10.8	18.7	**6.6**
5.2	3.42	na	0.00	**9.3**	2.7	1.81	16.26	4.22	46.3	**5.0**	33.2	6.7	**7.4**
8.8	2.63	na	0.94	**8.5**	3.2	1.79	7.66	3.89	41.7	**2.3**	48.2	44.1	**8.5**
4.4	1.16	4.6	0.35	**5.3**	1363.1	1.12	8.83	3.18	57.4	**3.2**	18.2	8.8	**9.7**
7.1	0.00	na	0.00	**8.2**	1.6	2.03	15.27	4.42	55.2	**1.5**	9.7	23.4	**9.7**
9.8	0.07	na	-0.01	**4.0**	0.7	0.71	3.40	3.23	69.8	**0.8**	24.1	57.1	**8.0**
5.8	0.13	0.3	0.00	**10.0**	160.4	1.90	11.12	4.41	38.5	**4.7**	13.4	3.6	**10.0**
6.8	0.49	4.0	-0.01	**4.0**	1.4	0.72	6.92	3.40	77.2	**1.4**	15.4	25.9	**5.1**
6.6	1.99	na	0.12	**5.8**	1.4	1.32	10.78	4.37	70.9	**3.1**	33.3	17.1	**8.5**
6.6	3.12	na	0.28	**5.3**	3.1	1.06	9.25	2.95	50.8	**1.5**	10.8	23.4	**6.8**
6.5	1.33	na	-0.01	**4.5**	0.6	0.80	6.54	3.71	71.8	**2.3**	12.4	17.1	**7.2**
5.8	1.16	na	0.05	**9.9**	3.0	1.72	13.43	4.97	44.7	**3.0**	18.1	14.2	**8.4**
4.1	2.27	na	0.07	**4.3**	8.4	0.82	6.81	3.52	69.0	**2.1**	17.3	13.9	**8.2**
6.9	0.38	2.1	0.13	**6.6**	4.5	1.30	13.31	3.63	60.4	**1.7**	18.4	22.0	**6.3**
7.9	0.18	na	0.17	**7.2**	2.7	1.64	10.18	3.84	55.7	**0.6**	17.4	47.7	**9.4**
9.9	0.00	na	0.00	**4.3**	0.3	1.13	3.96	3.02	69.4	**3.4**	55.1	21.0	**8.0**
8.3	1.15	4.2	0.00	**2.4**	0.3	0.29	2.42	2.82	89.3	**1.3**	26.7	32.1	**6.3**
9.6	0.47	0.7	-0.01	**8.4**	32.6	1.87	16.06	3.08	42.3	**6.9**	61.1	5.8	**9.1**
5.2	0.73	na	0.09	**5.3**	2.0	1.32	13.26	3.72	66.6	**1.0**	9.2	29.5	**6.2**
4.4	1.30	na	0.03	**5.6**	2.1	1.30	11.14	4.02	65.9	**1.2**	22.6	20.5	**7.9**
8.3	0.00	na	0.00	**9.2**	3.1	1.96	17.21	3.95	49.9	**4.6**	39.1	11.8	**8.8**
8.0	0.24	na	-0.93	**3.6**	0.3	0.79	8.98	3.71	80.0	**5.8**	43.1	5.5	**3.5**
2.5	1.68	na	0.07	**3.0**	0.7	0.48	7.01	4.01	87.3	**0.9**	10.5	31.4	**1.7**
6.1	1.20	4.5	0.01	**3.6**	1.3	0.62	5.16	3.68	80.5	**5.9**	37.8	2.7	**6.6**
9.1	0.01	na	-0.01	**3.9**	0.9	0.72	6.80	3.21	76.7	**4.7**	41.1	11.7	**6.2**
7.6	0.05	1.1	-0.01	**8.0**	15.2	1.89	16.65	3.90	54.1	**3.2**	17.3	13.5	**10.0**
8.8	0.00	0.0	0.01	**4.7**	3.2	1.06	9.35	3.40	61.9	**2.4**	25.6	18.2	**7.4**
8.6	0.68	na	0.02	**4.7**	0.8	1.20	10.46	4.16	69.1	**5.3**	48.0	9.5	**6.5**
8.0	0.64	na	0.19	**8.0**	5.3	3.33	26.00	4.15	41.8	**5.2**	43.5	9.6	**6.9**
5.2	2.94	na	0.10	**5.5**	2.6	1.10	6.49	3.32	56.1	**2.0**	26.9	20.8	**8.3**
6.4	0.74	na	0.00	**8.5**	13.0	2.04	20.59	3.89	53.0	**1.8**	6.6	10.4	**9.0**
6.4	2.07	na	-0.04	**3.3**	1.3	0.59	7.02	3.74	83.7	**6.1**	50.7	6.0	**3.8**
9.1	0.00	na	0.17	**7.1**	0.7	1.83	10.85	2.94	42.2	**3.1**	71.3	33.9	**7.9**
4.8	0.53	na	1.72	**3.3**	1.7	0.43	4.09	3.50	61.7	**2.3**	12.1	17.2	**7.7**
5.0	0.53	na	0.31	**4.3**	0.2	0.87	9.65	4.34	70.5	**5.2**	20.4	1.4	**3.7**
9.3	0.23	0.3	0.08	**5.1**	1.7	1.32	9.31	2.79	62.4	**6.7**	66.0	6.1	**7.8**
9.3	0.32	na	0.01	**4.3**	1.0	1.02	9.51	3.25	71.4	**5.0**	37.9	9.1	**7.0**
5.8	0.64	10.6	0.08	**5.0**	0.7	1.04	8.70	3.91	68.0	**3.6**	7.6	10.3	**6.9**
6.7	0.80	4.1	0.11	**7.9**	19.9	1.85	16.82	3.54	58.7	**2.1**	17.9	19.5	**10.0**
6.6	0.52	na	0.06	**6.8**	3.3	1.66	14.99	4.10	58.0	**1.9**	3.9	18.4	**7.7**
6.3	1.58	na	0.07	**5.8**	0.9	1.17	8.79	4.02	62.9	**1.2**	15.0	28.9	**7.4**
6.7	0.69	na	0.20	**6.0**	4.4	1.41	14.19	3.79	67.6	**2.4**	21.9	17.5	**6.7**
6.7	0.60	na	-0.06	**9.7**	21.2	2.55	23.55	5.09	53.9	**4.9**	14.1	2.7	**10.0**
9.9	0.00	na	0.00	**3.7**	0.8	0.79	11.93	2.95	67.2	**7.3**	58.7	1.2	**3.1**
6.8	0.71	na	0.09	**5.8**	9.1	1.22	11.12	4.04	62.4	**3.3**	16.6	13.2	**9.3**
2.7	0.22	na	0.37	**4.6**	1.2	0.99	8.09	4.46	74.1	**0.7**	13.4	43.5	**6.2**
10.0	0.36	na	0.01	**2.0**	0.3	0.25	1.17	2.74	89.8	**3.6**	46.2	18.8	**7.0**
7.1	0.77	na	0.01	**7.0**	1.4	1.60	14.35	3.85	55.6	**5.2**	32.5	5.1	**7.7**
9.5	0.00	0.3	-0.03	**4.4**	0.2	1.00	6.81	2.83	62.4	**5.6**	72.9	12.3	**7.0**

Name	City	State	Rating	2018 Rating	2017 Rating	Total Assets ($Mil)	One Year Asset Growth	Asset Mix (As a % of Total Assets): Comm-ercial Loans	Cons-umer Loans	Mort-gage Loans	Secur-ities	Capital-ization Index	Lever-age Ratio	Risk-Based Capital Ratio
Citizens Savings Bank	Marshalltown	IA	**C+**	C+	C+	59.1	-0.15	7.8	1.8	20.1	0.4	**6.8**	8.9	12.3
▲ Citizens Savings Bank	Spillville	IA	**A-**	B+	A	109.9	0.95	3.1	0.4	3.8	31.2	**10.0**	16.7	20.3
▲ Citizens Savings Bank	Bogalusa	LA	**B-**	C+	C+	234.0	2.98	1.9	5.1	41.8	9.5	**10.0**	14.4	22.5
Citizens Savings Bank	Clarks Summit	PA	**B-**	B-	B-	320.5	-2.84	0.0	0.1	75.8	12.4	**10.0**	15.5	32.6
Citizens Savings Bank and Trust Co.	Nashville	TN	**E+**	E+	D-	99.7	-4.86	4.6	2.2	9.1	9.2	**2.3**	6.6	9.3
▲ Citizens State Bank	Vernon	AL	**B**	B-	B-	71.5	2.76	7.8	5.1	10.6	52.4	**10.0**	15.0	38.4
Citizens State Bank	Monticello	IA	**A-**	A-	B+	414.8	4.66	5.9	0.9	3.1	37.3	**10.0**	11.3	16.5
▲ Citizens State Bank	Sheldon	IA	**A-**	B+	A-	125.9	6.24	8.2	6.6	15.1	11.7	**10.0**	13.3	18.2
Citizens State Bank	Wyoming	IA	**B**	B+	A	92.6	-2.23	10.2	2.6	4.3	32.3	**10.0**	23.4	37.1
Citizens State Bank	Lena	IL	**B-**	B	B+	263.6	4.87	8.7	5.8	11.9	17.0	**10.0**	11.7	16.3
▲ Citizens State Bank	Gridley	KS	**B**	B-	B-	202.0	6.35	9.2	2.7	14.7	15.2	**8.0**	9.7	16.4
Citizens State Bank	Hugoton	KS	**B-**	B-	B+	117.3	1.95	7.1	0.9	5.2	17.6	**10.0**	14.3	18.6
▲ Citizens State Bank	Marysville	KS	**A-**	B+	A-	349.3	-0.47	8.6	1.1	8.4	13.4	**7.5**	10.1	12.9
Citizens State Bank	Moundridge	KS	**B**	B	B	430.1	0.85	4.8	1.1	6.7	37.2	**7.9**	10.0	13.3
Citizens State Bank	Carleton	NE	**D+**	D	D+	23.5	5.12	8.7	4.9	2.0	0.0	**7.8**	9.5	14.3
▼ Citizens State Bank	Wisner	NE	**C**	B-	B-	306.0	-5.89	6.6	1.2	5.1	6.8	**8.5**	11.3	13.8
Citizens State Bank	Okemah	OK	**C+**	B-	B+	56.4	-34.06	4.7	3.4	13.5	35.3	**10.0**	20.9	41.8
Citizens State Bank	Anton	TX	**D+**	D	D	32.1	-2.44	9.6	1.7	0.0	3.4	**8.7**	10.1	15.5
Citizens State Bank	Buffalo	TX	**B+**	B+	A-	978.9	9.09	5.1	1.5	4.0	76.1	**10.0**	11.5	28.1
▲ Citizens State Bank	Corrigan	TX	**A-**	B+	A-	132.0	5.22	12.4	12.5	14.5	30.5	**10.0**	12.2	20.9
▲ Citizens State Bank	Ganado	TX	**D**	D-	D-	55.6	4.62	0.2	2.0	6.0	66.8	**6.1**	8.2	25.4
Citizens State Bank	Miles	TX	**B+**	A-	A-	155.2	10.57	11.5	2.8	30.1	0.0	**8.0**	9.7	14.8
Citizens State Bank	Roma	TX	**B-**	B-	B-	87.1	5.53	4.5	13.4	18.7	34.2	**8.0**	9.7	18.8
Citizens State Bank	Sealy	TX	**A-**	A-	A-	307.3	9.70	3.3	2.6	23.9	43.4	**9.9**	10.9	22.9
▲ Citizens State Bank	Somerville	TX	**B+**	B	B+	642.2	12.10	9.0	3.4	21.0	19.2	**10.0**	11.0	17.2
Citizens State Bank	Waco	TX	**C+**	C+	C+	143.0	-0.69	3.9	3.2	39.1	20.7	**8.1**	9.7	18.4
Citizens State Bank	Cadott	WI	**B-**	B-	B-	114.0	-2.78	5.8	3.4	16.8	14.8	**10.0**	12.0	17.9
Citizens State Bank	Hudson	WI	**B-**	B-	B-	216.3	6.07	7.1	1.0	27.4	12.2	**5.9**	8.3	11.7
Citizens State Bank and Trust Co.	Council Grove	KS	**D**	D+	D	47.9	-2.16	17.4	2.2	9.5	2.0	**5.3**	9.0	11.2
▲ Citizens State Bank and Trust Co.	Ellsworth	KS	**B**	B-	B	191.5	4.59	2.2	2.5	16.6	37.3	**7.0**	9.0	16.6
Citizens State Bank and Trust Co.	Hiawatha	KS	**A-**	A-	B	82.3	-5.85	4.1	2.9	15.1	18.9	**10.0**	18.5	25.8
Citizens State Bank at Mohall	Mohall	ND	**B-**	C	C+	60.3	-2.41	8.5	3.2	13.8	22.3	**10.0**	11.9	16.7
Citizens State Bank Midwest	Cavalier	ND	**B+**	B+	B+	129.4	5.27	14.2	1.6	4.6	11.5	**10.0**	13.2	16.1
Citizens State Bank Norwood Young Ameri	Norwood Young Ame	MN	**C**	C	B-	86.0	1.98	14.6	1.7	7.4	0.0	**10.0**	11.0	16.6
Citizens State Bank of Arlington	Arlington	SD	**B**	B-	B	107.4	-0.12	3.6	1.2	3.7	20.0	**10.0**	13.4	20.3
▲ Citizens State Bank of Cheney, Kansas	Cheney	KS	**B**	C+	B-	63.2	12.56	8.7	9.5	11.4	24.6	**9.7**	10.8	16.6
▲ Citizens State Bank of Finley	Finley	ND	**B+**	B-	C	132.7	-1.64	4.8	1.5	0.8	27.1	**10.0**	13.4	18.8
▲ Citizens State Bank of Glenville	Glenville	MN	**B**	C+	C+	41.4	2.75	4.6	5.0	5.1	24.4	**10.0**	11.8	31.9
Citizens State Bank of Hayfield	Hayfield	MN	**D+**	D+	D+	103.1	11.37	13.4	2.9	9.5	14.4	**5.2**	7.5	11.1
Citizens State Bank of La Crosse	La Crosse	WI	**B**	B	B	308.3	13.96	13.5	0.7	19.8	1.5	**5.3**	8.9	11.2
Citizens State Bank of Lankin	Lankin	ND	**C+**	C+	C-	48.1	9.15	11.0	4.7	1.6	25.1	**9.0**	10.9	14.1
▼ Citizens State Bank of Loyal	Loyal	WI	**B+**	B+	A-	207.5	2.89	2.3	0.2	8.0	23.0	**10.0**	13.2	17.9
Citizens State Bank of Luling	Luling	TX	**B**	B	B	70.5	7.60	5.7	0.8	8.9	7.1	**10.0**	15.2	19.8
Citizens State Bank of Milford	Milford	IL	**C-**	C-	D+	41.6	-4.15	7.9	1.8	0.7	18.4	**9.3**	10.5	14.6
Citizens State Bank of New Castle, Indiana	New Castle	IN	**B**	B	B	561.9	7.07	5.7	12.1	20.2	15.6	**8.5**	10.0	16.6
Citizens State Bank of Ontonagon	Ontonagon	MI	**C**	C+	C	56.6	-1.70	2.1	6.3	13.9	30.7	**10.0**	12.8	42.3
▲ Citizens State Bank of Ouray	Ouray	CO	**C**	C-	D	117.2	13.54	1.4	0.7	20.7	26.4	**8.1**	9.8	19.1
▲ Citizens State Bank of Roseau	Roseau	MN	**B+**	B	B+	221.0	7.99	7.2	5.9	7.1	39.7	**10.0**	13.0	16.9
▲ Citizens State Bank of Tyler, Inc.	Tyler	MN	**C-**	D+	D	21.8	-0.05	5.4	4.4	4.3	29.0	**8.5**	10.0	40.8
Citizens State Bank of Waverly	Waverly	MN	**B+**	B+	B-	79.3	8.34	4.8	1.3	20.6	14.5	**6.8**	8.8	13.6
Citizens Tri-County Bank	Dunlap	TN	**C**	C+	B-	907.6	7.77	2.1	9.3	21.5	22.8	**8.3**	9.9	19.1
Citizens Trust Bank	Atlanta	GA	**B+**	B+	B-	415.1	4.84	11.1	1.8	15.8	21.4	**10.0**	11.0	16.0
Citizens Union Bank of Shelbyville	Shelbyville	KY	**B**	B	B-	840.8	11.26	8.8	0.5	15.9	5.7	**9.8**	12.9	14.8
Citizens' Bank, Inc.	Robertsdale	AL	**B**	B	B-	107.0	0.46	7.6	1.7	18.8	21.1	**10.0**	12.6	19.8
Citizens-Farmers Bank of Cole Camp	Cole Camp	MO	**B+**	B+	A	134.9	3.14	4.2	7.4	28.0	23.3	**10.0**	16.1	28.4
▲ City Bank	Lubbock	TX	**B+**	B	B	2793.7	4.02	10.2	10.3	14.7	14.4	**8.6**	10.3	13.8
City Bank & Trust Co.	Natchitoches	LA	**B**	B	B-	255.4	5.45	2.6	2.7	11.4	63.5	**9.4**	10.6	20.0
City Bank & Trust Co.	Lincoln	NE	**B**	B	B-	178.4	19.14	11.0	2.1	12.4	13.0	**10.0**	13.7	19.5
City First Bank of D.C., N.A.	Washington	DC	**C+**	C+	B-	348.4	11.09	7.2	0.0	2.6	24.7	**7.4**	9.3	20.0
City National B&T Co. of Lawton, Oklahom	Lawton	OK	**A-**	A-	A-	365.7	1.41	3.2	3.1	19.6	21.6	**10.0**	14.3	24.2

Asset Quality Index	Adjusted Non-Performing Loans as a % of Total Loans	Adjusted Non-Performing Loans as a % of Capital	Net Charge-Offs Avg Loans	Profitability Index	Net Income ($Mil)	Return on Assets (R.O.A.)	Return on Equity (R.O.E.)	Net Interest Spread	Overhead Efficiency Ratio	Liquidity Index	Liquidity Ratio	Hot Money Ratio	Stability Index
8.5	0.00	na	0.06	**5.8**	0.6	1.41	16.27	3.88	61.4	**3.5**	15.3	11.4	**5.0**
7.7	0.07	na	-0.01	**7.1**	1.3	1.54	9.44	3.56	45.7	**2.5**	39.3	13.2	**9.2**
6.1	7.49	na	0.11	**4.5**	1.4	0.80	5.61	4.55	76.6	**1.5**	19.6	26.3	**7.6**
9.3	0.74	2.5	0.01	**2.9**	1.0	0.39	2.60	3.01	84.3	**2.6**	6.2	15.3	**7.7**
0.3	4.85	na	0.25	**1.7**	0.1	0.08	1.33	4.53	95.0	**0.7**	16.3	50.2	**2.6**
9.1	0.00	na	0.18	**4.7**	0.6	1.13	7.46	2.30	53.4	**2.2**	46.3	38.2	**6.5**
5.6	3.45	5.9	0.01	**7.3**	5.8	1.88	14.92	3.33	52.9	**2.4**	32.4	20.3	**9.2**
7.7	0.00	na	0.00	**6.5**	1.4	1.49	10.51	3.66	57.2	**4.5**	24.8	6.6	**9.2**
4.9	3.03	na	1.00	**4.8**	0.7	0.97	4.09	3.86	59.9	**4.0**	41.2	15.1	**8.2**
5.1	1.24	na	1.41	**3.9**	1.0	0.50	3.97	3.79	58.0	**1.9**	9.7	19.1	**8.6**
6.6	0.37	na	-0.01	**7.1**	2.2	1.42	15.75	4.24	56.8	**4.1**	22.1	8.8	**5.6**
2.9	3.99	na	-0.08	**6.2**	1.1	1.25	9.09	3.98	63.8	**0.8**	9.5	33.4	**8.2**
8.1	0.23	na	0.00	**9.7**	5.9	2.26	22.24	3.81	36.8	**0.9**	7.6	30.3	**8.6**
4.8	1.27	na	0.21	**5.0**	3.5	1.07	9.56	3.65	63.9	**3.8**	25.5	11.4	**7.2**
6.7	0.00	na	-0.01	**4.5**	0.2	0.96	9.93	4.15	72.8	**0.6**	11.7	36.0	**3.7**
2.6	1.15	9.9	-0.07	**5.7**	3.2	1.31	11.53	3.61	61.8	**1.3**	8.4	24.9	**7.0**
3.2	12.39	na	0.79	**1.2**	-4.1	-7.70	-39.07	3.16	237.5	**3.2**	34.5	17.1	**5.7**
9.0	4.48	na	2.03	**1.9**	0.1	0.29	2.91	3.87	77.4	**2.4**	43.2	31.2	**2.3**
8.6	1.91	2.1	0.13	**3.8**	6.8	0.95	7.76	2.55	66.8	**3.1**	62.8	36.8	**8.0**
5.6	0.00	na	0.00	**8.3**	1.9	1.99	16.82	4.17	57.2	**1.6**	22.6	25.2	**8.4**
9.9	0.00	na	0.07	**0.8**	0.0	0.03	0.39	2.67	99.9	**4.9**	86.3	17.4	**1.8**
6.9	0.23	na	0.08	**9.8**	2.6	2.30	24.01	4.32	45.3	**0.8**	22.0	46.4	**7.8**
4.6	1.15	6.4	0.64	**4.0**	0.4	0.67	7.08	5.04	81.9	**1.8**	38.9	46.1	**4.9**
9.3	0.00	na	0.01	**6.4**	3.2	1.47	14.16	3.30	47.7	**3.7**	53.5	20.1	**7.2**
5.0	1.43	na	0.22	**7.9**	7.3	1.59	14.77	4.50	54.8	**2.7**	18.4	15.8	**7.5**
4.5	2.26	na	0.06	**3.6**	0.9	0.78	8.33	4.65	80.8	**4.0**	16.4	8.8	**5.2**
5.1	1.75	na	0.28	**3.8**	0.5	0.55	4.66	3.81	82.9	**4.1**	20.9	8.5	**6.7**
7.9	0.19	na	0.00	**4.5**	1.4	0.89	10.93	3.82	69.4	**3.3**	13.6	12.3	**5.1**
5.1	0.62	na	0.00	**6.5**	0.6	1.52	16.30	4.81	60.4	**0.9**	6.8	30.9	**3.7**
6.7	0.90	na	0.04	**4.6**	1.6	1.08	11.28	3.14	69.4	**3.7**	17.5	10.5	**6.2**
8.4	0.73	2.5	0.00	**6.3**	0.9	1.42	8.05	4.29	61.1	**5.1**	19.8	2.1	**8.1**
5.6	1.95	na	0.22	**4.8**	0.5	1.09	9.19	3.93	70.8	**2.2**	4.8	17.0	**6.1**
7.4	0.89	na	0.00	**6.2**	1.7	1.72	12.40	4.49	56.3	**1.4**	4.3	22.6	**7.7**
1.0	4.07	na	0.07	**7.8**	1.1	1.77	12.19	5.07	61.3	**4.4**	29.8	9.4	**6.7**
6.4	0.45	na	0.01	**5.0**	0.7	0.93	6.96	3.65	64.8	**2.0**	30.5	23.2	**7.4**
7.4	0.33	na	-0.01	**6.7**	0.7	1.55	13.82	3.92	60.0	**3.1**	29.1	16.0	**7.0**
6.7	1.50	na	0.01	**7.6**	1.9	1.96	15.11	4.11	62.0	**1.6**	19.0	16.6	**8.1**
7.1	0.55	na	-0.01	**4.7**	0.4	1.20	10.50	3.19	61.6	**7.4**	72.8	1.2	**6.1**
1.4	5.63	47.6	2.63	**2.5**	0.1	0.17	2.10	4.18	67.9	**5.0**	27.8	4.4	**3.7**
6.0	0.16	na	0.01	**10.0**	6.2	2.86	32.89	4.28	46.5	**0.6**	10.3	27.1	**6.9**
4.6	1.57	8.7	0.00	**6.1**	0.5	1.42	12.91	4.51	70.3	**4.3**	12.9	6.5	**6.3**
8.5	0.98	na	0.02	**4.8**	1.7	1.08	8.31	3.46	74.5	**4.3**	18.8	6.9	**7.9**
7.3	0.10	na	-0.10	**5.0**	0.5	0.90	5.89	4.69	75.4	**3.3**	13.7	12.3	**7.8**
8.5	0.00	na	0.01	**3.2**	0.2	0.66	6.51	4.15	83.7	**4.7**	24.8	5.3	**4.1**
7.3	0.19	1.8	0.10	**4.8**	3.6	0.87	8.93	3.60	69.8	**5.5**	35.7	4.9	**6.2**
6.2	5.63	na	1.12	**2.3**	0.1	0.33	2.58	3.07	81.0	**7.3**	79.5	3.2	**5.2**
7.0	1.20	na	0.03	**2.7**	0.6	0.77	7.72	3.47	80.9	**4.9**	37.4	9.8	**4.8**
5.5	2.17	na	-0.06	**5.6**	2.3	1.44	11.10	3.26	58.4	**1.3**	10.7	25.6	**8.1**
7.8	0.21	na	-0.12	**3.4**	0.1	0.64	6.48	3.09	72.4	**6.8**	64.3	1.1	**3.0**
5.7	0.65	2.1	0.00	**6.9**	1.0	1.66	13.46	4.40	61.7	**4.3**	16.0	5.7	**5.7**
4.2	1.68	na	0.19	**8.0**	12.5	1.87	18.13	4.34	56.2	**1.7**	19.2	23.1	**8.3**
6.4	1.48	5.9	0.00	**5.3**	3.3	1.07	9.91	4.06	73.5	**1.9**	12.6	19.1	**6.8**
5.0	1.26	6.8	0.00	**6.2**	7.7	1.29	9.62	4.18	65.1	**3.7**	14.2	10.4	**8.9**
6.1	3.29	na	0.08	**3.4**	0.5	0.64	5.24	4.30	85.1	**3.1**	22.4	14.1	**7.2**
5.0	4.33	na	0.27	**5.2**	1.0	0.97	6.14	3.57	53.7	**2.3**	22.2	18.0	**8.8**
7.7	0.35	1.9	0.06	**5.5**	23.5	1.14	11.18	4.09	73.6	**3.2**	17.9	10.1	**8.9**
9.4	0.09	na	0.03	**4.6**	2.1	1.17	11.37	3.11	69.1	**7.1**	68.3	4.3	**5.9**
8.5	0.28	na	0.05	**4.2**	0.9	0.77	5.35	3.75	70.0	**4.4**	27.7	8.4	**7.2**
7.8	1.18	4.6	0.03	**3.2**	1.1	0.47	5.48	2.93	80.8	**5.4**	43.4	8.3	**5.3**
5.7	3.51	9.4	0.96	**8.9**	5.7	2.15	16.58	4.11	79.1	**6.0**	39.8	3.3	**8.7**

Name	City	State	Rating	2018 Rating	2017 Rating	Total Assets ($Mil)	One Year Asset Growth	Asset Mix (As a % of Total Assets) Comm-ercial Loans	Cons-umer Loans	Mort-gage Loans	Secur-ities	Capital-ization Index	Lever-age Ratio	Risk-Based Capital Ratio
City National Bank	Los Angeles	CA	**B+**	B	B	58193.1	20.25	14.1	1.4	20.1	21.2	**6.1**	8.1	12.6
City National Bank	Corsicana	TX	**B-**	B-	B	50.5	5.00	10.2	4.4	36.8	2.1	**10.0**	11.0	19.7
City National Bank of Colorado City	Colorado City	TX	**B-**	B	A-	135.2	9.49	5.1	7.5	22.6	25.6	**7.9**	9.6	15.6
City National Bank of Florida	Miami	FL	**B**	B	B	15248.3	9.29	13.6	0.5	11.8	18.4	**8.9**	10.8	14.1
City National Bank of Metropolis	Metropolis	IL	**B**	B	B	388.8	-0.12	3.8	3.5	20.1	46.0	**10.0**	13.8	39.1
City National Bank of San Saba	San Saba	TX	**C+**	C+	C+	60.0	-2.25	2.0	2.9	0.5	65.0	**10.0**	15.0	31.6
▲ City National Bank of Sulphur Springs	Sulphur Springs	TX	**B+**	B	B+	774.9	9.14	6.3	5.7	28.2	17.0	**9.1**	10.4	14.9
City National Bank of Taylor	Taylor	TX	**A-**	B+	B	199.9	-1.24	2.2	0.8	36.8	27.8	**10.0**	11.9	26.4
City National Bank of West Virginia	Charleston	WV	**B+**	B+	B+	4893.0	12.23	5.6	1.1	33.7	16.6	**8.1**	9.7	14.4
City State Bank	Norwalk	IA	**B**	B	B	428.1	4.44	9.1	1.3	12.5	8.7	**7.4**	9.2	12.9
City State Bank	Fort Scott	KS	**C+**	C+	C+	40.0	0.63	3.4	3.9	24.8	14.1	**8.3**	9.9	17.1
Citywide Banks	Denver	CO	**B+**	B+	B	2335.8	1.56	12.4	0.5	8.9	27.1	**9.0**	10.7	14.2
Civis Bank	Rogersville	TN	**E-**	E-	E-	88.9	-5.34	4.4	1.4	25.9	10.2	**0.0**	2.9	5.7
Civista Bank	Sandusky	OH	**A-**	A-	B+	2261.7	8.76	8.3	0.7	15.5	15.7	**9.4**	10.8	14.5
Clackamas County Bank	Sandy	OR	**A**	A	A	231.1	1.58	0.5	0.4	13.5	26.0	**10.0**	12.7	24.3
Clare Bank, N.A.	Platteville	WI	**B+**	B+	B+	264.6	0.38	2.7	1.2	23.7	32.6	**10.0**	12.2	28.2
Claremont Savings Bank	Claremont	NH	**C+**	C+	C+	427.7	2.71	2.2	1.3	59.2	10.5	**10.0**	14.4	21.0
Clarion County Community Bank	Clarion	PA	**B-**	B-	B-	173.5	8.78	8.4	2.1	32.5	12.8	**5.9**	10.2	11.7
▲ Clarkson Bank	Clarkson	NE	**B**	B	B+	57.4	5.41	5.2	1.3	0.1	36.8	**10.0**	14.1	20.0
Clarkston State Bank	Waterford	MI	**B-**	B-	B-	227.8	9.86	6.8	13.9	2.2	2.5	**6.3**	10.4	11.9
▲ Classic Bank, N.A.	Cameron	TX	**B-**	C+	B-	389.8	12.76	3.3	1.9	21.2	17.2	**7.5**	9.3	13.4
Claxton Bank	Claxton	GA	**C**	C+	B-	117.8	-3.00	3.3	1.3	11.0	22.9	**10.0**	11.0	17.6
Clay City Banking Co.	Clay City	IL	**C**	C+	C+	149.5	7.16	8.7	2.4	25.3	11.1	**8.7**	10.1	14.1
Clay County Bank, Inc.	Clay	WV	**A-**	A-	A-	95.7	1.73	1.1	13.3	39.9	18.0	**10.0**	14.9	37.2
Clay County Savings Bank	Liberty	MO	**C+**	C+	C+	111.5	0.05	2.6	0.4	26.4	5.1	**8.6**	10.1	16.8
▲ Clay County State Bank	Louisville	IL	**B-**	C+	B	78.5	-1.76	10.3	7.8	17.9	21.6	**10.0**	15.7	24.8
Clear Lake Bank and Trust Co.	Clear Lake	IA	**B+**	B+	B+	427.5	5.62	11.5	4.3	18.5	7.8	**6.5**	8.6	12.1
Clear Mountain Bank	Bruceton Mills	WV	**A-**	B+	B+	653.5	9.14	7.9	4.8	32.7	16.3	**10.0**	12.2	17.8
ClearPoint Federal Bank & Trust	Batesville	IN	**U**	U	U	103.0	5.16	0.0	0.0	0.0	92.5	**10.0**	16.5	63.5
Cleo State Bank	Cleo Springs	OK	**C+**	B-	B+	86.9	-2.50	16.8	2.7	0.1	54.9	**10.0**	18.2	47.5
▲ Cleveland State Bank	Cleveland	MS	**A-**	B+	B-	229.6	3.04	8.4	4.5	16.9	30.7	**10.0**	11.7	19.6
▲ Cleveland State Bank	Cleveland	WI	**B**	B	C+	130.1	13.51	6.8	5.0	25.4	26.3	**9.1**	10.7	14.3
Clinton Bank	Clinton	KY	**B-**	B-	B	65.2	7.70	4.7	1.9	10.6	35.4	**10.0**	18.0	26.7
Clinton National Bank	Clinton	IA	**B-**	B-	B-	397.8	-0.82	8.6	1.6	8.2	36.4	**10.0**	13.1	23.7
▲ Clinton Savings Bank	Clinton	MA	**B-**	C+	C+	584.6	4.50	2.9	2.0	36.6	15.7	**10.0**	11.2	17.1
▲ CNB Bank	Carlsbad	NM	**B+**	B+	B+	447.0	11.16	9.5	7.4	12.4	40.6	**6.4**	8.4	16.1
CNB Bank	Clearfield	PA	**B**	B	B	3521.8	13.26	13.4	2.9	19.9	15.0	**6.3**	9.0	12.0
▲ CNB Bank & Trust, N.A.	Carlinville	IL	**C**	C-	B-	1321.4	38.76	10.9	2.0	9.2	18.2	**6.5**	8.6	12.2
CNB Bank, Inc.	Berkeley Springs	WV	**B-**	B-	B-	412.7	6.52	3.0	1.3	45.2	14.4	**8.0**	9.7	15.6
Coastal Bank & Trust	Jacksonville	NC	**B-**	B-	B-	113.2	9.29	7.2	0.6	13.6	11.6	**10.0**	15.7	22.9
Coastal Carolina National Bank	Myrtle Beach	SC	**B-**	B-	B-	435.2	16.46	7.7	3.2	19.7	6.3	**7.5**	9.6	12.9
▲ Coastal Community Bank	Everett	WA	**A-**	B+	B	1089.4	18.81	8.2	0.3	8.2	3.0	**8.9**	11.5	14.1
Coastal Heritage Bank	Weymouth	MA	**C**	C	C	849.2	158.14	5.0	2.0	52.7	7.5	**8.2**	9.8	15.0
▲ Coastal States Bank	Hilton Head Island	SC	**D+**	D	D	689.7	23.49	23.5	6.8	9.3	8.7	**6.7**	10.5	12.3
▲ Coatesville Savings Bank	Coatesville	PA	**C**	C-	C-	219.4	6.24	3.2	0.1	47.2	9.5	**8.6**	10.1	15.9
▲ Coffee County Bank	Manchester	TN	**B**	B-	B+	198.1	4.51	8.8	6.5	30.2	6.6	**10.0**	11.7	15.4
▲ Cogent Bank	Orange City	FL	**E+**	E	E-	243.0	134.29	25.3	0.7	13.7	23.2	**10.0**	16.6	22.3
Colchester State Bank	Colchester	IL	**B**	B	B	68.8	6.66	3.9	3.6	7.3	55.5	**10.0**	15.2	29.8
Coleman County State Bank	Coleman	TX	**B**	B-	C+	121.9	11.21	9.8	2.1	12.8	5.6	**8.8**	10.2	16.0
Colfax Banking Co.	Colfax	LA	**B**	B	B	112.3	0.17	0.9	3.0	23.2	37.2	**8.8**	10.2	18.4
Collins State Bank	Collins	WI	**B-**	B-	C+	93.5	12.61	8.0	4.0	25.5	17.2	**7.0**	9.0	13.0
Collinsville Bank	Collinsville	CT	**C+**	C	C	165.8	1.38	8.9	2.6	42.9	7.1	**7.0**	9.0	13.3
▲ Collinsville Building and Loan Assn.	Collinsville	IL	**C**	C	D+	120.9	1.14	0.0	0.0	72.6	21.0	**10.0**	27.7	73.1
Colonial Federal Savings Bank	Quincy	MA	**B**	B	B	310.9	4.30	0.0	0.5	45.5	32.3	**10.0**	14.9	30.4
Colonial Savings, F.A.	Fort Worth	TX	**C**	C	D	1121.7	7.87	0.7	0.3	41.7	20.9	**9.3**	10.5	25.8
Colony Bank	Fitzgerald	GA	**B**	B	B	1473.5	24.42	5.2	1.5	13.3	25.0	**8.1**	9.8	14.2
Colorado Bank and Trust Co. of La Junta	La Junta	CO	**B+**	B	B-	152.9	10.54	11.3	2.6	12.2	24.4	**8.0**	9.6	16.9
Colorado Federal Savings Bank	Greenwood Village	CO	**B-**	B-	B-	2146.7	17.41	1.0	0.0	14.7	24.8	**9.4**	10.6	17.1
▲ Colorado National Bank	Denver	CO	**D**	D	D-	26.8	-52.28	0.0	0.0	0.0	4.6	**10.0**	24.7	177.3
▲ Columbia Bank	Lake City	FL	**C**	D+	D+	210.8	0.64	6.2	0.7	12.1	15.0	**9.8**	10.9	14.9

Asset Quality Index	Adjusted Non-Performing Loans as a % of Total Loans	Adjusted Non-Performing Loans as a % of Capital	Net Charge-Offs Avg Loans	Profitability Index	Net Income ($Mil)	Return on Assets (R.O.A.)	Return on Equity (R.O.E.)	Net Interest Spread	Overhead Efficiency Ratio	Liquidity Index	Liquidity Ratio	Hot Money Ratio	Stability Index
7.9	0.32	2.2	0.07	**5.9**	483.6	1.19	13.28	3.43	60.7	**5.8**	25.6	1.6	**7.9**
8.7	0.00	na	0.03	**4.2**	0.3	0.71	6.43	4.17	84.4	**1.6**	24.1	25.3	**6.3**
5.7	0.46	na	0.28	**5.0**	1.0	0.97	10.46	4.12	61.9	**1.8**	20.7	21.3	**6.0**
7.7	0.53	2.4	0.02	**5.2**	120.0	1.07	9.01	2.93	52.6	**3.2**	24.6	11.0	**9.0**
6.2	2.64	8.2	0.39	**3.8**	2.5	0.86	6.48	2.80	63.9	**2.2**	45.2	28.5	**6.6**
9.6	0.00	na	0.09	**3.2**	0.3	0.70	4.85	3.21	76.2	**6.9**	76.6	5.0	**7.2**
7.4	0.40	na	0.05	**8.3**	10.9	1.96	16.53	4.68	60.9	**3.1**	25.2	14.6	**8.9**
9.0	0.69	na	0.01	**6.3**	2.4	1.60	14.38	4.07	67.3	**6.3**	42.0	1.9	**7.4**
5.8	1.14	4.7	0.06	**9.4**	66.7	1.83	15.70	3.64	51.2	**2.6**	9.8	15.5	**9.5**
8.3	0.07	na	0.00	**5.3**	3.9	1.26	13.46	3.34	69.2	**2.9**	19.5	15.0	**6.4**
8.7	0.00	0.0	0.00	**4.7**	0.3	1.03	10.84	3.87	73.6	**2.4**	31.5	20.1	**5.7**
7.0	0.18	0.7	0.03	**6.2**	21.4	1.27	7.78	4.43	61.7	**5.8**	30.3	4.9	**8.2**
0.3	6.53	na	1.26	**1.1**	0.1	0.09	3.44	4.45	95.4	**3.6**	19.5	11.5	**0.5**
6.6	0.57	2.3	-0.03	**7.5**	26.8	1.60	11.66	4.42	60.9	**4.0**	14.6	7.0	**10.0**
9.1	0.00	0.0	-0.18	**7.1**	2.9	1.69	13.49	4.27	64.6	**5.2**	34.3	5.8	**8.8**
8.8	1.18	na	0.00	**4.9**	2.6	1.27	10.26	2.75	58.7	**4.8**	31.1	7.3	**7.9**
7.2	1.07	na	0.00	**3.2**	2.0	0.64	4.48	3.33	84.6	**1.7**	18.8	22.6	**7.5**
6.4	0.47	na	0.09	**3.4**	0.7	0.58	5.64	3.81	77.8	**0.8**	16.8	36.1	**5.4**
6.5	0.58	na	-0.51	**7.6**	0.8	1.94	14.04	3.72	48.8	**2.4**	29.1	19.2	**8.3**
6.3	0.08	0.3	0.00	**6.5**	2.2	1.31	12.76	3.96	58.7	**0.9**	6.1	30.6	**7.1**
5.0	1.05	na	0.24	**4.1**	2.5	0.90	9.67	3.53	77.3	**1.9**	13.3	19.2	**5.9**
4.2	2.85	na	0.34	**5.1**	1.1	1.18	11.38	4.75	74.8	**3.1**	22.2	14.2	**6.4**
3.3	2.51	na	0.02	**4.0**	0.7	0.64	6.36	3.72	79.7	**2.7**	12.7	15.4	**4.9**
8.3	0.18	na	0.12	**7.6**	1.0	1.41	9.63	4.18	60.4	**3.0**	35.4	18.4	**8.7**
9.0	0.00	na	0.00	**3.1**	0.5	0.59	5.97	3.41	86.9	**4.5**	23.6	6.4	**7.0**
4.5	2.90	na	0.07	**5.3**	0.8	1.34	8.85	3.44	62.9	**3.9**	14.0	9.4	**8.0**
7.2	0.40	1.6	0.01	**7.1**	4.9	1.52	17.54	3.78	61.6	**3.0**	12.3	13.8	**7.5**
6.4	1.02	4.5	0.15	**7.0**	6.5	1.37	11.52	4.08	61.6	**2.0**	24.9	20.0	**8.1**
10.0	na	na	na	**4.9**	0.8	1.04	6.07	2.45	82.9	**8.6**	116.7	0.9	**6.3**
3.5	22.19	na	0.74	**4.0**	0.7	1.03	5.81	3.40	67.4	**4.8**	65.3	15.1	**6.3**
8.4	0.86	na	0.13	**5.5**	1.9	1.10	10.85	4.02	67.1	**4.8**	33.4	8.8	**6.5**
4.9	0.89	na	0.03	**6.0**	1.1	1.20	11.35	3.87	65.5	**3.3**	33.3	8.3	**6.0**
4.6	3.25	na	0.01	**3.9**	0.4	0.81	4.33	3.33	71.4	**1.6**	8.5	20.8	**7.6**
8.2	0.80	2.1	0.03	**2.6**	1.1	0.38	2.80	2.89	87.6	**4.7**	37.8	10.7	**7.3**
6.2	1.39	6.8	0.01	**3.9**	3.7	0.85	7.89	3.29	73.6	**1.6**	21.7	20.3	**7.6**
7.4	0.37	na	0.09	**8.6**	6.8	2.16	26.84	4.07	48.6	**6.2**	41.9	3.0	**5.7**
5.8	0.76	5.0	0.17	**5.9**	29.8	1.20	12.14	3.68	61.2	**4.1**	6.1	7.1	**8.2**
3.7	1.93	na	0.10	**5.6**	10.5	1.07	11.29	3.68	62.6	**1.6**	15.9	22.7	**7.5**
7.0	0.90	na	0.07	**3.8**	2.3	0.77	8.87	3.46	79.1	**2.3**	14.9	17.6	**5.2**
8.8	0.81	na	0.04	**3.9**	0.6	0.70	4.36	4.16	79.8	**3.3**	29.2	14.7	**7.0**
5.9	0.79	na	0.00	**3.8**	2.0	0.66	6.14	3.69	75.0	**1.7**	17.5	21.9	**5.9**
7.4	0.15	0.4	0.04	**6.4**	10.2	1.34	12.43	4.29	61.4	**4.1**	17.4	7.3	**8.7**
6.1	0.66	na	0.00	**2.6**	1.4	0.27	2.96	3.72	88.0	**2.0**	11.2	18.6	**5.8**
3.5	1.44	8.6	0.14	**2.5**	2.0	0.41	3.49	4.24	85.5	**1.5**	9.9	17.7	**4.2**
3.1	2.79	na	0.00	**3.1**	0.7	0.41	4.13	3.24	78.8	**1.7**	14.1	20.2	**5.7**
4.8	2.53	na	0.02	**9.8**	3.5	2.38	20.43	4.46	47.5	**0.9**	14.4	33.6	**9.1**
7.3	0.74	na	-0.20	**0.0**	-1.3	-0.92	-5.13	3.54	120.2	**2.9**	27.5	16.6	**3.3**
6.4	3.12	na	-0.17	**4.5**	0.5	1.05	6.78	3.20	59.5	**3.6**	47.3	18.4	**6.4**
7.7	0.03	na	0.08	**9.3**	2.2	2.50	25.09	5.46	60.3	**3.4**	24.0	12.9	**7.3**
7.3	0.06	na	0.00	**4.9**	1.0	1.21	12.40	4.01	72.2	**1.3**	13.4	27.2	**6.3**
8.2	0.47	na	0.00	**5.7**	1.0	1.44	15.93	4.23	68.6	**3.6**	24.2	11.5	**5.2**
4.9	1.74	na	0.01	**2.9**	0.6	0.45	4.81	3.27	87.6	**2.1**	11.1	13.9	**5.8**
10.0	0.00	na	0.02	**2.4**	0.4	0.41	1.47	2.44	78.1	**2.0**	32.1	26.9	**7.4**
9.9	0.08	na	0.00	**3.6**	1.6	0.70	4.69	2.82	70.8	**2.8**	40.1	23.3	**7.9**
2.4	16.49	7.4	0.13	**2.8**	2.3	0.28	1.22	4.63	98.4	**6.2**	33.8	3.6	**9.2**
5.9	1.59	na	0.18	**4.7**	9.3	0.90	8.80	3.68	73.7	**3.6**	27.7	16.1	**8.0**
5.3	1.07	2.9	0.58	**9.2**	1.9	1.81	19.32	4.73	60.4	**4.7**	29.0	6.9	**5.7**
7.4	1.73	5.3	0.16	**3.6**	8.6	0.59	5.16	2.44	54.6	**5.0**	49.6	12.0	**8.7**
7.3	0.00	na	0.00	**3.0**	0.3	1.11	6.52	2.25	92.3	**7.6**	89.7	2.6	**3.9**
3.3	5.14	na	-0.18	**2.0**	0.4	0.26	2.47	3.73	93.5	**3.0**	18.3	14.4	**5.5**

Name	City	State	Rating	2018 Rating	2017 Rating	Total Assets ($Mil)	One Year Asset Growth	Asset Mix (As a % of Total Assets): Commercial Loans	Consumer Loans	Mortgage Loans	Securities	Capitalization Index	Leverage Ratio	Risk-Based Capital Ratio
Columbia Bank	Fair Lawn	NJ	B	B	B-	7055.5	7.58	5.3	0.0	30.4	20.0	10.0	12.2	18.0
Columbia S&L Assn.	Milwaukee	WI	E-	E-	E-	22.5	-4.55	0.0	1.9	48.0	0.1	7.0	9.0	14.2
Columbia State Bank	Tacoma	WA	B+	B+	B+	13753.8	6.22	15.7	0.3	2.7	24.5	8.0	10.4	13.3
Columbus Bank and Trust Co.	Columbus	NE	C+	C+	B-	142.5	5.87	15.0	1.6	4.5	13.1	5.6	9.7	11.4
Columbus State Bank	Columbus	TX	B-	B-	B-	105.0	-13.16	0.3	0.3	0.6	63.6	10.0	14.5	27.2
Comenity Bank	Wilmington	DE	D+	D+	D+	13836.2	0.52	0.0	81.4	0.0	1.0	10.0	13.0	16.3
Comenity Capital Bank	Draper	UT	C-	C-	C-	9708.5	7.56	0.1	80.1	0.0	1.0	10.0	13.9	17.7
Comerica Bank	Dallas	TX	A-	A-	B+	72895.0	1.91	36.8	0.8	2.9	17.1	6.5	10.1	12.2
Comerica Bank & Trust, N.A.	Ann Arbor	MI	U	U	U	69.2	-3.82	0.0	0.0	0.0	0.0	10.0	100.	280.3
▲ Commencement Bank	Tacoma	WA	B+	B	B	375.4	16.65	20.3	0.5	3.7	4.4	10.0	11.9	15.9
Commerce Bank	Evansville	IN	C	C	C-	187.7	6.18	17.7	0.5	11.6	6.4	8.9	11.8	14.1
▼ Commerce Bank	Edina	MN	B-	B+	B	210.4	4.68	9.7	0.1	7.9	7.0	9.4	12.7	14.5
Commerce Bank	Kansas City	MO	A	A-	A-	25781.9	3.26	12.4	9.5	9.7	33.6	8.8	10.2	14.0
▲ Commerce Bank	Corinth	MS	A-	B+	A	124.8	10.48	14.6	6.1	30.2	16.4	10.0	11.9	18.8
Commerce Bank	Laredo	TX	A	A	A	516.0	-4.41	4.2	1.1	19.2	52.9	10.0	17.3	35.9
Commerce Bank of Arizona, Inc.	Tucson	AZ	D+	D	E	251.4	20.92	13.3	0.1	6.9	9.3	9.1	11.1	14.2
Commerce Bank Texas	Stockdale	TX	B	B	B	55.2	6.36	14.3	0.4	17.0	20.0	10.0	14.0	21.2
▲ Commerce Community Bank	Oak Grove	LA	B	B-	B-	63.7	3.01	15.8	1.7	11.4	27.6	9.4	10.6	14.6
▲ Commerce National Bank & Trust	Winter Park	FL	A-	B	B	113.8	-0.13	3.9	0.8	20.1	8.8	10.0	12.6	19.4
Commerce State Bank	West Bend	WI	C+	C+	C+	706.8	9.09	24.6	0.0	15.4	4.6	5.8	9.9	11.6
CommerceWest Bank	Irvine	CA	B+	B+	A-	635.2	7.67	17.6	0.0	0.3	10.6	7.9	9.8	13.3
▲ Commercial & Savings Bank of Millersburg	Millersburg	OH	B	B-	B	786.6	10.68	13.3	2.4	18.1	13.3	8.7	10.1	14.9
Commercial Bank	Crawford	GA	A	A-	A-	217.6	28.59	5.8	2.2	22.4	9.8	10.0	11.2	16.4
Commercial Bank	Parsons	KS	B+	B+	B+	328.5	4.55	10.4	6.1	10.9	51.7	6.7	8.7	16.8
▼ Commercial Bank	West Liberty	KY	B-	B	B+	148.4	7.97	5.4	6.4	30.8	15.9	8.3	12.9	13.6
▲ Commercial Bank	Alma	MI	C+	C	C	511.6	-1.32	5.3	1.8	31.6	6.4	7.1	9.1	14.1
Commercial Bank	Saint Louis	MO	C	C	C-	220.2	8.88	16.0	2.0	12.2	33.1	5.9	7.9	12.1
Commercial Bank	De Kalb	MS	B	B	B	165.0	8.44	10.8	14.5	11.0	27.1	8.6	10.1	17.9
Commercial Bank	Nelson	NE	B	B	B	55.2	12.29	23.9	3.2	0.5	28.1	9.8	12.1	14.8
▲ Commercial Bank	Honea Path	SC	A-	B+	B+	189.9	1.68	2.9	3.7	14.1	38.1	10.0	14.8	49.7
Commercial Bank	Harrogate	TN	B	B	B	1328.1	10.11	8.2	1.3	23.2	6.1	8.1	9.8	13.4
▲ Commercial Bank	Mason	TX	B-	C+	C+	55.0	7.25	5.4	2.4	23.4	30.8	7.5	9.4	17.8
Commercial Bank & Trust Co.	Monticello	AR	B-	B-	B	211.9	-2.59	12.5	7.2	14.6	32.9	8.9	10.3	16.5
▲ Commercial Bank & Trust Co.	Paris	TN	A-	B+	A	789.4	7.46	11.2	3.8	18.1	23.2	10.0	11.0	17.1
Commercial Bank & Trust of PA	Latrobe	PA	B+	B+	A-	431.5	2.30	3.1	0.3	25.3	36.8	10.0	13.5	21.4
▲ Commercial Bank of California	Irvine	CA	B-	C+	B-	1016.7	10.90	8.1	2.3	1.6	9.0	7.4	9.8	12.8
Commercial Bank of Grayson	Grayson	KY	B	B	B-	180.4	1.17	6.9	7.9	16.1	42.4	10.0	15.0	26.2
▲ Commercial Bank of Mott	Mott	ND	A-	B+	A	108.3	4.43	3.0	1.7	2.4	12.3	10.0	14.2	16.8
Commercial Bank of Oak Grove	Oak Grove	MO	B+	B+	B+	77.7	11.71	5.2	0.9	26.0	19.5	10.0	15.8	28.3
Commercial Bank of Ozark	Ozark	AL	C	C-	C	91.5	0.41	2.8	5.4	17.5	33.4	6.7	8.7	19.4
▲ Commercial Bank of Texas, N.A.	Nacogdoches	TX	B	B-	B	786.7	12.53	11.5	4.5	15.5	26.5	8.7	10.1	15.3
▲ Commercial Banking Co.	Valdosta	GA	A-	B+	B	229.2	1.04	5.2	1.8	30.6	9.1	10.0	14.8	23.1
▲ Commercial Capital Bank	Delhi	LA	B-	B-	B-	174.0	2.35	5.9	2.0	17.0	3.9	10.0	13.0	17.1
▲ Commercial National Bank of Brady	Brady	TX	A	A-	A	147.9	-6.39	5.6	2.8	17.9	37.3	10.0	13.0	23.5
Commercial National Bank of Texarkana	Texarkana	TX	B+	B+	B	213.7	4.46	13.5	2.9	17.4	31.4	7.2	9.1	15.5
▲ Commercial Savings Bank	Carroll	IA	B	B-	B	191.7	4.67	9.9	3.2	27.4	7.0	6.6	8.6	12.5
Commercial State Bank	Donalsonville	GA	B-	B	B	90.4	8.47	8.6	4.7	8.1	23.5	10.0	16.6	28.1
▲ Commercial State Bank	Cedar Bluffs	NE	E	E-	E	19.5	-2.06	3.1	1.5	1.1	24.9	6.1	8.1	16.1
Commercial State Bank	Republican City	NE	A-	A-	A	62.5	7.78	2.8	0.5	0.0	50.9	10.0	30.7	38.2
Commercial State Bank	Wausa	NE	B-	B-	B-	129.2	14.64	22.0	5.0	4.3	3.4	6.9	10.0	12.5
▲ Commercial State Bank	Palmer	TX	C+	C	C	82.4	-0.71	11.5	3.7	9.6	29.6	6.7	8.7	18.5
▲ Commercial State Bank of Wagner	Wagner	SD	B-	C+	B+	187.0	6.99	6.0	2.5	8.0	24.2	8.3	9.9	15.7
▲ Commercial Trust Co. of Fayette	Fayette	MO	B+	B	B	130.7	1.41	2.1	5.9	43.8	8.4	9.6	10.7	18.9
Commodore Bank	Somerset	OH	D+	D+	D+	80.1	-2.00	4.5	6.1	35.2	28.0	6.2	8.2	15.2
Commonwealth Bank and Trust Co.	Louisville	KY	B-	B-	B-	1084.5	8.11	8.7	4.6	15.6	17.1	6.9	9.8	12.4
Commonwealth Business Bank	Los Angeles	CA	A-	A-	B+	1159.6	-3.71	12.3	0.4	0.9	8.4	10.0	12.1	15.8
Commonwealth Community Bank, Inc.	Hartford	KY	B-	B	B	143.7	0.76	0.2	2.9	17.4	62.4	10.0	16.8	42.8
Commonwealth Cooperative Bank	Hyde Park	MA	B	B	B	189.9	2.84	1.4	0.1	54.7	12.1	10.0	14.7	27.1
▲ Commonwealth National Bank	Mobile	AL	D+	D-	D-	48.6	3.95	5.0	1.1	8.8	35.2	9.6	10.7	29.5
Community 1st Bank Las Vegas	Las Vegas	NM	C	C-	D	141.5	5.68	2.0	1.0	10.8	36.8	8.3	9.9	21.8

Asset Quality Index	Adjusted Non-Performing Loans as a % of Total Loans	Adjusted Non-Performing Loans as a % of Capital	Net Charge-Offs Avg Loans	Profitability Index	Net Income ($Mil)	Return on Assets (R.O.A.)	Return on Equity (R.O.E.)	Net Interest Spread	Overhead Efficiency Ratio	Liquidity Index	Liquidity Ratio	Hot Money Ratio	Stability Index
9.0	0.43	1.5	0.04	**4.1**	41.2	0.81	7.13	2.55	62.4	**1.9**	16.3	20.3	**8.7**
1.7	4.72	na	0.31	**1.1**	-0.1	-0.29	-3.10	4.74	107.2	**0.7**	12.0	38.3	**0.7**
5.8	0.51	1.7	0.04	**7.4**	150.8	1.52	9.52	4.31	58.0	**5.7**	25.6	1.9	**10.0**
4.2	0.27	na	0.02	**6.4**	1.6	1.59	14.02	4.31	56.3	**1.5**	7.4	22.9	**7.4**
9.8	0.00	na	0.00	**3.9**	0.6	0.81	5.62	2.68	67.2	**6.9**	103.3	10.9	**6.8**
0.6	1.38	20.3	6.13	**10.0**	363.6	3.54	25.93	21.74	50.9	**0.4**	16.8	74.5	**9.5**
1.5	4.03	15.2	4.51	**10.0**	200.2	2.86	20.81	15.30	55.5	**0.9**	21.8	8.2	**9.3**
6.9	0.57	3.4	0.23	**9.0**	932.0	1.75	16.54	3.66	51.4	**5.3**	25.3	2.9	**10.0**
9.4	na	0.0	0.00	**10.0**	17.2	37.22	38.91	2.68	57.9	**4.0**	na	0.0	**7.0**
8.2	0.00	na	0.03	**6.6**	3.6	1.34	10.94	4.43	60.4	**1.7**	20.3	23.6	**7.2**
8.5	0.00	na	0.00	**3.3**	0.9	0.62	5.43	3.46	76.6	**2.6**	19.7	16.7	**6.1**
1.7	4.19	na	0.65	**3.9**	1.2	0.75	5.85	3.39	60.4	**0.6**	14.7	16.1	**8.4**
7.8	0.56	2.0	0.32	**8.6**	310.5	1.66	15.02	3.52	57.0	**5.2**	28.2	7.1	**9.8**
7.3	0.51	na	0.26	**8.2**	1.7	1.85	15.87	4.32	58.5	**2.0**	26.5	21.8	**8.5**
8.8	0.60	1.3	-0.16	**8.8**	7.2	1.68	9.91	3.18	42.6	**3.1**	63.4	34.4	**9.4**
1.2	4.61	na	-0.12	**4.4**	1.6	0.96	8.79	4.62	80.3	**3.1**	30.5	16.3	**4.6**
5.6	0.00	0.0	0.02	**4.9**	0.4	0.94	5.08	4.58	72.8	**2.5**	27.0	18.1	**8.1**
8.2	0.28	na	0.00	**6.2**	0.6	1.23	12.04	4.11	63.2	**1.6**	28.1	28.8	**5.9**
7.7	0.17	na	-0.01	**6.0**	0.8	0.93	7.49	3.69	77.2	**1.7**	28.6	27.5	**9.8**
4.6	0.89	na	0.34	**6.1**	5.6	1.12	11.59	3.59	54.1	**0.7**	11.6	24.0	**6.3**
7.5	0.12	0.1	0.00	**6.9**	6.1	1.40	13.09	3.85	54.4	**2.9**	26.1	8.7	**6.7**
6.0	1.14	na	0.00	**6.9**	8.0	1.42	13.49	4.05	57.3	**4.0**	14.8	8.4	**7.1**
7.7	0.16	na	-0.04	**10.0**	3.7	2.58	23.49	5.12	49.0	**3.3**	27.0	14.0	**7.9**
7.8	0.44	na	0.06	**4.7**	2.8	1.12	12.22	3.26	68.1	**3.4**	32.6	15.8	**6.3**
6.4	0.42	na	0.02	**3.8**	0.9	0.81	5.31	4.13	80.6	**1.8**	20.6	21.8	**8.0**
4.8	3.39	na	-0.03	**4.7**	4.1	1.06	11.30	3.12	62.2	**1.5**	18.7	5.7	**6.3**
4.9	1.35	na	-0.21	**2.8**	0.7	0.43	5.41	3.42	85.7	**4.0**	38.0	14.2	**4.0**
6.2	0.78	4.3	0.23	**4.6**	1.1	0.89	8.50	4.08	70.7	**2.4**	32.9	21.4	**6.6**
7.0	0.66	na	0.03	**6.3**	0.5	1.28	10.51	4.37	59.2	**1.3**	7.1	25.2	**7.4**
7.6	2.58	na	0.16	**5.6**	1.9	1.38	9.64	3.23	58.6	**5.8**	67.4	11.7	**8.5**
5.8	1.10	na	0.07	**6.4**	12.1	1.27	13.10	3.82	56.0	**1.0**	11.4	22.8	**8.4**
9.2	0.00	na	0.02	**6.4**	0.6	1.38	15.31	3.98	56.1	**2.7**	35.4	20.2	**5.9**
5.1	1.08	na	0.21	**4.8**	1.7	1.08	11.22	3.49	69.6	**0.9**	11.8	32.3	**6.7**
8.4	0.37	na	0.06	**8.3**	10.4	1.82	15.97	4.03	61.1	**4.1**	29.6	10.8	**9.1**
9.4	0.15	0.4	-0.01	**5.0**	3.5	1.13	7.41	4.08	71.2	**5.3**	40.9	8.0	**8.6**
6.5	0.56	na	0.05	**4.4**	5.4	0.72	7.22	4.28	79.8	**5.4**	23.9	3.3	**7.7**
6.3	0.80	5.9	0.14	**4.3**	1.1	0.84	5.79	3.90	76.9	**6.3**	47.6	4.1	**7.8**
5.9	0.62	na	0.00	**9.7**	2.0	2.58	18.34	4.14	39.9	**1.4**	7.2	22.3	**10.0**
6.4	2.57	na	0.00	**4.3**	0.5	0.78	5.05	2.87	72.6	**3.7**	24.9	11.3	**6.5**
4.5	2.18	na	0.08	**3.2**	0.4	0.60	7.02	3.78	83.0	**3.9**	23.2	10.4	**4.0**
5.5	0.90	na	0.11	**6.1**	6.8	1.22	11.90	4.09	63.7	**4.1**	19.0	8.6	**6.6**
7.8	1.23	na	-0.01	**6.0**	2.1	1.20	8.08	4.53	67.3	**2.5**	18.8	17.1	**8.1**
3.6	2.91	na	0.36	**9.1**	2.4	2.04	15.53	4.57	56.6	**0.8**	21.0	43.3	**8.2**
8.9	0.00	na	0.03	**7.1**	1.9	1.67	13.79	4.02	61.2	**4.2**	24.9	8.3	**8.6**
8.6	0.11	0.9	0.12	**7.3**	2.9	1.79	21.06	4.37	60.1	**3.0**	20.7	14.7	**6.6**
7.9	0.00	na	-0.02	**5.8**	2.1	1.46	17.86	3.45	54.1	**1.8**	18.7	20.6	**5.7**
3.5	6.30	17.7	0.00	**4.3**	0.7	0.98	5.80	3.92	72.1	**2.8**	27.7	17.0	**6.6**
5.2	4.31	na	-0.02	**1.5**	0.0	0.24	3.02	2.77	86.0	**3.5**	42.4	11.7	**1.0**
9.2	0.00	na	0.00	**6.7**	0.6	1.33	4.35	3.24	42.7	**3.8**	75.4	24.5	**8.4**
4.5	0.69	na	0.04	**5.5**	1.3	1.32	13.49	4.06	61.8	**1.1**	8.7	28.6	**6.8**
4.3	1.88	na	0.62	**6.8**	1.0	1.60	19.01	4.51	63.7	**5.1**	41.1	9.7	**4.2**
4.9	3.32	na	0.19	**9.3**	2.7	1.91	19.04	4.43	44.0	**0.7**	9.7	39.6	**8.4**
7.8	0.12	na	0.07	**5.3**	1.2	1.32	12.38	3.36	64.1	**3.1**	23.3	14.4	**6.8**
4.0	0.53	15.0	0.11	**1.4**	0.1	0.07	0.91	3.72	97.4	**5.1**	28.3	4.5	**3.4**
7.8	0.38	2.9	0.01	**4.0**	7.5	0.96	9.91	3.27	82.4	**1.5**	9.8	10.4	**8.5**
6.4	0.72	3.6	0.09	**8.0**	10.9	1.25	10.51	3.98	61.3	**0.7**	12.8	49.1	**10.0**
9.8	0.13	na	0.06	**3.2**	0.7	0.65	4.29	2.85	80.1	**4.2**	75.9	22.4	**7.9**
8.7	0.59	na	0.00	**3.6**	0.9	0.65	4.33	3.38	75.7	**1.2**	29.7	36.4	**7.9**
3.0	9.90	na	-0.38	**1.3**	0.1	0.15	1.66	3.71	94.8	**3.8**	41.1	16.4	**1.9**
7.7	0.58	1.6	0.02	**4.4**	1.1	1.02	10.39	3.87	74.8	**5.1**	40.2	9.5	**3.2**

Name	City	State	Rating	2018 Rating	2017 Rating	Total Assets ($Mil)	One Year Asset Growth	Asset Mix (As a % of Total Assets) Comm-ercial Loans	Cons-umer Loans	Mort-gage Loans	Secur-ities	Capital-ization Index	Lever-age Ratio	Risk-Based Capital Ratio
▲ Community Bank	Dunlap	IA	**B**	B	C+	89.1	0.70	2.6	3.9	16.8	12.6	**10.0**	13.0	16.9
Community Bank	Winslow	IL	**B+**	B+	B	217.3	5.17	6.3	1.4	19.9	33.6	**10.0**	14.3	25.6
▲ Community Bank	Liberal	KS	**B-**	C+	B	122.5	5.79	9.0	15.8	0.1	26.5	**10.0**	11.9	17.1
Community Bank	Topeka	KS	**B**	B	B	102.3	11.28	9.4	1.4	24.7	5.2	**6.2**	10.2	11.9
▲ Community Bank	Zanesville	OH	**B-**	C+	C+	454.4	4.67	6.9	4.9	37.5	13.3	**7.8**	9.6	15.8
Community Bank	Alva	OK	**A-**	A-	A-	107.2	2.85	10.9	2.0	5.4	52.3	**10.0**	12.0	19.4
▲ Community Bank	Bristow	OK	**A-**	B+	B+	88.2	4.00	5.8	4.2	32.8	9.1	**8.1**	9.7	16.2
▲ Community Bank	Joseph	OR	**B+**	B	B-	421.4	4.07	3.0	0.4	3.1	43.2	**8.5**	10.0	22.0
Community Bank	Carmichaels	PA	**B-**	B-	B-	1326.2	5.80	5.4	8.5	24.3	16.2	**6.1**	8.1	13.1
Community Bank	Avon	SD	**B-**	B	B	54.1	1.95	10.6	6.2	6.0	35.9	**10.0**	15.6	28.9
Community Bank	Lexington	TN	**B**	B	B	163.9	8.01	9.0	3.8	29.2	13.0	**7.9**	9.6	13.9
▲ Community Bank	Bridgeport	TX	**B-**	C+	C+	98.1	14.88	14.7	2.5	18.6	9.8	**8.9**	10.2	15.4
Community Bank	Longview	TX	**A**	A	A-	220.6	3.40	12.2	3.1	35.8	1.4	**10.0**	11.2	17.1
Community Bank & Trust	Ashland City	TN	**B**	B	B-	256.5	12.29	5.4	1.3	14.5	23.4	**9.7**	10.8	17.0
Community Bank & Trust - Alabama	Union Springs	AL	**D-**	D-	D-	45.6	-0.99	6.6	5.9	13.7	41.6	**6.7**	8.8	22.1
Community Bank & Trust - West Georgia	LaGrange	GA	**D-**	D-	E+	76.4	-9.66	6.5	1.5	19.3	11.2	**0.0**	3.1	6.0
▲ Community Bank & Trust, Waco, Texas	Waco	TX	**A-**	B+	A-	460.1	2.70	21.8	2.6	24.6	24.5	**10.0**	15.4	22.4
Community Bank and Trust	Neosho	MO	**B-**	B-	B-	311.2	-0.36	5.6	1.7	16.9	13.2	**6.4**	8.4	17.8
Community Bank and Trust Co.	Muscatine	IA	**D+**	C	C	229.9	-4.50	8.5	3.7	12.4	21.9	**7.6**	9.4	14.4
Community Bank Delaware	Lewes	DE	**B-**	B	B	202.8	2.42	2.7	0.4	37.5	4.7	**8.4**	9.9	14.4
Community Bank Mankato	Vernon Center	MN	**C-**	C	C	315.0	5.68	6.8	1.9	15.6	0.3	**5.4**	8.8	11.3
Community Bank of Cameron	Cameron	WI	**B**	B-	B	122.1	3.80	3.5	2.8	34.4	6.0	**7.5**	9.4	14.0
Community Bank of Easton	Easton	IL	**B+**	B+	A-	36.2	6.74	23.0	11.7	3.2	1.4	**10.0**	21.2	27.7
▲ Community Bank of El Dorado Springs	El Dorado Springs	MO	**A-**	B+	A	106.2	4.86	1.8	2.2	9.3	32.0	**10.0**	16.0	33.3
Community Bank of Elmhurst	Elmhurst	IL	**B-**	B-	C	145.8	1.06	6.0	0.2	12.9	40.6	**8.9**	10.3	17.1
Community Bank of Georgia	Baxley	GA	**C**	C+	B	126.8	49.54	6.4	1.4	11.0	5.7	**8.2**	10.9	13.5
Community Bank of Louisiana	Mansfield	LA	**B**	B	B	496.5	3.03	3.8	1.6	11.8	45.2	**7.1**	9.1	19.9
Community Bank of Marshall	Marshall	MO	**B**	B	B-	153.0	3.45	4.2	2.8	12.3	42.4	**10.0**	11.7	21.6
Community Bank of Memphis	Memphis	MO	**B-**	B-	B-	45.2	-5.40	2.5	3.5	15.0	22.7	**10.0**	12.6	23.4
Community Bank of Mississippi	Forest	MS	**B-**	B-	B-	3292.9	2.93	5.9	2.7	24.0	22.7	**6.2**	8.3	14.6
▲ Community Bank of Missouri	Richmond	MO	**B+**	B	B	53.1	0.92	4.8	1.3	21.9	4.3	**10.0**	14.4	20.3
Community Bank of Oelwein	Oelwein	IA	**B**	B	B	107.2	-0.60	7.3	3.1	9.9	34.1	**10.0**	12.6	22.7
Community Bank of Oklahoma	Verden	OK	**B-**	B-	B-	41.0	-7.63	17.0	6.5	4.5	11.7	**10.0**	13.9	18.3
Community Bank of Parkersburg	Parkersburg	WV	**B+**	B+	A-	253.3	7.01	3.0	7.2	56.7	11.4	**9.8**	10.8	17.8
Community Bank of Pickens County	Jasper	GA	**C**	C-	C-	361.1	3.56	4.8	2.0	16.6	9.5	**10.0**	11.9	16.9
Community Bank of Pleasant Hill	Pleasant Hill	MO	**B+**	B+	B+	82.3	14.79	9.8	1.2	6.8	35.4	**8.4**	9.9	17.4
Community Bank of Raymore	Raymore	MO	**B+**	B+	B+	271.4	10.42	16.1	0.6	2.0	28.9	**6.3**	8.3	13.1
▲ Community Bank of Santa Maria	Santa Maria	CA	**A-**	B+	B-	263.9	9.54	10.6	0.3	0.3	17.0	**9.7**	11.3	14.7
▲ Community Bank of Snyder	Snyder	TX	**C**	C	C-	110.3	0.57	1.6	2.1	4.8	23.0	**10.0**	11.6	30.0
Community Bank of the Bay	Oakland	CA	**B**	B-	B	491.4	19.80	20.5	0.1	5.0	3.0	**8.2**	12.0	13.5
Community Bank of the Chesapeake	Waldorf	MD	**B-**	B-	B	1854.3	10.83	5.1	0.1	15.4	11.9	**7.9**	10.6	13.3
Community Bank of the Midwest	Great Bend	KS	**B-**	B	B	177.2	-1.80	13.5	2.8	7.7	8.1	**6.5**	10.6	12.1
▲ Community Bank of the South	Merritt Island	FL	**B+**	C+	C	154.2	-2.57	3.6	0.9	5.9	21.5	**9.2**	10.4	26.3
▲ Community Bank of Trenton	Trenton	IL	**B**	B-	C+	84.5	4.38	7.6	4.0	29.6	13.3	**10.0**	11.9	17.8
Community Bank of Wichita, Inc.	Wichita	KS	**C+**	B-	B-	84.1	11.07	19.3	4.4	17.9	9.7	**7.1**	9.6	12.6
Community Bank Owatonna	Owatonna	MN	**C+**	C+	C+	59.4	4.55	10.7	1.4	18.9	13.4	**7.2**	9.2	13.1
Community Bank, N.A.	De Witt	NY	**B+**	B+	B+	11391.5	9.00	5.2	11.2	23.6	21.4	**6.7**	8.8	14.4
▲ Community Bankers' Bank	Midlothian	VA	**C+**	C-	C-	140.8	7.43	9.1	0.9	4.6	17.0	**10.0**	13.3	16.1
▲ Community Banking Co. of Fitzgerald	Fitzgerald	GA	**A-**	B+	A-	160.1	5.69	6.2	9.7	23.9	9.6	**10.0**	11.7	16.8
Community Banks of Shelby County	Cowden	IL	**C+**	C+	C	46.4	-0.48	9.5	3.5	11.4	20.8	**10.0**	11.9	22.5
Community Commerce Bank	Claremont	CA	**B+**	B+	B	276.8	15.46	0.0	12.7	6.0	0.1	**10.0**	19.1	25.7
Community Development Bank, FSB	Ogema	MN	**C+**	B-	B-	168.2	-1.88	8.2	2.9	11.9	15.8	**9.3**	10.5	14.8
Community Federal Savings Bank	New York	NY	**C-**	D	D-	175.6	11.64	4.4	6.7	19.0	5.3	**6.6**	8.6	15.9
▲ Community Financial Bank	Prentice	WI	**C+**	C+	C+	46.5	12.56	5.0	1.6	31.2	0.0	**9.0**	10.3	18.1
Community Financial Services Bank	Benton	KY	**C+**	C+	C+	1228.7	8.72	13.9	11.5	18.4	10.3	**6.1**	9.2	11.9
▲ Community First Bank	Kansas City	KS	**B+**	B	B	191.9	7.10	16.9	0.7	11.8	2.5	**6.7**	9.9	12.3
Community First Bank	New Iberia	LA	**B-**	B	B+	392.7	2.23	11.9	3.5	23.4	8.9	**8.9**	10.3	15.2
Community First Bank	Menahga	MN	**A-**	A-	A-	89.9	1.51	9.0	5.4	16.5	22.7	**10.0**	15.2	27.8
▲ Community First Bank	Butler	MO	**B**	B	B-	172.9	0.78	11.1	3.6	20.5	5.7	**7.6**	9.4	13.4
▼ Community First Bank	Maywood	NE	**D-**	D	D	122.0	-5.83	5.8	1.9	5.8	17.4	**8.9**	11.7	14.1

Asset Quality Index	Adjusted Non-Performing Loans as a % of Total Loans	Adjusted Non-Performing Loans as a % of Capital	Net Charge-Offs Avg Loans	Profitability Index	Net Income ($Mil)	Return on Assets (R.O.A.)	Return on Equity (R.O.E.)	Net Interest Spread	Overhead Efficiency Ratio	Liquidity Index	Liquidity Ratio	Hot Money Ratio	Stability Index
4.8	1.76	4.7	0.14	**4.0**	0.6	0.80	5.84	4.13	81.6	**4.0**	9.7	8.0	**7.1**
8.9	0.34	na	0.25	**5.3**	2.0	1.26	9.05	2.91	53.0	**2.7**	36.3	20.7	**8.2**
4.5	3.40	na	0.04	**6.0**	1.1	1.20	10.39	4.26	66.6	**1.6**	22.8	24.9	**7.2**
8.7	0.00	0.0	-0.11	**8.3**	1.2	1.64	16.32	4.30	58.1	**2.8**	15.4	15.0	**6.5**
4.3	2.07	na	0.03	**5.4**	4.0	1.17	12.19	4.13	68.9	**2.9**	9.5	13.9	**5.6**
8.8	0.08	na	-0.04	**5.3**	1.0	1.24	10.28	3.11	59.4	**1.8**	38.5	40.2	**8.0**
8.6	0.06	na	0.12	**10.0**	1.4	2.09	23.39	5.05	52.6	**3.7**	28.3	12.7	**7.1**
8.4	0.41	na	0.03	**5.2**	4.9	1.56	16.10	3.95	74.3	**6.3**	57.8	7.2	**6.5**
5.3	0.79	4.5	0.05	**4.8**	9.6	0.98	9.13	3.64	68.2	**3.5**	11.4	11.5	**8.0**
3.7	5.72	na	0.31	**2.9**	0.2	0.49	3.14	3.48	81.6	**2.8**	42.6	24.0	**7.0**
6.9	0.12	na	0.08	**4.7**	1.1	0.90	9.48	4.06	71.2	**0.8**	16.1	38.1	**5.9**
7.3	0.04	na	0.15	**4.1**	0.5	0.73	7.04	4.87	72.8	**3.4**	25.7	13.4	**4.8**
8.6	0.00	0.7	0.00	**9.7**	4.2	2.52	22.90	3.98	41.7	**2.5**	17.9	16.7	**8.6**
6.4	0.34	na	-0.20	**5.1**	2.0	1.06	10.14	3.78	79.4	**1.7**	19.4	22.9	**6.5**
4.3	2.96	na	-0.31	**2.9**	0.2	0.57	7.63	3.64	90.2	**2.6**	46.3	29.6	**1.7**
0.3	3.64	54.7	-0.02	**0.0**	-0.9	-1.44	-39.91	4.98	139.4	**5.0**	28.1	5.0	**0.8**
8.6	0.35	1.5	0.23	**5.8**	4.1	1.23	8.25	3.91	66.7	**2.7**	33.8	19.4	**7.1**
8.1	0.29	na	0.07	**4.3**	2.5	1.06	11.53	3.48	80.0	**6.0**	35.9	1.7	**5.4**
3.2	1.21	na	1.19	**1.7**	0.2	0.12	1.04	3.83	76.6	**3.7**	35.2	15.0	**4.7**
7.6	0.52	na	0.01	**3.7**	1.0	0.63	6.40	3.21	75.3	**0.6**	10.1	44.7	**6.1**
3.1	0.97	na	0.13	**5.5**	2.3	1.00	11.75	4.00	62.1	**1.6**	9.7	21.4	**5.0**
6.3	0.60	na	0.00	**6.3**	1.4	1.52	16.42	4.22	63.7	**2.4**	18.3	14.5	**6.9**
7.4	0.00	na	0.00	**10.0**	0.8	3.04	14.99	4.80	16.6	**3.6**	27.7	12.9	**9.3**
8.0	1.68	na	0.03	**7.6**	1.4	1.72	10.31	3.06	46.8	**4.5**	62.9	18.0	**10.0**
5.5	2.87	na	0.54	**4.3**	1.1	0.96	9.63	3.75	70.3	**5.8**	42.6	5.7	**4.7**
3.3	1.90	na	-0.17	**9.3**	1.3	1.60	14.06	5.18	47.3	**0.7**	16.4	40.7	**7.2**
9.1	0.30	na	-0.01	**6.3**	6.1	1.62	18.47	3.43	57.0	**2.2**	23.7	18.7	**6.3**
9.1	0.21	na	-0.03	**4.8**	1.2	1.08	9.25	3.07	60.8	**4.7**	37.0	10.4	**6.8**
8.1	0.02	na	-0.01	**5.1**	0.4	1.03	7.63	3.45	55.2	**3.1**	40.9	19.5	**6.7**
6.6	0.54	4.6	0.12	**4.8**	22.1	0.89	10.34	3.52	69.9	**1.8**	19.5	22.8	**7.2**
8.2	0.56	na	0.00	**7.1**	0.6	1.49	10.68	5.52	68.6	**3.5**	12.5	11.1	**7.3**
8.4	0.00	na	0.16	**4.8**	0.9	1.05	8.61	2.84	53.3	**2.4**	53.3	53.6	**6.9**
7.1	12.08	na	0.00	**6.7**	0.5	1.62	12.30	5.17	69.6	**3.2**	19.1	13.6	**6.3**
7.8	0.73	na	-0.01	**5.5**	2.4	1.27	11.63	3.98	71.9	**2.9**	9.1	13.7	**7.5**
4.9	3.97	na	0.15	**8.3**	4.4	1.64	14.37	4.13	53.5	**0.8**	19.2	40.4	**6.3**
7.8	0.00	na	0.06	**4.8**	0.6	0.97	9.74	3.03	73.1	**7.0**	57.7	0.7	**6.0**
8.1	0.24	na	0.00	**9.5**	5.0	2.58	31.12	3.46	51.8	**5.1**	29.2	4.5	**6.7**
8.6	0.27	na	-0.01	**6.2**	2.1	1.11	10.11	4.66	67.3	**4.8**	28.8	6.3	**6.6**
9.2	0.23	na	0.29	**3.4**	0.7	0.83	7.37	3.07	83.6	**5.5**	74.8	14.2	**5.4**
6.3	0.20	na	-0.04	**4.9**	3.0	0.93	7.74	4.32	64.6	**2.4**	19.5	17.6	**6.1**
4.0	1.14	7.9	0.10	**5.3**	13.8	1.07	9.54	3.43	55.7	**2.0**	17.7	16.0	**8.6**
8.1	0.21	na	0.90	**6.4**	1.9	1.50	14.24	4.05	51.3	**5.0**	35.8	8.3	**6.4**
8.4	0.00	na	-0.10	**6.6**	1.7	1.48	14.71	3.89	55.1	**5.9**	59.8	10.3	**6.0**
4.2	3.44	15.6	-0.03	**5.2**	0.8	1.33	11.07	3.47	64.2	**2.0**	20.5	19.7	**6.3**
4.7	1.36	na	0.00	**4.7**	0.5	0.84	9.02	4.60	75.5	**1.4**	16.3	27.0	**5.1**
7.3	0.65	2.8	0.00	**3.3**	0.3	0.56	6.14	3.73	81.5	**1.9**	25.7	21.1	**5.0**
6.2	0.39	1.8	0.14	**6.6**	104.9	1.31	9.18	3.84	60.7	**4.9**	18.7	3.8	**10.0**
8.5	0.00	na	0.21	**2.7**	0.5	0.49	3.64	3.11	87.7	**0.8**	18.6	17.4	**6.6**
6.3	0.81	na	0.14	**7.3**	1.8	1.47	11.59	4.40	55.3	**1.9**	15.4	19.5	**8.2**
8.7	0.17	na	-0.03	**3.1**	0.2	0.64	5.52	3.02	80.4	**4.1**	40.8	14.6	**5.9**
5.9	1.34	3.1	-0.10	**4.5**	1.4	0.68	3.52	3.31	72.3	**0.7**	22.9	73.3	**8.3**
3.9	1.85	8.3	0.28	**3.5**	0.6	0.49	3.81	3.81	80.3	**3.3**	23.4	13.2	**6.5**
8.2	0.13	0.5	0.00	**2.5**	0.8	0.62	6.80	3.48	90.3	**1.2**	28.6	35.8	**3.8**
8.4	0.38	na	0.00	**3.4**	0.2	0.69	6.85	3.10	77.5	**1.4**	31.0	33.9	**5.8**
1.9	3.14	na	0.16	**4.0**	6.9	0.76	8.40	3.43	67.8	**1.2**	10.0	24.2	**7.7**
8.4	0.00	na	0.00	**9.3**	2.3	1.63	17.16	4.75	54.4	**0.4**	2.6	49.6	**6.9**
5.6	0.88	na	0.03	**7.2**	5.0	1.68	17.04	4.53	62.0	**1.6**	16.2	23.1	**8.3**
8.1	0.57	na	0.02	**6.6**	1.1	1.64	10.30	4.13	62.6	**4.8**	46.2	10.7	**9.0**
5.1	0.66	na	0.37	**7.8**	2.5	1.90	20.41	4.36	51.9	**1.1**	10.3	26.6	**7.2**
0.0	6.64	na	0.03	**4.3**	0.6	0.63	5.04	4.77	74.7	**1.4**	5.9	17.4	**6.9**

Name	City	State	Rating	2018 Rating	2017 Rating	Total Assets ($Mil)	One Year Asset Growth	Asset Mix (As a % of Total Assets) Commercial Loans	Consumer Loans	Mortgage Loans	Securities	Capitalization Index	Leverage Ratio	Risk-Based Capital Ratio
Community First Bank	Walhalla	SC	**C**	C	C-	419.9	11.45	2.3	24.0	10.1	10.7	**9.3**	10.7	14.4
Community First Bank	Kennewick	WA	**B+**	B+	B+	338.0	11.37	4.7	0.8	10.1	16.1	**8.5**	10.0	15.7
Community First Bank	Boscobel	WI	**B+**	B+	B	427.5	3.27	8.7	1.4	16.6	21.1	**9.3**	10.6	15.0
▲ Community First Bank	Rosholt	WI	**B**	B-	C+	83.2	1.35	3.2	1.5	15.0	28.4	**9.3**	10.6	16.1
Community First Bank of Indiana	Kokomo	IN	**B-**	B-	B	298.1	12.37	15.0	1.4	10.6	2.3	**6.6**	10.9	12.2
Community First Bank of the Heartland	Mount Vernon	IL	**B**	B	B+	203.4	7.76	10.8	0.4	10.3	8.2	**5.9**	8.8	11.7
Community First Bank, N.A.	Forest	OH	**C-**	C-	C-	48.8	-8.28	7.2	1.9	29.2	13.7	**9.4**	10.6	19.3
Community First Banking Co.	West Plains	MO	**A-**	A-	A	190.6	7.43	6.9	3.9	24.9	22.2	**10.0**	11.8	17.7
Community First National Bank	Manhattan	KS	**C+**	C+	B-	294.4	10.65	11.8	2.1	19.7	0.0	**5.3**	9.2	11.3
▲ Community National B&T of Texas	Corsicana	TX	**B+**	B-	B+	746.5	0.17	5.9	1.5	12.3	11.6	**8.5**	10.1	13.7
Community National Bank	Seneca	KS	**B+**	A-	A-	475.1	8.52	3.1	0.4	6.1	57.2	**6.7**	8.7	18.4
Community National Bank	Monett	MO	**B+**	B+	B+	136.0	16.65	5.2	3.7	19.2	9.9	**7.5**	9.3	16.5
Community National Bank	Dayton	TN	**C+**	C+	B-	266.0	19.16	3.9	1.8	17.6	14.0	**9.0**	10.3	16.1
▲ Community National Bank	Hondo	TX	**B+**	B	B	212.6	4.17	6.6	1.9	8.9	24.6	**9.2**	10.5	17.0
Community National Bank	Midland	TX	**B+**	B	C+	1381.3	7.79	22.7	1.3	6.1	13.2	**8.9**	10.3	15.3
▲ Community National Bank	Newport	VT	**B-**	C+	B-	728.7	5.00	11.8	0.6	23.3	4.6	**8.2**	9.8	14.3
Community National Bank & Trust	Chanute	KS	**B-**	B-	B-	1259.5	9.57	8.6	2.8	16.5	14.1	**6.7**	8.8	12.3
Community National Bank in Monmouth	Monmouth	IL	**D**	D+	C	41.0	5.45	6.7	6.9	16.1	16.6	**10.0**	15.7	24.9
Community National Bank of Okarche	Okarche	OK	**A**	A	A	116.3	6.85	6.3	2.4	5.4	53.1	**10.0**	13.5	27.1
▲ Community Neighbor Bank	Camden	AL	**A-**	B+	A-	103.5	-2.30	13.7	8.0	16.6	16.5	**10.0**	15.7	24.4
▲ Community Partners Savings Bank	Salem	IL	**C+**	C	C	202.9	14.79	4.4	19.6	29.5	9.6	**10.0**	11.2	18.3
Community Point Bank	Russellville	MO	**B-**	B-	C+	139.2	9.14	5.3	3.2	22.2	11.6	**7.9**	9.6	13.7
Community Resource Bank	Northfield	MN	**A-**	A-	B-	309.6	2.80	10.0	0.9	18.5	11.4	**10.0**	12.6	16.6
Community Savings	Caldwell	OH	**D**	D	D	51.2	2.96	0.0	16.2	47.9	9.5	**10.0**	14.0	26.8
▼ Community Savings Bank	Edgewood	IA	**D**	C-	C	415.1	-0.21	10.4	2.3	9.2	18.6	**7.0**	9.0	12.5
Community Savings Bank	Chicago	IL	**C**	C	C	396.4	2.64	0.0	0.0	35.0	31.8	**10.0**	16.5	38.4
Community Savings Bank	Bethel	OH	**B-**	B	B	82.9	5.39	8.8	0.2	46.9	12.7	**10.0**	16.1	26.6
Community Shores Bank	Muskegon	MI	**C-**	D+	D+	203.8	13.22	25.9	0.5	10.6	8.1	**6.4**	9.0	12.1
Community Spirit Bank	Red Bay	AL	**B**	B	B	149.2	4.68	10.5	5.5	24.6	16.5	**9.9**	10.9	17.2
▲ Community State Bank	Bradley	AR	**C**	C-	D+	22.6	43.06	25.2	5.7	8.0	9.8	**10.0**	11.0	18.8
Community State Bank	Lamar	CO	**A-**	A-	A-	127.7	9.28	13.5	3.1	5.9	9.0	**10.0**	13.5	16.2
▲ Community State Bank	Starke	FL	**C+**	C	C+	125.8	-5.97	7.3	2.3	14.5	30.4	**6.5**	8.5	15.8
▲ Community State Bank	Ankeny	IA	**B+**	B	B+	802.8	9.23	18.1	0.2	8.7	16.8	**7.5**	10.4	12.9
Community State Bank	Paton	IA	**B**	B	B+	43.2	-0.04	3.2	2.3	1.9	51.4	**10.0**	19.6	36.8
Community State Bank	Spencer	IA	**B+**	B+	A-	209.2	4.91	13.4	1.4	4.8	39.2	**7.8**	9.5	18.8
▲ Community State Bank	Galva	IL	**C+**	C	C	237.3	0.32	5.9	1.7	9.7	15.6	**9.5**	10.7	14.6
▲ Community State Bank	Avilla	IN	**A-**	B+	A-	277.7	9.22	16.2	1.6	27.1	9.6	**9.6**	10.8	15.4
Community State Bank	Brook	IN	**B-**	C+	C	67.9	12.73	4.4	1.3	34.9	8.8	**10.0**	13.1	20.0
▲ Community State Bank	Royal Center	IN	**B-**	C+	C-	123.5	3.18	6.3	3.1	16.6	22.0	**10.0**	11.0	17.6
▲ Community State Bank	Coffeyville	KS	**A**	A-	A-	161.3	5.32	10.7	1.0	6.5	33.7	**10.0**	12.0	18.7
Community State Bank	Shelbina	MO	**C+**	B-	B-	78.0	13.77	5.1	11.9	26.5	22.8	**8.1**	9.7	16.8
▲ Community State Bank	Hennessey	OK	**C-**	D	D	68.7	-0.03	9.3	3.7	5.4	49.1	**4.8**	6.8	18.4
Community State Bank	Poteau	OK	**B-**	B-	B-	270.7	3.04	7.7	3.4	21.7	12.4	**7.6**	9.4	14.0
▲ Community State Bank	Union Grove	WI	**B-**	C+	C-	391.3	3.37	17.7	0.5	9.8	22.0	**6.7**	9.7	12.3
Community State Bank of Canton	Canton	OK	**B-**	C+	C+	48.0	0.37	10.7	9.3	5.9	18.5	**10.0**	11.5	16.3
Community State Bank of Missouri	Bowling Green	MO	**B+**	B+	B+	229.3	-3.98	6.6	0.6	19.1	26.4	**9.3**	13.7	14.4
Community State Bank of Orbisonia	Orbisonia	PA	**B**	B	B	328.3	-0.35	2.4	8.1	60.5	4.7	**10.0**	11.8	19.1
Community State Bank of Rock Falls	Rock Falls	IL	**C-**	C	D+	263.5	2.25	10.3	1.9	29.1	12.7	**8.8**	10.2	17.1
▲ Community State Bank Of Southwestern In	Poseyville	IN	**B**	B-	B-	84.3	7.09	12.6	2.0	24.9	3.5	**8.7**	10.2	16.1
Community Trust Bank	Irvington	IL	**B-**	B-	B-	78.2	-0.38	5.1	1.0	10.4	33.7	**10.0**	13.9	26.3
Community Trust Bank, Inc.	Pikeville	KY	**B**	B-	B-	4316.1	3.97	7.4	16.6	19.8	14.8	**10.0**	13.2	19.0
▲ Community Valley Bank	El Centro	CA	**A-**	B+	A-	189.6	4.32	13.0	0.0	4.9	1.1	**10.0**	11.6	15.7
▲ Community West Bank, N.A.	Goleta	CA	**C**	C-	C+	903.1	6.54	4.0	28.0	3.4	3.2	**5.2**	9.0	11.2
CommunityBank of Texas, N.A.	Beaumont	TX	**A-**	A-	B+	3432.1	7.59	15.2	1.1	8.1	6.6	**9.3**	12.0	14.5
▼ Compass Savings Bank	Wilmerding	PA	**D-**	D+	C-	50.9	-15.32	0.2	1.0	76.8	6.7	**7.1**	9.0	22.0
Computershare Trust Co., N.A.	Canton	MA	**U**	U	U	30.6	16.49	0.0	0.0	0.0	0.0	**10.0**	94.9	268.6
Concorde Bank	Blomkest	MN	**C+**	C+	B-	56.7	1.19	7.3	2.8	22.0	3.1	**9.3**	10.5	14.4
Concordia Bank	Concordia	MO	**B+**	B	B	73.7	4.71	3.6	1.4	21.6	10.3	**8.5**	10.7	13.7
Concordia Bank & Trust Co.	Vidalia	LA	**B**	B	B	523.8	5.17	5.0	2.3	13.1	35.4	**10.0**	12.4	18.7
Congressional Bank	Bethesda	MD	**C-**	C-	B-	1102.1	7.97	31.6	2.0	11.3	3.0	**8.5**	11.2	13.8

Arrows denote recent upgrades ▲ or downgrades ▼

Asset Quality Index	Adjusted Non-Performing Loans as a % of Total Loans	Adjusted Non-Performing Loans as a % of Capital	Net Charge-Offs Avg Loans	Profitability Index	Net Income ($Mil)	Return on Assets (R.O.A.)	Return on Equity (R.O.E.)	Net Interest Spread	Overhead Efficiency Ratio	Liquidity Index	Liquidity Ratio	Hot Money Ratio	Stability Index
5.5	1.07	na	0.00	**2.8**	1.1	0.37	3.76	3.79	88.5	**2.0**	19.2	19.5	**5.2**
7.9	0.40	2.1	0.04	**5.3**	3.2	1.32	12.19	3.85	76.5	**5.9**	35.0	1.8	**6.5**
5.0	1.61	7.3	0.01	**5.7**	4.3	1.36	11.50	3.96	66.0	**2.8**	22.3	14.1	**7.5**
8.2	0.25	na	-0.06	**4.6**	0.7	1.10	9.87	4.31	75.5	**6.3**	41.4	1.8	**6.7**
6.1	0.68	na	0.06	**5.7**	2.0	0.94	8.58	4.57	73.3	**1.1**	7.4	17.5	**7.0**
4.0	1.60	na	0.05	**8.0**	3.0	1.99	21.29	4.49	57.3	**1.9**	8.9	13.9	**7.5**
9.2	0.00	na	0.00	**2.4**	0.1	0.31	3.00	3.35	88.7	**5.8**	37.7	3.4	**4.5**
7.5	1.55	na	0.30	**6.2**	2.1	1.47	12.57	3.61	63.5	**3.2**	18.1	10.5	**8.8**
7.0	0.34	na	0.17	**4.6**	2.1	0.99	10.79	3.33	76.0	**0.9**	10.5	31.0	**5.4**
7.3	0.26	na	0.00	**7.8**	8.4	1.53	13.05	4.73	61.0	**3.6**	16.0	11.2	**8.3**
6.8	1.78	na	-0.01	**9.5**	7.8	2.21	25.32	3.40	45.5	**6.1**	48.4	5.4	**7.2**
8.5	0.07	na	0.01	**7.6**	1.8	1.88	19.91	3.93	58.8	**4.4**	33.1	10.7	**7.0**
3.3	1.55	na	-0.13	**4.1**	1.1	0.60	5.51	4.57	87.2	**2.2**	15.2	18.2	**7.3**
7.5	0.46	na	-0.01	**5.4**	2.1	1.31	11.48	4.13	71.1	**4.6**	38.4	11.5	**7.3**
5.5	1.60	7.3	0.32	**9.0**	19.3	1.87	17.31	4.47	46.3	**6.5**	36.1	1.9	**8.2**
4.5	0.93	na	0.11	**6.6**	7.1	1.35	12.26	4.12	61.3	**3.0**	8.5	10.7	**7.9**
4.8	1.41	8.7	0.20	**4.5**	7.8	0.85	8.65	3.91	72.6	**2.5**	11.9	16.5	**8.4**
5.6	1.33	5.4	2.03	**0.2**	-0.1	-0.38	-2.35	3.84	82.4	**4.2**	39.9	14.0	**5.1**
9.0	0.00	na	0.00	**7.6**	1.6	1.80	13.56	3.29	46.1	**0.7**	12.6	40.4	**9.4**
5.9	1.15	na	0.15	**7.4**	1.2	1.46	9.72	4.97	66.0	**2.7**	30.9	18.3	**8.6**
3.8	2.00	na	0.22	**3.9**	1.1	0.72	6.31	4.15	74.0	**2.0**	16.1	19.0	**5.3**
8.0	0.08	na	0.00	**4.2**	1.1	1.07	11.52	2.98	62.9	**1.2**	13.2	26.3	**6.2**
5.9	1.49	7.8	-0.18	**7.8**	3.3	1.42	10.71	4.23	57.6	**1.5**	10.3	19.7	**8.3**
5.1	1.94	na	0.08	**0.4**	-0.1	-0.16	-1.18	4.01	105.6	**4.2**	21.7	8.4	**5.6**
5.0	0.89	na	0.54	**0.6**	-0.4	-0.12	-1.24	3.46	84.8	**1.3**	18.9	22.8	**4.7**
8.5	2.71	na	-0.05	**2.5**	0.9	0.31	1.92	2.83	87.5	**3.1**	45.2	22.0	**7.4**
9.1	0.11	na	-0.04	**3.5**	0.4	0.61	3.78	3.74	81.3	**2.0**	19.4	19.3	**7.5**
2.2	3.82	19.8	0.14	**3.5**	0.9	0.58	6.07	3.94	82.5	**2.9**	20.6	12.6	**4.7**
8.2	1.13	na	0.13	**4.3**	0.9	0.80	7.36	4.41	77.9	**1.3**	21.8	29.0	**5.5**
7.2	0.00	na	-0.08	**4.5**	0.1	0.77	5.41	4.24	70.2	**2.5**	44.5	23.4	**4.3**
6.9	0.05	0.3	-0.12	**8.6**	1.9	2.09	15.82	4.69	51.5	**0.5**	8.0	48.2	**9.9**
3.7	2.20	na	0.16	**3.3**	0.5	0.46	5.17	4.22	86.0	**5.0**	25.9	3.6	**4.1**
7.9	0.10	na	-0.02	**6.0**	7.9	1.32	11.60	4.29	63.5	**3.0**	23.5	10.3	**7.9**
8.9	0.00	na	-0.15	**5.3**	0.4	1.19	6.24	3.18	52.7	**4.0**	65.7	19.4	**6.9**
8.5	0.02	na	0.02	**6.4**	2.2	1.44	13.27	3.54	52.7	**2.8**	30.4	9.4	**7.2**
4.0	2.14	na	0.00	**6.3**	2.4	1.40	12.77	4.10	59.6	**0.7**	8.7	25.4	**7.2**
8.2	0.48	na	0.03	**8.4**	3.2	1.54	14.32	4.48	55.9	**4.1**	19.5	8.5	**7.8**
4.4	5.52	na	0.12	**6.1**	0.6	1.23	9.70	4.06	59.5	**1.1**	26.4	27.7	**5.4**
4.1	2.32	11.7	0.01	**4.7**	0.9	0.96	8.46	4.08	72.5	**4.2**	15.0	7.1	**6.9**
8.7	3.68	na	-0.01	**8.4**	2.2	1.76	15.15	3.95	48.5	**4.5**	11.6	4.9	**8.0**
4.8	2.53	na	0.22	**7.3**	0.8	1.42	15.86	3.38	43.5	**2.6**	14.0	10.9	**6.0**
3.4	4.08	na	1.67	**5.4**	0.7	1.36	20.83	4.09	63.7	**6.7**	52.4	1.2	**3.6**
3.8	1.83	12.8	0.21	**5.0**	2.5	1.19	12.95	4.72	72.7	**0.8**	17.4	31.3	**6.3**
6.3	2.33	na	-0.04	**5.6**	3.9	1.32	14.43	4.11	70.5	**4.3**	25.1	7.2	**5.8**
7.8	0.24	na	0.65	**6.2**	0.4	1.12	10.01	4.91	72.0	**2.9**	11.5	14.0	**5.9**
8.0	0.21	na	0.00	**5.4**	2.4	1.37	10.49	3.43	63.0	**2.8**	14.1	15.0	**8.6**
5.1	2.25	na	0.10	**4.2**	1.8	0.75	6.42	3.93	78.1	**1.5**	6.6	21.8	**6.6**
2.4	3.25	na	0.38	**4.6**	1.7	0.88	8.48	3.64	62.9	**2.1**	15.9	18.5	**5.9**
7.8	0.00	na	0.13	**5.3**	0.8	1.34	13.56	4.10	67.9	**4.0**	29.0	11.4	**6.4**
5.7	3.13	na	2.14	**3.8**	0.5	0.75	5.46	3.82	77.0	**5.7**	44.9	6.4	**6.8**
4.0	2.07	8.7	0.17	**6.7**	44.8	1.39	9.81	3.71	59.6	**2.1**	9.7	17.3	**10.0**
5.7	1.17	na	0.17	**7.4**	1.9	1.32	11.60	5.01	59.3	**2.3**	16.2	17.4	**7.2**
3.4	1.26	na	-0.02	**4.9**	5.3	0.82	9.51	4.05	71.9	**0.6**	6.9	22.7	**6.2**
6.6	0.33	1.0	0.03	**7.7**	38.9	1.56	11.15	4.49	57.3	**3.6**	15.6	7.1	**10.0**
8.4	0.00	na	0.00	**0.0**	-0.5	-1.13	-12.72	1.60	248.1	**0.7**	13.5	45.0	**3.7**
6.5	na	na	na	**10.0**	4.8	22.50	24.51	2.14	63.0	**4.0**	na	0.0	**6.6**
2.8	2.92	na	0.00	**5.8**	0.6	1.33	12.70	4.85	67.1	**2.7**	22.9	16.2	**6.8**
3.1	6.10	na	0.00	**4.7**	0.5	0.90	8.77	4.36	72.5	**4.2**	14.1	5.6	**6.5**
7.0	0.34	na	0.10	**4.5**	4.3	1.13	8.97	3.48	70.2	**1.4**	14.8	25.6	**8.2**
1.9	3.59	na	0.08	**6.4**	6.1	0.79	5.81	5.35	77.3	**1.4**	21.6	15.2	**9.4**

Name	City	State	Rating	2018 Rating	2017 Rating	Total Assets ($Mil)	One Year Asset Growth	Asset Mix (As a % of Total Assets): Commercial Loans	Consumer Loans	Mortgage Loans	Securities	Capitalization Index	Leverage Ratio	Risk-Based Capital Ratio
Conneaut Savings Bank	Conneaut	OH	**C**	C	C	77.1	1.64	1.5	0.5	50.9	22.8	**10.0**	14.7	33.2
Connect Bank	Star City	AR	**B+**	A-	A-	98.3	3.95	10.9	1.4	17.0	22.9	**10.0**	15.9	23.0
Connecticut Community Bank, N.A.	Norwalk	CT	**C**	C	D	424.4	-4.65	24.8	0.1	3.7	2.4	**9.0**	10.4	16.3
Connection Bank	Fort Madison	IA	**B-**	B-	B-	308.0	10.44	12.4	2.0	31.7	8.5	**6.0**	8.8	11.7
Connections Bank	Kirksville	MO	**B**	C+	B-	88.7	69.79	3.2	1.0	38.2	10.7	**10.0**	11.1	16.8
ConnectOne Bank	Englewood Cliffs	NJ	**C+**	C	C-	6161.1	14.77	12.2	0.0	8.3	6.9	**7.0**	10.7	12.5
▲ Consumers National Bank	Minerva	OH	**B**	B-	C+	563.5	10.59	9.0	1.0	10.8	24.8	**6.9**	8.9	12.5
▲ Continental Bank	Salt Lake City	UT	**B**	B-	B+	153.0	-9.34	70.8	0.0	0.0	8.4	**10.0**	17.2	20.9
Converse County Bank	Douglas	WY	**B+**	B	B	629.8	10.72	7.9	4.5	5.5	58.5	**7.6**	9.4	25.9
Conway Bank	Conway Springs	KS	**D+**	D+	C-	98.7	-1.71	8.1	1.0	16.1	9.1	**5.5**	7.5	14.3
▲ Conway National Bank	Conway	SC	**B+**	B	B	1250.1	4.46	5.0	4.0	13.1	49.9	**8.7**	10.2	20.3
Cooperative Bank	Roslindale	MA	**C+**	C+	C+	439.2	4.32	2.0	1.0	44.6	9.7	**8.1**	9.7	14.4
Cooperative Bank of Cape Cod	Hyannis	MA	**C+**	C+	C+	958.7	3.62	2.9	0.1	52.9	5.6	**8.7**	10.1	16.1
Copiah Bank	Hazlehurst	MS	**B-**	B-	B-	233.2	2.26	8.4	2.9	19.0	10.6	**8.5**	10.0	14.1
▲ Corder Bank	Corder	MO	**C**	C-	D+	19.6	4.81	11.9	5.8	18.5	5.1	**10.0**	11.4	18.6
Core Bank	Omaha	NE	**C+**	B-	B-	601.2	13.68	19.1	0.4	15.6	4.8	**4.7**	8.1	10.9
▲ COREBANK	Waynoka	OK	**C-**	D	D-	62.7	61.32	15.7	0.4	23.5	8.3	**10.0**	12.6	19.0
CoreFirst Bank & Trust	Topeka	KS	**C+**	C+	C-	952.0	3.81	12.1	4.4	7.7	25.6	**8.1**	9.7	13.8
Corn City State Bank	Deshler	OH	**B+**	B+	B+	66.4	-3.14	1.1	2.8	28.5	42.1	**10.0**	15.6	38.1
▲ Corn Growers State Bank	Murdock	NE	**D**	D-	D-	25.4	-2.21	4.3	8.6	9.2	17.7	**6.1**	8.1	18.1
Cornerstone Bank	Eureka Springs	AR	**B-**	B-	B	325.0	17.31	5.0	3.9	19.6	10.2	**5.5**	8.2	11.3
Cornerstone Bank	Atlanta	GA	**D**	D+	E	192.8	-10.39	14.2	0.3	16.2	17.7	**9.0**	10.3	18.5
Cornerstone Bank	Clarinda	IA	**C-**	C-	C	41.3	9.63	4.8	6.6	33.9	7.0	**10.0**	13.6	27.7
▲ Cornerstone Bank	Overland Park	KS	**B+**	B	B	231.1	10.26	18.2	0.8	19.3	8.4	**8.1**	9.8	13.4
Cornerstone Bank	Worcester	MA	**C**	C	C	1149.9	-0.07	3.8	0.7	43.9	4.4	**9.0**	10.5	14.1
▲ Cornerstone Bank	South West City	MO	**B-**	C+	B-	140.6	1.13	10.8	9.6	27.1	11.7	**10.0**	14.4	22.2
▲ Cornerstone Bank	Fargo	ND	**C**	C	C-	969.8	9.18	9.5	2.3	10.4	19.4	**6.7**	8.7	12.6
Cornerstone Bank	York	NE	**B+**	B+	B-	1666.5	2.93	15.9	1.5	3.0	14.6	**8.3**	10.4	13.6
Cornerstone Bank	Mount Laurel	NJ	**D**	D	D-	258.8	-2.13	5.7	0.0	30.7	14.3	**4.6**	6.6	11.5
Cornerstone Bank	Watonga	OK	**C+**	C	C	211.4	4.16	5.7	3.9	8.4	48.9	**6.2**	8.2	16.6
Cornerstone Bank, Inc.	West Union	WV	**B**	B-	B-	191.9	11.26	3.0	1.2	7.6	49.2	**9.6**	10.7	27.6
CornerStone Bank, N.A.	Lexington	VA	**B-**	B	B	168.7	11.56	6.6	2.4	24.8	3.0	**8.8**	10.2	15.0
▲ Cornerstone Community Bank	Red Bluff	CA	**B**	B-	B	304.5	20.11	12.8	0.4	3.6	1.8	**6.8**	10.0	12.4
Cornerstone Community Bank	Grafton	WI	**C+**	C+	C+	205.9	6.87	9.0	0.0	11.9	0.1	**5.1**	9.1	11.1
Cornerstone National Bank & Trust Co.	Palatine	IL	**B-**	B-	B+	637.3	13.33	18.9	0.3	7.7	15.2	**5.5**	8.4	11.4
▲ CornerStone State Bank	Montgomery	MN	**A-**	B+	B	171.9	3.11	7.3	4.7	22.2	24.2	**10.0**	11.8	18.3
Cornhusker Bank	Lincoln	NE	**B-**	B-	B-	632.0	6.06	7.6	1.0	16.7	13.3	**7.1**	9.2	12.6
▲ Cortland Savings and Banking Co.	Cortland	OH	**B-**	C	B-	697.4	2.88	11.0	0.6	12.4	19.6	**8.6**	10.1	14.0
CorTrust Bank N.A.	Mitchell	SD	**B-**	B-	B-	1215.1	42.08	11.6	3.4	6.3	18.3	**8.0**	10.8	13.4
Corydon State Bank	Corydon	IA	**B+**	B+	A	100.0	-12.70	9.5	3.0	13.1	15.0	**10.0**	19.6	25.8
Cottonport Bank	Cottonport	LA	**B+**	B+	B	362.3	9.54	7.2	3.3	14.8	15.0	**10.0**	13.0	19.4
Cottonwood Valley Bank	Cedar Point	KS	**C+**	C+	C+	33.7	2.92	9.1	1.8	0.6	28.1	**10.0**	13.8	30.9
Coulee Bank	La Crosse	WI	**C+**	B-	B	386.7	2.16	15.4	1.6	10.3	17.6	**7.1**	9.1	12.9
Country Bank	New York	NY	**C**	C+	B-	786.3	10.66	1.4	0.4	15.2	19.8	**8.0**	9.8	13.3
Country Bank for Savings	Ware	MA	**B**	B	B	1692.9	6.15	1.6	0.5	31.6	19.7	**10.0**	14.3	19.8
Country Club Bank	Kansas City	MO	**A-**	A-	B+	1396.6	-1.38	17.9	0.7	9.4	26.5	**9.4**	10.6	15.3
Country Club Trust Co., N.A.	Kansas City	MO	**U**	U	U	22.9	12.20	0.0	0.0	0.0	86.7	**10.0**	101.	477.4
COUNTRY Trust Bank	Bloomington	IL	**U**	U	U	30.9	6.34	0.0	0.0	0.0	68.3	**10.0**	98.3	134.2
▲ Countryside Bank	Unadilla	NE	**B**	B	B	77.9	4.76	5.5	5.3	17.3	21.7	**10.0**	17.5	29.4
▲ County Bank	Rehoboth Beach	DE	**C+**	C-	C-	378.1	4.15	8.1	7.3	10.8	10.9	**10.0**	12.3	15.5
County Bank	Sigourney	IA	**C**	C+	B	174.4	9.29	12.7	2.2	10.5	5.7	**6.4**	10.0	12.0
County Bank	Brunswick	MO	**B-**	B-	B-	92.5	-3.49	6.4	4.2	23.4	13.2	**6.0**	8.0	13.9
▲ County National Bank	Hillsdale	MI	**B**	B-	B-	724.5	10.47	16.6	4.6	21.1	2.2	**7.6**	9.5	13.0
▲ County Savings Bank	Essington	PA	**C**	C-	D+	83.3	-0.90	0.0	0.2	37.2	9.0	**5.1**	7.1	22.4
Countybank	Greenwood	SC	**B-**	B-	B-	434.7	3.62	5.4	1.4	26.3	25.6	**6.1**	8.1	13.1
▲ Covenant Bank	Doylestown	PA	**B-**	C	D+	512.2	6.71	10.0	0.2	14.7	2.6	**7.8**	10.4	13.2
▲ Covington County Bank	Collins	MS	**C+**	C	C	76.1	-2.29	9.5	3.8	6.3	36.6	**6.9**	9.9	12.4
Covington S&L Assn.	Covington	OH	**B-**	B-	C	70.8	2.45	0.1	0.4	45.2	25.3	**10.0**	15.8	43.1
Cowboy Bank of Texas	Maypearl	TX	**A-**	A-	B+	87.1	9.81	0.7	4.1	25.8	16.2	**10.0**	11.0	17.4
Cowboy State Bank	Ranchester	WY	**D-**	D-	C-	50.0	5.07	4.4	3.6	9.8	19.6	**5.6**	8.0	11.5

Asset Quality Index	Adjusted Non-Performing Loans as a % of Total Loans	Adjusted Non-Performing Loans as a % of Capital	Net Charge-Offs Avg Loans	Profitability Index	Net Income ($Mil)	Return on Assets (R.O.A.)	Return on Equity (R.O.E.)	Net Interest Spread	Overhead Efficiency Ratio	Liquidity Index	Liquidity Ratio	Hot Money Ratio	Stability Index
9.7	0.42	na	0.01	**2.1**	0.1	0.20	1.35	3.18	93.6	**5.2**	40.7	8.9	**6.5**
6.2	2.53	na	0.14	**6.1**	0.9	1.30	8.43	4.47	70.6	**1.8**	24.2	22.3	**8.9**
4.2	2.15	na	0.11	**2.7**	1.4	0.41	4.04	4.12	90.9	**4.4**	28.6	8.7	**4.7**
6.6	0.17	1.6	0.06	**5.1**	2.6	1.16	11.37	3.67	70.2	**2.2**	11.7	7.1	**6.1**
8.2	0.29	na	0.06	**4.6**	0.6	0.84	6.59	4.25	67.3	**0.6**	10.8	35.8	**6.7**
3.2	1.38	7.7	0.10	**5.9**	56.9	1.27	9.95	3.45	47.0	**0.7**	9.5	20.0	**9.3**
7.7	0.23	na	0.00	**4.8**	4.1	1.02	11.27	3.61	70.1	**3.2**	16.3	12.9	**6.4**
4.9	4.70	na	1.19	**9.5**	2.5	2.06	12.17	5.85	59.5	**0.3**	16.0	96.3	**8.5**
9.1	0.01	na	0.14	**7.3**	8.6	1.89	19.87	2.81	42.4	**3.3**	52.8	25.0	**6.6**
2.1	4.66	na	1.35	**0.9**	-0.1	-0.18	-1.99	3.99	83.8	**1.6**	26.6	25.2	**4.9**
8.6	0.64	2.6	0.05	**5.5**	10.4	1.14	11.56	3.20	59.8	**5.1**	46.3	13.8	**8.2**
7.0	0.66	na	0.01	**3.1**	1.5	0.46	4.72	3.15	80.0	**1.4**	13.1	17.6	**6.1**
5.2	1.40	8.2	0.04	**3.7**	4.9	0.70	7.01	3.34	76.6	**3.1**	11.4	13.1	**6.7**
5.5	1.05	na	0.10	**4.5**	1.5	0.88	9.03	4.16	73.5	**2.5**	16.5	16.7	**6.1**
6.6	0.00	na	0.19	**5.4**	0.2	1.20	10.67	4.01	64.7	**4.2**	34.8	10.3	**4.4**
5.9	0.71	na	0.16	**4.2**	2.9	0.68	7.94	4.04	82.7	**3.8**	12.6	9.8	**5.5**
8.5	0.02	na	-0.01	**2.1**	0.2	0.42	2.91	3.61	79.7	**1.0**	27.2	59.6	**4.0**
3.4	2.69	na	0.06	**6.4**	11.1	1.59	16.96	3.54	65.9	**4.8**	14.9	3.7	**5.9**
9.2	0.15	na	0.00	**5.0**	0.7	1.39	9.18	2.84	57.5	**2.5**	35.7	23.2	**8.2**
5.2	0.79	na	-0.05	**2.9**	0.1	0.52	6.59	3.75	85.2	**5.2**	30.0	4.6	**2.5**
7.3	0.58	na	0.01	**5.8**	3.3	1.44	17.65	4.15	66.2	**0.9**	6.7	23.6	**6.0**
2.6	9.07	na	0.79	**0.6**	-0.7	-0.44	-4.55	3.71	104.2	**1.6**	19.6	25.1	**1.8**
7.0	0.44	1.6	0.04	**1.1**	0.0	-0.04	-0.29	2.97	103.0	**2.3**	38.5	29.3	**5.6**
8.4	0.00	na	0.02	**7.0**	2.8	1.67	17.45	3.54	51.5	**5.0**	14.1	2.2	**6.7**
8.3	0.48	2.4	-0.08	**3.2**	4.5	0.53	5.18	3.02	81.3	**1.4**	9.1	22.1	**7.3**
3.8	2.67	na	0.07	**6.7**	1.6	1.53	10.89	5.25	68.5	**0.9**	20.4	32.2	**7.8**
2.9	4.09	18.4	0.09	**4.9**	7.8	1.12	12.68	3.79	70.3	**2.0**	16.4	17.6	**5.9**
6.4	0.67	4.9	0.04	**6.0**	16.9	1.38	13.01	3.78	66.3	**1.1**	12.9	25.0	**8.9**
5.8	0.55	4.6	-0.04	**1.7**	0.5	0.25	3.78	2.95	96.6	**1.9**	26.7	23.3	**1.6**
8.9	0.11	0.4	0.11	**3.7**	1.2	0.75	9.94	3.47	78.0	**5.2**	43.4	9.8	**3.4**
9.5	0.00	na	0.09	**4.4**	1.2	0.94	9.03	1.85	60.1	**3.9**	60.9	21.6	**5.4**
3.2	3.11	na	0.00	**3.4**	0.6	0.49	4.57	3.90	81.0	**0.9**	20.2	35.4	**6.1**
7.4	0.06	na	0.05	**7.5**	2.8	1.36	13.36	4.46	55.5	**1.4**	18.6	21.4	**6.0**
5.3	0.54	na	0.00	**6.1**	1.7	1.10	12.13	3.95	61.0	**1.5**	9.3	18.5	**5.9**
5.3	0.89	na	-0.03	**5.3**	4.3	0.96	10.26	3.67	70.4	**3.9**	29.3	12.1	**6.8**
6.2	0.67	3.1	0.06	**5.7**	1.7	1.29	11.14	3.75	67.9	**4.3**	22.1	7.9	**7.2**
7.0	0.41	na	0.06	**4.8**	5.2	1.13	12.57	3.71	70.7	**2.0**	16.5	15.5	**7.1**
5.7	1.85	na	0.03	**5.8**	6.2	1.19	12.45	3.80	63.2	**2.6**	15.4	10.7	**6.7**
6.6	1.05	na	0.69	**4.1**	4.6	0.65	5.66	4.51	73.4	**3.3**	15.7	12.5	**7.5**
0.6	8.81	na	4.70	**1.9**	-2.2	-2.66	-12.77	3.83	24.1	**1.0**	26.3	32.4	**7.5**
6.0	1.43	na	0.17	**5.9**	3.3	1.27	9.78	4.45	67.2	**2.4**	26.4	18.3	**7.1**
9.5	0.00	na	-0.14	**2.6**	0.2	0.60	4.39	2.70	84.4	**5.0**	65.6	14.4	**6.9**
3.2	2.42	na	0.01	**4.1**	2.8	0.96	10.59	3.33	72.0	**2.8**	11.8	13.9	**6.5**
4.5	1.18	na	0.00	**7.0**	8.0	1.40	13.07	3.81	53.1	**0.8**	16.9	30.5	**7.5**
6.2	1.96	8.8	0.01	**4.0**	8.9	0.71	5.00	3.05	70.8	**2.3**	23.5	16.0	**9.6**
7.4	0.41	2.3	0.02	**6.6**	16.4	1.57	14.87	4.11	74.9	**5.2**	24.0	4.7	**9.5**
10.0	na	na	na	**9.5**	1.4	8.72	8.67	2.04	85.4	**4.0**	na	0.0	**7.0**
10.0	na	na	na	**10.0**	3.2	16.08	15.93	3.74	90.0	**4.0**	na	0.0	**7.0**
8.6	0.00	na	-0.01	**4.2**	0.6	1.01	5.84	3.33	73.7	**5.0**	38.3	9.5	**7.9**
6.2	4.10	na	-0.03	**7.2**	3.8	1.38	11.36	4.65	61.0	**4.9**	23.3	3.5	**7.0**
3.0	1.33	na	0.03	**6.5**	2.0	1.55	15.30	4.40	61.8	**2.2**	8.0	17.3	**7.2**
8.1	0.00	0.0	0.03	**5.0**	0.9	1.22	13.35	4.53	74.8	**3.3**	16.5	12.2	**5.5**
5.2	0.97	na	0.04	**7.0**	7.4	1.43	14.87	4.32	64.1	**3.7**	14.9	10.6	**6.7**
8.7	0.30	na	0.01	**2.9**	0.3	0.47	6.75	3.49	81.7	**5.9**	52.0	6.7	**3.5**
5.7	0.88	na	-0.01	**5.5**	4.2	1.32	16.99	3.74	81.2	**5.1**	18.0	1.6	**5.2**
4.6	0.82	3.2	0.27	**4.8**	3.6	0.98	9.55	3.65	60.1	**1.1**	13.8	28.7	**5.0**
5.4	0.97	4.7	0.43	**3.7**	0.4	0.62	6.75	3.33	75.3	**1.4**	24.9	29.6	**5.1**
10.0	0.32	na	0.00	**3.7**	0.4	0.75	4.72	3.24	72.6	**6.1**	43.6	3.5	**7.8**
7.4	0.31	5.3	0.00	**9.5**	1.5	2.32	22.21	3.87	55.1	**1.4**	17.0	23.2	**8.0**
4.3	3.24	na	0.10	**2.0**	0.1	0.26	3.30	4.52	89.2	**3.2**	32.9	16.6	**2.5**

Name	City	State	Rating	2018 Rating	2017 Rating	Total Assets ($Mil)	One Year Asset Growth	Asset Mix (As a % of Total Assets) Comm-ercial Loans	Cons-umer Loans	Mort-gage Loans	Secur-ities	Capital-ization Index	Lever-age Ratio	Risk-Based Capital Ratio
Crawford County Trust and Savings Bank	Denison	IA	**C+**	C+	B	192.9	1.63	5.7	3.6	10.3	10.7	**8.1**	9.9	13.4
Credit First N.A.	Brook Park	OH	**U**	U	U	31.1	-47.91	0.0	0.0	0.0	0.0	**10.0**	103.	455.3
Credit One Bank, N.A.	Las Vegas	NV	**U**	U	U	547.9	49.50	0.0	54.3	0.0	5.9	**10.0**	43.7	56.4
Crescent Bank & Trust	New Orleans	LA	**C-**	D	D	984.1	0.70	2.9	80.3	2.1	9.2	**10.0**	13.7	16.5
CresCom Bank	Charleston	SC	**A-**	A-	A-	3981.3	6.97	9.2	0.6	19.1	20.1	**10.0**	13.3	17.4
Crest Savings Bank	Wildwood	NJ	**C+**	C+	C+	485.9	-0.36	0.6	3.9	55.9	3.3	**6.1**	8.1	13.8
Crews Bank & Trust	Arcadia	FL	**A-**	A-	B+	154.9	9.28	1.2	2.9	19.9	22.2	**10.0**	12.0	24.9
▲ Crockett National Bank	San Antonio	TX	**A-**	B+	A-	651.6	0.43	3.4	0.1	30.5	3.0	**10.0**	11.9	16.0
Croghan Colonial Bank	Fremont	OH	**B+**	B+	B	878.2	7.69	6.0	9.9	10.3	15.3	**8.1**	11.3	13.4
Cross County Bank	Wynne	AR	**B+**	B+	B+	273.8	8.50	5.6	1.2	11.3	3.9	**10.0**	12.1	15.5
Cross County Savings Bank	Middle Village	NY	**B**	B	B	452.3	6.82	0.0	0.0	51.0	5.9	**10.0**	11.4	18.5
Cross Keys Bank	Saint Joseph	LA	**B+**	B+	B+	376.9	4.41	7.1	1.1	12.5	28.2	**10.0**	11.9	16.3
▲ Cross River Bank	Fort Lee	NJ	**B+**	B	A-	2000.0	69.13	3.1	45.4	4.4	0.9	**10.0**	11.9	16.8
CrossFirst Bank	Leawood	KS	**C+**	C	C	4650.6	25.36	36.1	0.5	6.4	15.7	**7.3**	11.5	12.8
Crossroads Bank	Effingham	IL	**B+**	A-	A-	175.6	6.16	9.2	1.3	9.4	21.1	**10.0**	14.2	18.5
▲ Crossroads Bank	Wabash	IN	**B-**	C+	C+	421.0	7.99	6.5	4.2	28.6	20.3	**7.7**	9.5	14.1
Crossroads Bank	Yoakum	TX	**A-**	A-	A-	210.8	6.47	10.5	7.7	22.9	30.1	**10.0**	12.1	22.6
▲ Crowell State Bank	Crowell	TX	**B-**	B-	B-	37.3	1.60	13.9	7.7	8.7	16.3	**10.0**	11.4	19.2
Crown Bank	Edina	MN	**C**	B-	B	215.4	7.56	32.5	1.0	8.0	0.0	**10.0**	11.7	16.0
▲ Crown Bank	Elizabeth	NJ	**C**	C-	D	522.8	4.04	4.1	0.1	2.8	10.1	**10.0**	20.7	24.5
Crystal Lake Bank & Trust Co., N.A.	Crystal Lake	IL	**B**	B	B-	1171.1	11.35	34.8	15.1	2.9	12.1	**6.0**	9.8	11.7
CTBC Bank Corp. (USA)	Los Angeles	CA	**A-**	A-	B	3563.0	1.81	8.3	0.0	36.5	10.0	**10.0**	14.4	20.9
▲ Culbertson Bank	Culbertson	NE	**C**	C-	D+	14.4	-0.54	6.1	0.9	0.2	47.1	**10.0**	15.6	27.9
Cullman Savings Bank	Cullman	AL	**A-**	B+	A-	301.4	2.22	8.4	1.0	42.9	7.8	**10.0**	15.8	23.1
Cumberland Federal Bank, FSB	Cumberland	WI	**B+**	A-	B	159.9	13.93	1.5	1.4	20.3	49.1	**10.0**	11.4	19.0
▲ Cumberland Security Bank, Inc.	Somerset	KY	**A**	B+	A	225.9	10.20	7.7	3.8	27.8	12.4	**10.0**	13.8	19.6
Cumberland Valley National B&T Co.	London	KY	**C+**	C+	C+	525.6	9.56	7.0	1.9	14.5	14.3	**8.6**	10.1	15.2
Currie State Bank	Currie	MN	**C-**	C-	C-	82.8	3.12	7.2	1.5	6.1	1.0	**6.7**	9.7	12.3
▲ CUSB Bank	Cresco	IA	**B+**	C+	C+	487.3	3.32	7.2	4.7	8.5	20.5	**10.0**	13.9	17.2
Custer Federal State Bank	Broken Bow	NE	**B-**	B	B-	116.1	-10.28	5.1	2.7	16.4	18.6	**10.0**	11.3	19.2
Customers Bank	Phoenixville	PA	**B-**	B	B	11724.3	10.44	12.5	5.8	6.7	5.0	**6.9**	9.8	12.4
▲ Cypress Bank, SSB	Pittsburg	TX	**B-**	C+	B-	192.4	2.44	6.9	7.5	31.4	22.9	**9.9**	11.0	18.6
D.A. Davidson Trust Co.	Great Falls	MT	**U**	U	U	9.6	18.67	0.0	0.0	0.0	73.2	**10.0**	73.8	161.8
D.L. Evans Bank	Burley	ID	**A-**	B+	B+	1677.4	10.40	7.7	2.1	5.9	20.1	**8.1**	9.7	14.6
Dacotah Bank	Aberdeen	SD	**B-**	B	B	2608.6	5.57	12.0	3.0	4.0	9.5	**9.3**	11.6	14.4
Dairy State Bank	Rice Lake	WI	**B**	B	B-	506.5	3.12	10.1	1.0	9.1	47.1	**10.0**	12.7	23.8
▲ Dakota Community Bank & Trust, N.A.	Hebron	ND	**B+**	B	B+	851.6	9.69	9.2	1.4	3.9	25.0	**6.5**	8.5	13.9
▼ Dakota Heritage Bank	Hunter	ND	**C+**	B+	A-	207.7	2.46	7.4	3.0	2.6	12.9	**8.6**	10.9	13.9
Dakota Prairie Bank	Fort Pierre	SD	**B+**	B+	B+	90.0	-2.46	11.2	2.7	2.0	6.9	**10.0**	12.4	16.9
▲ Dakota Western Bank	Bowman	ND	**B**	B	B+	280.0	4.18	8.7	3.0	1.4	21.5	**10.0**	11.4	15.1
Dalhart Federal S&L Assn., SSB	Dalhart	TX	**C+**	C+	C+	110.7	-0.73	0.5	2.2	49.0	29.7	**10.0**	12.0	27.8
Dallas Capital Bank, N.A.	Dallas	TX	**C**	C	C	988.4	18.67	12.3	0.4	8.1	12.0	**4.2**	8.9	10.6
Damariscotta Bank & Trust Co.	Damariscotta	ME	**C+**	C	C	193.3	-0.17	3.5	1.2	35.4	24.7	**8.3**	9.9	17.3
Danville State Savings Bank	Danville	IA	**B+**	B+	B+	146.0	2.14	3.7	4.4	20.8	51.2	**10.0**	12.8	25.6
▼ Dart Bank	Mason	MI	**C+**	B-	B-	480.0	10.95	5.5	1.1	30.8	8.2	**6.9**	8.9	13.3
▲ Davis Trust Co.	Elkins	WV	**B**	B-	B-	146.4	2.13	10.0	4.0	17.9	12.9	**10.0**	13.0	16.7
De Witt Bank & Trust Co.	De Witt	IA	**B**	B	B+	175.6	5.17	9.0	2.0	9.5	21.6	**6.6**	10.5	12.2
Dean Co-operative Bank	Franklin	MA	**C+**	C+	C+	331.4	5.42	4.3	1.1	49.7	16.0	**6.7**	8.7	15.0
Dearborn Federal Savings Bank	Dearborn	MI	**B+**	B+	B+	255.1	-3.31	0.0	0.0	73.7	3.6	**10.0**	29.5	60.9
Dearborn Savings Bank	Lawrenceburg	IN	**B-**	B	B	128.8	7.76	0.4	0.4	45.4	2.1	**8.4**	9.9	17.1
▲ Decatur County Bank	Decaturville	TN	**C-**	D+	C	132.0	16.13	13.4	7.8	22.4	12.1	**4.2**	7.7	10.6
Decorah Bank & Trust Co.	Decorah	IA	**A-**	A-	A-	488.8	9.37	14.4	2.4	9.5	18.6	**9.6**	10.9	14.7
Dedham Institution for Savings	Dedham	MA	**B**	B	B	1525.3	0.68	2.2	0.1	42.1	18.1	**10.0**	12.6	17.1
Dedicated Community Bank	Darlington	SC	**C**	C	C	70.9	3.35	13.5	2.8	18.2	15.5	**7.2**	9.1	13.8
▲ Deerwood Bank	Waite Park	MN	**B-**	C+	B	722.7	5.06	15.6	1.5	15.3	8.0	**5.5**	8.6	11.4
Defiance State Bank	Defiance	IA	**C-**	D+	C-	33.4	-3.96	8.6	7.4	8.2	8.3	**6.8**	9.8	12.4
▲ Del Norte Bank	Del Norte	CO	**B-**	C+	C+	107.3	13.41	5.4	1.0	24.1	8.1	**6.7**	8.7	14.1
▲ Delaware National Bank of Delhi	Delhi	NY	**B-**	C+	C+	304.8	3.14	6.6	1.6	24.3	23.6	**8.7**	10.2	28.5
Delta Bank	Vidalia	LA	**B-**	B-	B	308.8	4.40	5.2	2.3	19.3	17.9	**6.2**	8.2	12.9
Delta National Bank and Trust Co.	New York	NY	**C**	C	C-	409.0	20.34	23.6	5.8	0.0	19.1	**10.0**	15.8	28.3

Arrows denote recent upgrades ▲ or downgrades ▼

Asset Quality Index	Adjusted Non-Performing Loans as a % of Total Loans	Adjusted Non-Performing Loans as a % of Capital	Net Charge-Offs Avg Loans	Profitability Index	Net Income ($Mil)	Return on Assets (R.O.A.)	Return on Equity (R.O.E.)	Net Interest Spread	Overhead Efficiency Ratio	Liquidity Index	Liquidity Ratio	Hot Money Ratio	Stability Index
5.9	0.21	na	0.06	**7.9**	2.6	1.84	18.82	4.00	57.7	**2.9**	10.1	12.9	**7.1**
10.0	na	0.0	na	**10.0**	9.2	48.12	39.42	-0.01	68.8	**4.0**	na	100.0	**6.7**
5.3	0.00	2.9	7.35	**10.0**	162.7	51.07	108.30	14.95	68.6	**2.3**	55.3	99.9	**8.7**
1.3	2.88	17.0	6.18	**4.4**	5.7	0.76	5.67	12.48	48.3	**0.5**	13.5	62.1	**7.7**
6.5	0.71	3.1	0.02	**8.1**	48.1	1.66	10.31	4.09	55.8	**1.8**	20.3	18.0	**10.0**
8.2	0.29	na	0.00	**2.8**	1.2	0.34	4.13	3.01	84.1	**3.9**	11.5	8.8	**4.6**
6.1	1.96	7.2	0.15	**4.7**	1.2	1.02	8.68	4.08	77.6	**4.5**	43.0	13.2	**8.1**
8.2	0.04	na	0.01	**10.0**	12.4	3.56	28.97	4.06	72.6	**1.1**	5.8	28.1	**9.8**
5.7	0.65	2.0	0.07	**6.5**	8.9	1.40	10.15	4.26	64.5	**4.4**	11.0	5.7	**9.1**
6.6	0.65	na	0.17	**8.3**	3.0	1.56	12.25	5.12	58.8	**1.1**	8.6	27.9	**8.0**
7.8	1.06	na	0.00	**3.4**	1.4	0.43	3.79	4.07	85.3	**2.7**	16.6	15.4	**6.6**
6.1	2.86	na	0.63	**4.1**	2.4	0.84	6.87	3.72	70.4	**1.8**	30.5	27.3	**7.3**
5.7	0.13	0.8	1.34	**10.0**	26.9	2.14	17.05	7.48	42.5	**0.7**	14.4	52.3	**9.1**
5.7	1.52	8.4	0.21	**3.8**	29.6	0.90	8.13	3.36	59.2	**1.4**	20.5	20.3	**8.0**
7.5	0.00	na	0.00	**6.4**	1.7	1.29	9.21	3.07	47.8	**3.0**	32.5	17.5	**8.5**
5.0	1.84	na	0.04	**5.5**	3.4	1.11	11.06	3.62	67.1	**2.2**	22.2	18.9	**7.2**
7.9	0.58	na	0.07	**8.5**	3.3	2.19	18.80	4.18	50.3	**3.8**	41.7	16.6	**8.1**
6.9	0.32	na	0.05	**9.5**	0.7	2.38	22.50	4.75	53.6	**1.5**	21.7	26.7	**6.9**
8.2	0.52	na	-0.01	**0.8**	-1.1	-0.74	-6.46	4.04	115.0	**1.7**	30.2	22.9	**5.9**
3.6	3.24	9.2	0.09	**9.7**	16.4	4.29	22.25	4.79	40.3	**1.1**	28.0	41.5	**10.0**
7.1	0.25	1.8	0.04	**7.7**	12.9	1.53	15.99	3.42	40.3	**1.2**	10.0	19.9	**7.6**
8.1	0.70	3.7	0.00	**6.2**	31.9	1.20	8.48	3.40	54.4	**0.9**	17.3	34.0	**9.7**
6.2	1.76	6.0	0.00	**3.2**	0.1	0.70	4.68	3.78	80.5	**4.5**	49.3	12.5	**4.7**
8.3	1.04	na	0.00	**6.5**	2.8	1.27	8.24	3.98	61.5	**0.7**	11.6	33.0	**8.8**
9.3	0.74	1.9	0.00	**5.4**	1.2	1.07	9.07	3.18	56.3	**2.4**	44.0	7.8	**6.7**
8.5	0.08	na	0.12	**10.0**	4.8	2.98	21.96	4.88	46.9	**3.4**	22.8	12.9	**9.3**
5.0	1.40	na	0.09	**3.5**	2.7	0.70	6.99	3.49	79.4	**1.5**	23.4	27.6	**7.0**
1.6	1.71	na	-0.01	**8.8**	0.8	1.37	13.96	4.98	58.3	**0.6**	7.4	24.0	**7.5**
5.1	1.54	8.5	0.00	**6.0**	5.3	1.47	10.31	3.42	54.6	**0.9**	22.5	19.6	**8.3**
5.9	1.23	8.2	1.27	**2.7**	0.3	0.33	3.04	3.29	80.9	**1.1**	26.9	37.6	**6.4**
7.4	0.26	2.1	0.05	**3.9**	54.8	0.70	6.79	2.71	67.1	**1.1**	7.5	9.3	**7.1**
4.9	0.96	na	0.07	**4.5**	1.3	0.88	8.07	3.96	73.9	**1.7**	31.7	30.3	**6.4**
9.8	na	na	na	**10.0**	0.6	8.78	11.89	2.90	86.3	**10.0**	262.8	0.0	**6.1**
7.3	0.66	3.1	0.01	**7.7**	17.7	1.48	15.33	4.62	61.1	**3.8**	19.8	10.7	**8.7**
4.5	2.76	13.6	0.03	**6.1**	23.1	1.19	10.34	3.87	62.7	**2.3**	9.0	16.9	**9.6**
8.5	1.52	na	-0.01	**3.5**	2.7	0.74	5.73	2.79	75.2	**4.8**	42.3	11.5	**7.4**
7.2	0.33	na	0.04	**7.6**	11.2	1.83	21.31	3.74	57.5	**4.3**	29.4	7.9	**8.1**
3.3	0.31	na	0.01	**9.0**	3.3	2.19	18.59	4.84	51.3	**2.8**	8.1	14.4	**9.0**
7.0	0.25	na	0.00	**6.9**	1.0	1.52	12.75	4.58	63.9	**1.7**	14.8	21.3	**8.2**
6.8	0.18	na	0.01	**9.3**	4.6	2.24	19.54	4.43	46.6	**1.7**	7.9	18.5	**9.0**
8.9	0.29	na	-0.01	**2.3**	0.1	0.16	1.35	3.89	93.8	**2.1**	41.6	38.5	**6.4**
5.2	0.96	na	0.01	**3.3**	4.9	0.75	7.02	2.62	66.4	**0.9**	13.1	24.0	**5.9**
4.0	2.22	na	0.00	**3.5**	0.9	0.62	6.44	3.42	82.2	**3.0**	27.7	15.9	**5.5**
6.3	1.22	na	-0.03	**5.6**	1.4	1.30	9.69	2.51	63.3	**5.2**	61.8	14.1	**7.9**
2.9	3.05	16.2	0.00	**4.3**	2.6	0.75	8.55	3.95	80.9	**2.5**	19.4	17.0	**5.7**
6.3	7.56	na	0.17	**5.2**	1.2	1.10	11.04	4.80	70.8	**4.5**	20.9	6.3	**6.0**
5.8	0.45	na	0.01	**4.7**	1.6	1.23	11.55	3.39	75.8	**3.1**	24.1	14.4	**7.5**
6.3	0.96	4.6	0.08	**3.5**	1.5	0.59	6.87	3.62	80.7	**3.3**	16.4	12.8	**5.2**
9.2	2.21	na	0.00	**3.8**	1.0	0.50	1.72	2.96	76.5	**3.7**	27.0	12.0	**7.6**
8.0	0.76	na	0.00	**3.6**	0.7	0.70	6.90	3.05	73.9	**1.2**	18.3	30.4	**6.5**
4.7	0.44	na	0.06	**3.8**	0.6	0.64	9.41	4.88	83.2	**1.4**	11.1	22.5	**3.5**
7.9	0.16	0.9	0.09	**7.4**	6.2	1.72	14.46	3.70	56.4	**2.9**	21.9	15.1	**9.4**
9.2	0.30	1.9	0.00	**4.8**	11.9	1.04	9.00	3.27	73.1	**2.4**	24.8	12.0	**8.7**
6.4	1.54	na	0.07	**3.4**	0.3	0.47	5.26	3.88	83.9	**2.5**	17.5	16.6	**4.9**
5.3	0.33	na	-0.01	**7.4**	6.9	1.31	12.56	4.68	61.3	**4.8**	16.2	3.3	**7.5**
7.1	0.00	na	0.74	**4.1**	0.2	0.78	8.25	3.97	78.6	**2.2**	30.7	22.5	**4.6**
6.7	0.35	na	0.01	**5.1**	0.7	0.89	10.25	4.52	73.5	**1.2**	12.8	26.6	**5.3**
6.4	0.71	na	0.06	**4.2**	2.1	0.93	9.53	3.10	64.7	**2.6**	23.1	16.7	**5.3**
5.0	0.66	na	-0.13	**7.2**	3.9	1.70	20.48	4.44	64.6	**1.2**	7.9	27.4	**6.7**
8.6	0.00	0.0	0.00	**2.3**	0.7	0.30	1.81	2.18	92.5	**3.9**	60.0	10.7	**6.2**

Name	City	State	Rating	2018 Rating	2017 Rating	Total Assets ($Mil)	One Year Asset Growth	Asset Mix (As a % of Total Assets) Comm-ercial Loans	Cons-umer Loans	Mort-gage Loans	Secur-ities	Capital-ization Index	Lever-age Ratio	Risk-Based Capital Ratio
▲ DeMotte State Bank	Demotte	IN	B+	B	B	426.4	3.61	10.8	1.0	13.6	31.4	10.0	12.7	20.4
Denali State Bank	Fairbanks	AK	B-	B-	B-	304.7	4.55	15.0	8.0	8.3	25.3	8.7	10.1	15.7
▲ Denison State Bank	Holton	KS	A-	B+	A-	349.1	4.57	9.8	2.2	12.6	28.8	10.0	14.2	20.3
Denmark State Bank	Denmark	WI	B	B	B	522.2	6.85	15.2	1.9	9.7	6.2	8.9	10.5	14.0
Denver Savings Bank	Denver	IA	C	C+	B-	175.5	-1.29	11.6	1.6	17.3	19.8	7.3	9.2	13.0
Department Stores National Bank	Sioux Falls	SD	B+	B+	B+	326.2	0.35	0.0	18.0	0.0	0.0	10.0	19.2	52.0
Depository Trust Co.	New York	NY	U	U	U	4112.0	12.35	0.0	0.0	0.0	0.0	10.0	19.9	81.1
Desjardins Bank, N.A.	Hallandale Beach	FL	B-	B-	C+	210.7	-2.12	2.4	3.3	60.4	7.7	10.0	15.2	31.7
Deutsche Bank National Trust Co.	Los Angeles	CA	U	U	U	296.8	14.63	0.0	0.0	0.0	34.0	10.0	77.6	262.9
Deutsche Bank Trust Co. Americas	New York	NY	A	A-	B	40272.0	-1.61	5.4	0.3	5.0	0.0	10.0	24.4	76.3
▲ Deutsche Bank Trust Co. Delaware	Wilmington	DE	A+	A-	B+	310.6	0.72	11.3	0.2	0.0	0.7	10.0	94.5	146.5
Deutsche Bank Trust Co., N.A.	New York	NY	U	U	U	145.8	2.09	0.0	0.0	0.0	71.4	10.0	89.6	621.7
Devon Bank	Chicago	IL	C	C-	C	288.8	3.85	11.1	1.5	16.5	14.0	6.3	8.3	12.0
Dewey Bank	Dewey	IL	C-	D+	D+	21.9	0.46	7.5	2.0	7.7	29.9	6.9	8.9	12.6
DeWitt Savings Bank	Clinton	IL	B-	B	C+	117.4	9.34	0.0	22.0	28.7	26.8	10.0	12.3	23.8
▲ Diamond Bank	Glenwood	AR	B	B-	B+	639.3	8.40	5.7	2.2	19.1	21.2	8.6	10.0	16.0
▼ Dickinson County Bank	Enterprise	KS	E+	D+	C	17.1	21.10	11.1	7.7	36.8	4.2	6.7	8.7	13.7
▲ Dieterich Bank	Effingham	IL	B-	C+	C+	709.1	11.49	7.0	1.9	10.9	23.0	8.1	10.0	13.4
Dilley State Bank	Dilley	TX	B+	B+	B+	134.8	10.77	1.7	0.6	0.2	55.8	10.0	16.8	52.6
▲ Dime Bank	Norwich	CT	B-	C+	C-	878.1	3.42	6.0	0.1	34.7	14.6	10.0	12.3	17.3
▲ Dime Bank	Honesdale	PA	B-	C+	C	722.3	7.29	13.7	1.5	13.5	17.0	9.5	11.6	14.6
▼ Dime Community Bank	Brooklyn	NY	B	B+	B+	6417.5	2.09	4.8	0.0	2.1	8.1	6.8	9.8	12.4
Discover Bank	Greenwood	DE	D+	C-	C-	109168.6	4.64	0.2	83.5	1.0	9.8	8.9	10.2	14.2
Dixon Bank	Dixon	KY	B	B	B	82.7	1.32	4.3	3.1	3.9	62.4	10.0	25.2	58.2
DMB Community Bank	De Forest	WI	B+	B+	A-	494.1	2.14	1.0	0.5	20.1	10.6	10.0	12.3	18.7
DNB First, N.A.	Downingtown	PA	B	B	B	1113.7	-1.31	7.0	0.4	21.4	11.1	9.5	10.9	14.6
DNB National Bank	Clear Lake	SD	C+	C+	C+	78.7	0.10	5.8	1.2	6.9	49.4	7.0	9.0	21.7
▼ Dogwood State Bank	Raleigh	NC	D+	C	C	329.9	50.57	16.4	0.7	14.9	11.1	10.0	24.1	31.2
Dollar Bank, Federal Savings Bank	Pittsburgh	PA	B	B	B-	8998.3	7.04	8.3	3.1	53.3	12.9	10.0	12.0	19.3
▲ Dolores State Bank	Dolores	CO	A-	B+	A-	270.0	2.80	7.6	4.3	30.3	24.4	10.0	14.2	25.3
Dominion Bank	Grapeland	TX	C	C+	C+	102.2	201.50	27.2	2.3	10.0	3.4	10.0	51.3	98.7
Donley County State Bank	Clarendon	TX	C+	C	C	39.0	-2.05	4.9	1.6	0.1	23.9	10.0	20.3	63.2
Douglas National Bank	Douglas	GA	A-	A-	A	178.7	0.46	10.3	3.0	20.9	4.0	10.0	12.8	16.5
DR Bank	Darien	CT	D	D-	D	393.0	-36.82	0.2	15.0	22.5	20.5	7.7	10.9	13.1
Drake Bank	Saint Paul	MN	C+	B-	A-	130.5	17.38	22.9	0.8	17.8	2.3	6.9	8.9	12.8
Drummond Community Bank	Chiefland	FL	A-	A-	A-	632.8	23.38	5.1	2.5	16.6	32.3	10.0	11.5	18.6
DSRM National Bank	Albuquerque	NM	U	U	U	3.9	1.98	0.0	0.0	0.0	80.2	10.0	85.0	270.2
Du Quoin State Bank	Du Quoin	IL	B+	B+	B+	108.4	6.33	3.8	1.6	14.4	65.0	7.3	9.2	25.2
Dubuque Bank and Trust Co.	Dubuque	IA	B+	B+	B	1547.0	1.55	15.5	0.9	6.2	23.2	8.0	9.7	15.0
▲ Dundee Bank	Omaha	NE	C+	C-	C-	294.4	-4.94	12.8	0.5	23.1	8.9	6.8	9.0	12.4
▲ Durand State Bank	Durand	IL	B	B-	B-	105.9	1.81	6.6	2.3	13.2	25.6	10.0	11.5	18.2
Durden Banking Co., Inc.	Twin City	GA	A	A-	A-	178.9	2.17	4.6	5.4	29.0	28.3	10.0	16.8	29.0
▲ Dysart State Bank	Dysart	IA	D-	E	E	12.5	-9.75	1.3	1.2	19.9	6.0	8.0	9.7	15.8
E*TRADE Bank	Arlington	VA	B	B	B	45899.3	-6.20	0.0	0.5	2.1	93.5	5.4	7.4	37.5
E*TRADE Savings Bank	Arlington	VA	B	B	B	3821.7	-32.41	0.0	3.7	0.7	67.1	10.0	41.9	213.0
Eagle Bank	Everett	MA	B-	C	C-	459.8	2.24	9.6	0.0	28.3	15.7	10.0	12.1	15.3
Eagle Bank	Glenwood	MN	A	A	B+	152.7	1.59	8.9	3.8	14.1	16.3	10.0	14.0	21.7
▲ Eagle Bank	Polson	MT	B	C+	C+	69.3	5.31	13.5	3.6	11.7	18.6	10.0	11.2	15.4
▲ Eagle Bank and Trust Co.	Little Rock	AR	B	B-	B	420.8	4.84	2.9	0.5	26.3	33.2	10.0	12.5	22.5
▲ Eagle Community Bank	Maple Grove	MN	D	E	E	25.8	4.29	13.8	1.1	22.5	0.4	6.4	8.4	13.9
Eagle Savings Bank	Cincinnati	OH	B-	B	B	142.2	3.21	4.2	0.0	53.9	0.0	10.0	15.3	16.8
Eagle State Bank	Eagle	NE	D+	D+	C-	43.4	15.30	14.4	1.0	14.8	5.8	5.8	8.5	11.6
EagleBank	Bethesda	MD	A	A	A-	8994.7	11.73	13.1	0.0	4.0	7.8	10.0	13.9	15.4
Eaglemark Savings Bank	Carson City	NV	A-	A-	A-	53.4	48.96	0.0	47.1	0.0	37.4	10.0	24.1	29.0
Earlham Savings Bank	West Des Moines	IA	C-	C+	C+	300.9	4.29	13.0	2.0	12.4	29.8	6.6	8.6	16.5
▲ East Boston Savings Bank	East Boston	MA	B	B-	B-	6352.6	10.39	1.4	0.2	10.6	0.3	6.1	10.2	11.8
East Cambridge Savings Bank	Cambridge	MA	C+	C+	C	1136.8	9.02	2.1	0.9	45.5	10.2	9.5	10.7	17.1
East West Bank	Pasadena	CA	A-	A-	B+	43243.5	10.74	22.6	0.1	16.7	7.6	8.5	10.2	13.7
East Wisconsin Savings Bank	Kaukauna	WI	D+	D+	D+	241.5	-6.28	0.0	23.9	48.8	10.3	7.1	9.1	15.8
▼ Eastbank, N.A.	New York	NY	B-	B	B	177.9	-6.78	0.9	0.0	10.9	21.7	10.0	19.2	27.8

Asset Quality Index	Adjusted Non-Performing Loans as a % of Total Loans	Adjusted Non-Performing Loans as a % of Capital	Net Charge-Offs Avg Loans	Profitability Index	Net Income ($Mil)	Return on Assets (R.O.A.)	Return on Equity (R.O.E.)	Net Interest Spread	Overhead Efficiency Ratio	Liquidity Index	Liquidity Ratio	Hot Money Ratio	Stability Index
5.1	2.62	na	0.01	**5.2**	3.3	1.06	8.84	3.76	68.5	**4.0**	28.4	11.1	**7.0**
4.7	1.31	6.8	0.34	**5.0**	2.2	1.00	9.57	5.15	74.1	**4.8**	25.5	4.9	**6.3**
8.2	0.55	na	-0.15	**7.8**	4.5	1.74	12.34	3.69	56.4	**2.3**	9.9	17.0	**9.3**
7.1	0.43	2.8	-0.01	**4.9**	3.8	1.00	9.60	3.76	71.1	**3.2**	16.1	11.9	**7.5**
8.4	0.11	na	0.04	**3.2**	0.8	0.58	5.88	2.84	72.7	**0.9**	24.9	40.8	**5.4**
7.3	0.73	2.1	2.85	**5.4**	2.3	0.91	4.97	3.72	43.8	**3.3**	92.8	99.9	**8.3**
10.0	na	0.0	na	**9.8**	66.3	2.64	13.14	1.78	73.9	**4.0**	116.6	0.0	**7.0**
8.3	1.23	na	0.00	**3.7**	0.9	0.59	3.96	4.61	85.7	**5.1**	24.8	2.7	**7.7**
10.0	na	0.0	na	**5.3**	1.7	0.79	1.01	2.31	99.5	**4.0**	284.1	0.0	**7.0**
9.6	0.67	0.7	0.01	**8.0**	480.0	1.66	6.74	2.18	48.8	**8.4**	90.8	0.4	**10.0**
8.2	0.02	0.0	0.00	**9.5**	6.9	3.01	3.17	3.25	47.6	**4.0**	na	95.7	**9.7**
10.0	na	0.0	na	**3.6**	-0.7	-0.66	-0.74	2.13	101.8	**4.0**	na	0.0	**7.0**
4.9	1.90	na	0.26	**2.9**	0.8	0.38	4.25	3.90	91.5	**3.2**	22.7	13.8	**5.1**
4.0	1.18	na	0.20	**1.4**	0.0	0.24	1.86	4.17	92.2	**4.3**	17.8	6.8	**3.8**
7.3	0.84	na	0.04	**3.2**	0.5	0.60	4.81	3.32	77.4	**2.7**	38.1	19.2	**6.9**
5.1	1.69	na	0.20	**5.3**	6.0	1.28	12.68	3.62	64.9	**1.1**	14.5	31.0	**8.0**
2.5	2.66	14.5	-0.09	**2.4**	0.0	0.14	1.55	4.15	94.0	**1.3**	20.4	28.1	**1.0**
4.6	1.44	8.5	0.03	**4.2**	5.0	0.97	10.41	3.22	62.2	**3.4**	16.8	12.1	**6.1**
10.0	0.05	na	0.14	**4.2**	0.8	0.84	5.27	2.44	59.1	**7.1**	94.6	8.1	**7.8**
7.0	1.73	na	-0.02	**3.4**	4.4	0.68	5.87	3.07	77.6	**2.5**	19.7	15.4	**7.3**
5.0	2.14	na	0.06	**5.7**	6.7	1.27	11.05	4.19	65.3	**2.4**	8.6	16.3	**7.6**
6.7	0.30	2.4	0.14	**3.9**	32.1	0.67	6.35	2.43	55.2	**1.1**	10.5	21.3	**8.8**
1.2	3.71	18.9	3.16	**10.0**	2177.1	2.67	26.21	9.08	35.1	**0.9**	17.8	11.9	**10.0**
7.6	6.05	na	0.31	**3.9**	0.5	0.76	3.15	2.74	66.7	**3.9**	87.7	28.0	**7.7**
7.5	0.00	na	-0.13	**5.4**	4.1	1.09	9.05	2.82	53.8	**0.7**	13.9	30.3	**7.6**
4.9	1.06	5.8	0.06	**5.0**	8.7	1.01	8.64	3.50	65.5	**1.8**	8.9	12.9	**9.0**
9.4	0.00	na	0.00	**3.9**	0.5	0.87	9.88	2.98	76.1	**4.3**	45.8	14.2	**5.3**
7.5	0.12	na	0.00	**0.7**	-1.5	-0.64	-3.47	3.58	121.9	**1.6**	24.8	22.9	**6.2**
8.1	0.70	3.7	0.07	**4.1**	53.1	0.82	6.91	3.06	67.7	**2.6**	13.2	9.4	**9.0**
6.2	1.85	na	0.00	**8.3**	3.6	1.84	12.87	4.44	52.4	**5.0**	35.8	8.0	**8.6**
7.8	0.05	na	0.04	**1.0**	-1.6	-5.04	-16.72	3.59	240.8	**2.5**	51.3	36.2	**6.3**
9.6	0.39	na	0.00	**3.1**	0.2	0.64	3.32	2.53	80.6	**3.2**	70.5	31.8	**6.7**
7.6	0.27	na	-0.01	**10.0**	4.2	3.03	24.70	5.09	49.8	**1.3**	11.5	22.0	**9.2**
6.0	0.49	na	0.60	**0.4**	116.9	0.13	1.21	2.67	98.1	**1.0**	26.1	49.8	**3.8**
1.7	3.62	na	0.00	**3.3**	0.4	0.44	4.91	3.44	81.8	**2.1**	21.8	19.1	**4.8**
7.9	0.83	2.6	0.03	**6.3**	5.6	1.21	10.72	4.57	69.5	**4.6**	34.1	7.7	**8.2**
9.9	na	na	na	**7.9**	0.0	1.48	1.75	1.30	88.1	**4.0**	na	100.0	**5.3**
8.8	0.94	1.2	0.05	**4.8**	0.9	1.12	9.10	3.97	70.3	**5.3**	58.4	13.3	**7.9**
5.8	2.42	7.5	0.27	**8.1**	27.8	2.33	23.65	3.13	48.8	**6.6**	41.5	3.4	**8.0**
4.7	0.91	na	0.46	**4.8**	2.3	1.08	12.09	3.64	65.7	**0.7**	13.2	37.0	**5.2**
6.2	2.37	5.9	0.05	**3.9**	0.7	0.88	7.95	3.32	70.4	**2.6**	17.6	16.2	**6.2**
8.0	0.40	2.4	0.07	**9.5**	3.1	2.32	14.71	5.02	57.5	**2.7**	22.6	16.5	**9.6**
9.0	0.00	na	0.00	**2.9**	0.1	0.60	6.57	3.46	82.5	**5.5**	29.5	0.0	**2.9**
7.1	19.15	7.0	-1.54	**5.7**	387.0	1.04	13.51	2.80	49.0	**3.5**	80.1	0.0	**7.4**
7.8	1.02	0.1	0.01	**3.3**	5.8	0.15	0.46	2.42	68.9	**4.5**	156.9	0.0	**7.4**
8.9	0.13	na	0.00	**3.4**	2.3	0.67	5.84	3.35	83.2	**1.6**	24.3	20.9	**6.7**
8.4	0.02	0.6	0.00	**7.0**	1.9	1.71	12.06	4.01	61.5	**5.2**	27.3	3.4	**9.3**
8.3	0.09	na	0.03	**8.4**	0.8	1.62	15.21	4.66	55.9	**0.9**	24.7	24.8	**6.0**
8.3	0.93	na	0.01	**4.4**	3.0	0.96	7.67	3.94	85.7	**3.0**	26.1	10.9	**7.1**
7.1	0.00	0.0	0.00	**1.2**	0.0	0.11	1.24	5.05	97.3	**1.8**	18.3	21.7	**1.6**
8.7	0.86	na	0.03	**3.2**	0.5	0.50	3.29	3.60	86.9	**1.8**	9.8	19.6	**7.4**
5.0	0.11	na	0.00	**4.1**	0.4	1.07	12.64	3.00	65.0	**1.1**	14.9	30.1	**3.7**
6.0	0.54	4.1	0.12	**9.7**	116.3	1.79	11.88	4.02	38.2	**0.7**	8.6	10.3	**10.0**
5.8	0.00	0.0	0.00	**10.0**	3.3	11.36	45.45	14.54	74.2	**3.7**	56.3	19.4	**9.0**
8.7	0.00	na	0.39	**2.7**	0.9	0.41	4.81	3.17	82.8	**5.3**	43.1	9.2	**4.6**
7.1	0.12	0.7	0.01	**5.2**	50.0	1.07	10.53	2.87	54.2	**1.1**	7.8	16.9	**8.8**
9.2	0.17	1.2	0.00	**3.4**	4.7	0.56	5.57	3.04	76.7	**1.6**	20.0	26.1	**7.7**
7.6	0.54	2.9	0.18	**8.7**	497.8	1.59	14.29	3.71	42.4	**1.4**	17.9	20.7	**10.0**
6.4	0.68	na	0.02	**1.8**	0.3	0.14	1.55	2.61	96.2	**2.3**	19.1	17.8	**4.5**
7.9	0.00	0.0	0.00	**3.0**	0.5	0.37	2.09	3.39	84.5	**2.3**	42.2	31.9	**7.6**

Name	City	State	Rating	2018 Rating	2017 Rating	Total Assets ($Mil)	One Year Asset Growth	Asset Mix (As a % of Total Assets) Comm-ercial Loans	Cons-umer Loans	Mort-gage Loans	Secur-ities	Capital-ization Index	Lever-age Ratio	Risk-Based Capital Ratio
Eastern Bank	Boston	MA	**B+**	B	B	11507.0	2.63	15.0	3.6	16.0	11.9	**7.9**	11.2	13.2
▲ Eastern Colorado Bank	Cheyenne Wells	CO	**A-**	B+	A-	431.9	7.73	7.3	0.4	9.2	17.9	**9.5**	11.1	14.6
Eastern Connecticut Savings Bank	Norwich	CT	**D+**	D	D	181.7	1.06	5.8	3.0	37.2	0.2	**6.4**	8.4	12.4
Eastern International Bank	Los Angeles	CA	**B**	B	B-	122.9	9.49	0.0	0.0	0.2	4.6	**10.0**	18.2	23.3
Eastern Michigan Bank	Croswell	MI	**B**	B-	B-	400.2	14.87	8.7	3.5	7.5	25.5	**8.3**	9.8	18.3
▼ Eastern National Bank	Miami	FL	**D+**	C-	C	357.2	-13.82	17.7	0.7	23.8	1.3	**7.0**	9.0	13.4
▲ Eastern Savings Bank, FSB	Hunt Valley	MD	**B**	B-	C	315.7	-3.51	0.0	0.0	49.5	0.0	**10.0**	24.8	37.4
Easthampton Savings Bank	Easthampton	MA	**B-**	B-	B-	1421.1	5.32	8.2	0.6	35.2	11.9	**6.6**	8.6	13.1
Eaton Federal Savings Bank	Charlotte	MI	**B-**	C+	B-	371.5	7.52	2.0	1.4	41.1	26.7	**10.0**	14.8	23.6
Eclipse Bank, Inc.	Louisville	KY	**C+**	C+	C	159.7	4.97	6.8	1.7	8.8	6.1	**9.3**	13.1	14.5
Edgewater Bank	Saint Joseph	MI	**C+**	C-	C-	185.1	9.61	8.8	0.5	30.1	5.5	**7.8**	9.6	13.2
Edison National Bank	Fort Myers	FL	**B-**	B-	C+	302.0	0.93	2.3	2.4	24.6	7.3	**6.0**	8.1	19.3
▲ Edmonton State Bank	Edmonton	KY	**A-**	B+	A	547.4	5.23	7.4	7.6	17.9	10.6	**10.0**	14.7	20.3
Edon State Bank Co. of Edon, Ohio	Edon	OH	**B**	B	B	59.9	0.28	1.7	0.5	6.5	48.1	**10.0**	20.4	49.9
Edward Jones Trust Co.	Saint Louis	MO	**U**	U	U	95.2	14.25	0.0	0.0	0.0	0.1	**10.0**	94.2	366.0
EH National Bank	Beverly Hills	CA	**C**	C-	C	237.0	36.00	6.5	0.0	0.9	6.5	**10.0**	13.7	16.8
El Dorado Savings Bank, F.S.B.	Placerville	CA	**B**	B-	B-	2161.2	-1.72	0.0	0.0	24.4	55.6	**10.0**	11.3	37.9
Elberfeld State Bank	Elberfeld	IN	**B**	B	B-	80.2	-1.80	3.7	0.8	11.6	24.9	**10.0**	12.0	19.0
Elberton Federal S&L Assn.	Elberton	GA	**C-**	D+	C	24.1	1.44	0.0	1.2	74.0	16.2	**10.0**	20.8	42.5
▲ Elderton State Bank	Elderton	PA	**B+**	B	B	294.7	5.84	11.4	1.0	12.6	5.4	**10.0**	11.4	16.3
Elgin State Bank	Elgin	IA	**D-**	D-	D	22.9	-6.31	4.2	3.3	15.8	33.2	**5.9**	7.9	16.5
▲ Elizabethton Federal Savings Bank	Elizabethton	TN	**A**	A-	A-	296.8	-3.04	0.0	0.6	34.9	42.5	**10.0**	40.6	109.6
Elk State Bank	Clyde	KS	**C+**	C+	C+	97.1	-0.10	5.6	1.3	10.5	31.5	**9.1**	10.4	18.4
Elkhorn Valley Bank & Trust	Norfolk	NE	**B**	B	B	791.7	3.00	15.0	3.7	5.9	32.3	**10.0**	13.1	17.5
Elkton Bank & Trust Co.	Elkton	KY	**A-**	A-	B	139.6	2.26	4.3	4.6	16.1	41.7	**10.0**	13.2	26.8
Elmira Savings Bank	Elmira	NY	**C+**	C+	B-	615.9	7.86	4.9	6.7	52.2	3.5	**6.0**	8.0	12.2
▲ Elysian Bank	Elysian	MN	**B**	B-	B-	50.0	6.61	6.3	6.2	20.8	3.8	**10.0**	11.8	18.7
Embassy Bank for the Lehigh Valley	Bethlehem	PA	**B**	B	B	1161.8	7.87	4.3	0.1	50.8	8.3	**6.3**	8.3	12.6
Embassy National Bank	Lawrenceville	GA	**A**	A	A-	104.3	-1.65	2.4	0.1	2.7	0.0	**10.0**	17.2	24.0
Emerald Bank	Burden	KS	**C-**	C-	C-	18.0	6.98	4.8	8.6	34.2	4.2	**9.8**	10.8	21.6
Emigrant Bank	New York	NY	**B-**	B-	B-	5662.0	-0.32	30.8	0.4	17.0	10.2	**10.0**	20.0	20.5
Emigrant Mercantile Bank	New York	NY	**U**	U	U	3.4	0.38	0.0	0.0	0.0	0.0	**10.0**	85.3	427.4
Empire National Bank	Islandia	NY	**C+**	C+	B-	1012.5	2.76	9.6	0.1	8.3	25.1	**7.3**	9.2	15.4
▲ Empire State Bank	Newburgh	NY	**C**	D+	C-	421.8	15.27	4.4	0.0	38.6	3.8	**5.4**	7.4	11.6
Emprise Bank	Wichita	KS	**B+**	B+	B+	1778.8	5.98	10.8	3.1	18.9	17.8	**6.1**	8.1	11.9
Encore Bank	Little Rock	AR	**D+**	C-	C-	247.2	55.64	16.9	0.9	17.6	15.4	**10.0**	21.0	27.5
Endeavor Bank	San Diego	CA	**D**	D		115.9	54.32	27.0	2.1	7.2	0.0	**10.0**	17.0	18.7
▼ EnerBank USA	Salt Lake City	UT	**B+**	A-	B+	2681.5	50.58	0.0	93.1	0.0	0.9	**5.2**	10.2	11.2
Englewood Bank & Trust	Englewood	FL	**A-**	A-	B+	303.5	5.70	1.8	0.9	24.4	22.9	**8.6**	10.1	17.4
▲ Ennis State Bank	Ennis	TX	**B**	B-	B	250.1	8.58	11.7	0.7	9.8	15.6	**8.6**	10.1	14.6
Entegra Bank	Franklin	NC	**B-**	B-	B-	1702.7	2.05	1.8	0.4	20.1	20.5	**8.1**	9.7	14.7
Enterprise Bank	Omaha	NE	**C+**	C+	B-	329.6	11.88	11.8	0.7	5.5	1.7	**5.4**	9.0	11.3
▼ Enterprise Bank	Allison Park	PA	**D**	D	D-	310.8	9.00	11.2	0.0	4.2	0.0	**6.4**	9.3	12.1
Enterprise Bank & Trust	Clayton	MO	**B+**	B+	B+	7314.5	33.04	31.2	0.3	4.4	17.9	**7.0**	10.4	12.5
Enterprise Bank and Trust Co.	Lowell	MA	**B**	B-	B-	3138.7	8.58	14.3	0.3	13.2	15.4	**6.4**	9.1	12.0
Enterprise Bank of South Carolina	Ehrhardt	SC	**C-**	D	D-	334.2	1.03	7.0	2.5	18.6	29.6	**6.1**	8.1	15.2
▲ Envision Bank	Stoughton	MA	**C-**	D	D+	641.8	8.73	1.7	2.6	55.0	7.4	**10.0**	11.0	15.3
▲ Ephrata National Bank	Ephrata	PA	**B**	B-	C+	1145.4	7.89	4.8	0.5	23.1	26.6	**8.5**	10.0	14.6
Equitable Bank	Grand Island	NE	**C**	C	B-	336.7	16.16	11.7	1.3	20.2	2.2	**5.3**	9.3	11.3
▲ Equitable Bank, S.S.B.	Wauwatosa	WI	**D-**	E	E	316.8	2.72	0.6	0.1	47.5	6.6	**6.8**	8.8	14.1
Equitable S&L Assn.	Sterling	CO	**B**	B	B	164.3	1.42	0.0	0.7	84.9	3.5	**10.0**	16.3	31.6
Equitable S&L Co.	Cadiz	OH	**D+**	D	D+	13.3	2.98	0.0	0.5	50.7	23.7	**10.0**	20.6	44.3
Equity Bank	Andover	KS	**C+**	B-	B	4072.9	3.69	14.3	1.6	15.8	22.9	**6.4**	8.4	12.1
▲ Ergo Bank	Markesan	WI	**C+**	C	C+	91.1	5.64	14.3	1.1	11.3	12.3	**10.0**	12.8	16.9
▼ Ericson State Bank	Ericson	NE	**C-**	B-	B-	113.0	16.73	8.2	6.0	0.9	7.9	**4.3**	7.9	10.7
▲ ESB Bank	Caledonia	MN	**C+**	C	D+	113.3	5.71	12.9	4.1	9.3	10.7	**7.5**	9.4	13.0
ESB Financial	Emporia	KS	**B-**	B-	B	240.9	9.49	9.9	2.6	18.5	18.5	**9.0**	10.3	14.5
Escambia County Bank	Flomaton	AL	**B-**	B-	C+	74.4	1.87	9.5	5.9	15.5	55.4	**10.0**	15.8	34.8
▲ Esquire Bank, N.A.	Jericho	NY	**A-**	A-	A-	756.6	18.24	31.5	5.8	6.5	18.4	**10.0**	13.1	18.1
ESSA Bank & Trust	Stroudsburg	PA	**C+**	C+	C+	1796.0	-1.80	3.2	4.6	36.9	17.5	**8.0**	9.7	14.0

Asset Quality Index	Adjusted Non-Performing Loans as a % of Total Loans	Adjusted Non-Performing Loans as a % of Capital	Net Charge-Offs Avg Loans	Profitability Index	Net Income ($Mil)	Return on Assets (R.O.A.)	Return on Equity (R.O.E.)	Net Interest Spread	Overhead Efficiency Ratio	Liquidity Index	Liquidity Ratio	Hot Money Ratio	Stability Index
5.9	0.96	3.7	0.03	**5.9**	104.0	1.22	9.16	4.00	69.4	**4.9**	7.4	1.7	**10.0**
8.0	0.21	na	-0.05	**7.6**	5.7	1.88	15.87	4.51	60.1	**1.6**	13.2	21.8	**8.2**
1.8	3.89	na	0.07	**1.6**	0.1	0.04	0.52	3.57	97.5	**1.2**	9.1	27.1	**4.2**
7.4	0.00	na	0.00	**3.7**	0.5	0.56	3.00	4.13	79.0	**1.4**	32.3	46.4	**8.0**
6.8	2.45	5.7	0.10	**5.3**	3.3	1.19	12.27	3.49	60.4	**6.9**	53.6	2.1	**5.2**
3.6	3.35	15.2	0.12	**0.2**	-1.3	-0.45	-4.66	3.42	114.2	**0.8**	19.8	44.7	**3.8**
4.5	5.15	na	0.02	**5.7**	2.1	0.86	3.52	6.08	85.8	**3.2**	25.0	14.1	**8.6**
8.1	0.46	3.4	0.00	**4.2**	7.8	0.75	8.65	2.92	67.8	**1.4**	17.3	27.3	**7.1**
8.1	1.14	na	-0.02	**3.5**	1.6	0.58	3.89	3.44	79.3	**4.3**	36.4	11.8	**7.2**
3.8	2.65	na	-0.07	**4.1**	0.9	0.80	6.13	3.52	72.2	**0.7**	12.6	31.7	**7.2**
5.2	0.80	7.2	0.01	**4.1**	1.5	1.14	11.06	3.72	76.0	**3.5**	17.6	11.7	**5.9**
9.4	0.00	0.0	0.00	**4.4**	2.7	1.15	14.39	3.35	67.8	**6.4**	48.4	3.5	**5.1**
7.7	0.60	na	0.02	**8.5**	8.5	2.09	14.48	4.18	55.7	**2.8**	19.5	15.6	**10.0**
9.3	0.00	na	0.00	**3.9**	0.4	0.87	4.47	2.57	67.5	**6.5**	68.9	6.2	**7.8**
10.0	na	na	na	**10.0**	8.2	12.23	13.18	2.40	74.3	**4.0**	na	0.0	**6.7**
3.5	2.83	na	-0.09	**1.4**	-0.3	-0.16	-0.92	3.70	110.1	**0.8**	18.2	45.7	**6.9**
9.6	1.38	2.4	-0.02	**4.4**	14.6	0.90	8.02	2.49	57.9	**6.6**	78.3	10.7	**8.8**
9.2	3.21	na	0.27	**4.0**	0.5	0.75	6.43	3.60	74.4	**4.5**	40.1	12.5	**7.0**
9.1	0.97	na	0.00	**1.1**	0.0	-0.03	-0.16	3.48	104.1	**2.0**	22.1	19.2	**5.9**
5.1	4.18	na	0.08	**6.8**	3.0	1.38	11.96	3.80	48.2	**2.1**	13.7	18.2	**7.6**
8.8	0.03	na	0.00	**1.5**	0.0	0.03	0.47	3.38	98.1	**4.9**	37.9	6.6	**1.1**
9.8	0.00	na	0.00	**7.1**	3.1	1.42	3.54	3.20	40.2	**4.5**	85.3	22.2	**8.2**
3.4	2.94	na	0.10	**3.7**	0.5	0.69	6.71	3.40	73.3	**0.9**	22.1	26.2	**5.0**
7.7	0.37	na	0.47	**4.6**	5.9	1.00	7.90	2.92	53.6	**4.6**	33.9	9.8	**8.0**
8.5	0.69	na	0.25	**5.8**	1.3	1.20	9.21	3.92	62.5	**3.3**	46.2	19.9	**7.8**
4.1	0.91	na	0.10	**3.2**	2.6	0.56	5.83	3.06	77.6	**1.3**	7.2	24.5	**6.6**
6.9	1.03	na	-0.01	**9.1**	0.8	2.24	19.83	4.66	52.9	**6.1**	37.1	1.2	**7.0**
9.2	0.29	1.4	0.00	**4.6**	8.3	0.98	11.97	3.10	60.4	**2.1**	5.6	17.7	**7.3**
7.1	0.00	na	0.00	**9.9**	1.8	2.21	13.30	5.35	65.8	**1.2**	18.6	26.6	**9.7**
4.5	4.81	na	0.04	**3.6**	0.1	0.62	5.64	4.26	82.3	**3.6**	41.4	14.7	**5.0**
3.2	4.59	16.1	0.33	**5.3**	29.6	0.72	3.38	4.39	75.6	**4.5**	15.9	5.4	**10.0**
10.0	na	0.0	na	**1.3**	0.0	0.23	0.27	1.94	84.0	**4.0**	na	0.0	**6.5**
6.0	0.77	4.3	0.05	**3.0**	3.5	0.45	5.18	2.63	78.9	**4.6**	14.4	2.3	**6.9**
5.3	1.17	na	0.00	**3.1**	1.5	0.51	6.86	3.03	77.4	**0.9**	10.0	27.5	**3.2**
6.6	0.65	na	0.06	**7.1**	22.7	1.76	18.62	4.05	61.9	**4.3**	19.0	6.4	**9.4**
8.4	0.25	na	-0.02	**0.5**	-3.8	-2.65	-19.31	2.22	145.5	**0.6**	15.1	66.2	**4.1**
8.5	0.00	na	0.00	**0.0**	-2.6	-3.59	-17.89	3.71	172.7	**3.1**	32.6	16.8	**1.5**
5.3	0.02	2.4	1.23	**10.0**	32.6	1.88	17.76	6.69	40.1	**0.2**	6.4	8.0	**7.9**
8.0	0.50	1.7	0.00	**9.5**	5.4	2.38	25.26	4.14	51.9	**5.8**	36.3	3.0	**8.4**
6.1	0.81	na	-0.04	**8.0**	3.4	1.93	19.40	4.72	60.5	**4.3**	21.5	7.4	**7.1**
6.9	0.87	3.0	-0.01	**4.2**	10.6	0.85	7.59	3.18	70.3	**2.5**	22.5	13.7	**8.9**
7.2	0.00	na	0.00	**4.6**	2.1	0.91	9.89	2.92	62.6	**0.7**	17.9	43.6	**5.8**
0.0	5.94	na	-0.01	**3.5**	1.3	0.57	6.15	3.30	84.4	**0.6**	11.3	4.3	**5.1**
6.7	0.30	2.0	0.11	**7.6**	69.1	1.37	10.15	3.97	57.1	**2.6**	18.1	7.0	**10.0**
5.1	0.88	4.9	0.08	**5.7**	26.2	1.13	12.13	3.97	64.5	**4.0**	3.2	7.2	**8.0**
2.3	4.76	na	-0.07	**5.8**	3.1	1.24	16.73	3.77	71.0	**4.3**	27.7	9.5	**2.6**
6.4	1.01	na	0.03	**2.3**	2.6	0.55	4.97	2.94	91.3	**0.6**	9.6	28.3	**6.0**
8.8	0.45	na	0.01	**4.7**	8.7	1.04	10.73	3.57	69.1	**5.5**	27.4	4.7	**8.6**
4.2	1.14	na	0.01	**3.6**	1.6	0.65	6.43	3.38	76.8	**1.6**	4.2	19.9	**6.8**
6.1	0.44	na	0.00	**1.5**	0.4	0.18	2.87	3.51	96.5	**2.4**	8.1	16.2	**0.8**
9.9	0.00	na	0.00	**3.5**	0.8	0.62	3.86	3.24	78.3	**1.8**	15.8	20.3	**8.0**
8.3	0.00	na	0.00	**0.5**	0.0	-0.13	-0.64	3.27	104.2	**3.5**	30.4	12.5	**5.3**
3.2	1.95	10.3	0.55	**4.1**	18.3	0.61	5.22	3.50	64.2	**1.7**	9.4	19.9	**8.8**
3.7	5.21	na	0.26	**3.7**	0.5	0.71	5.29	4.25	73.5	**1.9**	24.3	14.0	**7.2**
0.0	7.36	na	1.17	**7.9**	1.5	1.90	24.65	3.98	36.5	**0.5**	13.6	67.6	**4.3**
7.3	0.00	na	-0.01	**6.3**	1.3	1.56	15.73	3.80	61.9	**2.4**	9.6	16.4	**7.7**
5.7	0.47	na	0.07	**4.5**	1.9	1.07	10.47	3.64	70.0	**4.1**	20.3	8.4	**6.2**
6.5	2.26	na	-0.42	**2.9**	0.3	0.57	3.75	3.47	90.9	**3.0**	61.0	30.2	**7.3**
8.0	0.20	na	0.04	**10.0**	11.2	2.11	16.57	4.86	50.9	**5.4**	30.5	2.8	**7.9**
5.9	1.23	na	0.08	**3.4**	9.5	0.70	7.05	2.72	69.1	**1.6**	10.6	10.8	**7.5**

Name	City	State	Rating	2018 Rating	2017 Rating	Total Assets ($Mil)	One Year Asset Growth	Asset Mix (As a % of Total Assets) Commercial Loans	Consumer Loans	Mortgage Loans	Securities	Capitalization Index	Leverage Ratio	Risk-Based Capital Ratio
Essex Bank	Richmond	VA	B	B	B-	1422.6	5.35	12.8	0.8	11.7	16.1	8.5	10.7	13.8
Essex Savings Bank	Essex	CT	B	B-	B-	406.5	3.37	3.3	0.5	46.7	0.3	9.2	10.4	17.5
ETHIC	Boston	MA	D	D-	D-	216.4	-6.42	1.5	19.8	15.1	0.0	10.0	15.9	19.8
Eureka Homestead	Metairie	LA	C	C	C-	108.7	8.87	0.0	0.2	71.2	6.3	10.0	17.7	38.5
Eureka Savings Bank	La Salle	IL	C+	C+	B-	316.0	-2.11	0.7	0.5	35.8	50.3	10.0	24.0	74.0
EvaBank	Cullman	AL	B-	B-	B	380.2	2.26	1.8	5.1	32.4	21.0	10.0	24.5	35.4
Evangeline Bank and Trust Co.	Ville Platte	LA	B	B	B	591.0	5.51	6.2	3.4	27.4	18.5	10.0	19.0	28.2
Evans Bank, N.A.	Hamburg	NY	B-	C+	B-	1439.9	5.45	16.4	0.1	12.6	9.5	7.5	10.0	12.9
Evercore Trust Co., N.A.	New York	NY	U	U	U	23.1	-1.58	0.0	0.0	0.0	87.2	0.0	100.	0.0
Everence Trust Co.	Goshen	IN	U	U	U	8.9	7.43	0.0	0.0	0.0	62.0	10.0	102.	311.1
Everett Co-operative Bank	Everett	MA	B+	B+	B+	513.8	3.52	0.5	0.1	40.7	8.1	10.0	13.1	19.3
▲ Evergreen Bank Group	Oak Brook	IL	B+	B	B	1071.1	7.99	2.7	50.6	4.0	8.9	8.2	11.0	13.5
Evergreen Federal Bank	Grants Pass	OR	B	B	B	470.0	2.00	1.6	0.3	29.0	8.6	10.0	12.5	17.5
Evergreen National Bank	Evergreen	CO	C+	C+	C-	118.4	2.46	2.3	0.6	16.4	24.9	8.0	9.6	20.0
EverTrust Bank	Pasadena	CA	A-	A-	A-	933.4	6.65	10.3	0.0	1.5	11.1	10.0	17.1	19.8
Evolve Bank & Trust	Memphis	TN	C+	C+	C+	518.8	6.05	18.4	0.7	21.7	3.9	6.2	8.5	11.9
▲ Exchange Bank	Santa Rosa	CA	A	A-	B+	2607.9	-0.24	8.0	0.7	10.5	27.6	8.8	10.2	15.4
Exchange Bank	Milledgeville	GA	B+	A-	A-	256.3	1.46	3.4	1.1	17.0	30.2	10.0	13.7	22.6
Exchange Bank	Gibbon	NE	B+	B+	B+	934.0	1.21	4.9	0.8	11.9	21.9	8.4	9.9	13.7
▲ Exchange Bank	Skiatook	OK	A-	B+	B	104.7	3.39	7.5	1.5	12.8	30.4	10.0	11.6	20.6
▲ Exchange Bank & Trust	Atchison	KS	A-	B+	B+	418.7	4.55	5.9	16.1	16.4	22.2	9.8	10.9	17.3
Exchange Bank and Trust Co.	Natchitoches	LA	A-	A-	A-	150.9	7.94	4.2	1.4	21.4	52.1	8.9	10.2	24.6
▼ Exchange Bank and Trust Co.	Perry	OK	B	A-	A-	294.0	7.79	6.3	5.1	21.5	28.2	8.9	10.3	17.9
Exchange Bank of Alabama	Altoona	AL	B+	A-	B+	288.4	2.92	3.3	3.4	15.2	24.5	10.0	14.3	22.0
Exchange Bank of Missouri	Fayette	MO	B+	B	B	213.9	11.26	7.2	1.5	10.4	7.9	8.1	11.1	13.4
▲ Exchange Bank of Northeast Missouri	Kahoka	MO	C+	C	B-	153.6	3.93	5.0	1.3	12.8	17.5	7.8	10.1	13.2
Exchange State Bank	Adair	IA	B	B	B	34.9	-2.18	4.2	2.3	8.4	17.5	10.0	13.1	24.1
Exchange State Bank	Collins	IA	B	B	B	112.3	1.50	10.1	0.8	13.8	6.6	8.3	10.4	13.6
Exchange State Bank	Springville	IA	B	B-	B-	43.9	-7.35	4.7	0.8	18.3	30.0	7.5	9.5	12.9
Exchange State Bank	Lanark	IL	B	B	B-	91.5	9.63	9.0	1.3	7.5	44.7	10.0	11.7	21.0
▲ Exchange State Bank	Carsonville	MI	A-	B+	A-	167.1	4.34	6.6	2.4	11.9	26.7	10.0	12.6	19.1
Exchange State Bank of St. Paul, Kansas	Saint Paul	KS	B-	B-	B-	73.5	5.89	10.4	2.4	13.9	24.6	9.1	10.4	20.2
Executive National Bank	Miami	FL	B	B-	B-	466.8	9.96	6.0	0.0	19.3	8.3	10.0	11.1	17.0
▲ Extraco Banks, N.A.	Temple	TX	B	B-	B-	1550.5	9.40	2.4	7.0	19.0	21.1	9.2	10.5	17.3
F & C Bank	Holden	MO	C+	B	B+	229.6	4.37	5.2	2.4	22.6	5.7	7.7	10.5	13.1
F & M Bank and Trust Co.	Manchester	GA	E-	E-	E-	68.0	-5.88	4.5	3.1	15.7	3.6	0.9	5.1	7.7
▲ F & M Bank Minnesota	Olivia	MN	B	B-	B-	127.4	2.91	4.9	0.3	1.9	28.3	6.4	8.7	12.1
F & M Community Bank, N.A.	Preston	MN	B-	B	B	140.1	9.00	6.6	1.7	14.1	14.0	9.1	11.3	14.2
F&M Bank	Washington	GA	B+	B+	B+	267.2	1.23	3.6	2.6	17.9	34.5	10.0	17.1	28.5
F&M Bank	Falls City	NE	B+	B+	B-	110.3	6.37	1.5	2.1	10.0	34.6	10.0	11.4	16.4
▲ F&M Bank	West Point	NE	B+	B	B+	276.9	0.08	5.1	1.1	7.5	9.4	9.0	10.9	14.2
F&M Bank	Edmond	OK	B+	B+	B	479.7	8.34	7.3	2.1	15.7	20.6	8.4	9.9	14.0
F&M Bank	Clarksville	TN	C+	B-	C+	1174.9	7.16	5.0	1.6	20.3	9.0	6.0	8.9	11.7
F&M Bank and Trust Co.	Hannibal	MO	B-	C+	C-	132.1	5.88	4.9	3.2	37.0	11.9	8.4	9.9	15.0
Fahey Banking Co.	Marion	OH	B+	B+	B+	291.6	3.33	1.7	0.5	8.7	17.1	10.0	16.3	21.6
Fairfax State Savings Bank	Fairfax	IA	B	B	B	168.4	14.82	5.8	2.0	10.8	30.3	10.0	12.1	23.3
Fairfield County Bank	Ridgefield	CT	B	B	B	1535.1	2.64	8.4	0.1	22.0	20.4	10.0	13.7	17.4
Fairfield Federal S&L Assn. of Lancaster	Lancaster	OH	C+	C+	C	265.7	1.64	0.0	0.4	80.8	3.4	10.0	11.4	23.7
Fairfield National Bank	Fairfield	IL	B+	B+	B+	551.3	-1.92	24.1	2.8	12.0	28.2	10.0	11.8	22.4
Fairmount State Bank	Fairmount	IN	C+	C+	C+	43.4	1.84	3.7	11.6	18.7	16.8	10.0	15.1	21.9
Fairport Savings Bank	Fairport	NY	C-	C-	C-	323.1	-0.66	2.3	0.0	67.8	7.5	7.2	9.1	16.5
Fairview S&L Assn.	Fairview	OK	B+	B+	B+	46.3	-3.22	3.0	2.2	30.6	1.6	10.0	19.7	30.0
Fairview State Banking Co.	Fairview	IL	C+	C+	C+	28.9	0.79	3.9	7.3	25.4	10.6	10.0	14.0	20.7
Falcon International Bank	Laredo	TX	A	A-	A-	1260.2	9.35	8.8	2.1	8.6	16.5	10.0	12.6	20.1
Falcon National Bank	Foley	MN	B	B	B+	568.9	21.47	26.7	0.6	8.3	9.3	7.2	9.8	12.7
Fall River Five Cents Savings Bank	Fall River	MA	C	C	C	1065.5	11.78	11.9	1.4	30.8	12.9	6.6	8.6	12.9
Falls City National Bank	Falls City	TX	B	B-	B	407.0	5.50	2.2	3.4	9.7	45.5	10.0	11.7	34.2
Family Bank	Pelham	GA	B	B	B-	100.2	5.24	5.5	7.9	50.2	7.9	10.0	12.7	19.9
▼ Family Federal Savings, F.A.	Fitchburg	MA	D+	C-	C-	95.6	-3.12	0.0	2.3	63.5	20.4	10.0	11.5	23.7
Fannin Bank	Bonham	TX	B	B	B-	110.7	11.77	10.4	3.2	18.7	24.8	7.2	9.2	15.1

Asset Quality Index	Adjusted Non-Performing Loans as a % of Total Loans	Adjusted Non-Performing Loans as a % of Capital	Net Charge-Offs Avg Loans	Profitability Index	Net Income ($Mil)	Return on Assets (R.O.A.)	Return on Equity (R.O.E.)	Net Interest Spread	Overhead Efficiency Ratio	Liquidity Index	Liquidity Ratio	Hot Money Ratio	Stability Index
6.4	0.54	4.3	0.09	**5.3**	12.1	1.14	10.95	3.86	65.0	**1.3**	16.7	29.8	**8.8**
3.7	2.98	na	0.00	**4.2**	2.3	0.76	5.98	3.65	86.6	**3.6**	18.7	11.2	**7.0**
3.4	1.06	na	0.26	**0.0**	-6.6	-3.72	-31.04	3.45	200.3	**1.3**	13.0	27.6	**4.8**
9.9	0.00	na	-0.02	**2.2**	0.2	0.23	1.73	2.07	90.1	**0.6**	20.6	70.2	**7.2**
7.3	3.45	na	0.02	**2.6**	0.9	0.36	1.54	2.66	87.6	**6.2**	76.1	11.2	**6.5**
4.1	6.31	na	0.49	**10.0**	7.4	2.73	10.30	6.39	40.1	**1.3**	31.3	42.3	**9.0**
6.1	1.62	na	0.09	**4.8**	4.2	0.98	5.16	4.22	70.1	**1.4**	17.6	26.7	**8.6**
4.0	1.49	8.3	-0.04	**6.1**	13.1	1.22	13.01	3.83	61.9	**2.4**	6.2	13.6	**8.7**
10.0	na	na	na	**7.7**	0.3	1.64	1.67	2.82	92.2	**4.0**	na	0.0	**0.0**
10.0	na	na	na	**8.6**	0.3	4.90	4.72	2.77	96.9	**4.0**	na	100.0	**5.5**
9.0	0.23	1.4	0.03	**4.4**	3.2	0.84	6.51	3.03	62.2	**0.9**	15.6	33.0	**8.3**
5.7	0.12	1.2	0.49	**7.0**	11.0	1.41	13.32	4.43	48.0	**0.8**	16.9	33.8	**8.2**
7.5	0.49	na	0.02	**5.0**	3.4	0.98	8.01	4.08	67.5	**4.2**	15.0	7.4	**7.4**
4.5	1.49	na	0.03	**3.5**	0.5	0.56	6.02	4.29	86.0	**6.7**	44.9	0.2	**5.1**
6.2	0.46	na	0.00	**9.3**	11.1	1.65	8.15	4.23	43.0	**0.8**	20.6	55.4	**9.4**
4.5	1.05	7.8	0.18	**5.1**	3.5	0.98	10.92	4.43	88.1	**1.8**	15.7	17.7	**5.6**
7.9	1.01	3.2	0.02	**8.0**	27.4	1.40	14.75	3.94	58.2	**5.6**	29.3	5.3	**9.2**
6.8	1.82	na	-0.01	**6.0**	2.3	1.24	9.09	4.23	66.1	**3.8**	31.4	13.4	**8.3**
6.6	0.83	3.8	0.03	**7.2**	12.9	1.83	17.56	3.19	45.1	**0.9**	20.9	38.3	**8.8**
8.4	2.24	na	-0.04	**5.9**	1.0	1.23	10.92	4.19	68.6	**2.7**	36.1	21.0	**7.3**
7.6	0.13	na	0.02	**7.4**	4.6	1.47	14.06	3.75	54.3	**4.3**	17.4	6.9	**6.5**
6.4	1.01	4.1	-0.03	**8.1**	2.3	1.97	20.14	3.74	50.9	**4.0**	17.0	9.1	**8.4**
3.3	3.60	17.6	0.07	**3.8**	0.8	0.34	3.02	4.39	66.0	**0.8**	13.6	32.7	**8.3**
8.6	0.04	0.5	0.03	**4.9**	2.1	0.97	6.91	3.68	69.1	**3.0**	18.6	14.3	**8.2**
5.8	0.14	3.3	0.27	**7.2**	2.1	1.34	11.65	4.22	53.7	**2.6**	3.5	15.0	**7.4**
3.7	1.22	na	0.87	**3.6**	0.7	0.59	5.20	4.04	71.3	**3.4**	15.3	12.2	**7.2**
7.8	0.00	na	0.00	**6.4**	0.4	1.48	9.57	3.73	60.7	**3.8**	32.8	13.4	**8.1**
8.2	0.00	na	0.00	**4.7**	0.9	1.05	10.29	3.55	68.7	**1.4**	8.2	24.0	**6.8**
8.7	0.21	na	0.00	**5.0**	0.3	1.01	10.99	3.72	64.4	**5.0**	33.3	7.3	**5.3**
7.4	1.31	na	0.13	**4.5**	0.9	1.43	11.29	3.13	70.6	**2.6**	40.0	23.9	**7.4**
8.7	0.47	na	0.11	**6.6**	1.9	1.58	12.89	3.92	58.3	**4.9**	38.5	10.1	**7.2**
8.2	0.40	na	0.00	**4.3**	0.5	0.89	8.60	3.64	69.9	**2.8**	39.7	22.3	**5.1**
7.1	0.49	na	0.05	**4.1**	2.2	0.66	5.99	3.76	76.2	**3.3**	17.4	12.7	**6.7**
8.3	0.06	0.3	0.03	**4.9**	13.4	1.21	11.61	3.60	72.2	**4.9**	26.1	5.8	**9.1**
4.9	1.82	na	-0.01	**8.8**	3.6	2.11	20.08	5.02	57.6	**3.0**	6.4	13.2	**8.1**
1.9	5.34	na	0.14	**1.4**	0.0	0.05	0.91	4.76	99.0	**1.5**	14.9	23.8	**0.2**
5.7	0.16	na	-0.08	**6.0**	1.4	1.49	15.39	4.22	61.4	**4.1**	13.5	7.6	**7.0**
5.5	1.75	na	0.00	**5.1**	1.3	1.26	11.43	4.15	71.6	**3.3**	6.9	10.0	**7.8**
7.5	0.71	na	0.41	**5.1**	2.0	1.01	5.93	4.03	69.3	**2.0**	28.2	21.8	**7.7**
8.8	0.18	na	0.15	**4.7**	0.9	1.16	10.33	3.04	59.1	**4.2**	30.3	8.6	**6.7**
8.3	0.17	na	0.02	**6.6**	3.3	1.57	15.21	3.70	63.0	**3.9**	20.2	10.1	**7.5**
5.9	0.18	na	0.05	**7.4**	6.5	1.80	18.67	4.22	62.1	**2.2**	10.5	17.6	**6.8**
7.4	0.29	2.2	0.09	**3.6**	5.1	0.60	5.46	3.42	83.0	**0.9**	17.9	30.3	**8.8**
7.6	0.65	na	0.07	**4.5**	0.8	0.84	8.07	3.57	71.0	**3.8**	11.7	9.8	**5.2**
7.0	0.45	na	-0.21	**4.3**	2.7	1.20	7.69	3.20	71.2	**0.6**	9.3	35.5	**7.2**
9.1	0.10	na	-0.16	**3.7**	0.9	0.75	6.04	3.05	74.1	**4.1**	55.4	18.1	**6.7**
7.6	1.23	na	0.13	**4.2**	8.8	0.77	5.62	3.75	78.1	**4.3**	24.1	7.0	**9.5**
7.0	0.99	na	0.03	**3.1**	1.0	0.49	4.35	3.31	81.5	**1.5**	8.4	22.3	**5.8**
3.6	3.38	16.1	0.27	**4.8**	4.8	1.13	9.46	2.74	48.1	**0.9**	17.2	30.4	**8.3**
4.7	2.21	na	0.92	**3.3**	0.2	0.51	3.64	4.28	72.1	**4.1**	16.2	7.9	**5.9**
8.4	0.37	na	0.00	**1.8**	0.3	0.11	1.22	2.71	94.1	**0.8**	9.5	33.2	**4.9**
8.8	0.00	na	0.00	**7.9**	0.7	1.88	10.02	4.18	53.4	**2.8**	24.8	16.1	**7.0**
4.9	2.45	9.6	0.53	**3.8**	0.2	0.73	5.32	4.41	75.6	**2.3**	25.2	18.5	**4.8**
7.1	1.16	3.5	-0.02	**8.7**	16.1	1.76	13.97	4.18	57.4	**2.0**	25.7	28.9	**10.0**
7.6	0.16	na	0.13	**4.9**	3.2	0.85	8.82	4.60	67.0	**1.2**	15.4	20.9	**7.1**
8.4	0.45	na	0.00	**3.2**	4.0	0.52	6.06	2.96	81.5	**1.6**	20.0	22.0	**6.5**
6.4	3.16	na	0.15	**10.0**	7.2	2.31	20.61	3.57	20.6	**5.7**	55.3	10.3	**7.1**
4.8	1.92	11.5	0.11	**5.3**	0.8	1.05	8.57	5.02	75.6	**2.2**	9.0	17.5	**6.7**
6.9	1.73	na	-0.01	**0.0**	-0.7	-0.96	-8.10	2.47	136.4	**1.4**	28.5	29.0	**5.9**
5.0	0.82	13.2	0.14	**4.8**	0.8	1.01	11.31	4.54	76.6	**2.0**	26.3	16.3	**5.8**

Name	City	State	Rating	2018 Rating	2017 Rating	Total Assets ($Mil)	One Year Asset Growth	Asset Mix (As a % of Total Assets): Commercial Loans	Consumer Loans	Mortgage Loans	Securities	Capitalization Index	Leverage Ratio	Risk-Based Capital Ratio
▲ Farm Bureau Bank, FSB	Sparks	NV	D+	D	C-	798.6	6.13	7.1	73.0	0.1	3.6	6.6	10.3	12.2
▲ Farmers & Mechanics Bank	Galesburg	IL	B+	B-	B	369.7	1.01	11.5	5.1	13.1	22.9	10.0	11.2	17.1
▲ Farmers & Merchants Bank	Piedmont	AL	B+	B	B	227.9	4.61	8.4	2.4	13.1	31.7	10.0	13.7	21.7
Farmers & Merchants Bank	Waterloo	AL	B+	B+	A-	88.6	7.06	1.6	2.1	0.2	79.9	10.0	21.7	51.4
Farmers & Merchants Bank	Stuttgart	AR	B+	B+	B+	1506.5	37.14	8.4	1.6	18.1	12.7	7.4	9.9	12.8
Farmers & Merchants Bank	Lodi	CA	A-	A-	A-	3569.1	12.47	10.5	0.4	7.7	15.4	6.8	10.0	12.3
▲ Farmers & Merchants Bank	Eatonton	GA	B-	C+	C+	181.4	4.11	11.2	2.0	12.3	26.1	10.0	14.9	24.6
Farmers & Merchants Bank	Lakeland	GA	E-	E-	E-	490.9	-2.56	8.4	6.0	20.0	10.5	2.6	6.1	9.6
▲ Farmers & Merchants Bank	Salisbury	NC	B+	B-	C+	633.0	0.60	4.1	0.3	14.3	0.6	10.0	11.4	18.2
▲ Farmers & Merchants Bank	Tolna	ND	C+	C	C	108.4	-0.40	8.5	2.7	2.6	25.5	6.7	9.8	12.3
Farmers & Merchants Bank	Miamisburg	OH	B+	B+	B	177.9	14.83	7.8	1.3	17.5	19.4	8.4	9.9	14.7
▲ Farmers & Merchants Bank	Duke	OK	C+	C	C	18.3	-1.81	7.9	2.1	0.0	15.3	10.0	11.5	26.6
▲ Farmers & Merchants Bank	Dyer	TN	C-	D+	D+	99.3	4.08	6.4	3.6	7.8	42.2	7.8	9.6	19.7
▲ Farmers & Merchants Bank	New Castle	VA	A-	B+	B+	61.0	1.34	0.9	5.0	31.6	36.3	10.0	19.9	48.9
Farmers & Merchants Bank	Timberville	VA	C+	B-	B	812.4	4.99	3.6	13.5	24.7	0.7	8.8	11.0	14.0
▲ Farmers & Merchants Bank	Berlin	WI	C+	C	B-	313.0	1.23	10.5	3.4	22.9	11.4	9.3	10.5	14.5
Farmers & Merchants Bank & Trust	Burlington	IA	C	C+	C+	205.2	7.15	7.8	1.8	29.0	13.4	8.1	9.7	15.4
Farmers & Merchants Bank & Trust	Marinette	WI	B-	C+	C+	139.1	-0.25	8.1	1.6	20.7	25.5	10.0	11.9	17.1
▲ Farmers & Merchants Bank of Colby	Colby	KS	A-	B+	A	244.6	16.03	9.0	0.3	0.9	25.4	10.0	13.8	16.5
Farmers & Merchants Bank of Hutsonville	Hutsonville	IL	B	B	B	45.6	6.43	6.5	8.1	25.7	6.0	10.0	18.6	32.9
Farmers & Merchants Bank of Long Beach	Long Beach	CA	A-	A-	A-	7597.1	3.94	0.7	0.3	8.3	38.2	10.0	14.1	20.7
Farmers & Merchants Bank of Orfordville	Orfordville	WI	B	B	B	54.4	4.49	4.1	6.0	29.1	17.9	10.0	13.2	24.8
Farmers & Merchants Savings Bank	Lone Tree	IA	B	B	B-	91.6	6.80	8.2	1.4	22.7	18.4	10.0	12.3	16.1
▲ Farmers & Merchants Savings Bank	Manchester	IA	B-	C+	B	599.4	2.35	33.2	0.7	6.3	3.5	9.7	13.4	14.8
Farmers & Merchants State Bank	Winterset	IA	B+	B+	A-	188.4	-0.68	4.0	3.1	10.2	27.0	8.7	10.1	14.9
Farmers & Merchants State Bank	New York Mills	MN	B	B	B	61.3	-4.26	10.7	3.9	6.6	33.8	10.0	16.0	25.9
Farmers & Merchants State Bank	Archbold	OH	A-	A-	B+	1551.2	43.23	8.4	3.2	7.7	11.2	7.7	10.2	13.0
Farmers & Merchants State Bank	Waterloo	WI	B-	C+	B-	182.0	8.53	1.6	0.9	15.9	8.1	10.0	11.5	15.1
Farmers & Merchants Union Bank	Columbus	WI	C+	B-	B	395.6	0.11	9.0	0.6	8.9	5.8	9.1	11.5	14.2
Farmers & Stockmens Bank	Clayton	NM	B-	B	B	218.0	-1.59	6.3	0.9	7.5	1.6	9.9	11.9	14.9
Farmers & Traders Bank of Campton	Campton	KY	B-	B-	B-	46.6	1.71	1.5	4.8	25.3	35.6	9.4	10.6	15.9
Farmers & Traders Savings Bank	Bancroft	IA	B-	B-	B-	55.7	-0.84	2.8	1.5	4.6	29.6	10.0	11.1	18.5
▲ Farmers and Drovers Bank	Council Grove	KS	A-	B+	B+	181.8	0.15	2.9	8.7	14.7	36.2	10.0	27.2	47.1
Farmers and Mechanics FSB	Bloomfield	IN	C-	C-	C-	74.0	0.77	0.1	0.1	33.7	44.3	10.0	17.2	54.2
Farmers and Merchants Bank	LaFayette	AL	A-	B+	B+	165.8	3.91	10.9	6.2	8.4	49.2	10.0	14.1	23.3
Farmers and Merchants Bank	Sylvania	GA	B	B	B-	114.5	4.04	1.8	3.1	11.9	35.2	10.0	16.2	39.2
Farmers and Merchants Bank	Boswell	IN	B	B	B	132.5	6.63	3.6	0.8	17.3	22.3	10.0	11.4	18.9
▲ Farmers and Merchants Bank	Laotto	IN	A-	B+	B+	159.3	4.71	9.1	2.8	27.1	19.4	9.8	10.9	17.0
▲ Farmers and Merchants Bank	Mound City	KS	D+	D	D	39.7	2.45	13.8	6.3	33.9	12.3	5.6	7.6	12.5
▲ Farmers and Merchants Bank	Upperco	MD	B-	C	B-	434.5	5.42	4.8	0.1	9.1	13.9	9.2	11.0	14.4
▲ Farmers and Merchants Bank	Baldwyn	MS	A-	B+	A-	342.2	2.35	4.6	8.5	19.2	29.6	10.0	15.0	24.6
Farmers and Merchants Bank	Axtell	NE	D+	D+	D	7.8	-2.97	4.7	4.5	0.4	54.3	9.0	10.3	33.9
Farmers and Merchants Bank	Milford	NE	B	B	B-	672.0	3.66	2.4	4.2	4.1	48.5	10.0	11.7	20.4
▲ Farmers and Merchants Bank	Milligan	NE	B	B-	B	118.5	3.40	9.2	1.1	3.2	0.0	8.5	11.4	13.7
▲ Farmers and Merchants Bank	Caldwell	OH	B-	C+	B	111.9	0.20	6.5	6.6	43.3	15.6	10.0	14.5	26.4
Farmers and Merchants Bank	Arnett	OK	B	B	B	52.3	-3.01	3.3	8.3	1.3	42.4	10.0	13.8	32.0
▲ Farmers and Merchants Bank	Maysville	OK	B-	C+	B-	19.0	-1.49	49.3	11.2	0.3	7.6	6.5	8.6	12.6
▲ Farmers and Merchants Bank	Holly Hill	SC	B+	B	B-	313.3	3.41	1.6	2.3	8.8	33.5	10.0	15.3	46.3
▲ Farmers and Merchants Bank	De Leon	TX	C+	C	D+	92.0	1.65	4.2	5.0	22.7	16.5	7.9	9.6	15.9
Farmers and Merchants Bank of Ashland	Ashland	NE	B	B	B-	81.6	5.93	5.5	1.3	17.0	9.8	9.6	10.7	15.5
Farmers and Merchants Bank of Kendall	Kendall	WI	C+	B-	B+	73.4	1.57	4.2	1.9	9.0	0.0	10.0	16.0	19.1
▲ Farmers and Merchants Bank of St. Clair	Saint Clair	MO	A-	B+	B	203.7	4.79	7.2	1.8	25.0	14.1	10.0	13.2	20.6
Farmers and Merchants National Bank	Nashville	IL	A-	A-	B	183.4	8.50	3.5	1.2	15.6	22.3	10.0	12.3	18.1
Farmers and Merchants National Bank	Fairview	OK	A	A	A	113.7	-2.22	3.4	2.6	9.4	52.4	10.0	12.5	26.7
▲ Farmers and Merchants State Bank	Bushnell	IL	B-	C+	C+	69.5	-0.70	4.5	6.4	11.6	21.6	8.1	9.8	19.5
Farmers and Merchants State Bank	Alpha	MN	D+	C-	D+	38.3	-3.10	5.1	3.2	13.0	2.1	10.0	11.7	18.1
▲ Farmers and Merchants State Bank	Appleton	MN	B-	C+	B+	46.3	-1.66	5.3	2.3	3.3	12.1	10.0	14.3	17.1
Farmers and Merchants State Bank	Blooming Prairie	MN	C+	C	C-	88.4	9.06	8.7	2.0	11.9	0.2	6.6	8.6	13.2
Farmers and Merchants State Bank	Pierz	MN	C+	B-	C+	222.7	-0.43	9.3	2.4	13.4	14.5	9.7	10.8	14.9
▲ Farmers and Merchants State Bank	Springfield	MN	C+	C+	B-	119.8	2.65	4.1	1.3	6.4	13.8	6.9	8.9	13.9

Asset Quality Index	Adjusted Non-Performing Loans as a % of Total Loans	as a % of Capital	Net Charge-Offs Avg Loans	Profitability Index	Net Income ($Mil)	Return on Assets (R.O.A.)	Return on Equity (R.O.E.)	Net Interest Spread	Overhead Efficiency Ratio	Liquidity Index	Liquidity Ratio	Hot Money Ratio	Stability Index
2.5	0.72	na	0.89	**3.2**	2.9	0.49	4.74	4.31	76.7	**0.4**	10.0	32.2	**5.6**
6.9	0.88	na	0.08	**5.1**	2.9	1.02	7.76	3.35	66.9	**4.0**	19.8	9.0	**8.1**
7.8	0.98	na	0.13	**5.1**	1.7	1.03	7.55	4.35	70.1	**4.2**	33.1	11.7	**7.4**
9.5	5.37	na	-0.04	**5.3**	0.9	1.36	6.38	2.54	41.8	**3.5**	85.7	33.3	**6.7**
6.0	0.48	na	0.11	**5.1**	10.6	1.02	8.09	3.98	66.6	**3.2**	5.1	12.0	**9.5**
8.4	0.46	1.4	0.03	**8.9**	42.8	1.67	16.56	4.37	51.0	**3.3**	15.8	12.9	**9.5**
4.4	5.41	na	-1.39	**5.8**	1.8	1.33	9.87	4.29	73.8	**2.9**	26.9	16.1	**6.0**
0.3	5.93	na	0.81	**2.4**	0.6	0.17	2.69	3.92	77.7	**0.7**	15.4	37.4	**1.2**
6.0	2.00	na	-0.03	**8.4**	7.9	1.69	14.85	4.50	59.6	**5.1**	33.3	6.1	**7.7**
5.6	0.80	na	0.24	**4.0**	0.7	0.82	7.35	3.82	71.6	**2.5**	25.8	16.9	**6.7**
5.3	1.21	5.8	0.18	**6.3**	1.6	1.31	13.19	4.41	62.7	**4.0**	9.6	8.0	**6.4**
8.8	0.00	na	0.00	**5.1**	0.2	1.36	12.50	3.34	56.2	**4.7**	59.5	13.2	**5.4**
6.5	2.62	na	0.25	**2.2**	0.4	0.58	6.37	3.43	88.5	**5.4**	41.6	7.8	**4.0**
9.1	0.00	na	0.21	**6.7**	0.6	1.35	6.82	4.25	59.4	**5.0**	43.0	10.6	**8.1**
3.4	1.24	8.9	0.59	**3.9**	2.7	0.47	4.19	4.44	68.7	**3.9**	4.7	8.1	**8.0**
3.6	2.42	na	0.19	**5.0**	2.5	1.06	10.17	3.92	60.0	**0.7**	11.4	25.1	**6.1**
3.7	1.89	na	0.67	**2.2**	0.4	0.25	2.71	3.72	89.9	**5.0**	22.9	2.8	**3.8**
5.9	1.75	na	-0.04	**3.5**	0.6	0.54	4.62	3.88	80.3	**4.0**	39.1	14.6	**5.9**
8.4	0.07	na	0.00	**9.9**	3.2	1.85	13.00	3.78	34.5	**0.7**	16.0	40.8	**9.2**
8.4	0.00	na	0.00	**7.2**	0.7	1.95	10.77	3.29	40.4	**2.2**	35.2	27.7	**7.0**
8.9	0.08	0.4	0.01	**5.6**	66.9	1.19	8.53	3.47	59.1	**4.4**	24.2	10.0	**10.0**
6.1	1.55	na	-0.02	**2.9**	0.1	0.21	1.59	3.57	91.8	**3.6**	37.2	15.4	**6.7**
8.1	0.00	na	0.00	**3.8**	0.5	0.75	5.36	3.27	72.4	**1.7**	14.1	16.4	**6.0**
5.8	0.92	na	0.02	**9.0**	12.5	2.83	24.16	4.06	43.2	**1.7**	21.4	24.0	**9.1**
8.6	0.34	na	0.25	**5.9**	1.7	1.19	12.01	3.53	56.3	**3.1**	25.9	14.8	**7.2**
8.7	0.00	na	-0.05	**4.1**	0.5	1.00	6.36	3.47	71.3	**4.2**	37.4	13.0	**7.0**
7.4	0.37	1.8	0.05	**6.2**	13.1	1.18	9.35	3.93	65.4	**3.4**	14.6	12.1	**9.3**
6.6	0.20	na	-0.49	**6.9**	1.8	1.33	11.97	3.52	56.2	**4.3**	19.6	7.0	**7.2**
3.4	3.34	13.8	-0.04	**7.3**	3.7	1.25	11.17	3.70	43.0	**0.7**	15.8	42.8	**8.1**
6.9	0.00	na	0.08	**9.1**	3.3	2.09	16.16	4.82	71.0	**3.6**	20.3	11.5	**9.2**
6.9	0.52	1.6	0.02	**3.8**	0.3	0.74	6.32	3.99	80.8	**1.7**	25.1	25.0	**5.4**
7.4	0.10	na	0.00	**3.9**	0.4	0.92	8.50	3.22	68.0	**2.4**	32.2	21.1	**6.5**
8.3	0.70	na	-0.25	**5.5**	1.6	1.17	4.34	3.35	55.8	**2.4**	28.9	19.4	**8.2**
10.0	0.15	na	0.00	**1.2**	0.2	0.35	2.03	2.41	105.3	**3.8**	74.1	17.2	**7.4**
8.1	0.60	3.5	0.08	**5.5**	1.5	1.18	8.43	3.90	62.8	**3.1**	41.7	19.8	**8.1**
9.0	2.26	na	0.02	**4.9**	0.9	1.09	6.87	3.78	64.7	**3.8**	48.0	18.0	**7.1**
8.9	0.45	1.8	-0.24	**4.3**	0.8	0.79	6.97	3.59	73.6	**2.0**	22.0	19.7	**6.8**
8.6	0.04	na	0.01	**5.9**	1.7	1.45	13.65	3.89	63.9	**5.4**	31.4	3.3	**7.1**
4.1	4.86	na	0.22	**5.8**	0.4	1.41	19.00	4.45	66.4	**1.5**	10.3	23.4	**3.7**
6.3	0.63	na	-0.01	**4.6**	2.8	0.86	8.00	3.69	71.3	**1.4**	18.7	19.7	**7.0**
6.5	1.92	na	0.19	**9.3**	4.9	1.91	12.95	4.98	60.9	**1.8**	25.5	24.0	**8.7**
9.1	0.00	1.1	0.00	**1.4**	0.0	0.25	2.50	3.44	99.0	**5.5**	55.9	4.4	**4.0**
8.3	0.10	na	0.34	**4.4**	6.4	1.30	10.82	2.70	61.0	**2.7**	51.6	4.1	**7.3**
6.5	0.00	na	-0.02	**8.1**	1.6	1.89	15.59	4.29	50.9	**0.6**	10.3	21.1	**8.6**
3.6	2.69	na	0.20	**6.0**	0.9	1.13	7.94	4.93	64.0	**3.3**	19.7	12.7	**8.1**
8.4	0.08	na	0.12	**4.9**	0.5	1.26	9.50	2.75	58.3	**3.6**	40.8	17.1	**7.6**
7.6	0.00	na	0.01	**9.0**	0.4	2.44	29.53	5.60	58.5	**4.1**	30.8	9.4	**5.1**
6.8	5.96	na	0.10	**5.1**	2.9	1.09	8.23	3.23	61.8	**6.0**	60.3	10.1	**6.8**
6.3	0.61	na	0.13	**3.4**	0.5	0.73	7.82	4.34	79.6	**4.9**	31.7	6.8	**5.3**
8.7	0.00	0.3	0.00	**4.1**	0.5	0.78	7.13	4.33	77.9	**4.3**	17.7	7.2	**6.6**
4.6	4.90	na	0.00	**10.0**	1.3	2.38	15.32	4.99	47.7	**1.6**	10.1	20.9	**9.0**
8.7	0.33	na	0.06	**5.3**	1.5	0.99	7.59	4.30	72.1	**3.4**	22.0	12.8	**7.3**
8.6	0.61	na	0.05	**6.0**	1.9	1.45	11.64	3.95	64.2	**4.4**	14.7	5.7	**8.1**
9.2	0.00	na	0.02	**7.6**	1.6	1.77	14.62	3.76	54.2	**3.4**	34.8	16.1	**9.3**
8.6	0.01	na	0.06	**5.0**	0.5	0.94	10.15	3.51	71.8	**5.5**	35.9	4.6	**4.9**
2.7	1.90	na	0.29	**3.2**	0.2	0.51	4.74	3.24	73.8	**1.5**	30.6	23.1	**1.6**
4.2	1.51	na	0.25	**8.3**	0.7	2.04	14.25	4.66	48.2	**2.3**	17.3	9.9	**8.6**
4.4	1.20	6.9	0.00	**9.2**	1.4	2.28	27.43	4.54	51.9	**4.7**	23.2	5.0	**5.0**
5.1	3.85	na	0.01	**9.0**	3.3	1.97	18.58	4.52	52.7	**3.8**	20.0	10.3	**8.6**
5.5	0.00	na	0.00	**5.2**	1.1	1.25	14.54	3.92	66.3	**2.9**	12.2	12.3	**4.8**

Name	City	State	Rating	2018 Rating	2017 Rating	Total Assets ($Mil)	One Year Asset Growth	Asset Mix (As a % of Total Assets) Comm-ercial Loans	Cons-umer Loans	Mort-gage Loans	Secur-ities	Capital-ization Index	Lever-age Ratio	Risk-Based Capital Ratio
Farmers and Merchants State Bank	Langdon	ND	**B**	B+	B+	106.4	0.55	4.6	2.2	1.2	26.6	**10.0**	14.5	22.1
▲ Farmers and Merchants State Bank	Bloomfield	NE	**B**	B-	B+	134.8	2.12	5.1	5.4	0.1	23.2	**7.8**	13.2	13.2
Farmers and Merchants State Bank	Plankinton	SD	**C+**	B-	B+	113.7	0.89	9.1	4.1	7.6	5.7	**7.8**	11.3	13.2
Farmers and Merchants State Bank	Scotland	SD	**B-**	B-	B-	29.2	6.82	6.0	11.1	2.0	37.5	**10.0**	11.3	21.4
▲ Farmers and Merchants Trust Co.	Chambersburg	PA	**B**	C+	B+	1302.3	8.97	6.5	0.5	12.1	11.3	**7.4**	9.3	15.5
▲ Farmers and Miners Bank	Pennington Gap	VA	**A-**	B+	B+	133.8	-2.65	2.6	7.7	20.6	20.9	**10.0**	14.4	31.9
Farmers Bank	Greenwood	AR	**B+**	B+	B	210.8	3.91	6.2	6.0	29.2	22.2	**10.0**	18.7	31.0
Farmers Bank	Ault	CO	**A**	A	A	253.4	6.18	5.5	0.6	5.5	0.0	**10.0**	13.7	18.4
Farmers Bank	Greensboro	GA	**B-**	B-	B-	95.3	4.25	10.4	0.8	15.9	39.6	**10.0**	15.8	28.9
▲ Farmers Bank	Buhl	ID	**A-**	A-	B+	461.7	2.29	13.2	1.9	5.6	33.8	**10.0**	15.1	23.0
Farmers Bank	Nicholasville	KY	**B**	B	B	155.3	13.33	1.8	0.9	28.6	20.5	**10.0**	11.1	20.3
Farmers Bank	Carnegie	OK	**D**	C-	D+	90.7	-2.37	8.0	2.7	27.1	3.3	**0.0**	2.2	4.3
Farmers Bank	Parsons	TN	**C+**	C+	C+	37.4	2.32	6.5	12.2	18.2	12.0	**10.0**	13.3	28.6
Farmers Bank	Portland	TN	**A-**	A-	A-	681.8	3.51	5.3	1.5	17.4	24.4	**10.0**	12.2	16.3
▲ Farmers Bank	Windsor	VA	**B**	B	B+	454.3	0.33	12.9	1.9	8.9	28.7	**8.6**	10.1	14.3
Farmers Bank & Trust	Atwood	KS	**B-**	C+	B	99.9	9.06	5.2	1.1	3.3	32.4	**7.4**	9.3	17.5
Farmers Bank & Trust	Great Bend	KS	**A**	A	A	871.7	9.73	2.0	0.2	5.7	54.3	**10.0**	18.1	28.5
Farmers Bank & Trust Co.	Magnolia	AR	**B**	B-	B-	1603.4	9.48	11.6	1.6	19.4	14.1	**7.4**	9.6	12.9
Farmers Bank and Savings Co.	Pomeroy	OH	**B-**	B-	B	335.1	2.61	3.7	5.6	36.5	16.3	**8.8**	10.2	16.8
Farmers Bank and Trust Co.	Blytheville	AR	**B**	B	B-	281.6	6.57	14.3	3.0	18.3	4.7	**6.9**	9.4	12.4
Farmers Bank and Trust Co.	Marion	KY	**B+**	B+	A	386.9	90.65	4.8	3.1	30.7	10.6	**8.4**	9.9	13.9
Farmers Bank and Trust Co.	Princeton	KY	**A**	A	A	136.0	9.11	5.5	1.4	15.9	14.1	**10.0**	14.6	20.7
▲ Farmers Bank of Appomattox	Appomattox	VA	**B+**	B	B+	236.2	0.70	5.3	17.0	23.9	23.8	**10.0**	14.6	21.2
Farmers Bank of Green City	Green City	MO	**C**	C-	C	55.4	4.86	19.5	5.2	13.0	15.0	**7.0**	9.1	12.5
Farmers Bank of Lincoln	Lincoln	MO	**A-**	A-	A-	126.0	5.30	3.4	3.3	37.1	7.5	**10.0**	11.3	19.8
Farmers Bank of Lohman	Jefferson City	MO	**B-**	B-	B-	67.8	3.06	6.1	3.2	12.6	54.0	**10.0**	15.7	35.9
Farmers Bank of Milton	Milton	KY	**B**	B	B	250.3	5.26	4.9	2.9	30.6	27.7	**10.0**	14.9	23.1
Farmers Bank of Mt. Pulaski	Mount Pulaski	IL	**C**	C	C	57.0	21.92	3.6	3.5	21.5	34.7	**10.0**	12.1	37.2
Farmers Bank of Northern Missouri	Unionville	MO	**B+**	B+	B+	369.6	0.64	3.8	1.8	9.7	28.2	**10.0**	12.9	19.2
▲ Farmers Bank of Osborne, Kansas	Osborne	KS	**B**	B-	B	66.7	2.90	1.6	1.6	2.5	19.2	**10.0**	12.7	18.1
▲ Farmers Bank of Willards	Willards	MD	**B-**	C	C	391.3	3.13	7.8	2.0	37.0	6.0	**9.9**	10.9	16.2
Farmers Bank, Frankfort, Indiana, Inc.	Frankfort	IN	**C+**	C+	B-	590.2	7.13	8.3	2.6	7.6	21.7	**8.9**	11.5	14.1
Farmers Building and Savings Bank	Rochester	PA	**B**	B+	B+	99.3	6.72	0.2	0.0	43.3	26.7	**10.0**	21.2	53.8
▲ Farmers Deposit Bank	Liberty	KY	**C**	D+	D	44.8	-0.83	8.8	9.2	22.9	2.2	**9.0**	10.3	15.1
Farmers National Bank	Prophetstown	IL	**A**	A	A	726.1	9.19	2.8	0.7	4.2	39.7	**10.0**	13.8	21.1
▲ Farmers National Bank	Phillipsburg	KS	**A-**	B+	A	144.5	6.84	19.6	3.0	7.9	14.6	**10.0**	17.1	19.7
▲ Farmers National Bank of Canfield	Canfield	OH	**B+**	B	B	2411.2	6.12	8.5	8.7	15.9	17.3	**7.4**	9.8	12.8
Farmers National Bank of Danville	Danville	KY	**B+**	B+	B+	557.9	6.83	4.3	1.6	26.5	20.3	**10.0**	11.3	16.3
Farmers National Bank of Emlenton	Emlenton	PA	**C+**	C+	C+	936.1	21.23	4.6	1.2	44.0	12.6	**6.1**	8.1	13.8
Farmers National Bank of Griggsville	Griggsville	IL	**C**	C	B-	91.3	-1.72	5.6	6.7	15.5	4.7	**9.4**	11.2	14.5
Farmers National Bank of Lebanon	Lebanon	KY	**B-**	C+	C	100.4	-0.58	6.0	2.6	8.8	37.6	**10.0**	11.9	19.2
▲ Farmers National Bank of Scottsville	Scottsville	KY	**A-**	B+	B+	251.2	0.84	6.2	1.5	18.8	20.1	**10.0**	16.2	22.0
▼ Farmers Savings Bank	Colesburg	IA	**B**	B+	B+	212.4	5.94	6.6	2.8	5.4	30.7	**10.0**	11.8	16.2
▲ Farmers Savings Bank	Fostoria	IA	**B**	B	B+	128.0	5.26	8.5	2.6	23.6	12.9	**10.0**	14.5	20.8
Farmers Savings Bank	Frederika	IA	**B**	B	B	45.7	1.54	4.6	3.1	11.4	19.6	**10.0**	18.9	28.6
▲ Farmers Savings Bank	Marshalltown	IA	**A-**	B+	B	111.3	5.81	6.5	1.7	12.1	23.1	**10.0**	14.8	21.6
▼ Farmers Savings Bank	Wever	IA	**C**	C+	B-	112.5	-10.08	15.8	2.1	32.0	7.0	**10.0**	15.1	23.2
▲ Farmers Savings Bank	Spencer	OH	**A-**	B+	A-	288.0	4.83	1.1	0.5	17.5	65.4	**10.0**	26.2	65.7
Farmers Savings Bank	Mineral Point	WI	**B**	B	B+	308.8	8.65	6.9	7.2	11.3	33.3	**6.7**	8.7	15.6
Farmers Savings Bank & Trust	Traer	IA	**A-**	B+	B+	168.5	0.33	3.9	1.4	10.2	28.1	**9.3**	10.6	16.9
▲ Farmers Security Bank	Washburn	ND	**B-**	C-	C+	55.8	3.99	8.9	2.7	2.2	19.5	**10.0**	11.5	15.9
▲ Farmers State Bank	Dublin	GA	**A-**	B+	B+	124.9	0.56	7.7	7.1	18.9	20.1	**10.0**	15.2	20.8
Farmers State Bank	Lincolnton	GA	**A**	A-	A-	127.3	6.39	3.1	7.2	23.9	17.3	**10.0**	17.7	26.7
Farmers State Bank	Algona	IA	**B+**	B+	C+	112.8	4.35	11.4	1.2	15.9	17.2	**10.0**	11.1	15.7
▲ Farmers State Bank	Lake View	IA	**B**	B-	C+	33.5	3.10	7.9	5.8	13.9	27.7	**10.0**	12.6	36.2
Farmers State Bank	Marcus	IA	**B+**	B+	A-	63.6	-7.03	8.8	3.6	5.6	27.0	**10.0**	14.3	20.6
Farmers State Bank	Marion	IA	**A**	A	A	821.8	9.19	7.9	1.3	8.4	11.8	**10.0**	14.2	19.2
▲ Farmers State Bank	Mason City	IA	**A-**	B+	A-	185.3	-2.29	5.1	2.1	17.4	40.5	**10.0**	12.6	22.6
Farmers State Bank	Waterloo	IA	**B**	B	B	1138.3	11.05	8.7	7.4	18.9	11.9	**6.7**	9.0	12.3
Farmers State Bank	Yale	IA	**B**	B-	B-	49.8	5.43	6.0	3.0	11.7	32.3	**10.0**	11.6	17.3

Asset Quality Index	Adjusted Non-Performing Loans as a % of Total Loans	Adjusted Non-Performing Loans as a % of Capital	Net Charge-Offs Avg Loans	Profitability Index	Net Income ($Mil)	Return on Assets (R.O.A.)	Return on Equity (R.O.E.)	Net Interest Spread	Overhead Efficiency Ratio	Liquidity Index	Liquidity Ratio	Hot Money Ratio	Stability Index
6.0	3.56	na	0.00	**9.1**	1.8	2.28	16.02	3.98	40.4	**1.9**	19.1	20.1	**9.9**
6.2	0.02	na	0.01	**8.9**	1.8	1.83	14.81	4.45	50.8	**4.2**	5.6	6.3	**7.9**
3.8	1.29	na	1.28	**8.5**	1.5	1.74	16.09	4.37	45.6	**0.8**	14.5	17.9	**8.6**
6.7	0.00	na	-0.02	**3.6**	0.2	0.69	6.16	3.99	79.7	**4.2**	31.6	11.4	**5.8**
5.9	1.46	6.9	0.06	**5.4**	11.8	1.26	12.93	3.88	65.7	**5.0**	16.6	3.1	**7.2**
7.1	1.68	na	0.12	**6.5**	1.4	1.33	9.49	5.08	70.1	**3.8**	50.9	18.9	**7.9**
8.2	0.43	1.7	-0.36	**4.7**	1.6	0.99	5.21	4.33	77.5	**3.3**	12.4	12.3	**7.8**
8.4	0.00	0.0	0.10	**9.9**	4.7	2.62	18.79	4.79	45.1	**2.0**	25.9	20.8	**9.6**
6.5	0.02	na	0.01	**3.4**	0.5	0.59	4.15	3.12	75.6	**2.1**	25.5	19.9	**6.5**
8.5	0.80	na	-0.05	**7.9**	5.3	1.58	10.27	3.99	52.9	**5.6**	46.0	8.4	**8.7**
9.1	0.04	na	-0.02	**4.6**	1.0	0.88	7.93	3.57	68.6	**1.7**	22.2	23.3	**6.6**
0.3	6.66	na	8.14	**0.0**	-6.2	-7.71	-117.13	3.34	104.8	**0.6**	17.3	65.5	**2.4**
2.4	4.89	na	0.36	**4.1**	0.2	0.62	4.62	4.33	78.2	**3.0**	44.1	22.2	**6.5**
8.4	1.06	na	0.01	**7.2**	7.0	1.39	11.75	4.15	62.3	**1.2**	17.9	29.3	**7.9**
6.8	0.65	na	0.04	**5.8**	4.3	1.34	11.08	3.85	72.3	**2.2**	21.3	18.5	**7.9**
5.9	3.77	na	0.00	**4.3**	0.9	1.26	13.57	3.15	69.7	**5.8**	40.5	4.9	**5.6**
9.3	1.52	na	-0.23	**8.0**	10.8	1.70	9.04	3.47	44.3	**2.1**	48.1	40.5	**10.0**
5.0	1.04	na	0.20	**6.0**	13.9	1.17	11.50	3.59	58.1	**0.9**	10.7	33.3	**9.7**
5.2	1.39	na	0.07	**4.6**	2.3	0.91	8.87	3.95	74.5	**1.7**	14.0	21.8	**6.6**
5.0	0.94	na	0.18	**8.9**	4.3	2.09	21.84	4.08	53.6	**0.6**	11.0	41.5	**8.0**
6.7	0.40	na	-0.01	**6.8**	3.2	1.64	15.29	5.93	74.3	**1.6**	14.6	22.3	**7.6**
8.7	0.07	na	0.03	**7.5**	1.8	1.81	12.53	4.38	61.5	**3.5**	15.2	11.6	**9.6**
6.7	0.81	na	0.16	**5.4**	2.0	1.15	8.29	4.15	66.5	**3.4**	27.6	13.7	**7.6**
4.1	1.42	na	0.11	**3.4**	0.2	0.49	5.40	3.78	71.8	**0.6**	10.7	41.9	**5.2**
8.9	0.16	na	0.02	**6.4**	1.3	1.43	12.98	3.68	62.3	**3.0**	21.0	14.5	**8.1**
9.6	0.00	na	-0.02	**3.6**	0.3	0.69	4.41	2.52	68.7	**6.1**	79.6	10.7	**7.3**
4.5	3.84	na	0.08	**4.6**	1.7	0.90	6.04	3.64	70.5	**1.7**	20.3	23.6	**8.0**
9.3	0.10	0.8	-0.06	**2.2**	0.1	0.36	2.82	2.88	86.9	**4.1**	46.6	15.5	**5.9**
7.6	0.30	1.3	0.01	**6.8**	4.0	1.44	10.77	3.95	53.2	**4.0**	25.2	10.0	**7.6**
5.6	2.55	na	-0.01	**6.6**	0.8	1.61	13.36	3.84	59.5	**2.9**	27.5	16.6	**7.7**
4.4	1.90	na	0.33	**5.5**	3.0	1.05	9.65	4.46	62.6	**1.4**	12.2	22.1	**6.0**
5.3	0.66	na	0.04	**6.9**	5.9	1.39	12.22	4.18	62.6	**4.0**	24.8	9.7	**8.1**
7.5	3.52	na	0.00	**3.3**	0.4	0.53	2.52	2.30	71.3	**7.3**	63.7	0.0	**8.2**
4.5	1.00	na	-0.15	**4.8**	0.4	1.21	9.81	5.31	76.1	**3.0**	21.3	14.6	**5.2**
6.7	0.96	4.9	0.00	**7.6**	8.1	1.55	10.78	3.53	38.6	**1.6**	34.7	37.4	**9.9**
7.7	0.24	na	-0.39	**6.8**	1.4	1.41	7.65	3.70	53.9	**1.3**	13.4	21.3	**8.4**
6.7	0.44	2.4	0.09	**6.8**	25.1	1.43	12.85	3.77	57.5	**1.7**	10.2	11.3	**8.7**
6.3	1.40	na	0.17	**4.8**	4.3	1.05	9.23	4.12	76.2	**4.2**	16.0	5.3	**7.8**
5.2	0.67	na	0.06	**4.7**	6.9	1.02	11.21	3.46	65.1	**2.5**	15.5	16.5	**5.4**
3.1	2.19	na	0.14	**7.0**	1.1	1.64	14.90	4.33	61.0	**0.9**	15.3	29.0	**7.9**
8.9	0.09	na	-0.03	**3.9**	0.6	0.81	7.58	3.79	76.7	**4.3**	37.0	12.4	**5.2**
8.4	0.57	na	0.03	**6.0**	2.4	1.27	7.96	4.18	66.0	**2.6**	19.5	16.4	**8.7**
5.8	3.20	na	0.09	**3.7**	1.3	0.87	7.09	3.11	66.5	**1.2**	28.8	38.9	**8.5**
4.9	1.74	na	0.11	**4.9**	1.0	0.99	6.94	3.42	60.0	**2.0**	19.6	19.4	**8.2**
8.5	0.35	na	-0.10	**5.6**	0.4	1.16	6.23	3.27	49.4	**4.5**	45.5	13.5	**6.7**
8.0	0.52	na	-0.03	**5.7**	1.0	1.25	8.64	3.70	63.0	**2.4**	33.1	16.4	**8.3**
1.7	7.01	na	-0.05	**5.0**	1.0	1.11	7.63	4.01	72.6	**3.7**	25.2	11.3	**7.2**
6.3	7.81	na	0.23	**6.2**	3.0	1.45	5.45	3.15	51.2	**4.3**	87.1	25.0	**9.9**
7.7	0.42	na	0.00	**5.0**	2.6	1.13	12.83	2.96	67.3	**5.5**	33.9	4.2	**6.4**
8.9	0.00	0.5	0.00	**6.6**	1.8	1.51	15.25	3.66	59.7	**5.3**	37.4	6.6	**6.2**
4.7	2.66	na	0.34	**4.7**	0.4	0.90	8.06	4.09	63.0	**3.7**	11.7	10.0	**5.5**
7.0	2.18	na	0.02	**5.7**	1.3	1.34	9.13	4.42	69.3	**2.7**	23.5	16.2	**8.6**
8.0	0.49	1.7	0.11	**8.6**	1.9	2.16	12.45	5.84	63.1	**2.8**	23.0	15.7	**8.8**
8.5	0.37	na	0.00	**5.0**	0.9	1.04	9.04	3.68	71.2	**4.4**	28.3	9.0	**7.6**
8.8	0.00	na	-0.10	**4.3**	0.3	0.97	7.96	3.20	59.4	**6.7**	66.1	4.3	**5.9**
8.2	0.06	na	0.77	**4.3**	0.4	0.83	5.82	3.43	49.4	**5.2**	40.8	8.9	**8.2**
8.3	0.24	na	0.02	**6.6**	9.7	1.61	11.41	3.47	56.8	**3.4**	19.5	12.3	**9.9**
8.2	0.85	na	0.08	**5.7**	1.6	1.16	9.29	3.57	60.0	**2.5**	42.3	29.0	**7.7**
8.0	0.01	na	0.04	**5.6**	10.9	1.33	14.95	3.17	53.0	**0.7**	9.0	20.2	**8.5**
7.7	1.19	na	0.00	**5.8**	0.5	1.35	11.71	3.69	57.4	**3.4**	43.9	18.8	**6.2**

Name	City	State	Rating	2018 Rating	2017 Rating	Total Assets ($Mil)	One Year Asset Growth	Asset Mix (As a % of Total Assets) Commercial Loans	Consumer Loans	Mortgage Loans	Securities	Capitalization Index	Leverage Ratio	Risk-Based Capital Ratio
▲ Farmers State Bank	Elmwood	IL	**C-**	C-	C-	55.4	5.79	2.8	1.3	22.0	33.4	**7.1**	9.0	16.7
▲ Farmers State Bank	Pittsfield	IL	**A-**	B+	B+	252.5	-0.43	2.1	1.1	4.4	15.4	**10.0**	13.8	16.6
▲ Farmers State Bank	Lagrange	IN	**B+**	B	B	786.2	10.85	4.7	2.0	34.0	12.9	**7.7**	9.4	15.6
Farmers State Bank	Dwight	KS	**C**	C-	C+	15.6	-0.04	4.3	1.5	8.1	0.0	**10.0**	12.8	25.4
Farmers State Bank	Fairview	KS	**D+**	D	D	21.2	-2.78	1.3	4.1	8.6	4.7	**8.6**	10.1	14.8
Farmers State Bank	Holton	KS	**B**	B	B	57.1	-1.10	4.4	1.5	25.4	20.7	**10.0**	13.0	21.5
Farmers State Bank	McPherson	KS	**A-**	A-	A-	120.5	10.28	8.6	4.1	18.3	37.7	**8.0**	9.7	15.6
Farmers State Bank	Phillipsburg	KS	**C**	C-	D+	36.2	-3.77	7.1	9.5	11.0	24.8	**9.8**	10.8	16.3
Farmers State Bank	Wathena	KS	**B**	B	B	60.5	2.79	8.3	5.0	17.0	49.9	**10.0**	17.2	35.0
Farmers State Bank	Westmoreland	KS	**B+**	B+	B+	185.0	11.93	9.3	2.5	13.8	13.7	**10.0**	14.6	15.3
Farmers State Bank	Booneville	KY	**B-**	B-	B-	51.0	1.52	4.3	6.1	18.5	44.0	**10.0**	12.4	19.0
Farmers State Bank	Cameron	MO	**B-**	B-	B-	242.9	4.65	2.5	2.9	42.2	11.8	**7.5**	9.4	12.9
▲ Farmers State Bank	Victor	MT	**B**	C+	B-	425.5	7.58	5.4	3.1	13.7	22.7	**8.3**	9.9	14.9
Farmers State Bank	Dodge	NE	**C+**	C+	C+	274.5	12.71	14.1	0.9	2.7	6.1	**6.0**	8.7	11.8
Farmers State Bank	New Madison	OH	**B**	B	B	181.3	2.39	3.5	4.2	26.1	14.5	**10.0**	12.4	19.0
▲ Farmers State Bank	West Salem	OH	**C+**	C+	C+	122.8	4.37	6.0	1.6	25.0	10.7	**7.6**	9.4	13.8
▲ Farmers State Bank	Quinton	OK	**B-**	C+	C+	116.2	12.03	8.3	9.7	17.3	26.2	**6.4**	8.5	13.3
Farmers State Bank	Hosmer	SD	**B-**	B-	B-	18.7	-1.25	33.8	4.2	0.0	4.9	**10.0**	16.4	17.6
Farmers State Bank	Parkston	SD	**B**	B	B	221.0	3.54	5.9	3.1	0.0	36.4	**8.3**	9.9	16.5
Farmers State Bank	Mountain City	TN	**B**	B	B	144.5	1.30	6.1	5.4	29.2	25.3	**10.0**	16.3	25.8
Farmers State Bank	Center	TX	**B-**	B-	C+	333.0	-8.98	17.9	2.4	7.5	19.0	**10.0**	13.8	21.5
Farmers State Bank	Groesbeck	TX	**B+**	B+	B+	132.5	-2.73	2.1	5.9	17.3	20.5	**8.3**	9.9	19.0
▲ Farmers State Bank	Winthrop	WA	**B-**	C+	C+	42.3	-1.51	3.3	1.2	0.9	51.4	**8.7**	10.1	78.5
▼ Farmers State Bank	Pine Bluffs	WY	**C-**	C+	C	25.7	-8.69	5.1	2.0	8.8	10.2	**7.0**	9.0	16.3
▲ Farmers State Bank & Trust Co.	Mount Sterling	IL	**B-**	C+	C+	97.0	7.86	12.2	3.4	15.9	16.0	**7.0**	9.0	13.3
Farmers State Bank & Trust Co.	Church Point	LA	**B-**	B-	B	116.4	0.04	10.9	2.6	9.8	23.8	**9.8**	10.9	16.2
▲ Farmers State Bank and Trust Co.	Jacksonville	IL	**B-**	C	C	196.7	-4.00	6.5	7.6	11.5	32.5	**10.0**	12.1	20.4
▲ Farmers State Bank Hillsboro	Hillsboro	WI	**A**	A-	A-	166.7	-0.19	2.4	1.9	9.2	42.3	**10.0**	19.4	35.5
▲ Farmers State Bank of Aliceville, Kansas	Westphalia	KS	**A-**	B+	A	145.1	-2.40	4.9	6.9	17.5	17.5	**10.0**	15.6	25.2
▼ Farmers State Bank of Alto Pass, Ill.	Harrisburg	IL	**C-**	C+	C-	234.8	11.20	15.8	2.2	15.9	9.2	**4.4**	8.8	10.7
Farmers State Bank of Blue Mound	Blue Mound	KS	**B-**	B-	B-	43.0	-3.24	7.9	3.4	1.4	7.2	**10.0**	19.1	24.8
▲ Farmers State Bank of Brush	Brush	CO	**A-**	B+	A-	108.5	3.54	2.8	1.5	3.3	27.0	**10.0**	19.2	32.0
▲ Farmers State Bank of Bucklin, Kansas	Bucklin	KS	**C**	C-	C	42.8	-2.28	6.2	1.1	1.6	24.3	**8.3**	9.8	21.0
Farmers State Bank of Calhan	Calhan	CO	**B**	B-	B	280.2	4.15	6.1	2.6	12.1	44.9	**9.3**	10.5	18.9
Farmers State Bank of Canton	Canton	SD	**B-**	B-	B-	47.8	-1.45	3.3	4.4	26.4	12.2	**10.0**	12.3	18.5
▲ Farmers State Bank of Danforth	Danforth	IL	**B+**	B	B	59.6	1.89	6.9	1.0	9.4	30.6	**10.0**	13.3	20.8
Farmers State Bank of Emden	Emden	IL	**B-**	B-	C+	35.0	2.43	3.9	1.3	2.1	57.7	**10.0**	27.7	60.2
▲ Farmers State Bank of Hamel	Hamel	MN	**B**	B-	B-	133.6	-3.15	3.2	0.5	12.0	36.7	**10.0**	11.1	25.5
▲ Farmers State Bank of Hartland	Hartland	MN	**B**	B-	B-	172.5	15.00	8.8	1.2	2.8	19.4	**9.3**	10.5	15.5
Farmers State Bank of Hoffman	Hoffman	IL	**B**	B	B	152.1	3.81	4.1	1.3	12.5	44.1	**10.0**	15.7	30.8
▲ Farmers State Bank of Hoffman	Hoffman	MN	**B**	B-	B+	30.4	7.07	6.1	3.5	9.5	35.3	**10.0**	12.7	23.8
Farmers State Bank of Medora	Medora	IL	**C**	C	C+	19.7	-1.10	11.1	7.5	2.3	46.1	**10.0**	17.2	31.3
Farmers State Bank of Munith	Munith	MI	**B-**	B-	B-	78.5	1.35	3.2	5.6	30.9	18.6	**9.3**	10.5	21.1
Farmers State Bank of Newcastle	Newcastle	TX	**B-**	B-	B-	48.1	2.43	6.1	2.9	8.1	34.3	**8.4**	9.9	20.6
▲ Farmers State Bank of Oakley, Kansas	Oakley	KS	**A-**	B+	A-	143.3	-0.26	6.5	0.5	1.1	21.8	**10.0**	16.2	19.2
▲ Farmers State Bank of Trimont	Trimont	MN	**B**	B-	B-	61.5	6.39	8.0	2.3	4.1	25.0	**10.0**	16.5	22.8
Farmers State Bank of Turton	Turton	SD	**B**	B	B	30.8	5.72	2.5	2.6	0.0	13.3	**10.0**	12.1	22.4
Farmers State Bank of Underwood	Underwood	MN	**B-**	C+	C+	72.0	3.03	11.4	4.3	14.6	7.0	**7.7**	9.4	13.9
Farmers State Bank of Watkins	Watkins	MN	**B**	B	B	43.5	4.17	5.2	5.5	15.0	33.4	**10.0**	13.4	24.4
Farmers State Bank of Waupaca	Waupaca	WI	**A-**	A-	A	204.3	7.18	7.5	4.0	23.6	26.5	**10.0**	13.8	18.6
Farmers State Bank of Western Illinois	Alpha	IL	**A-**	B+	B-	144.4	3.26	4.0	2.3	6.4	20.2	**10.0**	13.2	20.8
▲ Farmers State Bank, Allen, Oklahoma	Allen	OK	**B**	B-	C	41.6	-4.52	15.4	13.3	16.2	9.7	**10.0**	13.0	18.4
Farmers State Bank, S/B	Bolivar	MO	**C**	C+	C+	65.4	-2.16	1.2	2.8	29.9	8.4	**6.9**	8.9	13.1
Farmers Trust & Savings Bank	Earling	IA	**B**	B	B	93.4	5.50	8.7	1.7	8.5	1.1	**8.4**	9.9	14.0
▲ Farmers Trust & Savings Bank	Williamsburg	IA	**A**	A-	A+	147.6	10.83	6.6	3.5	13.7	35.9	**10.0**	25.2	38.1
▲ Farmers Trust and Savings Bank	Buffalo Center	IA	**A-**	B+	A-	258.7	1.14	13.7	1.1	5.8	1.3	**10.0**	12.4	15.8
Farmers Trust and Savings Bank	Spencer	IA	**C+**	C+	B-	457.5	6.57	11.0	1.1	7.8	13.7	**5.2**	8.8	11.2
Farmers-Merchants Bank & Trust Co.	Breaux Bridge	LA	**D**	D	D	321.2	3.62	4.9	5.1	16.2	10.7	**9.5**	13.2	14.5
▲ Farmers-Merchants Bank of Illinois	Paxton	IL	**B**	C+	C-	191.2	317.14	2.6	1.5	16.9	13.1	**9.1**	11.5	14.3
Farmington State Bank	Farmington	WA	**C-**	C-	C+	8.4	-3.86	11.6	2.2	0.5	1.1	**10.0**	24.4	42.7

Asset Quality Index	Adjusted Non-Performing Loans as a % of Total Loans	Adjusted Non-Performing Loans as a % of Capital	Net Charge-Offs Avg Loans	Profitability Index	Net Income ($Mil)	Return on Assets (R.O.A.)	Return on Equity (R.O.E.)	Net Interest Spread	Overhead Efficiency Ratio	Liquidity Index	Liquidity Ratio	Hot Money Ratio	Stability Index
5.4	2.37	na	0.41	**2.5**	0.2	0.43	5.09	3.33	86.9	**3.8**	34.9	14.5	**2.8**
7.4	0.16	na	0.02	**6.3**	3.0	1.58	11.78	3.91	63.5	**3.5**	13.1	11.3	**8.4**
7.7	0.40	na	-0.03	**7.6**	9.2	1.60	16.83	4.09	57.1	**4.1**	23.3	8.6	**6.6**
7.9	0.00	na	0.00	**3.1**	0.1	0.78	6.25	3.36	76.5	**4.9**	50.0	10.5	**5.2**
5.6	0.35	na	-0.12	**3.3**	0.1	0.61	6.34	3.69	83.2	**5.5**	31.1	0.7	**3.7**
8.7	0.09	na	0.11	**6.0**	0.5	1.10	8.77	4.31	66.3	**1.8**	17.9	20.7	**6.8**
8.8	0.14	na	0.04	**5.9**	1.2	1.32	13.51	3.87	62.6	**4.2**	41.7	14.4	**6.9**
3.1	2.52	na	0.15	**3.8**	0.2	0.69	6.36	3.71	80.2	**1.0**	21.1	31.9	**5.0**
8.6	0.14	na	-0.20	**3.7**	0.3	0.69	4.03	3.81	83.3	**5.7**	48.7	7.2	**7.6**
5.8	1.91	na	0.13	**5.3**	1.6	1.17	7.93	3.37	60.4	**1.8**	20.6	22.0	**7.6**
6.1	2.15	7.1	-0.01	**4.6**	0.4	1.06	8.70	4.15	78.1	**2.5**	29.9	19.0	**6.4**
7.1	0.34	2.5	0.03	**4.5**	1.6	0.88	8.55	4.21	74.4	**3.1**	17.7	13.6	**6.4**
6.0	0.82	na	0.02	**5.0**	3.5	1.17	11.59	4.49	76.0	**3.7**	28.2	12.4	**6.2**
4.3	1.11	na	0.04	**5.2**	2.3	1.18	12.34	3.69	63.8	**0.7**	13.9	36.3	**5.9**
8.5	0.13	1.8	-0.01	**4.9**	1.4	1.06	9.13	3.81	68.6	**1.3**	12.2	27.0	**7.2**
5.3	2.15	na	0.00	**3.8**	0.7	0.74	7.98	4.42	82.3	**5.0**	20.1	2.6	**5.6**
6.7	0.66	na	0.49	**4.6**	0.8	0.91	11.19	5.00	77.2	**4.6**	30.7	6.7	**4.5**
7.7	0.33	na	0.01	**7.0**	0.2	1.58	10.15	5.06	68.1	**1.2**	22.1	30.4	**5.7**
8.5	0.04	na	0.01	**4.9**	1.7	1.01	10.46	3.47	62.0	**4.4**	40.2	12.9	**6.1**
5.6	4.96	na	0.10	**4.1**	0.8	0.76	4.89	4.30	77.0	**2.7**	14.2	15.5	**7.5**
5.1	2.60	na	-0.54	**3.7**	1.6	0.66	4.90	3.84	81.1	**3.9**	38.2	15.0	**5.6**
8.2	0.59	na	0.04	**5.8**	1.4	1.40	14.00	4.09	70.2	**5.1**	38.1	8.6	**6.9**
9.7	0.00	na	0.24	**3.9**	0.3	0.81	8.16	2.92	59.5	**8.1**	94.0	0.0	**4.5**
8.6	0.00	na	0.00	**0.6**	-0.4	-2.07	-21.84	4.16	161.3	**5.1**	32.9	6.5	**3.6**
7.8	0.21	na	0.00	**6.1**	0.9	1.23	13.55	3.88	59.3	**1.6**	21.6	25.2	**5.4**
4.6	1.47	na	0.05	**6.9**	1.4	1.62	14.42	5.00	67.8	**2.8**	19.0	15.3	**8.1**
4.8	2.10	na	0.23	**3.4**	1.2	0.76	6.39	3.74	70.0	**5.4**	33.8	4.5	**5.7**
9.0	0.31	na	0.03	**8.0**	2.2	1.75	9.47	3.42	41.5	**5.4**	54.2	11.4	**9.4**
8.1	0.00	na	0.00	**6.9**	1.5	1.33	8.75	3.56	47.9	**1.2**	11.8	27.4	**8.8**
1.8	1.99	23.8	0.14	**5.0**	2.0	1.13	13.23	4.65	77.3	**2.7**	8.0	14.9	**4.4**
7.0	1.45	na	-0.01	**6.4**	0.5	1.47	8.04	5.33	70.2	**2.7**	20.9	16.2	**6.3**
7.6	0.05	na	0.00	**9.3**	1.5	1.83	9.64	4.36	52.6	**1.9**	24.4	21.8	**8.6**
8.5	0.00	na	0.00	**3.7**	0.2	0.69	5.98	3.73	80.1	**5.1**	40.6	9.6	**5.9**
6.8	0.51	na	0.03	**5.0**	2.6	1.23	11.74	3.82	69.9	**3.5**	33.4	15.5	**6.8**
8.3	0.46	na	-0.01	**3.6**	0.2	0.65	5.36	3.92	81.5	**4.2**	17.9	7.9	**6.0**
7.6	0.40	na	0.03	**5.7**	0.5	1.16	9.08	3.72	63.7	**5.7**	41.2	5.7	**6.7**
9.2	0.00	na	0.00	**3.8**	0.2	0.80	2.88	2.79	63.3	**3.5**	58.4	21.3	**7.0**
9.5	0.00	na	0.00	**4.4**	1.1	1.07	9.99	3.04	66.5	**5.7**	55.5	10.3	**6.6**
5.7	1.47	na	0.07	**7.6**	2.1	1.80	15.44	4.22	57.4	**4.3**	30.3	5.2	**8.1**
9.3	1.05	na	-0.01	**4.0**	0.8	0.74	4.70	3.18	71.4	**4.8**	43.0	11.9	**8.0**
8.7	0.00	na	0.00	**4.1**	0.2	0.97	7.14	3.34	70.8	**3.4**	53.5	20.7	**7.5**
4.0	0.00	na	0.19	**3.0**	0.1	0.40	2.26	3.57	84.2	**6.1**	75.1	8.1	**5.8**
4.8	2.17	na	-0.15	**4.7**	0.6	0.93	9.22	4.21	76.4	**5.9**	38.2	3.5	**6.2**
6.2	0.43	na	-0.07	**6.2**	0.5	1.35	13.53	3.85	58.8	**7.1**	58.0	0.0	**5.7**
7.3	0.00	na	-0.04	**7.8**	1.7	1.55	9.59	3.62	47.4	**0.8**	14.1	35.9	**9.3**
7.0	0.92	na	0.52	**5.9**	0.6	1.22	7.53	4.09	56.4	**1.5**	32.8	25.4	**7.2**
6.7	0.00	na	0.00	**7.0**	0.4	1.61	13.33	4.42	57.0	**2.2**	28.1	20.5	**6.3**
5.2	0.61	na	0.08	**7.5**	0.9	1.76	18.85	4.91	62.7	**1.4**	20.1	27.4	**7.0**
7.7	0.08	na	0.02	**6.6**	0.5	1.65	12.78	4.06	61.3	**6.0**	44.2	4.1	**7.4**
8.6	0.53	na	0.11	**6.9**	2.1	1.43	10.44	4.41	61.3	**3.6**	34.3	15.0	**8.1**
8.7	0.38	na	0.02	**5.5**	1.4	1.40	10.75	4.14	63.5	**5.2**	37.9	8.0	**7.2**
7.1	0.24	1.4	0.20	**6.8**	0.5	1.59	12.64	5.12	67.9	**1.6**	18.3	23.4	**6.3**
3.9	0.80	na	0.00	**2.8**	0.1	0.46	3.50	4.69	88.0	**2.4**	9.8	16.2	**6.9**
7.3	0.00	na	-0.02	**7.7**	1.3	1.87	19.17	4.35	57.0	**4.1**	20.8	8.9	**7.0**
8.4	1.25	na	0.04	**9.4**	2.4	2.30	9.03	4.07	43.3	**6.0**	52.6	7.4	**9.6**
5.8	0.20	na	0.02	**7.5**	3.3	1.67	13.20	4.01	51.9	**3.9**	11.7	9.2	**9.0**
4.7	1.85	na	0.00	**5.2**	4.0	1.18	13.42	3.18	53.3	**1.5**	8.3	10.1	**6.2**
1.3	4.98	na	0.05	**5.1**	2.9	1.20	9.24	4.30	72.7	**2.4**	18.8	17.3	**8.4**
3.5	0.65	na	0.00	**5.3**	1.5	1.13	6.72	3.68	58.7	**1.4**	7.1	24.1	**7.2**
8.5	0.00	na	0.00	**3.9**	0.1	1.03	5.08	4.34	79.2	**6.5**	50.0	0.0	**5.7**

Name	City	State	Rating	2018 Rating	2017 Rating	Total Assets ($Mil)	One Year Asset Growth	Asset Mix (As a % of Total Assets) Comm-ercial Loans	Cons-umer Loans	Mort-gage Loans	Secur-ities	Capital-ization Index	Lever-age Ratio	Risk-Based Capital Ratio
▲ Fauquier Bank	Warrenton	VA	B	B-	C+	725.8	8.44	3.9	1.9	30.4	10.0	**7.9**	9.6	13.7
▲ Fayette County National Bank of Fayettevill	Fayetteville	WV	B+	B	B	94.2	-1.34	1.1	4.0	48.8	26.4	**10.0**	12.7	25.2
Fayette Savings Bank, SSB	La Grange	TX	B	B	B	203.5	21.63	1.1	2.0	51.3	10.8	**8.3**	9.9	15.2
▼ Fayetteville Bank	Fayetteville	TX	B	B+	A-	545.5	10.33	4.2	0.9	4.1	76.3	**9.7**	10.8	25.4
▲ FBT Bank & Mortgage	Fordyce	AR	B+	B	B+	168.6	5.24	10.6	7.6	20.6	28.4	**10.0**	12.5	19.9
FCB Banks	Collinsville	IL	B	B	B-	1681.6	12.57	2.8	4.4	37.8	12.0	**6.5**	8.5	14.8
FCN Bank, N.A.	Brookville	IN	B+	B+	B	462.9	4.46	7.8	1.6	16.6	33.1	**9.7**	10.8	19.1
FDS Bank	Mason	OH	A+	A+	A+	107.5	-7.97	2.1	0.6	0.0	47.5	**10.0**	28.1	42.1
Federal Savings Bank	Chicago	IL	A	A	A	756.2	94.93	0.0	1.1	82.9	0.1	**10.0**	14.1	26.6
Federated Bank	Onarga	IL	C	C+	B-	97.1	9.12	6.2	2.6	11.8	33.4	**7.3**	9.2	20.1
▲ Federation Bank	Washington	IA	C+	C+	B-	134.2	12.12	10.1	4.2	14.1	15.1	**5.7**	8.8	11.5
▲ Feliciana Bank & Trust Co.	Clinton	LA	B+	B-	B+	127.4	-6.66	9.4	2.2	32.8	13.4	**10.0**	11.4	17.3
▲ Fidelity Bank	West Memphis	AR	A-	B+	B	395.8	3.61	3.6	1.0	5.1	41.5	**10.0**	12.6	20.6
Fidelity Bank	West Des Moines	IA	C+	C+	B-	99.6	22.72	0.3	0.2	53.3	3.6	**7.4**	9.2	13.3
▲ Fidelity Bank	New Orleans	LA	B	B	B-	790.6	-6.79	3.3	0.7	31.8	16.1	**10.0**	17.6	25.5
Fidelity Bank	Edina	MN	A-	A	A	614.3	35.10	23.6	0.7	0.0	8.5	**7.1**	11.7	12.6
Fidelity Bank	Fuquay-Varina	NC	A-	B+	B-	2057.3	5.36	4.6	0.5	3.4	26.9	**9.2**	10.5	16.5
Fidelity Bank & Trust	Dubuque	IA	B	B+	B	1204.7	47.58	10.5	1.7	11.1	15.0	**6.1**	9.2	11.9
Fidelity Bank of Texas	Waco	TX	B+	B+	B+	85.7	-9.72	1.4	1.9	26.5	1.8	**10.0**	18.5	43.2
Fidelity Bank, N.A.	Wichita	KS	B-	B-	B-	2380.2	3.02	9.0	3.8	16.7	11.9	**6.8**	9.5	12.3
Fidelity Co-operative Bank	Leominster	MA	C+	C+	C+	1002.0	9.13	12.3	0.2	31.0	10.3	**6.3**	8.4	12.0
Fidelity Deposit and Discount Bank	Dunmore	PA	B+	B+	B	1014.5	6.89	7.7	11.0	22.7	18.7	**8.8**	10.2	15.6
Fidelity Federal S&L Assn. of Delaware	Delaware	OH	C-	C-	C-	106.9	1.99	0.0	1.4	31.9	39.7	**10.0**	21.1	49.7
Fidelity Personal Trust Co., FSB	Boston	MA	U	U	U	98.2	4.26	0.0	0.0	0.0	0.0	**10.0**	95.5	95.0
Fidelity S&L Assn. of Bucks County	Bristol	PA	C+	C	C	85.9	-1.06	0.0	0.2	60.4	0.6	**10.0**	15.5	31.0
▲ Fidelity State Bank and Trust Co.	Dodge City	KS	A-	B+	B	170.3	1.03	3.5	0.3	1.4	29.3	**10.0**	19.6	74.4
▲ Fidelity State Bank and Trust Co.	Topeka	KS	C+	C	C+	140.1	4.74	8.1	18.5	8.6	23.0	**7.1**	9.1	15.8
▲ Field & Main Bank	Henderson	KY	C+	C	C+	456.8	9.04	12.1	0.9	21.9	7.8	**7.4**	9.6	12.9
Fieldpoint Private Bank & Trust	Greenwich	CT	B	B	B-	919.8	1.71	2.9	9.1	35.8	12.1	**10.0**	11.6	16.8
Fifth District Savings Bank	New Orleans	LA	B-	B-	B-	437.3	1.51	0.0	0.4	69.1	14.6	**10.0**	17.6	36.6
Fifth Third Bank, N.A.	Cincinnati	OH	B	B	B-	169489.5	21.08	26.5	9.6	10.6	21.6	**8.0**	10.3	13.4
Finance Factors, Ltd.	Honolulu	HI	B	B-	B-	588.1	2.67	0.0	1.0	30.4	17.8	**10.0**	11.7	17.3
▲ Financial Federal Bank	Memphis	TN	A-	B+	A	633.9	11.20	16.2	2.5	23.6	0.0	**10.0**	12.8	15.1
Financial Security Bank	Kerkhoven	MN	C	C	C+	100.9	8.28	13.6	0.7	9.9	5.3	**4.2**	9.0	10.6
FineMark National Bank & Trust	Fort Myers	FL	B-	B-	C+	2103.7	18.15	4.6	3.9	39.6	19.7	**7.8**	9.5	16.8
▲ Finwise Bank	Murray	UT	A-	B+	B+	161.7	58.94	5.2	18.5	9.7	0.3	**10.0**	17.6	20.8
First & Farmers National Bank, Inc.	Somerset	KY	B-	B+	B+	525.2	3.42	3.4	3.1	28.3	33.6	**9.7**	10.8	15.6
First & Peoples Bank and Trust Co.	Russell	KY	B	B	C	198.5	2.66	11.5	18.8	10.7	39.3	**10.0**	19.8	35.7
First Advantage Bank	Clarksville	TN	C+	C+	B-	732.8	15.89	8.8	20.1	10.4	5.7	**7.6**	10.8	13.0
▲ First American Bank	Fort Dodge	IA	B	B-	B	867.9	-6.76	3.9	0.1	20.9	11.2	**10.0**	14.1	27.8
First American Bank	Elk Grove Village	IL	C+	B-	B	4495.9	-9.43	11.2	1.7	5.4	53.2	**6.6**	8.6	17.0
First American Bank	Artesia	NM	A	A	A-	1203.5	8.51	10.7	0.2	7.5	38.2	**8.5**	10.0	18.0
First American Bank	Stonewall	OK	B	B	B	31.3	2.37	13.6	11.4	22.2	7.3	**10.0**	12.0	17.8
▲ First American Bank and Trust	Vacherie	LA	A	A-	A-	906.7	2.34	3.9	1.5	27.6	21.7	**10.0**	15.1	22.9
First American Bank and Trust Co.	Athens	GA	A-	A-	B	554.6	5.66	3.1	0.4	17.2	12.8	**10.0**	11.4	18.1
First American Bank, N.A.	Hudson	WI	B	B	B-	129.2	3.27	12.3	1.4	10.9	7.7	**10.0**	14.2	17.3
First American National Bank	Iuka	MS	B-	B-	B-	276.7	5.52	4.3	5.9	25.0	29.8	**10.0**	11.3	20.1
First American State Bank	Greenwood Village	CO	B-	B-	C	246.1	7.18	2.3	0.1	41.4	11.7	**7.6**	9.4	15.1
First American Trust, F.S.B.	Santa Ana	CA	U	U	U	4248.4	-12.76	0.0	0.0	0.0	78.3	**6.6**	8.6	36.5
First Arkansas Bank and Trust	Jacksonville	AR	B-	B-	B	752.8	0.89	17.9	7.1	9.8	23.3	**10.0**	18.3	24.4
▲ First Bank	Ketchikan	AK	B-	C+	C+	604.6	4.98	3.4	1.4	5.6	48.9	**7.5**	9.3	20.0
First Bank	Wadley	AL	B+	B+	B+	87.7	4.22	3.5	1.8	4.7	49.9	**7.7**	9.5	14.6
First Bank	Clewiston	FL	B	B-	B-	386.0	11.44	5.9	2.4	15.3	9.3	**7.7**	9.5	14.2
First Bank	Dalton	GA	B-	B-	B-	399.6	11.72	11.9	1.6	14.8	12.5	**6.3**	8.9	12.0
First Bank	Sterling	KS	B+	B+	A-	139.2	7.71	3.8	0.8	12.8	31.7	**10.0**	13.9	21.9
First Bank	Creve Coeur	MO	B+	B	B-	6111.5	-0.96	8.8	0.4	12.1	34.1	**7.9**	9.6	15.1
First Bank	McComb	MS	B	B	B	557.4	2.41	10.4	1.5	25.7	6.4	**9.1**	10.4	14.9
First Bank	Southern Pines	NC	B+	B	B	6069.5	6.25	5.1	1.2	18.6	12.9	**9.8**	11.1	14.9
First Bank	Hamilton	NJ	B	B	C+	2047.4	19.23	11.6	0.2	6.7	4.7	**6.8**	11.0	12.4
▲ First Bank	Erick	OK	A-	B+	A-	72.0	-4.29	18.5	4.9	10.4	6.6	**10.0**	12.5	17.1

Asset Quality Index	Adjusted Non-Performing Loans as a % of Total Loans	Adjusted Non-Performing Loans as a % of Capital	Net Charge-Offs Avg Loans	Profitability Index	Net Income ($Mil)	Return on Assets (R.O.A.)	Return on Equity (R.O.E.)	Net Interest Spread	Overhead Efficiency Ratio	Liquidity Index	Liquidity Ratio	Hot Money Ratio	Stability Index
7.3	0.35	na	0.01	**5.0**	5.7	1.08	11.39	3.80	71.1	**4.0**	17.8	6.7	**6.0**
6.3	1.58	na	0.00	**6.2**	0.9	1.30	10.27	4.32	64.0	**4.0**	15.6	8.7	**7.3**
5.8	0.53	5.2	0.00	**5.5**	1.9	1.37	15.58	3.26	57.4	**0.7**	7.7	34.4	**5.6**
9.9	0.00	0.0	0.02	**4.0**	4.0	1.05	9.51	2.25	59.3	**2.9**	59.1	41.4	**7.2**
6.7	3.80	na	0.06	**7.7**	2.2	1.76	15.46	4.25	63.9	**2.1**	29.5	22.4	**6.6**
5.8	1.00	6.7	0.00	**5.6**	11.9	0.96	11.20	2.70	59.6	**2.9**	15.8	15.0	**7.8**
6.4	1.17	3.4	0.70	**5.8**	4.1	1.21	10.54	3.78	61.5	**4.5**	39.2	12.4	**7.2**
10.0	0.00	na	0.32	**9.5**	427.7	443.84	2000.00	2.33	19.4	**8.8**	116.8	0.0	**8.8**
7.5	0.47	3.0	-0.74	**10.0**	34.2	8.41	50.49	2.64	79.9	**0.3**	9.7	27.1	**9.0**
7.0	0.00	na	0.03	**3.3**	0.4	0.55	4.40	3.67	86.6	**5.7**	52.8	7.9	**6.5**
4.3	0.81	na	0.41	**4.0**	0.8	0.80	8.28	4.05	69.5	**3.1**	19.2	12.7	**6.0**
6.3	0.98	na	0.10	**5.7**	1.3	1.34	12.29	4.16	66.8	**0.7**	10.1	40.5	**7.5**
8.2	0.24	na	0.00	**6.2**	4.6	1.60	12.92	3.42	58.1	**1.7**	17.3	22.1	**8.0**
5.2	0.18	na	0.02	**4.5**	0.8	1.24	11.05	3.57	88.5	**0.7**	11.2	39.5	**5.5**
8.0	0.89	na	0.04	**4.1**	4.1	0.68	3.85	4.80	89.1	**2.9**	18.4	8.1	**8.0**
6.8	0.02	na	0.04	**8.8**	8.2	2.15	12.11	5.66	58.3	**3.0**	3.2	0.8	**10.0**
8.0	1.65	na	-0.03	**7.2**	22.0	1.47	13.58	3.83	59.5	**6.5**	39.7	3.4	**9.3**
6.8	0.36	2.2	-0.03	**7.4**	10.7	1.50	13.56	4.55	57.7	**2.6**	20.9	17.7	**9.5**
6.6	2.05	na	0.02	**4.9**	0.6	0.91	5.13	4.01	73.7	**6.2**	55.6	5.6	**7.6**
5.0	2.25	7.6	0.07	**3.8**	12.1	0.69	6.99	3.35	73.7	**2.6**	6.3	14.8	**8.4**
5.8	1.82	9.1	0.01	**3.4**	4.5	0.62	7.31	3.44	77.2	**1.8**	9.3	11.3	**6.4**
6.5	0.64	3.7	0.21	**6.2**	9.6	1.32	12.90	3.65	60.1	**4.1**	14.6	8.4	**8.5**
9.7	0.31	0.7	0.00	**1.6**	0.1	0.15	0.71	3.19	97.8	**6.5**	62.5	7.0	**7.4**
10.0	na	na	na	**9.5**	30.7	42.93	48.71	3.18	45.3	**4.0**	na	100.0	**7.0**
7.0	1.77	7.7	0.00	**2.7**	0.2	0.31	2.11	3.30	87.7	**3.2**	30.7	15.3	**7.0**
9.8	0.59	0.6	0.03	**5.7**	1.6	1.25	6.55	3.04	53.8	**7.4**	75.3	3.1	**8.4**
4.6	0.62	na	0.04	**3.8**	0.9	0.89	9.74	3.22	71.8	**5.4**	31.9	3.9	**5.7**
3.7	1.26	na	0.15	**4.9**	3.8	1.11	9.95	4.07	75.3	**1.1**	8.9	28.5	**6.3**
5.0	1.45	9.8	0.00	**3.4**	3.4	0.48	4.24	2.58	83.2	**0.9**	4.0	30.8	**7.4**
9.9	0.29	1.6	0.00	**3.4**	1.9	0.58	3.34	2.81	75.1	**1.5**	24.9	26.7	**7.9**
5.0	1.16	4.1	0.33	**8.7**	1934.8	1.64	12.71	3.49	54.3	**5.0**	26.1	3.4	**10.0**
8.7	0.08	2.6	-0.14	**4.2**	3.4	0.80	6.75	3.78	73.5	**1.1**	22.4	32.9	**8.0**
7.2	0.17	na	-0.01	**6.9**	7.1	1.56	12.19	2.84	50.9	**0.3**	4.2	72.4	**10.0**
4.4	1.13	na	0.00	**4.2**	0.7	0.87	9.32	3.80	76.3	**1.3**	7.9	25.5	**6.4**
8.9	0.11	0.8	0.01	**4.3**	12.7	0.87	9.41	2.50	67.3	**4.6**	14.4	5.0	**7.5**
6.3	1.06	na	1.89	**10.0**	7.9	7.91	46.68	13.67	41.5	**1.1**	27.3	34.6	**9.3**
5.1	1.24	na	0.03	**3.5**	2.0	0.51	3.85	3.72	84.8	**2.2**	31.5	22.1	**8.5**
6.9	0.65	na	0.31	**4.0**	1.1	0.76	4.19	4.02	76.3	**4.4**	28.8	9.0	**7.6**
3.6	0.92	na	0.13	**5.6**	5.3	1.02	9.48	4.10	66.8	**1.2**	11.1	28.4	**8.0**
9.4	0.18	0.2	-0.03	**7.6**	20.6	2.96	24.50	2.63	48.3	**2.6**	35.8	22.0	**7.5**
5.5	2.78	9.2	0.51	**1.9**	28.0	0.77	9.23	2.64	126.7	**5.5**	42.6	9.0	**7.5**
8.7	0.46	na	0.86	**8.8**	19.7	2.21	21.38	4.48	54.9	**5.5**	29.6	6.3	**10.0**
4.8	1.19	5.5	0.00	**7.6**	0.4	1.77	15.04	4.98	63.8	**1.5**	19.8	26.0	**7.0**
7.4	1.93	na	0.00	**8.0**	11.4	1.66	11.46	4.28	59.3	**3.5**	21.4	12.3	**9.9**
8.3	0.78	3.0	-0.15	**6.8**	5.7	1.38	12.70	3.70	60.5	**4.5**	22.0	6.2	**8.0**
7.2	0.87	na	0.01	**4.3**	0.6	0.66	4.80	3.40	81.0	**0.7**	14.0	30.6	**6.8**
6.7	1.14	na	0.20	**3.0**	1.2	0.57	5.01	4.25	88.9	**4.4**	35.6	11.7	**6.2**
9.0	0.00	na	0.02	**3.3**	1.1	0.59	6.40	3.18	73.9	**0.7**	15.4	44.8	**4.7**
10.0	na	0.0	na	**8.6**	48.8	1.62	19.66	2.41	23.6	**8.7**	108.2	0.0	**7.0**
3.3	4.11	na	0.35	**7.7**	10.6	1.85	9.15	4.73	71.1	**4.7**	20.9	4.9	**8.4**
8.6	0.01	na	0.02	**4.2**	4.4	1.03	10.84	3.39	76.0	**4.2**	56.1	18.2	**6.5**
8.2	0.32	na	0.07	**6.4**	1.2	1.81	17.49	4.25	69.9	**5.4**	59.0	11.0	**6.6**
6.1	0.30	2.2	0.00	**4.9**	2.8	0.96	10.40	4.10	69.3	**4.1**	20.0	8.7	**5.8**
3.6	1.19	na	0.23	**7.1**	4.0	1.38	15.72	4.39	59.6	**1.7**	17.4	22.3	**6.7**
8.9	0.01	na	-0.01	**4.5**	1.0	0.87	6.21	3.54	69.9	**2.0**	27.0	18.8	**8.5**
7.8	0.72	3.4	-0.02	**5.9**	52.8	1.13	9.84	3.41	64.7	**5.4**	32.5	8.4	**9.9**
7.6	0.12	na	0.04	**4.5**	4.1	0.96	10.00	3.51	75.6	**1.5**	16.1	17.6	**7.6**
6.0	0.65	2.6	0.03	**8.3**	73.7	1.64	11.53	4.09	56.1	**3.1**	15.6	11.4	**9.9**
5.1	0.84	6.7	0.14	**4.1**	10.0	0.74	6.55	3.31	61.9	**1.1**	9.6	25.0	**8.4**
8.1	0.04	na	-0.21	**9.7**	1.4	2.47	20.23	5.56	55.7	**4.1**	25.0	8.4	**8.0**

Name	City	State	Rating	2018 Rating	2017 Rating	Total Assets ($Mil)	One Year Asset Growth	Asset Mix (As a % of Total Assets) Commercial Loans	Consumer Loans	Mortgage Loans	Securities	Capitalization Index	Leverage Ratio	Risk-Based Capital Ratio
First Bank	Burkburnett	TX	**B-**	B-	B+	469.0	11.27	13.0	1.1	30.2	0.8	**9.9**	11.5	14.9
First Bank	Strasburg	VA	**B+**	B+	B	776.7	4.08	6.3	1.5	24.7	17.1	**8.6**	10.1	14.6
First Bank & Trust	Brookings	SD	**B+**	B+	B+	1996.3	5.20	11.1	2.5	6.6	15.8	**7.1**	9.7	12.6
First Bank & Trust	Sioux Falls	SD	**B+**	B+	B+	1023.0	11.54	20.0	1.3	5.3	12.4	**8.4**	10.7	13.7
▲ First Bank & Trust	Lubbock	TX	**B+**	B	B	1158.3	4.12	14.2	1.1	11.7	26.0	**8.4**	10.8	13.7
First Bank & Trust	Seymour	TX	**C+**	C	C	127.4	-20.80	9.2	1.0	0.1	58.8	**10.0**	16.6	39.9
First Bank & Trust Co.	Duncan	OK	**A-**	A-	A-	563.2	-3.77	5.3	2.7	26.9	11.3	**10.0**	15.5	22.7
▼ First Bank & Trust Co.	Perry	OK	**A-**	A	A	146.5	0.25	4.7	7.7	17.3	31.0	**10.0**	13.4	19.9
First Bank and Trust	New Orleans	LA	**B-**	B-	B-	979.8	5.00	8.9	3.2	19.3	3.5	**6.7**	9.8	12.3
First Bank and Trust Co.	Minden	NE	**C+**	C+	C+	68.5	-4.86	6.5	2.7	14.1	30.7	**9.9**	11.0	20.0
▲ First Bank and Trust Co.	Clinton	OK	**B**	B-	B-	54.3	-5.91	2.2	10.8	17.7	33.7	**10.0**	13.4	35.6
First Bank and Trust Co.	Lebanon	VA	**A**	A	A	1927.6	9.87	6.8	3.0	15.3	1.7	**10.0**	11.7	16.4
First Bank and Trust Co. of Illinois	Palatine	IL	**C-**	C	B-	187.0	-1.04	17.2	0.0	1.8	1.1	**7.3**	9.2	13.6
First Bank and Trust Co. of Murphysboro	Murphysboro	IL	**D**	D+	C-	79.2	0.06	13.2	4.9	20.4	18.8	**6.8**	8.8	13.3
First Bank and Trust of Childress	Childress	TX	**C+**	C+	C-	115.7	5.70	13.4	3.6	9.4	35.2	**7.1**	9.1	20.3
▲ First Bank and Trust of Fullerton	Fullerton	NE	**B+**	B	B	93.5	5.85	3.8	1.0	0.3	13.5	**10.0**	14.7	18.2
▲ First Bank and Trust of Memphis	Memphis	TX	**B+**	B	B	56.2	-1.72	8.1	0.4	11.0	0.0	**10.0**	13.8	25.0
First Bank Blue Earth	Blue Earth	MN	**A-**	B+	B+	237.1	3.45	8.3	1.7	4.3	28.7	**8.9**	10.3	14.3
First Bank Elk River	Elk River	MN	**C+**	C	C+	298.3	7.53	18.1	0.6	4.3	30.6	**7.5**	9.3	13.2
First Bank Financial Centre	Oconomowoc	WI	**C+**	B-	B-	1248.8	7.96	4.9	0.1	16.4	11.5	**6.8**	9.2	12.4
▲ First Bank Hampton	Hampton	IA	**A-**	B+	A	167.2	8.75	16.6	4.0	13.5	16.2	**10.0**	12.6	16.9
▲ First Bank Kansas	Salina	KS	**B+**	B	B-	437.5	1.64	5.4	3.5	16.2	39.3	**7.4**	9.3	17.4
▲ First Bank of Alabama	Talladega	AL	**A-**	A-	A-	559.1	6.26	9.1	1.8	13.3	22.0	**10.0**	12.8	19.3
▲ First Bank of Baldwin	Baldwin	WI	**C+**	C	C	186.8	8.92	5.6	1.2	9.6	25.9	**8.0**	9.6	16.1
First Bank of Bancroft	Bancroft	NE	**B-**	B-	B-	23.0	0.65	5.7	1.9	4.1	18.9	**10.0**	17.5	31.2
▲ First Bank of Beloit	Beloit	KS	**B-**	C+	C	75.1	-1.76	8.3	1.8	14.1	26.1	**10.0**	13.6	21.9
▲ First Bank of Berne	Berne	IN	**B+**	B	A-	702.9	3.35	5.0	1.0	19.8	16.3	**9.0**	10.4	15.0
First Bank of Boaz	Boaz	AL	**A+**	A+	A+	241.3	0.95	3.7	1.8	5.9	70.4	**10.0**	17.3	35.6
▲ First Bank of Celeste	Celeste	TX	**C+**	C	C+	54.4	8.52	5.7	7.1	4.1	29.7	**5.9**	7.9	19.8
First Bank of Coastal Georgia	Pembroke	GA	**B-**	B	B	113.2	1.13	2.6	0.7	10.5	62.1	**10.0**	15.0	35.8
First Bank of Greenwich	Cos Cob	CT	**B-**	B-	B-	391.6	15.18	8.8	0.2	33.2	4.9	**7.6**	9.4	14.7
First Bank of Highland Park	Highland Park	IL	**C+**	C+	C	1825.8	7.03	41.6	0.1	3.5	13.2	**5.2**	10.3	11.2
First Bank of Linden	Linden	AL	**B**	B+	B+	80.5	2.11	8.5	7.3	4.7	45.6	**10.0**	14.9	25.0
▼ First Bank of Manhattan	Manhattan	IL	**B-**	B	B-	177.0	7.66	2.2	1.3	18.4	21.0	**8.8**	10.2	20.0
First Bank of Muleshoe	Muleshoe	TX	**B-**	B-	C+	89.2	-7.44	4.4	1.3	0.2	75.3	**10.0**	15.4	63.5
▲ First Bank of Ohio	Tiffin	OH	**B**	B+	A-	205.2	13.93	0.0	67.7	0.0	23.0	**10.0**	35.5	45.5
▲ First Bank of Okarche	Okarche	OK	**A**	A-	A	110.7	10.33	8.4	1.8	1.2	35.6	**10.0**	11.8	26.4
First Bank of Owasso	Owasso	OK	**A-**	A-	A-	432.2	13.22	2.4	0.4	10.2	2.7	**8.0**	10.9	13.4
First Bank of Pike	Molena	GA	**C-**	C-	C-	54.6	15.64	7.1	9.3	25.3	19.9	**6.3**	8.3	15.0
First Bank of the Lake	Osage Beach	MO	**C-**	C	C	111.0	41.02	20.3	0.4	6.8	5.7	**5.7**	7.7	20.4
First Bank of the Palm Beaches	West Palm Beach	FL	**C+**	C+	C-	189.1	8.67	1.9	0.3	29.8	0.3	**6.9**	8.9	12.5
First Bank of Thomas	Thomas	OK	**B+**	B+	B+	46.1	-4.49	1.2	1.0	9.8	26.4	**10.0**	15.2	33.4
First Bank of Utica	Utica	NE	**C+**	C+	C+	70.1	-0.18	9.9	4.0	11.3	2.4	**10.0**	12.5	15.1
▲ First Bank Richmond	Richmond	IN	**B-**	C+	C+	953.8	17.96	7.9	1.5	13.8	19.4	**10.0**	15.7	21.5
▲ First Bank, Upper Michigan	Gladstone	MI	**D+**	D	D+	474.9	2.36	13.0	10.2	17.8	11.7	**8.6**	10.4	13.8
▲ First Bankers Trust Co., N.A.	Quincy	IL	**B-**	C+	B-	906.6	-6.96	6.9	4.9	7.1	38.9	**7.6**	9.4	16.1
First Bethany Bank & Trust	Bethany	OK	**B**	B	B	223.9	6.43	6.0	0.5	11.0	38.5	**7.8**	9.5	16.0
▲ First Business Bank	Madison	WI	**B-**	C+	C+	2080.2	10.30	24.8	0.2	1.7	9.5	**5.9**	10.1	11.7
First Cahawba Bank	Selma	AL	**B**	B	B	127.0	21.82	18.5	2.2	17.3	12.1	**10.0**	11.6	17.2
▼ First Capital Bank	Laurinburg	NC	**C-**	C+	C+	110.5	28.62	4.1	2.0	20.1	9.0	**10.0**	23.0	34.3
First Capital Bank	Germantown	TN	**B-**	B-	B-	344.3	12.47	18.5	0.6	9.0	1.5	**6.3**	10.8	12.0
▲ First Capital Bank	Quanah	TX	**C-**	C-	C-	62.0	2.76	18.0	7.4	16.4	0.0	**6.3**	9.3	12.0
First Carolina Bank	Rocky Mount	NC	**B**	C+	C	593.2	35.84	6.4	0.3	10.0	29.7	**9.5**	10.9	14.6
First Central Bank	Cambridge	NE	**C-**	C	C+	111.3	7.86	12.9	3.8	2.9	10.8	**8.9**	10.3	16.3
First Central Bank McCook	McCook	NE	**C-**	C-	C-	121.0	2.50	24.7	2.3	3.8	8.1	**8.6**	10.8	13.8
First Central National Bank of Saint Paris	Saint Paris	OH	**B**	B	B	93.2	-0.83	2.8	2.3	14.2	28.6	**10.0**	18.0	31.4
First Central Savings Bank	Glen Cove	NY	**D+**	D+	C-	595.2	-1.24	14.4	0.0	14.6	7.9	**6.3**	8.8	12.0
First Central State Bank	De Witt	IA	**A-**	A-	B+	544.3	38.96	10.5	2.6	13.5	20.4	**10.0**	12.0	15.5
First Century Bank	Tazewell	TN	**B+**	B+	B-	412.3	4.93	7.6	1.5	28.4	1.7	**8.3**	9.9	13.7
First Century Bank, N.A.	Gainesville	GA	**B**	B	B	157.1	15.27	0.5	1.1	4.5	16.5	**10.0**	11.6	76.9

Arrows denote recent upgrades ▲ or downgrades ▼

Asset Quality Index	Adjusted Non-Performing Loans as a % of Total Loans	Adjusted Non-Performing Loans as a % of Capital	Net Charge-Offs Avg Loans	Profitability Index	Net Income ($Mil)	Return on Assets (R.O.A.)	Return on Equity (R.O.E.)	Net Interest Spread	Overhead Efficiency Ratio	Liquidity Index	Liquidity Ratio	Hot Money Ratio	Stability Index
4.1	1.45	na	0.06	**10.0**	7.6	2.38	20.92	5.25	68.2	**2.1**	16.0	18.6	**8.1**
6.9	0.27	na	0.07	**6.8**	7.7	1.32	13.41	4.01	65.5	**4.2**	17.3	7.9	**7.3**
4.9	1.11	5.9	0.01	**6.9**	18.6	1.27	11.40	3.84	62.1	**2.3**	8.8	14.9	**8.5**
4.6	1.29	9.0	0.12	**8.0**	10.4	1.41	11.54	4.76	64.3	**2.8**	16.0	12.3	**8.5**
5.2	0.57	1.3	0.57	**5.7**	8.8	1.07	5.03	4.48	67.2	**3.2**	35.1	20.4	**8.8**
8.2	0.13	na	0.00	**5.7**	1.5	1.30	8.58	2.44	57.7	**6.9**	67.1	5.2	**5.2**
5.7	1.85	na	0.04	**8.2**	8.5	1.93	12.97	4.32	58.6	**3.4**	12.6	11.6	**10.0**
5.1	3.90	10.2	-0.08	**8.7**	2.4	2.17	16.17	4.55	57.4	**3.9**	25.5	10.7	**9.2**
4.4	0.92	na	-0.03	**8.1**	14.7	2.03	20.60	4.46	62.6	**1.2**	7.9	26.3	**7.9**
7.0	4.06	na	0.01	**3.0**	0.3	0.59	5.54	3.20	84.9	**4.3**	31.7	10.5	**5.7**
8.5	0.00	na	0.44	**4.1**	0.4	0.92	7.18	4.01	80.3	**3.4**	31.4	15.0	**5.8**
7.0	0.19	5.4	0.01	**7.9**	20.7	1.48	12.88	3.93	56.1	**3.5**	14.3	11.6	**10.0**
7.4	0.00	na	0.00	**0.7**	-0.7	-0.52	-5.45	4.84	116.9	**0.9**	21.9	35.0	**4.3**
2.0	2.42	na	0.79	**1.3**	0.0	-0.06	-0.67	3.64	95.3	**2.1**	14.5	18.5	**4.2**
6.6	1.42	na	0.05	**3.0**	0.5	0.58	7.03	2.53	77.3	**0.7**	15.8	52.9	**4.7**
7.2	0.00	na	0.03	**5.1**	0.8	1.09	7.47	3.44	58.1	**1.4**	14.5	20.1	**8.1**
8.7	0.00	na	0.00	**5.8**	0.6	1.32	9.97	3.52	63.8	**2.3**	46.9	33.9	**8.4**
8.1	0.05	0.4	-0.31	**6.8**	2.9	1.69	16.37	3.47	53.4	**2.3**	13.9	17.2	**8.5**
7.4	0.49	na	0.01	**3.1**	1.3	0.61	5.91	3.25	82.7	**3.9**	26.8	10.2	**5.2**
3.2	1.31	na	0.05	**4.8**	9.6	1.07	11.61	3.61	76.5	**1.2**	11.9	22.3	**7.2**
7.3	0.80	na	0.85	**6.6**	1.8	1.44	11.33	4.01	49.2	**3.1**	15.5	13.5	**9.2**
8.5	0.02	1.3	0.08	**7.6**	5.8	1.78	19.47	3.67	64.8	**4.8**	35.0	9.2	**6.9**
7.4	2.25	na	0.14	**8.2**	6.5	1.60	11.74	4.48	53.1	**1.3**	15.1	27.0	**9.2**
4.0	2.53	na	-0.01	**5.1**	1.8	1.32	12.89	3.92	71.0	**5.1**	26.9	3.7	**6.5**
8.9	1.04	na	-0.07	**6.0**	0.2	1.21	7.02	3.89	59.4	**5.5**	50.0	7.0	**5.7**
8.8	0.17	na	-0.01	**3.4**	0.3	0.61	4.57	3.79	78.2	**4.1**	13.5	7.7	**6.8**
5.8	0.59	na	0.02	**8.6**	11.1	2.11	20.69	3.84	50.6	**4.8**	18.7	3.7	**8.7**
9.7	0.06	0.2	0.00	**7.8**	2.6	1.50	8.32	3.60	43.8	**4.7**	67.5	17.2	**9.5**
8.5	0.00	na	0.02	**4.2**	0.4	1.02	12.80	3.10	75.4	**5.5**	62.0	10.9	**4.6**
9.6	0.94	na	0.00	**2.7**	0.4	0.50	3.56	2.90	85.7	**4.2**	32.5	11.5	**6.6**
5.6	1.02	na	0.00	**3.2**	1.3	0.45	4.50	2.89	80.2	**0.8**	16.7	35.8	**5.6**
7.2	0.24	1.8	0.25	**3.2**	6.7	0.51	5.01	2.48	66.6	**0.6**	12.6	33.5	**8.3**
8.1	1.27	na	0.80	**4.1**	0.5	0.78	5.15	3.86	65.6	**2.8**	62.2	33.5	**7.5**
6.1	2.72	na	-0.08	**3.7**	1.0	0.80	7.61	3.47	79.1	**5.0**	32.7	6.6	**6.4**
9.7	0.70	0.6	0.00	**3.5**	0.5	0.67	4.44	3.07	76.2	**7.5**	91.2	3.3	**7.0**
5.6	0.11	na	0.71	**7.7**	2.3	1.62	4.42	4.76	43.7	**1.5**	39.3	61.0	**7.1**
8.9	0.56	na	-0.01	**9.0**	1.8	2.25	19.46	3.71	38.1	**5.1**	68.5	15.4	**8.6**
7.3	0.00	0.1	0.05	**9.5**	7.1	2.20	21.17	3.99	44.6	**0.8**	10.9	19.8	**9.1**
5.5	0.02	na	0.13	**3.3**	0.2	0.41	4.85	5.38	86.1	**3.3**	33.5	16.4	**2.9**
3.9	5.15	na	0.69	**6.2**	1.1	1.49	16.25	3.94	60.5	**2.1**	44.8	55.3	**5.4**
7.4	0.18	na	-0.01	**3.5**	0.9	0.63	7.25	4.15	77.2	**2.7**	18.7	16.0	**4.3**
7.9	1.27	3.5	0.02	**6.7**	0.6	1.58	10.74	3.59	57.7	**4.1**	55.0	16.8	**8.7**
3.8	1.62	9.2	0.00	**4.2**	0.4	0.73	5.71	4.09	73.8	**1.2**	7.0	27.3	**6.6**
7.4	0.28	na	0.08	**3.8**	5.4	0.77	7.46	3.41	67.8	**1.4**	19.7	16.8	**7.4**
2.3	3.77	na	0.09	**7.9**	6.3	1.80	13.94	4.40	62.8	**1.9**	18.4	19.2	**8.8**
4.2	1.42	6.3	0.87	**4.7**	6.4	0.92	9.40	3.09	61.2	**2.2**	7.4	16.9	**6.1**
8.7	0.22	na	0.00	**4.7**	1.8	1.10	11.69	3.16	65.9	**2.1**	25.2	16.1	**6.5**
4.1	1.33	6.2	0.07	**5.8**	20.9	1.38	13.11	3.76	67.9	**1.7**	11.6	9.4	**9.2**
8.6	0.01	na	0.01	**3.9**	0.6	0.67	5.79	4.48	78.6	**3.8**	24.6	10.9	**6.5**
7.8	1.90	na	0.05	**0.3**	-0.5	-0.67	-3.21	4.30	114.0	**2.7**	29.0	16.1	**6.3**
7.2	0.21	na	0.00	**4.9**	2.3	0.96	8.80	2.95	56.4	**0.5**	10.0	62.4	**5.8**
4.5	0.45	na	0.51	**4.9**	0.4	0.83	9.25	5.44	75.4	**1.0**	7.5	29.9	**4.3**
7.8	0.00	0.0	-0.01	**4.5**	4.2	1.04	9.48	2.95	51.8	**1.5**	37.5	44.9	**6.4**
0.0	5.93	na	0.37	**6.1**	0.8	1.00	9.96	4.00	66.8	**0.7**	14.5	34.3	**5.8**
0.0	8.50	na	0.44	**8.9**	1.5	1.59	15.42	5.02	49.7	**0.3**	9.0	49.5	**5.6**
8.9	0.13	1.9	0.00	**3.9**	0.6	0.79	4.54	3.14	70.6	**4.7**	48.1	13.0	**7.7**
0.9	4.63	24.2	0.01	**2.4**	2.2	0.49	5.27	3.40	78.0	**0.7**	13.6	40.3	**4.0**
8.3	0.57	na	0.08	**6.1**	4.9	1.17	10.22	3.30	57.5	**2.8**	20.5	14.8	**8.3**
8.3	0.23	1.3	0.00	**7.6**	4.4	1.48	14.81	4.15	56.6	**2.0**	11.1	12.7	**6.2**
10.0	0.00	na	2.35	**8.2**	3.0	2.55	23.93	3.87	50.7	**8.1**	82.8	0.0	**4.9**

Name	City	State	Rating	2018 Rating	2017 Rating	Total Assets ($Mil)	One Year Asset Growth	Asset Mix (As a % of Total Assets) Comm-ercial Loans	Cons-umer Loans	Mort-gage Loans	Secur-ities	Capital-ization Index	Lever-age Ratio	Risk-Based Capital Ratio
▲ First Chatham Bank	Savannah	GA	**D+**	D-	E-	377.1	2.19	6.1	0.6	7.6	7.1	**6.8**	8.8	13.4
First Choice Bank	Cerritos	CA	**A-**	B+	A-	1655.6	4.30	14.6	0.0	10.9	2.0	**9.2**	12.6	14.4
▲ First Choice Bank	Pontotoc	MS	**A-**	B+	B	310.5	4.35	8.1	6.7	25.2	25.0	**10.0**	13.0	20.8
First Citizens Bank	Luverne	AL	**A-**	A-	A-	244.3	-0.14	8.7	5.4	14.6	28.2	**10.0**	14.0	20.6
First Citizens Bank	Mason City	IA	**A-**	A-	A-	1276.9	1.94	12.1	1.0	9.5	23.9	**10.0**	12.7	15.8
▲ First Citizens Bank of Butte	Butte	MT	**B-**	B-	B-	69.6	8.03	9.9	4.4	19.0	14.7	**10.0**	11.1	22.0
First Citizens Bank of Polson, N.A.	Polson	MT	**D-**	E+	E-	18.2	0.46	5.9	4.7	11.9	8.4	**4.0**	6.0	12.8
First Citizens Community Bank	Mansfield	PA	**B**	B	B	1474.1	4.75	4.4	0.7	19.1	16.8	**7.2**	9.1	13.2
First Citizens National Bank	Dyersburg	TN	**B+**	B+	B+	1781.9	6.02	4.5	1.5	11.0	32.8	**9.0**	10.3	16.1
First Citizens National Bank of Upper Sand	Upper Sandusky	OH	**B-**	B-	B-	293.2	5.19	5.8	1.0	18.4	20.0	**10.0**	14.4	22.7
First Citizens State Bank	Whitewater	WI	**A-**	A-	B+	310.5	1.00	5.3	0.8	21.1	25.5	**10.0**	20.1	30.2
First Citrus Bank	Tampa	FL	**B-**	C+	C-	416.0	7.09	6.6	0.1	8.3	0.1	**6.5**	9.8	12.2
First City Bank	Columbus	OH	**C+**	C+	C+	64.2	-0.39	2.3	0.2	21.7	3.4	**10.0**	11.3	16.4
First City Bank of Florida	Fort Walton Beach	FL	**E-**	E-	E-	146.1	-12.62	5.1	0.7	16.1	6.1	**0.0**	2.4	4.6
▲ First Colony Bank of Florida	Maitland	FL	**B-**	B-	B+	231.5	12.95	13.2	0.2	1.3	11.8	**8.3**	9.9	13.6
▲ First Colorado National Bank	Paonia	CO	**B**	C+	B	72.9	7.78	10.3	0.3	1.9	0.0	**10.0**	16.7	21.6
First Columbia Bank & Trust Co.	Bloomsburg	PA	**B+**	B+	A-	753.8	4.26	3.0	0.8	31.5	23.9	**10.0**	11.8	21.2
▲ First Command Bank	Fort Worth	TX	**A-**	B+	B	786.5	-2.88	10.4	25.2	0.0	46.6	**7.2**	9.1	16.1
▲ First Commerce Bank	Marysville	KS	**B**	B-	B+	98.2	-0.33	10.2	5.2	29.3	7.3	**10.0**	11.3	18.3
First Commerce Bank	Lakewood	NJ	**C**	C-	C+	1004.1	6.15	5.2	0.0	24.3	12.4	**10.0**	14.0	19.2
First Commerce Bank	Lewisburg	TN	**B**	B	B+	432.4	10.70	8.6	3.2	14.4	12.7	**7.1**	9.1	13.4
First Commercial Bank	Jackson	MS	**B**	B	B	392.5	0.61	19.8	1.4	9.0	5.6	**10.0**	13.4	17.4
▲ First Commercial Bank (USA)	Alhambra	CA	**A-**	B+	A-	622.2	8.28	8.8	0.0	11.8	3.1	**10.0**	20.8	27.4
First Commercial Bank, N.A.	Seguin	TX	**B-**	B	B-	352.7	8.64	4.6	1.8	13.0	17.2	**7.4**	9.3	15.3
First Commonwealth Bank	Indiana	PA	**B+**	B+	B	8132.2	6.06	13.0	8.3	13.5	14.4	**8.0**	9.7	13.6
First Community Bank	Batesville	AR	**B-**	B-	B-	1506.0	5.67	13.2	4.0	19.3	14.7	**6.8**	9.5	12.4
▲ First Community Bank	Newell	IA	**B**	B-	C+	95.6	3.97	5.6	2.4	5.6	21.0	**8.3**	9.9	14.9
▲ First Community Bank	Harbor Springs	MI	**B+**	B	B+	317.5	2.84	11.5	0.6	9.2	8.1	**7.9**	10.0	13.3
First Community Bank	Lester Prairie	MN	**B-**	B-	C+	62.7	3.15	4.4	1.5	10.2	25.7	**9.4**	10.6	18.5
First Community Bank	Glasgow	MT	**B**	B-	C+	306.0	2.09	4.5	1.4	9.0	25.1	**9.9**	10.9	15.7
▲ First Community Bank	Beemer	NE	**B-**	C+	B-	146.3	0.05	7.3	1.5	6.4	7.9	**8.6**	10.2	13.8
First Community Bank	Lexington	SC	**B+**	B+	B-	1129.8	3.57	4.3	0.9	9.8	23.5	**8.7**	10.1	14.2
First Community Bank	Corpus Christi	TX	**A-**	B+	B	421.7	-1.96	12.9	2.9	16.6	15.4	**10.0**	12.1	17.5
First Community Bank	San Benito	TX	**B**	B	B	477.1	9.13	12.5	1.1	8.4	18.2	**6.7**	8.7	13.9
First Community Bank	Bluefield	VA	**B**	B	B	2202.1	-2.81	4.1	4.2	28.3	5.3	**9.0**	10.3	14.4
First Community Bank	Milton	WI	**B+**	B+	B+	106.6	5.55	5.9	1.3	15.7	21.2	**5.7**	10.4	11.5
▲ First Community Bank and Trust	Beecher	IL	**A-**	B+	B-	156.2	6.69	12.3	2.3	8.1	19.1	**10.0**	12.6	20.5
First Community Bank of Central Alabama	Wetumpka	AL	**B+**	B+	B+	377.8	6.85	8.1	5.3	17.1	25.1	**6.0**	8.1	11.9
First Community Bank of Cullman	Cullman	AL	**C+**	C	C+	124.8	13.86	5.0	2.7	36.1	4.5	**6.2**	8.3	11.9
First Community Bank of East Tennessee	Rogersville	TN	**B**	B-	B-	165.2	-7.25	7.9	2.6	22.7	12.1	**10.0**	12.0	17.8
▲ First Community Bank of Hillsboro	Hillsboro	IL	**B**	C+	B-	112.5	9.49	8.8	3.1	16.7	30.4	**7.6**	9.4	16.7
First Community Bank of Moultrie County	Sullivan	IL	**B**	C+	C+	90.1	6.95	4.4	5.5	26.1	8.3	**8.8**	10.2	18.5
First Community Bank of Tennessee	Shelbyville	TN	**B+**	B+	A-	600.7	21.86	5.2	0.8	40.1	11.7	**8.1**	11.9	13.4
▲ First Community Bank of the Heartland, Inc	Clinton	KY	**B-**	C+	B-	245.5	5.08	2.9	3.7	12.9	21.9	**6.0**	8.0	12.8
First Community Bank of the Ozarks	Branson	MO	**B+**	B+	B+	105.4	0.74	3.3	2.4	26.4	15.7	**10.0**	11.6	16.6
▲ First Community Bank, Xenia-Flora	Xenia	IL	**B**	B-	B	41.1	-7.14	3.9	6.2	23.2	28.6	**10.0**	11.9	23.7
▲ First Community National Bank	Cuba	MO	**D+**	D-	D-	130.3	-1.87	2.6	1.9	21.4	21.3	**7.3**	9.2	15.9
First Community Trust, N.A.	Dubuque	IA	**U**	U	U	12.2	57.76	0.0	0.0	0.0	40.1	**10.0**	95.6	55.4
First County Bank	Stamford	CT	**C+**	C+	C	1714.8	2.40	4.2	1.0	49.8	14.7	**7.7**	9.5	15.5
▼ First Covenant Bank	Commerce	GA	**B-**	B	C+	112.4	-12.31	1.9	0.3	1.7	19.0	**10.0**	15.7	39.4
▲ First Credit Bank	Los Angeles	CA	**B-**	C	C+	454.7	-6.47	1.3	0.0	12.2	6.3	**10.0**	44.6	49.9
First Dakota National Bank	Yankton	SD	**B**	B	B	1748.8	5.09	8.3	2.0	7.3	10.1	**7.0**	10.2	12.5
First Eagle Bank	Chicago	IL	**A**	A	A	528.8	3.40	1.7	0.1	19.3	24.8	**10.0**	17.4	23.8
▲ First Electronic Bank	Salt Lake City	UT	**B+**	B	B	55.9	106.60	13.9	14.4	0.0	0.1	**10.0**	28.6	80.4
▲ First Enterprise Bank	Oklahoma City	OK	**C+**	C-	C-	156.0	-3.64	15.8	0.8	17.2	0.0	**10.0**	12.9	16.9
First Exchange Bank	White Hall	WV	**C-**	C-	C-	289.3	14.21	7.4	3.9	42.0	6.3	**6.3**	8.3	12.1
▲ First FarmBank	Greeley	CO	**C**	C-	C	253.0	3.79	4.5	0.4	9.2	17.3	**6.6**	8.8	12.2
First Farmers & Merchants Bank	Cannon Falls	MN	**B+**	A-	A-	318.1	2.59	10.6	2.5	9.1	12.9	**10.0**	14.0	17.8
First Farmers & Merchants National Bank	Fairmont	MN	**B+**	B+	B+	103.6	-0.02	19.3	3.4	17.4	9.3	**10.0**	14.6	16.9
First Farmers & Merchants National Bank	Luverne	MN	**B**	B+	A-	177.8	4.08	13.0	1.9	2.5	1.8	**10.0**	16.8	17.2

Asset Quality Index	Adjusted Non-Performing Loans as a % of Total Loans	Adjusted Non-Performing Loans as a % of Capital	Net Charge-Offs Avg Loans	Profitability Index	Net Income ($Mil)	Return on Assets (R.O.A.)	Return on Equity (R.O.E.)	Net Interest Spread	Overhead Efficiency Ratio	Liquidity Index	Liquidity Ratio	Hot Money Ratio	Stability Index
4.9	2.86	na	0.18	**4.5**	2.9	1.05	10.38	4.47	77.4	**4.1**	26.0	10.1	**4.4**
5.8	0.59	na	0.03	**9.5**	22.6	1.92	11.42	5.42	47.9	**1.9**	15.2	9.5	**9.8**
8.2	0.40	na	0.14	**5.7**	2.7	1.14	9.01	3.97	63.4	**1.6**	19.0	24.0	**7.6**
6.8	1.16	4.6	0.12	**7.7**	2.9	1.57	11.44	4.53	58.3	**1.7**	19.8	22.7	**8.0**
7.7	0.32	na	0.07	**6.8**	15.2	1.62	12.86	3.38	54.1	**2.8**	16.6	15.2	**10.0**
7.8	2.72	na	0.00	**3.7**	0.4	0.79	7.21	4.26	82.3	**5.0**	33.4	7.2	**6.2**
8.1	0.10	na	0.45	**0.0**	-0.9	-6.77	-85.27	4.31	230.1	**6.1**	43.3	0.6	**1.4**
4.6	1.84	9.2	0.04	**6.6**	15.2	1.40	13.87	3.74	56.1	**3.1**	5.7	11.6	**9.5**
8.4	0.28	na	0.02	**5.3**	13.9	1.08	9.35	3.55	68.0	**1.9**	23.0	25.6	**9.7**
7.2	2.30	na	0.00	**3.6**	1.7	0.79	5.55	3.91	75.9	**4.1**	22.3	9.2	**7.0**
9.2	0.00	na	0.13	**6.0**	3.1	1.32	6.68	3.56	60.0	**3.8**	38.5	15.6	**8.5**
5.6	0.66	na	0.13	**5.5**	3.0	1.01	10.48	3.98	66.1	**1.9**	20.9	12.9	**5.4**
7.6	0.00	0.0	0.00	**3.0**	0.2	0.48	4.22	3.59	86.6	**1.5**	11.4	23.6	**6.7**
0.3	16.44	na	0.16	**0.4**	-0.6	-0.50	-20.35	4.19	113.9	**4.7**	18.6	4.6	**0.9**
6.9	0.20	na	0.65	**8.9**	3.5	2.11	21.21	4.25	47.4	**2.3**	32.9	22.7	**7.9**
5.3	2.17	na	0.24	**5.8**	0.5	0.84	4.28	5.26	86.7	**4.6**	43.3	12.7	**9.4**
6.5	1.27	na	0.03	**5.5**	6.8	1.25	9.91	3.26	60.6	**3.3**	7.9	11.9	**8.4**
7.1	0.30	1.0	0.38	**9.0**	12.9	2.24	27.47	3.52	58.1	**7.2**	58.4	1.5	**6.5**
6.8	0.54	na	-0.04	**7.6**	1.4	1.80	15.16	3.98	59.0	**2.6**	21.7	16.6	**7.9**
2.5	2.83	na	0.24	**5.8**	7.6	1.03	7.41	3.42	62.0	**1.4**	23.7	36.2	**9.3**
8.4	0.09	na	0.00	**7.2**	4.4	1.37	15.71	3.80	52.3	**0.8**	16.5	34.9	**6.1**
8.0	0.41	na	-0.01	**4.8**	3.2	1.06	8.02	3.57	69.8	**0.8**	12.4	19.6	**8.1**
7.1	0.00	na	0.00	**8.2**	5.8	1.28	6.03	3.58	50.3	**0.6**	8.4	50.2	**9.5**
5.8	1.03	na	-0.06	**5.4**	3.4	1.34	13.67	4.44	67.2	**5.6**	35.3	3.7	**6.0**
5.8	0.56	2.9	0.17	**6.9**	83.5	1.40	10.72	3.78	57.5	**4.2**	4.8	6.0	**9.8**
5.1	1.71	9.6	0.23	**5.1**	10.6	0.95	10.37	3.62	67.2	**0.9**	14.8	36.7	**7.5**
6.5	0.42	na	0.02	**5.3**	1.0	1.31	10.55	3.36	62.4	**3.5**	30.8	14.2	**7.2**
7.4	0.00	na	-0.21	**6.9**	3.8	1.63	16.68	4.61	67.1	**4.4**	15.9	6.1	**7.4**
9.0	0.00	na	0.00	**4.3**	0.5	0.98	9.31	3.71	74.1	**4.4**	39.8	12.8	**5.4**
4.6	1.51	7.3	0.01	**4.3**	1.7	0.77	6.80	3.97	77.7	**4.7**	30.6	7.9	**7.0**
5.9	0.56	na	0.00	**4.1**	0.8	0.70	6.53	4.16	75.1	**0.8**	17.1	37.6	**6.9**
6.5	0.56	2.4	-0.03	**5.3**	8.9	1.08	9.36	3.76	69.2	**4.1**	17.4	9.2	**9.0**
6.4	1.18	3.7	0.26	**6.1**	4.3	1.38	11.59	5.70	74.1	**2.7**	21.5	16.1	**7.9**
8.4	0.67	na	0.04	**7.0**	4.8	1.42	16.17	4.68	64.7	**2.3**	19.1	17.8	**6.1**
4.3	1.37	na	0.25	**9.6**	30.0	1.81	12.76	4.62	54.8	**4.1**	14.4	8.5	**10.0**
8.5	0.08	na	-0.21	**7.5**	1.4	1.79	17.71	3.69	59.3	**2.3**	32.0	20.6	**7.8**
5.9	1.94	7.7	-0.11	**6.8**	1.5	1.35	10.50	4.63	64.1	**5.4**	31.2	3.7	**6.0**
6.5	0.59	3.3	0.04	**9.6**	6.4	2.28	29.18	4.22	49.3	**2.3**	19.9	18.0	**6.9**
7.0	0.00	0.3	0.03	**3.5**	0.5	0.61	7.29	3.47	63.8	**0.5**	6.3	44.8	**4.5**
5.9	0.45	na	-0.06	**4.6**	1.3	0.94	7.95	4.16	78.9	**4.1**	8.8	7.2	**6.6**
6.8	0.66	na	0.00	**5.5**	1.1	1.42	15.53	3.25	58.4	**3.4**	12.1	11.5	**6.0**
6.3	0.38	na	0.04	**5.4**	0.9	1.35	12.62	3.83	66.6	**5.3**	35.8	6.4	**6.1**
8.2	0.17	0.9	-0.04	**6.2**	5.2	1.40	11.24	3.49	85.3	**0.6**	10.8	33.4	**7.5**
6.8	0.01	na	0.11	**4.0**	1.6	0.92	9.28	4.01	78.9	**1.1**	14.2	26.4	**6.3**
5.9	1.98	na	-0.06	**4.4**	0.8	0.98	8.47	4.02	75.4	**1.8**	14.2	20.2	**7.3**
8.6	0.51	na	0.01	**6.5**	0.5	1.56	13.22	3.68	59.5	**4.8**	34.3	8.8	**7.4**
5.2	2.42	na	0.24	**2.4**	0.6	0.61	6.93	4.14	102.8	**4.6**	41.0	12.1	**3.1**
10.0	na	na	na	**9.5**	1.2	15.58	17.99	2.08	64.1	**4.0**	na	0.0	**6.2**
6.3	1.44	9.0	0.02	**3.0**	6.1	0.48	5.47	2.92	80.7	**1.3**	15.0	22.2	**6.7**
9.5	0.83	na	0.33	**2.6**	0.6	0.60	3.97	4.23	111.1	**7.0**	54.1	0.5	**6.4**
3.8	5.57	na	0.00	**10.0**	15.5	4.52	10.25	6.24	12.4	**1.7**	38.8	43.2	**9.3**
5.0	1.01	7.0	0.24	**5.4**	13.2	1.05	10.11	4.12	68.5	**1.8**	13.6	15.1	**7.5**
8.8	0.17	na	0.02	**9.8**	9.5	2.49	14.37	4.00	40.6	**1.2**	23.2	25.9	**10.0**
7.7	0.00	na	0.00	**10.0**	1.8	5.82	17.93	12.83	77.0	**4.3**	93.1	10.5	**9.0**
3.5	2.12	na	0.00	**8.8**	2.2	1.81	14.12	5.39	68.1	**0.8**	10.4	28.2	**9.5**
2.0	2.94	24.6	0.10	**5.8**	2.9	1.38	16.72	4.05	62.3	**2.1**	8.5	17.8	**5.8**
3.7	1.01	na	-0.01	**4.7**	1.8	0.96	11.32	4.03	68.6	**1.1**	12.0	30.0	**5.0**
4.7	2.53	11.8	0.23	**8.3**	4.4	1.90	13.05	4.50	55.7	**4.1**	21.3	8.3	**8.3**
4.1	3.77	15.6	0.11	**5.4**	1.0	1.25	8.68	4.18	67.0	**0.8**	4.2	31.7	**7.6**
3.1	2.57	11.5	0.00	**8.9**	2.6	1.98	11.95	4.89	52.8	**2.5**	8.6	16.1	**8.3**

							One	Asset Mix (As a % of Total Assets)						Risk-
Name	City	State	Rating	2018 Rating	2017 Rating	Total Assets ($Mil)	Year Asset Growth	Comm-ercial Loans	Cons-umer Loans	Mort-gage Loans	Secur-ities	Capital-ization Index	Lever-age Ratio	Based Capital Ratio
First Farmers & Merchants State Bank	Brownsdale	MN	B+	B+	A-	73.5	0.27	8.6	0.8	4.1	16.9	10.0	18.6	22.5
▼ First Farmers & Merchants State Bank	Grand Meadow	MN	B	B+	A-	71.1	8.15	7.5	0.3	5.5	5.6	9.0	10.9	14.1
First Farmers and Commercial Bank	Pikeville	TN	B-	C+	B	131.3	14.29	12.5	3.9	12.0	18.9	10.0	11.8	15.7
First Farmers and Merchants Bank	Columbia	TN	B+	B	B-	1366.7	0.28	8.2	1.0	21.7	25.5	8.3	9.9	15.1
First Farmers Bank & Trust	Converse	IN	B-	B-	B-	1898.9	11.53	14.6	0.6	3.8	19.2	8.3	10.1	13.6
First Farmers National Bank of Waurika	Waurika	OK	B	B	B+	44.1	2.61	1.1	3.6	1.2	52.3	10.0	21.2	47.3
First Farmers State Bank	Minier	IL	A-	A-	A-	172.1	1.84	4.8	0.4	7.9	18.8	10.0	12.7	21.7
First Federal Bank	Lake City	FL	A-	A-	A-	2204.9	22.94	2.0	2.4	23.6	22.8	9.1	10.4	17.6
First Federal Bank	Dunn	NC	C+	C	D+	185.0	-1.79	6.3	0.7	36.5	20.2	10.0	11.5	20.3
First Federal Bank	Dickson	TN	A-	A-	A-	721.0	7.61	3.2	2.4	20.8	29.6	10.0	11.1	19.7
First Federal Bank & Trust	Sheridan	WY	B-	C+	C	327.0	9.31	7.8	1.0	27.0	24.4	10.0	15.9	20.4
First Federal Bank Littlefield, Texas	Littlefield	TX	B	B	B	50.3	-6.59	12.3	10.6	16.8	0.0	10.0	19.7	23.4
First Federal Bank Of Kansas City	Kansas City	MO	D+	C-	C	819.3	2.67	0.0	2.2	67.0	14.4	10.0	14.0	27.9
First Federal Bank of Louisiana	Lake Charles	LA	C+	C+	C	877.0	4.00	2.9	2.1	29.4	19.5	10.0	12.6	21.3
▲ First Federal Bank of Ohio	Galion	OH	C+	C	C-	238.8	1.89	0.1	1.2	28.7	32.8	10.0	15.7	35.6
First Federal Bank of the Midwest	Defiance	OH	B	B	B	3322.7	8.17	15.0	1.0	10.9	8.7	6.7	10.4	12.2
First Federal Bank of Wisconsin	Waukesha	WI	C+	C+	C-	258.0	-3.83	4.8	0.1	23.3	16.7	10.0	19.4	25.3
First Federal Bank, A FSB	Tuscaloosa	AL	C	C-	C-	141.1	18.77	0.1	0.3	69.7	0.6	10.0	11.3	16.1
First Federal Community Bank of Bucyrus	Bucyrus	OH	C+	C+	C+	177.7	19.79	4.9	5.1	50.7	6.9	6.2	8.2	13.1
First Federal Community Bank, N.A.	Dover	OH	B	B	B	443.2	15.18	8.2	2.5	25.9	4.0	7.2	9.1	12.8
First Federal Community Bank, SSB	Paris	TX	B	B	B-	447.7	5.27	10.5	2.6	40.4	3.5	10.0	11.4	17.0
▲ First Federal S&L Assn.	Hazard	KY	C+	C	B-	82.9	7.82	0.0	1.3	75.8	0.8	10.0	22.1	41.0
First Federal S&L Assn.	Morehead	KY	C+	C+	C	33.7	-4.02	1.4	1.3	56.9	0.0	10.0	29.4	52.4
First Federal S&L Assn.	Aberdeen	MS	B-	B-	B-	43.3	17.58	0.0	1.6	60.4	11.6	10.0	17.1	43.8
First Federal S&L Assn. of Bath	Bath	ME	B	B	B	135.8	3.95	0.9	1.2	74.0	2.3	10.0	17.0	29.7
First Federal S&L Assn. of Centerburg	Centerburg	OH	C+	C+	C+	23.7	2.11	0.0	0.3	56.8	9.1	10.0	19.3	41.5
First Federal S&L Assn. of Central Illinois,	Shelbyville	IL	B+	B+	B+	128.5	7.53	7.2	5.4	31.3	15.5	10.0	11.1	16.0
First Federal S&L Assn. of Delta	Delta	OH	C+	C-	C-	163.4	0.42	0.2	0.3	48.9	19.1	10.0	12.8	33.6
First Federal S&L Assn. of Greene County	Waynesburg	PA	B-	C+	C+	930.5	3.98	0.0	0.5	64.9	17.2	10.0	14.5	33.3
First Federal S&L Assn. of Greensburg	Greensburg	IN	C+	C	C	148.6	1.27	0.6	2.3	44.2	19.7	9.4	10.6	21.6
First Federal S&L Assn. of Lakewood	Lakewood	OH	C-	C-	C+	1918.8	0.36	2.1	3.9	65.7	6.6	9.4	10.6	16.4
First Federal S&L Assn. of Lorain	Lorain	OH	C	C	C	440.8	6.77	0.0	0.2	53.9	20.6	10.0	15.1	33.0
First Federal S&L Assn. of McMinnville	McMinnville	OR	B	B	B-	459.0	5.69	0.6	0.2	40.7	27.9	10.0	14.6	29.4
First Federal S&L Assn. of Newark	Newark	OH	C	C	C	221.8	-0.36	0.0	0.3	50.1	10.1	10.0	16.0	26.8
First Federal S&L Assn. of Pascagoula-Mo	Pascagoula	MS	C	C	C	311.3	1.73	0.0	0.4	79.2	9.9	7.6	9.4	20.1
First Federal S&L Assn. of Port Angeles	Port Angeles	WA	B-	C+	C+	1233.9	0.98	1.0	9.3	26.8	22.5	10.0	12.0	19.1
▲ First Federal S&L Assn. of Ravenswood	Ravenswood	WV	D+	D	C-	25.2	23.47	0.0	0.0	74.1	0.1	5.3	7.3	14.4
First Federal S&L Assn. of San Rafael	San Rafael	CA	B-	B-	B-	205.9	4.76	0.0	0.0	1.3	0.0	10.0	20.5	26.0
▲ First Federal S&L Assn. of Valdosta	Valdosta	GA	B-	C+	C	188.2	2.63	0.0	2.4	69.6	1.5	10.0	15.7	25.9
First Federal S&L Assn. of Van Wert	Van Wert	OH	C+	C+	C+	113.4	5.81	0.0	0.2	43.1	33.3	10.0	20.6	46.1
First Federal S&L Bank	Olathe	KS	B	B	C	97.0	12.86	0.2	0.1	77.4	0.0	10.0	12.2	23.1
First Federal Savings Bank	Ottawa	IL	C	C	C+	364.1	1.92	0.3	0.9	55.5	8.6	10.0	11.5	25.4
First Federal Savings Bank	Evansville	IN	C	C	C-	451.4	5.15	16.3	0.8	21.2	15.7	6.3	8.3	13.4
First Federal Savings Bank	Huntington	IN	B-	B	B+	351.6	7.61	15.0	2.9	14.9	17.7	10.0	11.2	16.2
▲ First Federal Savings Bank	Rochester	IN	B-	C	C+	425.2	-2.54	0.9	0.1	65.0	0.0	9.4	10.6	19.6
▲ First Federal Savings Bank of Angola	Angola	IN	B	B	B	128.7	-7.63	0.5	3.8	63.4	0.0	10.0	21.3	45.5
First Federal Savings Bank of Kentucky	Frankfort	KY	C	C	B-	246.8	2.87	0.8	0.4	61.9	0.4	10.0	12.8	21.0
▲ First Federal Savings of Middletown	Middletown	NY	C+	C-	C-	148.2	-3.19	0.0	0.0	0.6	32.1	10.0	37.0	75.7
First Fidelity Bank	Fort Payne	AL	C+	C+	C	101.7	5.36	7.5	1.7	25.0	35.8	8.0	9.7	20.7
First Fidelity Bank	Oklahoma City	OK	B	B	B-	1770.6	7.86	6.8	14.7	6.9	22.0	7.3	9.2	13.6
▲ First Fidelity Bank	Burke	SD	B	B	A-	371.5	4.96	4.3	2.5	1.9	28.3	9.0	10.3	14.4
First Financial Bank	Bessemer	AL	C+	B-	C-	168.4	5.93	7.4	1.7	12.1	33.9	7.8	9.6	15.6
First Financial Bank	El Dorado	AR	B+	B+	B+	1071.4	4.88	8.4	2.1	5.1	1.9	10.0	12.8	21.3
First Financial Bank	Cincinnati	OH	B+	B+	B	14409.5	4.64	15.3	0.7	9.7	20.8	7.6	10.2	13.0
First Financial Bank in Winnebago	Winnebago	MN	B	B	B	47.5	9.47	14.3	2.4	7.7	18.2	10.0	14.8	19.6
First Financial Bank, N.A.	Terre Haute	IN	A-	A-	A-	3888.4	33.89	15.4	7.6	11.6	24.1	10.0	12.8	15.3
First Financial Bank, N.A.	Abilene	TX	A	A	A-	8081.8	7.14	8.1	5.1	13.6	41.6	10.0	11.1	18.8
First Financial Northwest Bank	Renton	WA	B+	A-	B+	1308.1	6.10	1.8	1.3	27.1	10.6	8.7	10.1	14.4
First Financial Trust & Asset Mgmt Co.	Abilene	TX	U	U	U	28.9	23.84	0.0	0.0	0.0	72.6	10.0	104.	358.1
First Financial Trust, N.A.	Wellesley	MA	U	U	U	10.1	8.16	0.0	0.0	0.0	17.8	10.0	97.9	220.7

Asset Quality Index	Adjusted Non-Performing Loans as a % of Total Loans	Adjusted Non-Performing Loans as a % of Capital	Net Charge-Offs Avg Loans	Profitability Index	Net Income ($Mil)	Return on Assets (R.O.A.)	Return on Equity (R.O.E.)	Net Interest Spread	Overhead Efficiency Ratio	Liquidity Index	Liquidity Ratio	Hot Money Ratio	Stability Index
6.2	1.77	6.5	0.27	6.2	0.8	1.48	8.02	4.46	67.3	4.8	24.4	4.4	7.7
0.0	9.95	48.9	0.22	5.0	0.6	1.12	10.16	4.29	70.3	1.7	18.3	20.1	7.0
4.5	2.43	na	0.00	4.3	0.7	0.83	7.00	4.01	70.4	0.8	17.0	34.4	5.8
8.6	0.23	1.7	0.00	5.9	12.9	1.27	12.38	3.50	65.9	3.5	13.5	9.6	8.4
4.3	2.30	13.2	0.26	7.8	21.6	1.58	14.81	4.09	54.5	2.9	17.0	10.8	9.4
8.7	0.37	na	-0.15	6.3	0.5	1.55	7.64	3.84	59.4	2.0	27.9	22.6	7.4
7.5	0.00	0.0	-0.01	7.3	2.3	1.76	14.28	3.65	58.3	1.7	12.7	20.7	8.1
6.3	0.93	3.8	0.03	6.1	20.7	1.39	11.34	4.25	74.2	3.8	25.0	11.6	9.9
6.6	1.36	na	0.00	2.8	0.5	0.35	3.15	3.71	89.4	1.9	24.5	21.3	6.5
8.6	1.08	na	0.02	6.8	8.3	1.57	12.72	3.60	55.3	2.8	29.1	17.2	8.9
4.9	2.48	na	-0.18	4.1	2.2	0.97	6.37	3.21	74.3	3.3	20.1	13.1	7.4
6.6	0.12	0.6	0.00	4.8	0.3	0.70	3.54	5.04	75.3	0.7	10.4	34.9	7.3
9.0	0.21	na	0.00	0.5	-1.6	-0.26	-2.05	2.22	108.8	1.3	18.3	28.4	6.6
8.2	0.82	na	0.02	2.9	3.0	0.46	3.67	3.06	82.6	3.4	14.2	11.8	7.4
9.5	1.12	na	0.00	2.7	1.0	0.53	3.46	3.26	83.4	6.1	58.5	9.0	7.2
4.4	0.93	4.1	-0.01	7.3	35.7	1.48	11.68	3.99	58.2	3.3	8.2	12.1	10.0
7.4	1.63	na	0.04	3.1	1.2	0.61	3.18	3.48	74.1	1.1	23.1	24.4	6.6
6.5	1.69	na	0.07	6.3	1.9	2.06	19.14	3.28	82.7	0.6	9.6	49.3	4.7
5.5	1.88	na	0.02	3.8	0.8	0.66	7.78	3.98	83.0	2.3	11.5	17.0	4.0
6.3	0.38	2.6	0.03	7.6	4.7	1.57	17.03	4.01	52.2	2.3	15.2	15.8	6.1
6.2	0.86	na	0.04	4.4	2.8	0.84	7.50	3.61	70.0	1.2	12.0	28.6	6.8
4.6	2.77	na	0.10	3.9	0.5	0.79	3.54	3.11	67.2	1.1	6.2	27.7	6.0
7.0	4.10	na	0.00	2.6	0.1	0.27	0.93	3.72	91.1	1.5	17.6	24.7	6.8
9.7	0.00	na	0.00	2.8	0.1	0.39	2.27	2.02	73.3	1.4	33.7	52.3	6.6
4.4	6.14	na	-0.07	5.7	1.1	1.10	6.73	4.74	69.2	3.6	11.4	10.7	7.9
9.8	0.00	na	0.00	3.2	0.1	0.48	2.51	3.45	79.2	3.4	31.3	13.5	7.9
5.0	2.34	na	1.33	4.0	0.6	0.64	5.37	3.99	70.9	1.7	17.9	22.0	7.1
8.8	0.82	na	0.00	3.0	0.6	0.45	3.52	3.58	82.2	6.4	46.7	3.2	6.5
9.5	0.61	na	0.04	3.2	3.4	0.48	3.39	2.70	73.9	2.2	33.1	24.5	8.0
6.3	2.62	na	0.07	2.8	0.5	0.46	4.20	3.10	80.3	6.0	36.1	1.9	5.9
8.0	0.41	2.5	-0.01	2.4	4.4	0.30	2.90	2.31	87.8	1.6	7.5	14.5	7.5
5.1	6.33	na	-0.10	1.9	0.7	0.20	1.40	2.92	96.6	3.2	34.3	16.9	6.8
9.6	0.90	na	0.00	4.4	2.6	0.79	5.37	3.50	71.9	5.1	42.5	10.0	8.1
7.7	2.52	na	0.00	2.4	0.5	0.31	1.96	3.05	88.4	1.2	18.1	29.5	7.2
7.0	0.93	na	0.10	2.7	1.1	0.46	4.94	3.08	80.3	0.6	14.1	53.1	4.7
8.2	0.56	1.9	0.08	3.6	7.0	0.75	6.52	3.21	72.5	2.1	23.8	20.3	8.7
9.7	0.00	na	0.00	3.6	0.1	0.63	7.53	3.08	73.1	0.8	14.0	38.3	3.0
7.1	0.00	na	0.00	2.9	0.5	0.35	1.71	3.45	85.4	0.5	3.7	40.9	7.6
5.0	3.83	na	0.08	3.3	0.7	0.51	3.25	4.28	83.2	1.9	8.4	19.1	7.0
10.0	0.00	na	-0.02	3.3	0.6	0.71	3.42	3.30	76.1	5.1	45.2	10.9	7.8
4.7	3.41	na	-0.01	9.8	2.3	3.15	26.86	4.27	24.7	0.4	18.6	43.1	8.7
7.8	2.45	na	-0.02	2.3	0.6	0.22	1.90	2.65	93.8	2.3	32.5	22.5	6.4
5.7	0.92	6.0	0.01	2.5	1.5	0.45	4.69	3.28	84.4	1.7	19.5	8.1	5.3
4.4	2.20	na	0.06	6.6	3.7	1.38	12.45	3.60	59.9	1.2	20.6	16.0	7.6
6.0	4.85	na	0.01	5.1	4.0	1.16	11.33	3.98	77.3	1.4	12.8	25.1	6.4
9.5	0.17	na	0.00	4.3	1.0	0.98	4.79	3.29	72.2	4.2	35.6	12.5	7.6
3.3	1.89	na	0.06	2.2	0.4	0.22	1.20	3.14	90.0	0.9	7.0	31.5	6.7
10.0	0.29	na	0.00	2.9	0.6	0.55	1.51	2.94	70.7	6.0	105.0	15.2	7.3
7.9	1.05	na	0.00	3.5	0.6	0.76	8.14	3.19	73.7	3.6	53.1	20.0	5.4
5.8	0.84	3.5	0.02	5.0	15.1	1.19	12.26	3.33	68.1	5.1	22.3	3.5	9.8
7.4	0.07	na	0.11	8.2	4.8	1.75	17.47	4.17	56.9	4.2	26.7	8.6	7.4
6.2	2.47	na	0.11	1.7	-0.2	-0.17	-1.70	3.91	101.4	5.2	28.0	3.4	5.2
4.5	3.94	8.1	0.19	9.8	19.5	2.46	18.96	4.34	59.6	0.7	9.7	30.9	10.0
4.8	0.87	2.9	0.39	7.6	162.0	1.54	10.05	4.11	50.9	3.0	19.1	7.3	9.9
7.8	1.13	na	0.00	5.7	0.5	1.40	9.48	3.85	62.3	3.2	21.2	13.7	7.5
7.2	0.40	na	0.16	7.2	33.3	1.41	9.89	3.89	62.2	4.3	10.2	6.6	9.9
7.2	0.62	2.3	0.04	9.6	117.5	2.01	15.26	4.05	47.7	5.1	21.3	3.8	10.0
7.6	0.28	na	-0.01	4.5	8.6	0.89	8.77	3.18	67.2	0.7	11.6	33.3	9.9
10.0	na	0.0	na	10.0	10.4	55.08	55.38	6.91	40.2	4.0	na	0.0	7.0
6.5	na	na	na	9.5	0.5	7.11	7.28	2.54	71.3	4.0	na	0.0	5.7

Name	City	State	Rating	2018 Rating	2017 Rating	Total Assets ($Mil)	One Year Asset Growth	Asset Mix (As a % of Total Assets) Commercial Loans	Consumer Loans	Mortgage Loans	Securities	Capitalization Index	Leverage Ratio	Risk-Based Capital Ratio
▲ First Florida Integrity Bank	Naples	FL	**B**	B-	B-	1525.2	11.32	10.7	0.3	11.6	15.3	**6.0**	9.3	11.7
First Foundation Bank	Irvine	CA	**B-**	B-	B	6342.0	15.98	6.5	0.2	14.0	16.4	**5.2**	8.3	11.1
First Freedom Bank	Lebanon	TN	**C+**	C+	B-	484.4	4.58	18.1	4.0	11.4	0.0	**5.4**	10.3	11.3
First FSB of Champaign-Urbana	Champaign	IL	**B-**	C+	C+	167.7	1.12	5.9	1.1	26.1	0.1	**8.8**	10.2	21.9
▲ First FSB of Lincolnton	Lincolnton	NC	**A-**	B+	B+	392.2	1.48	0.6	0.6	64.6	5.8	**10.0**	16.4	29.1
First FSB of Mascoutah	Mascoutah	IL	**C**	C	C-	109.0	5.17	2.0	1.0	42.4	30.7	**10.0**	12.9	25.0
First FSB of Twin Falls	Twin Falls	ID	**A-**	B+	B	704.7	8.60	5.9	5.3	38.3	3.9	**10.0**	12.0	15.5
First FSB of Washington	Washington	IN	**C-**	C-	D+	76.9	22.60	6.5	2.5	50.3	1.7	**10.0**	12.0	22.1
▲ First General Bank	Rowland Heights	CA	**A-**	B+	B+	982.8	3.70	6.7	0.0	4.0	0.8	**10.0**	14.1	17.5
First Guaranty Bank	Hammond	LA	**B**	B	B	1800.9	3.08	11.9	1.1	10.3	14.9	**7.3**	9.7	12.8
▲ First Harrison Bank	Corydon	IN	**B**	B-	B+	818.0	4.02	4.8	7.0	14.9	31.2	**8.4**	9.9	14.9
First Hawaiian Bank	Honolulu	HI	**B+**	B	B	20601.4	3.08	11.3	7.4	17.2	20.2	**6.6**	8.6	13.0
First Heritage Bank	Shenandoah	IA	**B-**	B-	B	38.8	-1.47	15.3	3.4	23.9	20.7	**10.0**	11.5	17.4
First Heritage Bank	Centralia	KS	**B**	B	B	172.7	3.48	21.5	0.9	8.8	25.9	**7.6**	9.4	16.3
First Home Bank	Saint Petersburg	FL	**B+**	A-	A-	506.8	44.33	33.1	0.2	20.5	0.0	**9.7**	10.8	17.6
First Hope Bank, A National Banking Assn.	Hope	NJ	**C**	C	C	513.5	0.91	5.5	0.1	13.2	22.0	**7.5**	9.3	13.5
First Horizon Bank	Memphis	TN	**B-**	B-	B-	43532.7	7.69	18.5	0.8	11.7	10.1	**4.3**	9.3	10.7
First IC Bank	Doraville	GA	**B+**	A	A	702.5	50.55	7.1	0.0	6.9	7.4	**9.8**	10.9	16.1
First Independence Bank	Detroit	MI	**B-**	B-	C+	278.0	8.76	13.3	0.0	19.1	1.6	**6.6**	9.7	12.2
First Independent Bank	Russell	MN	**C**	C	B	283.3	-1.36	7.4	3.3	6.7	23.5	**10.0**	11.4	15.6
First Independent Bank	Aurora	MO	**B**	B	B	94.4	3.02	7.5	4.1	22.5	27.5	**10.0**	12.2	21.8
First International Bank & Trust	Watford City	ND	**B**	B	B	3184.8	12.61	15.2	3.2	11.9	13.4	**6.2**	9.0	11.9
First Internet Bank of Indiana	Fishers	IN	**B-**	B-	B-	4093.0	27.96	7.6	7.4	7.8	14.5	**6.3**	8.3	12.6
First Interstate Bank	Billings	MT	**B+**	B-	B-	14640.3	18.30	9.0	7.3	8.7	19.3	**6.8**	9.0	12.3
First Iowa State Bank	Albia	IA	**B**	B+	B+	139.5	0.60	6.1	1.6	11.7	24.7	**10.0**	13.0	20.1
First Iowa State Bank	Keosauqua	IA	**B+**	B+	B+	135.2	0.38	14.2	3.0	14.8	20.7	**9.5**	10.6	14.9
First Ipswich Bank	Ipswich	MA	**B-**	B-	B-	465.0	12.21	7.0	0.0	15.5	12.1	**8.6**	10.7	13.9
▲ First Jackson Bank, Inc.	Stevenson	AL	**A-**	B+	B+	276.3	6.68	6.4	3.7	17.1	21.2	**10.0**	12.5	17.6
▲ First Kansas Bank	Hoisington	KS	**B+**	B	C+	181.8	4.38	3.8	1.0	10.8	59.0	**6.6**	8.6	25.1
First Kentucky Bank, Inc.	Mayfield	KY	**B**	B	B	445.9	2.84	5.1	5.5	24.7	25.9	**7.2**	9.1	14.1
First Keystone Community Bank	Berwick	PA	**B**	B	B	1018.3	0.59	6.2	0.6	20.4	29.2	**7.8**	9.5	14.4
First Liberty Bank	Oklahoma City	OK	**B-**	B-	B-	440.2	6.79	26.6	0.2	18.1	2.3	**6.1**	9.0	11.8
First Liberty National Bank	Liberty	TX	**A-**	B+	B	323.6	6.42	6.2	6.0	18.3	19.0	**10.0**	12.2	21.0
First Merchants Bank	Muncie	IN	**A-**	A-	B+	12305.2	25.91	16.5	1.1	9.8	20.4	**7.7**	10.9	13.1
First Metro Bank	Muscle Shoals	AL	**A**	A	A	673.3	7.13	7.9	2.4	18.8	25.9	**10.0**	12.1	21.3
First Mid Bank & Trust, N.A.	Mattoon	IL	**B+**	B+	B+	3809.0	13.86	14.3	2.2	7.9	21.2	**8.9**	10.4	14.1
First Midwest Bank	Chicago	IL	**B**	B	B	17919.0	20.28	21.6	2.7	11.3	16.3	**5.4**	8.9	11.3
First Midwest Bank of Dexter	Dexter	MO	**C+**	B-	B	330.6	-1.14	22.0	2.4	12.5	3.7	**10.0**	11.3	15.0
First Midwest Bank of Poplar Bluff	Poplar Bluff	MO	**C+**	B-	B-	440.7	5.92	22.6	3.5	23.7	6.0	**7.4**	9.9	12.8
First Midwest Bank of the Ozarks	Piedmont	MO	**C+**	B-	B	124.7	1.15	12.3	5.8	14.9	9.2	**8.6**	11.2	13.8
▲ First Minnetonka City Bank	Minnetonka	MN	**A-**	B+	B+	215.6	0.14	11.7	1.6	14.8	31.0	**10.0**	11.3	19.0
First Missouri Bank	Brookfield	MO	**B-**	B-	B	286.8	16.22	8.2	1.2	14.5	7.2	**8.4**	9.9	13.8
First Missouri Bank of SEMO	Kennett	MO	**B+**	A-	B+	218.5	13.52	8.7	1.6	19.2	2.2	**6.4**	8.6	12.1
▼ First Missouri State Bank	Poplar Bluff	MO	**B+**	B+	B+	176.4	0.07	7.1	4.5	34.3	1.4	**8.5**	10.1	13.8
First Missouri State Bank of Cape County	Cape Girardeau	MO	**B-**	B-	C+	169.3	8.95	11.3	2.0	21.3	6.1	**5.9**	8.5	11.7
First Montana Bank, Inc.	Missoula	MT	**C+**	B-	B-	316.5	2.56	13.2	5.5	9.3	13.9	**8.4**	10.7	13.7
First Mutual Bank, FSB	Belpre	OH	**C-**	C-	C	89.9	-1.83	0.0	1.4	40.5	29.9	**6.6**	8.6	21.3
▲ First National B&T Co. of Ardmore	Ardmore	OK	**B**	B	B	558.9	8.16	11.5	3.3	9.6	30.5	**8.1**	9.8	15.1
First National B&T Co. of Bottineau	Bottineau	ND	**B-**	B-	C+	143.4	1.35	2.9	2.6	7.2	31.2	**10.0**	12.7	19.8
First National B&T Co. of Broken Arrow	Broken Arrow	OK	**B-**	C+	B-	185.5	-2.70	15.2	1.9	23.5	4.3	**10.0**	11.4	15.4
First National B&T Co. of Iron Mountain	Iron Mountain	MI	**C+**	C+	C+	325.2	2.54	12.2	2.5	13.7	33.5	**7.7**	9.4	15.0
▲ First National B&T Co. of McAlester	McAlester	OK	**B-**	C+	D+	469.3	1.84	4.5	2.2	10.7	33.4	**10.0**	11.8	19.0
▲ First National B&T Co. of Miami	Miami	OK	**B-**	C+	C+	131.9	-3.36	5.0	3.7	14.4	19.1	**9.1**	10.4	18.3
▲ First National B&T Co. of Newtown	Newtown	PA	**B+**	B-	C+	954.4	1.20	0.9	0.3	13.5	47.5	**8.5**	10.0	22.9
First National B&T Co. of Okmulgee	Okmulgee	OK	**B**	B+	B+	266.4	0.91	8.9	2.8	14.6	35.6	**10.0**	11.9	17.0
▲ First National B&T Co. of Vinita	Vinita	OK	**C+**	C	B-	442.1	-0.35	21.0	4.2	6.0	32.3	**7.1**	9.1	13.2
First National B&T Co. of Weatherford	Weatherford	OK	**B**	B+	B+	259.6	4.18	11.2	1.8	7.7	2.9	**10.0**	12.3	15.3
▲ First National B&T Co. of Williston	Williston	ND	**B+**	B	B-	457.3	6.97	5.4	1.2	2.8	56.3	**10.0**	13.2	25.7
▲ First National Bank	Hamilton	AL	**A**	A-	A-	283.7	2.07	5.5	9.4	11.8	41.7	**10.0**	17.9	34.2
First National Bank	Paragould	AR	**A-**	A-	A-	1665.3	2.10	6.9	2.4	27.0	8.4	**8.9**	10.3	14.3

Arrows denote recent upgrades ▲ or downgrades ▼

Asset Quality Index	Adjusted Non-Performing Loans as a % of Total Loans	Adjusted Non-Performing Loans as a % of Capital	Net Charge-Offs Avg Loans	Profitability Index	Net Income ($Mil)	Return on Assets (R.O.A.)	Return on Equity (R.O.E.)	Net Interest Spread	Overhead Efficiency Ratio	Liquidity Index	Liquidity Ratio	Hot Money Ratio	Stability Index
7.5	0.02	0.1	0.00	5.3	12.1	1.09	11.96	3.55	60.0	3.4	10.6	11.8	7.6
6.0	0.46	3.5	0.01	4.8	42.4	0.93	9.72	2.93	55.8	1.0	20.2	12.9	7.1
4.6	0.71	na	0.11	6.4	4.4	1.25	11.98	3.94	59.3	0.7	7.1	34.2	6.6
3.4	3.64	na	0.00	5.6	1.4	1.11	10.63	3.82	72.8	6.2	42.6	3.1	5.8
7.9	1.44	na	0.00	6.1	3.9	1.33	8.34	3.64	57.9	0.7	14.8	37.3	8.4
9.5	0.00	na	0.07	2.6	0.3	0.43	3.44	2.48	77.0	2.0	26.5	20.2	6.8
8.3	0.30	1.3	0.00	6.3	6.6	1.30	10.98	4.88	71.2	4.2	12.5	6.7	7.9
5.3	1.24	na	0.11	1.5	0.1	0.09	0.72	2.95	94.1	1.7	27.5	27.7	6.0
7.0	0.22	na	-0.01	9.8	16.1	2.24	16.47	4.49	28.9	0.4	4.7	47.8	9.9
7.5	0.85	3.3	0.27	4.5	11.6	0.84	8.75	3.37	63.3	1.1	17.4	28.3	8.1
6.3	0.71	na	0.09	5.8	7.4	1.22	11.63	4.03	63.4	5.6	34.2	3.1	7.0
7.1	0.20	0.8	0.19	7.6	222.3	1.45	11.34	3.21	46.7	3.7	20.2	11.5	10.0
8.5	0.01	na	0.11	4.1	0.2	0.80	6.92	4.25	78.4	3.6	17.4	11.2	6.9
8.4	0.06	na	0.00	5.0	1.6	1.20	12.28	3.54	64.1	1.0	20.2	19.4	7.2
4.5	1.22	6.8	1.30	5.8	4.0	1.23	10.33	4.49	75.0	1.2	23.5	30.9	6.8
4.5	0.98	6.2	0.08	3.1	1.7	0.45	5.06	3.32	86.0	4.3	14.2	6.4	5.4
4.8	1.07	5.1	0.11	6.2	378.2	1.22	9.81	3.36	62.2	2.9	10.9	8.1	10.0
7.4	0.60	na	-0.22	9.8	8.4	1.86	15.16	4.21	52.8	1.3	31.1	44.6	9.9
6.5	0.48	na	-0.01	7.4	2.3	1.60	19.19	4.43	83.9	1.8	12.3	15.7	4.5
4.2	3.05	na	0.14	6.6	3.2	1.55	13.15	4.16	58.5	3.4	27.5	13.8	7.8
5.8	1.76	na	-0.01	4.6	0.6	0.89	7.47	3.70	68.2	3.7	43.2	17.2	6.4
5.3	1.25	6.9	0.07	6.5	34.2	1.49	16.44	4.51	69.0	3.3	5.3	11.4	8.8
7.8	0.21	1.8	0.08	3.9	21.7	0.76	9.67	1.97	51.7	0.6	14.5	48.0	6.5
5.1	0.61	3.0	0.12	7.9	156.5	1.50	11.75	4.01	55.5	4.4	19.6	7.2	10.0
6.7	0.39	na	0.12	7.4	1.6	1.57	11.82	4.40	57.5	3.4	33.3	15.9	8.5
4.4	1.62	na	0.06	5.0	1.1	1.08	9.70	4.93	75.2	3.0	22.0	15.0	7.2
5.8	0.39	na	0.44	2.3	0.9	0.29	2.79	3.23	87.9	1.7	10.9	18.2	5.9
8.5	0.07	na	0.08	7.8	3.2	1.61	13.44	3.90	45.0	0.9	21.0	40.3	7.4
9.7	0.00	0.0	0.02	5.3	2.0	1.46	15.75	3.12	54.4	4.5	27.6	8.1	6.3
8.3	0.17	1.2	0.03	4.4	3.5	1.06	11.48	3.35	71.8	1.7	22.3	18.2	6.4
5.8	2.03	na	0.03	4.2	7.7	1.02	9.15	3.13	68.3	3.2	15.7	10.9	9.0
8.3	0.13	na	0.19	4.2	2.2	0.68	7.59	3.95	67.1	0.7	13.2	38.4	6.2
8.0	0.26	na	0.47	6.3	3.6	1.53	12.22	4.59	67.0	4.2	23.3	8.3	7.3
7.0	0.28	1.1	0.04	7.8	125.2	1.57	10.86	3.80	54.2	3.5	21.7	7.7	10.0
8.7	0.11	na	0.08	8.5	7.5	1.53	13.19	3.62	48.7	2.0	22.7	19.9	8.6
5.1	0.92	4.0	0.17	6.3	34.1	1.24	9.95	3.90	57.2	3.1	7.8	12.2	9.4
4.8	0.62	4.0	0.31	6.9	166.8	1.34	10.02	4.06	54.1	3.4	10.9	10.7	9.3
4.3	2.50	na	0.04	6.6	3.2	1.27	11.57	3.94	59.6	1.1	7.5	28.0	6.5
5.0	0.91	na	0.15	6.5	5.2	1.61	16.43	3.98	60.1	1.0	8.3	26.6	6.8
2.6	2.22	na	0.27	5.5	1.0	1.08	9.82	3.98	66.2	0.9	10.8	27.2	6.3
9.1	0.25	na	0.00	5.5	2.2	1.32	12.15	3.59	63.6	5.4	42.0	8.1	7.3
3.5	3.09	na	0.02	6.5	3.0	1.47	15.02	3.92	63.0	2.7	16.5	15.4	7.4
5.6	1.12	10.4	0.09	6.7	2.2	1.56	16.96	4.16	59.9	1.3	18.8	20.6	5.9
4.6	1.01	7.9	0.00	6.2	1.8	1.37	12.49	3.93	65.2	0.8	4.2	29.8	8.0
4.7	0.96	7.5	-0.01	3.9	1.1	0.88	10.50	3.25	74.2	0.6	11.6	39.0	5.6
3.5	0.87	na	0.13	5.9	2.5	1.08	9.96	4.63	67.8	4.5	10.7	4.6	6.7
3.5	2.06	6.8	0.25	1.2	0.1	0.12	0.88	3.67	97.9	5.4	51.7	10.0	5.6
6.3	1.26	na	0.02	5.2	4.8	1.19	12.08	3.86	70.1	2.3	14.5	17.7	7.2
4.5	2.73	na	-0.61	4.2	1.0	0.95	7.74	3.39	65.0	3.5	17.3	11.8	7.0
7.2	2.77	na	-0.02	6.4	1.7	1.22	10.85	4.81	65.7	4.2	14.4	7.3	7.0
5.0	3.28	na	1.16	2.9	1.0	0.44	4.44	3.94	74.1	5.2	43.4	9.8	5.0
4.5	4.28	na	0.02	6.8	5.8	1.64	13.69	3.44	57.5	3.3	26.6	14.1	8.5
6.5	0.42	na	0.05	5.5	1.1	1.05	11.59	4.79	70.7	4.8	14.4	3.2	5.5
7.9	0.44	na	-0.01	5.8	9.4	1.34	15.05	3.26	57.6	6.3	44.0	2.6	5.7
4.2	3.77	na	-0.09	6.3	3.1	1.54	12.54	3.74	61.8	2.5	29.5	17.4	8.6
3.7	2.20	na	0.21	4.2	3.3	0.97	11.36	3.48	73.2	1.1	13.3	17.4	5.8
5.6	1.30	na	0.22	7.8	3.6	1.82	14.24	4.72	61.5	1.5	15.2	24.4	8.1
6.4	2.67	na	0.49	8.4	7.4	2.14	15.97	3.49	45.7	5.5	49.0	9.7	8.7
8.5	0.02	na	0.24	7.3	3.7	1.72	9.93	4.13	58.2	5.9	54.4	9.1	8.8
7.9	0.44	2.8	0.06	6.1	15.8	1.29	12.37	3.40	53.2	0.8	9.7	34.6	8.8

Name	City	State	Rating	2018 Rating	2017 Rating	Total Assets ($Mil)	One Year Asset Growth	Asset Mix (As a % of Total Assets) Comm-ercial Loans	Cons-umer Loans	Mort-gage Loans	Secur-ities	Capital-ization Index	Lever-age Ratio	Risk-Based Capital Ratio
▼ First National Bank	Waverly	IA	**B+**	A-	B+	520.2	31.20	15.8	1.2	11.6	7.7	**7.6**	11.1	13.0
First National Bank	Mattoon	IL	**C-**	C-	C-	92.1	1.58	12.9	3.7	11.3	25.2	**6.7**	8.7	12.4
First National Bank	Cloverdale	IN	**C+**	C+	C+	296.1	1.42	4.4	1.5	19.0	21.9	**8.9**	10.2	21.3
▲ First National Bank	Arcadia	LA	**B-**	C-	C+	255.8	0.57	6.3	1.3	21.1	1.9	**5.6**	9.4	11.4
First National Bank	Damariscotta	ME	**B**	B	B	2001.1	2.62	8.3	1.3	24.3	31.7	**6.8**	8.8	15.4
▲ First National Bank	Alamogordo	NM	**A-**	B+	A	356.3	3.97	2.7	0.7	4.7	47.8	**10.0**	12.1	24.5
First National Bank	Heavener	OK	**B+**	B+	B+	84.2	2.79	3.2	3.5	17.3	11.5	**7.7**	9.5	16.7
First National Bank	Fort Pierre	SD	**A-**	A	A	1326.1	37.04	7.5	13.6	8.1	8.4	**10.0**	19.9	23.0
First National Bank	Oldham	SD	**A-**	A-	B	319.0	56.49	6.2	14.2	7.9	13.6	**10.0**	13.8	19.0
▲ First National Bank	Rotan	TX	**C+**	C	C-	72.8	-13.17	6.3	3.7	0.4	56.6	**10.0**	12.1	25.7
First National Bank	Spearman	TX	**B+**	B+	B+	225.7	-0.04	11.0	2.3	6.9	21.0	**10.0**	13.8	19.8
▲ First National Bank	Wichita Falls	TX	**B-**	C+	B	529.8	12.37	6.7	1.0	29.9	2.8	**7.1**	9.8	12.6
First National Bank	Altavista	VA	**B-**	B-	B-	480.5	1.94	11.4	20.8	14.3	9.7	**7.0**	9.6	12.5
▲ First National Bank & Trust of Elk City	Elk City	OK	**A-**	B+	B+	305.3	-2.03	8.6	0.7	13.2	36.3	**10.0**	11.3	21.1
First National Bank Alaska	Anchorage	AK	**A**	A	A	3845.1	2.33	8.8	0.5	2.6	41.9	**10.0**	13.9	21.1
First National Bank and Trust	Atmore	AL	**B-**	B-	B-	154.6	9.29	8.1	3.6	14.9	24.4	**10.0**	11.4	16.6
First National Bank and Trust	Phillipsburg	KS	**B-**	B-	B+	216.3	3.00	9.9	4.9	11.4	22.4	**10.0**	15.5	21.1
First National Bank and Trust	London	KY	**B-**	B-	C	211.6	2.53	6.8	5.0	22.0	22.5	**10.0**	11.1	17.5
First National Bank and Trust Co.	Clinton	IL	**C+**	B-	B-	193.0	7.35	0.7	0.2	5.1	82.8	**6.4**	8.4	16.8
▲ First National Bank and Trust Co.	Chickasha	OK	**B**	B-	B	659.2	6.88	10.9	1.4	7.0	29.5	**10.0**	12.4	18.9
First National Bank and Trust Co.	Shawnee	OK	**C+**	C	C	252.9	3.03	6.7	0.8	6.3	48.8	**10.0**	13.4	28.7
First National Bank and Trust Co.	Beloit	WI	**B-**	B-	B-	1117.2	-0.13	9.5	1.0	19.3	12.3	**8.3**	9.8	14.2
First National Bank at Darlington	Darlington	WI	**B+**	B+	A-	150.9	4.74	5.1	2.7	7.3	9.6	**10.0**	15.1	21.0
▲ First National Bank at Paris	Paris	AR	**B+**	B	B+	183.2	17.86	5.0	9.3	20.3	4.4	**10.0**	11.9	16.8
First National Bank at Saint James	Saint James	MN	**D+**	D	D+	29.2	-4.73	4.4	5.0	23.6	7.3	**7.1**	9.1	13.8
▲ First National Bank Baird	Baird	TX	**C+**	C+	B-	401.9	-3.17	17.0	1.8	14.5	1.1	**7.6**	10.1	13.0
First National Bank in Amboy	Amboy	IL	**B**	B	B	206.3	6.95	6.2	2.7	9.7	40.3	**10.0**	11.6	19.3
First National Bank in Carlyle	Carlyle	IL	**B**	B	C+	196.9	4.19	5.3	1.9	8.1	27.7	**10.0**	11.5	18.8
▲ First National Bank in Cimarron	Cimarron	KS	**B**	B-	B-	100.8	7.02	13.4	2.9	7.0	44.5	**6.2**	8.2	13.9
First National Bank in Cooper	Cooper	TX	**B**	B-	B-	44.8	-3.16	4.5	6.0	20.8	21.1	**10.0**	14.9	49.5
First National Bank in Creston	Creston	IA	**B+**	B+	B+	243.6	-4.03	7.8	2.8	11.9	18.8	**9.3**	10.6	15.7
First National Bank in DeRidder	DeRidder	LA	**B+**	B+	B+	299.8	25.80	6.1	2.7	25.7	18.6	**8.2**	9.8	19.5
▲ First National Bank in Fairfield	Fairfield	IA	**C+**	C	C+	145.5	-6.37	12.2	1.0	14.2	8.0	**8.7**	10.1	14.2
First National Bank in Falfurrias	Falfurrias	TX	**C+**	C+	C+	76.4	5.90	10.3	4.1	0.4	51.0	**9.5**	10.7	41.4
First National Bank in Frankfort	Frankfort	KS	**B-**	B-	B-	47.4	9.98	5.9	3.7	9.5	40.7	**8.2**	9.8	17.3
▲ First National Bank in Fredonia	Fredonia	KS	**A-**	B+	A-	88.1	-1.21	6.6	8.0	11.1	55.8	**10.0**	18.2	41.2
▲ First National Bank in Howell	Howell	MI	**B-**	B-	B-	430.9	9.63	5.7	12.5	13.3	9.0	**8.2**	11.8	13.5
First National Bank in Marlow	Marlow	OK	**C+**	C+	B-	57.3	-5.64	10.8	9.8	17.2	16.0	**8.3**	9.9	13.9
First National Bank in New Bremen	New Bremen	OH	**B+**	B+	B	298.3	3.29	5.8	0.9	10.3	30.3	**9.5**	10.7	23.9
First National Bank in Okeene	Okeene	OK	**C**	C+	B	84.9	13.30	3.8	0.2	0.0	35.2	**10.0**	17.2	27.5
First National Bank in Olney	Olney	IL	**B**	B+	B+	356.7	6.56	5.7	2.8	15.6	23.6	**10.0**	11.7	18.8
▲ First National Bank in Ord	Ord	NE	**B**	C+	C+	130.2	-0.76	4.3	2.1	11.6	35.1	**7.4**	9.3	17.2
▲ First National Bank in Philip	Philip	SD	**A-**	B+	A	271.3	1.24	5.6	0.7	0.1	16.3	**10.0**	13.4	17.6
First National Bank in Pinckneyville	Pinckneyville	IL	**A-**	A-	A-	104.8	-3.13	2.3	4.3	23.7	47.2	**10.0**	15.0	31.6
First National Bank in Port Lavaca	Port Lavaca	TX	**B**	B	B	330.7	5.38	2.9	1.8	31.6	37.9	**8.7**	10.1	23.0
▲ First National Bank in Sioux Falls	Sioux Falls	SD	**A-**	B	B	1221.2	2.13	12.2	0.8	20.7	19.8	**10.0**	13.2	17.5
First National Bank in Staunton	Staunton	IL	**B+**	B+	B+	543.3	1.95	5.7	4.5	24.7	20.3	**10.0**	11.8	16.9
First National Bank in Taylorville	Taylorville	IL	**A**	A	A	195.7	2.68	7.7	3.0	10.0	49.3	**10.0**	18.2	36.5
First National Bank in Tigerton	Tigerton	WI	**C+**	C+	C+	23.5	0.91	0.3	1.8	31.0	27.6	**10.0**	14.5	43.1
First National Bank in Tremont	Tremont	IL	**B**	B	B-	122.7	-0.61	6.5	1.8	23.0	25.6	**10.0**	12.2	20.0
▲ First National Bank in Trinidad	Trinidad	CO	**B-**	C+	C	210.1	-1.13	0.9	0.8	30.7	38.5	**10.0**	11.9	26.8
First National Bank Minnesota	Saint Peter	MN	**C+**	C+	C+	218.5	9.36	12.8	3.1	6.5	11.8	**8.3**	10.3	13.6
First National Bank North	Walker	MN	**A**	A-	A-	565.0	3.70	4.9	7.5	24.2	18.5	**9.9**	10.9	18.3
First National Bank Northwest Florida	Panama City	FL	**B+**	B+	B-	182.3	30.09	1.6	0.0	9.6	5.3	**8.9**	10.3	36.6
▲ First National Bank of Absecon	Absecon	NJ	**C+**	C	C	147.0	-2.67	4.5	0.2	25.1	39.2	**10.0**	11.2	24.7
▲ First National Bank of Albany	Albany	TX	**B+**	B+	A-	603.5	1.04	19.2	2.4	9.6	19.4	**9.8**	10.9	16.2
▲ First National Bank of Allendale	Allendale	IL	**B**	B-	B+	240.0	7.76	10.3	6.4	19.5	20.4	**9.8**	10.9	16.3
First National Bank of Alvin	Alvin	TX	**B+**	B+	B+	140.4	3.37	0.5	0.2	1.3	74.3	**10.0**	12.4	37.6
▲ First National Bank of America	East Lansing	MI	**B-**	C	C	2336.0	41.11	0.2	0.3	83.7	2.2	**7.7**	9.5	17.5
First National Bank of Anderson	Anderson	TX	**B**	B	B	181.4	5.35	10.5	4.7	13.7	14.7	**10.0**	11.4	17.7

Asset Quality Index	Adjusted Non-Performing Loans as a % of Total Loans	Adjusted Non-Performing Loans as a % of Capital	Net Charge-Offs Avg Loans	Profitability Index	Net Income ($Mil)	Return on Assets (R.O.A.)	Return on Equity (R.O.E.)	Net Interest Spread	Overhead Efficiency Ratio	Liquidity Index	Liquidity Ratio	Hot Money Ratio	Stability Index
5.0	1.18	7.1	0.26	**6.7**	4.4	1.36	10.40	3.78	51.4	**3.0**	11.9	13.8	**7.4**
4.3	1.55	na	0.14	**2.7**	0.3	0.41	4.79	3.20	82.9	**1.7**	25.8	25.5	**4.9**
7.0	1.41	na	-0.02	**3.7**	1.5	0.70	6.93	3.37	75.1	**6.1**	49.3	5.6	**6.1**
4.8	0.96	na	0.09	**8.0**	3.3	1.75	18.43	5.78	70.4	**2.9**	6.2	13.6	**7.5**
5.8	1.43	9.1	0.04	**5.9**	19.3	1.30	14.92	3.06	52.0	**1.4**	24.6	21.1	**8.1**
7.0	1.86	na	0.54	**6.5**	4.0	1.52	12.77	3.94	65.7	**6.2**	47.2	4.2	**8.9**
7.1	2.56	na	0.26	**6.5**	0.7	1.14	12.54	5.26	71.1	**3.2**	23.5	13.9	**6.9**
5.5	1.04	3.3	4.36	**10.0**	21.5	2.66	10.97	8.52	37.6	**2.7**	13.3	15.7	**9.3**
5.7	1.25	4.4	4.08	**6.3**	2.2	0.97	7.06	7.98	54.3	**3.4**	15.3	12.0	**6.5**
4.6	4.21	na	0.03	**3.1**	0.5	0.93	8.26	3.60	80.2	**4.8**	37.2	10.0	**4.9**
6.3	1.86	na	0.00	**6.5**	3.2	1.96	14.18	4.08	64.4	**1.0**	15.3	31.8	**8.8**
5.0	0.42	na	0.14	**5.5**	5.0	1.35	13.43	4.18	70.7	**1.0**	2.8	29.1	**7.6**
5.9	0.34	na	0.01	**5.0**	3.8	1.06	11.68	4.00	71.1	**4.2**	12.4	7.1	**5.6**
6.4	0.92	na	-0.07	**8.1**	4.6	1.95	17.02	3.84	51.0	**2.2**	34.3	25.5	**8.8**
7.8	1.38	3.2	0.01	**7.8**	41.4	1.47	10.49	3.72	53.1	**4.9**	14.4	3.1	**10.0**
4.9	2.24	na	0.25	**3.7**	0.9	0.78	6.98	3.70	81.6	**2.7**	25.2	16.8	**6.9**
4.0	2.27	na	0.26	**5.3**	2.1	1.25	8.09	4.05	70.7	**1.7**	9.8	20.5	**8.6**
5.6	0.87	na	0.79	**3.0**	0.7	0.45	4.00	3.85	76.3	**3.5**	16.5	11.7	**6.2**
10.0	0.50	na	0.04	**3.3**	2.8	2.02	21.49	3.26	98.3	**2.1**	45.0	39.3	**5.7**
6.5	1.65	na	0.65	**10.0**	9.2	1.92	14.54	4.78	47.9	**3.4**	28.3	10.6	**8.8**
8.7	0.42	na	0.10	**2.7**	0.8	0.43	2.97	3.54	89.4	**5.5**	43.0	7.9	**7.2**
7.8	0.34	1.7	0.03	**4.2**	6.9	0.82	7.02	3.62	79.9	**4.2**	22.3	9.9	**9.2**
5.5	0.27	1.2	0.17	**5.3**	1.1	0.97	6.49	3.67	57.8	**2.3**	32.3	23.5	**8.1**
6.0	0.25	na	0.11	**8.5**	2.5	1.88	13.46	4.76	63.0	**1.1**	16.2	30.3	**8.7**
4.5	1.16	na	0.01	**2.9**	0.1	0.43	4.90	4.55	89.6	**1.6**	19.2	23.7	**4.3**
3.0	2.16	na	0.99	**3.4**	0.9	0.27	2.79	5.27	78.9	**1.8**	11.2	19.6	**6.0**
8.7	0.29	na	0.04	**3.6**	1.2	0.79	6.73	3.48	76.5	**5.2**	35.9	6.6	**7.1**
8.5	0.10	na	0.00	**4.4**	1.3	0.91	8.10	3.24	64.8	**4.0**	20.8	9.0	**6.9**
8.7	0.00	0.1	-0.01	**5.9**	1.1	1.43	18.38	3.86	62.9	**2.2**	16.4	18.3	**5.2**
7.6	0.00	5.5	0.01	**5.1**	0.4	1.12	7.81	3.41	63.1	**4.7**	51.2	13.2	**6.6**
8.0	0.32	na	0.02	**7.5**	3.2	1.73	16.81	3.92	68.7	**3.3**	19.2	13.1	**7.9**
6.9	0.56	na	0.03	**4.3**	1.6	0.77	8.02	3.76	76.8	**5.1**	40.5	9.6	**5.5**
1.7	4.21	na	0.42	**1.6**	0.3	0.25	2.60	3.55	76.7	**2.4**	13.4	13.4	**4.1**
6.5	2.81	na	-0.13	**3.4**	0.5	0.84	8.28	2.76	74.0	**4.1**	33.3	12.3	**4.5**
8.7	0.00	na	0.31	**4.9**	0.4	1.09	11.36	3.57	64.4	**4.3**	37.6	12.9	**6.3**
7.5	1.52	na	0.22	**6.5**	1.0	1.51	8.53	3.71	57.8	**3.5**	55.7	21.0	**8.4**
5.9	0.58	na	-0.16	**6.7**	4.3	1.39	11.95	4.52	68.9	**4.3**	12.0	6.3	**7.3**
5.6	0.73	na	-0.01	**3.7**	0.3	0.63	6.50	4.54	86.0	**2.2**	19.7	18.5	**4.7**
8.2	0.72	na	0.03	**5.8**	3.2	1.46	14.07	2.98	52.6	**6.1**	53.7	7.3	**7.0**
8.6	0.00	na	1.00	**8.5**	1.3	2.00	12.07	3.65	42.8	**2.4**	40.4	28.1	**5.7**
6.5	1.10	na	0.05	**5.8**	3.2	1.26	9.97	3.53	59.8	**4.0**	25.7	10.4	**7.5**
8.8	0.01	0.1	0.00	**4.6**	1.2	1.19	13.42	3.36	64.0	**3.6**	14.1	7.4	**5.2**
7.2	0.05	na	0.01	**8.5**	3.7	1.87	13.84	3.84	45.3	**1.7**	14.5	8.3	**9.3**
8.1	1.04	na	0.06	**6.1**	1.1	1.42	9.11	4.16	61.7	**4.5**	23.9	6.7	**8.5**
8.6	0.54	na	0.01	**5.1**	2.6	1.08	10.72	3.07	56.4	**4.0**	28.7	11.3	**6.8**
5.4	1.92	na	-0.06	**6.0**	11.0	1.21	9.16	3.72	69.4	**2.4**	3.8	11.9	**9.9**
8.3	0.54	na	0.08	**5.3**	5.4	1.33	11.11	3.32	64.8	**4.1**	17.0	8.6	**8.7**
6.9	2.89	na	0.04	**6.8**	2.3	1.59	8.95	3.34	49.8	**4.8**	57.1	14.4	**9.6**
9.7	1.11	na	-0.01	**2.5**	0.1	0.41	2.93	3.41	87.6	**4.9**	41.7	8.1	**6.5**
7.2	0.69	na	0.03	**4.0**	0.7	0.72	5.83	3.78	78.5	**3.6**	29.6	13.6	**6.7**
5.7	4.72	na	0.11	**3.3**	1.1	0.67	5.59	3.82	81.6	**4.7**	29.1	6.9	**6.7**
4.4	1.47	na	0.01	**6.7**	2.6	1.61	15.15	4.52	67.2	**3.6**	13.9	10.7	**6.8**
8.2	0.17	1.1	0.04	**8.6**	8.6	2.11	18.78	4.14	53.1	**2.0**	26.0	20.9	**9.0**
9.5	0.00	na	0.00	**5.4**	1.8	1.37	13.23	3.17	56.8	**6.1**	68.6	10.6	**6.3**
8.5	1.15	na	0.00	**3.2**	0.6	0.52	4.85	3.55	83.1	**7.1**	59.0	2.1	**5.4**
6.0	0.56	na	0.34	**8.9**	10.0	2.28	19.93	4.48	39.9	**1.4**	31.7	19.7	**8.8**
4.9	1.37	na	0.03	**5.1**	1.8	1.00	9.22	3.72	59.2	**1.8**	15.3	20.6	**6.3**
10.0	0.00	na	-0.07	**5.2**	1.5	1.40	11.52	2.62	51.1	**5.1**	69.5	15.6	**7.8**
4.2	2.29	18.8	0.05	**10.0**	38.4	2.50	27.74	5.49	38.2	**0.4**	7.1	31.4	**9.1**
8.3	0.21	na	0.14	**4.9**	1.3	0.95	8.53	4.00	67.2	**1.4**	23.3	28.3	**6.4**

Name	City	State	Rating	2018 Rating	2017 Rating	Total Assets ($Mil)	One Year Asset Growth	Asset Mix (As a % of Total Assets) Comm-ercial Loans	Cons-umer Loans	Mort-gage Loans	Secur-ities	Capital-ization Index	Lever-age Ratio	Risk-Based Capital Ratio
▲ First National Bank of Anson	Anson	TX	**B-**	C+	C+	61.1	-2.91	12.2	11.1	21.3	27.2	**8.5**	10.0	18.3
First National Bank of Arenzville	Arenzville	IL	**B-**	B-	B-	86.9	5.33	9.7	4.7	13.4	13.9	**8.7**	10.7	13.9
First National Bank of Aspermont	Aspermont	TX	**B+**	B+	B+	60.4	-6.54	2.7	3.1	5.9	63.1	**10.0**	17.2	52.7
▲ First National Bank of Assumption	Assumption	IL	**C**	C-	C	20.9	-2.94	5.2	3.8	8.0	30.8	**9.2**	10.5	29.9
First National Bank of Ava	Ava	IL	**B**	B	B	63.6	2.25	4.8	3.8	19.5	42.3	**10.0**	13.2	22.1
First National Bank of Bagley	Bagley	MN	**C+**	C+	C+	91.9	5.27	8.7	9.0	22.7	15.2	**6.2**	8.2	13.1
First National Bank of Ballinger	Ballinger	TX	**B-**	B-	B-	182.6	7.29	10.9	1.6	12.2	13.1	**8.9**	10.3	15.6
▲ First National Bank of Bangor	Bangor	WI	**A-**	B+	A-	213.6	-2.16	4.2	1.6	20.8	16.1	**10.0**	32.6	41.6
▲ First National Bank of Bastrop	Bastrop	TX	**A-**	B+	A-	608.0	8.39	2.2	2.0	17.3	32.1	**10.0**	11.0	18.5
▲ First National Bank of Beardstown	Beardstown	IL	**A-**	B+	B+	128.8	8.28	4.0	6.0	11.8	10.8	**10.0**	12.1	20.0
▲ First National Bank of Bellevue	Bellevue	OH	**C+**	C+	B-	241.5	10.04	14.4	1.5	6.3	10.6	**6.3**	10.0	12.0
First National Bank of Bellville	Bellville	TX	**B+**	A-	A-	710.5	5.46	2.4	1.7	10.6	66.6	**10.0**	11.3	26.5
First National Bank of Bemidji	Bemidji	MN	**A**	A	A	670.5	1.79	12.7	12.5	13.4	33.8	**10.0**	13.7	19.2
▲ First National Bank of Benton	Benton	LA	**A-**	B+	B+	61.4	3.99	2.4	1.6	41.9	13.2	**10.0**	18.3	42.5
First National Bank of Blanchester	Blanchester	OH	**B+**	B+	B+	61.8	0.32	2.3	4.4	45.8	15.1	**10.0**	12.0	23.0
▲ First National Bank of Bosque County	Valley Mills	TX	**B+**	B-	B	120.1	-1.35	13.4	6.4	30.4	5.6	**10.0**	11.6	16.2
▲ First National Bank of Brookfield	Brookfield	IL	**A-**	B	B-	205.2	10.69	0.2	6.6	18.5	5.8	**10.0**	11.2	17.3
First National Bank of Brooksville	Brooksville	KY	**B-**	B-	C+	60.5	1.44	1.3	2.1	36.1	36.0	**10.0**	12.1	26.0
First National Bank of Brownstown	Brownstown	IL	**C+**	C	C	39.2	7.58	4.6	6.8	15.8	28.8	**10.0**	11.4	23.8
First National Bank of Brundidge	Brundidge	AL	**B-**	B-	B-	83.1	-4.07	4.8	3.9	15.0	16.0	**10.0**	17.3	28.6
▲ First National Bank of Buhl	Mountain Iron	MN	**D**	D-	D-	26.0	1.59	6.9	9.3	44.7	0.0	**6.0**	8.0	15.0
First National Bank of Burleson	Burleson	TX	**A-**	B+	B+	197.1	-3.52	7.7	2.5	2.4	47.0	**9.4**	10.6	29.5
First National Bank of Carmi	Carmi	IL	**B**	B-	B-	415.0	3.32	11.2	1.0	5.0	15.8	**7.6**	9.4	14.6
First National Bank of Central Texas	Waco	TX	**B+**	B+	B+	856.0	-2.93	17.6	1.1	14.2	5.5	**6.3**	9.9	12.0
▲ First National Bank of Chadron	Chadron	NE	**B+**	B	B+	126.3	2.57	3.6	1.1	0.2	31.9	**10.0**	14.2	20.9
First National Bank of Chisholm	Chisholm	MN	**D+**	D+	D	73.9	4.14	4.3	1.1	3.7	59.8	**7.3**	9.2	24.7
First National Bank of Clarksdale	Clarksdale	MS	**B+**	A-	A-	353.1	-2.91	6.2	3.3	7.6	28.6	**9.4**	14.3	14.5
First National Bank of Coffee County	Douglas	GA	**B+**	B+	A-	206.1	2.81	4.6	0.9	14.4	3.7	**8.0**	9.7	14.8
▲ First National Bank of Cokato	Cokato	MN	**B-**	C+	C+	60.8	-5.11	15.5	3.4	15.2	9.1	**7.7**	9.5	15.5
▲ First National Bank of Coleraine	Coleraine	MN	**C+**	C	C	88.7	-0.97	3.3	3.0	13.9	42.0	**6.4**	8.4	20.1
First National Bank of Decatur County	Bainbridge	GA	**B-**	B-	B-	171.8	8.46	12.4	3.6	22.9	12.1	**8.2**	9.8	14.3
▲ First National Bank of Dennison	Dennison	OH	**B**	B-	B-	233.7	1.18	4.0	21.2	15.3	25.7	**9.1**	10.4	18.5
First National Bank of Dighton	Dighton	KS	**B-**	B	B-	53.8	-6.75	6.7	2.7	1.9	27.3	**10.0**	21.3	30.9
First National Bank of Dozier	Dozier	AL	**B-**	B-	B-	36.4	7.12	5.6	2.1	5.8	47.3	**10.0**	14.2	38.8
First National Bank of Dryden	Dryden	NY	**B+**	B+	B+	187.1	11.52	3.5	5.5	15.2	44.2	**8.6**	10.1	31.1
▲ First National Bank of Dublin	Dublin	TX	**B+**	B	B+	92.2	3.33	12.3	9.2	4.5	2.4	**8.8**	11.3	14.0
First National Bank of Eagle Lake	Eagle Lake	TX	**B**	B+	B+	125.2	11.09	10.7	0.3	2.5	13.7	**9.5**	11.1	14.6
First National Bank of Eastern Arkansas	Forrest City	AR	**B+**	B+	B-	418.2	3.42	6.4	1.9	7.2	30.2	**9.5**	10.7	16.9
First National Bank of Eldorado	Eldorado	TX	**A-**	A-	A-	58.9	0.31	18.9	3.3	15.8	28.8	**10.0**	17.9	28.4
▲ First National Bank of Elmer	Elmer	NJ	**C**	D+	D+	285.4	-0.16	5.2	0.2	28.1	4.4	**7.7**	9.4	13.8
▲ First National Bank of Ely	Ely	NV	**B+**	B	C+	104.2	5.62	3.6	0.2	1.5	83.9	**10.0**	11.0	34.9
First National Bank of Evant	Evant	TX	**B**	B-	B	99.6	-0.22	8.4	7.1	36.2	12.4	**7.3**	9.2	16.1
▲ First National Bank of Fairfax	Fairfax	MN	**B+**	B	B	29.2	-3.27	8.8	0.5	1.0	21.3	**10.0**	39.6	39.3
First National Bank of Fleming	Fleming	CO	**C**	C-	C-	22.1	-0.56	5.0	2.1	4.5	8.6	**10.0**	13.8	28.6
First National Bank of Fletcher	Fletcher	OK	**B+**	B+	B	19.5	8.07	9.9	5.3	3.4	56.8	**10.0**	11.5	20.4
First National Bank of Floydada	Floydada	TX	**A-**	B+	A-	102.5	0.34	4.7	2.3	0.3	24.7	**10.0**	12.5	19.5
First National Bank of Fort Smith	Fort Smith	AR	**A-**	A-	B+	1375.9	5.38	11.9	1.0	11.3	19.4	**10.0**	11.3	15.1
▲ First National Bank of Fort Stockton	Fort Stockton	TX	**B**	B-	B-	132.7	4.78	14.3	1.7	5.3	33.4	**9.2**	10.4	16.6
First National Bank of Frederick	Frederick	SD	**C+**	C+	B-	22.7	15.71	3.5	0.3	0.0	21.6	**10.0**	13.8	26.7
First National Bank of Germantown	Germantown	OH	**C**	C-	D+	64.6	9.40	8.1	4.8	31.1	21.3	**6.8**	8.8	16.3
First National Bank of Giddings	Giddings	TX	**B**	B-	B-	206.1	1.31	4.7	2.8	22.3	31.0	**10.0**	11.9	19.8
First National Bank of Gilbert	Gilbert	MN	**C-**	C-	C	45.6	18.57	4.6	5.5	50.9	5.4	**6.0**	8.0	15.0
First National Bank of Gillette	Gillette	WY	**B-**	B-	B-	550.7	6.93	7.8	2.0	2.3	69.9	**10.0**	12.5	34.3
First National Bank of Gilmer	Gilmer	TX	**B-**	C+	B-	415.0	12.26	10.3	5.6	20.6	17.7	**9.5**	10.7	17.7
▲ First National Bank of Gordon	Gordon	NE	**B+**	B	B+	205.8	1.50	4.8	2.8	0.1	38.7	**10.0**	13.9	23.1
First National Bank of Granbury	Granbury	TX	**A-**	A-	A-	621.6	4.82	4.4	3.0	21.5	36.0	**10.0**	11.7	21.8
▲ First National Bank of Grayson	Grayson	KY	**B+**	B	B+	252.9	-0.13	4.3	14.3	23.3	22.6	**10.0**	12.2	22.0
First National Bank of Griffin	Griffin	GA	**C**	C	D+	282.7	5.26	2.8	1.6	7.1	34.4	**4.7**	6.7	13.4
▲ First National Bank of Groton	Groton	NY	**A-**	B+	A-	180.8	0.39	8.5	9.7	25.4	37.4	**10.0**	15.0	28.0
First National Bank of Hartford	Hartford	AL	**B**	B	B-	121.5	-1.17	5.8	5.2	23.9	25.7	**10.0**	14.8	24.3

Asset Quality Index	Adjusted Non-Performing Loans as a % of Total Loans	Adjusted Non-Performing Loans as a % of Capital	Net Charge-Offs Avg Loans	Profitability Index	Net Income ($Mil)	Return on Assets (R.O.A.)	Return on Equity (R.O.E.)	Net Interest Spread	Overhead Efficiency Ratio	Liquidity Index	Liquidity Ratio	Hot Money Ratio	Stability Index
7.1	0.00	na	-0.05	**9.0**	1.1	2.29	25.14	5.20	58.0	**4.5**	14.4	5.1	**5.6**
6.4	1.15	na	0.06	**5.2**	0.8	1.22	11.94	3.96	68.5	**2.9**	17.4	14.9	**6.3**
9.5	0.00	na	0.09	**5.7**	0.7	1.52	9.24	3.07	51.9	**3.6**	60.9	22.1	**7.8**
7.2	1.04	na	0.02	**3.6**	0.1	0.73	7.05	3.26	71.9	**5.1**	58.4	11.1	**4.8**
5.0	3.88	10.8	0.13	**6.5**	0.6	1.30	9.39	4.61	61.6	**5.0**	37.9	9.2	**8.1**
6.2	0.42	na	-0.02	**4.1**	0.6	0.92	11.31	3.91	73.8	**4.0**	17.9	9.0	**4.6**
4.5	1.24	na	0.01	**6.8**	2.1	1.59	15.20	4.57	62.5	**1.6**	16.8	23.7	**7.1**
7.5	2.72	na	0.00	**9.8**	4.2	2.59	8.34	4.46	24.4	**4.8**	20.4	3.8	**9.6**
7.6	0.37	na	0.04	**7.9**	8.1	1.81	17.17	4.06	58.5	**2.4**	25.4	18.0	**9.1**
8.2	0.17	na	0.00	**5.3**	1.3	1.34	11.12	4.12	68.0	**4.2**	26.2	9.1	**7.2**
4.0	2.16	na	0.02	**5.7**	2.0	1.14	11.04	4.16	67.4	**1.5**	13.8	9.8	**6.5**
8.5	0.03	0.0	0.03	**4.9**	6.8	1.29	9.18	2.61	58.1	**2.5**	50.0	40.1	**8.5**
6.1	1.41	4.2	0.04	**7.7**	9.4	1.90	13.19	3.53	51.4	**2.1**	26.5	20.3	**10.0**
9.1	0.68	na	0.02	**7.9**	0.7	1.59	8.71	4.26	53.3	**4.1**	23.6	9.4	**7.7**
8.1	0.77	na	0.04	**5.1**	0.5	1.04	8.87	4.06	68.4	**4.3**	23.4	7.5	**6.4**
6.0	0.51	na	0.01	**6.4**	1.4	1.56	14.00	4.37	65.4	**3.8**	17.9	10.4	**7.0**
8.5	0.00	na	-0.30	**5.9**	1.8	1.25	11.03	3.91	58.5	**3.5**	28.0	13.3	**6.6**
8.6	0.79	na	0.13	**3.9**	0.4	0.81	6.83	3.87	79.0	**4.2**	18.1	7.8	**6.6**
5.9	0.76	na	0.23	**3.6**	0.2	0.74	6.60	3.47	72.2	**4.2**	40.1	13.8	**5.3**
8.3	0.54	na	0.04	**3.9**	0.4	0.68	4.01	4.06	79.0	**1.3**	21.8	29.5	**7.6**
3.1	2.52	na	0.08	**2.2**	0.1	0.38	4.05	4.42	91.2	**2.2**	23.0	18.8	**3.7**
9.6	0.00	na	0.00	**6.5**	2.4	1.62	15.33	3.92	55.6	**6.9**	64.6	4.5	**6.8**
6.4	0.56	2.0	-0.17	**4.9**	2.9	0.93	9.55	3.77	71.6	**4.8**	30.6	7.1	**5.2**
8.2	0.01	na	-0.01	**9.6**	15.9	2.47	25.08	4.25	44.3	**2.5**	6.5	15.9	**8.6**
8.0	0.11	na	-0.01	**6.2**	1.1	1.18	7.47	4.08	65.1	**3.7**	34.7	14.7	**8.0**
7.4	1.21	3.5	0.01	**1.7**	0.2	0.30	3.20	3.47	96.5	**6.1**	48.6	4.8	**3.8**
5.5	2.97	na	0.07	**5.9**	3.6	1.34	9.98	3.59	61.9	**2.3**	22.1	18.2	**8.0**
8.7	0.07	na	-0.37	**5.8**	2.1	1.35	14.89	5.20	69.4	**4.3**	23.2	7.7	**6.4**
8.1	0.25	na	0.52	**7.1**	0.8	1.69	18.92	4.28	57.3	**5.7**	32.2	1.8	**5.5**
9.3	0.00	na	0.00	**3.4**	0.4	0.67	8.04	3.00	72.6	**4.9**	42.6	11.0	**4.0**
5.5	0.75	na	0.01	**4.4**	1.2	0.89	9.75	3.78	69.6	**1.6**	15.8	22.9	**5.0**
6.6	0.10	na	0.14	**4.9**	1.7	1.00	10.33	4.28	69.7	**4.8**	31.4	7.5	**5.9**
7.6	1.53	na	4.79	**1.5**	-0.5	-1.23	-5.87	3.60	71.9	**5.7**	37.1	4.3	**7.4**
9.6	0.00	na	-0.03	**2.6**	0.1	0.41	2.74	3.03	85.5	**4.2**	80.6	21.0	**7.0**
6.9	1.14	na	0.57	**6.1**	1.9	1.37	13.50	3.63	54.1	**6.3**	41.5	1.9	**6.8**
7.5	0.05	na	0.49	**7.2**	1.1	1.63	14.71	5.50	67.5	**4.5**	22.7	6.3	**7.7**
5.5	1.49	7.9	0.07	**5.1**	1.0	1.18	10.73	4.71	71.6	**3.9**	17.3	9.8	**6.6**
7.3	0.68	na	0.01	**5.8**	4.4	1.43	13.79	3.74	63.3	**3.0**	25.8	15.1	**7.2**
8.7	0.00	0.0	0.00	**9.8**	1.2	2.66	15.87	5.95	54.7	**5.3**	17.4	0.6	**9.3**
3.1	1.82	na	0.00	**4.1**	1.5	0.72	7.90	4.12	74.8	**3.5**	12.2	11.2	**5.8**
10.0	5.07	na	0.76	**5.4**	1.1	1.47	13.48	3.14	48.2	**7.8**	73.2	0.0	**5.9**
6.6	0.39	na	0.01	**8.1**	1.5	1.97	22.07	4.93	63.0	**3.6**	21.3	11.7	**6.8**
7.8	0.40	na	0.25	**7.8**	0.5	2.26	5.89	3.70	52.4	**6.7**	66.7	4.3	**6.9**
6.1	6.98	na	0.13	**4.8**	0.2	1.07	8.03	4.60	69.7	**0.5**	6.6	43.0	**4.3**
8.5	1.08	na	0.87	**3.3**	0.1	0.67	5.65	4.35	86.5	**6.4**	60.0	3.1	**6.2**
7.3	0.00	na	-0.21	**7.1**	1.4	1.73	15.21	3.45	48.9	**2.1**	32.5	25.2	**8.5**
6.4	0.84	3.6	0.18	**9.8**	18.9	1.88	14.88	4.26	50.0	**4.4**	22.5	8.7	**9.7**
8.4	0.11	0.5	-0.02	**4.8**	1.1	1.16	11.07	4.42	67.9	**2.7**	20.1	15.6	**6.2**
8.9	0.00	na	0.00	**3.6**	0.1	0.61	4.25	3.68	77.1	**5.9**	59.2	5.8	**7.0**
5.9	0.89	na	0.01	**4.7**	0.5	1.00	11.90	3.99	69.4	**4.7**	27.2	6.3	**4.0**
6.6	1.22	na	-0.06	**4.8**	1.8	1.14	10.04	3.37	63.5	**3.3**	15.9	12.4	**6.9**
7.6	0.02	na	0.01	**3.9**	0.3	0.86	10.72	4.13	76.6	**2.6**	21.0	16.6	**3.4**
5.9	6.33	na	0.41	**3.9**	3.2	0.80	6.41	2.56	61.8	**4.3**	71.4	20.4	**7.0**
3.9	1.61	na	0.13	**6.6**	4.9	1.65	13.64	4.10	62.5	**1.7**	25.2	24.1	**7.9**
5.3	2.22	na	1.44	**7.7**	2.8	1.89	13.71	4.36	45.1	**1.1**	11.7	23.6	**7.6**
8.3	0.60	2.3	0.07	**6.0**	6.2	1.35	11.83	3.81	61.2	**4.9**	42.1	10.8	**7.8**
5.6	1.08	na	0.07	**8.2**	3.1	1.63	13.95	4.24	61.9	**3.8**	24.1	10.9	**7.6**
5.8	1.25	6.1	0.06	**3.7**	1.5	0.70	9.42	3.77	78.9	**6.3**	49.4	4.2	**2.3**
6.8	0.99	na	0.20	**7.9**	2.2	1.60	11.14	4.67	56.2	**3.9**	15.9	9.4	**7.9**
7.6	1.50	na	-0.03	**3.9**	0.7	0.79	5.39	4.47	82.1	**1.7**	21.9	24.1	**7.5**

Name	City	State	Rating	2018 Rating	2017 Rating	Total Assets ($Mil)	One Year Asset Growth	Asset Mix (As a % of Total Assets) Commercial Loans	Consumer Loans	Mortgage Loans	Securities	Capitalization Index	Leverage Ratio	Risk-Based Capital Ratio
First National Bank of Hartford	Hartford	WI	**B**	B	B	229.8	12.21	10.7	0.3	18.2	10.2	**10.0**	11.4	15.7
First National Bank of Harveyville	Harveyville	KS	**D+**	D+	C-	14.4	1.32	8.7	5.9	25.1	0.0	**7.7**	9.4	17.3
First National Bank of Hebbronville	Hebbronville	TX	**B+**	A-	A-	89.6	-5.20	1.0	12.2	11.3	47.6	**10.0**	18.1	47.5
First National Bank of Henning	Ottertail	MN	**A-**	B+	A-	213.9	6.84	6.4	5.8	20.3	27.4	**10.0**	11.8	18.2
▲ First National Bank of Hereford	Hereford	TX	**B**	C+	D+	167.8	1.17	13.5	1.2	8.1	12.4	**8.3**	10.4	13.6
First National Bank of Hooker	Hooker	OK	**B-**	B+	A-	74.4	-1.30	6.9	3.3	13.2	28.0	**10.0**	14.3	20.9
▼ First National Bank of Hope	Hope	KS	**D**	D+	D+	84.2	1.55	5.4	1.8	2.7	17.6	**10.0**	11.8	15.2
First National Bank of Hughes Springs	Hughes Springs	TX	**B-**	B+	A-	264.0	-7.49	11.4	5.5	20.4	10.5	**10.0**	13.1	20.4
First National Bank of Hugo	Hugo	CO	**A-**	A-	B+	122.3	4.33	1.1	1.9	4.9	20.5	**10.0**	12.7	22.4
First National Bank of Huntsville	Huntsville	TX	**B**	B	B	465.6	1.11	6.7	5.7	21.5	32.4	**10.0**	12.2	24.1
▲ First National Bank of Hutchinson	Hutchinson	KS	**B+**	B	B	714.6	1.02	11.5	1.6	7.5	19.5	**10.0**	13.0	16.2
First National Bank of Izard County	Calico Rock	AR	**A**	A	A	165.2	2.16	2.2	5.5	18.0	33.8	**10.0**	35.2	67.5
First National Bank of Jasper	Jasper	TX	**B**	B	B	243.6	-4.08	3.3	4.2	8.3	61.9	**10.0**	13.5	43.8
▲ First National Bank of Jeanerette	Jeanerette	LA	**B**	C+	B-	263.6	7.95	8.8	2.7	27.9	7.6	**10.0**	11.6	15.4
First National Bank of Johnson	Johnson	NE	**C+**	C+	C	71.9	2.53	1.3	2.6	4.8	46.9	**10.0**	20.3	39.7
First National Bank of Kansas	Burlington	KS	**C+**	C+	C	85.0	-0.56	6.4	2.3	9.4	60.6	**6.3**	8.3	22.0
▲ First National Bank of Kemp	Kemp	TX	**B-**	C+	C	95.8	8.53	14.1	1.3	17.8	20.3	**7.5**	9.4	17.5
First National Bank of Kentucky	Carrollton	KY	**B+**	B+	B+	121.1	4.43	1.7	2.4	36.2	16.7	**10.0**	11.8	20.0
▲ First National Bank of Lacon	Lacon	IL	**C+**	C	C+	59.9	-4.29	8.8	7.8	14.3	11.7	**8.3**	9.8	14.6
First National Bank of Lake Jackson	Lake Jackson	TX	**B**	B	B	255.1	5.26	1.8	0.6	0.1	75.9	**8.7**	10.1	46.8
First National Bank of Las Animas	Las Animas	CO	**A**	A	A	382.2	6.85	5.5	1.2	11.2	18.1	**10.0**	11.8	16.5
First National Bank of Lawrence County	Walnut Ridge	AR	**B+**	B+	B	217.8	6.14	8.4	2.6	16.0	25.9	**10.0**	11.3	19.0
First National Bank of Le Center	Le Center	MN	**A-**	A-	B+	138.3	36.27	5.2	4.1	10.7	25.2	**8.8**	10.2	20.3
▲ First National Bank of Lindsay	Lindsay	OK	**B+**	B	B	64.8	8.89	24.5	3.5	13.2	15.2	**10.0**	12.5	17.8
▲ First National Bank of Lipan	Lipan	TX	**C-**	D+	D	21.4	0.52	3.3	12.7	12.0	12.8	**7.6**	9.4	28.9
First National Bank of Litchfield	Litchfield	IL	**B+**	B+	B+	96.7	-5.04	9.3	3.1	10.7	10.8	**10.0**	13.1	17.0
First National Bank of Livingston	Livingston	TX	**B+**	B+	B+	401.7	6.16	2.1	3.4	16.4	39.1	**10.0**	14.6	44.3
First National Bank of Long Island	Glen Head	NY	**B**	B	B	4160.7	-2.03	2.5	0.0	40.3	17.6	**7.4**	9.3	16.0
First National Bank of Louisburg	Louisburg	KS	**A-**	B+	B	119.9	2.54	3.0	0.7	27.2	40.6	**10.0**	13.7	25.1
▲ First National Bank of Louisiana	Crowley	LA	**A**	A-	A-	378.6	0.42	15.4	1.2	15.1	9.0	**10.0**	12.8	18.1
First National Bank of Manchester	Manchester	KY	**B**	B	B-	138.7	-0.31	6.0	3.4	14.7	33.3	**10.0**	14.2	24.9
▲ First National Bank of Manchester	Manchester	TN	**A-**	B+	A-	286.1	1.92	6.8	4.7	25.5	16.5	**10.0**	13.2	19.7
First National Bank of Manning	Manning	IA	**B+**	B	B	62.3	-3.88	5.4	1.8	8.7	15.7	**10.0**	19.4	32.7
First National Bank of McConnelsville	McConnelsville	OH	**C+**	C+	C+	149.9	2.19	0.6	4.5	34.8	19.9	**5.5**	7.5	17.1
▲ First National Bank of McGregor	McGregor	TX	**B+**	C+	B	488.9	23.65	10.3	3.5	35.1	0.0	**10.0**	12.3	16.6
First National Bank of McIntosh	McIntosh	MN	**B-**	B-	B-	26.3	-1.88	4.2	3.9	9.3	33.7	**10.0**	27.4	75.6
First National Bank of Mertzon	Mertzon	TX	**C+**	C	C-	478.1	14.32	3.2	0.7	1.4	57.3	**5.3**	7.3	37.2
First National Bank of Michigan	Kalamazoo	MI	**B-**	B-	B	594.2	8.64	17.3	0.3	3.9	5.6	**5.9**	10.3	11.7
▲ First National Bank of Middle Tennessee	McMinnville	TN	**A-**	B+	B+	520.1	3.31	4.1	0.4	27.8	23.6	**10.0**	13.0	22.6
▲ First National Bank of Milaca	Milaca	MN	**A-**	B	B+	213.6	1.44	13.9	5.2	17.4	20.0	**10.0**	11.7	21.0
First National Bank of Monterey	Monterey	IN	**B**	B	B	330.1	-0.29	3.4	1.3	11.8	28.5	**10.0**	13.0	18.7
First National Bank of Moody	Moody	TX	**B-**	B-	B	48.2	-0.10	2.8	3.6	16.6	40.6	**10.0**	20.8	40.6
▲ First National Bank of Moose Lake	Moose Lake	MN	**A-**	B+	B+	109.8	3.54	5.4	3.8	23.6	11.0	**10.0**	13.2	17.7
▲ First National Bank of Mount Dora	Mount Dora	FL	**A-**	B+	A-	245.0	4.78	2.0	2.1	13.6	43.1	**10.0**	15.6	27.4
First National Bank of Muscatine	Muscatine	IA	**B-**	B	B-	308.5	2.60	13.4	2.7	30.2	2.9	**10.0**	11.9	16.7
First National Bank of Nevada	Nevada	MO	**B**	B	B	95.4	-1.97	3.9	1.7	13.9	36.8	**10.0**	15.7	26.4
First National Bank of Nokomis	Nokomis	IL	**B**	B	C+	151.9	3.67	3.2	2.5	13.4	24.9	**10.0**	11.9	19.1
▲ First National Bank of North Arkansas	Berryville	AR	**B-**	C+	B	195.6	0.17	9.6	11.0	31.5	1.6	**10.0**	11.8	16.2
First National Bank of Northfield	Northfield	MN	**B+**	B+	B+	247.6	21.31	9.6	0.4	16.1	7.5	**9.6**	10.8	14.6
First National Bank of Okawville	Okawville	IL	**B**	B	B	59.9	-5.59	2.0	1.4	8.3	43.9	**10.0**	13.0	22.5
First National Bank of Oklahoma	Oklahoma City	OK	**B-**	B+	B+	546.2	15.16	10.4	1.6	19.2	4.4	**4.3**	7.9	10.7
First National Bank of Omaha	Omaha	NE	**B-**	B-	B-	22102.1	8.22	8.5	31.5	4.5	17.5	**7.6**	10.5	13.0
First National Bank of Oneida	Oneida	TN	**A-**	B+	B+	219.2	3.36	3.5	2.6	28.0	21.6	**10.0**	11.9	19.2
First National Bank of Orwell	Orwell	VT	**C-**	D+	D+	75.4	5.02	4.7	2.7	62.3	0.0	**6.8**	8.8	15.4
▼ First National Bank of Osakis	Osakis	MN	**B-**	B	B+	66.4	2.36	5.6	2.8	23.7	23.3	**5.7**	7.7	14.1
▲ First National Bank of Ottawa	Ottawa	IL	**B**	B-	B	378.9	20.29	13.4	1.0	23.4	10.9	**10.0**	12.5	16.4
▲ First National Bank of Pana	Pana	IL	**A-**	B+	B+	187.6	5.89	6.5	1.7	17.8	14.6	**10.0**	11.7	17.6
First National Bank of Pandora	Pandora	OH	**C+**	C+	C+	186.8	10.34	9.1	2.6	20.2	21.0	**6.4**	8.7	12.1
▲ First National Bank of Pasco	Dade City	FL	**C+**	C	C+	179.8	5.44	10.7	3.9	11.8	21.0	**10.0**	12.8	18.1
First National Bank of Pawnee	Pawnee	OK	**B**	B	B	58.2	-4.53	3.2	3.1	6.9	38.8	**10.0**	14.8	28.1

Asset Quality Index	Adjusted Non-Performing Loans as a % of Total Loans	Adjusted Non-Performing Loans as a % of Capital	Net Charge-Offs Avg Loans	Profitability Index	Net Income ($Mil)	Return on Assets (R.O.A.)	Return on Equity (R.O.E.)	Net Interest Spread	Overhead Efficiency Ratio	Liquidity Index	Liquidity Ratio	Hot Money Ratio	Stability Index
8.7	0.08	0.5	-0.01	**4.6**	1.5	0.90	7.77	3.85	70.8	**4.0**	20.6	9.3	**6.4**
7.5	0.00	na	0.00	**2.4**	0.0	0.26	2.83	3.53	90.4	**2.1**	35.7	22.8	**4.4**
8.2	1.08	na	0.52	**5.8**	0.9	1.36	7.80	3.50	63.2	**2.1**	44.3	40.4	**8.3**
7.9	0.36	na	0.01	**6.6**	2.5	1.59	12.71	3.84	60.3	**2.5**	21.3	17.0	**7.9**
4.9	1.36	na	-0.06	**6.6**	2.1	1.70	16.89	4.54	62.6	**2.8**	29.7	17.6	**5.3**
5.2	1.67	na	1.54	**4.8**	0.4	0.68	4.64	4.52	60.7	**2.3**	20.3	18.1	**8.8**
0.0	13.63	na	0.74	**3.3**	0.4	0.55	4.66	3.88	75.2	**2.7**	26.1	16.9	**5.2**
5.2	2.22	na	-0.13	**8.7**	5.3	2.57	19.84	5.53	62.4	**3.8**	14.7	10.0	**8.9**
8.5	0.27	1.7	0.01	**6.7**	1.5	1.67	12.91	4.43	61.0	**5.0**	30.7	5.6	**8.2**
8.3	0.12	na	0.04	**4.9**	3.8	1.08	8.45	3.47	66.1	**3.9**	26.8	11.0	**7.6**
8.4	0.21	na	0.05	**5.2**	6.4	1.17	9.23	3.52	69.9	**4.2**	11.3	7.1	**8.5**
8.8	1.27	1.6	0.04	**7.6**	2.0	1.57	4.61	4.30	53.9	**4.2**	60.8	19.1	**8.6**
8.2	0.31	0.5	0.85	**4.4**	1.8	0.95	7.38	3.29	65.8	**3.9**	25.1	10.5	**7.2**
5.1	1.09	na	0.03	**6.6**	2.9	1.50	13.49	4.77	63.4	**2.7**	15.4	15.7	**8.0**
8.8	0.01	na	-0.02	**2.9**	0.2	0.40	1.93	2.67	80.8	**6.8**	69.3	4.5	**6.7**
9.6	0.00	na	-0.03	**3.4**	0.5	0.73	8.91	2.74	79.3	**1.8**	24.8	22.6	**4.9**
8.3	0.00	na	0.06	**4.2**	0.6	0.89	7.94	4.15	74.7	**5.0**	34.5	7.5	**6.3**
7.7	0.41	na	0.29	**4.7**	1.0	1.12	9.88	3.94	74.2	**1.6**	18.5	24.1	**7.7**
6.0	0.07	na	-0.03	**4.7**	0.5	1.12	11.84	4.19	72.3	**3.1**	11.9	13.2	**4.9**
10.0	0.00	na	-0.59	**4.5**	2.3	1.14	12.49	2.19	49.5	**3.8**	31.1	13.0	**6.0**
8.5	0.10	0.3	0.00	**10.0**	7.2	2.55	20.75	4.77	46.8	**3.3**	21.6	12.6	**9.5**
8.7	0.40	na	0.12	**5.2**	1.9	1.19	10.91	4.10	70.1	**1.4**	17.8	26.9	**7.3**
5.4	0.84	6.8	-0.02	**6.3**	1.5	1.59	15.40	3.18	51.1	**3.7**	20.4	10.8	**6.7**
7.2	0.52	na	0.12	**8.9**	0.9	1.96	16.41	4.75	51.5	**1.9**	15.6	19.7	**7.0**
8.4	0.00	0.0	0.00	**2.7**	0.1	0.50	5.59	3.49	84.5	**6.4**	70.6	5.4	**3.5**
7.1	0.08	na	0.00	**5.7**	1.1	1.40	11.38	3.91	65.1	**1.6**	12.4	21.9	**7.3**
9.0	0.54	na	0.12	**5.4**	3.8	1.33	9.03	3.10	71.2	**6.9**	63.0	4.4	**8.6**
9.2	0.07	0.4	0.05	**5.2**	34.1	1.08	11.78	2.56	50.2	**3.0**	10.1	7.5	**7.8**
9.7	0.03	na	0.00	**5.6**	1.3	1.45	10.21	3.34	60.5	**5.0**	43.5	10.9	**8.6**
8.4	0.00	na	0.01	**8.2**	6.0	2.02	16.59	4.26	55.6	**4.4**	15.7	5.8	**9.3**
6.4	4.08	na	-0.01	**3.9**	1.0	0.91	6.42	3.49	75.1	**2.0**	33.3	28.1	**8.1**
7.8	0.74	na	0.10	**8.5**	3.3	1.50	11.88	4.28	51.5	**1.3**	12.6	25.8	**8.3**
8.6	0.00	0.0	0.00	**4.9**	0.5	1.09	5.82	3.43	59.8	**5.2**	44.7	9.6	**7.7**
4.9	0.58	2.9	0.04	**3.5**	0.8	0.65	6.01	3.28	78.4	**4.6**	21.1	5.4	**6.7**
7.8	0.10	na	0.10	**5.9**	3.6	1.04	8.95	4.71	65.8	**0.3**	9.5	50.7	**6.0**
9.0	0.00	na	0.15	**3.5**	0.2	0.77	2.86	3.03	76.1	**5.7**	68.6	11.4	**7.6**
9.8	0.00	0.0	-0.17	**5.3**	4.1	1.19	16.91	2.33	36.8	**7.2**	81.3	5.4	**3.5**
5.6	0.08	na	0.20	**5.3**	4.4	1.07	10.83	3.82	63.7	**1.4**	14.6	18.9	**7.1**
9.0	0.11	na	-0.01	**6.2**	5.1	1.33	10.44	3.40	66.8	**0.7**	9.3	31.3	**8.6**
5.7	2.28	na	0.34	**6.3**	2.3	1.43	12.09	3.97	62.9	**5.4**	32.1	4.0	**8.7**
8.0	0.74	na	-0.01	**4.1**	2.2	0.89	7.09	3.11	65.7	**3.9**	36.0	12.2	**7.5**
5.3	4.47	na	-0.08	**4.6**	0.4	1.02	4.97	3.92	72.9	**2.2**	49.0	12.0	**7.9**
7.1	1.04	na	0.01	**8.1**	1.5	1.91	14.56	4.49	60.1	**1.3**	25.5	19.4	**9.3**
6.1	4.91	na	0.05	**6.9**	2.6	1.47	9.18	3.88	70.4	**7.0**	60.5	3.8	**8.1**
4.7	2.83	na	0.12	**5.3**	2.5	1.06	9.14	3.29	62.0	**3.5**	14.6	11.6	**6.8**
5.2	2.91	na	0.08	**3.4**	0.5	0.62	4.07	3.48	77.0	**5.1**	45.6	10.4	**7.9**
6.4	2.52	na	0.03	**4.5**	1.0	0.92	7.54	3.73	67.7	**4.4**	37.3	12.1	**7.9**
4.8	1.65	na	0.05	**6.6**	2.2	1.52	13.26	5.60	75.4	**3.1**	13.5	13.3	**7.8**
7.6	0.00	na	0.01	**3.1**	0.2	1.00	10.15	3.25	58.0	**4.2**	26.8	9.7	**6.3**
9.5	0.00	0.0	0.03	**3.7**	0.4	0.76	6.19	3.24	73.6	**4.1**	56.6	12.0	**6.3**
7.4	0.31	2.9	0.16	**6.9**	6.2	1.56	19.72	3.78	55.5	**0.7**	12.8	41.2	**7.0**
4.6	1.19	5.4	1.98	**8.4**	259.6	1.62	15.29	6.46	55.6	**3.5**	10.0	7.0	**9.1**
6.8	0.60	na	-0.03	**6.7**	2.6	1.58	13.66	4.24	60.2	**1.7**	10.3	20.4	**7.4**
2.4	3.24	na	0.05	**5.2**	0.5	0.99	11.34	3.84	68.1	**0.7**	9.4	33.3	**5.3**
5.5	0.68	na	0.10	**4.2**	0.5	0.96	7.75	3.37	71.6	**3.8**	24.7	10.8	**6.1**
4.7	1.29	na	-0.10	**4.8**	1.9	0.76	5.49	4.16	76.2	**4.1**	2.9	6.2	**7.2**
7.3	1.11	na	-0.04	**6.6**	2.1	1.53	13.21	3.71	59.5	**3.0**	23.5	14.7	**8.1**
5.3	1.50	na	0.08	**3.9**	1.0	0.75	8.69	3.85	78.9	**2.1**	7.5	17.7	**4.7**
6.0	1.22	na	-0.01	**3.2**	0.7	0.52	4.70	4.38	79.8	**3.8**	19.3	10.7	**6.3**
6.2	1.91	7.2	0.60	**3.5**	0.3	0.67	4.56	4.06	75.4	**4.3**	32.2	10.9	**7.4**

Name	City	State	Rating	2018 Rating	2017 Rating	Total Assets ($Mil)	One Year Asset Growth	Asset Mix (As a % of Total Assets) Commercial Loans	Consumer Loans	Mortgage Loans	Securities	Capitalization Index	Leverage Ratio	Risk-Based Capital Ratio
First National Bank of Pennsylvania	Pittsburgh	PA	**B-**	B-	B-	34262.6	5.24	14.2	6.2	14.7	19.0	**5.1**	8.8	11.1
First National Bank of Peterstown	Peterstown	WV	**B**	B	B	67.7	9.59	4.0	4.5	40.2	16.9	**10.0**	12.4	22.9
First National Bank of Picayune	Picayune	MS	**B**	B	B	201.9	-1.74	5.2	6.1	28.0	22.6	**10.0**	14.7	23.1
First National Bank of Primghar	Primghar	IA	**B-**	B-	B-	32.9	5.98	6.4	1.6	1.6	20.9	**10.0**	17.8	23.3
First National Bank of Proctor	Proctor	MN	**D+**	C-	C-	25.2	3.44	1.4	4.0	34.8	9.0	**8.1**	9.7	25.0
First National Bank of Pulaski	Pulaski	TN	**A-**	B+	B+	872.4	4.65	5.1	2.8	12.8	24.3	**10.0**	11.2	15.5
First National Bank of Quitaque	Quitaque	TX	**B-**	C	B-	64.9	16.53	3.2	4.3	0.0	6.2	**10.0**	14.5	25.3
▼ First National Bank of Raymond	Raymond	IL	**C+**	B	B	149.6	5.10	4.0	2.2	9.0	39.1	**10.0**	11.1	17.9
▲ First National Bank of River Falls	River Falls	WI	**A-**	B+	B+	279.8	-0.16	5.6	1.6	13.4	32.3	**10.0**	11.5	20.4
First National Bank of Russell Springs	Russell Springs	KY	**B**	B	B	229.6	12.69	4.9	2.3	8.6	33.6	**10.0**	12.8	21.1
▲ First National Bank of Sandoval	Sandoval	IL	**B**	B-	B-	53.7	12.55	5.6	9.6	35.0	18.5	**10.0**	11.8	18.7
First National Bank of Scotia	Scotia	NY	**C+**	C+	C+	508.0	1.48	10.6	26.8	19.0	8.8	**6.3**	8.6	11.9
▲ First National Bank of Scott City	Scott City	KS	**B-**	C	D+	116.3	2.13	10.1	6.2	6.1	25.1	**10.0**	13.5	17.2
▲ First National Bank of Sedan	Sedan	KS	**C-**	D	D	55.0	-3.14	7.7	2.1	10.7	27.7	**10.0**	13.0	23.4
First National Bank of Shiner	Shiner	TX	**B+**	B+	B+	807.0	17.04	2.2	0.8	4.0	78.9	**9.7**	10.8	27.0
First National Bank of Sonora	Sonora	TX	**B**	B-	B-	439.6	4.51	6.3	3.7	18.1	2.6	**9.0**	10.3	16.5
First National Bank of South Carolina	Holly Hill	SC	**B**	B	B	201.3	3.26	2.2	1.6	10.3	26.6	**10.0**	12.8	30.7
First National Bank of South Miami	South Miami	FL	**B-**	B-	B-	804.4	14.58	2.7	0.1	12.5	10.8	**8.4**	9.9	15.7
First National Bank of South Padre Island	South Padre Island	TX	**B**	B	B	56.5	-3.28	1.8	0.5	38.0	11.5	**9.6**	10.7	24.3
▲ First National Bank of Sparta	Sparta	IL	**A-**	B+	B	78.8	-1.50	8.5	9.1	22.5	37.0	**10.0**	13.9	29.3
First National Bank of Spearville	Spearville	KS	**B**	B	B	37.8	4.76	9.3	3.9	0.0	7.6	**10.0**	15.3	25.9
First National Bank of St. Ignace	Saint Ignace	MI	**C-**	C-	C-	286.6	0.51	3.3	1.5	8.6	48.8	**5.2**	7.2	15.2
First National Bank of Stanton	Stanton	TX	**B+**	B-	B-	219.2	8.93	5.2	1.3	2.1	56.0	**9.0**	10.3	26.2
First National Bank of Steeleville	Steeleville	IL	**B+**	B+	B+	204.5	5.13	4.9	4.1	21.0	39.0	**10.0**	15.1	29.3
First National Bank of Sterling City	Sterling City	TX	**C**	C-	C+	181.8	-2.68	1.2	2.2	5.3	67.8	**6.7**	8.7	29.1
First National Bank of Stigler	Stigler	OK	**B**	B	B	113.3	5.70	4.8	2.4	6.1	51.6	**6.0**	8.0	19.1
First National Bank of Sycamore	Sycamore	OH	**C**	C	C+	152.3	1.92	6.3	1.7	20.2	32.4	**9.9**	10.9	18.1
First National Bank of Syracuse	Syracuse	KS	**B**	B	B+	368.6	6.51	11.4	1.9	6.1	10.3	**7.6**	11.4	13.0
▼ First National Bank of Tahoka	Tahoka	TX	**C+**	B-	B-	51.7	-4.99	1.0	3.2	1.9	36.9	**6.4**	11.3	12.1
▲ First National Bank of Tennessee	Livingston	TN	**A-**	B+	B	873.5	2.50	9.4	2.9	15.1	20.7	**10.0**	12.7	21.4
First National Bank of Tom Bean	Tom Bean	TX	**D+**	D+	C-	122.1	-5.21	17.4	11.8	25.8	11.2	**7.1**	9.0	13.9
▲ First National Bank of Trinity	Trinity	TX	**B**	B-	B-	60.9	6.25	5.5	14.1	13.0	39.1	**9.5**	10.6	19.2
▲ First National Bank of Wakefield	Wakefield	MI	**C+**	C	C	51.5	4.38	1.7	8.9	16.2	35.2	**7.9**	9.6	25.6
▲ First National Bank of Waseca	Waseca	MN	**B**	B-	B	140.0	7.71	7.5	2.4	32.3	7.1	**7.0**	9.5	12.5
First National Bank of Waterloo	Waterloo	IL	**C+**	C+	C+	485.5	4.27	3.9	0.6	16.3	34.0	**9.4**	10.6	15.8
First National Bank of Wauchula	Wauchula	FL	**C+**	C	C	71.7	-0.70	7.4	3.1	32.1	11.7	**10.0**	12.0	18.8
First National Bank of Waverly	Waverly	OH	**C**	C	C	155.3	-4.30	3.6	4.1	20.2	18.0	**7.7**	9.5	20.4
First National Bank of Waynesboro	Waynesboro	GA	**A**	A	A	135.6	1.87	5.0	10.0	29.4	11.6	**10.0**	18.6	30.7
▲ First National Bank of Weatherford	Weatherford	TX	**B-**	C+	B-	276.1	12.66	16.5	2.1	9.6	2.5	**7.7**	9.9	13.1
First National Bank of Williamson	Williamson	WV	**B**	B-	B-	85.2	6.67	5.7	7.2	37.6	12.8	**9.3**	10.5	21.3
First National Bank of Winnsboro	Winnsboro	TX	**B**	B	B	136.4	-1.21	6.3	2.3	16.0	15.3	**10.0**	20.6	31.1
First National Bank Texas	Killeen	TX	**B+**	B+	B	2033.1	10.81	0.3	15.1	12.2	30.2	**7.1**	9.1	24.2
First National Bank USA	Boutte	LA	**A-**	B+	B+	132.2	9.32	3.7	0.9	22.6	2.1	**10.0**	13.4	21.8
First National Bank, Ames, Iowa	Ames	IA	**A-**	A-	A-	872.8	5.37	2.7	0.5	10.7	31.3	**7.7**	9.5	13.9
First National Bank, Cortez	Cortez	CO	**B-**	B-	B-	109.8	3.95	6.0	3.6	9.2	34.0	**9.7**	10.8	17.8
First National Bankers Bank	Baton Rouge	LA	**B-**	C+	C+	905.4	0.99	4.7	0.0	1.4	4.2	**10.0**	15.7	21.6
First National Community Bank	Chatsworth	GA	**B**	B	B	288.2	77.25	5.2	1.0	16.2	8.1	**10.0**	11.3	17.1
First National Community Bank	New Richmond	WI	**C-**	C+	B-	206.9	3.72	6.0	3.2	18.0	22.2	**7.5**	9.3	14.9
First National Trust Co.	Pittsburgh	PA	**U**	U	U	31.4	15.73	0.0	0.0	0.0	0.0	**10.0**	90.2	145.4
First Nations Bank	Chicago	IL	**B+**	B+	A-	359.0	3.38	3.5	0.7	7.4	3.3	**10.0**	13.4	17.6
▲ First NaturalState Bank	McGehee	AR	**B-**	C+	C+	59.4	2.08	12.8	6.7	16.1	22.0	**10.0**	11.2	18.3
▲ First Nebraska Bank	Valley	NE	**B+**	B	B	283.8	2.31	7.5	1.4	9.7	16.5	**8.3**	10.2	13.6
▲ First Neighbor Bank, N.A.	Toledo	IL	**B-**	C+	C+	437.7	21.94	17.7	4.8	12.0	7.1	**8.1**	11.2	13.4
First Neighborhood Bank	Spencer	WV	**B-**	B-	B-	140.6	4.39	6.5	2.2	30.7	19.1	**10.0**	11.4	19.0
▲ First Neodesha Bank	Neodesha	KS	**B**	B	B	106.1	10.66	5.7	4.4	22.4	15.3	**8.2**	9.8	14.9
First New Mexico Bank	Deming	NM	**A**	A	A	203.8	-0.66	11.6	1.6	10.0	33.2	**10.0**	14.9	23.7
First New Mexico Bank of Silver City	Silver City	NM	**A**	A	A	113.4	1.46	1.9	1.0	10.1	34.8	**10.0**	12.5	24.9
First New Mexico Bank, Las Cruces	Las Cruces	NM	**A**	A	A	113.3	-2.16	4.4	2.5	17.2	18.5	**10.0**	15.2	25.1
▲ First Northeast Bank of Nebraska	Lyons	NE	**A-**	B	B	299.1	-2.15	5.6	1.3	1.9	30.8	**10.0**	13.9	15.5
First Northern Bank and Trust Co.	Palmerton	PA	**B**	B-	B-	717.4	0.33	5.7	0.5	30.7	19.7	**10.0**	14.5	21.0

Asset Quality Index	Adjusted Non-Performing Loans as a % of Total Loans	Adjusted Non-Performing Loans as a % of Capital	Net Charge-Offs Avg Loans	Profitability Index	Net Income ($Mil)	Return on Assets (R.O.A.)	Return on Equity (R.O.E.)	Net Interest Spread	Overhead Efficiency Ratio	Liquidity Index	Liquidity Ratio	Hot Money Ratio	Stability Index
5.2	0.45	2.4	0.13	**5.6**	307.9	1.24	8.65	3.28	54.4	**3.0**	8.5	10.3	**10.0**
6.1	1.57	na	-0.08	**4.1**	0.4	0.80	6.56	3.78	73.1	**3.2**	29.2	15.6	**6.3**
4.5	2.46	na	0.14	**10.0**	4.4	2.87	19.46	5.09	48.4	**2.1**	23.7	19.3	**9.8**
7.4	0.00	0.0	0.00	**4.5**	0.2	0.87	4.94	3.75	70.3	**2.0**	29.7	24.0	**7.2**
9.1	0.18	na	0.00	**2.3**	0.0	0.16	1.60	3.69	93.8	**5.6**	47.9	7.8	**4.6**
8.1	0.51	2.7	0.09	**6.3**	8.1	1.25	11.56	3.85	59.2	**1.7**	22.6	24.3	**7.8**
5.2	4.06	na	-0.08	**5.9**	0.6	1.29	8.94	4.18	63.3	**2.7**	40.4	24.5	**7.1**
7.2	0.80	3.7	1.38	**2.7**	0.3	0.23	2.12	3.56	70.5	**4.0**	44.5	16.4	**6.7**
8.9	0.11	na	-0.08	**5.4**	2.7	1.31	11.57	3.63	66.9	**5.3**	30.4	4.0	**7.2**
8.2	1.41	na	0.01	**4.2**	1.5	0.88	6.84	3.68	72.5	**1.9**	21.3	20.4	**6.4**
6.6	0.38	na	0.03	**5.5**	0.5	1.23	10.39	4.51	66.7	**2.3**	17.9	17.6	**6.4**
4.4	0.17	3.1	0.06	**4.2**	2.7	0.74	9.70	3.92	74.3	**4.6**	7.9	3.7	**4.4**
4.3	1.90	na	0.81	**4.9**	0.9	1.02	7.77	4.07	62.7	**4.1**	26.3	9.9	**6.1**
8.8	0.67	na	1.55	**1.3**	0.1	0.13	1.12	3.53	97.5	**3.4**	24.5	12.8	**4.3**
9.3	0.20	0.3	0.90	**4.5**	6.9	1.19	10.21	2.61	51.8	**3.1**	63.5	35.7	**7.4**
5.4	1.05	4.2	0.09	**4.8**	4.0	1.24	11.66	4.41	70.3	**1.8**	26.1	22.6	**6.6**
7.7	1.22	na	-0.01	**4.3**	1.2	0.78	6.13	3.63	75.8	**6.7**	59.4	5.0	**7.2**
6.7	0.12	na	-0.02	**4.3**	4.6	0.79	8.13	3.37	69.9	**3.4**	22.7	12.8	**6.3**
8.7	0.57	na	0.02	**4.4**	0.4	0.94	7.75	3.97	76.1	**5.7**	45.4	6.5	**6.6**
7.8	0.15	na	0.16	**6.9**	1.0	1.69	12.65	4.18	63.2	**4.8**	29.6	6.6	**7.7**
7.6	0.00	0.0	-0.06	**8.0**	0.5	1.59	9.52	3.68	46.0	**3.1**	47.8	19.2	**7.0**
3.2	4.66	na	0.02	**2.7**	0.9	0.45	5.26	2.89	83.7	**5.4**	67.2	13.7	**4.5**
9.5	0.08	na	0.02	**7.2**	2.5	1.55	15.44	3.76	46.5	**6.8**	57.5	4.0	**5.9**
8.1	1.15	na	0.04	**5.4**	2.4	1.60	10.64	3.43	66.9	**4.5**	39.4	12.1	**8.8**
9.3	0.49	na	0.13	**4.3**	1.6	1.13	17.75	2.63	58.6	**5.5**	60.3	12.3	**3.0**
8.4	0.33	1.2	0.01	**7.4**	1.6	1.85	23.03	3.63	52.5	**5.7**	50.8	9.2	**5.2**
5.8	0.42	6.7	-0.04	**3.2**	0.8	0.66	5.91	3.28	75.5	**3.4**	29.1	14.6	**6.7**
4.3	0.37	na	-0.19	**8.2**	4.0	1.60	13.95	4.64	54.3	**0.6**	12.3	43.9	**7.9**
6.8	0.86	na	0.13	**4.0**	0.3	0.84	7.90	4.09	76.3	**3.7**	64.2	21.5	**5.9**
7.7	1.91	na	0.00	**7.1**	10.9	1.72	14.00	3.71	57.5	**4.2**	40.6	14.1	**8.5**
1.3	1.93	na	0.02	**2.7**	0.4	0.41	4.71	4.33	82.3	**1.0**	13.0	31.4	**4.6**
7.2	0.37	na	0.17	**5.0**	0.5	1.24	12.48	4.19	74.3	**4.5**	37.6	11.8	**5.3**
6.8	2.14	na	0.07	**3.5**	0.3	0.66	7.00	3.87	82.0	**4.9**	62.5	14.5	**4.4**
5.7	0.43	na	0.01	**7.2**	1.7	1.71	16.97	4.60	65.0	**2.9**	9.2	12.1	**7.6**
6.2	1.49	na	-0.02	**3.9**	2.9	0.81	7.27	3.32	70.7	**4.3**	18.0	6.9	**6.6**
4.2	3.20	na	-0.07	**2.9**	0.2	0.35	3.10	4.88	93.6	**1.7**	18.2	22.3	**5.7**
4.2	2.53	na	0.07	**2.6**	0.4	0.33	3.51	3.88	91.4	**4.5**	20.9	6.3	**4.7**
7.6	0.66	3.3	0.13	**9.0**	1.8	1.70	9.61	4.92	58.3	**3.4**	21.1	12.6	**8.8**
7.1	0.09	na	0.05	**7.0**	2.8	1.46	14.79	5.01	63.6	**1.7**	19.4	23.4	**6.1**
6.4	0.34	2.2	0.34	**4.1**	0.5	0.80	7.63	4.38	80.2	**1.1**	23.4	32.9	**6.5**
7.4	3.45	na	0.01	**7.8**	1.7	1.64	8.47	5.02	60.2	**2.1**	20.1	19.2	**7.9**
8.2	0.14	na	1.75	**7.7**	29.1	1.93	21.67	3.68	83.5	**6.9**	42.0	1.1	**7.0**
6.0	1.14	6.4	-0.13	**6.3**	1.4	1.46	11.06	4.69	69.1	**2.2**	22.8	19.0	**8.1**
8.4	0.24	1.3	0.00	**5.8**	7.6	1.22	12.11	3.17	56.8	**5.0**	34.6	7.8	**7.8**
5.1	0.75	na	0.45	**4.7**	0.8	1.02	9.93	4.09	67.3	**4.0**	15.7	9.1	**6.2**
4.5	2.45	na	-0.08	**4.0**	5.4	0.80	4.89	3.27	79.8	**6.2**	35.6	0.1	**7.9**
5.9	1.77	na	-0.02	**4.8**	1.3	0.84	6.90	3.58	71.9	**3.9**	21.9	10.0	**8.0**
3.1	4.70	na	0.34	**4.1**	1.1	0.73	7.81	3.95	77.1	**4.5**	18.8	5.8	**5.9**
6.5	na	0.0	na	**9.5**	6.5	30.91	36.78	1.64	75.7	**4.0**	231.2	0.0	**6.3**
7.3	0.00	na	0.09	**6.2**	2.8	1.06	8.01	3.24	55.5	**0.7**	14.8	47.1	**8.3**
6.4	2.99	na	0.01	**3.8**	0.4	0.80	7.54	3.70	76.3	**3.2**	15.0	12.9	**5.8**
8.4	0.33	na	0.00	**5.6**	2.8	1.31	12.93	4.16	69.9	**4.2**	13.4	7.1	**6.8**
5.1	0.77	na	0.06	**5.0**	3.0	0.93	8.05	3.78	67.0	**1.2**	9.6	22.6	**7.0**
8.0	0.51	na	0.01	**3.4**	0.5	0.51	4.45	3.62	81.5	**4.0**	30.3	11.8	**6.3**
5.9	0.75	na	0.00	**7.3**	1.4	1.71	17.70	3.94	57.2	**1.3**	5.7	25.2	**6.7**
9.2	0.32	na	0.20	**7.7**	2.5	1.61	11.22	4.26	56.4	**6.6**	46.1	1.6	**8.5**
9.4	0.27	na	0.01	**8.5**	1.3	1.57	12.93	4.34	54.2	**7.2**	60.0	2.1	**8.2**
9.0	0.00	na	-0.02	**9.2**	1.4	1.60	10.80	5.16	60.1	**5.3**	46.4	10.2	**8.9**
8.5	0.00	na	-0.02	**5.3**	2.6	1.15	8.53	3.42	57.2	**2.8**	21.4	11.7	**8.2**
7.3	0.87	na	-0.04	**4.6**	4.7	0.89	6.10	3.72	70.8	**3.5**	11.8	11.0	**7.8**

Name	City	State	Rating	2018 Rating	2017 Rating	Total Assets ($Mil)	One Year Asset Growth	Asset Mix (As a % of Total Assets) Commercial Loans	Consumer Loans	Mortgage Loans	Securities	Capitalization Index	Leverage Ratio	Risk-Based Capital Ratio
First Northern Bank of Dixon	Dixon	CA	**A-**	B+	B	1287.3	3.48	7.7	0.1	5.0	25.3	**8.6**	10.0	15.2
First Northern Bank of Wyoming	Buffalo	WY	**C+**	C+	B-	370.9	6.65	8.9	4.0	14.5	19.7	**7.1**	9.0	13.7
First Oklahoma Bank	Jenks	OK	**C**	C-	C	739.8	18.57	16.5	0.4	15.7	0.1	**5.5**	9.0	11.3
First Option Bank	Osawatomie	KS	**B**	B	B	329.8	3.70	2.7	2.5	23.6	49.5	**9.9**	10.9	23.2
▲ First Palmetto Bank	Camden	SC	**B+**	B	B	725.9	6.02	2.0	1.0	14.9	19.9	**10.0**	11.1	18.4
▲ First Peoples Bank	Pine Mountain	GA	**A-**	B+	B+	151.6	17.43	4.5	1.8	21.5	20.1	**10.0**	11.6	18.4
▲ First Peoples Bank of Tennessee	Jefferson City	TN	**B-**	C+	C	154.4	2.78	10.5	1.2	9.5	16.5	**7.4**	9.3	13.1
First Piedmont Federal S&L Assn. of Gaffn	Gaffney	SC	**A**	A	A+	419.8	2.71	2.1	0.9	41.0	0.8	**10.0**	25.6	40.2
▲ First Pioneer National Bank	Wray	CO	**A-**	B+	A-	179.7	2.62	2.3	2.9	3.7	24.1	**10.0**	14.6	20.7
First Port City Bank	Bainbridge	GA	**B+**	B+	A-	216.0	15.72	9.2	1.5	18.9	10.4	**7.1**	9.1	13.0
First Premier Bank	Sioux Falls	SD	**A**	A	A	1972.6	16.80	6.0	40.4	3.1	11.6	**10.0**	14.3	21.5
First Progressive Bank	Brewton	AL	**C-**	C+	C-	30.3	-0.53	8.6	4.0	10.2	56.8	**10.0**	27.8	74.6
First Pryority Bank	Pryor	OK	**B**	B	B	201.6	20.87	27.5	7.0	5.0	4.9	**9.8**	10.9	16.4
First Reliance Bank	Florence	SC	**C**	C+	B-	654.7	16.38	8.4	12.6	21.7	7.2	**5.2**	9.1	11.1
First Republic Bank	San Francisco	CA	**B**	B	B+	111028.7	15.54	7.7	4.1	40.3	16.3	**6.5**	8.5	12.6
First Resource Bank	Lino Lakes	MN	**B-**	B-	B+	212.7	5.58	12.4	0.2	20.1	3.9	**8.1**	9.7	13.6
▲ First Resource Bank	Exton	PA	**C**	C-	C	322.3	18.93	7.4	0.3	22.4	5.6	**6.7**	8.7	13.1
First Robinson Savings Bank, N.A.	Robinson	IL	**B-**	B-	B-	338.0	4.89	5.3	4.2	19.7	25.0	**8.0**	9.7	17.6
First S&L Assn.	Mebane	NC	**C+**	C+	C+	55.3	11.93	0.0	0.0	59.7	18.8	**10.0**	22.4	53.2
First Savanna Savings Bank	Savanna	IL	**D-**	D	D-	11.8	-3.68	0.0	10.2	57.6	10.5	**8.1**	9.8	18.8
First Savings Bank	Danville	IL	**C+**	B-	B	36.4	8.70	0.0	0.9	29.9	56.8	**10.0**	25.8	90.1
▲ First Savings Bank	Clarksville	IN	**B+**	B-	B-	1218.6	18.24	5.2	1.3	22.8	14.8	**7.5**	9.3	12.9
First Savings Bank	Beresford	SD	**A-**	A-	B+	844.4	15.32	1.9	16.2	8.5	13.5	**10.0**	15.4	20.8
First Savings Bank of Hegewisch	Chicago	IL	**B**	B	B	673.2	2.10	0.0	0.1	48.5	31.1	**10.0**	16.2	47.8
First Seacoast Bank	Dover	NH	**C**	C	C	400.4	4.72	6.3	0.5	53.0	10.1	**10.0**	11.6	18.9
First Secure Bank and Trust Co.	Palos Hills	IL	**C+**	C	D+	169.4	30.75	7.5	0.1	16.5	6.7	**9.2**	10.5	14.4
▲ First Secure Community Bank	Sugar Grove	IL	**C+**	C	C+	361.1	20.37	17.0	1.9	4.5	14.9	**5.4**	9.7	11.3
First Security Bank	Searcy	AR	**A+**	A+	A+	5685.2	7.72	7.1	0.8	6.3	42.6	**10.0**	18.7	23.6
▲ First Security Bank	Mapleton	IA	**B+**	B+	A-	65.6	-3.55	2.9	3.1	3.0	13.9	**10.0**	13.1	18.8
First Security Bank	Mackinaw	IL	**D**	D	D	84.3	2.73	6.6	0.6	15.9	4.3	**7.9**	9.8	13.2
First Security Bank	Overbrook	KS	**C+**	C+	C+	66.0	8.36	7.8	1.8	21.1	5.5	**5.7**	8.0	11.5
First Security Bank	Byron	MN	**C**	C	C+	70.6	6.13	6.1	3.2	20.0	20.4	**6.5**	8.5	14.0
▲ First Security Bank	Union Star	MO	**C**	C-	C-	32.5	5.10	3.0	10.1	32.4	26.7	**6.3**	8.3	16.0
▲ First Security Bank	Batesville	MS	**A-**	B+	B+	572.4	2.33	7.7	4.0	19.0	22.7	**10.0**	11.2	17.7
First Security Bank	Beaver	OK	**C-**	C-	C+	114.9	-2.55	8.5	2.4	8.3	2.1	**6.5**	10.3	12.1
▲ First Security Bank & Trust Co.	Charles City	IA	**C**	C-	C-	493.6	3.07	5.0	1.4	13.1	29.1	**8.1**	9.7	15.3
First Security Bank - Canby	Canby	MN	**B+**	B+	A	64.2	-3.38	22.8	1.8	1.5	12.7	**10.0**	13.0	20.2
▲ First Security Bank - West	Beulah	ND	**A-**	B+	A-	65.8	-5.49	17.2	1.5	0.9	19.2	**10.0**	12.2	18.4
First Security Bank and Trust Co.	Oklahoma City	OK	**C-**	C	C	54.4	12.09	15.2	1.9	34.7	2.8	**6.7**	9.2	12.3
First Security Bank of Deer Lodge	Deer Lodge	MT	**B+**	B+	B	40.0	5.95	11.4	5.9	30.6	0.0	**9.1**	10.4	18.8
First Security Bank of Helena	Helena	MT	**B-**	C+	C+	57.8	16.62	14.7	2.4	19.6	4.8	**10.0**	13.1	21.1
First Security Bank of Nevada	Las Vegas	NV	**A**	A	A-	221.5	10.33	4.9	0.0	1.8	2.8	**10.0**	18.9	28.1
▲ First Security Bank of Roundup	Roundup	MT	**B**	B-	B+	61.8	2.52	8.9	4.6	4.2	32.6	**10.0**	12.0	20.6
First Security Bank-Hendricks	Hendricks	MN	**B+**	B+	B+	30.8	6.14	13.3	2.8	8.0	24.9	**10.0**	12.3	25.0
First Security Bank-Sleepy Eye	Sleepy Eye	MN	**B+**	B+	A	183.6	-2.38	10.7	1.9	9.0	18.9	**10.0**	13.3	19.9
▲ First Security State Bank	Evansdale	IA	**C**	C	B-	99.5	1.00	33.8	31.3	5.9	5.8	**8.9**	11.5	14.1
First Security State Bank	Cranfills Gap	TX	**B-**	B-	B-	119.5	5.01	3.8	4.1	21.8	42.4	**5.4**	7.4	16.5
First Security Trust and Savings Bank	Elmwood Park	IL	**C+**	C	C	332.8	4.32	9.2	2.9	4.4	14.2	**6.6**	8.6	18.2
First Sentinel Bank	Richlands	VA	**C+**	C+	B	282.5	6.71	4.8	33.1	20.2	0.0	**6.9**	8.9	13.0
First Service Bank	Greenbrier	AR	**B-**	B-	B	338.8	13.98	8.8	1.0	20.3	3.7	**6.9**	9.4	12.4
First Shore Federal S&L Assn.	Salisbury	MD	**B**	B	B-	314.9	5.09	2.5	8.8	54.3	5.7	**10.0**	15.5	26.0
First Sound Bank	Seattle	WA	**C-**	C-	C-	111.4	-15.87	28.6	0.6	2.1	3.0	**10.0**	12.6	17.9
First Southeast Bank	Harmony	MN	**D+**	D	D	101.4	-0.27	9.6	2.9	9.1	1.4	**5.5**	8.8	11.4
First Southern Bank	Florence	AL	**B**	B-	B-	265.9	13.41	12.1	1.8	24.5	8.5	**8.2**	9.8	13.9
First Southern Bank	Patterson	GA	**E**	E-	E-	123.5	16.26	8.3	2.6	9.9	16.3	**10.0**	15.8	21.7
First Southern Bank	Marion	IL	**A-**	A-	A-	702.9	2.42	7.6	7.1	13.4	23.4	**10.0**	12.6	18.5
▲ First Southern Bank	Columbia	MS	**B+**	B	B	197.3	-4.21	6.0	5.9	17.0	15.3	**10.0**	11.5	15.5
▲ First Southern National Bank	Lancaster	KY	**B-**	C+	B-	897.7	5.30	5.7	2.3	26.0	15.6	**7.4**	9.3	15.4
First Southern State Bank	Stevenson	AL	**B+**	B+	B+	403.9	8.99	4.5	6.5	21.4	32.5	**8.6**	10.1	17.6
▲ First Southwest Bank	Alamosa	CO	**B-**	C+	B-	331.7	9.87	10.0	1.1	8.4	12.9	**6.8**	8.8	15.1

Asset Quality Index	Adjusted Non-Performing Loans as a % of Total Loans	Adjusted Non-Performing Loans as a % of Capital	Net Charge-Offs Avg Loans	Profitability Index	Net Income ($Mil)	Return on Assets (R.O.A.)	Return on Equity (R.O.E.)	Net Interest Spread	Overhead Efficiency Ratio	Liquidity Index	Liquidity Ratio	Hot Money Ratio	Stability Index
7.7	0.62	na	0.10	**6.5**	11.3	1.22	12.75	4.01	61.5	**6.4**	37.7	3.3	**8.0**
4.0	1.33	na	0.08	**5.5**	3.4	1.25	14.12	4.29	69.0	**1.1**	12.8	22.8	**6.6**
5.3	0.84	na	0.25	**3.6**	3.2	0.61	6.81	3.55	73.7	**0.7**	17.0	58.8	**5.2**
7.8	1.03	na	-0.13	**5.5**	3.2	1.31	14.46	3.03	68.7	**2.5**	25.7	18.0	**6.3**
6.2	0.96	na	-0.02	**5.5**	6.1	1.14	10.04	3.28	57.2	**1.9**	31.9	28.2	**8.3**
7.6	0.87	na	0.00	**6.3**	1.4	1.26	11.44	5.19	65.8	**5.3**	35.9	6.2	**7.3**
7.1	0.00	na	0.05	**4.4**	1.0	0.87	9.49	4.37	75.3	**4.5**	21.1	6.2	**4.9**
9.3	0.47	na	0.00	**9.7**	5.4	1.76	6.43	4.76	54.8	**4.8**	32.2	8.1	**9.2**
7.4	0.00	na	0.00	**6.7**	1.9	1.44	9.98	3.80	53.5	**1.9**	12.6	19.4	**8.3**
8.1	0.29	na	0.00	**5.5**	1.4	0.85	9.33	3.92	73.0	**1.7**	17.3	21.8	**6.9**
6.8	0.41	1.3	0.21	**8.0**	27.3	1.87	12.96	3.72	59.5	**2.9**	25.3	2.8	**10.0**
8.9	2.65	na	0.00	**2.3**	0.0	0.15	0.55	2.93	83.9	**6.4**	98.2	11.6	**6.3**
5.3	1.01	na	0.22	**6.4**	1.9	1.38	12.42	4.00	53.3	**0.9**	24.6	41.7	**7.1**
4.6	0.87	na	0.08	**4.9**	4.5	0.98	9.21	4.10	75.3	**1.3**	10.0	24.7	**6.1**
8.7	0.18	1.5	0.01	**4.3**	684.0	0.89	10.01	2.91	64.4	**3.1**	17.0	10.9	**7.9**
6.9	0.20	na	0.00	**4.1**	1.1	0.76	6.90	3.85	69.6	**1.6**	13.8	15.2	**9.5**
3.6	1.15	na	0.12	**4.2**	1.7	0.75	8.60	3.84	68.4	**1.0**	10.0	28.4	**4.7**
5.2	1.13	na	0.14	**4.8**	2.3	0.93	9.85	3.60	69.4	**4.5**	25.7	6.7	**5.3**
9.2	0.00	na	0.00	**2.2**	0.0	0.08	0.37	2.68	91.9	**2.0**	42.7	52.8	**7.1**
2.9	1.44	17.6	0.02	**0.0**	-0.2	-2.62	-23.86	4.26	161.7	**1.1**	22.8	31.8	**3.9**
10.0	0.21	na	0.00	**1.6**	0.0	0.00	-0.01	2.44	100.8	**4.2**	92.3	25.0	**5.9**
6.3	1.34	na	0.11	**7.7**	13.4	1.62	15.46	3.97	73.5	**2.1**	19.2	7.4	**9.0**
5.8	1.17	3.8	4.30	**10.0**	13.5	2.18	14.24	9.03	45.1	**3.4**	15.3	11.8	**8.8**
9.9	0.17	na	0.08	**3.2**	2.3	0.46	2.84	2.52	75.1	**3.5**	54.6	23.7	**8.3**
9.0	0.33	na	0.01	**1.7**	0.4	0.15	1.62	3.06	96.8	**3.4**	14.0	11.7	**5.9**
5.6	0.83	2.7	0.00	**4.3**	1.0	0.83	7.14	3.44	66.6	**0.8**	19.0	48.7	**4.6**
5.1	0.45	na	0.29	**3.4**	1.3	0.55	5.58	3.40	73.3	**1.1**	27.0	37.5	**4.7**
9.0	0.18	0.4	0.09	**8.8**	76.7	1.90	9.42	3.98	46.0	**4.8**	26.7	8.6	**10.0**
5.9	0.00	na	0.00	**6.9**	0.8	1.60	8.95	3.97	57.3	**2.8**	30.6	17.8	**8.3**
1.2	2.15	15.9	0.70	**3.7**	0.6	0.91	8.79	3.79	75.2	**2.0**	14.0	19.0	**5.1**
7.4	0.00	0.0	-0.01	**4.2**	0.5	0.96	10.97	4.19	76.7	**1.6**	16.7	23.9	**5.1**
6.4	0.60	na	-0.03	**4.5**	0.6	1.05	12.59	3.79	72.2	**3.3**	33.3	16.1	**4.6**
8.3	0.00	na	0.22	**4.6**	0.2	0.92	11.61	4.22	68.2	**3.8**	19.8	10.4	**3.8**
7.1	1.62	na	0.07	**6.8**	6.1	1.41	12.44	4.46	64.4	**4.1**	17.1	8.5	**8.4**
0.7	3.24	na	0.35	**8.5**	1.8	2.11	21.13	4.38	42.4	**0.5**	7.4	48.5	**6.7**
3.2	4.43	na	0.08	**3.8**	3.0	0.82	7.40	3.43	77.7	**4.4**	30.0	8.5	**6.1**
7.7	0.27	na	0.00	**7.7**	0.9	1.74	10.84	4.16	55.7	**5.2**	30.1	4.0	**8.5**
6.6	0.00	na	0.00	**6.5**	0.8	1.67	12.37	3.79	54.2	**5.6**	28.8	1.1	**7.9**
3.5	1.73	na	0.13	**3.7**	0.2	0.58	6.20	4.98	89.6	**0.6**	6.0	43.1	**4.6**
8.4	0.00	na	0.00	**9.9**	0.8	2.79	26.89	4.66	44.3	**4.2**	22.1	8.0	**7.0**
5.7	1.35	na	0.00	**5.4**	0.4	1.04	6.95	5.03	63.9	**3.3**	29.9	15.0	**6.8**
6.6	0.00	0.0	0.00	**9.9**	4.6	2.73	12.93	4.50	39.4	**5.6**	38.1	5.3	**9.5**
4.6	0.96	na	0.39	**9.4**	1.0	2.25	18.96	4.63	51.2	**4.6**	28.2	7.7	**8.5**
8.9	0.03	na	0.00	**7.4**	0.4	1.82	15.19	3.55	52.7	**5.2**	50.5	10.8	**8.2**
5.9	0.14	na	1.33	**5.1**	1.4	1.03	7.27	4.27	60.4	**4.5**	24.7	6.4	**9.0**
3.7	1.10	na	0.15	**6.5**	1.1	1.45	13.05	3.76	58.3	**0.8**	14.5	29.1	**7.6**
8.9	0.08	na	0.06	**5.0**	1.1	1.20	16.19	3.58	70.5	**5.9**	54.8	8.8	**4.7**
5.3	1.86	na	0.45	**4.1**	2.4	0.98	11.74	2.54	64.8	**6.8**	60.0	4.8	**4.0**
4.1	0.76	na	0.73	**6.1**	2.3	1.10	12.36	4.54	59.7	**1.1**	16.6	30.4	**5.1**
6.4	0.85	na	0.06	**4.3**	1.9	0.77	7.95	4.31	81.0	**0.6**	7.6	19.4	**5.7**
5.8	1.32	na	0.00	**4.1**	1.7	0.74	4.81	3.54	70.6	**1.3**	15.6	27.6	**7.7**
4.3	2.07	na	-0.01	**2.0**	0.1	0.08	0.65	3.59	98.0	**4.1**	20.7	7.0	**5.9**
2.2	1.48	na	0.67	**4.0**	0.6	0.84	9.35	4.05	73.2	**1.2**	8.2	18.9	**6.8**
8.0	0.34	na	-0.03	**5.1**	2.0	1.09	11.07	3.87	63.5	**2.3**	16.8	17.6	**5.4**
4.4	2.75	na	0.98	**0.3**	-0.4	-0.41	-2.95	4.75	99.3	**4.1**	17.9	8.4	**0.3**
5.3	1.37	6.5	0.11	**6.9**	6.8	1.31	9.19	3.89	54.9	**2.9**	20.7	15.2	**8.8**
8.3	0.25	na	0.16	**5.2**	1.8	1.24	10.82	4.52	73.7	**2.9**	16.3	14.7	**6.7**
5.3	1.39	na	0.04	**6.5**	8.4	1.30	11.90	4.56	66.0	**4.1**	20.3	8.7	**7.5**
7.9	0.41	1.7	0.10	**6.7**	4.1	1.37	13.93	4.03	54.9	**2.3**	29.0	20.0	**6.4**
5.4	1.51	na	0.12	**4.6**	2.2	0.93	9.11	4.23	74.2	**3.2**	23.1	13.7	**6.0**

Name	City	State	Rating	2018 Rating	2017 Rating	Total Assets ($Mil)	One Year Asset Growth	Asset Mix (As a % of Total Assets) Comm-ercial Loans	Cons-umer Loans	Mort-gage Loans	Secur-ities	Capital-ization Index	Lever-age Ratio	Risk-Based Capital Ratio
▲ First State B&T Co. of Larned	Larned	KS	**A-**	A-	A	154.3	1.80	9.1	0.8	1.9	25.9	**10.0**	13.4	20.9
First State Bank	Crossett	AR	**B-**	B-	B-	33.0	-4.18	15.0	12.6	9.5	16.9	**10.0**	17.1	26.8
First State Bank	Lonoke	AR	**C**	C	D+	251.4	-6.77	1.7	0.5	12.8	37.2	**8.8**	10.2	18.1
First State Bank	Russellville	AR	**A-**	A-	A-	296.7	15.11	11.8	0.9	17.2	9.3	**10.0**	11.3	15.4
▲ First State Bank	Wrens	GA	**B**	B-	B-	155.2	10.75	11.8	2.9	30.5	11.6	**6.7**	8.7	13.2
First State Bank	Belmond	IA	**B**	B	B	95.1	-0.95	11.0	3.2	10.2	40.3	**10.0**	12.2	24.9
First State Bank	Britt	IA	**A**	A	A	108.0	-1.91	3.6	1.2	10.1	34.1	**10.0**	13.9	24.7
▲ First State Bank	Ida Grove	IA	**B**	B	A-	170.2	4.96	9.9	4.0	8.9	16.5	**8.9**	11.4	14.0
▲ First State Bank	Lynnville	IA	**B+**	B	A-	191.4	7.01	7.8	2.2	12.4	10.7	**10.0**	13.3	16.7
First State Bank	Nashua	IA	**B+**	B+	B+	52.9	5.08	8.7	2.9	23.1	8.0	**10.0**	11.5	17.5
▲ First State Bank	Stuart	IA	**B-**	B-	C+	100.3	-1.06	8.9	2.4	8.4	29.7	**10.0**	11.2	20.7
First State Bank	Sumner	IA	**C**	C	B-	103.9	-2.33	8.1	3.0	12.7	29.6	**10.0**	12.2	20.1
First State Bank	Webster City	IA	**A-**	A-	A-	477.9	9.87	9.4	0.6	8.4	9.3	**10.0**	13.8	16.4
First State Bank	Mendota	IL	**B-**	B-	C+	1136.7	6.08	8.3	0.9	24.5	8.6	**8.1**	9.8	13.4
▲ First State Bank	Monticello	IL	**B-**	C+	B-	271.9	3.72	5.2	1.4	9.2	28.0	**6.1**	8.1	13.9
First State Bank	Ness City	KS	**B+**	B+	B+	59.5	3.05	6.1	2.4	0.0	49.5	**10.0**	18.5	29.9
First State Bank	Norton	KS	**B-**	B-	B	444.5	1.93	9.2	2.4	1.9	38.0	**9.3**	10.5	16.0
First State Bank	Irvington	KY	**B+**	A-	A-	223.3	12.14	2.0	4.4	31.1	17.7	**9.6**	11.2	14.7
First State Bank	Saint Clair Shores	MI	**B**	B	B	798.8	9.75	9.0	0.5	15.5	19.4	**8.8**	10.2	14.5
First State Bank	Holly Springs	MS	**C**	C+	C+	118.5	-1.72	9.1	1.8	15.7	31.7	**10.0**	11.2	18.9
First State Bank	Waynesboro	MS	**B+**	B+	A-	791.5	-3.44	4.4	2.3	23.3	22.9	**10.0**	12.7	19.7
First State Bank	Buxton	ND	**B**	B+	B+	203.3	8.35	20.4	0.7	12.3	3.8	**6.9**	10.6	12.4
First State Bank	Farnam	NE	**A-**	B+	A-	146.8	0.08	7.9	2.5	4.4	20.9	**9.3**	12.2	14.4
▲ First State Bank	Gothenburg	NE	**C**	C	B-	539.4	6.59	6.8	0.8	2.4	18.2	**8.2**	11.4	13.5
▲ First State Bank	Hordville	NE	**B-**	C+	B-	40.0	-7.79	11.1	0.8	4.9	0.6	**10.0**	12.4	15.7
First State Bank	Loomis	NE	**C+**	C+	B	146.8	6.09	7.0	3.0	5.3	9.5	**8.4**	11.5	13.6
First State Bank	Randolph	NE	**B+**	B+	B+	65.4	4.96	1.5	1.4	2.3	2.8	**10.0**	13.3	17.6
▲ First State Bank	Scottsbluff	NE	**A-**	A-	A-	312.2	34.56	9.6	1.4	8.5	16.8	**7.5**	9.6	12.9
First State Bank	Socorro	NM	**B**	B	B	157.4	6.06	0.4	0.6	3.2	82.7	**8.8**	10.2	47.0
▲ First State Bank	Winchester	OH	**B**	B-	B	498.8	6.15	2.2	10.2	19.5	24.4	**8.6**	10.1	15.5
First State Bank	Anadarko	OK	**A-**	A-	A-	91.9	0.06	0.9	2.8	2.8	56.3	**10.0**	16.6	34.9
▲ First State Bank	Boise City	OK	**C+**	C	C+	83.0	2.28	6.6	6.0	1.5	12.4	**6.4**	10.2	12.0
▲ First State Bank	Elmore City	OK	**C+**	C-	C-	14.4	4.94	20.6	2.6	38.8	0.0	**10.0**	14.0	24.3
First State Bank	Noble	OK	**C+**	C+	C+	44.0	-5.96	2.3	5.3	19.3	35.3	**10.0**	11.0	31.6
▲ First State Bank	Oklahoma City	OK	**C+**	C	C	345.7	10.66	16.1	0.9	14.6	2.7	**5.5**	9.2	11.4
First State Bank	Tahlequah	OK	**C**	C+	C-	63.1	-1.96	11.4	2.3	12.8	21.3	**10.0**	12.4	18.3
▲ First State Bank	Valliant	OK	**C-**	D	C-	69.9	4.84	6.7	4.4	27.2	10.8	**6.9**	8.9	13.0
First State Bank	Watonga	OK	**B+**	B+	B+	74.8	-11.10	17.9	3.2	2.7	35.4	**9.2**	10.5	17.7
First State Bank	Abernathy	TX	**C+**	C+	C+	45.9	15.29	6.1	8.6	0.2	13.2	**6.9**	8.9	14.3
▲ First State Bank	Abilene	TX	**C**	D+	D	36.3	-13.10	7.2	1.4	3.5	23.4	**6.3**	8.3	24.5
▲ First State Bank	Athens	TX	**A-**	A-	A-	460.3	-1.35	5.3	3.3	30.7	23.2	**10.0**	11.7	21.1
First State Bank	Chico	TX	**C+**	C+	C-	185.0	4.42	4.5	2.0	14.1	32.3	**10.0**	11.9	20.8
First State Bank	Clute	TX	**C+**	B	B-	208.5	8.00	12.4	7.7	14.9	22.9	**7.4**	9.3	15.1
First State Bank	Columbus	TX	**B-**	B-	B-	148.1	3.99	1.4	3.7	4.1	51.1	**10.0**	14.5	32.4
First State Bank	Gainesville	TX	**B+**	B+	B+	1136.9	3.99	7.9	1.4	11.3	32.8	**7.7**	9.5	14.4
First State Bank	Graham	TX	**B+**	B+	A-	148.8	-1.32	16.0	2.0	12.5	15.1	**7.5**	9.3	16.9
▲ First State Bank	Junction	TX	**C+**	C-	C+	49.7	3.82	5.0	3.2	13.2	23.4	**8.6**	10.1	16.9
▲ First State Bank	Louise	TX	**A-**	B+	B+	499.7	7.16	10.1	0.9	9.4	17.4	**6.7**	9.3	12.3
First State Bank	Rice	TX	**B-**	B-	C	149.6	1.49	13.7	3.1	10.1	23.6	**10.0**	12.8	19.9
First State Bank	Shallowater	TX	**B-**	B+	A-	95.7	-10.04	8.3	1.5	3.6	12.3	**10.0**	17.0	24.8
▲ First State Bank	Spearman	TX	**B**	B-	B-	144.8	3.43	8.1	0.8	6.9	8.7	**7.9**	9.6	15.2
First State Bank	Stratford	TX	**A-**	A-	A-	250.2	6.84	8.0	1.5	5.5	28.7	**10.0**	11.7	15.0
First State Bank	New London	WI	**B-**	B-	B-	303.5	-0.15	4.1	4.5	12.0	34.5	**8.4**	9.9	16.1
First State Bank	Barboursville	WV	**E-**	E-	E-	157.7	-2.11	10.3	2.0	26.3	6.5	**0.0**	2.3	4.2
▲ First State Bank & Trust Co.	Fremont	NE	**B+**	B-	B-	254.8	5.76	20.6	2.1	21.0	8.6	**8.1**	9.7	13.5
First State Bank and Trust	Tonganoxie	KS	**C+**	C+	C+	299.6	6.51	5.3	2.4	16.4	19.5	**6.2**	8.2	12.6
▲ First State Bank and Trust	Bayport	MN	**B**	B-	B-	265.2	9.26	5.0	5.4	33.3	18.8	**6.9**	8.9	15.6
First State Bank and Trust Co.	Carthage	TX	**A-**	A-	A	505.2	2.92	2.1	5.1	18.4	57.0	**10.0**	16.1	37.3
First State Bank and Trust Co., Inc.	Caruthersville	MO	**A-**	A-	A-	383.6	4.40	7.5	3.6	15.7	16.7	**10.0**	12.7	16.4
First State Bank in Temple	Temple	OK	**B-**	C+	C+	25.0	6.13	4.5	3.9	3.1	33.4	**10.0**	20.4	33.2

Asset Quality Index	Adjusted Non-Performing Loans as a % of Total Loans	Adjusted Non-Performing Loans as a % of Capital	Net Charge-Offs Avg Loans	Profitability Index	Net Income ($Mil)	Return on Assets (R.O.A.)	Return on Equity (R.O.E.)	Net Interest Spread	Overhead Efficiency Ratio	Liquidity Index	Liquidity Ratio	Hot Money Ratio	Stability Index
6.6	1.54	na	0.23	5.8	1.6	1.43	10.76	3.49	59.0	3.2	28.2	11.4	8.9
6.1	1.81	na	0.08	5.6	0.3	1.24	7.38	5.33	74.4	1.7	25.9	25.1	6.2
9.0	0.00	na	0.00	3.0	1.9	0.96	9.49	2.82	77.5	1.6	30.3	31.1	4.2
8.6	0.13	na	0.01	7.1	2.9	1.32	12.02	3.94	58.0	1.9	19.2	19.1	7.5
6.1	0.72	na	0.04	7.6	1.6	1.44	17.27	5.26	62.3	1.2	15.5	28.0	5.6
9.0	0.20	na	0.10	4.6	0.8	1.03	8.60	2.68	57.2	4.2	57.1	16.7	6.8
9.0	0.00	0.0	0.00	7.4	1.2	1.44	10.63	2.99	40.5	3.7	42.5	17.2	8.8
7.4	0.58	na	0.03	6.7	2.0	1.60	14.13	3.68	53.2	1.0	25.1	36.5	7.8
5.9	0.58	na	0.50	8.5	2.6	1.89	13.79	4.38	52.2	1.7	13.4	16.0	9.1
8.5	0.00	0.0	-0.01	7.2	0.6	1.39	12.24	3.40	49.4	1.2	25.3	32.8	7.0
8.7	0.00	na	-0.07	3.3	0.4	0.56	5.24	3.17	77.1	5.2	41.1	8.8	6.6
6.0	1.54	5.8	1.45	2.0	0.2	0.21	1.61	3.30	70.8	4.7	45.2	12.8	5.4
8.2	0.01	na	0.00	5.9	3.9	1.13	8.06	3.31	67.1	1.4	16.9	24.1	8.5
6.3	0.64	na	0.02	4.5	7.8	0.93	9.11	3.29	69.6	1.0	8.6	25.6	7.9
5.0	1.99	na	-0.01	6.0	2.9	1.42	16.44	3.66	66.6	2.2	21.1	18.7	6.0
7.5	2.07	na	0.33	5.5	0.6	1.33	7.32	3.61	59.4	4.3	39.0	12.9	8.0
4.0	1.50	8.7	0.68	5.8	4.3	1.31	11.39	3.62	57.5	0.8	16.8	27.7	7.6
6.8	0.17	5.7	0.02	5.9	1.9	1.20	10.88	4.10	65.9	2.7	15.5	5.5	7.4
5.3	1.07	6.0	-0.07	5.0	5.9	1.03	9.93	3.82	68.9	3.1	25.1	14.8	7.5
5.7	1.66	na	0.02	2.3	0.6	0.60	5.56	3.34	93.1	2.3	11.9	17.1	6.5
6.5	0.96	na	0.15	4.8	5.8	0.95	7.23	3.37	63.3	1.4	10.9	24.4	8.5
8.1	0.00	0.0	0.01	6.2	2.1	1.46	13.53	3.83	60.3	0.9	2.9	23.3	8.4
4.0	1.75	na	-0.01	6.6	1.7	1.56	12.31	3.17	59.9	0.8	17.8	35.1	9.1
3.0	3.08	na	-0.05	7.9	6.5	1.69	13.83	3.66	48.9	1.5	12.3	17.2	8.4
7.0	0.00	na	0.01	3.9	0.2	0.60	4.97	3.57	67.5	3.6	17.0	11.0	6.1
6.2	0.03	na	0.00	8.4	1.7	1.63	12.13	4.38	53.4	0.6	6.5	25.8	8.6
7.1	0.23	na	0.00	7.6	0.9	1.77	13.43	3.85	51.0	0.9	19.9	26.9	7.0
8.5	0.05	na	-0.30	10.0	4.5	2.25	22.52	4.85	57.8	2.2	33.7	25.1	8.3
10.0	2.66	na	0.59	4.0	0.9	0.81	7.82	3.42	69.2	6.7	60.6	5.2	6.4
5.1	0.93	na	0.06	5.5	4.7	1.29	12.48	3.71	67.1	2.6	17.3	13.8	6.3
6.2	8.28	na	-0.11	6.8	1.3	1.73	12.00	3.38	51.7	5.0	37.1	8.6	7.7
4.4	0.45	na	-0.01	8.4	1.2	1.99	23.61	4.34	52.7	0.5	4.3	48.3	6.2
6.7	0.57	na	0.00	7.1	0.4	3.20	24.66	3.48	88.8	5.1	26.7	2.5	5.4
5.8	3.43	na	0.08	3.3	0.2	0.50	4.69	4.20	87.3	5.4	32.6	3.9	4.7
7.1	0.03	na	0.04	4.7	2.2	0.86	9.13	3.61	70.8	0.6	9.0	44.0	5.6
5.3	4.28	na	0.06	1.8	0.1	0.21	1.59	3.55	92.8	2.7	39.5	21.3	6.4
4.3	1.53	na	-0.08	3.7	0.4	0.76	9.29	4.66	83.4	1.0	12.8	31.4	5.2
4.9	0.77	na	0.37	9.0	1.3	2.18	21.91	4.62	51.7	4.8	43.3	11.7	7.4
4.7	1.41	na	0.50	5.9	0.5	1.42	13.80	6.14	73.7	1.4	15.0	26.0	4.3
8.6	0.00	na	0.00	4.2	0.2	0.83	9.07	3.61	70.7	5.5	56.1	10.1	3.4
7.0	1.06	na	0.35	5.6	3.8	1.06	9.78	3.83	60.8	3.6	16.4	10.9	7.5
6.0	1.72	na	-0.08	2.9	0.9	0.69	6.08	3.05	91.1	2.1	31.7	25.8	5.8
5.6	1.05	na	0.08	7.3	2.6	1.77	18.93	4.39	61.0	4.6	32.6	9.2	6.0
9.5	0.02	na	0.17	3.1	0.8	0.69	5.03	2.47	71.8	3.0	60.9	37.4	7.1
7.9	0.21	1.3	0.02	5.1	9.7	1.16	12.55	3.99	74.2	5.4	29.1	6.8	8.5
8.8	0.03	na	0.04	6.6	1.8	1.59	16.72	3.88	64.4	3.1	42.0	19.9	7.2
6.3	0.99	na	0.04	5.9	0.5	1.42	14.79	4.53	67.2	4.6	30.1	8.5	5.4
8.3	0.13	na	0.03	9.7	8.4	2.30	24.78	5.32	56.5	4.3	23.9	7.6	7.5
6.9	0.49	na	0.25	3.5	0.7	0.61	4.63	4.32	84.2	3.3	21.7	13.1	7.3
2.8	3.78	12.5	0.21	9.9	1.9	2.42	13.53	5.19	53.4	1.8	13.4	19.7	9.0
8.5	0.13	na	0.00	6.3	1.7	1.57	19.45	3.96	61.3	1.4	24.0	28.1	5.0
8.5	0.00	na	0.00	7.2	3.1	1.71	14.69	3.63	56.9	3.2	33.8	17.1	8.4
4.7	3.73	na	-0.03	4.1	1.9	0.83	6.40	3.25	68.8	4.2	37.2	9.3	6.9
0.0	20.62	na	0.40	0.0	-2.2	-1.90	-74.19	3.22	147.0	1.0	18.3	29.7	0.3
6.6	0.22	na	0.01	8.1	3.7	1.97	20.81	4.55	58.5	3.5	16.0	11.5	7.0
6.8	0.90	4.4	0.02	4.0	1.6	0.72	8.40	4.00	81.6	4.0	12.8	8.5	5.3
8.6	0.07	na	0.03	5.5	2.6	1.33	14.71	3.91	74.0	4.1	23.7	9.1	6.0
8.6	1.46	na	0.05	5.5	4.2	1.12	7.03	2.93	56.1	1.9	36.7	33.7	9.1
8.3	0.16	na	0.10	6.9	4.6	1.66	13.05	4.25	64.7	1.6	10.2	22.3	8.4
8.2	0.18	na	0.07	6.2	0.3	1.69	8.56	4.43	60.9	1.6	23.1	23.9	6.4

Name	City	State	Rating	2018 Rating	2017 Rating	Total Assets ($Mil)	One Year Asset Growth	Asset Mix (As a % of Total Assets) Comm-ercial Loans	Cons-umer Loans	Mort-gage Loans	Secur-ities	Capital-ization Index	Lever-age Ratio	Risk-Based Capital Ratio
▲ First State Bank Minnesota	Le Roy	MN	**B**	B-	B-	66.9	-2.64	7.7	2.8	5.4	7.3	**10.0**	11.7	17.2
First State Bank Nebraska	Lincoln	NE	**B-**	B-	B	594.0	9.39	10.4	1.3	13.3	10.6	**6.1**	8.5	11.8
▲ First State Bank of Ashby	Ashby	MN	**B-**	B-	C	36.3	0.72	9.2	6.2	20.8	6.4	**5.5**	7.6	11.4
First State Bank of Bedias	Bedias	TX	**A**	A	A	160.6	3.46	11.3	4.7	10.4	22.7	**10.0**	16.6	27.7
First State Bank of Beecher City	Beecher City	IL	**B+**	B	B	72.7	4.40	7.9	11.8	20.7	6.9	**10.0**	18.5	25.1
First State Bank of Ben Wheeler, Texas	Ben Wheeler	TX	**A-**	A-	A	151.5	3.90	6.4	4.1	21.1	40.4	**10.0**	13.7	25.1
▲ First State Bank of Bigfork	Bigfork	MN	**D+**	D	D	80.6	4.32	9.4	11.6	36.5	1.5	**10.0**	11.1	15.8
▲ First State Bank of Blakely	Blakely	GA	**B+**	B+	A	520.7	1.53	6.7	2.4	14.3	11.5	**10.0**	14.4	20.6
First State Bank of Bloomington	Bloomington	IL	**C**	C+	B-	121.5	1.91	6.6	2.1	26.6	13.4	**7.4**	9.3	15.2
▲ First State Bank of Brownsboro	Brownsboro	TX	**B-**	C+	B	102.2	1.87	6.6	9.0	20.4	36.8	**9.7**	10.8	18.7
First State Bank of Burnet	Burnet	TX	**A-**	A-	B+	246.2	0.12	4.2	1.6	8.1	60.9	**10.0**	13.6	29.2
First State Bank of Campbell Hill	Campbell Hill	IL	**B+**	B	B-	115.8	1.22	6.3	3.6	29.0	16.8	**10.0**	11.5	20.5
First State Bank of Cando	Cando	ND	**C+**	C+	C+	60.8	4.08	5.1	5.9	4.5	32.2	**7.8**	9.5	15.6
First State Bank of Claremont	Groton	SD	**B-**	B-	C+	57.7	3.13	6.8	1.2	0.0	20.1	**10.0**	12.4	21.9
▲ First State Bank of Colfax	Colfax	IA	**B+**	B+	A	63.5	-2.50	3.2	0.8	10.6	49.5	**10.0**	24.4	50.2
First State Bank of Decatur	Decatur	MI	**B**	B	B	52.2	-3.29	14.2	3.9	39.8	31.4	**10.0**	21.2	45.9
▲ First State Bank of DeKalb County	Fort Payne	AL	**C+**	C+	B	193.3	7.10	7.6	6.3	19.6	21.9	**9.9**	11.2	14.9
First State Bank of DeQueen	De Queen	AR	**B+**	B+	B+	265.4	10.31	9.1	3.9	14.6	16.5	**8.8**	10.2	14.4
First State Bank of Dongola	Dongola	IL	**C**	C	C-	25.1	-1.29	3.6	11.9	30.4	4.3	**10.0**	11.6	20.9
First State Bank of Forrest	Forrest	IL	**C-**	C-	C	229.3	9.84	14.2	5.2	32.2	9.3	**6.1**	8.1	12.8
▲ First State Bank of Forsyth	Forsyth	MT	**B**	B-	B	118.8	-3.66	4.6	4.3	9.8	38.0	**10.0**	12.2	19.7
First State Bank of Fountain	Fountain	MN	**D**	D+	D+	32.4	-4.01	4.8	1.5	10.2	36.6	**8.7**	10.2	17.4
First State Bank of Golva	Golva	ND	**B+**	B+	B+	77.5	0.45	4.7	2.8	4.0	39.7	**8.2**	9.8	15.4
First State Bank of Grove City	Grove City	MN	**B-**	B	B-	31.2	31.23	9.7	2.8	20.9	0.8	**10.0**	11.8	23.0
▲ First State Bank of Harvey	Harvey	ND	**B**	B-	B-	80.9	-1.48	3.0	2.7	5.7	51.7	**10.0**	11.1	21.9
▲ First State Bank of Healy	Healy	KS	**C+**	C	C-	77.1	3.87	11.8	1.0	1.3	32.3	**10.0**	20.6	28.3
▲ First State Bank of Kiester	Kiester	MN	**D+**	D	C-	20.5	7.51	13.7	2.6	7.8	1.3	**9.6**	10.8	19.0
▲ First State Bank of Le Center	Le Center	MN	**B+**	B	B+	87.2	2.15	12.3	7.1	20.2	13.9	**10.0**	11.0	16.9
First State Bank of Livingston	Livingston	TX	**B**	B	B	335.5	1.13	2.0	3.1	4.5	44.7	**10.0**	15.6	38.4
First State Bank of Malta	Malta	MT	**D**	D+	B-	135.6	-4.81	3.9	1.8	0.0	25.0	**10.0**	16.7	19.5
▲ First State Bank of Middlebury	Middlebury	IN	**B**	B-	B	594.2	9.36	14.3	1.9	22.9	17.6	**10.0**	11.2	16.4
First State Bank of Mobeetie	Mobeetie	TX	**B**	B	B	76.7	-3.58	5.2	2.9	0.3	5.8	**10.0**	13.5	82.1
First State Bank of Newcastle	Newcastle	WY	**B**	B	B	148.9	9.77	5.8	2.5	7.8	55.5	**10.0**	13.7	39.6
First State Bank of Odem	Odem	TX	**A-**	A-	A-	145.7	1.27	11.0	1.8	5.4	25.0	**10.0**	12.5	22.2
First State Bank of Olmsted	Olmsted	IL	**B-**	B-	B-	50.9	2.93	13.0	4.0	31.4	19.8	**10.0**	13.4	21.8
▲ First State Bank of Paint Rock	Paint Rock	TX	**B+**	B	B	105.2	4.12	6.9	4.1	4.0	34.0	**10.0**	12.9	23.0
First State Bank of Porter	Porter	IN	**B+**	A-	A-	143.4	2.20	1.1	0.3	23.5	32.9	**10.0**	16.3	27.6
▲ First State Bank of Purdy	Monett	MO	**C+**	C	C+	152.8	-7.23	15.3	1.1	10.8	6.9	**6.7**	8.7	13.3
▼ First State Bank of Randolph County	Cuthbert	GA	**D+**	C-	C+	77.4	2.99	7.7	3.6	4.8	44.5	**8.6**	10.1	17.8
First State Bank of Ransom	Ransom	KS	**B**	B	B+	41.0	-3.31	8.5	1.4	1.1	48.8	**10.0**	23.9	45.3
First State Bank of Red Wing	Red Wing	MN	**D+**	D+	D+	75.9	-2.28	3.6	4.3	11.6	43.4	**7.1**	9.1	27.5
▲ First State Bank of Roscoe	Roscoe	SD	**A-**	B+	A-	109.8	4.65	7.4	0.6	0.3	3.9	**10.0**	12.2	15.8
First State Bank of Rosemount	Rosemount	MN	**D-**	D-	D-	72.3	3.47	5.3	7.9	16.6	23.2	**4.8**	6.8	12.4
First State Bank of San Diego	San Diego	TX	**C+**	C+	C+	60.5	2.74	13.3	4.7	4.1	40.1	**7.7**	9.4	24.0
▲ First State Bank of Sauk Centre	Sauk Centre	MN	**A-**	B+	B+	111.8	2.10	11.8	4.7	18.5	12.9	**10.0**	12.7	18.8
First State Bank of Shelby	Shelby	MT	**A**	A	A	127.9	-0.84	4.0	0.6	0.0	71.0	**10.0**	23.2	23.2
First State Bank of St. Charles, Missouri	Saint Charles	MO	**A-**	A-	A-	391.5	6.99	8.9	0.1	49.4	12.1	**10.0**	13.2	17.0
First State Bank of St. Peter	Saint Peter	IL	**B+**	B+	A-	28.6	4.27	0.8	4.8	3.8	58.5	**10.0**	17.3	39.1
First State Bank of Swanville	Swanville	MN	**C+**	C+	D+	24.9	-2.53	14.5	3.3	16.0	1.9	**10.0**	15.7	24.2
First State Bank of Texas	Orange	TX	**B-**	B-	C-	169.8	6.17	16.5	11.3	14.1	7.5	**10.0**	11.6	15.4
▲ First State Bank of the Florida Keys	Key West	FL	**B**	B-	B	968.1	5.05	5.3	0.8	18.7	29.2	**6.9**	8.9	16.3
First State Bank of the South, Inc.	Sulligent	AL	**B+**	B+	B+	103.4	0.05	6.9	7.9	13.2	39.3	**10.0**	16.0	25.9
First State Bank of the Southeast, Inc.	Middlesboro	KY	**C+**	B-	C+	346.8	-0.77	8.3	3.1	27.9	9.5	**6.9**	8.9	12.9
First State Bank of Uvalde	Uvalde	TX	**B+**	B	B	1784.8	7.79	2.2	0.6	4.7	49.9	**7.2**	9.2	30.0
▲ First State Bank of Van Orin	Van Orin	IL	**C**	C-	C-	40.5	-1.25	3.3	1.5	2.2	37.2	**8.3**	9.9	24.8
First State Bank of Warren	Warren	AR	**B-**	C+	C	107.2	-2.52	11.7	2.3	6.0	51.1	**10.0**	11.4	21.4
▲ First State Bank of Wyoming	Wyoming	MN	**A-**	B+	B+	181.6	-0.84	4.1	1.7	13.8	51.3	**10.0**	17.7	40.4
First State Bank Shannon-Polo	Shannon	IL	**C+**	C+	B	165.2	3.99	8.1	2.9	9.3	29.5	**6.1**	9.3	11.8
First State Bank Southwest	Worthington	MN	**A-**	A-	A	262.2	4.48	9.6	3.2	3.5	32.8	**10.0**	11.6	19.4
▲ First State Bank, Pond Creek, Oklahoma	Pond Creek	OK	**B**	B-	C	48.0	-4.47	17.3	4.0	17.3	17.5	**10.0**	11.9	20.2

Asset Quality Index	Adjusted Non-Performing Loans as a % of Total Loans	Adjusted Non-Performing Loans as a % of Capital	Net Charge-Offs Avg Loans	Profitability Index	Net Income ($Mil)	Return on Assets (R.O.A.)	Return on Equity (R.O.E.)	Net Interest Spread	Overhead Efficiency Ratio	Liquidity Index	Liquidity Ratio	Hot Money Ratio	Stability Index
4.5	3.88	na	-0.02	6.2	0.7	1.44	12.56	3.93	62.4	5.3	22.0	1.2	7.4
6.6	0.43	na	0.04	5.3	6.1	1.39	13.87	3.41	58.2	1.6	11.2	22.2	7.4
2.2	0.16	na	0.01	4.8	0.3	1.16	9.14	4.43	66.8	3.9	29.6	12.0	5.9
7.3	0.31	4.9	0.05	8.6	2.5	2.14	13.39	4.25	47.9	2.5	41.1	28.0	9.7
5.3	1.52	5.8	0.25	9.6	1.3	2.28	12.78	4.40	50.0	3.1	18.2	13.9	9.0
8.5	0.37	na	0.02	6.6	1.8	1.62	11.93	3.45	59.2	1.5	28.8	31.1	9.2
1.2	4.35	33.1	0.01	5.3	0.7	1.11	10.33	4.39	66.1	1.6	13.3	18.6	6.3
5.4	2.38	na	0.36	7.3	5.2	1.38	9.35	4.35	54.6	0.7	11.3	26.6	9.4
4.2	0.91	na	0.02	5.2	1.1	1.26	13.09	3.97	74.8	4.0	22.5	9.7	6.1
6.3	0.99	na	0.12	5.1	0.9	1.22	11.97	3.96	71.3	3.2	23.2	13.7	6.3
9.4	0.45	na	0.00	5.4	2.4	1.29	9.86	3.83	62.1	5.7	65.3	12.0	8.3
5.5	0.98	8.0	0.01	6.1	1.1	1.25	11.31	3.92	59.6	4.5	26.0	7.1	6.4
6.6	0.91	na	-0.01	3.9	0.4	0.80	8.03	3.67	72.0	2.5	26.6	18.0	5.5
5.1	3.31	8.6	1.95	4.2	0.4	0.89	7.43	4.03	70.9	5.1	40.5	9.2	5.9
9.8	0.00	na	0.00	9.2	1.0	1.99	8.51	3.76	35.9	5.7	84.7	12.1	7.0
7.4	1.14	na	0.16	4.4	0.4	0.90	4.36	3.88	73.7	4.7	52.2	13.5	7.5
4.1	0.86	na	0.28	6.4	1.9	1.34	11.17	4.93	59.6	2.7	28.4	17.9	6.7
4.8	0.96	na	0.17	5.8	2.6	1.35	13.92	3.86	64.9	0.8	17.2	17.3	6.9
6.0	2.63	na	-0.03	4.9	0.2	1.16	10.28	4.52	76.3	5.1	38.0	8.3	5.5
2.1	1.97	na	0.54	2.5	0.6	0.38	4.48	2.81	70.1	1.2	16.2	27.4	5.0
5.7	2.44	na	0.23	6.9	1.2	1.31	10.30	3.78	51.6	3.8	38.5	15.4	8.1
8.9	0.00	na	0.00	1.1	0.0	0.02	0.16	2.95	104.9	5.1	43.9	10.1	4.7
7.7	1.13	na	0.00	8.9	1.4	2.35	22.67	4.46	47.6	4.8	27.0	5.5	8.3
4.9	1.90	na	0.07	5.3	0.2	1.44	7.55	3.65	61.1	4.8	47.7	12.3	7.9
6.9	0.09	6.3	-0.04	4.5	0.7	1.13	10.36	3.19	67.6	6.0	58.1	7.3	6.9
4.0	6.44	na	-0.10	5.5	0.7	1.27	5.96	3.93	73.5	1.1	22.9	30.1	7.0
3.7	0.18	na	0.33	3.9	0.2	1.04	8.91	3.91	71.4	5.0	41.4	7.5	2.1
5.3	1.98	na	0.18	8.8	1.6	2.43	22.17	4.39	49.7	3.1	18.8	13.8	8.1
7.8	0.78	na	0.03	4.8	2.7	1.08	6.79	3.52	69.4	4.6	37.0	10.9	8.1
0.0	27.44	na	1.10	2.8	-0.1	-0.08	-0.50	2.65	60.4	2.7	14.9	15.5	8.3
5.3	1.81	na	-0.01	6.8	6.5	1.50	13.32	4.31	64.3	1.7	22.7	22.0	8.1
6.3	4.98	na	-0.14	3.3	0.9	1.50	11.88	2.71	96.3	4.4	93.5	22.9	6.3
9.1	1.92	na	0.03	3.3	0.7	0.66	4.66	2.67	73.8	3.5	58.9	26.1	7.8
8.7	0.00	na	0.21	7.7	1.6	1.54	12.72	5.15	62.1	5.3	34.0	5.1	7.3
5.4	0.72	na	0.00	4.8	0.4	0.94	7.47	3.78	67.6	2.8	12.2	14.6	7.0
6.4	1.88	na	-0.02	8.2	1.6	2.04	16.32	4.17	51.9	4.0	46.4	16.6	8.0
8.5	1.46	na	0.29	5.0	1.1	1.08	6.55	4.02	68.2	2.6	38.1	24.7	8.3
4.5	2.05	na	0.08	4.4	1.4	1.10	13.27	4.12	74.4	3.0	20.3	9.4	5.2
1.1	6.85	na	0.01	3.0	0.3	0.54	6.07	3.42	82.1	5.1	41.2	9.7	4.9
8.9	0.21	0.5	-0.20	5.8	0.4	1.39	6.08	3.33	53.1	5.9	61.7	8.9	6.4
9.0	0.04	na	-0.37	1.8	0.1	0.22	2.44	2.21	90.1	3.5	57.8	21.9	4.2
7.1	0.04	na	0.04	6.1	1.1	1.34	10.39	3.73	54.0	2.2	13.8	18.1	9.0
4.5	2.29	na	0.12	2.6	0.2	0.41	6.06	3.44	82.6	5.5	37.7	5.4	1.8
6.7	0.77	3.3	-0.16	5.2	0.6	1.27	13.64	3.55	69.7	4.3	41.3	13.6	5.1
7.9	0.00	na	0.08	7.4	1.5	1.80	13.12	3.88	52.0	2.3	16.3	17.4	8.3
9.9	1.58	na	0.02	5.9	1.1	1.15	5.12	3.24	51.8	6.4	99.6	13.1	9.1
6.8	0.74	3.7	-0.02	8.5	4.8	1.71	13.09	3.82	79.8	2.1	12.3	18.1	7.8
9.2	0.00	na	0.03	7.2	0.3	1.46	8.92	3.80	50.3	6.5	77.1	7.9	8.0
6.9	2.31	na	-0.03	3.6	0.1	0.69	4.36	4.70	87.6	4.4	36.5	9.6	6.1
6.5	0.45	na	0.62	3.3	0.8	0.61	4.44	4.54	75.2	2.7	21.0	16.0	7.3
6.9	1.53	na	-0.01	5.7	9.7	1.35	15.77	3.58	65.7	4.6	22.2	5.5	7.1
8.2	0.02	na	0.15	4.0	0.6	0.75	4.72	3.95	77.9	3.3	52.6	24.7	8.0
3.4	1.92	15.3	0.54	1.7	-0.5	-0.19	-2.07	3.68	97.0	1.3	11.1	23.0	4.5
9.8	0.21	na	0.04	6.0	17.5	1.32	14.75	2.35	34.4	3.1	60.4	54.1	7.2
5.4	1.14	na	0.07	2.6	0.2	0.48	4.64	2.75	78.3	5.6	65.8	11.5	4.5
7.7	0.87	na	0.02	3.3	0.6	0.67	6.23	3.01	79.3	3.5	43.7	18.3	5.9
7.9	3.33	na	0.03	5.5	1.6	1.15	6.60	3.18	58.4	6.4	67.4	8.7	8.0
3.1	1.57	na	1.20	2.1	0.1	0.05	0.51	3.42	74.4	3.2	18.9	13.5	6.5
8.4	0.36	na	0.00	8.0	3.6	1.83	16.21	3.97	60.4	3.9	23.2	10.2	8.8
7.9	0.00	3.1	-0.31	7.0	0.6	1.74	14.84	4.98	64.8	3.6	28.2	12.9	4.9

Name	City	State	Rating	2018 Rating	2017 Rating	Total Assets ($Mil)	One Year Asset Growth	Asset Mix (As a % of Total Assets) Comm-ercial Loans	Cons-umer Loans	Mort-gage Loans	Secur-ities	Capital-ization Index	Lever-age Ratio	Risk-Based Capital Ratio
First State Community Bank	Farmington	MO	**B+**	B	B	2566.0	6.80	6.4	2.2	21.8	10.3	**7.0**	10.4	12.5
First Summit Bank	Ryan	OK	**C+**	C+	C	27.2	2.19	9.9	3.7	7.7	0.0	**10.0**	13.3	18.5
▲ First Texas Bank	Georgetown	TX	**B+**	B-	C+	651.9	0.86	2.5	1.2	3.1	54.7	**6.9**	8.9	17.7
First Texas Bank	Killeen	TX	**B**	B-	C+	315.6	1.78	0.7	0.4	11.4	45.1	**10.0**	11.3	23.3
First Texas Bank	Lampasas	TX	**B+**	B-	B-	138.1	-0.59	2.6	1.5	14.6	42.2	**10.0**	11.8	22.5
▲ First Texoma National Bank	Durant	OK	**A-**	B+	B	184.0	1.72	4.7	5.5	28.2	11.1	**10.0**	11.5	16.8
▲ First Tri-County Bank	Swanton	NE	**C**	C	C+	55.1	1.90	9.3	5.2	19.4	3.9	**7.9**	10.8	13.3
▲ First Trust & Savings Bank of Albany	Albany	IL	**B+**	B	B	172.6	-4.71	5.5	1.3	24.3	14.2	**10.0**	13.7	21.6
▼ First Trust and Savings Bank	Coralville	IA	**C**	C+	C	46.1	-14.06	3.6	1.7	3.7	65.6	**10.0**	12.7	26.9
▲ First Trust and Savings Bank	Wheatland	IA	**B-**	B-	C+	187.9	5.75	14.3	3.4	5.2	4.4	**7.1**	10.4	12.6
First Trust and Savings Bank of Watseka	Watseka	IL	**A**	A	A	256.0	5.65	8.4	1.2	5.6	34.3	**10.0**	16.0	30.0
First Trust Bank of Illinois	Kankakee	IL	**B**	B	B+	233.6	-3.01	13.7	1.2	6.6	44.7	**9.8**	10.9	16.3
▲ First United Bank	Park River	ND	**C**	C-	C+	261.7	6.06	5.0	2.0	4.0	18.3	**8.2**	10.4	13.5
First United Bank	Dimmitt	TX	**A-**	A-	A-	1358.4	5.64	12.4	0.5	7.3	21.3	**8.8**	10.3	14.0
▲ First United Bank & Trust	Oakland	MD	**B**	B-	B-	1422.2	7.10	7.5	2.5	26.2	16.0	**9.9**	10.9	16.3
▲ First United Bank and Trust Co.	Madisonville	KY	**A-**	A-	A	323.5	3.93	9.2	2.7	26.0	15.7	**10.0**	12.4	17.3
First United Bank and Trust Co.	Durant	OK	**B**	B	B+	7849.1	16.19	6.7	2.2	20.7	16.5	**6.5**	9.3	12.1
First United National Bank	Fryburg	PA	**B**	B	B	268.2	1.49	3.9	6.5	43.4	21.3	**7.8**	9.6	19.1
First US Bank	Birmingham	AL	**B-**	C+	B-	771.6	-3.85	7.6	14.9	12.1	14.8	**7.8**	9.6	13.6
▲ First Utah Bank	Salt Lake City	UT	**C+**	C	B	437.6	17.75	14.3	1.1	2.3	4.8	**9.6**	10.8	14.7
First Vision Bank of Tennessee	Tullahoma	TN	**B+**	B+	A-	270.9	19.97	5.4	2.9	20.3	6.5	**8.8**	10.2	15.0
First Volunteer Bank	Chattanooga	TN	**A-**	B+	B-	1012.3	2.02	7.2	2.2	14.1	2.3	**10.0**	12.4	16.6
▲ First Western Bank	Booneville	AR	**B-**	C+	C+	449.2	7.02	2.7	1.1	36.2	4.7	**6.5**	8.5	12.4
▼ First Western Bank & Trust	Minot	ND	**B**	B+	B+	1076.4	-1.82	17.1	3.2	4.0	21.3	**8.3**	11.2	13.6
First Western Federal Savings Bank	Rapid City	SD	**A-**	A-	A-	61.4	9.70	0.0	0.2	84.6	0.0	**10.0**	14.5	28.3
First Western Trust Bank	Denver	CO	**C+**	C+	C	1261.4	21.49	14.6	6.2	28.9	4.9	**6.2**	8.2	11.9
First Westroads Bank, Inc.	Omaha	NE	**A**	A	A-	270.4	2.82	9.8	0.3	8.0	11.5	**10.0**	13.2	17.0
First Whitney Bank and Trust	Atlantic	IA	**B**	B+	A-	222.5	5.22	18.6	1.4	5.3	21.6	**5.2**	11.2	11.1
First, A National Banking Assn.	Hattiesburg	MS	**B+**	A-	B	3472.9	38.59	9.7	1.1	15.2	17.8	**10.0**	12.0	16.1
First-Citizens Bank & Trust Co.	Raleigh	NC	**B+**	B+	B+	37665.3	8.12	8.7	4.7	13.7	18.8	**7.6**	9.4	13.0
First-Lockhart National Bank	Lockhart	TX	**B**	B	B	274.9	2.84	2.1	0.6	23.2	15.3	**8.4**	9.9	15.5
▲ Firstar Bank	Sallisaw	OK	**B-**	C+	B-	633.4	12.40	19.3	2.0	21.6	5.8	**4.3**	8.6	10.6
FirstBank	Lakewood	CO	**A-**	A-	A-	19526.9	6.28	0.9	0.4	31.8	33.0	**6.6**	8.6	16.9
▲ FirstBank	Antlers	OK	**B**	B-	B	315.9	-3.54	7.8	11.6	32.8	0.7	**7.2**	9.1	13.9
FirstBank	Nashville	TN	**B+**	B+	B+	6084.6	20.41	16.4	3.6	16.7	11.0	**6.0**	9.8	11.7
▲ FirstBank of Nebraska	Wahoo	NE	**B**	B-	B+	282.1	8.26	6.3	1.2	7.8	32.4	**8.3**	10.1	13.6
▲ FirstBank Puerto Rico	San Juan	PR	**C-**	D+	D	12523.1	2.66	9.3	14.3	24.0	14.8	**10.0**	17.2	24.8
▲ FirstBank Southwest	Amarillo	TX	**B+**	B	B-	1008.8	3.77	16.4	3.5	8.8	28.4	**8.1**	9.7	14.5
FirstCapital Bank of Texas, N.A.	Midland	TX	**B-**	C+	B	1691.1	50.65	17.2	0.9	15.2	6.6	**7.3**	10.9	12.8
▲ FirsTier Bank	Kimball	NE	**A-**	B+	A	402.6	22.81	33.1	1.9	3.1	6.6	**9.9**	14.0	15.0
▲ FirstOak Bank	Independence	KS	**A-**	B+	A-	180.4	-3.73	10.5	1.4	15.0	6.8	**8.1**	9.8	14.4
Firstrust Savings Bank	Conshohocken	PA	**B+**	B+	B	3652.0	4.09	23.7	7.0	14.9	6.6	**6.2**	10.6	11.9
▲ FirstState Bank	Lineville	AL	**A-**	B+	A-	245.3	11.37	3.0	4.8	10.7	38.2	**10.0**	12.2	19.0
▲ Fisher National Bank	Fisher	IL	**A-**	B+	A-	127.8	4.00	4.3	2.4	41.5	11.8	**10.0**	13.3	20.1
Five Points Bank	Grand Island	NE	**A**	A	A	1200.9	11.95	17.1	1.4	6.4	23.4	**9.0**	10.9	14.2
Five Points Bank of Hastings	Hastings	NE	**A**	A	A	311.1	2.76	10.3	0.7	5.6	31.2	**10.0**	13.2	19.1
Five Star Bank	Rancho Cordova	CA	**B**	B	B+	1423.4	27.05	7.3	0.7	2.2	6.0	**5.4**	9.4	11.3
Five Star Bank	Warsaw	NY	**B**	B	B	4299.4	1.85	10.9	20.5	13.9	18.3	**6.7**	9.5	12.3
▲ Flagler Bank	West Palm Beach	FL	**B**	B-	B	321.8	9.31	16.8	0.0	10.0	16.3	**8.7**	10.1	15.1
▲ Flagship Bank	Clearwater	FL	**B**	B-	B-	115.8	-2.22	9.7	0.3	5.0	4.3	**10.0**	14.0	19.5
▲ Flagship Bank Minnesota	Wayzata	MN	**B-**	C+	C+	249.3	15.14	7.8	0.3	22.8	3.5	**7.1**	9.8	12.6
Flagstar Bank, FSB	Troy	MI	**B+**	B+	A-	21989.1	17.99	5.4	3.1	36.6	10.6	**6.3**	8.4	12.1
▲ Flanagan State Bank	Flanagan	IL	**B-**	C+	B-	187.7	0.44	4.7	2.2	26.4	22.9	**9.1**	10.4	15.7
Flatirons Bank	Boulder	CO	**B**	B+	B+	178.9	5.26	12.7	0.4	35.7	28.8	**8.3**	9.9	16.4
Flatwater Bank	Gothenburg	NE	**C+**	B+	A-	218.3	37.74	11.7	2.0	4.3	20.9	**7.3**	9.4	12.7
Fleetwood Bank	Fleetwood	PA	**C+**	C+	C	255.4	0.66	2.9	0.2	40.7	21.3	**7.8**	9.6	16.9
▲ Flint Community Bank	Albany	GA	**C**	C	B-	261.5	17.02	8.4	1.4	26.3	1.8	**5.7**	8.4	11.5
▲ Flint Hills Bank	Eskridge	KS	**A-**	B+	A-	128.4	-2.44	5.5	3.5	13.3	34.7	**10.0**	12.8	23.8
Flora Bank & Trust	Flora	IL	**B-**	B-	B-	69.3	-6.62	6.7	10.7	22.1	6.0	**10.0**	12.5	20.1
Florence Bank	Florence	MA	**B**	B	B	1415.6	4.97	3.0	0.0	44.1	19.8	**10.0**	11.4	17.5

Arrows denote recent upgrades ▲ or downgrades ▼

Asset Quality Index	Adjusted Non-Performing Loans as a % of Total Loans	Adjusted Non-Performing Loans as a % of Capital	Net Charge-Offs Avg Loans	Profitability Index	Net Income ($Mil)	Return on Assets (R.O.A.)	Return on Equity (R.O.E.)	Net Interest Spread	Overhead Efficiency Ratio	Liquidity Index	Liquidity Ratio	Hot Money Ratio	Stability Index
7.2	0.41	2.4	0.06	**7.4**	29.5	1.56	13.37	3.87	60.2	**1.9**	6.2	14.9	**10.0**
7.3	0.58	2.8	-0.04	**2.1**	0.0	0.14	1.07	4.70	96.5	**1.5**	21.4	25.7	**6.4**
9.4	0.00	na	0.00	**5.9**	6.4	1.32	15.12	3.11	53.4	**6.9**	65.5	4.9	**6.3**
9.6	0.05	na	0.00	**3.9**	1.9	0.86	7.82	3.42	70.9	**7.2**	64.5	2.5	**7.2**
9.3	0.25	na	-0.57	**7.2**	1.6	1.56	13.37	3.78	60.0	**6.8**	58.3	4.1	**7.8**
8.2	0.30	na	0.01	**5.9**	1.6	1.19	10.28	4.57	72.6	**2.3**	17.0	17.7	**7.4**
4.3	0.00	na	0.19	**3.3**	0.2	0.49	4.25	4.04	77.1	**4.0**	8.0	7.8	**5.7**
6.4	1.15	na	0.05	**6.6**	2.1	1.63	10.92	3.72	58.1	**2.5**	20.6	15.5	**8.6**
6.6	3.85	na	0.58	**1.8**	0.0	0.07	0.61	2.92	95.5	**2.1**	32.3	24.9	**5.5**
4.6	0.45	3.6	0.09	**5.9**	1.9	1.37	13.42	3.79	57.6	**1.2**	8.1	25.4	**7.6**
8.6	1.41	2.4	0.12	**7.1**	2.6	1.40	8.81	3.09	47.2	**4.6**	38.4	11.5	**8.8**
5.3	2.02	na	0.00	**4.6**	1.7	0.95	8.78	3.08	58.8	**2.8**	27.0	16.6	**7.0**
3.7	0.91	na	0.01	**7.8**	3.6	1.92	17.98	4.43	53.0	**2.0**	13.9	8.6	**8.2**
8.2	0.19	na	0.01	**8.1**	20.1	1.99	18.78	4.02	54.1	**1.5**	10.1	24.0	**8.0**
6.2	1.56	8.4	-0.03	**5.0**	10.6	1.02	10.15	3.69	69.9	**1.7**	13.0	15.2	**8.5**
7.9	0.63	na	-0.01	**5.7**	3.1	1.28	10.30	3.99	69.4	**3.8**	6.6	8.8	**8.9**
5.4	0.93	5.5	0.09	**5.6**	36.1	0.65	6.33	4.01	66.9	**1.3**	10.4	23.5	**9.0**
6.6	0.53	na	0.07	**4.6**	1.9	0.96	10.06	3.58	68.5	**4.6**	31.7	9.2	**5.7**
6.1	0.29	1.7	0.38	**4.1**	4.1	0.69	6.60	5.21	77.3	**1.8**	15.2	19.4	**6.4**
5.4	2.16	na	0.13	**7.3**	4.3	1.39	11.83	5.10	71.4	**1.4**	22.4	28.7	**8.2**
5.0	0.91	na	0.08	**6.3**	2.3	1.17	11.78	3.81	64.0	**0.8**	16.8	36.6	**6.5**
6.0	0.66	na	0.05	**10.0**	15.4	2.06	16.92	5.30	54.8	**3.7**	16.4	11.0	**10.0**
7.5	0.33	na	0.03	**4.3**	2.7	0.81	9.38	3.83	74.4	**0.7**	9.8	27.7	**5.0**
4.5	2.11	12.2	0.16	**4.8**	8.0	0.96	8.44	3.29	64.9	**1.5**	20.4	19.8	**8.4**
9.2	0.19	0.6	0.00	**9.6**	1.0	2.22	15.19	5.08	55.2	**0.4**	7.8	68.9	**8.0**
4.4	1.29	na	0.00	**3.9**	7.2	0.83	8.99	3.08	81.6	**2.1**	17.6	14.8	**6.7**
7.3	0.16	1.1	-0.01	**7.9**	3.2	1.59	12.46	4.06	55.3	**4.6**	19.3	5.0	**9.5**
8.3	0.00	na	0.00	**9.5**	3.5	2.19	20.06	3.66	35.7	**2.1**	19.1	19.0	**8.5**
4.4	1.77	7.3	-0.01	**7.2**	37.3	1.48	9.59	4.14	53.9	**3.4**	12.0	12.1	**9.6**
6.3	0.76	4.6	0.10	**6.4**	353.0	1.28	13.52	3.83	66.0	**4.5**	14.3	5.7	**8.6**
8.9	0.00	na	0.01	**4.3**	1.7	0.82	8.46	3.67	74.9	**2.2**	15.0	18.0	**6.5**
5.4	0.41	na	0.04	**8.2**	7.0	1.49	14.06	4.67	62.2	**1.5**	6.3	18.5	**8.1**
9.6	0.15	1.3	0.03	**8.6**	225.9	1.60	18.16	3.70	50.4	**6.1**	36.5	5.1	**8.6**
6.2	0.18	na	0.27	**7.0**	3.9	1.56	17.14	5.92	73.9	**0.6**	10.8	43.5	**6.8**
5.8	0.56	2.9	0.05	**8.6**	63.9	1.51	11.84	4.43	67.1	**2.6**	11.0	15.6	**10.0**
5.1	1.06	na	0.03	**8.4**	4.2	2.06	19.99	3.88	41.8	**1.5**	15.0	7.5	**7.9**
1.8	6.84	19.0	0.92	**7.6**	135.9	1.46	8.02	5.01	55.1	**1.5**	18.7	19.9	**9.4**
7.6	0.45	na	0.11	**5.4**	9.9	1.31	13.83	3.60	66.8	**2.2**	22.8	20.5	**7.7**
4.1	1.79	7.4	0.17	**7.5**	14.7	1.52	14.41	5.68	63.5	**1.0**	12.0	30.8	**9.2**
7.9	0.15	na	0.01	**9.0**	5.6	2.03	14.27	4.61	53.1	**0.7**	11.3	37.5	**9.5**
7.7	0.26	na	0.00	**9.4**	2.9	2.14	20.13	5.23	55.7	**2.5**	18.5	16.8	**7.7**
7.0	0.43	2.4	0.06	**6.3**	36.4	1.44	13.46	4.22	67.3	**1.9**	5.1	13.3	**10.0**
8.0	0.98	na	0.28	**5.6**	2.1	1.18	9.42	4.14	64.9	**1.9**	31.1	28.2	**7.4**
7.8	1.26	na	0.03	**8.1**	1.8	1.85	14.07	4.00	57.4	**2.2**	16.7	18.1	**9.2**
7.8	0.15	3.3	0.18	**6.7**	13.2	1.54	13.42	3.34	53.4	**3.4**	17.4	12.6	**9.6**
8.7	0.01	0.0	-0.01	**5.7**	3.1	1.32	10.55	3.05	51.3	**4.4**	22.1	7.2	**8.7**
7.2	0.08	0.5	0.17	**9.7**	23.6	2.34	26.81	4.10	35.9	**4.2**	17.7	8.4	**9.3**
6.9	0.31	1.7	0.33	**5.6**	39.7	1.25	12.67	3.35	54.6	**1.4**	4.0	20.6	**8.0**
7.5	0.07	na	-0.08	**7.6**	4.2	1.78	18.91	3.37	46.7	**0.7**	15.6	44.1	**7.5**
6.5	1.42	na	0.20	**4.6**	0.4	0.40	2.94	3.65	83.8	**1.6**	30.7	31.3	**7.4**
6.6	0.45	na	-0.02	**5.9**	1.9	1.12	10.74	4.24	62.9	**2.2**	12.3	17.6	**5.6**
6.7	2.70	2.8	0.33	**5.6**	178.1	1.20	12.44	3.23	73.6	**2.6**	11.7	12.0	**8.7**
4.3	1.68	na	0.19	**6.6**	2.5	1.79	17.67	3.64	84.7	**3.5**	21.6	12.3	**5.6**
9.1	0.00	na	0.00	**4.5**	1.4	1.00	10.11	3.69	74.6	**1.3**	28.5	26.7	**7.2**
2.7	2.22	na	0.29	**6.0**	2.1	1.32	12.32	4.09	62.7	**1.9**	9.7	19.1	**8.1**
8.2	0.33	na	-0.01	**3.8**	1.4	0.70	7.50	3.63	78.1	**4.4**	22.1	7.2	**5.5**
2.7	1.41	na	0.10	**5.9**	2.3	1.35	15.65	3.88	62.9	**2.0**	19.4	17.5	**5.2**
8.7	0.05	na	0.00	**6.6**	1.6	1.65	13.34	3.18	53.0	**2.0**	19.3	19.5	**8.2**
7.2	0.86	na	-0.08	**3.8**	0.3	0.64	5.27	3.91	79.4	**4.2**	27.0	9.6	**5.9**
9.3	0.41	2.3	0.01	**4.6**	8.1	0.79	7.19	3.55	72.7	**4.1**	27.1	13.2	**8.6**

Name	City	State	Rating	2018 Rating	2017 Rating	Total Assets ($Mil)	One Year Asset Growth	Asset Mix (As a % of Total Assets): Commercial Loans	Consumer Loans	Mortgage Loans	Securities	Capitalization Index	Leverage Ratio	Risk-Based Capital Ratio
▲ Florida Business Bank	Melbourne	FL	**A-**	B+	A-	146.9	14.27	6.2	0.1	1.8	13.5	**10.0**	13.8	17.8
▲ Florida Capital Bank, N.A.	Jacksonville	FL	**C-**	C-	C-	536.7	45.53	5.9	0.0	30.5	3.9	**4.5**	8.5	10.8
▼ Flushing Bank	Uniondale	NY	**B**	B+	B+	7110.9	8.73	10.9	0.0	10.6	12.3	**7.9**	9.7	13.2
FMB Bank	Wright City	MO	**D**	D+	D	37.7	3.19	9.1	3.9	16.5	32.8	**7.5**	9.4	15.9
FMS Bank	Fort Morgan	CO	**C**	B-	B+	193.2	3.73	15.5	13.6	12.0	12.8	**5.7**	10.5	11.6
FNB Bank	Scottsboro	AL	**C+**	C+	B+	688.3	29.36	8.6	2.5	15.2	14.7	**9.7**	10.8	14.8
FNB Bank	Fontanelle	IA	**B+**	B+	A-	200.6	0.88	5.3	0.9	8.4	7.1	**10.0**	14.3	17.3
FNB Bank	Goodland	KS	**B+**	B+	B+	191.8	0.59	3.5	1.1	1.6	29.1	**10.0**	13.6	19.9
▲ FNB Bank, Inc.	Mayfield	KY	**B-**	C+	B	510.4	1.98	7.3	11.2	20.5	18.8	**6.6**	8.7	12.4
▲ FNB Bank, Inc.	Romney	WV	**B**	B-	B-	200.7	5.93	7.3	3.7	28.3	13.7	**9.5**	10.7	14.9
▲ FNB Community Bank	Vandalia	IL	**A-**	B+	A-	351.3	8.89	4.8	1.2	14.6	27.6	**10.0**	13.2	20.0
FNB Community Bank	Midwest City	OK	**B-**	B-	C+	463.6	-1.51	5.5	3.8	6.9	38.3	**9.1**	10.4	19.0
FNB Coweta	Coweta	OK	**C+**	C+	C+	76.5	-1.16	8.8	2.1	13.3	39.9	**8.9**	10.2	21.9
FNB Oxford Bank	Oxford	MS	**B+**	A-	A-	365.4	17.03	5.4	1.3	18.6	35.4	**9.7**	10.8	17.3
▲ FNB South	Alma	GA	**A-**	B+	A	386.7	4.41	7.8	5.9	16.8	6.7	**10.0**	16.9	25.2
FNB Washington	Washington	KS	**B+**	B+	B+	69.4	-6.69	0.7	1.9	12.9	36.9	**10.0**	27.2	56.8
▲ FNBC Bank	Ash Flat	AR	**C**	C	B-	528.5	17.17	8.5	4.8	15.2	24.8	**8.1**	9.7	14.1
▲ FNBC Bank and Trust	La Grange	IL	**B**	B-	B-	520.2	1.06	3.1	0.5	17.2	31.5	**8.7**	10.2	18.2
FNBT Bank	Fort Walton Beach	FL	**A-**	B	B	451.2	6.64	3.1	0.8	11.3	1.4	**10.0**	11.0	19.9
▲ FNCB Bank	Dunmore	PA	**B**	B-	C+	1193.7	-4.43	13.7	11.3	14.0	21.2	**10.0**	11.0	15.4
▼ FNNB Bank	Newton	IA	**C-**	C	C-	82.3	-0.93	8.2	0.8	10.2	24.6	**6.7**	8.7	14.0
▲ Focus Bank	Charleston	MO	**B+**	B-	B-	764.5	2.47	7.2	2.0	25.3	6.1	**10.0**	11.0	15.3
Forcht Bank, N.A.	Lexington	KY	**B-**	B-	B	1225.8	16.86	4.3	1.9	29.0	17.5	**8.1**	9.7	15.5
Ford County State Bank	Spearville	KS	**C+**	B-	B-	38.7	3.43	19.7	1.7	2.7	5.1	**10.0**	13.1	18.8
▲ Foresight Bank	Plainview	MN	**B-**	C	B-	262.6	7.77	5.2	1.8	26.0	14.3	**7.8**	9.5	13.2
Forest Park National Bank and Trust Co.	Forest Park	IL	**B-**	B-	C+	237.5	1.63	4.5	0.3	20.3	7.3	**6.6**	8.6	12.3
Forreston State Bank	Forreston	IL	**B+**	B+	B+	221.4	11.34	4.7	0.3	7.1	29.0	**10.0**	11.5	16.2
Fort Davis State Bank	Fort Davis	TX	**C+**	C+	C+	91.5	8.64	11.5	4.3	5.9	30.3	**7.8**	9.5	17.8
▲ Fort Hood National Bank	Fort Hood	TX	**B+**	B	B	297.6	5.81	0.0	15.9	16.1	35.9	**7.0**	9.0	41.2
Fort Jennings State Bank	Fort Jennings	OH	**B**	B	A-	192.5	9.95	10.3	3.7	22.5	2.9	**9.8**	10.9	15.9
▲ Fortifi Bank	Berlin	WI	**C+**	C	B-	438.4	9.84	14.5	1.9	15.1	12.1	**5.9**	10.0	11.7
▲ Fortis Private Bank	Denver	CO	**C-**	D+	D+	804.7	15.06	4.8	9.7	29.1	20.9	**7.1**	9.0	12.8
Fortress Bank	Peoria	IL	**C**	C	C	446.6	6.43	14.5	1.6	15.9	12.9	**5.9**	8.6	11.7
FortuneBank	Arnold	MO	**C-**	C-	D	187.4	0.38	15.8	0.3	16.4	4.5	**5.5**	8.8	11.4
Forward Bank	Marshfield	WI	**C+**	B-	B-	593.2	30.99	11.5	2.3	16.2	7.7	**5.4**	8.4	11.3
Foundation One Bank	Omaha	NE	**C+**	C+	B-	109.4	3.89	21.6	3.4	27.1	8.5	**10.0**	11.6	15.4
▲ Fountain Trust Co.	Covington	IN	**A-**	B+	B+	386.0	7.31	5.2	1.3	21.6	20.2	**10.0**	12.2	21.8
▼ Four Corners Community Bank	Farmington	NM	**C-**	C-	B-	370.9	3.21	11.0	0.7	6.4	15.0	**10.0**	12.1	16.1
▲ Four County Bank	Allentown	GA	**B+**	B	B	70.9	2.72	11.0	9.0	21.7	16.1	**10.0**	14.8	22.3
▲ Fowler State Bank	Fowler	CO	**B**	B	B	84.8	7.71	3.3	1.1	5.0	28.7	**10.0**	15.5	26.1
Fowler State Bank	Fowler	IN	**A-**	A-	A-	163.6	0.28	7.7	5.4	9.0	45.8	**10.0**	14.9	21.8
▼ Fowler State Bank	Fowler	KS	**D+**	D+	D+	77.2	-5.81	17.0	2.7	3.8	24.2	**7.8**	9.5	14.8
Fox Valley Savings Bank	Fond du Lac	WI	**B**	B	B-	341.5	-2.78	2.5	1.0	28.6	39.2	**10.0**	14.4	21.9
Foxboro Federal Savings	Foxborough	MA	**B-**	B-	C+	165.7	-1.09	0.0	0.8	65.5	12.7	**10.0**	17.0	35.7
Frandsen Bank & Trust	Lonsdale	MN	**B**	B	B	1737.0	3.21	9.7	2.1	16.1	19.8	**5.8**	8.5	11.6
Franklin Bank	Pilesgrove	NJ	**C+**	C+	C-	259.1	-0.13	4.3	1.7	44.3	13.5	**8.6**	10.1	17.9
▲ Franklin Bank & Trust Co.	Franklin	KY	**A-**	B+	B+	542.6	5.57	23.6	1.3	15.2	0.8	**10.0**	12.5	15.5
Franklin Savings Bank	Farmington	ME	**B+**	B+	A-	444.0	7.42	8.0	3.3	39.0	1.9	**10.0**	25.4	32.4
Franklin Savings Bank	Franklin	NH	**C+**	C+	C+	522.5	7.10	5.0	0.2	24.7	21.7	**9.1**	10.4	16.2
Franklin State Bank	Franklin	MN	**B-**	B	B	32.2	6.16	2.7	3.6	10.7	8.5	**10.0**	15.6	26.9
▲ Franklin State Bank & Trust Co.	Winnsboro	LA	**B+**	B	C+	172.5	4.98	3.3	5.3	17.5	14.2	**8.7**	10.1	17.6
▼ Franklin Synergy Bank	Franklin	TN	**B**	B+	B+	3813.3	-8.45	15.5	0.1	13.7	16.1	**9.5**	11.2	14.6
▼ Frazer Bank	Altus	OK	**C-**	C+	B	298.0	-4.56	10.5	1.1	7.6	32.2	**8.0**	9.7	15.2
Frederick Community Bank	Cissna Park	IL	**B+**	B	B-	140.5	-5.49	7.7	2.2	6.9	36.9	**9.0**	10.3	18.1
Frederick County Bank	Frederick	MD	**B-**	B-	C	452.1	6.96	10.8	0.4	12.1	5.1	**7.0**	10.2	12.5
Fredonia Valley Bank	Fredonia	KY	**B+**	B+	B+	81.1	1.48	4.3	3.4	43.8	18.3	**10.0**	17.9	28.0
Freedom Bank	Saint Petersburg	FL	**B-**	B-	C+	306.2	11.66	18.1	1.0	2.3	1.7	**5.2**	9.1	11.1
Freedom Bank	Huntingburg	IN	**B+**	A-	A-	440.2	5.93	4.9	4.2	40.0	0.6	**8.3**	10.6	13.6
Freedom Bank	Overland Park	KS	**C+**	B-	B-	168.0	-11.77	13.9	0.0	6.7	15.9	**8.3**	11.4	13.6
Freedom Bank	Columbia Falls	MT	**C**	C+	B	85.3	3.67	20.5	1.9	13.2	0.0	**9.4**	10.6	15.2

Asset Quality Index	Adjusted Non-Performing Loans as a % of Total Loans	Adjusted Non-Performing Loans as a % of Capital	Net Charge-Offs Avg Loans	Profitability Index	Net Income ($Mil)	Return on Assets (R.O.A.)	Return on Equity (R.O.E.)	Net Interest Spread	Overhead Efficiency Ratio	Liquidity Index	Liquidity Ratio	Hot Money Ratio	Stability Index
7.5	0.00	na	0.12	**6.6**	1.2	1.14	8.32	3.90	61.6	**2.2**	31.2	23.7	**8.6**
4.8	1.17	na	0.09	**5.2**	5.1	1.58	17.49	3.28	80.3	**0.6**	10.2	17.5	**3.7**
6.7	0.37	2.7	0.05	**3.8**	34.5	0.66	6.88	2.61	63.5	**1.3**	12.1	18.9	**8.3**
5.1	5.66	na	0.19	**3.0**	0.2	0.49	5.42	3.58	84.6	**2.9**	19.2	14.7	**4.7**
4.1	1.13	na	0.79	**5.3**	1.4	1.03	9.79	5.50	72.3	**1.6**	14.6	22.9	**6.5**
3.9	2.06	na	0.08	**6.1**	6.1	1.25	10.01	4.57	67.5	**2.9**	16.2	14.4	**7.8**
4.0	1.14	na	0.00	**5.9**	2.0	1.32	8.53	4.02	65.3	**2.6**	9.7	15.4	**9.2**
6.6	0.74	2.0	0.07	**4.4**	1.2	0.89	6.65	4.21	77.0	**3.3**	10.8	11.9	**8.3**
6.2	0.79	na	0.07	**4.3**	3.0	0.79	7.71	3.50	74.6	**1.7**	11.5	12.2	**7.8**
6.8	1.78	na	0.05	**5.5**	1.6	1.10	10.64	4.01	65.8	**1.6**	19.5	24.6	**6.4**
7.2	0.48	na	0.02	**6.3**	3.3	1.30	9.33	3.86	59.9	**3.8**	23.8	11.1	**8.1**
4.5	4.30	18.8	0.05	**3.8**	3.2	0.85	8.59	3.43	70.9	**4.6**	23.3	5.7	**7.1**
8.6	0.25	na	0.02	**3.7**	0.5	0.77	8.02	3.53	79.1	**4.4**	37.0	12.2	**5.1**
8.1	0.61	na	0.01	**4.9**	2.9	1.12	9.59	3.27	67.0	**1.9**	22.6	13.9	**7.2**
8.2	0.02	na	-0.16	**10.0**	8.3	2.89	17.86	5.13	46.3	**3.0**	17.5	14.2	**8.6**
8.2	2.70	na	0.00	**5.8**	0.6	1.13	4.28	3.23	53.6	**3.9**	29.4	11.9	**7.8**
3.0	1.80	na	0.28	**5.2**	4.6	1.28	13.44	4.11	63.9	**2.0**	21.1	19.8	**6.1**
6.4	1.47	na	-0.02	**5.2**	4.8	1.23	11.75	3.54	71.8	**5.6**	36.4	4.2	**6.8**
8.6	1.34	na	-0.36	**6.6**	5.8	1.72	15.78	3.21	65.0	**6.3**	59.7	7.7	**7.5**
5.2	1.66	6.5	0.17	**4.0**	8.1	0.90	8.38	3.28	69.0	**3.5**	5.8	10.8	**9.7**
8.8	0.08	na	0.91	**1.4**	0.0	-0.06	-0.65	3.52	89.2	**5.1**	38.9	8.7	**4.3**
6.9	0.77	na	0.24	**5.6**	7.5	1.32	12.10	3.56	65.6	**0.7**	12.3	34.5	**7.9**
5.9	1.12	3.7	0.04	**3.4**	5.7	0.60	4.82	3.82	83.5	**3.8**	15.4	10.3	**8.8**
2.4	5.55	na	0.52	**3.2**	0.0	-0.14	-1.02	4.42	50.5	**3.8**	25.9	11.3	**7.8**
4.3	5.89	na	0.00	**5.8**	2.5	1.35	13.67	3.53	62.7	**0.9**	22.7	35.2	**7.8**
4.6	0.92	7.1	-0.04	**5.2**	2.1	1.17	13.55	4.72	74.3	**4.1**	11.5	7.6	**5.8**
8.4	0.96	na	0.01	**4.7**	2.0	1.23	10.75	3.07	61.3	**1.4**	30.0	28.4	**7.0**
6.0	0.55	na	0.20	**3.8**	0.6	0.83	8.68	4.31	81.1	**5.8**	46.3	6.3	**5.1**
8.6	0.12	na	0.24	**4.3**	2.1	1.02	11.34	3.04	82.5	**7.0**	60.3	3.3	**6.3**
5.0	0.88	na	0.09	**6.0**	1.5	1.11	9.83	4.54	62.9	**1.7**	17.9	22.6	**7.0**
4.3	1.21	na	0.07	**3.8**	2.0	0.63	6.48	4.23	80.0	**1.4**	17.2	18.0	**5.3**
8.4	0.06	na	0.01	**2.4**	2.3	0.40	4.47	2.76	79.6	**1.6**	25.0	13.1	**5.0**
2.7	0.93	na	-0.03	**4.1**	2.7	0.82	7.86	3.43	68.6	**0.7**	13.4	26.6	**6.7**
3.4	0.41	na	0.60	**3.6**	0.9	0.63	6.80	3.70	84.1	**0.7**	10.1	28.2	**4.7**
5.9	0.54	na	0.00	**3.7**	2.5	0.63	5.83	4.05	79.4	**3.1**	18.2	13.8	**6.6**
8.0	0.37	na	0.17	**2.4**	0.1	0.16	1.34	3.34	83.7	**0.8**	16.6	40.2	**6.3**
7.0	0.66	na	0.07	**7.3**	4.5	1.62	12.59	4.42	60.3	**5.5**	40.1	6.6	**8.1**
0.2	6.30	na	0.72	**6.9**	3.7	1.37	11.35	4.34	59.8	**1.9**	16.7	19.6	**8.8**
7.5	0.29	na	-0.07	**8.2**	1.0	1.91	13.46	4.48	56.8	**1.0**	24.5	36.4	**8.9**
5.7	2.09	na	0.17	**5.9**	0.8	1.32	8.93	3.33	50.5	**2.3**	43.9	31.9	**7.7**
8.0	0.73	na	0.10	**6.6**	2.1	1.68	11.37	4.37	65.2	**6.2**	45.5	4.0	**8.7**
0.7	10.21	na	0.32	**1.1**	-0.4	-0.64	-6.72	3.60	87.8	**0.9**	14.7	30.9	**4.7**
7.5	1.75	na	0.01	**3.8**	1.9	0.73	5.04	2.82	71.3	**3.6**	36.7	15.9	**7.4**
10.0	0.00	na	0.00	**3.9**	1.1	0.88	5.23	3.19	69.0	**3.6**	31.7	14.4	**8.0**
5.7	0.71	3.4	-0.01	**6.8**	21.4	1.68	13.87	4.31	64.8	**4.9**	13.8	2.5	**10.0**
7.4	0.48	na	0.02	**3.7**	1.1	0.59	5.97	3.63	79.2	**4.1**	21.8	9.1	**5.0**
7.1	0.88	na	0.51	**6.5**	5.0	1.27	10.53	3.67	57.0	**0.9**	9.7	31.4	**8.0**
7.3	1.29	na	0.03	**5.5**	3.2	1.02	4.24	4.57	73.8	**3.0**	4.9	9.9	**8.1**
6.7	1.26	na	0.00	**3.4**	2.2	0.59	5.65	3.30	80.3	**2.8**	26.4	16.3	**6.9**
6.8	2.66	na	0.14	**4.3**	0.2	0.69	4.40	3.26	66.9	**3.5**	42.9	17.8	**7.6**
6.3	0.16	5.1	0.12	**7.9**	2.3	1.82	18.75	4.57	63.2	**1.1**	18.8	32.0	**5.7**
8.5	0.11	0.6	0.47	**4.2**	25.2	0.82	7.55	2.95	57.2	**0.9**	13.4	14.6	**8.2**
5.2	2.76	na	0.57	**2.0**	0.8	0.35	3.91	3.45	81.7	**0.8**	15.7	29.9	**4.3**
8.8	0.08	na	0.00	**6.1**	1.7	1.58	15.27	3.27	57.5	**4.3**	29.1	9.7	**5.8**
5.2	0.95	5.6	0.01	**3.4**	1.8	0.56	5.45	3.44	78.9	**1.9**	17.6	16.1	**6.3**
4.4	5.53	na	0.18	**7.1**	0.8	1.34	7.67	4.44	61.8	**4.9**	24.3	4.0	**8.2**
6.1	0.42	3.0	-0.02	**7.9**	3.5	1.58	17.85	4.20	58.4	**1.5**	16.8	22.7	**6.1**
6.5	0.31	na	0.06	**9.2**	7.0	2.17	20.75	3.35	43.5	**2.3**	10.8	17.1	**8.8**
6.9	0.54	na	-0.16	**3.5**	1.0	0.67	6.76	2.90	79.3	**2.9**	8.7	8.9	**6.3**
4.5	2.05	na	-0.01	**8.9**	1.0	1.69	16.18	5.39	60.2	**1.3**	19.7	28.9	**8.2**

Name	City	State	Rating	2018 Rating	2017 Rating	Total Assets ($Mil)	One Year Asset Growth	Asset Mix (As a % of Total Assets): Comm-ercial Loans	Cons-umer Loans	Mort-gage Loans	Secur-ities	Capital-ization Index	Lever-age Ratio	Risk-Based Capital Ratio
Freedom Bank	Maywood	NJ	**B-**	B-	B	458.4	13.35	1.9	0.0	19.7	0.4	**9.0**	10.4	14.2
Freedom Bank	Freer	TX	**C+**	C-	C	46.7	6.25	11.8	4.6	6.4	11.8	**10.0**	11.0	17.5
Freedom Bank of Southern Missouri	Cassville	MO	**B**	B+	B+	292.2	4.29	9.1	3.1	19.4	5.5	**9.0**	10.3	14.5
▲ Freedom Bank of Virginia	Fairfax	VA	**B-**	C+	B-	507.4	-2.07	15.3	4.5	15.0	8.9	**10.0**	12.8	15.8
▲ Freedom Bank, Inc.	Belington	WV	**C-**	D+	D+	167.5	7.51	8.8	9.7	39.9	8.2	**9.5**	10.7	17.1
Freedom Financial Bank	West Des Moines	IA	**B**	B	B+	192.4	0.40	10.4	0.2	11.1	2.8	**7.3**	10.1	12.8
Freedom National Bank	Greenville	RI	**C**	C	C-	123.0	0.99	13.2	0.0	14.2	7.6	**9.0**	10.4	15.0
FreedomBank	Elkader	IA	**C+**	B	B+	401.5	50.27	7.5	2.5	16.3	9.8	**5.6**	8.7	11.5
Freehold Savings Bank	Freehold	NJ	**C+**	C+	C+	287.1	-4.56	0.5	0.0	20.0	47.7	**10.0**	13.4	24.0
Freeland State Bank	Freeland	MI	**C-**	C-	C-	51.6	2.09	0.1	0.4	10.9	47.4	**10.0**	18.1	82.2
▲ Freeport State Bank	Freeport	MN	**B**	B-	B	119.4	5.63	9.3	2.6	9.0	13.7	**8.7**	10.4	13.9
Fremont Bank	Fremont	CA	**B+**	B+	B+	4507.2	11.89	6.0	0.1	29.5	8.7	**5.0**	7.7	11.0
▲ Fresno First Bank	Fresno	CA	**B+**	B-	B	538.7	21.49	24.1	0.0	1.6	18.5	**7.9**	9.6	16.4
▲ Friend Bank	Slocomb	AL	**B**	B-	B	132.7	4.88	6.0	4.5	22.4	12.3	**8.3**	9.8	16.2
Friendly Hills Bank	Whittier	CA	**B**	B-	C+	160.3	3.10	5.3	0.0	12.9	21.5	**10.0**	11.6	19.4
▲ Friendship State Bank	Friendship	IN	**A-**	B+	B+	378.6	3.97	2.1	3.0	45.0	12.6	**9.0**	10.4	18.1
Frontier Bank	Lamar	CO	**A-**	A	A	310.0	0.67	1.6	0.7	9.0	43.2	**9.6**	10.7	18.8
Frontier Bank	Omaha	NE	**C+**	C+	C+	877.3	9.66	11.3	1.5	16.5	7.3	**4.8**	9.5	10.9
Frontier Bank	Sioux Falls	SD	**C+**	C+	C+	220.4	1.32	5.2	1.0	14.1	21.5	**6.9**	8.9	12.4
Frontier Bank of Texas	Elgin	TX	**B+**	A-	A-	360.7	39.98	6.2	2.2	22.0	4.4	**8.8**	10.9	14.0
Frontier Community Bank	Waynesboro	VA	**C+**	C+	C+	136.5	9.73	9.8	1.5	30.8	0.4	**8.5**	10.0	15.3
▲ Frontier State Bank	Oklahoma City	OK	**C**	C	D+	590.8	-4.92	13.0	0.4	15.9	14.1	**10.0**	12.5	17.3
Frost Bank	San Antonio	TX	**A-**	B+	B+	33171.6	5.87	17.2	1.5	2.8	40.5	**7.5**	9.3	13.5
Frost State Bank	Frost	MN	**D+**	C	C+	54.0	9.24	11.4	3.5	1.7	1.3	**10.0**	12.6	15.4
FSNB, N.A.	Lawton	OK	**A**	A	A	373.0	-0.47	2.0	2.3	13.3	34.8	**10.0**	15.5	34.7
Fulton Bank, N.A.	Lancaster	PA	**B**	B	B	21564.4	83.96	11.2	2.2	14.4	12.6	**6.3**	9.7	12.0
Fulton Savings Bank	Fulton	NY	**A-**	B+	B+	378.5	-0.02	0.4	1.0	26.2	31.9	**10.0**	28.6	57.2
▲ FVCbank	Fairfax	VA	**B+**	B	B	1562.1	33.21	7.1	1.6	7.9	8.7	**8.1**	12.1	13.4
G.W. Jones Exchange Bank	Marcellus	MI	**C+**	C+	C-	59.0	4.23	2.3	1.5	16.6	21.4	**10.0**	11.7	27.5
Galion Building and Loan Bank	Galion	OH	**C**	C	C	62.4	0.53	0.9	1.9	67.3	13.7	**10.0**	12.0	26.1
Garden Plain State Bank	Wichita	KS	**A-**	B+	B+	100.6	7.40	7.0	1.7	12.4	38.6	**10.0**	15.5	23.4
Garfield County Bank	Jordan	MT	**D-**	D	D	88.9	0.52	3.7	2.6	2.0	8.3	**10.0**	12.6	15.0
▲ Garrett State Bank	Garrett	IN	**B**	B-	B+	246.6	8.67	4.8	2.6	51.1	21.2	**9.2**	10.5	19.5
Garrison State Bank and Trust	Garrison	ND	**B-**	C+	B-	143.0	4.53	4.3	4.0	2.4	19.5	**10.0**	12.5	18.0
Gary State Bank	Gary	MN	**B-**	B-	B-	15.0	8.61	9.1	5.7	1.1	0.0	**10.0**	13.9	19.7
Gate City Bank	Fargo	ND	**B**	B	B	2325.8	4.97	2.4	28.6	50.1	3.8	**10.0**	11.4	16.4
Gates Banking and Trust Co.	Gates	TN	**B**	B+	B+	49.0	5.25	9.9	0.5	2.9	52.7	**9.6**	10.7	19.8
Gateway Bank	Rison	AR	**C+**	B-	C+	76.1	6.57	12.7	3.3	34.5	4.8	**10.0**	11.5	16.8
Gateway Bank	Mendota Heights	MN	**A-**	A-	A-	193.4	7.71	25.9	2.6	13.0	1.2	**7.5**	9.3	13.1
▲ Gateway Bank, F.S.B.	Oakland	CA	**D-**	E	E-	118.5	3.72	3.4	0.0	45.3	5.0	**10.0**	13.4	26.1
Gateway Commercial Bank	Mesa	AZ	**A-**	A-	B+	125.1	5.49	15.9	0.3	2.4	27.9	**10.0**	14.1	19.4
GBC International Bank	Los Angeles	CA	**B-**	B-	B	582.6	9.32	15.0	0.0	0.4	7.2	**9.3**	10.8	14.4
Geauga Savings Bank	Newbury	OH	**B-**	B-	B	274.8	-2.16	7.0	0.8	19.1	26.1	**10.0**	14.7	21.7
▼ Geddes Federal S&L Assn.	Syracuse	NY	**B-**	B	B+	558.4	5.09	0.0	0.1	85.3	6.3	**10.0**	16.4	29.1
▲ Generations Bank	Rogers	AR	**B**	B-	B-	524.9	5.78	6.2	2.9	24.3	12.0	**7.8**	9.5	13.3
Generations Bank	Exeter	NE	**C-**	C-	D+	37.0	-1.77	11.5	2.4	10.1	13.8	**8.6**	11.2	13.8
Generations Bank	Seneca Falls	NY	**D+**	D	D+	323.2	-3.50	4.4	14.1	43.3	6.7	**7.1**	9.0	13.4
▲ Genesee Regional Bank	Rochester	NY	**B+**	B-	B	596.5	2.50	21.2	0.8	11.3	16.1	**9.7**	10.8	15.9
Genoa Banking Co.	Genoa	OH	**C+**	C+	C+	392.3	6.62	4.2	5.0	28.2	13.5	**6.4**	8.4	12.9
▲ Genoa Community Bank	Genoa	NE	**B**	C+	B-	63.8	5.93	3.5	1.2	4.3	9.1	**10.0**	11.8	17.1
Geo. D. Warthen Bank	Sandersville	GA	**C+**	C+	C-	177.6	-0.95	11.2	8.9	24.3	18.8	**7.4**	9.3	15.1
▼ Georgia Banking Co.	Sandy Springs	GA	**C+**	B	C+	575.2	36.36	2.7	4.2	71.4	3.0	**6.1**	8.1	11.8
Georgia Community Bank	Dawson	GA	**B-**	B	B-	173.4	8.72	8.8	2.9	36.9	8.6	**8.5**	10.0	15.8
Georgia Primary Bank	Atlanta	GA	**C**	C-	D	219.8	18.04	13.6	0.4	4.1	13.1	**9.7**	11.6	14.7
Gerber State Bank	Argenta	IL	**B-**	B-	B-	77.3	-3.56	7.5	1.3	11.5	47.6	**10.0**	12.3	25.1
German American Bank	Jasper	IN	**A-**	A-	A-	4343.8	29.34	10.4	1.1	13.0	19.5	**7.7**	10.4	13.1
German-American State Bank	German Valley	IL	**B**	B	B-	246.6	-0.39	14.5	4.3	6.6	20.7	**8.6**	10.5	13.8
Germantown Trust & Savings Bank	Breese	IL	**A-**	A-	A	394.1	6.21	1.4	1.0	15.3	42.3	**10.0**	12.9	22.9
Gibraltar Bank	Parsippany	NJ	**C**	C-	D	103.1	-1.77	0.0	0.0	60.1	7.4	**10.0**	11.3	19.7
▲ Gibsland Bank & Trust Co.	Gibsland	LA	**C**	D+	D	448.1	8.06	13.0	2.7	13.3	12.8	**8.9**	10.9	14.0

Asset Quality Index	Adjusted Non-Performing Loans as a % of Total Loans	Adjusted Non-Performing Loans as a % of Capital	Net Charge-Offs Avg Loans	Profitability Index	Net Income ($Mil)	Return on Assets (R.O.A.)	Return on Equity (R.O.E.)	Net Interest Spread	Overhead Efficiency Ratio	Liquidity Index	Liquidity Ratio	Hot Money Ratio	Stability Index
7.5	0.00	na	0.05	**4.6**	2.6	0.77	7.43	3.29	65.7	**0.7**	11.2	43.8	**6.4**
7.1	0.06	1.0	-0.03	**2.5**	0.2	0.54	3.36	4.43	89.0	**2.9**	41.3	21.4	**5.1**
5.5	0.95	na	0.20	**5.9**	3.0	1.35	13.69	3.77	60.0	**1.2**	11.6	26.6	**7.0**
5.4	0.52	4.1	0.09	**3.4**	2.0	0.54	4.28	3.53	85.6	**0.7**	15.0	37.4	**6.0**
2.3	4.51	na	0.22	**4.9**	1.0	0.80	7.60	4.05	66.8	**3.9**	19.0	9.9	**5.9**
7.4	0.00	na	0.00	**5.2**	1.7	1.22	12.07	3.12	57.8	**0.7**	16.9	40.3	**7.6**
5.9	1.74	na	0.30	**2.6**	0.2	0.26	2.56	3.79	86.7	**1.2**	11.4	16.3	**5.4**
1.1	1.14	na	0.02	**5.4**	3.4	1.26	11.12	3.58	63.0	**1.9**	10.4	15.5	**7.4**
9.1	0.08	0.1	0.00	**2.6**	0.6	0.28	2.15	1.80	78.4	**2.0**	32.3	26.9	**6.7**
9.0	12.02	na	-0.37	**1.5**	0.1	0.21	1.19	2.40	90.5	**7.6**	105.3	4.9	**7.1**
8.0	0.97	na	-0.02	**5.4**	0.9	1.04	10.29	4.57	70.0	**1.7**	20.8	16.1	**6.3**
8.0	0.52	3.0	-0.06	**5.3**	36.1	1.17	14.73	4.04	75.7	**4.8**	20.9	5.2	**8.1**
6.8	0.21	na	0.06	**9.6**	6.7	1.89	19.93	4.85	49.4	**4.7**	30.1	7.7	**5.6**
5.1	0.80	na	-0.01	**7.3**	1.6	1.66	17.01	4.80	58.4	**2.7**	26.0	16.9	**6.5**
8.9	0.00	na	0.00	**4.2**	0.9	0.79	6.91	3.79	72.4	**5.4**	35.0	4.9	**7.2**
8.3	0.26	na	0.05	**7.2**	3.9	1.39	12.95	4.53	66.3	**2.4**	20.2	17.4	**6.8**
9.1	0.07	0.2	-0.12	**8.0**	4.4	1.90	17.46	3.60	51.0	**3.5**	27.5	13.2	**8.8**
3.2	1.76	12.1	0.34	**4.9**	7.1	1.14	10.09	3.26	55.3	**1.0**	11.9	20.6	**7.6**
7.0	1.18	na	0.21	**3.6**	1.1	0.67	7.35	3.61	77.1	**1.3**	19.2	13.0	**5.9**
8.2	0.03	0.4	0.27	**4.7**	1.9	0.82	7.16	4.12	71.4	**0.9**	20.3	36.2	**6.8**
8.7	0.00	na	0.00	**3.7**	0.7	0.72	7.19	3.12	74.2	**0.8**	18.1	36.7	**5.9**
2.8	5.24	25.5	0.60	**2.5**	2.6	0.56	4.83	2.38	71.8	**0.7**	21.4	62.6	**5.3**
7.2	0.71	2.9	0.20	**6.7**	347.5	1.47	12.74	3.70	59.2	**6.8**	43.5	2.7	**10.0**
2.4	2.39	na	1.01	**7.4**	0.5	1.34	10.58	3.75	33.4	**0.5**	13.8	61.3	**7.0**
9.6	0.00	0.2	2.28	**9.8**	11.3	3.90	24.61	3.86	72.0	**7.0**	56.0	2.3	**9.0**
5.1	1.07	6.1	0.09	**6.8**	189.7	1.50	14.32	4.25	64.1	**4.0**	16.3	8.2	**9.5**
9.9	1.43	na	0.10	**5.9**	4.5	1.60	5.68	4.37	73.7	**7.3**	81.2	4.9	**8.1**
5.7	0.78	na	0.04	**6.4**	13.8	1.29	10.07	3.67	52.4	**1.6**	17.2	19.7	**9.1**
9.5	0.30	na	-0.01	**3.2**	0.3	0.59	5.23	4.09	84.8	**6.2**	59.1	6.1	**5.9**
7.4	1.14	na	-0.03	**1.9**	0.1	0.21	1.74	3.36	92.7	**3.4**	24.6	12.9	**5.6**
8.6	1.18	na	0.11	**8.5**	1.3	1.79	11.56	3.62	54.0	**5.6**	62.5	12.4	**7.8**
0.0	6.68	na	1.15	**4.5**	0.5	0.80	6.56	3.83	55.2	**0.6**	10.5	48.9	**7.3**
5.4	1.50	na	0.01	**7.2**	3.2	1.73	16.05	3.80	55.3	**2.4**	25.9	11.2	**7.7**
3.1	0.04	na	0.15	**6.2**	1.3	1.23	10.12	4.11	57.1	**3.6**	21.9	11.5	**7.0**
6.9	0.00	0.2	-0.07	**7.9**	0.2	1.78	12.63	4.84	66.8	**5.1**	28.1	2.6	**6.3**
6.9	0.24	2.0	0.10	**4.3**	14.8	0.87	7.75	3.26	75.5	**4.4**	6.7	5.4	**8.6**
9.4	0.32	na	0.00	**3.7**	0.3	0.76	7.02	2.91	70.1	**0.8**	21.5	58.2	**6.7**
8.3	0.62	na	-0.03	**2.8**	0.2	0.37	3.23	3.83	83.9	**0.6**	12.2	42.6	**5.4**
8.3	0.11	0.5	0.00	**6.5**	2.2	1.58	16.75	3.86	57.8	**1.7**	23.2	19.1	**7.7**
4.3	5.98	na	0.00	**0.0**	-0.5	-0.57	-3.90	3.44	123.9	**2.1**	28.7	22.3	**3.5**
8.8	0.00	0.0	-0.03	**5.3**	1.0	1.04	7.67	3.54	58.0	**3.5**	31.3	14.6	**7.5**
6.8	0.24	na	0.00	**4.3**	3.6	0.84	7.68	3.39	67.8	**0.7**	12.9	42.2	**7.5**
4.4	6.86	na	0.21	**4.2**	1.4	0.68	4.65	3.24	67.8	**0.8**	22.0	48.4	**8.0**
9.9	0.27	1.9	0.02	**2.9**	1.6	0.39	2.37	2.09	73.8	**0.7**	12.0	39.9	**8.7**
5.9	0.64	na	0.01	**5.1**	4.1	1.04	11.22	3.76	66.4	**0.7**	12.5	38.0	**6.1**
4.1	3.25	na	0.03	**4.2**	0.2	0.76	6.25	4.22	74.7	**2.1**	11.7	11.8	**5.9**
2.3	2.58	19.1	0.05	**1.4**	0.2	0.09	1.02	3.58	100.5	**1.5**	6.9	21.3	**3.7**
7.2	0.28	na	0.10	**6.6**	5.8	1.31	12.40	3.86	61.0	**1.3**	20.6	22.0	**7.0**
8.4	0.05	na	0.04	**3.7**	1.9	0.65	7.93	3.78	79.0	**1.4**	11.1	18.3	**4.9**
7.1	1.63	na	0.75	**6.0**	0.7	1.42	12.09	3.68	70.9	**1.2**	26.8	34.0	**7.9**
4.3	1.76	na	0.17	**4.2**	1.0	0.75	8.33	4.73	77.0	**4.5**	21.0	6.4	**4.6**
4.2	1.01	13.1	0.12	**3.9**	2.1	0.63	6.88	3.40	81.8	**0.5**	1.5	33.9	**4.9**
4.1	2.01	14.3	0.00	**5.9**	1.9	1.49	15.26	4.23	62.6	**0.7**	14.6	44.6	**5.4**
5.7	0.08	na	0.01	**4.8**	1.4	0.96	8.01	3.94	69.4	**1.3**	30.9	41.3	**6.1**
7.1	5.92	na	0.05	**3.5**	0.4	0.72	6.05	3.14	73.6	**4.8**	35.2	9.0	**6.2**
6.9	0.44	2.3	0.17	**7.3**	45.5	1.50	12.04	3.96	58.7	**3.6**	18.2	10.7	**9.8**
5.6	0.66	3.5	0.02	**6.3**	2.1	1.16	11.39	3.59	59.8	**1.7**	12.7	20.1	**7.3**
7.8	0.88	na	0.11	**7.9**	5.6	1.93	14.65	2.95	35.3	**3.2**	39.9	18.9	**9.4**
9.6	0.29	na	0.00	**2.0**	0.1	0.18	1.54	2.91	92.6	**1.3**	20.3	29.6	**6.4**
3.2	3.12	na	0.79	**4.1**	2.2	0.68	6.57	4.42	63.1	**0.7**	15.4	37.8	**4.6**

Name	City	State	Rating	2018 Rating	2017 Rating	Total Assets ($Mil)	One Year Asset Growth	Asset Mix (As a % of Total Assets) Commercial Loans	Consumer Loans	Mortgage Loans	Securities	Capitalization Index	Leverage Ratio	Risk-Based Capital Ratio
Gifford State Bank	Gifford	IL	**D+**	D+	C-	155.1	2.27	7.0	4.5	29.8	2.1	**7.6**	10.0	13.0
▲ Gilmer National Bank	Gilmer	TX	**B**	B-	B+	226.8	4.68	7.8	10.3	19.9	13.5	**10.0**	14.3	22.0
Glacier Bank	Kalispell	MT	**A-**	A-	A-	13707.2	15.24	7.4	1.3	9.2	19.7	**9.5**	11.8	14.6
▲ Glasford State Bank	Glasford	IL	**B-**	C+	C+	41.7	-1.56	0.8	11.0	26.6	23.9	**6.8**	8.8	19.0
Glen Burnie Mutual Savings Bank	Glen Burnie	MD	**C-**	C-	C-	99.5	2.72	0.0	0.0	76.1	2.0	**5.7**	7.7	17.4
Glen Rock Savings Bank	Glen Rock	NJ	**D+**	D+	D	269.1	3.45	1.0	0.0	49.2	24.0	**10.0**	11.8	24.5
Glenmede Trust Co., N.A.	Philadelphia	PA	**U**	U	U	109.1	2.58	0.0	0.0	0.0	19.4	**10.0**	69.0	114.8
Glennville Bank	Glennville	GA	**A-**	B+	A-	255.8	7.68	3.4	4.0	21.5	22.2	**10.0**	12.1	18.9
Glens Falls National Bank and Trust Co.	Glens Falls	NY	**B+**	B+	B+	2526.4	4.55	2.6	27.2	23.1	20.3	**7.8**	9.6	14.4
Glenview State Bank	Glenview	IL	**B**	B	B-	1269.3	1.16	4.5	17.6	8.7	56.5	**10.0**	11.1	18.1
▲ Glenwood State Bank	Glenwood	IA	**B-**	C	C-	219.8	27.89	3.5	2.4	11.3	35.2	**10.0**	11.0	22.4
▲ Glenwood State Bank	Glenwood	MN	**C+**	C	C-	318.5	9.07	18.2	1.9	15.2	0.1	**4.2**	9.2	10.6
Global Bank	New York	NY	**C+**	C	C	179.1	4.90	1.0	0.0	19.7	2.2	**10.0**	13.5	16.9
▼ GN Bank	Chicago	IL	**D-**	D	D-	137.0	-3.62	0.8	1.3	19.9	32.5	**7.7**	9.4	23.7
GNB Bank	Grundy Center	IA	**B**	B	B	559.9	-0.30	22.7	1.0	5.3	12.3	**10.0**	12.6	15.2
▲ GNBank, N.A.	Girard	KS	**B-**	C	C+	720.0	14.52	13.3	2.1	9.7	23.6	**9.1**	10.4	14.6
▲ Gogebic Range Bank	Ironwood	MI	**C+**	C	B	125.1	1.90	17.9	6.7	11.7	24.8	**9.7**	10.8	16.5
Gold Coast Bank	Chicago	IL	**A-**	B+	A	379.0	1.00	4.1	0.3	22.1	0.0	**10.0**	12.9	20.2
Gold Coast Bank	Islandia	NY	**B-**	B-	C+	561.7	3.66	1.6	0.2	21.3	12.3	**9.2**	10.4	15.3
Golden Bank, N.A.	Houston	TX	**A-**	A-	A-	991.9	10.67	2.3	0.1	10.1	8.7	**10.0**	13.4	16.9
Golden Belt Bank, FSA	Ellis	KS	**B**	B+	B+	246.2	4.57	9.1	2.8	33.2	11.2	**9.0**	12.1	14.2
▲ Golden Pacific Bank, N.A.	Sacramento	CA	**C**	C-	C	131.8	3.99	15.0	0.9	6.5	1.4	**9.0**	10.3	16.2
Golden State Bank	Glendale	CA	**C**	B-	C-	352.5	34.26	11.5	0.1	1.8	0.0	**6.2**	9.2	11.9
Golden Valley Bank	Chico	CA	**B+**	B+	B+	343.8	39.59	5.5	0.2	6.9	26.0	**6.1**	8.1	14.5
Goldman Sachs Bank USA	New York	NY	**B+**	A-	A-	211831.0	18.18	7.1	4.1	5.2	3.4	**8.0**	13.7	13.3
Goldman Sachs Trust Co., N.A.	New York	NY	**U**	U	U	66.9	-2.40	0.0	0.0	0.0	36.0	**10.0**	46.5	207.9
Goldwater Bank, N.A.	Phoenix	AZ	**C-**	C-	D+	195.5	23.75	2.5	0.3	64.1	2.1	**8.9**	10.2	19.0
▲ Goodfield State Bank	Goodfield	IL	**A-**	B+	A	129.2	10.95	15.2	2.0	22.3	11.9	**10.0**	13.3	17.1
▲ Goose River Bank	Mayville	ND	**B-**	C+	B	119.6	-0.65	21.7	3.7	1.1	11.7	**8.0**	10.8	13.4
Goppert Financial Bank	Lathrop	MO	**B-**	B-	C+	176.4	2.35	8.0	0.7	10.2	29.8	**9.4**	10.6	15.2
Goppert State Service Bank	Garnett	KS	**B**	B	C+	184.7	10.08	18.9	5.6	14.9	13.9	**9.6**	10.9	14.7
Gorham Savings Bank	Gorham	ME	**C+**	C+	C+	1223.2	5.23	9.5	0.4	19.0	13.2	**8.0**	10.1	13.3
▼ Gorham State Bank	Gorham	KS	**C+**	B-	B-	28.2	0.16	10.9	3.8	13.1	2.2	**10.0**	12.4	19.5
▼ Gouverneur S&L Assn.	Gouverneur	NY	**B**	B+	B+	125.3	-4.98	1.6	2.1	58.9	13.6	**10.0**	22.3	38.0
Graham S&L, SSB	Graham	TX	**B+**	B+	B+	138.5	7.44	2.9	1.9	45.5	7.6	**10.0**	11.6	21.2
▲ Grand Bank	Tulsa	OK	**C+**	B-	B+	387.4	12.56	17.6	0.2	12.2	5.9	**7.8**	10.5	13.2
Grand Bank for Savings, FSB	Hattiesburg	MS	**B+**	B+	B+	86.0	5.46	0.0	0.5	74.2	0.0	**10.0**	12.9	28.7
▲ Grand Marais State Bank	Grand Marais	MN	**B**	B-	B	96.5	7.21	9.4	1.7	28.5	34.9	**5.6**	7.6	15.3
Grand Mountain Bank, FSB	Granby	CO	**C+**	B-	C+	130.6	12.08	3.7	1.7	34.1	3.6	**7.0**	9.0	17.1
Grand Rapids State Bank	Grand Rapids	MN	**B-**	B-	C+	227.5	1.57	11.5	3.9	10.0	20.7	**8.1**	9.7	13.8
Grand Ridge National Bank	Grand Ridge	IL	**A-**	A-	A-	223.7	17.75	9.6	0.0	10.0	0.3	**9.7**	11.9	14.7
Grand River Bank	Grandville	MI	**C+**	C+	C+	320.7	27.47	7.8	0.1	15.6	1.9	**7.3**	11.0	12.8
Grand Rivers Community Bank	Grand Chain	IL	**E-**	E-	E	31.8	-18.19	8.3	1.1	14.5	4.8	**1.5**	4.6	8.5
▲ Grand Savings Bank	Grove	OK	**B**	B-	B	510.6	12.28	6.5	8.0	21.7	6.6	**7.6**	9.4	13.3
Grand Timber Bank	McGregor	MN	**B-**	C+	C+	43.9	2.17	8.3	7.4	31.1	15.1	**10.0**	14.7	22.5
Grand Valley Bank	Heber City	UT	**B+**	B+	B	439.6	13.25	1.4	0.4	7.6	48.1	**7.7**	9.5	18.3
GrandSouth Bank	Greenville	SC	**B**	B	B+	887.2	19.98	21.7	4.7	11.5	6.5	**7.6**	10.1	13.0
Grandview Bank	Grandview	TX	**A-**	B+	B+	229.2	10.03	13.6	6.8	15.8	22.2	**8.1**	9.7	17.4
▲ Granger National Bank	Granger	TX	**B**	B-	B-	31.9	-2.10	1.9	2.5	5.6	44.0	**10.0**	18.0	40.3
▲ Granite Community Bank	Cold Spring	MN	**C+**	C	C+	123.9	4.16	7.1	1.8	9.0	7.4	**4.2**	8.2	10.6
▲ Granite Falls Bank	Granite Falls	MN	**B+**	B-	B	136.5	-2.03	5.0	0.5	2.1	43.7	**9.6**	10.7	16.9
▲ Granite Mountain Bank, Inc.	Philipsburg	MT	**B**	B-	B-	85.9	8.95	10.9	2.4	14.6	10.5	**7.4**	9.3	19.2
▲ Grant County Bank	Ulysses	KS	**B-**	C+	C+	227.5	2.34	8.7	1.9	21.9	26.4	**10.0**	14.7	23.7
Grant County Bank	Medford	OK	**C**	C	C+	56.2	-4.96	4.4	6.2	1.7	38.2	**10.0**	16.8	33.9
Grant County Bank	Petersburg	WV	**B-**	B-	B	257.9	1.23	6.9	3.1	30.5	6.9	**10.0**	14.0	19.4
▲ Grant County State Bank	Swayzee	IN	**B-**	C+	B	193.9	9.07	9.9	6.6	39.0	0.0	**10.0**	11.7	18.4
Grant County State Bank	Carson	ND	**A-**	A-	A-	33.3	-2.15	1.6	0.1	0.0	0.0	**10.0**	13.4	19.4
Granville National Bank	Granville	IL	**B-**	B-	C	88.7	5.12	3.3	4.9	24.0	37.5	**9.9**	10.9	28.3
Gratz Bank	Gratz	PA	**B**	B	B	358.9	6.78	5.7	0.6	28.3	19.5	**6.9**	8.9	13.8
▲ Great American Bank	Lawrence	KS	**B**	B-	B+	218.1	8.33	8.0	0.4	25.7	0.9	**7.8**	10.0	13.2

Asset Quality Index	Adjusted Non-Performing Loans as a % of Total Loans	Adjusted Non-Performing Loans as a % of Capital	Net Charge-Offs Avg Loans	Profitability Index	Net Income ($Mil)	Return on Assets (R.O.A.)	Return on Equity (R.O.E.)	Net Interest Spread	Overhead Efficiency Ratio	Liquidity Index	Liquidity Ratio	Hot Money Ratio	Stability Index
3.1	1.59	na	2.23	**3.5**	0.7	0.62	6.08	4.15	67.1	**2.4**	11.2	16.5	**5.4**
4.5	1.57	na	0.29	**5.8**	2.0	1.18	8.41	3.76	56.8	**1.7**	34.0	33.5	**7.6**
6.2	0.76	2.8	0.09	**8.7**	164.5	1.76	12.52	4.42	58.6	**4.4**	13.9	5.2	**10.0**
5.2	0.00	na	0.36	**3.7**	0.2	0.72	7.95	3.69	75.9	**6.0**	37.5	2.3	**5.1**
5.4	1.05	na	0.00	**2.1**	0.2	0.31	4.09	1.07	70.4	**5.5**	23.9	0.0	**4.0**
6.7	1.77	na	0.00	**0.8**	0.0	0.00	0.02	2.40	103.7	**1.7**	13.8	21.5	**5.6**
10.0	na	0.0	na	**9.5**	24.7	32.83	63.51	2.72	80.6	**4.0**	104.4	0.0	**7.0**
7.0	0.64	3.1	0.07	**7.4**	2.5	1.37	11.17	4.51	62.7	**1.5**	23.9	26.9	**7.6**
6.8	0.19	1.7	0.04	**5.9**	22.0	1.20	12.47	3.08	60.7	**3.4**	6.7	5.7	**8.4**
7.9	0.03	0.3	0.02	**4.7**	11.2	1.18	10.42	2.64	63.5	**6.2**	53.8	9.6	**9.4**
8.7	0.00	na	0.02	**4.1**	1.5	0.92	9.19	3.16	65.1	**6.5**	54.3	4.8	**4.9**
4.2	1.30	na	-0.01	**7.0**	3.6	1.57	16.84	4.00	60.8	**1.6**	4.0	17.8	**7.5**
7.5	0.00	na	0.00	**3.1**	0.6	0.43	3.32	3.79	85.7	**0.5**	7.1	47.4	**7.0**
3.1	8.49	24.3	-0.06	**0.1**	-0.3	-0.29	-3.09	2.83	120.3	**3.6**	39.6	17.0	**2.6**
7.7	0.76	na	0.13	**7.6**	7.0	1.68	12.76	4.23	60.9	**0.7**	12.4	27.9	**9.4**
4.4	0.97	na	0.06	**5.5**	5.9	1.13	9.24	4.03	67.4	**3.3**	14.1	10.4	**8.0**
4.7	1.54	na	0.25	**5.8**	1.0	1.07	9.91	4.73	66.3	**4.3**	34.8	11.7	**6.7**
8.2	0.66	na	0.28	**7.8**	3.8	1.31	10.59	3.85	58.3	**1.2**	30.7	44.9	**8.8**
6.3	0.61	na	-0.02	**3.5**	2.7	0.64	6.22	2.68	67.2	**0.7**	12.4	32.3	**6.2**
7.3	0.35	1.9	0.00	**8.3**	11.3	1.60	12.02	3.94	48.4	**1.0**	26.3	45.8	**9.4**
4.6	1.38	na	0.05	**7.8**	3.5	1.96	14.90	3.96	56.6	**3.7**	10.4	9.9	**9.0**
3.4	1.34	na	0.21	**3.2**	0.2	0.24	1.97	4.89	88.0	**2.9**	17.8	14.6	**6.5**
4.4	1.35	na	-0.03	**4.3**	1.8	0.73	6.91	3.92	68.5	**1.4**	26.7	31.2	**6.7**
9.1	0.05	na	0.00	**5.3**	3.2	1.28	15.83	3.47	61.6	**5.9**	52.1	8.1	**5.3**
8.7	0.62	1.7	0.50	**4.2**	1116.0	0.74	5.26	1.52	48.6	**3.3**	66.2	12.1	**10.0**
10.0	na	0.0	na	**9.5**	27.9	44.32	60.25	2.16	49.5	**4.0**	225.8	0.0	**5.7**
7.9	0.70	2.2	-0.03	**5.9**	6.3	5.28	61.42	2.97	87.6	**0.5**	9.1	59.3	**2.2**
7.3	0.00	na	0.22	**9.4**	2.0	2.15	16.49	3.99	53.1	**1.8**	17.8	20.3	**8.9**
5.0	0.34	na	-0.04	**7.3**	1.8	2.01	19.07	4.79	65.0	**2.8**	7.2	14.2	**7.3**
8.3	0.04	na	0.18	**4.0**	1.0	0.76	7.46	3.65	71.9	**4.2**	19.4	8.1	**5.6**
8.0	0.05	na	-0.05	**5.3**	1.5	1.07	10.01	3.84	64.6	**2.4**	6.1	16.2	**6.5**
7.1	0.81	na	0.00	**3.4**	6.1	0.67	7.12	3.39	77.2	**1.4**	4.7	6.8	**7.5**
1.7	9.13	na	0.00	**4.9**	0.2	1.01	8.62	3.61	61.3	**5.3**	33.6	4.9	**5.8**
7.2	1.79	na	0.28	**1.9**	-0.3	-0.32	-1.37	4.57	118.1	**4.4**	15.8	5.8	**7.9**
9.0	0.45	na	0.00	**4.0**	0.8	0.81	6.91	3.54	74.7	**1.3**	29.0	35.1	**7.9**
4.8	1.45	na	0.09	**6.7**	3.8	1.34	12.59	3.97	54.9	**0.7**	13.5	38.5	**7.5**
7.7	1.30	na	0.05	**5.5**	0.8	1.20	9.39	6.31	82.2	**0.6**	19.1	47.8	**6.8**
9.1	0.00	na	0.04	**6.8**	1.1	1.68	21.76	3.77	57.6	**4.6**	17.0	4.6	**5.5**
7.0	0.66	na	-0.04	**3.7**	0.6	0.65	6.68	4.00	79.9	**5.6**	33.5	3.4	**5.9**
8.1	0.24	1.5	0.01	**4.6**	1.8	1.07	10.60	3.98	75.1	**4.5**	14.5	5.4	**6.1**
7.2	0.11	na	0.00	**10.0**	3.0	1.90	15.47	5.61	52.3	**1.2**	16.0	29.0	**8.7**
7.3	0.00	na	0.00	**3.4**	1.3	0.59	5.88	3.05	74.0	**0.8**	12.6	26.8	**6.0**
1.1	5.05	37.8	0.91	**1.1**	-0.4	-1.78	-25.60	3.74	150.9	**1.4**	31.1	37.1	**0.2**
7.3	0.44	na	-0.01	**7.6**	6.7	1.82	19.37	4.44	62.1	**1.1**	12.7	29.2	**6.6**
3.8	5.11	na	0.26	**8.8**	0.7	2.31	15.86	4.85	60.8	**4.7**	25.7	5.6	**8.6**
8.3	0.32	na	0.02	**6.0**	3.8	1.23	11.98	3.93	61.7	**5.5**	49.1	9.7	**6.3**
7.4	0.30	1.9	0.24	**5.2**	6.6	1.05	10.41	5.13	66.4	**1.1**	18.1	32.0	**6.6**
8.2	0.02	0.6	0.07	**8.2**	2.9	1.74	18.06	4.34	50.7	**3.5**	33.4	15.3	**6.6**
7.9	0.98	na	0.10	**4.1**	0.2	0.79	4.42	3.70	77.5	**5.4**	79.2	14.2	**7.3**
6.8	0.93	na	0.00	**5.5**	1.0	1.09	12.80	4.01	67.5	**0.9**	15.6	31.1	**5.6**
7.8	0.36	na	0.00	**7.4**	1.8	1.73	14.62	4.00	51.7	**4.1**	19.3	8.4	**7.5**
8.8	0.00	na	0.00	**5.9**	0.7	1.17	12.57	4.57	67.3	**6.0**	41.9	3.6	**5.2**
3.6	4.57	na	0.30	**6.0**	2.6	1.52	10.27	3.55	65.0	**1.2**	20.5	29.3	**8.4**
6.9	2.53	na	0.75	**2.1**	0.1	0.27	1.69	2.67	88.1	**2.2**	45.8	36.1	**5.1**
4.4	2.59	na	0.11	**5.6**	1.9	0.99	7.64	4.57	70.6	**2.1**	10.6	17.9	**7.3**
3.4	2.91	na	0.56	**9.7**	3.5	2.54	21.90	4.26	30.7	**0.8**	17.5	40.4	**8.9**
7.2	0.00	0.0	0.00	**9.4**	0.6	2.39	18.73	5.05	51.7	**3.3**	18.4	12.7	**7.0**
7.1	0.52	na	0.22	**3.5**	0.4	0.67	5.73	2.85	70.8	**5.9**	52.2	6.9	**6.3**
6.9	0.35	2.4	-0.01	**5.5**	2.9	1.13	11.96	3.57	59.5	**3.2**	22.2	13.8	**5.9**
5.4	0.09	na	0.02	**8.3**	3.1	1.95	14.66	4.71	56.6	**0.9**	6.0	30.9	**9.0**

Name	City	State	Rating	2018 Rating	2017 Rating	Total Assets ($Mil)	One Year Asset Growth	Asset Mix (As a % of Total Assets) Commercial Loans	Consumer Loans	Mortgage Loans	Securities	Capitalization Index	Leverage Ratio	Risk-Based Capital Ratio
▲ Great Midwest Bank, S.S.B.	Brookfield	WI	**B+**	B	B	851.3	9.26	0.0	0.1	66.3	6.1	**10.0**	15.2	22.2
Great Nations Bank	Norman	OK	**B-**	B-	B-	67.4	9.24	24.8	0.8	11.1	1.8	**10.0**	13.8	15.9
Great North Bank	Florence	WI	**C-**	C-	C+	142.3	0.03	24.0	2.5	14.1	14.8	**6.7**	8.7	13.6
▲ Great Plains Bank	Eureka	SD	**D**	D-	D	114.0	5.24	11.0	1.0	4.4	6.4	**10.0**	13.2	15.4
Great Plains National Bank	Hollis	OK	**B**	B+	B+	809.9	11.47	19.8	3.8	18.5	6.8	**8.2**	10.0	13.5
Great Plains State Bank	Petersburg	NE	**C**	C	C+	297.8	48.77	11.6	0.5	0.1	5.1	**8.3**	9.9	14.2
Great Rivers Bank	Barry	IL	**C+**	C+	C-	132.2	32.24	9.6	2.3	7.6	11.6	**9.7**	11.1	14.7
Great Southern Bank	Springfield	MO	**A-**	B+	B-	4976.2	8.50	4.7	4.5	11.2	7.0	**8.3**	12.2	13.6
Great Southern Bank	Meridian	MS	**B**	B	B	301.0	4.69	4.4	10.9	12.3	47.8	**7.7**	9.4	22.4
Great Western Bank	Sioux Falls	SD	**C+**	C+	C+	12775.3	5.51	11.0	0.4	4.2	14.0	**6.6**	9.9	12.2
Greater Community Bank	Rome	GA	**B+**	B	B-	220.7	22.00	10.8	7.3	10.4	2.7	**8.0**	10.2	13.4
Greater State Bank	McAllen	TX	**C**	C	C	87.3	7.31	9.6	1.7	14.1	6.9	**7.7**	9.5	17.3
▲ Green Belt Bank & Trust	Iowa Falls	IA	**C-**	C-	C	496.7	6.60	9.1	2.2	6.5	12.1	**5.5**	8.9	11.4
Green Dot Bank	Provo	UT	**A**	A	A	1325.6	-15.75	0.0	1.5	0.1	18.1	**10.0**	15.1	102.8
Greene County Commercial Bank	Catskill	NY	**U**	U	U	595.4	32.81	0.0	0.0	0.0	77.6	**8.1**	9.7	41.3
Greeneville Federal Bank, FSB	Greeneville	TN	**B-**	B	B+	153.9	-4.26	8.9	1.2	29.0	1.1	**10.0**	14.5	21.2
Greenfield Banking Co.	Greenfield	IN	**A-**	A-	B	577.2	5.58	3.8	0.9	7.6	24.6	**10.0**	11.0	17.1
Greenfield Banking Co.	Greenfield	TN	**D+**	C-	C+	64.2	4.68	16.0	9.5	17.8	6.3	**5.8**	9.7	11.6
Greenfield Co-operative Bank	Greenfield	MA	**B**	B	C+	656.9	7.43	5.2	0.5	40.4	20.7	**10.0**	11.8	22.7
Greenfield Savings Bank	Greenfield	MA	**B**	B	B	874.5	3.97	3.8	0.1	54.6	10.3	**10.0**	12.0	20.1
Greenleaf Wayside Bank	Greenleaf	WI	**B**	B	C+	95.8	5.01	4.7	1.1	22.3	28.4	**8.6**	10.1	17.4
Greenville Federal	Greenville	OH	**C+**	C+	B-	186.2	2.68	8.2	0.9	54.2	0.9	**10.0**	11.2	15.7
Greenville National Bank	Greenville	OH	**B+**	B+	B+	484.4	7.69	2.7	11.7	20.9	15.7	**9.8**	10.9	16.4
Greenville Savings Bank	Greenville	PA	**B**	B	B	243.3	1.09	0.7	0.8	58.8	12.3	**10.0**	14.6	25.9
Greenwoods State Bank	Lake Mills	WI	**C-**	C	B-	311.8	75.22	7.5	1.4	16.3	4.9	**6.2**	9.2	11.9
▲ Grinnell State Bank	Grinnell	IA	**B**	B	B+	318.8	3.12	5.2	0.5	5.6	14.5	**10.0**	12.6	16.1
▼ Grove Bank & Trust	Miami	FL	**B**	B+	B+	714.5	12.37	5.1	0.5	4.4	41.8	**10.0**	16.6	29.9
▲ Grundy Bank	Morris	IL	**B**	B-	B+	277.9	-11.26	5.9	0.6	19.0	11.5	**7.3**	9.2	17.8
Grundy National Bank	Grundy	VA	**C**	C-	C-	303.0	-1.88	5.9	5.1	8.0	36.1	**10.0**	22.3	39.4
GSL Savings Bank	Guttenberg	NJ	**D+**	D+	C-	104.6	3.45	1.8	0.0	61.2	1.9	**9.9**	11.0	18.0
▲ Guadalupe Bank	Kerrville	TX	**B+**	B	B	168.8	7.59	5.2	1.6	24.1	0.3	**6.9**	8.9	15.6
Guaranty Bank	Springfield	MO	**C**	C	C	1014.8	5.10	10.0	0.6	12.1	10.5	**7.6**	10.2	13.0
Guaranty Bank & Trust Co. of Delhi	Delhi	LA	**B+**	B+	A-	275.1	12.80	3.9	2.1	27.8	5.5	**6.4**	8.4	13.7
▲ Guaranty Bank & Trust, N.A.	Mount Pleasant	TX	**B+**	B	B	2325.5	3.71	8.4	2.3	17.5	16.5	**7.5**	10.0	12.9
▲ Guaranty Bank and Trust Co.	New Roads	LA	**A-**	B+	A-	218.7	6.86	2.9	2.3	31.5	15.5	**10.0**	13.5	20.4
▲ Guaranty Bank and Trust Co.	Belzoni	MS	**B**	B-	B	896.4	8.79	9.7	1.2	10.2	16.5	**8.5**	10.4	13.7
Guaranty State Bank and Trust Co.	Beloit	KS	**C+**	C	C-	285.1	4.51	7.6	1.1	8.0	7.5	**10.0**	12.8	15.8
▲ Guardian Bank	Valdosta	GA	**B+**	B	B+	418.9	2.21	8.6	2.0	14.5	25.2	**9.4**	10.6	18.6
Guardian Savings Bank	Granite City	IL	**D**	D+	C	37.4	0.45	0.0	0.3	23.2	46.8	**10.0**	19.4	90.7
Guardian Savings Bank, F.S.B.	West Chester	OH	**B**	B	B-	1002.7	6.83	0.0	0.0	66.0	0.0	**10.0**	11.4	24.0
Guilford Savings Bank	Guilford	CT	**B**	B-	B-	835.1	11.12	2.5	0.8	38.2	11.8	**10.0**	12.2	17.3
▲ Gulf Coast Bank	Abbeville	LA	**B+**	B	B+	370.3	1.41	5.0	9.6	17.2	11.4	**10.0**	14.5	22.5
Gulf Coast Bank and Trust Co.	New Orleans	LA	**B-**	C+	C+	1862.3	9.34	25.1	2.2	15.8	10.3	**6.6**	9.1	12.2
▲ Gunnison Bank and Trust Co.	Gunnison	CO	**A-**	B	B	123.7	25.54	2.2	0.3	24.9	4.5	**7.5**	9.3	14.8
Gunnison S&L Assn.	Gunnison	CO	**B-**	C+	C-	102.9	1.75	0.0	1.0	48.0	0.5	**10.0**	12.2	33.4
Guthrie County State Bank	Panora	IA	**C+**	C+	B-	123.6	5.57	6.7	3.4	17.4	18.5	**10.0**	11.5	16.6
Gwinnett Community Bank	Duluth	GA	**E-**	E-	E-	223.2	-7.02	6.4	0.4	12.3	15.4	**0.9**	5.0	7.8
▲ H. F. Gehant Banking Co.	West Brooklyn	IL	**B+**	B	B	58.5	4.06	4.9	2.7	14.6	8.5	**10.0**	15.9	21.9
Habib American Bank	New York	NY	**B+**	B+	B+	1834.7	21.45	2.8	0.4	6.7	3.5	**6.3**	8.3	17.4
Haddon Savings Bank	Haddon Heights	NJ	**C**	C	C	328.1	-0.50	6.9	0.0	25.9	52.5	**9.0**	10.3	21.9
▲ Halstead Bank	Halstead	KS	**B-**	B-	C+	117.7	-2.34	9.6	7.6	18.7	6.8	**7.7**	9.6	13.1
▲ Hamilton Bank	Hamilton	MO	**B-**	C+	B-	80.3	3.35	3.2	3.1	17.2	27.2	**8.4**	10.0	13.9
Hamler State Bank	Hamler	OH	**B+**	B+	B+	85.0	5.36	6.6	1.1	16.5	22.6	**10.0**	16.3	24.5
▲ Hamlin Bank and Trust Co.	Smethport	PA	**A-**	B+	A	388.5	-5.08	1.3	4.7	50.5	27.7	**10.0**	20.6	28.9
Hancock Bank and Trust Co.	Hawesville	KY	**B-**	C+	C	287.0	-1.15	6.7	1.4	24.6	6.6	**9.9**	10.9	15.8
Hancock County Savings Bank, FSB	Chester	WV	**B**	B	B	373.5	2.31	0.1	2.8	75.0	9.9	**10.0**	18.5	36.8
Hancock Whitney Bank	Gulfport	MS	**B-**	C+	C+	30529.4	8.94	21.6	3.4	11.4	21.2	**5.3**	9.0	11.2
▼ Hanmi Bank	Los Angeles	CA	**B+**	A-	A-	5512.6	0.55	16.7	0.1	8.1	11.3	**9.6**	11.9	14.7
Hanover Community Bank	Garden City Park	NY	**B+**	B+	B-	848.8	30.60	0.9	0.1	52.9	1.5	**9.2**	10.5	19.1
Happy State Bank	Amarillo	TX	**A-**	A-	B+	3677.4	7.30	14.1	0.9	10.2	16.6	**10.0**	13.9	17.3

Asset Quality Index	Adjusted Non-Performing Loans as a % of Total Loans	Adjusted Non-Performing Loans as a % of Capital	Net Charge-Offs Avg Loans	Profitability Index	Net Income ($Mil)	Return on Assets (R.O.A.)	Return on Equity (R.O.E.)	Net Interest Spread	Overhead Efficiency Ratio	Liquidity Index	Liquidity Ratio	Hot Money Ratio	Stability Index
6.9	1.55	na	-0.01	**5.1**	6.7	1.09	7.12	2.58	60.4	**0.5**	9.8	40.3	**8.5**
8.2	0.10	na	0.06	**2.7**	0.2	0.36	2.56	3.52	89.1	**0.5**	10.1	62.8	**7.3**
3.1	2.46	11.4	0.04	**2.1**	0.5	0.50	5.58	3.52	87.7	**1.1**	31.3	50.2	**4.4**
0.8	3.86	na	0.00	**8.6**	1.8	2.14	16.74	4.35	44.0	**0.6**	9.1	33.1	**8.8**
4.0	1.26	na	0.35	**9.4**	11.8	1.98	19.79	5.85	72.4	**1.3**	12.4	26.3	**8.7**
4.9	0.85	na	0.00	**2.4**	0.5	0.25	2.36	2.84	73.2	**0.9**	26.2	22.1	**5.2**
4.0	1.51	na	0.33	**3.2**	0.6	0.71	5.48	3.61	72.7	**3.2**	24.0	14.1	**6.2**
6.8	0.29	1.7	0.11	**8.2**	60.3	1.67	13.11	4.13	51.6	**0.7**	8.8	30.5	**10.0**
6.9	0.35	na	0.38	**4.4**	2.0	0.87	9.43	4.40	77.4	**5.6**	58.9	11.5	**5.0**
3.5	1.43	6.5	0.42	**7.7**	130.7	1.37	9.16	3.76	44.0	**2.6**	10.8	8.9	**10.0**
7.1	0.20	1.4	0.12	**5.8**	2.1	1.36	13.60	4.52	68.5	**1.9**	22.1	18.1	**6.0**
5.3	1.16	na	0.52	**3.1**	0.2	0.40	4.30	4.55	89.5	**1.7**	34.0	34.1	**4.3**
3.3	1.46	na	0.11	**6.1**	5.9	1.56	17.03	3.46	48.2	**1.8**	15.2	18.6	**7.2**
9.8	16.92	na	7.39	**10.0**	40.3	3.26	26.00	3.00	14.4	**3.8**	105.4	0.3	**9.0**
10.0	na	na	na	**7.8**	5.6	1.50	15.77	2.54	10.1	**5.5**	25.9	0.1	**7.0**
4.9	2.75	na	-0.01	**3.7**	0.7	0.57	4.03	3.95	80.3	**1.2**	15.5	25.1	**8.0**
6.4	0.70	na	0.11	**6.5**	5.3	1.28	12.39	3.87	59.6	**6.5**	45.4	1.8	**7.2**
2.4	2.27	na	0.00	**4.1**	0.4	0.95	9.91	4.21	68.7	**0.7**	14.0	38.6	**3.4**
7.8	0.85	na	0.08	**3.8**	3.4	0.71	6.06	3.05	70.3	**3.1**	31.1	16.7	**7.0**
8.2	0.53	na	0.04	**4.3**	5.4	0.84	7.13	3.43	72.5	**1.1**	13.8	25.9	**7.7**
8.9	0.04	na	-0.03	**5.0**	0.9	1.22	12.46	3.61	69.4	**6.0**	41.4	3.4	**6.2**
8.9	0.22	na	0.01	**2.5**	0.4	0.31	2.77	3.31	89.4	**0.7**	10.6	36.4	**6.5**
4.6	1.19	8.0	0.17	**6.3**	4.6	1.31	12.39	3.71	57.7	**3.3**	15.8	12.6	**7.0**
8.1	0.56	na	0.06	**3.8**	1.1	0.63	4.43	2.88	71.4	**1.9**	23.7	20.7	**7.5**
4.7	1.49	na	0.01	**4.0**	1.3	0.73	6.47	4.21	79.6	**2.3**	18.8	16.4	**6.5**
5.0	1.12	na	-0.02	**5.7**	2.8	1.18	9.44	3.72	61.1	**3.9**	12.8	9.2	**6.7**
9.3	0.25	0.4	0.00	**2.6**	1.3	0.27	1.55	2.85	92.3	**6.2**	51.1	5.9	**8.5**
7.1	1.44	na	0.01	**9.7**	5.1	2.45	22.05	4.34	50.7	**4.9**	23.3	3.9	**8.1**
5.0	4.11	8.0	0.61	**2.1**	0.6	0.28	1.26	2.93	83.8	**3.1**	49.5	25.7	**6.5**
9.3	0.04	0.3	0.00	**1.7**	0.2	0.19	1.66	2.77	91.4	**0.7**	10.8	35.5	**6.5**
7.4	0.01	na	0.09	**7.4**	1.9	1.53	17.31	4.41	62.2	**4.8**	36.3	9.4	**6.2**
4.7	2.05	na	0.11	**5.9**	8.7	1.19	10.84	3.64	64.7	**2.8**	20.6	16.2	**8.9**
7.6	0.23	na	0.04	**10.0**	4.7	2.36	28.07	4.76	57.3	**1.7**	28.7	28.2	**6.5**
7.6	1.04	2.8	-0.04	**5.6**	20.3	1.17	10.37	3.74	63.1	**1.7**	9.7	20.1	**9.1**
7.3	0.43	na	0.02	**7.8**	2.4	1.50	11.59	4.74	58.6	**3.2**	11.3	12.6	**7.9**
5.4	1.34	na	-0.14	**7.8**	12.4	1.93	18.61	4.16	59.8	**1.5**	11.6	22.9	**8.5**
2.4	2.96	19.3	0.67	**4.2**	1.4	0.65	4.97	4.07	60.5	**1.8**	16.5	11.3	**6.6**
5.5	1.02	na	0.08	**6.0**	4.5	1.45	14.47	3.61	60.1	**1.8**	23.7	23.1	**7.8**
10.0	1.50	na	0.02	**0.0**	-0.5	-1.80	-9.28	2.18	176.6	**4.0**	79.4	24.0	**6.9**
7.4	0.82	na	-0.03	**7.9**	13.7	1.90	15.62	2.65	45.3	**1.8**	23.1	27.5	**10.0**
7.8	0.82	na	0.04	**3.8**	4.8	0.80	6.57	3.12	79.6	**2.5**	21.1	17.1	**7.8**
6.1	1.17	na	0.10	**6.2**	3.4	1.19	8.71	4.77	73.3	**4.7**	28.9	7.1	**7.6**
4.1	1.71	14.5	0.05	**7.6**	21.8	1.67	18.19	7.73	76.6	**1.9**	21.7	18.2	**8.4**
8.9	0.10	na	-0.02	**9.3**	1.4	1.77	18.54	5.23	61.5	**3.7**	27.6	9.3	**6.0**
9.7	0.43	na	0.00	**3.4**	0.5	0.67	5.60	3.17	72.9	**3.1**	46.2	22.6	**6.4**
8.2	0.47	na	-0.06	**3.2**	0.5	0.57	5.03	3.96	85.2	**3.0**	16.3	14.1	**6.4**
8.8	0.01	0.1	-0.26	**3.6**	1.2	0.72	16.74	4.01	79.9	**1.7**	21.8	23.5	**1.1**
8.2	0.42	na	-0.03	**5.5**	0.6	1.35	8.53	3.74	63.0	**1.7**	27.7	27.1	**8.3**
8.8	0.23	1.3	-0.03	**7.2**	16.5	1.27	14.80	2.16	48.7	**2.8**	49.1	50.6	**7.7**
8.6	1.06	na	0.13	**2.4**	0.7	0.27	2.70	1.89	80.5	**3.0**	50.7	15.5	**5.1**
7.7	0.27	na	0.07	**4.1**	0.8	0.85	9.09	4.25	75.4	**1.8**	10.5	11.0	**5.3**
4.6	0.31	na	0.07	**6.9**	1.0	1.68	16.85	4.31	62.2	**3.5**	24.1	12.5	**6.7**
8.8	0.06	na	0.00	**5.5**	0.9	1.41	8.90	3.33	56.3	**2.3**	28.1	19.8	**8.6**
7.0	0.84	na	0.23	**7.6**	6.4	2.14	9.76	3.94	54.9	**4.9**	39.8	10.6	**7.6**
6.8	1.24	na	-0.09	**3.6**	1.6	0.76	6.71	3.83	82.7	**2.5**	9.7	16.2	**6.0**
9.1	0.92	na	0.02	**4.8**	2.6	0.92	5.02	3.52	68.6	**3.2**	16.5	13.0	**7.9**
4.0	1.35	7.4	0.25	**5.3**	240.8	1.12	9.85	3.46	63.3	**3.2**	14.8	9.1	**9.3**
4.5	1.47	9.1	0.02	**5.6**	36.1	0.88	7.26	3.53	55.9	**0.9**	15.3	31.2	**9.9**
8.5	0.37	na	0.00	**5.7**	6.3	1.18	10.64	3.38	58.6	**0.7**	12.4	38.0	**7.3**
6.7	0.80	3.2	0.35	**5.5**	34.4	1.31	8.66	4.39	67.7	**1.8**	12.3	7.3	**9.9**

Name	City	State	Rating	2018 Rating	2017 Rating	Total Assets ($Mil)	One Year Asset Growth	Asset Mix (As a % of Total Assets) Comm-ercial Loans	Cons-umer Loans	Mort-gage Loans	Secur-ities	Capital-ization Index	Lever-age Ratio	Risk-Based Capital Ratio
Harbor Bank of Maryland	Baltimore	MD	**D-**	D-	D-	305.8	7.64	9.5	0.7	16.8	10.0	**4.4**	6.8	10.7
▲ HarborOne Bank	Brockton	MA	**C+**	C	C	3818.8	33.82	5.0	11.7	28.8	6.1	**10.0**	12.1	15.4
Hardin County Bank	Savannah	TN	**C+**	C+	C	502.6	0.51	27.6	3.8	17.1	10.2	**6.9**	9.8	12.5
Hardin County Savings Bank	Eldora	IA	**B-**	B-	B-	221.4	5.13	7.2	1.1	9.3	35.1	**7.5**	9.3	14.0
Harford Bank	Aberdeen	MD	**B-**	C	C	389.7	8.49	3.8	2.4	17.0	10.7	**10.0**	11.2	15.6
Harleysville Bank	Harleysville	PA	**B-**	B-	B-	780.3	1.34	1.0	0.1	46.7	15.2	**8.1**	9.7	14.9
Harrison Building and Loan Assn.	Harrison	OH	**B**	B-	B-	224.0	2.53	2.0	0.2	37.2	35.4	**10.0**	15.6	29.3
Harrison County Bank	Lost Creek	WV	**B**	B	B	114.9	3.33	0.9	5.5	26.9	41.0	**10.0**	11.1	22.6
Hart County Bank and Trust Co.	Munfordville	KY	**B**	B	B	27.0	0.99	19.2	1.5	1.6	26.3	**10.0**	23.7	30.4
▲ Hartsburg State Bank	Hartsburg	IL	**C+**	C	C	16.2	10.10	6.3	1.5	4.9	27.2	**10.0**	13.3	19.6
Harvard State Bank	Harvard	IL	**B-**	B-	B-	254.5	10.15	5.7	1.3	20.9	26.9	**7.5**	9.3	15.9
▼ Harvest Bank	Kimball	MN	**B-**	B	B-	144.1	1.30	9.0	3.0	18.9	13.8	**7.9**	9.6	14.3
▲ Harwood State Bank	Harwood	ND	**C**	C-	C-	40.2	-0.92	11.8	3.6	2.0	4.2	**8.0**	9.7	14.6
Haskell National Bank	Haskell	TX	**B**	B-	B-	71.9	3.03	4.9	3.9	12.6	38.6	**10.0**	12.8	29.9
Hatboro Federal Savings, FA	Hatboro	PA	**B**	B	B-	513.3	3.66	0.0	0.0	67.5	16.5	**10.0**	22.9	43.9
▼ Hatch Bank	San Marcos	CA	**C+**	B	B+	68.5	-5.54	0.0	56.6	36.0	0.0	**10.0**	41.7	42.8
Havana National Bank	Havana	IL	**D+**	C-	B-	254.2	3.42	7.2	1.5	8.3	17.0	**9.0**	10.9	14.2
Haven Savings Bank	Hoboken	NJ	**C-**	C-	C	1009.0	1.44	0.4	0.0	59.2	9.6	**8.6**	10.1	17.2
Haverford Trust Co.	Radnor	PA	**A**	A	A	162.4	24.70	1.1	37.6	0.5	26.9	**10.0**	17.6	17.2
Haverhill Bank	Haverhill	MA	**C+**	C	C	412.9	4.35	8.6	0.2	45.6	15.4	**9.6**	10.7	16.9
Haviland State Bank	Haviland	KS	**B**	B	B	39.2	1.88	4.1	1.0	1.1	22.0	**10.0**	14.2	20.6
Hawaii National Bank	Honolulu	HI	**C+**	C	C-	643.9	3.51	20.9	0.4	18.2	17.5	**8.3**	9.9	14.2
Hawthorn Bank	Jefferson City	MO	**B+**	B	B	1441.5	-0.21	9.9	2.2	15.1	12.5	**9.1**	11.3	14.3
Headwaters State Bank	Land O'Lakes	WI	**B+**	B+	B+	66.9	-0.18	2.4	2.5	34.0	26.3	**10.0**	15.2	30.5
▲ Heartland Bank	Somers	IA	**A-**	B+	A	158.9	6.33	14.9	1.4	7.7	17.1	**10.0**	13.4	16.2
Heartland Bank	Geneva	NE	**C**	C+	C+	616.3	39.29	6.1	1.2	2.2	18.1	**7.7**	9.9	13.1
▲ Heartland Bank	Whitehall	OH	**A-**	B+	B	1136.4	11.27	6.9	0.8	17.7	12.4	**9.2**	10.7	14.3
Heartland Bank and Trust Co.	Bloomington	IL	**A-**	A-	A-	2818.1	-0.53	11.3	0.6	8.9	20.3	**9.2**	11.0	14.3
Heartland National Bank	Sebring	FL	**A-**	B+	B	415.3	10.36	2.1	1.5	9.9	22.9	**8.6**	10.1	23.2
▲ Heartland State Bank	Edgeley	ND	**C+**	C+	C+	60.2	-3.96	2.8	2.5	0.6	19.5	**10.0**	11.6	17.4
Heartland State Bank	Redfield	SD	**C+**	B	A-	88.7	0.98	9.4	1.6	0.1	7.3	**8.1**	11.8	13.5
▲ Heartland Tri-State Bank	Elkhart	KS	**B-**	C+	B	118.3	26.31	4.0	2.8	3.2	28.7	**8.1**	9.7	16.6
Hebron Savings Bank	Hebron	MD	**C-**	D+	D+	609.2	3.10	7.0	0.8	25.2	5.5	**7.0**	9.7	12.5
Helm Bank USA	Miami	FL	**B**	B	C+	838.0	4.55	0.6	1.6	59.8	29.8	**10.0**	11.5	29.0
Henderson Federal Savings Bank	Henderson	TX	**B**	B	B+	105.7	-2.30	2.7	4.4	55.2	10.4	**10.0**	22.1	41.0
▲ Henderson State Bank	Henderson	NE	**C-**	C-	D+	268.5	1.19	9.4	0.5	0.2	17.0	**8.4**	10.9	13.7
Hendricks County Bank and Trust Co.	Brownsburg	IN	**B-**	B-	B-	169.7	4.13	5.6	1.9	19.4	24.9	**10.0**	11.8	17.6
Henry County Bank	Napoleon	OH	**C**	C	C	292.1	3.40	3.2	4.1	10.9	45.6	**8.3**	9.8	21.2
Heritage Bank	Marion	IA	**C-**	D+	D+	35.9	1.76	6.2	2.3	20.3	35.4	**9.1**	10.4	23.9
Heritage Bank	Topeka	KS	**C**	C-	C+	60.6	4.22	11.1	1.1	22.5	5.1	**8.8**	10.2	15.5
▲ Heritage Bank	Wood River	NE	**A**	B+	A	515.3	-0.36	3.9	1.0	3.4	53.2	**10.0**	15.4	25.3
Heritage Bank	Pearland	TX	**C**	C+	B	298.3	9.79	6.2	0.4	13.3	1.3	**9.4**	12.3	14.5
Heritage Bank	Olympia	WA	**B+**	B	B	5510.9	4.53	9.8	5.3	4.3	17.5	**7.1**	10.6	12.6
▲ Heritage Bank & Trust	Columbia	TN	**B-**	C+	B-	181.5	9.91	6.2	2.0	24.3	13.0	**6.8**	9.0	12.3
Heritage Bank Minnesota	West Concord	MN	**B-**	B-	C+	55.7	9.24	7.6	7.6	38.0	8.9	**9.1**	10.4	16.0
Heritage Bank of Commerce	San Jose	CA	**A-**	A-	A-	3181.1	-0.31	15.0	0.4	3.0	21.3	**9.5**	10.7	15.3
▲ Heritage Bank of Schaumburg	Schaumburg	IL	**C+**	C	C-	137.0	-4.08	3.2	0.0	9.6	15.3	**7.1**	9.1	23.5
Heritage Bank of St. Tammany	Covington	LA	**B-**	B-	C+	131.3	13.47	1.9	0.2	51.9	5.4	**10.0**	14.2	23.9
Heritage Bank of the Ozarks	Lebanon	MO	**B-**	B-	B-	157.9	8.95	4.7	3.6	17.6	17.7	**6.9**	8.9	12.8
Heritage Bank, Inc.	Burlington	KY	**C+**	C+	B-	922.4	11.38	9.4	0.7	9.8	15.6	**6.4**	9.3	12.1
Heritage Bank, N.A.	Spicer	MN	**C-**	C-	C+	431.0	2.97	9.1	2.7	14.1	12.3	**6.7**	9.2	12.3
Heritage Community Bank	Chamois	MO	**B-**	B-	B	148.6	5.87	10.1	1.6	26.3	4.4	**6.6**	9.4	12.2
Heritage Community Bank	Greeneville	TN	**B-**	B-	C+	117.6	15.61	6.4	4.4	37.4	3.0	**8.1**	9.8	14.5
Heritage First Bank	Rome	GA	**B-**	B-	B-	145.4	9.97	10.7	4.6	17.4	8.2	**8.1**	11.2	13.4
▼ Heritage Southeast Bank	Jonesboro	GA	**C+**	B-	B-	1287.1	156.67	12.2	1.4	9.5	8.1	**4.5**	14.0	10.7
Heritage State Bank	Lawrenceville	IL	**C-**	C-	B	82.2	-10.42	4.1	0.0	0.6	0.0	**9.2**	11.7	14.3
Herring Bank	Amarillo	TX	**C+**	B-	B	448.2	5.11	8.8	5.9	8.9	12.8	**8.4**	10.0	13.9
Hershey State Bank	Hershey	NE	**B+**	B+	A-	77.6	2.14	12.8	7.8	17.0	5.3	**10.0**	13.9	17.4
Hertford Savings Bank, SSB	Hertford	NC	**C**	C	C	12.9	-1.59	0.0	3.1	56.1	0.1	**10.0**	16.5	29.1
Hiawatha Bank and Trust Co.	Hiawatha	IA	**B**	B-	B-	52.5	-9.28	6.6	1.6	35.8	0.5	**10.0**	11.9	17.0

Asset Quality Index	Adjusted Non-Performing Loans as a % of Total Loans	Adjusted Non-Performing Loans as a % of Capital	Net Charge-Offs Avg Loans	Profitability Index	Net Income ($Mil)	Return on Assets (R.O.A.)	Return on Equity (R.O.E.)	Net Interest Spread	Overhead Efficiency Ratio	Liquidity Index	Liquidity Ratio	Hot Money Ratio	Stability Index
2.3	4.29	na	0.17	**0.3**	-1.0	-0.47	-6.59	3.46	113.6	**1.3**	22.6	29.3	**2.7**
4.4	1.34	6.5	0.05	**3.2**	16.2	0.59	5.36	3.21	82.6	**2.3**	10.4	15.2	**7.4**
4.0	1.67	11.3	0.09	**5.7**	4.4	1.15	12.60	3.75	63.5	**0.6**	5.3	29.0	**5.8**
6.5	0.18	5.1	-0.06	**4.7**	1.9	1.20	13.70	3.02	60.0	**2.3**	30.6	21.0	**5.3**
3.6	1.90	12.2	0.00	**4.8**	2.6	0.93	8.45	3.84	68.7	**2.4**	18.4	16.0	**6.7**
4.9	1.62	na	0.00	**5.4**	6.5	1.11	11.67	3.24	54.8	**3.6**	15.0	10.8	**6.4**
6.9	2.18	na	0.00	**3.6**	1.1	0.64	3.99	4.28	79.5	**4.5**	46.8	14.2	**7.3**
9.0	0.00	na	-0.10	**4.7**	0.8	0.92	8.61	3.73	68.5	**5.8**	50.2	8.0	**6.2**
8.5	0.00	na	-0.12	**5.3**	0.3	1.31	5.47	3.69	67.2	**5.8**	46.0	6.1	**7.9**
8.7	0.00	na	-0.45	**5.2**	0.1	1.22	9.51	3.52	66.4	**1.9**	27.0	21.0	**5.0**
3.6	2.46	na	0.36	**3.1**	1.2	0.64	6.06	3.28	80.9	**2.8**	22.3	15.9	**5.0**
2.7	4.35	21.9	0.00	**6.4**	1.6	1.52	15.93	4.01	62.1	**4.5**	14.3	5.3	**6.5**
6.9	0.13	na	0.00	**4.0**	0.2	0.71	7.46	3.66	74.1	**3.0**	34.0	18.2	**4.7**
9.0	0.19	na	0.06	**4.0**	0.5	0.89	7.18	3.57	77.8	**5.5**	56.1	10.1	**6.5**
7.0	4.29	na	0.00	**4.3**	3.4	0.89	3.92	2.87	59.9	**1.3**	24.0	30.9	**8.7**
5.7	0.00	na	1.35	**0.6**	-0.5	-1.04	-2.39	2.89	101.8	**0.3**	12.1	98.5	**6.3**
1.8	0.52	na	0.06	**6.8**	2.5	1.34	12.14	3.71	53.5	**2.6**	7.0	14.9	**7.1**
7.1	0.62	na	0.03	**1.9**	0.9	0.11	1.05	2.17	93.1	**0.7**	12.5	42.3	**8.1**
6.8	0.00	0.0	0.00	**9.5**	6.1	5.90	31.80	1.61	82.1	**2.7**	61.3	83.1	**9.5**
8.0	0.24	na	0.06	**3.4**	1.9	0.63	5.73	3.32	78.2	**1.6**	24.0	26.1	**6.4**
7.3	0.00	na	0.00	**5.9**	0.4	1.20	8.50	4.26	62.9	**3.7**	12.3	10.1	**8.1**
6.1	1.02	na	0.03	**3.9**	3.1	0.66	6.62	4.23	83.1	**4.5**	22.6	6.4	**5.8**
7.2	0.62	3.3	0.04	**6.1**	14.1	1.27	12.13	3.60	60.3	**2.2**	9.0	15.0	**8.8**
7.2	1.01	na	0.27	**5.9**	0.7	1.43	9.63	3.96	66.0	**4.7**	45.6	12.2	**8.4**
6.1	0.07	na	-0.17	**9.1**	2.5	2.21	16.19	4.60	53.7	**1.1**	5.4	19.9	**9.6**
4.8	0.92	na	0.00	**7.7**	6.7	1.46	12.23	3.99	55.9	**3.5**	20.3	11.9	**8.5**
8.4	0.30	na	0.02	**6.1**	10.0	1.23	11.32	3.95	61.0	**1.6**	12.0	21.7	**8.8**
5.9	0.96	5.3	0.08	**9.6**	48.7	2.27	19.37	4.64	53.8	**4.9**	19.1	4.0	**9.5**
9.3	0.55	na	-0.05	**6.6**	4.1	1.37	14.41	3.41	51.2	**6.3**	61.8	8.5	**5.9**
5.3	0.80	na	0.13	**3.9**	0.4	0.84	6.71	3.85	78.1	**1.9**	16.2	16.8	**7.2**
3.9	1.59	na	0.00	**9.8**	1.4	2.14	18.00	5.30	56.8	**1.2**	12.6	20.6	**8.9**
4.1	0.49	na	0.01	**4.4**	0.7	0.83	8.35	3.69	72.5	**1.9**	17.8	19.7	**5.9**
2.1	4.33	26.5	0.25	**4.9**	4.2	0.93	9.79	3.87	62.6	**1.6**	9.4	21.2	**6.0**
6.2	2.67	11.2	0.02	**4.8**	6.2	0.97	8.49	3.69	70.0	**2.8**	41.3	24.2	**8.0**
5.8	2.19	na	0.31	**5.0**	0.8	1.04	4.76	3.76	58.5	**0.8**	17.4	44.1	**8.1**
3.0	1.83	na	2.07	**4.1**	0.6	0.31	2.85	3.65	46.7	**0.6**	18.0	52.9	**7.7**
7.6	2.02	na	0.05	**2.8**	0.5	0.38	3.20	3.87	90.6	**3.5**	36.2	16.4	**6.3**
6.1	3.05	na	0.00	**2.9**	1.0	0.48	4.88	3.04	83.5	**1.1**	27.6	30.7	**4.4**
7.5	0.50	na	0.00	**2.1**	0.1	0.24	2.46	3.76	92.0	**5.5**	49.2	9.0	**4.4**
6.1	1.12	5.1	0.02	**2.8**	0.2	0.43	4.22	3.89	87.9	**1.1**	15.3	31.3	**4.5**
8.4	0.20	na	-0.01	**9.2**	7.7	2.00	13.30	3.49	37.8	**4.9**	27.9	3.5	**10.0**
6.0	1.95	na	0.10	**8.0**	3.4	1.56	11.91	5.04	57.1	**0.9**	5.3	30.4	**7.6**
4.8	1.55	5.6	0.05	**6.3**	53.8	1.34	9.08	4.32	61.4	**4.4**	20.2	7.8	**9.6**
6.1	0.45	na	-0.42	**4.3**	1.2	0.92	10.60	3.84	78.5	**2.1**	22.9	16.4	**5.8**
7.0	0.42	na	0.22	**3.5**	0.3	0.65	6.18	4.43	83.3	**4.3**	9.0	5.8	**5.9**
6.1	0.74	3.2	-0.03	**8.8**	37.4	1.61	12.46	4.41	51.7	**6.2**	38.2	4.9	**9.7**
4.4	0.81	na	-0.01	**4.4**	1.2	1.16	8.26	3.29	61.8	**5.9**	46.1	6.2	**7.7**
8.5	0.73	na	0.02	**3.2**	0.5	0.53	3.60	3.35	81.3	**0.8**	16.0	37.0	**6.9**
7.1	0.52	na	0.01	**5.2**	1.1	1.00	11.63	4.18	71.6	**0.9**	21.3	24.1	**5.4**
3.9	1.89	8.0	0.01	**4.8**	6.4	0.96	10.49	3.77	69.3	**3.2**	18.0	12.8	**6.4**
2.7	2.22	na	0.14	**4.2**	3.0	0.94	10.09	4.11	80.8	**2.4**	13.5	8.9	**5.4**
6.4	0.39	3.2	0.00	**4.8**	1.1	1.04	11.03	3.92	72.2	**1.2**	8.6	27.6	**5.4**
7.4	0.19	1.3	0.01	**3.9**	0.6	0.74	7.47	3.96	81.4	**0.9**	10.5	32.8	**5.5**
4.8	0.89	5.8	0.29	**4.7**	1.0	1.01	9.20	5.29	76.6	**1.3**	14.0	22.8	**6.5**
7.0	0.60	na	0.08	**2.4**	-0.4	-0.08	-0.78	4.51	98.7	**1.9**	15.1	19.4	**7.0**
0.4	4.94	na	2.96	**1.1**	-1.0	-1.56	-14.30	4.26	56.5	**3.3**	12.3	12.4	**6.6**
5.9	1.09	na	0.20	**3.6**	2.3	0.73	7.84	4.26	84.9	**2.9**	18.3	15.0	**6.1**
5.0	2.10	na	-0.05	**6.6**	0.2	1.75	9.40	5.73	53.8	**0.4**	8.5	49.3	**8.3**
5.9	0.79	na	0.00	**2.3**	0.0	0.07	0.43	3.75	92.6	**1.5**	20.7	24.6	**6.6**
8.0	0.04	na	0.02	**6.4**	0.5	1.19	10.09	3.96	60.2	**0.5**	3.0	15.3	**6.7**

	Name	City	State	Rating	2018 Rating	2017 Rating	Total Assets ($Mil)	One Year Asset Growth	Asset Mix (As a % of Total Assets) Comm-ercial Loans	Cons-umer Loans	Mort-gage Loans	Secur-ities	Capital-ization Index	Lever-age Ratio	Risk-Based Capital Ratio
▲	Hiawatha National Bank	Hager City	WI	**C**	C	C	235.7	17.02	14.3	1.1	11.5	9.8	**8.5**	10.0	13.7
	Hibernia Bank	New Orleans	LA	**B-**	C	C	202.7	2.82	1.6	0.1	48.2	3.8	**10.0**	13.2	22.5
	Hickory Point Bank and Trust	Decatur	IL	**B**	B-	B-	639.6	2.57	9.8	1.2	6.2	19.5	**8.8**	10.7	14.0
	Hicksville Bank	Hicksville	OH	**B-**	B-	B-	120.5	6.31	5.9	1.6	17.1	31.6	**10.0**	13.2	21.5
	High Country Bank	Salida	CO	**A-**	A-	A-	285.6	3.76	9.7	0.9	27.4	10.9	**6.5**	9.4	12.1
	High Plains Bank	Flagler	CO	**A-**	A-	A-	194.6	12.56	5.7	1.2	13.1	7.2	**8.9**	10.3	14.1
▲	High Plains Bank	Keyes	OK	**B-**	B-	B+	150.1	63.40	7.3	2.7	6.9	9.9	**9.8**	11.2	14.9
▲	Highland Bank	Saint Michael	MN	**B**	B-	B-	526.5	0.17	17.9	0.4	6.5	27.9	**8.6**	10.1	13.9
	Highland Federal S&L Assn.	Crossville	TN	**C+**	C	C-	62.2	-0.51	0.0	0.1	33.9	1.6	**10.0**	22.7	52.4
▲	Highland State Bank	Highland	WI	**B-**	C+	C+	32.8	0.28	3.6	6.6	28.8	7.6	**10.0**	11.3	25.3
▲	Highlands Community Bank	Covington	VA	**B+**	B	B+	152.0	6.29	4.0	15.0	20.1	33.9	**10.0**	13.0	20.6
▲	Highlands Union Bank	Abingdon	VA	**C+**	C-	C	575.3	-3.11	9.3	2.0	28.7	9.8	**8.2**	9.8	14.1
	Highpoint Community Bank	Hastings	MI	**C+**	C+	C+	331.2	2.91	3.6	3.5	28.0	17.0	**8.7**	10.2	17.7
	Hill Bank & Trust Co.	Weimar	TX	**B**	B	B	143.3	3.35	1.2	0.7	3.2	83.2	**10.0**	17.0	26.9
	Hill-Dodge Banking Co.	Warsaw	IL	**B-**	B-	B-	41.5	2.97	18.0	3.8	3.8	4.5	**10.0**	15.3	24.1
	Hills Bank and Trust Co.	Hills	IA	**A**	A	A	3356.5	8.25	6.5	1.0	30.2	9.6	**10.0**	12.5	18.0
	Hillsboro Bank	Plant City	FL	**A**	A	A	154.2	13.55	6.0	1.1	21.6	18.4	**10.0**	13.4	25.0
	Hillsboro State Bank	Hillsboro	KS	**D+**	D	D	18.3	-0.60	8.7	1.7	14.6	5.3	**8.3**	9.8	18.0
	Hilltop National Bank	Casper	WY	**A-**	B+	B+	759.5	5.98	4.5	2.4	11.9	52.8	**10.0**	12.5	29.1
	Hingham Institution for Savings	Hingham	MA	**B+**	B+	B+	2480.4	4.63	0.0	0.0	41.4	0.0	**7.4**	9.2	13.8
	Hinsdale Bank & Trust Co.	Hinsdale	IL	**B**	B	B-	2659.3	9.16	34.1	11.7	4.6	9.5	**5.9**	10.1	11.7
▲	HNB First Bank	Headland	AL	**A-**	B+	B	157.7	7.82	10.1	3.1	16.7	10.3	**9.2**	10.5	14.4
▲	HNB National Bank	Hannibal	MO	**A-**	B+	A	505.4	7.81	6.0	1.6	18.1	6.2	**10.0**	13.4	18.1
	Hocking Valley Bank	Athens	OH	**B**	B	B-	270.5	2.55	5.5	1.1	29.9	17.4	**9.7**	10.8	18.1
	Hodge Bank & Trust Co.	Hodge	LA	**B-**	B-	B+	70.9	2.01	13.6	10.0	30.0	12.8	**10.0**	19.2	32.3
▲	Holcomb Bank	Rochelle	IL	**C+**	C	C-	187.8	5.07	14.2	2.0	14.5	15.0	**8.7**	10.4	13.9
	Holladay Bank & Trust	Salt Lake City	UT	**A-**	A-	A-	57.7	-4.10	5.3	3.9	11.4	3.5	**10.0**	16.7	27.9
▲	Holmes County Bank & Trust Co.	Lexington	MS	**B**	B-	C	120.1	2.75	8.5	2.5	6.6	38.5	**10.0**	13.1	28.9
▲	Home Bank and Trust Co.	Eureka	KS	**B-**	C+	C+	105.4	4.32	11.9	3.2	36.9	4.5	**5.4**	8.2	11.3
▲	Home Bank of California	San Diego	CA	**A-**	B+	A	175.8	7.26	0.3	0.0	28.5	0.0	**10.0**	13.7	19.1
	Home Bank SB	Martinsville	IN	**B-**	B-	B-	321.7	12.03	3.7	1.1	32.8	26.0	**10.0**	12.4	20.4
	Home Bank, N.A.	Lafayette	LA	**B**	B-	B	2213.7	3.58	6.9	2.2	20.5	11.9	**10.0**	11.1	15.3
	Home Banking Co.	Selmer	TN	**C+**	C+	C+	87.0	-3.07	8.0	6.9	12.6	39.3	**10.0**	11.2	20.0
▼	Home Exchange Bank	Jamesport	MO	**A-**	A	A	173.3	6.72	3.3	0.4	3.1	52.7	**9.7**	10.8	21.6
	Home Federal Bank	Shreveport	LA	**B+**	B+	B+	461.2	7.58	7.7	0.1	28.6	14.1	**10.0**	11.3	17.3
	Home Federal Bank Corp.	Middlesboro	KY	**B**	B	B	391.1	4.63	3.5	1.9	41.7	16.7	**10.0**	11.4	18.5
	Home Federal Bank of Hollywood	Hallandale Beach	FL	**D**	D	D	57.5	8.36	5.6	0.0	50.1	4.0	**10.0**	12.5	20.8
	Home Federal Bank of Tennessee	Knoxville	TN	**B**	B	B	2231.3	3.79	2.1	0.4	19.8	46.1	**10.0**	18.9	33.9
	Home Federal S&L Assn.	Bamberg	SC	**C+**	C+	B-	42.6	3.98	0.0	3.7	63.3	3.4	**10.0**	12.7	22.9
	Home Federal S&L Assn. of Grand Island	Grand Island	NE	**B-**	C+	B-	295.0	6.35	10.3	4.4	13.0	24.5	**10.0**	12.2	17.7
▲	Home Federal S&L Assn. of Niles Ohio	Niles	OH	**C+**	C	C	95.2	-3.03	2.8	0.1	32.7	25.9	**10.0**	13.0	21.4
▲	Home Federal Savings Bank	Rochester	MN	**A-**	B+	B+	762.5	3.42	7.6	3.1	18.0	11.1	**9.5**	11.0	14.6
▲	Home Loan Investment Bank, F.S.B.	Warwick	RI	**D+**	D	D	346.0	17.59	0.0	34.5	43.4	0.4	**6.1**	9.0	11.8
	Home Loan Savings Bank	Coshocton	OH	**B**	B+	A-	220.2	6.48	15.3	2.9	42.0	1.6	**10.0**	11.9	16.3
▲	Home Loan State Bank	Grand Junction	CO	**C+**	C	C	126.5	3.68	16.6	2.6	3.3	33.7	**6.2**	8.2	13.7
	Home National Bank	Racine	OH	**C-**	C-	C-	70.4	9.28	3.5	11.3	36.6	25.3	**10.0**	13.1	21.8
	Home National Bank of Thorntown	Thorntown	IN	**B-**	B-	B-	114.2	5.19	14.3	2.6	13.4	41.1	**8.3**	9.9	17.3
	Home S&L Assn. of Carroll County, F.A.	Norborne	MO	**C+**	C+	C+	85.6	-1.36	0.8	3.3	47.0	10.1	**10.0**	20.8	40.5
	Home S&L Co. of Kenton, Ohio	Kenton	OH	**B**	B	B-	129.1	1.46	10.3	0.7	22.2	18.6	**10.0**	27.7	41.3
	Home Savings Bank	Chanute	KS	**B-**	B-	C+	78.2	6.80	6.8	4.6	31.2	32.6	**10.0**	18.1	32.6
	Home Savings Bank	Youngstown	OH	**B+**	B+	B	2895.3	4.20	9.3	3.4	37.2	10.9	**8.5**	10.0	13.7
▲	Home Savings Bank	Salt Lake City	UT	**A-**	B+	A-	127.1	4.30	0.0	0.0	29.8	2.1	**10.0**	14.8	20.4
	Home Savings Bank	Madison	WI	**D+**	D	D	154.0	6.10	1.4	0.4	41.6	1.0	**7.8**	9.6	16.7
	Home Savings Bank of Wapakoneta	Wapakoneta	OH	**B-**	B-	B-	37.3	-2.46	0.0	0.2	61.3	15.8	**10.0**	13.5	23.8
▼	Home Savings Bank, FSB	Ludlow	KY	**D**	D+	D+	26.2	2.33	0.0	0.0	36.5	13.3	**10.0**	14.8	38.4
▲	Home State Bank	Jefferson	IA	**B-**	C+	B	260.1	2.95	13.6	1.4	4.3	9.1	**4.4**	8.9	10.7
	Home State Bank	Royal	IA	**B+**	B+	A-	45.9	1.64	0.8	0.5	2.8	32.5	**10.0**	29.5	42.8
	Home State Bank	Litchfield	MN	**B+**	B+	B+	152.7	2.47	10.8	2.7	8.4	27.3	**9.6**	11.2	14.7
	Home State Bank, N.A.	Crystal Lake	IL	**B**	B-	B-	603.7	5.00	6.4	0.7	22.9	20.4	**10.0**	12.8	19.6
	Home Trust & Savings Bank	Osage	IA	**B+**	B+	A-	238.8	0.94	5.5	1.9	16.8	23.9	**9.2**	10.5	16.3

Asset Quality Index	Adjusted Non-Performing Loans as a % of Total Loans	Adjusted Non-Performing Loans as a % of Capital	Net Charge-Offs Avg Loans	Profitability Index	Net Income ($Mil)	Return on Assets (R.O.A.)	Return on Equity (R.O.E.)	Net Interest Spread	Overhead Efficiency Ratio	Liquidity Index	Liquidity Ratio	Hot Money Ratio	Stability Index
4.8	6.02	na	-0.01	**4.0**	1.5	0.93	8.87	3.66	74.0	**1.0**	19.7	9.6	**5.7**
7.1	0.45	na	0.00	**3.2**	0.2	0.16	0.96	3.39	89.7	**0.8**	16.9	42.4	**7.3**
7.3	0.40	na	-0.02	**5.4**	5.2	1.09	10.23	3.60	69.1	**3.7**	12.9	10.5	**6.8**
5.6	1.94	na	-0.01	**4.0**	0.7	0.77	5.80	3.88	76.5	**3.9**	23.5	10.1	**7.1**
7.1	0.00	na	0.00	**9.2**	3.5	1.68	18.13	5.60	62.3	**4.3**	11.0	6.3	**6.7**
8.1	0.13	0.9	0.18	**7.1**	2.3	1.68	16.60	5.08	64.2	**2.9**	18.9	13.6	**7.3**
5.6	0.56	na	0.33	**8.4**	1.8	1.82	16.80	4.55	51.0	**0.9**	21.7	41.3	**7.9**
6.2	0.68	na	-0.05	**4.8**	3.8	0.98	9.19	3.93	73.2	**3.6**	26.9	6.7	**7.8**
9.8	0.00	na	0.00	**3.2**	0.3	0.54	2.33	3.82	85.0	**5.2**	52.8	11.3	**7.1**
8.1	0.04	na	-0.17	**4.5**	0.3	1.05	9.58	3.75	71.7	**5.3**	44.7	8.9	**5.6**
5.2	1.43	na	0.16	**5.4**	1.2	1.10	8.22	4.31	68.0	**2.6**	43.7	28.1	**7.5**
4.1	2.69	na	0.50	**3.7**	2.5	0.56	5.68	3.82	74.8	**3.1**	8.4	12.7	**5.8**
8.3	0.52	na	0.01	**3.7**	1.7	0.72	7.16	3.71	81.4	**5.4**	31.5	3.5	**5.5**
9.7	0.00	na	0.00	**4.8**	1.2	1.14	6.52	2.44	53.0	**5.0**	95.8	19.6	**8.5**
4.5	3.37	na	0.01	**5.5**	0.5	1.50	9.72	4.00	58.5	**5.4**	43.8	8.3	**7.1**
7.7	0.66	3.3	0.03	**7.0**	34.1	1.41	11.38	3.14	53.7	**2.8**	21.3	11.5	**10.0**
9.2	0.33	na	0.01	**8.5**	1.8	1.61	11.84	4.23	50.2	**4.8**	51.6	13.7	**8.7**
6.6	10.04	na	0.02	**2.2**	0.1	0.34	3.53	3.18	88.6	**5.5**	49.4	6.6	**3.8**
9.4	0.88	na	0.02	**5.6**	8.4	1.46	12.34	3.09	63.6	**6.4**	61.6	7.9	**7.8**
9.0	0.13	0.8	0.00	**7.9**	27.6	1.47	16.30	2.67	30.7	**0.8**	12.4	32.2	**8.1**
5.8	0.47	2.8	0.23	**8.2**	28.0	1.49	11.36	3.66	45.6	**1.4**	12.3	17.1	**8.5**
8.3	0.09	0.6	-0.02	**6.5**	1.8	1.60	15.64	4.00	64.0	**1.5**	14.1	23.6	**7.5**
7.8	0.78	na	-0.02	**10.0**	9.7	2.68	19.54	4.53	50.0	**3.5**	17.5	11.7	**9.1**
7.5	0.48	na	0.08	**4.9**	2.1	1.02	9.72	3.62	67.5	**3.9**	16.4	9.4	**6.8**
4.2	4.53	na	-0.01	**10.0**	1.6	3.00	16.12	5.07	42.5	**1.7**	25.8	25.9	**8.9**
4.6	1.69	na	-0.07	**3.5**	1.0	0.70	6.84	3.81	79.2	**1.8**	15.6	20.0	**5.0**
7.6	0.71	1.3	-0.05	**8.6**	0.6	1.45	8.87	5.33	62.8	**2.9**	38.9	20.6	**8.2**
4.6	9.04	na	0.05	**4.5**	1.2	1.32	10.46	3.32	69.0	**3.1**	34.1	17.3	**6.8**
8.2	0.06	na	0.02	**6.2**	1.2	1.51	18.95	4.28	68.6	**1.5**	9.4	23.4	**5.5**
7.6	0.00	na	0.00	**10.0**	3.6	2.75	19.71	4.82	40.6	**0.5**	9.2	58.9	**9.7**
7.1	0.55	na	0.06	**3.6**	1.7	0.72	5.70	3.75	82.6	**4.4**	35.2	11.3	**7.0**
4.1	1.57	8.8	0.08	**6.5**	21.4	1.31	9.56	4.34	63.1	**3.4**	8.0	11.6	**9.9**
7.0	1.55	na	0.00	**2.8**	0.2	0.33	3.01	3.70	86.6	**3.5**	44.9	18.4	**5.7**
9.2	0.00	na	0.00	**6.0**	1.8	1.39	12.61	2.63	45.4	**1.9**	41.7	12.6	**9.3**
6.6	2.04	na	0.13	**5.8**	3.7	1.14	10.05	3.64	62.5	**1.2**	23.3	26.1	**7.2**
8.8	0.80	na	0.02	**4.1**	2.1	0.72	6.38	3.68	76.4	**1.6**	17.5	23.8	**7.0**
8.6	0.52	na	0.00	**0.0**	-0.6	-1.52	-11.16	3.45	134.8	**0.6**	19.7	69.2	**6.1**
9.1	0.81	2.0	0.00	**3.3**	8.7	0.53	2.87	2.49	75.9	**4.4**	53.6	18.5	**9.2**
7.5	0.62	na	0.18	**3.0**	0.1	0.44	3.47	3.65	87.6	**0.7**	16.3	56.8	**5.9**
7.7	0.44	na	-0.01	**3.6**	1.5	0.67	5.59	3.86	81.5	**4.2**	23.0	8.6	**6.9**
7.1	0.84	na	0.00	**2.9**	0.4	0.57	4.56	2.33	77.1	**0.8**	18.1	42.3	**6.8**
7.2	0.27	na	-0.21	**6.7**	7.0	1.29	11.28	4.04	68.8	**4.0**	18.1	9.3	**8.5**
1.7	3.99	na	0.48	**4.8**	2.2	0.90	9.92	4.61	74.6	**0.5**	7.6	53.7	**5.1**
4.1	2.72	na	0.39	**9.5**	2.8	1.75	14.62	4.64	48.8	**1.9**	5.1	17.5	**8.5**
5.2	11.15	na	0.11	**4.7**	0.8	0.91	11.44	4.15	69.0	**4.8**	19.5	4.3	**4.8**
1.7	5.90	28.1	0.50	**5.1**	0.6	1.24	9.42	5.26	70.5	**2.0**	9.4	18.3	**7.3**
4.2	2.75	11.2	0.03	**4.1**	0.6	0.74	7.67	3.68	75.5	**3.2**	25.9	14.6	**5.6**
6.8	1.83	na	0.01	**2.2**	0.1	0.20	1.00	2.70	90.5	**2.8**	40.3	23.3	**6.9**
8.8	0.96	na	0.03	**4.0**	0.8	0.85	3.19	3.25	63.1	**1.9**	35.6	22.9	**7.9**
8.9	0.09	na	0.01	**3.5**	0.5	0.81	4.20	3.46	81.1	**1.4**	27.9	26.0	**7.4**
6.4	0.97	5.4	0.07	**6.1**	28.4	1.33	13.13	3.26	57.7	**3.0**	8.0	12.6	**8.9**
7.8	0.28	na	0.00	**6.9**	1.1	1.21	8.43	3.82	58.1	**0.6**	18.2	53.5	**8.5**
7.8	0.74	na	0.01	**1.7**	0.3	0.25	2.94	3.24	92.2	**1.2**	18.1	19.6	**4.6**
9.9	0.00	na	0.00	**2.9**	0.1	0.30	2.25	3.66	87.0	**3.4**	23.2	12.8	**7.3**
3.7	6.11	na	0.00	**0.1**	-0.1	-0.50	-3.26	2.50	118.8	**2.5**	56.1	34.2	**6.2**
4.7	1.25	na	0.03	**6.4**	2.8	1.45	16.57	3.78	62.1	**1.0**	15.4	16.6	**6.4**
7.5	0.00	na	0.10	**8.3**	0.8	2.14	7.45	4.02	40.5	**5.6**	53.1	9.0	**7.0**
8.7	0.17	0.8	0.13	**4.9**	1.4	1.24	11.35	3.95	74.2	**4.7**	24.5	4.9	**7.8**
6.5	1.05	na	0.22	**4.3**	4.7	1.05	8.25	4.01	79.0	**3.6**	23.1	11.9	**7.5**
6.2	0.21	na	-0.01	**5.7**	2.6	1.44	14.28	2.62	44.4	**3.0**	26.9	15.6	**6.3**

Name	City	State	Rating	2018 Rating	2017 Rating	Total Assets ($Mil)	One Year Asset Growth	Asset Mix (As a % of Total Assets): Comm-ercial Loans	Cons-umer Loans	Mort-gage Loans	Secur-ities	Capital-ization Index	Lever-age Ratio	Risk-Based Capital Ratio
HOMEBANK	Palmyra	MO	**B-**	B-	B	398.6	5.18	17.4	2.1	11.4	7.3	**6.2**	9.8	11.9
HomeBank of Arkansas	Portland	AR	**C-**	C	C+	71.1	0.34	12.1	3.5	25.2	3.3	**9.5**	10.7	16.1
▲ HomeBank Texas	Seagoville	TX	**A-**	B+	B	205.3	6.65	9.8	1.0	30.4	5.8	**9.8**	10.9	15.6
Homeland Community Bank	McMinnville	TN	**C+**	C	C-	151.9	2.96	7.4	3.3	23.0	17.9	**7.5**	9.3	14.5
▲ Homeland Federal Savings Bank	Columbia	LA	**B-**	C+	B	335.1	16.90	8.3	9.3	30.0	4.5	**8.2**	9.8	14.4
HomePride Bank	Mansfield	MO	**D-**	D-	D-	97.6	1.29	3.1	2.2	53.3	7.7	**6.9**	8.9	15.3
Homestead Bank	Cozad	NE	**B**	B	B+	263.0	2.30	6.2	0.9	1.2	21.4	**10.0**	16.2	23.2
▲ Homestead Savings Bank	Albion	MI	**D-**	E-	E-	64.9	-1.17	2.5	1.4	52.1	6.0	**5.0**	7.0	13.6
HomeStreet Bank	Seattle	WA	**C+**	B-	B	6794.9	-2.69	5.6	0.2	20.0	12.7	**8.8**	10.2	14.4
Hometown Bank	Oxford	MA	**B-**	B-	B-	797.0	3.66	5.5	0.3	26.3	17.9	**6.9**	8.9	13.8
▲ HomeTown Bank	Redwood Falls	MN	**A-**	B+	A-	353.4	13.91	10.6	2.5	18.8	17.3	**8.7**	10.1	15.1
Hometown Bank	Kent	OH	**C-**	C-	C-	204.7	2.58	9.6	1.4	31.8	4.8	**5.9**	8.6	11.7
▲ Hometown Bank	Fond du Lac	WI	**B+**	B+	A	500.7	65.57	19.9	0.4	10.9	3.8	**9.8**	11.5	14.8
HomeTown Bank of Alabama	Oneonta	AL	**A-**	A-	A	382.1	9.16	4.5	9.9	38.9	19.8	**10.0**	14.6	24.3
Hometown Bank of Corbin, Inc.	Corbin	KY	**B-**	C+	C+	177.4	7.92	4.6	3.1	25.7	23.3	**6.9**	8.9	14.7
Hometown Bank of Pennsylvania	Bedford	PA	**B-**	B-	B-	219.8	23.04	10.3	0.8	28.5	5.8	**6.4**	8.4	12.7
HomeTown Bank, N.A.	Galveston	TX	**A-**	B+	B+	632.9	6.84	6.1	1.6	15.8	22.0	**10.0**	12.5	18.1
▲ Hometown Community Bank	Cyrus	MN	**C+**	C	D+	61.7	1.68	7.0	2.3	17.9	2.9	**9.1**	10.4	16.0
▼ Hometown National Bank	LaSalle	IL	**B+**	B+	A-	218.9	-4.03	13.9	0.4	7.2	20.2	**10.0**	11.5	17.1
HomeTrust Bank	Asheville	NC	**C+**	B-	C	3652.9	9.07	11.0	4.4	18.3	11.5	**6.1**	10.2	11.8
Homewood Federal Savings Bank	Baltimore	MD	**B-**	B-	B	61.1	9.84	0.1	3.0	60.0	4.6	**10.0**	26.7	44.9
Hondo National Bank	Hondo	TX	**B+**	B+	B+	270.4	8.42	11.8	2.6	14.3	19.6	**9.1**	10.4	15.1
Honesdale National Bank	Honesdale	PA	**A-**	A-	A	706.2	9.32	11.2	3.9	24.5	15.4	**10.0**	15.0	19.5
▲ Honor Bank	Honor	MI	**B-**	C+	C+	249.2	1.82	10.6	2.7	11.8	9.3	**6.8**	9.2	12.4
Hoosier Heartland State Bank	Crawfordsville	IN	**B-**	B-	B-	203.8	-1.04	3.9	4.7	10.8	30.4	**6.9**	8.9	13.6
Hopeton State Bank	Hopeton	OK	**D+**	C	C-	26.1	-4.74	5.9	4.1	0.0	49.0	**8.7**	10.1	15.6
▲ Horatio State Bank	Horatio	AR	**B**	B-	B+	217.7	8.17	6.3	20.5	29.6	9.8	**10.0**	11.9	18.0
Horicon Bank	Horicon	WI	**C**	C+	B-	780.2	7.35	13.8	0.8	13.9	2.7	**5.9**	10.5	11.7
Horizon Bank	Michigan City	IN	**B+**	B+	B+	5189.1	25.45	7.8	7.5	16.6	19.0	**6.4**	9.4	12.1
▲ Horizon Bank	Waverly	NE	**A-**	B+	A	338.5	19.29	7.3	0.5	10.7	7.8	**10.0**	14.7	15.9
Horizon Bank, SSB	Austin	TX	**B+**	B+	B+	1178.2	21.97	18.2	0.1	10.5	7.6	**5.5**	8.2	11.4
Horizon Community Bank	Lake Havasu City	AZ	**B-**	B-	B-	344.7	19.45	15.5	0.3	7.6	8.2	**6.8**	8.8	12.7
Horizon Financial Bank	Munich	ND	**B**	B+	B+	144.1	1.05	4.7	1.7	4.7	9.9	**10.0**	12.8	17.2
▲ Houghton State Bank	Red Oak	IA	**B**	B-	B+	176.0	-3.09	5.3	0.9	4.9	11.6	**10.0**	11.3	15.8
Howard Bank	Baltimore	MD	**C+**	C+	B-	2293.1	6.49	16.4	2.1	20.4	7.6	**6.9**	10.3	12.4
▲ Howard State Bank	Howard	KS	**B**	B-	C+	50.9	0.29	3.0	2.9	4.9	28.7	**10.0**	11.7	23.0
Hoyne Savings Bank	Chicago	IL	**C-**	D+	D	443.4	-0.85	0.0	0.0	31.2	37.5	**10.0**	16.8	39.8
▼ HSBC Bank USA, N.A.	McLean	VA	**C**	C	C+	182096.0	5.64	15.2	0.8	9.7	30.2	**10.0**	11.2	18.9
HSBC Trust Co. (Delaware), N.A.	Wilmington	DE	**U**	U	U	56.2	1.58	0.0	0.0	0.0	0.0	**0.0**	95.2	0.0
Huntingdon Savings Bank	Huntingdon	PA	**C**	C+	C+	16.6	3.12	0.0	0.0	73.2	0.0	**10.0**	21.1	46.5
Huntingdon Valley Bank	Huntingdon Valley	PA	**C-**	C-	C	353.4	19.25	2.4	1.8	71.2	4.6	**6.6**	8.6	15.9
▼ Huntington Federal Savings Bank	Huntington	WV	**C+**	B-	B	537.6	0.28	0.0	0.2	34.9	52.9	**10.0**	17.0	50.6
Huntington National Bank	Columbus	OH	**B-**	B-	B-	108790.4	2.83	20.7	16.0	12.3	21.0	**8.2**	9.9	13.5
Huron Community Bank	East Tawas	MI	**B**	B	B	235.1	4.66	9.9	1.2	10.3	15.0	**10.0**	11.4	18.3
Huron National Bank	Rogers City	MI	**C+**	C	C+	63.9	-2.35	2.5	4.5	36.1	5.9	**10.0**	15.7	27.1
Huron Valley State Bank	Milford	MI	**B**	B	B-	159.5	7.50	10.8	0.6	5.1	1.1	**7.8**	10.3	13.2
Hustisford State Bank	Hustisford	WI	**B+**	B+	B+	55.9	6.52	4.4	1.9	51.3	9.4	**10.0**	19.2	29.3
Hyden Citizens Bank	Hyden	KY	**B-**	B-	B-	126.5	-1.74	10.3	4.0	23.2	29.3	**7.8**	9.5	14.5
▲ Hyperion Bank	Philadelphia	PA	**D+**	D	D-	170.8	76.54	9.2	0.2	34.1	1.3	**10.0**	12.6	18.4
IBERIABANK	Lafayette	LA	**B**	B-	B-	31647.6	5.40	14.8	1.7	18.2	14.0	**5.8**	9.5	11.6
Idabel National Bank	Idabel	OK	**B+**	B+	A-	131.8	8.78	4.7	6.1	19.2	36.5	**8.6**	10.1	17.6
Idaho First Bank	McCall	ID	**C**	C-	D+	214.4	8.44	14.3	3.1	12.4	9.0	**7.6**	9.4	13.1
Idaho Trust Bank	Boise	ID	**C**	C	B-	145.7	17.11	12.7	1.7	0.6	0.4	**8.7**	10.3	13.9
▲ Illini State Bank	Oglesby	IL	**B**	B-	B-	125.5	5.95	6.4	1.0	10.0	26.9	**10.0**	13.8	20.9
Illinois Bank & Trust	Rockford	IL	**B+**	B+	B	871.5	9.60	16.3	1.6	6.4	28.9	**7.0**	9.0	12.7
▲ Impact Bank	Wellington	KS	**B-**	B-	B-	137.9	7.28	14.6	2.3	3.6	26.5	**10.0**	11.1	16.4
INB, N.A.	Springfield	IL	**C+**	C+	C+	1185.3	20.18	10.6	0.1	11.2	8.4	**6.7**	8.7	12.7
▼ InBank	Raton	NM	**C+**	B	B+	365.0	11.22	9.4	0.6	6.3	30.5	**9.6**	13.0	14.7
Incommons Bank, N.A.	Mexia	TX	**B-**	B-	B-	177.0	3.31	10.0	4.3	24.3	18.5	**6.9**	8.9	14.3
IncredibleBank	Wausau	WI	**B-**	B-	B-	1379.1	4.17	21.8	4.6	8.3	14.6	**4.9**	8.3	10.9

Asset Quality Index	Adjusted Non-Performing Loans as a % of Total Loans	Adjusted Non-Performing Loans as a % of Capital	Net Charge-Offs Avg Loans	Profitability Index	Net Income ($Mil)	Return on Assets (R.O.A.)	Return on Equity (R.O.E.)	Net Interest Spread	Overhead Efficiency Ratio	Liquidity Index	Liquidity Ratio	Hot Money Ratio	Stability Index
5.2	0.58	na	0.03	**4.9**	3.4	1.12	11.65	4.01	72.4	**2.9**	11.1	14.2	**6.6**
4.6	1.48	9.4	0.03	**0.4**	-0.7	-1.18	-10.84	4.12	174.3	**0.7**	18.8	50.0	**5.8**
8.6	0.05	na	0.00	**9.0**	3.1	2.15	19.83	4.77	54.0	**1.9**	21.7	15.7	**7.5**
4.0	2.21	na	0.02	**4.2**	1.0	0.91	10.26	3.43	69.9	**1.9**	24.6	20.6	**5.1**
4.3	1.37	na	0.38	**5.9**	3.1	1.33	13.21	4.46	67.7	**0.7**	12.6	47.1	**7.3**
3.4	2.20	14.4	0.22	**0.5**	-0.1	-0.14	-1.63	4.36	97.0	**1.3**	10.9	25.6	**2.9**
4.9	0.91	na	0.02	**7.7**	3.0	1.57	9.81	4.34	56.4	**4.3**	19.3	7.3	**8.5**
3.8	3.19	na	0.08	**2.5**	0.4	0.68	10.24	3.98	95.5	**4.6**	22.1	5.4	**2.0**
5.8	1.28	5.0	-0.01	**3.6**	12.2	0.62	5.65	3.11	79.0	**1.3**	12.8	15.8	**8.4**
4.6	1.52	na	0.03	**4.3**	5.3	0.90	8.58	3.46	68.7	**2.2**	16.7	18.2	**6.8**
7.1	0.40	na	-0.01	**7.8**	3.6	1.48	13.20	4.43	59.5	**4.6**	23.1	5.6	**7.7**
2.7	2.13	na	0.02	**3.3**	1.0	0.62	7.44	3.76	85.3	**1.2**	10.2	27.0	**3.9**
6.2	0.39	na	0.02	**8.9**	5.4	1.48	12.29	4.38	57.9	**3.9**	15.5	7.3	**8.8**
8.2	0.40	na	0.15	**9.7**	5.1	1.84	12.77	4.52	58.2	**2.3**	12.8	17.5	**9.2**
6.2	0.51	na	0.07	**5.1**	1.5	1.14	12.86	4.06	73.2	**3.3**	24.8	13.6	**5.3**
6.7	0.58	3.0	-0.03	**3.9**	1.2	0.77	8.72	3.34	70.9	**1.8**	25.7	23.6	**4.8**
8.7	0.23	na	0.12	**6.9**	6.2	1.39	11.37	4.13	57.3	**2.1**	27.3	20.3	**8.6**
8.1	0.08	na	0.00	**4.5**	0.5	1.06	9.61	3.75	70.2	**1.6**	17.4	24.3	**4.9**
8.3	1.01	na	0.03	**5.0**	1.5	0.87	7.46	3.73	80.1	**4.3**	27.9	8.8	**7.7**
6.1	1.13	5.3	0.30	**3.8**	20.1	0.77	6.92	3.35	69.4	**1.9**	15.1	12.8	**8.7**
8.3	1.08	na	0.10	**3.6**	0.3	0.65	2.37	3.37	70.6	**1.3**	30.7	51.0	**7.2**
8.5	0.00	na	0.01	**5.8**	2.7	1.37	13.32	4.28	66.8	**2.0**	21.8	19.6	**6.8**
8.1	0.66	na	0.48	**6.2**	6.4	1.27	8.45	4.21	62.5	**3.2**	17.2	13.5	**9.4**
5.2	0.50	na	0.07	**5.3**	2.0	1.10	12.04	4.20	71.4	**3.5**	19.0	10.3	**5.7**
5.0	1.95	na	0.04	**4.5**	1.6	1.00	11.72	4.15	76.4	**4.4**	18.9	6.7	**5.7**
5.4	0.00	4.0	0.12	**2.1**	0.0	0.10	0.92	3.86	96.8	**2.6**	57.4	37.1	**6.1**
4.7	0.71	na	0.33	**9.0**	2.5	1.55	13.38	4.40	46.0	**0.6**	11.5	46.4	**7.9**
4.8	2.31	na	0.02	**6.3**	8.6	1.52	14.09	4.07	62.1	**2.5**	6.5	9.0	**8.1**
6.1	0.52	2.6	0.06	**6.6**	50.2	1.39	10.88	3.80	59.6	**2.6**	18.1	16.6	**9.3**
7.3	0.00	na	0.00	**9.8**	5.2	2.18	15.84	4.07	37.4	**1.5**	14.7	24.2	**9.2**
8.3	0.00	0.0	0.19	**9.7**	16.4	2.00	24.04	4.76	55.0	**4.5**	22.1	6.9	**8.6**
7.0	0.91	na	0.05	**4.7**	2.2	0.93	10.31	4.48	75.5	**2.6**	24.8	16.8	**5.4**
4.8	0.78	na	-0.06	**5.6**	1.2	1.14	8.98	4.15	62.8	**1.6**	7.5	15.6	**7.4**
6.0	1.08	na	0.02	**6.4**	1.7	1.28	9.52	3.93	56.1	**1.8**	14.0	20.0	**7.8**
4.2	1.12	na	0.29	**3.7**	12.4	0.74	5.11	3.63	72.1	**0.9**	12.0	23.3	**7.1**
7.6	0.75	na	0.64	**5.3**	0.5	1.30	11.54	3.85	65.7	**5.9**	40.8	4.1	**5.9**
9.6	0.98	na	0.08	**1.5**	0.5	0.15	0.89	2.41	95.1	**3.5**	59.2	26.5	**6.5**
7.4	1.70	4.2	0.12	**1.9**	134.8	0.10	0.81	1.42	86.4	**3.2**	59.1	22.8	**8.8**
10.0	na	0.0	na	**9.3**	1.1	2.65	2.73	2.43	31.1	**4.0**	na	0.0	**5.9**
6.7	2.40	na	0.00	**3.5**	0.1	0.52	2.46	3.10	76.3	**1.0**	24.4	33.4	**7.9**
5.6	1.23	na	0.20	**2.4**	0.8	0.34	3.96	2.62	85.9	**1.7**	12.2	9.1	**3.5**
9.5	1.00	na	0.01	**2.4**	1.0	0.25	1.54	2.11	83.9	**3.5**	68.7	31.1	**8.4**
4.3	1.49	6.3	0.34	**7.0**	1226.8	1.53	13.88	3.44	52.8	**4.8**	22.1	3.4	**9.6**
7.2	1.41	na	0.04	**4.9**	1.7	1.01	8.69	4.03	70.2	**4.5**	28.8	8.1	**7.1**
4.5	4.76	na	0.86	**3.0**	0.1	0.27	1.76	3.95	73.5	**4.4**	44.6	13.6	**6.7**
6.6	0.45	1.7	0.00	**6.0**	1.4	1.19	11.71	4.19	64.5	**1.8**	15.2	16.4	**6.8**
8.0	4.60	na	0.00	**6.1**	0.4	1.07	5.48	4.47	65.7	**3.2**	14.5	11.2	**7.7**
6.6	0.63	3.5	0.13	**4.2**	0.8	0.88	9.19	4.07	77.4	**1.8**	14.5	20.2	**5.7**
6.0	2.05	na	0.00	**0.8**	0.1	0.07	0.52	3.37	89.3	**0.7**	18.1	51.9	**4.5**
5.1	0.90	4.3	0.14	**6.3**	304.6	1.30	9.92	3.54	53.0	**2.5**	12.4	10.1	**10.0**
6.3	0.26	na	0.10	**8.7**	2.0	2.11	21.99	4.00	51.0	**1.2**	24.4	32.3	**7.8**
7.7	0.10	na	0.26	**3.2**	0.8	0.48	5.30	3.92	82.3	**1.7**	24.1	21.4	**4.9**
8.6	0.14	na	-0.01	**3.0**	0.6	0.65	4.38	4.07	88.8	**5.0**	35.3	8.2	**7.3**
7.3	0.33	na	0.00	**4.1**	0.9	1.01	6.30	3.22	64.2	**2.5**	26.2	5.1	**8.1**
7.5	0.32	2.0	0.00	**5.5**	6.6	1.08	12.25	3.58	67.3	**5.1**	23.1	2.4	**6.5**
5.7	1.13	na	0.01	**4.2**	1.0	0.99	9.01	3.65	75.6	**1.8**	17.5	20.6	**7.0**
5.3	1.13	na	-0.01	**4.0**	7.7	0.96	10.63	3.39	75.7	**2.5**	22.9	3.4	**7.5**
4.9	2.65	na	-0.01	**1.3**	-0.7	-0.26	-1.62	4.26	105.3	**1.8**	13.2	19.9	**6.3**
7.0	0.48	na	0.07	**4.1**	1.0	0.79	8.50	4.45	80.1	**3.6**	11.4	10.7	**5.4**
4.6	1.43	7.4	0.10	**6.4**	15.7	1.53	16.35	4.00	65.8	**1.9**	18.1	9.3	**9.1**

Name	City	State	Rating	2018 Rating	2017 Rating	Total Assets ($Mil)	One Year Asset Growth	Asset Mix (As a % of Total Assets) Commercial Loans	Consumer Loans	Mortgage Loans	Securities	Capitalization Index	Leverage Ratio	Risk-Based Capital Ratio
▲ Independence Bank	Havre	MT	**A-**	B+	A-	787.1	8.49	5.8	2.1	6.8	8.1	**10.0**	12.9	15.4
Independence Bank	Independence	OH	**B**	B	B	169.9	-10.45	24.3	0.6	4.7	18.4	**10.0**	13.3	19.9
Independence Bank	East Greenwich	RI	**B**	B	B	64.8	1.69	87.0	0.3	3.1	0.0	**10.0**	26.6	39.5
Independence Bank of Kentucky	Owensboro	KY	**B+**	B+	A-	2568.4	11.81	4.5	0.4	13.3	42.1	**6.2**	8.2	13.0
Independence State Bank	Independence	WI	**D**	D	D	68.4	2.73	10.3	1.1	9.1	11.3	**6.4**	8.5	12.2
Independent Bank	Grand Rapids	MI	**B-**	B-	C+	3549.8	7.85	9.2	12.7	27.9	12.4	**7.3**	9.4	12.8
Independent Bank	Memphis	TN	**C+**	C+	B-	1055.9	5.93	8.7	46.3	1.4	0.7	**6.5**	11.6	12.1
Independent Bank	McKinney	TX	**B+**	B+	B+	14954.2	51.30	9.3	0.2	9.8	7.3	**6.2**	10.7	11.9
Independent Farmers Bank	Maysville	MO	**B**	B	B	123.3	5.55	6.1	3.7	10.4	40.2	**8.5**	10.0	17.0
Industrial & Commerc. Bank of China (USA	New York	NY	**B**	B	B-	2822.0	7.60	25.8	0.0	7.8	0.5	**10.0**	13.4	16.2
Industrial Bank	Washington	DC	**D+**	D+	D+	425.1	0.93	7.5	0.1	24.8	14.4	**6.7**	8.7	13.0
Industry State Bank	Industry	TX	**A-**	A-	A	835.6	9.14	5.0	1.3	4.6	69.6	**9.7**	10.8	23.2
Inez Deposit Bank	Inez	KY	**C+**	C	C	140.6	0.82	2.7	3.2	24.5	43.2	**10.0**	13.4	38.6
Infinity Bank	Santa Ana	CA	**D**	D		110.1	84.90	31.5	0.6	0.7	31.6	**10.0**	26.3	41.2
InFirst Bank	Indiana	PA	**B-**	B-	B-	420.3	6.62	6.5	0.7	51.3	7.2	**8.3**	9.9	14.6
Inland Bank and Trust	Oak Brook	IL	**B**	B	B	1112.4	-0.46	9.1	0.1	12.8	20.3	**10.0**	12.5	15.6
InsBank	Nashville	TN	**B**	B-	C+	536.7	5.41	22.1	1.6	5.9	3.6	**7.7**	11.4	13.1
INSOUTH Bank	Brownsville	TN	**B-**	B-	B-	341.3	5.50	16.7	2.8	16.4	10.5	**7.2**	10.0	12.7
▲ Institution for Savings	Newburyport	MA	**B+**	C+	C+	3609.6	4.00	0.3	0.4	60.3	5.9	**8.8**	10.6	14.0
Integrity Bank & Trust	Monument	CO	**B-**	B-	B-	215.0	2.57	3.3	0.7	17.5	12.4	**6.5**	8.5	12.4
▲ Integrity Bank Plus	Wabasso	MN	**C+**	C+	B-	63.6	6.03	2.8	1.1	6.1	15.5	**10.0**	12.1	17.6
Interamerican Bank, A FSB	Miami	FL	**C**	C-	D+	199.2	-1.41	0.4	0.6	28.1	0.0	**10.0**	13.9	19.2
Interaudi Bank	New York	NY	**B+**	B	B-	2051.7	4.87	6.0	0.3	18.1	24.8	**6.5**	8.5	22.4
InterBank	Oklahoma City	OK	**C+**	C+	B-	3604.9	-0.23	16.4	0.6	6.2	0.0	**6.1**	10.3	11.8
▲ Intercity State Bank	Schofield	WI	**A-**	B+	A-	188.4	2.02	10.0	1.4	19.7	9.1	**10.0**	22.1	28.5
Intercredit Bank, N.A.	Miami	FL	**C-**	C	C+	376.2	1.43	8.5	2.8	27.5	14.0	**8.8**	10.2	14.9
International Bank of Amherst	Amherst	WI	**A-**	A-	A-	72.4	2.78	6.1	1.0	10.9	33.0	**10.0**	14.1	30.9
▲ International Bank of Chicago	Chicago	IL	**B-**	C	C+	648.7	5.96	6.0	0.0	21.8	23.7	**10.0**	12.4	21.4
International Bank of Commerce	Brownsville	TX	**A**	A	A	1055.3	5.58	14.9	0.5	3.1	30.2	**10.0**	16.4	23.6
International Bank of Commerce	Laredo	TX	**A**	A	A	8525.8	1.64	9.7	0.7	10.4	25.1	**10.0**	14.8	18.1
International Bank of Commerce	Zapata	TX	**A**	A	A	397.5	-9.33	4.4	1.5	23.5	43.3	**10.0**	18.2	35.7
International Bank of Commerce Oklahoma	Oklahoma City	OK	**A-**	A-	A-	1412.3	-7.61	20.7	0.2	1.5	20.9	**10.0**	14.3	17.3
▼ International City Bank	Long Beach	CA	**B+**	A-	A-	327.2	24.41	1.2	0.0	2.4	49.4	**7.4**	9.3	20.1
International Finance Bank	Miami	FL	**C+**	C+	C+	753.1	38.19	32.1	1.0	20.9	10.9	**3.1**	6.8	10.0
▲ Interstate Bank, SSB	Perryton	TX	**B-**	C+	B-	202.2	12.06	11.4	2.0	11.4	31.2	**8.8**	10.2	16.3
Interstate Federal S&L Assn. of McGregor	McGregor	IA	**C-**	C	C	7.8	0.41	0.0	0.5	75.7	0.0	**10.0**	21.4	49.3
Intracoastal Bank	Palm Coast	FL	**B**	B	B+	338.7	3.41	7.0	0.4	2.0	23.4	**6.2**	9.0	11.9
INTRUST Bank, N.A.	Wichita	KS	**B**	B	B	5142.3	1.45	24.8	4.6	2.8	27.3	**4.7**	8.3	10.8
Investar Bank, N.A.	Baton Rouge	LA	**B**	B	B	2019.9	16.52	14.3	1.5	14.2	13.7	**7.7**	10.6	13.1
Investment Savings Bank	Altoona	PA	**C+**	C+	C+	101.5	-2.26	0.5	0.8	40.2	40.4	**10.0**	21.1	43.8
Investors Bank	Short Hills	NJ	**B**	B+	B+	26721.8	4.78	3.2	1.4	21.0	14.2	**8.0**	9.7	14.1
Investors Community Bank	Chillicothe	MO	**B+**	B+	B+	70.5	3.15	1.5	4.1	21.8	56.1	**10.0**	13.3	32.7
Investors Community Bank	Manitowoc	WI	**B-**	B-	B-	1406.8	-6.71	5.7	0.0	1.5	11.0	**10.0**	13.8	17.9
Inwood National Bank	Dallas	TX	**A-**	A-	A-	2959.5	7.57	3.7	0.3	11.6	30.0	**8.6**	10.1	14.9
▲ Ion Bank	Naugatuck	CT	**B-**	C+	C+	1335.7	1.75	9.1	12.2	28.9	5.2	**9.2**	10.7	14.4
▲ Iowa Falls State Bank	Iowa Falls	IA	**B-**	B-	B+	134.9	-1.23	13.0	2.4	14.2	27.2	**9.9**	11.7	14.9
Iowa Prairie Bank	Brunsville	IA	**D**	D+	C-	60.2	-5.29	9.2	3.0	0.9	45.0	**5.7**	7.7	14.3
Iowa Savings Bank	Carroll	IA	**B**	B	B	195.4	-0.04	13.0	0.7	6.1	15.2	**7.0**	9.3	12.5
Iowa State Bank	Algona	IA	**A-**	A-	A-	321.6	-0.69	9.9	1.7	9.9	20.7	**10.0**	11.9	17.2
Iowa State Bank	Clarksville	IA	**D**	D+	C-	380.7	4.19	9.7	0.7	2.8	14.5	**6.6**	8.6	12.4
Iowa State Bank	Des Moines	IA	**A**	A	A+	393.9	2.54	3.2	0.5	11.7	40.5	**10.0**	17.6	28.7
▲ Iowa State Bank	Hull	IA	**A-**	B+	A	592.5	1.63	6.8	1.3	4.1	13.4	**10.0**	14.1	15.7
▲ Iowa State Bank	Sac City	IA	**A-**	B+	A-	132.3	6.38	8.3	4.8	20.1	6.0	**10.0**	12.8	17.2
Iowa State Bank and Trust Co.	Fairfield	IA	**B**	B	B	132.5	-2.91	8.2	1.8	21.3	8.5	**8.9**	10.3	14.6
Iowa State Savings Bank	Creston	IA	**C**	C-	C-	207.3	3.43	6.0	1.6	12.8	16.7	**7.1**	9.1	13.8
Iowa Trust & Savings Bank	Emmetsburg	IA	**B+**	B+	B+	314.4	35.37	2.6	0.5	9.3	20.1	**8.1**	10.4	13.4
Iowa Trust and Savings Bank	Centerville	IA	**A-**	B+	A-	171.5	1.24	3.4	1.9	6.5	50.5	**10.0**	11.1	18.4
Ipava State Bank	Ipava	IL	**B+**	B+	B+	142.5	10.67	7.2	3.7	22.9	16.6	**6.8**	8.8	15.0
Ipswich State Bank	Ipswich	SD	**B**	B	B	53.4	-2.91	5.3	1.1	0.0	19.3	**10.0**	16.6	23.5
▲ Ireland Bank	Malad City	ID	**B+**	B-	B-	248.6	8.14	14.5	1.2	4.0	26.0	**9.8**	10.9	19.2

Asset Quality Index	Adjusted Non-Performing Loans as a % of Total Loans	Adjusted Non-Performing Loans as a % of Capital	Net Charge-Offs Avg Loans	Profitability Index	Net Income ($Mil)	Return on Assets (R.O.A.)	Return on Equity (R.O.E.)	Net Interest Spread	Overhead Efficiency Ratio	Liquidity Index	Liquidity Ratio	Hot Money Ratio	Stability Index
6.2	1.43	na	0.00	9.8	10.8	1.86	14.47	4.47	41.9	0.6	6.9	19.5	10.0
7.8	1.36	na	0.05	4.9	1.6	1.09	8.79	3.43	58.8	0.7	15.2	47.7	7.0
4.1	3.13	6.1	6.62	10.0	2.9	5.87	21.25	7.95	32.9	0.9	25.5	50.5	8.5
8.3	0.51	3.0	0.05	4.6	19.8	1.07	13.00	3.21	68.0	2.3	12.6	6.2	8.1
2.0	3.09	na	0.00	2.8	0.2	0.47	5.01	3.71	84.6	2.1	22.0	19.2	3.8
4.3	1.88	7.7	-0.01	6.5	33.7	1.32	12.82	3.91	65.6	3.2	16.1	7.2	9.2
3.3	0.38	4.3	0.40	6.7	10.3	1.33	10.58	4.73	63.2	1.2	2.5	14.1	9.2
5.8	0.19	0.6	0.09	8.4	179.1	1.66	10.05	4.10	46.1	2.1	11.9	12.1	10.0
5.9	0.87	na	0.74	6.2	1.2	1.29	12.90	4.48	59.4	3.0	23.8	15.1	6.3
6.1	1.02	2.9	0.00	4.6	18.9	0.86	5.92	3.05	61.7	0.6	10.5	40.3	9.2
2.0	3.00	na	-0.02	2.6	0.9	0.30	3.42	4.27	92.2	1.8	11.7	19.5	5.2
9.3	0.02	0.2	0.00	6.4	9.9	1.64	13.70	2.58	57.4	3.0	60.3	39.4	8.5
6.2	1.82	na	0.09	2.9	0.6	0.54	4.18	3.16	81.2	4.1	46.9	16.2	6.5
9.2	0.00	0.0	0.00	0.0	-1.5	-2.30	-7.59	3.41	153.4	7.8	73.6	0.0	1.5
5.5	1.10	na	0.06	3.7	1.6	0.51	5.14	3.59	77.3	1.2	11.4	24.5	6.2
4.8	1.55	7.8	0.02	4.2	6.9	0.83	6.81	3.21	77.4	2.2	15.5	16.9	8.0
6.5	0.24	1.6	0.04	4.8	3.7	0.95	8.43	3.26	57.0	0.6	11.9	52.9	7.0
4.9	0.92	na	0.10	6.9	3.3	1.36	13.62	4.66	67.9	2.4	4.3	15.7	6.2
9.5	0.12	0.7	0.01	5.9	51.5	1.94	18.61	2.00	69.4	0.9	17.5	39.5	8.7
5.8	0.32	na	0.04	5.6	1.7	1.06	12.78	4.51	68.5	4.4	15.6	6.3	5.2
2.9	7.52	na	-0.30	6.6	0.7	1.59	12.45	4.79	65.5	3.6	24.0	12.1	7.6
2.4	5.88	na	-0.36	4.8	1.6	1.08	7.88	4.80	80.1	2.2	15.8	18.2	7.5
9.6	0.06	0.3	0.00	6.9	19.2	1.29	15.80	2.76	43.8	3.2	60.8	44.2	6.5
2.0	1.25	8.1	1.03	7.7	42.0	1.57	12.14	4.37	43.0	3.9	16.3	10.0	10.0
7.5	0.93	na	-0.01	9.2	2.3	1.62	7.51	3.55	43.8	3.6	24.5	12.1	9.1
5.8	0.87	6.5	0.01	0.8	-0.4	-0.14	-1.40	2.87	102.1	0.9	19.6	31.7	6.4
8.6	0.91	na	0.00	6.8	0.9	1.70	12.29	3.90	59.7	6.2	52.0	4.8	8.5
4.1	4.20	na	0.29	7.0	7.6	1.60	12.90	3.81	52.4	1.4	32.1	30.7	8.7
6.9	1.16	4.3	0.13	9.8	18.1	2.28	13.04	4.38	43.6	3.0	34.5	22.8	9.4
8.0	0.16	0.7	0.12	9.5	123.5	1.93	11.36	4.42	52.0	3.2	23.5	15.7	9.5
7.8	0.70	2.3	0.63	5.3	3.5	1.12	6.20	3.43	69.1	2.5	33.1	20.2	8.4
5.8	0.13	0.6	1.84	4.7	9.8	0.88	5.74	4.15	62.8	4.4	8.6	5.2	7.0
9.5	0.05	na	-0.05	2.8	-1.1	-0.51	-3.90	2.44	142.8	3.0	44.6	19.0	8.1
6.3	0.40	2.5	0.01	4.0	3.4	0.64	8.93	3.57	72.1	1.0	22.0	33.7	5.7
6.4	1.23	na	0.05	6.9	2.5	1.74	16.83	4.07	58.2	3.7	43.8	17.5	6.2
10.0	0.68	1.1	0.00	1.4	0.0	-0.08	-0.38	3.02	100.6	2.8	26.7	15.5	6.1
7.5	0.84	na	0.09	7.8	4.7	1.86	20.16	4.01	51.7	2.7	28.0	17.8	7.1
7.3	0.73	4.1	0.17	6.3	57.2	1.46	18.84	3.50	63.3	2.6	14.1	15.2	7.7
6.4	0.38	2.4	0.03	4.9	14.8	1.02	8.74	3.62	63.9	1.2	12.8	29.1	8.6
10.0	0.46	na	0.00	2.7	0.3	0.33	1.58	2.93	85.7	4.0	57.6	19.5	7.6
6.0	0.48	3.4	0.03	4.2	145.6	0.73	7.28	2.51	60.2	1.8	12.6	10.4	8.5
8.7	0.11	na	-0.01	4.0	0.5	0.94	7.02	3.33	72.0	5.3	59.1	11.8	8.1
3.4	4.54	14.1	0.22	6.9	15.3	1.39	10.56	3.19	50.5	1.0	20.6	29.8	9.7
8.5	0.03	0.2	-0.02	8.3	41.2	1.95	17.71	3.32	43.2	4.6	31.9	12.7	10.0
5.0	1.81	na	0.06	4.0	8.6	0.86	9.32	3.41	75.6	3.7	14.3	7.8	7.4
4.2	2.00	na	0.14	6.1	1.5	1.45	12.48	3.66	60.1	3.4	32.4	15.3	7.5
4.6	0.78	na	0.05	1.7	0.2	0.34	4.75	3.41	91.6	3.5	10.8	10.8	1.3
7.7	0.65	na	0.01	6.2	2.2	1.52	16.22	3.47	58.4	3.7	14.8	8.6	6.8
7.0	2.12	na	0.00	5.9	3.0	1.22	9.77	4.07	60.0	2.9	16.2	14.7	8.1
0.6	8.86	na	1.23	3.0	1.3	0.45	5.20	3.02	46.1	1.2	28.8	32.3	3.9
9.4	0.27	na	-0.02	7.0	4.5	1.57	8.85	3.35	63.8	6.2	57.1	7.7	10.0
7.1	0.17	na	0.04	7.1	7.0	1.54	10.88	3.28	52.0	3.4	14.3	12.1	9.3
6.1	0.03	na	0.06	8.5	1.9	1.94	14.83	3.75	47.7	2.9	18.7	14.8	9.4
8.4	1.22	na	0.00	4.6	0.9	0.88	9.05	3.54	67.1	1.4	18.9	26.4	6.1
5.1	0.60	na	0.19	3.7	1.1	0.72	7.78	3.75	81.6	2.6	13.9	15.9	5.5
8.1	0.00	na	-0.02	8.0	3.7	1.89	17.26	4.44	54.2	0.8	17.6	29.4	8.0
9.1	0.00	na	0.04	6.4	2.0	1.51	14.29	3.49	56.6	4.6	42.8	12.5	7.8
8.6	0.01	0.1	-0.08	7.1	1.9	1.80	20.74	4.22	61.2	2.7	15.0	15.4	6.4
7.5	0.00	na	0.01	5.7	0.5	1.30	8.11	3.73	60.0	1.3	21.8	29.2	8.2
7.2	1.16	na	-0.04	5.8	2.0	1.12	10.31	5.23	72.4	5.3	32.9	5.0	6.6

Name	City	State	Rating	2018 Rating	2017 Rating	Total Assets ($Mil)	One Year Asset Growth	Asset Mix (As a % of Total Assets): Commercial Loans	Consumer Loans	Mortgage Loans	Securities	Capitalization Index	Leverage Ratio	Risk-Based Capital Ratio
Iron Workers Savings Bank	Aston	PA	C	C	C	177.0	2.03	0.7	0.0	46.8	6.4	8.5	10.0	16.4
Iroquois Farmers State Bank	Iroquois	IL	B-	B-	B-	113.3	4.71	2.6	3.1	13.1	16.0	7.9	9.6	14.5
Iroquois Federal S&L Assn.	Watseka	IL	C+	B-	B-	678.2	3.47	9.2	1.1	18.6	21.8	10.0	11.2	16.2
Isabella Bank	Mount Pleasant	MI	B-	B-	B	1761.0	-1.13	8.4	4.1	17.1	25.3	6.5	8.5	12.3
▲ Islanders Bank	Friday Harbor	WA	A-	B+	B+	294.9	-0.30	5.5	1.0	16.3	19.6	10.0	11.7	19.0
Israel Discount Bank of New York	New York	NY	B+	B+	C+	9701.6	8.15	29.6	0.4	0.8	24.5	9.8	10.9	15.1
▲ Itasca Bank & Trust Co.	Itasca	IL	B+	B-	B-	579.2	10.13	21.9	0.2	12.7	17.6	8.2	9.8	14.0
ITS Bank	Johnston	IA	U	U	U	8.1	7.24	0.0	0.0	0.0	25.6	10.0	93.0	458.2
▲ Iuka State Bank	Salem	IL	C	D+	C	97.6	3.25	11.2	11.7	12.8	4.8	6.6	10.0	12.2
▲ Ixonia Bank	Ixonia	WI	B-	C+	C+	371.1	6.78	21.4	0.2	4.4	25.4	9.7	11.0	14.7
Jacksboro National Bank	Jacksboro	TX	B+	B+	B+	235.9	3.39	6.5	3.1	11.0	46.2	10.0	12.2	22.6
Jackson County Bank	Seymour	IN	B-	B-	B-	593.5	6.64	3.9	1.0	21.6	15.2	7.6	9.4	13.0
Jackson County Bank	McKee	KY	A-	A-	A	133.7	1.65	1.7	10.6	20.3	39.3	10.0	28.0	51.7
▼ Jackson County Bank	Black River Falls	WI	D-	C-	B-	200.4	-9.43	0.8	1.3	12.2	26.8	7.3	9.2	17.0
Jackson Federal S&L Assn.	Jackson	MN	C	C	C+	37.1	-5.34	5.2	3.7	29.1	39.4	10.0	24.0	40.8
Jackson Parish Bank	Jonesboro	LA	B-	B-	C+	64.8	0.75	5.4	5.1	12.7	60.4	10.0	15.6	44.4
Jackson Savings Bank, SSB	Sylva	NC	B-	C+	C	32.6	-1.16	0.0	0.6	66.4	0.0	10.0	20.9	41.5
▲ James Polk Stone Community Bank	Portales	NM	A-	B+	A-	233.7	8.85	5.5	4.6	22.0	31.3	10.0	11.1	20.3
Janesville State Bank	Janesville	MN	B+	B+	A-	72.7	7.42	2.9	2.5	21.8	10.9	10.0	13.1	17.5
Jarrettsville Federal S&L Assn.	Jarrettsville	MD	B-	B-	B-	127.9	5.15	0.8	0.0	57.9	7.4	10.0	14.1	30.0
▲ JD Bank	Jennings	LA	B+	B	B-	870.7	2.85	7.9	4.1	18.7	16.9	10.0	11.3	16.2
▲ Jeff Bank	Jeffersonville	NY	B+	B	B+	512.1	0.68	5.8	0.6	21.9	20.1	10.0	11.7	19.8
Jefferson Bank	Greenville	MS	B+	B+	A-	125.6	-8.61	10.8	0.3	1.9	18.6	10.0	18.5	21.8
Jefferson Bank	San Antonio	TX	B+	B+	B+	1863.3	-1.00	7.4	1.4	25.2	16.6	7.8	9.6	13.5
Jefferson Bank and Trust Co.	Saint Louis	MO	B	B	B-	619.4	-0.92	11.3	0.5	4.9	20.9	8.7	11.9	13.9
Jefferson Bank of Missouri	Jefferson City	MO	B+	B+	B	649.3	9.27	8.3	21.8	16.1	18.2	7.3	9.2	12.8
Jefferson Security Bank	Shepherdstown	WV	C+	C+	C+	320.5	4.52	1.4	1.2	34.5	26.7	7.7	9.4	15.9
Jersey Shore State Bank	Williamsport	PA	B-	B-	B-	1243.2	0.06	3.7	11.6	21.5	9.7	5.4	8.1	11.3
Jersey State Bank	Jerseyville	IL	B+	B+	B+	154.9	-1.51	6.9	0.6	7.7	46.9	10.0	13.8	26.9
Jewett City Savings Bank	Jewett City	CT	B	B-	C+	293.6	1.84	9.1	2.3	37.8	6.4	10.0	16.1	23.3
Jim Thorpe Neighborhood Bank	Jim Thorpe	PA	C+	C+	C+	201.6	2.54	1.4	0.6	23.8	35.2	9.1	10.4	20.8
John Deere Financial, F.S.B.	Madison	WI	A-	A-	A-	3922.4	3.71	5.1	13.1	0.0	0.0	10.0	15.4	15.6
John Marshall Bank	Reston	VA	B+	B+	B+	1512.8	14.35	4.7	0.1	9.6	7.1	8.4	11.9	13.7
Johnson Bank	Racine	WI	A-	A-	B	5256.6	6.19	18.5	1.7	18.1	10.9	10.0	12.4	16.4
Johnson City Bank	Johnson City	TX	B+	A-	A-	122.5	4.17	6.8	8.3	22.6	7.0	10.0	12.1	23.1
Johnson County Bank	Mountain City	TN	B	B	B+	120.2	1.24	3.7	4.6	32.7	29.9	10.0	15.6	31.7
Johnson State Bank	Johnson	KS	B	B	B+	78.4	6.67	4.0	2.6	4.5	37.8	10.0	16.3	28.3
▲ Jonah Bank of Wyoming	Casper	WY	B	B-	B+	334.5	0.89	14.9	0.5	10.1	9.5	9.6	10.9	14.6
Jones Bank	Seward	NE	B	B-	B+	323.3	37.26	10.2	1.4	8.3	30.9	10.0	12.9	16.9
Jonesboro State Bank	Jonesboro	LA	A-	A	A	314.0	16.95	0.9	1.1	4.7	88.0	10.0	14.4	48.3
Jonesburg State Bank	Jonesburg	MO	B-	B-	B-	99.4	4.69	5.1	2.3	22.3	2.3	6.3	8.3	14.7
Jonestown Bank and Trust Co.	Jonestown	PA	C	C	C	630.5	9.72	3.4	24.6	18.2	6.2	6.8	9.1	12.4
JPMorgan Chase Bank, Dearborn	Dearborn	MI	U	U	B	60.6	1.16	0.0	0.0	0.0	0.0	10.0	99.7	512.8
JPMorgan Chase Bank, N.A.	Columbus	OH	B+	B+	B	2367127.0	7.85	7.3	8.6	9.2	16.7	6.8	8.8	15.4
Junction National Bank	Junction	TX	B	B+	B+	69.0	17.24	4.0	2.7	6.0	63.0	8.1	9.7	32.1
Juniata Valley Bank	Mifflintown	PA	B-	B-	B-	665.9	7.42	7.1	1.4	21.5	30.0	7.9	9.6	15.9
▲ Kahoka State Bank	Kahoka	MO	B-	C+	C	50.2	2.32	5.3	5.4	23.7	31.1	10.0	11.0	19.3
▲ Kalamazoo County State Bank	Schoolcraft	MI	C+	C	C	95.3	-3.61	3.5	16.1	12.3	43.6	10.0	12.2	23.5
Kansas State Bank	Ottawa	KS	B	B-	B-	145.1	-0.28	5.9	1.7	13.4	50.9	7.1	9.0	20.0
Kansas State Bank Overbrook Kansas	Overbrook	KS	B+	B+	B+	63.1	6.98	9.2	3.3	7.6	36.6	10.0	14.1	21.9
▼ KansasLand Bank	Quinter	KS	C-	C+	C	52.7	-3.35	5.2	2.0	10.8	22.5	6.3	8.3	14.0
Kanza Bank	Kingman	KS	B-	B-	B-	221.1	-1.76	9.8	0.8	22.5	14.5	8.6	10.0	15.1
Karnes County National Bank	Karnes City	TX	B-	C	C+	407.7	6.10	1.7	0.8	3.2	76.4	9.7	10.8	36.4
Katahdin Trust Co.	Patten	ME	B-	B-	C+	844.9	6.65	19.2	1.0	18.8	10.6	7.7	9.5	13.5
▲ Kaw Valley Bank	Topeka	KS	B-	C+	C	315.9	1.66	15.2	2.8	20.0	5.2	8.8	10.4	14.0
▲ Kaw Valley State Bank	Eudora	KS	C+	C	C-	50.9	4.54	5.6	5.7	21.3	40.7	7.2	9.1	19.2
Kaw Valley State Bank and Trust Co.	Wamego	KS	A	A	A	184.2	6.39	8.3	2.1	15.8	31.5	10.0	12.0	21.5
Kearney Trust Co.	Kearney	MO	A-	A-	A-	198.0	5.89	5.7	4.0	17.0	22.7	9.2	10.5	16.9
Kearny Bank	Fairfield	NJ	B-	B-	C+	6621.3	-0.28	1.0	0.1	20.7	19.0	10.0	11.9	20.2
▲ Kearny County Bank	Lakin	KS	A-	B+	A	203.1	3.06	14.8	1.8	13.3	16.6	10.0	17.5	23.8

Asset Quality Index	Adjusted Non-Performing Loans as a % of Total Loans	Adjusted Non-Performing Loans as a % of Capital	Net Charge-Offs Avg Loans	Profitability Index	Net Income ($Mil)	Return on Assets (R.O.A.)	Return on Equity (R.O.E.)	Net Interest Spread	Overhead Efficiency Ratio	Liquidity Index	Liquidity Ratio	Hot Money Ratio	Stability Index
9.0	0.19	na	0.00	**2.6**	0.4	0.30	2.97	3.24	88.0	**1.7**	18.9	21.9	**5.2**
5.7	0.44	na	0.38	**4.0**	0.8	0.95	10.10	3.48	65.7	**4.0**	25.6	10.3	**5.6**
8.6	0.34	na	0.01	**3.3**	3.0	0.58	5.26	2.70	75.4	**0.9**	15.6	28.0	**7.4**
4.9	2.31	10.5	0.03	**4.4**	13.1	0.99	11.63	3.05	67.8	**1.6**	16.7	20.2	**7.7**
5.9	2.09	6.2	0.08	**8.8**	3.7	1.76	15.06	4.38	51.6	**5.8**	36.4	3.1	**8.8**
8.2	0.29	1.3	-0.02	**5.1**	79.2	1.12	10.60	2.84	58.2	**1.2**	23.3	29.2	**8.4**
7.6	0.73	na	-0.02	**7.0**	5.5	1.32	13.42	4.22	58.8	**1.7**	22.7	23.3	**6.6**
10.0	na	na	na	**10.0**	0.4	5.94	6.41	6.98	20.9	**4.0**	na	100.0	**5.8**
3.3	1.58	na	0.31	**4.5**	0.7	0.96	9.84	4.47	64.3	**1.2**	11.9	23.3	**3.4**
8.6	0.01	na	-0.03	**3.9**	1.8	0.66	5.43	3.69	77.1	**2.4**	31.8	13.4	**6.1**
7.1	1.35	na	0.12	**4.7**	1.9	1.06	8.73	3.83	75.6	**3.9**	34.6	13.8	**6.8**
5.1	1.70	na	0.05	**4.3**	4.0	0.92	9.39	3.34	73.9	**3.2**	22.0	13.6	**6.6**
8.3	1.29	na	0.23	**7.3**	1.5	1.48	5.36	4.23	57.9	**4.5**	51.8	15.6	**8.4**
2.5	20.54	na	3.37	**0.1**	-1.7	-1.07	-11.28	2.72	91.9	**2.4**	40.4	12.1	**3.7**
7.9	0.54	1.1	0.00	**2.1**	0.1	0.41	1.73	3.48	88.4	**3.7**	35.7	15.1	**6.1**
7.8	1.03	na	0.37	**3.8**	0.5	0.96	6.60	3.26	70.0	**5.8**	40.9	5.1	**6.3**
6.9	0.74	5.5	0.00	**3.0**	0.2	0.62	2.97	3.42	77.6	**0.8**	24.1	56.6	**6.9**
6.5	1.95	na	0.09	**6.9**	2.8	1.60	14.38	4.80	68.1	**6.0**	35.9	1.8	**7.5**
8.5	0.00	na	0.00	**7.6**	1.0	1.84	14.06	3.91	53.4	**3.0**	5.4	13.0	**8.4**
9.0	0.72	na	0.04	**2.9**	0.4	0.37	2.64	2.59	80.4	**2.0**	32.1	26.4	**7.5**
5.0	2.04	9.7	0.06	**5.7**	7.5	1.16	10.19	4.68	73.5	**4.1**	24.7	9.5	**7.3**
5.2	3.05	na	0.04	**6.6**	5.4	1.40	12.98	4.47	61.1	**5.1**	29.7	5.1	**7.8**
5.2	2.03	na	0.05	**8.7**	2.4	2.65	14.58	5.04	42.6	**0.5**	13.7	46.4	**8.4**
8.5	0.32	2.3	0.02	**5.4**	18.5	1.30	15.20	3.67	70.0	**2.6**	23.6	17.3	**8.0**
7.4	0.01	0.5	0.00	**5.1**	4.9	1.05	8.95	2.95	52.8	**1.1**	12.6	25.6	**8.0**
4.7	0.59	3.5	0.01	**9.7**	8.8	1.93	20.42	4.13	47.4	**3.7**	24.2	10.3	**7.6**
4.3	2.95	na	-0.01	**4.1**	2.1	0.88	10.81	3.42	70.9	**4.5**	14.7	5.5	**4.6**
4.0	1.61	13.3	0.08	**5.1**	10.7	1.15	14.96	3.18	59.3	**1.2**	8.6	18.7	**6.9**
8.5	1.21	na	0.01	**4.1**	1.0	0.90	6.34	3.29	70.1	**5.4**	40.0	7.6	**7.7**
5.6	2.73	9.2	0.42	**3.8**	1.5	0.71	4.23	4.08	76.8	**4.1**	17.0	8.4	**7.2**
7.8	0.55	2.1	0.06	**3.2**	1.0	0.71	7.09	3.23	79.6	**3.4**	27.9	14.2	**5.3**
5.8	0.18	na	1.42	**10.0**	87.1	3.50	20.00	6.19	31.7	**0.0**	0.1	99.4	**10.0**
7.4	0.18	1.0	0.02	**5.8**	12.5	1.16	9.68	3.54	56.1	**0.8**	13.0	32.3	**9.1**
7.8	0.50	2.7	0.14	**6.1**	45.5	1.20	9.39	3.78	67.4	**4.6**	15.2	5.3	**10.0**
8.2	1.22	na	0.21	**5.6**	1.2	1.35	11.14	3.97	66.4	**2.6**	42.1	28.3	**7.8**
5.5	4.35	na	0.10	**4.6**	0.7	0.82	5.14	3.75	73.5	**2.3**	37.8	28.1	**8.0**
4.8	5.43	na	0.10	**5.0**	0.7	1.15	7.23	3.59	66.2	**2.7**	31.7	18.7	**8.1**
5.2	0.87	na	0.00	**7.2**	3.5	1.43	13.68	4.11	63.1	**4.4**	17.6	6.3	**7.3**
7.2	0.59	na	-0.02	**7.9**	3.4	1.82	16.41	4.93	61.3	**3.6**	17.9	11.0	**7.0**
9.4	4.57	na	0.17	**5.2**	4.7	2.34	15.77	2.70	84.1	**2.9**	75.5	61.3	**8.9**
7.7	0.39	na	0.00	**7.5**	1.3	1.78	22.31	4.12	59.8	**3.4**	29.5	14.8	**6.2**
3.3	0.94	6.5	0.17	**4.4**	4.0	0.88	9.71	3.61	69.5	**2.2**	10.4	17.3	**6.3**
10.0	na	0.0	0.00	**9.0**	1.2	2.42	2.61	2.92	0.1	**4.0**	na	100.0	**7.0**
6.4	1.15	3.8	0.60	**6.3**	23875.0	1.37	13.58	2.81	57.3	**6.5**	54.1	5.6	**9.1**
9.6	0.45	na	0.10	**5.8**	0.8	1.52	16.29	3.05	58.3	**4.9**	73.3	15.9	**5.5**
5.1	1.06	na	-0.17	**4.2**	4.4	0.93	8.55	3.63	79.5	**4.5**	26.2	7.3	**6.7**
7.4	1.03	na	-0.02	**4.3**	0.3	0.86	7.95	3.50	66.7	**1.9**	28.9	25.7	**5.5**
8.1	0.02	na	0.00	**3.0**	0.3	0.40	3.45	3.59	85.2	**6.2**	59.2	6.1	**5.9**
9.1	0.32	1.4	0.04	**4.7**	1.4	1.24	14.06	3.20	64.1	**3.5**	11.4	11.0	**5.4**
6.9	2.33	na	-0.08	**6.3**	0.6	1.32	9.65	4.08	60.4	**2.9**	40.6	21.3	**8.3**
0.8	9.72	41.9	3.42	**0.3**	-1.0	-2.42	-25.72	3.66	83.4	**0.9**	9.7	31.4	**5.5**
7.9	0.15	na	0.22	**3.6**	1.2	0.72	6.87	3.79	77.7	**2.2**	9.6	17.6	**6.7**
7.0	11.33	na	-1.76	**4.8**	3.8	1.24	13.04	3.05	61.7	**7.2**	74.2	4.3	**4.6**
4.8	0.93	6.0	-0.01	**5.0**	6.6	1.08	10.84	3.69	65.3	**0.6**	9.6	19.3	**6.6**
5.5	4.17	na	-0.19	**6.6**	3.3	1.43	12.98	4.71	57.0	**0.9**	11.9	32.5	**7.5**
4.3	1.06	na	-0.01	**5.4**	0.5	1.30	14.06	4.09	68.1	**4.8**	27.8	5.9	**6.0**
8.8	0.21	na	-0.01	**7.4**	2.4	1.76	14.72	3.51	58.2	**2.9**	25.5	15.8	**8.4**
8.6	0.06	na	0.06	**6.0**	2.1	1.47	13.79	3.71	60.4	**4.5**	32.6	9.9	**7.6**
6.2	0.60	2.4	0.02	**3.5**	31.6	0.63	4.22	2.52	65.7	**1.1**	18.8	29.3	**8.7**
6.1	1.30	na	0.00	**9.2**	3.6	2.36	13.33	4.59	54.3	**1.8**	11.2	17.2	**9.9**

Name	City	State	Rating	2018 Rating	2017 Rating	Total Assets ($Mil)	One Year Asset Growth	Asset Mix (As a % of Total Assets) Commercial Loans	Consumer Loans	Mortgage Loans	Securities	Capitalization Index	Leverage Ratio	Risk-Based Capital Ratio
KEB Hana Bank USA, N.A.	New York	NY	**D**	D	D	237.3	-18.62	0.0	0.0	1.0	22.1	**10.0**	15.9	30.4
▼ Kendall State Bank	Valley Falls	KS	**C-**	C	C+	36.1	-1.52	6.8	3.8	13.1	0.2	**6.8**	8.9	14.5
Kennebec Federal S&L Assn. of Waterville	Waterville	ME	**C**	C-	C	98.4	2.63	0.0	0.2	77.9	2.6	**6.7**	8.7	15.1
Kennebec Savings Bank	Augusta	ME	**B+**	B+	B+	1122.8	6.69	3.7	0.3	57.9	12.3	**10.0**	12.9	17.5
Kennebunk Savings Bank	Kennebunk	ME	**B**	B	B	1317.6	7.81	3.0	0.1	26.7	9.1	**10.0**	11.7	15.4
Kennett Trust Bank	Kennett	MO	**B-**	C+	C+	107.3	-6.16	9.7	3.4	32.6	21.1	**10.0**	12.0	19.4
▼ Kensington Bank	Kensington	MN	**C-**	C+	B	273.1	59.25	9.9	1.1	9.8	7.3	**5.1**	9.1	11.1
▲ Kentland Bank	Kentland	IN	**A**	A-	A-	306.1	0.32	9.7	1.6	8.6	30.3	**10.0**	14.5	20.5
Kentland Federal S&L Assn.	Kentland	IN	**D**	D	D	4.1	-8.19	0.6	0.0	90.9	1.7	**10.0**	13.7	28.6
Kentucky Bank	Paris	KY	**B+**	B+	B	1079.5	2.82	4.7	2.1	21.1	22.8	**7.7**	9.5	14.4
Kentucky Farmers Bank Corp.	Ashland	KY	**A**	A	A	187.3	8.57	3.9	5.5	26.1	40.2	**10.0**	23.7	35.4
▲ Kerndt Brothers Savings Bank	Lansing	IA	**C+**	C+	B	287.4	1.95	10.8	0.8	7.9	18.8	**9.5**	10.8	14.6
Key Community Bank	Inver Grove Heights	MN	**C+**	C+	C	51.4	9.59	8.4	3.9	7.0	1.0	**9.3**	10.5	18.3
Key National Trust Co. of Delaware	Wilmington	DE	**U**	U	U	4.6	9.47	0.0	0.0	0.0	0.0	**10.0**	97.7	443.9
KeyBank N.A.	Cleveland	OH	**B**	B	B	145183.6	6.05	25.9	6.4	7.2	22.7	**7.1**	9.8	12.6
KeySavings Bank	Wisconsin Rapids	WI	**C-**	C-	C-	77.2	2.55	0.6	1.3	46.2	23.6	**10.0**	14.7	32.8
Keystone Bank, N.A.	Austin	TX	**C**	C	C+	178.7	331.86	6.3	1.2	11.1	9.4	**10.0**	14.3	18.6
Keystone Savings Bank	Keystone	IA	**B-**	B	B+	147.5	42.04	6.5	2.2	19.5	22.8	**6.5**	9.9	12.2
Killbuck Savings Bank Co.	Killbuck	OH	**A-**	A-	B+	557.7	5.77	10.1	1.2	21.5	22.5	**9.5**	10.6	14.8
▲ Kindred State Bank	Kindred	ND	**C-**	D+	D+	28.4	3.60	4.4	8.4	4.5	6.3	**7.3**	9.2	16.8
Kingston National Bank	Kingston	OH	**B**	B	B	376.0	10.73	8.4	2.0	20.2	21.0	**6.5**	8.5	12.8
Kingstree Federal S&L Assn.	Kingstree	SC	**C+**	C+	C+	33.8	6.94	0.7	0.3	43.3	13.4	**10.0**	16.6	37.2
▲ Kinmundy Bank	Kinmundy	IL	**B**	B-	B+	48.6	3.22	7.7	17.8	28.0	13.9	**10.0**	11.2	17.2
▲ Kirkpatrick Bank	Edmond	OK	**B**	B-	B	797.9	1.36	7.9	1.1	6.1	16.6	**10.0**	11.7	15.6
Kirkwood Bank and Trust Co.	Bismarck	ND	**B**	B-	B-	252.0	4.98	10.6	3.4	10.5	13.7	**7.8**	9.6	13.2
▲ Kirkwood Bank of Nevada	Las Vegas	NV	**B+**	B	B	130.8	57.72	3.1	0.0	1.2	0.0	**10.0**	16.3	18.2
Kish Bank	Belleville	PA	**C+**	C+	C+	900.3	7.15	11.2	0.8	24.5	14.0	**5.9**	8.6	11.7
Kitsap Bank	Port Orchard	WA	**A-**	B	B	1191.3	3.82	8.4	0.4	9.0	23.8	**8.5**	10.0	14.3
▲ Kleberg Bank, N.A.	Kingsville	TX	**C+**	C	B-	563.5	4.13	8.5	15.6	12.1	18.4	**7.3**	9.2	13.9
▲ KodaBank	Drayton	ND	**B**	C+	B-	148.9	1.75	10.7	7.3	10.5	12.3	**9.5**	13.4	14.5
Kress National Bank	Kress	TX	**B-**	B-	B-	38.7	1.89	10.0	3.4	0.6	29.3	**10.0**	12.0	25.1
KS Bank, Inc.	Smithfield	NC	**C+**	B-	B-	404.0	3.76	3.3	0.4	22.2	16.2	**8.1**	9.8	14.2
KS StateBank	Manhattan	KS	**A-**	A-	A-	2097.7	9.82	14.8	0.4	17.8	15.8	**7.6**	9.4	13.7
La Monte Community Bank	La Monte	MO	**B+**	B+	B+	32.1	8.55	3.8	2.2	18.2	23.4	**9.3**	10.5	17.3
Labette Bank	Altamont	KS	**B+**	B+	B	396.5	-2.40	2.6	2.8	26.0	20.6	**10.0**	11.9	18.5
▲ Ladysmith Federal S&L Assn.	Ladysmith	WI	**B-**	C	C-	53.3	1.05	12.2	6.5	50.9	8.1	**10.0**	11.1	21.2
Lafayette State Bank	Mayo	FL	**E**	E-	E-	105.5	15.47	5.6	3.0	15.3	7.8	**6.0**	8.0	13.7
Lake Area Bank	Lindstrom	MN	**B-**	B	B-	360.6	8.50	7.3	0.1	23.2	19.0	**7.2**	10.1	12.6
▲ Lake Bank	Two Harbors	MN	**B-**	C	D+	133.6	0.15	7.1	1.3	36.0	22.8	**8.6**	10.1	16.4
Lake Central Bank	Annandale	MN	**A**	A-	A-	157.9	5.63	7.4	0.7	16.5	37.6	**10.0**	13.7	17.6
Lake City Bank	Warsaw	IN	**A-**	A-	A-	4936.9	4.12	29.0	1.8	4.0	12.4	**9.2**	11.7	14.3
▲ Lake City Federal Bank	Lake City	MN	**B**	C	D+	69.3	-3.30	1.0	3.0	49.3	14.9	**10.0**	12.9	23.4
▲ Lake Community Bank	Long Lake	MN	**B**	B	B+	120.0	-1.01	4.8	0.8	8.5	13.3	**10.0**	13.0	17.0
Lake Country Community Bank	Morristown	MN	**C**	C-	D	27.2	8.62	10.5	1.1	17.9	13.7	**8.0**	9.7	17.8
Lake Elmo Bank	Lake Elmo	MN	**B+**	B	B	376.4	-1.87	6.1	2.8	26.4	17.2	**8.6**	10.0	15.6
Lake Forest Bank & Trust Co., N.A.	Lake Forest	IL	**B+**	B+	B+	4296.6	16.10	45.1	6.9	2.5	10.2	**6.5**	9.9	12.2
Lake Region Bank	New London	MN	**C+**	B-	C+	114.0	3.12	16.8	4.2	9.2	27.8	**8.3**	9.8	18.1
Lake Shore Savings Bank	Dunkirk	NY	**B**	B	B	596.9	9.26	3.5	0.2	27.9	12.6	**10.0**	13.2	17.9
Lake-Osceola State Bank	Baldwin	MI	**C+**	C+	C+	280.2	5.23	6.1	20.8	21.1	6.6	**7.7**	9.5	13.1
Lakeland Bank	Oak Ridge	NJ	**B+**	B+	B	6487.8	15.55	5.9	0.2	9.7	13.4	**7.6**	10.1	13.0
Lakeside Bank	Chicago	IL	**A-**	A-	A	1775.8	9.50	5.5	0.0	8.5	2.6	**9.4**	12.0	14.5
Lakeside Bank	Lake Charles	LA	**B-**	B-	B-	210.8	17.01	7.6	2.6	18.0	18.5	**10.0**	11.9	18.3
Lakeside Bank of Salina	Salina	OK	**B**	B	B	39.0	15.25	16.4	19.1	22.7	11.5	**10.0**	13.0	20.3
Lakeside National Bank	Rockwall	TX	**B**	C+	C	83.9	29.64	1.2	1.4	8.5	5.4	**10.0**	27.3	58.9
▲ Lakeside State Bank	Oologah	OK	**C**	C	C+	66.0	-8.93	8.9	11.1	18.2	25.1	**7.6**	9.4	17.7
Lakestone Bank & Trust	Lapeer	MI	**B+**	B+	B+	672.2	8.59	9.4	1.8	16.5	27.9	**8.1**	9.8	14.6
Lakeview Bank	Lakeville	MN	**B**	B	B-	103.2	18.02	16.7	0.2	27.0	7.4	**7.4**	9.3	13.6
▲ Lamar Bank and Trust Co.	Lamar	MO	**B+**	B+	A	162.8	4.49	12.0	2.7	19.0	11.2	**10.0**	11.2	16.2
Lamar National Bank	Paris	TX	**C**	C+	B	174.0	10.61	6.1	3.0	32.5	8.8	**10.0**	11.5	18.6
Lamesa National Bank	Lamesa	TX	**B**	B	B-	347.4	2.77	3.0	0.3	0.0	52.4	**9.3**	10.5	21.6

Asset Quality Index	Adjusted Non-Performing Loans as a % of Total Loans	Adjusted Non-Performing Loans as a % of Capital	Net Charge-Offs Avg Loans	Profitability Index	Net Income ($Mil)	Return on Assets (R.O.A.)	Return on Equity (R.O.E.)	Net Interest Spread	Overhead Efficiency Ratio	Liquidity Index	Liquidity Ratio	Hot Money Ratio	Stability Index
7.4	1.52	na	-0.07	**0.0**	-4.1	-2.44	-13.57	2.89	176.9	**6.5**	56.8	5.7	**5.1**
8.5	0.06	0.3	1.59	**0.9**	-0.2	-0.87	-9.11	4.61	99.1	**2.4**	31.4	20.4	**4.2**
7.3	0.39	na	0.03	**2.9**	0.3	0.41	4.76	3.50	85.2	**0.7**	8.0	29.1	**4.4**
8.7	0.56	3.2	0.01	**4.4**	8.4	1.03	7.75	3.22	65.0	**2.9**	14.9	6.3	**9.9**
7.9	0.54	3.4	0.05	**4.3**	7.3	0.77	7.04	3.90	77.6	**4.8**	10.4	1.2	**9.0**
6.0	1.22	na	0.20	**3.7**	0.5	0.57	5.16	3.57	78.4	**0.9**	22.6	31.2	**5.7**
2.7	2.05	na	0.02	**2.7**	0.6	0.27	2.56	4.13	91.1	**3.2**	15.0	13.2	**5.9**
8.8	0.38	na	0.03	**7.8**	3.6	1.58	10.96	4.46	57.7	**2.9**	39.4	21.2	**9.2**
4.2	1.45	na	0.00	**0.6**	0.0	-0.37	-2.76	3.77	110.0	**1.0**	8.7	30.2	**6.3**
7.7	0.21	3.0	0.13	**5.2**	9.2	1.12	10.77	3.68	71.3	**1.4**	12.1	13.3	**9.1**
8.6	0.57	na	0.10	**8.7**	2.4	1.75	7.32	4.78	62.0	**5.6**	56.2	11.0	**9.4**
4.8	2.31	na	0.03	**4.5**	2.1	1.01	8.45	3.76	70.8	**3.5**	28.8	13.8	**7.4**
8.6	0.06	na	0.00	**3.8**	0.3	0.90	8.54	3.90	77.2	**5.9**	45.6	5.0	**5.6**
10.0	na	0.0	na	**10.0**	0.2	6.50	6.71	7.53	56.3	**4.0**	na	0.0	**7.0**
5.3	0.95	4.9	0.47	**6.1**	1364.7	1.28	11.20	3.16	56.1	**4.8**	23.1	6.0	**10.0**
8.2	0.99	na	0.04	**1.3**	0.0	0.07	0.51	2.55	99.9	**4.3**	46.0	14.7	**6.6**
8.0	0.05	na	0.01	**1.4**	-0.1	-0.16	-0.65	4.92	94.6	**5.1**	42.5	10.3	**6.2**
6.3	0.89	na	0.19	**3.9**	0.9	0.85	7.80	4.25	73.3	**3.5**	26.3	12.8	**6.3**
8.8	0.04	na	0.14	**6.8**	5.7	1.41	12.29	4.00	57.4	**3.7**	21.6	11.2	**7.9**
7.4	0.28	na	-0.02	**4.0**	0.3	1.15	13.71	3.46	69.8	**5.8**	37.2	3.2	**3.2**
8.7	0.12	0.8	0.02	**4.1**	2.3	0.86	10.19	3.36	69.3	**1.4**	17.1	27.0	**5.0**
6.1	2.63	na	0.01	**2.8**	0.1	0.40	2.43	2.81	83.4	**1.2**	28.2	37.7	**7.4**
6.3	0.07	na	0.23	**10.0**	0.7	2.00	15.03	4.99	41.3	**3.9**	16.6	9.3	**8.5**
5.6	0.65	na	-0.01	**7.4**	10.8	1.78	16.00	3.93	54.1	**4.2**	15.0	7.4	**8.4**
7.3	0.14	na	0.10	**5.0**	1.8	1.01	10.43	3.60	69.5	**3.9**	18.9	10.0	**6.0**
6.4	0.00	na	0.00	**5.2**	0.4	1.37	9.40	4.46	65.4	**2.7**	45.4	28.2	**8.2**
8.0	0.16	na	-0.09	**3.8**	5.5	0.84	9.68	3.48	76.6	**1.5**	9.3	22.3	**6.0**
8.2	0.04	0.2	0.01	**6.0**	12.3	1.42	12.56	4.59	70.2	**6.1**	30.9	2.7	**9.7**
4.3	0.78	na	0.16	**4.6**	4.3	1.08	8.88	3.97	73.5	**3.0**	19.4	14.6	**7.8**
4.0	2.26	na	0.18	**10.0**	3.1	2.79	21.49	4.60	40.3	**1.4**	4.0	21.7	**8.2**
8.5	0.49	na	0.81	**4.6**	0.3	1.03	9.30	3.61	69.8	**2.6**	47.3	29.4	**6.4**
6.3	1.12	na	-0.01	**5.4**	3.2	1.07	11.16	3.70	67.8	**1.5**	18.3	21.7	**6.5**
6.8	0.81	6.8	0.02	**6.6**	24.3	1.60	17.24	3.15	50.8	**0.8**	17.8	39.7	**9.3**
5.0	0.00	na	-0.01	**3.7**	0.2	0.65	6.15	3.55	75.7	**3.6**	5.7	9.9	**6.3**
8.3	0.64	na	-0.02	**5.1**	3.1	1.03	8.85	3.89	70.3	**2.6**	9.1	15.5	**7.3**
5.7	2.37	na	0.09	**3.9**	0.3	0.71	6.48	3.82	75.1	**1.4**	22.1	28.1	**5.4**
1.7	8.18	48.1	-0.21	**3.9**	0.7	0.95	12.62	4.57	82.8	**5.1**	29.9	5.1	**0.8**
6.0	2.17	na	-0.04	**6.2**	3.7	1.47	13.58	3.96	76.5	**1.8**	21.8	18.0	**7.4**
8.5	0.23	na	-0.01	**7.2**	1.3	1.34	13.81	3.77	60.6	**1.3**	14.5	24.2	**6.2**
6.6	1.51	5.6	0.00	**9.1**	2.8	2.48	18.52	4.02	53.8	**5.5**	31.7	3.2	**8.5**
7.5	0.61	3.4	0.03	**9.3**	67.3	1.83	15.91	3.44	42.5	**1.5**	15.7	25.1	**10.0**
8.2	0.59	na	-0.09	**5.4**	0.6	1.18	9.52	3.48	75.6	**2.7**	22.7	16.3	**6.8**
7.5	0.62	na	-0.01	**6.5**	1.1	1.24	9.57	4.02	58.6	**3.4**	23.2	12.9	**7.6**
6.8	4.97	na	-0.15	**3.0**	0.1	0.48	4.67	3.46	82.5	**5.6**	53.9	9.3	**4.4**
6.3	0.71	3.1	-0.06	**7.3**	5.0	1.79	18.44	4.01	59.4	**4.5**	19.7	5.6	**6.7**
5.1	0.76	4.9	0.60	**9.8**	67.1	2.21	20.91	3.85	42.2	**2.0**	18.6	8.0	**8.5**
3.8	4.46	na	-0.05	**5.0**	1.0	1.24	12.04	4.60	79.7	**6.6**	50.3	2.9	**5.8**
7.6	0.75	na	0.01	**3.9**	3.1	0.72	5.25	3.61	73.5	**2.1**	15.3	18.4	**8.5**
3.1	1.56	9.8	0.22	**5.5**	2.4	1.20	12.77	4.15	67.0	**2.0**	14.4	16.1	**6.0**
6.0	0.42	2.9	0.00	**5.9**	55.2	1.17	9.66	3.43	56.1	**3.4**	10.4	10.8	**9.5**
6.2	0.48	3.2	-0.03	**7.4**	21.7	1.66	14.10	3.70	56.2	**0.8**	13.2	18.9	**10.0**
8.7	0.10	na	0.06	**3.4**	0.6	0.42	3.44	3.72	83.7	**1.8**	26.3	23.6	**7.1**
4.4	3.84	na	0.08	**7.9**	0.4	1.38	10.63	5.70	64.8	**2.5**	20.3	17.2	**6.8**
7.3	0.49	na	na	**1.5**	0.0	0.00	0.00	na	81.1	**7.2**	103.5	7.4	**5.8**
7.1	0.99	na	0.10	**2.9**	0.1	0.17	2.02	4.49	89.5	**3.7**	24.3	11.2	**4.4**
8.0	0.20	1.1	-0.05	**5.6**	5.7	1.16	11.66	3.78	67.9	**5.1**	27.1	3.8	**6.6**
6.4	0.62	4.7	0.04	**6.8**	0.9	1.18	12.73	4.50	65.2	**3.3**	22.3	11.1	**6.4**
7.5	0.46	na	0.02	**8.1**	2.1	1.74	16.23	3.93	60.1	**3.9**	11.5	8.8	**8.4**
4.0	3.32	19.3	0.11	**5.4**	1.5	1.22	11.59	4.68	73.7	**3.6**	25.9	12.2	**6.9**
5.4	3.09	na	-0.22	**5.5**	4.4	1.66	16.68	2.28	42.3	**3.5**	55.0	23.2	**4.5**

Name	City	State	Rating	2018 Rating	2017 Rating	Total Assets ($Mil)	One Year Asset Growth	Asset Mix (As a % of Total Assets) Comm-ercial Loans	Cons-umer Loans	Mort-gage Loans	Secur-ities	Capital-ization Index	Lever-age Ratio	Risk-Based Capital Ratio
Lamont Bank of St. John	Saint John	WA	B	B	B	50.9	11.34	4.1	10.7	0.1	48.8	10.0	13.4	23.3
▲ Landmark Bank	Clinton	LA	C+	C	D+	138.4	7.17	7.7	2.8	29.6	16.6	8.8	10.2	15.4
Landmark Bank	Columbia	MO	B+	B+	B+	3276.0	8.84	8.4	2.1	16.8	30.5	6.6	8.6	13.7
Landmark Community Bank	Pittston	PA	D+	D+	D+	321.4	-2.82	9.5	8.5	11.6	16.1	8.2	9.8	14.0
Landmark Community Bank	Collierville	TN	B	B	B	968.8	-1.58	5.5	0.7	50.1	12.2	7.3	9.2	15.5
Landmark National Bank	Manhattan	KS	B	B+	B+	1005.6	4.85	10.2	0.2	15.5	36.4	9.1	10.4	16.8
Laona State Bank	Laona	WI	B-	B	B	205.7	14.83	5.8	3.7	26.5	28.2	10.0	11.6	21.5
LaSalle State Bank	La Salle	IL	C+	C+	C+	141.1	-5.25	7.3	1.6	10.9	38.5	8.4	9.9	17.4
Latimer State Bank	Wilburton	OK	B	B-	B-	69.2	2.75	8.3	3.7	5.3	11.5	10.0	20.4	57.9
Lauderdale County Bank	Halls	TN	C+	C+	C+	50.3	2.97	18.0	6.9	14.3	27.9	10.0	11.4	21.4
Laurens State Bank	Laurens	IA	B+	B+	B+	68.2	1.91	4.5	2.0	7.3	33.5	10.0	12.2	25.7
Lawrenceburg Federal Bank	Lawrenceburg	TN	B	B	B+	71.3	9.33	0.0	3.1	80.0	0.0	10.0	22.0	38.5
LCA Bank Corp.	Park City	UT	A-	A	A	162.9	-6.80	1.8	0.0	0.0	0.8	10.0	15.9	18.5
LCNB National Bank	Lebanon	OH	B	B	B	1641.8	1.49	4.4	1.5	17.7	13.7	7.2	10.0	12.7
▲ Lea County State Bank	Hobbs	NM	A-	B	B	345.7	4.14	13.5	4.8	0.9	65.6	9.9	10.9	23.5
Lead Bank	Garden City	MO	C	C+	C	356.8	38.54	11.0	20.4	10.1	0.8	6.5	8.5	13.4
Leader Bank, N.A.	Arlington	MA	A	A	A	1545.3	12.41	1.3	0.0	42.5	2.2	10.0	11.8	15.7
Leaders Bank	Oak Brook	IL	C	C-	D	335.7	7.47	17.6	1.1	6.5	6.0	10.0	11.9	15.7
Ledyard National Bank	Norwich	VT	B	B	B	504.4	1.89	7.8	2.5	24.4	28.1	7.8	9.5	16.0
Lee Bank	Lee	MA	C	C	C	400.4	7.22	4.1	0.2	39.9	8.6	7.2	9.1	13.5
Lee Bank and Trust Co.	Pennington Gap	VA	B	B	B	144.4	-4.03	12.4	3.9	24.3	9.7	10.0	16.7	27.2
Lee County Bank	Fort Madison	IA	A-	A-	A-	188.0	5.78	9.5	4.5	45.3	1.1	10.0	12.2	18.6
Legacy Bank	Wiley	CO	B+	B+	B+	367.8	13.90	10.4	0.6	9.1	15.3	10.0	14.7	17.8
Legacy Bank	Altoona	IA	C	C-	D+	112.5	5.96	16.5	2.8	22.5	10.9	5.6	7.6	11.6
Legacy Bank	Wichita	KS	C+	C	B-	465.3	6.03	8.8	0.5	19.0	10.4	9.6	11.1	14.7
Legacy Bank	Hinton	OK	B-	B-	B-	457.1	-1.22	10.8	1.1	11.6	22.3	6.9	8.9	13.5
Legacy Bank & Trust Co.	Rogersville	MO	B	B	B-	284.9	14.59	13.2	2.3	23.6	1.8	6.7	9.8	12.3
▲ Legacy Bank of Florida	Boca Raton	FL	B-	C+	C+	457.8	12.32	11.5	0.2	11.4	6.0	6.3	10.8	12.0
▲ Legacy National Bank	Springdale	AR	B-	C+	B+	545.4	7.89	9.4	1.1	16.5	3.1	7.0	9.5	12.5
Legacy State Bank	Loganville	GA	D+	D	E	110.8	11.73	7.0	0.2	6.1	11.1	7.5	10.3	12.9
Legacy Trust Co., N.A.	Houston	TX	U	U	U	31.6	14.44	0.0	0.0	0.0	77.2	10.0	91.0	143.5
▲ Legence Bank	Eldorado	IL	B	B	B+	477.2	3.97	18.7	3.9	4.3	20.7	7.5	9.3	13.5
▲ Legend Bank, N.A.	Bowie	TX	B	B	B+	765.4	13.23	10.1	0.9	12.8	22.1	8.1	9.8	14.2
▲ Legends Bank	Linn	MO	A-	B+	A-	385.1	4.87	5.2	8.0	20.5	18.7	10.0	14.0	21.5
Legends Bank	Clarksville	TN	B	B	B	506.2	5.03	9.6	1.0	8.8	16.6	7.5	10.0	12.9
Leighton State Bank	Pella	IA	B+	B+	A-	188.4	7.29	11.3	1.3	16.6	11.2	10.0	11.1	15.1
Lemont National Bank	Lemont	IL	D+	D+	D+	51.9	-5.31	0.0	0.0	8.2	63.3	4.6	6.6	24.0
▲ Lena State Bank	Lena	IL	B+	B	B-	89.9	1.53	17.6	0.4	3.8	27.6	10.0	12.2	17.6
Level One Bank	Farmington Hills	MI	B	B	B-	1506.1	4.31	24.0	0.1	12.6	13.6	7.9	10.6	13.2
▲ Lewis & Clark Bank	Oregon City	OR	B	B-	B+	267.3	35.86	7.0	0.1	8.2	6.9	10.0	12.3	15.3
▲ Lewisburg Banking Co.	Lewisburg	KY	B+	B	A-	134.6	12.96	6.3	4.6	26.6	26.6	8.9	10.3	17.5
Liberty Bank	Geraldine	AL	B	B	B	148.0	6.66	5.2	6.8	18.2	28.5	10.0	11.7	17.9
▲ Liberty Bank	South San Francisco	CA	B	B-	C+	271.2	2.10	4.8	0.1	1.7	17.2	10.0	13.6	15.3
▲ Liberty Bank	Middletown	CT	A-	B	B	5294.4	7.14	10.5	0.1	18.4	14.8	10.0	15.0	18.1
▲ Liberty Bank	Liberty	IL	B	B-	B-	101.2	10.09	5.4	6.2	17.5	15.2	10.0	12.9	18.8
Liberty Bank	Ironton	OH	B-	B-	B-	52.2	-2.57	2.9	4.7	44.2	10.9	10.0	16.6	29.1
Liberty Bank and Trust Co.	New Orleans	LA	B-	C+	C+	627.8	5.21	3.3	4.6	23.5	29.2	7.6	9.4	17.2
Liberty Bank for Savings	Chicago	IL	C+	C+	C+	825.7	0.75	0.0	0.0	52.2	39.5	10.0	23.5	56.0
Liberty Bank Minnesota	Saint Cloud	MN	A	A	A	222.0	3.19	0.1	2.8	33.6	19.6	10.0	12.2	25.4
▼ Liberty Bank, Inc.	Salt Lake City	UT	E+	E+	E	8.9	-1.46	3.5	29.2	13.7	12.1	5.8	7.8	18.0
Liberty Bay Bank	Poulsbo	WA	C	C	C-	117.3	3.44	6.2	0.2	11.6	11.2	7.5	9.3	15.8
▲ Liberty Capital Bank	Addison	TX	A-	B+	A-	267.6	10.59	9.8	0.1	13.2	0.0	8.5	10.0	13.9
Liberty First Bank	Monroe	GA	B+	B+	B+	133.8	2.83	5.8	0.8	17.7	28.6	10.0	11.4	16.5
Liberty National Bank	Sioux City	IA	B	B	B	432.0	9.34	12.3	0.6	12.6	14.8	7.9	9.9	13.3
▲ Liberty National Bank	Ada	OH	B+	B	B-	342.5	4.74	8.5	0.2	13.3	14.0	10.0	12.9	17.9
Liberty National Bank	Lawton	OK	A-	A-	A-	564.8	11.35	13.8	1.7	11.2	13.7	9.5	10.6	15.9
Liberty National Bank in Paris	Paris	TX	A-	A-	B+	295.3	3.91	5.0	7.0	28.1	31.1	10.0	17.0	29.4
Liberty Savings Assn., FSA	Fort Scott	KS	C+	C+	C	31.7	-1.40	0.3	3.6	19.8	61.3	10.0	20.8	84.1
Liberty Savings Bank, F.S.B.	Wilmington	OH	B-	B-	B	709.5	7.00	0.1	2.4	66.2	24.9	7.4	9.2	19.2
Liberty State Bank	Powers Lake	ND	A-	A-	A-	95.2	6.55	2.5	2.6	7.9	44.9	10.0	12.1	23.0

Asset Quality Index	Adjusted Non-Performing Loans as a % of Total Loans	Adjusted Non-Performing Loans as a % of Capital	Net Charge-Offs Avg Loans	Profitability Index	Net Income ($Mil)	Return on Assets (R.O.A.)	Return on Equity (R.O.E.)	Net Interest Spread	Overhead Efficiency Ratio	Liquidity Index	Liquidity Ratio	Hot Money Ratio	Stability Index
8.2	0.62	na	1.47	6.0	0.5	1.23	9.51	3.48	44.2	6.6	44.0	0.0	6.2
3.9	1.77	na	0.23	3.4	0.6	0.56	5.41	4.55	82.2	2.6	20.7	11.3	5.9
8.0	0.63	2.8	0.08	5.0	28.0	1.16	13.37	3.17	67.1	1.2	19.9	21.3	7.3
4.4	0.66	na	0.09	1.9	0.9	0.34	3.65	3.24	90.4	2.4	10.3	16.5	4.2
6.1	0.77	5.5	0.06	4.7	6.7	0.92	10.11	2.47	52.5	0.8	17.3	34.9	5.9
5.8	1.68	5.8	0.13	4.8	7.8	1.05	8.82	3.53	69.3	1.5	15.9	16.1	9.0
3.5	5.34	na	-0.23	4.1	1.2	0.83	6.88	3.30	64.8	3.7	41.4	16.7	6.6
7.2	0.77	na	0.02	4.0	1.0	0.99	10.73	3.20	73.2	3.3	13.5	12.6	5.1
7.3	3.84	4.5	0.17	4.7	0.6	1.16	5.68	2.79	52.4	3.4	87.0	35.2	6.8
5.9	1.53	na	0.47	3.5	0.2	0.47	4.18	3.97	81.5	2.2	42.1	32.8	5.3
9.0	0.00	na	0.01	5.3	0.6	1.22	10.38	3.18	60.8	5.2	55.1	11.6	7.2
6.5	1.19	na	0.02	4.1	0.3	0.60	2.67	3.60	75.1	0.7	11.1	40.2	7.6
8.9	0.49	na	1.12	10.0	2.6	2.08	13.84	6.77	44.1	0.3	12.5	0.0	7.8
5.5	0.84	na	0.01	5.4	14.1	1.15	8.59	3.67	65.4	3.2	5.7	12.1	9.5
7.8	0.06	0.1	-1.03	6.4	7.6	2.97	27.87	3.64	63.7	5.7	61.8	8.4	6.2
2.3	1.67	na	0.85	5.4	2.5	1.06	12.12	11.37	84.1	0.7	11.6	13.1	5.1
8.6	0.36	1.6	0.07	9.6	22.2	2.08	17.74	3.16	47.0	1.6	8.4	18.5	9.8
5.6	2.80	na	0.00	3.8	2.6	1.03	8.30	3.46	68.3	0.7	17.4	47.8	5.6
5.9	0.86	3.7	0.00	5.4	4.6	1.22	12.83	3.63	75.3	5.2	31.0	4.8	7.1
5.1	1.70	na	0.04	3.3	1.9	0.66	7.82	3.49	80.4	3.5	12.9	7.2	5.5
6.8	0.29	4.5	0.15	4.4	1.0	0.86	5.60	4.09	72.7	1.3	16.0	27.8	7.1
8.6	0.03	na	0.06	7.0	2.3	1.67	13.89	3.69	55.1	4.9	13.0	2.2	8.3
4.1	3.11	na	0.07	8.9	5.1	2.01	12.30	4.53	49.9	1.5	16.4	25.2	9.4
2.7	0.30	na	0.11	4.6	0.9	1.03	13.54	4.22	78.4	4.8	24.4	4.6	4.6
3.5	2.75	na	0.16	6.2	4.5	1.32	11.61	4.13	58.1	2.0	11.8	16.0	5.7
7.4	0.72	3.0	-0.01	4.1	2.7	0.77	8.81	4.77	85.9	4.9	26.1	4.6	4.6
7.5	0.30	na	0.02	8.3	3.0	1.51	13.80	4.57	57.6	1.5	4.4	16.2	7.1
7.3	0.21	na	0.02	4.6	3.1	0.94	8.75	3.21	64.8	0.8	10.4	33.5	6.7
4.4	2.30	na	-0.09	5.9	4.5	1.13	11.98	3.92	60.4	1.6	10.8	18.2	6.5
7.5	0.00	na	0.00	4.5	0.9	1.16	11.49	3.87	63.8	1.6	16.4	22.8	4.2
10.0	na	0.0	na	9.5	2.4	10.61	11.59	2.79	74.7	4.0	na	0.0	6.7
6.1	0.75	na	0.09	6.2	5.4	1.54	13.60	5.46	72.3	3.6	16.7	11.1	7.1
6.0	0.61	na	-0.02	6.8	8.7	1.62	14.78	4.53	66.1	2.7	19.9	16.1	8.1
7.3	0.26	na	0.10	8.7	4.7	1.65	11.98	4.11	50.0	2.1	4.8	17.6	8.6
7.4	0.08	0.4	0.09	5.4	4.1	1.10	11.36	3.87	66.5	1.7	12.3	9.4	6.3
6.5	0.73	na	0.06	6.0	1.8	1.31	10.49	3.50	68.3	2.2	18.4	18.5	8.8
9.8	0.00	0.0	0.00	2.4	0.1	0.32	4.61	3.38	87.3	7.6	84.1	1.7	2.7
8.4	0.40	1.2	0.00	6.5	0.8	1.15	9.47	3.21	55.3	1.3	20.4	28.8	8.2
5.1	1.02	6.1	0.01	5.5	12.2	1.09	9.84	3.69	67.8	0.9	16.1	29.1	8.8
6.2	0.11	na	0.00	5.2	1.7	0.95	8.03	4.46	69.7	2.5	14.5	16.4	7.3
5.7	1.58	na	-0.01	8.0	1.8	1.88	17.99	4.29	58.7	2.7	21.1	15.9	8.2
7.0	0.83	na	0.03	4.0	0.9	0.82	7.24	4.43	75.8	2.5	38.1	25.9	6.8
6.9	1.29	na	0.00	4.1	1.3	0.69	4.98	4.02	77.0	3.9	23.4	10.4	7.5
8.5	0.26	1.2	0.02	5.8	49.6	1.28	8.61	3.13	68.4	3.6	25.8	15.1	10.0
5.6	0.94	na	0.00	7.3	1.0	1.41	11.17	4.18	54.5	3.5	24.9	12.3	6.8
6.6	1.95	na	0.01	3.3	0.2	0.54	3.32	4.24	84.9	4.2	24.4	8.3	7.1
4.7	2.28	8.4	0.23	4.1	4.0	0.89	9.63	4.16	80.4	2.7	14.8	12.5	5.2
10.0	0.76	na	-0.01	2.8	2.4	0.38	1.61	2.47	81.3	4.0	53.2	18.1	8.2
8.3	0.00	0.0	0.04	5.7	1.4	0.87	6.59	3.37	80.8	6.5	47.5	2.3	9.1
4.2	2.23	na	-0.15	0.0	-0.2	-3.43	-34.56	3.27	121.3	1.6	46.3	62.7	3.0
5.4	0.80	na	0.00	2.4	0.1	0.16	1.65	3.73	93.0	3.9	18.6	9.5	5.7
8.7	0.00	na	0.00	7.8	3.7	1.84	19.44	3.92	49.3	5.0	28.3	5.0	7.4
8.0	0.90	na	0.00	4.9	1.1	1.13	10.28	4.01	72.6	2.4	31.4	20.8	7.2
7.7	0.00	na	0.32	5.6	3.4	1.07	9.06	3.94	58.6	1.0	16.5	26.2	7.8
6.9	0.77	na	0.00	5.5	3.0	1.13	8.75	4.09	63.9	1.1	9.6	19.1	7.1
5.8	0.87	3.7	0.01	7.3	6.6	1.58	13.77	4.57	65.1	2.1	15.0	18.5	9.2
8.7	0.41	na	0.18	6.3	3.0	1.38	8.24	3.51	54.1	4.1	31.6	11.8	8.5
9.8	0.00	na	0.00	2.7	0.1	0.48	2.39	2.91	79.1	4.2	89.5	23.5	6.5
5.6	2.01	na	-0.54	4.2	4.8	1.01	10.37	2.45	81.2	1.1	27.2	40.2	6.7
8.8	0.00	na	0.00	8.4	1.3	1.87	14.83	3.65	46.9	2.4	32.7	21.2	9.0

Name	City	State	Rating	2018 Rating	2017 Rating	Total Assets ($Mil)	One Year Asset Growth	Asset Mix (As a % of Total Assets) Commercial Loans	Consumer Loans	Mortgage Loans	Securities	Capitalization Index	Leverage Ratio	Risk-Based Capital Ratio
Liberty Trust & Savings Bank	Durant	IA	A	A	A	147.4	-0.06	6.1	2.1	10.0	34.5	10.0	20.4	34.4
Libertyville Bank & Trust Co., N.A.	Libertyville	IL	B	B	B	1684.6	8.73	32.2	11.2	4.6	13.5	5.6	9.8	11.5
Libertyville Savings Bank	Fairfield	IA	B-	C+	B	367.0	7.52	7.1	1.4	11.1	23.7	9.6	10.8	15.9
Lifestore Bank	West Jefferson	NC	B	B	C+	305.0	7.94	4.2	0.8	30.3	21.3	10.0	11.1	18.1
▲ Limestone Bank, Inc.	Louisville	KY	C	C-	D	1126.0	7.63	12.1	4.7	12.6	18.1	9.9	11.3	14.9
Lincoln 1st Bank	Lincoln Park	NJ	D	D	D	306.8	-10.18	3.1	0.1	42.7	31.1	4.9	6.9	13.2
▲ Lincoln FSB of Nebraska	Lincoln	NE	C+	C-	C-	310.7	-3.11	0.0	0.0	58.1	15.1	10.0	13.3	24.7
▲ Lincoln National Bank	Hodgenville	KY	A-	B+	A-	313.5	10.02	3.8	5.5	40.6	10.0	10.0	12.8	20.7
Lincoln Savings Bank	Reinbeck	IA	B-	B	C+	1342.9	10.26	13.5	0.9	11.2	9.7	6.8	10.1	12.4
▲ Lincoln State Bank	Hankinson	ND	B	C+	C	75.8	0.71	6.7	6.2	3.7	38.8	9.3	10.5	17.0
▼ LincolnWay Community Bank	New Lenox	IL	C	C+	B-	225.2	10.31	9.6	0.0	13.9	2.5	10.0	11.6	15.0
▲ Lindell Bank & Trust Co.	Saint Louis	MO	A	A-	A	515.2	-3.13	7.3	0.5	16.3	39.5	10.0	18.8	38.2
LINKBANK	Camp Hill	PA	E	E-	E-	195.1	283.16	10.7	0.2	16.6	0.0	10.0	20.5	29.3
▲ Lisle Savings Bank	Lisle	IL	A-	B	B	505.7	-1.75	0.5	0.0	41.8	39.6	10.0	24.3	57.9
Litchfield Bancorp	Litchfield	CT	C+	C	C	253.2	0.38	7.0	1.8	40.2	13.2	6.5	8.5	13.8
Litchfield National Bank	Litchfield	IL	C+	C+	C+	107.3	4.70	2.1	5.5	17.0	25.2	7.1	9.1	15.0
Little Horn State Bank	Hardin	MT	B-	B-	C+	109.0	16.42	7.2	2.3	10.6	4.0	5.3	9.7	11.2
Live Oak Banking Co.	Wilmington	NC	A-	A-	A-	4578.8	34.81	24.9	0.0	0.7	12.5	8.5	10.0	15.1
▲ Llano National Bank	Llano	TX	B+	B	B	185.8	3.02	2.9	3.9	20.6	29.6	10.0	13.0	22.8
LNB Community Bank	Lynnville	IN	C+	C+	C+	116.6	4.70	6.0	3.8	48.0	9.1	9.0	10.4	18.3
Logan Bank & Trust Co.	Logan	WV	B-	B-	C+	268.3	5.00	8.7	3.9	20.9	43.5	7.9	9.6	21.4
Logan County Bank	Scranton	AR	B+	B+	B	82.0	1.02	3.8	7.6	22.0	55.2	10.0	20.7	49.0
▲ Logan State Bank	Logan	IA	C-	D+	C+	66.5	11.23	4.1	2.9	9.1	1.7	5.1	7.1	11.4
Logansport Savings Bank	Logansport	IN	A-	A-	A-	186.1	7.11	10.9	1.0	17.5	23.9	10.0	12.1	18.6
▲ Lone Star Bank	Houston	TX	B-	B-	B-	135.2	7.05	5.1	0.2	19.4	0.0	10.0	11.4	15.4
Lone Star Capital Bank, N.A.	San Antonio	TX	B-	B-	C	256.2	6.62	11.8	1.2	19.8	14.1	10.0	11.2	15.2
Lone Star National Bank	McAllen	TX	B+	B+	B-	2172.2	6.03	3.9	1.1	9.6	31.7	10.0	12.6	20.5
▲ Lone Star State Bank of West Texas	Lubbock	TX	C+	C	C	968.2	6.18	20.6	0.5	4.4	10.6	9.4	11.7	14.5
Longview Bank	Ogden	IL	C+	C+	B-	207.4	9.63	9.4	1.3	12.8	9.6	7.7	9.4	13.8
▲ Longview Bank & Trust	Chrisman	IL	C	C-	C+	186.6	15.70	6.2	0.8	6.7	2.4	6.4	8.4	12.2
Loomis Federal S&L Assn.	Chicago	IL	C-	C-	C-	61.5	-9.06	2.0	0.0	35.9	14.4	10.0	28.5	117.4
Lorraine State Bank	Lorraine	KS	C+	C+	C+	22.5	-0.18	4.4	8.4	9.4	12.9	10.0	18.0	22.5
▲ Lovelady State Bank	Lovelady	TX	B-	C	C	44.1	-6.79	10.4	12.0	12.4	20.4	10.0	12.1	20.8
Lowell Five Cent Savings Bank	Tewksbury	MA	B+	B	B+	1181.3	6.23	5.0	0.2	25.3	7.9	10.0	13.3	17.6
Lowry State Bank	Lowry	MN	C	C	D+	54.8	7.96	16.5	5.7	24.5	0.1	5.2	8.4	11.1
Luana Savings Bank	Luana	IA	B+	B+	B+	1496.6	35.40	1.1	1.2	25.5	12.1	5.2	8.1	11.2
▲ Lumbee Guaranty Bank	Pembroke	NC	B	B-	B-	346.2	1.69	2.5	2.2	14.2	30.1	10.0	12.0	19.9
Lusitania Savings Bank	Newark	NJ	B+	B+	B+	328.9	5.06	0.1	0.5	38.0	17.4	10.0	15.4	39.3
Lusk State Bank	Lusk	WY	B+	B+	A-	52.6	-8.12	2.2	3.4	0.5	13.3	10.0	14.1	21.0
Luther Burbank Savings	Santa Rosa	CA	B	B+	B+	7158.6	6.99	0.0	0.0	29.1	9.0	9.0	10.4	19.5
Luzerne Bank	Luzerne	PA	C+	C+	C+	461.2	8.04	9.3	5.1	14.4	6.2	5.2	8.6	11.2
▲ Lyndon State Bank	Lyndon	KS	C	C	C-	74.0	3.78	5.1	3.4	34.4	14.2	9.1	10.4	16.1
Lyon County State Bank	Emporia	KS	B	B	C+	141.7	0.68	3.5	1.9	17.0	46.3	7.0	9.0	22.2
Lyons Federal Bank	Lyons	KS	B	B	B-	117.4	1.51	3.8	2.8	22.6	2.7	10.0	13.2	18.7
Lyons National Bank	Lyons	NY	B	B	B	1152.5	7.92	8.8	2.8	25.3	20.2	6.3	8.3	12.3
Lytle State Bank of Lytle, Texas	Lytle	TX	B+	B+	B+	86.4	0.30	5.9	21.1	4.4	47.1	10.0	17.3	30.6
M C Bank & Trust Co.	Morgan City	LA	C+	B	B+	309.1	1.65	6.4	2.2	11.5	22.1	10.0	23.1	30.5
M.Y. Safra Bank, FSB	New York	NY	C-	D	D	431.9	18.95	0.6	16.6	20.3	34.5	10.0	11.3	22.1
M1 Bank	Macks Creek	MO	B-	B-	C-	283.4	188.66	30.9	0.3	1.9	0.4	6.0	9.3	11.8
Mabrey Bank	Bixby	OK	B-	B-	B-	1168.8	3.32	20.4	1.7	19.1	16.5	5.8	8.4	11.6
Macatawa Bank	Holland	MI	A	A	A-	2143.0	11.75	20.8	0.3	11.1	13.8	10.0	11.9	16.4
Machias Savings Bank	Machias	ME	B	B	B	1502.6	4.89	15.5	1.0	24.4	6.6	10.0	13.2	16.1
Macon Bank and Trust Co.	Lafayette	TN	B	B	B	416.0	10.06	1.6	4.7	11.7	43.2	10.0	12.8	24.0
▲ Macon-Atlanta State Bank	Macon	MO	B	C+	C-	278.1	-1.44	5.0	2.7	7.5	33.4	9.5	10.7	17.2
Madison Bank of Maryland	Forest Hill	MD	C	C-	D+	144.0	-4.15	1.5	0.0	52.0	18.2	10.0	18.3	34.2
▲ Madison County Bank	Madison	NE	A-	B+	A	422.1	5.54	0.6	1.5	14.8	17.1	10.0	17.1	20.4
Madison County Community Bank	Madison	FL	B-	C+	C+	126.8	0.37	5.0	1.6	8.9	31.3	7.5	9.3	17.7
▲ Madison Valley Bank	Ennis	MT	B	B-	B	183.4	8.58	4.5	4.5	18.5	29.0	7.1	9.1	15.3
▲ Magnolia Bank	Magnolia	KY	A-	B+	A-	321.0	36.08	3.9	0.8	37.0	7.4	9.6	10.8	17.8
Magnolia State Bank	Bay Springs	MS	B-	B-	B-	336.4	0.06	6.5	4.5	25.3	8.5	8.4	10.0	14.3

Asset Quality Index	Adjusted Non-Performing Loans as a % of Total Loans	Adjusted Non-Performing Loans as a % of Capital	Net Charge-Offs Avg Loans	Profitability Index	Net Income ($Mil)	Return on Assets (R.O.A.)	Return on Equity (R.O.E.)	Net Interest Spread	Overhead Efficiency Ratio	Liquidity Index	Liquidity Ratio	Hot Money Ratio	Stability Index
8.7	0.00	na	0.01	**8.5**	2.5	2.23	10.70	3.58	43.3	**5.5**	52.6	4.4	**8.8**
6.1	0.46	4.1	0.06	**7.2**	17.4	1.46	14.66	3.38	42.8	**1.6**	11.2	14.4	**8.2**
4.7	1.86	na	0.02	**5.1**	3.1	1.18	9.64	3.90	69.7	**5.4**	39.8	6.9	**7.2**
7.6	0.61	3.2	0.07	**4.9**	2.4	1.09	9.88	3.63	69.4	**2.3**	33.0	23.1	**6.5**
8.2	0.32	na	0.00	**5.1**	8.9	1.09	9.75	3.60	66.0	**1.3**	18.9	29.8	**7.4**
7.1	0.69	na	0.00	**0.3**	-0.9	-0.37	-5.57	1.88	132.2	**0.5**	3.9	34.8	**2.0**
7.0	0.82	na	0.00	**3.2**	1.6	0.67	5.01	2.54	77.4	**1.3**	18.8	28.5	**7.3**
8.1	0.40	na	0.04	**6.5**	3.1	1.35	10.20	4.38	62.5	**2.2**	17.1	18.2	**8.1**
3.9	2.30	12.3	0.27	**5.3**	9.6	1.01	8.84	3.74	69.8	**0.7**	12.8	28.9	**9.2**
5.7	0.63	na	0.00	**6.1**	0.9	1.49	15.12	3.84	62.3	**3.5**	12.9	11.2	**5.3**
1.4	3.49	na	0.00	**6.8**	1.8	1.12	9.48	4.67	67.2	**2.0**	20.9	19.3	**7.4**
8.4	0.59	na	-0.52	**8.3**	7.7	1.95	10.20	4.09	56.5	**5.0**	35.2	7.6	**10.0**
9.0	0.17	0.5	-0.06	**0.0**	-4.2	-4.80	-16.93	3.53	213.5	**2.4**	48.0	39.6	**4.9**
7.2	4.85	na	-0.08	**5.8**	5.9	1.52	6.43	2.57	51.2	**3.5**	57.4	25.8	**8.7**
5.9	0.57	na	-0.02	**2.5**	0.6	0.30	3.70	3.37	88.1	**2.0**	14.1	15.9	**5.0**
3.8	1.09	na	0.11	**4.3**	0.7	0.85	9.61	3.66	72.7	**2.8**	38.5	21.3	**5.5**
5.0	0.60	na	0.01	**5.7**	0.7	0.99	10.05	5.09	70.7	**2.2**	14.2	17.8	**6.2**
5.8	3.10	6.0	0.13	**5.3**	16.7	0.54	4.92	3.99	76.0	**0.8**	20.1	40.4	**9.7**
6.8	0.99	na	-0.10	**7.2**	2.1	1.55	12.33	4.57	61.4	**4.3**	43.4	14.3	**8.3**
7.0	0.38	na	0.01	**4.0**	0.8	0.88	8.51	3.64	79.6	**4.9**	20.3	3.3	**6.4**
9.1	0.17	na	0.09	**4.5**	1.9	0.94	10.19	3.12	63.2	**4.1**	42.4	14.9	**5.7**
8.8	0.50	na	0.03	**4.5**	0.6	0.95	4.81	2.93	59.3	**3.1**	49.5	22.7	**7.4**
7.1	0.00	na	0.11	**4.6**	0.5	1.03	14.56	3.94	68.6	**1.1**	9.8	11.3	**4.3**
8.3	1.11	na	-0.02	**6.2**	1.7	1.23	9.71	3.60	63.8	**4.2**	29.9	10.4	**8.4**
7.0	0.44	na	0.13	**4.6**	1.0	0.96	7.84	4.00	68.7	**0.7**	14.2	46.0	**7.6**
7.7	0.00	na	0.00	**3.3**	0.9	0.49	3.50	4.04	85.5	**2.0**	20.7	16.9	**7.4**
5.4	2.42	8.5	-0.03	**5.1**	18.7	1.14	9.20	3.61	71.5	**1.8**	19.3	22.7	**9.8**
4.4	1.00	na	0.41	**7.5**	12.4	1.81	14.34	3.96	48.5	**1.4**	23.8	28.0	**8.2**
2.5	2.61	na	0.02	**6.4**	1.8	1.20	12.69	3.73	55.1	**1.4**	14.3	26.1	**5.5**
5.1	0.54	na	-0.10	**6.7**	1.8	1.31	14.79	3.71	54.2	**2.3**	26.3	19.2	**4.7**
6.9	7.37	na	0.82	**0.0**	-0.3	-0.63	-2.26	2.97	123.6	**6.8**	83.1	6.8	**6.3**
6.8	0.00	na	-0.10	**6.4**	0.2	1.08	6.21	3.72	52.7	**2.9**	20.7	14.9	**5.0**
6.4	0.71	na	0.20	**6.7**	0.5	1.58	13.94	5.07	67.3	**4.2**	42.4	14.5	**5.0**
8.6	0.93	na	0.01	**5.4**	8.9	1.02	8.13	3.81	70.9	**3.3**	19.2	13.5	**8.8**
4.5	0.55	na	0.16	**9.3**	0.8	2.13	22.12	4.85	52.7	**1.6**	8.7	18.2	**6.0**
8.5	0.09	0.5	0.00	**7.9**	17.2	1.72	19.74	2.66	32.3	**0.5**	11.7	11.6	**8.8**
5.0	4.30	na	-0.01	**4.4**	2.3	0.90	7.67	4.15	76.2	**3.5**	21.1	12.3	**6.7**
9.3	0.88	na	0.00	**4.4**	2.0	0.82	5.37	2.65	56.3	**3.8**	56.4	20.2	**7.9**
6.8	0.00	na	0.00	**8.0**	0.7	1.80	13.16	4.34	60.5	**4.9**	28.9	5.8	**8.7**
7.6	0.25	1.8	-0.01	**4.4**	41.2	0.78	7.51	1.97	44.0	**0.6**	12.8	49.2	**8.4**
4.0	0.81	4.9	0.01	**4.9**	3.3	0.99	8.56	3.60	65.4	**2.7**	14.6	14.9	**7.1**
6.9	0.49	na	0.01	**3.1**	0.3	0.46	4.17	4.43	89.1	**3.2**	16.6	12.9	**5.6**
9.5	0.01	na	0.01	**4.8**	1.3	1.24	13.93	3.55	71.0	**6.6**	50.8	3.2	**6.4**
8.2	0.31	na	0.00	**3.9**	0.8	0.83	6.30	3.45	72.1	**2.1**	16.5	18.8	**7.5**
7.6	0.66	na	0.09	**5.0**	8.1	0.97	12.12	3.59	68.3	**2.5**	15.7	16.5	**7.3**
6.9	1.70	na	0.41	**5.0**	0.8	1.13	6.86	3.98	67.6	**4.7**	47.7	12.7	**7.1**
4.0	5.61	na	0.18	**5.2**	2.4	1.05	4.62	4.25	64.2	**2.1**	30.2	22.5	**7.9**
8.1	0.03	na	0.43	**1.4**	0.7	0.20	1.78	2.24	82.1	**1.2**	29.5	36.9	**6.4**
8.5	0.00	na	0.00	**4.9**	1.9	1.07	11.27	3.45	53.3	**1.6**	35.9	34.5	**4.7**
7.9	0.43	3.4	0.02	**4.6**	7.9	0.91	11.14	3.88	71.5	**1.2**	9.5	19.4	**7.2**
8.1	0.97	na	-0.07	**8.4**	25.6	1.71	14.51	3.58	51.6	**6.1**	34.9	4.2	**9.6**
4.9	2.52	9.8	0.11	**5.5**	12.6	1.15	8.95	4.35	70.1	**2.6**	12.3	10.0	**9.4**
8.4	0.28	na	0.03	**3.6**	2.0	0.67	5.32	3.12	78.7	**2.4**	46.3	34.5	**6.9**
5.6	0.43	3.5	-0.04	**4.9**	2.6	1.27	11.85	3.39	65.4	**2.5**	19.2	16.8	**5.9**
8.5	2.69	na	-0.38	**2.0**	0.2	0.22	1.20	2.62	98.9	**1.2**	28.5	35.2	**7.2**
6.9	0.67	na	0.00	**6.8**	4.4	1.41	8.10	3.27	53.5	**4.8**	17.0	3.9	**9.0**
4.6	2.44	11.3	0.02	**4.6**	0.9	0.98	11.08	3.82	63.9	**3.9**	38.9	15.3	**4.5**
6.3	0.48	na	-0.09	**5.4**	1.6	1.29	14.75	4.13	68.8	**5.5**	41.2	7.2	**5.8**
8.4	0.10	0.8	-0.02	**8.4**	8.0	3.89	39.19	3.09	83.1	**0.5**	10.1	41.7	**7.4**
6.9	0.27	na	0.05	**4.4**	2.8	1.08	11.15	4.00	73.0	**1.8**	16.1	21.0	**6.1**

Name	City	State	Rating	2018 Rating	2017 Rating	Total Assets ($Mil)	One Year Asset Growth	Commercial Loans	Consumer Loans	Mortgage Loans	Securities	Capitalization Index	Leverage Ratio	Risk-Based Capital Ratio
								Asset Mix (As a % of Total Assets)						
Magyar Bank	New Brunswick	NJ	**C**	C	C-	630.3	1.02	7.7	0.8	29.9	7.3	**7.1**	9.0	13.0
Mahopac Bank	Brewster	NY	**B**	B	B	1341.8	-3.57	11.2	2.0	18.1	20.6	**6.8**	8.8	12.8
▲ Main Bank	Albuquerque	NM	**B+**	B	A-	166.3	18.40	6.4	0.1	6.7	4.3	**7.1**	9.1	13.9
Main Street Bank	Marlborough	MA	**C**	C	C	1032.8	0.38	3.9	1.3	32.3	7.8	**9.8**	11.5	14.8
Main Street Bank	Bingham Farms	MI	**C+**	B-	B	291.5	12.99	13.0	0.4	36.2	1.7	**5.5**	8.7	11.3
Main Street Bank Corp.	Wheeling	WV	**C**	C	C-	455.6	1.14	12.1	3.7	40.9	7.6	**8.0**	9.7	14.7
Mainstreet Bank	Cook	NE	**B-**	B-	B-	94.5	-3.19	3.5	2.5	12.5	25.0	**9.4**	10.6	16.0
▲ MainStreet Bank	Fairfax	VA	**B+**	C+	C+	1233.6	16.76	9.4	6.7	10.4	9.1	**8.4**	12.1	13.7
Mainstreet Community Bank of Florida	Deland	FL	**C+**	C+	B-	464.8	17.53	9.5	0.8	9.2	8.6	**4.9**	8.4	10.9
Malaga Bank F.S.B.	Palos Verdes Estates	CA	**A-**	B+	A	1231.3	15.23	0.1	0.0	8.8	0.0	**10.0**	13.0	22.9
▲ Malvern Bank	Malvern	IA	**C**	C-	C	141.9	-0.53	24.1	16.2	16.0	0.6	**7.7**	9.5	13.0
Malvern Bank, N.A.	Paoli	PA	**B**	B	B	1264.1	22.23	8.2	0.2	20.7	3.3	**10.0**	12.2	16.4
Malvern National Bank	Malvern	AR	**C**	C	C-	564.3	6.01	5.5	0.8	7.5	35.6	**8.5**	10.0	14.3
Manasquan Bank	Manasquan	NJ	**B**	B	B	1728.2	32.01	8.5	0.1	34.4	4.0	**7.6**	9.7	13.0
Manhattan Bank	Manhattan	MT	**B+**	B+	B-	184.3	7.49	4.4	2.5	15.5	30.5	**7.4**	9.2	15.4
Mansfield Co-operative Bank	Mansfield	MA	**C+**	C+	C+	527.2	1.49	3.2	0.0	34.0	9.0	**9.4**	10.6	15.9
Manson State Bank	Manson	IA	**B-**	B-	B-	33.7	-1.06	9.7	1.3	7.2	35.8	**10.0**	12.5	20.3
Manufacturers and Traders Trust Co.	Buffalo	NY	**C+**	C+	C+	125040.6	7.45	14.8	8.5	13.2	8.0	**6.7**	9.2	12.3
Manufacturers Bank	Los Angeles	CA	**B**	B	C+	4492.0	73.55	19.7	0.0	0.6	14.7	**6.2**	8.2	14.1
Manufacturers Bank & Trust Co.	Forest City	IA	**A-**	A-	A-	356.3	5.13	13.3	2.3	12.4	19.5	**10.0**	13.3	15.4
▼ Maple Bank	Champlin	MN	**D+**	C	D+	58.5	10.10	19.8	0.5	8.3	1.7	**8.6**	10.8	13.9
Maple City Savings Bank, FSB	Hornell	NY	**C-**	C-	C	84.2	10.67	4.4	1.0	65.6	1.2	**6.7**	8.7	14.7
MapleMark Bank	Dallas	TX	**D**	D	D	511.5	99.16	41.1	0.4	7.0	12.0	**10.0**	14.1	17.0
Maquoketa State Bank	Maquoketa	IA	**A-**	A-	A-	341.8	3.69	8.5	2.9	5.8	30.7	**10.0**	17.6	22.1
Marathon Bank	Wausau	WI	**B-**	B-	B-	148.9	-2.07	3.5	0.3	32.6	15.1	**10.0**	13.1	17.1
▲ Marblehead Bank	Marblehead	MA	**C**	C-	D+	214.9	3.37	2.0	0.3	47.7	5.4	**7.7**	9.5	14.4
Marblehead Bank	Marblehead	OH	**C**	C	C	50.2	3.44	1.4	7.1	25.5	52.8	**9.6**	10.7	28.3
Maries County Bank	Vienna	MO	**B+**	B+	B	463.2	-1.39	3.3	8.2	15.2	31.7	**10.0**	15.7	23.4
▲ Marine Bank	Springfield	IL	**C**	C-	C+	630.7	-0.77	7.4	0.4	7.5	11.2	**8.7**	11.3	13.9
Marine Bank & Trust Co.	Vero Beach	FL	**B-**	C+	C+	277.8	3.53	6.2	0.4	40.5	8.7	**7.1**	9.1	14.2
▲ Mariner's Bank	Edgewater	NJ	**C**	C-	C	391.9	-0.04	9.0	2.8	15.4	1.3	**7.0**	9.2	12.5
Marion Bank and Trust Co.	Marion	AL	**B**	B	B	287.9	6.41	6.7	2.6	10.3	27.7	**10.0**	11.6	17.4
Marion Center Bank	Indiana	PA	**C**	C	C	320.1	4.78	11.0	2.8	27.6	16.5	**5.6**	7.6	12.1
Marion County State Bank	Pella	IA	**B+**	B+	A	314.6	3.12	15.6	1.1	15.8	21.0	**5.2**	8.1	11.2
▲ Marion National Bank	Marion	KS	**C+**	C	C	22.5	5.56	5.2	0.8	7.1	35.7	**10.0**	13.2	28.1
Marion State Bank	Marion	LA	**B**	B	B-	180.6	12.21	9.9	3.6	19.8	11.5	**10.0**	11.3	15.6
▲ Marion State Bank	Marion	TX	**A-**	B+	A-	111.6	7.00	9.8	8.4	0.1	38.9	**10.0**	14.0	23.6
Marlin Business Bank	Salt Lake City	UT	**A-**	A-	A	1078.8	21.68	50.6	0.0	0.0	0.6	**10.0**	13.8	16.9
Marquette Bank	Orland Park	IL	**C+**	B-	C+	1598.8	4.07	1.1	0.0	15.2	12.3	**7.1**	9.1	14.0
Marquette Farmers State Bank	Marquette	KS	**C**	C	B-	28.8	-6.61	6.2	5.1	12.6	20.4	**10.0**	16.3	27.1
Marquette Savings Bank	Erie	PA	**B+**	B+	B+	915.8	6.04	4.6	0.2	42.3	31.0	**10.0**	18.0	33.6
Marquis Bank	Coral Gables	FL	**B**	B-	B	676.8	5.16	10.8	0.7	4.5	4.1	**6.6**	9.7	12.2
Mars Bank	Mars	PA	**C**	C	C-	403.4	2.40	2.6	0.1	35.7	26.5	**7.4**	9.3	15.9
Marseilles Bank	Marseilles	IL	**B-**	B	B	63.6	10.43	0.6	10.6	28.3	44.8	**8.5**	10.0	20.3
Marshall County State Bank	Newfolden	MN	**B**	B	B	31.8	-2.40	2.0	3.7	9.1	56.4	**10.0**	18.2	100.5
Martha's Vineyard Savings Bank	Edgartown	MA	**B+**	B+	B+	832.1	2.93	1.8	0.3	45.4	7.3	**10.0**	12.9	20.4
Martinsville First Savings Bank	Martinsville	VA	**C+**	C+	C+	39.0	-2.34	0.0	0.4	50.3	19.6	**10.0**	17.5	43.1
Mascoma Bank	Lebanon	NH	**C+**	C+	C+	1884.0	8.46	6.4	0.4	41.4	9.6	**7.4**	9.3	13.3
▲ Mason Bank	Mason	TX	**A**	A-	A-	119.4	-2.41	6.0	5.1	9.4	60.2	**10.0**	18.2	43.4
▲ Mason City National Bank	Mason City	IL	**B+**	B	B	71.5	1.20	0.8	1.2	10.3	50.7	**10.0**	17.9	39.6
Maspeth Federal S&L Assn.	Maspeth	NY	**A-**	A-	A-	1967.0	5.92	0.0	0.0	48.2	1.6	**10.0**	33.0	43.7
Massena S&L	Massena	NY	**B**	B	B	165.5	4.14	1.6	8.0	75.1	0.0	**10.0**	13.3	21.1
MassMutual Trust Co., FSB	Enfield	CT	**U**	U	U	90.1	4.38	0.0	0.0	0.0	81.8	**10.0**	38.1	45.1
Mauch Chunk Trust Co.	Jim Thorpe	PA	**C+**	C+	C+	459.8	2.97	4.7	5.2	21.1	43.5	**6.9**	8.9	15.2
▲ Maxwell State Bank	Maxwell	IA	**B+**	B+	A	28.5	2.24	1.9	0.4	4.5	37.5	**10.0**	19.0	46.1
▲ Maynard Savings Bank	Maynard	IA	**A-**	B+	B	60.4	2.11	5.9	5.5	23.3	13.3	**10.0**	15.7	24.5
Mayville Savings Bank	Mayville	WI	**B-**	B-	C+	66.5	11.39	5.9	1.4	52.6	5.6	**9.8**	10.9	20.1
Mayville State Bank	Mayville	MI	**B-**	C+	C+	84.9	-3.04	1.0	4.3	31.7	26.7	**10.0**	11.3	24.4
mBank	Manistique	MI	**B**	B-	B-	1352.0	8.05	15.4	1.5	17.6	7.9	**7.4**	9.7	12.8
MCBank	Goldthwaite	TX	**C**	C+	B-	316.2	-0.24	5.4	2.9	13.6	44.9	**7.8**	9.5	19.4

Asset Quality Index	Adjusted Non-Performing Loans as a % of Total Loans	Adjusted Non-Performing Loans as a % of Capital	Net Charge-Offs Avg Loans	Profitability Index	Net Income ($Mil)	Return on Assets (R.O.A.)	Return on Equity (R.O.E.)	Net Interest Spread	Overhead Efficiency Ratio	Liquidity Index	Liquidity Ratio	Hot Money Ratio	Stability Index
4.5	2.32	na	-0.01	**3.3**	2.4	0.51	5.99	3.54	77.2	**2.8**	11.5	13.4	**4.9**
6.1	0.87	4.6	0.03	**5.7**	11.6	1.14	11.49	3.50	60.1	**4.1**	4.2	6.2	**7.9**
7.7	0.00	na	0.00	**9.0**	2.4	2.06	22.22	4.09	46.6	**2.3**	31.4	22.5	**7.3**
6.3	1.17	5.7	0.02	**3.3**	4.4	0.57	4.82	3.45	80.0	**1.7**	15.4	17.2	**8.3**
7.1	0.49	na	0.11	**3.6**	1.3	0.62	7.13	3.68	88.5	**0.5**	3.9	36.7	**4.7**
3.3	2.25	na	0.20	**5.8**	3.7	1.08	11.32	3.95	58.5	**1.2**	13.2	20.0	**6.3**
8.7	0.04	na	0.04	**3.4**	0.4	0.61	5.71	4.09	83.9	**1.9**	22.4	20.8	**6.4**
6.9	0.01	0.1	0.10	**6.0**	11.0	1.28	10.60	3.63	55.3	**0.6**	16.8	52.4	**8.8**
5.6	0.46	na	-0.03	**5.7**	4.9	1.50	18.17	4.48	64.2	**4.1**	20.1	6.7	**5.6**
7.3	0.05	na	0.00	**7.9**	11.5	1.36	10.25	2.97	34.3	**0.9**	7.4	32.5	**10.0**
3.4	0.67	na	0.24	**4.2**	1.0	0.87	9.23	3.74	70.7	**0.7**	13.9	31.2	**5.2**
6.5	1.37	na	0.01	**4.5**	8.5	0.95	7.68	2.65	52.1	**1.4**	16.6	20.8	**8.9**
7.3	0.47	na	0.03	**2.9**	2.4	0.60	6.04	3.25	81.7	**1.2**	17.4	23.7	**6.3**
7.5	0.43	3.2	0.04	**4.1**	8.5	0.73	7.69	3.48	69.4	**1.7**	12.8	21.2	**7.9**
7.9	0.02	2.5	0.00	**5.3**	1.7	1.26	14.02	4.05	68.2	**5.4**	35.7	5.6	**6.7**
7.7	0.28	na	0.06	**3.5**	2.3	0.59	5.70	3.18	78.4	**1.9**	20.7	20.3	**7.0**
5.7	3.57	na	0.06	**4.8**	0.3	1.14	8.93	3.61	62.2	**5.8**	50.9	6.9	**6.7**
3.5	1.35	7.7	0.15	**9.1**	1467.0	1.66	12.96	3.92	53.0	**4.7**	20.6	3.0	**10.0**
8.7	0.34	1.0	0.05	**4.1**	23.8	0.72	8.63	2.18	52.8	**4.2**	52.8	11.5	**8.2**
8.2	0.32	na	0.04	**7.3**	4.6	1.74	13.28	3.79	60.4	**2.0**	20.7	17.5	**8.9**
3.2	2.66	11.1	-0.01	**1.3**	0.0	-0.06	-0.47	4.14	93.9	**1.4**	19.1	6.0	**6.0**
2.7	2.19	na	-0.14	**3.2**	0.5	0.85	8.72	3.90	75.4	**1.5**	5.2	16.6	**3.8**
8.1	0.00	na	0.00	**0.0**	-2.9	-0.93	-5.22	2.87	128.2	**0.9**	17.6	34.3	**5.2**
8.0	0.91	na	-0.02	**6.3**	3.4	1.35	7.74	3.47	59.0	**4.9**	37.7	9.3	**9.2**
6.0	3.05	na	-0.05	**3.0**	1.2	1.05	8.20	3.26	91.3	**1.7**	21.7	19.0	**6.3**
7.9	0.53	na	0.01	**2.7**	0.6	0.35	3.85	3.81	88.4	**4.3**	10.8	6.2	**5.1**
8.9	0.36	1.3	0.00	**2.9**	0.2	0.54	5.41	3.10	84.5	**5.6**	51.9	9.0	**5.4**
7.4	1.14	na	0.14	**5.3**	3.7	1.06	6.75	4.00	68.0	**3.1**	19.4	13.7	**8.0**
3.3	1.66	na	0.51	**4.8**	5.6	1.14	10.32	3.49	69.8	**2.2**	15.0	11.2	**8.0**
8.7	0.40	na	-0.01	**4.0**	1.3	0.63	7.20	3.92	77.4	**3.7**	12.9	10.1	**5.1**
4.1	1.12	na	0.12	**3.5**	2.4	0.80	8.99	3.34	73.1	**1.5**	12.7	23.6	**5.3**
4.9	3.98	11.0	0.08	**5.5**	2.9	1.37	11.72	3.55	60.3	**1.0**	24.0	34.3	**6.6**
3.9	1.58	na	0.17	**3.9**	1.7	0.73	9.70	3.52	74.2	**1.8**	19.9	21.0	**4.0**
4.4	0.62	na	0.00	**8.8**	4.6	1.96	19.93	3.66	47.8	**4.2**	22.4	8.5	**8.3**
7.8	0.00	na	-0.03	**3.6**	0.1	0.77	4.61	3.20	71.7	**4.4**	53.4	13.5	**6.5**
6.4	0.83	4.5	0.14	**3.8**	0.9	0.67	5.96	4.40	78.7	**2.2**	20.0	18.5	**6.1**
6.7	0.66	na	0.74	**6.3**	1.2	1.41	10.41	3.56	59.0	**2.1**	32.5	26.7	**8.9**
7.3	0.75	na	1.78	**8.1**	11.8	1.49	10.83	8.24	61.8	**0.4**	14.5	49.3	**9.3**
3.1	1.98	11.1	0.07	**4.2**	8.7	0.74	6.69	3.63	74.1	**3.8**	11.9	9.7	**8.4**
2.1	7.52	na	0.02	**2.4**	0.1	0.56	3.51	3.41	86.7	**2.7**	49.7	29.3	**4.9**
8.9	0.84	na	0.03	**4.0**	5.1	0.76	4.20	3.19	71.3	**3.2**	37.5	18.3	**8.7**
7.4	0.02	0.2	-0.02	**6.4**	6.1	1.23	12.92	3.58	53.9	**0.8**	17.7	39.3	**6.3**
9.5	0.02	na	0.00	**2.9**	1.4	0.47	5.09	2.95	83.9	**4.1**	18.6	8.6	**5.4**
6.7	0.59	na	0.09	**4.3**	0.5	1.01	10.35	2.67	62.7	**2.6**	42.8	26.8	**5.7**
9.3	0.07	na	0.00	**4.3**	0.3	1.01	5.62	2.60	61.6	**7.2**	76.3	3.2	**7.7**
8.0	0.79	4.5	0.01	**5.4**	6.5	1.03	8.42	3.53	63.5	**4.1**	13.4	3.4	**8.1**
4.0	6.99	na	0.31	**3.5**	0.2	0.66	3.88	3.05	75.6	**2.7**	52.5	30.1	**7.4**
8.6	0.40	2.0	0.02	**3.7**	9.7	0.71	7.52	3.48	77.0	**2.6**	11.4	14.2	**7.7**
8.9	0.43	na	0.03	**6.6**	1.4	1.59	8.93	3.51	56.5	**4.9**	72.4	17.2	**9.2**
9.2	0.42	na	0.01	**5.5**	0.8	1.49	8.39	3.10	52.8	**5.4**	63.3	11.8	**8.1**
6.4	2.24	5.9	0.00	**7.2**	18.2	1.27	3.85	3.65	53.4	**1.8**	10.9	20.0	**10.0**
5.0	3.28	na	0.15	**3.8**	0.9	0.76	5.78	3.42	68.1	**0.8**	3.6	31.6	**6.9**
10.0	na	na	na	**9.5**	2.6	4.19	12.65	1.68	86.0	**3.9**	136.3	100.0	**7.0**
7.6	1.50	na	0.28	**3.2**	2.1	0.61	6.94	2.85	76.0	**4.2**	20.7	8.4	**5.2**
9.5	0.00	na	0.00	**5.7**	0.3	1.32	6.90	3.11	48.4	**5.8**	90.5	13.1	**8.2**
8.1	0.00	2.4	0.36	**6.4**	0.6	1.39	8.94	3.63	58.9	**3.5**	32.1	14.8	**7.6**
5.2	1.51	7.9	-0.03	**3.8**	0.4	0.72	6.61	3.35	68.5	**2.9**	23.3	15.5	**5.3**
9.2	1.40	na	0.01	**3.6**	0.4	0.64	5.83	3.40	80.2	**6.2**	51.5	4.4	**6.0**
5.6	1.06	5.0	0.03	**5.8**	11.3	1.14	9.92	4.56	67.2	**2.6**	14.2	9.0	**8.1**
3.2	3.70	na	0.37	**4.8**	2.7	1.14	11.13	3.99	69.3	**5.2**	43.9	9.8	**6.7**

Name	City	State	Rating	2018 Rating	2017 Rating	Total Assets ($Mil)	One Year Asset Growth	Asset Mix (As a % of Total Assets) Commercial Loans	Consumer Loans	Mortgage Loans	Securities	Capitalization Index	Leverage Ratio	Risk-Based Capital Ratio
McClain Bank	Purcell	OK	**A-**	A-	A-	224.2	3.80	8.1	1.9	21.8	5.5	**10.0**	12.2	18.6
▲ McClave State Bank	McClave	CO	**B**	B-	B-	43.9	8.54	11.0	1.7	3.6	10.8	**10.0**	13.4	15.6
▲ McCurtain County National Bank	Broken Bow	OK	**A-**	B+	A-	256.6	0.65	2.7	6.4	30.6	15.0	**10.0**	13.6	28.0
▲ McFarland State Bank	McFarland	WI	**B+**	B+	A-	502.4	0.96	6.0	0.1	16.5	8.4	**9.9**	11.5	14.9
McGehee Bank	McGehee	AR	**A-**	A-	A-	137.2	-2.57	13.1	1.1	2.4	16.1	**10.0**	14.4	16.6
McHenry Savings Bank	McHenry	IL	**E**	E	E-	230.3	15.00	4.1	20.9	27.8	24.0	**7.2**	9.1	13.7
▲ McIntosh County Bank	Ashley	ND	**C**	C-	C	86.6	-1.10	4.2	2.4	0.2	22.3	**10.0**	12.9	17.4
McKenzie Banking Co.	McKenzie	TN	**B-**	B+	A-	129.6	0.68	10.4	6.6	21.5	10.0	**10.0**	15.3	28.2
▲ MCNB Bank and Trust Co.	Welch	WV	**C+**	C-	C-	297.8	1.09	6.3	1.0	16.0	14.7	**10.0**	11.4	16.3
MCS Bank	Lewistown	PA	**C+**	C+	C+	147.1	3.23	9.5	8.2	36.9	6.4	**10.0**	13.5	19.0
Meade County Bank	Brandenburg	KY	**B+**	B+	B+	212.8	7.31	1.6	3.3	37.9	17.0	**7.7**	9.5	13.2
▲ Meadows Bank	Las Vegas	NV	**B**	B-	B+	950.6	10.82	15.9	0.0	4.5	1.8	**8.4**	11.9	13.7
▲ Mechanics and Farmers Bank	Durham	NC	**C-**	D	D-	267.2	1.97	6.1	0.4	5.7	17.7	**6.2**	8.2	12.3
▼ Mechanics Bank	Walnut Creek	CA	**B-**	B	B-	17299.3	188.11	3.2	11.1	11.1	20.9	**7.9**	14.8	13.3
▲ Mechanics Bank	Water Valley	MS	**B**	B-	C+	233.7	5.30	8.2	2.2	26.8	17.3	**10.0**	11.1	17.0
▲ Mechanics Bank	Mansfield	OH	**B-**	C+	C+	554.8	4.75	2.2	1.3	67.8	9.4	**6.3**	8.3	16.6
▲ Mechanics Cooperative Bank	Taunton	MA	**B+**	B-	B-	612.0	4.59	5.9	0.9	29.0	11.6	**8.9**	10.3	15.1
Mechanics Savings Bank	Auburn	ME	**B**	B	B	423.3	3.76	7.3	1.1	41.1	9.7	**10.0**	13.4	17.9
▲ Medallion Bank	Salt Lake City	UT	**C+**	C-	D	1162.2	3.79	9.7	81.5	0.0	4.1	**10.0**	15.9	17.4
▲ Mediapolis Savings Bank	Mediapolis	IA	**C**	D+	C-	171.9	4.89	7.0	1.9	19.9	8.7	**9.1**	10.6	14.2
Mega Bank	San Gabriel	CA	**B**	B	B	349.9	-7.44	3.0	0.0	22.2	7.7	**10.0**	12.7	19.8
Melrose Bank	Melrose	MA	**C+**	C+	C+	336.9	5.77	0.0	0.0	60.3	5.8	**7.4**	9.2	14.5
Melvin Savings Bank	Melvin	IA	**B**	B	B	70.3	-0.16	4.3	1.6	3.2	44.2	**10.0**	18.3	38.8
MEMBERS Trust Co.	Tampa	FL	**U**	U	U	40.2	8.05	0.0	0.0	0.0	65.0	**10.0**	90.7	567.5
Menard Bank	Menard	TX	**B-**	B-	B-	41.8	17.29	3.6	1.1	7.9	44.6	**10.0**	13.5	26.9
Mer Rouge State Bank	Mer Rouge	LA	**C+**	C+	C+	39.3	0.93	17.2	0.8	4.2	8.1	**10.0**	13.6	17.1
▲ Meramec Valley Bank	Ellisville	MO	**C**	C-	C-	120.9	4.97	12.5	1.1	19.3	11.8	**5.0**	8.4	11.0
▲ Mercantile Bank of Louisiana, Missouri	Louisiana	MO	**A-**	A-	B+	110.1	3.23	1.3	1.6	13.8	17.3	**10.0**	21.2	27.4
Mercantile Bank of Michigan	Grand Rapids	MI	**A-**	A-	B+	3692.6	12.57	21.8	0.7	10.0	9.4	**7.0**	11.0	12.5
Mercer County State Bank	Sandy Lake	PA	**B-**	B-	B	437.4	6.95	6.6	1.0	20.2	32.0	**8.0**	9.7	16.2
Mercer Savings Bank	Celina	OH	**C+**	C+	C-	133.3	1.93	1.0	0.7	58.1	3.5	**8.3**	9.9	15.6
Merchants & Citizens Bank	McRae	GA	**B-**	B-	B-	103.4	2.43	2.6	3.1	14.9	50.0	**10.0**	15.4	35.3
Merchants & Farmers Bank	Eutaw	AL	**C+**	B-	C+	71.7	18.49	13.5	10.4	14.7	17.9	**9.2**	10.5	15.8
Merchants & Farmers Bank	Holly Springs	MS	**B-**	C	B-	102.7	1.91	6.2	4.5	10.2	42.1	**10.0**	11.4	20.4
Merchants & Farmers Bank & Trust Co.	Leesville	LA	**B-**	B-	B-	410.4	0.28	3.9	1.1	26.2	31.5	**10.0**	11.3	19.8
Merchants & Marine Bank	Pascagoula	MS	**B-**	B	B	574.1	4.13	6.3	4.7	14.1	28.9	**10.0**	12.4	20.0
▼ Merchants & Planters Bank	Clarendon	AR	**C**	C+	C+	38.7	-13.46	10.7	1.9	1.9	58.4	**10.0**	13.2	28.7
Merchants & Planters Bank	Newport	AR	**C**	C+	B-	267.0	-0.17	6.9	4.4	10.2	18.3	**9.7**	11.1	14.8
Merchants and Farmers Bank	Dumas	AR	**C+**	B-	B-	160.6	5.36	12.7	2.9	11.2	6.1	**5.5**	8.9	11.4
▲ Merchants and Farmers Bank of Salisbury	Salisbury	MO	**C+**	C	C	94.2	0.42	3.7	2.5	15.5	28.0	**8.0**	9.7	16.1
Merchants and Manufacturers Bank	Joliet	IL	**C+**	C+	C+	283.5	11.60	25.3	35.5	6.4	2.9	**4.4**	8.3	10.7
▲ Merchants and Planters Bank	Raymond	MS	**B**	C	C-	93.8	3.83	6.6	1.4	14.4	22.2	**8.4**	9.9	15.6
▲ Merchants Bank	Rugby	ND	**B**	C+	B	169.6	6.63	8.0	2.6	3.4	25.1	**6.3**	9.1	12.0
▲ Merchants Bank of Alabama	Cullman	AL	**B**	B-	B-	303.5	3.27	6.8	4.0	20.1	24.5	**9.2**	10.5	17.7
▲ Merchants Bank of Bangor	Bangor	PA	**B**	B-	C+	412.8	3.29	3.7	0.8	22.5	34.1	**7.5**	9.4	16.1
Merchants Bank of Commerce	Redding	CA	**B**	B	B	1471.7	11.84	10.1	2.5	7.0	18.5	**10.0**	11.7	15.3
▼ Merchants Bank of Indiana	Carmel	IN	**B+**	A	A	6145.3	63.41	5.1	0.2	1.2	4.6	**5.2**	10.3	11.2
Merchants Bank, N.A.	Winona	MN	**B**	B	B+	1854.3	8.74	20.7	2.3	12.5	7.0	**5.8**	10.1	11.6
Merchants Commercial Bank	Saint Thomas	VI	**C-**	C-	D-	255.7	19.60	4.0	0.4	14.1	51.1	**6.6**	8.6	21.9
Merchants National Bank	Hillsboro	OH	**B-**	B-	B	933.3	31.25	5.9	3.5	32.9	2.9	**5.4**	8.6	11.3
▲ Merchants State Bank	Freeman	SD	**B-**	C+	B-	171.0	2.52	5.9	1.7	2.1	14.8	**10.0**	13.5	17.0
Meredith Village Savings Bank	Meredith	NH	**B**	B	B	1001.5	5.20	4.9	6.7	45.3	6.0	**10.0**	11.2	17.3
Merit Bank	Huntsville	AL	**C**	C+	C+	64.1	135.31	7.1	3.0	9.3	7.7	**10.0**	34.6	77.9
Merrick Bank Corp.	South Jordan	UT	**C**	C	C	3927.7	4.17	0.0	95.3	0.0	2.5	**10.0**	21.8	24.9
Merrimack County Savings Bank	Concord	NH	**B-**	B-	B-	914.4	4.63	10.8	7.3	31.7	8.9	**8.3**	9.8	14.0
MetaBank	Sioux Falls	SD	**B+**	B+	B+	6190.2	6.34	26.7	6.4	3.7	22.7	**7.6**	9.7	13.0
Metairie Bank and Trust Co.	Metairie	LA	**B-**	B-	B-	405.4	1.89	4.0	1.3	35.0	11.1	**8.9**	10.3	15.2
Metamora State Bank	Metamora	OH	**C**	C	C+	82.7	10.79	5.5	1.1	19.4	17.1	**7.1**	9.1	14.5
Methuen Co-operative Bank	Methuen	MA	**C**	C-	D+	93.2	-0.64	0.5	1.4	45.2	15.0	**9.8**	10.8	24.3
▲ Metro Bank	Pell City	AL	**A-**	B+	A-	762.1	4.64	8.8	2.0	10.6	28.1	**10.0**	15.8	24.2

Arrows denote recent upgrades ▲ or downgrades ▼

Asset Quality Index	Adjusted Non-Performing Loans as a % of Total Loans	Adjusted Non-Performing Loans as a % of Capital	Net Charge-Offs Avg Loans	Profitability Index	Net Income ($Mil)	Return on Assets (R.O.A.)	Return on Equity (R.O.E.)	Net Interest Spread	Overhead Efficiency Ratio	Liquidity Index	Liquidity Ratio	Hot Money Ratio	Stability Index
5.6	2.94	na	0.06	**7.9**	2.5	1.47	12.59	4.44	61.4	**4.2**	20.7	8.0	**7.6**
5.7	1.38	na	0.22	**9.8**	0.6	1.72	13.15	5.15	54.3	**0.5**	11.2	46.7	**7.9**
6.9	1.29	na	0.08	**8.6**	3.2	1.69	13.03	3.76	45.8	**3.6**	39.6	16.6	**8.1**
7.4	0.02	na	-0.01	**6.7**	5.7	1.49	13.46	3.76	68.4	**1.3**	9.0	17.6	**9.1**
6.3	1.16	3.0	0.04	**7.5**	1.6	1.76	12.32	4.38	59.3	**2.4**	5.2	15.8	**8.9**
2.7	2.03	na	0.13	**0.8**	0.0	0.02	0.25	3.26	96.8	**1.0**	24.0	31.0	**0.4**
4.2	3.68	na	0.81	**7.6**	1.2	1.85	15.19	4.24	51.8	**3.4**	8.8	11.3	**8.9**
3.9	3.72	na	0.21	**9.8**	2.2	2.25	15.64	6.52	63.0	**5.1**	47.8	11.2	**9.4**
3.9	5.27	na	0.21	**4.0**	1.8	0.82	7.42	3.75	73.3	**3.5**	17.6	12.0	**6.3**
4.7	1.65	na	0.07	**2.8**	0.5	0.47	3.50	3.35	80.3	**1.0**	11.2	24.2	**6.7**
8.2	0.15	1.2	0.01	**5.2**	1.6	1.05	11.21	3.56	65.4	**2.5**	9.5	15.8	**5.9**
6.5	0.81	na	0.00	**10.0**	13.7	2.03	17.32	4.94	48.2	**1.6**	12.2	21.9	**9.2**
3.9	2.55	na	-0.04	**2.4**	0.7	0.37	4.78	3.51	91.7	**0.9**	18.9	32.1	**3.1**
6.3	0.45	2.0	0.43	**3.1**	17.0	0.31	2.04	4.40	80.7	**4.6**	25.4	8.3	**9.1**
5.2	1.66	9.6	0.12	**5.1**	1.9	1.10	10.06	3.79	70.9	**1.3**	19.5	27.6	**6.2**
6.7	0.84	na	0.02	**4.1**	3.4	0.84	10.34	3.41	73.5	**3.3**	10.8	12.0	**5.6**
8.3	0.24	na	0.00	**5.6**	4.6	1.05	10.60	3.67	63.3	**1.1**	8.4	23.9	**6.6**
6.8	1.72	na	0.00	**4.7**	2.9	0.91	7.19	3.56	71.7	**0.8**	13.0	19.9	**7.3**
2.8	1.82	na	4.63	**8.0**	13.8	1.70	10.69	9.56	33.0	**0.2**	8.2	0.0	**8.0**
3.5	1.57	na	0.17	**4.5**	1.4	1.04	10.06	3.28	62.5	**1.6**	14.8	23.4	**7.0**
7.6	0.00	na	-0.04	**4.1**	2.0	0.75	6.16	2.88	74.4	**0.8**	23.3	60.0	**6.6**
9.6	0.06	na	0.00	**2.9**	0.9	0.37	3.61	2.27	78.6	**0.8**	14.3	36.5	**6.0**
6.6	2.59	6.4	0.00	**3.6**	0.4	0.80	4.46	2.94	67.7	**6.0**	69.3	9.8	**7.6**
9.3	na	0.0	na	**9.5**	0.5	1.82	1.92	2.70	95.1	**4.0**	na	0.0	**7.0**
9.6	0.00	na	0.00	**3.5**	0.3	0.87	6.54	3.48	78.4	**3.3**	52.7	22.5	**6.4**
6.8	0.23	na	0.01	**4.3**	0.2	0.82	6.18	4.90	70.1	**1.9**	26.1	22.2	**5.1**
8.6	0.00	na	0.00	**3.0**	0.6	0.61	7.35	3.44	82.5	**2.6**	16.5	15.2	**4.7**
7.7	8.17	na	-0.02	**6.0**	1.2	1.43	6.63	3.98	63.1	**3.8**	33.7	13.7	**9.1**
6.8	1.05	3.7	0.02	**7.6**	40.9	1.55	13.20	3.89	54.2	**2.3**	10.4	11.6	**9.7**
6.0	2.48	na	0.00	**4.4**	2.9	0.94	9.25	3.64	70.1	**3.4**	28.1	14.2	**6.5**
7.8	0.09	0.7	0.02	**3.5**	0.6	0.59	6.05	3.57	77.7	**3.6**	12.0	10.7	**5.5**
5.9	3.31	na	0.03	**3.4**	0.7	0.84	4.95	3.41	75.3	**2.8**	39.8	22.0	**7.6**
3.5	2.08	na	0.51	**4.7**	0.5	0.92	8.55	5.18	76.5	**1.6**	14.5	22.3	**4.9**
4.6	4.40	na	0.53	**3.6**	0.5	0.65	5.92	3.73	84.3	**2.5**	33.6	20.9	**6.3**
6.9	1.09	na	0.05	**4.0**	2.4	0.78	6.70	3.63	75.6	**1.9**	26.6	16.0	**6.7**
5.2	2.58	na	0.14	**3.7**	2.9	0.65	5.30	3.44	76.9	**3.0**	15.8	13.9	**7.4**
6.8	3.14	na	3.32	**1.0**	-0.1	-0.25	-2.00	3.10	86.2	**5.2**	47.6	10.4	**5.1**
4.1	2.08	na	0.15	**4.3**	1.8	0.89	8.10	4.18	77.7	**1.4**	7.1	19.4	**6.2**
4.5	1.77	na	0.09	**4.4**	0.9	0.79	8.45	4.48	74.6	**1.4**	8.5	24.2	**5.7**
8.8	0.00	na	0.00	**3.5**	0.5	0.73	7.80	3.59	80.6	**3.0**	22.5	14.7	**5.3**
6.8	0.00	na	-0.03	**4.9**	1.8	0.88	10.77	4.53	74.9	**1.7**	9.4	10.1	**4.8**
7.9	0.22	na	-0.07	**5.7**	0.9	1.35	13.01	4.17	68.5	**4.5**	27.2	7.4	**5.1**
6.9	0.00	na	0.05	**8.4**	2.3	1.80	18.81	4.44	43.3	**2.8**	8.6	14.2	**5.7**
5.9	1.37	na	0.22	**6.0**	2.8	1.26	12.51	4.09	65.1	**3.8**	34.8	14.1	**6.1**
6.5	0.90	na	0.01	**4.6**	2.9	0.96	10.77	3.60	69.1	**4.8**	24.2	4.8	**5.1**
4.6	1.71	7.6	0.00	**5.9**	12.4	1.15	9.36	4.11	63.4	**4.3**	22.2	9.8	**9.5**
7.6	0.10	1.6	0.04	**8.3**	49.1	1.42	12.90	2.55	37.3	**0.7**	10.8	1.9	**9.4**
4.4	1.61	8.9	0.11	**6.5**	16.2	1.22	9.94	4.35	64.4	**3.1**	6.1	12.5	**9.1**
2.5	6.24	na	0.36	**8.9**	3.5	1.92	23.58	4.55	44.5	**7.0**	55.9	1.9	**4.6**
4.6	0.75	na	0.03	**5.7**	6.7	1.04	10.93	3.97	67.3	**2.2**	5.7	14.2	**7.1**
3.7	1.49	na	0.01	**8.4**	2.5	1.97	15.23	4.44	49.5	**3.2**	7.7	12.0	**8.7**
6.6	1.02	6.0	0.02	**4.5**	5.8	0.80	7.24	3.59	72.1	**2.4**	3.0	14.3	**7.4**
5.8	2.63	na	-0.07	**0.5**	-2.3	-8.18	-26.72	4.42	281.0	**7.5**	92.7	3.8	**5.6**
1.7	2.47	13.5	11.17	**10.0**	168.7	5.82	27.79	20.22	25.7	**0.5**	14.4	15.3	**9.3**
6.4	0.46	2.7	0.03	**3.9**	4.4	0.66	6.47	3.56	74.3	**3.5**	2.1	9.7	**6.7**
5.5	0.57	3.1	1.40	**7.8**	85.0	1.86	13.14	5.27	66.2	**0.6**	9.8	3.2	**8.1**
8.8	0.17	na	0.05	**4.6**	2.9	0.97	9.80	4.33	73.4	**4.3**	16.3	6.8	**6.2**
7.3	1.56	na	0.03	**2.9**	0.2	0.32	3.34	3.68	90.9	**2.5**	29.9	18.6	**4.2**
5.9	0.83	na	0.00	**3.1**	0.3	0.48	4.55	3.02	79.9	**4.5**	48.5	14.0	**5.6**
7.3	0.75	na	0.17	**8.3**	9.1	1.65	10.68	4.17	53.6	**2.6**	35.5	20.8	**9.0**

Name	City	State	Rating	2018 Rating	2017 Rating	Total Assets ($Mil)	One Year Asset Growth	Asset Mix (As a % of Total Assets) Commercial Loans	Consumer Loans	Mortgage Loans	Securities	Capitalization Index	Leverage Ratio	Risk-Based Capital Ratio
Metro Bank	Louisville	KY	**D**	D+	D+	25.8	-2.96	2.1	0.2	5.0	25.7	**10.0**	18.5	31.6
Metro City Bank	Doraville	GA	**A**	A	A	1647.7	14.17	2.9	0.1	44.5	1.0	**10.0**	11.6	19.3
▲ Metro Phoenix Bank	Phoenix	AZ	**A-**	B+	A-	223.8	19.23	18.8	0.0	6.0	1.2	**10.0**	15.3	20.9
▲ Metropolitan Bank	Oakland	CA	**B**	B-	B+	179.8	5.39	2.6	0.0	21.3	7.0	**10.0**	12.0	19.4
▲ Metropolitan Capital Bank & Trust	Chicago	IL	**D+**	D-	D+	229.9	-16.00	52.4	0.3	3.5	6.9	**7.5**	9.3	14.7
Metropolitan Commercial Bank	New York	NY	**A-**	A-	B	3241.1	68.10	13.2	2.4	4.3	7.9	**7.7**	10.3	13.1
Metz Banking Co.	Nevada	MO	**B+**	B+	B+	75.4	3.68	7.1	1.2	11.8	15.9	**10.0**	12.3	18.5
▲ Miami Savings Bank	Miamitown	OH	**A-**	B+	B	128.5	1.57	4.6	0.4	37.8	7.0	**10.0**	16.7	27.6
▲ Mid America Bank	Jefferson City	MO	**A-**	B+	A-	505.9	11.14	10.2	1.8	18.9	4.9	**9.6**	10.7	15.1
Mid Penn Bank	Millersburg	PA	**B-**	B-	C+	2248.6	10.11	11.9	0.3	17.3	10.1	**6.4**	8.5	12.0
▲ Mid-America Bank	Baldwin City	KS	**B-**	B-	B	226.7	24.19	3.6	1.1	41.0	1.8	**5.3**	9.9	11.2
Mid-Central Federal Savings Bank	Wadena	MN	**B-**	B-	B-	116.1	0.55	3.2	16.5	52.0	0.9	**7.8**	9.6	16.3
Mid-Missouri Bank	Springfield	MO	**B**	B	B	660.7	4.22	5.8	1.1	20.7	4.8	**7.3**	9.4	12.7
MidAmerica National Bank	Canton	IL	**B-**	B-	B	424.3	1.99	6.3	6.8	11.4	27.6	**10.0**	11.2	17.3
MidCoast Community Bank	Wilmington	DE	**C**	C	D+	265.6	12.92	6.3	0.0	19.5	5.4	**6.8**	9.9	12.3
MidCountry Bank	Minneapolis	MN	**C+**	C+	B	802.2	0.40	9.4	0.2	13.8	6.0	**8.9**	12.5	14.1
▲ Middlefield Banking Co.	Middlefield	OH	**B**	B-	B-	1280.3	6.21	6.3	1.2	18.5	8.2	**6.8**	10.0	12.4
Middlesex Federal Savings, F.A.	Somerville	MA	**C**	C-	C-	426.1	4.43	1.9	0.1	33.8	8.0	**8.8**	10.2	15.1
Middlesex Savings Bank	Natick	MA	**B**	B	B	4941.0	3.05	8.0	0.2	24.4	26.8	**10.0**	13.1	17.5
Middletown State Bank	Middletown	IL	**B-**	B	B+	37.4	1.93	4.1	1.4	30.7	10.3	**3.0**	9.5	10.0
Middletown Valley Bank	Middletown	MD	**B-**	B-	B-	484.0	12.85	19.0	0.4	20.3	7.7	**7.2**	9.4	12.7
MidFirst Bank	Oklahoma City	OK	**B**	B	B	21611.4	31.23	7.6	0.6	34.0	12.4	**6.8**	8.8	14.9
▲ Midland Community Bank	Kincaid	IL	**B+**	B	B	62.4	15.36	9.7	2.5	40.9	23.0	**10.0**	11.5	15.4
Midland Federal S&L Assn.	Bridgeview	IL	**D+**	D+	D+	115.8	2.10	0.1	0.5	32.3	36.9	**7.8**	9.5	35.5
Midland National Bank	Newton	KS	**B**	B	C+	139.9	2.23	6.7	12.9	21.4	25.5	**10.0**	11.6	15.8
Midland States Bank	Effingham	IL	**B-**	B-	B-	5712.8	-0.05	13.1	11.1	9.4	10.3	**7.4**	10.6	12.8
MidSouth Bank	Dothan	AL	**B+**	B+	B	416.0	5.66	10.9	0.7	8.9	11.1	**10.0**	12.4	16.6
Midstates Bank, N.A.	Council Bluffs	IA	**C+**	C+	C	575.1	51.09	4.1	0.9	9.6	29.8	**6.6**	8.6	13.2
Midwest Bank	Monmouth	IL	**B-**	B-	B-	522.3	4.75	8.5	2.6	8.2	28.3	**7.4**	9.2	15.5
Midwest Bank	Detroit Lakes	MN	**B**	B	B+	508.8	11.76	19.4	2.1	15.9	4.1	**5.1**	9.4	11.1
Midwest Bank N.A.	Pierce	NE	**B+**	B+	A-	788.2	7.62	7.7	1.9	2.7	17.9	**7.2**	9.2	13.1
Midwest BankCentre	Saint Louis	MO	**C+**	B-	B-	2007.4	5.13	13.0	2.4	18.5	17.6	**6.3**	9.4	12.0
Midwest Community Bank	Freeport	IL	**B-**	B-	B-	246.3	11.83	1.6	0.2	29.9	0.7	**10.0**	11.0	15.2
Midwest Heritage Bank, FSB	West Des Moines	IA	**A**	A	A	284.8	7.21	5.7	14.9	25.1	10.0	**10.0**	13.1	18.0
Midwest Independent Bank	Jefferson City	MO	**B+**	B+	B	274.6	-1.79	2.3	0.0	3.1	15.8	**10.0**	15.1	23.8
Midwest Regional Bank	Festus	MO	**C-**	C	C	644.3	4.26	18.5	0.3	7.6	4.9	**5.6**	9.4	11.5
MidWestOne Bank	Iowa City	IA	**B**	B	B	4640.3	42.30	12.9	1.5	9.7	15.0	**5.0**	9.7	11.0
▲ Mifflinburg Bank & Trust Co.	Mifflinburg	PA	**B**	B-	B	452.1	0.69	10.6	3.1	18.7	17.6	**8.6**	10.1	14.5
▲ Milford Bank	Milford	CT	**C+**	C	C	448.4	3.02	7.9	4.1	40.7	4.8	**10.0**	11.1	15.9
Milford Building and Loan Assn., SB	Milford	IL	**D+**	C-	C-	30.1	5.82	0.0	0.0	59.1	0.0	**6.9**	8.9	19.1
Milford Federal Bank	Milford	MA	**C+**	C+	C+	418.6	9.23	0.2	1.0	73.5	4.0	**10.0**	12.0	20.3
Millbury National Bank	Millbury	MA	**C**	C	C	95.8	9.56	5.8	0.9	28.9	14.1	**9.1**	10.4	15.2
Milledgeville State Bank	Milledgeville	IL	**B+**	A-	A	148.6	9.65	13.2	0.7	5.9	24.6	**9.8**	10.8	16.3
▲ Millennial Bank	Leeds	AL	**D-**	E	E-	79.0	19.73	11.7	1.0	14.3	15.1	**9.9**	11.9	14.9
Millennium Bank	Des Plaines	IL	**A-**	A-	B+	144.9	26.73	9.4	0.1	3.5	0.0	**10.0**	11.3	15.7
Millennium Bank	Ooltewah	TN	**B-**	B	B+	188.0	6.30	11.8	0.3	15.5	6.7	**9.6**	11.2	14.7
Millington Bank	Millington	NJ	**B-**	B-	C+	591.2	0.14	12.7	0.1	24.8	6.4	**7.1**	10.5	12.6
Millville Savings Bank	Millville	NJ	**C+**	C	C	130.9	-0.34	0.0	0.0	22.3	42.0	**10.0**	14.3	29.5
Milton Savings Bank	Milton	PA	**B**	B	B	62.2	-3.68	0.0	1.7	60.9	14.4	**10.0**	24.8	66.7
Minden Exchange Bank & Trust Co.	Minden	NE	**A-**	A-	A-	144.7	-2.58	5.5	2.9	1.3	26.4	**10.0**	19.6	25.8
▲ Mineola Community Bank, SSB	Mineola	TX	**C+**	C+	C+	263.5	15.68	1.6	1.6	47.7	18.3	**10.0**	11.5	21.2
Miners and Merchants Bank	Thomas	WV	**B-**	B-	B-	54.1	-3.66	0.2	1.9	23.1	52.0	**10.0**	16.4	48.9
Miners Exchange Bank	Coeburn	VA	**B-**	B-	B-	100.8	11.08	1.4	5.6	30.7	14.7	**10.0**	12.9	22.2
▲ Miners National Bank of Eveleth	Eveleth	MN	**C+**	C-	C	70.0	1.05	2.2	4.2	23.3	24.7	**6.4**	8.4	20.4
Miners State Bank	Iron River	MI	**B**	B-	C+	138.4	11.39	11.9	0.4	4.8	18.6	**7.5**	10.0	13.0
Minnesota Bank & Trust	Edina	MN	**B**	B	B	722.6	11.30	20.8	2.6	6.6	19.8	**8.3**	11.3	13.6
Minnesota First Credit and Savings, Inc.	Rochester	MN	**C+**	C+	B-	26.7	0.63	1.7	36.0	48.8	0.0	**10.0**	15.4	23.2
Minnesota Lakes Bank	Delano	MN	**C+**	C+	C+	104.0	4.83	12.3	2.2	8.3	15.2	**7.6**	9.4	13.0
▲ Minnesota National Bank	Sauk Centre	MN	**B+**	B	B	211.8	6.13	11.8	3.0	15.7	18.9	**8.9**	10.2	15.2
MinnStar Bank N.A.	Lake Crystal	MN	**B-**	B-	C+	127.3	1.86	7.7	0.6	21.6	2.1	**7.8**	9.6	13.1

Asset Quality Index	Adjusted Non-Performing Loans as a % of Total Loans	Adjusted Non-Performing Loans as a % of Capital	Net Charge-Offs / Avg Loans	Profitability Index	Net Income ($Mil)	Return on Assets (R.O.A.)	Return on Equity (R.O.E.)	Net Interest Spread	Overhead Efficiency Ratio	Liquidity Index	Liquidity Ratio	Hot Money Ratio	Stability Index
7.1	2.35	na	-0.15	**0.0**	-0.5	-2.48	-12.95	2.63	185.0	**1.9**	49.2	87.1	**7.1**
6.4	1.11	6.5	-0.02	**9.8**	34.1	2.98	25.61	4.25	39.3	**1.1**	21.0	39.1	**10.0**
7.3	0.04	na	-0.06	**9.8**	2.7	1.71	11.26	5.27	57.0	**3.3**	22.3	13.4	**7.5**
6.2	1.14	na	-0.10	**5.4**	1.3	0.96	8.30	3.86	64.8	**1.7**	19.9	22.5	**8.7**
5.5	1.88	na	-0.46	**4.1**	1.5	0.83	9.49	6.02	87.0	**1.6**	35.9	29.3	**4.2**
6.9	0.22	na	-0.21	**7.3**	24.4	1.21	10.23	3.53	52.7	**3.3**	16.1	3.7	**9.1**
8.7	0.12	na	-0.01	**6.0**	0.7	1.33	10.70	3.65	63.9	**2.4**	31.7	21.3	**8.4**
7.5	1.42	na	-0.01	**5.6**	1.1	1.12	6.84	3.51	61.5	**1.2**	21.4	30.4	**8.4**
7.0	0.37	na	0.07	**7.5**	6.3	1.74	16.45	3.83	51.7	**3.5**	19.8	12.2	**8.0**
6.3	0.32	2.0	0.02	**4.6**	14.8	0.92	8.02	3.67	69.3	**2.1**	10.8	12.9	**7.6**
7.1	0.00	na	0.26	**6.4**	1.9	1.21	11.97	4.14	61.7	**0.8**	17.5	35.2	**6.7**
6.7	0.32	na	0.16	**4.0**	0.8	0.87	9.46	3.75	80.0	**2.6**	8.9	15.5	**5.4**
4.8	1.32	9.4	0.03	**6.3**	6.0	1.22	13.41	3.96	66.7	**1.8**	12.6	12.3	**6.9**
6.5	1.49	na	0.03	**6.3**	4.1	1.32	10.37	4.05	60.0	**4.1**	18.4	8.3	**7.7**
6.5	0.00	na	0.29	**2.7**	0.7	0.37	3.61	2.97	78.3	**0.7**	12.0	29.0	**4.0**
3.2	2.27	na	0.10	**4.2**	5.8	0.66	5.06	4.38	75.3	**1.7**	12.6	14.6	**8.5**
5.2	1.30	8.0	0.11	**6.0**	11.4	1.26	11.41	3.72	59.5	**1.1**	14.0	26.4	**8.8**
7.5	0.29	2.1	0.00	**2.6**	1.1	0.34	3.65	2.78	94.8	**0.7**	16.3	33.5	**5.5**
8.8	0.30	1.3	0.02	**4.3**	32.3	0.89	6.81	3.00	67.1	**3.6**	34.4	18.2	**9.7**
8.1	0.00	na	0.04	**7.9**	0.5	1.93	19.91	3.41	39.3	**1.5**	17.2	25.7	**6.9**
5.9	0.46	3.2	0.04	**3.7**	2.0	0.58	6.12	3.73	75.4	**2.7**	11.5	14.0	**5.1**
5.5	0.29	2.3	-0.01	**6.4**	205.1	1.49	15.91	3.39	59.9	**2.9**	21.5	11.0	**9.5**
8.7	0.00	na	0.02	**7.6**	0.6	1.37	12.10	3.45	54.2	**1.5**	23.6	27.0	**6.2**
5.4	3.94	na	0.01	**1.4**	0.0	0.04	0.42	2.77	98.9	**6.1**	67.5	10.6	**4.6**
7.8	0.47	na	0.01	**4.2**	1.0	1.02	8.83	3.96	77.6	**5.2**	34.4	6.3	**6.9**
4.2	1.05	5.6	0.25	**5.5**	47.1	1.12	8.13	3.95	63.1	**3.6**	10.6	8.4	**8.7**
8.8	0.38	na	0.01	**4.8**	3.2	1.06	8.52	3.92	72.2	**3.8**	31.0	13.2	**7.4**
4.2	2.13	na	0.03	**4.7**	3.8	1.04	9.95	3.81	67.7	**4.0**	34.3	13.1	**7.8**
3.2	2.18	9.4	0.03	**4.7**	3.5	0.90	7.40	3.57	68.1	**2.0**	13.8	11.4	**7.5**
5.2	0.96	6.5	0.01	**9.6**	8.1	2.24	23.48	4.45	44.0	**1.9**	6.3	18.4	**8.3**
8.0	0.15	na	0.02	**7.5**	8.7	1.51	15.61	3.68	53.2	**1.3**	11.9	26.8	**7.6**
7.8	0.29	2.0	0.03	**3.2**	7.8	0.53	5.24	2.89	79.7	**2.6**	10.0	15.1	**8.4**
7.7	0.49	na	0.01	**8.1**	4.0	2.74	25.04	3.69	80.2	**1.0**	6.2	16.7	**6.5**
6.7	0.48	1.7	0.22	**9.6**	4.1	1.96	14.85	3.73	68.0	**4.6**	21.6	5.6	**8.9**
8.8	0.00	na	0.00	**4.2**	1.6	0.74	5.24	2.93	78.1	**3.8**	42.8	11.2	**8.0**
4.0	0.91	na	0.51	**3.7**	3.2	0.66	6.88	3.17	67.8	**1.2**	7.5	26.5	**5.6**
5.1	1.04	5.6	0.19	**5.2**	34.1	1.09	9.81	3.85	61.4	**3.1**	12.8	13.7	**8.7**
6.8	1.22	na	0.04	**5.5**	4.0	1.21	12.20	3.28	58.9	**2.6**	11.7	15.3	**6.7**
7.2	0.83	na	0.01	**2.8**	1.0	0.30	2.85	3.51	90.3	**3.8**	9.6	9.2	**5.9**
5.3	0.59	na	0.00	**2.6**	0.1	0.31	3.53	2.43	75.2	**1.5**	32.6	38.1	**4.6**
7.7	0.60	na	0.00	**2.8**	1.2	0.39	3.19	2.97	84.9	**2.1**	11.2	18.2	**6.6**
2.9	2.64	31.4	0.14	**3.3**	0.3	0.44	4.45	4.19	82.2	**0.7**	13.9	45.5	**5.3**
7.8	0.25	na	0.34	**5.8**	1.5	1.36	12.14	3.36	50.5	**1.3**	32.8	45.9	**8.6**
7.3	0.00	na	0.03	**1.8**	0.2	0.39	3.08	5.35	89.3	**2.6**	18.2	16.2	**2.4**
6.7	0.11	3.3	0.00	**10.0**	3.0	3.05	26.60	4.08	55.1	**0.5**	19.2	62.8	**7.9**
5.4	0.79	na	-0.11	**4.9**	1.4	0.99	8.78	4.47	76.6	**0.9**	20.9	31.4	**7.1**
4.3	2.38	11.8	0.00	**4.2**	3.2	0.74	7.02	3.16	67.5	**0.7**	9.4	22.5	**7.4**
9.1	1.67	3.1	0.00	**2.8**	0.5	0.45	3.24	3.12	81.8	**6.7**	63.6	6.1	**6.9**
9.5	0.00	na	0.00	**4.6**	0.5	0.96	3.94	3.45	63.2	**5.6**	44.8	7.4	**7.6**
7.2	0.00	0.0	0.00	**6.9**	1.6	1.41	7.47	3.73	54.8	**4.3**	6.6	5.8	**8.9**
9.0	0.48	na	0.01	**2.6**	0.7	0.38	3.20	3.08	86.4	**2.3**	31.2	22.3	**6.9**
7.8	2.19	na	0.02	**2.9**	0.2	0.39	2.43	2.89	82.6	**6.9**	77.4	5.6	**7.3**
7.8	2.26	na	0.38	**3.0**	0.2	0.34	2.75	5.15	89.4	**5.4**	42.7	8.3	**5.4**
9.2	0.00	na	0.00	**4.3**	0.4	0.86	9.82	4.48	73.0	**5.4**	39.7	7.0	**4.0**
6.3	0.04	0.2	-0.01	**5.2**	1.2	1.22	12.07	4.22	69.2	**2.9**	19.6	14.4	**5.7**
2.9	1.91	6.1	0.13	**6.8**	6.7	1.37	8.49	4.53	61.5	**4.9**	33.4	7.4	**7.4**
6.8	0.24	na	-0.05	**3.0**	0.1	0.29	1.91	5.19	93.8	**1.7**	12.9	13.8	**6.6**
7.4	0.06	0.5	0.09	**3.2**	0.4	0.48	4.02	4.61	86.8	**4.9**	17.6	3.1	**6.3**
6.6	0.55	2.4	0.00	**5.5**	2.1	1.39	11.70	3.88	67.3	**3.6**	20.8	11.6	**7.3**
7.6	0.10	na	0.15	**4.3**	0.9	0.91	9.75	4.13	75.0	**2.2**	7.4	17.1	**5.6**

Name	City	State	Rating	2018 Rating	2017 Rating	Total Assets ($Mil)	One Year Asset Growth	Asset Mix (As a % of Total Assets) Commercial Loans	Consumer Loans	Mortgage Loans	Securities	Capitalization Index	Leverage Ratio	Risk-Based Capital Ratio
▲ Minnwest Bank	Redwood Falls	MN	**B+**	B	B	1995.6	8.89	6.3	0.9	3.3	7.1	**8.8**	11.0	14.0
Minster Bank	Minster	OH	**B+**	B+	B+	509.6	7.26	5.7	0.6	7.6	24.0	**7.0**	9.0	16.9
▲ MINT National Bank	Kingwood	TX	**B-**	C+	B+	249.8	19.71	5.3	0.6	11.2	0.0	**10.0**	11.8	16.6
Mission Bank	Kingman	AZ	**B-**	B-	C+	124.3	9.12	4.7	0.4	4.4	37.2	**6.9**	8.9	15.5
▲ Mission Bank	Bakersfield	CA	**B+**	B	B	800.4	19.30	10.9	0.0	3.8	7.7	**6.3**	9.6	12.0
▲ Mission National Bank	San Francisco	CA	**B+**	B	B-	243.1	-9.96	1.9	0.1	29.4	0.0	**10.0**	12.8	20.7
▲ Mission Valley Bank	Sun Valley	CA	**B+**	B+	A	338.3	10.53	21.7	0.1	0.9	4.4	**10.0**	11.7	15.8
▲ Mississippi River Bank	Belle Chasse	LA	**A-**	B+	A-	110.6	-6.35	17.8	1.0	8.5	15.8	**10.0**	14.4	32.7
Missouri Bank	Warrenton	MO	**A-**	A-	A-	214.1	0.28	4.8	0.9	18.3	25.6	**10.0**	12.7	17.3
Missouri Bank II	Sedalia	MO	**A-**	A-	A-	101.8	7.25	1.1	1.5	29.6	14.7	**9.7**	10.8	17.0
▲ Mitchell Bank	Milwaukee	WI	**C+**	C-	C-	48.8	1.74	6.4	0.1	11.0	0.0	**10.0**	17.0	61.3
▲ Mizuho Bank (USA)	New York	NY	**B**	B	B-	6072.5	10.28	37.0	0.0	0.0	0.0	**10.0**	22.9	23.2
▲ MNB Bank	McCook	NE	**C+**	C	C+	361.4	0.35	3.9	0.7	5.9	24.7	**10.0**	15.2	20.0
Modern Bank, N.A.	New York	NY	**C**	C+	C+	782.7	-9.50	41.2	0.0	4.8	16.9	**8.1**	10.2	13.4
Monona Bank	Monona	WI	**C+**	C+	B-	939.8	6.24	10.5	0.6	12.6	8.3	**6.0**	9.8	11.8
Monroe Federal S&L Assn.	Tipp City	OH	**C**	C	C	103.6	7.53	6.5	0.8	30.1	12.5	**10.0**	11.8	17.0
Monroe Savings Bank	Williamstown	NJ	**B-**	C+	C+	92.9	1.42	0.5	11.2	50.8	14.3	**10.0**	13.8	27.0
Monson Savings Bank	Monson	MA	**B-**	B-	B-	436.2	8.00	8.9	0.7	29.8	9.5	**7.7**	9.4	13.9
Montecito Bank & Trust	Santa Barbara	CA	**B+**	B+	B+	1537.9	10.15	7.0	1.2	13.9	29.3	**9.5**	10.7	15.0
Monterey County Bank	Monterey	CA	**C-**	D+	C+	171.6	3.65	14.6	0.2	7.2	21.1	**8.8**	10.5	14.0
▲ Montezuma State Bank	Montezuma	IA	**B-**	C+	B-	37.5	4.48	11.9	9.2	14.8	28.0	**10.0**	13.3	24.2
Montgomery Bank	Sikeston	MO	**C+**	C+	C+	929.2	3.17	14.6	0.6	24.2	9.1	**5.6**	8.7	11.5
Monticello Banking Co.	Monticello	KY	**B**	B	B	764.2	2.60	5.2	3.5	21.5	13.0	**8.3**	10.5	13.6
Montrose Savings Bank	Montrose	MO	**B**	B	B	42.3	-0.29	6.7	3.8	15.5	23.2	**10.0**	15.2	23.6
Moody National Bank	Galveston	TX	**A-**	A-	B	1194.8	15.75	7.6	0.8	7.1	16.9	**10.0**	15.1	18.9
Morgan Stanley Bank, N.A.	Salt Lake City	UT	**A**	A	A	138262.0	-1.95	6.6	6.0	0.4	40.5	**10.0**	11.9	20.3
Morgan Stanley Private Bank, N.A.	New York	NY	**A**	A	A	78786.0	11.89	4.6	12.3	36.9	19.6	**9.6**	10.8	27.5
Morganton Savings Bank, S.S.B.	Morganton	NC	**B**	B-	C	95.4	18.76	0.3	0.2	26.2	8.9	**10.0**	27.0	33.1
Morgantown Bank & Trust Co., Inc.	Morgantown	KY	**B-**	B-	B-	205.2	7.14	4.9	4.0	38.5	17.1	**6.8**	8.8	14.5
▲ Morris Bank	Dublin	GA	**C**	C-	C+	958.5	33.54	8.3	3.0	15.5	12.2	**9.6**	11.1	14.7
Morris County National Bank	Naples	TX	**C-**	C	B-	89.7	-10.21	7.1	7.8	16.9	26.7	**9.8**	10.9	15.8
Morris Plan Co. of Terre Haute, Inc.	Terre Haute	IN	**A-**	A-	A-	91.5	22.47	0.2	91.2	2.8	4.1	**10.0**	28.1	30.0
Morton Community Bank	Morton	IL	**B**	B	B	3870.9	3.86	11.1	2.2	9.0	19.7	**8.3**	10.3	13.6
Mound City Bank	Platteville	WI	**C+**	B-	B	371.3	3.83	1.9	0.7	18.4	10.5	**10.0**	11.0	15.6
Mount Vernon Bank	Mount Vernon	GA	**B**	B+	A-	131.1	-4.32	4.4	2.4	14.4	26.0	**10.0**	11.9	20.0
Mount Vernon Bank and Trust Co.	Mount Vernon	IA	**A-**	A-	A	130.6	5.36	6.3	4.0	33.2	19.0	**10.0**	13.8	21.9
Mountain Commerce Bank	Knoxville	TN	**B+**	B+	B	909.3	9.66	8.0	1.4	20.8	5.7	**8.3**	11.3	13.6
Mountain Pacific Bank	Everett	WA	**C+**	C	C+	344.8	3.98	7.3	0.2	7.7	3.9	**8.1**	11.5	13.4
Mountain Valley Bank	Walden	CO	**B-**	B-	B-	235.4	21.45	9.6	1.4	18.1	11.3	**7.8**	9.5	13.5
▲ Mountain Valley Bank	Dunlap	TN	**C**	C-	C	106.3	4.48	4.0	7.9	40.3	16.7	**7.3**	9.2	15.5
▲ Mountain Valley Bank, N.A.	Elkins	WV	**A-**	B	B	145.5	3.15	5.6	2.1	29.6	25.6	**10.0**	14.3	27.0
Mountain View Bank of Commerce	Westminster	CO	**C**	C	C	125.5	7.58	9.7	0.0	7.3	0.0	**6.1**	9.6	11.8
▲ MountainOne Bank	North Adams	MA	**B**	B-	B-	898.9	1.98	10.2	1.0	26.5	10.7	**10.0**	12.0	15.2
▲ Movement Bank	Danville	VA	**D**	E	E	45.5	11.17	7.2	2.4	12.9	10.5	**10.0**	16.7	22.7
MRV Banks	Sainte Genevieve	MO	**B**	B-	B-	385.6	15.76	24.0	0.4	7.9	1.4	**6.1**	10.2	11.9
Mt. McKinley Bank	Fairbanks	AK	**A-**	B+	A-	459.4	9.02	6.7	0.2	4.3	50.9	**10.0**	20.4	38.4
Mt. Victory State Bank	Mount Victory	OH	**C**	C	C	18.1	10.20	3.9	8.2	15.7	23.5	**10.0**	11.2	25.8
Muenster State Bank	Muenster	TX	**A-**	A-	A	165.0	1.68	2.7	2.1	9.3	63.8	**10.0**	16.2	38.6
▼ MUFG Union Bank, N.A.	New York	NY	**C+**	B	B-	134715.5	8.66	11.8	3.4	28.1	20.0	**9.1**	10.4	14.9
Muncy Bank and Trust Co.	Muncy	PA	**B**	B	B+	493.2	6.73	4.4	2.2	43.2	15.2	**8.2**	9.8	15.6
▲ Municipal Trust and Savings Bank	Bourbonnais	IL	**A**	A-	A	317.9	6.20	0.8	0.5	21.7	8.8	**10.0**	16.9	33.8
Murphy Bank	Fresno	CA	**B+**	B+	A-	309.3	9.64	26.0	17.5	13.6	0.0	**9.3**	10.8	14.4
Murphy-Wall State Bank and Trust Co.	Pinckneyville	IL	**C+**	B-	B-	128.5	8.71	6.8	2.0	18.6	29.5	**10.0**	11.2	19.9
Murray Bank	Murray	KY	**B**	B	B	312.2	3.91	6.9	3.4	26.9	15.3	**7.9**	9.6	15.0
▲ Mutual Federal Bank	Chicago	IL	**C-**	C-	C+	71.8	-5.06	0.0	0.0	48.4	1.8	**10.0**	19.2	21.1
Mutual of Omaha Bank	Omaha	NE	**B-**	B-	C+	8827.9	5.68	9.6	0.2	27.3	19.7	**7.5**	10.1	12.9
Mutual S&L Assn.	Metairie	LA	**B-**	B-	B	50.0	8.90	0.0	0.2	80.7	0.0	**10.0**	27.1	49.6
▲ Mutual Savings Assn.	Leavenworth	KS	**B+**	B	B	214.9	1.22	4.6	1.2	36.1	22.8	**10.0**	30.5	52.6
Mutual Savings Bank	Franklin	IN	**B-**	B-	B-	172.7	9.23	3.9	2.1	21.1	21.8	**7.9**	10.1	13.3
▲ Mutual Savings Bank	Hartsville	SC	**C-**	C-	D+	50.9	18.46	5.8	4.6	26.0	6.6	**10.0**	28.2	42.6

Asset Quality Index	Adjusted Non-Performing Loans as a % of Total Loans	Adjusted Non-Performing Loans as a % of Capital	Net Charge-Offs Avg Loans	Profitability Index	Net Income ($Mil)	Return on Assets (R.O.A.)	Return on Equity (R.O.E.)	Net Interest Spread	Overhead Efficiency Ratio	Liquidity Index	Liquidity Ratio	Hot Money Ratio	Stability Index
5.8	1.36	5.4	0.11	**5.9**	16.0	1.08	9.59	3.97	58.9	**1.4**	14.5	11.8	**9.0**
8.8	0.37	na	0.03	**6.3**	5.1	1.38	15.81	3.44	57.9	**5.4**	37.8	6.4	**5.8**
4.6	1.05	na	0.15	**9.1**	2.8	1.65	13.81	3.87	56.6	**1.2**	29.6	54.9	**8.3**
7.0	0.50	na	-0.02	**4.4**	0.8	0.87	9.67	4.39	74.9	**6.2**	50.4	5.3	**5.4**
7.4	0.03	na	0.00	**9.5**	9.3	1.66	17.59	4.80	52.6	**4.1**	19.1	7.8	**7.0**
8.0	0.00	na	-0.16	**5.3**	2.0	1.05	8.34	3.69	71.3	**1.0**	23.5	35.1	**7.1**
6.5	0.70	na	0.13	**7.6**	3.4	1.33	10.18	4.89	67.2	**4.6**	25.7	6.5	**8.1**
6.3	1.36	na	0.29	**10.0**	2.5	3.06	22.41	5.74	52.7	**5.8**	49.9	7.7	**8.8**
8.4	0.00	na	0.07	**6.6**	2.5	1.51	12.21	4.02	59.9	**3.8**	8.4	9.4	**8.4**
7.7	0.54	na	0.00	**5.1**	0.9	1.15	10.74	3.52	68.8	**1.6**	14.3	22.4	**8.3**
8.2	11.30	na	0.00	**3.0**	0.2	0.43	2.45	3.55	85.1	**7.6**	82.6	1.4	**7.0**
5.6	2.36	8.3	0.17	**4.8**	45.1	0.98	4.26	1.75	83.2	**0.8**	16.8	7.4	**8.9**
3.2	3.53	12.9	0.00	**5.5**	3.1	1.16	7.69	3.74	59.7	**2.2**	20.9	18.4	**6.4**
7.4	0.00	na	0.00	**2.6**	1.7	0.29	2.67	2.10	79.4	**0.2**	6.3	78.8	**6.4**
4.8	0.39	na	0.00	**4.9**	6.6	0.97	8.50	3.50	64.1	**1.5**	10.7	14.3	**7.3**
7.1	1.04	na	-0.01	**2.2**	0.2	0.20	1.67	3.38	93.8	**1.9**	20.0	19.1	**6.5**
6.1	1.90	6.3	0.00	**3.6**	0.5	0.63	4.71	3.27	70.8	**1.8**	27.3	24.7	**6.8**
7.9	0.43	na	0.02	**4.6**	2.8	0.86	9.40	3.68	70.2	**2.0**	17.1	18.5	**5.9**
6.9	0.89	na	0.00	**4.4**	8.5	0.74	6.78	3.91	75.3	**5.5**	30.0	6.4	**9.6**
2.4	4.50	na	0.01	**3.6**	1.2	0.92	9.32	4.44	85.6	**3.7**	26.8	12.0	**3.9**
4.1	2.81	na	0.00	**5.7**	0.3	1.21	8.73	3.58	59.2	**5.3**	38.2	7.3	**6.3**
6.0	0.95	na	0.10	**4.5**	7.2	1.05	12.00	3.62	70.7	**3.1**	7.5	12.9	**6.0**
7.0	0.35	na	0.12	**4.8**	5.5	0.99	8.97	3.98	70.3	**1.2**	9.7	26.8	**7.6**
7.0	0.94	na	-0.07	**7.3**	0.6	1.83	12.39	4.29	52.7	**4.3**	29.4	9.8	**7.0**
6.3	0.77	3.4	0.08	**7.6**	12.4	1.53	10.25	3.92	60.7	**3.0**	25.6	17.8	**10.0**
8.1	0.74	2.8	0.01	**9.5**	2198.0	2.06	18.28	2.27	13.1	**3.5**	52.1	0.0	**9.6**
8.0	0.17	1.2	0.00	**7.8**	882.0	1.56	15.19	2.48	24.0	**2.0**	25.7	0.0	**8.7**
7.0	1.50	na	-0.65	**4.6**	0.6	0.93	3.55	4.22	73.5	**2.5**	22.7	17.5	**6.5**
7.2	0.35	na	0.02	**3.6**	0.8	0.55	6.25	3.64	85.1	**1.7**	14.5	21.6	**5.5**
4.0	1.95	na	0.25	**8.7**	11.1	1.69	15.11	4.64	59.0	**2.1**	23.1	18.1	**8.7**
2.7	3.02	18.9	0.85	**2.5**	0.2	0.24	2.40	4.14	80.1	**1.6**	13.8	23.1	**5.1**
5.0	1.01	na	2.26	**10.0**	2.4	3.83	13.08	12.11	34.8	**0.3**	1.4	60.0	**8.8**
4.5	1.69	12.0	0.12	**6.4**	44.8	1.58	14.69	3.06	47.5	**1.8**	16.4	13.3	**10.0**
4.5	4.35	na	0.57	**5.8**	3.1	1.12	10.27	3.26	60.4	**1.6**	15.9	20.9	**7.1**
4.2	3.41	na	0.00	**5.9**	1.4	1.43	12.73	4.11	69.0	**2.8**	35.8	19.6	**7.5**
8.7	0.00	na	0.01	**5.4**	1.1	1.09	8.00	3.25	57.8	**3.2**	25.6	12.2	**8.3**
7.2	0.21	1.5	0.05	**7.6**	9.5	1.47	13.38	3.49	48.1	**1.2**	10.1	27.4	**7.0**
3.4	2.24	na	0.00	**5.7**	2.7	1.10	9.38	4.18	65.2	**1.1**	13.2	29.7	**7.6**
5.1	1.81	na	0.06	**5.3**	1.7	1.02	9.93	4.03	68.9	**1.5**	16.6	22.7	**6.4**
3.7	1.48	na	0.06	**3.5**	0.4	0.50	5.52	4.66	81.5	**1.8**	6.5	17.8	**4.4**
8.9	0.09	na	0.06	**5.6**	1.2	1.16	8.68	4.29	68.6	**5.0**	29.3	5.4	**7.7**
6.0	0.12	na	0.10	**3.2**	0.4	0.42	4.27	3.67	85.9	**0.8**	16.2	42.9	**5.0**
6.6	1.03	na	0.08	**5.0**	6.3	0.94	7.82	3.63	72.1	**0.8**	14.9	25.4	**7.5**
5.5	1.58	na	0.51	**0.0**	-0.3	-0.99	-6.74	5.45	109.0	**4.6**	23.3	5.6	**3.1**
8.4	0.00	na	0.05	**7.4**	4.1	1.47	15.76	3.92	45.8	**1.0**	11.7	24.0	**5.9**
8.7	1.10	na	0.30	**5.2**	3.5	1.05	5.14	4.04	66.7	**6.5**	63.0	7.1	**8.3**
8.6	0.00	na	0.12	**3.1**	0.1	0.57	5.28	3.40	77.9	**4.1**	41.7	12.5	**4.3**
7.3	2.66	na	0.60	**7.3**	2.3	1.89	12.22	3.16	42.7	**5.7**	67.5	12.7	**9.6**
6.3	1.02	4.6	0.17	**1.1**	-957.7	-0.97	-8.24	2.47	118.0	**3.5**	31.4	12.5	**9.9**
7.3	0.98	na	0.00	**5.1**	4.0	1.10	11.19	3.68	66.8	**0.7**	11.1	26.3	**6.4**
8.3	0.52	na	0.00	**9.7**	5.3	2.28	13.65	3.54	37.2	**3.2**	46.2	17.5	**9.6**
5.6	0.19	2.4	0.04	**8.4**	4.0	1.75	16.47	4.10	51.8	**0.4**	15.2	73.0	**8.2**
3.1	4.80	na	0.13	**3.6**	0.6	0.62	5.22	4.04	79.5	**3.1**	14.6	8.9	**6.6**
6.3	0.56	na	0.05	**5.4**	3.1	1.35	14.42	3.32	61.0	**1.7**	17.3	22.0	**6.3**
3.1	6.86	na	0.59	**3.1**	0.3	0.52	2.77	4.26	93.6	**1.8**	19.6	21.4	**7.0**
4.5	1.74	8.9	0.04	**5.5**	70.3	1.11	9.41	3.91	76.1	**3.6**	20.4	12.1	**9.2**
9.7	0.38	na	0.00	**3.0**	0.2	0.40	1.51	2.60	82.5	**0.5**	7.3	59.6	**7.9**
6.8	2.93	na	-0.21	**6.5**	2.2	1.37	4.54	3.86	62.4	**2.8**	37.2	20.8	**7.7**
8.6	0.07	na	-0.02	**3.8**	0.7	0.60	5.88	3.72	79.7	**2.6**	25.5	17.3	**5.7**
8.5	0.41	na	0.00	**1.7**	0.1	0.23	0.79	3.74	93.9	**0.7**	17.9	28.1	**5.2**

Name	City	State	Rating	2018 Rating	2017 Rating	Total Assets ($Mil)	One Year Asset Growth	Comm-ercial Loans	Cons-umer Loans	Mort-gage Loans	Secur-ities	Capital-ization Index	Lever-age Ratio	Risk-Based Capital Ratio
								Asset Mix (As a % of Total Assets)						
MutualBank	Muncie	IN	B-	B-	B-	2068.6	2.57	6.4	14.1	24.2	18.5	7.9	9.6	13.4
▲ MutualOne Bank	Framingham	MA	A-	B+	A-	983.3	13.99	19.3	0.6	15.5	5.8	10.0	16.9	20.3
MVB Bank, Inc.	Fairmont	WV	B+	B	B	1958.3	14.05	16.9	0.2	18.5	11.5	7.1	9.9	12.6
Nano Banc	Irvine	CA	C+	C+	B	910.4	98.91	29.2	0.0	3.5	0.8	6.3	9.5	12.0
▲ Nantahala Bank & Trust Co.	Franklin	NC	E+	E-	E-	162.2	4.11	3.4	1.1	23.4	11.7	6.5	8.5	12.1
Napoleon State Bank	Napoleon	IN	B+	B+	A-	273.0	10.90	8.2	7.5	21.3	5.6	10.0	11.4	15.2
Nashville Savings Bank	Nashville	IL	B	B	B	60.7	2.39	8.1	2.8	24.8	12.4	10.0	13.7	20.3
Natbank, N.A.	Hollywood	FL	B	B-	B-	177.5	7.02	0.8	1.5	77.3	1.6	10.0	17.7	31.1
National Advisors Trust Co.	Kansas City	MO	U	U	U	13.2	24.35	0.0	0.0	0.0	13.3	10.0	87.7	237.6
National Bank & Trust	La Grange	TX	B-	B-	B-	211.1	-14.62	1.1	4.7	26.3	50.9	10.0	11.8	28.6
▲ National Bank of Adams County	West Union	OH	B	B-	C+	82.1	1.70	1.9	3.2	26.4	20.4	10.0	12.0	28.7
National Bank of Andrews	Andrews	TX	C+	B-	B+	224.5	10.23	25.1	2.6	7.9	16.3	8.8	10.2	14.2
National Bank of Blacksburg	Blacksburg	VA	A	A	A	1269.3	1.16	3.3	2.7	12.9	26.3	10.0	14.6	23.4
National Bank of Commerce	Superior	WI	B-	B	B+	633.6	3.81	11.2	3.2	10.5	16.8	10.0	11.6	15.3
National Bank of Coxsackie	Coxsackie	NY	C	C	C	335.5	15.02	3.1	2.7	29.3	34.0	7.3	9.2	16.7
National Bank of Indianapolis	Indianapolis	IN	B	B	B-	2149.3	5.65	15.4	1.7	11.9	16.9	6.5	8.5	12.5
▲ National Bank of Malvern	Malvern	PA	B+	B	B+	151.6	2.31	0.7	0.3	21.3	16.7	10.0	15.5	22.3
National Bank of Middlebury	Middlebury	VT	B	B-	C+	382.9	7.42	5.4	2.3	37.5	19.5	7.7	9.4	15.4
National Bank of New York City	Flushing	NY	B	B+	A-	228.1	-2.21	0.9	0.0	19.2	2.1	10.0	17.5	22.4
National Bank of St. Anne	Saint Anne	IL	B-	B-	C+	74.8	30.90	5.9	4.5	13.7	2.8	8.8	10.3	14.0
National Bank of Texas at Fort Worth	Fort Worth	TX	B-	B	B	285.3	3.08	16.1	4.9	26.5	10.7	10.0	11.8	20.1
National Capital Bank of Washington	Washington	DC	B-	B	B+	514.3	14.20	5.2	0.1	29.1	19.2	8.3	9.8	15.9
National Cooperative Bank, N.A.	Hillsboro	OH	B-	B	B	2621.2	12.39	18.4	0.9	20.4	7.3	9.4	11.2	14.5
National Exchange Bank and Trust	Fond du Lac	WI	A	A	A	1943.1	4.31	11.8	1.3	6.1	27.4	10.0	20.7	26.7
National Grand Bank of Marblehead	Marblehead	MA	A-	A-	A-	340.2	4.14	1.2	0.5	66.9	17.5	10.0	11.6	21.9
National Iron Bank	Salisbury	CT	C	C	C	142.0	9.29	0.9	0.6	49.9	16.8	5.8	7.8	17.7
National United	Gatesville	TX	B-	B	B-	644.6	4.08	4.0	7.0	13.2	20.4	9.7	10.8	14.9
Nationwide Trust Co., FSB	Columbus	OH	U	U	C-	193.2	-96.39	0.0	0.0	0.0	58.5	10.0	19.6	45.8
Native American Bank, N.A.	Denver	CO	C-	C-	C	126.5	12.49	58.8	0.5	0.7	7.6	8.9	10.3	26.2
NBC Oklahoma	Oklahoma City	OK	B-	C+	C+	676.5	-2.13	19.6	0.8	11.8	9.6	6.3	8.4	12.0
NBH Bank	Greenwood Village	CO	B	B	C+	5982.4	7.32	23.5	0.4	14.5	14.2	5.5	8.8	11.4
▲ NBKC Bank	Kansas City	MO	B+	B+	A	814.3	24.91	3.4	2.2	38.5	16.6	10.0	12.5	15.1
NBT Bank, N.A.	Norwich	NY	B	B	B	9591.4	1.29	9.8	18.6	16.8	16.9	7.1	9.5	12.6
NBW Bank	Waupun	WI	A-	A-	B+	151.3	-0.26	9.8	4.2	13.3	11.9	4.1	7.7	10.5
Nebraska Bank of Commerce	Lincoln	NE	C	C	C	151.8	5.97	13.3	0.5	16.9	3.3	6.4	8.9	12.0
Nebraska State Bank	Bristow	NE	C	C	C+	18.2	3.56	10.8	2.3	1.5	0.0	10.0	15.6	25.6
▲ Nebraska State Bank	Lynch	NE	C	C-	D+	15.1	9.77	6.4	2.3	2.3	0.0	10.0	15.3	26.0
▲ Nebraska State Bank	Oshkosh	NE	A-	B+	A-	50.3	0.35	0.8	0.0	0.0	0.0	10.0	17.6	21.3
Nebraska State Bank and Trust Co.	Broken Bow	NE	B	B	B+	247.0	0.53	9.9	2.6	8.8	7.0	6.6	9.9	12.2
NebraskaLand National Bank	North Platte	NE	B	B	B	747.5	5.99	13.1	0.6	5.5	26.2	10.0	12.0	17.7
Needham Bank	Needham	MA	B-	B-	B-	2345.5	12.05	3.3	0.5	43.6	8.4	10.0	12.5	15.3
Neffs National Bank	Neffs	PA	A-	A-	A	370.4	1.53	1.8	2.5	22.0	49.8	10.0	18.5	37.0
Neighborhood National Bank	San Diego	CA	D	D+	C-	68.1	15.13	13.7	0.0	7.1	0.2	10.0	16.9	27.1
▲ Neighborhood National Bank	Mora	MN	A-	B+	B+	224.5	0.00	12.2	3.8	18.8	26.4	10.0	11.8	16.9
▼ Neighbors Bank	Clarence	MO	C-	C+	C-	31.1	19.71	1.7	1.1	8.8	13.5	10.0	13.5	24.4
▲ Nekoosa Port Edwards State Bank	Nekoosa	WI	A-	B+	B+	214.7	1.23	3.0	2.2	31.7	19.3	10.0	14.2	31.5
Nelsonville Home & Savings Bank	Nelsonville	OH	B-	B-	B-	30.7	4.85	0.0	3.2	53.2	4.3	10.0	12.3	28.1
Neuberger Berman Trust Co. of Delaware	Wilmington	DE	U	U	U	6.8	2.80	0.0	0.0	0.0	0.0	10.0	92.0	228.0
Neuberger Berman Trust Co., N.A.	New York	NY	U	U	U	26.8	1.71	0.0	0.0	0.0	0.0	10.0	46.1	124.0
Nevada Bank and Trust Co.	Caliente	NV	C+	C+	C+	142.4	11.04	6.0	4.9	3.4	50.6	8.7	10.1	22.1
New Albin Savings Bank	New Albin	IA	A	A	A+	255.2	9.57	2.3	1.0	10.7	69.9	10.0	17.7	56.2
▲ New Buffalo Savings Bank	New Buffalo	MI	C	C-	C	121.9	3.19	1.1	0.2	21.9	0.0	10.0	12.9	18.1
New Carlisle Federal Savings Bank	New Carlisle	OH	C+	C+	C+	130.3	12.83	7.6	1.7	38.7	2.1	8.4	9.9	13.8
▼ New Century Bank	Belleville	KS	B	B+	B+	59.7	20.11	2.1	2.7	34.0	0.2	6.5	9.5	12.1
New Covenant Trust Co., N.A.	Jeffersonville	IN	U	U	U	6.7	-4.73	0.0	0.0	0.0	21.6	10.0	88.9	294.2
New Era Bank	Fredericktown	MO	A-	A-	A-	350.6	0.85	4.9	1.2	27.1	15.7	9.2	10.5	15.8
▲ New Foundation Savings Bank	Cincinnati	OH	C+	C	C+	19.1	-1.76	4.6	0.3	64.2	1.9	10.0	11.6	21.1
▲ New Frontier Bank	Saint Charles	MO	C+	C	D+	97.5	19.13	8.0	0.2	8.8	12.9	6.1	9.2	11.9
New Haven Bank	New Haven	CT	C	C	C-	145.7	2.91	3.1	4.3	42.8	4.9	8.9	10.3	16.2
New Horizon Bank, N.A.	Powhatan	VA	C+	C+	C+	87.7	7.08	8.6	1.8	15.0	8.1	7.6	10.6	13.0

Asset Quality Index	Adjusted Non-Performing Loans as a % of Total Loans	Adjusted Non-Performing Loans as a % of Capital	Net Charge-Offs Avg Loans	Profitability Index	Net Income ($Mil)	Return on Assets (R.O.A.)	Return on Equity (R.O.E.)	Net Interest Spread	Overhead Efficiency Ratio	Liquidity Index	Liquidity Ratio	Hot Money Ratio	Stability Index
6.1	0.46	2.6	0.11	**4.7**	17.1	1.10	10.21	3.49	68.2	**2.0**	22.5	16.6	**8.8**
6.7	1.48	na	0.00	**9.0**	11.7	1.65	9.74	3.74	47.3	**0.9**	23.1	39.6	**9.0**
6.2	0.84	4.3	0.06	**8.2**	27.2	1.99	18.13	3.57	70.5	**2.0**	12.8	11.1	**8.9**
7.8	0.03	na	0.00	**2.0**	0.3	0.07	0.62	4.76	88.6	**5.7**	27.8	0.1	**6.5**
3.7	1.76	na	-0.05	**2.2**	0.3	0.30	4.33	3.81	90.8	**2.8**	21.2	15.7	**1.9**
7.2	0.48	na	0.25	**6.3**	2.1	1.08	9.56	4.23	62.7	**2.1**	17.2	17.5	**7.3**
8.6	0.00	na	0.01	**5.6**	0.5	1.12	8.53	3.27	55.0	**1.3**	12.8	26.5	**7.3**
8.9	0.74	na	0.00	**3.8**	0.7	0.59	3.30	4.18	82.2	**2.5**	18.4	11.0	**7.7**
8.7	na	na	na	**10.0**	1.1	13.27	14.93	1.91	89.2	**5.0**	326.4	100.0	**6.1**
9.3	0.08	na	0.02	**3.4**	1.3	0.73	7.04	2.15	67.4	**2.4**	32.9	21.4	**5.9**
4.7	0.84	na	0.00	**6.5**	1.0	1.64	14.02	3.90	55.3	**4.8**	34.0	8.4	**6.9**
1.8	4.24	na	0.00	**10.0**	5.0	3.06	28.82	4.96	57.3	**5.1**	31.0	5.7	**7.4**
8.1	0.80	2.7	0.09	**6.4**	13.1	1.40	9.59	3.30	55.2	**5.2**	25.0	5.5	**10.0**
5.6	1.28	na	0.01	**7.0**	7.2	1.57	12.71	4.19	62.0	**1.8**	19.9	8.9	**9.7**
7.1	0.84	4.3	-0.01	**3.1**	1.2	0.53	5.92	3.17	79.2	**4.7**	10.8	3.3	**4.0**
7.5	0.60	3.1	-0.01	**5.3**	18.1	1.12	13.32	3.28	63.7	**5.0**	23.5	6.0	**7.4**
5.3	2.37	na	0.00	**5.7**	1.4	1.24	7.98	3.66	59.4	**2.5**	20.7	16.4	**7.9**
7.0	0.71	4.7	0.08	**4.7**	2.9	1.03	11.04	3.90	70.0	**4.6**	16.5	4.6	**5.4**
7.5	0.00	na	0.01	**3.5**	1.0	0.58	3.27	2.65	75.8	**0.4**	12.3	54.9	**8.3**
7.5	0.10	na	0.00	**5.4**	0.4	0.88	7.01	4.06	69.5	**1.0**	25.5	45.8	**6.7**
8.4	0.32	na	0.31	**3.1**	1.0	0.48	4.32	3.90	78.5	**2.6**	32.3	19.3	**6.3**
9.1	0.07	na	0.00	**3.8**	2.1	0.56	5.92	3.53	79.2	**3.8**	23.2	10.7	**5.1**
6.6	0.77	4.2	-0.03	**4.0**	17.5	0.90	8.13	3.11	75.6	**3.6**	23.8	11.3	**8.6**
7.5	1.98	3.7	0.00	**8.9**	24.3	1.69	8.28	3.94	52.8	**6.2**	33.6	3.2	**9.7**
9.8	0.51	na	-0.01	**5.4**	2.5	1.02	8.59	3.19	61.6	**3.4**	23.6	13.0	**7.4**
9.7	0.00	na	0.01	**3.2**	0.7	0.72	9.09	3.12	78.3	**3.7**	33.2	14.0	**4.1**
5.5	0.84	na	0.03	**4.5**	4.4	0.93	8.76	4.17	70.8	**4.2**	29.7	10.8	**6.8**
10.0	na	na	na	**7.0**	17.5	10.38	43.16	-0.52	88.8	**8.3**	91.5	0.0	**3.8**
3.7	3.68	na	0.08	**2.3**	0.2	0.17	1.50	4.29	95.1	**0.1**	3.3	68.3	**6.8**
5.2	0.54	4.4	0.16	**5.2**	6.6	1.25	15.28	3.97	67.8	**2.7**	19.6	15.8	**5.8**
5.9	0.70	4.0	0.23	**6.6**	62.6	1.44	13.38	3.99	61.0	**3.8**	8.3	9.7	**8.8**
6.8	1.22	na	0.00	**8.6**	35.3	6.43	51.21	2.53	67.3	**1.0**	24.2	36.3	**9.5**
5.7	0.55	2.9	0.38	**6.1**	88.3	1.24	10.77	3.65	58.5	**4.0**	5.7	4.6	**9.2**
7.1	0.00	3.3	2.65	**3.3**	-0.6	-0.52	-4.51	4.67	76.0	**3.3**	22.2	13.3	**7.3**
7.4	0.04	na	0.00	**3.0**	0.5	0.49	5.56	3.00	78.7	**0.9**	15.0	33.8	**5.2**
7.4	0.00	na	0.00	**4.5**	0.1	0.99	6.51	4.06	73.8	**1.7**	45.0	26.9	**6.5**
7.3	0.00	na	-0.14	**4.1**	0.1	0.96	6.37	3.65	71.3	**4.5**	56.1	9.8	**5.8**
7.3	0.00	na	0.00	**10.0**	1.5	3.93	23.66	5.02	41.1	**2.4**	21.3	17.6	**9.5**
7.0	0.08	na	0.01	**7.3**	3.2	1.78	17.27	3.94	54.6	**1.1**	13.9	15.8	**7.4**
8.7	0.02	0.0	0.00	**4.2**	5.3	0.98	8.38	3.32	70.3	**1.0**	9.3	20.9	**7.9**
6.6	0.90	5.4	0.00	**3.9**	11.9	0.70	5.64	2.95	66.6	**0.8**	12.8	32.7	**8.9**
9.0	1.16	na	0.00	**5.7**	3.8	1.38	7.58	3.00	54.2	**4.0**	56.0	18.9	**8.7**
7.6	0.59	na	-0.05	**0.0**	-1.7	-3.49	-21.14	4.70	143.2	**2.3**	33.5	24.3	**5.7**
8.5	0.32	1.5	0.00	**5.3**	2.2	1.36	11.64	4.12	70.4	**3.8**	19.3	10.4	**7.5**
9.1	0.00	na	0.00	**0.3**	-0.2	-0.85	-5.69	3.18	110.4	**7.0**	64.3	1.9	**6.5**
8.3	1.70	na	-0.06	**6.1**	2.5	1.57	10.83	2.99	46.3	**2.7**	44.6	27.5	**8.3**
9.2	0.19	na	0.00	**4.9**	0.2	0.93	7.75	3.64	60.2	**2.3**	30.2	20.6	**6.6**
10.0	na	na	na	**10.0**	0.2	4.18	4.18	82.17	96.8	**4.0**	413.5	0.0	**5.8**
10.0	na	na	na	**10.0**	1.0	4.98	11.53	89.22	95.7	**4.0**	112.4	0.0	**7.0**
8.9	0.00	na	-0.02	**3.9**	0.8	0.81	7.95	3.76	75.0	**7.4**	60.4	1.0	**6.2**
9.7	0.05	na	-0.02	**6.0**	2.4	1.33	7.28	2.49	32.8	**4.3**	77.1	22.7	**9.4**
4.0	3.51	na	0.00	**3.6**	0.7	0.75	5.84	3.19	84.6	**0.9**	19.3	27.9	**6.4**
7.1	0.46	na	0.02	**4.0**	0.7	0.72	7.30	3.65	78.1	**1.2**	13.3	28.0	**5.6**
5.0	1.23	na	0.19	**9.0**	0.8	1.75	18.19	5.53	65.9	**0.6**	14.1	53.5	**7.2**
10.0	na	na	na	**10.0**	0.3	5.02	5.63	2.01	88.8	**4.0**	na	0.0	**5.8**
8.4	0.02	0.4	0.02	**8.4**	5.4	2.04	18.52	3.41	48.4	**3.3**	16.8	11.2	**8.6**
9.8	0.43	na	-0.08	**3.9**	0.0	0.77	6.58	3.60	94.2	**1.6**	14.3	22.1	**6.0**
2.5	5.47	na	-0.02	**4.3**	0.8	1.17	11.85	4.67	65.6	**3.0**	23.6	14.7	**5.8**
8.3	0.17	na	0.00	**3.0**	0.6	0.57	5.61	2.84	81.7	**0.6**	11.5	47.1	**5.4**
5.4	0.55	na	0.09	**3.3**	0.2	0.37	3.58	4.32	85.8	**0.7**	12.7	32.5	**6.1**

Name	City	State	Rating	2018 Rating	2017 Rating	Total Assets ($Mil)	One Year Asset Growth	Asset Mix (As a % of Total Assets) Commercial Loans	Consumer Loans	Mortgage Loans	Securities	Capitalization Index	Leverage Ratio	Risk-Based Capital Ratio
New Market Bank	Elko New Market	MN	**C+**	C+	C	119.5	6.70	8.1	0.9	9.3	22.8	**6.0**	8.0	13.6
New Mexico Bank & Trust	Albuquerque	NM	**A-**	A-	B	1607.5	9.73	13.1	0.5	6.0	27.4	**8.1**	9.8	13.5
▲ New Millennium Bank	Fort Lee	NJ	**C+**	C	C	448.6	24.77	11.5	0.0	12.0	0.7	**6.4**	8.4	13.5
New OMNI Bank, N.A.	Alhambra	CA	**A-**	A-	A-	482.7	5.20	0.2	0.2	34.8	5.6	**10.0**	14.5	24.5
New Peoples Bank, Inc.	Honaker	VA	**C**	C-	C	705.8	4.02	7.3	3.4	33.0	7.6	**7.8**	9.5	14.7
New Republic Savings Bank	Roanoke Rapids	NC	**C-**	C	B-	63.4	-5.22	3.7	0.5	49.2	0.0	**8.6**	10.1	16.1
▼ New Tripoli Bank	New Tripoli	PA	**B**	B+	A-	499.1	5.00	5.4	0.4	46.2	17.0	**9.9**	10.9	17.0
▲ New Washington State Bank	New Washington	IN	**B**	B-	B	339.8	4.66	12.7	12.1	15.8	11.1	**8.7**	10.2	13.9
▼ New York Community Bank	Westbury	NY	**B**	B+	B	52513.9	9.86	3.4	0.0	0.8	11.2	**7.8**	9.6	13.2
NewBank	Flushing	NY	**A-**	B+	A	447.9	19.41	23.1	0.0	0.2	0.2	**10.0**	11.5	19.3
Newburyport Five Cents Savings Bank	Newburyport	MA	**C+**	B-	B	1012.4	15.21	4.4	3.1	31.0	10.8	**10.0**	12.8	16.7
Newfield National Bank	Newfield	NJ	**C+**	C	C	688.2	5.25	6.9	0.4	19.5	27.1	**7.8**	9.5	17.2
NewFirst National Bank	El Campo	TX	**B**	B	B	727.6	3.09	9.4	0.7	8.6	6.1	**10.0**	11.5	16.2
Newport Federal Bank	Newport	TN	**B**	B	B	214.1	5.40	0.3	1.0	39.1	36.5	**10.0**	11.1	24.7
▼ Newton Federal Bank	Covington	GA	**C+**	B-	B-	310.3	0.74	8.6	8.3	38.6	1.3	**10.0**	20.1	29.2
Newtown Savings Bank	Newtown	CT	**C+**	C+	C+	1339.7	2.35	5.9	2.0	44.9	11.0	**6.3**	8.3	13.0
▼ NexBank SSB	Dallas	TX	**B+**	A-	B+	10157.5	25.81	5.1	0.1	44.9	20.1	**5.7**	7.7	12.2
NexTier Bank, N.A.	Butler	PA	**B+**	B	B	1396.1	8.02	7.5	8.6	24.0	7.7	**7.3**	10.4	12.8
Nicolet National Bank	Green Bay	WI	**B+**	B+	B+	3098.7	3.24	22.6	0.9	12.1	13.5	**4.7**	9.3	10.8
Ninnescah Valley Bank	Cunningham	KS	**B**	B	B	31.2	4.69	4.5	2.2	5.1	51.0	**10.0**	12.8	21.2
Noah Bank	Elkins Park	PA	**C-**	C	B-	444.3	6.33	9.5	0.0	0.5	1.0	**6.6**	8.6	15.5
NobleBank & Trust	Anniston	AL	**B**	B-	B-	266.8	3.93	12.0	1.9	12.7	24.2	**7.7**	9.5	14.3
Nodaway Valley Bank	Maryville	MO	**A-**	A-	A	911.6	6.65	6.4	0.9	6.7	21.2	**10.0**	12.9	18.0
▼ Nokomis Savings Bank	Nokomis	IL	**C**	C+	B-	28.7	9.63	18.3	5.0	15.4	29.9	**10.0**	17.2	71.0
Normangee State Bank	Normangee	TX	**C+**	C+	C	121.3	0.76	5.5	12.1	26.5	27.6	**10.0**	16.6	28.8
North Adams State Bank	Ursa	IL	**B-**	B-	B-	38.5	2.74	14.5	5.7	15.7	16.0	**10.0**	15.0	23.3
North Alabama Bank	Hazel Green	AL	**C+**	C+	B-	114.2	11.12	3.5	1.8	12.5	6.6	**9.0**	10.9	14.2
North American Banking Co.	Roseville	MN	**A-**	B+	B+	596.7	15.66	13.5	0.3	6.4	15.4	**7.8**	9.5	13.5
North American Savings Bank, F.S.B.	Kansas City	MO	**A-**	A-	A-	2592.4	26.63	0.4	0.1	74.6	5.0	**9.0**	10.4	14.4
North Arundel Savings Bank	Pasadena	MD	**C**	C	C	43.5	0.83	0.0	3.2	58.0	1.5	**10.0**	13.3	27.9
North Brookfield Savings Bank	North Brookfield	MA	**B-**	B-	B-	319.9	2.19	0.7	2.2	51.1	16.3	**10.0**	11.7	21.5
North Cambridge Co-operative Bank	Cambridge	MA	**C+**	C+	C+	91.6	2.89	0.0	0.2	54.1	17.8	**10.0**	22.1	49.6
North Central Bank	Hennepin	IL	**B**	B	B	124.9	0.80	7.5	4.3	17.2	30.6	**10.0**	12.8	20.1
North Country Savings Bank	Canton	NY	**B-**	B-	B-	264.8	2.64	0.1	3.1	72.6	0.7	**10.0**	15.9	24.8
North County Savings Bank	Red Bud	IL	**C+**	C+	C+	54.3	5.81	0.0	3.3	41.2	16.2	**7.1**	9.0	24.5
North Dallas Bank & Trust Co.	Dallas	TX	**B**	B	C+	1280.4	-1.45	3.9	0.6	19.8	39.3	**10.0**	12.4	27.5
North Easton Savings Bank	South Easton	MA	**C**	C	C	1135.3	105.25	4.2	3.3	41.4	12.7	**6.6**	8.6	13.6
North Georgia National Bank	Calhoun	GA	**B-**	B-	C+	122.8	-1.34	6.2	1.4	17.6	29.8	**10.0**	11.9	20.6
North Salem State Bank	North Salem	IN	**B**	B-	B-	365.6	10.06	6.6	4.2	16.7	7.9	**6.8**	9.0	12.4
North Shore Bank of Commerce	Duluth	MN	**B**	B	B-	288.1	4.81	3.0	0.5	31.2	12.5	**6.8**	8.8	15.6
North Shore Bank, a Co-operative Bank	Peabody	MA	**B-**	C+	C+	906.9	6.02	10.2	0.2	19.4	11.5	**9.9**	11.0	15.5
North Shore Bank, FSB	Brookfield	WI	**B**	B-	B-	2048.7	4.89	1.5	21.6	16.8	7.0	**10.0**	11.9	16.4
North Shore Trust and Savings	Waukegan	IL	**C**	C	C	224.5	1.71	0.0	0.0	39.4	30.5	**10.0**	20.0	57.4
▲ North Side Bank and Trust Co.	Cincinnati	OH	**A-**	B+	A-	715.2	14.58	21.2	1.0	11.9	16.1	**8.5**	12.7	13.7
North Side Federal S&L Assn. of Chicago	Chicago	IL	**D+**	D	D	39.7	-1.29	0.1	0.0	44.3	19.2	**10.0**	11.2	25.0
▲ North Star Bank	Roseville	MN	**B+**	B	B-	293.6	6.98	18.6	2.4	4.8	18.7	**8.9**	10.6	14.1
▲ North State Bank	Raleigh	NC	**B**	B-	B-	947.6	7.58	8.4	0.4	22.1	2.9	**5.5**	8.6	11.4
▲ North Valley Bank	Thornton	CO	**A**	A	A	177.9	4.44	1.1	0.1	40.3	0.0	**10.0**	12.1	18.0
North Valley Bank	Zanesville	OH	**B-**	B-	C+	208.7	-2.20	6.5	4.3	20.8	17.2	**9.7**	10.8	15.6
Northbrook Bank & Trust Co., N.A.	Northbrook	IL	**B**	B	B-	2872.6	25.47	29.7	7.3	3.8	12.4	**6.2**	9.5	11.9
▲ Northeast Bank	Lewiston	ME	**C+**			1123.1	-7.39	1.3	0.2	6.2	6.6	**10.0**	14.1	19.1
Northeast Bank	Minneapolis	MN	**A-**	A-	A-	510.2	10.11	22.0	0.2	7.9	14.7	**7.8**	10.8	13.2
▲ NorthEast Community Bank	White Plains	NY	**B-**	B-	B	1031.3	21.90	8.1	0.0	0.9	0.6	**8.8**	12.4	14.0
Northeast Georgia Bank	Lavonia	GA	**A-**	A-	B	460.4	1.08	4.4	6.9	6.7	22.9	**10.0**	12.3	20.9
Northeast Missouri State Bank	Kirksville	MO	**A-**	A-	A-	110.3	6.93	2.2	3.8	10.6	41.6	**10.0**	13.8	26.0
▲ Northeast Security Bank	Sumner	IA	**A-**	A-	A-	268.2	6.60	6.8	0.6	10.5	27.6	**10.0**	12.4	18.4
Northern Bank & Trust Co.	Woburn	MA	**B**	B-	B+	2148.4	0.28	33.4	0.0	12.2	2.4	**8.9**	11.9	14.1
▲ Northern California National Bank	Chico	CA	**B+**	B	B-	264.8	15.27	5.0	0.3	7.3	21.6	**7.6**	9.4	23.4
Northern Interstate Bank, N.A.	Norway	MI	**B**	B-	B	157.5	-1.23	7.2	3.9	26.6	28.8	**10.0**	11.4	21.0
▲ Northern Sky Bank	Crookston	MN	**C+**	C+	B-	77.1	9.16	9.4	1.9	14.8	19.0	**9.4**	10.6	17.5

Asset Quality Index	Adjusted Non-Performing Loans as a % of Total Loans	Adjusted Non-Performing Loans as a % of Capital	Net Charge-Offs Avg Loans	Profitability Index	Net Income ($Mil)	Return on Assets (R.O.A.)	Return on Equity (R.O.E.)	Net Interest Spread	Overhead Efficiency Ratio	Liquidity Index	Liquidity Ratio	Hot Money Ratio	Stability Index
5.3	2.18	na	0.00	**3.9**	0.6	0.65	8.12	4.59	81.2	**5.8**	34.9	1.8	**4.5**
8.2	0.22	1.3	0.02	**9.5**	21.9	1.91	18.50	4.22	50.6	**4.9**	22.9	5.7	**8.0**
5.4	0.54	na	0.06	**5.3**	3.3	0.98	11.71	3.19	61.7	**1.3**	32.3	60.0	**5.2**
9.1	0.00	na	0.00	**5.7**	3.5	1.02	6.98	3.97	63.7	**0.7**	23.4	73.8	**7.7**
4.6	1.41	8.4	0.35	**3.2**	2.2	0.42	4.40	3.96	84.2	**2.0**	14.9	19.0	**6.0**
6.1	0.72	na	0.03	**1.7**	-0.1	-0.11	-1.07	3.80	102.9	**0.4**	8.2	64.4	**5.1**
6.7	0.96	na	-0.03	**4.1**	3.5	0.94	8.37	3.17	66.0	**1.4**	4.3	23.3	**7.4**
6.2	0.53	na	0.07	**7.1**	4.1	1.63	16.12	4.54	66.3	**4.7**	20.5	4.6	**7.9**
6.0	0.15	0.8	0.05	**4.4**	319.8	0.82	5.99	2.09	47.1	**0.7**	11.1	24.7	**10.0**
8.0	0.22	na	1.51	**6.8**	3.5	1.11	9.74	3.79	49.7	**2.1**	44.7	46.7	**7.8**
8.7	0.23	na	-0.01	**2.3**	2.2	0.31	2.34	3.04	87.2	**1.8**	15.1	18.1	**8.4**
5.8	0.87	4.7	0.13	**3.5**	3.7	0.72	7.69	3.48	72.9	**5.3**	31.6	4.6	**5.9**
6.0	0.91	na	0.10	**10.0**	15.0	2.82	23.93	4.95	50.3	**5.1**	27.2	3.8	**9.1**
7.9	1.47	na	0.14	**4.1**	1.1	0.68	6.35	2.88	68.4	**1.2**	25.6	32.8	**6.4**
7.3	1.48	na	-0.07	**2.2**	0.5	0.20	1.01	4.20	96.1	**1.7**	15.6	21.0	**7.2**
5.4	1.74	11.5	0.18	**3.0**	4.4	0.45	5.66	3.25	80.8	**2.9**	15.3	14.7	**6.4**
9.0	0.12	1.7	0.02	**5.0**	48.4	0.77	9.77	2.02	43.1	**5.0**	11.0	2.2	**6.6**
6.2	0.47	3.4	0.00	**6.9**	15.2	1.56	14.47	4.16	57.4	**4.0**	10.3	8.4	**9.2**
6.9	0.43	2.1	0.03	**9.3**	42.2	1.84	14.17	4.31	56.4	**4.3**	16.2	6.9	**9.6**
7.0	19.52	na	0.00	**4.6**	0.3	1.09	8.63	4.05	68.9	**5.1**	47.1	10.6	**6.9**
2.6	2.44	na	1.43	**0.9**	-8.0	-2.48	-23.59	3.32	111.8	**0.8**	25.4	59.6	**4.3**
5.2	1.75	na	0.15	**2.3**	-0.1	-0.07	-0.66	4.26	73.2	**2.9**	30.6	17.1	**6.2**
8.0	0.07	na	0.07	**8.6**	14.2	2.11	15.39	4.13	56.5	**4.2**	24.6	8.8	**10.0**
8.2	0.40	1.5	0.08	**1.9**	0.0	0.10	0.55	2.53	90.3	**2.9**	38.9	20.8	**6.7**
2.6	4.20	na	2.07	**3.9**	0.5	0.57	3.49	4.76	55.3	**2.4**	31.6	20.1	**7.2**
8.0	0.14	na	0.00	**4.6**	0.2	0.88	5.80	4.22	70.6	**3.3**	27.7	14.6	**6.9**
5.8	2.09	na	-0.01	**5.8**	0.8	1.03	8.15	5.49	71.2	**1.0**	19.1	29.2	**7.5**
8.0	0.00	0.0	0.14	**9.2**	9.7	2.37	25.31	3.71	49.3	**3.3**	33.8	11.9	**7.6**
6.2	1.23	7.9	-0.09	**9.8**	35.6	1.99	18.88	3.67	57.8	**0.6**	7.9	28.7	**10.0**
6.5	0.80	2.3	0.23	**2.7**	0.1	0.18	1.35	4.06	87.3	**1.3**	29.4	37.6	**6.3**
8.3	0.75	3.5	0.01	**2.7**	0.8	0.35	3.00	3.06	88.0	**3.0**	21.5	14.8	**6.7**
9.2	1.08	na	0.00	**3.0**	0.3	0.48	2.03	2.82	77.1	**2.8**	49.2	28.1	**7.6**
6.4	1.40	na	-0.01	**4.6**	1.0	1.14	8.21	3.47	70.1	**4.5**	36.1	11.2	**8.5**
7.5	0.78	na	0.10	**3.4**	1.0	0.52	3.98	4.08	83.2	**4.5**	6.9	4.5	**6.9**
9.6	0.00	0.0	0.00	**3.0**	0.2	0.46	5.20	2.62	79.6	**2.8**	50.4	28.3	**4.2**
9.4	0.07	na	-0.06	**3.7**	6.9	0.71	5.88	2.67	69.2	**5.9**	50.6	10.4	**9.4**
7.6	0.83	na	0.03	**2.9**	2.8	0.44	4.70	3.54	84.9	**3.6**	18.8	12.1	**6.1**
8.1	1.83	na	-0.03	**3.4**	0.5	0.48	4.17	3.89	83.7	**3.5**	9.6	10.8	**7.0**
7.5	1.08	na	-0.01	**6.5**	3.6	1.35	15.54	4.32	60.5	**1.7**	13.2	19.3	**5.8**
6.7	0.62	3.4	0.00	**7.0**	3.6	1.74	19.72	4.81	73.7	**4.9**	24.0	4.2	**5.0**
6.8	0.47	na	0.01	**4.3**	4.9	0.74	6.69	3.70	70.8	**2.2**	19.2	18.3	**7.1**
6.2	0.39	2.1	0.00	**3.9**	9.1	0.60	4.79	3.66	79.9	**3.4**	14.6	12.1	**8.9**
9.9	1.88	na	-0.01	**2.1**	0.5	0.27	1.37	2.61	91.3	**4.4**	60.1	17.8	**7.0**
8.4	0.11	na	0.01	**7.4**	7.6	1.50	11.77	3.52	51.5	**2.3**	17.6	17.2	**8.4**
3.7	6.77	na	0.00	**1.1**	0.0	-0.11	-1.09	3.71	103.9	**5.1**	37.8	8.4	**5.1**
7.9	0.60	na	-0.01	**5.5**	2.8	1.34	12.99	4.00	64.1	**3.8**	28.9	12.5	**6.6**
7.3	0.12	na	-0.01	**6.0**	10.3	1.47	17.23	4.27	70.9	**4.7**	12.3	3.4	**6.7**
8.8	0.00	na	0.00	**10.0**	3.9	2.96	24.88	5.62	48.0	**3.4**	9.1	11.4	**9.0**
6.5	0.46	na	-0.11	**3.5**	1.0	0.66	6.21	4.10	83.9	**2.9**	13.1	12.6	**6.2**
5.6	0.77	5.2	0.02	**9.1**	31.9	1.63	16.34	3.47	41.3	**2.2**	24.5	13.9	**8.0**
4.0	3.25	na	0.08	**10.0**	16.1	1.82	13.15	5.72	56.4	**0.6**	7.7	41.4	**6.7**
5.7	0.35	2.8	-0.02	**7.7**	6.9	1.87	17.77	4.45	57.6	**4.5**	9.8	4.5	**8.2**
6.8	0.52	na	0.06	**7.8**	9.7	1.38	10.60	4.54	58.1	**1.2**	23.6	47.4	**9.0**
8.0	0.42	na	0.05	**7.0**	6.2	1.79	16.67	3.73	57.2	**3.9**	31.3	12.4	**7.4**
8.1	0.00	na	0.00	**6.0**	1.2	1.48	9.74	3.36	55.0	**3.6**	43.8	17.9	**9.1**
8.4	0.01	na	0.00	**5.4**	2.3	1.11	8.60	3.30	59.5	**3.2**	25.5	14.2	**7.8**
4.8	1.07	5.6	0.18	**9.6**	28.2	1.76	15.67	4.47	42.6	**0.9**	5.8	22.0	**9.8**
8.8	0.53	na	-0.01	**5.7**	2.3	1.16	12.78	3.20	49.7	**5.0**	44.5	7.3	**5.3**
7.3	1.82	na	0.05	**4.2**	1.0	0.83	7.16	3.95	74.8	**5.2**	39.4	8.5	**6.5**
7.9	0.00	na	0.00	**4.7**	0.4	1.83	15.58	3.42	44.5	**3.6**	30.2	13.8	**6.0**

Name	City	State	Rating	2018 Rating	2017 Rating	Total Assets ($Mil)	One Year Asset Growth	Asset Mix (As a % of Total Assets) Commercial Loans	Consumer Loans	Mortgage Loans	Securities	Capitalization Index	Leverage Ratio	Risk-Based Capital Ratio
▲ Northern State Bank	Ashland	WI	B	B-	B-	235.9	0.25	6.5	1.4	29.5	22.2	8.0	9.7	18.6
▲ Northern State Bank of Gonvick	Gonvick	MN	B	B-	C+	34.5	-6.95	3.4	5.2	5.7	58.9	10.0	19.1	102.4
▲ Northern State Bank of Thief River Falls	Thief River Falls	MN	B+	B-	B-	341.4	9.58	3.3	4.4	11.4	22.5	8.8	10.2	27.0
▲ Northern State Bank of Virginia	Virginia	MN	B-	C	C	74.5	6.13	13.0	3.1	31.1	7.4	7.6	9.4	14.4
Northern Trust Co.	Chicago	IL	B+	B	B	123824.3	-6.12	3.2	0.3	4.5	40.6	6.0	8.0	14.9
Northfield Bank	Woodbridge	NJ	B	B	B	4810.4	12.21	1.3	0.0	7.5	22.2	10.0	12.4	15.8
Northfield Savings Bank	Berlin	VT	B-	B-	B-	1053.8	3.85	7.4	0.2	43.3	14.1	10.0	11.8	17.3
▲ Northmark Bank	North Andover	MA	A-	B+	B+	365.7	1.64	5.8	0.3	41.8	7.3	10.0	13.0	20.0
Northpointe Bank	Grand Rapids	MI	B	B	C	2086.8	78.32	0.4	0.0	56.1	0.1	6.2	8.2	12.8
Northrim Bank	Anchorage	AK	B	B	B	1603.8	7.49	20.8	0.4	7.3	16.0	8.6	11.0	13.8
Northside Community Bank	Gurnee	IL	B	B-	B	240.8	9.36	3.4	0.6	7.7	1.0	10.0	22.9	27.5
▲ NorthStar Bank	Estherville	IA	A-	B+	A-	189.9	6.90	5.9	1.1	13.9	8.3	10.0	11.6	17.1
▲ Northstar Bank	Bad Axe	MI	C+	C-	C-	666.6	2.94	10.9	1.6	10.7	8.5	7.6	10.0	13.0
Northumberland National Bank	Northumberland	PA	C+	C+	C+	543.6	2.27	11.0	0.9	36.4	24.3	9.0	10.4	17.7
▲ Northview Bank	Sandstone	MN	B-	C+	B	325.2	3.17	7.1	4.0	23.0	14.8	10.0	11.9	16.3
Northway Bank	Berlin	NH	B-	C+	C+	895.6	-7.16	4.6	1.5	20.3	18.6	9.8	10.9	16.9
Northwest Bank	Spencer	IA	B+	B+	B+	1666.7	6.31	16.1	1.7	14.5	8.2	5.9	9.7	11.7
Northwest Bank	Boise	ID	A-	A-	A-	788.9	17.66	40.0	0.0	0.2	4.8	8.7	11.2	13.9
Northwest Bank	Warren	PA	B	B	B-	10724.9	11.12	5.9	10.4	35.8	7.7	9.6	11.3	14.7
Northwest Bank & Trust Co.	Davenport	IA	C+	B-	B	160.2	-2.14	15.1	0.8	13.3	6.7	8.1	10.9	13.4
▲ Northwest Bank of Rockford	Rockford	IL	B	B-	C+	285.9	4.72	20.9	3.0	11.0	13.3	7.3	9.7	12.7
Northwest Community Bank	Winsted	CT	B-	B-	C+	416.2	5.06	3.8	2.3	46.5	15.1	10.0	11.7	19.4
▲ Northwestern Bank	Orange City	IA	A-	B+	A-	220.5	1.59	4.2	1.0	8.5	9.2	10.0	15.5	18.0
▲ Northwestern Bank	Chippewa Falls	WI	A	A-	A-	448.8	1.76	17.1	0.8	7.4	16.6	9.5	11.1	14.5
Northwestern Bank, N.A.	Dilworth	MN	C+	C+	C+	146.4	10.96	15.5	3.4	8.9	9.8	7.3	10.0	12.7
Northwestern Mutual Wealth Mgmt Co.	Milwaukee	WI	U	U	U	313.0	5.21	0.0	0.0	0.0	95.8	10.0	61.9	218.9
Northwoods Bank of Minnesota	Park Rapids	MN	B-	B-	B	121.2	0.37	4.6	1.9	19.6	34.6	9.1	10.4	18.6
▲ Norway Savings Bank	Norway	ME	A	B+	B	1240.6	4.07	5.0	6.4	31.4	4.9	10.0	15.0	17.3
Norwood Co-operative Bank	Norwood	MA	B	B	B-	571.6	9.74	2.2	0.0	37.8	9.8	10.0	14.0	19.9
NSB Bank	Mason City	IA	A-	A-	A-	209.8	3.47	20.3	1.3	6.8	12.7	8.7	11.2	13.9
NVE Bank	Englewood	NJ	B	B	B-	662.0	2.60	0.1	0.1	39.0	12.2	10.0	16.3	27.1
NXT Bank	Central City	IA	B-	B-	C+	263.0	-0.32	10.0	0.3	13.8	9.3	10.0	11.5	15.4
O'Bannon Banking Co.	Buffalo	MO	B-	B-	B-	214.3	7.18	9.6	1.9	23.8	9.6	7.0	9.0	12.5
Oak Bank	Fitchburg	WI	B-	B+	A-	316.1	2.17	14.1	0.8	13.1	12.4	10.0	11.2	15.0
Oak Valley Community Bank	Oakdale	CA	B+	B+	B	1101.1	2.35	5.2	0.1	2.7	17.6	6.5	9.5	12.1
Oak View National Bank	Warrenton	VA	B-	C+	C+	255.6	6.13	9.7	2.2	36.3	1.0	7.5	9.4	13.9
Oakdale State Bank	Oakdale	IL	C+	C+	C+	21.0	4.72	6.5	3.9	26.6	3.1	10.0	12.4	17.9
▲ OakStar Bank	Springfield	MO	B-	C+	B	1013.2	11.33	14.0	1.7	20.6	1.8	8.3	10.1	13.6
Oakwood Bank	Dallas	TX	D	D+	C-	373.4	74.99	27.2	0.2	6.6	1.0	6.1	9.8	11.8
Oakwood Bank	Pigeon Falls	WI	C	C+	B	88.8	2.71	5.9	0.5	11.6	1.6	5.3	9.0	11.2
Oakworth Capital Bank	Birmingham	AL	A-	A-	A-	646.9	12.75	34.9	2.2	2.2	9.0	8.3	11.9	13.6
Ocean Bank	Miami	FL	B+	B+	B	4306.1	12.55	6.5	0.6	4.7	11.6	9.4	10.8	14.5
OceanFirst Bank, N.A.	Toms River	NJ	B	B	B-	8133.9	7.52	4.2	1.3	31.8	11.7	8.5	10.4	13.8
Oconee Federal S&L Assn.	Seneca	SC	B+	B+	A-	524.0	5.08	0.9	1.1	55.9	16.8	10.0	15.5	29.7
Oconee State Bank	Watkinsville	GA	C+	C+	C+	355.9	7.46	6.2	1.2	7.4	16.9	7.7	9.7	13.1
Odin State Bank	Odin	MN	D	D	D+	45.8	-0.37	9.0	7.0	12.0	10.3	9.5	10.7	14.7
Ohana Pacific Bank	Honolulu	HI	B	B	B	174.1	13.76	8.7	0.5	14.8	0.0	10.0	11.3	17.3
Ohio Valley Bank Co.	Gallipolis	OH	B-	C+	C+	1030.5	1.25	6.1	10.8	30.2	12.1	10.0	11.1	16.5
Ohnward Bank & Trust	Cascade	IA	A-	A-	B+	296.3	9.43	9.7	2.4	9.1	13.4	10.0	12.2	15.2
Oklahoma Bank and Trust Co.	Clinton	OK	A-	B+	A-	159.4	-2.22	3.0	0.8	9.0	49.3	10.0	15.3	36.4
Oklahoma Capital Bank	Tulsa	OK	B	B	C+	181.3	10.38	20.8	1.5	11.2	6.2	10.0	16.7	21.4
▲ Oklahoma Heritage Bank	Stratford	OK	C+	C-	D	85.6	12.15	8.5	5.4	28.9	13.0	9.2	10.5	17.4
▲ Oklahoma State Bank	Buffalo	OK	B+	B	B+	53.1	-1.96	7.0	11.3	5.2	25.9	10.0	11.1	16.6
Oklahoma State Bank	Guthrie	OK	C-	C-	C-	151.2	3.18	21.4	0.4	11.6	1.5	9.6	11.4	14.7
▲ Oklahoma State Bank	Vinita	OK	A-	B	B-	149.1	-3.90	9.1	2.7	24.1	8.8	10.0	12.0	18.3
Old Dominion National Bank	North Garden	VA	D	D	D	356.3	41.02	21.9	0.4	14.3	5.2	10.0	17.8	18.8
▲ Old Exchange National Bank of Okawville	Okawville	IL	B+	B-	B-	68.5	3.78	1.1	0.6	8.1	40.0	10.0	11.5	22.3
Old Fort Banking Co.	Old Fort	OH	B	B	B	561.5	5.20	10.5	0.6	13.6	24.1	6.3	8.3	13.9
Old Line Bank	Bowie	MD	B	B	B-	3095.4	5.65	9.5	1.2	12.8	8.7	6.3	10.7	12.0
Old Mission Bank	Sault Sainte Marie	MI	B	B	B	120.8	3.24	7.3	3.3	9.5	38.4	10.0	11.3	19.9

Asset Quality Index	Adjusted Non-Performing Loans as a % of Total Loans	Adjusted Non-Performing Loans as a % of Capital	Net Charge-Offs Avg Loans	Profitability Index	Net Income ($Mil)	Return on Assets (R.O.A.)	Return on Equity (R.O.E.)	Net Interest Spread	Overhead Efficiency Ratio	Liquidity Index	Liquidity Ratio	Hot Money Ratio	Stability Index
7.4	0.87	na	0.01	**6.4**	2.7	1.53	16.03	3.72	60.3	**4.7**	24.9	5.3	**6.1**
8.7	1.41	na	-0.03	**4.4**	0.3	1.09	6.09	2.70	57.9	**7.2**	87.8	5.3	**6.7**
7.4	0.36	na	-0.04	**5.6**	3.7	1.45	14.58	2.84	51.4	**6.6**	56.1	4.8	**6.9**
8.1	0.00	na	-0.02	**5.8**	0.8	1.39	12.01	4.87	70.5	**2.3**	15.6	17.8	**5.4**
9.4	0.45	1.4	-0.01	**6.1**	1100.8	1.26	15.03	1.57	67.4	**6.8**	43.6	2.3	**6.7**
6.3	0.71	3.3	-0.05	**4.5**	30.0	0.87	6.38	2.54	58.5	**1.8**	14.0	13.1	**9.6**
7.8	0.62	na	0.01	**3.3**	4.9	0.63	5.38	3.10	77.3	**1.8**	10.9	20.3	**8.8**
9.0	0.00	na	0.00	**5.7**	2.8	1.04	8.30	3.99	64.1	**1.1**	12.3	30.0	**7.8**
5.9	0.74	4.8	-0.01	**9.5**	23.4	1.86	23.05	2.52	78.2	**0.9**	9.0	23.8	**8.3**
4.9	1.67	na	-0.08	**7.7**	16.7	1.47	12.11	4.90	73.4	**4.5**	22.5	8.0	**10.0**
6.9	0.00	na	-3.08	**8.8**	5.0	2.81	12.02	4.07	62.7	**1.5**	13.9	20.9	**8.3**
7.8	0.00	na	0.00	**6.4**	2.0	1.44	10.74	3.42	57.8	**3.3**	24.4	13.6	**8.9**
3.8	2.49	na	-0.07	**7.4**	9.0	1.87	18.02	4.50	62.8	**3.1**	20.7	12.8	**8.2**
6.7	0.66	na	0.01	**3.4**	2.7	0.68	6.73	3.20	77.3	**2.8**	15.1	15.2	**6.5**
5.2	1.05	na	0.07	**8.4**	4.8	2.01	15.90	4.83	61.9	**3.1**	15.6	11.0	**8.6**
6.2	0.74	3.4	0.01	**4.7**	7.5	1.08	9.72	3.50	79.5	**3.9**	7.5	8.6	**6.5**
7.5	0.28	3.1	0.17	**6.7**	20.0	1.63	16.70	3.71	63.5	**1.5**	9.5	18.8	**8.8**
7.8	0.30	0.4	0.07	**8.9**	8.4	1.51	12.59	4.84	55.3	**1.8**	26.9	15.0	**9.0**
4.7	0.97	5.1	0.26	**5.7**	88.4	1.12	8.85	4.04	64.2	**4.3**	10.1	6.3	**9.3**
3.9	2.95	na	1.82	**6.3**	1.6	1.33	12.97	4.53	65.6	**4.1**	12.1	7.8	**6.9**
2.6	2.24	15.6	0.10	**4.2**	1.5	0.71	7.35	3.83	77.7	**1.6**	12.6	22.2	**6.6**
8.8	0.74	na	-0.01	**4.7**	3.1	1.00	8.63	2.93	71.8	**2.2**	22.8	16.8	**6.6**
5.4	2.35	na	-0.07	**10.0**	3.5	2.17	14.45	4.05	39.8	**2.9**	17.6	12.4	**9.3**
8.3	0.02	0.1	0.13	**8.5**	6.9	2.07	18.47	3.97	48.5	**4.6**	21.1	5.3	**9.2**
4.8	0.63	na	0.07	**3.3**	0.6	0.52	4.76	4.81	88.2	**2.3**	12.8	8.8	**6.4**
10.0	na	na	na	**10.0**	60.0	24.36	43.06	1.93	88.1	**5.0**	311.7	100.0	**7.0**
4.9	2.11	7.4	-0.02	**4.7**	1.0	1.11	10.24	3.94	71.4	**3.1**	30.4	16.1	**6.7**
8.1	0.21	1.1	0.02	**7.3**	15.0	1.65	10.95	4.29	71.6	**4.2**	11.9	7.5	**10.0**
8.5	0.20	0.9	0.00	**4.4**	3.6	0.86	6.23	3.30	64.5	**0.8**	12.7	27.8	**9.0**
7.4	0.44	1.6	-0.07	**9.4**	3.3	2.13	19.23	4.14	47.0	**3.2**	7.2	12.1	**8.4**
7.5	0.96	na	0.01	**4.2**	3.9	0.79	4.89	3.24	67.3	**3.6**	15.0	11.1	**8.8**
7.2	0.04	na	0.00	**4.0**	1.5	0.76	6.52	2.86	67.0	**1.0**	10.2	30.1	**7.0**
5.2	0.82	na	-0.05	**5.4**	1.7	1.04	11.86	4.12	64.9	**1.5**	12.4	23.0	**5.8**
5.4	0.55	na	0.01	**8.0**	3.6	1.53	13.79	3.87	51.7	**2.6**	19.2	10.9	**7.8**
7.5	0.16	1.0	0.00	**6.2**	9.7	1.22	12.47	4.19	61.5	**5.1**	18.6	2.7	**8.0**
8.8	0.01	0.1	0.01	**4.2**	1.5	0.82	8.84	3.52	72.4	**1.3**	12.8	27.1	**5.8**
6.1	1.15	na	0.00	**7.1**	0.2	1.23	10.09	4.84	61.4	**2.5**	24.4	17.2	**5.0**
6.2	1.55	na	0.15	**4.4**	6.4	0.88	7.89	3.75	74.1	**1.6**	8.0	15.9	**8.0**
8.2	0.00	na	0.03	**0.9**	0.4	0.19	1.68	3.15	84.4	**2.2**	28.1	20.9	**4.5**
4.7	3.43	na	0.00	**4.8**	0.7	1.13	7.98	3.96	66.2	**0.8**	14.2	37.0	**7.6**
8.2	0.00	na	0.03	**6.6**	6.0	1.29	11.08	3.76	64.6	**1.4**	16.3	26.7	**8.2**
5.3	1.20	5.0	-0.07	**4.7**	25.4	0.81	7.21	3.72	72.7	**1.2**	22.4	35.7	**9.5**
5.4	0.80	3.2	0.03	**5.4**	68.3	1.14	7.67	3.73	62.3	**4.2**	8.7	7.0	**8.9**
7.1	1.08	na	0.00	**4.2**	3.1	0.79	5.03	3.12	69.1	**1.6**	23.3	24.7	**9.1**
6.8	0.25	na	0.00	**3.9**	1.9	0.73	7.80	3.90	78.2	**2.9**	15.1	10.9	**5.5**
0.3	4.10	na	0.08	**4.2**	0.3	0.90	8.57	3.96	62.4	**1.2**	17.8	23.7	**4.8**
7.7	0.09	na	0.00	**4.5**	1.1	0.84	7.51	3.44	65.1	**0.9**	20.8	41.7	**7.2**
4.2	2.19	10.6	0.43	**4.1**	5.7	0.75	6.49	4.33	76.0	**2.5**	12.1	11.6	**8.9**
8.1	0.12	na	0.02	**5.7**	2.5	1.14	9.08	3.52	59.1	**1.5**	20.0	22.1	**8.6**
8.6	0.62	na	0.03	**5.8**	1.8	1.47	9.71	3.08	53.9	**2.0**	28.4	23.7	**8.8**
7.7	0.76	na	0.00	**4.3**	1.0	0.77	4.54	3.68	70.7	**0.9**	23.0	41.2	**5.7**
3.9	1.76	10.4	0.37	**3.5**	0.4	0.70	6.79	4.55	78.7	**0.9**	23.4	37.1	**3.7**
7.6	0.06	na	0.04	**10.0**	1.1	2.72	26.02	5.30	52.1	**1.9**	7.9	18.6	**7.1**
4.2	0.65	na	0.37	**1.8**	0.3	0.28	2.21	3.50	90.6	**0.9**	16.1	33.5	**4.5**
7.7	0.67	na	0.04	**7.5**	1.9	1.66	14.12	4.52	64.2	**0.7**	12.5	35.8	**8.9**
6.6	0.53	na	0.09	**0.0**	-0.8	-0.33	-1.71	3.37	108.5	**2.3**	11.7	16.4	**4.8**
9.2	0.60	na	0.00	**5.2**	0.7	1.32	11.27	3.29	58.4	**3.9**	57.4	18.5	**6.8**
8.6	0.37	na	0.01	**6.5**	6.8	1.66	20.78	3.45	57.4	**4.2**	26.0	8.8	**6.6**
6.0	0.39	2.2	0.02	**6.7**	29.0	1.28	9.27	3.54	51.9	**1.3**	7.3	26.0	**9.4**
5.6	2.23	na	0.06	**4.0**	0.7	0.84	7.33	3.81	79.7	**4.7**	50.5	14.0	**6.9**

Name	City	State	Rating	2018 Rating	2017 Rating	Total Assets ($Mil)	One Year Asset Growth	Asset Mix (As a % of Total Assets) Comm-ercial Loans	Cons-umer Loans	Mort-gage Loans	Secur-ities	Capital-ization Index	Lever-age Ratio	Risk-Based Capital Ratio
Old Missouri Bank	Springfield	MO	C+	C	C+	521.8	18.63	12.0	1.6	16.0	6.0	6.2	9.3	11.9
Old National Bank	Evansville	IN	B-	B-	C+	20333.0	16.39	11.3	5.2	12.8	26.1	7.9	9.6	13.5
Old Plank Trail Community Bank, N.A.	Mokena	IL	B	B	B-	1655.9	8.45	31.8	13.9	2.2	13.7	5.7	9.3	11.5
▲ Old Point National Bank of Phoebus	Hampton	VA	C+	C-	C	1044.3	2.40	6.4	13.6	12.5	13.4	7.4	9.7	12.9
Old Point Trust & Financial Services, N.A.	Newport News	VA	U	U	U	6.5	7.35	0.0	0.0	0.0	89.1	10.0	94.6	394.3
Old Second National Bank	Aurora	IL	A-	A-	A-	2611.1	0.51	15.9	0.2	8.4	18.7	10.0	12.7	15.7
▲ Olpe State Bank	Olpe	KS	B	B-	B-	41.1	-4.02	4.7	2.3	17.8	23.4	10.0	15.2	29.6
Olympia Federal S&L Assn.	Olympia	WA	B-	B-	B-	702.7	8.84	0.3	0.5	66.9	6.3	10.0	14.8	23.7
▲ OmniBank	Bay Springs	MS	D+	D-	D-	46.9	-2.78	7.5	7.6	25.1	10.4	7.7	9.5	14.7
ONB Bank	Rochester	MN	B	B	B	114.6	21.94	14.6	1.0	16.8	3.7	8.1	11.2	13.4
▲ One American Bank	Sioux Falls	SD	C	C	C	135.1	53.08	8.5	9.6	35.6	1.1	9.0	10.9	14.2
▼ One Florida Bank	Orlando	FL	C	B-	C	351.5	614.16	17.7	0.3	7.6	0.1	10.0	35.6	53.8
One South Bank	Blakely	GA	C+	C+	C	143.4	7.80	4.7	1.7	13.6	0.6	9.3	10.6	15.9
▲ One World Bank	Dallas	TX	B-	C+	C+	116.5	28.07	3.3	0.1	1.4	3.6	10.0	12.0	18.9
OneUnited Bank	Boston	MA	D	D-	D-	650.2	0.18	0.0	0.4	4.9	13.9	4.0	6.0	11.8
Oostburg State Bank	Oostburg	WI	B	B	B	239.6	7.68	14.7	0.7	18.4	20.2	10.0	14.0	18.6
▲ Open Bank	Los Angeles	CA	A-	B+	A-	1151.6	11.27	10.1	0.3	10.7	4.5	10.0	11.8	15.0
Opportunity Bank of Montana	Helena	MT	B-	B	B	1012.3	21.98	7.2	1.9	14.2	12.5	10.0	11.2	15.7
▼ OptimumBank	Plantation	FL	C-	C	D+	118.5	22.17	4.0	3.8	22.6	10.4	7.2	9.8	12.7
▲ Optum Bank, Inc.	Salt Lake City	UT	A+	A	A	10664.1	20.25	2.4	0.0	0.0	77.5	10.0	11.0	21.5
▲ Optus Bank	Columbia	SC	C-	D	D-	72.0	20.53	23.9	0.5	7.9	13.9	8.6	10.1	16.5
▲ Opus Bank	Irvine	CA	B-	C+	C	7771.3	5.09	7.4	0.0	0.7	13.0	8.1	9.7	15.3
Orange Bank & Trust Co.	Middletown	NY	B-	C+	C-	1235.4	16.40	17.8	0.1	7.3	20.9	6.9	9.0	13.4
▲ Oregon Coast Bank	Newport	OR	A-	B+	B+	248.6	4.89	3.9	1.2	11.4	40.9	10.0	11.6	18.3
▲ Oregon Community Bank	Oregon	WI	A-	B+	A-	524.5	15.10	5.4	0.4	16.2	6.5	10.0	14.5	15.4
▲ Oregon Pacific Banking Co.	Florence	OR	B+	B	B	360.2	19.03	17.4	0.3	10.3	7.5	10.0	11.1	15.7
▲ Oriental Bank	San Juan	PR	C-	D+	D+	6284.7	-4.83	10.9	26.3	17.8	8.3	10.0	14.8	20.8
Origin Bank	Choudrant	LA	B	B-	C	5365.9	15.78	23.1	0.4	9.9	9.7	6.4	10.5	12.1
Oritani Bank	Township of Washing	NJ	A-	A-	A-	3988.7	-2.95	0.5	0.0	6.5	8.9	9.8	12.4	14.8
Ormsby State Bank	Ormsby	MN	B+	B+	B+	26.5	3.75	4.2	6.4	2.1	27.7	10.0	15.7	32.4
Orrstown Bank	Shippensburg	PA	B-	B-	C+	2311.4	34.51	7.4	1.7	21.5	20.8	6.9	8.9	13.7
▲ Osgood State Bank	Osgood	OH	B+	B	B	264.3	7.78	24.8	2.1	8.7	23.0	8.1	10.3	13.4
Ossian State Bank	Ossian	IN	B	C+	C+	107.0	0.30	7.5	1.2	6.5	15.2	8.7	10.2	16.1
Ottawa Savings Bank	Ottawa	IL	B	B	B	304.0	9.64	7.4	11.8	42.3	7.9	10.0	15.1	21.6
Ottoville Bank Co.	Ottoville	OH	A-	A-	A-	78.4	-4.38	5.9	0.5	13.1	28.2	10.0	21.5	34.2
Our Community Bank	Spencer	IN	C+	C	B-	72.3	-1.42	0.0	0.8	60.9	11.6	10.0	11.6	19.7
Owen County State Bank	Spencer	IN	B-	B-	B	235.3	11.47	6.1	3.7	30.8	12.5	7.7	9.5	15.3
Owingsville Banking Co.	Owingsville	KY	C-	D+	C-	69.8	0.12	1.5	5.6	37.7	19.7	8.1	9.7	17.2
▲ Oxford Bank	Oxford	MI	B-	C+	C	476.8	9.00	12.9	1.0	8.3	11.0	7.7	9.5	13.3
▲ Oxford Bank & Trust	Oak Brook	IL	C	C-	C-	583.2	6.67	2.6	13.9	6.0	27.6	7.9	9.6	13.9
Oxford University Bank	Oxford	MS	B	B	B-	163.7	7.39	7.1	4.8	31.9	13.4	8.8	10.2	15.3
▲ Ozark Bank	Ozark	MO	B	B-	B-	239.8	0.89	5.2	0.9	25.1	17.5	9.7	10.8	16.1
Ozarks Federal S&L Assn.	Farmington	MO	B-	B-	B-	251.3	1.40	0.0	0.2	66.0	4.1	10.0	14.8	21.9
Ozona National Bank	Ozona	TX	B-	B	B-	273.2	5.80	4.6	1.0	11.8	31.6	10.0	11.0	23.3
Pacific Alliance Bank	Rosemead	CA	B+	B+	B+	276.8	1.55	12.5	0.0	11.5	10.4	10.0	13.5	18.9
Pacific City Bank	Los Angeles	CA	A	A	A-	1699.4	2.14	13.0	1.4	14.8	9.2	10.0	12.7	17.1
Pacific Coast Bankers' Bank	Walnut Creek	CA	B+	B+	B	879.9	11.60	2.0	0.0	0.1	13.0	7.8	9.5	16.7
▲ Pacific Crest Savings Bank	Lynnwood	WA	B+	B-	B	225.5	0.34	0.0	0.1	17.2	9.0	10.0	11.7	17.1
▼ Pacific Enterprise Bank	Irvine	CA	B	B+	B+	486.7	-5.29	14.9	0.0	3.2	0.0	9.3	10.5	15.0
Pacific Global Bank	Chicago	IL	A-	A-	A-	224.5	12.42	0.8	0.0	63.2	7.2	10.0	11.3	23.3
▼ Pacific Mercantile Bank	Costa Mesa	CA	B-	B	C	1437.7	8.97	30.0	6.5	3.4	1.7	7.8	10.9	13.2
Pacific National Bank	Miami	FL	B-	B-	B	586.1	29.62	8.2	0.2	13.5	17.5	10.0	12.3	17.4
Pacific Premier Bank	Irvine	CA	A-	A-	A-	11811.5	2.69	14.1	0.3	2.2	11.0	8.1	12.2	13.4
▲ Pacific Valley Bank	Salinas	CA	B-	C+	B-	340.4	20.94	10.8	0.4	4.0	0.0	9.6	10.7	14.9
Pacific West Bank	West Linn	OR	C	C+	C+	104.2	59.67	6.7	0.5	12.0	6.6	10.0	33.7	45.0
Pacific Western Bank	Beverly Hills	CA	B+	B	B-	26682.7	7.82	15.9	1.5	0.5	14.3	5.7	10.7	11.5
▼ Paducah Bank and Trust Co.	Paducah	KY	A-	A	A	713.2	11.58	11.1	1.5	22.0	15.5	9.6	10.9	14.7
Palmetto State Bank	Hampton	SC	A-	B+	A	549.7	-1.85	4.4	2.7	8.6	58.4	10.0	17.1	38.0
Palo Savings Bank	Palo	IA	B	B+	A-	38.6	23.00	1.4	2.8	27.3	31.8	10.0	12.4	24.5
Pan American Bank & Trust	Melrose Park	IL	C	C	C	378.6	4.54	7.4	0.2	19.5	15.6	6.8	8.8	12.6

Asset Quality Index	Adjusted Non-Performing Loans as a % of Total Loans	Adjusted Non-Performing Loans as a % of Capital	Net Charge-Offs Avg Loans	Profitability Index	Net Income ($Mil)	Return on Assets (R.O.A.)	Return on Equity (R.O.E.)	Net Interest Spread	Overhead Efficiency Ratio	Liquidity Index	Liquidity Ratio	Hot Money Ratio	Stability Index
5.4	0.31	na	0.23	**4.7**	3.3	0.89	9.34	3.59	61.1	**0.6**	6.6	43.4	**6.5**
4.2	1.22	4.3	0.02	**6.2**	198.3	1.33	9.20	3.63	59.9	**4.3**	20.8	7.7	**10.0**
6.5	0.37	2.9	0.05	**5.4**	13.6	1.13	11.10	3.39	61.2	**3.2**	12.7	11.5	**8.1**
4.3	1.19	7.5	0.09	**3.6**	5.8	0.75	7.65	3.65	77.6	**2.9**	17.5	15.3	**7.3**
10.0	na	na	na	**10.0**	0.5	11.32	11.94	2.22	81.6	**4.0**	na	0.0	**5.0**
6.4	0.80	3.8	0.05	**9.0**	35.3	1.80	14.10	4.22	55.9	**3.8**	9.5	9.8	**10.0**
9.0	0.00	na	0.00	**5.1**	0.4	1.29	8.95	3.17	61.3	**3.7**	41.6	16.9	**7.2**
9.0	0.41	na	0.00	**3.5**	2.8	0.55	3.69	3.59	80.0	**1.5**	10.4	23.3	**8.4**
4.4	1.17	7.4	-0.57	**1.6**	0.1	0.18	1.81	4.82	99.1	**3.9**	22.5	10.0	**3.9**
7.9	0.00	na	0.07	**5.4**	1.0	1.27	10.82	4.14	68.8	**1.1**	16.7	29.9	**6.9**
4.1	0.55	3.4	3.76	**4.2**	0.8	0.99	6.98	15.06	85.2	**2.1**	9.7	16.3	**5.6**
7.3	0.23	na	0.00	**0.8**	-3.6	-2.47	-6.41	2.83	158.2	**4.4**	57.6	17.5	**7.3**
4.6	0.97	na	0.35	**3.6**	0.7	0.70	6.82	4.54	79.2	**1.4**	19.6	26.9	**5.6**
5.2	1.18	na	-0.14	**3.7**	0.7	0.82	6.30	3.73	83.9	**2.2**	46.4	46.1	**7.6**
3.1	1.16	10.6	-0.03	**1.0**	0.7	0.14	2.13	1.85	119.8	**0.6**	12.5	50.7	**3.5**
7.7	1.20	na	0.00	**6.1**	2.2	1.28	9.12	4.03	64.9	**3.5**	26.9	10.4	**8.0**
7.1	0.16	na	0.10	**8.7**	13.2	1.62	13.30	4.24	57.0	**0.8**	14.3	34.3	**9.7**
6.8	0.48	na	0.07	**7.0**	10.6	1.44	11.49	4.52	67.0	**2.1**	13.5	16.8	**8.3**
3.3	1.83	9.8	0.30	**2.0**	-0.2	-0.19	-1.89	3.16	106.2	**1.7**	18.6	22.5	**6.4**
8.6	0.13	0.1	0.02	**9.8**	212.5	2.74	21.08	2.90	29.4	**8.6**	99.2	0.0	**10.0**
4.5	2.53	7.7	-0.14	**3.2**	0.4	0.74	7.26	4.06	85.2	**0.8**	24.4	55.1	**2.7**
5.4	0.13	0.7	0.17	**4.0**	41.6	0.73	5.24	2.94	70.5	**3.7**	19.4	11.2	**7.8**
6.0	1.56	7.2	0.00	**4.6**	8.4	0.97	11.38	3.95	66.5	**4.4**	12.7	5.8	**6.5**
6.9	1.19	na	0.05	**5.5**	2.5	1.36	11.98	3.83	65.1	**4.2**	38.8	13.5	**8.0**
7.3	0.25	na	0.00	**9.9**	7.6	2.09	14.31	4.08	41.7	**3.8**	8.0	7.4	**9.6**
5.7	1.01	na	-0.05	**5.3**	2.7	1.05	9.23	4.43	72.4	**4.9**	18.9	3.5	**6.4**
1.6	4.15	17.7	1.75	**6.2**	56.2	1.16	7.42	5.41	49.3	**1.9**	19.6	15.8	**8.8**
5.7	0.82	5.5	0.10	**5.1**	41.3	1.10	10.13	3.68	63.3	**1.6**	12.9	15.1	**8.2**
7.3	0.18	1.2	0.00	**6.6**	37.3	1.22	10.20	2.55	36.7	**0.7**	9.8	26.2	**10.0**
8.5	1.87	na	-0.04	**5.1**	0.3	1.32	8.57	3.06	58.2	**2.8**	64.5	30.7	**8.2**
7.0	0.52	4.2	0.01	**4.3**	16.4	1.00	10.53	3.51	78.0	**2.8**	17.9	14.1	**8.3**
8.2	0.29	na	-0.02	**5.3**	2.2	1.15	10.81	4.08	66.3	**3.4**	23.1	13.0	**6.4**
6.2	0.91	4.7	-0.01	**5.0**	1.0	1.22	12.53	3.67	69.6	**5.8**	40.9	4.8	**6.3**
6.5	0.86	na	0.14	**4.1**	1.4	0.65	4.20	3.60	72.9	**1.2**	16.4	28.8	**7.0**
8.9	0.00	na	0.08	**6.0**	0.8	1.31	6.20	3.86	55.5	**2.5**	25.6	17.6	**8.5**
6.1	2.42	na	0.13	**3.3**	0.4	0.65	5.61	4.03	84.4	**1.7**	15.8	21.3	**5.7**
5.3	0.81	na	0.13	**4.7**	1.5	0.88	9.25	3.90	72.4	**2.9**	25.6	15.5	**5.9**
4.7	1.47	13.2	0.37	**3.0**	0.2	0.34	5.18	4.28	83.0	**1.3**	19.5	28.8	**2.6**
6.4	1.68	na	0.00	**5.2**	3.7	1.08	11.52	4.21	70.0	**4.9**	20.7	3.4	**6.3**
3.2	2.00	na	0.07	**4.7**	5.1	1.18	12.07	4.37	71.9	**2.4**	20.2	14.5	**6.7**
7.2	0.14	2.4	0.12	**4.6**	1.1	0.88	8.61	3.67	68.8	**0.9**	19.5	35.5	**5.9**
8.9	0.00	na	-0.04	**4.6**	2.0	1.10	10.54	3.59	69.6	**1.9**	6.8	18.5	**6.5**
7.7	0.89	4.4	0.01	**3.1**	0.9	0.49	3.55	2.80	79.4	**1.6**	9.8	21.5	**7.4**
7.1	1.65	na	-0.26	**5.9**	2.8	1.41	12.81	4.46	71.9	**6.4**	52.7	5.1	**7.3**
7.5	0.00	na	0.00	**5.1**	1.8	0.87	6.49	2.99	64.8	**1.0**	28.4	65.6	**8.0**
7.2	0.18	0.9	0.03	**9.3**	20.4	1.58	12.51	4.15	51.8	**0.7**	12.1	41.8	**9.8**
8.8	0.00	0.0	-0.01	**6.0**	7.9	1.22	13.38	2.37	70.0	**4.8**	29.8	1.8	**7.0**
7.1	0.60	na	-0.02	**5.8**	2.4	1.43	12.37	3.46	57.1	**1.1**	26.6	27.1	**8.1**
5.2	0.29	na	0.03	**4.5**	2.6	0.72	6.78	5.20	80.9	**0.9**	23.2	36.5	**6.8**
9.0	0.12	na	-0.27	**7.8**	2.3	1.38	12.50	3.78	61.0	**1.4**	24.3	26.1	**7.3**
5.8	1.13	na	0.84	**4.0**	6.6	0.62	5.65	3.66	64.6	**2.0**	17.9	19.5	**8.3**
8.7	0.00	0.0	0.00	**3.0**	1.7	0.42	3.22	3.04	74.5	**1.2**	27.9	38.7	**7.6**
5.8	0.09	0.3	0.08	**7.7**	127.1	1.47	7.95	4.50	51.8	**3.3**	16.4	9.3	**9.9**
5.3	0.44	na	-0.01	**4.8**	2.0	0.85	7.87	3.91	69.9	**3.4**	27.1	13.9	**6.6**
8.9	0.19	na	0.00	**0.2**	-0.6	-0.82	-2.23	4.03	123.4	**3.9**	50.2	18.0	**6.9**
5.9	0.62	1.7	0.12	**10.0**	369.2	1.90	9.66	4.74	41.9	**3.0**	18.9	5.6	**10.0**
6.4	0.58	3.0	0.13	**6.2**	7.4	1.46	12.66	3.63	66.3	**1.4**	13.9	9.3	**9.2**
8.3	2.70	na	-0.20	**6.5**	5.2	1.25	7.56	3.47	54.1	**5.7**	61.0	11.5	**9.4**
9.2	0.36	na	0.00	**4.3**	0.2	0.86	6.71	3.49	72.3	**2.7**	48.9	27.6	**7.9**
6.7	0.04	na	0.30	**3.1**	1.9	0.69	7.74	3.61	81.3	**1.0**	25.2	36.0	**4.7**

Name	City	State	Rating	2018 Rating	2017 Rating	Total Assets ($Mil)	One Year Asset Growth	Asset Mix (As a % of Total Assets) Comm-ercial Loans	Cons-umer Loans	Mort-gage Loans	Secur-ities	Capital-ization Index	Lever-age Ratio	Risk-Based Capital Ratio
Panola National Bank	Carthage	TX	**B-**	B-	C+	115.2	0.63	3.1	5.6	29.2	41.1	**5.4**	11.0	11.3
Paper City Savings Assn.	Wisconsin Rapids	WI	**B+**	B	B	167.6	6.10	0.0	2.6	53.6	1.2	**10.0**	14.3	20.6
Paradise Bank	Boca Raton	FL	**A**	A	A	318.8	2.57	8.7	0.4	13.4	11.4	**10.0**	11.0	16.7
Paragon Bank	Memphis	TN	**B-**	B-	C+	413.5	4.78	17.4	4.1	17.8	11.7	**9.8**	11.0	14.9
Paramount Bank	Saint Louis	MO	**D+**	C-	D-	126.7	282.10	1.4	1.7	66.6	0.0	**8.2**	9.8	14.8
Park Bank	Holmen	WI	**B-**	B-	B-	57.3	2.27	6.0	4.1	22.1	23.0	**10.0**	15.9	27.3
Park Bank	Madison	WI	**C+**	B-	B-	1044.4	8.56	12.3	0.6	17.4	8.3	**7.0**	10.6	12.5
Park Bank	Milwaukee	WI	**B+**	A-	A-	1011.8	7.15	27.6	0.9	1.4	14.5	**10.0**	11.9	15.3
Park National Bank	Newark	OH	**C+**	C+	C+	8680.8	12.63	8.9	16.2	17.5	14.5	**6.5**	8.5	12.4
▲ Park Ridge Community Bank	Park Ridge	IL	**A-**	A-	A	320.6	-0.92	2.6	0.0	13.0	26.4	**10.0**	14.1	21.2
▲ Park State Bank	Duluth	MN	**B-**	B-	B	139.2	-4.36	24.1	2.3	24.9	2.4	**10.0**	13.1	15.5
Park State Bank & Trust	Woodland Park	CO	**B-**	C+	C+	102.8	-0.11	1.3	1.1	24.2	10.8	**9.2**	10.4	15.1
Parke Bank	Sewell	NJ	**A-**	A-	B-	1598.1	19.12	1.5	0.8	37.6	1.9	**10.0**	11.6	16.4
▲ Parkside Financial Bank & Trust	Clayton	MO	**B+**	B	B	526.9	8.56	41.9	0.1	2.8	6.5	**8.0**	11.1	13.4
Parkway Bank and Trust Co.	Harwood Heights	IL	**B-**	B-	B	2620.9	-1.47	8.4	0.1	1.6	9.9	**9.5**	11.5	14.5
Partners Bank	Helena	AR	**C+**	C+	B-	205.2	22.80	13.1	0.8	2.8	28.9	**10.0**	13.7	20.0
▲ Partners Bank	Spencer	WI	**B+**	B	B	214.5	1.14	13.4	2.1	16.0	22.5	**10.0**	14.0	20.0
Partners Bank of California	Mission Viejo	CA	**B**	B	B-	284.7	18.86	14.9	0.1	7.8	2.1	**9.0**	12.1	14.2
Partners Bank of New England	Sanford	ME	**B**	B-	B-	586.1	0.03	6.3	0.9	40.4	5.0	**10.0**	12.5	16.4
▲ Passumpsic Bank	Saint Johnsbury	VT	**C**	C-	C-	678.8	5.20	4.3	11.2	40.7	5.8	**9.4**	10.6	15.3
Pataskala Banking Co.	Pataskala	OH	**D**	D	D	33.7	4.05	1.6	4.0	32.0	18.6	**5.7**	7.7	14.5
Pathfinder Bank	Oswego	NY	**U**	U		1052.3	14.31	14.3	4.6	23.7	22.4	**5.8**	7.8	12.1
Pathway Bank	Cairo	NE	**C-**	C-	C+	171.0	3.21	7.0	1.4	4.4	8.3	**8.0**	10.8	13.4
Patriot Bank	Millington	TN	**B**	B	B	361.8	8.70	3.5	1.8	12.5	43.3	**7.6**	9.4	13.8
Patriot Bank, N.A.	Stamford	CT	**D+**	D+	C+	972.2	6.20	18.1	6.3	19.3	5.2	**6.1**	9.5	11.8
Patriot Community Bank	Woburn	MA	**B+**	B+	B+	187.2	9.29	3.7	0.0	15.8	0.0	**10.0**	13.8	21.3
▲ Patriots Bank	Garnett	KS	**B-**	C+	C+	125.8	3.48	5.7	2.3	15.3	14.9	**8.5**	10.0	13.9
Patterson State Bank	Patterson	LA	**B**	B	B	227.0	2.67	4.5	2.2	41.6	24.5	**9.3**	10.5	19.5
▲ Pauls Valley National Bank	Pauls Valley	OK	**B-**	C+	B-	245.9	0.56	16.4	10.2	4.7	30.7	**9.2**	10.5	15.0
Pavillion Bank	Richardson	TX	**B**	B	B	75.6	-2.03	6.8	1.1	18.4	12.5	**10.0**	13.3	20.9
Payne County Bank	Perkins	OK	**A**	A	A	172.0	6.82	8.9	6.6	23.1	26.3	**10.0**	18.5	28.7
▲ PBK Bank, Inc.	Stanford	KY	**B+**	B+	B+	117.7	0.73	0.9	6.0	24.3	7.5	**10.0**	13.2	22.7
PCSB Bank	Clarinda	IA	**C+**	B-	B-	253.9	9.62	10.0	3.7	8.7	20.6	**9.2**	10.5	14.7
PCSB Bank	Yorktown Heights	NY	**B-**	B-	C+	1655.5	12.36	4.5	0.0	16.1	23.1	**10.0**	12.9	17.6
▲ Peach State Bank & Trust	Gainesville	GA	**B+**	B	B-	263.4	14.70	9.1	3.2	14.4	11.5	**10.0**	11.4	15.7
Peapack-Gladstone Bank	Bedminster	NJ	**B+**	B+	B	4920.8	11.02	14.2	0.8	12.1	7.1	**9.1**	11.1	14.2
▲ Pearland State Bank	Pearland	TX	**A-**	B+	B+	188.6	4.50	3.2	0.7	4.4	68.9	**10.0**	11.5	32.4
Pecos County State Bank	Fort Stockton	TX	**B**	B	B	262.0	7.94	6.4	4.6	9.1	52.7	**6.7**	8.7	17.5
▲ Pedestal Bank	Houma	LA	**A-**	B	B	1240.4	2.18	18.7	2.4	15.2	22.2	**10.0**	11.7	17.0
▲ Pee Dee Federal Savings Bank	Marion	SC	**C-**	D+	D	36.4	3.21	12.0	6.2	6.4	46.5	**10.0**	18.0	43.4
Pegasus Bank	Dallas	TX	**B+**	B-	B-	726.3	10.46	22.0	3.7	10.0	5.6	**5.7**	7.7	13.4
▲ Pendleton Community Bank, Inc.	Franklin	WV	**B**	B	B+	339.4	9.21	5.8	3.4	27.9	9.2	**10.0**	14.2	19.1
Penn Community Bank	Doylestown	PA	**B-**	B-	B-	2299.4	9.69	3.7	0.2	34.5	21.5	**10.0**	12.3	17.5
PennCrest BANK	Altoona	PA	**B-**	B-	B-	182.8	0.72	0.2	7.6	52.6	23.5	**10.0**	16.1	28.7
Pennian Bank	Mifflintown	PA	**B-**	B	B-	536.4	5.56	9.6	0.2	23.2	26.2	**8.3**	9.9	17.9
Pennsville National Bank	Pennsville	NJ	**C**	C	C	202.8	2.13	1.7	0.9	16.4	60.7	**7.5**	9.3	17.0
Pentucket Bank	Haverhill	MA	**B-**	C+	C+	793.7	5.72	9.9	0.2	38.7	9.9	**10.0**	12.3	16.5
▲ People's B&T Co. of Clinton County	Albany	KY	**C+**	C	C	40.9	6.78	13.6	23.8	28.9	1.8	**8.2**	9.8	13.5
▲ People's B&T Co. of Pickett County	Byrdstown	TN	**C+**	C	C	125.0	4.60	17.3	10.0	22.0	9.6	**10.0**	13.1	19.9
People's Bank of Commerce	Medford	OR	**B-**	B-	B-	363.9	8.14	8.8	1.2	10.1	6.4	**6.3**	9.6	11.9
People's Bank of Seneca	Seneca	MO	**B-**	B-	B-	205.1	6.07	9.0	1.6	31.8	6.8	**6.2**	10.0	11.9
People's United Bank, N.A.	Bridgeport	CT	**B**	B	B-	51819.3	18.08	16.9	0.1	19.7	13.4	**6.7**	8.8	12.2
PeopleFirst Bank	Joliet	IL	**B**	C+	C+	138.5	-2.68	5.0	0.1	7.2	4.5	**10.0**	12.6	17.5
Peoples B&T Co. of Madison County	Berea	KY	**B**	B	B-	402.5	0.52	2.2	2.8	21.2	23.9	**10.0**	12.9	20.7
▲ Peoples B&T Co. of Pointe Coupee Parish	New Roads	LA	**B**	B-	B+	320.7	11.59	5.1	1.5	37.1	1.6	**10.0**	13.5	21.2
Peoples Bank	Magnolia	AR	**C+**	C+	B-	202.3	-6.85	2.7	21.9	43.6	10.1	**8.8**	10.2	17.8
Peoples Bank	Sheridan	AR	**A**	A	A	169.2	9.11	10.4	3.0	7.7	30.3	**10.0**	15.0	23.8
Peoples Bank	Eatonton	GA	**E**	E	E-	130.0	4.74	1.1	4.1	25.0	14.4	**4.6**	6.6	11.3
Peoples Bank	Lyons	GA	**B-**	B-	C+	103.1	12.29	5.7	2.0	17.1	2.3	**8.0**	9.7	15.6
Peoples Bank	Willacoochee	GA	**B**	B	B	74.2	-2.58	3.8	4.4	14.6	21.8	**10.0**	14.1	24.5

Asset Quality Index	Adjusted Non-Performing Loans as a % of Total Loans	Adjusted Non-Performing Loans as a % of Capital	Net Charge-Offs Avg Loans	Profitability Index	Net Income ($Mil)	Return on Assets (R.O.A.)	Return on Equity (R.O.E.)	Net Interest Spread	Overhead Efficiency Ratio	Liquidity Index	Liquidity Ratio	Hot Money Ratio	Stability Index
8.7	0.75	na	0.03	**3.4**	0.6	0.65	5.96	3.55	84.3	**5.3**	49.8	11.2	**6.2**
6.3	1.49	6.4	0.06	**5.2**	1.3	1.06	7.39	3.47	66.0	**1.8**	15.2	20.0	**7.6**
7.6	0.00	0.0	0.54	**9.2**	4.7	2.00	17.93	4.96	63.0	**4.7**	28.0	6.6	**8.7**
7.0	1.08	na	0.20	**4.4**	2.3	0.77	7.13	3.66	74.5	**1.4**	15.3	10.6	**6.7**
8.9	0.00	na	0.00	**1.3**	0.0	0.07	0.56	2.31	98.6	**0.4**	11.5	41.2	**5.2**
6.5	3.96	na	0.11	**3.8**	0.3	0.62	3.84	4.89	87.1	**4.9**	17.7	2.7	**5.9**
6.3	0.72	na	-0.01	**5.1**	7.6	0.99	9.56	3.44	65.1	**3.4**	9.5	4.7	**9.4**
6.3	1.07	na	0.15	**8.3**	14.1	1.93	16.90	3.73	48.6	**4.7**	33.1	12.2	**9.5**
3.4	1.64	10.4	0.04	**6.9**	87.0	1.39	14.47	3.83	60.7	**4.0**	13.5	8.0	**8.3**
8.9	0.31	na	0.00	**9.7**	5.6	2.38	16.90	4.26	41.1	**3.6**	14.7	10.7	**9.9**
7.5	0.22	na	-0.08	**10.0**	2.0	2.00	15.23	5.65	53.4	**3.9**	13.4	8.9	**6.3**
4.2	2.51	12.6	0.01	**5.0**	0.8	1.12	11.14	4.82	80.7	**5.4**	28.6	2.0	**5.7**
5.4	1.66	6.4	0.00	**9.8**	22.9	2.02	17.72	3.80	28.4	**0.8**	12.8	31.6	**10.0**
8.1	0.00	na	0.11	**8.3**	6.0	1.61	14.75	3.81	56.7	**1.6**	16.7	5.3	**7.8**
3.9	2.75	9.6	0.00	**5.7**	21.7	1.10	9.69	2.92	50.6	**1.1**	15.0	25.7	**9.4**
8.6	0.41	na	0.03	**2.9**	0.6	0.43	3.01	3.65	90.2	**1.3**	13.7	26.8	**6.6**
6.7	1.45	na	0.28	**6.0**	2.1	1.31	8.98	3.61	67.0	**1.9**	22.1	17.9	**7.2**
6.8	0.25	na	-0.05	**4.4**	1.4	0.73	6.09	4.33	71.5	**3.7**	19.3	6.2	**6.7**
8.7	0.28	na	0.01	**4.0**	4.3	0.99	8.33	3.94	78.4	**2.7**	7.8	11.7	**7.6**
3.6	1.39	na	0.31	**5.4**	7.0	1.42	11.47	3.64	74.5	**1.5**	6.7	8.1	**7.2**
5.8	1.81	na	-0.01	**2.9**	0.1	0.44	5.88	4.63	90.1	**5.9**	37.8	3.2	**2.4**
6.6	1.07	7.1	0.07	**3.0**	3.1	0.42	5.26	3.08	78.9	**0.8**	15.2	32.4	**5.8**
0.8	2.13	na	-0.13	**3.8**	0.8	0.60	5.55	3.45	81.0	**1.7**	15.3	21.5	**7.5**
6.7	0.78	na	-0.04	**5.2**	3.1	1.21	12.68	3.16	68.8	**0.5**	3.8	39.3	**5.8**
1.9	3.75	na	0.40	**1.7**	-0.1	-0.01	-0.07	3.07	86.3	**0.6**	11.4	28.2	**6.3**
5.9	2.78	8.9	0.00	**5.5**	1.5	1.11	7.97	3.26	65.1	**1.2**	28.6	44.8	**7.8**
6.8	2.69	na	0.01	**5.0**	1.1	1.14	11.55	4.41	72.9	**1.8**	9.9	19.7	**7.0**
5.1	1.72	na	0.07	**3.9**	1.4	0.78	7.63	3.83	74.3	**2.4**	11.1	16.8	**6.0**
5.0	1.48	na	0.05	**4.3**	1.5	0.81	7.61	4.04	73.4	**2.2**	32.0	23.8	**6.3**
5.5	4.25	na	0.05	**6.3**	0.7	1.27	9.61	4.94	63.2	**2.3**	33.8	25.0	**6.8**
8.4	0.26	1.6	0.19	**8.9**	2.9	2.29	12.15	4.42	49.4	**2.6**	33.3	19.6	**9.6**
5.6	2.39	na	0.02	**10.0**	1.9	2.10	15.61	5.47	58.5	**4.2**	25.4	8.6	**8.5**
3.0	3.04	16.0	0.62	**2.9**	0.9	0.46	4.37	3.18	74.6	**4.5**	31.6	9.4	**6.0**
7.3	0.59	na	0.00	**3.4**	6.4	0.55	4.09	2.94	73.1	**1.4**	15.2	21.7	**8.3**
8.4	0.00	na	0.11	**5.2**	1.8	1.00	9.72	4.56	71.5	**4.2**	22.7	8.5	**6.0**
5.0	0.77	5.0	-0.03	**5.5**	38.5	1.09	9.23	2.71	58.8	**2.4**	5.6	11.1	**8.7**
9.8	0.11	na	0.00	**6.5**	2.4	1.65	14.48	2.88	46.3	**3.9**	70.9	25.7	**7.8**
7.6	0.65	na	0.06	**6.1**	3.0	1.51	17.93	3.78	63.4	**3.8**	19.3	10.6	**5.7**
5.7	0.70	4.1	0.30	**8.0**	16.6	1.78	14.17	4.53	61.4	**2.2**	23.4	21.8	**10.0**
7.9	1.94	na	0.62	**3.2**	0.2	0.60	3.41	4.06	85.0	**5.3**	82.8	15.2	**5.3**
7.9	0.30	2.2	0.07	**3.0**	0.7	0.13	1.80	3.57	93.1	**5.8**	46.0	6.6	**6.3**
5.1	2.79	na	0.11	**6.3**	2.9	1.24	9.67	4.50	65.4	**3.3**	13.6	12.6	**7.9**
8.8	0.48	1.9	0.01	**3.0**	7.5	0.45	3.53	2.99	80.9	**2.2**	19.9	14.4	**8.3**
8.9	0.29	2.0	0.08	**2.8**	0.6	0.44	2.75	3.19	83.8	**4.8**	32.8	8.0	**7.5**
7.1	0.63	2.7	0.12	**3.5**	2.7	0.67	6.76	3.11	75.1	**2.1**	18.0	18.6	**7.0**
4.8	2.06	na	0.53	**3.1**	0.9	0.57	6.36	2.88	74.3	**7.1**	64.0	3.1	**4.5**
8.6	0.79	na	-0.01	**3.7**	4.3	0.74	6.16	2.93	89.2	**1.3**	15.7	27.7	**7.6**
3.1	0.82	na	0.12	**5.0**	0.3	0.86	8.83	4.95	77.6	**0.5**	10.5	56.7	**5.1**
3.7	3.68	na	0.48	**6.2**	1.0	1.14	8.59	5.03	65.1	**0.9**	20.2	38.2	**6.8**
6.2	0.38	1.3	-0.01	**5.3**	2.7	1.01	9.77	4.50	74.6	**4.6**	11.4	4.0	**6.5**
4.9	1.37	na	0.33	**7.6**	2.0	1.31	13.70	4.55	53.0	**1.3**	5.9	18.2	**5.7**
5.0	0.72	3.1	0.06	**5.0**	398.7	1.06	7.89	3.21	61.5	**2.0**	9.5	9.4	**10.0**
6.4	1.66	na	-0.19	**4.4**	1.0	0.93	7.78	3.79	70.3	**1.4**	23.1	21.7	**6.6**
4.9	3.27	8.2	0.15	**6.7**	4.6	1.54	10.83	4.18	62.6	**4.0**	18.1	8.8	**7.8**
5.4	2.32	na	0.11	**9.7**	4.0	1.82	13.29	4.40	49.8	**0.7**	13.5	38.4	**9.0**
3.2	2.03	na	0.68	**5.4**	1.9	1.21	11.93	4.00	62.0	**0.7**	20.5	33.7	**5.5**
8.8	0.07	na	0.11	**9.6**	2.2	1.85	12.69	4.03	41.8	**4.0**	25.2	10.1	**9.3**
1.9	5.58	na	0.12	**3.1**	0.5	0.53	8.34	4.40	86.0	**4.4**	24.7	7.5	**1.8**
5.3	0.61	4.4	0.01	**6.9**	1.0	1.39	14.73	5.00	64.8	**1.9**	19.9	20.5	**5.9**
8.8	0.38	na	0.01	**5.0**	0.7	1.20	9.21	3.77	72.3	**1.8**	25.0	23.7	**7.3**

Name	City	State	Rating	2018 Rating	2017 Rating	Total Assets ($Mil)	One Year Asset Growth	Asset Mix (As a % of Total Assets) Comm-ercial Loans	Cons-umer Loans	Mort-gage Loans	Secur-ities	Capital-ization Index	Lever-age Ratio	Risk-Based Capital Ratio
▼ Peoples Bank	Clive	IA	**C-**	C	B-	335.1	-0.76	4.2	1.2	12.6	21.5	**5.2**	8.6	11.1
▲ Peoples Bank	Rock Valley	IA	**C**	C-	C-	592.9	1.29	11.8	1.6	5.4	7.1	**8.9**	11.7	14.1
Peoples Bank	Brownstown	IN	**C+**	C+	C+	207.5	0.66	2.4	5.9	19.0	50.2	**10.0**	11.0	24.2
▲ Peoples Bank	Coldwater	KS	**B+**	B	B	52.0	1.10	4.7	1.4	8.2	39.3	**10.0**	12.3	19.5
Peoples Bank	Pratt	KS	**C+**	B-	C+	348.9	1.00	8.1	1.5	9.1	22.8	**10.0**	12.2	19.4
Peoples Bank	Lebanon	KY	**B-**	B-	B-	59.5	8.55	9.0	3.6	5.8	26.3	**9.2**	10.5	14.4
Peoples Bank	Marion	KY	**D+**	C-	D+	71.8	24.49	33.9	5.7	8.7	2.2	**4.8**	9.3	10.9
▲ Peoples Bank	Taylorsville	KY	**B+**	B	B+	102.8	1.77	2.7	2.8	23.6	22.9	**10.0**	12.7	22.0
▼ Peoples Bank	Chatham	LA	**D+**	C-	C-	91.1	4.08	16.1	8.3	25.3	1.9	**7.4**	9.8	12.8
Peoples Bank	Chestertown	MD	**C+**	B-	C	246.2	1.58	3.7	0.4	34.2	6.8	**8.9**	10.3	16.8
▲ Peoples Bank	Cuba	MO	**B+**	B+	B+	206.5	-1.85	3.6	2.9	37.9	18.1	**9.2**	10.5	17.0
Peoples Bank	Mendenhall	MS	**C-**	C	C-	311.0	5.63	10.1	4.1	18.8	11.1	**8.3**	9.8	15.3
Peoples Bank	Ripley	MS	**B**	B+	B+	425.2	6.72	12.2	7.3	16.5	48.2	**9.5**	10.7	22.5
Peoples Bank	Newton	NC	**A**	A-	A-	1221.8	11.18	7.1	0.7	16.0	15.2	**10.0**	12.7	16.0
Peoples Bank	Gambier	OH	**C**	C	C	57.4	2.64	2.7	4.1	42.8	18.5	**8.9**	10.3	19.0
Peoples Bank	Marietta	OH	**B**	B	B-	4392.9	9.90	13.1	11.5	15.3	23.3	**8.0**	9.6	14.3
▲ Peoples Bank	Tulsa	OK	**B**	B-	B-	100.4	-16.45	24.0	6.7	15.1	0.0	**10.0**	12.3	15.1
Peoples Bank	Westville	OK	**B**	B+	B+	46.5	1.08	13.6	5.5	12.1	17.9	**8.6**	11.4	13.9
Peoples Bank	Iva	SC	**B**	B	B	293.4	3.86	1.6	2.4	17.1	30.2	**10.0**	12.5	20.3
Peoples Bank	Clifton	TN	**D+**	D+	C+	208.9	-0.22	26.2	7.9	14.3	6.5	**6.6**	9.2	12.2
▲ Peoples Bank	Sardis	TN	**A-**	B+	B+	86.4	2.49	3.4	5.3	28.3	12.8	**8.2**	9.8	14.9
Peoples Bank	Lubbock	TX	**A-**	A-	B+	542.9	12.43	8.9	2.5	8.0	14.4	**9.4**	10.6	14.5
Peoples Bank	Paris	TX	**B-**	B-	B	148.3	-2.74	7.4	1.0	30.2	20.3	**6.0**	8.1	15.4
Peoples Bank	Bellingham	WA	**A-**	A-	B+	1922.3	13.05	4.4	7.4	8.7	4.5	**10.0**	11.5	15.2
Peoples Bank & Trust	Buford	GA	**B**	B	B-	334.0	7.84	3.6	0.9	10.9	34.1	**9.0**	10.4	18.9
Peoples Bank & Trust	Pana	IL	**C-**	C+	B	429.2	0.24	13.1	0.3	4.1	14.2	**8.5**	10.1	13.7
Peoples Bank & Trust Co.	Owenton	KY	**B**	B	B+	51.5	-4.45	3.5	3.2	34.8	13.9	**10.0**	14.9	22.6
▲ Peoples Bank & Trust Co.	Troy	MO	**B-**	C+	C+	455.6	5.40	11.7	0.5	9.4	27.6	**9.0**	10.4	14.6
Peoples Bank & Trust Co.	Ryan	OK	**B-**	B	B	46.8	11.45	12.3	0.3	4.5	2.7	**10.0**	12.9	17.9
▲ Peoples Bank & Trust Co.	Manchester	TN	**A-**	B+	B-	100.6	0.30	7.1	5.2	32.2	12.2	**10.0**	12.4	19.1
Peoples Bank & Trust Co. of Hazard	Hazard	KY	**E**	E+	D-	235.1	-7.75	14.6	2.5	22.2	7.2	**3.9**	5.9	11.0
Peoples Bank and Trust Co.	McPherson	KS	**B+**	B+	B+	612.6	26.09	17.2	2.7	4.7	29.8	**9.0**	11.4	14.2
▲ Peoples Bank Co.	Coldwater	OH	**A**	A-	A	563.6	11.72	3.5	2.1	14.4	37.0	**9.6**	10.7	18.8
▲ Peoples Bank MT. Washington	Mount Washington	KY	**B+**	B	B	86.3	-1.82	5.9	0.3	7.0	15.6	**10.0**	12.7	16.9
Peoples Bank of Alabama	Cullman	AL	**B-**	B-	B-	826.1	7.02	14.9	2.5	9.5	9.3	**7.5**	9.5	12.9
▲ Peoples Bank of Altenburg	Altenburg	MO	**B-**	C+	C+	63.4	1.55	5.5	2.0	33.5	15.1	**8.8**	10.2	15.5
▲ Peoples Bank of Deer Lodge	Deer Lodge	MT	**C-**	C-	C+	35.4	1.02	9.4	4.9	16.6	27.5	**7.5**	9.3	16.3
Peoples Bank of East Tennessee	Madisonville	TN	**A-**	B+	B	228.2	5.91	5.5	3.5	30.0	15.7	**10.0**	11.4	16.7
▲ Peoples Bank of Georgia	Talbotton	GA	**B-**	C+	C+	82.0	-0.80	9.7	9.9	30.7	15.8	**10.0**	11.1	16.9
Peoples Bank of Graceville	Graceville	FL	**A-**	A-	A-	95.3	7.09	3.2	1.8	14.6	47.0	**10.0**	12.1	40.9
Peoples Bank of Greensboro	Greensboro	AL	**B-**	B-	B-	91.1	4.95	6.8	8.5	14.6	35.1	**7.6**	9.4	17.7
Peoples Bank of Kankakee County	Bourbonnais	IL	**C**	C	B-	220.9	10.79	6.6	2.8	10.3	36.9	**6.9**	8.9	13.0
▲ Peoples Bank of Kentucky, Inc.	Flemingsburg	KY	**B**	B-	B	318.7	2.20	6.8	7.0	18.8	6.5	**10.0**	11.8	15.2
Peoples Bank of Macon	Macon	IL	**C+**	C+	C+	20.7	0.95	10.0	6.5	6.2	44.9	**10.0**	14.0	31.5
Peoples Bank of Middle Tennessee	Shelbyville	TN	**A-**	A-	B+	154.2	3.39	3.7	5.1	17.7	16.7	**10.0**	12.1	17.8
▲ Peoples Bank of Moniteau County	Jamestown	MO	**C-**	D+	D-	57.1	-2.62	3.0	4.4	21.0	28.8	**7.4**	9.3	14.6
Peoples Bank of Red Level	Red Level	AL	**C**	C	C	15.0	-3.73	0.9	20.3	12.3	35.5	**10.0**	13.7	28.1
Peoples Bank of the South	La Follette	TN	**C**	C	C+	151.3	2.70	1.9	1.6	35.7	0.1	**9.9**	13.8	14.9
Peoples Bank of Wyaconda	Kahoka	MO	**B**	B	B	96.3	-4.51	3.2	4.3	18.8	24.3	**9.9**	10.9	17.8
Peoples Bank SB	Munster	IN	**B-**	B	B	1328.8	24.20	8.4	1.1	23.1	19.7	**6.2**	8.2	12.4
Peoples Bank, Biloxi, Mississippi	Biloxi	MS	**C-**	C-	C-	614.8	-0.26	5.3	0.8	8.7	45.0	**10.0**	14.3	24.8
▲ Peoples Community Bank	Greenville	MO	**A-**	B+	A-	483.1	4.30	3.3	6.0	35.0	22.8	**10.0**	16.9	25.0
Peoples Community Bank	Montross	VA	**C**	C+	B-	191.8	-7.19	6.6	7.2	37.4	10.6	**8.7**	10.1	16.2
Peoples Community Bank	Mazomanie	WI	**B+**	B+	B+	295.5	7.99	4.0	1.3	8.3	21.7	**10.0**	12.9	19.0
▲ Peoples Community Bank SB	Monticello	IN	**C+**	C-	C+	27.3	-7.21	0.3	1.6	74.8	3.6	**10.0**	45.8	90.4
▲ Peoples Exchange Bank	Monroeville	AL	**B**	B-	B-	69.4	2.59	17.6	6.9	17.3	19.0	**10.0**	14.8	20.4
▲ Peoples Exchange Bank	Winchester	KY	**B**	B-	B-	415.1	6.16	5.3	1.4	30.7	4.7	**7.4**	9.3	13.6
Peoples Federal S&L Assn.	Sidney	OH	**B-**	B-	B-	115.2	4.33	2.6	1.3	47.0	7.8	**10.0**	13.2	25.0
Peoples First Savings Bank	Mason	OH	**C**	B-	C-	71.2	2.97	0.0	0.3	47.4	2.0	**10.0**	11.0	19.0
Peoples Independent Bank	Boaz	AL	**B**	B	B+	305.5	-0.08	7.0	1.6	9.0	37.5	**8.5**	10.0	15.5

Asset Quality Index	Adjusted Non-Performing Loans as a % of Total Loans	Adjusted Non-Performing Loans as a % of Capital	Net Charge-Offs Avg Loans	Profitability Index	Net Income ($Mil)	Return on Assets (R.O.A.)	Return on Equity (R.O.E.)	Net Interest Spread	Overhead Efficiency Ratio	Liquidity Index	Liquidity Ratio	Hot Money Ratio	Stability Index
2.5	1.92	na	-0.02	3.3	1.8	0.71	5.35	3.86	77.4	1.7	16.1	22.3	3.4
4.4	0.43	na	-0.04	8.9	9.0	2.09	16.26	4.15	49.8	1.4	10.4	18.1	10.0
6.9	0.79	2.7	0.05	3.9	1.3	0.82	7.94	3.22	70.1	6.4	65.6	8.2	5.4
8.3	0.18	na	0.00	4.2	0.4	0.93	6.94	3.37	72.0	0.9	19.9	26.9	7.2
1.5	5.39	na	1.49	5.6	3.3	1.24	8.61	4.59	64.0	1.5	19.9	25.3	8.2
8.5	0.00	na	0.00	4.3	0.4	0.92	9.03	3.85	72.9	4.2	34.7	12.3	5.5
3.8	1.60	na	0.11	5.2	0.4	0.86	9.34	4.51	72.7	1.0	14.5	32.5	3.7
5.7	3.69	na	-0.07	5.8	1.2	1.45	11.54	4.34	69.7	3.7	22.8	11.1	8.2
1.5	0.76	na	0.24	4.4	0.6	0.84	9.10	4.07	66.9	0.3	10.1	65.8	4.7
4.8	2.04	na	-0.21	5.4	2.0	1.10	9.95	3.96	78.9	4.3	21.6	7.5	7.0
6.3	1.29	na	0.11	8.0	3.0	1.89	17.85	4.28	60.0	3.3	7.1	11.9	8.1
2.0	4.26	na	0.42	10.0	5.7	2.45	25.14	5.42	63.3	1.1	17.1	31.7	7.5
7.6	0.69	na	1.01	4.7	3.5	1.12	10.30	3.23	60.9	3.0	46.5	24.2	6.6
8.6	0.38	2.1	0.09	6.9	12.0	1.43	11.17	4.66	68.6	4.8	23.4	6.7	9.5
8.9	0.00	na	0.06	3.2	0.2	0.49	4.79	4.16	84.6	2.9	21.8	15.2	5.0
4.6	0.92	4.4	0.00	6.6	43.0	1.37	10.65	3.75	64.8	1.8	13.4	13.3	9.4
6.8	0.19	na	0.23	5.8	1.1	1.36	8.39	5.49	57.8	1.6	7.1	21.3	7.2
4.5	1.16	na	-0.12	9.7	0.9	2.53	21.53	5.70	61.0	0.8	13.9	37.7	7.6
6.8	2.33	na	0.01	4.8	2.4	1.11	8.63	3.63	72.3	3.4	41.4	18.1	7.4
2.0	3.54	na	0.94	4.0	1.3	0.84	9.47	4.44	62.9	0.6	11.5	36.3	5.1
6.6	0.69	na	0.08	4.7	0.6	0.90	9.40	4.32	70.7	1.4	14.6	25.5	6.2
8.2	0.11	0.7	0.01	6.7	5.3	1.38	12.85	4.10	63.7	2.1	27.2	20.9	7.3
5.3	0.38	na	0.10	4.5	1.2	1.07	13.26	3.43	75.6	0.8	11.2	17.3	6.1
7.9	0.44	1.5	0.00	6.7	17.5	1.30	11.14	4.13	66.6	3.3	22.5	14.8	9.5
9.3	0.09	na	-0.26	5.0	2.5	1.03	10.09	3.69	68.8	2.5	44.9	31.1	6.2
2.4	2.48	na	1.49	6.8	4.4	1.45	14.14	4.53	50.8	2.0	25.9	18.6	7.3
5.9	1.44	na	-0.01	7.2	0.9	2.13	15.26	4.65	69.9	3.9	10.4	8.9	8.4
5.3	1.70	na	-0.27	5.0	4.3	1.27	12.34	3.54	74.5	4.3	21.0	7.4	7.2
4.4	2.99	na	0.00	5.4	0.1	0.25	1.93	4.84	83.9	1.7	37.0	51.1	8.3
8.5	0.03	na	0.03	6.9	1.1	1.38	11.83	4.62	65.1	3.0	15.3	14.2	7.6
0.3	6.67	55.0	0.64	1.0	0.3	0.16	2.52	3.56	86.2	1.4	23.4	27.9	1.0
6.9	1.08	na	0.01	4.9	3.9	0.97	7.26	3.69	68.8	2.9	17.0	14.5	8.0
8.9	0.01	na	0.01	8.7	7.2	1.79	16.33	3.26	39.8	5.6	43.1	7.0	8.0
7.3	2.90	na	-0.01	6.6	1.0	1.59	12.47	4.82	71.4	4.8	24.9	4.9	8.6
4.7	1.48	5.6	-0.05	6.8	10.4	1.72	17.91	4.59	69.4	4.2	19.4	8.0	7.1
6.2	1.18	na	-0.53	5.4	0.7	1.36	13.61	3.93	73.3	4.4	22.6	7.3	6.7
3.2	2.55	na	-0.02	4.5	0.3	0.94	10.95	4.18	73.7	5.4	31.1	3.5	5.4
7.6	0.95	na	0.06	6.0	2.0	1.24	10.89	5.04	69.8	3.7	22.1	11.1	6.6
4.5	1.35	na	0.32	4.9	0.6	0.92	8.66	5.49	73.2	1.2	8.5	27.1	5.8
8.7	1.93	na	0.04	5.2	1.0	1.30	11.02	2.85	58.0	4.0	61.6	18.8	7.8
5.5	0.95	na	0.14	5.0	0.8	1.21	13.45	3.76	67.0	2.7	36.7	20.6	5.5
3.5	3.27	na	0.00	4.4	1.7	1.12	13.23	3.22	71.1	4.5	31.2	9.2	4.4
4.5	1.48	na	0.02	5.8	2.7	1.14	9.63	4.15	63.0	1.0	6.8	28.9	7.5
8.6	0.00	na	0.00	3.4	0.1	0.63	4.56	2.85	72.5	4.6	37.0	8.7	6.4
7.4	0.57	3.1	0.11	6.5	1.3	1.15	9.70	3.92	60.3	0.9	20.2	25.8	7.7
2.2	3.39	na	0.60	2.7	0.2	0.56	6.16	3.17	74.2	4.1	32.3	12.1	3.4
4.0	3.61	na	0.34	7.0	0.2	1.39	10.74	5.53	60.7	6.6	66.5	3.4	5.2
1.6	3.23	na	0.05	9.0	2.0	1.79	12.83	4.78	61.8	1.3	12.7	26.5	9.6
8.5	0.00	na	0.01	5.1	0.7	0.90	8.56	3.50	60.5	1.8	14.2	19.8	6.6
5.6	1.10	7.0	0.02	4.5	9.4	0.98	10.38	3.82	71.0	3.1	22.0	15.5	7.8
5.6	3.97	na	0.56	1.8	0.7	0.16	1.12	3.24	95.3	3.4	9.6	11.6	6.7
6.4	0.93	na	0.13	10.0	11.4	3.11	18.14	4.89	39.3	1.8	20.8	22.3	9.1
5.4	2.23	na	0.87	3.5	1.1	0.72	7.52	3.69	76.1	1.6	19.7	24.2	4.3
7.1	1.62	na	-0.06	5.7	2.3	1.07	8.05	3.58	64.4	3.7	16.1	10.5	7.5
9.3	1.41	na	0.00	2.9	0.1	0.68	1.52	3.87	82.0	4.5	27.4	7.8	5.2
5.8	1.24	na	0.01	4.9	0.5	1.00	6.82	5.20	76.4	4.1	22.7	9.2	7.2
7.2	0.37	na	0.05	4.8	3.2	1.03	11.28	3.79	71.7	1.6	12.8	22.4	6.2
7.3	0.97	na	-0.03	4.0	0.6	0.73	5.52	3.77	77.4	4.2	25.8	8.7	7.3
9.3	0.00	na	0.08	2.5	0.2	0.37	3.37	3.34	86.1	1.6	17.5	23.9	6.3
8.6	0.40	1.1	0.04	4.9	3.1	1.37	12.34	4.01	73.2	5.5	46.1	8.8	6.4

Name	City	State	Rating	2018 Rating	2017 Rating	Total Assets ($Mil)	One Year Asset Growth	Asset Mix (As a % of Total Assets) Comm-ercial Loans	Cons-umer Loans	Mort-gage Loans	Secur-ities	Capital-ization Index	Lever-age Ratio	Risk-Based Capital Ratio
Peoples National Bank of Checotah	Checotah	OK	**A-**	A-	B+	139.0	-0.64	0.9	11.2	10.3	43.6	**10.0**	17.1	44.1
Peoples National Bank of Kewanee	Kewanee	IL	**B+**	B+	A-	360.7	0.71	3.7	1.3	7.6	38.9	**10.0**	13.3	24.1
Peoples National Bank of Mount Pleasant	Mount Pleasant	OH	**B**	B-	B-	72.4	0.23	1.7	22.3	35.3	6.5	**10.0**	11.4	20.9
▼ Peoples National Bank, N.A.	Mount Vernon	IL	**C+**	B-	B-	1211.6	1.70	15.5	0.4	5.1	4.4	**5.7**	9.8	11.5
Peoples S&L Co.	Bucyrus	OH	**C+**	B-	B-	140.0	2.23	0.0	0.9	35.3	39.9	**10.0**	21.1	62.8
Peoples S&L Co.	West Liberty	OH	**B-**	B-	B-	50.3	2.33	1.8	2.6	59.8	6.6	**10.0**	14.8	24.9
Peoples Savings Bank	Crawfordsville	IA	**B**	B-	B-	34.9	5.52	9.0	1.2	9.3	48.3	**8.7**	10.2	14.3
Peoples Savings Bank	Indianola	IA	**B**	B	B	328.5	12.89	14.8	0.9	8.2	22.8	**8.2**	9.8	13.7
Peoples Savings Bank	Montezuma	IA	**B-**	B-	B-	38.9	6.14	9.9	7.3	14.3	35.0	**10.0**	11.9	20.7
Peoples Savings Bank	Wellsburg	IA	**C**	C	C+	94.5	-0.43	11.9	2.2	5.8	21.8	**7.8**	9.5	13.2
Peoples Savings Bank	New Matamoras	OH	**B**	B	B	63.4	0.39	3.5	3.9	27.9	50.5	**10.0**	12.4	37.5
Peoples Savings Bank	Urbana	OH	**C**	C	C	120.8	2.05	1.5	1.9	59.1	1.3	**8.6**	10.1	16.6
Peoples Savings Bank of Rhineland	Rhineland	MO	**B-**	B-	B-	271.3	1.20	11.5	1.9	24.3	8.4	**6.1**	8.9	11.8
▲ Peoples Security Bank and Trust Co.	Scranton	PA	**B+**	B	B	2372.1	5.16	13.1	4.5	14.6	11.7	**7.6**	10.1	13.0
Peoples State Bank	Albia	IA	**B**	B	B	119.7	0.18	7.1	2.1	19.7	27.4	**10.0**	13.2	21.5
Peoples State Bank	Ellettsville	IN	**B**	B	B+	299.0	9.75	4.7	1.0	8.0	43.0	**9.1**	10.4	17.4
Peoples State Bank	Cherryvale	KS	**C**	C-	C+	17.6	5.36	15.4	4.2	14.9	1.7	**10.0**	26.9	33.6
Peoples State Bank	Manhattan	KS	**C**	C+	B-	260.5	12.34	10.3	0.6	11.0	3.1	**6.1**	10.1	11.8
▲ Peoples State Bank	Fairmount	ND	**D+**	D+	D+	27.7	6.10	16.1	3.8	4.9	27.0	**5.1**	7.9	11.0
Peoples State Bank	Westhope	ND	**B+**	B+	B+	61.6	-3.54	2.0	1.7	0.4	18.6	**10.0**	14.3	18.4
▲ Peoples State Bank	New Lexington	OH	**B-**	C+	C+	134.2	4.98	4.0	10.1	41.0	10.3	**8.1**	9.7	15.6
▲ Peoples State Bank	Blair	OK	**B-**	C+	C+	16.7	3.69	34.8	8.1	2.7	9.6	**8.0**	9.7	14.3
▲ Peoples State Bank	Rocksprings	TX	**A-**	B+	A-	80.9	5.81	1.2	1.4	11.8	41.4	**10.0**	12.8	23.1
Peoples State Bank	Shepherd	TX	**B-**	B-	B-	119.8	-4.59	3.4	3.9	5.9	45.4	**8.1**	9.7	23.2
Peoples State Bank	Prairie Du Chien	WI	**C**	C+	B	792.3	0.75	8.5	0.6	8.3	22.5	**8.7**	10.1	15.3
▲ Peoples State Bank	Wausau	WI	**B+**	B	B	948.8	7.43	10.8	0.5	16.0	17.5	**9.1**	10.4	14.5
▲ Peoples State Bank of Colfax	Colfax	IL	**B+**	B	B	34.8	3.44	9.0	7.5	18.4	12.6	**10.0**	12.7	21.7
Peoples State Bank of Hallettsville	Hallettsville	TX	**B-**	B-	B-	276.8	3.69	1.0	1.6	10.9	38.7	**10.0**	12.0	39.2
▲ Peoples State Bank of Munising	Munising	MI	**A-**	B+	B+	145.8	0.70	9.0	6.0	13.5	22.7	**10.0**	12.1	17.5
▲ Peoples State Bank of Newton, Illinois	Newton	IL	**B-**	B-	B+	461.9	2.76	10.9	2.6	11.7	23.9	**8.6**	10.1	14.2
Peoples State Bank of Plainview	Plainview	MN	**B-**	B-	B	282.0	6.90	9.3	3.2	15.5	23.4	**6.8**	8.8	13.8
Peoples State Bank of Velva	Velva	ND	**C-**	C	C+	115.2	-0.84	12.5	2.7	6.6	7.3	**7.0**	9.7	12.5
▲ Peoples State Bank of Wells	Wells	MN	**C+**	C	B	55.1	6.25	4.8	1.6	10.9	5.5	**10.0**	11.1	15.3
Peoples Trust & Savings Bank	Boonville	IN	**B**	B	B	195.5	4.60	3.4	0.8	34.3	27.1	**10.0**	15.6	24.3
Peoples Trust and Savings Bank	Riverside	IA	**B**	B-	B-	28.0	-6.06	3.0	0.9	13.3	43.2	**10.0**	11.9	17.1
Peoples Trust Co. of St. Albans	Saint Albans	VT	**B**	B-	B-	272.3	-0.55	3.0	2.1	25.8	18.2	**10.0**	12.3	19.0
PeoplesBank	Holyoke	MA	**B-**	B-	C+	2926.9	17.35	9.0	0.4	30.5	11.9	**6.8**	9.2	12.4
PeoplesBank, A Codorus Valley Co.	York	PA	**B+**	B+	B	1865.7	3.82	13.8	0.6	12.9	8.7	**8.8**	10.3	14.0
▲ PeoplesSouth Bank	Colquitt	GA	**B**	B-	B	816.1	8.25	3.9	3.5	14.9	23.9	**7.5**	9.4	15.3
PeoplesTrust Bank	Hamilton	AL	**B-**	B-	B-	104.4	5.19	21.6	6.7	12.5	17.7	**9.8**	12.0	14.9
▲ Perennial Bank	Darwin	MN	**B**	B-	B-	103.2	-2.74	3.6	5.1	12.2	42.1	**7.6**	9.4	24.8
▲ Perpetual Federal Savings Bank	Urbana	OH	**A**	A-	A-	391.7	-0.80	2.1	0.9	52.0	0.3	**10.0**	19.4	34.3
▲ Perryton National Bank	Perryton	TX	**A-**	B+	B+	174.1	2.96	9.2	4.9	5.7	56.4	**10.0**	14.0	33.7
Persons Banking Co.	Forsyth	GA	**D+**	D	E+	316.7	1.46	3.9	1.4	15.8	21.2	**5.0**	7.0	11.5
Peru Federal Savings Bank	Peru	IL	**B-**	B-	B-	150.7	4.48	2.8	2.1	32.5	34.6	**10.0**	13.7	27.9
▼ Peshtigo National Bank	Peshtigo	WI	**B-**	B	B+	215.5	10.76	5.4	1.9	16.5	31.3	**10.0**	11.0	21.0
▲ Petefish, Skiles & Co.	Virginia	IL	**A-**	B+	A-	198.1	11.48	4.1	8.2	11.5	22.1	**10.0**	11.8	15.6
▲ Petit Jean State Bank	Morrilton	AR	**A-**	B+	A-	186.9	0.51	13.5	2.2	13.1	33.2	**10.0**	15.0	27.1
Phelps County Bank	Rolla	MO	**B**	B	B	375.4	7.87	3.1	1.5	31.3	26.0	**6.0**	8.0	15.5
Phenix-Girard Bank	Phenix City	AL	**B**	B	B	190.6	11.01	1.1	0.4	9.9	50.3	**10.0**	15.4	29.5
Philadelphia Trust Co.	Philadelphia	PA	**B+**	B+	B+	22.1	-0.34	3.5	7.8	2.0	18.0	**10.0**	72.8	160.4
▲ Philo Exchange Bank	Philo	IL	**B+**	B	B	97.4	3.52	2.3	1.7	8.7	24.9	**10.0**	11.3	16.5
Phoenixville Federal Bank and Trust	Phoenixville	PA	**B-**	B-	C	456.5	2.38	3.6	0.0	40.9	12.8	**10.0**	12.4	18.4
Pickens S&L Assn., FA	Pickens	SC	**B-**	B-	C+	95.7	3.15	1.0	1.0	38.2	33.7	**10.0**	11.9	23.3
▲ Piedmont Bank	Peachtree Corners	GA	**B-**	C+	B-	1028.6	10.08	12.2	0.9	5.3	4.9	**7.1**	10.7	12.6
Piedmont Federal Savings Bank	Winston-Salem	NC	**C+**	C+	C+	881.9	-1.05	0.0	0.0	56.4	31.3	**10.0**	26.3	69.3
Piggott State Bank	Piggott	AR	**B**	B	B+	84.8	-0.07	8.8	4.5	19.9	37.4	**8.0**	9.6	16.7
Pike National Bank	McComb	MS	**B+**	B+	B+	256.5	5.41	6.6	4.0	17.5	20.3	**10.0**	14.0	23.1
Pikes Peak National Bank	Colorado Springs	CO	**B-**	C+	B-	92.6	-1.85	4.4	0.4	4.4	0.0	**10.0**	14.2	34.5
Pilgrim Bank	Pittsburg	TX	**B**	B-	B-	555.7	-5.03	4.5	1.0	11.1	24.1	**10.0**	12.1	18.0

Asset Quality Index	Adjusted Non-Performing Loans as a % of Total Loans	Adjusted Non-Performing Loans as a % of Capital	Net Charge-Offs Avg Loans	Profitability Index	Net Income ($Mil)	Return on Assets (R.O.A.)	Return on Equity (R.O.E.)	Net Interest Spread	Overhead Efficiency Ratio	Liquidity Index	Liquidity Ratio	Hot Money Ratio	Stability Index
8.5	0.58	na	-0.06	**5.5**	1.5	1.38	8.25	3.32	65.0	**5.4**	61.3	13.3	**8.6**
6.0	2.24	na	0.20	**5.8**	2.9	1.09	7.45	4.71	60.1	**5.1**	48.0	11.3	**8.0**
7.4	0.17	na	0.11	**5.0**	0.6	1.04	9.57	4.37	65.2	**3.0**	27.9	16.2	**5.8**
2.8	2.88	21.4	0.10	**5.1**	10.7	1.20	12.60	4.15	71.3	**2.5**	5.6	15.1	**8.4**
8.2	0.51	na	0.13	**2.3**	0.3	0.31	1.46	3.38	88.5	**5.2**	71.2	15.3	**7.7**
9.2	0.00	na	-0.03	**3.1**	0.2	0.40	2.69	3.67	87.4	**3.1**	14.7	13.7	**7.2**
9.4	0.00	na	0.00	**5.2**	0.4	1.33	13.47	3.35	60.0	**6.5**	61.4	4.8	**6.1**
8.1	0.25	na	0.09	**5.2**	2.4	1.10	10.85	3.65	60.5	**2.8**	22.8	12.0	**6.0**
6.6	1.47	na	0.62	**3.7**	0.2	0.66	5.64	3.77	72.9	**5.8**	52.9	7.3	**5.7**
2.2	3.15	na	0.69	**3.4**	0.5	0.74	7.89	3.41	77.0	**1.2**	19.2	29.6	**3.9**
8.4	0.81	na	-0.02	**4.6**	0.5	0.95	7.69	3.92	70.7	**6.6**	55.4	2.8	**6.7**
3.1	2.49	na	0.05	**3.2**	0.4	0.44	4.94	4.10	84.4	**1.4**	7.1	24.4	**4.7**
4.7	1.05	na	-0.01	**4.4**	1.9	0.91	10.51	4.03	68.6	**3.2**	8.3	12.4	**5.3**
6.2	0.57	3.2	0.08	**5.4**	20.8	1.19	9.83	3.61	62.2	**2.3**	8.8	14.4	**10.0**
8.5	0.36	na	0.02	**4.2**	0.8	0.88	6.38	3.60	75.1	**2.7**	35.6	20.6	**7.9**
8.8	0.10	na	-0.01	**4.3**	2.3	1.03	9.94	3.27	76.3	**4.8**	43.4	11.7	**7.0**
1.8	2.63	na	0.07	**9.6**	0.3	2.27	8.55	5.50	57.2	**1.7**	29.6	24.2	**7.8**
3.0	1.67	na	0.06	**3.9**	1.0	0.53	5.11	4.83	84.0	**0.9**	16.8	33.4	**5.9**
5.6	1.34	na	0.03	**4.2**	0.2	0.73	9.89	4.11	75.3	**4.9**	24.1	4.1	**2.4**
7.5	0.00	na	-0.02	**6.3**	0.8	1.59	11.45	4.14	59.8	**4.0**	32.4	12.4	**8.2**
4.3	1.74	na	0.03	**4.5**	0.8	0.86	8.54	4.55	76.2	**3.2**	9.1	12.6	**5.9**
7.7	0.00	na	0.02	**7.6**	0.2	1.78	18.34	5.56	71.5	**5.0**	35.6	5.5	**5.6**
9.4	0.00	na	-0.02	**6.6**	1.0	1.69	13.73	3.04	42.8	**5.0**	47.2	11.4	**8.1**
8.1	0.52	na	0.02	**4.0**	0.8	0.82	9.39	3.32	74.2	**3.3**	42.5	19.1	**5.8**
1.6	5.12	na	0.58	**4.2**	4.7	0.80	7.43	3.45	61.8	**2.3**	25.3	18.6	**7.9**
6.0	0.70	na	0.03	**6.6**	8.8	1.30	12.63	3.76	58.4	**3.2**	14.1	9.0	**7.2**
8.3	0.00	na	0.02	**7.9**	0.4	1.55	12.47	4.31	52.9	**4.7**	33.7	9.0	**7.0**
5.7	4.51	na	0.01	**3.9**	1.9	0.92	7.75	2.41	55.1	**3.0**	62.4	35.2	**6.9**
6.1	1.42	na	0.02	**6.9**	1.6	1.49	11.48	4.29	60.5	**3.1**	22.2	14.2	**8.3**
4.3	1.43	na	0.09	**6.8**	4.4	1.30	11.90	3.66	53.5	**3.1**	11.9	12.0	**7.2**
6.3	0.68	na	0.01	**5.9**	2.9	1.40	14.82	3.68	63.9	**2.2**	22.9	16.2	**6.6**
3.2	5.74	na	-1.02	**5.2**	1.1	1.25	12.98	4.46	67.0	**1.3**	10.7	26.1	**5.5**
6.3	0.29	na	-1.23	**7.3**	0.8	1.87	15.11	4.12	65.2	**1.4**	12.6	25.1	**6.4**
9.3	0.57	na	0.02	**3.6**	1.1	0.76	4.58	3.39	77.9	**2.6**	36.1	21.4	**8.2**
6.1	2.31	na	-0.15	**2.5**	0.1	0.53	4.50	2.83	84.4	**5.2**	40.9	9.0	**4.8**
5.7	2.32	na	0.01	**4.3**	1.7	0.86	6.84	4.13	79.0	**4.0**	24.5	10.1	**7.0**
7.2	0.40	2.9	0.05	**4.0**	17.6	0.82	8.37	3.03	66.4	**2.2**	11.0	7.6	**7.3**
4.4	2.07	14.9	0.02	**5.6**	14.7	1.07	10.28	3.69	64.2	**2.5**	8.7	15.2	**9.2**
5.4	1.39	na	-0.01	**7.2**	9.4	1.52	17.17	4.05	56.5	**3.2**	30.5	15.9	**6.8**
4.6	1.11	na	0.00	**6.7**	1.0	1.31	10.79	4.12	59.4	**1.2**	19.9	30.9	**7.3**
7.3	0.08	na	-0.03	**4.9**	1.0	1.22	13.58	3.17	62.0	**7.2**	58.9	1.6	**5.1**
8.9	0.53	na	-0.03	**8.1**	4.6	1.55	8.13	2.94	34.7	**0.7**	14.8	42.2	**8.8**
6.7	2.03	na	0.01	**6.4**	2.2	1.64	12.33	3.15	49.4	**5.0**	63.1	15.4	**8.5**
6.2	1.22	2.7	0.72	**2.4**	0.6	0.25	3.73	4.35	91.3	**3.5**	21.6	12.4	**1.4**
8.4	1.25	na	0.00	**3.1**	0.6	0.52	3.80	2.89	79.7	**3.6**	41.3	17.6	**7.2**
7.4	0.77	na	-0.04	**3.9**	1.2	0.77	6.62	3.63	79.4	**4.3**	36.2	8.0	**6.8**
6.7	0.66	na	0.07	**6.5**	2.2	1.51	11.42	3.92	63.9	**3.4**	16.0	11.4	**8.2**
8.0	1.66	na	0.31	**7.9**	2.2	1.56	10.76	3.82	44.4	**2.3**	33.0	23.0	**8.4**
7.8	0.25	na	0.08	**7.3**	4.7	1.76	23.35	3.66	63.0	**5.0**	24.7	3.3	**4.8**
9.0	1.56	2.1	0.11	**4.7**	1.7	1.15	7.47	3.26	68.1	**5.0**	30.4	5.6	**7.7**
8.8	0.00	0.0	0.00	**9.5**	1.0	6.26	8.70	1.70	77.9	**5.2**	219.4	69.7	**7.0**
8.1	0.55	na	0.00	**5.4**	1.0	1.33	10.96	3.59	62.4	**4.1**	23.2	9.3	**7.5**
7.9	0.48	na	0.01	**3.7**	2.7	0.81	6.60	3.46	72.3	**3.2**	16.9	13.3	**7.0**
9.2	0.51	na	0.00	**3.5**	0.5	0.64	5.40	3.54	80.4	**3.1**	44.7	20.2	**6.4**
6.7	0.30	na	0.00	**8.6**	11.8	1.60	14.25	4.51	51.2	**1.0**	12.8	32.9	**9.5**
10.0	0.04	na	0.01	**2.3**	1.7	0.25	0.96	2.37	86.3	**2.6**	51.4	34.9	**8.2**
8.3	0.16	na	0.18	**5.2**	0.8	1.25	13.08	3.88	68.1	**3.3**	33.5	16.1	**6.5**
6.3	2.49	na	0.05	**5.9**	2.2	1.17	8.65	4.42	70.7	**1.8**	22.4	22.1	**7.7**
6.3	2.26	5.5	-0.01	**6.2**	1.0	1.38	9.62	5.61	66.8	**6.8**	63.2	3.2	**8.3**
8.2	0.04	na	0.16	**4.2**	4.5	1.04	8.13	3.46	69.6	**2.3**	21.5	18.2	**7.8**

Name	City	State	Rating	2018 Rating	2017 Rating	Total Assets ($Mil)	One Year Asset Growth	Asset Mix (As a % of Total Assets) Comm-ercial Loans	Cons-umer Loans	Mort-gage Loans	Secur-ities	Capital-ization Index	Lever-age Ratio	Risk-Based Capital Ratio
▲ Pilot Bank	Tampa	FL	**C**	C-	C-	426.1	23.84	30.0	18.5	4.9	9.3	**6.7**	9.8	12.2
Pilot Grove Savings Bank	Pilot Grove	IA	**A-**	A-	B+	617.4	5.01	8.2	3.3	29.4	4.9	**8.3**	10.1	13.6
▲ Pine Country Bank	Little Falls	MN	**B**	B-	B	179.0	2.40	9.1	0.7	6.8	16.9	**7.7**	10.0	13.1
Pine Island Bank	Pine Island	MN	**B+**	B+	B	106.4	10.67	5.2	1.6	30.5	9.2	**8.9**	10.2	14.9
▲ Pine River State Bank	Pine River	MN	**B-**	C+	C+	119.4	2.72	6.0	2.0	19.9	15.1	**6.9**	8.9	16.1
Pineland Bank	Alma	GA	**B**	B-	C+	288.1	5.05	5.5	2.4	10.0	7.2	**10.0**	11.2	16.2
Pineries Bank	Stevens Point	WI	**B**	B	B	101.8	5.11	1.9	2.2	35.8	6.9	**8.4**	9.9	19.3
Pinnacle Bank	Jasper	AL	**A-**	A-	B+	235.6	6.77	14.5	2.2	6.9	41.5	**10.0**	12.9	20.0
▼ Pinnacle Bank	Scottsdale	AZ	**C+**	B	B+	269.2	21.00	3.5	0.1	19.9	0.0	**8.7**	10.1	15.8
▲ Pinnacle Bank	Gilroy	CA	**B+**	B	B	399.5	8.18	8.9	0.2	6.3	0.3	**10.0**	12.9	15.5
Pinnacle Bank	Elberton	GA	**B+**	B+	B	960.3	10.35	7.1	2.3	7.0	12.5	**6.4**	9.7	12.1
▲ Pinnacle Bank	Marshalltown	IA	**A-**	B+	A	202.7	1.79	17.4	2.6	6.8	26.1	**10.0**	15.9	21.7
Pinnacle Bank	Lincoln	NE	**A-**	A-	A-	5193.9	10.76	6.1	1.4	10.0	12.6	**7.3**	10.4	12.7
Pinnacle Bank	Nashville	TN	**B+**	B+	B+	27417.5	12.28	21.2	1.1	7.4	13.1	**6.4**	10.4	12.1
Pinnacle Bank	Fort Worth	TX	**B+**	B+	B+	1483.7	9.20	7.2	1.4	12.8	22.9	**7.9**	9.6	14.7
▲ Pinnacle Bank - Wyoming	Torrington	WY	**A-**	B+	B+	955.7	13.12	5.7	1.9	14.8	18.9	**7.9**	9.7	13.2
Pinnacle Bank, Inc.	Vanceburg	KY	**B-**	B-	B-	50.0	0.81	3.7	5.5	37.6	8.9	**10.0**	14.7	20.9
Pioneer Bank	Sioux City	IA	**B**	B	B	179.4	1.29	11.4	0.8	24.3	7.6	**7.7**	9.5	13.1
Pioneer Bank	Mapleton	MN	**C**	C+	B	651.1	45.53	11.7	1.5	10.9	10.0	**7.6**	9.4	14.2
Pioneer Bank	Roswell	NM	**B-**	B-	C+	819.7	2.43	4.2	2.0	20.8	44.2	**7.8**	9.6	19.6
▲ Pioneer Bank	Stanley	VA	**B-**	C-	D+	220.1	7.87	4.7	12.1	28.5	5.4	**10.0**	11.8	16.1
▼ Pioneer Bank	Auburndale	WI	**B-**	B	B-	157.4	6.11	6.7	0.8	11.1	5.8	**8.1**	10.7	13.5
Pioneer Bank & Trust	Spearfish	SD	**A**	A	A-	671.1	4.44	9.2	1.8	5.6	32.0	**10.0**	11.9	18.8
Pioneer Bank, SSB	Austin	TX	**C+**	C	C+	1687.3	10.87	6.8	1.6	17.1	17.4	**5.8**	7.8	11.7
Pioneer Commercial Bank	Albany	NY	**U**	U	U	355.1	6.44	0.0	0.0	0.0	3.9	**6.4**	8.4	38.0
Pioneer Community Bank, Inc.	Iaeger	WV	**B**	B	B	113.5	4.69	11.7	3.3	52.9	3.7	**10.0**	14.6	26.7
▼ Pioneer Federal S&L Assn.	Dillon	MT	**B-**	B	B	90.1	-0.23	3.8	1.7	54.3	23.0	**10.0**	18.8	37.2
Pioneer Savings Bank	Cleveland	OH	**C+**	C+	C	39.1	5.39	0.0	0.4	42.7	31.1	**10.0**	17.0	36.7
Pioneer State Bank	Earlville	IL	**C**	C	B-	107.7	-1.10	5.8	1.0	13.9	12.5	**10.0**	11.4	17.7
▲ Pioneer Trust Bank, N.A.	Salem	OR	**A**	A	A+	536.3	5.94	12.3	0.4	7.1	19.5	**10.0**	12.8	18.1
▲ Piqua State Bank	Piqua	KS	**B**	C+	C	27.6	-4.88	7.2	3.0	10.5	26.6	**10.0**	11.5	21.8
Piscataqua Savings Bank	Portsmouth	NH	**B-**	B-	B-	291.7	5.60	0.0	0.4	58.7	18.4	**10.0**	16.4	27.3
Pitney Bowes Bank, Inc.	Salt Lake City	UT	**A-**	B+	B+	743.6	5.06	29.2	0.0	0.0	51.2	**7.9**	9.6	19.0
Pittsfield Co-operative Bank	Pittsfield	MA	**B**	B	C+	322.6	4.14	4.0	0.5	43.9	12.4	**10.0**	13.7	19.4
▲ Plains Commerce Bank	Hoven	SD	**C**	D+	D+	694.7	4.28	7.2	0.8	12.3	7.5	**10.0**	13.2	15.8
Plains State Bank	Plains	KS	**C**	C	D+	210.6	0.41	12.6	1.3	19.3	22.7	**9.3**	11.1	14.5
▲ Plains State Bank	Humble	TX	**C-**	C-	C	561.8	20.13	13.4	0.4	5.6	8.4	**8.7**	10.5	13.9
PlainsCapital Bank	Dallas	TX	**A-**	A-	A	11095.8	10.61	9.8	0.3	23.4	11.7	**8.6**	11.8	13.9
Planters and Citizens Bank	Camilla	GA	**B-**	B-	C	99.8	5.69	3.5	2.3	3.8	40.2	**10.0**	11.8	20.3
Planters Bank & Trust Co.	Indianola	MS	**B**	B	B	1091.0	4.31	9.0	2.1	14.5	32.6	**8.9**	10.3	16.7
Planters Bank, Inc.	Hopkinsville	KY	**B+**	B+	B+	1132.7	10.03	6.9	0.9	14.0	19.3	**7.8**	10.8	13.2
Planters First Bank	Hawkinsville	GA	**B-**	C+	C-	303.9	-10.27	7.4	1.6	10.6	11.6	**8.7**	10.8	13.9
Plaquemine Bank and Trust Co.	Plaquemine	LA	**B-**	B-	B-	159.4	5.80	9.5	3.1	11.5	32.0	**10.0**	11.6	20.3
Platinum Bank	Oakdale	MN	**B**	B	C+	276.7	16.17	33.2	2.3	9.8	3.0	**6.9**	8.9	12.7
▲ Platte Valley Bank	North Bend	NE	**A-**	B+	B+	86.4	5.70	10.2	2.7	3.3	16.7	**10.0**	14.4	22.8
▲ Platte Valley Bank	Scottsbluff	NE	**B-**	C+	B	741.9	11.77	13.3	6.3	20.9	6.9	**6.8**	9.3	12.4
▲ Platte Valley Bank	Torrington	WY	**B-**	C+	B	452.1	10.33	25.8	4.7	14.1	4.4	**7.8**	10.4	13.1
Platte Valley Bank of Missouri	Platte City	MO	**A-**	A-	A-	597.2	9.31	6.9	1.0	15.7	15.7	**8.6**	10.3	13.8
Plattsmouth State Bank	Plattsmouth	NE	**C+**	C+	C	101.7	10.32	5.3	0.7	5.0	51.9	**6.6**	9.3	12.2
▼ Pleasants County Bank	Saint Marys	WV	**C**	B-	C+	64.7	-0.77	5.7	7.5	25.2	18.5	**10.0**	11.0	19.6
Plumas Bank	Quincy	CA	**B-**	B	B	887.9	15.29	4.9	10.4	1.6	19.1	**8.8**	10.2	14.1
Plus International Bank	Miami	FL	**C-**	D+	D+	82.7	-0.47	29.2	0.0	24.4	14.3	**10.0**	17.0	28.6
▲ PNB Community Bank	Niceville	FL	**B-**	C	C-	104.6	7.41	4.3	0.9	27.0	29.6	**10.0**	11.5	22.4
PNC Bank, N.A.	Wilmington	DE	**B-**	B-	B-	395783.0	7.37	23.5	7.6	8.2	22.3	**6.1**	8.3	11.8
▲ Poca Valley Bank, Inc.	Walton	WV	**B-**	C+	B-	376.2	5.01	11.4	7.2	36.0	8.8	**6.9**	8.9	13.5
Pocahontas State Bank	Pocahontas	IA	**B+**	B+	A	104.9	2.14	5.7	0.4	4.3	41.8	**10.0**	27.5	47.1
Pointbank	Pilot Point	TX	**B**	B	B	543.3	2.01	12.1	2.5	9.3	30.8	**9.9**	10.9	17.8
▲ Points West Community Bank	Windsor	CO	**A-**	B+	B+	253.8	0.90	6.9	0.6	7.6	27.5	**8.6**	10.1	15.9
▲ Points West Community Bank	Sidney	NE	**B+**	B	B+	406.9	3.59	3.4	1.9	8.1	37.8	**8.2**	9.8	18.2
POINTWEST Bank	West	TX	**B**	B-	B-	98.3	-2.03	1.4	8.2	22.3	26.6	**9.8**	10.8	23.2

Asset Quality Index	Adjusted Non-Performing Loans as a % of Total Loans	Adjusted Non-Performing Loans as a % of Capital	Net Charge-Offs Avg Loans	Profitability Index	Net Income ($Mil)	Return on Assets (R.O.A.)	Return on Equity (R.O.E.)	Net Interest Spread	Overhead Efficiency Ratio	Liquidity Index	Liquidity Ratio	Hot Money Ratio	Stability Index
5.4	1.16	na	0.00	**3.1**	1.5	0.51	5.02	3.25	76.4	**0.8**	15.4	21.3	**5.0**
5.9	0.06	3.4	-0.03	**8.6**	8.5	1.92	17.04	3.65	50.4	**3.5**	11.2	11.0	**8.7**
5.3	1.43	na	0.06	**6.4**	1.7	1.29	13.12	4.44	62.8	**3.5**	16.0	9.1	**6.1**
6.3	0.37	4.5	0.00	**8.7**	1.7	2.19	19.49	3.91	44.1	**0.6**	4.9	26.4	**7.6**
5.4	1.26	na	-0.18	**4.9**	1.0	1.18	13.24	4.30	71.8	**5.1**	34.1	6.5	**5.0**
5.9	1.43	7.7	0.10	**4.7**	1.8	0.83	7.47	5.03	77.5	**3.2**	21.5	13.5	**5.3**
9.1	0.00	na	-0.01	**5.1**	0.9	1.17	11.57	3.33	63.1	**2.6**	37.7	24.0	**7.3**
8.8	0.16	0.5	0.08	**6.3**	2.3	1.35	10.27	4.02	62.6	**4.3**	32.3	10.8	**8.0**
4.8	1.59	na	0.29	**3.2**	0.9	0.50	4.60	4.13	93.5	**3.2**	30.4	15.8	**5.2**
7.0	0.29	na	0.04	**8.5**	4.2	1.44	11.37	5.46	63.0	**2.5**	15.8	15.0	**7.4**
6.6	0.18	0.8	0.11	**7.0**	9.2	1.28	11.28	4.61	64.8	**4.2**	23.0	8.3	**8.1**
7.7	0.42	na	0.00	**9.9**	2.8	1.89	11.35	4.24	41.5	**5.2**	30.9	1.4	**9.2**
8.1	0.12	1.7	0.04	**7.5**	54.3	1.47	13.83	3.59	55.8	**3.3**	11.2	12.6	**8.9**
5.9	0.41	1.6	0.09	**8.3**	306.7	1.58	9.57	3.52	46.2	**1.8**	14.8	10.3	**10.0**
7.2	0.04	0.3	0.00	**5.8**	12.3	1.17	8.49	4.05	62.4	**3.8**	30.2	15.9	**8.9**
6.2	0.32	2.2	0.03	**8.1**	10.7	1.58	16.41	3.95	53.9	**1.6**	16.4	23.1	**8.3**
5.4	1.29	na	0.33	**5.2**	0.4	0.97	5.86	4.93	70.9	**0.7**	11.2	31.7	**7.5**
8.5	0.09	0.7	0.00	**4.5**	1.4	1.04	11.18	3.41	68.0	**1.7**	10.9	20.5	**6.6**
3.8	1.72	na	0.47	**5.9**	5.0	1.28	12.90	4.65	65.7	**2.7**	20.8	16.2	**7.9**
8.0	1.47	na	0.21	**4.0**	6.1	0.96	10.59	2.79	71.1	**4.4**	34.2	11.2	**6.1**
4.7	1.57	na	0.11	**5.3**	1.7	1.04	8.84	4.72	74.4	**3.1**	14.5	11.4	**7.0**
5.9	1.37	4.9	0.00	**2.8**	0.2	0.18	1.61	4.36	94.4	**2.8**	16.7	15.0	**6.0**
8.7	0.27	1.1	0.00	**8.8**	8.5	1.70	15.01	3.58	45.1	**4.6**	31.0	8.8	**8.2**
8.1	0.28	1.5	0.09	**3.4**	7.4	0.61	6.84	2.80	73.4	**2.0**	31.2	36.4	**6.6**
10.0	na	0.0	na	**5.3**	2.6	1.11	14.65	1.70	11.0	**8.6**	103.4	0.0	**7.0**
6.3	1.12	na	1.01	**3.7**	0.5	0.53	3.60	4.79	86.5	**3.9**	18.5	9.9	**7.4**
9.7	0.06	na	0.02	**1.6**	-0.1	-0.14	-0.75	3.77	108.3	**3.5**	37.6	16.8	**7.6**
9.1	0.00	na	-0.10	**2.3**	0.1	0.34	1.95	2.70	90.2	**1.9**	39.4	46.8	**7.1**
5.1	2.79	na	0.18	**2.1**	0.1	0.14	1.15	4.08	89.4	**3.7**	19.2	10.8	**6.1**
8.5	0.44	na	-0.01	**9.8**	9.7	2.54	19.89	4.12	36.3	**5.8**	37.5	3.2	**9.4**
9.0	0.01	na	0.05	**5.1**	0.2	1.13	10.51	4.31	72.1	**6.5**	57.4	4.1	**5.8**
10.0	0.22	na	0.00	**3.0**	0.9	0.45	2.88	2.38	82.4	**2.4**	32.4	21.3	**7.7**
6.5	1.58	4.1	1.85	**10.0**	47.3	8.66	87.74	10.55	3.5	**7.8**	72.6	0.0	**7.4**
7.4	1.26	na	0.00	**4.0**	1.8	0.77	4.84	3.58	73.2	**1.9**	23.6	18.8	**7.7**
2.4	4.09	na	0.07	**7.4**	8.6	1.74	12.32	4.28	74.9	**1.0**	14.6	28.9	**10.0**
7.3	0.66	na	0.05	**2.9**	0.8	0.50	4.22	3.56	81.7	**1.8**	11.5	19.9	**6.8**
3.1	3.48	na	0.01	**7.6**	5.5	1.37	12.91	4.16	57.4	**0.7**	16.1	33.6	**7.9**
6.7	0.42	2.5	0.07	**9.3**	148.8	2.00	13.63	4.06	74.6	**2.8**	10.6	14.6	**10.0**
9.1	0.06	na	0.11	**3.5**	0.5	0.69	6.08	3.68	77.8	**6.5**	54.8	3.4	**5.8**
5.9	1.43	6.4	0.20	**5.2**	9.2	1.13	10.89	3.48	63.6	**2.7**	27.8	21.9	**8.3**
7.1	1.09	4.4	-0.01	**6.4**	11.4	1.38	13.03	3.49	53.7	**1.5**	7.0	16.6	**9.9**
4.3	1.93	10.5	0.00	**5.6**	3.3	1.40	14.01	4.48	74.5	**3.8**	11.5	9.8	**6.5**
6.0	2.14	na	0.12	**3.9**	0.8	0.66	5.73	3.88	73.8	**2.2**	26.2	19.3	**6.3**
6.9	1.28	2.7	0.32	**7.0**	3.0	1.57	17.22	4.06	57.4	**4.5**	18.0	4.6	**6.2**
8.4	0.18	na	0.01	**6.2**	0.8	1.34	9.61	3.86	55.4	**6.3**	46.3	3.1	**7.8**
4.5	0.83	na	0.06	**5.9**	6.1	1.16	12.05	3.80	61.3	**1.5**	13.1	23.0	**7.1**
5.3	0.67	na	0.49	**9.4**	6.7	2.03	19.90	5.55	50.7	**0.7**	13.3	33.4	**7.5**
8.6	0.11	na	0.02	**8.1**	8.8	1.96	19.86	4.36	62.3	**3.4**	6.9	11.1	**8.0**
9.2	0.02	0.1	-0.06	**4.2**	1.1	1.51	17.25	3.58	86.6	**3.5**	46.1	19.0	**5.2**
2.5	2.39	na	0.10	**3.8**	0.3	0.69	6.44	3.68	75.6	**4.7**	37.5	10.6	**5.9**
6.4	0.58	na	0.14	**10.0**	12.1	1.90	19.13	4.89	49.3	**5.1**	20.4	2.2	**7.5**
3.7	3.24	20.3	0.00	**1.6**	0.1	0.07	0.42	3.85	98.9	**0.8**	26.8	71.7	**7.5**
7.6	2.54	na	0.27	**3.4**	0.4	0.56	5.10	4.31	85.5	**4.9**	40.9	10.9	**6.2**
4.6	1.13	5.7	0.25	**5.4**	3357.8	1.18	11.09	2.93	62.2	**5.9**	31.3	2.8	**9.7**
5.1	1.08	na	0.13	**4.2**	2.0	0.73	7.80	4.39	79.0	**3.0**	17.9	14.3	**5.2**
8.4	0.00	na	-0.01	**9.5**	1.6	2.11	7.38	3.61	27.1	**4.3**	80.6	20.7	**8.0**
8.7	0.42	na	0.03	**5.0**	4.7	1.14	10.61	4.03	74.2	**4.5**	19.5	5.9	**8.1**
7.0	1.57	na	-0.12	**9.6**	4.2	2.21	20.73	4.55	52.0	**3.0**	17.6	14.1	**8.7**
8.4	0.21	na	0.01	**6.0**	4.2	1.41	13.54	3.64	61.6	**2.5**	19.6	17.0	**7.9**
8.8	0.02	0.0	0.10	**5.7**	1.0	1.37	14.16	3.65	69.8	**5.8**	55.1	8.3	**4.7**

Name	City	State	Rating	2018 Rating	2017 Rating	Total Assets ($Mil)	One Year Asset Growth	Asset Mix (As a % of Total Assets) Commercial Loans	Consumer Loans	Mortgage Loans	Securities	Capitalization Index	Leverage Ratio	Risk-Based Capital Ratio
Ponce Bank	Bronx	NY	**C+**	C+	C+	1098.5	11.97	1.0	0.1	35.7	4.7	**10.0**	13.6	19.3
▲ Pony Express Bank	Liberty	MO	**B**	B	B+	179.1	8.74	13.2	2.0	15.6	6.8	**9.8**	10.8	15.2
Poplar Grove State Bank	Poplar Grove	IL	**A**	A	A	86.5	2.42	6.0	0.7	7.6	53.4	**10.0**	26.8	61.2
Poppy Bank	Santa Rosa	CA	**A**	A	B+	2347.2	22.78	4.4	0.0	8.4	8.0	**10.0**	11.0	16.2
▲ Popular Bank	New York	NY	**C+**	C	C+	10095.2	7.53	2.7	3.1	9.8	14.9	**10.0**	12.5	17.4
Port Austin State Bank	Port Austin	MI	**B+**	B+	B+	52.4	2.06	3.8	4.2	40.9	7.7	**10.0**	18.3	30.2
▲ Port Richmond Savings	Philadelphia	PA	**A-**	B	B	80.4	9.71	5.3	0.0	64.3	0.0	**10.0**	18.9	32.8
Port Washington State Bank	Port Washington	WI	**B-**	B-	B-	601.1	4.93	7.7	3.1	17.2	21.1	**7.4**	9.3	13.8
Portage Community Bank	Ravenna	OH	**B**	B	B	355.6	7.97	7.0	0.7	30.6	17.8	**10.0**	12.0	17.8
Portage County Bank	Almond	WI	**B-**	B	B-	162.2	2.00	7.0	0.8	17.3	13.2	**10.0**	11.2	17.5
▲ Potter State Bank of Potter	Potter	NE	**B**	B-	B-	41.9	8.18	11.4	2.2	1.3	23.5	**10.0**	14.6	22.6
▲ Powell State Bank	Powell	TX	**D+**	D	C-	30.5	-33.99	12.3	13.3	5.2	41.0	**8.2**	9.8	23.3
▼ Powell Valley National Bank	Jonesville	VA	**B**	B+	B+	295.0	6.01	5.2	4.6	27.4	13.6	**10.0**	13.4	19.8
Prairie Bank of Kansas	Stafford	KS	**C**	C+	C-	103.6	-3.88	5.8	1.8	5.8	30.5	**7.8**	9.5	14.5
Prairie Community Bank	Marengo	IL	**C+**	C-	D+	125.1	10.44	13.4	1.1	19.5	5.7	**8.9**	10.2	14.6
Prairie State Bank & Trust	Springfield	IL	**A-**	A-	A-	692.5	-2.20	8.8	0.8	16.8	20.4	**10.0**	11.4	16.7
▲ Prairie Sun Bank	Milan	MN	**D+**	D	D	50.2	52.38	7.5	4.5	2.7	8.8	**5.7**	9.5	11.5
Preferred Bank	Los Angeles	CA	**B+**	B+	A-	4497.1	10.29	23.3	0.0	9.5	5.6	**8.2**	10.3	13.5
Preferred Bank	Casey	IL	**C-**	C-	C	59.0	6.42	20.1	4.7	18.0	17.5	**7.6**	9.4	14.1
Preferred Bank	Rothville	MO	**B-**	B-	B	107.2	1.61	4.3	2.7	11.9	50.9	**6.2**	8.2	20.6
Premier Bank	Dubuque	IA	**B**	B	B	339.8	7.24	11.1	1.1	15.2	22.5	**6.9**	9.0	12.6
▲ Premier Bank	Rock Valley	IA	**C**	C	C+	580.5	7.91	9.3	1.7	5.7	8.4	**7.9**	10.3	13.3
Premier Bank	Maplewood	MN	**C+**	C+	C+	866.6	15.77	8.3	0.4	5.1	8.0	**8.1**	10.6	13.4
▲ Premier Bank	Omaha	NE	**B+**	B	B	306.3	13.84	10.5	0.2	7.2	8.8	**7.2**	11.0	12.7
▲ Premier Bank Minnesota	Farmington	MN	**B**	B	B	262.8	14.81	12.5	0.3	6.4	8.2	**6.6**	10.0	12.2
Premier Bank of Arkansas	Marion	AR	**A-**	A-	B+	164.6	5.47	9.9	1.3	15.8	9.8	**10.0**	14.7	20.4
Premier Bank of the South	Cullman	AL	**B**	B	B	195.5	1.48	9.7	6.3	29.8	17.3	**7.4**	9.3	15.4
▲ Premier Bank Rochester	Rochester	MN	**B-**	C+	B	235.9	17.51	7.4	0.1	9.9	6.0	**6.5**	9.6	12.1
Premier Bank, Inc.	Huntington	WV	**B**	B-	B-	1227.9	11.49	7.0	1.3	19.8	16.2	**10.0**	11.3	16.2
Premier Community Bank	Marion	WI	**C+**	C+	C+	310.3	7.02	4.9	2.5	11.4	14.4	**7.5**	9.7	12.9
Premier Valley Bank	Fresno	CA	**A-**	B+	B+	888.4	4.35	15.8	0.2	3.5	24.4	**8.1**	10.7	13.5
▲ PremierBank	Fort Atkinson	WI	**B-**	C+	B	423.9	3.71	7.6	1.1	15.0	29.2	**8.7**	10.1	16.4
Prescott State Bank	Prescott	KS	**B-**	B-	B-	12.8	-1.19	5.8	3.4	13.8	15.0	**10.0**	16.5	30.9
Presidential Bank, FSB	Bethesda	MD	**B**	B-	C	630.3	22.06	4.0	2.0	36.5	5.4	**10.0**	11.1	16.1
▲ Primary Bank	Bedford	NH	**C+**	C	D	263.8	24.47	18.5	0.0	5.1	0.7	**8.6**	11.6	13.8
Prime Alliance Bank	Woods Cross	UT	**B-**	C+	C	477.3	23.10	35.1	0.0	0.5	9.6	**7.3**	11.0	12.8
▼ Prime Bank	Edmond	OK	**A-**	A	A	283.0	4.51	18.7	0.5	19.2	0.0	**10.0**	12.8	15.1
Prime Meridian Bank	Tallahassee	FL	**B+**	B+	B	484.0	19.25	13.0	1.6	19.8	11.5	**7.4**	9.2	14.2
▲ Prime Security Bank	Karlstad	MN	**B-**	C	B-	82.1	7.87	9.1	0.5	14.2	1.0	**7.4**	9.4	12.8
▼ Primebank	Le Mars	IA	**B**	B+	A-	473.2	8.97	11.4	1.3	16.3	9.2	**9.5**	11.7	14.6
PrimeSouth Bank	Waycross	GA	**B-**	B	B+	669.3	19.98	11.2	3.2	24.1	10.2	**9.2**	10.5	15.0
▲ Princeville State Bank	Princeville	IL	**C**	C-	C+	86.3	6.29	7.7	3.7	4.8	39.1	**6.7**	8.7	13.7
Principal Bank	Des Moines	IA	**B+**	B+	B+	3748.6	37.30	0.0	0.0	28.3	67.5	**5.6**	7.6	14.6
PrinsBank	Prinsburg	MN	**B+**	B+	A	136.0	4.07	3.8	0.6	3.4	4.4	**10.0**	16.0	20.7
Priority Bank	Fayetteville	AR	**B-**	C+	C	85.3	0.16	3.4	1.0	72.3	0.2	**6.9**	8.9	16.0
PriorityOne Bank	Magee	MS	**B**	B+	B+	687.8	5.22	8.4	3.9	17.1	11.3	**9.2**	10.4	14.7
Private Trust Co., N.A.	Cleveland	OH	**U**	U	U	23.1	10.27	0.0	0.0	0.0	56.7	**10.0**	93.2	308.8
▲ Produce State Bank	Hollandale	MN	**B**	B-	C+	59.5	-6.52	18.4	5.1	5.4	8.8	**10.0**	11.0	16.7
Professional Bank	Coral Gables	FL	**C+**	C+	C+	962.8	36.45	10.6	0.8	33.7	3.0	**6.3**	8.3	12.4
Profile Bank	Rochester	NH	**C**	C	C	220.2	6.14	3.3	1.8	28.8	15.2	**10.0**	12.6	21.3
▲ Profinium, Inc.	Truman	MN	**B-**	C+	B-	390.8	5.71	7.8	0.8	9.6	14.2	**8.0**	9.7	13.7
Progress Bank and Trust	Huntsville	AL	**B**	B	B	1209.2	5.20	18.9	1.7	11.6	4.5	**7.1**	11.6	12.6
Progressive Bank	Monroe	LA	**B**	B	B	572.4	-0.85	12.1	1.1	14.8	9.3	**8.0**	10.9	13.3
▲ Progressive National Bank	Mansfield	LA	**C+**	D+	D+	72.3	22.25	4.7	3.2	23.8	17.2	**6.0**	8.0	15.7
Progressive Ozark Bank	Salem	MO	**A-**	A-	A-	112.5	-1.23	4.5	6.2	52.8	6.1	**10.0**	11.1	18.6
Progressive Savings Bank	Jamestown	TN	**B-**	B-	B-	292.0	0.34	5.2	2.3	22.9	10.4	**8.8**	10.2	14.6
▲ ProGrowth Bank	Nicollet	MN	**B**	C+	C	118.6	0.14	6.2	1.1	14.6	23.4	**8.6**	10.1	17.2
▲ PromiseOne Bank	Duluth	GA	**A-**	B+	A-	435.5	17.90	8.4	0.0	1.5	10.0	**10.0**	12.6	18.9
Prospect Bank	Paris	IL	**B-**	B-	B	545.7	6.56	12.5	0.5	8.4	32.5	**7.2**	9.1	13.8
Prosperity Bank	El Campo	TX	**A-**	A-	B+	22083.2	-2.34	5.4	0.5	11.9	38.6	**9.7**	10.8	17.3

Arrows denote recent upgrades ▲ or downgrades ▼

Asset Quality Index	Adjusted Non-Performing Loans as a % of Total Loans	Adjusted Non-Performing Loans as a % of Capital	Net Charge-Offs Avg Loans	Profitability Index	Net Income ($Mil)	Return on Assets (R.O.A.)	Return on Equity (R.O.E.)	Net Interest Spread	Overhead Efficiency Ratio	Liquidity Index	Liquidity Ratio	Hot Money Ratio	Stability Index
5.1	1.98	na	0.10	**3.3**	4.1	0.52	4.06	3.77	81.7	**0.8**	10.3	26.9	**8.5**
6.1	0.56	na	-0.02	**9.7**	3.2	2.40	19.35	5.04	51.8	**2.8**	14.8	7.7	**9.1**
8.4	3.45	na	0.00	**8.4**	1.3	2.09	7.81	3.84	45.5	**6.7**	73.5	6.2	**8.8**
7.2	0.76	2.1	0.00	**9.8**	35.2	2.23	20.25	3.62	35.6	**1.0**	20.3	34.1	**10.0**
4.3	0.64	4.7	0.47	**3.4**	41.3	0.57	3.13	3.36	66.5	**1.6**	20.9	21.1	**7.4**
8.5	0.06	na	0.00	**6.1**	0.6	1.51	8.28	4.02	59.2	**3.7**	23.3	11.1	**8.1**
8.9	0.37	na	0.00	**8.2**	1.1	1.81	9.74	4.49	56.5	**2.1**	5.7	17.4	**7.7**
7.4	0.61	na	0.02	**4.6**	4.1	0.92	10.02	3.40	68.2	**3.9**	14.7	9.2	**5.9**
6.9	1.53	na	-0.01	**4.3**	2.2	0.85	7.16	3.47	73.0	**2.3**	15.2	17.2	**7.1**
8.5	0.34	1.5	0.00	**3.7**	0.9	0.77	6.72	3.83	80.2	**2.0**	36.9	19.4	**6.8**
8.6	0.00	na	-0.04	**4.8**	0.3	1.03	7.13	4.20	70.1	**3.8**	56.1	18.6	**6.8**
4.4	1.99	na	0.29	**3.8**	0.2	0.77	9.15	3.69	74.6	**4.6**	25.1	5.8	**3.9**
6.6	0.90	4.3	0.14	**3.6**	1.2	0.54	3.97	3.84	82.6	**1.5**	14.8	24.4	**8.3**
4.2	1.44	na	0.06	**2.9**	0.4	0.44	4.50	3.49	79.3	**2.2**	12.7	17.6	**4.6**
1.6	6.65	30.2	0.23	**1.9**	-0.7	-0.75	-6.50	3.89	70.1	**1.5**	19.8	25.4	**6.5**
8.0	0.38	2.3	0.09	**6.5**	8.1	1.53	13.63	3.76	61.5	**3.4**	8.8	11.3	**8.9**
3.5	0.60	na	-0.01	**6.4**	0.6	1.77	17.89	5.37	63.7	**3.5**	13.8	11.3	**4.5**
5.7	0.10	1.4	-0.01	**9.7**	58.8	1.84	17.79	4.00	32.8	**0.7**	11.1	33.8	**9.5**
2.5	0.75	na	0.03	**1.8**	0.1	0.15	1.61	3.11	96.7	**1.4**	17.0	25.9	**4.3**
7.5	0.15	na	0.01	**4.4**	0.9	1.11	14.08	3.30	68.1	**6.2**	50.0	5.0	**5.0**
8.7	0.03	0.1	0.04	**4.3**	2.7	1.11	12.43	2.92	69.0	**2.6**	25.2	9.5	**6.0**
2.9	0.32	na	0.06	**9.2**	8.8	2.11	18.77	3.73	36.7	**0.7**	15.5	39.1	**9.0**
4.1	1.00	na	0.32	**9.6**	11.4	1.90	18.48	4.09	41.1	**3.2**	16.9	13.0	**8.3**
7.3	0.00	0.0	0.00	**7.3**	3.2	1.50	13.55	4.21	56.5	**2.6**	22.4	15.4	**7.0**
5.9	0.41	na	0.24	**7.3**	3.2	1.70	17.20	4.29	61.5	**2.5**	13.4	16.3	**7.8**
8.6	0.21	1.5	0.03	**6.4**	1.5	1.28	8.77	4.39	62.1	**2.0**	13.5	18.8	**8.1**
7.7	0.46	na	0.21	**5.6**	1.8	1.21	13.15	4.55	70.8	**2.9**	9.8	14.0	**6.3**
4.8	0.83	na	0.30	**6.6**	2.5	1.51	15.17	3.94	56.7	**1.5**	14.3	24.9	**7.4**
4.1	1.51	7.7	0.15	**8.5**	15.6	1.67	11.98	4.48	49.7	**3.3**	16.3	12.8	**8.9**
6.0	2.52	na	0.02	**4.0**	1.7	0.73	7.44	3.87	77.9	**3.9**	25.5	8.2	**6.3**
6.6	0.70	0.5	0.26	**6.8**	8.5	1.32	7.96	4.60	58.3	**5.0**	33.2	6.8	**8.8**
5.4	1.95	na	0.15	**5.1**	3.5	1.10	9.19	3.43	71.1	**4.6**	23.2	5.6	**7.4**
8.7	0.00	na	0.00	**3.4**	0.1	0.56	3.45	3.88	83.4	**2.3**	40.2	23.6	**6.3**
6.7	1.60	na	0.14	**4.8**	3.7	0.90	8.10	4.28	82.7	**3.2**	6.5	11.9	**6.5**
4.5	1.57	8.6	0.00	**3.8**	1.8	0.99	8.42	3.50	67.0	**0.8**	20.7	33.2	**4.6**
4.3	1.65	9.6	0.78	**9.8**	8.3	2.49	23.74	4.48	27.0	**0.5**	16.2	78.3	**8.2**
5.5	0.77	5.2	0.02	**9.8**	5.3	2.60	20.23	4.35	39.9	**0.6**	8.6	35.7	**9.3**
6.6	0.98	6.2	0.11	**5.0**	2.9	0.87	9.70	3.68	65.3	**4.1**	30.2	11.1	**5.7**
7.4	0.02	na	0.00	**5.4**	0.8	1.24	13.45	4.38	70.8	**1.4**	9.2	16.4	**5.9**
4.3	0.09	na	-0.02	**7.0**	5.5	1.61	13.73	3.48	54.0	**1.2**	12.0	26.0	**8.8**
6.4	0.55	na	0.22	**7.8**	6.9	1.44	12.58	4.58	59.2	**1.7**	11.4	20.2	**8.5**
3.0	5.24	na	0.14	**3.2**	0.4	0.61	6.78	3.63	76.8	**2.6**	34.9	9.8	**4.6**
9.2	0.71	2.1	-0.28	**7.8**	30.8	1.26	17.31	2.08	27.7	**4.4**	76.4	6.5	**6.9**
4.9	0.95	na	-1.29	**10.0**	3.6	3.48	21.39	5.41	44.0	**2.1**	21.0	18.9	**8.7**
4.3	1.52	13.1	-0.04	**8.4**	1.6	2.48	27.05	4.19	71.1	**0.6**	7.1	43.8	**7.2**
5.4	0.55	na	0.56	**6.6**	7.6	1.51	13.92	4.23	67.2	**1.7**	12.7	19.5	**8.9**
7.0	na	na	na	**10.0**	2.9	17.71	19.39	1.94	53.6	**4.0**	na	0.0	**5.8**
6.4	0.00	na	-0.04	**7.8**	0.9	1.91	17.49	3.90	54.1	**5.4**	36.8	6.2	**5.6**
6.5	0.25	na	0.00	**2.8**	2.0	0.31	3.74	3.38	84.6	**3.2**	16.3	12.7	**4.8**
8.6	1.77	na	0.01	**2.4**	0.5	0.29	2.40	3.32	89.3	**3.4**	33.9	16.1	**6.4**
4.9	1.15	na	-0.12	**4.9**	2.5	0.88	8.24	3.60	68.9	**3.5**	16.3	9.9	**6.4**
7.9	0.42	1.7	0.09	**4.8**	8.5	0.97	7.64	3.46	63.9	**1.6**	14.4	24.2	**8.9**
8.3	0.19	na	0.06	**4.3**	3.2	0.74	6.87	4.16	77.0	**2.3**	14.9	17.4	**7.7**
8.6	0.19	na	0.06	**4.6**	0.6	1.10	13.92	3.99	76.0	**2.7**	30.6	18.6	**4.1**
8.3	0.26	na	0.02	**7.9**	1.5	1.71	15.17	4.61	70.5	**4.8**	9.1	2.6	**8.6**
5.5	0.62	na	0.22	**3.4**	1.1	0.47	4.62	4.07	87.9	**1.6**	20.0	23.9	**5.9**
7.1	0.31	na	0.11	**5.1**	0.9	0.99	10.09	4.42	69.2	**4.4**	12.4	5.4	**4.6**
6.5	2.55	na	0.00	**9.8**	9.1	2.95	22.41	4.35	50.7	**1.1**	28.2	48.1	**8.8**
5.9	0.84	na	-0.07	**4.1**	3.6	0.91	9.71	2.83	72.3	**0.9**	23.2	22.5	**7.0**
6.7	0.47	1.2	0.03	**7.4**	254.1	1.51	8.28	3.17	41.7	**4.4**	20.9	7.8	**10.0**

Name	City	State	Rating	2018 Rating	2017 Rating	Total Assets ($Mil)	One Year Asset Growth	Asset Mix (As a % of Total Assets) Commercial Loans	Consumer Loans	Mortgage Loans	Securities	Capitalization Index	Leverage Ratio	Risk-Based Capital Ratio
Providence Bank	Columbia	MO	**B**	B	B	1066.2	10.99	22.4	3.3	7.6	13.6	**10.0**	13.6	16.1
▲ Providence Bank	Rocky Mount	NC	**B+**	B	B+	482.9	9.56	5.9	0.4	10.0	3.5	**8.5**	10.8	13.7
▲ Providence Bank & Trust	South Holland	IL	**B**	B	B	1035.1	65.09	13.1	0.0	5.7	10.9	**9.9**	11.0	15.0
▲ Providence Bank of Texas	Southlake	TX	**B**	B-	B	152.5	3.03	4.0	0.4	14.0	0.0	**10.0**	13.4	17.3
Provident Bank	Amesbury	MA	**B+**	B+	B	1077.9	17.84	39.1	1.4	5.5	4.2	**8.8**	12.0	14.0
Provident Bank	Iselin	NJ	**B-**	B-	B-	9917.5	2.15	7.2	0.2	13.5	15.4	**7.0**	9.6	12.5
Provident Savings Bank, F.S.B.	Riverside	CA	**C**	C+	C	1105.3	-4.51	0.0	0.0	29.9	8.2	**8.8**	10.2	17.4
▲ Provident State Bank, Inc.	Preston	MD	**B-**	C+	C+	457.3	4.46	3.4	0.6	21.2	12.5	**8.1**	9.7	13.7
Prudential Bank	Philadelphia	PA	**B-**	B	C+	1289.1	19.32	1.5	0.1	20.2	45.2	**9.2**	10.5	18.9
Prudential Bank & Trust, FSB	Hartford	CT	**U**	U	U	25.6	1.48	0.0	0.0	0.0	93.3	**10.0**	90.4	251.2
PS Bank	Wyalusing	PA	**B**	B	B	405.7	7.51	8.3	0.6	20.8	26.3	**7.3**	9.2	15.4
Pueblo Bank and Trust Co.	Pueblo	CO	**B+**	A-	B+	432.4	5.96	4.5	0.2	5.5	29.6	**10.0**	11.9	17.8
Pulaski Savings Bank	Chicago	IL	**D**	D-	D-	49.0	6.32	0.0	0.7	62.4	19.9	**5.2**	7.2	17.1
▲ Putnam 1st Mercantile Bank	Cookeville	TN	**A-**	B+	B+	127.2	2.96	17.0	3.1	22.1	14.0	**10.0**	11.7	17.0
Putnam Bank	Putnam	CT	**B-**	B-	C+	538.1	5.09	1.6	0.1	39.1	16.9	**10.0**	12.5	18.9
Putnam County Bank	Hurricane	WV	**B-**	C+	B-	595.1	-2.31	2.8	0.9	35.4	27.7	**10.0**	15.7	34.0
▲ Putnam County National Bank of Carmel	Carmel	NY	**B**	B-	D+	166.7	-0.07	1.7	0.3	22.5	14.6	**10.0**	21.3	56.8
Putnam County State Bank	Unionville	MO	**B-**	B+	A-	220.1	5.47	12.5	1.8	7.6	2.8	**10.0**	13.7	16.2
▲ PyraMax Bank, FSB	Greenfield	WI	**D+**	D	C-	439.0	-8.62	7.7	0.2	20.3	15.1	**8.4**	9.9	13.9
QNB Bank	Quakertown	PA	**B-**	B-	B-	1234.3	5.16	12.9	0.5	13.7	28.8	**6.8**	8.8	12.6
Quad City Bank and Trust Co.	Bettendorf	IA	**B**	B	B	1662.8	4.30	23.1	0.8	8.5	13.2	**6.0**	9.9	11.7
▼ Quail Creek Bank, N.A.	Oklahoma City	OK	**C-**	C	B-	689.5	2.26	3.3	1.0	20.7	13.3	**7.8**	9.5	14.8
Quaint Oak Bank	Southampton	PA	**B**	C+	C+	292.5	13.29	11.9	0.0	22.5	3.2	**9.4**	10.7	14.5
Quantum National Bank	Suwanee	GA	**A**	A	A-	510.6	8.43	3.7	0.0	10.1	3.0	**9.9**	11.3	14.9
Quarry City S&L Assn.	Warrensburg	MO	**C+**	B-	B-	57.4	4.48	0.5	1.5	35.0	0.0	**10.0**	16.1	20.9
Queensborough National Bank & Trust Co.	Louisville	GA	**C-**	C	C+	1209.2	8.24	5.9	1.2	12.0	19.8	**8.3**	9.9	14.8
▲ Queenstown Bank of Maryland	Queenstown	MD	**B+**	B+	B+	473.8	0.60	3.0	1.5	35.4	3.1	**10.0**	14.2	19.6
Quoin Financial Bank	Miller	SD	**A-**	A-	A-	171.7	7.63	11.2	1.7	6.0	13.5	**10.0**	12.5	16.3
Quontic Bank	New York	NY	**B-**	B	B+	392.7	-3.48	0.6	0.0	47.9	1.7	**7.3**	9.2	22.8
R Bank	Round Rock	TX	**B-**	C+	C+	547.0	13.30	18.8	0.6	15.5	12.1	**9.8**	11.3	14.8
Rabun County Bank	Clayton	GA	**B**	B	C	183.5	3.83	2.9	5.3	31.5	2.4	**10.0**	13.0	21.9
Raccoon Valley Bank	Perry	IA	**C+**	C+	B-	285.0	6.41	11.8	0.6	7.5	22.0	**5.1**	7.9	11.1
Radius Bank	Boston	MA	**C+**	C+	C-	1356.0	4.81	6.6	22.0	14.3	17.3	**7.2**	9.1	12.8
Ramsey National Bank	Devils Lake	ND	**A-**	A-	A	263.9	4.51	12.4	1.1	8.1	16.8	**10.0**	13.4	18.4
Randall State Bank	Randall	MN	**C+**	C+	B	46.9	2.53	6.9	2.3	22.5	4.4	**10.0**	11.7	17.9
Range Bank, N.A.	Marquette	MI	**C+**	C+	B-	389.2	-1.60	11.7	0.8	14.4	22.1	**7.8**	9.5	14.7
▲ Raritan State Bank	Raritan	IL	**C+**	C+	C+	182.2	5.90	9.3	5.7	26.4	19.8	**10.0**	11.8	17.8
Raymond Federal Bank	Raymond	WA	**C-**	D+	C	58.4	-2.86	0.0	0.4	76.2	8.9	**10.0**	11.0	24.0
Raymond James Bank, N.A.	Saint Petersburg	FL	**A-**	A-	A-	25705.5	10.78	31.7	10.5	17.3	12.0	**6.8**	8.8	14.5
Raymond James Trust, N.A.	Saint Petersburg	FL	**U**	U	U	35.3	14.35	0.0	0.0	0.0	3.4	**10.0**	92.9	267.0
Rayne Building and Loan Assn.	Rayne	LA	**B-**	B	B	54.2	-4.38	4.4	1.2	25.1	41.1	**10.0**	27.9	65.0
▲ Rayne State Bank & Trust Co.	Rayne	LA	**A**	A-	A-	382.0	0.62	9.8	0.5	19.6	20.1	**10.0**	13.1	20.1
RBC Bank (Georgia), N.A.	Raleigh	NC	**B+**	B+	B-	4580.4	-6.44	0.0	3.1	25.5	64.8	**7.4**	9.3	30.2
RCB Bank	Claremore	OK	**B**	B	B	3119.5	14.00	4.9	5.7	8.7	23.8	**6.7**	8.7	13.4
Reading Cooperative Bank	Reading	MA	**B-**	B-	B-	591.5	5.22	3.7	0.1	48.0	14.0	**7.1**	9.1	15.3
Readlyn Savings Bank	Readlyn	IA	**A-**	A-	A-	75.2	2.12	8.6	1.7	22.2	21.2	**10.0**	15.8	21.5
ReconTrust Co., N.A.	Simi Valley	CA	**U**	U	U	352.4	-2.55	0.0	0.0	0.0	0.0	**10.0**	99.3	467.1
Red River Bank	Alexandria	LA	**A-**	A-	B	1938.8	6.77	12.6	1.7	20.7	17.6	**10.0**	11.4	16.0
Red River State Bank	Halstad	MN	**B**	B+	B+	92.3	13.10	37.8	11.2	7.6	7.0	**7.8**	9.5	14.7
▲ Red Rock Bank	Sanborn	MN	**A-**	B	B	39.1	7.84	10.2	2.8	13.1	5.3	**6.1**	8.1	14.9
▲ Redstone Bank	Centennial	CO	**A-**	B+	A-	157.8	7.83	6.8	0.0	18.6	12.7	**10.0**	13.3	19.4
Redwood Capital Bank	Eureka	CA	**B**	B	B	374.9	0.42	7.1	0.4	7.0	8.1	**7.3**	9.2	13.6
Regal Bank	Livingston	NJ	**C**	C	C	523.7	2.03	1.2	0.1	2.4	9.6	**8.0**	9.6	16.3
Regent Bank	Tulsa	OK	**C+**	C+	C	650.0	18.57	24.9	0.6	14.3	2.2	**5.1**	10.0	11.1
Regional Missouri Bank	Marceline	MO	**C-**	C	C	242.5	3.17	7.4	2.2	18.4	9.6	**7.4**	10.4	12.8
Regions Bank	Birmingham	AL	**B**	B-	C+	127543.0	2.92	19.7	5.8	13.9	19.1	**7.6**	10.3	13.0
Reliabank Dakota	Estelline	SD	**B-**	B-	B	454.9	22.17	12.9	1.8	7.5	23.3	**5.2**	9.3	11.2
Reliance Bank	Faribault	MN	**B-**	B	B	164.9	15.36	21.4	1.1	11.9	11.6	**8.1**	9.8	13.4
Reliance Savings Bank	Altoona	PA	**C+**	C+	C+	558.8	7.32	3.9	1.5	25.5	19.0	**8.9**	10.4	14.1
Reliance State Bank	Story City	IA	**A-**	A-	A-	229.6	3.51	6.1	1.1	10.8	23.3	**10.0**	12.1	15.7

Arrows denote recent upgrades ▲ or downgrades ▼

Asset Quality Index	Adjusted Non-Performing Loans as a % of Total Loans	Adjusted Non-Performing Loans as a % of Capital	Net Charge-Offs Avg Loans	Profitability Index	Net Income ($Mil)	Return on Assets (R.O.A.)	Return on Equity (R.O.E.)	Net Interest Spread	Overhead Efficiency Ratio	Liquidity Index	Liquidity Ratio	Hot Money Ratio	Stability Index
5.8	0.83	na	0.15	**4.1**	7.0	0.91	6.04	3.53	74.2	**1.1**	8.7	24.6	**8.4**
7.1	0.01	na	0.02	**7.9**	5.6	1.57	13.55	3.99	45.9	**0.8**	15.4	35.1	**7.4**
5.5	0.96	4.3	-0.27	**8.4**	26.5	3.34	31.41	4.69	53.9	**3.2**	21.9	13.3	**9.2**
6.2	2.96	na	0.00	**4.2**	0.9	0.78	5.93	4.02	75.3	**0.9**	20.8	36.2	**7.9**
6.1	0.83	na	0.43	**5.5**	8.2	1.08	8.96	4.44	58.0	**3.5**	5.2	3.9	**9.6**
4.4	1.13	4.3	0.16	**5.7**	86.5	1.18	8.57	3.38	54.4	**3.6**	19.1	7.6	**9.9**
5.2	2.18	na	-0.01	**3.3**	3.9	0.47	4.53	3.62	85.3	**3.3**	5.6	11.9	**8.1**
5.8	0.78	na	0.09	**4.4**	2.6	0.77	8.12	3.73	73.8	**2.2**	12.4	17.6	**5.1**
5.6	2.46	10.0	-0.03	**3.8**	7.9	0.88	7.99	2.22	58.5	**2.4**	42.0	34.1	**9.2**
9.5	na	na	na	**10.0**	4.2	24.31	27.68	2.70	23.0	**4.0**	na	100.0	**6.7**
6.9	0.49	na	0.01	**5.6**	3.4	1.17	12.83	3.35	60.7	**2.1**	26.5	17.2	**6.1**
8.8	0.78	na	-0.18	**4.9**	3.5	1.11	9.74	3.98	75.5	**5.8**	36.6	3.3	**7.9**
5.6	2.11	14.6	0.00	**0.4**	0.0	-0.06	-0.82	2.57	101.9	**4.2**	27.2	9.9	**2.0**
7.5	0.05	na	0.28	**6.5**	1.3	1.43	12.50	3.99	56.9	**0.8**	16.8	41.9	**7.3**
6.5	1.07	na	0.00	**3.8**	2.8	0.70	5.24	3.02	71.2	**1.9**	18.7	15.2	**7.8**
5.3	3.79	na	0.39	**3.9**	3.8	0.85	5.65	2.97	57.4	**1.6**	34.6	39.2	**6.4**
6.0	7.13	na	0.00	**4.2**	1.1	0.93	4.33	3.47	66.5	**6.1**	50.5	6.4	**6.5**
4.9	0.04	na	-0.07	**9.6**	2.8	1.75	13.25	3.66	34.3	**0.6**	12.1	50.6	**7.9**
6.3	0.58	na	0.09	**1.3**	0.5	0.15	1.54	2.78	94.9	**1.6**	19.4	16.2	**4.6**
5.5	1.70	11.0	0.04	**4.4**	8.4	0.93	10.96	3.16	64.8	**3.7**	15.4	10.8	**7.4**
6.5	0.54	3.8	0.27	**6.0**	15.5	1.23	12.96	3.28	55.9	**4.8**	20.5	5.1	**7.5**
1.7	4.33	na	0.10	**8.3**	9.5	1.86	19.17	3.86	50.9	**2.6**	28.7	18.1	**8.5**
5.0	0.31	3.4	0.00	**5.2**	2.2	1.06	10.05	3.39	68.3	**0.6**	9.7	43.0	**5.7**
7.3	0.02	0.3	0.01	**10.0**	11.5	3.13	27.70	5.24	43.1	**2.6**	12.4	11.9	**9.3**
5.2	1.80	na	0.00	**3.3**	0.2	0.50	3.12	3.85	85.6	**2.0**	13.0	18.9	**7.2**
2.1	3.77	na	0.08	**6.1**	11.2	1.27	12.89	4.12	69.0	**3.6**	21.1	12.4	**9.0**
6.0	2.24	na	0.03	**8.9**	5.7	1.65	12.04	4.31	49.6	**1.7**	14.0	20.9	**8.2**
7.9	0.63	2.5	0.00	**8.4**	2.1	1.62	13.85	4.64	55.1	**1.4**	13.5	23.5	**7.7**
5.3	1.88	na	0.02	**6.1**	3.8	1.30	13.27	3.52	81.2	**1.1**	27.3	46.7	**6.9**
8.1	0.01	0.1	0.13	**4.0**	2.7	0.69	6.44	3.97	76.2	**0.9**	13.8	31.8	**7.1**
6.5	1.12	na	-0.42	**6.1**	1.7	1.26	9.32	4.35	66.2	**4.6**	29.4	7.9	**8.8**
8.0	0.41	na	0.00	**5.3**	2.7	1.25	15.93	3.58	63.7	**1.7**	15.7	21.9	**5.3**
3.8	1.32	9.0	0.33	**2.9**	4.9	0.50	5.39	3.09	76.8	**1.7**	15.2	7.5	**7.1**
8.1	0.01	na	-0.18	**8.4**	4.0	2.10	15.93	3.95	55.0	**3.0**	9.0	10.9	**9.3**
3.3	4.48	na	0.00	**8.8**	0.7	1.95	16.96	5.20	60.7	**2.7**	26.8	17.2	**8.3**
4.5	2.43	na	0.02	**4.0**	2.1	0.75	7.61	3.78	75.9	**5.0**	35.9	8.1	**5.6**
3.5	5.78	na	0.16	**4.6**	1.1	0.84	7.23	3.48	64.6	**1.7**	22.1	23.6	**6.9**
9.2	0.59	na	0.00	**2.3**	0.1	0.28	2.63	3.77	90.2	**1.7**	18.8	22.5	**5.9**
7.6	0.25	2.0	0.04	**8.7**	316.0	1.68	19.46	3.37	36.1	**4.9**	18.5	1.3	**9.0**
10.0	na	0.0	na	**10.0**	6.0	25.07	29.86	2.57	81.2	**4.0**	462.1	0.0	**7.0**
9.0	0.95	na	0.00	**3.6**	0.3	0.71	2.52	3.51	80.4	**2.9**	72.0	56.1	**7.5**
8.7	0.14	na	-0.02	**7.1**	4.8	1.69	13.08	4.36	62.1	**4.5**	22.1	6.2	**9.2**
9.9	0.30	1.1	0.22	**7.7**	58.1	1.61	19.58	2.71	37.0	**7.9**	75.3	1.4	**6.7**
6.4	0.41	2.2	0.07	**5.2**	28.4	1.25	12.75	3.65	68.5	**3.0**	14.1	12.2	**9.0**
6.7	0.49	na	0.11	**3.8**	3.0	0.69	7.75	3.30	73.8	**1.5**	17.8	12.9	**5.6**
8.5	0.03	0.5	0.00	**8.2**	1.0	1.84	11.61	3.55	42.8	**1.1**	23.1	32.7	**8.0**
10.0	na	0.0	na	**1.7**	-7.3	-2.76	-2.76	4.00	192.7	**4.0**	na	0.0	**7.0**
7.6	0.56	3.2	0.00	**6.3**	18.5	1.31	11.96	3.57	60.0	**3.2**	20.8	14.5	**9.4**
4.4	0.78	6.7	-0.01	**6.5**	1.1	1.59	15.92	4.42	62.3	**0.8**	15.7	34.0	**7.0**
7.0	0.00	na	0.00	**5.2**	0.4	1.26	11.17	3.76	63.7	**4.9**	40.1	10.8	**6.5**
7.7	0.00	na	0.00	**5.9**	1.3	1.10	6.80	5.03	52.7	**1.8**	28.0	25.6	**7.6**
7.1	0.15	na	-0.31	**7.6**	3.9	1.41	15.64	4.27	60.4	**3.8**	17.5	10.0	**6.3**
7.1	0.10	na	0.00	**2.5**	1.1	0.27	2.80	2.87	86.1	**1.1**	20.3	31.8	**6.1**
6.8	0.57	na	0.05	**4.2**	3.4	0.74	7.36	3.69	69.2	**0.6**	9.7	37.1	**6.4**
3.3	1.38	na	0.01	**8.2**	3.5	1.89	18.35	4.18	55.8	**1.7**	4.9	15.1	**8.4**
4.9	1.09	4.4	0.42	**7.2**	1335.0	1.43	11.00	3.57	55.7	**4.9**	20.2	3.9	**10.0**
5.9	0.72	na	0.53	**5.6**	3.6	1.15	12.10	4.01	64.1	**2.4**	7.7	16.2	**7.1**
4.6	1.37	na	1.15	**4.3**	0.9	0.75	7.61	3.72	64.2	**1.8**	26.0	21.9	**7.2**
6.6	1.42	na	0.69	**3.4**	2.5	0.61	5.74	3.10	73.2	**2.2**	11.9	15.4	**7.2**
5.3	1.83	8.3	0.00	**6.5**	2.1	1.26	8.97	3.28	51.9	**4.3**	26.1	8.5	**8.7**

Name	City	State	Rating	2018 Rating	2017 Rating	Total Assets ($Mil)	One Year Asset Growth	Asset Mix (As a % of Total Assets) Comm-ercial Loans	Cons-umer Loans	Mort-gage Loans	Secur-ities	Capital-ization Index	Lever-age Ratio	Risk-Based Capital Ratio
Reliant Bank	Brentwood	TN	**B**	B+	B+	1854.9	10.52	11.9	1.0	12.8	16.0	**6.5**	9.6	12.2
▲ Relyance Bank, N.A.	Pine Bluff	AR	**B**	C+	B	866.6	3.58	7.3	1.2	10.4	11.8	**9.0**	12.0	14.2
Renasant Bank	Tupelo	MS	**A-**	A-	B+	13020.6	2.34	9.7	2.1	18.8	9.5	**8.4**	11.2	13.7
Republic Bank & Trust	Norman	OK	**C+**	C+	C+	589.4	5.22	8.3	1.5	14.9	30.2	**9.2**	10.6	14.4
Republic Bank & Trust Co.	Louisville	KY	**A-**	A-	A-	6093.2	16.85	6.6	4.1	21.3	10.4	**8.3**	11.6	13.6
Republic Bank of Arizona	Phoenix	AZ	**B+**	B+	B+	106.1	-5.01	7.8	0.1	9.9	25.3	**10.0**	14.4	24.4
Republic Bank of Chicago	Oak Brook	IL	**B+**	B	B	2027.6	1.68	19.4	0.1	7.0	11.4	**7.9**	11.0	13.2
▲ Republic Banking Co.	Republic	OH	**B-**	B-	B-	48.8	2.58	5.7	10.0	41.8	6.9	**10.0**	16.3	24.5
▼ Republic First Bank	Philadelphia	PA	**D+**	C	C-	3077.4	16.11	4.3	0.1	10.2	35.1	**6.2**	8.2	13.0
▲ Resource Bank	Covington	LA	**B-**	C+	B-	758.3	1.87	3.7	1.1	22.8	6.0	**9.9**	12.0	14.9
Resource Bank, N.A.	DeKalb	IL	**C**	C+	C+	526.9	12.61	5.0	0.6	14.3	31.5	**7.0**	9.0	14.2
Revere Bank	Rockville	MD	**B+**	B+	B-	2835.2	22.33	11.9	0.0	11.6	6.4	**8.0**	9.8	13.3
Reynolds State Bank	Reynolds	IL	**A**	A	A+	106.7	5.15	2.8	0.1	0.8	71.7	**10.0**	24.6	59.9
▲ Rhinebeck Bank	Poughkeepsie	NY	**C**	D+	C	945.9	15.41	12.0	36.0	7.0	12.2	**8.1**	11.0	13.4
Richland County Bank	Richland Center	WI	**B**	B-	B-	99.5	2.60	4.9	3.5	11.7	43.1	**10.0**	18.7	36.2
▲ Richland State Bank	Bruce	SD	**B+**	B+	A-	36.1	-5.38	6.9	6.7	2.3	37.7	**10.0**	11.3	21.3
Richton Bank & Trust Co.	Richton	MS	**B**	B	B	57.1	3.82	15.4	3.3	9.7	29.5	**10.0**	16.0	29.4
Richwood Banking Co., Inc.	Richwood	OH	**B-**	B-	B	736.4	40.76	4.7	0.6	21.1	20.1	**7.5**	9.3	12.9
▲ Riddell National Bank	Brazil	IN	**C+**	C	C	233.2	4.45	11.2	5.8	36.5	11.0	**7.3**	9.3	12.8
Ridgewood Savings Bank	Ridgewood	NY	**B**	C+	C+	5737.3	4.83	0.0	0.1	35.1	21.0	**10.0**	13.0	21.1
Riley State Bank of Riley, Kansas	Riley	KS	**B**	B	B	90.4	5.35	13.6	4.8	7.2	23.9	**10.0**	11.3	17.2
▲ Rio Bank	McAllen	TX	**B-**	C+	B-	554.4	2.73	11.7	1.5	8.6	21.3	**7.4**	9.3	13.8
Rio Grande S&L Assn.	Monte Vista	CO	**C+**	C+	C+	108.4	6.04	1.5	2.8	55.7	8.1	**10.0**	11.3	19.7
▲ River Bank	La Crosse	WI	**B**	B-	B	517.1	7.23	5.5	0.3	12.0	6.8	**7.8**	10.7	13.2
River Bank & Trust	Prattville	AL	**B+**	B+	B	1139.0	30.72	9.1	3.3	16.7	20.7	**8.9**	10.3	14.4
River City Bank	Sacramento	CA	**B+**	B+	B+	2460.8	12.70	4.0	0.0	5.6	22.0	**7.0**	9.3	12.5
▲ River City Bank	Rome	GA	**A-**	B	C+	162.5	4.67	7.9	1.9	13.9	23.1	**10.0**	11.9	17.8
River City Bank, Inc.	Louisville	KY	**B+**	A-	A-	312.2	6.75	0.6	1.0	28.8	16.1	**10.0**	13.8	18.4
▲ River Falls State Bank	River Falls	WI	**B+**	B-	B-	93.2	3.47	1.1	2.7	34.9	14.1	**10.0**	14.9	23.4
▲ River Valley Community Bank	Yuba City	CA	**B**	B-	B-	419.3	15.13	8.5	0.1	2.3	40.1	**6.5**	8.5	12.4
▲ RiverBank	Pocahontas	AR	**B-**	C+	B	104.9	17.84	8.0	1.3	10.2	5.3	**9.2**	10.5	16.9
RiverBank	Spokane	WA	**C+**	C	C	141.9	3.49	10.2	0.2	8.6	1.8	**8.6**	10.2	13.8
▲ RiverHills Bank	Vicksburg	MS	**B**	B-	B	338.5	9.20	7.7	1.6	11.2	30.0	**10.0**	11.0	17.9
RiverHills Bank	Milford	OH	**C+**	C+	B-	175.0	7.76	7.4	0.2	8.4	15.8	**7.8**	11.5	13.1
Riverland Bank	Jordan	MN	**C+**	C+	C+	142.5	5.40	16.2	3.0	23.3	1.4	**10.0**	13.3	15.9
Rivers Edge Bank	Marion	SD	**C-**	C	C	207.9	11.39	5.6	2.6	6.5	2.5	**7.2**	9.1	12.8
Riverside Bank	Sparkman	AR	**B-**	B-	B-	60.2	-3.75	15.2	8.2	51.7	2.0	**6.6**	8.6	12.2
▲ Riverview Bank	Marysville	PA	**C**	C	D	1109.7	-4.10	7.6	0.8	14.8	9.6	**6.1**	8.8	11.8
Riverview Community Bank	Vancouver	WA	**A**	A-	B	1172.2	2.18	6.0	0.5	8.4	14.0	**10.0**	11.8	17.3
▲ Riverwind Bank	Augusta	AR	**B**	B-	B-	102.6	0.48	17.0	3.2	16.5	18.8	**10.0**	11.2	16.2
▲ RiverWood Bank	Baxter	MN	**C+**	C	C+	433.1	5.06	11.3	6.1	15.0	14.0	**6.5**	8.5	12.3
RNB State Bank	Rawlins	WY	**C+**	C+	C+	179.9	-0.44	9.0	1.8	6.0	20.3	**8.8**	10.2	15.6
▲ Roanoke Rapids Savings Bank, SSB	Roanoke Rapids	NC	**C+**	C-	D+	71.6	56.66	0.8	1.9	34.4	14.7	**10.0**	24.5	48.5
▲ Robert Lee State Bank	Robert Lee	TX	**B-**	C+	C+	44.9	10.21	4.7	5.7	16.6	43.5	**10.0**	14.8	29.8
Robertson Banking Co.	Demopolis	AL	**A-**	A-	A-	336.8	8.36	7.1	1.5	19.5	7.9	**9.1**	10.8	14.3
▼ Rochelle State Bank	Rochelle	GA	**C+**	B-	B-	27.2	1.72	4.7	5.6	0.5	42.1	**10.0**	17.6	34.7
Rochester State Bank	Rochester	IL	**C**	C	C-	95.1	5.40	1.5	2.0	10.3	70.8	**9.2**	10.5	19.0
Rock Canyon Bank	Provo	UT	**B+**	B+	B	471.1	16.35	12.2	0.2	4.5	0.0	**7.2**	11.4	12.7
Rockefeller Trust Co., N.A.	New York	NY	**U**	U	U	14.9	12.92	0.0	0.0	0.0	85.7	**10.0**	88.8	331.4
Rockford Bank and Trust Co.	Rockford	IL	**B-**	B-	B-	519.5	7.30	23.1	0.9	12.6	12.7	**4.5**	9.1	10.7
▼ Rockhold Bank	Bainbridge	OH	**D-**	D	D+	40.8	7.59	5.3	0.8	46.1	0.0	**6.9**	8.9	13.9
▲ Rockland Savings Bank, FSB	Rockland	ME	**C+**	D+	D	83.4	13.06	7.9	2.0	50.8	0.1	**10.0**	11.8	17.8
Rockland Trust Co.	Rockland	MA	**B+**	B+	B+	11540.3	37.80	12.4	0.2	21.5	10.3	**9.4**	11.3	14.5
▲ Rockwood Bank	Eureka	MO	**B+**	B	B	250.3	0.90	4.5	0.9	22.0	0.0	**10.0**	15.0	19.4
Rocky Mountain Bank	Billings	MT	**B**	B	B	528.1	6.53	12.8	2.3	9.1	22.3	**7.7**	9.4	13.6
Rocky Mountain Bank	Jackson	WY	**B+**	B+	B+	323.7	1.60	6.8	13.4	22.2	4.3	**10.0**	12.0	17.1
▲ Rocky Mountain Bank & Trust	Florence	CO	**C+**	C-	D+	73.5	10.75	17.2	1.4	16.1	21.0	**8.0**	9.7	17.0
Rolette State Bank	Rolette	ND	**D**	D	D	40.1	4.17	14.6	2.2	3.7	9.4	**5.4**	9.8	11.3
▼ Rolling Hills Bank & Trust	Atlantic	IA	**D+**	C	B-	303.3	7.93	6.0	0.8	3.9	0.6	**6.5**	10.2	12.1
Rollstone Bank & Trust	Fitchburg	MA	**C+**	B-	C+	690.8	9.05	4.8	0.1	22.1	19.1	**10.0**	11.0	16.2

Asset Quality Index	Adjusted Non-Performing Loans as a % of Total Loans	Adjusted Non-Performing Loans as a % of Capital	Net Charge-Offs Avg Loans	Profitability Index	Net Income ($Mil)	Return on Assets (R.O.A.)	Return on Equity (R.O.E.)	Net Interest Spread	Overhead Efficiency Ratio	Liquidity Index	Liquidity Ratio	Hot Money Ratio	Stability Index
7.2	0.36	2.0	-0.06	**4.0**	13.9	0.71	5.67	3.54	74.7	**0.7**	17.8	44.8	**9.1**
5.1	1.04	na	0.16	**5.3**	6.6	1.04	7.95	3.72	67.5	**1.5**	5.9	21.4	**8.0**
6.4	0.36	1.7	0.03	**7.5**	138.3	1.44	8.04	4.22	60.0	**3.0**	11.5	13.6	**10.0**
2.6	3.92	18.4	0.06	**6.3**	5.6	1.34	12.03	4.49	67.8	**3.9**	37.1	14.6	**7.3**
6.6	0.84	4.3	0.68	**7.9**	65.2	1.56	13.23	4.64	55.5	**3.5**	10.9	7.8	**9.1**
7.8	0.80	na	-0.04	**4.0**	0.4	0.53	3.66	4.09	83.5	**2.1**	37.9	31.4	**7.2**
5.9	1.06	5.8	0.09	**7.6**	20.6	1.38	13.08	3.95	55.0	**2.7**	22.5	16.6	**9.0**
3.7	3.72	na	0.00	**8.5**	0.7	1.93	12.31	4.30	47.4	**2.3**	8.2	16.9	**7.3**
6.7	1.14	5.9	0.08	**1.6**	1.6	0.07	0.90	2.98	98.0	**4.3**	14.1	6.7	**5.5**
6.2	0.59	na	0.00	**6.4**	7.1	1.27	10.80	4.46	64.5	**2.8**	12.1	14.5	**8.2**
3.2	4.64	na	0.01	**4.6**	4.0	1.07	11.36	3.92	76.5	**4.0**	25.4	10.1	**6.6**
7.1	0.12	1.7	0.02	**6.4**	23.7	1.22	11.25	3.63	49.2	**1.3**	11.9	23.7	**8.2**
10.0	0.00	na	-1.30	**6.2**	1.0	1.31	5.24	2.59	29.6	**7.3**	96.3	7.2	**9.4**
3.3	1.14	na	0.14	**3.9**	4.8	0.72	7.02	3.79	71.6	**2.5**	12.8	16.2	**5.2**
9.0	0.00	na	0.03	**4.7**	0.9	1.22	6.62	3.45	65.4	**5.4**	56.4	10.5	**7.6**
8.1	0.00	na	0.14	**7.9**	0.7	2.48	19.04	4.23	61.2	**4.7**	70.2	16.5	**8.1**
8.6	0.00	na	0.24	**4.3**	0.4	1.01	6.18	4.32	80.5	**5.5**	52.2	9.1	**7.6**
5.5	0.97	na	-0.01	**4.4**	4.9	0.90	8.78	3.74	70.1	**1.9**	10.8	19.1	**6.4**
4.2	1.60	na	0.08	**4.5**	1.4	0.84	9.69	3.80	71.1	**1.3**	14.5	24.6	**4.7**
6.6	0.79	4.0	0.00	**4.1**	35.8	0.85	6.35	2.28	72.1	**2.7**	29.3	23.9	**9.2**
8.1	0.02	na	0.15	**4.8**	0.7	1.09	9.96	3.52	66.2	**1.7**	16.1	21.7	**6.9**
4.5	0.91	na	0.08	**5.9**	4.5	1.11	10.54	4.96	72.0	**3.6**	20.1	11.6	**6.2**
5.0	1.89	na	0.01	**2.5**	0.2	0.28	2.50	3.99	91.0	**1.6**	14.9	23.2	**6.2**
4.6	0.83	na	0.03	**7.7**	7.1	1.86	16.58	3.20	44.1	**0.8**	6.2	31.7	**8.7**
7.2	0.61	2.3	0.11	**5.9**	9.7	1.18	9.72	4.05	61.5	**3.7**	20.6	11.9	**8.8**
7.5	0.00	0.0	-0.02	**6.2**	19.5	1.12	11.81	2.73	39.7	**4.1**	10.9	7.6	**8.4**
8.8	0.38	na	-0.19	**6.5**	1.5	1.27	11.12	4.50	65.7	**3.9**	29.8	12.1	**6.4**
6.1	1.08	8.9	-0.03	**4.3**	1.8	0.71	5.39	3.91	77.2	**2.4**	22.1	17.6	**8.4**
9.0	0.00	na	-0.01	**5.0**	0.8	1.18	8.05	3.75	68.4	**5.3**	28.2	3.0	**7.8**
9.1	0.00	na	0.00	**5.2**	3.4	1.12	13.07	3.28	55.9	**3.5**	36.5	16.4	**5.2**
5.0	1.01	na	0.04	**9.4**	1.2	1.53	14.71	4.31	39.9	**0.5**	9.9	56.7	**7.9**
6.3	0.59	na	0.02	**3.3**	0.6	0.58	5.58	4.25	86.4	**1.5**	22.7	26.1	**5.9**
5.7	0.84	na	0.00	**6.9**	4.3	1.74	16.37	3.41	52.3	**2.4**	31.7	21.3	**7.2**
6.3	0.12	na	0.01	**7.7**	2.0	1.64	15.38	5.23	69.2	**1.4**	12.8	4.9	**6.8**
4.6	2.18	na	0.00	**3.1**	0.9	0.81	6.33	3.86	78.4	**0.6**	8.2	48.3	**6.0**
4.1	0.90	na	0.01	**5.2**	1.9	1.24	11.61	3.92	63.0	**3.7**	20.0	9.0	**7.1**
7.2	0.20	1.9	-0.03	**9.8**	1.1	2.40	28.01	4.04	54.4	**0.6**	5.1	41.9	**6.3**
6.9	0.33	na	0.23	**2.8**	3.5	0.41	3.82	4.22	83.2	**3.5**	6.8	10.7	**7.7**
6.3	0.63	2.0	0.01	**8.3**	13.8	1.59	11.69	4.55	60.4	**4.4**	20.5	8.0	**10.0**
7.3	0.68	na	0.06	**4.3**	0.7	0.89	8.61	4.01	71.2	**1.4**	22.1	27.7	**6.0**
4.1	0.80	na	0.02	**4.5**	2.8	0.88	9.96	3.77	68.5	**1.4**	14.2	19.5	**5.6**
7.6	0.60	na	0.01	**3.6**	1.0	0.74	7.33	4.10	85.1	**3.3**	23.6	10.8	**5.6**
8.6	0.41	na	-0.01	**2.9**	0.4	0.61	2.45	4.18	80.6	**3.0**	32.1	17.5	**6.2**
8.8	0.57	na	0.03	**3.8**	0.3	0.80	5.63	3.64	81.1	**2.7**	26.2	16.7	**6.0**
8.6	0.14	0.9	0.00	**8.1**	4.6	1.92	18.34	4.32	54.6	**1.5**	17.4	23.0	**7.8**
8.7	0.00	0.0	0.10	**1.1**	-0.2	-1.08	-5.89	3.60	84.1	**2.4**	49.5	33.3	**6.5**
9.1	1.31	na	0.01	**3.1**	0.5	0.77	7.55	3.21	73.4	**7.5**	77.5	1.1	**5.4**
6.3	0.13	2.4	0.07	**10.0**	7.3	2.23	20.36	6.61	59.0	**1.7**	12.3	16.4	**7.5**
10.0	na	na	na	**9.5**	0.8	7.59	8.58	2.12	86.6	**4.0**	na	0.0	**6.4**
4.9	1.17	na	0.33	**2.8**	1.7	0.44	4.94	2.87	81.0	**0.9**	16.7	27.9	**5.9**
3.0	2.67	na	0.15	**0.5**	-0.1	-0.43	-4.51	3.99	109.2	**0.7**	12.1	29.2	**2.8**
8.3	1.06	na	-0.01	**2.9**	0.3	0.49	3.89	3.94	91.5	**0.9**	19.7	32.0	**5.1**
5.6	0.71	3.0	-0.01	**8.0**	121.4	1.52	11.13	4.18	56.9	**3.8**	11.8	7.5	**10.0**
7.6	0.16	na	-0.30	**8.4**	3.6	1.98	13.39	4.82	59.3	**4.2**	18.4	7.6	**7.5**
4.6	3.14	9.2	0.24	**4.9**	2.9	0.76	7.27	4.34	68.7	**3.8**	24.4	10.8	**7.6**
7.0	0.63	na	1.35	**5.3**	2.5	1.09	8.80	4.35	52.3	**4.2**	21.8	6.2	**6.9**
6.4	0.34	na	0.09	**7.2**	1.0	1.89	19.20	4.59	69.2	**5.3**	34.7	5.6	**3.5**
0.8	9.40	na	0.22	**3.8**	0.2	0.67	7.02	5.02	85.0	**1.6**	7.5	14.5	**4.7**
1.3	2.18	na	0.00	**5.6**	2.3	1.02	8.47	3.81	58.6	**2.1**	10.7	16.0	**7.8**
8.0	1.20	na	0.08	**2.6**	2.7	0.53	4.85	2.61	88.8	**1.1**	24.2	19.4	**7.4**

Name	City	State	Rating	2018 Rating	2017 Rating	Total Assets ($Mil)	One Year Asset Growth	Asset Mix (As a % of Total Assets) Commercial Loans	Consumer Loans	Mortgage Loans	Securities	Capitalization Index	Leverage Ratio	Risk-Based Capital Ratio
Rondout Savings Bank	Kingston	NY	**C**	C+	C+	389.7	4.34	5.8	0.2	45.7	12.1	**9.5**	10.6	17.8
Root River State Bank	Chatfield	MN	**C+**	C+	C+	69.3	-0.09	6.0	1.1	9.3	34.2	**10.0**	12.4	21.8
▲ Roscoe State Bank	Roscoe	TX	**A-**	B+	B	166.5	6.93	5.0	1.6	12.8	45.0	**9.6**	10.8	19.7
Rosedale Federal S&L Assn.	Baltimore	MD	**B**	B	B+	961.5	2.04	0.0	0.0	44.0	13.5	**10.0**	25.4	42.2
Roselle Bank	Roselle	NJ	**D**	D	D	442.1	9.37	1.3	0.1	36.6	47.2	**10.0**	13.0	35.5
Round Top State Bank	Round Top	TX	**A-**	A-	A-	596.3	8.10	2.9	2.2	25.7	25.7	**10.0**	11.8	19.9
Roundbank	Waseca	MN	**B-**	B	B	322.2	6.48	9.7	1.2	23.8	20.5	**10.0**	11.3	15.9
▲ Rowley Savings Bank	Rowley	IA	**C-**	D	D	15.4	-1.86	6.2	5.0	8.9	0.0	**7.3**	9.2	44.3
Roxboro Savings Bank, SSB	Roxboro	NC	**B+**	B+	B+	224.6	1.63	0.7	0.5	27.6	36.3	**10.0**	21.9	47.6
▲ Royal Bank	Elroy	WI	**B+**	B	B+	450.2	6.56	7.7	4.6	16.7	16.6	**9.0**	10.4	15.0
Royal Banks of Missouri	Saint Louis	MO	**C+**	C	C-	668.0	-5.66	10.4	1.1	5.4	7.0	**10.0**	15.2	16.4
Royal Business Bank	Los Angeles	CA	**A**	A	A	2815.7	31.98	7.0	0.0	42.5	2.9	**10.0**	15.0	21.5
Royal Savings Bank	Chicago	IL	**B+**	B+	B+	394.5	-2.88	2.0	0.4	32.7	10.1	**8.8**	10.2	16.6
RSI Bank	Rahway	NJ	**B-**	B-	B-	542.4	0.62	1.9	0.1	40.1	23.9	**10.0**	16.2	29.2
▲ RSNB Bank	Rock Springs	WY	**A**	A-	A-	361.2	3.79	3.5	0.9	3.9	57.4	**10.0**	11.6	23.2
▲ Rushford State Bank (Inc.)	Rushford	MN	**C-**	D+	C-	56.1	3.88	4.3	3.2	15.8	8.0	**6.5**	8.5	12.7
▲ Rushville State Bank	Rushville	IL	**A-**	B+	A-	105.2	6.27	7.1	2.1	3.9	42.9	**10.0**	14.5	26.1
▼ S&T Bank	Indiana	PA	**B**	B+	B-	7555.3	6.61	16.8	1.0	12.3	8.8	**7.0**	9.8	12.5
Sabal Palm Bank	Sarasota	FL	**C+**	C+	C+	238.0	18.34	4.2	0.7	25.8	6.2	**7.0**	9.0	14.2
Sabine State Bank and Trust Co.	Many	LA	**B**	B	B	956.8	6.05	12.3	1.8	10.1	9.6	**6.3**	10.2	12.0
Saco & Biddeford Savings Institution	Saco	ME	**B**	B	B	1031.5	4.62	1.4	0.7	53.7	9.9	**10.0**	11.6	18.2
▲ Sacramento Deposit Bank	Sacramento	KY	**A-**	B+	A-	109.9	5.97	5.0	5.2	21.1	25.1	**10.0**	12.1	17.9
Safra National Bank of New York	New York	NY	**B+**	B+	B	7707.0	7.12	12.1	0.0	0.1	43.4	**7.7**	9.4	20.6
Sage Capital Bank	Gonzales	TX	**B**	B	B	406.5	2.69	3.3	0.6	10.7	14.4	**9.4**	10.6	15.6
Sainte Marie State Bank	Sainte Marie	IL	**D**	D+	C	17.1	-14.63	5.3	1.3	0.8	7.7	**10.0**	22.4	26.7
▲ Saints Avenue Bank	New London	MO	**C-**	D+	D+	93.5	12.91	15.8	12.6	16.9	10.7	**5.1**	8.5	11.1
Salem Co-operative Bank	Salem	NH	**C**	C+	C+	459.3	6.11	2.2	0.0	60.2	14.5	**10.0**	14.9	25.5
▲ Salem Five Cents Savings Bank	Salem	MA	**A-**	B	B	5243.0	6.03	10.7	2.1	29.6	16.7	**9.0**	10.3	14.5
Salisbury Bank and Trust Co.	Lakeville	CT	**B-**	B-	B-	1144.2	4.09	13.6	0.5	29.5	8.3	**7.1**	9.3	12.6
Sallie Mae Bank	Salt Lake City	UT	**D+**	D+	D+	31019.8	21.07	0.0	81.0	0.0	1.5	**7.4**	10.3	12.8
▼ Salyersville National Bank	Salyersville	KY	**B**	B+	B+	109.2	-1.02	3.3	2.7	14.4	36.2	**10.0**	15.5	28.9
▲ Samson Banking Co., Inc.	Samson	AL	**A-**	B+	B	79.9	3.00	3.9	5.9	18.9	50.1	**10.0**	14.0	29.8
San Luis Valley Federal Bank	Alamosa	CO	**B**	B	B	284.7	5.02	2.5	1.8	40.4	16.7	**10.0**	17.1	24.1
Sanborn Savings Bank	Sanborn	IA	**C+**	C+	B	67.3	5.74	4.9	3.2	15.8	10.3	**8.3**	9.8	14.4
Sandhills Bank	North Myrtle Beach	SC	**C**	C	C	196.0	11.88	4.1	1.9	35.6	10.3	**7.7**	9.4	13.8
▲ Sandhills State Bank	Bassett	NE	**C+**	C	B-	295.3	25.62	7.6	1.0	0.9	15.3	**6.1**	8.7	11.8
Sandy Spring Bank	Olney	MD	**B-**	B	B+	8425.1	5.06	7.5	0.3	18.9	10.5	**6.6**	9.9	12.2
Sanger Bank	Sanger	TX	**A**	A	A	141.4	6.31	7.9	2.1	13.2	20.5	**10.0**	15.0	29.4
Sanibel Captiva Community Bank	Sanibel	FL	**B-**	B-	B-	460.2	9.28	3.2	2.0	45.2	1.8	**4.5**	7.6	10.8
Santa Anna National Bank	Santa Anna	TX	**B+**	B+	A-	54.3	10.93	17.1	7.6	1.2	41.2	**10.0**	12.0	19.1
Santa Cruz County Bank	Santa Cruz	CA	**A**	A-	B+	722.9	8.72	9.2	0.2	4.3	7.6	**9.7**	10.8	16.2
Santander Bank, N.A.	Boston	MA	**C+**	C+	C+	83543.3	12.59	18.0	8.0	10.5	16.3	**10.0**	13.4	17.0
Saratoga National Bank and Trust Co.	Saratoga Springs	NY	**B+**	B+	B+	603.5	12.18	4.3	19.8	27.6	9.9	**8.5**	10.0	13.9
Sargent County Bank	Forman	ND	**A-**	A-	A-	187.7	4.39	2.2	2.3	0.7	45.2	**10.0**	11.4	16.9
Sauk Valley Bank & Trust Co.	Sterling	IL	**B-**	B-	B-	450.2	8.31	14.9	0.4	8.7	22.1	**7.4**	9.5	12.9
Savanna-Thomson State Bank	Savanna	IL	**B**	B	B	93.9	2.19	11.4	0.4	6.4	22.6	**10.0**	12.1	19.0
Savannah Bank, N.A.	Savannah	NY	**B-**	B-	B-	146.4	0.27	8.4	0.8	22.1	41.0	**6.9**	8.9	19.3
Savers Co-operative Bank	Southbridge	MA	**B-**	B-	B-	581.4	2.09	3.7	5.2	36.4	8.6	**10.0**	11.5	15.3
SaviBank	Burlington	WA	**C+**	C+	C+	309.9	25.57	11.2	4.3	11.4	3.5	**6.1**	10.1	11.8
Savings Bank	Primghar	IA	**A-**	B	C+	215.7	7.51	13.9	2.1	6.7	12.5	**9.9**	12.3	14.9
Savings Bank	Wakefield	MA	**C+**	C+	C+	615.3	2.15	1.3	0.1	53.0	10.1	**10.0**	11.3	20.6
Savings Bank	Circleville	OH	**B-**	B-	B-	350.4	2.70	9.3	3.9	34.3	28.4	**10.0**	11.5	20.8
▲ Savings Bank of Danbury	Danbury	CT	**A-**	B+	B+	1096.7	2.81	4.9	0.1	44.1	7.3	**10.0**	12.6	17.5
Savings Bank of Mendocino County	Ukiah	CA	**A**	A	A-	1109.4	-0.89	2.7	0.5	5.5	46.2	**10.0**	17.0	28.3
▲ Savings Bank of Walpole	Walpole	NH	**B-**	C+	C-	441.8	8.61	6.8	0.3	37.0	19.8	**6.3**	8.4	14.8
▲ Savoy Bank	New York	NY	**C-**	D+	C	381.7	14.07	7.1	0.0	13.5	0.8	**9.0**	10.3	14.1
Sawyer Savings Bank	Saugerties	NY	**C-**	C-	C-	251.0	-0.43	3.6	0.1	46.8	21.6	**9.1**	10.4	22.0
SB One Bank	Paramus	NJ	**C+**	C+	B	1933.3	32.66	5.5	0.1	17.4	10.9	**7.1**	10.2	12.6
Schaumburg Bank & Trust Co., N.A.	Schaumburg	IL	**B**	B	B-	1220.0	5.59	31.8	12.8	3.0	15.5	**5.9**	9.6	11.7
▲ Schertz Bank & Trust	Schertz	TX	**A-**	B+	B+	407.0	5.55	4.8	0.6	4.8	2.8	**10.0**	12.8	15.0

Asset Quality Index	Adjusted Non-Performing Loans as a % of Total Loans	Adjusted Non-Performing Loans as a % of Capital	Net Charge-Offs Avg Loans	Profitability Index	Net Income ($Mil)	Return on Assets (R.O.A.)	Return on Equity (R.O.E.)	Net Interest Spread	Overhead Efficiency Ratio	Liquidity Index	Liquidity Ratio	Hot Money Ratio	Stability Index
6.5	1.34	na	0.03	**2.9**	1.1	0.38	3.90	3.12	86.1	**1.5**	9.9	23.6	**5.9**
8.9	0.00	na	-0.01	**2.8**	0.2	0.43	3.47	3.30	83.9	**4.8**	31.6	7.9	**6.1**
9.0	0.13	0.3	0.08	**6.2**	1.9	1.56	14.29	4.01	65.6	**3.3**	39.6	18.6	**7.6**
5.3	6.30	na	-0.04	**3.7**	4.6	0.64	2.54	2.95	71.3	**2.1**	29.4	22.7	**8.9**
10.0	1.22	na	0.00	**0.0**	-2.7	-0.85	-5.94	1.37	160.1	**2.7**	52.6	33.8	**6.2**
8.9	0.11	na	0.02	**6.2**	5.7	1.31	11.59	3.23	53.3	**1.9**	30.8	28.0	**8.1**
5.8	1.56	na	-0.25	**7.2**	4.2	1.77	15.62	3.91	71.9	**2.0**	19.3	16.2	**8.3**
9.3	0.00	na	-0.24	**4.0**	0.1	0.99	11.05	3.41	71.4	**7.1**	82.9	2.9	**3.6**
8.0	2.64	na	0.00	**5.0**	2.0	1.16	5.72	3.41	60.6	**3.1**	51.4	27.5	**8.3**
5.7	0.68	na	0.04	**6.6**	4.3	1.31	12.20	4.24	60.1	**3.8**	20.6	10.4	**7.2**
5.6	0.59	na	0.22	**5.3**	5.2	0.98	6.27	3.54	57.5	**0.6**	9.4	38.3	**8.0**
7.9	0.36	0.8	0.00	**9.3**	33.2	1.56	9.80	3.50	47.2	**0.6**	9.3	43.8	**10.0**
6.5	0.54	na	0.03	**5.5**	3.0	0.99	8.47	3.83	61.3	**1.1**	18.3	22.8	**8.2**
6.7	2.24	7.5	-0.09	**3.2**	2.0	0.49	3.08	2.83	76.6	**3.8**	34.5	14.1	**8.3**
9.5	0.28	na	-0.04	**7.2**	4.9	1.82	15.74	3.53	54.1	**5.4**	42.0	8.4	**8.0**
4.0	2.93	na	-0.03	**3.9**	0.3	0.83	9.79	4.50	78.6	**2.1**	16.1	18.7	**4.1**
6.1	2.22	na	0.01	**6.4**	1.2	1.55	11.09	3.50	54.8	**4.7**	37.9	11.0	**8.7**
4.3	1.42	6.6	0.26	**7.2**	79.4	1.46	11.21	3.68	52.2	**2.7**	9.4	10.3	**10.0**
8.8	0.00	na	-0.05	**4.0**	1.3	0.72	7.97	3.89	73.8	**3.2**	21.0	13.6	**5.2**
7.6	0.33	na	0.09	**7.8**	12.9	1.78	18.37	4.57	67.1	**4.4**	10.6	5.7	**8.2**
6.5	1.12	na	0.00	**3.7**	5.6	0.73	6.44	2.76	80.5	**0.8**	11.8	24.5	**8.6**
6.5	0.52	na	0.14	**7.8**	1.5	1.82	15.17	4.40	57.8	**2.4**	34.7	23.1	**8.5**
9.2	0.00	0.0	0.00	**5.5**	56.2	0.97	8.32	1.76	58.1	**1.4**	26.0	12.5	**9.0**
8.3	0.08	na	0.04	**5.2**	3.1	1.01	8.92	4.16	68.9	**2.5**	22.1	17.2	**7.2**
7.3	0.00	na	2.06	**0.0**	-0.1	-0.86	-4.02	2.64	121.2	**1.7**	14.2	20.8	**4.9**
6.5	0.30	na	0.15	**2.4**	0.3	0.37	4.48	3.95	85.4	**2.1**	4.3	11.9	**3.9**
8.9	0.72	na	0.00	**2.1**	0.5	0.16	1.04	2.59	92.2	**0.8**	18.4	28.5	**7.6**
7.8	0.38	2.5	0.01	**6.2**	48.9	1.28	12.24	2.94	55.9	**2.5**	15.7	14.9	**8.8**
6.1	0.99	na	-0.07	**4.5**	8.7	1.04	10.12	3.28	65.8	**3.6**	5.7	10.2	**8.5**
0.8	5.27	21.4	1.03	**10.0**	449.8	2.10	20.01	5.95	32.2	**0.7**	14.9	8.5	**9.9**
8.2	0.26	na	1.29	**3.5**	0.4	0.50	3.36	3.81	69.1	**1.5**	25.9	28.5	**8.2**
8.5	0.00	na	0.08	**6.4**	0.9	1.52	11.15	3.75	61.1	**4.8**	51.8	13.1	**8.1**
8.1	1.07	na	0.00	**4.4**	1.6	0.80	4.73	3.85	77.0	**4.0**	28.5	11.4	**7.9**
4.7	1.64	na	0.00	**4.6**	0.5	1.02	10.09	3.45	62.0	**2.6**	17.6	16.1	**5.1**
6.8	0.21	na	0.00	**3.1**	0.5	0.39	3.69	3.65	87.9	**0.9**	17.6	34.1	**5.5**
4.4	0.13	na	-0.01	**4.6**	2.2	1.01	9.01	4.07	70.8	**1.7**	11.3	17.7	**6.3**
4.0	0.77	4.0	0.03	**7.2**	89.4	1.44	10.79	3.52	52.2	**1.8**	9.2	16.4	**9.8**
9.0	0.00	na	0.00	**5.8**	1.2	1.15	7.71	3.87	66.7	**3.2**	44.7	21.0	**8.7**
4.6	1.60	na	0.00	**9.4**	5.3	1.61	22.28	4.70	56.3	**4.1**	11.5	7.5	**5.2**
7.3	0.95	na	0.03	**9.0**	0.7	1.85	15.80	4.88	55.2	**3.3**	39.2	18.4	**7.1**
7.1	0.31	1.8	0.00	**9.9**	9.3	1.78	16.88	4.83	49.3	**3.4**	23.2	12.9	**8.0**
4.8	1.16	3.8	0.38	**2.7**	247.8	0.42	2.42	3.07	79.0	**4.1**	20.1	4.3	**8.0**
7.4	0.03	0.3	0.04	**7.0**	6.0	1.41	14.34	3.26	47.1	**3.8**	10.0	9.3	**7.3**
8.4	0.00	na	0.04	**7.8**	2.6	1.90	15.29	3.80	44.3	**4.3**	34.3	11.8	**9.1**
3.9	1.53	10.3	0.03	**4.4**	2.6	0.79	8.80	3.57	69.2	**1.9**	18.1	14.0	**5.5**
5.1	1.11	na	0.19	**3.8**	0.6	0.92	6.14	3.47	69.1	**5.2**	24.9	2.1	**7.8**
7.7	0.61	3.0	-0.02	**3.4**	0.8	0.71	8.19	3.21	76.6	**1.8**	19.2	21.5	**5.4**
6.9	1.09	na	0.03	**3.6**	2.9	0.69	6.25	3.27	73.5	**2.3**	15.3	16.0	**7.1**
6.4	0.49	na	0.02	**3.8**	1.4	0.62	5.69	4.41	79.6	**0.8**	13.7	25.3	**6.9**
7.0	0.00	0.8	0.00	**8.1**	3.1	1.93	16.03	3.48	40.0	**1.2**	10.1	26.8	**8.7**
8.5	0.40	na	0.00	**3.0**	2.3	0.51	4.08	3.08	83.7	**1.6**	18.5	22.6	**7.7**
7.1	1.40	na	0.06	**3.6**	1.7	0.65	5.69	3.27	78.7	**3.2**	21.9	13.7	**6.6**
5.8	1.79	10.0	0.07	**5.8**	9.6	1.19	9.87	3.63	63.0	**1.1**	10.2	23.2	**9.4**
9.1	0.61	1.1	0.01	**7.5**	11.6	1.40	8.54	3.87	52.4	**6.7**	49.0	5.0	**10.0**
6.0	0.87	5.4	0.01	**4.0**	2.6	0.84	10.29	3.37	73.2	**4.9**	28.5	5.9	**5.8**
2.4	1.73	na	1.06	**7.7**	3.7	1.34	13.13	4.57	53.0	**0.6**	15.2	59.9	**7.7**
6.4	1.96	na	0.30	**2.1**	0.5	0.26	2.48	2.66	90.5	**1.0**	26.6	27.8	**5.9**
3.8	1.04	6.8	0.09	**5.9**	18.2	1.30	11.29	3.46	56.0	**1.0**	14.9	15.2	**8.0**
4.7	1.08	7.2	0.09	**5.6**	10.2	1.14	10.65	3.20	54.3	**1.3**	14.5	24.3	**8.4**
7.3	0.55	na	0.02	**7.6**	4.5	1.46	11.80	3.88	50.4	**0.7**	13.7	38.3	**7.7**

Name	City	State	Rating	2018 Rating	2017 Rating	Total Assets ($Mil)	One Year Asset Growth	Asset Mix (As a % of Total Assets) Commercial Loans	Consumer Loans	Mortgage Loans	Securities	Capitalization Index	Leverage Ratio	Risk-Based Capital Ratio
Schuyler Savings Bank	Kearny	NJ	**C**	C	C	120.3	4.79	0.0	0.1	54.9	18.3	**10.0**	16.2	35.7
▼ Scotiabank de Puerto Rico	San Juan	PR	**C**	C	D	3508.5	-14.91	6.8	7.4	39.1	21.4	**10.0**	20.6	41.2
Scott State Bank	Bethany	IL	**B-**	B-	B-	162.9	-0.92	8.8	3.4	13.6	33.1	**10.0**	15.0	25.3
Scottsburg Building and Loan Assn.	Scottsburg	IN	**C+**	C+	C+	89.6	-1.42	1.2	0.2	43.4	35.1	**10.0**	14.9	33.6
▲ Scribner Bank	Scribner	NE	**A-**	B+	A-	65.6	6.29	7.9	1.0	3.0	12.7	**10.0**	15.2	20.6
Seacoast Commerce Bank	San Diego	CA	**C+**	B	B+	1082.5	5.86	1.9	0.0	1.3	0.0	**6.7**	8.7	14.9
Seacoast National Bank	Stuart	FL	**B+**	B+	B-	6890.6	16.17	10.0	3.0	16.7	17.4	**9.5**	11.3	14.6
Seamen's Bank	Provincetown	MA	**C+**	C	C	401.7	-0.26	2.4	0.1	44.1	16.0	**9.8**	10.9	18.1
▲ Seaside National Bank & Trust	Orlando	FL	**B-**	B-	C+	1857.2	-1.38	35.3	1.6	8.8	23.0	**6.6**	8.8	12.2
▲ Seattle Bank	Seattle	WA	**B**	B-	C+	661.8	9.74	9.7	1.3	9.4	0.5	**7.8**	9.5	16.9
Sebree Deposit Bank	Sebree	KY	**D+**	D+	D+	21.9	0.50	4.9	7.3	32.6	17.3	**10.0**	11.4	21.7
Second Federal S&L Assn. of Philadelphia	Philadelphia	PA	**D**	D	D	14.7	18.57	0.0	0.0	50.9	16.6	**10.0**	45.4	82.0
Securian Trust Co., N.A.	Saint Paul	MN	**U**	U	U	16.0	13.21	0.0	0.0	0.0	83.5	**10.0**	92.5	101.9
Security Bank	Stephens	AR	**B**	B	B-	69.3	2.62	5.0	5.1	54.6	6.7	**8.1**	9.7	16.7
▲ Security Bank	Laurel	NE	**B+**	B-	A-	221.7	2.85	8.2	2.5	3.3	20.6	**10.0**	11.7	16.4
▼ Security Bank	Tulsa	OK	**B-**	B+	A-	567.2	5.01	27.8	1.0	8.2	3.7	**9.5**	12.1	14.6
Security Bank	Dyersburg	TN	**B-**	B	B	202.8	4.40	6.5	1.7	5.7	54.4	**9.7**	10.8	18.3
▲ Security Bank	Midland	TX	**B+**	B	C+	921.7	8.72	21.7	0.5	2.4	21.6	**10.0**	11.3	18.0
▲ Security Bank	New Auburn	WI	**B**	C+	B	111.3	11.72	8.6	1.3	16.4	8.7	**10.0**	13.5	17.2
Security Bank & Trust Co.	Glencoe	MN	**B+**	B+	B+	570.0	11.96	7.4	0.6	6.1	24.4	**8.2**	9.8	16.4
Security Bank and Trust Co.	Maysville	KY	**B+**	B+	B+	54.4	1.43	3.6	1.7	17.6	39.3	**10.0**	20.2	38.1
Security Bank and Trust Co.	Miami	OK	**B-**	B-	B	94.5	2.83	5.9	3.9	27.5	14.3	**7.5**	9.3	14.8
Security Bank and Trust Co.	Paris	TN	**B+**	B+	A-	475.7	21.78	22.1	1.8	13.9	13.2	**5.1**	9.1	11.1
Security Bank Minnesota	Albert Lea	MN	**B+**	B+	B+	134.1	5.02	55.1	3.8	3.7	8.5	**7.2**	10.4	12.7
Security Bank of Crawford	Crawford	TX	**C**	C	C	77.3	47.24	5.2	3.0	36.5	0.0	**6.9**	8.9	14.8
Security Bank of Kansas City	Kansas City	KS	**A-**	A-	A-	3226.0	4.86	6.6	0.4	2.1	33.6	**10.0**	14.2	21.3
Security Bank of Pulaski County	Waynesville	MO	**C+**	C+	C+	108.1	3.37	6.7	4.4	21.1	20.6	**7.1**	9.1	13.5
▲ Security Bank of Southwest Missouri	Cassville	MO	**B+**	B	B	78.9	-3.89	5.8	5.8	33.2	19.4	**10.0**	12.0	28.9
Security Bank of the Ozarks	Eminence	MO	**C+**	C	C+	93.8	-1.66	8.7	7.5	13.4	12.3	**6.5**	8.5	12.1
Security Bank USA	Bemidji	MN	**B**	B-	B-	161.1	8.13	16.7	5.1	18.6	5.5	**7.6**	9.4	13.8
Security Bank, s.b.	Springfield	IL	**C**	C-	D+	196.4	63.65	5.3	3.1	20.6	9.9	**8.8**	10.2	14.1
Security Federal Bank	Aiken	SC	**B-**	B-	B-	991.1	9.87	2.6	2.2	9.6	46.4	**7.4**	9.3	17.0
Security Federal Bank	Elizabethton	TN	**B-**	B-	B+	62.7	-9.26	2.4	1.9	36.2	16.1	**10.0**	15.0	26.7
Security Federal Savings Bank	Jasper	AL	**C+**	C	C	35.4	-13.39	0.0	8.8	32.4	19.5	**10.0**	13.6	26.8
Security Federal Savings Bank	Logansport	IN	**B-**	B-	B-	277.8	12.39	3.9	1.0	30.5	11.1	**10.0**	12.1	17.7
Security Financial Bank	Durand	WI	**B-**	B	B	499.3	5.28	13.9	0.2	8.3	15.1	**6.5**	9.3	12.1
Security First Bank	Lincoln	NE	**C**	C+	B-	1124.4	6.85	5.8	9.1	8.5	17.8	**6.4**	9.0	12.0
▲ Security First Bank of North Dakota	Center	ND	**A-**	B+	A-	182.3	0.80	11.5	2.5	9.0	4.7	**10.0**	14.2	16.7
▲ Security First National Bank of Hugo	Hugo	OK	**A-**	B+	B+	112.9	-0.80	2.5	1.8	27.0	8.1	**8.4**	10.0	14.6
▲ Security FSB of McMinnville	McMinnville	TN	**A-**	B+	B	217.8	5.96	13.6	6.4	24.8	15.9	**10.0**	11.2	15.5
Security Home Bank	Malmo	NE	**B-**	B-	B-	38.0	-5.59	5.6	3.4	17.4	1.5	**10.0**	13.8	18.9
▲ Security National Bank	Witt	IL	**B**	B-	B-	81.6	2.77	7.0	3.2	21.8	15.4	**9.5**	10.7	16.7
Security National Bank of Enid	Enid	OK	**B+**	B+	B+	318.7	-0.96	3.5	1.4	20.3	37.1	**6.6**	8.6	14.7
▲ Security National Bank of Omaha	Omaha	NE	**A**	A-	A-	855.4	-13.65	17.9	3.2	6.7	23.7	**10.0**	12.2	15.8
Security National Bank of Sioux City, Iowa	Sioux City	IA	**A-**	B+	A-	1037.4	3.14	5.8	1.6	14.2	26.3	**10.0**	12.1	18.5
Security National Bank of South Dakota	Dakota Dunes	SD	**A-**	A-	A-	195.4	5.96	5.2	2.1	12.7	22.9	**10.0**	12.5	20.9
Security National Trust Co.	Wheeling	WV	**U**	U	U	6.6	0.70	0.0	0.0	0.0	72.2	**10.0**	120.	153.8
Security Savings Bank	Gowrie	IA	**B+**	B+	B+	126.6	1.34	4.6	2.4	13.8	26.0	**10.0**	11.2	16.0
Security Savings Bank	Monmouth	IL	**B-**	C+	C	198.4	6.26	2.4	6.5	12.2	15.9	**10.0**	11.3	16.5
Security Savings Bank	Canton	SD	**C+**	B-	B	451.5	97.11	3.8	1.0	5.9	12.4	**7.3**	9.2	13.1
▲ Security State Bank	McRae	GA	**A-**	B+	A-	46.7	2.58	15.5	2.8	6.1	29.7	**10.0**	15.8	32.3
Security State Bank	Algona	IA	**B+**	B+	A-	101.1	-4.87	11.4	1.0	2.6	2.4	**10.0**	17.8	20.9
▲ Security State Bank	Radcliffe	IA	**C-**	C-	C+	94.2	-0.19	7.0	1.8	15.5	23.3	**8.1**	9.7	18.7
▲ Security State Bank	Sutherland	IA	**B**	B-	B	223.9	61.93	8.3	2.1	4.5	0.3	**6.9**	10.6	12.4
▲ Security State Bank	Waverly	IA	**A-**	B+	B+	81.6	9.61	1.0	2.5	11.7	40.0	**10.0**	12.2	20.4
▲ Security State Bank	Scott City	KS	**A-**	B+	A-	302.0	4.01	13.1	2.2	2.2	18.3	**10.0**	15.1	17.4
▲ Security State Bank	Wellington	KS	**C+**	C	C-	53.0	-9.61	3.8	0.6	7.3	50.7	**10.0**	14.1	26.9
▲ Security State Bank	Cheyenne	OK	**A-**	A-	A	167.6	-2.22	5.6	3.7	20.3	27.9	**10.0**	14.6	21.9
▲ Security State Bank	Alexandria	SD	**B**	B-	B	86.3	5.00	6.9	4.5	2.2	23.4	**9.8**	10.9	16.2
Security State Bank	Emery	SD	**B**	B	B	50.7	12.28	17.3	2.8	0.0	4.2	**10.0**	14.3	29.3

Asset Quality Index	Adjusted Non-Performing Loans as a % of Total Loans	Adjusted Non-Performing Loans as a % of Capital	Net Charge-Offs Avg Loans	Profitability Index	Net Income ($Mil)	Return on Assets (R.O.A.)	Return on Equity (R.O.E.)	Net Interest Spread	Overhead Efficiency Ratio	Liquidity Index	Liquidity Ratio	Hot Money Ratio	Stability Index
8.4	1.32	na	-0.02	**2.3**	0.3	0.30	1.89	2.69	86.7	**1.2**	26.5	34.2	**7.3**
1.6	9.70	22.6	0.17	**8.2**	50.8	1.78	8.03	3.96	55.0	**3.5**	44.6	23.0	**8.2**
8.8	0.17	na	-0.12	**4.0**	1.2	0.96	6.46	3.43	74.5	**5.0**	34.5	7.6	**7.6**
10.0	0.35	na	0.02	**2.6**	0.3	0.38	2.59	2.53	82.8	**1.6**	35.9	46.9	**7.3**
7.1	0.27	na	-0.01	**9.9**	1.1	2.22	14.95	4.48	60.1	**4.8**	19.0	4.2	**8.9**
5.9	0.57	na	0.04	**7.7**	10.9	1.35	11.65	6.17	67.8	**4.9**	7.5	2.1	**9.2**
5.9	0.74	3.1	0.14	**7.3**	73.7	1.45	10.44	3.98	54.2	**2.5**	18.5	9.0	**9.5**
3.5	4.50	na	0.01	**3.1**	1.5	0.52	4.73	3.37	79.1	**2.9**	29.8	16.9	**6.4**
7.2	0.64	4.6	0.41	**4.1**	10.2	0.72	8.59	2.75	61.4	**1.2**	19.7	19.2	**7.3**
5.8	1.59	na	0.07	**5.9**	6.0	1.26	12.23	4.10	55.2	**0.5**	9.7	44.4	**8.7**
8.7	0.00	na	0.00	**0.7**	0.0	-0.22	-1.86	3.60	107.0	**1.5**	29.3	27.0	**4.7**
10.0	0.00	na	0.00	**0.0**	-0.1	-1.26	-2.60	3.70	135.1	**2.7**	75.0	45.6	**6.2**
10.0	na	0.0	na	**9.5**	0.2	1.80	1.97	3.19	93.6	**4.0**	na	0.0	**6.4**
6.3	0.13	na	0.14	**5.3**	0.5	0.95	10.17	3.99	63.1	**0.5**	11.9	49.9	**5.8**
6.7	0.42	na	0.57	**6.6**	2.6	1.52	12.85	4.52	65.1	**3.8**	23.3	8.0	**8.5**
2.7	1.24	na	0.85	**9.2**	8.8	2.07	17.04	3.88	42.4	**0.7**	16.1	38.1	**9.7**
6.7	2.10	na	0.00	**4.2**	1.4	0.93	8.37	3.19	76.8	**1.8**	29.7	27.8	**7.3**
7.8	0.07	na	0.02	**9.3**	14.8	2.28	16.53	5.28	58.9	**5.7**	36.5	3.9	**9.4**
5.8	1.04	na	0.00	**7.0**	1.0	1.27	9.42	3.91	59.6	**1.4**	18.4	15.5	**7.5**
5.5	1.62	6.3	0.04	**6.5**	6.1	1.56	15.64	3.14	58.9	**4.2**	27.8	9.9	**8.2**
9.1	0.21	na	-0.08	**6.2**	0.6	1.56	7.93	3.67	58.7	**4.6**	37.7	11.1	**8.2**
4.7	0.62	na	0.43	**3.6**	0.5	0.73	7.47	3.94	79.9	**1.2**	20.7	29.9	**6.2**
8.4	0.02	na	0.01	**7.1**	4.9	1.47	15.32	3.70	59.4	**1.2**	12.3	18.5	**7.0**
6.9	0.32	na	-0.13	**7.4**	1.6	1.60	14.90	4.52	61.1	**1.5**	10.4	22.5	**8.4**
7.7	0.05	na	-0.32	**4.3**	0.4	0.84	9.36	3.95	67.0	**1.1**	29.7	54.8	**4.2**
6.4	2.14	4.2	0.11	**7.1**	32.5	1.42	8.74	3.57	50.8	**5.4**	34.7	8.8	**9.6**
5.1	1.21	6.5	0.04	**3.7**	0.6	0.71	7.72	4.29	80.4	**1.2**	14.1	22.0	**5.0**
5.3	0.50	na	0.11	**9.8**	1.4	2.24	17.62	4.52	56.4	**2.8**	21.2	15.6	**8.4**
5.6	0.31	na	0.00	**4.8**	0.8	1.07	11.29	5.03	74.7	**2.4**	12.6	16.8	**5.1**
4.9	1.08	7.6	-0.05	**7.4**	2.1	1.84	19.91	4.47	63.6	**4.2**	14.4	7.1	**7.0**
2.4	3.73	21.1	0.12	**3.6**	0.7	0.57	5.63	3.56	78.5	**6.4**	51.8	4.4	**4.1**
6.0	1.06	na	0.18	**4.2**	6.6	0.93	9.31	3.40	74.3	**2.4**	34.4	16.5	**6.5**
6.9	2.42	na	-0.02	**2.7**	0.2	0.36	2.44	3.27	89.7	**0.8**	15.8	34.5	**6.6**
8.9	0.00	na	0.19	**3.3**	0.2	0.64	5.02	3.70	84.9	**2.3**	40.6	30.2	**5.7**
7.3	1.22	na	0.13	**3.4**	1.2	0.59	4.80	3.92	82.4	**3.2**	19.8	13.5	**6.2**
4.4	1.50	na	0.00	**6.4**	5.8	1.60	14.89	3.94	58.9	**4.0**	19.2	8.2	**7.5**
4.0	1.03	na	1.37	**3.9**	5.5	0.69	6.96	3.65	64.5	**2.0**	19.1	19.8	**8.7**
7.6	0.01	na	-0.10	**8.0**	2.7	2.02	14.04	4.93	62.3	**3.5**	7.1	10.5	**9.3**
8.7	0.14	na	-0.01	**10.0**	2.0	2.36	25.45	6.01	51.1	**1.7**	6.1	19.8	**7.5**
8.0	0.27	1.7	0.00	**5.9**	1.9	1.20	11.18	3.86	62.5	**1.8**	15.3	20.3	**6.6**
7.1	0.00	na	0.00	**5.4**	0.3	1.10	8.23	3.63	62.4	**1.6**	17.7	24.0	**6.4**
4.8	2.59	9.3	0.26	**3.8**	0.3	0.55	5.11	3.81	74.2	**3.2**	30.8	16.1	**6.0**
6.7	0.41	3.3	0.19	**7.0**	4.3	1.72	18.60	3.27	50.5	**4.4**	17.7	6.3	**7.6**
8.4	0.11	0.4	-0.01	**6.3**	8.7	1.28	11.22	3.70	65.4	**4.9**	22.5	3.4	**8.7**
7.1	1.47	na	-0.01	**7.9**	12.0	1.62	13.97	3.20	56.4	**4.5**	25.1	8.2	**9.5**
8.7	0.03	na	0.00	**8.9**	2.3	1.64	13.71	2.76	52.3	**2.3**	30.5	17.0	**9.0**
10.0	na	na	na	**9.5**	1.0	27.78	23.78	2.14	74.7	**4.0**	na	0.0	**5.7**
8.3	0.60	na	0.33	**5.0**	1.1	1.19	10.81	3.36	61.7	**2.0**	18.1	19.5	**7.6**
6.7	0.49	na	0.09	**3.4**	0.9	0.59	5.38	3.00	74.0	**1.9**	19.6	19.8	**6.2**
4.5	0.58	na	0.02	**3.6**	2.6	0.75	8.35	3.09	74.3	**1.5**	14.6	23.4	**5.3**
8.8	0.01	na	-0.06	**7.5**	0.6	1.78	11.81	4.72	63.7	**5.9**	56.5	8.0	**7.9**
6.4	0.64	na	0.01	**8.7**	1.3	1.67	9.81	4.41	46.8	**2.6**	18.9	16.3	**8.7**
2.9	2.99	na	0.01	**2.3**	0.2	0.23	2.37	2.68	89.9	**3.7**	35.9	15.0	**4.9**
6.6	0.04	na	0.06	**10.0**	3.3	2.65	27.91	5.37	43.1	**1.4**	5.6	11.7	**7.8**
9.0	0.00	0.0	0.01	**5.0**	0.8	1.21	9.96	3.06	58.2	**5.8**	43.6	5.3	**7.2**
7.1	0.00	na	-0.01	**8.4**	3.7	1.64	10.92	3.53	44.1	**0.4**	9.5	52.1	**8.8**
5.8	1.81	na	0.06	**2.8**	0.2	0.57	4.38	3.37	84.1	**6.1**	46.0	4.0	**4.8**
5.6	0.80	na	0.22	**9.7**	3.4	2.66	18.09	4.39	44.0	**0.8**	6.8	32.2	**9.5**
7.6	0.26	na	0.01	**4.7**	0.7	1.08	9.82	3.59	66.8	**2.3**	34.1	24.7	**6.6**
8.7	0.00	0.0	0.00	**5.1**	0.4	0.99	7.04	3.45	56.8	**5.1**	66.6	14.2	**7.0**

Name	City	State	Rating	2018 Rating	2017 Rating	Total Assets ($Mil)	One Year Asset Growth	Asset Mix (As a % of Total Assets) Comm-ercial Loans	Cons-umer Loans	Mort-gage Loans	Secur-ities	Capital-ization Index	Lever-age Ratio	Risk-Based Capital Ratio
▲ Security State Bank	Tyndall	SD	**B-**	C+	B-	230.0	5.85	9.9	0.7	2.4	7.9	**7.4**	9.6	12.9
Security State Bank	Farwell	TX	**A-**	A-	A-	151.5	0.03	18.9	0.5	11.8	18.8	**10.0**	14.8	21.4
▲ Security State Bank	Pearsall	TX	**A-**	B	B+	631.7	4.78	3.0	0.9	2.4	32.5	**10.0**	13.2	18.3
▲ Security State Bank	Winters	TX	**B-**	C+	C+	61.7	1.02	8.9	8.0	8.7	28.6	**7.7**	9.5	17.8
▲ Security State Bank	Centralia	WA	**A**	A-	A-	488.1	8.04	5.0	1.3	4.7	2.6	**10.0**	13.2	28.9
▲ Security State Bank	Iron River	WI	**B-**	C	C	104.3	8.09	16.0	1.3	12.0	18.7	**10.0**	18.3	23.8
Security State Bank	Basin	WY	**B**	B+	B+	358.5	5.36	5.9	3.3	9.5	26.3	**10.0**	11.5	18.6
Security State Bank & Trust	Fredericksburg	TX	**A**	A	A-	1090.2	8.51	10.1	2.2	10.5	19.5	**10.0**	13.3	18.3
▲ Security State Bank of Aitkin	Aitkin	MN	**A-**	B+	A-	101.7	3.44	18.4	2.3	11.3	22.5	**10.0**	12.5	20.0
▲ Security State Bank of Fergus Falls	Fergus Falls	MN	**B+**	B-	B-	121.4	-1.62	6.9	0.3	6.0	21.6	**8.3**	10.2	13.6
▲ Security State Bank of Hibbing	Hibbing	MN	**B**	C+	C+	135.2	8.69	14.9	1.5	11.7	18.9	**9.8**	10.8	20.6
Security State Bank of Kenyon	Kenyon	MN	**D-**	D-	D	55.1	0.56	5.6	1.5	16.9	1.8	**9.8**	11.7	14.8
▲ Security State Bank of Marine	Marine On Saint Croi	MN	**A-**	B+	B+	144.9	0.69	4.3	2.1	38.4	3.8	**9.6**	10.8	17.8
Security State Bank of Oklahoma	Wewoka	OK	**C**	C	B-	255.8	6.73	15.8	10.8	16.8	13.3	**10.0**	11.2	15.1
▲ Security State Bank of Oklee	Oklee	MN	**B+**	B	B	30.6	-2.27	3.5	6.1	14.5	42.3	**10.0**	17.9	46.7
▲ Security State Bank of Wanamingo	Wanamingo	MN	**B+**	B	B	66.6	1.33	6.2	1.3	3.6	18.4	**10.0**	12.2	18.0
▼ Security State Bank of Warroad	Warroad	MN	**D+**	D+	D+	101.9	5.38	12.7	13.1	2.3	31.2	**10.0**	16.3	22.3
Security State Bank, Wishek, North Dakota	Wishek	ND	**B**	B	B-	72.8	-0.76	6.6	2.7	0.8	38.9	**10.0**	13.5	25.4
Security Trust & Savings Bank	Storm Lake	IA	**B-**	B-	C+	231.9	20.39	4.5	1.1	8.0	42.4	**9.9**	10.9	21.7
SEI Private Trust Co.	Oaks	PA	**U**	U	U	183.6	-0.02	0.0	0.0	0.0	49.2	**10.0**	91.7	286.1
▲ Seiling State Bank	Seiling	OK	**B**	B-	C+	113.0	-0.16	11.4	2.8	9.1	24.8	**7.5**	9.4	15.3
Select Bank	Forest	VA	**B-**	B-	B-	244.0	10.60	30.8	2.4	26.1	0.5	**7.1**	9.1	16.6
Select Bank & Trust Co.	Dunn	NC	**B**	B	B-	1268.7	1.40	4.1	0.4	12.3	6.1	**10.0**	13.0	15.6
▲ Senath State Bank	Senath	MO	**A-**	A-	A-	75.2	-0.70	7.0	8.9	29.8	8.2	**10.0**	16.1	29.4
SENB Bank	Moline	IL	**B-**	B-	B-	297.4	35.61	12.2	1.2	17.9	21.3	**7.5**	9.3	12.9
Seneca Savings	Baldwinsville	NY	**C**	C	C	210.5	9.27	7.5	0.4	48.8	13.3	**8.6**	10.1	16.2
▲ Sentry Bank	Saint Joseph	MN	**C+**	C+	B	229.7	3.89	9.7	3.1	14.8	17.4	**7.3**	9.2	13.3
ServisFirst Bank	Birmingham	AL	**A-**	A-	B+	9004.8	19.78	28.1	0.7	4.9	7.6	**6.7**	9.6	12.2
▲ Settlers Bank	Marietta	OH	**A-**	B+	B+	126.7	2.16	4.3	4.0	41.5	4.7	**10.0**	13.4	22.3
Settlers bank	Windsor	WI	**B-**	B-	B-	314.4	12.16	23.0	1.0	14.7	2.6	**6.8**	10.3	12.3
Severn Savings Bank, FSB	Annapolis	MD	**A-**	B+	B	822.4	-7.15	4.0	0.3	33.1	4.8	**10.0**	13.5	19.7
Sevier County Bank	Sevierville	TN	**E-**	E-	E-	326.0	3.00	5.4	0.8	12.5	9.9	**8.0**	9.7	15.3
Sewickley Savings Bank	Sewickley	PA	**B-**	B-	B-	319.2	2.26	1.8	0.1	6.3	60.4	**10.0**	28.7	66.7
Seymour Bank	Seymour	MO	**B**	B	B	148.5	8.28	2.6	5.9	19.2	27.1	**10.0**	13.4	16.6
Shamrock Bank, N.A.	Coalgate	OK	**A-**	A-	A-	314.9	2.55	6.6	4.4	18.1	21.3	**10.0**	12.6	18.4
Sharon Bank	Springfield	PA	**D+**	D+	C-	173.4	11.32	2.4	0.2	31.8	26.4	**8.3**	9.9	14.6
▲ Shelby County State Bank	Harlan	IA	**C+**	C+	B	268.5	3.68	3.1	1.3	5.7	16.4	**10.0**	11.5	15.6
▲ Shelby County State Bank	Shelbyville	IL	**B+**	B	B	257.4	4.14	7.7	2.6	16.6	15.6	**8.4**	10.0	14.0
Shelby Savings Bank, SSB	Center	TX	**A-**	B+	A-	302.1	-0.40	12.0	4.6	15.2	11.4	**10.0**	12.3	16.6
Shelby State Bank	Shelby	MI	**B-**	B-	B-	269.7	8.82	5.0	1.4	13.4	23.0	**6.5**	8.5	12.6
Shell Lake State Bank	Shell Lake	WI	**A-**	A	A	213.6	-0.29	3.3	3.4	26.6	39.7	**10.0**	16.6	31.4
▲ Sherburne State Bank	Becker	MN	**B-**	C+	B	126.9	7.27	10.5	1.7	15.3	12.9	**5.3**	8.4	11.2
▲ Sherwood Community Bank	Creighton	MO	**C+**	C	C	48.8	2.36	3.4	1.2	27.3	17.1	**8.8**	10.2	19.0
Sherwood State Bank	Sherwood	OH	**C+**	C	C+	72.9	9.66	7.9	6.1	32.2	17.0	**10.0**	11.3	16.9
▼ Shinhan Bank America	New York	NY	**C**	C+	B+	1581.5	12.08	17.4	0.2	14.1	3.1	**10.0**	13.6	17.9
Shore United Bank	Easton	MD	**B+**	B+	B+	1562.3	7.24	6.1	0.8	22.8	9.5	**8.4**	10.7	13.7
▲ Sibley State Bank	Sibley	IA	**B**	C	D+	80.7	6.02	2.9	1.5	3.6	6.0	**10.0**	12.4	16.3
Sicily Island State Bank	Sicily Island	LA	**B-**	B-	B	63.0	6.54	9.2	4.7	31.0	6.1	**10.0**	13.5	20.6
Sidney Federal S&L Assn.	Sidney	NE	**D-**	D-	E+	15.6	-8.51	6.1	3.1	64.5	20.5	**7.3**	9.2	17.7
Sidney State Bank	Sidney	MI	**C**	C	B-	80.2	10.71	4.3	4.5	50.4	6.7	**6.5**	8.5	14.4
▲ Signature Bank	Rosemont	IL	**A-**	B+	B-	891.2	14.91	38.0	0.1	2.7	10.2	**7.3**	10.3	12.7
Signature Bank	New York	NY	**B+**	B+	B+	49424.9	7.75	15.7	0.4	1.1	18.3	**7.8**	9.7	13.2
Signature Bank of Arkansas	Fayetteville	AR	**B**	B	B	659.9	5.16	10.7	3.5	18.1	8.5	**9.2**	11.6	14.4
Signature Bank of Georgia	Sandy Springs	GA	**D+**	D	D	144.8	39.78	8.3	0.2	3.1	18.7	**10.0**	13.0	20.0
▲ Signature Bank, N.A.	Toledo	OH	**A-**	B+	B	958.2	10.51	24.9	0.8	9.6	1.1	**8.2**	10.9	13.5
Silex Banking Co.	Silex	MO	**B+**	B+	B	70.7	-3.44	4.2	0.8	9.1	42.7	**10.0**	17.1	36.3
Silicon Valley Bank	Santa Clara	CA	**A-**	B+	B	67059.6	17.07	16.5	0.3	4.4	40.9	**5.5**	7.5	12.4
▲ Silver Lake Bank	Topeka	KS	**B+**	B	B	289.9	8.51	10.0	1.2	20.4	17.2	**10.0**	11.1	15.3
Silvergate Bank	La Jolla	CA	**A-**	B+	B	2133.3	-0.61	0.7	0.0	25.0	42.7	**8.5**	10.0	25.0
▲ Simmesport State Bank	Simmesport	LA	**B-**	C+	B-	96.7	14.90	4.8	14.2	41.6	3.9	**10.0**	14.2	20.7

Asset Quality Index	Adjusted Non-Performing Loans as a % of Total Loans	Adjusted Non-Performing Loans as a % of Capital	Net Charge-Offs Avg Loans	Profitability Index	Net Income ($Mil)	Return on Assets (R.O.A.)	Return on Equity (R.O.E.)	Net Interest Spread	Overhead Efficiency Ratio	Liquidity Index	Liquidity Ratio	Hot Money Ratio	Stability Index
6.0	0.38	na	-0.23	**7.9**	3.4	1.91	20.69	4.20	48.9	**0.8**	19.6	28.6	**6.5**
8.6	0.00	na	-0.03	**9.4**	3.4	2.99	22.12	4.05	30.9	**1.3**	13.6	27.6	**8.6**
8.5	0.92	na	0.01	**6.0**	5.8	1.24	9.61	3.19	53.8	**1.1**	19.4	32.4	**8.1**
8.6	0.05	na	0.06	**6.2**	0.8	1.59	17.67	4.28	63.7	**4.6**	26.6	6.9	**4.4**
8.4	1.13	na	0.03	**9.1**	12.0	3.42	25.76	4.16	41.6	**6.8**	63.0	5.3	**9.1**
3.9	5.05	na	-0.01	**5.5**	0.9	1.17	6.29	4.23	66.7	**1.5**	28.5	27.6	**7.0**
5.8	1.01	na	0.58	**4.0**	1.7	0.67	5.85	3.56	70.1	**1.4**	19.9	25.8	**6.7**
6.4	1.51	na	0.01	**8.3**	15.7	1.98	14.91	4.70	67.4	**3.5**	18.1	12.2	**10.0**
7.9	0.21	na	0.13	**6.7**	1.3	1.68	13.63	4.36	58.1	**4.6**	21.7	5.8	**8.1**
5.8	1.87	na	0.00	**5.9**	1.4	1.50	13.84	4.13	63.8	**3.7**	4.5	8.3	**7.0**
4.9	3.66	na	0.05	**4.9**	1.0	0.97	9.68	4.12	64.7	**5.0**	43.8	10.7	**5.3**
0.0	11.49	na	0.06	**2.6**	0.1	0.33	2.91	4.27	86.4	**3.1**	13.3	13.3	**6.0**
6.9	1.31	na	-0.03	**9.5**	2.4	2.29	21.78	4.83	53.5	**3.7**	27.9	12.6	**8.5**
4.3	1.70	na	0.10	**9.3**	3.7	1.95	17.94	4.79	49.4	**0.6**	6.8	34.1	**6.5**
8.2	0.00	na	0.31	**7.1**	0.5	1.88	11.17	2.96	52.7	**6.5**	57.2	3.7	**7.0**
8.5	0.00	na	0.02	**6.5**	0.8	1.64	13.61	3.98	59.3	**4.3**	33.4	11.3	**7.5**
6.1	1.82	na	4.72	**0.0**	-1.4	-1.90	-10.98	3.92	76.7	**5.1**	41.3	10.0	**5.4**
8.7	0.00	0.4	0.14	**4.9**	0.7	1.24	9.31	3.53	62.2	**5.6**	52.9	8.9	**7.4**
8.7	0.08	na	-0.07	**3.5**	1.2	0.72	6.28	2.57	66.6	**5.4**	56.4	11.9	**5.8**
10.0	na	na	na	**10.0**	65.3	47.99	53.92	2.93	56.0	**4.0**	na	100.0	**7.0**
8.5	0.14	na	-0.07	**6.1**	1.4	1.55	16.94	4.27	63.7	**1.7**	9.8	19.9	**6.0**
5.4	0.69	na	-0.01	**3.9**	1.2	0.70	7.57	3.19	72.8	**0.6**	8.8	49.2	**4.7**
4.0	1.51	7.2	0.10	**5.8**	11.0	1.16	7.81	4.13	63.8	**1.1**	12.9	30.0	**9.6**
8.1	0.00	2.4	-0.01	**9.0**	1.3	2.20	14.62	4.17	52.4	**5.4**	30.5	2.9	**9.5**
8.4	0.22	na	0.01	**4.3**	2.1	0.99	10.78	4.24	71.1	**2.6**	14.0	15.9	**5.6**
6.4	1.02	na	0.14	**3.3**	1.0	0.64	7.43	3.19	74.8	**0.7**	10.1	32.0	**4.7**
5.7	0.13	na	0.01	**7.2**	2.3	1.35	11.55	3.76	48.1	**1.7**	29.1	27.7	**6.7**
6.9	0.51	4.3	0.31	**9.3**	110.4	1.73	17.82	3.55	32.8	**4.2**	16.3	8.0	**9.0**
6.8	0.91	na	0.01	**7.4**	1.3	1.46	10.99	4.13	54.7	**2.8**	21.3	15.7	**8.3**
5.7	0.71	na	0.09	**3.5**	1.3	0.60	5.97	3.48	77.1	**0.6**	11.6	43.2	**5.3**
6.1	1.88	7.3	0.02	**5.8**	7.9	1.15	8.80	3.69	67.0	**2.0**	16.0	19.2	**8.6**
6.0	0.75	na	-0.04	**0.0**	-2.1	-0.91	-14.73	3.67	147.1	**1.6**	19.5	24.3	**1.7**
10.0	0.06	0.0	0.00	**3.6**	1.8	0.74	2.62	1.86	54.8	**4.3**	106.2	32.6	**8.0**
8.5	0.15	na	-0.36	**4.4**	1.0	0.91	7.03	4.11	80.4	**2.6**	22.9	16.4	**7.4**
8.4	0.31	na	0.01	**6.0**	3.4	1.42	11.75	4.47	67.0	**2.2**	27.8	20.1	**7.7**
8.7	0.31	na	0.00	**1.4**	0.3	0.20	1.96	2.79	90.5	**2.3**	32.7	23.8	**4.5**
6.3	1.36	na	0.11	**6.8**	2.7	1.38	11.28	3.75	53.6	**4.6**	25.9	6.6	**7.6**
8.4	0.00	na	0.00	**5.7**	2.6	1.38	14.06	3.63	63.2	**3.7**	17.8	10.6	**7.0**
7.9	0.35	3.0	0.10	**6.1**	3.4	1.50	11.39	4.26	69.2	**1.6**	21.8	24.6	**7.8**
3.9	3.18	12.9	0.00	**3.9**	1.4	0.73	8.16	4.06	82.8	**4.5**	26.8	7.2	**5.2**
9.0	0.69	na	0.00	**6.0**	2.5	1.55	9.47	3.33	63.8	**4.4**	35.3	7.9	**8.6**
4.7	0.93	na	0.07	**8.6**	1.5	1.63	20.55	4.50	55.7	**3.4**	20.0	12.4	**6.2**
6.6	0.09	na	0.01	**3.5**	0.2	0.59	5.95	4.19	86.8	**5.2**	33.8	5.9	**5.1**
3.9	2.08	na	0.30	**3.5**	0.3	0.63	5.77	4.43	80.5	**3.9**	17.6	9.5	**5.7**
7.2	0.24	1.3	-0.06	**2.0**	1.1	0.10	0.67	3.40	96.3	**0.8**	12.8	36.4	**8.4**
4.8	1.37	8.1	0.04	**6.0**	12.4	1.12	9.91	3.52	61.2	**3.8**	13.9	9.2	**8.8**
6.6	1.60	na	0.03	**6.5**	0.8	1.31	10.96	3.59	55.7	**1.4**	19.2	26.7	**6.9**
4.3	5.82	na	0.09	**4.6**	0.4	0.94	7.57	4.55	74.8	**0.7**	17.3	50.7	**7.6**
7.1	0.54	na	0.00	**0.0**	-0.2	-1.70	-18.05	3.37	145.7	**2.6**	26.5	16.5	**2.0**
4.6	1.94	12.9	0.17	**3.9**	0.4	0.68	8.12	4.23	77.3	**3.3**	17.1	12.8	**4.8**
8.2	0.32	na	-0.04	**9.9**	12.2	1.93	18.87	4.57	45.6	**3.8**	25.5	5.3	**6.3**
7.0	0.26	1.4	0.00	**5.8**	440.7	1.20	12.78	2.76	39.8	**4.2**	16.1	6.4	**8.1**
7.2	0.02	0.2	-0.01	**4.9**	4.5	0.92	8.00	4.04	71.8	**0.7**	11.2	28.7	**7.6**
6.3	3.95	na	-0.01	**1.0**	0.0	0.03	0.22	4.00	95.8	**5.3**	39.3	8.0	**4.5**
8.2	0.04	0.3	0.01	**7.2**	9.9	1.42	13.43	3.59	50.2	**2.9**	22.4	13.2	**7.8**
9.0	0.00	na	-0.02	**5.4**	0.6	1.14	6.94	3.59	61.5	**6.0**	58.0	7.5	**8.0**
8.7	0.42	2.3	0.26	**9.3**	783.1	1.75	21.80	3.63	43.7	**7.5**	49.7	0.1	**7.0**
7.1	3.34	na	0.00	**5.3**	2.3	1.08	9.55	3.59	59.6	**1.4**	12.4	24.6	**7.2**
8.9	0.72	2.4	0.01	**7.9**	23.1	1.49	14.35	3.70	54.0	**4.7**	56.4	0.1	**7.7**
3.6	2.71	na	0.27	**7.2**	1.0	1.42	9.96	4.81	58.0	**0.7**	15.6	52.1	**6.8**

Name	City	State	Rating	2018 Rating	2017 Rating	Total Assets ($Mil)	One Year Asset Growth	Asset Mix (As a % of Total Assets) Commercial Loans	Consumer Loans	Mortgage Loans	Securities	Capitalization Index	Leverage Ratio	Risk-Based Capital Ratio
▲ Simmons Bank	Pine Bluff	AR	**B+**	B	B-	17716.1	8.97	12.6	2.0	10.5	12.7	**6.7**	10.4	12.3
▲ Simply Bank	Spring City	TN	**C+**	C-	C-	368.1	11.82	9.9	1.6	19.8	7.6	**6.5**	9.1	12.1
Siouxland Bank	South Sioux City	NE	**C+**	C	C	55.4	6.32	8.9	2.9	18.3	0.0	**8.8**	10.2	20.2
▼ SJN Bank of Kansas	Saint John	KS	**B**	B+	B+	173.7	20.44	9.2	2.3	4.3	31.2	**6.1**	8.1	13.0
▲ Skowhegan Savings Bank	Skowhegan	ME	**B+**	B	B	603.6	1.03	7.1	9.5	34.3	12.4	**10.0**	15.2	21.7
▲ Skyline National Bank	Independence	VA	**B-**	C+	B-	694.2	2.18	4.2	1.1	25.6	5.0	**8.1**	10.8	13.5
Sloan State Bank	Sloan	IA	**B+**	B+	A-	54.0	-2.29	4.3	8.1	16.7	39.5	**10.0**	12.1	22.5
Slovenian S&L Assn. of Canonsburg	Strabane	PA	**B+**	B+	A-	431.0	9.36	0.0	0.3	35.9	55.3	**10.0**	15.1	24.4
Slovenian S&L Assn. of Franklin-Conemau	Conemaugh	PA	**C+**	C+	C+	146.3	8.58	0.0	2.2	48.7	31.5	**10.0**	11.7	19.3
Smackover State Bank	Smackover	AR	**B**	B	B	182.2	-0.40	2.9	4.3	19.4	45.5	**10.0**	13.3	29.8
Small Business Bank	Lenexa	KS	**C**	C	C-	65.9	2.74	21.8	8.8	13.8	13.5	**10.0**	14.7	22.0
SmartBank	Pigeon Forge	TN	**B**	B	B-	2392.8	16.69	13.4	0.4	13.2	7.2	**7.8**	11.2	13.2
▲ SNB Bank, N.A.	Shattuck	OK	**C+**	C	C+	114.6	-1.34	13.1	14.6	2.3	12.8	**7.6**	9.4	13.9
▲ Solera National Bank	Lakewood	CO	**A-**	B+	B	277.8	28.93	6.9	5.8	10.8	12.1	**10.0**	14.8	20.2
Solomon State Bank	Solomon	KS	**A-**	A-	A	203.1	2.08	3.3	1.7	48.2	5.8	**10.0**	16.8	32.1
Solon State Bank	Solon	IA	**A-**	A-	A-	96.1	-0.40	20.9	2.1	11.5	34.2	**10.0**	23.0	26.6
Solutions North Bank	Stockton	KS	**B+**	B+	B+	246.8	5.17	7.8	2.0	5.5	17.0	**10.0**	11.4	16.1
Solvay Bank	Solvay	NY	**B**	B	B	969.6	7.49	9.0	9.7	26.4	28.7	**8.0**	9.6	16.8
Somerset Savings Bank, SLA	Bound Brook	NJ	**B-**	C+	C+	582.4	3.82	0.0	0.0	54.6	24.2	**10.0**	20.8	48.0
Somerset Trust Co.	Somerset	PA	**B-**	B-	B-	1310.4	8.21	18.8	3.3	13.3	23.2	**5.5**	8.8	11.4
Somerville Bank	Somerville	OH	**B-**	C+	C	196.2	8.53	5.0	1.3	17.9	14.0	**9.6**	10.8	15.9
▲ Sonabank	Glen Allen	VA	**A-**	B+	B+	2703.6	-0.08	6.4	1.0	21.3	9.0	**10.0**	11.6	15.0
▲ Sooner State Bank	Tuttle	OK	**A**	A-	A	209.1	1.20	2.6	2.2	16.9	17.3	**10.0**	12.6	19.6
▲ Sound Banking Co.	Lakewood	WA	**B+**	B-	B-	56.9	5.57	7.7	0.6	22.5	0.0	**8.4**	9.9	18.1
Sound Community Bank	Seattle	WA	**C+**	C+	B	715.3	0.11	4.8	9.6	25.8	1.1	**5.9**	10.4	11.7
▲ South Atlantic Bank	Myrtle Beach	SC	**B-**	C+	C+	709.5	15.94	6.0	1.0	25.3	10.2	**5.3**	8.7	11.3
▲ South Central Bank, Inc.	Glasgow	KY	**B+**	B	B	1180.6	2.54	6.9	1.8	15.9	14.2	**10.0**	11.0	15.0
▼ South Central Bank, N.A.	Chicago	IL	**C-**	C+	C+	292.2	-1.94	12.9	2.3	10.0	29.4	**6.6**	8.6	21.0
▲ South Central State Bank	Campbell	NE	**A-**	B+	B+	135.6	-0.36	3.5	0.9	0.7	19.6	**9.8**	12.2	14.8
South Coast Bank & Trust	Brunswick	GA	**B**	B	B	137.6	8.51	5.3	0.9	21.7	9.7	**9.3**	10.6	15.8
South Georgia Bank	Glennville	GA	**A**	A	A-	157.7	2.86	3.1	4.6	18.9	20.0	**10.0**	12.9	21.0
▲ South Georgia Banking Co.	Tifton	GA	**A-**	B+	A-	443.1	2.65	4.4	2.1	11.5	16.7	**10.0**	12.5	20.7
South Lafourche Bank & Trust Co.	Larose	LA	**D+**	D	D-	145.8	2.66	10.2	4.1	39.6	7.9	**10.0**	13.3	22.6
▲ South Louisiana Bank	Houma	LA	**A-**	B+	A	487.5	5.61	18.6	1.8	9.1	12.9	**10.0**	14.9	23.7
South Ottumwa Savings Bank	Ottumwa	IA	**B+**	B+	B+	394.2	-4.06	5.5	1.1	17.5	35.0	**10.0**	13.5	22.7
South Porte Bank	Marion	IL	**C+**	C	C	105.4	2.83	6.2	2.2	27.8	8.8	**7.1**	9.1	13.7
South Shore Bank	South Weymouth	MA	**C+**	C+	C+	1540.4	10.59	9.9	0.4	22.4	15.8	**8.9**	10.3	15.4
South State Bank	Columbia	SC	**A-**	A-	B+	15748.6	8.47	6.3	4.2	19.6	11.5	**7.0**	9.6	12.5
▲ South Story Bank & Trust	Slater	IA	**B**	C+	B-	201.2	2.73	14.8	1.2	19.1	8.8	**7.2**	9.6	12.7
▲ SouthCrest Bank, N.A.	Atlanta	GA	**B**	B-	B-	522.1	-3.67	6.4	0.5	13.2	26.2	**8.0**	9.7	13.5
SouthEast Bank	Farragut	TN	**B**	B	C+	1709.8	23.70	7.1	54.2	6.1	0.0	**6.6**	8.7	13.2
▼ Southeast First National Bank	Summerville	GA	**C**	C+	C	60.0	4.58	0.6	2.1	11.6	59.1	**10.0**	11.8	35.1
▲ Southeastern Bank	Darien	GA	**A**	A-	A-	421.1	0.00	5.6	2.1	13.8	28.8	**10.0**	13.2	22.1
Southern Bancorp Bank	Arkadelphia	AR	**B-**	B-	B-	1461.8	10.43	9.3	2.6	17.2	12.0	**7.3**	9.2	13.4
Southern Bank	Sardis	GA	**B-**	B-	B-	78.9	-0.11	0.6	8.3	29.8	24.1	**10.0**	12.4	23.4
Southern Bank	Poplar Bluff	MO	**B+**	B+	B+	2238.0	15.68	11.4	1.5	16.4	7.6	**7.4**	10.5	12.9
▲ Southern Bank & Trust	Clarkesville	GA	**B-**	C+	B-	224.6	20.68	5.6	4.2	20.7	9.3	**7.1**	9.1	12.9
Southern Bank and Trust Co.	Mount Olive	NC	**A-**	A-	B	2854.3	10.02	6.8	1.0	11.3	25.7	**8.0**	9.6	13.3
Southern Bank Co.	Gadsden	AL	**C**	C-	D-	96.6	1.70	14.1	1.7	8.6	17.5	**9.7**	10.8	18.1
Southern Bank of Tennessee	Mount Juliet	TN	**B+**	B+	B-	288.8	6.52	7.4	1.6	23.7	9.9	**10.0**	13.1	16.4
Southern First Bank	Greenville	SC	**B+**	B+	B+	2201.5	18.35	10.4	1.2	23.2	4.1	**7.9**	10.5	13.2
▲ Southern Heritage Bank	Jonesville	LA	**A-**	B+	A-	301.1	1.36	9.5	5.1	29.7	19.4	**10.0**	11.8	20.4
Southern Hills Community Bank	Leesburg	OH	**C**	C-	C-	159.6	-0.49	2.4	3.4	44.0	1.9	**10.0**	15.4	25.6
Southern Illinois Bank	Johnston City	IL	**B+**	B+	A-	117.1	10.74	6.9	1.7	16.3	23.4	**10.0**	12.6	18.8
▲ Southern Independent Bank	Opp	AL	**B+**	B	B	242.0	6.71	15.4	3.0	15.1	32.9	**10.0**	12.3	19.7
Southern Michigan Bank & Trust	Coldwater	MI	**B**	B	B	808.8	5.77	12.0	0.5	7.5	15.6	**7.4**	9.8	12.8
▼ Southern States Bank	Anniston	AL	**B-**	B+	B+	1127.6	33.86	11.2	1.2	9.1	5.0	**8.1**	12.1	13.4
SouthernTrust Bank	Goreville	IL	**C**	C	C-	56.0	5.75	4.5	1.6	20.5	34.4	**8.4**	9.9	21.8
▼ SouthFirst Bank	Sylacauga	AL	**D+**	C+	C+	78.9	-6.36	3.4	0.7	41.1	13.7	**10.0**	11.8	20.7
SouthPoint Bank	Birmingham	AL	**B-**	B-	B	407.3	8.65	19.1	1.0	10.9	9.1	**5.0**	9.2	11.0

Asset Quality Index	Adjusted Non-Performing Loans as a % of Total Loans	Adjusted Non-Performing Loans as a % of Capital	Net Charge-Offs Avg Loans	Profitability Index	Net Income ($Mil)	Return on Assets (R.O.A.)	Return on Equity (R.O.E.)	Net Interest Spread	Overhead Efficiency Ratio	Liquidity Index	Liquidity Ratio	Hot Money Ratio	Stability Index
5.4	0.58	2.4	0.30	**7.7**	196.3	1.53	10.20	3.96	55.7	**1.8**	11.1	12.4	**9.3**
4.2	1.65	na	-0.03	**4.1**	1.9	0.71	7.51	4.46	84.2	**1.5**	11.2	23.7	**6.6**
5.7	0.00	na	0.27	**3.6**	0.3	0.83	8.14	3.18	64.7	**3.0**	42.3	20.6	**4.7**
6.9	0.61	na	0.28	**5.1**	1.3	1.02	10.92	4.32	64.3	**3.3**	21.0	13.3	**5.8**
6.0	1.18	na	0.06	**5.2**	4.9	1.09	7.14	3.70	74.1	**3.5**	16.1	11.5	**8.6**
4.6	1.76	na	0.05	**5.4**	5.5	1.08	9.54	4.55	69.6	**2.3**	9.8	16.7	**6.3**
5.2	0.76	na	0.06	**8.1**	0.8	1.90	15.67	3.70	46.3	**5.1**	34.6	6.7	**8.3**
6.1	2.96	na	0.10	**6.2**	3.5	1.13	7.52	2.69	35.2	**3.0**	65.3	52.7	**8.6**
8.1	0.01	na	0.08	**2.4**	0.3	0.29	2.58	2.86	87.1	**2.9**	47.5	27.1	**6.3**
9.1	0.12	na	0.04	**4.2**	1.2	0.86	6.58	2.77	64.7	**3.0**	53.9	30.7	**7.6**
6.9	1.90	na	0.22	**2.3**	0.1	0.25	1.69	3.52	95.7	**2.1**	23.9	19.2	**5.9**
6.5	0.14	0.9	0.03	**5.2**	18.2	1.04	7.58	4.10	63.4	**1.3**	12.0	16.4	**9.0**
5.0	0.81	na	0.12	**4.6**	0.9	1.01	11.15	3.92	71.3	**0.6**	12.3	42.2	**5.0**
8.2	0.01	na	0.03	**7.3**	2.7	1.52	10.05	3.89	48.9	**3.3**	28.2	14.2	**7.7**
8.0	1.13	na	0.05	**6.4**	2.2	1.47	8.71	3.28	48.9	**1.5**	23.0	25.2	**7.1**
6.1	1.42	3.6	0.09	**10.0**	2.0	2.69	11.10	5.21	45.6	**5.7**	49.3	7.4	**8.7**
8.2	0.00	na	0.04	**4.9**	1.9	1.01	9.09	3.68	64.2	**1.5**	16.2	25.5	**7.1**
7.5	0.45	na	0.05	**4.4**	6.6	0.94	10.13	2.84	62.5	**2.1**	17.4	18.5	**6.2**
10.0	0.00	na	0.00	**3.4**	2.5	0.58	2.86	2.54	69.4	**4.7**	48.3	13.7	**8.4**
5.5	1.33	7.5	0.23	**4.1**	8.6	0.90	10.73	4.47	78.1	**2.8**	19.3	10.9	**7.4**
6.1	0.59	4.4	0.00	**4.1**	1.4	1.02	9.37	3.40	69.5	**2.0**	26.9	22.4	**6.7**
7.4	0.21	0.2	0.09	**6.4**	26.7	1.31	8.78	3.55	56.4	**0.9**	7.3	25.0	**9.4**
8.7	0.11	na	0.04	**8.1**	3.1	1.93	15.91	4.40	57.9	**3.2**	22.9	13.9	**8.8**
8.9	0.00	na	0.00	**9.6**	1.1	2.59	26.46	5.20	50.1	**2.2**	31.1	23.0	**7.0**
5.1	1.72	na	0.00	**5.3**	5.3	1.01	9.92	4.11	71.9	**1.3**	10.4	26.5	**7.0**
8.3	0.18	na	0.00	**4.4**	4.8	0.93	9.49	4.22	74.0	**2.3**	14.3	16.5	**5.8**
5.9	1.23	5.5	0.04	**5.4**	10.3	1.17	10.54	3.59	66.4	**2.3**	12.0	17.6	**8.4**
6.6	2.22	na	0.05	**1.8**	0.1	0.03	0.39	2.86	93.2	**4.7**	53.6	12.5	**4.5**
7.2	0.01	0.1	0.00	**6.0**	1.4	1.34	11.24	3.78	56.5	**2.6**	18.1	14.7	**7.9**
7.6	0.00	na	0.02	**5.0**	1.2	1.18	11.45	4.04	69.5	**1.5**	21.4	25.4	**7.4**
8.4	0.28	1.6	-0.42	**9.9**	2.8	2.38	19.15	4.95	56.2	**1.4**	29.2	33.3	**9.3**
7.8	0.59	na	0.08	**6.0**	4.3	1.27	8.95	4.06	62.7	**3.7**	35.0	14.7	**8.3**
2.7	3.88	na	0.81	**1.4**	0.2	0.16	1.26	4.04	83.6	**1.8**	24.4	23.4	**5.1**
6.6	1.27	na	0.08	**8.5**	5.8	1.62	11.14	4.59	57.8	**2.0**	27.0	22.5	**8.5**
8.4	0.66	na	0.03	**5.2**	3.8	1.24	8.97	3.10	58.9	**2.5**	35.2	21.3	**8.4**
5.5	0.40	na	-0.01	**4.2**	0.7	0.90	9.73	3.15	60.4	**0.7**	17.1	49.0	**5.0**
6.7	0.82	na	-0.01	**3.9**	8.6	0.79	7.30	3.41	67.9	**3.9**	24.3	12.6	**8.1**
6.2	0.28	1.6	0.05	**6.4**	142.4	1.24	7.71	3.86	62.2	**4.3**	14.1	7.3	**10.0**
6.9	0.15	na	-0.02	**7.8**	2.8	1.83	17.48	4.32	54.3	**1.4**	7.6	19.0	**6.3**
5.0	1.58	9.2	0.00	**4.7**	3.7	0.92	9.00	3.82	72.1	**4.0**	20.3	9.7	**5.6**
4.6	0.27	na	0.07	**5.7**	14.2	1.17	13.31	3.75	61.5	**0.5**	4.7	27.6	**7.6**
9.1	0.00	na	0.03	**1.9**	0.1	0.12	1.03	2.62	94.8	**2.1**	43.4	41.9	**5.5**
8.7	0.69	na	-0.65	**8.1**	5.1	1.61	12.53	4.31	60.6	**5.2**	30.4	4.4	**7.9**
4.4	1.64	7.5	0.30	**4.8**	10.7	1.03	8.94	3.87	62.4	**1.6**	15.0	19.2	**8.8**
5.1	2.86	na	0.25	**3.2**	0.3	0.53	4.42	4.35	82.6	**2.1**	28.0	21.4	**6.0**
5.4	1.40	na	0.02	**7.1**	23.5	1.43	13.58	3.81	55.9	**1.3**	4.3	22.1	**8.9**
5.2	1.06	na	0.00	**6.6**	2.0	1.27	14.13	4.58	65.1	**1.4**	16.9	26.3	**5.7**
7.0	0.57	3.6	-0.02	**6.6**	27.4	1.35	13.12	3.88	65.0	**4.6**	19.3	6.0	**8.4**
4.0	2.31	10.7	0.44	**3.1**	0.3	0.47	4.04	4.93	86.1	**1.3**	27.3	33.1	**4.8**
8.5	0.01	0.1	0.00	**5.1**	2.5	1.16	8.60	3.91	71.8	**0.8**	17.1	35.2	**7.6**
7.0	0.68	4.1	0.09	**6.9**	21.2	1.39	14.39	3.55	54.6	**2.7**	11.4	12.4	**8.2**
5.9	1.22	na	0.06	**6.7**	3.6	1.58	13.68	4.68	68.1	**2.3**	17.3	17.6	**8.3**
6.0	3.31	na	0.16	**1.6**	0.1	0.09	0.58	4.44	95.8	**2.5**	24.6	17.2	**6.4**
7.5	0.33	na	0.54	**4.9**	0.8	0.97	7.77	3.88	64.0	**4.1**	17.5	8.2	**6.8**
8.6	0.55	na	0.01	**5.1**	2.0	1.12	9.43	3.24	58.6	**2.0**	41.3	37.5	**6.8**
5.8	0.97	2.6	0.04	**5.7**	7.0	1.21	10.67	3.78	67.3	**2.8**	23.2	14.8	**8.1**
4.5	1.99	na	0.62	**3.8**	3.0	0.42	3.68	3.82	68.0	**1.3**	19.4	24.9	**8.7**
4.7	2.70	na	-0.03	**3.6**	0.2	0.52	5.48	3.59	81.1	**3.5**	38.1	16.8	**4.4**
4.7	4.36	na	0.60	**0.8**	-0.2	-0.30	-2.55	4.00	101.7	**2.0**	25.2	19.9	**5.5**
5.1	0.39	3.5	0.07	**6.8**	3.8	1.33	14.46	3.93	66.8	**1.1**	9.2	29.1	**6.7**

Name	City	State	Rating	2018 Rating	2017 Rating	Total Assets ($Mil)	One Year Asset Growth	Asset Mix (As a % of Total Assets) Commercial Loans	Consumer Loans	Mortgage Loans	Securities	Capitalization Index	Leverage Ratio	Risk-Based Capital Ratio
Southside Bank	Tyler	TX	A-	A-	A-	6537.5	7.18	5.2	1.5	12.1	36.5	10.0	11.7	18.1
SouthStar Bank, S.S.B.	Moulton	TX	A-	A-	A-	860.6	21.56	2.1	0.5	21.9	8.9	9.2	11.6	14.3
SouthTrust Bank, N.A.	George West	TX	B-	B-	C-	401.2	9.97	3.1	1.1	4.5	16.3	10.0	11.1	19.6
Southwest Bank	Odessa	TX	B+	B+	B+	448.4	9.23	28.6	0.7	6.8	13.7	6.2	8.2	12.4
Southwest Bank of Weatherford	Weatherford	OK	B+	B+	B+	75.7	3.81	2.5	3.2	14.2	22.5	10.0	12.3	21.9
Southwest Capital Bank	Albuquerque	NM	C-	C	B-	344.3	-6.66	13.4	0.2	7.8	14.8	8.2	9.8	14.7
Southwest Georgia Bank	Moultrie	GA	B-	B-	B-	545.9	6.24	7.6	0.7	18.5	18.9	6.5	8.5	12.7
Southwest Missouri Bank	Carthage	MO	B	B	B	748.1	4.83	8.3	7.9	21.3	30.8	7.7	9.5	16.3
▲ Southwest National Bank	Wichita	KS	B-	B-	B	448.1	0.17	9.1	38.6	6.2	9.4	6.2	9.7	11.9
▲ Southwestern National Bank	Houston	TX	B+	B	B	516.9	25.01	2.3	0.0	1.5	7.5	10.0	14.3	16.3
Southwind Bank	Natoma	KS	B	B-	B	130.1	6.68	5.2	3.2	11.0	42.0	8.8	10.2	16.1
▼ Spectra Bank	Fort Worth	TX	C	B-	B	83.0	30.50	15.8	0.5	2.3	2.5	5.1	7.1	11.5
▲ Spencer County Bank	Santa Claus	IN	B	B-	B-	109.1	4.32	5.7	5.7	30.3	23.8	10.0	12.9	20.9
Spencer Savings Bank, SLA	Elmwood Park	NJ	B-	B-	B-	3034.1	7.32	0.9	0.2	25.0	14.8	10.0	11.1	16.2
Spirit of Texas Bank, SSB	Conroe	TX	B+	B	B	1959.5	77.92	12.3	0.5	16.2	8.5	8.6	11.3	13.8
SpiritBank	Tulsa	OK	C-	C	C-	624.5	-3.58	13.1	1.6	9.3	10.5	8.7	10.6	13.9
Spiro State Bank	Spiro	OK	C+	C	C-	51.5	3.52	4.3	3.8	9.8	45.1	10.0	12.7	35.4
Spratt Savings Bank	Chester	SC	C+	C+	C+	120.0	3.12	1.6	0.5	13.8	53.1	10.0	24.3	67.8
Spring Bank	Bronx	NY	B+	B+	A-	193.2	9.13	8.4	0.9	13.0	19.6	10.0	12.5	20.0
▲ Spring Bank	Brookfield	WI	C+	C	C+	315.8	11.24	11.1	0.1	12.3	4.3	9.3	11.6	14.4
▲ Spring Hill State Bank	Longview	TX	B+	B-	B	204.5	-2.36	6.3	4.8	45.8	3.2	10.0	11.7	23.6
Spring Valley Bank	Wyoming	OH	B+	A-	A-	80.3	10.82	0.8	0.1	41.8	0.1	10.0	41.6	43.9
Spring Valley City Bank	Spring Valley	IL	B+	B+	B+	189.7	2.48	6.4	3.7	17.2	38.9	10.0	15.1	29.9
▲ Springfield First Community Bank	Springfield	MO	B	B-	B	695.0	11.38	13.0	0.6	10.8	1.8	7.8	10.6	13.2
Springfield State Bank	Springfield	KY	A-	B+	B+	321.4	4.31	2.8	2.6	26.4	38.2	10.0	15.9	26.0
▲ Springfield State Bank	Springfield	NE	B+	B	B	60.0	11.73	4.4	3.6	7.3	17.7	9.3	10.6	25.7
Springs Valley Bank & Trust Co.	Jasper	IN	B-	B-	B-	453.0	13.47	5.5	2.8	21.0	12.7	9.1	10.4	14.5
Spur Security Bank	Spur	TX	C+	C+	C+	45.0	6.81	2.1	3.6	0.9	65.8	10.0	12.4	37.1
SSB Bank	Pittsburgh	PA	C	C	C	201.2	9.69	11.2	1.1	31.8	4.2	6.9	8.9	12.7
▲ SSB Community Bank	Strasburg	OH	C+	C+	C+	103.5	15.00	11.8	1.3	34.5	0.0	5.2	7.8	11.2
St. Ansgar State Bank	Saint Ansgar	IA	A-	A-	B	117.5	5.22	7.7	1.8	8.5	23.7	10.0	12.1	18.0
St. Charles Bank & Trust Co.	Saint Charles	IL	B	B	B-	1273.1	7.45	25.0	17.9	3.5	10.9	5.5	9.6	11.4
St. Clair County State Bank	Osceola	MO	A-	A-	A-	142.8	3.08	6.5	3.8	19.5	8.3	10.0	14.0	18.7
St. Clair State Bank (Inc.)	Saint Clair	MN	B+	B+	A-	95.2	6.49	9.8	6.3	11.3	1.4	8.8	10.6	14.0
St. Henry Bank	Saint Henry	OH	A	A	A+	299.0	-0.35	5.4	0.9	16.0	19.3	10.0	15.7	21.7
St. Johns Bank and Trust Co.	Saint Louis	MO	C+	C+	C-	293.2	2.40	4.6	0.5	7.4	14.6	8.4	9.9	15.2
▼ St. Landry Bank and Trust Co.	Opelousas	LA	C+	B	B-	279.9	-2.47	6.2	0.8	4.3	59.1	7.7	9.5	25.5
St. Landry Homestead FSB	Opelousas	LA	B	B	B	220.0	-4.41	1.4	2.5	51.7	14.0	10.0	23.0	41.3
▲ St. Louis Bank	Town And Country	MO	C	C	C	437.6	2.25	13.7	0.2	6.4	12.1	7.1	9.2	12.5
St. Martin National Bank	Saint Martin	MN	B	B	B	21.6	-3.43	6.6	3.9	23.9	16.7	10.0	15.7	31.2
▲ Stafford Savings Bank	Stafford Springs	CT	B+	B-	B	296.5	2.68	0.0	0.4	19.5	15.2	10.0	41.8	33.3
Standard Bank, PaSB	Monroeville	PA	B	B	B-	990.7	0.93	4.5	0.1	42.5	16.4	10.0	11.4	17.4
▲ Standing Stone Bank	Lancaster	OH	C+	C	C-	102.5	-5.49	8.4	18.9	22.5	13.6	6.7	8.7	13.3
▲ Stanley Bank	Overland Park	KS	A-	B+	A-	120.6	8.48	33.0	2.5	4.5	0.0	10.0	18.3	29.0
▲ Stanton State Bank	Stanton	NE	C+	C	C	48.6	5.68	11.9	3.1	15.2	27.7	8.4	9.9	18.6
Star Bank	Maple Lake	MN	C+	B-	B+	281.6	1.83	7.9	2.5	10.6	1.6	6.8	9.5	12.3
STAR Financial Bank	Fort Wayne	IN	B+	B	B	2032.5	7.58	19.8	1.8	10.2	17.5	8.1	11.1	13.4
Starion Bank	Bismarck	ND	B+	A-	A-	1391.7	5.26	11.0	2.0	8.5	25.5	9.6	10.7	14.7
State Bank	La Junta	CO	B	B	B	105.4	0.05	2.1	2.6	9.4	20.6	10.0	14.8	21.4
State Bank	Spencer	IA	C	C	C	69.5	4.76	7.4	3.6	16.9	11.6	6.6	8.6	13.3
State Bank	Spirit Lake	IA	C+	B-	B-	71.9	-4.94	5.5	0.8	12.9	27.9	10.0	12.3	24.0
▲ State Bank	Freeport	IL	B+	B	B-	262.7	-1.23	16.4	0.2	5.0	27.2	10.0	11.1	15.4
State Bank	Wonder Lake	IL	C	C	C-	224.0	-2.91	6.9	0.6	24.9	16.0	8.7	10.1	16.0
State Bank	Fenton	MI	B+	B	B-	977.1	7.36	6.2	0.9	30.4	5.4	8.1	10.4	13.4
State Bank	Richmond	MO	B	B	B	33.2	4.02	4.0	3.4	24.0	26.5	6.5	8.5	20.9
▼ State Bank	Green River	WY	D-	D+	D+	28.3	-10.50	3.8	1.9	9.3	1.8	8.0	12.8	13.3
State Bank & Trust	Winfield	AL	B-	B-	C+	240.6	5.07	1.9	7.4	13.6	61.0	9.8	10.8	23.6
▲ State Bank & Trust Co.	Nevada	IA	A-	B+	B+	160.1	1.56	11.6	0.5	11.5	25.4	10.0	11.4	15.9
State Bank & Trust Co.	Golden Meadow	LA	C	D+	D-	118.2	-3.72	20.2	4.5	19.0	12.7	10.0	11.8	18.1
State Bank & Trust Co.	Ridgeland	MS	B-	B-	B-	1151.0	1.25	4.9	1.9	16.3	9.8	6.4	9.2	12.1

Asset Quality Index	Adjusted Non-Performing Loans as a % of Total Loans	Adjusted Non-Performing Loans as a % of Capital	Net Charge-Offs Avg Loans	Profitability Index	Net Income ($Mil)	Return on Assets (R.O.A.)	Return on Equity (R.O.E.)	Net Interest Spread	Overhead Efficiency Ratio	Liquidity Index	Liquidity Ratio	Hot Money Ratio	Stability Index
6.5	0.76	2.3	0.18	**6.1**	64.0	1.36	9.37	3.22	52.4	**2.8**	29.1	13.4	**9.5**
6.7	0.24	4.2	-0.14	**5.8**	6.4	1.16	9.70	4.74	70.9	**1.6**	12.0	19.5	**6.7**
6.5	1.26	na	0.17	**3.6**	2.1	0.72	6.47	3.97	80.4	**4.1**	43.6	15.3	**6.5**
5.9	0.63	na	0.54	**8.0**	5.7	1.78	20.73	5.28	66.9	**4.8**	35.9	9.9	**6.4**
5.1	3.23	12.7	-0.01	**4.9**	0.5	0.92	7.56	3.74	70.9	**4.8**	50.4	12.8	**7.5**
0.4	6.56	na	0.32	**2.6**	-0.2	-0.05	-0.56	4.73	79.0	**3.9**	25.9	10.7	**6.9**
6.7	0.49	3.9	0.23	**4.7**	4.1	0.99	12.28	3.98	70.2	**2.9**	13.1	14.2	**5.8**
7.1	1.11	na	0.11	**4.5**	5.1	0.92	9.99	3.92	74.4	**4.0**	23.6	9.9	**6.0**
6.2	0.37	na	0.19	**5.0**	3.9	1.16	12.13	3.73	67.3	**1.2**	10.5	14.1	**6.0**
7.0	0.00	na	-0.03	**5.1**	3.7	1.06	7.92	3.59	65.7	**0.8**	16.5	36.5	**8.0**
5.9	0.66	na	-0.01	**5.3**	1.1	1.16	10.98	3.55	57.9	**4.4**	40.7	13.1	**6.1**
7.5	0.00	na	3.59	**1.2**	-2.2	-3.90	-40.33	4.56	99.4	**2.9**	32.4	17.5	**5.0**
6.0	1.61	na	0.05	**4.3**	0.6	0.81	6.43	3.50	74.1	**2.8**	33.3	18.7	**6.7**
5.8	1.19	6.2	0.09	**3.4**	12.4	0.55	4.96	2.58	66.3	**1.6**	17.0	25.2	**8.3**
6.4	0.62	3.3	0.18	**6.0**	17.5	1.34	10.55	4.66	65.8	**1.0**	10.6	30.9	**9.1**
3.9	2.36	na	-0.34	**2.7**	2.6	0.53	4.71	3.36	95.1	**0.8**	19.5	38.8	**6.7**
9.5	0.00	na	0.03	**2.5**	0.2	0.43	3.33	3.47	88.0	**6.3**	64.0	6.4	**6.3**
9.9	0.73	0.9	0.00	**2.9**	0.4	0.47	1.95	2.82	75.6	**5.0**	85.4	18.3	**7.5**
5.5	1.30	na	-0.59	**9.0**	2.4	1.66	13.10	4.73	65.5	**0.8**	21.5	37.2	**7.8**
4.1	0.94	na	0.07	**7.4**	3.1	1.38	11.88	3.44	45.9	**0.8**	18.6	42.5	**7.7**
6.6	0.46	na	0.04	**5.4**	1.7	1.14	10.06	3.76	62.1	**1.9**	25.7	22.1	**7.3**
7.6	0.25	na	0.07	**10.0**	2.8	4.72	11.48	6.51	25.8	**0.8**	18.6	45.2	**9.1**
7.9	1.05	na	0.01	**4.5**	1.3	0.94	6.30	3.09	64.8	**3.7**	46.9	18.0	**8.1**
5.8	0.08	na	0.01	**6.4**	5.9	1.27	7.03	3.76	49.4	**1.3**	15.1	21.9	**8.0**
9.1	0.54	na	0.07	**5.4**	3.1	1.32	8.71	3.39	62.2	**2.1**	33.9	27.6	**8.2**
8.8	0.00	na	-0.01	**5.9**	0.6	1.50	14.21	3.44	54.8	**6.8**	55.4	1.5	**6.9**
4.8	1.70	na	0.07	**4.1**	2.8	0.86	7.90	3.51	75.5	**1.3**	21.2	16.8	**6.3**
9.4	0.00	na	0.02	**3.0**	0.3	0.97	8.70	2.69	82.4	**3.0**	69.7	38.2	**5.2**
1.4	4.63	39.3	0.10	**2.3**	0.3	0.22	2.52	2.44	87.2	**0.6**	16.6	52.3	**4.4**
5.8	1.15	na	0.00	**5.6**	1.0	1.38	18.00	3.73	65.9	**1.3**	12.9	27.2	**5.1**
8.5	0.00	na	-0.03	**5.4**	1.1	1.30	10.85	3.49	60.0	**5.0**	34.7	7.5	**7.3**
4.0	1.19	7.5	0.58	**4.4**	7.1	0.77	6.84	3.27	55.4	**1.4**	15.1	17.3	**8.4**
7.5	0.02	na	0.00	**8.2**	1.7	1.59	11.56	4.23	50.9	**2.1**	13.9	18.3	**8.8**
7.9	0.06	na	0.02	**9.2**	1.7	2.34	21.10	3.75	36.9	**1.6**	23.8	25.6	**9.1**
8.8	0.00	na	0.00	**9.7**	5.4	2.45	15.88	4.05	40.3	**4.4**	25.4	7.6	**10.0**
7.6	0.15	na	0.05	**3.9**	1.6	0.74	7.43	4.08	74.0	**4.9**	18.6	3.0	**5.5**
3.7	4.44	na	0.05	**0.9**	-4.7	-2.15	-19.58	2.77	59.4	**5.8**	49.7	7.9	**6.9**
6.1	6.23	na	0.06	**3.2**	0.7	0.42	1.87	3.36	83.4	**1.2**	17.7	29.1	**7.5**
3.6	1.52	na	0.22	**3.1**	1.8	0.53	5.80	2.83	74.3	**0.5**	16.6	49.7	**4.8**
8.8	0.00	na	0.00	**7.8**	0.3	1.89	12.53	3.63	60.4	**5.7**	46.8	4.1	**6.3**
10.0	0.78	0.4	0.00	**7.4**	13.1	6.02	14.78	2.65	66.0	**7.6**	129.0	8.9	**8.8**
8.0	0.33	na	0.04	**4.4**	6.8	0.92	6.57	3.17	63.7	**2.8**	19.4	15.2	**8.2**
5.4	0.37	na	0.10	**3.6**	0.5	0.70	8.27	3.73	79.8	**1.7**	22.6	7.4	**4.1**
8.2	0.00	na	0.21	**5.9**	0.8	0.91	4.88	4.30	76.3	**5.4**	39.3	6.9	**7.8**
6.6	0.00	na	0.00	**3.4**	0.3	0.75	7.61	3.31	77.6	**5.2**	26.1	2.8	**4.8**
1.4	4.19	na	0.00	**7.5**	3.5	1.61	16.35	4.64	66.3	**3.6**	9.5	10.2	**8.1**
5.5	1.04	5.4	0.10	**6.1**	19.2	1.26	11.53	3.94	64.5	**4.4**	14.0	4.0	**8.8**
5.3	2.06	9.6	-0.04	**5.7**	13.9	1.34	12.38	3.43	61.2	**1.7**	15.3	18.0	**10.0**
7.1	0.81	na	0.17	**5.9**	0.9	1.16	7.96	4.76	67.9	**4.1**	18.9	8.4	**8.4**
7.1	0.02	na	0.01	**3.9**	0.4	0.76	8.69	3.59	78.9	**2.1**	26.3	20.1	**4.0**
3.7	9.75	na	2.24	**2.9**	0.3	0.53	4.40	3.18	62.0	**3.1**	47.9	22.9	**5.5**
6.9	1.24	5.6	0.15	**8.3**	3.1	1.55	14.46	3.50	45.7	**1.7**	17.3	21.8	**8.0**
3.2	2.62	na	0.10	**2.7**	0.4	0.23	1.97	4.11	92.6	**4.6**	22.7	5.9	**6.7**
8.3	0.08	na	0.00	**6.9**	9.8	1.38	13.12	3.96	59.7	**1.7**	9.2	18.2	**7.2**
4.7	1.86	10.0	0.00	**5.3**	0.3	1.27	14.64	3.77	69.8	**6.4**	45.0	1.8	**5.6**
7.8	0.07	na	0.45	**0.0**	-0.8	-3.90	-29.44	3.92	568.3	**5.0**	50.6	11.7	**4.9**
5.1	2.15	na	0.32	**3.7**	1.5	0.82	7.87	2.79	70.8	**2.7**	57.3	49.7	**5.9**
5.9	1.06	5.3	0.41	**7.1**	1.7	1.36	11.80	3.27	44.6	**3.7**	20.8	6.9	**8.4**
2.3	3.55	18.9	0.44	**3.2**	0.6	0.63	5.41	3.91	79.8	**1.7**	18.7	22.8	**5.5**
6.9	0.45	2.6	0.07	**4.6**	8.1	0.92	8.47	3.71	69.1	**1.7**	10.4	20.8	**8.7**

Name	City	State	Rating	2018 Rating	2017 Rating	Total Assets ($Mil)	One Year Asset Growth	Asset Mix (As a % of Total Assets) Comm-ercial Loans	Cons-umer Loans	Mort-gage Loans	Secur-ities	Capital-ization Index	Lever-age Ratio	Risk-Based Capital Ratio
State Bank & Trust of Kenmare	Kenmare	ND	B-	C	C+	127.7	-4.68	10.9	2.5	8.2	33.7	7.0	9.0	16.4
State Bank and Trust Co.	Defiance	OH	B+	B+	B-	1036.9	6.12	12.4	1.3	23.0	7.4	7.6	11.1	13.0
State Bank Financial	La Crosse	WI	B	B	C+	345.9	6.32	8.4	0.4	7.1	32.6	9.0	10.3	15.5
▲ State Bank Northwest	Spokane Valley	WA	B-	C+	C	136.8	-2.29	15.2	0.1	12.0	3.7	10.0	12.3	17.1
State Bank of Arcadia	Arcadia	WI	B-	B-	B-	173.5	0.07	4.7	1.9	19.1	18.2	10.0	11.6	24.6
State Bank of Arizona	Lake Havasu City	AZ	B	B	B-	676.8	5.28	4.4	1.3	7.3	24.9	9.5	10.7	15.4
State Bank of Belle Plaine	Belle Plaine	MN	B-	B-	B-	121.6	-1.18	1.9	1.5	13.1	43.8	9.1	10.4	23.4
State Bank of Bellingham	Bellingham	MN	C-	C	B	48.9	-7.29	2.9	0.6	0.0	13.0	10.0	12.3	16.7
State Bank of Bement	Bement	IL	B-	B-	B-	104.3	0.94	22.2	12.4	9.4	19.7	10.0	11.6	15.7
▲ State Bank of Bern	Bern	KS	A-	B+	A-	94.6	2.70	3.0	2.4	1.1	41.3	10.0	17.2	23.7
State Bank of Bottineau	Bottineau	ND	C+	C+	B-	78.9	-1.01	6.3	2.5	19.9	1.4	6.2	9.5	11.9
State Bank of Brooks	Corning	IA	C	C	C	18.3	10.53	2.6	4.9	10.0	32.1	10.0	11.8	38.3
▼ State Bank of Burnettsville	Burnettsville	IN	D-	D+	D-	40.2	14.00	4.9	7.2	23.8	17.1	7.8	9.5	17.6
▲ State Bank of Burrton	Burrton	KS	C	C-	C-	10.7	-3.73	15.4	4.3	18.1	26.6	10.0	11.7	26.5
▲ State Bank of Bussey	Bussey	IA	C	C-	C-	43.8	-1.62	7.1	1.9	30.2	2.9	7.0	9.0	14.5
State Bank of Canton	Canton	KS	B-	C+	C+	30.4	1.07	13.2	1.0	2.1	22.3	10.0	20.6	42.0
State Bank of Cerro Gordo	Cerro Gordo	IL	B-	B-	B-	31.1	7.76	14.8	4.9	11.0	27.2	10.0	13.2	25.2
State Bank of Ceylon	Ceylon	MN	D+	D+	D	14.2	19.25	2.1	2.7	9.0	15.2	10.0	13.3	30.7
State Bank of Chandler	Chandler	MN	B-	B-	B	48.2	11.03	3.5	3.6	2.9	8.7	10.0	12.7	18.1
State Bank of Cherry	Cherry	IL	B+	A-	A-	90.7	6.38	6.8	3.7	13.7	17.5	10.0	14.2	20.4
State Bank of Chilton	Chilton	WI	B	B	B-	280.8	1.19	9.3	1.0	13.1	5.5	10.0	12.0	16.9
▲ State Bank of Cochran	Cochran	GA	B+	B	B	207.9	-1.59	4.9	7.6	17.6	11.4	10.0	17.0	29.9
State Bank of Cold Spring	Cold Spring	MN	C+	C+	C+	63.3	0.44	3.8	5.4	25.8	16.6	7.8	9.5	18.0
▲ State Bank of Colon	Colon	NE	D	D	D+	18.1	6.65	2.3	0.5	0.5	10.0	7.1	9.1	18.3
State Bank of Cross Plains	Cross Plains	WI	C	C	D+	1317.8	34.83	10.2	1.1	15.5	11.5	6.5	10.2	12.1
▲ State Bank of Danvers	Benson	MN	B+	B	B-	46.2	-1.54	4.2	0.7	0.3	36.5	10.0	12.8	21.7
State Bank of Davis	Davis	IL	B+	B	C+	161.2	5.18	15.9	0.8	3.3	32.8	10.0	11.6	18.1
State Bank of De Kalb	De Kalb	TX	B+	B+	A	260.0	16.21	15.7	1.5	16.6	0.0	8.9	10.3	14.0
State Bank of Downs	Downs	KS	C+	C-	C+	92.5	6.24	16.1	1.6	23.3	5.7	10.0	13.5	18.7
▲ State Bank of Eagle Butte	Eagle Butte	SD	D+	D+	C-	66.2	6.14	6.8	23.2	3.2	40.8	7.5	9.4	14.9
▲ State Bank of Easton	Easton	MN	C-	D+	C-	20.3	3.29	14.6	4.8	3.5	8.2	10.0	12.8	19.7
▼ State Bank of Fairmont	Fairmont	MN	C+	B-	C	112.7	4.63	22.4	4.9	4.1	12.6	9.5	11.0	14.6
▲ State Bank of Faribault	Faribault	MN	B	B-	B	208.9	-1.75	7.9	3.1	17.3	21.2	9.6	11.1	14.7
State Bank of Geneva	Geneva	IL	C-	D+	D-	80.3	-1.69	4.2	1.1	11.4	16.5	7.9	9.6	16.6
State Bank of Graymont	Graymont	IL	B	B	B	211.8	5.17	8.0	1.9	7.5	19.8	10.0	12.3	16.8
▲ State Bank of Herscher	Herscher	IL	B+	B	C+	146.2	-0.29	11.3	0.2	7.1	33.3	10.0	13.5	21.3
▲ State Bank of India (California)	Los Angeles	CA	B+	B	C	839.4	13.65	21.4	0.0	0.0	9.7	10.0	17.1	20.3
State Bank of Industry	Industry	IL	B	B	B	51.5	-6.01	9.3	4.0	18.4	15.9	10.0	15.3	22.9
▲ State Bank of Jeffers	Jeffers	MN	B	B-	B-	27.5	1.74	8.4	3.3	2.1	18.7	10.0	13.1	17.0
▲ State Bank of Lake Park	Lake Park	MN	C+	C	C	38.1	2.43	8.8	6.8	28.0	8.7	10.0	11.2	21.3
▲ State Bank of Lakota	Lakota	ND	B-	C+	C+	49.9	3.01	8.3	5.4	11.5	14.2	9.8	10.8	14.8
▲ State Bank of Lincoln	Lincoln	IL	A-	B+	A-	344.7	-0.03	6.6	0.3	3.7	42.7	8.4	10.0	19.9
State Bank of Lismore	Lismore	MN	C	C	C+	61.6	4.77	6.8	2.7	0.0	0.2	6.3	10.3	12.0
▲ State Bank of Lizton	Lizton	IN	B+	B	B	503.4	1.43	8.7	1.0	8.1	13.7	9.0	10.4	14.2
State Bank of Medora	Medora	IN	B	B	B	91.1	4.86	1.4	4.9	16.4	55.7	10.0	15.0	34.3
State Bank of Missouri	Concordia	MO	B	B	B-	98.8	-0.12	5.9	1.8	24.5	30.3	6.5	8.5	18.1
▼ State Bank of Nauvoo	Nauvoo	IL	D+	C-	C-	33.7	12.99	6.6	8.9	30.2	0.0	7.0	9.0	16.1
▲ State Bank of New Richland	New Richland	MN	C	C-	C-	115.9	7.76	4.3	1.6	16.5	11.2	6.3	9.3	11.9
▲ State Bank of Newburg	Newburg	WI	B+	B	B	186.7	5.93	2.3	0.7	29.8	10.1	10.0	19.6	28.0
State Bank of Odell	Odell	NE	C	C	C	26.7	5.81	4.2	10.0	3.3	3.3	9.1	10.4	17.8
▲ State Bank of Pearl City	Pearl City	IL	B-	C	B-	58.2	-5.55	2.3	43.8	6.8	16.5	10.0	11.4	19.5
State Bank of Reeseville	Reeseville	WI	B-	B-	B	101.7	19.93	8.2	2.0	10.1	50.6	7.9	9.6	19.0
State Bank of Saunemin	Saunemin	IL	B-	B-	B-	35.2	0.50	11.3	2.5	3.8	28.2	10.0	11.6	16.4
State Bank of Schaller	Schaller	IA	B	B	B+	30.3	-5.42	4.0	1.4	1.3	52.6	10.0	15.4	29.2
State Bank of Scotia	Scotia	NE	B-	B-	B	47.0	9.68	5.1	2.2	8.1	6.8	10.0	22.5	28.4
State Bank of Southern Utah	Cedar City	UT	A	A	A	1249.8	15.67	6.6	3.1	3.7	23.1	10.0	13.4	18.4
State Bank of Southwest Missouri	Springfield	MO	C+	C+	C+	131.2	12.49	4.8	5.5	35.5	7.7	4.4	7.0	10.7
▲ State Bank of Spring Hill	Spring Hill	KS	C+	C	C	45.2	0.31	4.1	1.0	5.1	44.4	7.3	9.2	23.5
State Bank of St. Jacob	Saint Jacob	IL	B+	B+	B+	65.1	2.64	5.7	9.7	15.1	30.6	10.0	16.5	35.5
State Bank of Table Rock	Table Rock	NE	C-	D+	D+	93.7	6.44	7.8	3.2	10.2	1.7	6.4	8.4	12.4

Arrows denote recent upgrades ▲ or downgrades ▼

Asset Quality Index	Adjusted Non-Performing Loans as a % of Total Loans	Adjusted Non-Performing Loans as a % of Capital	Net Charge-Offs Avg Loans	Profitability Index	Net Income ($Mil)	Return on Assets (R.O.A.)	Return on Equity (R.O.E.)	Net Interest Spread	Overhead Efficiency Ratio	Liquidity Index	Liquidity Ratio	Hot Money Ratio	Stability Index
4.4	0.56	na	0.03	**4.0**	1.0	0.98	10.33	3.20	64.3	**2.8**	34.2	18.9	**6.0**
7.1	0.49	2.6	0.03	**6.2**	9.2	1.20	9.36	3.79	69.1	**1.6**	7.7	19.6	**10.0**
6.9	2.10	3.0	0.02	**4.2**	2.6	1.03	9.18	3.19	70.4	**4.5**	27.1	7.5	**6.9**
5.7	0.81	na	-0.02	**7.6**	2.0	1.85	15.69	5.49	68.1	**3.2**	17.6	13.5	**8.2**
8.5	1.18	na	0.03	**3.9**	1.2	0.93	7.31	2.77	64.1	**5.5**	42.0	7.7	**7.2**
5.3	1.45	4.8	-0.12	**6.9**	6.7	1.33	11.93	3.88	60.9	**4.5**	35.8	11.0	**7.5**
8.4	0.00	na	0.30	**2.9**	0.4	0.49	4.61	3.39	79.4	**5.1**	39.7	9.1	**5.8**
3.2	0.00	na	0.05	**7.6**	0.7	1.72	14.80	3.55	52.0	**0.9**	22.0	33.8	**7.5**
6.2	0.25	na	0.04	**2.7**	0.3	0.42	3.60	3.25	85.9	**3.2**	16.9	13.3	**6.6**
8.4	1.00	na	0.12	**7.5**	1.2	1.69	9.96	3.67	45.8	**3.3**	48.4	20.1	**8.3**
7.1	0.00	na	0.00	**5.6**	0.8	1.33	13.63	4.67	67.0	**2.3**	5.3	16.4	**6.5**
5.5	0.82	na	-0.07	**3.6**	0.1	0.74	6.25	2.58	66.8	**7.2**	84.8	2.6	**5.0**
4.8	1.20	6.4	0.07	**0.0**	-0.2	-0.80	-7.38	4.08	126.0	**2.2**	31.9	23.5	**3.3**
9.0	0.00	na	0.33	**3.5**	0.1	0.79	7.01	3.92	79.9	**2.6**	27.6	16.7	**5.2**
8.1	0.50	na	-0.01	**3.3**	0.2	0.62	7.15	4.14	84.5	**2.9**	18.5	14.8	**4.6**
9.0	0.39	na	0.00	**3.3**	0.2	0.66	3.23	3.25	79.0	**7.4**	74.7	1.7	**6.6**
8.2	0.02	na	0.01	**3.4**	0.1	0.64	4.49	3.55	79.1	**5.8**	50.5	7.1	**5.9**
5.7	2.41	na	0.14	**0.4**	-0.1	-0.94	-7.39	3.87	135.8	**3.0**	60.3	24.9	**3.6**
6.6	0.29	na	0.00	**5.5**	0.4	1.12	8.77	4.16	63.3	**4.3**	32.6	11.1	**6.4**
7.9	0.73	na	-0.01	**6.5**	1.0	1.51	10.66	3.85	55.4	**3.4**	36.8	16.8	**8.5**
3.3	3.26	na	-0.11	**7.8**	4.2	1.96	16.44	3.88	52.1	**3.2**	18.5	13.2	**7.8**
5.2	3.79	na	-0.11	**9.8**	3.8	2.40	14.77	4.70	52.3	**3.8**	33.3	13.7	**9.4**
4.3	2.77	na	-0.03	**4.8**	0.6	1.22	12.85	3.43	66.2	**4.8**	31.5	7.5	**5.1**
7.3	0.28	na	0.00	**1.2**	0.0	0.09	1.00	2.24	96.4	**2.1**	44.6	19.3	**4.1**
7.1	0.54	3.2	0.03	**4.7**	7.7	0.86	7.79	3.43	68.2	**3.0**	10.8	13.9	**9.1**
8.8	0.05	na	-0.33	**8.3**	0.8	2.15	17.29	3.64	52.1	**4.2**	23.3	8.3	**7.7**
5.3	3.01	9.2	0.00	**6.6**	1.5	1.32	11.28	3.16	48.1	**1.8**	27.8	26.1	**7.8**
5.0	0.53	na	-0.01	**8.3**	3.8	1.91	18.68	4.40	61.2	**2.2**	14.6	18.1	**8.8**
3.5	4.63	na	-0.17	**7.9**	1.4	2.06	15.62	4.26	55.9	**3.9**	19.0	9.4	**7.5**
2.1	1.72	9.5	4.09	**1.9**	0.0	-0.02	-0.18	5.85	66.2	**0.9**	3.8	29.4	**4.0**
4.5	2.87	na	0.19	**3.4**	0.2	1.07	8.69	3.48	72.0	**2.0**	35.7	24.5	**3.5**
2.9	2.53	15.8	-0.03	**5.9**	1.3	1.49	13.98	3.77	54.7	**2.0**	18.2	19.5	**6.4**
7.9	0.23	na	0.02	**6.0**	2.3	1.48	13.59	4.30	72.2	**3.9**	17.4	9.9	**7.2**
7.8	1.11	na	0.00	**2.4**	0.2	0.35	3.61	3.74	91.9	**2.2**	28.2	20.5	**4.6**
7.2	1.05	4.6	0.00	**4.9**	1.7	1.07	8.77	3.20	60.9	**3.7**	26.3	12.1	**7.2**
5.2	2.22	6.7	0.05	**6.7**	1.5	1.38	10.28	3.75	69.3	**4.3**	28.3	9.8	**7.2**
7.1	0.11	na	-0.03	**5.8**	6.2	1.05	5.96	3.61	59.2	**0.7**	16.3	38.0	**7.8**
8.3	0.20	na	0.03	**5.9**	0.6	1.49	10.32	3.43	55.5	**0.8**	16.3	44.3	**7.3**
8.2	0.00	na	0.00	**4.2**	0.2	0.88	6.86	3.47	66.5	**5.7**	47.3	7.2	**6.5**
4.6	3.47	na	-0.01	**5.9**	0.4	1.49	13.81	4.49	66.7	**3.5**	32.7	15.0	**5.6**
5.9	0.00	na	0.07	**6.1**	0.6	1.53	14.40	4.09	60.3	**1.6**	7.6	20.1	**5.7**
8.8	0.24	na	-0.23	**6.5**	4.1	1.51	14.56	3.56	62.3	**4.9**	37.0	9.3	**8.2**
3.4	1.11	na	0.14	**5.9**	0.6	1.34	12.90	4.30	63.9	**0.8**	8.6	32.5	**6.6**
6.0	0.67	3.6	0.00	**6.2**	5.2	1.34	12.93	3.98	62.3	**2.3**	16.4	17.6	**7.3**
8.1	1.37	na	0.00	**3.9**	0.6	0.82	5.56	2.75	64.8	**3.7**	70.3	25.0	**7.5**
6.7	0.69	3.8	0.02	**5.6**	1.1	1.44	16.10	3.49	63.1	**4.6**	27.9	7.3	**6.0**
2.2	3.21	19.7	1.13	**4.1**	0.2	0.81	8.40	4.13	66.6	**5.0**	35.4	7.8	**3.6**
3.3	0.93	na	-0.01	**9.7**	1.9	2.30	24.58	3.74	41.1	**0.6**	9.7	19.2	**7.5**
7.5	5.38	na	0.00	**8.7**	2.2	1.62	8.40	3.81	43.3	**1.0**	25.9	29.6	**9.2**
4.3	0.63	na	-0.39	**3.7**	0.2	0.84	8.37	3.94	78.9	**4.7**	51.2	13.6	**4.5**
6.7	0.35	na	0.30	**3.4**	0.3	0.72	6.21	3.36	77.9	**2.2**	28.0	19.9	**4.8**
9.0	0.09	na	0.06	**3.6**	0.6	0.79	7.51	3.10	72.2	**2.9**	59.2	12.5	**6.1**
8.5	0.00	na	0.00	**3.3**	0.2	0.72	6.33	3.16	62.4	**4.7**	40.1	11.8	**6.5**
7.1	0.00	na	0.01	**6.1**	0.3	1.38	9.22	3.01	60.8	**5.7**	64.3	10.7	**7.4**
6.4	0.85	na	0.32	**7.7**	0.5	1.47	6.42	4.00	44.5	**0.9**	22.3	36.5	**6.3**
6.6	1.48	6.5	0.02	**10.0**	17.1	1.91	14.43	4.52	50.3	**4.5**	29.7	12.5	**10.0**
6.8	0.34	na	-0.02	**5.5**	1.0	1.04	14.29	3.57	77.0	**3.9**	17.0	9.4	**4.6**
8.3	0.00	na	2.10	**3.5**	0.2	0.52	5.39	3.54	69.5	**5.9**	45.7	5.1	**5.2**
8.0	1.00	na	0.01	**6.1**	0.7	1.46	8.97	3.40	49.9	**5.3**	57.1	11.4	**7.7**
3.4	1.41	na	-0.01	**3.6**	0.5	0.73	8.75	3.72	78.6	**2.3**	22.4	18.3	**4.8**

Name	City	State	Rating	2018 Rating	2017 Rating	Total Assets ($Mil)	One Year Asset Growth	Asset Mix (As a % of Total Assets) Comm-ercial Loans	Cons-umer Loans	Mort-gage Loans	Secur-ities	Capital-ization Index	Lever-age Ratio	Risk-Based Capital Ratio
▲ State Bank of Taunton	Taunton	MN	**C+**	D+	C	47.7	1.21	5.8	0.5	5.3	10.7	**8.9**	11.0	14.1
State Bank of Texas	Dallas	TX	**B+**	B+	A	823.0	-2.39	1.1	0.1	6.9	7.5	**10.0**	16.7	20.8
State Bank of the Lakes, N.A.	Antioch	IL	**B**	B	B	1321.0	9.15	29.3	19.8	3.0	11.8	**5.9**	9.4	11.7
▼ State Bank of Toledo	Toledo	IA	**D**	D+	C-	114.2	-3.73	4.4	4.8	29.6	0.0	**4.3**	9.5	10.7
▲ State Bank of Toulon	Toulon	IL	**B-**	B-	B+	229.2	3.67	7.9	1.3	5.9	24.5	**8.5**	10.5	13.7
State Bank of Wapello	Wapello	IA	**B**	B-	B-	38.1	0.37	1.5	4.9	10.3	19.8	**10.0**	14.4	28.4
State Bank of Waterloo	Waterloo	IL	**C**	C	D+	190.3	12.70	3.0	1.0	17.6	13.0	**6.4**	8.8	12.0
▲ State Bank of Wheaton	Wheaton	MN	**B+**	B+	A-	84.2	6.73	5.8	0.8	1.0	0.9	**10.0**	24.5	29.7
▲ State Bank of Whittington	Benton	IL	**B-**	C+	B-	133.0	3.16	6.4	15.9	16.2	26.6	**9.9**	11.0	16.5
State Bank of Wynnewood	Wynnewood	OK	**B+**	A-	A	92.5	3.68	7.9	1.8	9.8	43.3	**10.0**	14.9	23.6
State Central Bank	Bonaparte	IA	**D+**	D+	D-	37.7	-0.91	22.8	2.3	14.6	32.0	**8.8**	10.3	14.0
▲ State Exchange Bank	Mankato	KS	**B-**	C+	C+	34.6	-1.18	3.8	3.8	6.2	38.2	**10.0**	13.5	21.5
State Exchange Bank	Lamont	OK	**D**	D-	D	66.1	-0.18	14.1	0.9	5.0	5.6	**9.9**	12.0	14.9
State Farm Bank, FSB	Bloomington	IL	**C**	C-	C-	15959.1	-6.69	0.9	38.3	20.1	34.2	**10.0**	11.8	20.4
▲ State National Bank of Big Spring	Big Spring	TX	**A-**	B	C+	400.0	6.49	4.8	0.7	1.3	56.9	**10.0**	11.2	29.2
State National Bank of Groom	Groom	TX	**C**	C	C-	37.1	2.00	9.2	1.8	3.8	11.8	**9.4**	10.6	16.0
▲ State Nebraska Bank & Trust	Wayne	NE	**A-**	B+	B+	157.0	-1.57	11.8	2.2	10.7	31.0	**10.0**	13.2	19.4
▼ State Savings Bank	Creston	IA	**B**	B+	B-	124.7	7.93	9.5	4.9	20.1	0.2	**6.6**	9.8	12.2
State Savings Bank	Rake	IA	**D-**	D-	D-	75.6	2.65	11.5	0.8	0.7	2.4	**8.1**	11.5	13.4
State Savings Bank	West Des Moines	IA	**B+**	B+	A-	150.5	9.56	9.4	0.7	16.5	0.6	**7.2**	9.8	12.7
State Savings Bank	Frankfort	MI	**D+**	C-	D	223.5	60.22	7.4	0.9	28.7	3.1	**9.5**	11.0	14.6
State Savings Bank of Manistique	Manistique	MI	**B**	B	B-	130.9	2.95	6.9	4.8	16.1	41.3	**10.0**	11.6	19.1
State Street B&T Co. of California, N.A.	Los Angeles	CA	**U**	U	U	15.9	0.50	0.0	0.0	0.0	0.0	**10.0**	99.4	380.7
State Street Bank and Trust Co.	Quincy	IL	**B-**	B-	B-	224.4	2.72	3.8	25.1	24.9	15.4	**7.5**	9.3	13.1
State Street Bank and Trust Co.	Boston	MA	**B+**	B+	B	241364.0	4.50	1.7	0.0	0.0	39.0	**6.3**	8.3	17.1
State Street Bank and Trust Co., N.A.	New York	NY	**U**	U	U	34.4	3.45	0.0	0.0	0.0	0.0	**10.0**	98.4	323.4
Stearns Bank Holdingford N.A.	Holdingford	MN	**A-**	A-	A-	103.2	23.42	77.0	0.2	0.8	2.6	**10.0**	16.4	19.6
Stearns Bank N.A.	Saint Cloud	MN	**A-**	A-	A-	2172.8	12.36	66.4	0.1	1.3	0.8	**10.0**	20.2	21.7
Stearns Bank Upsala N.A.	Upsala	MN	**A-**	A-	A-	88.7	29.30	68.8	0.1	0.7	3.8	**10.0**	15.1	18.8
▲ Stephenson National Bank and Trust	Marinette	WI	**B-**	C+	B-	531.2	3.38	12.9	2.8	13.7	25.2	**7.9**	9.6	14.7
Sterling Bank	Poplar Bluff	MO	**A-**	A-	A-	1252.3	1.94	39.4	0.6	4.0	4.9	**9.7**	11.0	14.8
Sterling Bank	Barron	WI	**B**	B	B+	249.8	5.41	4.4	0.4	12.5	21.6	**6.9**	8.9	13.5
Sterling Bank and Trust, FSB	Southfield	MI	**A-**	A-	A-	3323.0	3.93	0.1	0.0	75.7	4.5	**8.6**	10.1	18.5
Sterling Federal Bank, F.S.B.	Sterling	IL	**D+**	C-	C-	454.0	-2.24	5.4	0.5	28.0	37.4	**6.5**	8.6	16.3
Sterling National Bank	Montebello	NY	**B**	B	B	30019.5	-3.80	17.4	0.0	8.2	17.1	**8.6**	10.1	14.0
Sterling State Bank	Austin	MN	**C+**	C+	C	353.2	-0.22	9.5	1.1	9.6	34.8	**7.0**	9.0	15.9
▲ Steuben Trust Co.	Hornell	NY	**A-**	B+	A-	576.0	2.80	3.4	3.6	14.1	33.2	**10.0**	11.8	19.2
Stifel Bank	Clayton	MO	**B**	B	B+	2103.8	250.40	10.3	24.3	1.5	40.2	**5.0**	7.0	19.1
Stifel Bank and Trust	Saint Louis	MO	**B+**	B+	B+	13901.3	-15.33	24.4	6.4	22.8	35.7	**5.3**	7.3	14.3
Stifel Trust Co. Delaware, N.A.	Wilmington	DE	**U**	U	U	14.4	9.94	0.0	0.0	0.0	2.8	**10.0**	87.4	324.0
Stifel Trust Co., N.A.	Saint Louis	MO	**U**	U	U	558.3	3308.7	0.0	0.0	0.0	88.4	**5.7**	7.7	30.7
Stillman BancCorp, N.A.	Stillman Valley	IL	**B-**	B-	C+	464.2	7.06	3.8	1.4	8.3	53.6	**6.8**	8.8	19.8
▲ Stock Exchange Bank	Caldwell	KS	**C+**	C	C	54.2	4.99	4.2	3.8	44.7	11.1	**7.4**	9.2	15.3
Stock Exchange Bank	Woodward	OK	**A**	A-	A-	247.2	2.87	6.4	4.2	7.2	42.8	**10.0**	15.8	26.1
Stock Growers Bank	Napoleon	ND	**A-**	A-	A-	65.1	7.41	2.4	1.8	3.0	37.7	**10.0**	15.5	22.4
Stock Yards Bank & Trust Co.	Louisville	KY	**A**	A	A	3529.9	6.22	23.2	1.2	10.1	10.6	**6.2**	10.6	11.9
Stockgrowers State Bank	Ashland	KS	**B+**	B	B	134.4	5.77	6.9	0.9	1.4	30.7	**10.0**	14.4	19.6
Stockgrowers State Bank	Maple Hill	KS	**B+**	B+	A-	81.3	-2.32	8.0	1.3	14.1	38.3	**10.0**	11.6	19.6
Stockman Bank of Montana	Miles City	MT	**A-**	A-	A-	3814.6	7.46	3.8	0.8	6.3	19.3	**8.3**	10.2	13.6
▲ Stockmans Bank	Altus	OK	**C**	C-	C	257.5	6.36	4.6	0.6	9.0	3.6	**7.3**	9.9	12.7
▲ Stockmens Bank	Colorado Springs	CO	**B**	B-	B	360.0	1.78	11.1	0.6	20.5	11.2	**7.4**	9.3	13.9
Stockmens Bank	Cascade	MT	**B-**	B-	B-	38.9	12.45	3.3	2.1	4.7	10.4	**10.0**	11.8	25.2
Stockmens National Bank in Cotulla	Cotulla	TX	**B+**	B+	B-	95.8	-5.08	1.7	4.4	3.6	57.5	**10.0**	12.1	41.4
▲ Stone Bank	Mountain View	AR	**C+**	C	B-	471.8	38.40	10.1	0.7	6.9	10.2	**10.0**	12.4	15.2
StonehamBank	Stoneham	MA	**C+**	C+	B-	615.6	2.48	13.5	0.1	34.9	10.0	**8.6**	10.1	14.9
Stoughton Co-operative Bank	Stoughton	MA	**C-**	C-	C-	119.1	4.30	0.4	1.7	62.9	19.1	**6.7**	8.7	16.3
Strasburg State Bank	Strasburg	ND	**C+**	C+	B-	65.8	9.73	3.0	0.5	0.0	17.2	**6.8**	8.8	13.5
Streator Home Savings Bank	Streator	IL	**B-**	B-	B-	162.9	-2.97	0.0	1.4	23.1	66.4	**10.0**	25.3	90.7
▲ Stride Bank, N.A.	Enid	OK	**C**	C-	D+	684.0	4.68	28.5	2.2	6.2	10.1	**5.1**	9.5	11.1
Stroud National Bank	Stroud	OK	**C+**	C+	C+	75.7	-3.13	6.9	5.6	21.7	26.7	**10.0**	12.2	21.0

Asset Quality Index	Adjusted Non-Performing Loans as a % of Total Loans	Adjusted Non-Performing Loans as a % of Capital	Net Charge-Offs Avg Loans	Profitability Index	Net Income ($Mil)	Return on Assets (R.O.A.)	Return on Equity (R.O.E.)	Net Interest Spread	Overhead Efficiency Ratio	Liquidity Index	Liquidity Ratio	Hot Money Ratio	Stability Index
8.5	0.00	na	-0.06	**4.0**	0.4	1.06	10.37	3.95	80.5	**3.2**	25.0	13.9	**4.0**
5.1	0.91	na	0.40	**10.0**	32.1	4.90	30.41	6.37	22.7	**0.9**	25.3	44.8	**10.0**
4.7	1.03	5.1	0.21	**4.6**	7.9	0.85	6.33	3.36	53.2	**2.0**	12.0	15.9	**8.5**
0.7	5.72	na	0.02	**6.8**	1.4	1.60	17.39	4.26	63.1	**1.8**	7.4	13.4	**7.0**
5.1	1.09	na	0.22	**4.6**	1.9	1.12	9.84	3.64	63.2	**2.6**	21.1	16.6	**6.2**
9.0	0.34	0.9	0.06	**4.4**	0.3	1.09	7.78	3.09	64.9	**7.1**	60.4	0.5	**6.4**
7.3	1.41	na	-0.09	**2.8**	0.6	0.44	4.88	3.27	84.9	**2.9**	24.7	15.7	**4.3**
6.9	0.92	na	0.00	**10.0**	1.7	2.72	11.17	4.53	40.2	**2.1**	26.9	20.9	**9.8**
4.8	0.36	na	0.21	**5.3**	1.2	1.27	12.05	4.40	68.9	**4.9**	27.7	5.2	**5.9**
8.2	1.01	na	0.00	**5.0**	1.0	1.41	9.36	3.43	64.1	**2.0**	34.2	29.4	**8.2**
0.3	43.51	na	-1.00	**0.5**	-0.4	-1.53	-11.34	3.75	79.6	**6.4**	38.8	0.3	**5.5**
7.9	0.67	na	0.05	**4.7**	0.3	1.12	8.53	3.59	65.0	**4.5**	24.4	6.9	**5.7**
1.3	9.37	na	0.46	**6.4**	0.7	1.49	12.91	4.28	60.1	**0.8**	20.6	43.7	**6.1**
4.0	1.76	7.3	1.06	**2.8**	49.7	0.40	3.51	2.91	68.4	**1.3**	27.7	27.0	**6.9**
9.7	0.05	na	0.00	**6.1**	4.7	1.61	15.01	2.86	44.4	**7.2**	77.1	4.8	**6.6**
4.1	2.61	na	0.35	**3.3**	0.2	0.54	5.05	4.21	86.0	**4.1**	19.7	8.3	**5.2**
6.4	0.83	na	0.13	**7.0**	1.7	1.42	10.99	3.57	49.1	**4.3**	14.5	6.4	**8.3**
3.0	2.56	17.9	0.00	**8.6**	1.7	1.91	19.61	4.01	49.4	**1.7**	10.9	20.1	**8.0**
0.0	6.12	na	0.57	**3.8**	0.4	0.68	6.09	3.23	36.8	**0.6**	15.3	55.2	**4.9**
6.7	0.44	na	-0.01	**6.3**	1.5	1.38	14.03	3.81	64.6	**3.6**	10.8	10.7	**8.1**
5.4	1.64	na	0.08	**1.2**	-0.1	-0.06	-0.57	4.12	103.0	**4.5**	21.2	6.2	**5.9**
6.4	2.07	na	0.08	**4.2**	0.9	0.94	8.01	3.78	69.0	**5.8**	52.9	9.0	**6.3**
10.0	na	0.0	na	**8.2**	0.2	1.53	1.54	1.18	90.3	**4.0**	na	0.0	**7.0**
6.8	0.09	na	0.03	**6.4**	2.7	1.58	17.46	3.95	65.8	**3.9**	19.9	9.7	**6.2**
8.4	0.00	0.1	0.01	**5.2**	1707.0	1.05	8.65	1.81	74.0	**3.2**	56.6	31.7	**9.1**
10.0	na	0.0	na	**9.5**	0.6	2.38	2.43	1.18	93.9	**4.0**	na	0.0	**7.0**
7.3	0.53	na	0.42	**5.6**	0.8	1.13	6.72	3.30	27.0	**0.6**	19.1	53.0	**8.0**
5.6	2.72	5.4	0.77	**10.0**	38.4	2.43	12.08	6.59	49.1	**0.4**	4.3	12.5	**9.5**
6.8	0.67	na	0.65	**5.3**	0.6	1.06	6.62	3.11	30.0	**0.8**	27.5	55.9	**8.1**
5.5	0.88	na	0.10	**5.1**	4.6	1.15	11.34	3.50	72.1	**3.5**	18.3	10.7	**7.4**
7.3	0.47	2.9	0.03	**7.0**	12.5	1.34	11.34	3.63	49.6	**0.9**	17.7	18.3	**9.4**
7.3	0.43	na	0.00	**6.8**	2.9	1.60	18.15	3.76	58.1	**2.6**	31.4	18.6	**6.7**
9.0	0.42	3.1	0.00	**9.8**	46.3	1.88	19.28	3.92	38.1	**1.1**	10.1	28.5	**9.0**
5.4	2.77	na	0.25	**1.1**	-0.1	-0.04	-0.47	2.96	96.2	**3.0**	41.0	21.4	**4.5**
4.5	1.03	4.4	0.17	**7.4**	336.0	1.49	9.92	3.55	41.7	**3.4**	12.9	6.6	**10.0**
8.8	0.08	0.5	-0.01	**2.9**	1.3	0.49	5.61	3.27	86.9	**4.3**	16.2	6.9	**5.3**
7.8	0.47	na	0.06	**6.2**	5.3	1.24	11.12	3.73	62.7	**1.6**	12.3	20.4	**8.0**
7.0	0.02	na	0.00	**6.2**	21.3	1.45	22.14	3.21	35.9	**5.8**	35.1	3.6	**6.8**
8.4	0.19	1.4	0.00	**9.4**	199.9	1.80	24.80	3.12	21.7	**4.7**	27.0	1.3	**6.7**
10.0	na	na	na	**9.5**	0.8	7.19	8.26	2.17	74.5	**4.0**	na	0.0	**7.0**
10.0	na	na	na	**7.0**	1.7	1.12	9.96	1.77	78.2	**8.6**	104.4	0.1	**7.0**
9.3	0.09	na	-0.04	**4.5**	3.8	1.14	12.51	2.82	69.1	**3.9**	48.6	17.7	**5.8**
7.3	0.00	na	-0.01	**5.2**	0.4	1.01	11.32	4.55	69.7	**1.0**	14.5	31.4	**4.6**
8.8	0.09	0.5	0.09	**7.4**	2.8	1.47	9.61	3.67	53.3	**5.0**	31.9	6.2	**8.5**
8.8	0.00	na	0.00	**8.2**	1.0	2.06	13.68	3.95	45.3	**4.2**	35.9	12.5	**8.0**
8.2	0.10	0.7	-0.02	**9.5**	49.1	1.94	17.59	3.83	53.5	**4.0**	6.9	6.8	**10.0**
7.3	0.17	na	0.26	**5.9**	1.4	1.40	9.59	3.61	70.3	**1.0**	24.6	30.0	**7.9**
8.7	0.37	na	0.02	**5.9**	0.9	1.46	12.17	3.81	58.6	**2.6**	17.8	16.3	**7.4**
7.1	0.79	4.6	0.04	**8.2**	52.5	1.90	18.16	3.99	53.5	**3.1**	18.4	12.1	**10.0**
3.8	0.72	na	0.03	**6.7**	2.9	1.53	15.74	4.88	68.8	**0.7**	9.2	36.8	**6.6**
7.4	0.30	na	0.01	**5.3**	2.9	1.09	11.33	3.83	56.5	**3.2**	10.6	12.8	**6.1**
9.1	0.00	na	-0.01	**3.8**	0.2	0.87	7.02	3.27	73.7	**4.7**	69.3	16.5	**6.0**
9.6	0.00	0.0	-0.01	**5.2**	0.9	1.31	11.35	2.61	55.0	**3.6**	46.9	18.4	**6.0**
5.5	1.82	na	0.45	**4.6**	2.6	0.87	7.73	3.38	66.4	**0.7**	16.3	42.7	**6.6**
5.6	0.47	na	0.00	**3.7**	2.8	0.61	6.14	3.25	82.2	**1.4**	8.8	21.0	**6.8**
7.8	0.46	na	0.00	**2.1**	0.3	0.28	3.45	2.54	89.6	**1.1**	24.7	34.1	**4.4**
6.0	0.00	na	0.00	**4.5**	0.4	0.90	10.29	3.49	64.7	**4.0**	36.3	13.9	**4.9**
9.7	2.05	na	0.15	**2.7**	0.6	0.45	1.83	2.16	79.3	**4.7**	93.7	22.5	**7.6**
3.4	1.54	na	0.30	**5.8**	6.2	1.24	13.22	4.84	74.0	**2.7**	7.4	7.3	**6.6**
4.8	2.91	na	0.19	**3.2**	0.4	0.62	5.16	4.46	84.6	**4.2**	26.6	9.7	**6.3**

Name	City	State	Rating	2018 Rating	2017 Rating	Total Assets ($Mil)	One Year Asset Growth	Asset Mix (As a % of Total Assets) Comm-ercial Loans	Cons-umer Loans	Mort-gage Loans	Secur-ities	Capital-ization Index	Lever-age Ratio	Risk-Based Capital Ratio
Sturdy Savings Bank	Cape May Court Hou	NJ	C+	C+	C+	893.5	0.54	2.8	0.0	26.4	25.0	7.8	9.5	15.5
▲ Sturgis Bank & Trust Co.	Sturgis	MI	B-	C+	C+	473.1	5.73	7.8	1.3	24.4	11.8	6.7	8.7	13.3
▲ Success Bank	Bloomfield	IA	B-	C+	B	197.6	4.93	7.3	1.9	13.8	5.8	9.9	12.0	14.9
Sugar River Bank	Newport	NH	B-	B-	C+	313.2	3.27	4.6	2.6	45.9	19.8	10.0	14.3	24.7
▲ Sumitomo Mitsui Trust Bank (U.S.A.) Ltd.	Hoboken	NJ	B+	B-	C+	2918.9	-12.11	0.0	0.0	0.0	0.0	10.0	11.8	24.0
▲ Summit Bank	Oakland	CA	A-	B+	A-	250.9	-10.56	15.7	0.2	1.5	0.2	10.0	13.0	17.0
Summit Bank	Eugene	OR	B-	B-	B+	498.7	25.42	23.6	0.4	1.9	0.8	5.3	9.8	11.2
Summit Community Bank, Inc.	Moorefield	WV	B+	B	B	2321.7	8.90	8.2	1.6	18.5	11.4	7.4	10.4	12.9
▲ Summit National Bank	Hulett	WY	C-	D+	D+	74.4	1.01	5.9	3.9	6.5	13.8	7.7	9.5	13.6
Summit State Bank	Santa Rosa	CA	B	B+	B+	680.8	14.38	8.0	0.0	7.4	9.8	7.1	9.4	12.6
▲ Sumner Bank & Trust	Gallatin	TN	B	B-	B-	181.6	10.26	4.7	0.9	19.8	12.7	7.4	9.3	14.0
▼ Suncrest Bank	Visalia	CA	B+	B+	B+	997.4	9.42	5.4	0.0	4.5	18.7	9.6	10.9	14.7
▲ Sundance State Bank	Sundance	WY	B-	C	B	193.3	6.71	13.1	4.2	9.1	27.0	10.0	11.7	16.6
▲ Sundown State Bank	Sundown	TX	B+	B	B+	159.3	3.82	13.6	0.8	0.9	11.1	8.3	11.4	13.6
Sunflower Bank, N.A.	Denver	CO	C	C	C-	4026.3	7.65	19.2	0.5	17.5	14.9	8.1	10.6	13.4
SunMark Community Bank	Hawkinsville	GA	B	B+	B+	267.7	2.64	5.8	2.9	21.8	8.9	10.0	11.6	17.8
Sunnyside Federal S&L Assn. of Irvington	Irvington	NY	D+	D+	D+	87.9	6.65	1.4	7.6	25.6	44.4	10.0	13.6	26.6
▲ Sunrise Bank	Cocoa Beach	FL	A-	B+	B+	233.5	13.51	3.9	0.9	8.7	17.5	10.0	11.6	16.4
▼ Sunrise Bank Dakota	Onida	SD	D+	D+	C	52.2	-11.39	7.0	1.4	4.8	12.5	10.0	12.7	20.5
Sunrise Banks, N.A.	Saint Paul	MN	B-	B	C+	1123.9	0.88	7.2	3.5	10.4	13.2	7.4	9.3	13.4
Sunset Bank & Savings	Waukesha	WI	C+	C+	C-	130.4	2.29	5.2	0.9	38.2	7.4	10.0	11.1	17.2
SunSouth Bank	Dothan	AL	E	E	E-	107.1	-12.64	28.8	0.5	11.8	35.8	4.8	6.8	17.8
▲ Sunstate Bank	Miami	FL	B	C+	C	458.1	7.20	0.8	0.4	28.3	16.9	6.3	9.6	12.0
SunTrust Bank	Atlanta	GA	B-	B-	C+	221424.2	7.73	19.3	15.8	14.3	14.1	6.7	9.8	12.3
Sunwest Bank	Irvine	CA	B+	B+	A-	1346.6	-0.98	11.5	2.4	3.3	5.1	9.3	12.8	14.4
▲ Superior National Bank & Trust Co.	Hancock	MI	A-	B+	B+	586.1	2.26	5.6	8.0	21.7	33.8	10.0	13.1	24.5
Superior Savings Bank	Superior	WI	B	B-	B-	66.3	0.15	6.0	0.8	45.7	0.0	10.0	19.7	38.2
Surety Bank	Deland	FL	B-	B-	B	131.3	12.40	2.2	0.2	7.2	14.7	10.0	11.4	19.0
▲ Surrey Bank & Trust	Mount Airy	NC	A-	B+	A	331.6	6.99	24.6	1.2	7.0	2.1	10.0	14.6	20.9
Susquehanna Community Bank	West Milton	PA	B+	B+	B+	473.7	15.13	5.0	3.5	8.4	36.6	7.0	9.0	13.3
Sutton Bank	Attica	OH	B	B	B+	561.3	9.45	8.3	1.1	5.3	23.8	9.4	10.6	18.5
Swedish-American State Bank	Courtland	KS	C	C-	D	41.5	-0.85	8.7	3.1	10.8	17.2	10.0	12.2	16.3
▲ Sweet Water State Bank	Sweet Water	AL	B-	C+	C	97.9	1.65	15.0	3.9	8.1	15.9	10.0	11.5	15.4
Sycamore Bank	Senatobia	MS	B	B	B	227.4	0.11	5.9	3.0	20.1	14.1	8.9	10.3	15.5
Synchrony Bank	Draper	UT	C	C	C	91937.0	1.93	1.3	85.2	0.0	7.4	10.0	12.7	15.9
Synergy Bank	Houma	LA	B-	C+	D+	552.8	6.90	14.0	2.1	12.5	26.5	10.0	11.9	18.9
Synovus Bank	Columbus	GA	B+	B+	B+	47572.4	48.73	17.5	5.2	13.0	14.5	6.1	9.9	11.9
Synovus Trust Co., N.A.	Columbus	GA	U	U	U	97.5	6.26	0.0	0.0	0.0	20.3	10.0	94.8	132.3
Systematic Savings Bank	Springfield	MO	D	D	D	36.8	-9.86	3.4	0.6	53.2	6.8	10.0	13.4	24.0
▲ T Bank, N.A.	Dallas	TX	B	B-	B+	351.0	21.01	37.0	1.0	1.5	4.6	10.0	11.3	15.3
▲ Table Grove State Bank	Table Grove	IL	B	B-	B-	46.3	-0.01	1.7	9.5	1.6	24.6	10.0	12.5	18.6
Table Rock Community Bank	Kimberling City	MO	B-	C+	C+	90.1	2.77	4.0	5.9	29.6	8.0	7.4	9.3	14.0
▲ Talbot State Bank	Woodland	GA	D+	D	D	60.0	-2.50	0.0	0.4	43.7	32.0	9.5	10.7	29.9
Tampa State Bank	Tampa	KS	C+	C+	B	55.9	-0.97	9.9	2.8	18.8	25.3	6.2	10.5	11.9
Tarboro Savings Bank, SSB	Tarboro	NC	B-	B-	B	49.3	5.49	0.0	0.1	61.7	0.1	10.0	14.5	25.9
▲ Taylor County Bank	Campbellsville	KY	A-	B+	A	182.0	0.73	12.7	5.0	21.3	19.4	10.0	15.1	22.0
▲ Taylorsville Savings Bank, SSB	Taylorsville	NC	B-	C+	C+	107.6	6.68	1.1	1.1	56.5	5.3	10.0	11.1	18.3
TBK Bank, SSB	Dallas	TX	B	B-	B-	5014.6	11.40	35.9	0.5	3.1	6.0	5.6	10.8	11.5
TC Federal Bank	Thomasville	GA	C+	C+	B	310.7	6.23	1.7	0.4	35.6	7.6	10.0	12.8	18.8
TCF National Bank	Sioux Falls	SD	B+	B	B-	45687.8	99.32	21.4	6.1	14.5	12.5	6.6	10.7	12.2
▲ TCM Bank, N.A.	Tampa	FL	C+	C+	B	312.0	7.03	22.3	68.2	0.0	0.9	10.0	17.0	19.0
TD Bank USA, N.A.	Wilmington	DE	B-	C+	C+	16812.6	-12.40	2.4	55.3	0.0	23.4	10.0	17.5	28.3
TD Bank, N.A.	Wilmington	DE	B-	C+	C+	311037.5	5.68	10.9	9.5	8.8	40.1	7.1	9.1	15.6
Tecumseh Federal Bank	Tecumseh	NE	B	B	B-	49.0	-3.22	2.8	1.4	42.1	16.2	10.0	21.3	44.6
▲ Tejas Bank	Monahans	TX	A-	B+	B+	183.6	12.02	20.6	2.8	2.2	20.3	8.7	10.1	16.8
Templeton Savings Bank	Templeton	IA	A-	A-	A-	124.2	4.12	10.8	2.8	16.0	12.7	10.0	14.4	19.6
Tempo Bank	Trenton	IL	C-	C-	C	94.9	-1.45	0.0	1.3	84.8	0.0	10.0	11.6	21.9
▼ Tennessee Bank & Trust	Nashville	TN	D	D+		265.9	-4.05	27.1	0.1	7.1	0.8	5.3	8.6	11.2
▲ Tennessee State Bank	Pigeon Forge	TN	A-	B	C+	662.9	4.14	1.4	4.3	18.0	18.4	10.0	11.3	16.1
Tensas State Bank	Newellton	LA	B	B	B+	155.8	-0.08	16.8	1.3	11.3	32.0	10.0	12.8	19.6

Asset Quality Index	Adjusted Non-Performing Loans as a % of Total Loans	Adjusted Non-Performing Loans as a % of Capital	Net Charge-Offs Avg Loans	Profitability Index	Net Income ($Mil)	Return on Assets (R.O.A.)	Return on Equity (R.O.E.)	Net Interest Spread	Overhead Efficiency Ratio	Liquidity Index	Liquidity Ratio	Hot Money Ratio	Stability Index
7.1	0.78	na	0.01	**3.4**	3.1	0.49	4.78	3.64	82.7	**5.4**	28.4	2.0	**6.5**
5.7	1.88	na	0.02	**5.3**	3.9	1.18	12.39	4.01	69.2	**3.0**	16.5	8.6	**5.9**
5.1	0.63	na	0.24	**8.1**	2.6	1.78	15.42	4.88	57.7	**1.7**	8.2	16.8	**8.6**
8.1	1.01	na	0.26	**3.7**	1.4	0.62	4.47	3.65	79.2	**3.1**	27.9	15.6	**7.5**
10.0	0.00	0.0	0.00	**5.0**	20.9	1.00	8.51	0.91	69.7	**8.8**	110.4	0.0	**8.3**
6.0	0.72	na	0.00	**8.4**	2.8	1.48	11.83	5.29	59.0	**4.4**	29.6	9.3	**7.7**
5.7	0.30	na	0.35	**7.8**	4.2	1.29	13.21	5.40	57.2	**3.4**	13.9	10.4	**6.1**
5.9	0.72	4.8	0.09	**6.4**	23.4	1.38	12.58	3.71	56.8	**1.4**	11.3	13.0	**9.5**
2.7	1.55	na	0.31	**4.3**	0.5	0.80	8.19	3.76	77.5	**3.4**	7.0	11.2	**6.0**
6.2	0.11	na	-0.01	**5.1**	4.6	0.97	9.66	3.62	63.2	**0.7**	12.3	28.3	**6.8**
8.9	0.08	na	0.04	**5.1**	1.4	0.99	10.92	3.98	67.5	**3.9**	24.6	10.6	**5.3**
4.8	1.08	4.7	0.00	**7.2**	8.9	1.26	8.48	4.53	53.7	**4.8**	31.8	8.0	**8.2**
4.2	2.66	na	0.55	**5.9**	1.8	1.27	11.09	4.00	51.6	**2.8**	27.0	16.5	**6.4**
7.2	0.00	na	-0.01	**6.8**	1.7	1.44	13.37	4.85	61.9	**1.9**	15.0	19.3	**6.3**
5.6	0.72	4.5	0.07	**3.3**	16.6	0.57	4.86	3.62	85.7	**3.4**	7.2	8.4	**7.9**
6.1	0.81	na	0.29	**6.6**	3.3	1.59	14.48	4.68	71.2	**3.3**	16.9	12.6	**7.6**
8.5	1.49	na	0.00	**0.2**	-0.2	-0.34	-2.74	2.66	115.2	**3.1**	46.3	21.6	**5.8**
7.6	0.00	na	0.00	**5.4**	2.3	1.35	12.05	4.15	67.8	**1.2**	26.8	31.5	**7.7**
0.7	18.01	na	1.01	**2.0**	0.2	0.44	3.60	2.95	87.0	**1.8**	19.9	16.9	**5.1**
7.0	0.16	1.4	0.41	**4.4**	7.9	0.95	10.81	4.69	78.5	**1.0**	21.4	2.0	**8.3**
7.5	1.13	na	0.01	**2.3**	0.3	0.27	2.25	3.28	88.9	**1.2**	14.2	28.3	**6.3**
6.0	1.57	na	0.09	**2.0**	0.3	0.38	5.86	2.71	95.6	**1.1**	27.5	34.2	**0.3**
7.7	0.10	na	-0.12	**6.7**	5.2	1.58	14.48	3.43	52.6	**2.3**	47.1	46.2	**6.5**
4.3	1.43	5.2	0.28	**5.7**	1940.3	1.21	10.18	3.22	60.6	**4.2**	20.7	5.6	**10.0**
4.5	0.93	5.1	-0.12	**9.5**	16.7	1.68	13.52	4.48	52.2	**3.8**	13.4	4.0	**10.0**
7.3	2.72	na	-0.12	**6.0**	5.2	1.23	9.69	3.78	63.8	**4.4**	48.3	15.1	**8.0**
6.4	3.91	7.3	0.00	**5.3**	0.5	1.01	5.16	3.97	68.0	**5.5**	40.6	7.1	**7.0**
6.9	1.97	na	-0.03	**6.2**	1.4	1.47	13.11	4.09	73.4	**3.9**	44.7	16.7	**7.5**
7.7	0.79	na	0.10	**9.1**	3.8	1.64	11.09	4.70	56.4	**3.3**	25.7	12.5	**9.2**
8.1	0.29	na	0.02	**4.9**	3.9	1.11	11.78	3.12	68.1	**4.7**	30.4	7.9	**6.6**
5.0	2.39	7.7	0.98	**9.8**	12.8	3.18	30.40	4.12	47.4	**4.7**	37.7	1.5	**8.5**
3.1	2.74	na	0.41	**5.6**	0.5	1.53	12.82	4.41	68.2	**1.4**	7.0	23.0	**3.8**
3.7	2.15	na	0.34	**4.5**	0.7	0.96	8.54	5.32	77.3	**1.2**	19.1	30.2	**6.4**
5.9	0.84	3.2	0.01	**4.9**	1.7	1.00	10.21	4.23	72.3	**3.8**	14.2	9.3	**5.8**
1.8	1.05	12.6	6.04	**10.0**	2547.0	3.73	27.72	12.48	32.8	**0.8**	18.2	32.7	**10.0**
5.7	2.93	na	-0.03	**6.9**	5.9	1.47	12.61	4.06	59.2	**2.3**	30.9	21.4	**7.3**
6.7	0.67	3.1	0.18	**7.0**	431.4	1.24	11.87	3.75	54.4	**1.7**	16.1	14.8	**9.7**
6.6	na	0.0	na	**9.5**	6.4	8.91	9.34	1.62	77.4	**4.0**	na	0.0	**7.0**
7.1	0.20	na	0.18	**0.1**	-0.1	-0.43	-3.21	3.45	112.2	**0.7**	23.7	58.0	**5.1**
5.6	2.30	na	0.41	**7.0**	3.3	1.38	9.80	4.19	72.0	**0.4**	6.3	65.3	**8.7**
6.8	0.05	na	0.03	**6.4**	0.6	1.64	13.87	4.23	68.2	**4.8**	27.9	5.8	**6.3**
5.4	0.86	na	0.06	**6.1**	0.7	1.13	12.33	4.86	71.0	**3.4**	17.2	12.0	**5.2**
4.9	4.00	na	0.04	**2.3**	0.5	1.19	10.73	3.88	101.9	**2.2**	51.6	44.9	**4.8**
5.4	0.61	na	0.11	**3.5**	0.4	0.81	7.90	3.31	79.3	**1.5**	14.0	23.5	**6.3**
6.4	1.32	na	0.12	**3.2**	0.2	0.42	2.86	3.50	81.4	**0.8**	18.9	41.3	**7.7**
6.2	1.23	na	-0.02	**9.0**	2.9	2.09	14.36	4.68	58.5	**3.1**	21.2	14.2	**9.6**
6.0	3.17	na	0.03	**4.2**	0.6	0.72	7.23	4.27	77.1	**1.6**	14.1	21.1	**5.5**
4.3	0.83	6.4	0.12	**7.6**	46.8	1.34	9.09	6.13	69.0	**0.9**	8.0	23.2	**10.0**
6.9	1.64	na	0.07	**2.7**	0.9	0.39	2.96	3.36	86.5	**1.8**	18.9	21.6	**6.5**
5.1	0.80	4.7	0.51	**5.3**	240.5	1.14	11.11	4.36	71.6	**2.2**	15.7	11.9	**9.3**
4.0	0.20	na	2.99	**6.7**	2.9	1.29	7.35	7.51	70.8	**0.2**	9.8	100.0	**6.9**
3.1	1.17	7.1	5.21	**7.6**	214.6	1.58	10.31	10.64	62.2	**2.7**	48.3	0.0	**7.4**
4.9	1.08	3.9	0.39	**4.1**	2027.0	0.90	6.80	2.53	55.3	**2.8**	46.3	1.8	**9.0**
9.1	0.48	na	-0.04	**4.0**	0.3	0.68	3.24	3.59	79.3	**4.1**	42.5	15.0	**7.1**
8.1	0.00	na	0.08	**9.4**	3.7	2.74	24.59	4.39	44.5	**5.5**	37.3	5.8	**7.8**
7.1	0.04	3.7	0.02	**6.9**	1.3	1.33	8.53	3.86	53.6	**2.7**	19.5	16.2	**8.7**
5.9	1.46	na	0.00	**1.7**	0.1	0.10	0.87	2.64	94.0	**1.2**	7.9	27.6	**5.9**
4.7	3.07	na	0.95	**0.6**	-0.5	-0.23	-2.62	3.64	83.8	**1.5**	20.9	25.6	**1.9**
6.1	1.21	na	0.34	**6.4**	6.0	1.24	10.83	4.05	72.4	**4.2**	18.8	7.0	**6.4**
5.7	3.06	na	0.37	**5.0**	1.3	1.15	8.72	3.63	65.5	**1.7**	31.3	29.2	**8.0**

Name	City	State	Rating	2018 Rating	2017 Rating	Total Assets ($Mil)	One Year Asset Growth	Asset Mix (As a % of Total Assets) Commercial Loans	Consumer Loans	Mortgage Loans	Securities	Capitalization Index	Leverage Ratio	Risk-Based Capital Ratio
Terrabank, N.A.	Miami	FL	C+	C+	C+	425.2	7.39	3.4	0.6	16.4	23.0	7.5	9.4	15.0
Terre Haute Savings Bank	Terre Haute	IN	C	C	C	330.6	1.56	7.1	1.2	28.4	23.3	7.7	9.4	14.3
Territorial Savings Bank	Honolulu	HI	B+	B+	A-	2085.5	2.96	0.4	0.1	74.1	18.5	10.0	11.3	24.1
Teutopolis State Bank	Teutopolis	IL	A	A	A	246.5	9.59	6.4	2.5	10.4	25.1	10.0	13.8	21.1
Texan Bank, N.A.	Houston	TX	C	C	D+	329.2	13.02	10.4	0.3	5.3	1.3	9.6	12.1	14.7
Texana Bank, N.A.	Linden	TX	C-	D+	D	216.0	0.56	26.8	2.1	23.2	7.9	5.9	8.5	11.7
▲ Texas Advantage Community Bank, N.A.	Alvin	TX	B-	B-	C	123.4	11.92	19.7	2.6	4.3	9.1	8.6	10.1	15.3
Texas Bank	Henderson	TX	B-	B	B	489.1	-0.44	6.8	4.9	15.4	29.2	9.5	10.7	15.9
Texas Bank and Trust Co.	Longview	TX	A-	B+	B+	2635.5	3.99	14.9	2.0	22.1	4.3	10.0	11.5	15.0
Texas Bank Financial	Weatherford	TX	B	B+	A-	420.7	29.49	0.8	0.1	65.1	0.5	8.3	9.8	16.8
Texas Brand Bank	Dallas	TX	B+	B+	B+	210.5	1.11	11.8	0.3	6.5	2.2	10.0	13.1	17.5
Texas Capital Bank, N.A.	Dallas	TX	B-	B-	B-	33506.6	23.63	23.1	0.2	9.4	0.6	4.2	8.4	10.6
Texas Champion Bank	Corpus Christi	TX	C-	D+	D	318.4	0.30	7.6	1.0	5.2	9.6	10.0	12.0	17.0
▲ Texas Citizens Bank, N.A.	Pasadena	TX	C-	C-	C	520.9	-3.90	18.3	2.3	8.3	0.2	7.2	9.8	12.7
▲ Texas Community Bank	Laredo	TX	A	A-	B+	1433.5	4.20	11.0	1.2	11.4	20.3	9.9	10.9	20.5
Texas Exchange Bank, SSB	Crowley	TX	A	A	A	1079.0	-14.75	18.8	0.0	0.0	34.6	10.0	13.9	22.6
▲ Texas Financial Bank	Eden	TX	A-	B+	B+	102.1	-2.92	1.9	1.0	0.4	39.0	9.9	10.9	28.7
Texas First Bank	Texas City	TX	B+	A-	A-	1096.6	1.61	9.4	0.8	5.1	31.8	9.3	10.6	15.8
Texas First State Bank	Riesel	TX	C	C	C+	398.2	0.43	4.5	0.5	11.1	44.0	6.6	8.6	16.3
▼ Texas Gulf Bank, N.A.	Houston	TX	B-	B+	B+	694.1	13.66	9.7	0.7	15.2	27.4	8.1	9.7	14.3
▲ Texas Heritage Bank	Boerne	TX	B	B-	B	146.5	-3.23	7.9	2.0	20.2	1.8	7.6	9.4	13.7
▲ Texas Heritage National Bank	Daingerfield	TX	B	B	B+	143.1	6.17	4.9	4.7	20.7	8.6	10.0	11.1	15.1
Texas Hill Country Bank	Bandera	TX	B	B	B	153.4	14.48	15.7	1.4	17.5	2.4	7.0	9.9	12.5
Texas National Bank	Mercedes	TX	B	B	B	295.1	13.45	11.2	1.8	19.7	13.9	7.7	9.4	14.5
Texas National Bank	Sweetwater	TX	C+	C+	C+	142.8	8.23	5.4	1.7	5.9	54.4	8.3	9.9	23.2
Texas National Bank of Jacksonville	Jacksonville	TX	B	B-	B-	559.0	5.02	12.2	3.2	29.2	3.1	8.8	10.2	15.0
▲ Texas Regional Bank	Harlingen	TX	B-	C+	C+	987.2	13.92	10.7	1.2	8.7	25.9	8.8	10.2	14.3
▲ Texas Republic Bank, N.A.	Frisco	TX	A-	B+	A-	297.6	13.41	8.3	0.3	36.6	0.0	10.0	11.1	16.2
Texas Security Bank	Dallas	TX	A-	A-	A-	488.6	7.99	20.3	0.2	14.8	5.5	10.0	13.0	16.7
▲ Texas State Bank	San Angelo	TX	A	A-	B+	274.2	1.94	7.3	1.0	13.5	29.4	10.0	12.6	21.9
▲ TexasBank	Brownwood	TX	A-	B+	A+	497.4	2.53	3.6	1.4	15.0	9.1	10.0	13.6	18.9
Texico State Bank	Texico	IL	D-	D-	D-	8.2	11.64	1.7	1.9	28.4	0.0	7.0	9.0	22.5
▲ TexStar National Bank	Universal City	TX	B+	B	B	282.1	9.74	11.4	0.5	8.0	7.1	10.0	11.0	15.5
▲ Thayer County Bank	Hebron	NE	C	C-	C	64.3	13.02	16.4	3.5	15.5	24.3	10.0	11.5	23.9
The Bank	Oberlin	KS	D+	C-	C-	330.7	-3.34	3.0	0.4	0.5	12.4	10.0	13.2	20.3
▲ The Bank	Jennings	LA	A-	B+	B+	243.3	3.60	11.3	12.6	28.5	6.6	10.0	11.4	15.8
▲ The Bank of Soperton	Soperton	GA	B-	C+	B-	91.7	17.22	18.9	8.3	23.9	6.8	8.9	10.3	15.0
The Bankers Bank	Oklahoma City	OK	B-	B-	C+	319.6	9.03	4.8	0.3	2.0	0.0	10.0	12.4	18.2
Think Mutual Bank	Rochester	MN	B+	B+	B	1662.4	2.16	1.1	14.5	43.8	25.0	10.0	16.7	29.0
▲ Third Coast Bank, SSB	Humble	TX	C	C-	C+	933.9	15.10	22.5	0.4	6.5	0.1	5.6	9.1	11.5
Third Federal S&L Assn. of Cleveland	Cleveland	OH	B-	B-	B-	14495.1	2.80	0.0	0.0	78.8	3.8	9.3	10.5	19.6
Thomaston Savings Bank	Thomaston	CT	C+	C+	C+	1121.0	7.42	6.2	1.2	27.7	23.6	10.0	11.2	17.2
▲ Thomasville National Bank	Thomasville	GA	A-	A-	B+	953.9	9.60	13.6	1.8	24.3	6.2	7.2	9.2	12.7
Three Rivers Bank of Montana	Kalispell	MT	B+	A-	A-	169.4	10.14	15.1	3.0	9.5	10.1	10.0	11.8	15.9
Thrivent Trust Co.	Appleton	WI	U	U	U	64.2	6.42	0.0	0.0	0.0	41.8	10.0	34.2	143.5
Thumb Bank & Trust	Pigeon	MI	C+	C+	C	267.6	6.96	7.1	1.3	7.3	22.5	7.0	9.0	13.9
TIAA, FSB	Jacksonville	FL	C+	B-	C+	41159.0	19.56	2.1	0.0	42.9	6.5	5.7	7.7	12.8
TIB The Independent BankersBank, N.A.	Farmers Branch	TX	B	B-	B-	2633.5	3.56	5.1	3.1	1.0	13.5	9.1	10.4	16.9
Tilden Bank	Tilden	NE	C	C	C+	84.5	2.61	3.6	2.5	1.6	15.1	7.2	11.4	12.7
Timberland Bank	Hoquiam	WA	A	A	A-	1244.9	22.56	5.2	0.4	12.2	4.4	10.0	12.5	19.3
Timberline Bank	Grand Junction	CO	B-	B-	B-	307.9	5.53	12.1	1.7	10.6	15.1	5.7	8.6	11.6
Timberwood Bank	Tomah	WI	A-	A-	A-	191.8	8.13	8.5	0.6	9.7	20.4	10.0	11.2	16.1
Time Federal Savings Bank	Medford	WI	B-	B+	B+	586.5	-0.30	0.0	0.3	59.8	19.4	10.0	23.6	56.4
Tioga Franklin Savings Bank	Philadelphia	PA	C	B-	B-	45.3	9.32	1.7	0.5	55.1	3.1	10.0	11.1	19.1
▲ Tioga State Bank	Spencer	NY	A-	B+	B+	481.9	-0.05	10.5	1.8	24.5	25.1	10.0	12.2	19.9
Tipton Latham Bank, N.A.	Tipton	MO	B	B	B+	139.4	6.49	7.9	3.0	20.1	19.5	10.0	11.1	16.5
Titan Bank, N.A.	Mineral Wells	TX	A-	A-	A-	142.3	29.83	5.3	0.2	28.2	12.7	9.1	10.4	23.3
Titonka Savings Bank	Titonka	IA	B-	B-	C+	181.1	1.41	3.7	1.5	9.6	39.3	10.0	11.8	21.7
TNB Bank	Tuscola	IL	C+	C	C	85.9	3.78	3.5	1.7	7.0	17.3	10.0	12.9	21.4
TNBANK	Oak Ridge	TN	C	C	C-	235.4	8.84	4.5	1.4	18.8	12.2	5.2	8.8	11.2

Asset Quality Index	Adjusted Non-Performing Loans as a % of Total Loans	Adjusted Non-Performing Loans as a % of Capital	Net Charge-Offs Avg Loans	Profitability Index	Net Income ($Mil)	Return on Assets (R.O.A.)	Return on Equity (R.O.E.)	Net Interest Spread	Overhead Efficiency Ratio	Liquidity Index	Liquidity Ratio	Hot Money Ratio	Stability Index
7.8	0.01	na	0.01	**3.2**	1.5	0.50	5.38	3.49	82.6	**2.4**	33.3	21.0	**5.6**
5.9	0.73	na	0.03	**2.6**	1.0	0.40	4.15	3.49	89.2	**2.1**	19.5	18.7	**5.2**
9.9	0.09	0.5	0.00	**5.0**	17.4	1.12	10.45	2.94	58.6	**1.7**	11.7	22.0	**9.0**
8.7	0.00	na	0.00	**7.5**	2.7	1.49	10.94	3.37	43.4	**5.0**	35.5	8.3	**8.3**
3.6	1.25	na	0.23	**3.3**	0.9	0.35	2.76	4.01	84.3	**0.8**	13.7	37.3	**5.7**
6.4	0.25	2.3	0.07	**2.6**	0.8	0.51	6.09	3.92	86.7	**0.6**	9.7	29.1	**4.1**
7.9	0.00	na	-0.01	**4.4**	0.8	0.88	8.85	4.08	73.1	**1.6**	32.2	32.8	**5.2**
6.3	0.76	na	0.09	**4.4**	3.7	1.01	9.71	4.12	73.9	**1.9**	26.4	23.6	**6.2**
6.6	0.71	3.7	0.08	**7.7**	29.9	1.54	12.94	3.87	54.9	**3.1**	17.0	14.1	**10.0**
5.9	0.73	na	0.01	**10.0**	6.9	2.39	25.61	4.74	60.1	**0.7**	13.6	38.2	**7.5**
7.3	0.00	na	-0.03	**4.9**	1.4	0.89	6.81	4.30	71.2	**0.8**	17.7	35.4	**7.4**
6.4	0.44	5.1	0.32	**5.8**	257.3	1.16	13.04	3.41	51.2	**2.3**	17.9	2.2	**7.8**
7.0	0.59	na	-0.12	**3.9**	1.2	0.51	4.17	4.78	88.6	**4.1**	21.3	8.6	**6.0**
2.3	1.97	13.9	0.60	**2.5**	0.9	0.21	2.38	4.51	79.6	**1.7**	14.5	19.1	**4.9**
8.7	0.19	0.6	0.03	**7.0**	15.3	1.42	13.42	3.70	56.4	**2.4**	28.2	26.1	**9.2**
9.3	0.00	0.0	0.00	**8.2**	21.7	3.64	27.59	2.55	17.2	**2.9**	62.9	39.9	**9.1**
9.3	0.00	na	0.02	**6.1**	1.1	1.34	13.45	3.43	60.5	**4.9**	49.8	13.0	**7.1**
5.7	2.19	na	0.06	**7.3**	14.5	1.77	16.56	4.25	58.9	**4.8**	27.0	9.3	**10.0**
9.1	0.00	na	0.02	**2.4**	0.9	0.31	3.63	2.62	87.4	**3.0**	35.3	18.7	**4.4**
4.0	2.24	na	0.01	**5.2**	5.7	1.23	11.26	3.73	68.1	**3.7**	31.2	13.7	**6.9**
8.3	0.12	na	0.01	**5.8**	1.6	1.49	16.02	4.43	69.2	**2.2**	20.4	18.4	**6.8**
4.6	1.12	na	0.00	**4.8**	1.1	1.02	9.16	4.12	73.6	**1.5**	20.1	25.9	**7.3**
8.5	0.00	na	0.00	**4.6**	1.0	0.86	8.91	4.07	72.2	**1.1**	13.0	30.5	**6.2**
6.9	0.39	na	-0.07	**6.3**	2.9	1.33	14.29	5.10	70.9	**1.0**	14.7	31.6	**6.2**
9.3	0.17	na	-0.01	**3.4**	0.8	0.72	7.22	2.97	77.3	**5.7**	47.9	7.9	**6.1**
5.7	0.64	4.9	0.01	**5.8**	4.8	1.17	11.69	3.83	59.5	**0.6**	8.3	45.4	**7.5**
7.3	0.66	na	0.02	**4.1**	6.6	0.92	8.38	4.23	78.5	**2.6**	28.8	18.3	**6.7**
7.8	0.00	na	0.03	**9.2**	3.6	1.69	14.89	4.93	55.6	**0.8**	17.2	35.4	**7.6**
7.4	0.22	0.7	-0.04	**7.1**	5.3	1.45	11.43	3.91	53.3	**2.4**	18.5	14.9	**6.5**
9.1	0.00	na	0.00	**6.8**	3.5	1.70	14.06	3.89	62.2	**5.6**	36.3	4.2	**8.3**
6.9	0.23	na	0.02	**10.0**	9.4	2.53	18.77	4.63	53.0	**3.5**	25.0	12.3	**9.6**
6.8	1.15	na	0.00	**2.2**	0.0	0.31	3.42	3.75	92.0	**7.1**	67.0	0.0	**1.7**
7.1	0.22	na	0.01	**5.6**	2.8	1.37	12.06	4.14	64.6	**0.9**	22.8	27.8	**7.7**
2.4	5.14	na	0.03	**4.6**	0.4	0.89	8.13	3.58	67.0	**1.7**	13.1	21.2	**4.7**
0.6	10.89	na	-0.01	**9.0**	5.5	2.13	16.18	4.15	46.9	**2.9**	25.2	8.7	**9.4**
6.5	0.59	na	0.29	**8.3**	2.7	1.52	12.98	5.46	61.8	**2.3**	17.7	17.8	**7.2**
6.0	0.68	na	0.07	**7.8**	1.1	1.69	18.71	5.37	65.2	**1.0**	17.4	33.4	**7.5**
6.0	1.55	na	0.37	**3.1**	1.1	0.50	4.03	2.76	87.9	**2.5**	42.8	10.9	**7.0**
8.1	0.06	na	0.06	**4.2**	9.6	0.78	4.75	3.12	72.8	**6.3**	35.6	2.9	**9.8**
4.1	0.58	na	-0.01	**3.7**	3.5	0.56	6.06	4.17	79.9	**0.8**	15.1	34.7	**5.2**
7.1	1.24	7.9	-0.05	**3.5**	57.5	0.54	5.25	1.84	67.0	**0.6**	6.3	29.9	**7.7**
6.1	2.08	9.1	0.07	**2.8**	4.1	0.50	4.68	3.19	83.4	**2.9**	30.6	21.7	**7.6**
6.5	0.64	na	0.02	**9.8**	14.3	2.01	21.68	3.65	46.4	**3.0**	11.3	11.3	**8.8**
5.1	1.22	10.3	0.28	**6.9**	1.7	1.37	11.70	5.28	64.7	**2.4**	20.3	16.3	**7.4**
6.5	na	na	na	**0.0**	-1.2	-2.15	-4.06	-0.71	103.0	**4.2**	152.3	100.0	**1.5**
7.2	0.50	na	0.02	**3.8**	1.7	0.83	9.01	3.77	81.9	**2.7**	29.4	18.1	**5.9**
4.4	1.05	6.8	0.08	**3.2**	135.1	0.46	4.67	2.35	77.2	**0.7**	9.4	24.0	**7.3**
8.5	0.14	0.6	0.21	**4.3**	17.2	0.94	8.65	1.92	77.9	**4.0**	41.2	8.6	**8.2**
5.6	2.12	na	-0.10	**7.6**	1.0	1.62	14.51	4.28	59.2	**4.5**	10.3	4.5	**7.3**
6.8	0.66	2.5	-0.02	**10.0**	18.6	2.02	15.39	4.53	53.8	**4.5**	23.7	8.5	**10.0**
8.4	0.33	na	0.06	**4.3**	1.7	0.77	8.92	4.67	80.9	**4.9**	20.0	3.6	**5.5**
7.8	0.74	1.9	-0.04	**7.0**	2.0	1.39	11.15	3.61	54.4	**1.6**	25.5	20.8	**8.5**
10.0	0.50	na	0.02	**3.0**	1.9	0.43	1.82	2.21	78.1	**2.8**	45.4	26.1	**8.6**
7.4	2.88	na	0.00	**1.9**	0.0	0.03	0.30	4.10	92.5	**0.6**	17.1	50.7	**6.1**
8.6	1.25	na	0.07	**5.8**	4.6	1.27	11.02	4.09	65.3	**2.5**	14.5	11.6	**7.3**
7.0	1.25	na	0.00	**5.0**	1.4	1.40	13.15	2.91	56.1	**1.3**	30.0	41.6	**6.7**
7.7	0.13	0.7	0.02	**8.9**	2.3	2.00	20.38	4.00	59.6	**4.9**	33.5	5.6	**8.0**
6.7	1.85	na	0.02	**3.1**	0.6	0.45	4.09	2.91	79.3	**3.5**	45.4	18.9	**6.5**
8.5	0.29	na	0.01	**2.4**	0.2	0.34	2.59	3.40	83.3	**3.0**	41.6	21.4	**6.9**
4.6	2.07	na	0.00	**3.5**	0.9	0.49	5.67	3.72	82.6	**1.3**	11.8	26.4	**5.2**

Name	City	State	Rating	2018 Rating	2017 Rating	Total Assets ($Mil)	One Year Asset Growth	Asset Mix (As a % of Total Assets) Comm-ercial Loans	Cons-umer Loans	Mort-gage Loans	Secur-ities	Capital-ization Index	Lever-age Ratio	Risk-Based Capital Ratio
Today's Bank	Huntsville	AR	**C+**	C	D+	242.2	4.03	9.1	1.7	16.8	21.2	**7.3**	9.2	13.6
▲ Tolleson Private Bank	Dallas	TX	**A-**	B	B	541.7	0.10	13.5	5.2	37.6	14.7	**7.3**	9.2	16.1
▲ Tomahawk Community Bank, SSB	Tomahawk	WI	**B**	B-	B-	144.0	4.88	8.9	5.3	39.9	6.9	**10.0**	13.5	16.1
Tompkins State Bank	Avon	IL	**B-**	B-	B-	217.2	3.11	8.4	1.5	8.0	24.8	**7.6**	9.4	13.6
Tompkins Trust Co.	Ithaca	NY	**B+**	B+	B+	2048.7	-3.30	4.8	1.7	26.3	25.1	**7.1**	9.1	14.1
Torrington Savings Bank	Torrington	CT	**B**	B-	B-	823.6	0.59	0.4	0.2	55.8	19.7	**10.0**	20.0	40.3
▲ Touchmark National Bank	Alpharetta	GA	**B**	B-	A-	407.7	1.83	13.9	0.0	2.1	5.2	**10.0**	12.4	23.2
Touchstone Bank	Prince George	VA	**C+**	C+	B-	471.6	11.21	6.0	0.9	23.1	10.5	**8.2**	9.8	14.2
Towanda State Bank	Towanda	KS	**E+**	E+	E+	10.3	3.37	1.3	7.9	55.1	14.0	**6.0**	8.0	15.4
▲ Tower Community Bank	Jasper	TN	**C+**	C-	D+	208.0	9.53	4.4	3.4	16.9	9.5	**6.1**	9.4	11.8
Town & Country Bank	Salem	MO	**A-**	A-	A-	520.7	2.28	2.4	3.7	34.9	16.3	**10.0**	11.6	17.7
Town & Country Bank	Ravenna	NE	**A-**	A-	A-	170.2	3.43	4.2	1.7	2.9	25.1	**10.0**	12.9	16.0
▲ Town & Country Bank	Las Vegas	NV	**B+**	B+	A-	163.1	0.31	4.9	0.0	1.3	0.1	**10.0**	13.7	19.6
Town & Country Bank and Trust Co.	Bardstown	KY	**A**	A-	B+	315.3	2.98	4.8	1.0	22.8	18.6	**10.0**	12.5	17.7
Town and Country Bank	Springfield	IL	**B-**	B-	B-	826.1	7.80	10.1	0.7	16.4	17.2	**7.3**	9.4	12.7
▲ Town and Country Bank Midwest	Quincy	IL	**A-**	B+	A-	188.3	12.34	17.8	1.3	14.3	6.6	**10.0**	11.0	16.2
Town Bank, N.A.	Hartland	WI	**B**	B	B	2393.1	17.22	23.1	19.9	6.0	7.4	**5.5**	9.7	11.4
Town Center Bank	New Lenox	IL	**C**	C	C-	101.6	2.02	12.2	2.3	1.9	18.0	**7.6**	10.9	13.0
▲ Town-Country National Bank	Camden	AL	**B+**	B	A-	109.5	3.52	14.9	13.8	13.9	29.0	**10.0**	18.9	28.7
TowneBank	Portsmouth	VA	**A-**	A-	A-	12021.3	8.09	9.9	2.6	13.4	11.5	**8.2**	9.8	14.7
Toyota Financial Savings Bank	Henderson	NV	**C**	C+	B-	1011.6	5.84	0.0	0.0	83.0	0.9	**10.0**	16.8	35.3
TPNB Bank	Paris	MO	**B+**	B+	B+	80.4	2.82	3.3	1.2	9.5	33.3	**10.0**	15.1	24.9
Traders & Farmers Bank	Haleyville	AL	**B**	B	B	367.3	3.17	3.5	4.4	19.2	47.5	**10.0**	16.4	30.1
Tradition Capital Bank	Wayzata	MN	**C+**	B-	B	850.2	17.08	12.7	0.9	13.7	12.0	**6.3**	10.0	12.0
Traditional Bank, Inc.	Mount Sterling	KY	**A-**	A-	A-	1618.1	6.01	5.1	0.4	23.8	23.0	**8.7**	10.1	14.5
Traditions Bank	Cullman	AL	**B**	B	B	372.1	5.65	15.1	8.3	32.8	6.6	**9.1**	10.4	14.3
Traditions First Bank	Erin	TN	**B-**	B-	B	151.8	6.74	2.9	1.6	20.4	24.4	**6.9**	8.9	14.2
TrailWest Bank	Lolo	MT	**B**	B	B+	668.2	19.77	9.2	2.2	28.3	3.2	**7.4**	9.3	13.4
▲ TransCapital Bank	Sunrise	FL	**A-**	B+	B+	208.5	4.45	0.1	0.0	17.5	1.2	**10.0**	18.8	25.5
TransPecos Banks, SSB	Pecos	TX	**C+**	B-	B	242.6	15.26	19.5	1.5	15.1	21.0	**6.4**	8.4	13.1
Transportation Alliance Bank, Inc.	Ogden	UT	**C**	C+	B	757.2	-3.49	71.6	2.9	0.0	7.6	**10.0**	13.9	15.7
Treynor State Bank	Treynor	IA	**D**	D+	D-	358.4	-6.67	5.8	0.7	2.6	49.6	**7.1**	9.1	13.6
Tri City National Bank	Oak Creek	WI	**A-**	B+	B	1445.4	3.37	2.6	0.3	11.3	23.7	**10.0**	11.6	17.9
▲ Tri Counties Bank	Chico	CA	**A**	A-	A-	6383.1	1.04	3.9	1.2	8.5	21.7	**10.0**	11.2	15.1
Tri Valley Bank	Talmage	NE	**C**	C	C	48.7	5.17	10.1	0.9	12.1	2.7	**4.6**	8.4	10.8
Tri-County Bank	Brown City	MI	**A-**	A-	A-	318.7	10.01	7.3	1.4	9.3	14.3	**10.0**	12.2	16.0
Tri-County Bank	Stuart	NE	**B-**	C+	B-	137.5	8.94	10.2	2.5	16.0	15.8	**6.6**	9.2	12.2
Tri-County Bank & Trust Co.	Roachdale	IN	**B**	B	B	216.8	13.25	3.3	4.0	13.8	38.8	**10.0**	12.0	25.7
Tri-County Trust Co.	Glasgow	MO	**C+**	B	B	58.6	3.23	7.2	6.6	26.2	21.5	**10.0**	12.4	15.8
Tri-State Bank of Memphis	Memphis	TN	**C-**	C-	D+	89.5	7.59	7.1	3.5	7.8	19.5	**8.6**	10.1	17.4
▲ Tri-Valley Bank	Randolph	IA	**B-**	C+	C	59.9	0.84	6.9	1.6	11.1	23.2	**10.0**	11.8	17.7
Triad Bank	Frontenac	MO	**C+**	C	B-	384.2	15.12	13.1	0.3	16.5	8.6	**6.2**	9.5	11.9
▲ Triad Bank, N.A.	Tulsa	OK	**B**	B-	B+	181.6	9.31	11.4	2.4	30.0	0.0	**10.0**	11.3	19.7
TriCentury Bank	De Soto	KS	**A-**	B+	B	100.7	-4.38	13.5	0.1	20.2	0.0	**10.0**	12.0	17.4
Trinity Bank, N.A.	Fort Worth	TX	**A-**	A	A	295.0	16.58	29.4	0.2	6.2	24.2	**10.0**	12.8	21.8
▲ TriStar Bank	Dickson	TN	**C+**	C	B-	304.3	3.74	5.5	9.8	21.3	15.0	**5.4**	8.4	11.3
TriState Capital Bank	Pittsburgh	PA	**B-**	B-	B-	7114.0	29.84	32.9	25.8	0.6	6.3	**5.2**	7.2	11.4
Triumph Bank	Memphis	TN	**C+**	B-	B-	840.0	7.16	19.6	0.5	22.3	17.4	**5.9**	9.1	11.7
Triumph State Bank	Trimont	MN	**C+**	C+	C+	73.0	18.33	7.7	4.1	1.8	11.8	**8.3**	9.9	15.0
Troy Bank & Trust Co.	Troy	AL	**B+**	B+	B	946.1	5.15	10.3	2.8	15.7	25.7	**10.0**	11.0	16.6
TruBank	Indianola	IA	**B-**	B	B	305.6	3.29	7.0	1.0	11.5	18.3	**9.8**	10.9	15.3
▲ TruPoint Bank	Grundy	VA	**B-**	C	C-	449.2	5.76	15.8	4.5	17.9	17.8	**8.1**	9.7	15.0
Trust Bank	Lenox	GA	**C-**	C	C	38.4	3.30	4.5	6.9	17.1	5.4	**9.1**	10.4	17.8
Trust Co. of Toledo, N.A.	Holland	OH	**U**	U	U	5.7	-4.28	0.0	0.0	0.0	81.4	**10.0**	93.3	331.4
TrustBank	Olney	IL	**B**	B+	A-	234.1	1.13	7.2	2.9	17.0	10.4	**9.4**	10.7	14.5
TrustCo Bank	Glenville	NY	**B+**	B+	B	5222.1	6.91	0.4	0.2	67.4	13.1	**8.3**	9.9	19.5
▲ Trustmark National Bank	Jackson	MS	**B+**	B	B	13582.7	1.09	11.0	1.3	12.8	17.3	**7.6**	10.2	13.0
TrustTexas Bank, SSB	Cuero	TX	**B-**	B-	B-	343.0	5.32	4.3	1.1	25.5	32.9	**10.0**	12.3	22.7
Truxton Trust Co.	Nashville	TN	**A**	A	A-	515.2	1.80	6.6	4.1	14.9	22.6	**10.0**	11.3	15.8
▲ TSB Bank	Lomira	WI	**A-**	B+	B+	142.5	7.97	8.6	1.2	18.3	12.6	**10.0**	12.3	15.8

Asset Quality Index	Adjusted Non-Performing Loans as a % of Total Loans	Adjusted Non-Performing Loans as a % of Capital	Net Charge-Offs Avg Loans	Profitability Index	Net Income ($Mil)	Return on Assets (R.O.A.)	Return on Equity (R.O.E.)	Net Interest Spread	Overhead Efficiency Ratio	Liquidity Index	Liquidity Ratio	Hot Money Ratio	Stability Index
4.9	0.81	na	0.01	4.3	1.8	1.02	11.28	4.33	78.8	0.9	22.3	41.9	5.3
8.1	0.01	na	0.02	9.2	10.4	2.56	28.02	3.02	44.8	4.8	26.8	5.6	7.5
7.7	0.46	na	0.04	4.4	0.9	0.86	6.36	4.23	75.9	4.2	13.3	7.3	7.1
5.4	0.25	na	0.01	4.2	1.5	0.97	9.01	3.45	70.3	2.4	13.1	12.5	6.8
7.7	0.79	6.1	0.08	8.0	23.5	1.51	20.76	3.17	68.6	3.9	3.7	7.2	6.8
9.7	0.74	na	0.04	4.3	5.6	0.91	4.52	2.63	74.1	2.9	37.9	19.6	8.4
4.8	2.57	na	0.00	6.6	4.2	1.33	11.32	2.81	50.0	0.5	14.5	59.5	8.1
6.4	0.72	na	0.00	3.9	2.2	0.66	6.49	4.23	82.4	2.5	20.5	17.3	4.8
0.3	3.62	75.3	0.07	0.1	-0.1	-0.63	-7.84	4.13	107.0	3.7	13.0	10.1	2.6
6.2	0.11	na	0.09	3.8	1.1	0.75	7.67	4.14	81.2	1.3	9.1	22.5	4.9
7.5	0.55	3.1	0.02	6.7	6.1	1.60	12.77	4.11	64.1	3.1	7.9	12.8	9.3
7.3	0.11	0.5	0.00	7.9	2.0	1.62	12.85	4.13	53.0	2.9	19.8	14.8	8.2
5.9	5.09	na	-0.03	9.2	2.5	1.99	15.20	4.38	53.2	4.5	31.0	9.3	9.0
8.8	0.68	2.1	-0.02	6.6	3.2	1.36	10.96	4.10	66.0	5.0	26.9	4.1	8.6
5.6	0.59	3.9	0.12	5.0	6.2	1.03	10.17	3.63	66.8	1.8	16.6	15.3	7.0
7.8	0.24	na	0.03	9.4	3.3	2.37	21.53	4.17	49.5	2.6	29.3	18.4	8.3
6.5	0.16	1.0	0.04	4.6	14.6	0.88	7.06	3.23	63.8	3.9	17.6	7.4	8.4
5.5	0.36	na	0.05	2.2	0.2	0.32	2.72	3.69	94.1	1.1	11.8	28.8	6.7
5.9	1.31	na	0.14	9.7	1.8	2.24	12.25	5.26	55.4	1.7	36.5	36.1	9.4
7.2	0.35	1.4	0.04	6.4	103.7	1.25	9.12	3.53	71.7	2.0	17.5	14.6	9.9
10.0	0.33	0.8	-0.01	1.8	0.9	0.12	0.68	1.24	83.2	0.5	12.9	37.9	8.5
6.4	2.52	7.6	0.07	4.5	0.5	0.88	5.92	3.29	67.6	3.4	30.0	14.7	8.0
8.6	1.00	na	0.08	4.1	2.3	0.82	5.34	3.70	71.0	3.0	46.9	24.8	7.7
7.5	0.30	1.8	0.01	3.5	5.7	0.94	10.71	3.37	65.7	1.5	15.5	13.1	6.8
8.2	0.43	na	0.06	6.3	17.0	1.46	14.24	3.31	56.2	1.8	19.2	17.5	10.0
5.4	0.76	4.9	0.54	6.7	3.5	1.25	12.22	5.80	64.9	1.3	11.7	18.0	6.1
8.9	0.00	na	0.00	4.3	0.9	0.79	8.66	3.60	73.1	1.5	26.4	27.8	5.9
6.8	0.26	na	0.11	6.0	6.4	1.35	14.69	3.73	59.2	2.4	18.1	15.0	7.9
7.4	1.10	na	0.02	9.8	3.7	2.37	13.10	4.01	42.4	0.8	20.0	49.4	9.7
3.8	1.20	13.8	0.97	4.3	1.4	0.79	8.91	5.31	67.1	1.2	26.2	9.5	4.8
3.4	2.71	na	2.40	4.2	3.2	0.59	4.18	7.34	66.8	0.6	18.5	40.5	9.7
3.7	3.04	na	0.81	0.7	2.2	0.77	8.24	3.10	129.3	2.1	43.9	29.4	3.4
5.4	2.03	6.4	-0.01	6.2	14.0	1.31	11.61	3.92	67.6	5.8	25.5	1.8	9.2
6.5	0.59	2.1	-0.01	8.2	71.5	1.48	10.41	4.52	58.8	4.8	20.9	5.6	10.0
8.2	0.00	na	0.00	8.3	0.7	1.87	20.76	3.66	46.0	0.7	13.5	35.4	6.5
7.1	0.89	4.6	0.02	8.4	3.8	1.64	13.81	4.58	58.0	4.0	17.6	9.2	7.4
7.3	0.17	na	0.00	4.9	1.0	0.99	10.91	4.41	70.6	3.5	18.7	12.0	5.8
6.6	1.16	na	0.36	4.4	1.5	0.98	7.88	3.41	64.3	6.1	65.0	10.1	6.9
4.7	2.02	na	0.17	4.8	0.5	1.15	9.44	3.94	69.0	0.8	19.3	38.4	7.6
3.4	12.84	na	0.02	2.5	0.1	0.18	1.37	3.96	92.2	3.5	26.6	13.3	5.7
7.5	0.29	na	0.03	3.6	0.3	0.56	4.59	4.08	79.5	2.3	24.5	16.7	5.6
6.1	1.26	na	-0.01	5.6	3.1	1.10	11.89	3.72	58.1	1.7	16.5	6.4	6.2
4.8	0.83	na	0.91	7.5	2.2	1.76	15.11	5.03	59.4	5.0	23.7	3.3	8.0
8.6	0.00	0.0	-0.01	6.9	1.0	1.37	11.94	3.73	52.7	2.0	23.3	19.7	7.0
8.7	0.27	na	0.38	6.7	2.8	1.43	10.84	3.95	46.4	5.1	52.2	12.8	8.1
7.1	0.21	na	0.02	4.2	1.7	0.77	9.32	3.88	75.0	1.2	11.4	27.2	5.1
6.8	0.00	0.0	-0.05	4.3	43.8	0.91	12.78	2.04	53.9	1.3	12.5	17.5	5.3
4.2	1.67	12.2	-0.05	4.0	4.5	0.75	8.14	2.81	73.0	0.7	17.7	34.8	6.2
4.3	1.52	na	0.02	4.2	0.4	0.68	6.91	4.04	73.7	5.1	41.0	9.6	5.0
5.9	1.89	8.5	0.18	5.4	7.1	1.03	8.77	3.60	65.1	2.1	26.9	20.8	7.5
8.3	0.13	na	0.00	4.8	2.2	0.95	8.30	3.69	68.3	1.3	11.6	26.3	6.7
8.1	0.15	1.5	-0.02	4.3	3.0	0.89	9.31	3.53	72.3	3.1	7.9	12.7	4.6
2.0	3.64	na	0.17	3.7	0.0	0.12	1.10	5.88	97.9	2.8	29.8	17.6	5.4
10.0	na	0.0	na	10.0	1.8	48.32	54.18	2.34	71.6	4.0	na	0.0	5.8
5.9	0.64	na	0.03	7.1	3.1	1.73	15.59	4.13	67.9	4.0	7.4	7.8	8.3
7.9	0.82	4.8	0.01	6.1	45.7	1.19	12.34	3.12	55.9	2.7	19.0	16.4	8.5
5.8	0.63	3.3	0.05	5.3	118.6	1.17	9.57	3.60	68.7	4.1	8.2	7.4	9.6
7.8	0.15	na	0.15	3.1	1.6	0.63	5.31	3.57	87.5	4.6	45.5	13.6	6.8
8.6	0.21	0.6	0.00	9.1	6.7	1.81	16.28	3.32	57.9	4.9	33.6	5.3	8.0
8.6	0.10	na	-0.04	6.5	1.3	1.22	10.37	3.81	58.6	1.0	13.2	24.1	7.1

Name	City	State	Rating	2018 Rating	2017 Rating	Total Assets ($Mil)	One Year Asset Growth	Asset Mix (As a % of Total Assets): Comm-ercial Loans	Cons-umer Loans	Mort-gage Loans	Secur-ities	Capital-ization Index	Lever-age Ratio	Risk-Based Capital Ratio
Tucumcari Federal S&L Assn.	Tucumcari	NM	C+	C+	C+	34.1	1.03	0.0	0.8	51.9	20.4	10.0	15.1	33.6
Turbotville National Bank	Turbotville	PA	B	B+	A	150.6	6.29	5.8	1.9	27.8	17.8	10.0	17.0	24.4
▲ Turtle Mountain State Bank	Belcourt	ND	C	D+	D+	33.5	1.22	25.6	6.2	4.1	7.4	8.5	10.0	39.8
Tustin Community Bank	Tustin	CA	B	B+	B+	74.2	-5.01	2.4	45.3	4.9	0.0	10.0	14.9	18.6
▲ Twin City Bank	Longview	WA	B-	C+	C	57.5	7.42	16.1	0.1	15.7	0.0	8.5	10.0	15.1
▲ Twin River Bank	Lewiston	ID	B	B-	B-	103.0	1.33	12.5	3.4	13.9	3.5	6.9	8.9	15.3
Twin Valley Bank	West Alexandria	OH	C+	C+	B-	79.5	15.60	9.9	2.7	18.2	18.9	8.2	9.8	14.5
▲ Two River Community Bank	Tinton Falls	NJ	B-	C+	B-	1146.2	5.55	4.9	0.0	11.6	5.5	7.0	10.1	12.5
▲ Two Rivers Bank	Blair	NE	B+	B	B	143.0	0.49	7.2	1.7	15.7	25.8	10.0	13.7	20.5
Two Rivers Bank & Trust	Burlington	IA	B-	B-	C+	841.9	2.14	16.9	1.2	18.5	11.6	7.5	9.6	12.9
U.S. Bank N.A.	Minneapolis	MN	B	B-	B-	477393.6	4.69	16.8	12.1	15.7	25.0	6.7	8.7	12.6
U.S. Bank Trust Co., N.A.	Portland	OR	U	U	U	18.8	4.71	0.0	0.0	0.0	0.0	10.0	101.	499.0
U.S. Bank Trust N.A.	Wilmington	DE	U	U	U	653.0	3.96	0.0	0.0	0.0	0.0	10.0	98.5	495.0
U.S. Bank Trust N.A. SD	Sioux Falls	SD	U	U	U	101.4	9.34	0.0	0.0	0.0	0.0	10.0	100.	404.5
U.S. Century Bank	Doral	FL	B-	B-	C+	1283.3	10.85	5.0	0.1	20.3	14.9	7.2	9.1	12.7
UBank	Jellico	TN	B	B	B	67.0	0.34	6.4	8.9	18.8	15.2	10.0	14.1	20.1
▲ UBank	Huntington	TX	B+	B-	B-	240.2	2.69	13.5	2.8	20.2	7.9	10.0	11.2	16.4
UBS Bank USA	Salt Lake City	UT	A	A	A-	56853.2	5.85	9.5	40.4	29.0	11.4	10.0	11.8	39.3
Uinta Bank	Mountain View	WY	B-	B-	B-	218.7	15.44	10.2	0.6	1.6	60.8	6.2	8.2	20.8
Ulster Savings Bank	Kingston	NY	C	C-	C-	944.8	7.21	4.0	2.7	43.6	7.2	9.5	10.7	15.3
▲ Ultima Bank Minnesota	Winger	MN	C+	C	C	189.3	4.58	10.7	1.5	6.4	0.0	8.0	10.5	13.4
UMB Bank & Trust, N.A.	Saint Louis	MO	U	U	U	3.0	0.07	0.0	0.0	0.0	0.0	10.0	99.5	102.5
UMB Bank, N.A.	Kansas City	MO	B-	B-	B-	23964.7	12.85	24.6	1.4	3.5	35.5	6.4	8.8	12.0
Umpqua Bank	Roseburg	OR	B+	B+	B+	28904.5	8.72	11.8	1.7	14.4	9.9	7.5	10.3	12.9
UNB Bank	Mount Carmel	PA	C-	D+	D+	146.8	3.31	2.4	1.1	44.2	27.0	8.0	9.7	24.1
▲ UniBank	Lynnwood	WA	A-	B+	B+	337.1	13.85	5.2	0.0	0.0	13.7	10.0	14.8	19.2
UniBank for Savings	Whitinsville	MA	B-	B-	B-	1763.8	7.42	4.4	24.3	24.1	14.7	6.9	8.9	13.7
UNICO Bank	Mineral Point	MO	C+	C+	B+	337.7	10.93	5.6	3.5	29.3	12.6	6.1	8.1	12.0
▲ Unified Bank	Martins Ferry	OH	B+	B	B	674.7	28.86	15.1	1.5	12.8	29.8	8.8	10.3	14.0
Unified Trust Co., N.A.	Lexington	KY	U	U	U	17.2	6.96	0.0	0.0	0.0	18.7	10.0	102.	86.6
▲ Union Bank	Lake Odessa	MI	C	C	C	191.9	10.04	11.7	0.9	9.1	7.6	4.5	9.3	10.7
Union Bank	Greenville	NC	B	B	B	787.6	7.69	5.6	0.4	16.9	18.8	7.0	9.0	13.7
Union Bank	Halliday	ND	C+	C+	C+	153.4	0.70	4.0	6.3	12.9	18.2	8.6	10.1	14.6
Union Bank	Jamestown	TN	B-	B-	B-	198.2	-1.23	7.9	4.9	20.5	24.0	10.0	12.5	23.0
Union Bank	Morrisville	VT	B	B	B	844.2	8.39	5.3	0.4	23.1	10.2	6.2	8.2	12.9
Union Bank & Trust Co.	Monticello	AR	C+	C-	D+	211.4	-0.18	14.9	4.7	18.7	16.2	9.1	10.4	14.2
▲ Union Bank & Trust Co.	Livingston	TN	B	B-	B	83.5	-1.83	7.5	6.4	28.1	17.3	10.0	14.2	23.5
Union Bank and Trust Co.	Minneapolis	MN	B-	B-	B-	168.2	-1.83	6.0	0.2	0.1	22.3	6.9	8.9	22.6
Union Bank and Trust Co.	Lincoln	NE	B+	B+	B+	4397.0	7.64	14.4	14.9	3.6	12.9	9.0	11.0	14.2
Union Bank Co.	Columbus Grove	OH	B	B-	B-	875.5	7.24	6.7	1.1	18.1	20.6	7.3	9.3	12.7
▲ Union Bank of Blair	Blair	WI	C	C	C-	109.7	2.18	13.9	2.3	11.5	7.8	10.0	14.2	17.8
▲ Union Bank of Mena	Mena	AR	B	B	B+	268.1	2.38	4.5	12.6	31.0	24.1	9.1	10.4	19.0
▲ Union Bank of Sparta	Sparta	WI	B-	B-	B+	143.3	2.85	3.9	1.7	18.0	12.3	10.0	15.6	20.6
▲ Union Bank, Inc.	Middlebourne	WV	B+	B	B	266.4	3.01	5.6	2.9	17.2	41.5	8.0	9.6	19.9
Union Banking Co.	West Mansfield	OH	B+	B+	B+	57.6	4.19	0.2	0.3	5.3	84.4	10.0	11.2	42.0
▼ Union County Savings Bank	Elizabeth	NJ	C+	B-	B-	1769.7	0.96	0.0	0.1	5.4	77.3	10.0	14.1	51.7
Union Federal S&L Assn.	Kewanee	IL	B-	B-	B-	150.1	1.38	2.0	0.2	48.0	11.4	10.0	14.7	25.2
Union National Bank	Elgin	IL	B+	A-	B+	314.2	0.74	8.9	0.0	3.0	1.5	10.0	12.4	18.7
▲ Union S&L Assn.	Connersville	IN	C+	C+	C+	164.5	5.09	1.7	13.5	42.4	0.4	9.3	10.5	15.3
▲ Union Savings Bank	Danbury	CT	B+	B	B-	2194.8	2.00	3.3	0.2	30.7	10.9	10.0	12.7	17.4
UNION Savings BANK	Freeport	IL	C	C	C-	151.8	-1.38	5.9	3.5	32.5	19.3	9.4	10.6	17.5
Union Savings Bank	Cincinnati	OH	A-	B+	B	3067.3	9.83	0.3	0.8	68.1	0.2	8.2	9.8	16.0
Union State Bank	Pell City	AL	D+	D-	D-	206.2	-2.30	4.9	1.4	6.7	26.9	5.4	7.4	12.3
Union State Bank	Greenfield	IA	C-	C-	B	80.2	8.13	2.8	1.7	18.1	10.4	5.4	10.4	11.3
Union State Bank	Winterset	IA	C+	C+	C+	89.3	0.00	4.7	2.6	28.7	19.3	6.5	8.5	15.5
Union State Bank	Arkansas City	KS	B	B	B	335.6	3.07	6.6	2.6	16.4	16.2	7.4	9.3	13.8
Union State Bank	Clay Center	KS	B-	B-	C+	144.0	1.85	2.5	1.0	11.4	46.4	10.0	11.3	20.2
▼ Union State Bank	Olsburg	KS	C+	B	B	30.9	-5.18	13.3	4.5	4.3	17.2	10.0	13.2	27.3
▲ Union State Bank	Uniontown	KS	C	D+	D+	49.4	-1.99	7.5	4.1	27.1	11.0	6.8	8.8	13.3
Union State Bank of Browns Valley	Browns Valley	MN	C+	C+	B-	21.2	-0.21	8.7	2.1	0.6	10.9	10.0	11.5	18.6

Asset Quality Index	Adjusted Non-Performing Loans as a % of Total Loans	Adjusted Non-Performing Loans as a % of Capital	Net Charge-Offs Avg Loans	Profitability Index	Net Income ($Mil)	Return on Assets (R.O.A.)	Return on Equity (R.O.E.)	Net Interest Spread	Overhead Efficiency Ratio	Liquidity Index	Liquidity Ratio	Hot Money Ratio	Stability Index
5.9	2.18	na	0.00	**2.4**	0.1	0.25	1.66	3.56	89.3	**0.7**	14.7	45.5	**6.5**
4.9	3.23	na	0.03	**7.2**	1.7	1.57	9.36	3.47	45.7	**2.7**	32.6	19.0	**8.7**
5.2	7.10	na	0.56	**5.8**	0.4	1.59	17.07	3.88	69.0	**3.9**	62.4	19.1	**3.9**
5.7	0.06	na	0.87	**4.8**	0.5	0.89	6.30	6.21	74.1	**0.8**	19.0	48.1	**6.5**
6.5	1.54	na	0.01	**4.6**	0.3	0.84	8.24	4.96	80.8	**3.1**	18.2	13.7	**5.7**
7.7	0.00	na	0.00	**7.7**	1.5	1.95	22.91	4.62	56.6	**5.3**	37.5	6.8	**5.3**
5.7	0.71	4.3	0.42	**3.2**	0.4	0.72	7.08	4.00	79.0	**3.0**	18.8	14.3	**4.9**
6.3	0.66	na	0.03	**5.5**	8.4	0.99	8.69	3.58	61.6	**1.5**	10.2	16.7	**9.8**
8.8	0.11	1.3	0.04	**5.5**	1.6	1.46	11.15	3.81	67.1	**1.8**	19.2	12.4	**7.3**
6.4	0.85	na	-0.11	**4.6**	5.1	0.82	8.22	3.50	73.3	**4.2**	12.5	6.9	**7.0**
4.8	1.21	5.2	0.49	**7.7**	5432.6	1.57	14.96	3.18	53.7	**4.6**	30.5	3.9	**9.9**
10.0	na	0.0	na	**9.8**	0.6	4.61	4.59	4.44	17.0	**4.0**	na	0.0	**6.3**
9.2	na	0.0	na	**9.8**	18.5	3.84	3.92	2.46	21.8	**4.0**	na	0.0	**7.0**
10.0	na	0.0	na	**9.5**	6.8	9.23	9.35	2.39	21.5	**4.0**	na	0.0	**7.0**
8.6	0.52	1.6	-0.13	**3.9**	7.2	0.78	6.26	3.32	70.8	**2.0**	20.1	20.7	**8.4**
6.4	0.67	na	0.24	**5.2**	0.5	1.08	7.70	4.76	73.6	**0.9**	14.3	32.7	**7.0**
6.7	1.24	na	0.19	**5.0**	1.8	1.00	8.60	4.80	79.1	**3.8**	15.9	9.9	**7.1**
6.8	0.07	0.5	0.00	**9.4**	756.4	1.78	15.71	2.85	16.1	**1.9**	17.2	0.0	**10.0**
7.1	0.00	na	0.04	**4.5**	1.5	0.97	11.75	2.47	52.1	**1.9**	39.8	28.9	**4.9**
4.1	2.38	11.9	0.04	**3.0**	3.6	0.53	4.73	3.49	82.9	**2.1**	11.3	15.5	**6.4**
4.6	0.80	na	0.06	**10.0**	3.2	2.34	22.66	5.02	53.1	**0.7**	4.8	31.2	**8.0**
10.0	na	na	na	**2.3**	0.0	0.13	0.13	5.93	99.9	**4.0**	0.0	0.0	**7.0**
7.7	0.67	3.4	0.29	**4.5**	178.6	1.03	11.23	3.34	67.4	**4.6**	19.6	3.0	**7.2**
6.3	0.21	1.5	0.28	**7.0**	283.7	1.37	8.49	3.91	59.4	**2.3**	10.9	11.1	**10.0**
9.4	0.01	na	0.02	**2.1**	0.3	0.27	2.82	2.61	88.4	**3.2**	26.6	14.7	**5.3**
7.1	0.18	na	-0.04	**8.6**	4.3	1.82	12.47	4.32	54.2	**1.3**	23.9	28.8	**8.5**
5.1	0.75	4.8	0.28	**3.4**	8.1	0.60	7.06	3.01	71.1	**4.1**	19.5	9.3	**6.9**
2.0	3.34	na	0.17	**3.4**	1.3	0.55	6.29	3.52	84.1	**1.4**	15.7	26.8	**4.6**
6.5	0.62	na	0.08	**6.9**	6.9	1.48	14.39	3.83	56.6	**4.4**	29.2	9.0	**6.8**
10.0	na	na	na	**10.0**	4.1	41.00	50.06	2.14	83.3	**4.0**	140.2	0.0	**6.8**
3.4	3.81	na	0.01	**4.0**	1.1	0.78	7.81	4.50	80.6	**4.1**	9.4	6.4	**5.2**
6.3	0.15	2.5	-0.04	**4.6**	5.3	0.92	8.67	3.82	68.4	**1.6**	22.2	16.8	**6.6**
5.8	0.56	na	0.16	**3.3**	0.6	0.52	4.88	4.03	81.2	**4.2**	14.6	7.6	**6.0**
4.7	7.52	na	0.26	**2.9**	0.3	0.23	1.89	3.60	83.0	**1.5**	33.0	35.4	**5.9**
5.9	0.43	3.6	0.06	**6.6**	8.2	1.36	16.25	4.04	66.8	**2.8**	16.0	11.6	**6.2**
5.5	1.11	na	0.02	**6.9**	2.6	1.64	16.05	3.94	61.8	**1.1**	14.4	26.8	**6.8**
5.3	2.02	na	0.44	**10.0**	1.3	2.19	16.44	5.75	49.7	**3.2**	24.4	14.2	**8.9**
9.5	0.00	na	0.00	**5.0**	1.1	1.03	11.44	3.12	73.8	**7.8**	77.3	1.1	**4.7**
5.8	0.57	3.8	0.07	**7.9**	46.0	1.44	13.12	3.56	60.8	**1.4**	14.9	15.8	**10.0**
6.1	0.48	1.8	-0.01	**5.6**	7.5	1.18	9.49	3.94	70.4	**3.2**	23.4	11.9	**8.5**
2.9	11.00	na	0.36	**5.6**	0.8	1.03	7.08	3.51	52.9	**0.9**	24.4	36.3	**7.0**
6.1	0.77	na	0.15	**8.9**	4.0	2.02	19.37	4.43	58.2	**2.5**	18.9	16.9	**8.3**
6.4	2.56	na	0.10	**5.6**	1.2	1.10	6.05	3.52	53.4	**0.7**	9.9	22.8	**8.1**
6.4	0.72	na	0.03	**6.9**	3.3	1.72	14.26	3.90	54.6	**5.5**	33.2	3.4	**8.1**
10.0	0.25	na	0.00	**4.3**	0.4	0.98	7.60	3.08	60.3	**1.5**	21.1	26.6	**8.1**
9.4	2.73	0.1	0.00	**2.5**	3.1	0.23	1.65	0.76	55.9	**4.0**	107.9	63.0	**9.1**
6.3	1.81	na	0.07	**3.4**	0.6	0.55	3.73	3.48	76.7	**3.4**	23.7	13.0	**7.5**
7.1	0.39	2.1	-0.02	**4.9**	2.2	0.95	7.82	2.89	58.2	**0.7**	14.8	50.9	**7.6**
5.8	0.98	na	0.06	**4.5**	1.0	0.85	8.29	3.75	72.1	**1.3**	9.6	26.5	**6.1**
6.1	1.41	na	0.00	**5.1**	17.6	1.08	8.79	3.68	67.5	**4.0**	6.2	7.4	**9.3**
5.4	0.60	na	0.12	**2.9**	0.5	0.44	4.34	3.43	86.5	**4.2**	26.0	9.0	**5.1**
7.0	0.75	na	-0.08	**8.4**	41.9	1.97	17.79	2.82	49.9	**0.9**	9.1	32.7	**10.0**
4.1	3.12	na	-0.12	**2.7**	0.7	0.45	6.48	3.62	89.8	**4.9**	29.0	5.6	**1.7**
2.7	0.26	na	-0.02	**6.4**	0.8	1.40	8.99	4.55	64.4	**0.7**	9.6	30.3	**8.7**
7.6	0.00	na	0.04	**4.1**	0.6	0.92	10.79	3.84	77.1	**2.6**	17.8	16.4	**4.9**
7.5	0.04	na	0.04	**4.0**	2.0	0.81	6.75	3.70	77.9	**2.0**	21.8	19.5	**7.8**
6.0	6.33	na	-0.01	**3.5**	0.7	0.63	5.61	2.81	70.6	**0.7**	11.9	31.4	**6.3**
3.7	20.65	na	1.89	**1.0**	-0.5	-2.28	-15.14	2.46	83.2	**5.3**	45.1	9.0	**6.5**
5.3	0.46	na	0.04	**4.7**	0.4	1.00	11.67	5.18	78.3	**3.6**	11.0	10.5	**4.3**
8.8	0.00	na	0.03	**5.4**	0.2	1.40	12.49	3.20	54.7	**4.9**	53.2	10.9	**6.1**

Name	City	State	Rating	2018 Rating	2017 Rating	Total Assets ($Mil)	One Year Asset Growth	Asset Mix (As a % of Total Assets) Commercial Loans	Consumer Loans	Mortgage Loans	Securities	Capitalization Index	Leverage Ratio	Risk-Based Capital Ratio
▲ Union State Bank of Everest	Everest	KS	B-	C+	B	307.7	0.04	7.0	2.7	18.7	25.1	8.7	10.2	15.4
Union State Bank of Fargo	Fargo	ND	B-	B-	B-	107.0	5.65	9.0	5.2	25.1	5.7	8.4	10.1	13.7
Union State Bank of Hazen	Hazen	ND	C+	B-	B+	147.8	7.83	5.7	5.5	13.9	28.8	8.5	10.0	15.3
Union State Bank of West Salem	West Salem	WI	B-	B-	C+	84.8	-0.99	6.4	5.0	26.3	17.9	10.0	12.0	19.2
Unison Bank	Jamestown	ND	B-	B+	B+	320.8	8.51	3.5	10.0	19.7	13.9	9.1	10.7	14.2
▲ United Bank	Atmore	AL	B	B-	B-	692.1	9.60	16.2	2.9	11.0	19.6	7.4	9.3	13.6
United Bank	Springdale	AR	B+	B+	B+	201.3	5.42	9.8	1.5	33.9	2.2	10.0	12.4	15.3
United Bank	Zebulon	GA	A	A	A-	1459.0	7.25	4.0	2.4	11.9	28.5	9.5	10.7	19.4
United Bank	Vienna	VA	B	B	B	19734.5	2.92	7.5	5.7	18.3	12.3	8.7	11.1	13.9
United Bank & Trust	Marysville	KS	A-	A-	A-	608.9	0.37	7.4	1.7	8.3	14.1	10.0	11.9	15.8
United Bank & Trust N.A.	Marshalltown	IA	A-	A-	A-	102.8	-7.65	4.2	0.8	10.1	33.1	10.0	13.3	18.9
▲ United Bank and Trust Co.	Hampton	IA	A	A-	A-	164.9	4.68	4.9	3.4	12.4	27.6	10.0	15.4	25.5
United Bank of El Paso del Norte	El Paso	TX	C	C+	B-	254.7	5.17	15.1	0.5	3.0	7.7	9.3	11.8	14.4
United Bank of Iowa	Ida Grove	IA	A-	A-	B+	1653.8	4.94	3.7	3.0	7.3	17.1	9.5	10.9	14.6
▲ United Bank of Michigan	Grand Rapids	MI	C	C-	C	695.3	8.83	3.8	1.3	11.2	0.5	6.9	9.8	12.5
United Bank of Philadelphia	Philadelphia	PA	E-	E-	E-	49.6	-8.30	9.2	1.3	8.5	9.2	3.7	5.7	12.2
▲ United Bank of Union	Union	MO	C	C-	C-	372.7	5.87	14.1	0.9	17.1	17.4	8.6	10.5	13.8
United Bankers' Bank	Bloomington	MN	B-	B-	B-	834.3	-9.24	9.1	0.4	1.2	1.8	10.0	13.0	15.1
United Business Bank	Walnut Creek	CA	A-	B+	B+	1769.9	31.72	8.6	0.1	6.8	5.6	10.0	12.0	17.0
▲ United Citizens Bank & Trust Co.	Campbellsburg	KY	B+	B	B	110.2	0.61	1.7	1.8	23.7	15.7	10.0	13.0	21.9
▲ United Citizens Bank of Southern Kentucky	Columbia	KY	A-	B+	A-	171.5	9.87	9.5	5.4	32.2	7.3	10.0	12.3	16.6
United Community Bank	Blairsville	GA	A-	A-	B+	12785.2	3.29	15.1	2.0	11.2	19.7	9.8	11.4	14.8
United Community Bank	Milford	IA	B-	B-	B	209.0	-3.60	8.0	1.3	12.2	2.0	6.5	9.4	12.1
United Community Bank	Chatham	IL	B-	B	B	2601.1	30.99	10.4	2.1	9.7	24.7	6.3	8.3	12.7
▲ United Community Bank	Raceland	LA	C	C-	D+	534.1	-0.02	19.2	0.7	11.3	3.5	10.0	14.7	18.2
▲ United Community Bank	Perham	MN	B+	B	B	260.3	7.62	12.9	3.2	11.7	25.7	10.0	11.1	17.1
United Community Bank of North Dakota	Leeds	ND	B-	B-	B+	351.8	-2.86	17.8	1.6	4.9	12.0	10.0	11.3	15.0
United Community Bank of W Kentucky	Morganfield	KY	A-	A-	A	267.1	4.88	12.7	5.9	17.4	22.4	10.0	14.2	20.8
▲ United Cumberland Bank	Whitley City	KY	B-	C+	B	297.3	3.10	7.9	11.2	27.0	19.7	10.0	13.5	23.0
United Farmers State Bank	Adams	MN	B-	B+	A	155.5	3.30	5.1	1.1	4.2	4.0	8.9	12.0	14.1
United Fidelity Bank, FSB	Evansville	IN	B+	B+	B+	965.7	22.58	0.9	0.1	7.5	62.2	6.9	8.9	27.7
▲ United Midwest Savings Bank, N.A.	De Graff	OH	C-	D+	D	281.5	9.72	23.9	17.3	11.3	0.6	7.3	9.2	16.5
▲ United Minnesota Bank	New London	MN	C	D+	C	32.0	5.10	12.7	11.1	27.9	2.3	6.1	8.1	13.0
United Mississippi Bank	Natchez	MS	C+	C+	B-	356.4	-0.90	7.3	3.8	13.6	17.4	8.6	10.6	13.8
▲ United National Bank	Cairo	GA	B	B	B	224.2	3.52	12.6	3.8	15.0	4.9	10.0	14.2	18.9
United Orient Bank	New York	NY	B	B	B	86.3	-7.00	1.2	0.0	20.9	2.3	10.0	15.9	23.0
United Pacific Bank	City of Industry	CA	B	B	B	143.6	5.40	2.7	0.0	0.3	0.3	10.0	17.0	21.8
United Prairie Bank	Mountain Lake	MN	C	C+	B-	595.8	2.95	12.0	0.7	5.3	12.6	6.0	9.7	11.7
United Republic Bank	Elkhorn	NE	D+	C-	C+	137.8	8.58	7.7	0.3	12.2	7.1	6.3	10.8	12.0
United Roosevelt Savings Bank	Carteret	NJ	C-	D+	D+	144.0	13.90	7.4	0.1	52.4	6.2	10.0	11.7	19.3
United Savings Bank	Philadelphia	PA	B-	B-	B-	370.6	3.94	0.2	0.0	27.1	24.9	10.0	16.7	37.0
United Security Bank	Fresno	CA	B+	B+	B+	956.2	5.90	7.4	7.3	5.8	8.1	10.0	12.3	18.2
United Security Bank	Auxvasse	MO	B+	B+	A-	61.3	-5.59	5.7	7.4	34.6	26.3	10.0	14.2	21.5
▲ United Southern Bank	Umatilla	FL	B	B-	B-	533.4	2.51	2.6	1.3	14.2	30.6	8.5	10.0	16.5
▲ United Southern Bank	Hopkinsville	KY	B	B-	C+	218.4	-1.75	5.8	2.5	24.0	16.2	10.0	12.1	16.4
▲ United Southwest Bank	Cottonwood	MN	C	C-	C-	47.5	4.89	2.6	2.2	0.4	36.4	6.8	8.8	16.7
United State Bank	Lewistown	MO	B-	B-	C+	183.7	5.63	5.8	1.5	7.4	8.5	6.7	9.5	12.3
United Texas Bank	Dallas	TX	B-	B-	B-	645.5	31.44	19.2	0.1	9.1	10.0	7.4	9.3	14.1
United Trust Bank	Palos Heights	IL	E	E	E-	26.3	-6.52	0.0	0.6	28.4	0.4	10.0	12.0	18.3
▲ United Valley Bank	Cavalier	ND	C+	B-	B	360.1	37.45	12.6	2.7	8.0	15.6	7.7	9.5	13.1
Unity Bank	Clinton	NJ	A-	B+	B	1658.8	7.13	4.7	0.1	29.9	3.7	8.5	10.1	13.8
Unity Bank	Augusta	WI	D+	C-	C+	506.3	182.81	7.2	2.6	14.7	6.3	6.3	8.9	12.0
Unity National Bank of Houston	Houston	TX	D-	D-	D+	97.1	8.46	15.3	0.7	14.5	8.1	6.9	8.9	13.3
▼ Universal Bank	West Covina	CA	C+	B	B	406.5	9.58	0.5	0.0	4.0	4.3	10.0	14.4	21.7
University Bank	Ann Arbor	MI	B+	B+	B+	383.2	44.24	0.5	0.1	49.6	3.3	6.1	8.6	11.9
University National Bank of Lawrence	Lawrence	KS	B-	C+	C+	80.2	1.34	4.7	0.8	40.8	3.5	7.7	9.4	16.0
Univest Bank and Trust Co.	Souderton	PA	B	B	B	5333.0	11.61	15.4	0.6	14.4	8.4	5.9	9.9	11.7
Upper Peninsula State Bank	Escanaba	MI	A-	A-	A-	201.1	-0.13	5.6	5.6	17.4	21.0	10.0	17.7	24.4
Upstate National Bank	Ogdensburg	NY	C	C+	B-	156.8	12.67	4.0	0.1	26.9	9.7	7.7	9.4	13.3
US Metro Bank	Garden Grove	CA	B+	B+	A-	507.3	36.82	11.0	0.0	0.5	0.0	10.0	11.2	15.0

Asset Quality Index	Adjusted Non-Performing Loans as a % of Total Loans	Adjusted Non-Performing Loans as a % of Capital	Net Charge-Offs Avg Loans	Profitability Index	Net Income ($Mil)	Return on Assets (R.O.A.)	Return on Equity (R.O.E.)	Net Interest Spread	Overhead Efficiency Ratio	Liquidity Index	Liquidity Ratio	Hot Money Ratio	Stability Index
4.6	1.60	na	-0.01	**5.3**	2.7	1.13	10.31	3.98	73.2	**3.9**	13.4	9.0	**7.5**
5.1	0.78	2.2	-0.09	**4.5**	0.6	0.72	5.33	4.36	72.3	**2.4**	20.0	17.1	**6.2**
3.3	2.58	na	1.03	**4.5**	1.0	0.92	9.10	4.06	69.6	**4.4**	24.9	7.1	**6.7**
5.9	1.45	na	0.10	**3.0**	0.2	0.37	3.19	3.68	78.4	**2.5**	26.0	13.7	**5.9**
7.2	0.51	na	-0.01	**7.6**	3.5	1.48	12.93	4.31	55.6	**1.4**	7.7	16.1	**8.1**
5.6	0.66	na	0.12	**6.6**	6.7	1.35	14.90	4.09	62.0	**3.5**	27.6	11.7	**6.7**
6.5	1.36	na	-0.01	**4.4**	1.5	1.02	8.42	3.63	76.2	**0.8**	14.4	34.0	**8.5**
7.3	1.12	na	-0.06	**9.6**	26.7	2.52	23.98	4.04	54.6	**6.0**	34.3	4.9	**10.0**
4.4	0.92	3.7	0.14	**7.3**	202.7	1.39	7.70	3.48	51.2	**3.2**	11.4	11.2	**9.8**
7.9	0.12	na	0.00	**6.8**	6.3	1.36	10.90	3.61	52.4	**1.6**	8.0	18.2	**8.9**
8.9	0.09	0.4	-0.01	**4.5**	0.7	0.91	6.87	2.93	67.1	**4.9**	37.9	9.8	**8.3**
8.6	0.34	na	0.07	**6.6**	1.9	1.56	10.25	3.46	50.0	**5.3**	47.3	10.5	**9.1**
4.0	1.07	na	0.03	**6.6**	2.4	1.30	11.54	5.49	64.2	**2.6**	21.3	15.4	**6.7**
5.6	0.89	4.0	0.05	**7.0**	19.3	1.58	13.81	3.24	53.5	**1.3**	19.5	29.2	**10.0**
5.7	0.99	na	0.10	**5.1**	5.3	1.03	10.49	3.99	70.8	**3.7**	12.2	7.8	**7.2**
0.3	11.72	na	0.11	**0.0**	-1.4	-3.91	-79.64	4.81	198.3	**5.4**	34.7	5.3	**0.0**
3.0	3.03	na	0.19	**6.1**	4.1	1.46	14.09	3.65	59.5	**1.3**	11.5	23.9	**7.5**
7.8	0.72	3.2	0.01	**3.5**	3.6	0.58	4.70	3.00	81.2	**0.9**	24.6	1.3	**7.1**
6.9	0.60	na	0.00	**5.8**	13.0	1.03	8.38	4.19	64.8	**3.2**	28.8	18.6	**9.2**
6.2	3.27	na	0.00	**6.9**	1.2	1.48	11.88	4.44	60.9	**4.4**	25.0	7.2	**7.7**
7.3	0.97	na	0.02	**7.8**	1.9	1.56	13.02	4.19	56.6	**0.8**	12.0	34.1	**7.9**
6.8	0.78	2.6	0.13	**7.8**	139.3	1.48	11.25	4.19	54.8	**3.7**	19.5	9.5	**10.0**
6.5	1.21	na	0.00	**5.9**	2.2	1.32	12.95	4.05	60.8	**3.3**	7.0	11.7	**8.1**
4.7	1.82	10.2	0.26	**5.5**	21.7	1.21	13.28	3.47	62.5	**3.8**	18.0	8.0	**8.0**
2.7	3.59	14.6	-0.33	**6.8**	8.2	2.01	14.64	4.71	54.9	**2.8**	17.8	15.1	**6.9**
7.3	1.23	na	0.03	**5.1**	2.3	1.21	10.75	3.94	69.2	**2.8**	27.6	16.8	**7.1**
4.3	0.24	5.9	2.18	**5.2**	2.2	0.80	6.87	4.22	47.7	**2.6**	8.9	15.4	**7.1**
8.3	0.37	na	0.10	**8.4**	3.3	1.65	11.91	4.06	55.9	**1.7**	16.9	14.9	**9.3**
3.8	3.05	na	0.32	**8.3**	4.2	1.90	14.59	4.74	59.3	**1.8**	20.6	21.6	**7.9**
6.9	0.05	na	0.33	**8.5**	2.0	1.79	14.81	4.21	48.6	**3.2**	10.5	11.3	**8.9**
6.2	5.00	5.8	0.02	**6.0**	8.9	1.36	11.03	2.21	64.4	**5.9**	48.4	6.8	**7.8**
2.8	3.67	na	1.71	**9.2**	3.6	1.56	15.72	4.73	68.2	**0.9**	23.0	47.1	**7.5**
6.7	0.00	na	0.27	**6.1**	0.3	1.45	18.50	4.63	68.4	**4.6**	22.1	5.4	**4.0**
3.9	1.17	na	-0.06	**4.2**	2.4	0.90	8.66	4.44	81.0	**2.8**	12.8	14.4	**6.5**
5.1	3.68	na	-0.03	**8.3**	2.4	1.48	10.49	4.80	54.4	**1.2**	5.1	24.1	**8.0**
7.6	0.01	1.6	0.00	**4.3**	0.4	0.59	3.89	5.69	86.4	**2.6**	20.9	16.4	**7.2**
7.2	0.05	na	0.00	**3.7**	0.7	0.66	3.82	3.43	77.0	**0.8**	20.2	53.2	**8.4**
2.9	1.67	na	0.02	**5.8**	6.6	1.48	13.74	4.35	68.6	**1.7**	12.8	17.0	**7.5**
6.4	0.00	na	-0.02	**3.0**	0.5	0.47	3.36	3.52	73.9	**0.7**	16.6	45.4	**2.7**
8.6	0.57	4.3	0.00	**1.6**	0.2	0.15	1.50	2.51	87.9	**1.5**	15.2	22.4	**5.1**
9.9	0.00	na	0.00	**4.0**	2.3	0.84	4.89	2.90	61.7	**3.7**	48.8	18.8	**8.0**
4.4	2.59	na	0.04	**9.3**	11.6	1.60	12.75	4.32	48.9	**5.0**	31.5	6.2	**10.0**
8.5	0.00	na	0.02	**5.4**	0.6	1.36	9.84	4.10	67.9	**2.9**	23.5	15.5	**8.0**
5.3	1.64	na	-0.14	**5.2**	4.0	1.00	10.45	3.96	69.7	**6.3**	40.2	1.7	**7.3**
5.2	2.03	na	-0.44	**5.3**	2.1	1.26	10.98	4.26	72.9	**2.3**	18.6	18.0	**6.6**
8.9	0.00	na	0.00	**3.1**	0.2	0.56	6.39	3.51	81.4	**6.4**	55.3	4.1	**3.7**
4.4	0.61	4.3	0.01	**6.7**	2.1	1.51	16.20	3.75	56.3	**1.1**	14.3	22.0	**6.9**
8.7	0.00	0.0	0.00	**4.1**	3.7	0.90	8.99	2.54	54.9	**2.3**	48.7	47.9	**4.7**
5.3	2.10	na	0.00	**0.0**	-0.9	-4.92	-36.42	4.21	231.7	**1.7**	21.1	23.1	**2.6**
4.5	1.56	na	-0.01	**5.3**	3.2	1.19	10.63	4.29	67.5	**2.5**	5.3	12.1	**6.9**
7.3	0.46	3.5	0.11	**7.5**	16.8	1.47	14.90	4.07	53.8	**1.6**	14.8	16.6	**8.2**
1.8	2.55	na	0.06	**4.2**	3.5	0.95	11.70	4.48	76.8	**1.2**	7.2	22.1	**5.7**
2.9	2.44	na	0.53	**0.1**	-0.5	-0.61	-6.74	3.68	104.8	**3.1**	15.0	7.9	**4.1**
7.4	0.83	na	-0.04	**2.4**	0.2	0.08	0.54	2.80	96.8	**0.8**	19.0	46.0	**8.5**
5.8	1.25	2.7	0.04	**7.2**	2.4	1.29	12.44	5.67	93.6	**5.5**	25.8	0.5	**5.2**
6.4	1.00	na	-0.22	**6.0**	0.9	1.47	15.20	4.08	68.5	**3.5**	20.7	12.3	**5.8**
5.0	0.89	5.6	0.06	**6.7**	54.6	1.41	11.09	3.75	59.4	**3.2**	6.3	8.8	**9.2**
7.9	0.43	2.7	0.03	**7.1**	2.3	1.49	9.03	4.14	58.7	**3.0**	28.9	11.9	**8.3**
7.7	0.00	na	0.00	**3.2**	1.0	0.90	7.92	2.97	74.6	**0.6**	17.9	70.9	**7.0**
7.1	0.06	na	0.12	**6.6**	3.6	1.06	8.80	4.01	62.5	**1.0**	25.6	43.7	**8.4**

Name	City	State	Rating	2018 Rating	2017 Rating	Total Assets ($Mil)	One Year Asset Growth	Asset Mix (As a % of Total Assets) Commercial Loans	Consumer Loans	Mortgage Loans	Securities	Capitalization Index	Leverage Ratio	Risk-Based Capital Ratio
USAA Federal Savings Bank	San Antonio	TX	**C+**	C+	C+	88536.6	7.76	0.0	47.4	4.7	31.7	**8.4**	10.0	16.8
USAA Savings Bank	Las Vegas	NV	**U**	U	U	1747.9	-4.66	0.0	0.0	0.0	18.1	**10.0**	19.2	69.3
▲ USNY Bank	Geneva	NY	**B-**	B-	B+	435.9	11.33	13.5	0.7	10.9	4.5	**7.4**	10.4	12.9
▲ Utah Independent Bank	Salina	UT	**A-**	B+	A-	83.1	0.57	16.5	6.0	13.0	16.9	**10.0**	16.2	22.5
Uwharrie Bank	Albemarle	NC	**C+**	C+	C+	658.9	3.72	6.1	2.0	11.5	15.6	**6.9**	8.9	13.7
Valley Bank of Commerce	Roswell	NM	**A-**	A-	B+	169.9	-1.06	19.3	0.5	5.9	0.2	**9.9**	11.0	24.0
▲ Valley Bank of Kalispell	Kalispell	MT	**B**	C+	B	134.5	13.54	14.1	4.9	19.4	13.2	**9.1**	11.3	14.2
Valley Bank of Nevada	North Las Vegas	NV	**D**	D	D	143.2	9.21	12.4	0.3	1.0	3.5	**7.4**	9.3	12.9
▼ Valley Bank of Ronan	Ronan	MT	**C-**	C+	B	104.2	-1.39	12.3	5.6	13.3	8.0	**9.6**	10.8	17.4
Valley Central Bank	Liberty Township	OH	**C**	C	C+	166.2	49.20	2.4	0.5	47.9	3.1	**10.0**	22.0	31.8
Valley Exchange Bank	Lennox	SD	**B**	B	C+	66.8	5.69	2.9	1.5	0.9	11.4	**10.0**	12.3	34.4
Valley National Bank	Wayne	NJ	**B-**	B-	B-	33736.6	9.43	12.5	6.6	12.4	11.1	**4.9**	8.1	11.0
Valley Premier Bank	Hawley	MN	**B**	B	B	111.1	0.24	14.2	3.0	11.1	30.8	**8.2**	9.8	17.1
▲ Valley Republic Bank	Bakersfield	CA	**B+**	B-	B-	915.0	17.40	10.7	0.2	4.1	16.0	**8.2**	10.1	13.5
Valley State Bank	Russellville	AL	**B**	B	B-	124.1	6.10	6.6	2.7	20.0	37.8	**10.0**	17.5	35.6
Valley State Bank	Belle Plaine	KS	**B**	B	B	134.8	7.31	8.1	10.1	16.8	21.2	**10.0**	13.5	22.4
Valley State Bank	Syracuse	KS	**B-**	B-	C+	152.6	11.08	10.8	5.0	13.1	9.3	**5.7**	9.4	11.5
Valliance Bank	Oklahoma City	OK	**C**	C	C+	456.8	0.20	20.5	0.3	11.7	7.4	**4.3**	9.2	10.6
Valor Bank	Edmond	OK	**B**	B	C	95.4	17.61	3.8	0.1	46.8	0.5	**6.9**	8.9	12.8
ValueBank Texas	Corpus Christi	TX	**A-**	B+	B+	243.7	-0.94	3.2	0.5	13.9	16.8	**9.7**	10.8	21.5
Van Wert Federal Savings Bank	Van Wert	OH	**C+**	C+	C+	116.4	5.20	0.0	0.8	47.2	20.9	**10.0**	21.3	48.2
Vanguard National Trust Co., N.A.	Malvern	PA	**U**	U	U	109.5	21.80	0.0	0.0	0.0	76.4	**10.0**	60.7	316.4
▲ Vantage Bank	Alexandria	MN	**C-**	D+	D+	32.5	16.57	7.4	6.2	32.2	0.0	**4.7**	8.7	10.8
▲ Vantage Bank Texas	San Antonio	TX	**B-**		B-	1995.4	273.82	11.3	0.5	4.9	6.2	**10.0**	13.9	16.3
Vast Bank, N.A.	Tulsa	OK	**B-**	B-	C+	651.2	0.59	18.9	1.7	9.2	1.2	**7.8**	10.6	13.2
▼ VCC Bank	Richmond	VA	**D**	D	C-	214.2	16.05	8.8	0.0	10.5	8.3	**8.6**	10.8	13.9
VeraBank, N.A.	Henderson	TX	**B**	B	B	2398.8	31.58	8.4	3.7	15.7	20.5	**6.8**	8.8	14.9
Vergas State Bank	Vergas	MN	**B-**	B-	B-	50.1	4.59	3.2	2.2	10.5	21.2	**10.0**	15.7	39.5
Veritex Community Bank	Dallas	TX	**B**	B	B+	7959.0	142.58	20.4	0.2	6.6	12.9	**6.3**	10.6	12.0
▲ Vermilion Bank & Trust Co.	Kaplan	LA	**B-**	C+	B-	109.8	-0.57	8.1	5.2	21.8	20.4	**10.0**	11.1	18.0
▲ Vermilion Valley Bank	Piper City	IL	**A-**	B+	A	130.7	4.69	2.8	1.4	10.7	18.0	**10.0**	16.0	23.7
Vermillion State Bank	Vermillion	MN	**A+**	A+	A+	591.9	8.35	14.8	1.5	12.1	37.3	**10.0**	16.0	27.7
▲ Vermont State Bank	Vermont	IL	**D**	D	D	29.9	3.94	8.3	21.2	31.6	9.1	**10.0**	13.3	20.0
Versailles S&L Co.	Versailles	OH	**B**	B-	C+	54.9	3.15	1.9	2.4	54.3	0.1	**10.0**	20.7	36.8
▲ Verus Bank of Commerce	Fort Collins	CO	**A-**	B+	A	268.9	10.97	2.9	0.0	9.0	0.0	**10.0**	13.6	16.0
▲ Victor State Bank	Victor	IA	**A-**	A-	A	37.3	0.68	12.4	1.7	7.9	40.1	**10.0**	12.2	22.9
Victory Bank	Limerick	PA	**B-**	C	C	267.3	10.42	13.8	2.3	13.5	3.8	**5.6**	9.5	11.4
▲ Victory Community Bank	Fort Mitchell	KY	**A-**	B+	A-	179.2	2.66	0.0	0.4	66.5	0.5	**10.0**	14.6	26.1
Victory State Bank	Staten Island	NY	**B**	B	B-	378.0	0.27	5.5	0.1	4.6	43.6	**7.8**	9.6	20.0
▼ Vidalia Federal Savings Bank	Vidalia	GA	**C+**	B-	B-	201.6	-6.94	0.1	2.0	27.6	50.4	**10.0**	15.8	54.8
▲ Viking Bank	Alexandria	MN	**B-**	B-	B-	185.6	8.06	10.5	1.5	20.1	2.8	**8.8**	10.8	14.0
Villa Grove State Bank	Villa Grove	IL	**B+**	B+	B+	72.2	2.63	8.1	2.2	43.7	15.1	**10.0**	11.8	23.7
Village Bank	Saint Libory	IL	**B-**	B-	B-	89.2	4.37	5.1	6.4	21.5	21.0	**8.0**	9.7	20.7
Village Bank	Auburndale	MA	**B**	B	B	1249.5	7.26	3.2	0.3	43.9	11.5	**10.0**	11.1	16.9
▲ Village Bank	Saint Francis	MN	**C+**	C	D+	302.0	1.55	13.6	1.2	12.3	15.1	**7.4**	9.3	13.5
▲ Village Bank	Midlothian	VA	**C**	C-	C	557.4	9.23	7.2	6.6	15.4	8.3	**7.2**	9.4	12.6
Village Bank & Trust, N.A.	Arlington Heights	IL	**B**	B	B-	1754.8	18.11	42.0	11.1	3.6	11.2	**5.7**	9.2	11.5
Vinings Bank	Smyrna	GA	**C+**	B-	B	375.7	28.60	5.6	0.1	1.9	49.8	**6.1**	8.1	12.8
Vintage Bank Kansas	Leon	KS	**B-**	B	B	141.5	10.19	7.6	3.2	14.7	21.3	**8.9**	10.3	15.4
Vinton County National Bank	McArthur	OH	**B**	B	B	1006.1	6.68	3.6	18.7	30.7	14.8	**10.0**	11.1	16.4
Virginia Bank and Trust Co.	Danville	VA	**B**	B+	B+	221.4	14.02	10.5	8.3	20.3	13.7	**10.0**	11.6	18.7
Virginia Commonwealth Bank	Richmond	VA	**C+**	C+	C	1107.6	8.10	15.1	1.3	27.8	7.3	**7.4**	10.3	12.9
Virginia Community Bank	Louisa	VA	**B**	B	B	251.5	-1.21	10.9	1.6	12.1	20.0	**8.2**	10.8	13.5
▲ Virginia National Bank	Charlottesville	VA	**B+**	B-	B	660.3	5.38	12.3	11.6	12.4	11.8	**10.0**	11.3	15.5
Virginia Partners Bank	Fredericksburg	VA	**C+**	C+	C	441.8	5.18	10.4	0.8	20.4	15.1	**9.1**	11.0	14.3
Vision Bank, N.A.	Ada	OK	**B-**	B-	B-	680.3	5.07	6.3	6.7	24.7	21.8	**8.1**	9.8	14.9
VisionBank	Topeka	KS	**C+**	B-	B-	182.9	4.63	22.5	2.0	20.2	1.9	**5.4**	8.7	11.3
VisionBank	Saint Louis Park	MN	**B+**	B+	B+	92.8	16.73	25.8	0.8	16.8	0.0	**9.2**	10.8	14.3
VISIONBank	Fargo	ND	**D**	D	D	197.6	1.70	25.3	4.8	21.0	0.0	**7.1**	10.1	12.6
▲ VisionBank of Iowa	Ames	IA	**B**	B-	B-	489.0	-1.51	6.9	0.1	10.9	1.6	**7.8**	11.1	13.2

Asset Quality Index	Adjusted Non-Performing Loans as a % of Total Loans	Adjusted Non-Performing Loans as a % of Capital	Net Charge-Offs Avg Loans	Profitability Index	Net Income ($Mil)	Return on Assets (R.O.A.)	Return on Equity (R.O.E.)	Net Interest Spread	Overhead Efficiency Ratio	Liquidity Index	Liquidity Ratio	Hot Money Ratio	Stability Index
3.6	1.80	5.3	1.45	**6.7**	799.5	1.29	12.87	5.30	70.3	**5.1**	48.0	4.4	**8.2**
10.0	na	0.0	0.00	**10.0**	176.0	15.15	79.10	2.20	69.8	**3.6**	89.5	50.3	**6.3**
4.8	1.05	na	0.07	**6.1**	3.6	1.11	10.92	3.71	52.6	**0.6**	11.6	39.2	**7.1**
6.2	0.97	na	0.00	**9.8**	2.0	3.08	19.92	5.90	49.1	**5.5**	34.3	4.0	**9.7**
5.6	1.74	8.1	-0.10	**3.8**	3.3	0.69	7.94	3.56	83.3	**3.6**	30.1	13.7	**5.6**
8.0	0.00	na	-0.01	**9.5**	3.3	2.54	25.28	4.07	40.6	**6.4**	59.2	7.0	**7.2**
4.7	1.51	na	0.06	**8.5**	2.5	2.68	23.80	5.01	53.1	**1.6**	21.1	23.2	**6.6**
0.9	5.77	22.6	0.11	**2.7**	0.3	0.30	2.75	4.28	87.5	**4.7**	34.1	9.4	**6.5**
2.2	6.47	na	-0.09	**5.1**	0.6	0.82	7.58	4.68	74.8	**5.7**	38.5	4.9	**6.9**
9.0	0.49	1.5	-0.01	**2.3**	0.2	0.15	0.66	4.45	96.7	**0.7**	10.7	21.3	**7.1**
9.1	0.00	na	-0.10	**4.9**	0.5	1.02	8.53	3.54	62.2	**6.8**	68.0	4.4	**6.2**
4.2	1.10	6.1	0.05	**5.9**	295.8	1.20	10.85	2.98	50.1	**1.2**	6.5	12.9	**9.2**
6.0	0.39	na	0.00	**4.8**	0.9	1.11	11.24	3.53	69.6	**5.6**	40.9	6.4	**6.5**
8.4	0.00	na	0.00	**5.4**	7.8	1.24	12.17	3.40	56.3	**4.6**	29.1	7.7	**6.8**
8.9	0.23	na	0.02	**4.2**	0.9	0.90	5.23	3.35	62.2	**1.7**	36.4	37.7	**8.1**
6.7	0.75	na	0.13	**4.8**	1.0	0.98	7.36	4.18	66.6	**1.7**	21.0	20.5	**7.2**
8.1	0.05	0.4	0.04	**6.5**	1.7	1.48	15.90	4.08	65.1	**0.7**	11.1	43.9	**6.2**
5.0	0.21	na	0.04	**3.7**	2.3	0.71	7.79	3.86	79.5	**0.7**	11.1	39.5	**5.2**
9.0	0.00	0.0	0.01	**8.0**	1.1	1.76	18.97	3.68	68.8	**0.6**	10.6	42.7	**5.7**
9.2	0.00	na	-0.03	**8.7**	4.0	2.18	20.64	4.54	59.9	**5.5**	44.9	8.1	**6.9**
9.9	0.07	na	0.00	**2.7**	0.4	0.46	2.15	2.73	79.9	**3.2**	44.1	20.6	**7.6**
10.0	na	na	na	**10.0**	14.2	18.90	22.54	2.33	66.1	**4.0**	199.1	0.0	**6.5**
8.0	0.00	na	0.00	**4.4**	0.2	1.01	10.45	4.09	78.0	**2.5**	9.5	16.1	**3.7**
4.9	0.94	na	-0.03	**6.7**	18.2	1.25	8.70	4.53	63.3	**1.6**	19.1	25.6	**9.3**
5.7	0.44	2.8	0.36	**4.7**	3.9	0.81	7.77	3.62	69.5	**0.8**	19.4	48.5	**6.5**
0.8	3.85	na	0.38	**3.0**	0.9	0.57	5.20	2.48	59.2	**0.5**	13.5	69.5	**6.4**
6.0	0.87	4.3	0.09	**5.1**	18.1	1.04	10.24	4.05	70.3	**5.2**	26.1	6.1	**8.1**
7.1	0.00	5.3	-0.05	**3.6**	0.2	0.65	4.16	2.91	70.6	**3.6**	64.5	23.1	**7.3**
4.5	0.18	3.3	0.25	**6.2**	69.0	1.16	8.17	4.08	55.8	**1.3**	17.4	20.6	**10.0**
4.6	3.57	na	0.35	**6.0**	1.2	1.39	13.18	4.39	63.5	**1.8**	20.0	21.1	**6.7**
7.2	0.04	na	0.01	**8.3**	2.0	2.07	12.10	3.80	42.2	**1.8**	13.5	19.9	**9.5**
7.5	1.24	3.6	0.07	**10.0**	11.2	2.67	16.84	3.54	26.8	**5.6**	51.4	9.9	**10.0**
1.0	6.50	na	0.63	**1.8**	0.0	0.06	0.68	3.41	79.1	**0.5**	11.4	52.3	**4.4**
9.2	0.00	na	0.00	**4.7**	0.4	0.97	4.73	3.63	65.0	**3.0**	25.1	15.2	**7.5**
7.3	0.00	na	-0.01	**9.8**	4.1	2.03	15.39	4.24	40.7	**1.3**	9.9	9.3	**9.3**
2.9	2.00	na	0.00	**5.6**	0.3	1.07	5.85	3.91	55.1	**5.0**	66.0	12.6	**8.1**
6.8	0.12	0.8	0.17	**5.0**	1.9	0.99	10.69	4.36	67.2	**3.9**	10.0	8.6	**5.2**
7.2	0.66	na	-0.15	**9.5**	4.3	3.35	22.75	3.35	51.5	**1.4**	13.2	25.3	**9.6**
6.6	1.37	5.8	-0.07	**4.6**	2.8	0.94	10.28	3.32	69.8	**3.7**	36.3	15.2	**5.7**
7.9	0.89	na	0.03	**2.3**	0.3	0.22	1.40	2.36	89.3	**3.6**	77.1	32.8	**7.2**
5.5	0.27	na	0.00	**6.1**	1.9	1.41	8.72	3.64	54.4	**1.8**	13.6	20.2	**9.1**
9.0	0.16	na	0.01	**6.2**	0.8	1.46	12.70	3.70	59.3	**3.7**	19.9	10.9	**7.7**
7.5	0.20	na	0.17	**4.6**	0.7	1.05	11.11	3.57	63.0	**5.8**	40.6	5.1	**5.0**
8.9	0.38	2.2	0.00	**4.3**	7.6	0.83	7.72	3.08	65.6	**1.1**	13.9	31.9	**9.1**
3.8	2.58	na	-0.32	**5.7**	2.6	1.20	13.38	4.44	75.7	**3.5**	27.3	13.1	**7.2**
4.0	2.30	na	-0.02	**4.5**	3.7	0.94	9.92	3.92	77.1	**2.4**	16.7	17.1	**6.3**
6.1	0.51	2.9	0.30	**6.6**	16.6	1.35	12.24	3.42	44.3	**1.5**	18.5	19.5	**8.4**
7.0	0.79	3.1	0.16	**3.5**	2.2	0.89	10.05	3.44	80.9	**5.3**	33.3	5.1	**4.6**
6.3	0.73	na	0.00	**5.5**	1.3	1.26	11.20	4.47	63.4	**3.0**	16.5	10.0	**7.0**
6.4	0.50	na	0.15	**4.7**	6.5	0.91	7.67	3.80	71.8	**2.1**	11.9	18.3	**8.5**
7.1	1.19	na	0.18	**4.7**	1.4	0.94	8.07	4.33	72.0	**5.3**	34.8	5.5	**6.9**
5.6	1.30	na	0.19	**3.8**	6.3	0.77	7.10	3.53	70.2	**1.1**	10.4	26.8	**7.1**
7.5	0.96	na	-0.02	**5.6**	2.0	1.09	10.63	4.81	71.9	**4.3**	22.7	7.5	**6.2**
7.4	0.50	na	0.36	**6.6**	6.1	1.26	11.20	3.65	61.2	**2.7**	17.2	15.8	**7.6**
8.6	0.02	na	0.00	**3.6**	2.2	0.71	6.67	3.42	74.0	**0.8**	17.9	38.3	**5.2**
4.5	1.25	7.9	0.29	**4.9**	5.9	1.16	11.92	4.23	72.8	**1.8**	5.5	19.3	**7.3**
4.6	1.31	na	1.25	**3.0**	0.3	0.24	2.55	3.83	67.2	**1.5**	4.4	21.4	**5.4**
8.1	0.34	na	0.00	**8.5**	1.3	1.90	17.95	4.11	52.5	**0.6**	12.4	50.3	**7.8**
1.0	4.33	28.8	0.63	**3.9**	0.9	0.59	5.64	4.08	77.6	**1.3**	6.9	24.6	**6.6**
7.3	0.08	na	-0.02	**5.2**	4.8	1.29	11.91	3.37	62.8	**1.5**	11.7	9.1	**7.3**

Name	City	State	Rating	2018 Rating	2017 Rating	Total Assets ($Mil)	One Year Asset Growth	Asset Mix (As a % of Total Assets) Comm-ercial Loans	Cons-umer Loans	Mort-gage Loans	Secur-ities	Capital-ization Index	Lever-age Ratio	Risk-Based Capital Ratio
VIST Bank	Wyomissing	PA	**B**	B	B	1817.3	7.28	6.7	0.2	17.9	12.7	**6.1**	8.7	11.8
Vista Bank	Dallas	TX	**B-**	B+	B+	863.6	11.08	16.6	0.7	10.2	2.9	**6.5**	9.8	12.2
Volunteer Federal Savings Bank	Madisonville	TN	**B**	B-	B-	214.6	5.05	0.6	4.8	45.0	9.1	**10.0**	13.7	27.5
Volunteer State Bank	Portland	TN	**B-**	B	B+	729.5	5.59	8.9	0.7	11.9	0.9	**5.4**	9.5	11.3
Wabash Savings Bank	Mount Carmel	IL	**D-**	D-	D	9.1	-4.58	1.8	6.8	29.9	9.3	**10.0**	12.9	30.2
Wadena State Bank	Wadena	MN	**B+**	A-	B+	175.5	3.99	11.2	2.9	16.4	21.1	**8.2**	9.8	15.1
▲ Waggoner National Bank of Vernon	Vernon	TX	**A-**	A-	A+	286.7	-0.61	5.9	5.3	7.0	26.6	**10.0**	14.5	21.1
Wahoo State Bank	Wahoo	NE	**C+**	B-	B-	90.6	12.18	9.0	4.3	21.6	18.0	**6.1**	8.1	12.2
▲ Wake Forest Federal S&L Assn.	Wake Forest	NC	**A**	A-	A-	104.4	0.51	0.0	0.1	32.1	1.8	**10.0**	23.2	39.0
Wakefield Co-operative Bank	Wakefield	MA	**C**	C	C	249.2	12.71	0.2	0.0	58.3	14.9	**5.7**	7.7	14.1
Walcott Trust and Savings Bank	Walcott	IA	**B-**	B	B	124.3	-1.24	6.6	0.5	13.4	9.6	**10.0**	13.7	19.5
▲ Walden Savings Bank	Montgomery	NY	**B-**	C+	C	603.4	4.55	7.4	0.5	34.3	14.5	**8.1**	9.8	16.6
Waldo State Bank	Waldo	WI	**B**	B	B	82.3	1.42	10.4	1.9	42.1	11.5	**10.0**	12.5	18.2
Walker State Bank	Walker	IA	**B**	B-	B-	43.0	4.03	4.2	1.8	11.1	24.1	**9.7**	10.8	15.4
Wallis Bank	Wallis	TX	**A**	A-	B+	779.7	14.18	9.7	0.4	1.3	1.5	**9.7**	11.8	14.7
▲ Wallkill Valley Federal S&L Assn.	Wallkill	NY	**C**	C-	C	329.6	1.16	4.8	1.5	50.6	6.8	**8.2**	9.8	15.0
Walpole Co-operative Bank	Walpole	MA	**B**	B	B	510.3	2.19	2.8	0.0	21.1	12.3	**10.0**	18.9	24.6
Walters Bank and Trust Co.	Walters	OK	**B**	B	B-	53.4	-7.06	2.8	5.3	20.5	32.7	**10.0**	22.8	59.9
Walton State Bank	Walton	KS	**D-**	D-	D-	9.0	1.02	3.9	4.8	11.3	31.0	**6.0**	8.0	21.5
Wanda State Bank	Wanda	MN	**B+**	B+	B+	139.6	9.55	3.1	0.5	2.9	18.0	**10.0**	16.8	24.0
Warren Bank and Trust Co.	Warren	AR	**B-**	B	B	127.7	4.56	4.7	5.3	16.3	53.8	**10.0**	17.7	44.6
▲ Warren-Boynton State Bank	New Berlin	IL	**A-**	B+	A-	174.2	3.78	9.3	2.1	16.6	22.7	**10.0**	13.7	19.0
Warrington Bank	Pensacola	FL	**C**	C-	C-	88.0	4.36	0.0	0.3	1.8	47.9	**10.0**	18.8	47.1
Warsaw Federal S&L Assn.	Cincinnati	OH	**D**	D	D+	55.4	-11.50	0.0	0.0	55.2	21.9	**10.0**	12.9	21.2
▲ Washington Business Bank	Olympia	WA	**B+**	B-	B	91.5	7.78	28.4	0.0	14.4	0.1	**9.7**	11.2	14.8
▲ Washington County Bank	Blair	NE	**B+**	B	B+	433.5	15.50	5.8	1.3	7.1	12.8	**7.9**	9.6	13.4
Washington Federal Bank, N.A.	Seattle	WA	**A-**	A-	A-	16471.0	3.73	6.0	0.8	35.6	17.9	**8.9**	10.2	15.1
Washington Financial Bank	Washington	PA	**B**	B	B	1189.3	1.88	5.9	0.7	35.0	14.5	**10.0**	12.9	20.9
Washington Savings Bank	Effingham	IL	**B-**	B-	C+	399.0	9.53	5.7	1.6	25.5	23.7	**10.0**	16.8	27.4
Washington Savings Bank	Lowell	MA	**C**	C	C	252.1	3.85	0.6	0.1	56.0	8.8	**7.1**	9.0	16.2
Washington Savings Bank	Philadelphia	PA	**D**	D+	D+	159.4	-0.88	1.4	2.5	60.8	2.0	**6.1**	8.1	12.5
▲ Washington State Bank	Washington	IA	**A-**	B+	A-	330.1	6.75	5.7	1.0	27.1	25.4	**10.0**	13.1	20.1
Washington State Bank	Washington	IL	**B-**	C+	C	62.3	0.34	3.5	5.2	34.3	37.7	**10.0**	11.0	24.5
▼ Washington State Bank	Washington	LA	**B-**	B	B	205.3	7.91	12.1	2.0	15.9	9.9	**8.9**	10.2	14.3
Washington Trust Bank	Spokane	WA	**A-**	A-	B+	6802.0	6.31	18.2	1.9	9.3	28.8	**8.4**	10.1	13.6
Washington Trust Co. of Westerly	Westerly	RI	**B+**	B+	B+	5198.7	8.96	4.0	0.4	27.9	17.1	**6.9**	8.9	12.9
Washita State Bank	Burns Flat	OK	**C+**	B	B	106.2	0.17	4.1	3.8	10.2	32.7	**10.0**	12.7	27.2
Washita Valley Bank	Fort Cobb	OK	**B**	B+	B+	42.3	2.48	6.5	8.8	1.1	25.3	**10.0**	17.6	23.7
▲ Waterford Bank, N.A.	Toledo	OH	**B+**	B	B+	795.5	10.71	26.8	1.2	4.2	5.4	**7.7**	10.6	13.1
Waterford Commercial and Savings Bank	Waterford	OH	**B**	B	B	46.4	0.81	2.5	11.7	33.4	28.5	**10.0**	13.8	25.5
Waterman State Bank	Waterman	IL	**C-**	D+	E+	33.6	-1.92	12.2	1.7	5.2	32.6	**10.0**	11.3	18.2
WaterStone Bank, SSB	Wauwatosa	WI	**A**	A	A	2002.4	4.54	1.5	0.0	36.6	9.4	**10.0**	17.1	22.9
Watertown Savings Bank	Watertown	MA	**C+**	C+	C+	1258.3	8.12	0.4	0.1	36.3	40.2	**9.6**	10.8	23.7
▲ Watertown Savings Bank	Watertown	NY	**B**	B-	B+	691.0	3.18	7.3	1.4	15.4	15.9	**10.0**	14.5	20.6
Watkins Savings Bank	Watkins	IA	**B+**	B+	B+	69.6	3.26	0.6	1.1	6.5	53.4	**10.0**	17.4	34.0
▲ Wauchula State Bank	Wauchula	FL	**B+**	B	B-	691.9	5.80	1.9	0.7	15.8	24.3	**10.0**	12.7	21.1
Waukesha State Bank	Waukesha	WI	**A**	A	A	986.3	3.33	9.3	0.7	18.8	22.4	**10.0**	12.0	16.1
▲ Waukon State Bank	Waukon	IA	**A-**	A-	A	296.1	8.77	8.8	2.2	17.6	12.4	**10.0**	12.3	15.5
Waumandee State Bank	Waumandee	WI	**B-**	B	C	184.7	1.96	8.7	2.2	20.7	11.4	**9.2**	10.5	15.1
▲ Waycross Bank & Trust	Waycross	GA	**B+**	B	B	179.4	8.18	6.1	0.5	10.8	31.5	**10.0**	11.1	22.8
Wayland State Bank	Mount Pleasant	IA	**A-**	A-	A-	109.8	-3.34	9.1	2.1	13.3	29.2	**10.0**	17.0	26.9
Wayne Bank	Honesdale	PA	**B+**	B+	B	1216.6	5.12	6.3	12.0	19.3	17.4	**8.4**	9.9	13.7
Wayne Bank and Trust Co.	Cambridge City	IN	**B-**	B-	B-	164.3	3.67	6.2	5.2	22.7	12.2	**10.0**	11.4	16.3
▲ Wayne County Bank	Waynesboro	TN	**C+**	C+	C+	314.3	0.41	10.0	7.8	17.2	8.8	**10.0**	14.8	20.0
▲ Wayne Savings Community Bank	Wooster	OH	**B**	B-	B-	494.4	4.75	5.7	0.6	36.1	10.8	**7.5**	9.3	13.1
▲ Waypoint Bank	Cozad	NE	**A-**	B+	A-	269.6	-0.03	8.2	1.7	1.3	16.5	**10.0**	12.5	15.7
▲ WCF Financial Bank	Webster City	IA	**C**	C	C	125.7	8.32	0.0	5.0	44.5	33.1	**10.0**	15.9	35.6
▲ WebBank	Salt Lake City	UT	**B+**	B+	A	889.2	17.21	28.1	53.3	0.0	5.1	**10.0**	17.4	19.6
Webster Bank, N.A.	Waterbury	CT	**B**	B	B	29927.1	9.38	20.3	0.7	18.9	27.6	**7.1**	9.0	13.4
Webster Five Cents Savings Bank	Webster	MA	**B**	B	B	882.4	7.64	5.3	1.3	26.6	14.8	**10.0**	12.4	16.3

Asset Quality Index	Adjusted Non-Performing Loans as a % of Total Loans	Adjusted Non-Performing Loans as a % of Capital	Net Charge-Offs Avg Loans	Profitability Index	Net Income ($Mil)	Return on Assets (R.O.A.)	Return on Equity (R.O.E.)	Net Interest Spread	Overhead Efficiency Ratio	Liquidity Index	Liquidity Ratio	Hot Money Ratio	Stability Index
5.5	0.64	4.1	0.32	**4.0**	10.7	0.82	7.48	3.20	68.4	**4.2**	11.2	6.3	**7.8**
6.1	0.55	3.0	0.04	**4.6**	7.0	1.15	11.54	4.42	64.5	**1.4**	16.7	22.0	**5.2**
9.0	0.08	na	0.02	**4.6**	1.4	0.88	6.51	3.81	72.4	**3.6**	27.9	13.1	**7.6**
5.0	0.64	2.0	0.01	**5.3**	5.5	0.96	6.29	5.20	75.9	**1.4**	14.4	21.4	**9.2**
7.1	0.67	na	0.31	**0.0**	-0.1	-0.87	-6.58	3.07	125.5	**3.3**	60.8	20.8	**4.5**
5.7	2.50	na	-0.10	**6.6**	2.1	1.64	14.75	4.08	58.4	**4.9**	37.5	9.3	**8.4**
7.9	0.31	na	-0.04	**9.8**	6.2	2.86	21.14	4.46	44.5	**2.1**	16.3	18.7	**9.8**
7.1	2.16	na	0.00	**3.0**	0.3	0.40	4.74	3.67	87.6	**4.8**	26.2	5.1	**4.2**
9.4	0.00	na	0.00	**7.8**	1.2	1.55	6.81	3.66	44.8	**2.4**	41.9	30.1	**8.5**
6.0	0.64	6.3	0.00	**3.4**	1.0	0.55	6.94	2.97	74.9	**0.9**	17.9	23.5	**4.0**
7.4	0.64	na	0.04	**3.8**	0.4	0.42	2.94	3.52	77.8	**1.8**	28.7	22.1	**7.7**
5.9	2.75	na	-0.01	**4.7**	4.5	1.00	10.55	3.87	72.2	**4.7**	20.8	4.9	**6.3**
6.5	1.68	na	-0.02	**4.3**	0.5	0.84	6.76	3.73	70.6	**0.7**	13.1	27.5	**7.1**
8.0	0.00	na	0.00	**5.9**	0.4	1.17	10.73	3.54	57.5	**3.2**	27.1	15.0	**6.4**
7.1	0.68	1.1	0.08	**10.0**	14.9	2.72	22.57	5.45	53.9	**1.0**	23.1	34.9	**9.0**
4.0	2.90	na	0.06	**3.9**	2.1	0.85	7.44	4.07	72.2	**1.6**	11.0	17.5	**6.7**
6.2	0.98	na	-0.02	**3.3**	2.0	0.54	2.84	3.21	76.5	**0.9**	14.0	33.9	**8.0**
8.8	0.00	na	0.05	**4.6**	0.5	1.11	4.99	3.69	72.2	**5.1**	44.6	10.1	**6.9**
2.9	4.70	na	0.00	**1.8**	0.0	0.26	3.39	3.29	92.4	**5.5**	58.0	8.1	**1.0**
5.7	0.12	5.6	0.00	**4.6**	1.1	1.06	6.20	3.15	57.3	**3.4**	39.8	17.7	**8.1**
9.1	4.33	na	0.05	**2.9**	0.5	0.49	2.86	2.86	83.1	**3.9**	54.2	19.1	**8.0**
8.1	0.42	na	0.01	**6.1**	1.5	1.21	8.71	3.91	61.4	**1.7**	15.2	21.2	**8.7**
9.6	0.00	na	0.00	**2.6**	0.3	0.42	2.22	2.64	80.5	**7.2**	81.4	4.1	**6.1**
8.8	3.21	na	0.00	**0.0**	-0.6	-1.49	-10.96	2.68	140.6	**2.3**	40.7	31.0	**5.9**
8.3	0.00	na	-0.01	**5.6**	0.8	1.17	10.78	4.17	64.4	**0.8**	14.6	34.7	**7.1**
7.8	0.16	na	0.09	**6.7**	4.2	1.31	13.56	3.61	54.5	**3.8**	14.9	9.9	**6.4**
7.4	0.58	2.4	-0.02	**6.3**	157.6	1.27	10.59	3.13	51.6	**1.8**	19.5	21.2	**10.0**
8.7	0.55	2.9	0.06	**4.0**	7.7	0.88	7.00	3.38	68.1	**4.4**	13.6	6.1	**9.1**
8.7	0.37	1.7	0.03	**3.4**	1.6	0.56	3.27	2.64	76.2	**4.4**	40.5	13.0	**7.6**
6.1	1.00	6.0	-0.01	**3.3**	1.1	0.58	6.73	3.08	77.9	**1.2**	14.0	23.5	**5.4**
8.4	0.13	na	0.01	**0.5**	-0.5	-0.38	-4.57	2.82	109.0	**2.3**	9.1	17.1	**4.2**
7.4	0.44	na	0.16	**6.5**	3.3	1.34	10.55	3.60	55.5	**2.1**	29.9	18.3	**8.1**
4.9	0.66	na	-0.06	**4.2**	0.4	0.86	8.07	2.88	62.0	**4.0**	26.2	10.3	**4.8**
4.8	1.52	na	0.70	**3.7**	1.2	0.76	7.28	4.37	70.6	**1.4**	15.2	26.4	**6.9**
8.4	0.39	2.2	-0.13	**6.5**	62.5	1.28	13.29	4.00	62.5	**5.8**	27.2	2.5	**9.0**
7.6	0.40	2.8	0.06	**7.1**	54.5	1.41	14.67	2.83	53.5	**1.5**	13.5	12.9	**9.3**
5.3	2.97	na	3.97	**0.9**	-0.4	-0.49	-3.78	1.65	68.4	**2.1**	43.2	41.0	**6.4**
7.5	0.51	na	0.30	**6.0**	0.3	0.89	5.17	5.28	54.0	**2.8**	34.7	19.3	**7.9**
6.6	1.50	na	0.00	**6.7**	7.6	1.33	12.58	3.72	59.9	**3.6**	18.1	10.4	**7.6**
8.0	0.08	na	-0.05	**4.9**	0.4	1.05	7.79	4.24	73.2	**4.0**	18.3	9.2	**6.5**
7.1	7.73	na	0.00	**1.9**	0.1	0.27	2.51	3.47	97.0	**2.4**	27.5	18.9	**2.9**
8.7	0.58	2.2	0.00	**9.5**	27.1	1.83	9.98	3.01	74.2	**1.4**	14.6	26.4	**10.0**
9.8	0.66	2.4	0.00	**2.9**	4.0	0.44	4.21	2.76	79.6	**4.6**	50.4	17.0	**7.5**
5.3	1.11	na	0.10	**6.7**	7.2	1.42	9.04	3.96	55.5	**4.8**	17.0	3.5	**8.6**
9.1	0.00	na	0.00	**5.0**	0.6	1.08	6.23	2.92	54.0	**3.7**	62.6	20.8	**8.2**
4.8	3.16	12.3	0.11	**9.3**	11.5	2.25	18.71	4.44	50.8	**3.4**	35.4	16.5	**8.9**
8.9	0.27	1.1	0.00	**8.8**	13.7	1.84	15.61	4.27	59.2	**5.1**	14.5	1.3	**9.4**
8.4	0.21	na	-0.02	**9.3**	4.6	2.16	17.18	3.64	42.6	**2.9**	21.1	15.1	**9.7**
7.6	0.14	na	0.19	**4.7**	1.2	0.86	7.98	3.91	67.9	**2.2**	19.4	18.5	**6.6**
7.4	0.69	na	0.00	**7.0**	2.1	1.69	15.41	3.39	71.3	**4.8**	44.3	12.2	**7.8**
8.2	0.14	na	0.07	**7.3**	1.3	1.49	8.65	3.76	42.2	**5.8**	49.8	7.7	**8.5**
7.6	0.15	na	0.17	**5.7**	10.9	1.20	11.40	3.51	59.3	**1.6**	1.9	20.0	**8.8**
6.6	0.63	na	0.14	**3.1**	0.6	0.51	4.45	3.98	88.2	**3.2**	17.6	4.9	**6.8**
3.1	5.40	na	0.26	**5.4**	2.2	0.92	6.31	4.34	67.7	**0.9**	22.7	39.3	**7.1**
5.7	0.82	na	0.01	**6.0**	4.8	1.33	13.80	3.61	55.3	**2.4**	7.0	11.4	**5.9**
5.9	1.16	na	0.03	**7.6**	3.4	1.70	13.18	4.11	55.8	**3.0**	23.6	13.8	**9.3**
8.9	0.54	2.4	0.10	**2.0**	0.2	0.22	1.41	2.77	89.6	**3.2**	47.0	22.5	**7.2**
5.1	0.00	na	3.58	**10.0**	34.3	5.15	30.43	11.13	28.3	**0.5**	13.4	7.6	**9.1**
5.2	1.50	6.6	0.25	**7.0**	308.9	1.44	13.75	3.66	55.4	**4.1**	21.2	7.3	**9.5**
8.4	0.42	2.1	0.02	**4.0**	5.1	0.79	6.31	3.59	75.3	**3.5**	13.1	3.2	**7.9**

Name	City	State	Rating	2018 Rating	2017 Rating	Total Assets ($Mil)	One Year Asset Growth	Asset Mix (As a % of Total Assets) Comm-ercial Loans	Cons-umer Loans	Mort-gage Loans	Secur-ities	Capital-ization Index	Lever-age Ratio	Risk-Based Capital Ratio
Welch State Bank of Welch, Oklahoma	Welch	OK	A-	A	A-	275.8	4.84	5.7	2.8	15.2	18.6	10.0	12.8	18.3
▲ Welcome State Bank	Welcome	MN	B+	C+	B	30.2	-0.66	11.5	7.5	12.9	3.7	10.0	11.6	16.4
Wellesley Bank	Wellesley	MA	B-	B-	B-	979.2	17.14	9.0	0.0	40.6	3.5	5.7	8.0	11.5
Wellington State Bank	Wellington	TX	B	B	B	386.0	0.72	4.6	1.9	4.9	24.1	10.0	12.3	16.7
Wellington Trust Co., N.A.	Boston	MA	U	U	U	87.3	-13.55	0.0	0.0	0.0	0.0	10.0	43.9	45.1
Wells Bank	Platte City	MO	A-	A-	A-	229.0	5.10	3.2	0.7	25.0	10.1	8.3	9.8	14.3
Wells Fargo Bank South Central, N.A.	Houston	TX	A-	B	B-	5594.7	-24.65	0.0	0.0	90.5	0.0	10.0	14.2	29.0
Wells Fargo Bank, Ltd.	Los Angeles	CA	U	U	U	908.9	16.73	0.0	0.0	0.0	0.0	10.0	80.2	54.6
Wells Fargo Bank, N.A.	Sioux Falls	SD	B	B	B-	1708548.0	2.60	11.2	6.5	16.8	24.2	6.7	8.7	14.3
Wells Fargo Delaware Trust Co., N.A.	Wilmington	DE	U	U	U	239.0	-37.06	0.0	0.0	0.0	0.0	10.0	99.3	487.0
Wells Fargo National Bank West	Las Vegas	NV	A-	A-	B+	14785.0	70.11	0.0	0.0	82.6	0.0	8.1	9.7	21.8
Wells Fargo Trust Co., N.A.	Salt Lake City	UT	U	U	B+	1285.3	-1.45	0.0	0.0	0.0	0.9	10.0	93.7	422.3
Wells River Savings Bank	Wells River	VT	C-	D+	C-	184.9	0.90	4.2	5.5	44.4	21.0	9.7	10.8	17.1
Wenona State Bank	Wenona	IL	C+	C+	C+	34.3	1.73	10.3	3.7	5.7	32.6	10.0	14.9	23.1
WesBanco Bank, Inc.	Wheeling	WV	A-	B+	B	12560.4	-0.05	7.9	2.6	16.1	24.6	8.7	10.1	14.6
▲ West Alabama Bank & Trust	Reform	AL	A-	B+	A-	636.1	5.72	7.6	1.7	12.5	29.4	10.0	13.0	19.7
West Bank	West Des Moines	IA	B+	B+	B+	2456.4	13.21	13.2	0.1	2.1	16.7	6.3	9.7	12.0
West Central Bank	Ashland	IL	C+	C	C	182.0	-2.70	12.7	7.5	23.8	8.1	8.8	10.2	14.0
West Central Georgia Bank	Thomaston	GA	A-	A-	A-	119.8	-6.19	2.9	4.3	17.8	48.1	10.0	27.2	59.4
▲ West End Bank, S.B.	Richmond	IN	C	C-	C+	299.2	-2.98	4.1	32.8	20.7	5.1	9.0	10.3	14.4
West Gate Bank	Lincoln	NE	B+	B+	A-	741.0	25.88	11.8	0.2	34.6	4.6	7.9	9.6	13.2
West Iowa Bank	West Bend	IA	A-	B+	A-	135.5	-0.95	7.5	1.3	8.9	21.3	10.0	12.9	19.1
West Michigan Community Bank	Hudsonville	MI	B-	C+	C+	597.9	14.26	23.8	0.7	9.8	7.3	6.0	10.2	11.7
▲ West Plains Bank	Ainsworth	NE	A-	B+	A-	113.8	8.38	16.6	1.8	0.6	15.0	10.0	14.6	17.7
▲ West Plains Bank and Trust Co.	West Plains	MO	A-	B+	A-	386.8	1.92	13.4	3.0	11.2	12.4	10.0	12.2	15.5
▼ West Plains S&L Assn.	West Plains	MO	B-	B	B	82.9	7.24	1.1	1.3	60.0	10.6	10.0	21.7	43.8
▼ West Point Bank	Radcliff	KY	B	B+	B+	295.3	17.32	0.4	1.9	31.2	34.1	6.4	8.4	12.4
West Pointe Bank	Oshkosh	WI	C+	C	C-	283.3	-0.22	13.4	0.2	18.7	12.8	10.0	17.5	20.8
West Shore Bank	Ludington	MI	B-	B-	B-	485.0	7.67	11.4	4.5	20.4	16.4	6.7	8.7	12.7
West Suburban Bank	Lombard	IL	B-	B-	B-	2263.4	1.41	16.2	0.4	6.2	38.8	7.9	9.6	15.5
▲ West Texas National Bank	Midland	TX	A-	B+	B	1306.9	-5.66	27.3	0.7	11.7	31.7	9.5	10.7	16.9
▲ West Texas State Bank	Snyder	TX	B-	C-	D+	133.1	8.55	6.3	3.1	6.5	34.8	10.0	12.5	20.8
▲ West Town Bank & Trust	North Riverside	IL	B-	C	C	275.2	-10.78	31.2	0.0	16.9	4.3	10.0	13.1	16.6
West Union Bank	West Union	WV	B-	C+	C+	191.3	2.03	6.3	9.8	8.1	43.6	7.4	9.3	16.5
West Valley National Bank	Goodyear	AZ	D-	D	D-	76.7	31.88	16.0	0.3	3.9	3.5	8.1	9.7	15.4
▲ West View Savings Bank	Pittsburgh	PA	B-	C+	C+	357.0	2.04	0.1	0.0	22.3	68.6	7.3	9.2	17.4
WestAmerica Bank	San Rafael	CA	B+	B+	B	5589.3	1.77	2.7	4.8	0.6	67.7	5.6	7.6	13.0
Westbury Bank	West Bend	WI	B-	B-	C	853.7	4.47	9.4	0.7	18.8	12.2	7.4	9.6	12.8
Westchester Bank	White Plains	NY	A-	A-	B+	886.2	2.12	29.2	0.6	3.6	8.7	10.0	13.3	16.5
Western Alliance Bank	Phoenix	AZ	A-	A-	A-	26344.7	18.77	18.4	0.1	6.4	15.1	5.8	10.1	11.6
▲ Western Bank	Lordsburg	NM	A-	B+	A-	188.9	9.67	4.3	1.9	6.6	49.4	10.0	12.0	24.9
Western Bank	Lubbock	TX	B-	B-	B	347.8	44.24	13.4	0.9	12.1	17.3	6.2	9.1	11.9
Western Bank of Clovis	Clovis	NM	B+	B+	B+	71.0	2.98	3.3	0.6	2.9	18.0	10.0	14.7	20.6
Western Bank of Wolf Point	Wolf Point	MT	B	B	B+	104.8	8.22	2.7	1.5	4.4	42.6	9.7	10.8	20.4
▲ Western Bank, Artesia, New Mexico	Artesia	NM	C+	C+	B	213.4	7.63	27.3	1.5	1.6	37.0	8.3	9.9	19.6
Western Commerce Bank	Carlsbad	NM	B+	B+	B+	524.6	11.32	12.1	0.5	15.4	27.5	5.5	7.5	17.2
▲ Western Dakota Bank	Timber Lake	SD	C-	D+	D	37.9	2.55	5.0	3.7	0.1	5.1	6.4	8.5	18.2
▲ Western Heritage Bank	Las Cruces	NM	C+	C-	C	254.5	26.19	19.8	1.3	8.9	2.9	8.3	11.3	13.6
▲ Western National Bank	Duluth	MN	C	C	B-	106.7	-3.59	10.1	2.6	20.4	1.6	9.2	10.5	15.4
Western National Bank	Chester	NE	B	B	B	133.4	1.45	8.6	2.4	13.6	0.3	6.5	9.1	12.1
▲ Western National Bank of Cass Lake	Cass Lake	MN	C	C	B-	33.8	-5.48	1.7	2.3	27.7	5.1	6.6	8.6	16.4
Western Nebraska Bank	Curtis	NE	C-	D+	C-	120.4	-0.95	15.0	1.8	7.3	11.0	5.6	10.0	11.4
Western State Bank	Garden City	KS	A-	A	A	466.6	6.85	11.1	0.4	5.6	19.7	10.0	12.7	17.7
▲ Western State Bank	Devils Lake	ND	B	B-	B	1242.7	18.48	40.4	1.3	7.1	4.9	7.7	10.7	13.1
Western States Bank	Laramie	WY	C+	C	B-	473.1	-8.92	10.2	0.9	9.5	11.4	10.0	12.2	17.0
▼ Westfield Bank	Westfield	MA	B-	B	B	2171.2	1.10	10.4	0.2	29.6	10.7	8.0	9.9	13.3
Westfield Bank, FSB	Westfield Center	OH	B	B	B	1493.8	6.48	20.4	11.7	16.8	8.2	8.9	10.3	14.3
Westmoreland Federal S&L Assn.	Latrobe	PA	C+	C+	C+	171.5	2.41	0.0	0.0	37.2	48.9	10.0	24.6	59.9
WestSide Bank	Hiram	GA	C+	C-	D	138.1	8.37	3.5	0.6	7.8	6.2	8.0	9.7	15.8
Westside State Bank	Westside	IA	B-	B-	B-	119.6	11.84	12.1	1.8	23.4	4.3	4.6	7.8	10.8

Arrows denote recent upgrades ▲ or downgrades ▼

Asset Quality Index	Adjusted Non-Performing Loans as a % of Total Loans	Adjusted Non-Performing Loans as a % of Capital	Net Charge-Offs Avg Loans	Profitability Index	Net Income ($Mil)	Return on Assets (R.O.A.)	Return on Equity (R.O.E.)	Net Interest Spread	Overhead Efficiency Ratio	Liquidity Index	Liquidity Ratio	Hot Money Ratio	Stability Index
8.3	0.11	na	0.22	**5.4**	2.6	1.27	9.95	4.33	71.9	**0.7**	10.9	38.3	**9.3**
7.8	0.00	na	-1.47	**9.7**	0.6	2.68	23.73	4.36	49.4	**4.0**	17.2	8.9	**7.7**
8.3	0.19	na	0.00	**4.4**	5.7	0.82	10.15	3.00	63.7	**1.3**	12.8	19.9	**5.4**
7.8	0.13	na	0.21	**4.4**	2.9	1.00	8.14	4.42	74.5	**2.3**	17.6	17.9	**6.5**
10.0	na	na	na	**10.0**	2.3	3.66	8.65	na	98.6	**4.0**	10.6	0.0	**6.7**
7.2	0.58	4.4	0.00	**9.1**	3.7	2.19	22.25	4.39	50.9	**3.3**	6.9	6.7	**7.4**
6.8	1.96	8.3	-0.04	**10.0**	249.2	5.64	44.08	3.76	9.6	**3.7**	3.5	0.0	**8.6**
6.6	na	0.0	na	**9.5**	29.2	4.64	5.68	2.36	91.2	**9.7**	316.8	1.8	**7.0**
5.3	1.29	5.4	0.29	**6.0**	16212.0	1.29	12.92	3.15	60.6	**5.2**	40.2	4.7	**9.2**
10.0	na	0.0	na	**10.0**	6.8	3.43	3.52	2.47	27.2	**4.0**	na	0.0	**7.0**
10.0	0.02	0.2	0.00	**9.5**	233.4	2.14	22.66	2.50	12.0	**4.3**	17.3	0.0	**8.0**
10.0	na	0.0	na	**5.8**	67.0	6.95	7.47	6.05	77.3	**4.0**	na	0.0	**8.1**
5.9	0.56	na	0.06	**2.3**	0.5	0.35	3.24	3.83	88.7	**4.0**	29.9	3.6	**5.6**
5.6	2.21	na	0.18	**3.1**	0.2	0.64	4.43	3.43	76.4	**4.5**	44.5	7.9	**6.4**
6.0	0.52	1.9	0.05	**6.6**	127.8	1.37	8.32	3.70	56.5	**4.3**	12.5	6.3	**9.9**
7.4	1.36	na	0.08	**6.1**	5.8	1.23	8.92	3.57	59.7	**1.8**	32.2	29.9	**8.7**
7.4	0.03	0.2	0.00	**6.5**	22.3	1.26	13.07	3.02	50.3	**2.1**	17.9	12.6	**8.9**
4.1	0.76	na	0.37	**3.9**	1.2	0.86	8.04	4.09	80.1	**1.4**	14.5	26.1	**5.7**
9.3	0.00	na	-0.02	**6.3**	1.2	1.28	5.09	3.79	62.7	**6.2**	75.3	10.8	**8.4**
3.4	0.93	na	0.66	**3.4**	1.2	0.54	5.34	4.15	74.3	**1.1**	6.8	28.6	**5.1**
7.9	0.00	na	0.03	**7.6**	7.7	1.54	15.27	4.94	67.1	**0.7**	7.0	27.5	**7.9**
8.4	0.00	na	0.02	**6.5**	1.3	1.31	10.19	3.73	53.7	**3.9**	20.2	9.7	**7.8**
7.4	0.32	na	-0.01	**5.7**	5.0	1.20	11.89	3.93	61.2	**2.6**	13.3	12.7	**6.5**
6.0	1.97	na	0.15	**8.1**	1.3	1.49	10.30	4.11	51.2	**2.3**	19.2	18.1	**8.8**
7.1	1.00	na	0.01	**7.4**	4.9	1.69	14.01	3.86	61.6	**3.7**	6.8	9.9	**9.1**
6.4	2.17	na	0.00	**3.2**	0.3	0.46	2.10	3.21	65.0	**1.4**	31.8	38.7	**7.7**
7.9	0.30	2.5	-0.03	**4.2**	1.6	0.76	9.14	2.72	66.1	**0.6**	4.4	17.3	**6.0**
3.1	5.87	na	-0.62	**6.5**	2.9	1.37	7.87	3.77	48.7	**0.7**	16.8	54.0	**7.2**
4.9	1.03	5.1	0.06	**3.9**	2.6	0.76	8.32	3.79	84.0	**3.3**	16.4	12.9	**5.3**
5.4	2.07	9.0	-0.02	**4.0**	12.1	0.71	7.47	3.33	73.0	**6.4**	42.3	4.9	**7.8**
8.1	0.65	2.9	1.27	**6.6**	15.3	1.52	14.14	3.97	47.7	**6.4**	45.3	6.0	**9.2**
3.5	5.59	na	0.28	**5.6**	1.5	1.52	12.09	3.73	61.9	**3.5**	33.5	15.5	**6.4**
3.6	2.52	na	0.24	**9.2**	3.4	1.70	13.37	4.70	64.1	**0.7**	13.9	26.1	**8.0**
7.9	0.16	na	-0.03	**4.8**	1.5	1.08	12.19	3.80	64.0	**5.2**	27.7	2.9	**4.6**
8.6	0.05	0.3	0.00	**0.0**	-0.5	-1.00	-9.47	4.60	115.5	**5.2**	37.8	7.8	**4.7**
10.0	0.00	na	0.00	**4.1**	2.2	0.81	9.01	2.11	48.1	**3.8**	40.3	13.0	**5.4**
8.3	0.65	1.1	0.17	**7.2**	60.8	1.46	14.90	3.11	47.8	**7.7**	69.1	1.7	**8.6**
7.6	0.12	0.8	0.00	**4.2**	5.5	0.88	9.19	3.31	66.5	**3.5**	19.0	11.7	**6.4**
7.1	0.13	0.7	0.00	**7.5**	9.9	1.47	11.58	3.93	50.0	**2.5**	12.9	10.4	**8.1**
7.7	0.45	2.3	0.02	**10.0**	374.7	2.04	18.20	4.62	43.0	**3.9**	16.7	6.7	**10.0**
8.0	2.11	na	0.05	**7.7**	3.3	2.39	19.76	4.07	61.8	**6.3**	58.6	7.2	**8.1**
8.5	0.00	na	0.00	**4.9**	2.6	1.21	14.16	4.47	70.6	**0.7**	10.3	31.8	**5.6**
9.1	0.27	0.6	0.00	**5.7**	0.6	1.11	9.19	4.13	61.2	**3.7**	25.3	11.5	**6.8**
8.3	0.16	2.3	0.35	**5.0**	1.0	1.40	12.91	3.19	63.2	**2.7**	44.7	9.4	**7.2**
4.9	2.36	na	-0.03	**9.6**	4.0	2.43	25.35	3.91	37.2	**5.9**	59.9	10.6	**7.8**
9.3	0.34	na	0.00	**8.9**	8.9	2.29	30.92	4.40	44.8	**5.1**	39.2	8.9	**7.0**
8.8	0.00	na	0.03	**3.3**	0.2	0.68	8.42	3.54	78.3	**6.2**	56.9	6.1	**3.3**
7.9	0.21	na	0.05	**3.8**	1.3	0.77	6.22	4.44	76.5	**2.0**	26.0	20.6	**5.9**
2.7	0.46	na	0.81	**3.0**	0.4	0.43	3.44	4.49	76.5	**0.7**	16.7	34.3	**6.5**
6.6	0.01	0.1	0.01	**5.8**	1.3	1.34	12.14	3.53	55.6	**0.6**	11.1	41.1	**7.2**
8.4	0.00	na	-0.05	**3.3**	0.2	0.57	5.99	3.71	85.5	**1.4**	33.5	29.1	**4.3**
3.4	0.72	11.6	1.48	**2.2**	0.1	0.13	1.33	3.69	79.0	**0.6**	5.2	22.7	**5.9**
5.2	1.87	8.5	0.83	**9.4**	7.1	2.07	16.40	4.82	48.5	**2.8**	15.0	15.1	**9.3**
5.3	1.63	na	0.25	**9.2**	14.1	1.59	14.96	4.83	53.1	**1.3**	13.5	20.8	**9.8**
5.1	3.42	na	0.03	**6.5**	4.9	1.39	11.38	3.99	63.0	**2.3**	20.2	18.0	**6.7**
6.2	0.85	5.6	0.04	**3.8**	11.0	0.69	6.72	2.92	68.7	**1.7**	11.5	20.2	**8.3**
4.9	1.02	6.0	0.07	**4.5**	10.6	0.94	8.40	3.27	65.5	**2.4**	13.7	17.4	**8.9**
9.6	1.57	2.3	0.00	**2.1**	0.2	0.17	0.70	1.72	87.7	**5.1**	81.4	17.3	**7.5**
8.9	0.00	na	0.37	**3.7**	0.8	0.74	7.92	5.01	79.4	**3.6**	31.4	14.4	**4.6**
7.0	0.00	na	0.09	**3.7**	0.6	0.67	7.69	3.88	79.6	**1.3**	18.2	24.5	**4.8**

Name	City	State	Rating	2018 Rating	2017 Rating	Total Assets ($Mil)	One Year Asset Growth	Asset Mix (As a % of Total Assets): Commercial Loans	Consumer Loans	Mortgage Loans	Securities	Capitalization Index	Leverage Ratio	Risk-Based Capital Ratio
WestStar Bank	El Paso	TX	**A-**	A-	A-	1863.7	4.17	15.7	0.1	2.7	19.8	**8.1**	11.4	13.4
WEX Bank	Midvale	UT	**B+**	B+	B+	3032.0	0.41	86.0	0.0	0.0	0.0	**7.3**	11.1	12.7
Wheatland Bank	Spokane	WA	**B**	B-	B-	453.5	7.14	5.4	0.4	4.7	6.8	**6.8**	10.4	12.3
Wheaton Bank & Trust Co., N.A.	Wheaton	IL	**B**	B	B-	1984.7	16.74	22.6	18.2	3.8	16.2	**5.5**	9.3	11.4
Wheaton College Trust Co., N.A.	Wheaton	IL	**U**	U	U	3.6	5.38	0.0	0.0	0.0	93.5	**0.0**	95.8	0.0
Wheeler County State Bank	Alamo	GA	**B+**	B+	B+	92.3	0.03	10.3	6.9	15.0	11.2	**10.0**	17.6	27.0
Whitaker Bank, Inc.	Lexington	KY	**B**	B	B-	1168.1	-5.74	3.0	3.0	17.7	34.6	**10.0**	15.0	27.1
White State Bank	South English	IA	**B**	B-	B-	40.1	9.16	11.0	2.2	13.9	27.1	**10.0**	14.4	18.4
Whitesville State Bank	Whitesville	WV	**C+**	B-	B-	110.0	8.71	1.2	15.3	25.3	31.5	**9.0**	10.4	22.3
▲ Wilcox County State Bank	Abbeville	GA	**B-**	C+	B	111.0	4.16	4.4	6.0	35.0	10.6	**10.0**	11.0	17.1
Wilkinson County Bank	Irwinton	GA	**B**	B	B	46.9	0.66	5.9	6.7	43.3	33.0	**10.0**	17.2	35.2
Willamette Community Bank	Albany	OR	**C+**	B-	C+	155.0	10.37	13.2	0.1	2.0	13.1	**9.5**	12.9	14.6
▲ Willamette Valley Bank	Salem	OR	**A-**	B+	A	265.4	12.80	4.3	0.1	32.4	0.0	**10.0**	13.7	17.8
William Penn Bank,	Levittown	PA	**A-**	B+	B+	417.8	2.78	0.5	0.2	53.9	9.0	**10.0**	16.6	25.7
Williamstown Bank, Inc.	Williamstown	WV	**B+**	B+	A-	166.9	2.89	9.4	15.5	36.5	8.2	**10.0**	12.6	18.2
Williamsville State Bank & Trust	Williamsville	IL	**C**	C	C	98.2	-1.73	6.8	3.9	22.7	43.6	**10.0**	13.4	31.1
Wilmington Savings Bank	Wilmington	OH	**B-**	C+	C+	161.9	3.28	1.0	1.5	60.9	5.2	**10.0**	18.0	28.2
Wilmington Savings Fund Society, FSB	Wilmington	DE	**B+**	B+	B+	12254.6	72.62	10.9	3.3	15.1	16.7	**8.2**	11.1	13.5
Wilmington Trust, N.A.	Wilmington	DE	**B-**	B	B	3739.8	1.49	0.0	0.0	1.2	0.2	**10.0**	15.4	66.2
Wilson & Muir Bank & Trust Co.	Bardstown	KY	**B**	B	B	550.1	10.21	9.8	2.4	16.5	28.7	**5.9**	7.9	14.0
Wilson Bank and Trust	Lebanon	TN	**A-**	A-	A-	2741.8	12.22	3.3	1.3	17.9	15.9	**10.0**	12.0	15.3
Wilson State Bank	Wilson	KS	**C+**	C	C	86.9	-1.30	20.3	3.1	22.2	11.8	**6.3**	9.6	12.0
Winchester Co-operative Bank	Winchester	MA	**B**	B	B	683.0	8.77	0.0	0.2	60.1	12.0	**10.0**	13.3	25.6
Winchester Savings Bank	Winchester	MA	**C+**	C+	C+	552.2	1.83	1.0	0.1	53.0	14.1	**10.0**	12.9	20.6
Windsor Federal S&L Assn.	Windsor	CT	**B-**	B-	B-	531.5	7.21	7.6	0.1	26.5	16.3	**10.0**	12.0	16.0
WinFirst Bank	Winchester	KY	**B+**	B+	A-	143.8	7.55	0.5	0.5	55.6	3.5	**10.0**	14.0	22.5
▼ Winnsboro State Bank & Trust Co.	Winnsboro	LA	**C**	C+	B-	227.5	17.32	4.9	3.2	14.2	8.5	**7.6**	9.4	13.6
Winter Hill Bank, FSB	Somerville	MA	**C**	C	C	366.5	0.92	0.0	0.3	50.2	9.6	**7.8**	9.6	15.1
Winter Park National Bank	Winter Park	FL	**B**	C		342.5	50.76	12.2	0.2	0.8	30.8	**10.0**	12.8	21.0
Wintrust Bank, N.A.	Chicago	IL	**B**	B	B-	6444.8	15.49	36.1	6.5	5.7	5.2	**6.0**	10.4	11.8
Wisconsin Bank & Trust	Madison	WI	**B+**	B+	B	1032.0	-1.82	18.2	1.2	6.5	14.5	**9.3**	10.9	14.4
▲ Wisconsin River Bank	Sauk City	WI	**B**	B-	B+	141.9	14.61	3.6	0.4	28.8	7.8	**8.9**	10.2	15.3
WNB Financial, N.A.	Winona	MN	**B+**	B+	B+	417.5	39.13	7.3	1.8	16.7	30.1	**9.7**	10.8	16.4
▲ Wolf River Community Bank	Hortonville	WI	**A-**	A-	A-	197.7	11.28	10.5	2.0	26.0	12.5	**10.0**	12.3	16.8
▲ Wood & Huston Bank	Marshall	MO	**A-**	B+	A-	733.4	3.20	11.4	1.8	16.4	18.1	**10.0**	11.9	15.3
▲ Woodford State Bank	Monroe	WI	**B+**	B	B	246.2	9.41	8.2	0.8	13.9	21.5	**6.9**	8.9	12.6
Woodforest National Bank	The Woodlands	TX	**B+**	B+	A-	6307.6	8.00	30.1	1.0	9.6	16.0	**7.4**	9.7	12.8
Woodland Bank	Grand Rapids	MN	**B-**	B	B	107.8	7.85	14.2	5.4	24.4	4.6	**9.9**	11.0	15.2
Woodlands Bank	Williamsport	PA	**B-**	B-	B-	424.3	4.90	9.6	0.3	27.0	16.4	**9.4**	10.6	14.8
▲ Woodlands National Bank	Onamia	MN	**A-**	B+	A-	206.1	3.29	17.1	4.7	6.3	23.0	**10.0**	11.9	16.9
Woodruff Federal S&L Assn.	Woodruff	SC	**B-**	C+	C+	94.7	6.87	0.0	0.0	47.8	3.4	**10.0**	33.4	70.1
Woodsboro Bank	Woodsboro	MD	**C**	C	C	260.3	3.29	6.4	0.5	19.0	31.1	**6.7**	8.7	14.3
▲ Woodsfield Savings Bank	Woodsfield	OH	**C-**	C-	C-	69.0	9.09	3.2	8.3	35.7	19.0	**6.1**	8.1	17.2
Woodsville Guaranty Savings Bank	Woodsville	NH	**C+**	C+	C+	506.3	0.44	7.0	1.8	47.2	13.3	**7.5**	9.4	17.1
WoodTrust Bank	Wisconsin Rapids	WI	**B-**	B-	B-	418.0	6.11	11.6	0.9	8.4	21.1	**10.0**	11.6	15.1
Woori America Bank	New York	NY	**B+**	A-	B+	2053.2	3.34	7.5	0.1	17.6	10.1	**10.0**	13.9	17.4
Worthington Federal Savings Bank, FSB	Worthington	MN	**B**	B	B	77.7	3.95	0.8	2.7	64.2	11.4	**10.0**	16.4	39.6
Worthington National Bank	Arlington	TX	**B**	B-	B-	293.1	9.07	10.4	1.5	24.6	4.4	**9.1**	10.4	15.5
Wray State Bank	Wray	CO	**D+**	D+	C-	152.4	-2.89	8.9	3.4	9.9	7.9	**8.3**	10.2	13.6
Wrentham Co-operative Bank	Wrentham	MA	**C+**	C+	C+	115.0	-1.11	0.1	2.0	57.6	3.8	**10.0**	14.2	31.4
WSB Municipal Bank	Watertown	NY	**U**	U	U	109.3	-4.82	0.0	0.0	0.0	81.1	**10.0**	12.9	74.5
▲ Wyoming Bank & Trust	Cheyenne	WY	**A**	A-	A	218.1	3.41	4.1	2.6	6.6	32.1	**10.0**	11.7	17.4
Wyoming Community Bank	Riverton	WY	**B**	B	B	150.3	1.53	8.0	4.9	9.0	29.2	**8.1**	9.7	15.7
Yakima Federal S&L Assn.	Yakima	WA	**A-**	A-	B+	1802.6	1.42	0.0	0.0	35.8	41.6	**10.0**	25.8	69.0
▲ Yampa Valley Bank	Steamboat Springs	CO	**B+**	B-	B	319.2	5.86	6.7	2.1	19.5	13.7	**7.0**	9.7	12.5
▲ Yellowstone Bank	Laurel	MT	**A**	A	A	780.1	7.15	10.2	1.0	10.8	15.5	**10.0**	18.5	25.1
▲ YNB	Yukon	OK	**C+**	C	C-	231.6	3.74	3.5	4.5	19.8	23.2	**5.4**	7.4	11.5
Yoakum National Bank	Yoakum	TX	**A-**	A-	A-	220.5	0.44	6.7	5.7	18.1	43.7	**10.0**	14.7	32.3
▲ York State Bank	York	NE	**C+**	C	B-	149.0	-0.75	9.1	2.2	4.6	7.6	**9.1**	10.8	14.3
▲ York Traditions Bank	York	PA	**B**	B-	B-	538.5	15.68	12.4	0.1	21.9	12.6	**9.1**	10.4	15.3

Arrows denote recent upgrades ▲ or downgrades ▼

Asset Quality Index	Adjusted Non-Performing Loans as a % of Total Loans	Adjusted Non-Performing Loans as a % of Capital	Net Charge-Offs Avg Loans	Profitability Index	Net Income ($Mil)	Return on Assets (R.O.A.)	Return on Equity (R.O.E.)	Net Interest Spread	Overhead Efficiency Ratio	Liquidity Index	Liquidity Ratio	Hot Money Ratio	Stability Index
6.6	0.40	na	-0.04	**9.8**	37.0	2.62	20.30	4.32	47.0	**4.0**	20.8	10.2	**10.0**
5.4	0.03	7.5	1.33	**10.0**	200.4	8.96	82.01	21.48	63.5	**0.6**	10.9	1.6	**9.2**
7.4	0.08	na	-0.01	**6.1**	3.9	1.19	11.56	4.94	72.5	**4.7**	14.2	3.8	**6.5**
6.5	0.41	2.1	0.60	**6.2**	16.1	1.18	9.72	3.46	43.5	**2.3**	11.9	12.2	**8.5**
10.0	na	na	na	**9.2**	0.1	3.47	3.68	2.39	85.2	**4.0**	na	0.0	**0.0**
7.0	0.99	na	-0.30	**5.0**	0.8	1.12	6.45	4.41	74.9	**2.2**	26.5	19.6	**8.2**
3.9	5.80	14.9	0.14	**4.6**	9.2	1.04	6.63	3.84	76.7	**5.3**	31.7	8.9	**7.9**
7.9	0.00	na	0.00	**8.0**	0.4	1.52	9.12	3.67	46.3	**3.8**	39.3	15.7	**7.0**
6.4	0.67	2.8	0.35	**3.4**	0.5	0.62	6.06	3.99	84.8	**3.5**	50.8	19.6	**5.1**
4.4	2.20	na	0.09	**6.9**	1.0	1.26	11.81	4.61	64.5	**1.1**	10.7	29.1	**7.0**
8.0	2.52	na	0.22	**6.5**	0.4	1.18	7.22	4.50	65.1	**3.6**	16.0	11.1	**7.6**
3.4	1.32	na	0.00	**3.2**	0.5	0.47	3.64	4.37	82.9	**4.3**	10.9	6.2	**6.6**
7.7	0.00	na	-0.01	**10.0**	8.9	4.68	38.04	4.13	70.0	**0.6**	8.6	31.7	**8.9**
7.2	0.95	na	0.00	**5.2**	3.3	1.08	5.99	3.62	64.0	**1.8**	16.8	20.4	**8.0**
6.8	0.39	na	0.07	**5.3**	1.2	0.96	7.64	4.45	72.2	**3.9**	16.1	9.8	**7.5**
6.0	4.96	na	0.31	**2.1**	0.2	0.24	1.74	2.98	91.7	**5.8**	56.3	8.0	**6.4**
5.3	6.05	na	-0.05	**3.2**	0.7	0.62	3.30	2.94	74.4	**1.8**	19.2	21.4	**6.7**
5.5	0.78	3.8	0.27	**6.5**	95.8	1.14	7.75	4.38	70.7	**4.0**	13.3	6.3	**9.9**
10.0	4.64	0.9	0.17	**4.1**	8.6	0.30	1.98	4.90	95.7	**8.8**	109.8	0.1	**8.0**
4.9	1.65	9.2	0.06	**9.1**	8.9	2.22	26.39	4.35	51.1	**5.4**	33.2	4.2	**7.1**
7.5	0.18	1.3	0.01	**7.6**	28.7	1.44	12.33	3.64	57.5	**2.7**	16.4	16.1	**9.8**
4.0	0.71	4.8	0.10	**4.8**	0.7	1.12	10.90	4.19	68.9	**1.6**	6.3	19.2	**6.2**
7.5	0.36	na	0.00	**3.8**	3.1	0.64	4.79	2.42	65.0	**1.2**	27.8	36.4	**7.9**
9.3	0.35	na	0.00	**2.8**	1.6	0.38	3.11	2.67	81.7	**1.5**	23.9	27.3	**7.2**
5.6	2.31	8.5	0.00	**3.8**	3.0	0.76	6.48	3.42	73.9	**3.3**	20.8	13.1	**7.5**
7.3	1.15	na	0.00	**5.1**	1.2	1.19	8.49	3.32	64.1	**0.7**	13.4	40.1	**8.5**
2.6	1.61	17.3	0.26	**4.1**	1.3	0.84	9.08	4.11	75.5	**1.0**	16.0	32.1	**5.3**
9.0	0.25	na	0.00	**2.6**	1.1	0.40	4.31	3.08	87.3	**1.3**	14.2	16.6	**5.5**
9.0	0.00	na	0.00	**4.8**	3.0	1.35	9.66	3.02	47.2	**6.5**	45.4	1.9	**5.8**
6.3	0.46	2.7	0.06	**8.8**	74.9	1.68	15.36	3.67	51.7	**2.3**	13.6	11.8	**8.2**
4.8	1.61	6.4	0.10	**6.8**	10.4	1.34	9.98	4.16	62.4	**4.4**	20.4	5.8	**8.5**
6.0	1.20	na	0.00	**5.1**	1.0	0.97	9.08	3.48	55.3	**0.7**	14.5	39.8	**7.0**
7.2	0.71	na	0.10	**4.8**	3.9	1.26	10.09	3.90	74.6	**4.4**	27.0	8.5	**7.9**
7.2	0.79	na	0.00	**5.7**	1.6	1.14	9.29	4.21	64.9	**3.5**	13.3	11.2	**7.7**
8.5	0.14	na	0.08	**7.5**	8.7	1.61	13.80	3.78	63.4	**2.0**	9.1	18.3	**9.4**
7.7	0.24	na	0.00	**7.7**	3.2	1.82	19.95	3.98	57.4	**3.1**	25.1	14.7	**7.6**
5.3	1.30	7.0	0.46	**8.9**	107.6	2.30	24.50	3.93	78.2	**6.4**	31.1	1.1	**8.9**
5.1	1.50	na	0.01	**4.7**	0.6	0.81	7.40	4.62	76.4	**1.4**	11.2	22.1	**6.9**
4.3	2.47	na	-0.24	**6.5**	4.4	1.42	13.85	3.88	65.5	**4.1**	13.9	8.1	**6.6**
6.3	0.61	1.8	0.06	**6.6**	1.9	1.28	9.64	4.08	61.3	**2.4**	38.4	3.7	**7.9**
8.1	3.20	na	0.00	**3.7**	0.5	0.74	2.19	2.87	67.5	**2.1**	44.7	41.1	**7.5**
7.3	0.61	na	-0.02	**3.2**	1.0	0.50	5.72	3.57	83.6	**4.5**	35.8	11.2	**5.0**
4.5	1.75	na	-0.01	**2.6**	0.2	0.40	4.89	3.47	82.9	**5.1**	40.4	9.5	**3.9**
7.6	0.24	na	0.05	**3.7**	2.9	0.77	8.27	3.47	75.6	**3.3**	15.3	10.3	**6.3**
5.7	2.02	na	-0.07	**10.0**	10.5	3.46	30.70	3.67	42.4	**5.3**	28.4	2.8	**7.7**
7.4	0.05	na	0.04	**4.8**	14.5	0.96	7.07	3.35	65.7	**1.1**	16.8	25.1	**9.4**
9.6	0.38	1.6	0.00	**4.3**	0.5	0.78	4.80	3.24	64.2	**4.3**	34.1	11.7	**8.0**
8.6	0.04	na	0.00	**4.9**	2.2	1.03	10.41	4.24	69.8	**1.8**	24.5	22.4	**6.5**
1.5	3.70	na	0.28	**5.8**	1.3	1.10	10.00	4.58	63.2	**1.3**	6.0	24.4	**6.6**
9.8	0.43	na	0.00	**2.7**	0.4	0.43	3.04	2.81	81.9	**3.9**	34.6	14.0	**7.2**
10.0	na	na	na	**5.9**	1.1	1.31	11.10	1.74	3.1	**5.1**	26.3	3.5	**6.7**
8.7	0.01	na	0.08	**9.6**	4.0	2.76	23.31	3.83	80.5	**5.7**	44.8	4.6	**8.8**
7.5	0.62	2.3	-0.01	**4.8**	1.2	1.07	11.16	3.99	75.0	**3.0**	28.6	16.0	**6.7**
10.0	0.24	na	0.00	**5.7**	16.8	1.25	4.93	2.57	43.7	**3.8**	74.7	32.5	**10.0**
7.0	0.19	na	-0.13	**10.0**	5.8	2.43	25.44	4.80	51.7	**3.7**	17.3	10.9	**8.1**
7.2	0.53	na	-0.01	**10.0**	16.4	2.91	15.44	4.72	39.3	**4.5**	24.0	6.6	**10.0**
7.8	0.08	na	0.03	**3.4**	1.3	0.75	10.15	3.78	80.8	**2.1**	13.3	18.6	**4.4**
8.9	0.04	0.1	-0.01	**5.7**	2.3	1.40	9.77	2.87	52.5	**3.1**	47.9	24.3	**8.6**
5.3	0.19	na	0.04	**5.6**	1.3	1.16	8.67	3.87	62.5	**2.4**	10.5	14.4	**7.9**
6.8	0.66	na	0.03	**5.2**	4.1	1.08	10.23	3.59	69.8	**2.8**	12.4	12.7	**6.7**

Name	City	State	Rating	2018 Rating	2017 Rating	Total Assets ($Mil)	One Year Asset Growth	Asset Mix (As a % of Total Assets) Comm-ercial Loans	Cons-umer Loans	Mort-gage Loans	Secur-ities	Capital-ization Index	Lever-age Ratio	Risk-Based Capital Ratio
Yorktown Bank	Pryor	OK	**B-**	B-	B-	118.5	26.47	14.5	1.6	21.9	0.1	**9.1**	10.4	16.6
Young Americans Bank	Denver	CO	**D-**	D-	D-	20.5	2.62	0.0	0.4	0.0	0.5	**5.1**	7.1	242.0
▲ Zapata National Bank	Zapata	TX	**B**	B-	B	81.2	-0.31	6.3	5.6	18.0	30.9	**10.0**	14.1	41.2
Zavala County Bank	Crystal City	TX	**B+**	B+	B+	69.2	10.37	1.7	4.7	0.3	63.6	**10.0**	14.6	53.2
Zions BanCorp., N.A.	Salt Lake City	UT	**A-**	A-	B+	70360.8	5.44	17.9	0.9	11.2	20.9	**7.1**	9.3	12.6

Asset Quality Index	Adjusted Non-Performing Loans as a % of Total Loans	Adjusted Non-Performing Loans as a % of Capital	Net Charge-Offs Avg Loans	Profitability Index	Net Income ($Mil)	Return on Assets (R.O.A.)	Return on Equity (R.O.E.)	Net Interest Spread	Overhead Efficiency Ratio	Liquidity Index	Liquidity Ratio	Hot Money Ratio	Stability Index
7.6	0.00	na	-0.02	**4.6**	0.8	0.89	6.69	3.79	67.7	**1.6**	30.6	32.2	**7.4**
10.0	0.00	na	4.94	**0.0**	-0.9	-6.12	-80.19	2.46	345.3	**8.1**	106.0	0.5	**0.8**
4.7	8.55	na	0.00	**5.8**	0.8	1.26	9.08	3.17	65.0	**1.7**	36.2	43.2	**8.7**
9.4	0.07	na	0.06	**4.4**	0.6	1.14	8.30	3.10	72.2	**5.7**	75.2	12.1	**7.1**
6.8	0.65	3.4	0.04	**6.4**	632.6	1.21	11.13	3.53	59.9	**4.9**	24.7	2.8	**10.0**

Section II

Weiss Recommended Banks by State

A compilation of those

U.S. Commercial Banks and Savings Banks

receiving a Weiss Safety Rating
of A+, A, A-, or B+.

Institutions are ranked by Safety Rating
in each state where they have a branch location.

Section II Contents

This section provides a list of Weiss Recommended Banks by State and contains all financial institutions receiving a Safety Rating of A+, A, A-, or B+. Recommended institutions are listed in each state in which they currently operate one or more branches. If a company is not on this list, it should not be automatically assumed that the firm is weak. Indeed, there are many firms that have not achieved a B+ or better rating but are in good condition with adequate resources to weather an average recession. Not being included in this list should not be construed as a recommendation to immediately withdraw deposits or cancel existing financial arrangements.

Institutions are ranked within each state by their Weiss Safety Rating, and then listed alphabetically by name. Institutions with the same rating should be viewed as having the same relative safety regardless of their ranking in this table.

- **State** The state in which the institution currently operates one or more branches. With the adoption of interstate branching laws, some institutions operating in your area may actually be headquartered in another state. Even so, there are no restrictions on your ability to do business with an out-of-state institution.

- **Institution Name** The name under which the institution was chartered. A bank's name can be very similar to, or the same as, the name of other banks which may not be on our Recommended List, so make sure you note the exact name.

- **Telephone** The telephone number for the institution's headquarters, or main office.

- **Safety Rating** Weiss rating assigned to the institution at the time of publication. Our ratings are designed to distinguish levels of insolvency risk and are measured on a scale from A to F based upon a wide range of factors. Highly rated companies are, in our opinion, less likely to experience financial difficulties than lower rated firms. See *About Weiss Safety Ratings* for more information and a description of what each rating means.

Weiss Safety Ratings are not deemed to be a recommendation concerning the purchase or sale of the securities of any bank that is publicly owned.

Alabama

Name	Telephone
Rating: A+	
First Bank of Boaz	(256) 593-8670
Rating: A	
Cheaha Bank	(256) 835-8855
Citizens Bank of Winfield	(205) 487-4277
First Metro Bank	(256) 386-0600
First National Bank	(205) 921-7435
Metro City Bank	(770) 455-4989
Rating: A-	
Armed Forces Bank, N.A.	(913) 682-9090
AuburnBank	(334) 821-9200
Bank of Vernon	(205) 695-7141
Bank OZK	(501) 978-2265
BankSouth	(334) 677-2265
Bryant Bank	(205) 464-4646
Central State Bank	(205) 668-0711
Citizens Bank	(334) 624-8888
Citizens Bank & Trust, Inc.	(706) 657-5678
Community Neighbor Bank	(334) 682-4215
Cullman Savings Bank	(256) 734-1740
Farmers and Merchants Bank	(334) 864-9941
First Bank of Alabama	(256) 362-2334
First Citizens Bank	(334) 335-3346
First Jackson Bank, Inc.	(256) 437-2107
First National Bank of Pulaski	(931) 363-2585
FirstState Bank	(256) 396-2187
HNB First Bank	(334) 693-3352
HomeTown Bank of Alabama	(205) 625-4434
Metro Bank	(205) 884-2265
Oakworth Capital Bank	(205) 263-4700
Pinnacle Bank	(205) 221-4111
Renasant Bank	(800) 680-1601
Robertson Banking Co.	(334) 289-3564
Samson Banking Co., Inc.	(334) 898-7107
ServisFirst Bank	(205) 949-0302
West Alabama Bank & Trust	(205) 375-6261
Rating: B+	
Ameris Bank	(404) 814-8114
BancorpSouth Bank	(662) 680-2000
Branch Banking and Trust Co.	(336) 776-5342
Brantley Bank and Trust Co.	(334) 527-3206
Cadence Bank, N.A.	(800) 636-7622
CCB Community Bank	(334) 222-2561
Centennial Bank	(501) 328-4663
CenterState Bank, N.A.	(863) 293-4710
Citizens Bank of Fayette	(205) 932-8911
Citizens Trust Bank	(678) 406-4000
Exchange Bank of Alabama	(205) 589-6334
Farmers & Merchants Bank	(256) 766-2579
Farmers & Merchants Bank	(256) 447-9041
First Bank	(256) 395-2255
First Community Bank of Central Alabama	(334) 567-0081
First Southern State Bank	(256) 437-2171
First State Bank of the South, Inc.	(205) 698-8116
First, A National Banking Assn.	(601) 268-8998
FirstBank	(615) 313-0080
JPMorgan Chase Bank, N.A.	(614) 248-5800
MidSouth Bank	(334) 702-7774
River Bank & Trust	(334) 290-1012
Southern Independent Bank	(334) 493-2265
Synovus Bank	(706) 649-4900
Town-Country National Bank	(334) 682-4155
Troy Bank & Trust Co.	(334) 566-4000
Trustmark National Bank	(601) 208-5111
Woodforest National Bank	(832) 375-2505

Alaska

Name	Telephone
Rating: A	
First National Bank Alaska	(907) 777-4362
Rating: A-	
Mt. McKinley Bank	(907) 452-1751

Arizona

Rating: A-

Name	Telephone
Academy Bank, N.A.	(816) 472-0081
Alerus Financial, N.A.	(701) 795-3200
Armed Forces Bank, N.A.	(913) 682-9090
Comerica Bank	(214) 462-4000
First Savings Bank	(605) 763-2009
FirstBank	(303) 232-2000
Gateway Commercial Bank	(480) 358-1000
Glacier Bank	(406) 756-4200
Johnson Bank	(262) 619-2700
KS StateBank	(785) 587-4000
Metro Phoenix Bank	(602) 346-1800
Pacific Premier Bank	(949) 864-8000
Stearns Bank N.A.	(320) 253-6607
Washington Federal Bank, N.A.	(206) 204-3446
Western Alliance Bank	(602) 389-3500
Western Bank	(575) 542-3521
Zions BanCorp., N.A.	(801) 844-7637

Rating: B+

Name	Telephone
Arizona Bank & Trust	(602) 381-2090
Bank of America, N.A.	(704) 386-5681
Bell Bank	(701) 298-1500
Enterprise Bank & Trust	(314) 725-5500
First National Bank Texas	(254) 554-4236
First-Citizens Bank & Trust Co.	(919) 716-7050
JPMorgan Chase Bank, N.A.	(614) 248-5800
Northern Trust Co.	(312) 630-6000
Republic Bank of Arizona	(602) 277-2500
Sunwest Bank	(714) 730-4444
TCF National Bank	(952) 745-2760

Arkansas

Name	Telephone
Rating: A+	
First Security Bank	(501) 279-3400
Rating: A	
First National Bank of Izard County	(870) 297-3711
FSNB, N.A.	(580) 357-9880
Peoples Bank	(870) 942-5707
Rating: A-	
Bank of Delight	(870) 379-2293
Bank OZK	(501) 978-2265
Citizens Bank & Trust Co.	(479) 474-1201
Fidelity Bank	(870) 735-8700
First National Bank	(870) 215-4000
First National Bank of Fort Smith	(479) 782-2041
First State Bank	(479) 498-2400
Great Southern Bank	(417) 895-5234
McGehee Bank	(870) 222-3151
Petit Jean State Bank	(501) 354-4988
Premier Bank of Arkansas	(870) 739-7300
Rating: B+	
BancorpSouth Bank	(662) 680-2000
Bank of America, N.A.	(704) 386-5681
Bank of England	(501) 842-2555
Bank of Lake Village	(870) 265-2241
Bank of Salem	(870) 895-2591
Centennial Bank	(501) 328-4663
Commercial National Bank of Texarkana	(903) 831-4561
Connect Bank	(870) 628-4286
Cross County Bank	(870) 238-8171
Farmers & Merchants Bank	(870) 673-6911
Farmers Bank	(479) 996-4171
FBT Bank & Mortgage	(870) 352-3107
First Financial Bank	(870) 863-7000
First Missouri Bank of SEMO	(573) 717-7177
First National Bank at Paris	(479) 963-2121
First National Bank of Eastern Arkansas	(870) 633-3112
First National Bank of Lawrence County	(870) 886-5959
First National Bank Texas	(254) 554-4236
First State Bank of DeQueen	(870) 642-4423
Focus Bank	(573) 683-3712
Logan County Bank	(479) 938-2511
Simmons Bank	(870) 541-1000
Southern Bank	(573) 778-1800
United Bank	(479) 756-8811

California

Rating: A

Name	Telephone
Bank of Stockton	(209) 929-1600
California First National Bank	(800) 735-2465
California Pacific Bank	(415) 399-8000
Central Valley Community Bank	(559) 298-1775
Exchange Bank	(707) 524-3000
Pacific City Bank	(213) 210-2000
Poppy Bank	(707) 636-9000
Royal Business Bank	(213) 627-9888
Santa Cruz County Bank	(831) 457-5000
Savings Bank of Mendocino County	(707) 462-6613
Tri Counties Bank	(530) 898-0300
Wallis Bank	(979) 478-6151

Rating: A-

Name	Telephone
American Continental Bank	(626) 363-8988
American First National Bank	(713) 596-2888
American Plus Bank, N.A.	(626) 821-9188
Armed Forces Bank, N.A.	(913) 682-9090
Axos Bank	(858) 350-6200
Bank of America California, N.A.	(925) 988-4801
Bank of Marin	(415) 763-4520
Bank of San Francisco	(415) 744-6700
Bank of the Sierra	(559) 782-4900
Cathay Bank	(213) 625-4791
Citizens Business Bank	(909) 980-4030
Comerica Bank	(214) 462-4000
Commonwealth Business Bank	(323) 988-3000
Community Bank of Santa Maria	(805) 922-2900
Community Valley Bank	(760) 352-7777
CTBC Bank Corp. (USA)	(424) 277-4612
East West Bank	(626) 768-6000
EverTrust Bank	(626) 993-3800
Farmers & Merchants Bank	(209) 367-2300
Farmers & Merchants Bank of Long Beach	(562) 437-0011
First Choice Bank	(562) 345-9092
First Commercial Bank (USA)	(626) 300-6000
First General Bank	(626) 820-1234
First Northern Bank of Dixon	(707) 678-3041
FirstBank	(303) 232-2000
Golden Bank, N.A.	(713) 777-3838
Heritage Bank of Commerce	(408) 947-6900
Home Bank of California	(858) 270-5881
Malaga Bank F.S.B.	(310) 375-9000
New OMNI Bank, N.A.	(626) 284-5555
Open Bank	(213) 892-9999
Pacific Premier Bank	(949) 864-8000
Premier Valley Bank	(559) 438-2002
Silicon Valley Bank	(408) 654-7400
Silvergate Bank	(858) 362-6300
Sterling Bank and Trust, FSB	(248) 355-2400
Summit Bank	(510) 839-8800
United Business Bank	(925) 476-1800
Western Alliance Bank	(602) 389-3500
Zions BanCorp., N.A.	(801) 844-7637

Rating: B+

Name	Telephone
1st Capital Bank	(831) 264-4000
Avidbank	(408) 200-7390
Bank of America, N.A.	(704) 386-5681
Bank of Feather River	(530) 755-3700
Bank of Hemet	(951) 248-2000
Bank of Santa Clarita	(661) 362-6000
Banner Bank	(509) 527-3636
C3bank, N.A.	(760) 759-1130
Chino Commercial Bank, N.A.	(909) 393-8880
CIT Bank, N.A.	(855) 462-2652
Citibank, N.A.	(605) 370-6261
City National Bank	(800) 773-7100
CommerceWest Bank	(949) 251-6959
Community Commerce Bank	(909) 450-2050
First Bank	(314) 995-8700
First-Citizens Bank & Trust Co.	(919) 716-7050
Flagstar Bank, FSB	(248) 312-5400
Fremont Bank	(510) 505-5226
Fresno First Bank	(559) 439-0200
Golden Valley Bank	(530) 894-1000
Habib American Bank	(212) 532-4444
Hanmi Bank	(213) 382-2200
International City Bank	(562) 436-9800
Israel Discount Bank of New York	(212) 551-8500
JPMorgan Chase Bank, N.A.	(614) 248-5800
Mission Bank	(661) 859-2500
Mission National Bank	(415) 826-3627
Mission Valley Bank	(818) 394-2300
Montecito Bank & Trust	(805) 564-0256
Murphy Bank	(559) 225-0225
Northern California National Bank	(530) 879-5900
Northern Trust Co.	(312) 630-6000
Oak Valley Community Bank	(209) 844-7500
Pacific Alliance Bank	(626) 773-8888
Pacific Coast Bankers' Bank	(415) 399-1900
Pacific Western Bank	(310) 887-8500
Pinnacle Bank	(408) 842-8200

California

Name	Telephone
Preferred Bank	(213) 891-1188
River City Bank	(916) 567-2600
Signature Bank	(646) 822-1500
Southwestern National Bank	(713) 771-9700
State Bank of India (California)	(213) 225-5700
Suncrest Bank	(559) 802-1000
Sunwest Bank	(714) 730-4444
Umpqua Bank	(541) 440-3961
United Security Bank	(559) 248-4944
US Metro Bank	(714) 620-8888
Valley Republic Bank	(661) 371-2000
WestAmerica Bank	(415) 257-8057
Woori America Bank	(212) 244-1500

Colorado

Rating: A

Name	Telephone
Commerce Bank	(816) 234-2000
Farmers Bank	(970) 834-2121
First National Bank of Las Animas	(719) 456-1512
North Valley Bank	(303) 452-5500

Rating: A-

Name	Telephone
5Star Bank	(719) 574-2777
Academy Bank, N.A.	(816) 472-0081
Alamosa State Bank	(719) 589-2564
Alpine Bank	(970) 945-2424
AMG National Trust Bank	(303) 694-2190
Armed Forces Bank, N.A.	(913) 682-9090
Bank of Colorado	(970) 206-1160
Bank of Estes Park	(970) 586-4485
Bankers' Bank of the West	(303) 291-3700
Champion Bank	(303) 840-8484
Community State Bank	(719) 336-3272
Dolores State Bank	(970) 882-7600
Eastern Colorado Bank	(719) 767-5652
Farmers State Bank of Brush	(970) 842-5101
First National Bank	(605) 223-2521
First National Bank of Hugo	(719) 743-2415
First Pioneer National Bank	(970) 332-4824
First State Bank	(308) 632-4158
FirstBank	(303) 232-2000
FirsTier Bank	(308) 235-4633
FirstOak Bank	(620) 331-2265
Frontier Bank	(719) 336-4351
Glacier Bank	(406) 756-4200
Gunnison Bank and Trust Co.	(970) 641-0320
High Country Bank	(719) 539-2516
High Plains Bank	(719) 765-4000
Points West Community Bank	(970) 686-0878
Redstone Bank	(720) 880-5000
Solera National Bank	(303) 209-8600
United Business Bank	(925) 476-1800
Verus Bank of Commerce	(970) 204-1010
Waypoint Bank	(308) 784-2515
Zions BanCorp., N.A.	(801) 844-7637

Rating: B+

Name	Telephone
Adams Bank & Trust	(308) 284-4071
ANB Bank	(303) 394-5143
Bank of America, N.A.	(704) 386-5681
Bank of Burlington	(719) 346-5376
Central Trust Bank	(573) 634-1302
Citywide Banks	(303) 365-3800
Colorado Bank and Trust Co. of La Junta	(719) 384-8131
First-Citizens Bank & Trust Co.	(919) 716-7050
FNB Bank	(785) 890-2000
Grand Valley Bank	(435) 654-7400
Independent Bank	(972) 562-9004
JPMorgan Chase Bank, N.A.	(614) 248-5800
Legacy Bank	(719) 829-4811
Northern Trust Co.	(312) 630-6000
Pacific Western Bank	(310) 887-8500
Pueblo Bank and Trust Co.	(719) 545-1834
Simmons Bank	(870) 541-1000
TCF National Bank	(952) 745-2760
United Fidelity Bank, FSB	(812) 424-0921
Yampa Valley Bank	(970) 879-2993

Connecticut

Name	Telephone
Rating: A	
Bessemer Trust Co., N.A.	(212) 708-9100
Rating: A-	
Chelsea Groton Bank	(860) 823-4800
Liberty Bank	(860) 638-2922
Savings Bank of Danbury	(203) 743-3849
Rating: B+	
Bank of America, N.A.	(704) 386-5681
Citibank, N.A.	(605) 370-6261
JPMorgan Chase Bank, N.A.	(614) 248-5800
Northern Trust Co.	(312) 630-6000
Signature Bank	(646) 822-1500
Stafford Savings Bank	(860) 684-4261
Union Savings Bank	(203) 830-4200
Washington Trust Co. of Westerly	(401) 348-1200

Delaware

Name	Telephone
Rating: A+	
Deutsche Bank Trust Co. Delaware	(302) 636-3301
Rating: A	
Applied Bank	(888) 839-7952
Calvin B. Taylor Banking Co.	(410) 641-1700
FSNB, N.A.	(580) 357-9880
Morgan Stanley Private Bank, N.A.	(212) 762-1803
Rating: A-	
Bank of Ocean City	(410) 213-0173
Rating: B+	
Bank of America, N.A.	(704) 386-5681
Bryn Mawr Trust Co.	(610) 581-4839
Citibank, N.A.	(605) 370-6261
JPMorgan Chase Bank, N.A.	(614) 248-5800
Shore United Bank	(410) 822-1400
Wilmington Savings Fund Society, FSB	(302) 792-6000

District of Columbia

Name	Telephone
Rating: A	
EagleBank	(240) 497-2075
Rating: B+	
Bank of America, N.A.	(704) 386-5681
Branch Banking and Trust Co.	(336) 776-5342
Citibank, N.A.	(605) 370-6261
City National Bank	(800) 773-7100
FVCbank	(703) 436-4740
John Marshall Bank	(703) 584-0840
JPMorgan Chase Bank, N.A.	(614) 248-5800
Northern Trust Co.	(312) 630-6000

Federated States of Micronesia

Name	Telephone
Rating: A-	
Bank of the Federated States of Micronesia	

Florida

Name	Telephone
Rating: A	
Citizens First Bank	(352) 753-9515
Hillsboro Bank	(813) 707-6506
Metro City Bank	(770) 455-4989
Paradise Bank	(561) 392-5444
Southeastern Bank	(912) 437-4141
Rating: A-	
1st Source Bank	(574) 235-2000
Armed Forces Bank, N.A.	(913) 682-9090
Bank OZK	(501) 978-2265
Busey Bank	(217) 351-6500
Charlotte State Bank & Trust	(941) 624-5400
Comerica Bank	(214) 462-4000
Commerce National Bank & Trust	(407) 622-8181
Crews Bank & Trust	(863) 494-2220
Drummond Community Bank	(352) 493-2277
Englewood Bank & Trust	(941) 475-6771
Esquire Bank, N.A.	(516) 535-2002
First Federal Bank	(386) 755-0600
First National Bank of Mount Dora	(352) 383-2111
Florida Business Bank	(321) 253-1555
FNBT Bank	(850) 796-2000
Heartland National Bank	(863) 386-1300
Peoples Bank of Graceville	(850) 263-3267
Raymond James Bank, N.A.	(727) 567-8000
Renasant Bank	(800) 680-1601
Republic Bank & Trust Co.	(502) 584-3600
ServisFirst Bank	(205) 949-0302
Stearns Bank N.A.	(320) 253-6607
Sunrise Bank	(321) 784-8333
TransCapital Bank	(954) 452-3516
Rating: B+	
Amerasia Bank	(718) 463-3600
American Momentum Bank	(979) 774-1111
American National Bank	(954) 491-7788
Ameris Bank	(404) 814-8114
BAC Florida Bank	(305) 789-7000
BancorpSouth Bank	(662) 680-2000
Bank of America, N.A.	(704) 386-5681
Bank of Central Florida	(863) 701-2685
Bank of Tampa	(813) 872-1216
BankUnited, N.A.	(786) 313-1010
Branch Banking and Trust Co.	(336) 776-5342
Cadence Bank, N.A.	(800) 636-7622
CCB Community Bank	(334) 222-2561
Centennial Bank	(501) 328-4663
CenterState Bank, N.A.	(863) 293-4710
Citibank, N.A.	(605) 370-6261
City National Bank	(800) 773-7100
Community Bank of the South	(321) 452-0420
First Home Bank	(727) 440-6848
First National Bank Northwest Florida	(850) 769-3207
First National Bank of Coffee County	(912) 384-1100
First Port City Bank	(229) 246-6200
First, A National Banking Assn.	(601) 268-8998
First-Citizens Bank & Trust Co.	(919) 716-7050
Interaudi Bank	(212) 833-1000
Israel Discount Bank of New York	(212) 551-8500
JPMorgan Chase Bank, N.A.	(614) 248-5800
Lake Forest Bank & Trust Co., N.A.	(847) 234-2882
MidSouth Bank	(334) 702-7774
Northern Trust Co.	(312) 630-6000
Ocean Bank	(305) 442-2660
Prime Meridian Bank	(850) 907-2301
Safra National Bank of New York	(212) 704-5500
Seacoast National Bank	(772) 221-2760
Synovus Bank	(706) 649-4900
TrustCo Bank	(518) 377-3311
Trustmark National Bank	(601) 208-5111
United Fidelity Bank, FSB	(812) 424-0921
Wauchula State Bank	(863) 773-4151
Woodforest National Bank	(832) 375-2505

Georgia

Rating: A

Name	Telephone
Commercial Bank	(706) 743-8184
Durden Banking Co., Inc.	(478) 763-2121
Embassy National Bank	(770) 822-9111
Farmers State Bank	(706) 359-3131
First National Bank of Waynesboro	(706) 554-8100
FSNB, N.A.	(580) 357-9880
Metro City Bank	(770) 455-4989
Quantum National Bank	(770) 945-8300
South Georgia Bank	(912) 654-1051
Southeastern Bank	(912) 437-4141
United Bank	(770) 567-7211
Wallis Bank	(979) 478-6151

Rating: A-

Name	Telephone
American Pride Bank	(478) 784-1448
Armed Forces Bank, N.A.	(913) 682-9090
Bank of Dade	(706) 657-6842
Bank OZK	(501) 978-2265
BankSouth	(706) 453-2943
Century Bank of Georgia	(770) 387-1922
Citizens Bank & Trust, Inc.	(706) 657-5678
Commercial Banking Co.	(229) 242-7600
Community Banking Co. of Fitzgerald	(229) 423-4321
Douglas National Bank	(912) 384-2233
East West Bank	(626) 768-6000
Farmers State Bank	(478) 275-3223
First American Bank and Trust Co.	(706) 354-5000
First Peoples Bank	(706) 663-2700
First Volunteer Bank	(423) 668-4509
FNB South	(912) 632-7262
Glennville Bank	(912) 654-3471
Northeast Georgia Bank	(706) 356-4444
Peoples Bank of East Tennessee	(423) 442-7262
PromiseOne Bank	(678) 385-0800
Renasant Bank	(800) 680-1601
River City Bank	(706) 236-2123
Security State Bank	(229) 868-6431
ServisFirst Bank	(205) 949-0302
South Georgia Banking Co.	(229) 382-4211
South State Bank	(803) 771-2265
Thomasville National Bank	(229) 226-3300
United Community Bank	(706) 745-2151
West Central Georgia Bank	(706) 647-8951

Rating: B+

Name	Telephone
Ameris Bank	(404) 814-8114
Atlantic Capital Bank, N.A.	(404) 995-6050
Bank of Alapaha	(229) 532-6115
Bank of America, N.A.	(704) 386-5681
Bank of Camilla	(229) 336-5225
Bank of Dawson	(229) 995-2141
Bank of Dudley	(478) 277-1500
Bank of Hancock County	(706) 444-5781
Bank of Madison	(706) 342-1953
Branch Banking and Trust Co.	(336) 776-5342
Cadence Bank, N.A.	(800) 636-7622
CenterState Bank, N.A.	(863) 293-4710
Citizens Bank of Americus	(229) 924-4011
Citizens Bank of The South	(478) 552-5116
Citizens Community Bank	(229) 794-2111
Citizens National Bank of Quitman	(229) 263-7575
Citizens Trust Bank	(678) 406-4000
City National Bank	(800) 773-7100
Exchange Bank	(478) 452-4531
F&M Bank	(706) 678-2187
First Community Bank	(803) 951-2265
First IC Bank	(770) 451-7200
First National Bank of Coffee County	(912) 384-1100
First Port City Bank	(229) 246-6200
First State Bank of Blakely	(229) 723-3711
First, A National Banking Assn.	(601) 268-8998
FirstBank	(615) 313-0080
First-Citizens Bank & Trust Co.	(919) 716-7050
Four County Bank	(478) 962-3221
Greater Community Bank	(706) 295-9300
Guardian Bank	(229) 241-9444
JPMorgan Chase Bank, N.A.	(614) 248-5800
Liberty First Bank	(770) 207-3000
Northern Trust Co.	(312) 630-6000
Oconee Federal S&L Assn.	(864) 882-2765
Peach State Bank & Trust	(770) 536-1100
Pinnacle Bank	(706) 283-2854
RBC Bank (Georgia), N.A.	(919) 206-1060
Southern First Bank	(864) 679-9000
State Bank of Cochran	(478) 934-4501
Synovus Bank	(706) 649-4900
Waycross Bank & Trust	(912) 283-0001
Wheeler County State Bank	(912) 568-7191
Woodforest National Bank	(832) 375-2505

Guam

Name	Telephone
Rating: B+	
First Hawaiian Bank	(808) 525-6340

Hawaii

Name	Telephone
Rating: A-	
Central Pacific Bank	(808) 544-0500
Rating: B+	
American Savings Bank, F.S.B.	(808) 627-6900
First Hawaiian Bank	(808) 525-6340
Territorial Savings Bank	(808) 946-1400

Idaho

Name	Telephone
Rating: A	
Altabank	(801) 756-7681
Bank of Commerce	(208) 525-9108
Rating: A-	
bankcda	(208) 665-5999
D.L. Evans Bank	(208) 678-8615
Farmers Bank	(208) 543-4351
First FSB of Twin Falls	(208) 733-4222
Glacier Bank	(406) 756-4200
Northwest Bank	(208) 332-0700
Washington Federal Bank, N.A.	(206) 204-3446
Washington Trust Bank	(509) 353-4204
Zions BanCorp., N.A.	(801) 844-7637
Rating: B+	
Bank of America, N.A.	(704) 386-5681
Banner Bank	(509) 527-3636
Bell Bank	(701) 298-1500
Columbia State Bank	(253) 305-1900
First Interstate Bank	(406) 255-5000
Ireland Bank	(208) 766-2211
JPMorgan Chase Bank, N.A.	(614) 248-5800
Sunwest Bank	(714) 730-4444
Umpqua Bank	(541) 440-3961

Illinois

Rating: A

Name	Telephone
Commerce Bank	(816) 234-2000
Farmers National Bank	(815) 537-2348
Federal Savings Bank	(312) 738-8422
First Eagle Bank	(312) 850-2900
First National Bank in Taylorville	(217) 824-2241
First Trust and Savings Bank of Watseka	(815) 432-2494
Lindell Bank & Trust Co.	(314) 645-7700
Municipal Trust and Savings Bank	(815) 935-8000
Poplar Grove State Bank	(815) 765-3333
Reynolds State Bank	(309) 372-4242
Teutopolis State Bank	(217) 857-3166

Rating: A-

Name	Telephone
AMG National Trust Bank	(303) 694-2190
Armed Forces Bank, N.A.	(913) 682-9090
Bank of Advance	(573) 722-3517
Bank of O'Fallon	(618) 632-3595
Blackhawk Bank & Trust	(309) 787-4451
Buena Vista National Bank	(618) 826-2331
Burling Bank	(312) 408-8400
Busey Bank	(217) 351-6500
Cathay Bank	(213) 625-4791
Farmers and Merchants National Bank	(618) 327-4401
Farmers State Bank	(217) 285-5585
Farmers State Bank of Western Illinois	(309) 629-4361
First Community Bank and Trust	(708) 946-2246
First Farmers State Bank	(309) 392-2623
First Financial Bank, N.A.	(812) 238-6000
First Merchants Bank	(765) 747-1500
First National Bank	(605) 482-8293
First National Bank in Pinckneyville	(618) 357-9393
First National Bank of Beardstown	(217) 323-4105
First National Bank of Brookfield	(708) 485-2770
First National Bank of Pana	(217) 562-3961
First National Bank of Sparta	(618) 443-2187
First Southern Bank	(618) 997-4341
Fisher National Bank	(217) 897-1136
FNB Community Bank	(618) 283-1141
Germantown Trust & Savings Bank	(618) 526-4202
Gold Coast Bank	(312) 587-3200
Goodfield State Bank	(309) 965-2221
Grand Ridge National Bank	(815) 249-6414
Heartland Bank and Trust Co.	(309) 662-4444
Lakeside Bank	(312) 435-5100
Lisle Savings Bank	(630) 852-3710
Millennium Bank	(847) 296-9500
Old Second National Bank	(630) 892-0202
Pacific Global Bank	(312) 225-2323
Park Ridge Community Bank	(847) 384-9200
Petefish, Skiles & Co.	(217) 452-3041
Prairie State Bank & Trust	(217) 993-6260
Rushville State Bank	(217) 322-3323
Signature Bank	(847) 268-1001
State Bank of Lincoln	(217) 735-5551
Sterling Bank	(573) 778-3333
Town and Country Bank Midwest	(217) 222-0015
Vermilion Valley Bank	(815) 686-2258
Warren-Boynton State Bank	(217) 488-6091

Rating: B+

Name	Telephone
Albany Bank and Trust Co., N.A.	(773) 267-7300
American Community Bank & Trust	(815) 338-2300
Anna State Bank	(618) 833-2151
Anna-Jonesboro National Bank	(618) 833-8506
Apple River State Bank	(815) 594-2351
Bank of America, N.A.	(704) 386-5681
Bank of Bourbonnais	(815) 933-0570
Bank of Carbondale	(618) 549-2181
Bank of Pontiac	(815) 844-6155
BankChampaign, N.A.	(217) 351-2870
BankFinancial, N.A.	(800) 894-6900
Bradford National Bank of Greenville	(618) 664-2200
CBI Bank & Trust	(563) 263-3131
Central Bank of St. Louis	(314) 862-8300
Citibank, N.A.	(605) 370-6261
Citizens Community Bank	(618) 566-8800
Community Bank	(815) 367-5011
Community Bank of Easton	(309) 562-7420
Crossroads Bank	(217) 347-7751
Du Quoin State Bank	(618) 542-2111
Evergreen Bank Group	(630) 413-9580
Fairfield National Bank	(618) 842-2107
Farmers & Mechanics Bank	(309) 343-7141
Farmers State Bank of Danforth	(815) 269-2570
First Bank	(314) 995-8700
First Federal S&L Assn. of Central Illinois, S.B.	(217) 774-3322
First Financial Bank	(877) 322-9530
First Mid Bank & Trust, N.A.	(217) 234-7454
First National Bank in Staunton	(618) 635-2234
First National Bank of Litchfield	(217) 324-2105
First National Bank of Steeleville	(618) 965-3441
First Nations Bank	(773) 594-5900
First State Bank of Beecher City	(618) 487-5161

Illinois

Name	Telephone	Name	Telephone
First State Bank of Campbell Hill	(618) 426-3396		
First State Bank of St. Peter	(618) 349-8343		
First Trust & Savings Bank of Albany	(309) 887-4335		
Forreston State Bank	(815) 938-3121		
Frederick Community Bank	(815) 457-2111		
H. F. Gehant Banking Co.	(815) 628-3121		
Hanmi Bank	(213) 382-2200		
Hometown National Bank	(815) 223-7300		
Illinois Bank & Trust	(815) 637-7000		
Ipava State Bank	(309) 753-8202		
Itasca Bank & Trust Co.	(630) 773-0350		
Jersey State Bank	(618) 498-6466		
JPMorgan Chase Bank, N.A.	(614) 248-5800		
Lake Forest Bank & Trust Co., N.A.	(847) 234-2882		
Lena State Bank	(815) 369-4901		
Mason City National Bank	(217) 482-3246		
Midland Community Bank	(217) 237-4324		
Milledgeville State Bank	(815) 225-7171		
Northern Trust Co.	(312) 630-6000		
Old Exchange National Bank of Okawville	(618) 243-5234		
Peoples National Bank of Kewanee	(309) 853-3333		
Peoples State Bank of Colfax	(309) 723-2111		
Philo Exchange Bank	(217) 684-2600		
Republic Bank of Chicago	(630) 570-7700		
Royal Savings Bank	(773) 768-4800		
Shelby County State Bank	(217) 774-3911		
Simmons Bank	(870) 541-1000		
Southern Bank	(573) 778-1800		
Southern Illinois Bank	(618) 983-8433		
Spring Valley City Bank	(815) 663-2211		
State Bank	(815) 297-0900		
State Bank of Cherry	(815) 894-2345		
State Bank of Davis	(815) 865-5125		
State Bank of Herscher	(815) 426-2156		
State Bank of St. Jacob	(618) 644-5555		
State Bank of Texas	(972) 252-6000		
TCF National Bank	(952) 745-2760		
Union National Bank	(847) 888-7500		
United Fidelity Bank, FSB	(812) 424-0921		
Villa Grove State Bank	(217) 832-2631		
Woodforest National Bank	(832) 375-2505		

Indiana

Name	Telephone
Rating: A	
Kentland Bank	(219) 474-5155
Stock Yards Bank & Trust Co.	(502) 582-2571
Rating: A-	
1st Source Bank	(574) 235-2000
Alliance Bank	(219) 567-9151
Busey Bank	(217) 351-6500
Civista Bank	(419) 625-4121
Community State Bank	(260) 897-3361
Farmers & Merchants State Bank	(419) 446-2501
Farmers and Merchants Bank	(260) 637-5546
First Financial Bank, N.A.	(812) 238-6000
First Merchants Bank	(765) 747-1500
Fountain Trust Co.	(765) 793-2237
Fowler State Bank	(765) 884-1200
Friendship State Bank	(812) 667-5101
German American Bank	(812) 482-1314
Greenfield Banking Co.	(317) 462-1431
Lake City Bank	(574) 267-6144
Logansport Savings Bank	(574) 722-3855
Morris Plan Co. of Terre Haute, Inc.	(812) 238-6063
Republic Bank & Trust Co.	(502) 584-3600
Union Savings Bank	(513) 247-0300
WesBanco Bank, Inc.	(304) 234-9000
Rating: B+	
Bank of America, N.A.	(704) 386-5681
Bank of Wolcott	(219) 279-2185
Branch Banking and Trust Co.	(336) 776-5342
Centier Bank	(219) 755-6100
CentreBank	(765) 294-2228
DeMotte State Bank	(219) 987-4141
Farmers State Bank	(260) 463-7111
FCN Bank, N.A.	(765) 647-4116
First Bank of Berne	(260) 589-2151
First Financial Bank	(877) 322-9530
First Savings Bank	(812) 283-0724
First State Bank of Porter	(219) 926-2136
Flagstar Bank, FSB	(248) 312-5400
Freedom Bank	(812) 683-8998
Greenville National Bank	(937) 548-1114
Horizon Bank	(219) 874-9245
JPMorgan Chase Bank, N.A.	(614) 248-5800
Merchants Bank of Indiana	(317) 324-4660
Napoleon State Bank	(812) 852-4002
STAR Financial Bank	(260) 467-5500
State Bank and Trust Co.	(419) 783-8950
State Bank of Lizton	(317) 994-5115
TCF National Bank	(952) 745-2760
United Fidelity Bank, FSB	(812) 424-0921
Woodforest National Bank	(832) 375-2505

Iowa

Name	Telephone
Rating: A	
Citizens First National Bank	(712) 732-5440
Farmers State Bank	(319) 377-4891
Farmers Trust & Savings Bank	(319) 668-2525
First State Bank	(641) 843-4411
Hills Bank and Trust Co.	(319) 679-2291
Iowa State Bank	(515) 288-0111
Liberty Trust & Savings Bank	(563) 785-4441
Midwest Heritage Bank, FSB	(515) 278-6541
New Albin Savings Bank	(563) 544-4214
Security National Bank of Omaha	(402) 344-7300
United Bank and Trust Co.	(641) 456-5587
Rating: A-	
Bank 1st	(563) 422-3883
Bellevue State Bank	(563) 872-4911
Blackhawk Bank & Trust	(309) 787-4451
Boone Bank & Trust Co.	(515) 432-6200
Breda Savings Bank	(712) 673-2321
Chelsea Savings Bank	(319) 444-3144
Citizens Savings Bank	(563) 427-3255
Citizens Savings Bank	(563) 562-3674
Citizens State Bank	(319) 465-5921
Citizens State Bank	(712) 324-2519
Decorah Bank & Trust Co.	(563) 382-9661
Farmers Savings Bank	(641) 752-2525
Farmers Savings Bank & Trust	(319) 478-2148
Farmers State Bank	(641) 424-3053
Farmers Trust and Savings Bank	(641) 562-2696
First Bank Hampton	(641) 456-4793
First Central State Bank	(563) 659-3141
First Citizens Bank	(641) 423-1600
First National Bank	(605) 482-8293
First National Bank, Ames, Iowa	(515) 232-5561
First State Bank	(515) 832-2520
Great Southern Bank	(417) 895-5234
Heartland Bank	(515) 467-5561
Home Federal Savings Bank	(507) 535-1309
Iowa State Bank	(515) 295-3595
Iowa State Bank	(712) 662-4721
Iowa State Bank	(712) 439-1025
Iowa Trust and Savings Bank	(641) 437-4500
Lee County Bank	(319) 372-2243
Manufacturers Bank & Trust Co.	(641) 585-2825
Maquoketa State Bank	(563) 652-2491
Maynard Savings Bank	(563) 637-2289
Mount Vernon Bank and Trust Co.	(319) 895-8835
Northeast Security Bank	(563) 578-3251
NorthStar Bank	(712) 362-3322
Northwestern Bank	(712) 737-4911
NSB Bank	(641) 423-7638
Ohnward Bank & Trust	(563) 852-7696
Pilot Grove Savings Bank	(319) 469-3951
Pinnacle Bank	(641) 752-2393
Readlyn Savings Bank	(319) 279-3321
Reliance State Bank	(515) 733-4396
Savings Bank	(712) 957-6815
Security National Bank of Sioux City, Iowa	(712) 277-6500
Security State Bank	(319) 352-3500
Solon State Bank	(319) 624-3405
St. Ansgar State Bank	(641) 713-4501
State Bank & Trust Co.	(515) 382-2191
Templeton Savings Bank	(712) 669-3322
United Bank & Trust N.A.	(641) 753-5900
United Bank of Iowa	(712) 364-3393
Victor State Bank	(319) 647-2231
Washington State Bank	(319) 653-2151
Waukon State Bank	(563) 568-3451
Wayland State Bank	(319) 385-8189
West Iowa Bank	(515) 887-7811
Rating: B+	
American Savings Bank	(319) 882-4279
Atkins Savings Bank & Trust	(319) 446-7700
Availa Bank	(712) 792-3567
Bank of America, N.A.	(704) 386-5681
BankFirst	(402) 371-8005
Bridge Community Bank	(319) 895-8200
CBI Bank & Trust	(563) 263-3131
Cedar Rapids Bank and Trust Co.	(319) 862-2728
Charter Bank	(515) 331-2265
Citizens Savings Bank	(319) 462-3561
Clear Lake Bank and Trust Co.	(641) 357-7121
Community State Bank	(515) 331-3100
Community State Bank	(712) 262-3030
Corydon State Bank	(641) 872-2212
CUSB Bank	(563) 547-2040
Danville State Savings Bank	(319) 392-4261
Dubuque Bank and Trust Co.	(563) 589-2000
F&M Bank	(402) 372-5331
Farmers & Merchants State Bank	(515) 462-4242
Farmers Bank of Northern Missouri	(660) 947-2474
Farmers State Bank	(515) 295-7221
Farmers State Bank	(712) 376-4154

Iowa

Name	Telephone
First Iowa State Bank	(319) 293-3794
First National Bank	(319) 352-1340
First National Bank in Creston	(641) 782-2195
First National Bank of Manning	(712) 655-3557
First Security Bank	(712) 881-1131
First Security Bank-Sleepy Eye	(507) 794-3911
First State Bank	(641) 527-2535
First State Bank	(641) 435-4943
First State Bank of Colfax	(515) 674-3533
FNB Bank	(641) 745-2141
Home State Bank	(712) 933-5511
Home Trust & Savings Bank	(641) 732-3763
Iowa Trust & Savings Bank	(712) 852-3451
Laurens State Bank	(712) 845-2627
Leighton State Bank	(641) 628-1566
Luana Savings Bank	(563) 539-2166
Marion County State Bank	(641) 628-2191
Maxwell State Bank	(515) 387-1175
MetaBank	(605) 361-4347
Northwest Bank	(712) 580-4100
Pocahontas State Bank	(712) 335-3567
Principal Bank	(800) 672-3343
Security Savings Bank	(515) 352-3333
Security State Bank	(515) 295-9501
Sloan State Bank	(712) 428-3344
South Ottumwa Savings Bank	(641) 682-7541
State Savings Bank	(515) 457-9533
Watkins Savings Bank	(319) 227-7773
West Bank	(515) 222-2300

Kansas

Name	Telephone
Rating: A	
Bank7	(405) 810-8600
CBW Bank	(620) 396-8221
Commerce Bank	(816) 234-2000
Community State Bank	(620) 251-1313
Farmers Bank & Trust	(620) 792-2411
Kaw Valley State Bank and Trust Co.	(785) 456-2021
Rating: A-	
Academy Bank, N.A.	(816) 472-0081
Armed Forces Bank, N.A.	(913) 682-9090
Bank of Prairie Village	(913) 713-0300
Bank of Tescott	(785) 283-4217
Citizens State Bank	(785) 562-2186
Citizens State Bank and Trust Co.	(785) 742-2101
City National B&T Co. of Lawton, Oklahoma	(866) 385-3444
Country Club Bank	(816) 931-4060
Denison State Bank	(785) 364-3131
Eastern Colorado Bank	(719) 767-5652
Exchange Bank & Trust	(913) 367-6000
Farmers & Merchants Bank of Colby	(785) 460-3321
Farmers and Drovers Bank	(620) 767-5138
Farmers National Bank	(785) 543-6541
Farmers State Bank	(620) 241-3090
Farmers State Bank of Aliceville, Kansas	(785) 489-2468
Farmers State Bank of Oakley, Kansas	(785) 672-3251
Fidelity State Bank and Trust Co.	(620) 227-8586
First National Bank in Fredonia	(620) 378-2151
First National Bank of Louisburg	(913) 837-5191
First State B&T Co. of Larned	(620) 285-6931
FirstOak Bank	(620) 331-2265
Flint Hills Bank	(785) 449-2266
Garden Plain State Bank	(316) 721-1500
Great Southern Bank	(417) 895-5234
Kearny County Bank	(620) 355-6222
KS StateBank	(785) 587-4000
Pinnacle Bank	(402) 434-3127
Security Bank of Kansas City	(913) 281-3165
Security State Bank	(620) 872-7224
Solomon State Bank	(785) 655-2941
Stanley Bank	(913) 681-8800
State Bank of Bern	(785) 336-6121
TriCentury Bank	(913) 583-3222
United Bank & Trust	(785) 562-2333
Western State Bank	(620) 275-4128
Rating: B+	
Adams Bank & Trust	(308) 284-4071
Alliance Bank	(785) 271-1800
ANB Bank	(303) 394-5143
Bank of America, N.A.	(704) 386-5681
Bank of Blue Valley	(913) 338-1000
Bank of Holyrood	(785) 252-3239
Bankers' Bank of Kansas	(316) 681-2265
Bankwest of Kansas	(785) 899-2342
Central Bank of the Midwest	(816) 525-5300
City Bank	(806) 792-7101
Commercial Bank	(620) 421-1000
Community First Bank	(913) 371-1242
Community National Bank	(785) 336-6143
Cornerstone Bank	(913) 353-4130
Emprise Bank	(316) 383-4301
Enterprise Bank & Trust	(314) 725-5500
Exchange Bank	(308) 468-5741
Farmers State Bank	(785) 457-3316
First Bank	(620) 278-2161
First Bank Kansas	(785) 825-2211
First Kansas Bank	(620) 653-4921
First National Bank of Hutchinson	(620) 663-1521
First State Bank	(785) 798-3347
First-Citizens Bank & Trust Co.	(919) 716-7050
FNB Bank	(785) 890-2000
FNB Washington	(785) 325-2221
JPMorgan Chase Bank, N.A.	(614) 248-5800
Kansas State Bank Overbrook Kansas	(785) 665-7121
Labette Bank	(620) 784-5311
Mutual Savings Assn.	(913) 682-3491
NBKC Bank	(816) 965-1400
Peoples Bank	(620) 582-2166
Peoples Bank and Trust Co.	(620) 241-2100
Silver Lake Bank	(785) 232-0102
Simmons Bank	(870) 541-1000
Solutions North Bank	(785) 425-6721
Stockgrowers State Bank	(620) 635-4032
Stockgrowers State Bank	(785) 256-4241
Union Bank and Trust Co.	(402) 323-1828

Kentucky

Rating: A

Name	Telephone
Cumberland Security Bank, Inc.	(606) 679-9361
Farmers Bank and Trust Co.	(270) 365-5526
Kentucky Farmers Bank Corp.	(606) 929-5000
Stock Yards Bank & Trust Co.	(502) 582-2571
Town & Country Bank and Trust Co.	(502) 348-3911

Rating: A-

Name	Telephone
Armed Forces Bank, N.A.	(913) 682-9090
Bank of the Bluegrass & Trust Co.	(859) 233-4500
Citizens Deposit Bank of Arlington, Inc.	(270) 655-6921
Edmonton State Bank	(270) 432-3231
Elkton Bank & Trust Co.	(270) 265-9841
Farmers National Bank of Scottsville	(270) 237-3141
First Financial Bank, N.A.	(812) 238-6000
First United Bank and Trust Co.	(270) 821-5555
Franklin Bank & Trust Co.	(270) 586-7121
German American Bank	(812) 482-1314
Jackson County Bank	(606) 287-8484
Lincoln National Bank	(270) 358-4116
Magnolia Bank	(270) 324-3226
Paducah Bank and Trust Co.	(270) 575-5700
Republic Bank & Trust Co.	(502) 584-3600
Sacramento Deposit Bank	(270) 736-2212
Springfield State Bank	(859) 336-3939
Taylor County Bank	(270) 465-4196
Traditional Bank, Inc.	(859) 498-0414
United Citizens Bank of Southern Kentucky, Inc.	(270) 384-2265
United Community Bank of W Kentucky	(270) 389-3232
Victory Community Bank	(859) 341-2265
WesBanco Bank, Inc.	(304) 234-9000

Rating: B+

Name	Telephone
Bank of Clarkson	(270) 242-2111
Bank of Maysville	(606) 564-4001
Branch Banking and Trust Co.	(336) 776-5342
Cecilian Bank	(270) 862-3294
Central Bank & Trust Co.	(859) 253-6013
City National Bank of West Virginia	(304) 769-1100
Farmers Bank and Trust Co.	(270) 965-3106
Farmers National Bank of Danville	(859) 236-2926
First Financial Bank	(877) 322-9530
First National Bank of Grayson	(606) 474-2000
First National Bank of Kentucky	(502) 732-4406
First State Bank	(270) 547-2271
Fredonia Valley Bank	(270) 545-3301
Independence Bank of Kentucky	(270) 686-1776
JPMorgan Chase Bank, N.A.	(614) 248-5800
Kentucky Bank	(859) 987-1795
Lewisburg Banking Co.	(270) 755-4818
Meade County Bank	(270) 422-4141
PBK Bank, Inc.	(606) 365-7098
Peoples Bank	(502) 477-2244
Peoples Bank MT. Washington	(502) 538-7301
Planters Bank, Inc.	(270) 886-9030
River City Bank, Inc.	(502) 585-4600
Security Bank and Trust Co.	(731) 642-6644
Security Bank and Trust Co.	(606) 564-3304
South Central Bank, Inc.	(270) 651-7466
United Citizens Bank & Trust Co.	(502) 532-7392
WinFirst Bank	(859) 744-1900
Woodforest National Bank	(832) 375-2505

Louisiana

Name	Telephone
Rating: A	
First American Bank and Trust	(225) 265-2265
First National Bank of Louisiana	(337) 783-4014
FSNB, N.A.	(580) 357-9880
Rayne State Bank & Trust Co.	(337) 334-3191
Rating: A-	
American Bank & Trust Co.	(337) 948-3056
Exchange Bank and Trust Co.	(318) 352-8141
First National Bank of Benton	(318) 965-9691
First National Bank USA	(985) 785-8411
Guaranty Bank and Trust Co.	(225) 638-8621
Jonesboro State Bank	(318) 259-4411
Mississippi River Bank	(504) 392-1111
Pedestal Bank	(985) 580-2265
Red River Bank	(318) 561-4000
South Louisiana Bank	(985) 851-3434
Southern Heritage Bank	(318) 339-8505
The Bank	(337) 824-0033
Rating: B+	
BancorpSouth Bank	(662) 680-2000
Bank of Sunset and Trust Co.	(337) 662-5222
Beauregard Federal Savings Bank	(337) 463-4493
Citizens National Bank, N.A.	(318) 747-6000
Cottonport Bank	(318) 253-9612
Cross Keys Bank	(318) 766-3246
Feliciana Bank & Trust Co.	(225) 683-8565
First National Bank in DeRidder	(337) 463-6231
First, A National Banking Assn.	(601) 268-8998
Franklin State Bank & Trust Co.	(318) 435-3711
Guaranty Bank & Trust Co. of Delhi	(318) 878-3703
Gulf Coast Bank	(337) 893-7733
Home Federal Bank	(318) 841-1170
JD Bank	(337) 824-3424
JPMorgan Chase Bank, N.A.	(614) 248-5800
Woodforest National Bank	(832) 375-2505

Maine

Name	Telephone
Rating: A	
Norway Savings Bank	(207) 743-7986
Rating: A-	
Bath Savings Institution	(207) 442-7711
Rating: B+	
Bank of America, N.A.	(704) 386-5681
Camden National Bank	(207) 236-8821
Franklin Savings Bank	(207) 778-3339
Kennebec Savings Bank	(207) 622-5801
Skowhegan Savings Bank	(207) 474-9511

Maryland

Name	Telephone
Rating: A	
Calvin B. Taylor Banking Co.	(410) 641-1700
EagleBank	(240) 497-2075
Rating: A-	
ACNB Bank	(717) 334-3161
Bank of Ocean City	(410) 213-0173
Cathay Bank	(213) 625-4791
Clear Mountain Bank	(304) 379-2265
Severn Savings Bank, FSB	(410) 260-2000
Sonabank	(804) 528-4754
Rating: B+	
1880 Bank	(410) 228-5600
Atlantic Union Bank	(804) 327-5720
Bank of America, N.A.	(704) 386-5681
Branch Banking and Trust Co.	(336) 776-5342
Chesapeake Bank & Trust Co.	(410) 778-1600
Citibank, N.A.	(605) 370-6261
First-Citizens Bank & Trust Co.	(919) 716-7050
FVCbank	(703) 436-4740
John Marshall Bank	(703) 584-0840
JPMorgan Chase Bank, N.A.	(614) 248-5800
PeoplesBank, A Codorus Valley Co.	(717) 846-1970
Queenstown Bank of Maryland	(410) 827-8881
Revere Bank	(301) 841-9600
Shore United Bank	(410) 822-1400
Woodforest National Bank	(832) 375-2505
Woori America Bank	(212) 244-1500

Massachusetts

Rating: A

Name	Telephone
Leader Bank, N.A.	(781) 646-3900

Rating: A-

Name	Telephone
Boston Trust Walden Co.	(617) 726-7250
Cape Ann Savings Bank	(978) 283-0246
Cathay Bank	(213) 625-4791
East West Bank	(626) 768-6000
MutualOne Bank	(508) 820-4000
National Grand Bank of Marblehead	(781) 631-6000
Northmark Bank	(978) 686-9100
Salem Five Cents Savings Bank	(978) 745-5555

Rating: B+

Name	Telephone
Bank of America, N.A.	(704) 386-5681
Cambridge Trust Co.	(617) 876-5500
Community Bank, N.A.	(315) 445-2282
Eastern Bank	(617) 897-1100
Everett Co-operative Bank	(617) 387-1110
Goldman Sachs Bank USA	(212) 902-1000
Hingham Institution for Savings	(781) 749-2200
Institution for Savings	(978) 462-3106
JPMorgan Chase Bank, N.A.	(614) 248-5800
Lowell Five Cent Savings Bank	(978) 452-1300
Martha's Vineyard Savings Bank	(774) 310-2001
Mechanics Cooperative Bank	(508) 823-7744
Northern Trust Co.	(312) 630-6000
Patriot Community Bank	(781) 935-3318
Provident Bank	(978) 834-8555
Rockland Trust Co.	(781) 982-6110
State Street Bank and Trust Co.	(617) 786-3000
TrustCo Bank	(518) 377-3311

Michigan

Name	Telephone
Rating: A	
Chelsea State Bank	(734) 475-1355
Macatawa Bank	(616) 820-1444
Rating: A-	
1st Source Bank	(574) 235-2000
Ann Arbor State Bank	(734) 761-1475
Bank of Ann Arbor	(734) 662-1600
Comerica Bank	(214) 462-4000
Exchange State Bank	(810) 657-9333
First Merchants Bank	(765) 747-1500
Mercantile Bank of Michigan	(616) 242-7760
Peoples State Bank of Munising	(906) 387-2006
Sterling Bank and Trust, FSB	(248) 355-2400
Superior National Bank & Trust Co.	(906) 482-0404
Tri-County Bank	(810) 346-2745
Upper Peninsula State Bank	(906) 789-7000
Rating: B+	
Alden State Bank	(231) 331-4481
Bank of America, N.A.	(704) 386-5681
Charlevoix State Bank	(231) 547-4411
Dearborn Federal Savings Bank	(313) 565-3100
Farmers State Bank	(260) 463-7111
First Community Bank	(231) 526-2114
Flagstar Bank, FSB	(248) 312-5400
Horizon Bank	(219) 874-9245
JPMorgan Chase Bank, N.A.	(614) 248-5800
Lakestone Bank & Trust	(810) 664-2977
Nicolet National Bank	(920) 430-1400
Northern Trust Co.	(312) 630-6000
Port Austin State Bank	(989) 738-5235
State Bank	(810) 629-2263
TCF National Bank	(952) 745-2760
University Bank	(734) 741-5858

Minnesota

Rating: A+

Name	Telephone
Vermillion State Bank	(651) 437-4433

Rating: A

Name	Telephone
Bank of Alma	(608) 685-4461
Charter Bank	(715) 832-4254
Eagle Bank	(320) 634-4545
First National Bank North	(218) 547-1160
First National Bank of Bemidji	(218) 751-2430
Lake Central Bank	(320) 274-8216
Liberty Bank Minnesota	(320) 252-2841

Rating: A-

Name	Telephone
1st United Bank	(507) 334-2201
Alerus Financial, N.A.	(701) 795-3200
American Heritage National Bank	(320) 732-6131
Bridgewater Bank	(952) 893-6868
Castle Rock Bank	(651) 463-7590
Center National Bank	(320) 693-3255
Community First Bank	(218) 564-4171
Community Resource Bank	(507) 645-4441
CornerStone State Bank	(507) 364-2265
Farmers Trust and Savings Bank	(641) 562-2696
Fidelity Bank	(952) 831-6600
First Bank Blue Earth	(507) 526-3241
First Citizens Bank	(641) 423-1600
First Minnetonka City Bank	(952) 935-8663
First National Bank	(605) 482-8293
First National Bank of Henning	(218) 367-2735
First National Bank of Le Center	(507) 357-2273
First National Bank of Milaca	(320) 983-3101
First National Bank of Moose Lake	(218) 485-4441
First State Bank of Sauk Centre	(320) 352-5771
First State Bank of Wyoming	(651) 462-7611
First State Bank Southwest	(507) 376-9747
Gateway Bank	(651) 209-4800
Great Southern Bank	(417) 895-5234
Home Federal Savings Bank	(507) 535-1309
HomeTown Bank	(507) 637-1000
Manufacturers Bank & Trust Co.	(641) 585-2825
Neighborhood National Bank	(320) 679-3100
North American Banking Co.	(651) 636-9654
Northeast Bank	(612) 379-8811
Red Rock Bank	(507) 648-3871
Security State Bank of Aitkin	(218) 927-3765
Security State Bank of Marine	(651) 433-2424
Stearns Bank Holdingford N.A.	(320) 746-2261
Stearns Bank N.A.	(320) 253-6607
Stearns Bank Upsala N.A.	(320) 573-2111
Woodlands National Bank	(320) 384-6191

Rating: B+

Name	Telephone
Bank of America, N.A.	(704) 386-5681
Bank of Elk River	(763) 441-1000
Bank of Maple Plain	(763) 479-1931
Bank of Zumbrota	(507) 732-7555
BANKWEST	(763) 477-5231
Bell Bank	(701) 298-1500
Bremer Bank, N.A.	(651) 288-3751
Choice Financial Group	(701) 356-9700
Citizens National Bank of Park Rapids	(218) 732-3393
Citizens State Bank Midwest	(701) 265-8484
Citizens State Bank of Roseau	(218) 463-2135
Citizens State Bank of Waverly	(763) 658-4417
City National Bank	(800) 773-7100
First Bank & Trust	(605) 696-2265
First Farmers & Merchants Bank	(507) 263-3030
First Farmers & Merchants National Bank	(507) 235-5556
First Farmers & Merchants State Bank	(507) 567-2219
First National Bank of Fairfax	(507) 426-7242
First Security Bank - Canby	(507) 223-7231
First Security Bank-Hendricks	(507) 275-3141
First Security Bank-Sleepy Eye	(507) 794-3911
First State Bank of Le Center	(507) 357-2225
Granite Falls Bank	(320) 564-2111
Home State Bank	(320) 593-2001
Janesville State Bank	(507) 234-5108
JPMorgan Chase Bank, N.A.	(614) 248-5800
Lake Elmo Bank	(651) 777-8365
Minnesota National Bank	(320) 352-5211
Minnwest Bank	(507) 637-5731
North Star Bank	(651) 489-8811
Northern State Bank of Thief River Falls	(218) 681-4020
Northern Trust Co.	(312) 630-6000
Ormsby State Bank	(507) 736-2941
Pine Island Bank	(507) 356-8328
PrinsBank	(320) 978-6351
Security Bank & Trust Co.	(320) 864-3107
Security Bank Minnesota	(507) 373-1481
Security State Bank of Fergus Falls	(218) 736-5485
Security State Bank of Oklee	(218) 796-5157
Security State Bank of Wanamingo	(507) 824-2265
St. Clair State Bank (Inc.)	(507) 245-3636
State Bank of Danvers	(320) 843-3828

Minnesota

Name	Telephone
State Bank of Wheaton	(320) 563-8142
TCF National Bank	(952) 745-2760
Think Mutual Bank	(507) 288-3425
United Community Bank	(218) 346-5700
VisionBank	(952) 920-8400
Wadena State Bank	(218) 631-1860
Wanda State Bank	(507) 550-1678
Welcome State Bank	(507) 728-8251
West Bank	(515) 222-2300
WNB Financial, N.A.	(507) 454-8800

Mississippi

Name	Telephone
Rating: A	
FSNB, N.A.	(580) 357-9880
Rating: A-	
Bank of Franklin	(601) 384-2305
Bank of Vernon	(205) 695-7141
Bank OZK	(501) 978-2265
BNA Bank	(662) 534-8171
Citizens National Bank of Meridian	(601) 484-5269
Cleveland State Bank	(662) 843-9461
Commerce Bank	(662) 286-5577
Farmers and Merchants Bank	(662) 365-1200
First Choice Bank	(662) 489-1631
First Security Bank	(662) 563-9311
Renasant Bank	(800) 680-1601
Rating: B+	
BancorpSouth Bank	(662) 680-2000
Bank of Brookhaven	(601) 835-3033
Bank of Commerce	(662) 453-4142
Bank of Forest	(601) 469-3663
Bank of Kilmichael	(662) 262-7844
Bank of Morton	(601) 732-8944
Bank of Wiggins	(601) 928-5233
BankPlus	(662) 247-1811
Cadence Bank, N.A.	(800) 636-7622
Citizens Bank	(662) 838-2146
First Financial Bank	(870) 863-7000
First National Bank of Clarksdale	(662) 627-3261
First Southern Bank	(601) 736-6378
First State Bank	(601) 735-3124
First, A National Banking Assn.	(601) 268-8998
FNB Oxford Bank	(662) 234-2821
Grand Bank for Savings, FSB	(601) 264-1467
Jefferson Bank	(662) 332-7545
Pike National Bank	(601) 684-7575
Trustmark National Bank	(601) 208-5111
Woodforest National Bank	(832) 375-2505

Missouri

Name	Telephone
Rating: A	
Bank of Old Monroe	(636) 665-5601
Central Bank of Kansas City	(816) 483-1210
Commerce Bank	(816) 234-2000
Lindell Bank & Trust Co.	(314) 645-7700
Rating: A-	
Academy Bank, N.A.	(816) 472-0081
Armed Forces Bank, N.A.	(913) 682-9090
Bank Northwest	(816) 583-2154
Bank of Advance	(573) 722-3517
Bank of Grain Valley	(816) 373-1905
Bank of Monticello	(573) 767-5264
Bank of New Madrid	(573) 748-5551
Bank of St. Elizabeth	(573) 493-2313
Busey Bank	(217) 351-6500
Cass Commercial Bank	(314) 506-5544
Citizens Bank of Charleston	(573) 683-3373
Citizens Bank of Eldon	(573) 392-3381
Community Bank of El Dorado Springs	(417) 876-6811
Community First Banking Co.	(417) 255-2265
Country Club Bank	(816) 931-4060
Exchange Bank & Trust	(913) 367-6000
Farmers and Merchants Bank of St. Clair	(636) 629-2225
Farmers Bank of Lincoln	(660) 547-3311
First State Bank and Trust Co., Inc.	(573) 333-1700
First State Bank of St. Charles, Missouri	(636) 940-5555
Great Southern Bank	(417) 895-5234
HNB National Bank	(573) 221-0050
Home Exchange Bank	(660) 684-6114
Kearney Trust Co.	(816) 628-6666
Legends Bank	(573) 897-2204
Mercantile Bank of Louisiana, Missouri	(573) 754-6221
Mid America Bank	(573) 635-0019
Missouri Bank	(636) 456-3441
Missouri Bank II	(660) 827-5520
New Era Bank	(573) 783-3336
Nodaway Valley Bank	(660) 562-3232
North American Savings Bank, F.S.B.	(866) 599-9800
Northeast Missouri State Bank	(660) 665-6161
Peoples Community Bank	(573) 224-3267
Pinnacle Bank	(402) 434-3127
Platte Valley Bank of Missouri	(816) 858-5400
Progressive Ozark Bank	(573) 729-4146
Security Bank of Kansas City	(913) 281-3165
Senath State Bank	(573) 738-2646
St. Clair County State Bank	(417) 646-8128
Sterling Bank	(573) 778-3333
Town & Country Bank	(573) 729-3155
Town and Country Bank Midwest	(217) 222-0015
Wells Bank	(816) 858-2121
West Plains Bank and Trust Co.	(417) 256-2147
Wood & Huston Bank	(660) 886-6825
Rating: B+	
Adrian Bank	(816) 297-2194
Alliance Bank	(573) 334-1010
Alliant Bank	(660) 291-3041
Alton Bank	(417) 778-7211
BancorpSouth Bank	(662) 680-2000
Bank of America, N.A.	(704) 386-5681
Bank of Blue Valley	(913) 338-1000
Bank of Kirksville	(660) 665-7766
Bank of Missouri	(573) 547-6541
Bank of Odessa	(816) 230-4512
Central Bank of Boone County	(573) 874-8100
Central Bank of Branson	(417) 334-4125
Central Bank of Lake of the Ozarks	(573) 348-2761
Central Bank of Sedalia	(660) 827-3333
Central Bank of St. Louis	(314) 862-8300
Central Bank of the Midwest	(816) 525-5300
Central Bank of the Ozarks	(417) 881-3100
Central Trust Bank	(573) 634-1302
Century Bank of the Ozarks	(417) 679-3321
Citizens-Farmers Bank of Cole Camp	(660) 668-4416
Commercial Bank of Oak Grove	(816) 690-4416
Commercial Trust Co. of Fayette	(660) 248-2222
Community Bank of Missouri	(816) 470-2265
Community Bank of Pleasant Hill	(816) 540-2525
Community Bank of Raymore	(816) 322-2100
Community National Bank	(417) 235-2265
Community State Bank of Missouri	(573) 324-2233
Concordia Bank	(660) 463-7911
Enterprise Bank & Trust	(314) 725-5500
Exchange Bank of Missouri	(660) 248-3388
Farmers Bank of Northern Missouri	(660) 947-2474
First Bank	(314) 995-8700
First Community Bank of the Ozarks	(417) 336-6310
First Mid Bank & Trust, N.A.	(217) 234-7454
First Missouri Bank of SEMO	(573) 717-7177
First Missouri State Bank	(573) 785-6800
First State Community Bank	(573) 756-4547
First-Citizens Bank & Trust Co.	(919) 716-7050
Focus Bank	(573) 683-3712

Missouri

Name	Telephone
Hawthorn Bank	(573) 761-6100
Investors Community Bank	(660) 646-3733
Jefferson Bank of Missouri	(573) 634-0888
La Monte Community Bank	(660) 347-5656
Lamar Bank and Trust Co.	(417) 682-3348
Landmark Bank	(573) 499-7333
Maries County Bank	(573) 422-3323
Metz Banking Co.	(417) 667-4550
Midwest Independent Bank	(573) 636-9555
NBKC Bank	(816) 965-1400
Northern Trust Co.	(312) 630-6000
Parkside Financial Bank & Trust	(314) 290-8600
Peoples Bank	(573) 885-2511
Rockwood Bank	(636) 938-9222
Security Bank of Southwest Missouri	(417) 847-4794
Silex Banking Co.	(573) 384-5221
Simmons Bank	(870) 541-1000
Southern Bank	(573) 778-1800
State Street Bank and Trust Co.	(617) 786-3000
Stifel Bank and Trust	(314) 342-2000
TPNB Bank	(660) 327-4181
United Security Bank	(573) 386-2233

Montana

Name	Telephone
Rating: A	
Bank of Commerce	(208) 525-9108
First State Bank of Shelby	(406) 434-5567
Yellowstone Bank	(406) 628-7951
Rating: A-	
1st Bank	(406) 436-2611
American Bank	(406) 587-1234
Bank of Montana	(406) 829-2662
Glacier Bank	(406) 756-4200
Independence Bank	(406) 265-1241
Stockman Bank of Montana	(406) 234-8420
Rating: B+	
First Interstate Bank	(406) 255-5000
First Security Bank of Deer Lodge	(406) 846-2300
Manhattan Bank	(406) 284-3255
Three Rivers Bank of Montana	(406) 755-4271

Nebraska

Name	Telephone
Rating: A	
American Interstate Bank	(402) 289-2551
First Westroads Bank, Inc.	(402) 330-7200
Five Points Bank	(308) 384-5350
Five Points Bank of Hastings	(402) 462-2228
Heritage Bank	(308) 583-2262
Security National Bank of Omaha	(402) 344-7300
Rating: A-	
Auburn State Bank	(402) 274-4342
Cattle Bank & Trust	(402) 643-3636
Commercial State Bank	(308) 799-3995
First Northeast Bank of Nebraska	(402) 687-2640
First Savings Bank	(605) 763-2009
First State Bank	(308) 569-2311
First State Bank	(308) 632-4158
FirsTier Bank	(308) 235-4633
Great Southern Bank	(417) 895-5234
Horizon Bank	(402) 786-2555
Madison County Bank	(402) 454-6511
Minden Exchange Bank & Trust Co.	(308) 832-1600
Nebraska State Bank	(308) 772-3234
Pinnacle Bank	(402) 434-3127
Pinnacle Bank - Wyoming	(307) 532-2181
Platte Valley Bank	(402) 652-3221
Scribner Bank	(402) 664-2561
South Central State Bank	(402) 756-8601
State Nebraska Bank & Trust	(402) 375-1130
Town & Country Bank	(308) 452-3225
Waypoint Bank	(308) 784-2515
West Plains Bank	(402) 387-2381
Rating: B+	
Adams Bank & Trust	(308) 284-4071
Adams State Bank	(402) 988-2255
Bank of Prague	(402) 663-4317
BankFirst	(402) 371-8005
Chambers State Bank	(402) 482-5222
Cornerstone Bank	(402) 363-7411
Exchange Bank	(308) 468-5741
F&M Bank	(402) 372-5331
F&M Bank	(402) 245-2491
First Bank and Trust of Fullerton	(308) 536-2492
First National Bank of Chadron	(308) 432-5552
First National Bank of Gordon	(308) 282-0050
First Nebraska Bank	(402) 359-2281
First State Bank	(402) 337-0323
First State Bank & Trust Co.	(402) 721-2500
Hershey State Bank	(308) 368-5555
Midwest Bank N.A.	(402) 329-6221
Northwest Bank	(712) 580-4100
Points West Community Bank	(308) 254-7110
Premier Bank	(402) 558-8000
Security Bank	(402) 256-3247
Springfield State Bank	(402) 253-2222
Two Rivers Bank	(402) 426-9500
Union Bank and Trust Co.	(402) 323-1828
Washington County Bank	(402) 426-2111
West Gate Bank	(402) 434-3453

Nevada

Name	Telephone
Rating: A	
First Security Bank of Nevada	(702) 853-0900
Royal Business Bank	(213) 627-9888
Rating: A-	
American First National Bank	(713) 596-2888
Armed Forces Bank, N.A.	(913) 682-9090
Bank of George	(702) 851-4200
Cathay Bank	(213) 625-4791
Eaglemark Savings Bank	(775) 886-3000
East West Bank	(626) 768-6000
First Savings Bank	(605) 763-2009
Glacier Bank	(406) 756-4200
Pacific Premier Bank	(949) 864-8000
Washington Federal Bank, N.A.	(206) 204-3446
Wells Fargo National Bank West	(702) 952-6650
Western Alliance Bank	(602) 389-3500
Zions BanCorp., N.A.	(801) 844-7637
Rating: B+	
Bank of America, N.A.	(704) 386-5681
Charles Schwab Bank	(775) 689-6800
Citibank, N.A.	(605) 370-6261
City National Bank	(800) 773-7100
First National Bank of Ely	(775) 289-4441
JPMorgan Chase Bank, N.A.	(614) 248-5800
Kirkwood Bank of Nevada	(702) 912-0700
Northern Trust Co.	(312) 630-6000
Town & Country Bank	(702) 252-8777
Umpqua Bank	(541) 440-3961
Wilmington Savings Fund Society, FSB	(302) 792-6000

New Hampshire

Rating: B+

Name	Telephone
Bank of America, N.A.	(704) 386-5681
Cambridge Trust Co.	(617) 876-5500
Camden National Bank	(207) 236-8821
Eastern Bank	(617) 897-1100
Lowell Five Cent Savings Bank	(978) 452-1300
Provident Bank	(978) 834-8555

New Jersey

Name	Telephone
Rating: A	
Metro City Bank	(770) 455-4989
Pacific City Bank	(213) 210-2000
Rating: A-	
AMG National Trust Bank	(303) 694-2190
Armed Forces Bank, N.A.	(913) 682-9090
Bessemer Trust Co.	(212) 708-9100
Cathay Bank	(213) 625-4791
Cenlar FSB	(609) 883-3900
CTBC Bank Corp. (USA)	(424) 277-4612
NewBank	(718) 353-9100
Oritani Bank	(201) 664-5400
Parke Bank	(856) 256-2500
Unity Bank	(908) 730-7630
William Penn Bank,	(215) 269-1200
Rating: B+	
Bank of America, N.A.	(704) 386-5681
Bank of Princeton	(609) 921-1700
Branch Banking and Trust Co.	(336) 776-5342
Bryn Mawr Trust Co.	(610) 581-4839
Citibank, N.A.	(605) 370-6261
Cross River Bank	(201) 808-7000
First IC Bank	(770) 451-7200
Firstrust Savings Bank	(610) 238-5001
Goldman Sachs Bank USA	(212) 902-1000
Habib American Bank	(212) 532-4444
Hanmi Bank	(213) 382-2200
Israel Discount Bank of New York	(212) 551-8500
JPMorgan Chase Bank, N.A.	(614) 248-5800
Lakeland Bank	(973) 697-2000
Lusitania Savings Bank	(973) 344-5125
Peapack-Gladstone Bank	(908) 234-0700
State Street Bank and Trust Co.	(617) 786-3000
Sumitomo Mitsui Trust Bank (U.S.A.) Ltd.	(201) 420-9470
TrustCo Bank	(518) 377-3311
Wilmington Savings Fund Society, FSB	(302) 792-6000
Woori America Bank	(212) 244-1500

New Mexico

Rating: A

Name	Telephone
First American Bank	(575) 746-8000
First New Mexico Bank	(575) 546-2691
First New Mexico Bank of Silver City	(575) 388-3121
First New Mexico Bank, Las Cruces	(575) 556-3000

Rating: A-

Name	Telephone
AimBank	(806) 385-4441
Bank of Clovis	(575) 769-9000
Bank of Colorado	(970) 206-1160
Centinel Bank of Taos	(575) 758-6700
Citizens Bank	(505) 599-0100
Citizens Bank of Clovis	(575) 769-1911
First National Bank	(575) 437-4880
First Savings Bank	(605) 763-2009
James Polk Stone Community Bank	(575) 356-6601
Lea County State Bank	(575) 397-4511
New Mexico Bank & Trust	(505) 830-8100
United Business Bank	(925) 476-1800
Valley Bank of Commerce	(575) 623-2265
Washington Federal Bank, N.A.	(206) 204-3446
Western Bank	(575) 542-3521
WestStar Bank	(915) 532-1000
Zions BanCorp., N.A.	(801) 844-7637

Rating: B+

Name	Telephone
American Heritage Bank	(575) 762-2800
Bank of America, N.A.	(704) 386-5681
Century Bank	(505) 995-1200
Citizens Bank	(806) 350-5600
Citizens Bank of Las Cruces	(575) 647-4100
City Bank	(806) 792-7101
CNB Bank	(575) 234-2500
Enterprise Bank & Trust	(314) 725-5500
First National Bank Texas	(254) 554-4236
First-Citizens Bank & Trust Co.	(919) 716-7050
Main Bank	(505) 880-1700
Western Bank of Clovis	(575) 769-1975
Western Commerce Bank	(575) 887-6686

New York

Name	Telephone
Rating: A	
Alpine Capital Bank	(212) 328-2555
Bessemer Trust Co., N.A.	(212) 708-9100
Deutsche Bank Trust Co. Americas	(212) 250-2500
Metro City Bank	(770) 455-4989
Morgan Stanley Private Bank, N.A.	(212) 762-1803
Pacific City Bank	(213) 210-2000
Royal Business Bank	(213) 627-9888
Rating: A-	
Armed Forces Bank, N.A.	(913) 682-9090
Bank OZK	(501) 978-2265
Cathay Bank	(213) 625-4791
Citizens & Northern Bank	(570) 724-3411
CTBC Bank Corp. (USA)	(424) 277-4612
East West Bank	(626) 768-6000
Esquire Bank, N.A.	(516) 535-2002
First National Bank of Groton	(607) 898-5871
Fulton Savings Bank	(315) 592-4201
Hamlin Bank and Trust Co.	(814) 887-5555
Maspeth Federal S&L Assn.	(718) 335-1300
Metropolitan Commercial Bank	(212) 659-0600
NewBank	(718) 353-9100
Sterling Bank and Trust, FSB	(248) 355-2400
Steuben Trust Co.	(607) 324-5010
Tioga State Bank	(607) 589-7000
Westchester Bank	(914) 368-9919
Rating: B+	
Amerasia Bank	(718) 463-3600
Bank of America, N.A.	(704) 386-5681
Bank of Greene County	(518) 943-2600
Bank of Utica	(315) 797-2700
BankUnited, N.A.	(786) 313-1010
BNB Bank	(631) 537-8834
Canandaigua National Bank and Trust Co.	(585) 394-4260
Centennial Bank	(501) 328-4663
Citibank, N.A.	(605) 370-6261
City National Bank	(800) 773-7100
Community Bank, N.A.	(315) 445-2282
First IC Bank	(770) 451-7200
First National Bank of Dryden	(607) 844-8141
Genesee Regional Bank	(585) 249-1540
Glens Falls National Bank and Trust Co.	(518) 793-4121
Goldman Sachs Bank USA	(212) 902-1000
Habib American Bank	(212) 532-4444
Hanmi Bank	(213) 382-2200
Hanover Community Bank	(516) 248-4868
Interaudi Bank	(212) 833-1000
Israel Discount Bank of New York	(212) 551-8500
Jeff Bank	(845) 482-4000
JPMorgan Chase Bank, N.A.	(614) 248-5800
Lakeland Bank	(973) 697-2000
Northern Trust Co.	(312) 630-6000
Peoples Security Bank and Trust Co.	(570) 955-1700
Preferred Bank	(213) 891-1188
Safra National Bank of New York	(212) 704-5500
Saratoga National Bank and Trust Co.	(518) 583-3114
Signature Bank	(646) 822-1500
Spring Bank	(718) 879-5000
Tompkins Trust Co.	(607) 273-3210
TrustCo Bank	(518) 377-3311
Wayne Bank	(570) 253-1455
Woodforest National Bank	(832) 375-2505
Woori America Bank	(212) 244-1500

North Carolina

Name	Telephone
Rating: A	
FSNB, N.A.	(580) 357-9880
Peoples Bank	(828) 464-5620
Wake Forest Federal S&L Assn.	(919) 556-5146
Rating: A-	
Bank OZK	(501) 978-2265
Benchmark Community Bank	(434) 676-9054
BlueHarbor Bank	(704) 662-7700
CresCom Bank	(855) 273-7266
Fidelity Bank	(919) 552-2242
First FSB of Lincolnton	(704) 735-0416
Live Oak Banking Co.	(910) 790-5867
South State Bank	(803) 771-2265
Southern Bank and Trust Co.	(919) 658-7000
Surrey Bank & Trust	(336) 783-3900
TowneBank	(757) 638-7500
United Community Bank	(706) 745-2151
Rating: B+	
American National Bank and Trust Co.	(434) 792-5111
Atlantic Union Bank	(804) 327-5720
Bank of America, N.A.	(704) 386-5681
Branch Banking and Trust Co.	(336) 776-5342
Farmers & Merchants Bank	(704) 633-1772
First Bank	(910) 692-6222
First-Citizens Bank & Trust Co.	(919) 716-7050
JPMorgan Chase Bank, N.A.	(614) 248-5800
Pacific Western Bank	(310) 887-8500
Pinnacle Bank	(615) 744-3705
Providence Bank	(252) 443-9477
Roxboro Savings Bank, SSB	(336) 599-2137
Southern First Bank	(864) 679-9000
Woodforest National Bank	(832) 375-2505

North Dakota

Name	Telephone
Rating: A-	
Alerus Financial, N.A.	(701) 795-3200
Commercial Bank of Mott	(701) 824-2593
First Security Bank - West	(701) 873-4301
Grant County State Bank	(701) 622-3491
Liberty State Bank	(701) 464-5421
Ramsey National Bank	(701) 662-4024
Sargent County Bank	(701) 724-3216
Security First Bank of North Dakota	(701) 794-8758
Stock Growers Bank	(701) 754-2226
Rating: B+	
American State Bank & Trust Co	(701) 774-4100
Bell Bank	(701) 298-1500
Bremer Bank, N.A.	(651) 288-3751
Choice Financial Group	(701) 356-9700
Citizens State Bank Midwest	(701) 265-8484
Citizens State Bank of Finley	(701) 524-1921
Dakota Community Bank & Trust, N.A.	(701) 878-4416
First National B&T Co. of Williston	(701) 577-2113
First State Bank of Golva	(701) 872-3656
Peoples State Bank	(701) 245-6407
Starion Bank	(701) 223-6050

Northern Mariana Islands

Name	Telephone
Rating: B+	
First Hawaiian Bank	(808) 525-6340

Ohio

Name	Telephone
Rating: A+	
FDS Bank	(513) 573-2265
Rating: A	
Peoples Bank Co.	(419) 678-2385
Perpetual Federal Savings Bank	(937) 653-1700
St. Henry Bank	(419) 678-2358
Stock Yards Bank & Trust Co.	(502) 582-2571
Rating: A-	
Citizens Bank Co.	(740) 984-2381
Civista Bank	(419) 625-4121
Farmers & Merchants State Bank	(419) 446-2501
Farmers Savings Bank	(330) 648-2441
First Merchants Bank	(765) 747-1500
Heartland Bank	(614) 416-4601
Killbuck Savings Bank Co.	(330) 276-4881
Miami Savings Bank	(513) 353-1339
North Side Bank and Trust Co.	(513) 542-7800
Ottoville Bank Co.	(419) 453-3313
Republic Bank & Trust Co.	(502) 584-3600
Settlers Bank	(740) 373-9200
Signature Bank, N.A.	(419) 841-7773
Union Savings Bank	(513) 247-0300
WesBanco Bank, Inc.	(304) 234-9000
Rating: B+	
Bank of America, N.A.	(704) 386-5681
Branch Banking and Trust Co.	(336) 776-5342
Buckeye Community Bank	(440) 233-8800
City National Bank of West Virginia	(304) 769-1100
Corn City State Bank	(419) 278-0015
Croghan Colonial Bank	(419) 332-7301
Fahey Banking Co.	(740) 382-8231
Farmers & Merchants Bank	(937) 866-2455
Farmers National Bank of Canfield	(330) 533-3341
FCN Bank, N.A.	(765) 647-4116
First Bank of Berne	(260) 589-2151
First Commonwealth Bank	(724) 463-8555
First Financial Bank	(877) 322-9530
First National Bank in New Bremen	(419) 629-2761
First National Bank of Blanchester	(937) 783-2451
Flagstar Bank, FSB	(248) 312-5400
Greenville National Bank	(937) 548-1114
Hamler State Bank	(419) 274-3955
Home Savings Bank	(330) 742-0500
JPMorgan Chase Bank, N.A.	(614) 248-5800
Liberty National Bank	(419) 634-5015
Minster Bank	(419) 628-2351
Northern Trust Co.	(312) 630-6000
Osgood State Bank	(419) 582-2681
Spring Valley Bank	(513) 761-6688
State Bank and Trust Co.	(419) 783-8950
TCF National Bank	(952) 745-2760
Unified Bank	(740) 633-0445
Union Banking Co.	(937) 355-6511
Waterford Bank, N.A.	(419) 720-3900
Woodforest National Bank	(832) 375-2505

Oklahoma

Name	Telephone
Rating: A	
Bank of the West	(580) 661-3541
Bank7	(405) 810-8600
Commerce Bank	(816) 234-2000
Community National Bank of Okarche	(405) 263-7491
Farmers and Merchants National Bank	(580) 227-3773
First Bank of Okarche	(405) 263-7215
FSNB, N.A.	(580) 357-9880
Payne County Bank	(405) 547-2436
Sooner State Bank	(405) 381-2326
Stock Exchange Bank	(580) 256-3314
Rating: A-	
1st Bank & Trust	(580) 584-9123
American Bank and Trust Co.	(918) 481-3000
BancFirst	(405) 270-1086
Bank of Hydro	(405) 663-2214
Bank of the Panhandle	(580) 338-2593
Bank, N.A.	(918) 423-2265
City National B&T Co. of Lawton, Oklahoma	(866) 385-3444
Community Bank	(918) 367-3343
Community Bank	(580) 327-5500
Exchange Bank	(918) 396-2345
First Bank	(580) 526-3332
First Bank & Trust Co.	(580) 255-1810
First Bank & Trust Co.	(580) 336-5562
First Bank of Owasso	(918) 272-5301
First National Bank & Trust of Elk City	(580) 225-2580
First National Bank of Fort Smith	(479) 782-2041
First State Bank	(405) 247-2471
First Texoma National Bank	(580) 924-4242
Great Southern Bank	(417) 895-5234
International Bank of Commerce Oklahoma	(405) 841-2100
Liberty National Bank	(580) 351-2265
McClain Bank	(405) 527-6503
McCurtain County National Bank	(580) 584-6262
Oklahoma Bank and Trust Co.	(580) 323-2345
Oklahoma State Bank	(918) 256-5585
Peoples National Bank of Checotah	(918) 473-2237
Prime Bank	(405) 340-2775
Prosperity Bank	(979) 543-2200
Security First National Bank of Hugo	(580) 326-9641
Security State Bank	(580) 497-3354
Shamrock Bank, N.A.	(580) 927-2311
Welch State Bank of Welch, Oklahoma	(918) 788-3373
Rating: B+	
American Exchange Bank	(405) 756-3101
Anchor D Bank	(580) 423-7541
Bank of America, N.A.	(704) 386-5681
Bank of Commerce	(918) 789-2567
Bank of Cushing	(918) 225-2010
F&M Bank	(405) 715-1100
Fairview S&L Assn.	(580) 227-3735
First Bank of Thomas	(580) 661-3515
First National Bank	(918) 653-3200
First National Bank of Fletcher	(580) 549-6106
First National Bank of Lindsay	(405) 756-4433
First State Bank	(580) 623-4945
First-Citizens Bank & Trust Co.	(919) 716-7050
Idabel National Bank	(580) 286-7656
JPMorgan Chase Bank, N.A.	(614) 248-5800
Landmark Bank	(573) 499-7333
Oklahoma State Bank	(580) 735-2545
Security National Bank of Enid	(580) 234-5151
Simmons Bank	(870) 541-1000
Southwest Bank of Weatherford	(580) 774-0900
State Bank of Wynnewood	(405) 665-2001

Oregon

Name	Telephone
Rating: A	
Citizens Bank	(541) 752-5161
Clackamas County Bank	(503) 668-5501
Pioneer Trust Bank, N.A.	(503) 363-3136
Riverview Community Bank	(360) 693-6650
Rating: A-	
Bank of the Pacific	(360) 537-4052
Northwest Bank	(208) 332-0700
Oregon Coast Bank	(541) 265-9000
Washington Federal Bank, N.A.	(206) 204-3446
Washington Trust Bank	(509) 353-4204
Willamette Valley Bank	(503) 485-2222
Zions BanCorp., N.A.	(801) 844-7637
Rating: B+	
Baker-Boyer National Bank	(509) 525-2000
Bank of America, N.A.	(704) 386-5681
Banner Bank	(509) 527-3636
Columbia State Bank	(253) 305-1900
Community Bank	(541) 432-9050
First Interstate Bank	(406) 255-5000
First-Citizens Bank & Trust Co.	(919) 716-7050
Heritage Bank	(360) 943-1500
JPMorgan Chase Bank, N.A.	(614) 248-5800
Oregon Pacific Banking Co.	(541) 997-7121
Umpqua Bank	(541) 440-3961

Pennsylvania

Name	Telephone
Rating: A	
Haverford Trust Co.	(610) 995-8700
Rating: A-	
ACNB Bank	(717) 334-3161
Citizens & Northern Bank	(570) 724-3411
Hamlin Bank and Trust Co.	(814) 887-5555
Honesdale National Bank	(570) 253-3355
Neffs National Bank	(610) 767-3875
Parke Bank	(856) 256-2500
Port Richmond Savings	(215) 634-7000
Union Savings Bank	(513) 247-0300
Unity Bank	(908) 730-7630
WesBanco Bank, Inc.	(304) 234-9000
William Penn Bank,	(215) 269-1200
Rating: B+	
American Bank	(610) 366-1800
Bank of America, N.A.	(704) 386-5681
Bank of Landisburg	(717) 789-3213
Bank of Princeton	(609) 921-1700
Branch Banking and Trust Co.	(336) 776-5342
Bryn Mawr Trust Co.	(610) 581-4839
Centric Bank	(717) 657-7727
Commercial Bank & Trust of PA	(724) 539-3501
Community Bank, N.A.	(315) 445-2282
Elderton State Bank	(724) 354-2111
Farmers National Bank of Canfield	(330) 533-3341
Fidelity Deposit and Discount Bank	(570) 342-8281
First Columbia Bank & Trust Co.	(570) 784-1660
First Commonwealth Bank	(724) 463-8555
First National B&T Co. of Newtown	(215) 860-9100
Firstrust Savings Bank	(610) 238-5001
Home Savings Bank	(330) 742-0500
JPMorgan Chase Bank, N.A.	(614) 248-5800
Marquette Savings Bank	(814) 455-4481
National Bank of Malvern	(610) 647-0100
NexTier Bank, N.A.	(724) 543-1125
Peoples Security Bank and Trust Co.	(570) 955-1700
PeoplesBank, A Codorus Valley Co.	(717) 846-1970
Philadelphia Trust Co.	(215) 979-3434
Slovenian S&L Assn. of Canonsburg	(724) 745-5000
Susquehanna Community Bank	(570) 568-6851
Wayne Bank	(570) 253-1455
Wilmington Savings Fund Society, FSB	(302) 792-6000
Woodforest National Bank	(832) 375-2505
Woori America Bank	(212) 244-1500

Puerto Rico

Name	Telephone
Rating: B+	
Citibank, N.A.	(605) 370-6261

Rhode Island

Rating: B+

Name	Telephone
Bank of America, N.A.	(704) 386-5681
BankNewport	(401) 846-3400
JPMorgan Chase Bank, N.A.	(614) 248-5800
Washington Trust Co. of Westerly	(401) 348-1200

South Carolina

Name	Telephone
Rating: A	
Bank of Clarendon	(803) 433-4451
Bank of South Carolina	(843) 724-1500
First Piedmont Federal S&L Assn. of Gaffney	(864) 489-6046
Rating: A-	
Bank OZK	(501) 978-2265
Commercial Bank	(864) 369-7326
CresCom Bank	(855) 273-7266
First Federal Bank	(386) 755-0600
Palmetto State Bank	(803) 943-2671
ServisFirst Bank	(205) 949-0302
South State Bank	(803) 771-2265
United Community Bank	(706) 745-2151
Rating: B+	
Ameris Bank	(404) 814-8114
Arthur State Bank	(864) 427-1213
Bank of America, N.A.	(704) 386-5681
Bank of Travelers Rest	(864) 834-9031
Bank of York	(803) 684-4249
Branch Banking and Trust Co.	(336) 776-5342
Carolina Bank & Trust Co.	(843) 413-9978
Citizens Building and Loan, SSB	(864) 877-2054
Conway National Bank	(843) 248-5721
Farmers and Merchants Bank	(803) 496-3430
First Bank	(910) 692-6222
First Community Bank	(803) 951-2265
First Palmetto Bank	(803) 432-2265
First-Citizens Bank & Trust Co.	(919) 716-7050
JPMorgan Chase Bank, N.A.	(614) 248-5800
Oconee Federal S&L Assn.	(864) 882-2765
Pinnacle Bank	(615) 744-3705
Southern First Bank	(864) 679-9000
Synovus Bank	(706) 649-4900
Woodforest National Bank	(832) 375-2505

South Dakota

Name	Telephone
Rating: A	
First Premier Bank	(605) 357-3000
Pioneer Bank & Trust	(605) 717-2265
Rating: A-	
First National Bank	(605) 223-2521
First National Bank	(605) 482-8293
First National Bank in Philip	(605) 859-2525
First National Bank in Sioux Falls	(605) 335-5200
First Savings Bank	(605) 763-2009
First State Bank of Roscoe	(605) 287-4451
First Western Federal Savings Bank	(605) 341-1203
Quoin Financial Bank	(605) 853-2473
Security National Bank of South Dakota	(605) 232-6060
Rating: B+	
Bryant State Bank	(605) 628-2171
Campbell County Bank, Inc.	(605) 437-2294
Citibank, N.A.	(605) 370-6261
Dakota Prairie Bank	(605) 223-2337
Department Stores National Bank	
First Bank & Trust	(605) 978-9300
First Bank & Trust	(605) 696-2265
First Interstate Bank	(406) 255-5000
MetaBank	(605) 361-4347
Minnwest Bank	(507) 637-5731
Richland State Bank	(605) 627-5671
TCF National Bank	(952) 745-2760

Tennessee

Name	Telephone
Rating: A	
Citizens Bank	(423) 543-2265
Citizens Bank	(615) 735-1490
Citizens National Bank	(865) 453-9031
Elizabethton Federal Savings Bank	(423) 543-5050
First Bank and Trust Co.	(276) 889-4622
FSNB, N.A.	(580) 357-9880
Truxton Trust Co.	(615) 515-1700
Rating: A-	
Andrew Johnson Bank	(423) 783-1000
Bank of Lincoln County	(931) 433-1708
Bank of Marion	(276) 783-3116
Bank of Waynesboro	(931) 722-2265
Commercial Bank & Trust Co.	(731) 642-3341
Farmers Bank	(615) 325-2265
Financial Federal Bank	(901) 756-2848
First Federal Bank	(615) 446-2822
First Financial Bank, N.A.	(812) 238-6000
First Jackson Bank, Inc.	(256) 437-2107
First National Bank of Manchester	(931) 728-3518
First National Bank of Middle Tennessee	(931) 473-4402
First National Bank of Oneida	(423) 569-8586
First National Bank of Pulaski	(931) 363-2585
First National Bank of Tennessee	(931) 823-1261
First Volunteer Bank	(423) 668-4509
Peoples Bank	(731) 858-2661
Peoples Bank & Trust Co.	(931) 728-3381
Peoples Bank of East Tennessee	(423) 442-7262
Peoples Bank of Middle Tennessee	(931) 684-7222
Putnam 1st Mercantile Bank	(931) 528-6372
Renasant Bank	(800) 680-1601
Republic Bank & Trust Co.	(502) 584-3600
Security FSB of McMinnville	(931) 473-4483
ServisFirst Bank	(205) 949-0302
Tennessee State Bank	(865) 453-0873
United Community Bank	(706) 745-2151
Wilson Bank and Trust	(615) 444-2265
Rating: B+	
BancorpSouth Bank	(662) 680-2000
Bank of America, N.A.	(704) 386-5681
Bank of Cleveland	(423) 478-5656
Bank of Crockett	(731) 663-2031
Bank of Gleason	(731) 648-5506
Branch Banking and Trust Co.	(336) 776-5342
Cadence Bank, N.A.	(800) 636-7622
Citizens B&T Co. of Grainger County	(865) 828-5237
Citizens Bank	(615) 374-2265
Citizens Bank of Lafayette	(615) 666-2195
City National Bank	(800) 773-7100
First Century Bank	(423) 626-7261
First Citizens National Bank	(731) 285-4410
First Community Bank of Tennessee	(931) 684-5800
First Farmers and Merchants Bank	(931) 388-3145
First National Bank of Eastern Arkansas	(870) 633-3112
First Vision Bank of Tennessee	(931) 454-0500
FirstBank	(615) 313-0080
First-Citizens Bank & Trust Co.	(919) 716-7050
Mountain Commerce Bank	(865) 694-5725
Pinnacle Bank	(615) 744-3705
Planters Bank, Inc.	(270) 886-9030
Security Bank and Trust Co.	(731) 642-6644
Simmons Bank	(870) 541-1000
Southern Bank of Tennessee	(615) 758-6600
Synovus Bank	(706) 649-4900
Trustmark National Bank	(601) 208-5111

Texas

Rating: A+

Name	Telephone
Citizens 1st Bank	(903) 581-1900

Rating: A

Name	Telephone
Austin Bank, Texas N.A.	(903) 586-1526
Bank and Trust of Bryan/College Station	(979) 260-2100
Bank7	(405) 810-8600
Bessemer Trust Co., N.A.	(212) 708-9100
Commerce Bank	(956) 724-1616
Commercial National Bank of Brady	(325) 597-2961
Community Bank	(903) 236-4422
Falcon International Bank	(956) 723-2265
First Financial Bank, N.A.	(325) 627-7200
First State Bank of Bedias	(936) 395-2141
FSNB, N.A.	(580) 357-9880
International Bank of Commerce	(956) 765-8361
International Bank of Commerce	(956) 547-1000
International Bank of Commerce	(956) 722-7611
Mason Bank	(325) 347-5911
Metro City Bank	(770) 455-4989
Sanger Bank	(940) 458-4600
Security State Bank & Trust	(830) 997-7575
Texas Community Bank	(956) 722-8333
Texas Exchange Bank, SSB	(817) 297-4331
Texas State Bank	(325) 949-3721
Wallis Bank	(979) 478-6151

Rating: A-

Name	Telephone
AimBank	(806) 385-4441
American First National Bank	(713) 596-2888
American National Bank of Mount Pleasant	(903) 572-1776
Amistad Bank	(830) 775-0295
Armed Forces Bank, N.A.	(913) 682-9090
Arrowhead Bank	(325) 247-5741
Bank of Texas	(432) 221-6100
Bank OZK	(501) 978-2265
Big Bend Banks, N.A.	(432) 729-4344
BOC Bank	(806) 373-1720
BTH Bank, N.A.	(903) 763-2264
Buckholts State Bank	(254) 593-3661
Cathay Bank	(213) 625-4791
Central National Bank	(254) 776-3800
Citizens National Bank at Brownwood	(325) 643-3545
Citizens State Bank	(936) 398-2566
Citizens State Bank	(979) 885-3571
City National Bank of Taylor	(512) 671-2265
Comerica Bank	(214) 462-4000
Commonwealth Business Bank	(323) 988-3000
Community Bank & Trust, Waco, Texas	(254) 753-1521
CommunityBank of Texas, N.A.	(409) 861-7200
Cowboy Bank of Texas	(972) 435-2131
Crockett National Bank	(210) 467-5391
Crossroads Bank	(361) 293-3572
East West Bank	(626) 768-6000
First Command Bank	(888) 763-7600
First Community Bank	(361) 888-9310
First Liberty National Bank	(936) 336-6471
First National Bank of Bastrop	(512) 321-2561
First National Bank of Burleson	(817) 295-0461
First National Bank of Eldorado	(325) 853-2561
First National Bank of Floydada	(806) 983-3717
First National Bank of Granbury	(817) 573-2655
First Savings Bank	(605) 763-2009
First State Bank	(903) 676-1900
First State Bank	(979) 648-2691
First State Bank	(806) 396-5521
First State Bank and Trust Co.	(903) 693-6606
First State Bank of Ben Wheeler, Texas	(903) 833-5861
First State Bank of Burnet	(512) 756-2191
First State Bank of Odem	(361) 368-2651
First Texoma National Bank	(580) 924-4242
First United Bank	(806) 647-4151
Frost Bank	(210) 220-4011
Golden Bank, N.A.	(713) 777-3838
Grandview Bank	(817) 866-3316
Happy State Bank	(806) 558-2265
HomeBank Texas	(972) 287-2030
HomeTown Bank, N.A.	(409) 763-1271
Industry State Bank	(979) 357-4437
International Bank of Commerce Oklahoma	(405) 841-2100
Inwood National Bank	(214) 358-5281
Liberty Capital Bank	(469) 375-6600
Liberty National Bank in Paris	(903) 785-5555
Marion State Bank	(830) 420-2331
Moody National Bank	(409) 632-5016
Muenster State Bank	(940) 759-2257
Open Bank	(213) 892-9999
Pearland State Bank	(281) 485-3211
Peoples Bank	(806) 794-0044
Peoples State Bank	(830) 683-2119
Perryton National Bank	(806) 435-9641
PlainsCapital Bank	(214) 525-9100
Prosperity Bank	(979) 543-2200
Roscoe State Bank	(325) 766-3311

Texas

Name	Telephone
Round Top State Bank	(979) 249-3151
Schertz Bank & Trust	(210) 945-7400
Security State Bank	(806) 481-3327
Security State Bank	(830) 334-3606
Shelby Savings Bank, SSB	(936) 598-5688
Southside Bank	(903) 531-7111
SouthStar Bank, S.S.B.	(361) 596-4611
State National Bank of Big Spring	(432) 264-2100
Tejas Bank	(432) 943-4230
Texas Bank and Trust Co.	(903) 237-5500
Texas Financial Bank	(325) 869-5511
Texas Republic Bank, N.A.	(972) 334-0700
Texas Security Bank	(469) 398-4800
TexasBank	(325) 649-9200
Titan Bank, N.A.	(940) 325-9821
Tolleson Private Bank	(214) 252-3033
Trinity Bank, N.A.	(817) 763-9966
ValueBank Texas	(361) 888-4451
Waggoner National Bank of Vernon	(940) 552-2511
Washington Federal Bank, N.A.	(206) 204-3446
Wells Fargo Bank South Central, N.A.	(713) 802-2717
West Texas National Bank	(432) 685-6500
WestStar Bank	(915) 532-1000
Yoakum National Bank	(361) 293-5225
Zions BanCorp., N.A.	(801) 844-7637

Rating: B+

Name	Telephone
Amarillo National Bank	(806) 378-8000
American Momentum Bank	(979) 774-1111
American National Bank of Texas	(972) 524-3411
Anahuac National Bank	(409) 267-3106
Austin Capital Bank SSB	(512) 693-3600
Austin County State Bank	(979) 865-4200
BancorpSouth Bank	(662) 680-2000
Bandera Bank	(830) 796-3711
Bank and Trust, SSB	(830) 774-2555
Bank of America, N.A.	(704) 386-5681
Bank of DeSoto, N.A.	(972) 780-7777
Benchmark Bank	(972) 673-4000
Branch Banking and Trust Co.	(336) 776-5342
Brazos National Bank	(979) 265-1911
Brenham National Bank	(979) 836-4571
Broadway National Bank	(210) 283-6500
Cadence Bank, N.A.	(800) 636-7622
Capital Bank of Texas	(830) 876-5221
Cendera Bank, N.A.	(903) 965-7755
Central Bank	(832) 485-2300
Citibank, N.A.	(605) 370-6261
Citizens Bank	(806) 350-5600
Citizens Bank of Las Cruces	(575) 647-4100
Citizens Bank, N.A.	(325) 695-3000
Citizens National Bank of Crosbyton	(806) 675-2376
Citizens National Bank of Hillsboro	(254) 582-2531
Citizens State Bank	(979) 596-1421
Citizens State Bank	(903) 322-4256
Citizens State Bank	(325) 468-3311
City Bank	(806) 792-7101
City National Bank of Sulphur Springs	(903) 885-7523
Commercial National Bank of Texarkana	(903) 831-4561
Community National B&T of Texas	(903) 654-4500
Community National Bank	(830) 426-3066
Community National Bank	(432) 262-1600
Dilley State Bank	(830) 965-1511
Farmers State Bank	(254) 729-3272
Fidelity Bank of Texas	(254) 755-6555
First Bank & Trust	(806) 788-0800
First Bank and Trust of Memphis	(806) 259-3556
First IC Bank	(770) 451-7200
First National Bank	(806) 659-5544
First National Bank of Albany	(325) 762-2222
First National Bank of Alvin	(281) 331-3151
First National Bank of Aspermont	(940) 989-3505
First National Bank of Bellville	(979) 865-3181
First National Bank of Bosque County	(254) 932-5345
First National Bank of Central Texas	(254) 772-9330
First National Bank of Dublin	(254) 445-4400
First National Bank of Hebbronville	(361) 527-3221
First National Bank of Livingston	(936) 327-1234
First National Bank of McGregor	(254) 840-2836
First National Bank of Shiner	(361) 594-3317
First National Bank of Stanton	(432) 756-3361
First National Bank Texas	(254) 554-4236
First State Bank	(940) 549-8880
First State Bank	(940) 665-1711
First State Bank of Paint Rock	(325) 732-4386
First State Bank of Uvalde	(830) 278-6231
First Texas Bank	(512) 556-3691
First Texas Bank	(512) 863-2567
FirstBank Southwest	(806) 355-9661
First-Citizens Bank & Trust Co.	(919) 716-7050
Fort Hood National Bank	(254) 532-1026
Frontier Bank of Texas	(512) 281-1500
Graham S&L, SSB	(940) 549-2066
Guadalupe Bank	(830) 792-1950

Texas

Name	Telephone	Name	Telephone
Guaranty Bank & Trust, N.A.	(903) 572-9881		
Hanmi Bank	(213) 382-2200		
Hondo National Bank	(830) 426-3355		
Horizon Bank, SSB	(512) 637-5730		
Independent Bank	(972) 562-9004		
Jacksboro National Bank	(940) 567-5551		
Jefferson Bank	(210) 734-4311		
Johnson City Bank	(830) 868-7131		
JPMorgan Chase Bank, N.A.	(614) 248-5800		
Landmark Bank	(573) 499-7333		
Llano National Bank	(325) 247-5701		
Lone Star National Bank	(956) 984-2991		
Lytle State Bank of Lytle, Texas	(830) 709-3601		
NexBank SSB	(972) 934-4700		
Northern Trust Co.	(312) 630-6000		
Pegasus Bank	(214) 353-3000		
Pinnacle Bank	(817) 810-9110		
Santa Anna National Bank	(325) 348-3108		
Security Bank	(432) 570-9330		
Simmons Bank	(870) 541-1000		
Southwest Bank	(432) 552-5000		
Southwestern National Bank	(713) 771-9700		
Spirit of Texas Bank, SSB	(936) 538-1000		
Spring Hill State Bank	(903) 759-0751		
State Bank of De Kalb	(903) 667-2553		
State Bank of Texas	(972) 252-6000		
Stockmens National Bank in Cotulla	(830) 879-2331		
Sundown State Bank	(806) 229-2111		
Texas Brand Bank	(214) 219-0003		
Texas First Bank	(409) 948-1990		
TexStar National Bank	(210) 659-4000		
Trustmark National Bank	(601) 208-5111		
UBank	(936) 639-5566		
Woodforest National Bank	(832) 375-2505		
Zavala County Bank	(830) 374-5866		

Utah

Name	Telephone
Rating: A+	
Optum Bank, Inc.	(866) 234-8913
Rating: A	
Altabank	(801) 756-7681
Bank of Utah	(801) 409-5000
Green Dot Bank	(801) 344-7020
Morgan Stanley Bank, N.A.	(801) 236-3600
State Bank of Southern Utah	(435) 865-2300
UBS Bank USA	(801) 741-0310
Rating: A-	
BMW Bank of North America	(801) 461-6500
Brighton Bank	(801) 943-6500
Central Bank	(801) 375-1000
D.L. Evans Bank	(208) 678-8615
Finwise Bank	(801) 545-6000
Glacier Bank	(406) 756-4200
Holladay Bank & Trust	(801) 272-4275
Home Savings Bank	(801) 523-3878
LCA Bank Corp.	(435) 658-4824
Marlin Business Bank	(888) 479-9111
Pitney Bowes Bank, Inc.	(801) 832-4440
Utah Independent Bank	(435) 529-7459
Washington Federal Bank, N.A.	(206) 204-3446
Zions BanCorp., N.A.	(801) 844-7637
Rating: B+	
Ally Bank	(801) 790-5000
Bank of America, N.A.	(704) 386-5681
EnerBank USA	(801) 832-0700
First Electronic Bank	(801) 572-4004
Goldman Sachs Bank USA	(212) 902-1000
Grand Valley Bank	(435) 654-7400
JPMorgan Chase Bank, N.A.	(614) 248-5800
Rock Canyon Bank	(801) 426-0150
WebBank	(801) 456-8350
WEX Bank	(801) 568-4345

Vermont

Name	Telephone
Rating: B+	
Community Bank, N.A.	(315) 445-2282
TrustCo Bank	(518) 377-3311

Virgin Islands of the U.S.

Name	Telephone
Rating: B+	
United Fidelity Bank, FSB	(812) 424-0921

Virginia

Rating: A

Name	Telephone
Calvin B. Taylor Banking Co.	(410) 641-1700
EagleBank	(240) 497-2075
First Bank and Trust Co.	(276) 889-4622
Metro City Bank	(770) 455-4989
National Bank of Blacksburg	(540) 951-6205

Rating: A-

Name	Telephone
AMG National Trust Bank	(303) 694-2190
Armed Forces Bank, N.A.	(913) 682-9090
Bank of Charlotte County	(434) 542-5111
Bank of Marion	(276) 783-3116
Bank of Southside Virginia	(434) 246-5211
Benchmark Community Bank	(434) 676-9054
Citizens and Farmers Bank	(804) 843-2360
Citizens Bank and Trust Co.	(434) 292-8100
Farmers & Merchants Bank	(540) 864-5156
Farmers and Miners Bank	(276) 546-4692
Fidelity Bank	(919) 552-2242
Sonabank	(804) 528-4754
South State Bank	(803) 771-2265
Southern Bank and Trust Co.	(919) 658-7000
Surrey Bank & Trust	(336) 783-3900
TowneBank	(757) 638-7500

Rating: B+

Name	Telephone
American National Bank and Trust Co.	(434) 792-5111
Atlantic Union Bank	(804) 327-5720
Bank of America, N.A.	(704) 386-5681
Bank of Clarke County	(540) 955-2510
Branch Banking and Trust Co.	(336) 776-5342
Burke & Herbert Bank & Trust Co.	(703) 684-1655
Chesapeake Bank	(804) 435-1181
Citibank, N.A.	(605) 370-6261
City National Bank of West Virginia	(304) 769-1100
Farmers Bank of Appomattox	(434) 352-7171
First Bank	(540) 465-9121
First-Citizens Bank & Trust Co.	(919) 716-7050
FVCbank	(703) 436-4740
Hanmi Bank	(213) 382-2200
Highlands Community Bank	(540) 962-2265
John Marshall Bank	(703) 584-0840
JPMorgan Chase Bank, N.A.	(614) 248-5800
MainStreet Bank	(703) 481-4567
MVB Bank, Inc.	(304) 363-4800
Pinnacle Bank	(615) 744-3705
Shore United Bank	(410) 822-1400
Summit Community Bank, Inc.	(304) 530-1000
Virginia National Bank	(434) 817-8621
Woodforest National Bank	(832) 375-2505
Woori America Bank	(212) 244-1500

Washington

Name	Telephone
Rating: A	
1st Security Bank of Washington	(800) 683-0973
Bessemer Trust Co., N.A.	(212) 708-9100
Cashmere Valley Bank	(509) 782-2624
Riverview Community Bank	(360) 693-6650
Security State Bank	(360) 736-0763
Timberland Bank	(360) 533-4747
Rating: A-	
American Continental Bank	(626) 363-8988
Armed Forces Bank, N.A.	(913) 682-9090
Bank of the Pacific	(360) 537-4052
Cathay Bank	(213) 625-4791
Coastal Community Bank	(425) 257-9000
East West Bank	(626) 768-6000
Glacier Bank	(406) 756-4200
Islanders Bank	(360) 378-3658
Kitsap Bank	(360) 876-7834
Northwest Bank	(208) 332-0700
Pacific Premier Bank	(949) 864-8000
Peoples Bank	(360) 715-4200
Sterling Bank and Trust, FSB	(248) 355-2400
UniBank	(425) 275-9700
United Business Bank	(925) 476-1800
Washington Federal Bank, N.A.	(206) 204-3446
Washington Trust Bank	(509) 353-4204
Yakima Federal S&L Assn.	(509) 248-2634
Zions BanCorp., N.A.	(801) 844-7637
Rating: B+	
Baker-Boyer National Bank	(509) 525-2000
Bank of America, N.A.	(704) 386-5681
Banner Bank	(509) 527-3636
Columbia State Bank	(253) 305-1900
Commencement Bank	(253) 284-1800
Community Bank	(541) 432-9050
Community First Bank	(509) 783-3435
First Financial Northwest Bank	(425) 255-4400
First Interstate Bank	(406) 255-5000
First-Citizens Bank & Trust Co.	(919) 716-7050
Heritage Bank	(360) 943-1500
JPMorgan Chase Bank, N.A.	(614) 248-5800
Northern Trust Co.	(312) 630-6000
Pacific Crest Savings Bank	(425) 670-9600
Sound Banking Co.	(253) 588-0100
Umpqua Bank	(541) 440-3961
Washington Business Bank	(360) 754-1945

West Virginia

Rating: A-

Name	Telephone
Bank of Monroe	(304) 772-3034
Clay County Bank, Inc.	(304) 587-4221
Clear Mountain Bank	(304) 379-2265
Mountain Valley Bank, N.A.	(304) 637-2265
WesBanco Bank, Inc.	(304) 234-9000

Rating: B+

Name	Telephone
Branch Banking and Trust Co.	(336) 776-5342
Citizens Bank of Weston, Inc.	(304) 269-2862
City National Bank of West Virginia	(304) 769-1100
Community Bank of Parkersburg	(304) 485-7991
Fayette County National Bank of Fayetteville	(304) 574-1212
First-Citizens Bank & Trust Co.	(919) 716-7050
JPMorgan Chase Bank, N.A.	(614) 248-5800
MVB Bank, Inc.	(304) 363-4800
Summit Community Bank, Inc.	(304) 530-1000
Union Bank, Inc.	(304) 758-2191
Williamstown Bank, Inc.	(304) 375-6262
Woodforest National Bank	(832) 375-2505

Wisconsin

Name	Telephone
Rating: A+	
Bank of Prairie Du Sac	(608) 643-3393
Rating: A	
Bank of Alma	(608) 685-4461
Charter Bank	(715) 832-4254
Farmers State Bank Hillsboro	(608) 489-2621
National Exchange Bank and Trust	(920) 921-7700
Northwestern Bank	(715) 723-4461
WaterStone Bank, SSB	(414) 761-1000
Waukesha State Bank	(262) 549-8500
Rating: A-	
Advantage Community Bank	(715) 654-5100
American National Bank-Fox Cities	(920) 739-1040
Badger Bank	(920) 563-2478
Bank of Cashton	(608) 654-5121
Bank of Deerfield	(608) 764-5411
Bank of Lake Mills	(920) 648-8336
Bank of Mauston	(608) 847-6200
BLC Community Bank	(920) 788-4141
Capitol Bank	(608) 836-1616
Farmers State Bank of Waupaca	(715) 258-1400
First Citizens State Bank	(262) 473-2112
First National Bank of Bangor	(608) 486-2386
First National Bank of River Falls	(715) 425-2401
Home Federal Savings Bank	(507) 535-1309
Intercity State Bank	(715) 359-4231
International Bank of Amherst	(715) 824-3325
John Deere Financial, F.S.B.	(608) 821-2000
Johnson Bank	(262) 619-2700
NBW Bank	(920) 324-5551
Nekoosa Port Edwards State Bank	(715) 886-3104
Oregon Community Bank	(608) 835-3168
Shell Lake State Bank	(715) 468-7858
Timberwood Bank	(608) 372-2265
Tri City National Bank	(414) 761-1610
TSB Bank	(920) 269-7777
Wolf River Community Bank	(920) 779-7000
Rating: B+	
Bank of Brodhead	(608) 897-2121
Bank of Sun Prairie	(608) 837-4511
Bank of Wisconsin Dells	(608) 253-1111
Bay Bank	(920) 490-7600
Black River Country Bank	(715) 284-9448
Bluff View Bank	(608) 582-2233
Bonduel State Bank	(715) 758-2141
Bremer Bank, N.A.	(651) 288-3751
Citizens State Bank of Loyal	(715) 255-8526
Clare Bank, N.A.	(608) 348-2727
Community First Bank	(608) 375-4117
Cumberland Federal Bank, FSB	(715) 822-2249
DMB Community Bank	(608) 846-3711
First Community Bank	(608) 868-7644
First National Bank at Darlington	(608) 776-4071
First-Citizens Bank & Trust Co.	(919) 716-7050
Flagstar Bank, FSB	(248) 312-5400
Great Midwest Bank, S.S.B.	(262) 784-4400
Headwaters State Bank	(715) 547-3383
Hometown Bank	(920) 907-0788
Hustisford State Bank	(920) 349-3241
JPMorgan Chase Bank, N.A.	(614) 248-5800
McFarland State Bank	(608) 838-3141
Nicolet National Bank	(920) 430-1400
Northern Trust Co.	(312) 630-6000
Paper City Savings Assn.	(715) 423-8100
Park Bank	(414) 466-8000
Partners Bank	(715) 659-2430
Peoples Community Bank	(608) 795-2120
Peoples State Bank	(715) 842-2191
River Falls State Bank	(715) 425-6782
Royal Bank	(608) 462-8401
Starion Bank	(701) 223-6050
State Bank of Newburg	(262) 675-2306
TCF National Bank	(952) 745-2760
Wisconsin Bank & Trust	(608) 203-1200
WNB Financial, N.A.	(507) 454-8800
Woodford State Bank	(608) 325-7766

Wyoming

Rating: A

Name	Telephone
RSNB Bank	(307) 362-8801
Wyoming Bank & Trust	(307) 632-7733

Rating: A-

Name	Telephone
AMG National Trust Bank	(303) 694-2190
Bank of Commerce	(307) 324-2265
First State Bank	(308) 632-4158
FirsTier Bank	(308) 235-4633
Glacier Bank	(406) 756-4200
Hilltop National Bank	(307) 265-2740
Pinnacle Bank - Wyoming	(307) 532-2181
Zions BanCorp., N.A.	(801) 844-7637

Rating: B+

Name	Telephone
ANB Bank	(303) 394-5143
Bank of Star Valley	(307) 885-0000
Converse County Bank	(307) 358-5300
First Interstate Bank	(406) 255-5000
Lusk State Bank	(307) 334-2500
Points West Community Bank	(308) 254-7110
Rocky Mountain Bank	(307) 739-9000

Section III

Rating Upgrades and Downgrades

A list of all

U.S. Commercial Banks and Savings Banks

receiving a rating upgrade or downgrade
during the current quarter.

Section III Contents

This section identifies those institutions receiving a rating change since the previous edition of this publication, whether it be a rating upgrade, rating downgrade, newly-rated company or the withdrawal of a rating. A rating upgrade or downgrade may entail a change from one letter grade to another, or it may mean the addition or deletion of a plus or minus sign within the same letter grade previously assigned to the company. Ratings are normally updated once each quarter of the year. In some instances, however, an institution's rating may be downgraded outside of the normal updates due to overriding circumstances.

1. **Institution Name** The name under which the institution was chartered. A company's name can be very similar to, or the same as, that of another, so verify the company's exact name, city, and state to make sure you are looking at the correct company.

2. **New Safety Rating** Weiss rating assigned to the institution at the time of publication. Our ratings are designed to distinguish levels of insolvency risk and are measured on a scale from A to F based upon a wide range of factors. Highly rated companies are, in our opinion, less likely to experience financial difficulties than lower rated firms. See *About Weiss Safety Ratings* for more information and a description of what each rating means.

3. **State** The state in which the institution's headquarters or main office is located.

4. **Date of Change** Date that rating was finalized.

New Ratings

Name	State	Date of Change
Rating: B+		
BankLiberty	MO	12/04/19

Rating Upgrades

Rating: A+

Name	State	Date of Change
Deutsche Bank Trust Co. Delaware	DE	12/04/19
Optum Bank, Inc.	UT	12/04/19

Rating: A

Name	State	Date of Change
Alpine Capital Bank	NY	12/04/19
Bank and Trust of Bryan/College Station	TX	12/04/19
Bank of Alma	WI	12/04/19
Bank of Clarendon	SC	12/04/19
Bank of the West	OK	12/04/19
Bessemer Trust Co., N.A.	NY	12/04/19
Calvin B. Taylor Banking Co.	MD	12/04/19
Cashmere Valley Bank	WA	12/04/19
CBW Bank	KS	12/04/19
Chelsea State Bank	MI	12/04/19
Citizens Bank	OR	12/04/19
Citizens First National Bank	IA	12/04/19
Commercial National Bank of Brady	TX	12/04/19
Community State Bank	KS	12/04/19
Cumberland Security Bank, Inc.	KY	12/04/19
Elizabethton Federal Savings Bank	TN	12/04/19
Exchange Bank	CA	12/04/19
Farmers State Bank Hillsboro	WI	12/04/19
Farmers Trust & Savings Bank	IA	12/04/19
First American Bank and Trust	LA	12/04/19
First Bank of Okarche	OK	12/04/19
First National Bank	AL	12/04/19
First National Bank of Louisiana	LA	12/04/19
Heritage Bank	NE	12/04/19
Kentland Bank	IN	12/04/19
Lindell Bank & Trust Co.	MO	12/04/19
Mason Bank	TX	12/04/19
Municipal Trust and Savings Bank	IL	12/04/19
North Valley Bank	CO	12/04/19
Northwestern Bank	WI	12/04/19
Norway Savings Bank	ME	12/04/19
Peoples Bank Co.	OH	12/04/19
Perpetual Federal Savings Bank	OH	12/04/19
Pioneer Trust Bank, N.A.	OR	12/04/19
Rayne State Bank & Trust Co.	LA	12/04/19
RSNB Bank	WY	12/04/19
Security National Bank of Omaha	NE	12/04/19
Security State Bank	WA	12/04/19
Sooner State Bank	OK	12/04/19
Southeastern Bank	GA	12/04/19
Texas Community Bank	TX	12/04/19
Texas State Bank	TX	12/04/19
Tri Counties Bank	CA	12/04/19
United Bank and Trust Co.	IA	12/04/19
Wake Forest Federal S&L Assn.	NC	12/04/19
Wyoming Bank & Trust	WY	12/04/19
Yellowstone Bank	MT	12/04/19

Rating: A-

Name	State	Date of Change
1st Bank & Trust	OK	12/04/19
1st United Bank	MN	12/04/19
Alliance Bank	IN	12/04/19
American Bank and Trust Co.	OK	12/04/19
American Continental Bank	CA	12/04/19
American National Bank of Mount Pleasant	TX	12/04/19
American National Bank-Fox Cities	WI	12/04/19
American Plus Bank, N.A.	CA	12/04/19
American Pride Bank	GA	12/04/19
Amistad Bank	TX	12/04/19
Auburn State Bank	NE	12/04/19
AuburnBank	AL	12/04/19
Badger Bank	WI	12/04/19
Bank of Advance	MO	12/04/19
Bank of Clovis	NM	12/04/19
Bank of Dade	GA	12/04/19
Bank of Deerfield	WI	12/04/19
Bank of Estes Park	CO	12/04/19
Bank of Franklin	MS	12/04/19
Bank of George	NV	12/04/19
Bank of Hydro	OK	12/04/19
Bank of Lake Mills	WI	12/04/19
Bank of Lincoln County	TN	12/04/19
Bank of Marion	VA	12/04/19
Bank of Montana	MT	12/04/19
Bank of Monticello	MO	12/04/19
Bank of Southside Virginia	VA	12/04/19
Bank of St. Elizabeth	MO	12/04/19
Bank of Tescott	KS	12/04/19
Bank of the Bluegrass & Trust Co.	KY	12/04/19
Bank of the Federated States of Micronesia	FM	12/04/19
Bank of the Panhandle	OK	12/04/19
Bank of Waynesboro	TN	12/04/19
Bank OZK	AR	12/04/19
Bank, N.A.	OK	12/04/19
bankcda	ID	12/04/19
Bankers' Bank of the West	CO	12/04/19
Bellevue State Bank	IA	12/04/19
Benchmark Community Bank	VA	12/04/19
Bessemer Trust Co.	NY	12/04/19
Blackhawk Bank & Trust	IL	12/04/19
BlueHarbor Bank	NC	12/04/19
Breda Savings Bank	IA	12/04/19
Brighton Bank	UT	12/04/19
Buena Vista National Bank	IL	12/04/19

Rating Upgrades

Name	State	Date of Change
Burling Bank	IL	12/04/19
Capitol Bank	WI	12/04/19
Cass Commercial Bank	MO	12/04/19
Castle Rock Bank	MN	12/04/19
Cattle Bank & Trust	NE	12/04/19
Centinel Bank of Taos	NM	12/04/19
Central Bank	UT	12/04/19
Central National Bank	TX	12/04/19
Champion Bank	CO	12/04/19
Chelsea Groton Bank	CT	12/04/19
Chelsea Savings Bank	IA	12/04/19
Citizens Bank	NM	12/04/19
Citizens Bank & Trust, Inc.	GA	12/04/19
Citizens Bank of Charleston	MO	12/04/19
Citizens Bank of Clovis	NM	12/04/19
Citizens Deposit Bank of Arlington, Inc.	KY	12/04/19
Citizens National Bank at Brownwood	TX	12/04/19
Citizens Savings Bank	IA	12/04/19
Citizens Savings Bank	IA	12/04/19
Citizens State Bank	KS	12/04/19
Citizens State Bank	TX	12/04/19
Citizens State Bank	IA	12/04/19
Cleveland State Bank	MS	12/04/19
Coastal Community Bank	WA	12/04/19
Commerce Bank	MS	12/04/19
Commerce National Bank & Trust	FL	12/04/19
Commercial Bank	SC	12/04/19
Commercial Bank & Trust Co.	TN	12/04/19
Commercial Bank of Mott	ND	12/04/19
Commercial Banking Co.	GA	12/04/19
Community Bank	OK	12/04/19
Community Bank & Trust, Waco, Texas	TX	12/04/19
Community Bank of El Dorado Springs	MO	12/04/19
Community Bank of Santa Maria	CA	12/04/19
Community Banking Co. of Fitzgerald	GA	12/04/19
Community Neighbor Bank	AL	12/04/19
Community State Bank	IN	12/04/19
Community Valley Bank	CA	12/04/19
CornerStone State Bank	MN	12/04/19
Crockett National Bank	TX	12/04/19
Denison State Bank	KS	12/04/19
Dolores State Bank	CO	12/04/19
Eastern Colorado Bank	CO	12/04/19
Edmonton State Bank	KY	12/04/19
Esquire Bank, N.A.	NY	12/04/19
Exchange Bank	OK	12/04/19
Exchange Bank & Trust	KS	12/04/19
Exchange State Bank	MI	12/04/19
Farmers & Merchants Bank	VA	12/04/19
Farmers & Merchants Bank of Colby	KS	12/04/19
Farmers and Drovers Bank	KS	12/04/19
Farmers and Merchants Bank	IN	12/04/19
Farmers and Merchants Bank	MS	12/04/19
Farmers and Merchants Bank of St. Clair	MO	12/04/19
Farmers and Miners Bank	VA	12/04/19
Farmers Bank	ID	12/04/19
Farmers National Bank	KS	12/04/19
Farmers National Bank of Scottsville	KY	12/04/19
Farmers Savings Bank	OH	12/04/19
Farmers Savings Bank	IA	12/04/19
Farmers State Bank	GA	12/04/19
Farmers State Bank	IA	12/04/19
Farmers State Bank	IL	12/04/19
Farmers State Bank of Aliceville, Kansas	KS	12/04/19
Farmers State Bank of Brush	CO	12/04/19
Farmers State Bank of Oakley, Kansas	KS	12/04/19
Farmers Trust and Savings Bank	IA	12/04/19
Fidelity Bank	AR	12/04/19
Fidelity State Bank and Trust Co.	KS	12/04/19
Financial Federal Bank	TN	12/04/19
Finwise Bank	UT	12/04/19
First Bank	OK	12/04/19
First Bank Hampton	IA	12/04/19
First Bank of Alabama	AL	12/04/19
First Choice Bank	MS	12/04/19
First Command Bank	TX	12/04/19
First Commercial Bank (USA)	CA	12/04/19
First Community Bank and Trust	IL	12/04/19
First FSB of Lincolnton	NC	12/04/19
First General Bank	CA	12/04/19
First Jackson Bank, Inc.	AL	12/04/19
First Minnetonka City Bank	MN	12/04/19
First National Bank	NM	12/04/19
First National Bank & Trust of Elk City	OK	12/04/19
First National Bank in Fredonia	KS	12/04/19
First National Bank in Philip	SD	12/04/19
First National Bank in Sioux Falls	SD	12/04/19
First National Bank of Bangor	WI	12/04/19
First National Bank of Bastrop	TX	12/04/19
First National Bank of Beardstown	IL	12/04/19
First National Bank of Benton	LA	12/04/19
First National Bank of Brookfield	IL	12/04/19
First National Bank of Groton	NY	12/04/19
First National Bank of Manchester	TN	12/04/19
First National Bank of Middle Tennessee	TN	12/04/19
First National Bank of Milaca	MN	12/04/19
First National Bank of Moose Lake	MN	12/04/19
First National Bank of Mount Dora	FL	12/04/19
First National Bank of Pana	IL	12/04/19
First National Bank of River Falls	WI	12/04/19

Rating Upgrades

Name	State	Date of Change	Name	State	Date of Change
First National Bank of Sparta	IL	12/04/19	Liberty Bank	CT	12/04/19
First National Bank of Tennessee	TN	12/04/19	Liberty Capital Bank	TX	12/04/19
First Northeast Bank of Nebraska	NE	12/04/19	Lincoln National Bank	KY	12/04/19
First Peoples Bank	GA	12/04/19	Lisle Savings Bank	IL	12/04/19
First Pioneer National Bank	CO	12/04/19	Madison County Bank	NE	12/04/19
First Security Bank	MS	12/04/19	Magnolia Bank	KY	12/04/19
First Security Bank - West	ND	12/04/19	Marion State Bank	TX	12/04/19
First State B&T Co. of Larned	KS	12/04/19	Maynard Savings Bank	IA	12/04/19
First State Bank	TX	12/04/19	McCurtain County National Bank	OK	12/04/19
First State Bank	NE	12/04/19	Mercantile Bank of Louisiana, Missouri	MO	12/04/19
First State Bank	TX	12/04/19	Metro Bank	AL	12/04/19
First State Bank of Roscoe	SD	12/04/19	Metro Phoenix Bank	AZ	12/04/19
First State Bank of Sauk Centre	MN	12/04/19	Miami Savings Bank	OH	12/04/19
First State Bank of Wyoming	MN	12/04/19	Mid America Bank	MO	12/04/19
First Texoma National Bank	OK	12/04/19	Mississippi River Bank	LA	12/04/19
First United Bank and Trust Co.	KY	12/04/19	Mountain Valley Bank, N.A.	WV	12/04/19
FirsTier Bank	NE	12/04/19	MutualOne Bank	MA	12/04/19
FirstOak Bank	KS	12/04/19	Nebraska State Bank	NE	12/04/19
FirstState Bank	AL	12/04/19	Neighborhood National Bank	MN	12/04/19
Fisher National Bank	IL	12/04/19	Nekoosa Port Edwards State Bank	WI	12/04/19
Flint Hills Bank	KS	12/04/19	North Side Bank and Trust Co.	OH	12/04/19
Florida Business Bank	FL	12/04/19	Northeast Security Bank	IA	12/04/19
FNB Community Bank	IL	12/04/19	Northmark Bank	MA	12/04/19
FNB South	GA	12/04/19	NorthStar Bank	IA	12/04/19
Fountain Trust Co.	IN	12/04/19	Northwestern Bank	IA	12/04/19
Franklin Bank & Trust Co.	KY	12/04/19	Oklahoma State Bank	OK	12/04/19
Friendship State Bank	IN	12/04/19	Open Bank	CA	12/04/19
Goodfield State Bank	IL	12/04/19	Oregon Coast Bank	OR	12/04/19
Guaranty Bank and Trust Co.	LA	12/04/19	Oregon Community Bank	WI	12/04/19
Gunnison Bank and Trust Co.	CO	12/04/19	Park Ridge Community Bank	IL	12/04/19
Hamlin Bank and Trust Co.	PA	12/04/19	Pearland State Bank	TX	12/04/19
Heartland Bank	IA	12/04/19	Pedestal Bank	LA	12/04/19
Heartland Bank	OH	12/04/19	Peoples Bank	TN	12/04/19
HNB First Bank	AL	12/04/19	Peoples Bank & Trust Co.	TN	12/04/19
HNB National Bank	MO	12/04/19	Peoples Community Bank	MO	12/04/19
Home Bank of California	CA	12/04/19	Peoples State Bank	TX	12/04/19
Home Federal Savings Bank	MN	12/04/19	Peoples State Bank of Munising	MI	12/04/19
Home Savings Bank	UT	12/04/19	Perryton National Bank	TX	12/04/19
HomeBank Texas	TX	12/04/19	Petefish, Skiles & Co.	IL	12/04/19
HomeTown Bank	MN	12/04/19	Petit Jean State Bank	AR	12/04/19
Horizon Bank	NE	12/04/19	Pinnacle Bank	IA	12/04/19
Independence Bank	MT	12/04/19	Pinnacle Bank - Wyoming	WY	12/04/19
Intercity State Bank	WI	12/04/19	Platte Valley Bank	NE	12/04/19
Iowa State Bank	IA	12/04/19	Points West Community Bank	CO	12/04/19
Iowa State Bank	IA	12/04/19	Port Richmond Savings	PA	12/04/19
Islanders Bank	WA	12/04/19	PromiseOne Bank	GA	12/04/19
James Polk Stone Community Bank	NM	12/04/19	Putnam 1st Mercantile Bank	TN	12/04/19
Kearny County Bank	KS	12/04/19	Red Rock Bank	MN	12/04/19
Lea County State Bank	NM	12/04/19	Redstone Bank	CO	12/04/19
Legends Bank	MO	12/04/19	River City Bank	GA	12/04/19

Rating Upgrades

Name	State	Date of Change
Roscoe State Bank	TX	12/04/19
Rushville State Bank	IL	12/04/19
Sacramento Deposit Bank	KY	12/04/19
Salem Five Cents Savings Bank	MA	12/04/19
Samson Banking Co., Inc.	AL	12/04/19
Savings Bank of Danbury	CT	12/04/19
Schertz Bank & Trust	TX	12/04/19
Scribner Bank	NE	12/04/19
Security First Bank of North Dakota	ND	12/04/19
Security First National Bank of Hugo	OK	12/04/19
Security FSB of McMinnville	TN	12/04/19
Security State Bank	IA	12/04/19
Security State Bank	GA	12/04/19
Security State Bank	KS	12/04/19
Security State Bank	TX	12/04/19
Security State Bank	OK	12/04/19
Security State Bank of Aitkin	MN	12/04/19
Security State Bank of Marine	MN	12/04/19
Senath State Bank	MO	12/04/19
Settlers Bank	OH	12/04/19
Signature Bank	IL	12/04/19
Signature Bank, N.A.	OH	12/04/19
Solera National Bank	CO	12/04/19
Sonabank	VA	12/04/19
South Central State Bank	NE	12/04/19
South Georgia Banking Co.	GA	12/04/19
South Louisiana Bank	LA	12/04/19
Southern Heritage Bank	LA	12/04/19
Stanley Bank	KS	12/04/19
State Bank & Trust Co.	IA	12/04/19
State Bank of Bern	KS	12/04/19
State Bank of Lincoln	IL	12/04/19
State National Bank of Big Spring	TX	12/04/19
State Nebraska Bank & Trust	NE	12/04/19
Steuben Trust Co.	NY	12/04/19
Summit Bank	CA	12/04/19
Sunrise Bank	FL	12/04/19
Superior National Bank & Trust Co.	MI	12/04/19
Surrey Bank & Trust	NC	12/04/19
Taylor County Bank	KY	12/04/19
Tejas Bank	TX	12/04/19
Tennessee State Bank	TN	12/04/19
Texas Financial Bank	TX	12/04/19
Texas Republic Bank, N.A.	TX	12/04/19
TexasBank	TX	12/04/19
The Bank	LA	12/04/19
Thomasville National Bank	GA	12/04/19
Tioga State Bank	NY	12/04/19
Tolleson Private Bank	TX	12/04/19
Town and Country Bank Midwest	IL	12/04/19
TransCapital Bank	FL	12/04/19
TSB Bank	WI	12/04/19
UniBank	WA	12/04/19
United Citizens Bank of Southern Kentucky, Inc.	KY	12/04/19
Utah Independent Bank	UT	12/04/19
Vermilion Valley Bank	IL	12/04/19
Verus Bank of Commerce	CO	12/04/19
Victor State Bank	IA	12/04/19
Victory Community Bank	KY	12/04/19
Waggoner National Bank of Vernon	TX	12/04/19
Warren-Boynton State Bank	IL	12/04/19
Washington State Bank	IA	12/04/19
Waukon State Bank	IA	12/04/19
Waypoint Bank	NE	12/04/19
West Alabama Bank & Trust	AL	12/04/19
West Plains Bank	NE	12/04/19
West Plains Bank and Trust Co.	MO	12/04/19
West Texas National Bank	TX	12/04/19
Western Bank	NM	12/04/19
Willamette Valley Bank	OR	12/04/19
Wolf River Community Bank	WI	12/04/19
Wood & Huston Bank	MO	12/04/19
Woodlands National Bank	MN	12/04/19

Rating: B+

Name	State	Date of Change
1880 Bank	MD	12/04/19
Adams Bank & Trust	NE	12/04/19
Adrian Bank	MO	12/04/19
Alliance Bank	KS	12/04/19
American Heritage Bank	NM	12/04/19
Anna-Jonesboro National Bank	IL	12/04/19
Apple River State Bank	IL	12/04/19
Atlantic Capital Bank, N.A.	GA	12/04/19
Baker-Boyer National Bank	WA	12/04/19
Bandera Bank	TX	12/04/19
Bank of America, N.A.	NC	12/04/19
Bank of Burlington	CO	12/04/19
Bank of Central Florida	FL	12/04/19
Bank of Clarke County	VA	12/04/19
Bank of Cleveland	TN	12/04/19
Bank of Commerce	MS	12/04/19
Bank of Commerce	OK	12/04/19
Bank of DeSoto, N.A.	TX	12/04/19
Bank of Dudley	GA	12/04/19
Bank of Elk River	MN	12/04/19
Bank of England	AR	12/04/19
Bank of Hemet	CA	12/04/19
Bank of Kirksville	MO	12/04/19
Bank of Prague	NE	12/04/19
Bank of Santa Clarita	CA	12/04/19

Rating Upgrades

Name	State	Date of Change
Bank of Star Valley	WY	12/04/19
Bank of Sunset and Trust Co.	LA	12/04/19
Bank of Travelers Rest	SC	12/04/19
Bank of Wisconsin Dells	WI	12/04/19
Bank of Wolcott	IN	12/04/19
Bank of York	SC	12/04/19
BankChampaign, N.A.	IL	12/04/19
BankFirst	NE	12/04/19
Bankwest of Kansas	KS	12/04/19
Black River Country Bank	WI	12/04/19
Bradford National Bank of Greenville	IL	12/04/19
Broadway National Bank	TX	12/04/19
Bryant State Bank	SD	12/04/19
Carolina Bank & Trust Co.	SC	12/04/19
CBI Bank & Trust	IA	12/04/19
Cecilian Bank	KY	12/04/19
Cendera Bank, N.A.	TX	12/04/19
Century Bank	NM	12/04/19
Century Bank of the Ozarks	MO	12/04/19
Charlevoix State Bank	MI	12/04/19
Chesapeake Bank & Trust Co.	MD	12/04/19
Chino Commercial Bank, N.A.	CA	12/04/19
Citizens Bank	MS	12/04/19
Citizens Bank	TX	12/04/19
Citizens Bank	TN	12/04/19
Citizens Bank of Americus	GA	12/04/19
Citizens Bank of Las Cruces	NM	12/04/19
Citizens Bank of Weston, Inc.	WV	12/04/19
Citizens Bank, N.A.	TX	12/04/19
Citizens National Bank of Crosbyton	TX	12/04/19
Citizens National Bank of Hillsboro	TX	12/04/19
Citizens National Bank of Park Rapids	MN	12/04/19
Citizens National Bank of Quitman	GA	12/04/19
Citizens State Bank	TX	12/04/19
Citizens State Bank of Finley	ND	12/04/19
Citizens State Bank of Roseau	MN	12/04/19
City Bank	TX	12/04/19
City National Bank of Sulphur Springs	TX	12/04/19
CNB Bank	NM	12/04/19
Commencement Bank	WA	12/04/19
Commercial Trust Co. of Fayette	MO	12/04/19
Community Bank	OR	12/04/19
Community Bank of Missouri	MO	12/04/19
Community Bank of the South	FL	12/04/19
Community First Bank	KS	12/04/19
Community National B&T of Texas	TX	12/04/19
Community National Bank	TX	12/04/19
Community State Bank	IA	12/04/19
Conway National Bank	SC	12/04/19
Cornerstone Bank	KS	12/04/19
Cross River Bank	NJ	12/04/19
CUSB Bank	IA	12/04/19
Dakota Community Bank & Trust, N.A.	ND	12/04/19
DeMotte State Bank	IN	12/04/19
Elderton State Bank	PA	12/04/19
Evergreen Bank Group	IL	12/04/19
F&M Bank	NE	12/04/19
Farmers & Mechanics Bank	IL	12/04/19
Farmers & Merchants Bank	NC	12/04/19
Farmers & Merchants Bank	AL	12/04/19
Farmers and Merchants Bank	SC	12/04/19
Farmers Bank of Appomattox	VA	12/04/19
Farmers National Bank of Canfield	OH	12/04/19
Farmers State Bank	IN	12/04/19
Farmers State Bank of Danforth	IL	12/04/19
Fayette County National Bank of Fayetteville	WV	12/04/19
FBT Bank & Mortgage	AR	12/04/19
Feliciana Bank & Trust Co.	LA	12/04/19
First Bank & Trust	TX	12/04/19
First Bank and Trust of Fullerton	NE	12/04/19
First Bank and Trust of Memphis	TX	12/04/19
First Bank Kansas	KS	12/04/19
First Bank of Berne	IN	12/04/19
First Community Bank	MI	12/04/19
First Electronic Bank	UT	12/04/19
First Kansas Bank	KS	12/04/19
First National B&T Co. of Newtown	PA	12/04/19
First National B&T Co. of Williston	ND	12/04/19
First National Bank at Paris	AR	12/04/19
First National Bank of Albany	TX	12/04/19
First National Bank of Bosque County	TX	12/04/19
First National Bank of Chadron	NE	12/04/19
First National Bank of Dublin	TX	12/04/19
First National Bank of Ely	NV	12/04/19
First National Bank of Fairfax	MN	12/04/19
First National Bank of Gordon	NE	12/04/19
First National Bank of Grayson	KY	12/04/19
First National Bank of Hutchinson	KS	12/04/19
First National Bank of Lindsay	OK	12/04/19
First National Bank of McGregor	TX	12/04/19
First Nebraska Bank	NE	12/04/19
First Palmetto Bank	SC	12/04/19
First Savings Bank	IN	12/04/19
First Security Bank	IA	12/04/19
First Southern Bank	MS	12/04/19
First State Bank	IA	12/04/19
First State Bank & Trust Co.	NE	12/04/19
First State Bank of Blakely	GA	12/04/19
First State Bank of Colfax	IA	12/04/19
First State Bank of Le Center	MN	12/04/19

Rating Upgrades

Name	State	Date of Change
First State Bank of Paint Rock	TX	12/04/19
First Texas Bank	TX	12/04/19
First Trust & Savings Bank of Albany	IL	12/04/19
FirstBank Southwest	TX	12/04/19
Focus Bank	MO	12/04/19
Fort Hood National Bank	TX	12/04/19
Four County Bank	GA	12/04/19
Franklin State Bank & Trust Co.	LA	12/04/19
Fresno First Bank	CA	12/04/19
FVCbank	VA	12/04/19
Genesee Regional Bank	NY	12/04/19
Granite Falls Bank	MN	12/04/19
Great Midwest Bank, S.S.B.	WI	12/04/19
Guadalupe Bank	TX	12/04/19
Guaranty Bank & Trust, N.A.	TX	12/04/19
Guardian Bank	GA	12/04/19
Gulf Coast Bank	LA	12/04/19
H. F. Gehant Banking Co.	IL	12/04/19
Highlands Community Bank	VA	12/04/19
Hometown Bank	WI	12/04/19
Institution for Savings	MA	12/04/19
Ireland Bank	ID	12/04/19
Itasca Bank & Trust Co.	IL	12/04/19
JD Bank	LA	12/04/19
Jeff Bank	NY	12/04/19
Kirkwood Bank of Nevada	NV	12/04/19
Lamar Bank and Trust Co.	MO	12/04/19
Lena State Bank	IL	12/04/19
Lewisburg Banking Co.	KY	12/04/19
Liberty National Bank	OH	12/04/19
Llano National Bank	TX	12/04/19
Main Bank	NM	12/04/19
MainStreet Bank	VA	12/04/19
Mason City National Bank	IL	12/04/19
Maxwell State Bank	IA	12/04/19
McFarland State Bank	WI	12/04/19
Mechanics Cooperative Bank	MA	12/04/19
Midland Community Bank	IL	12/04/19
Minnesota National Bank	MN	12/04/19
Minnwest Bank	MN	12/04/19
Mission Bank	CA	12/04/19
Mission National Bank	CA	12/04/19
Mission Valley Bank	CA	12/04/19
Mutual Savings Assn.	KS	12/04/19
National Bank of Malvern	PA	12/04/19
NBKC Bank	MO	12/04/19
North Star Bank	MN	12/04/19
Northern California National Bank	CA	12/04/19
Northern State Bank of Thief River Falls	MN	12/04/19
Oklahoma State Bank	OK	12/04/19

Name	State	Date of Change
Old Exchange National Bank of Okawville	IL	12/04/19
Oregon Pacific Banking Co.	OR	12/04/19
Osgood State Bank	OH	12/04/19
Pacific Crest Savings Bank	WA	12/04/19
Parkside Financial Bank & Trust	MO	12/04/19
Partners Bank	WI	12/04/19
PBK Bank, Inc.	KY	12/04/19
Peach State Bank & Trust	GA	12/04/19
Peoples Bank	KY	12/04/19
Peoples Bank	MO	12/04/19
Peoples Bank	KS	12/04/19
Peoples Bank MT. Washington	KY	12/04/19
Peoples Security Bank and Trust Co.	PA	12/04/19
Peoples State Bank	WI	12/04/19
Peoples State Bank of Colfax	IL	12/04/19
Philo Exchange Bank	IL	12/04/19
Pinnacle Bank	CA	12/04/19
Points West Community Bank	NE	12/04/19
Premier Bank	NE	12/04/19
Providence Bank	NC	12/04/19
Queenstown Bank of Maryland	MD	12/04/19
Richland State Bank	SD	12/04/19
River Falls State Bank	WI	12/04/19
Rockwood Bank	MO	12/04/19
Royal Bank	WI	12/04/19
Security Bank	NE	12/04/19
Security Bank	TX	12/04/19
Security Bank of Southwest Missouri	MO	12/04/19
Security State Bank of Fergus Falls	MN	12/04/19
Security State Bank of Oklee	MN	12/04/19
Security State Bank of Wanamingo	MN	12/04/19
Shelby County State Bank	IL	12/04/19
Silver Lake Bank	KS	12/04/19
Simmons Bank	AR	12/04/19
Skowhegan Savings Bank	ME	12/04/19
Sound Banking Co.	WA	12/04/19
South Central Bank, Inc.	KY	12/04/19
Southern Independent Bank	AL	12/04/19
Southwestern National Bank	TX	12/04/19
Spring Hill State Bank	TX	12/04/19
Springfield State Bank	NE	12/04/19
Stafford Savings Bank	CT	12/04/19
State Bank	IL	12/04/19
State Bank of Cochran	GA	12/04/19
State Bank of Danvers	MN	12/04/19
State Bank of Herscher	IL	12/04/19
State Bank of India (California)	CA	12/04/19
State Bank of Lizton	IN	12/04/19
State Bank of Newburg	WI	12/04/19
State Bank of Wheaton	MN	12/04/19

Rating Upgrades

Name	State	Date of Change
Sumitomo Mitsui Trust Bank (U.S.A.) Ltd.	NJ	12/04/19
Sundown State Bank	TX	12/04/19
TexStar National Bank	TX	12/04/19
Town & Country Bank	NV	12/04/19
Town-Country National Bank	AL	12/04/19
Trustmark National Bank	MS	12/04/19
Two Rivers Bank	NE	12/04/19
UBank	TX	12/04/19
Unified Bank	OH	12/04/19
Union Bank, Inc.	WV	12/04/19
Union Savings Bank	CT	12/04/19
United Citizens Bank & Trust Co.	KY	12/04/19
United Community Bank	MN	12/04/19
Valley Republic Bank	CA	12/04/19
Virginia National Bank	VA	12/04/19
Washington Business Bank	WA	12/04/19
Washington County Bank	NE	12/04/19
Waterford Bank, N.A.	OH	12/04/19
Wauchula State Bank	FL	12/04/19
Waycross Bank & Trust	GA	12/04/19
WebBank	UT	12/04/19
Welcome State Bank	MN	12/04/19
Woodford State Bank	WI	12/04/19
Yampa Valley Bank	CO	12/04/19

Rating: B

Name	State	Date of Change
1st Bank Yuma	AZ	12/04/19
AB&T	GA	12/04/19
Adams County Bank	NE	12/04/19
Altamaha Bank and Trust Co.	GA	12/04/19
Amalgamated Bank	NY	12/04/19
American B&T of the Cumberlands	TN	12/04/19
American Bank, N.A.	TX	12/04/19
Anderson State Bank	IL	12/04/19
Arlington State Bank	MN	12/04/19
Associated Bank, N.A.	WI	12/04/19
Audubon State Bank	IA	12/04/19
Bank of Cordell	OK	12/04/19
Bank of Greeleyville	SC	12/04/19
Bank of Gueydan	LA	12/04/19
Bank of Hazelton	ND	12/04/19
Bank of Holly Springs	MS	12/04/19
Bank of Mead	NE	12/04/19
Bank of Millbrook	NY	12/04/19
Bank of New Cambria	MO	12/04/19
Bank of Putnam County	TN	12/04/19
Bank of Romney	WV	12/04/19
Bank of St. Francisville	LA	12/04/19
Bank of the Lowcountry	SC	12/04/19
Bank of Weston	MO	12/04/19
Bank of Winona	MS	12/04/19
Bank Star	MO	12/04/19
Bankers Trust Co.	IA	12/04/19
BayVanguard Bank	MD	12/04/19
Belgrade State Bank	MO	12/04/19
Blackhawk Bank	WI	12/04/19
BMO Harris Bank, N.A.	IL	12/04/19
BNC National Bank	AZ	12/04/19
BOM Bank	LA	12/04/19
Brookville Building and Savings Assn.	OH	12/04/19
BTC Bank	MO	12/04/19
Burton State Bank	TX	12/04/19
Calwest Bank	CA	12/04/19
Casey County Bank, Inc.	KY	12/04/19
Castroville State Bank	TX	12/04/19
Celtic Bank	UT	12/04/19
CenBank	MN	12/04/19
CenterBank	OH	12/04/19
Central Bank	TN	12/04/19
Central Bank and Trust	WY	12/04/19
Central Bank Illinois	IL	12/04/19
Central Savings, F.S.B.	IL	12/04/19
Century Bank	IA	12/04/19
Charter Bank	TX	12/04/19
Citizens Bank	SC	12/04/19
Citizens Bank	GA	12/04/19
Citizens Bank & Trust	AL	12/04/19
Citizens Bank of Ada	OK	12/04/19
Citizens Bank of Cumberland County	KY	12/04/19
Citizens Bank of Swainsboro	GA	12/04/19
Citizens Community Bank	TN	12/04/19
Citizens Community Bank	MO	12/04/19
Citizens State Bank	KS	12/04/19
Citizens State Bank	AL	12/04/19
Citizens State Bank and Trust Co.	KS	12/04/19
Citizens State Bank of Cheney, Kansas	KS	12/04/19
Citizens State Bank of Glenville	MN	12/04/19
Clarkson Bank	NE	12/04/19
Cleveland State Bank	WI	12/04/19
Coffee County Bank	TN	12/04/19
Commerce Community Bank	LA	12/04/19
Commercial & Savings Bank of Millersburg	OH	12/04/19
Commercial Bank of Texas, N.A.	TX	12/04/19
Commercial Savings Bank	IA	12/04/19
Community Bank	IA	12/04/19
Community Bank of Trenton	IL	12/04/19
Community First Bank	MO	12/04/19
Community First Bank	WI	12/04/19
Community State Bank Of Southwestern Indiana	IN	12/04/19
Consumers National Bank	OH	12/04/19

Rating Upgrades

Name	State	Date of Change
Continental Bank	UT	12/04/19
Cornerstone Community Bank	CA	12/04/19
Countryside Bank	NE	12/04/19
County National Bank	MI	12/04/19
Dakota Western Bank	ND	12/04/19
Davis Trust Co.	WV	12/04/19
Diamond Bank	AR	12/04/19
Durand State Bank	IL	12/04/19
Eagle Bank	MT	12/04/19
Eagle Bank and Trust Co.	AR	12/04/19
East Boston Savings Bank	MA	12/04/19
Eastern Savings Bank, FSB	MD	12/04/19
Elysian Bank	MN	12/04/19
Ennis State Bank	TX	12/04/19
Ephrata National Bank	PA	12/04/19
Extraco Banks, N.A.	TX	12/04/19
F & M Bank Minnesota	MN	12/04/19
Farmers and Merchants Bank	NE	12/04/19
Farmers and Merchants State Bank	NE	12/04/19
Farmers and Merchants Trust Co.	PA	12/04/19
Farmers Bank	VA	12/04/19
Farmers Bank of Osborne, Kansas	KS	12/04/19
Farmers Savings Bank	IA	12/04/19
Farmers State Bank	IA	12/04/19
Farmers State Bank	MT	12/04/19
Farmers State Bank of Hamel	MN	12/04/19
Farmers State Bank of Hartland	MN	12/04/19
Farmers State Bank of Hoffman	MN	12/04/19
Farmers State Bank of Trimont	MN	12/04/19
Farmers State Bank, Allen, Oklahoma	OK	12/04/19
Farmers-Merchants Bank of Illinois	IL	12/04/19
Fauquier Bank	VA	12/04/19
Fidelity Bank	LA	12/04/19
First American Bank	IA	12/04/19
First Bank and Trust Co.	OK	12/04/19
First Bank of Ohio	OH	12/04/19
First Colorado National Bank	CO	12/04/19
First Commerce Bank	KS	12/04/19
First Community Bank	IA	12/04/19
First Community Bank of Hillsboro	IL	12/04/19
First Community Bank, Xenia-Flora	IL	12/04/19
First Federal Savings Bank of Angola	IN	12/04/19
First Fidelity Bank	SD	12/04/19
First Florida Integrity Bank	FL	12/04/19
First Harrison Bank	IN	12/04/19
First National B&T Co. of Ardmore	OK	12/04/19
First National Bank and Trust Co.	OK	12/04/19
First National Bank in Cimarron	KS	12/04/19
First National Bank in Ord	NE	12/04/19
First National Bank of Allendale	IL	12/04/19
First National Bank of Dennison	OH	12/04/19
First National Bank of Fort Stockton	TX	12/04/19
First National Bank of Hereford	TX	12/04/19
First National Bank of Jeanerette	LA	12/04/19
First National Bank of Ottawa	IL	12/04/19
First National Bank of Sandoval	IL	12/04/19
First National Bank of Trinity	TX	12/04/19
First National Bank of Waseca	MN	12/04/19
First Neodesha Bank	KS	12/04/19
First Security Bank of Roundup	MT	12/04/19
First State Bank	GA	12/04/19
First State Bank	OH	12/04/19
First State Bank	TX	12/04/19
First State Bank	IA	12/04/19
First State Bank and Trust	MN	12/04/19
First State Bank Minnesota	MN	12/04/19
First State Bank of Forsyth	MT	12/04/19
First State Bank of Harvey	ND	12/04/19
First State Bank of Middlebury	IN	12/04/19
First State Bank of the Florida Keys	FL	12/04/19
First State Bank, Pond Creek, Oklahoma	OK	12/04/19
First United Bank & Trust	MD	12/04/19
FirstBank	OK	12/04/19
FirstBank of Nebraska	NE	12/04/19
Flagler Bank	FL	12/04/19
Flagship Bank	FL	12/04/19
FNB Bank, Inc.	WV	12/04/19
FNBC Bank and Trust	IL	12/04/19
FNCB Bank	PA	12/04/19
Fowler State Bank	CO	12/04/19
Freeport State Bank	MN	12/04/19
Friend Bank	AL	12/04/19
Garrett State Bank	IN	12/04/19
Generations Bank	AR	12/04/19
Genoa Community Bank	NE	12/04/19
Gilmer National Bank	TX	12/04/19
Grand Marais State Bank	MN	12/04/19
Grand Savings Bank	OK	12/04/19
Granger National Bank	TX	12/04/19
Granite Mountain Bank, Inc.	MT	12/04/19
Great American Bank	KS	12/04/19
Grinnell State Bank	IA	12/04/19
Grundy Bank	IL	12/04/19
Guaranty Bank and Trust Co.	MS	12/04/19
Highland Bank	MN	12/04/19
Holmes County Bank & Trust Co.	MS	12/04/19
Horatio State Bank	AR	12/04/19
Houghton State Bank	IA	12/04/19
Howard State Bank	KS	12/04/19
Illini State Bank	IL	12/04/19

Rating Upgrades

Name	State	Date of Change
Jonah Bank of Wyoming	WY	12/04/19
Kinmundy Bank	IL	12/04/19
Kirkpatrick Bank	OK	12/04/19
KodaBank	ND	12/04/19
Lake City Federal Bank	MN	12/04/19
Lake Community Bank	MN	12/04/19
Legence Bank	IL	12/04/19
Legend Bank, N.A.	TX	12/04/19
Lewis & Clark Bank	OR	12/04/19
Liberty Bank	IL	12/04/19
Liberty Bank	CA	12/04/19
Lincoln State Bank	ND	12/04/19
Lumbee Guaranty Bank	NC	12/04/19
Macon-Atlanta State Bank	MO	12/04/19
Madison Valley Bank	MT	12/04/19
McClave State Bank	CO	12/04/19
Meadows Bank	NV	12/04/19
Mechanics Bank	MS	12/04/19
Merchants and Planters Bank	MS	12/04/19
Merchants Bank	ND	12/04/19
Merchants Bank of Alabama	AL	12/04/19
Merchants Bank of Bangor	PA	12/04/19
Metropolitan Bank	CA	12/04/19
Middlefield Banking Co.	OH	12/04/19
Mifflinburg Bank & Trust Co.	PA	12/04/19
Mizuho Bank (USA)	NY	12/04/19
MountainOne Bank	MA	12/04/19
National Bank of Adams County	OH	12/04/19
New Washington State Bank	IN	12/04/19
North State Bank	NC	12/04/19
Northern State Bank	WI	12/04/19
Northern State Bank of Gonvick	MN	12/04/19
Northwest Bank of Rockford	IL	12/04/19
Olpe State Bank	KS	12/04/19
Ozark Bank	MO	12/04/19
Pendleton Community Bank, Inc.	WV	12/04/19
Peoples B&T Co. of Pointe Coupee Parish	LA	12/04/19
Peoples Bank	OK	12/04/19
Peoples Bank of Kentucky, Inc.	KY	12/04/19
Peoples Exchange Bank	KY	12/04/19
Peoples Exchange Bank	AL	12/04/19
PeoplesSouth Bank	GA	12/04/19
Perennial Bank	MN	12/04/19
Pine Country Bank	MN	12/04/19
Piqua State Bank	KS	12/04/19
Pony Express Bank	MO	12/04/19
Potter State Bank of Potter	NE	12/04/19
Premier Bank Minnesota	MN	12/04/19
Produce State Bank	MN	12/04/19
ProGrowth Bank	MN	12/04/19
Providence Bank & Trust	IL	12/04/19
Providence Bank of Texas	TX	12/04/19
Putnam County National Bank of Carmel	NY	12/04/19
Relyance Bank, N.A.	AR	12/04/19
River Bank	WI	12/04/19
River Valley Community Bank	CA	12/04/19
RiverHills Bank	MS	12/04/19
Riverwind Bank	AR	12/04/19
Seattle Bank	WA	12/04/19
Security Bank	WI	12/04/19
Security National Bank	IL	12/04/19
Security State Bank	IA	12/04/19
Security State Bank	SD	12/04/19
Security State Bank of Hibbing	MN	12/04/19
Seiling State Bank	OK	12/04/19
Sibley State Bank	IA	12/04/19
South Story Bank & Trust	IA	12/04/19
SouthCrest Bank, N.A.	GA	12/04/19
Spencer County Bank	IN	12/04/19
Springfield First Community Bank	MO	12/04/19
State Bank of Faribault	MN	12/04/19
State Bank of Jeffers	MN	12/04/19
Stockmens Bank	CO	12/04/19
Sumner Bank & Trust	TN	12/04/19
Sunstate Bank	FL	12/04/19
T Bank, N.A.	TX	12/04/19
Table Grove State Bank	IL	12/04/19
Texas Heritage Bank	TX	12/04/19
Texas Heritage National Bank	TX	12/04/19
Tomahawk Community Bank, SSB	WI	12/04/19
Touchmark National Bank	GA	12/04/19
Triad Bank, N.A.	OK	12/04/19
Twin River Bank	ID	12/04/19
Union Bank & Trust Co.	TN	12/04/19
Union Bank of Mena	AR	12/04/19
United Bank	AL	12/04/19
United National Bank	GA	12/04/19
United Southern Bank	FL	12/04/19
United Southern Bank	KY	12/04/19
Valley Bank of Kalispell	MT	12/04/19
VisionBank of Iowa	IA	12/04/19
Watertown Savings Bank	NY	12/04/19
Wayne Savings Community Bank	OH	12/04/19
Western State Bank	ND	12/04/19
Wisconsin River Bank	WI	12/04/19
York Traditions Bank	PA	12/04/19
Zapata National Bank	TX	12/04/19

Rating: B-

Name	State	Date of Change
1st Federal Savings Bank of SC, Inc.	SC	12/04/19

Rating Upgrades

Name	State	Date of Change
Abington Bank	MA	12/04/19
American State Bank of Grygla	MN	12/04/19
Apex Bank	TN	12/04/19
Apollo Bank	FL	12/04/19
Athol Savings Bank	MA	12/04/19
Auburn Banking Co.	KY	12/04/19
Balboa Thrift and Loan Assn.	CA	12/04/19
Bank of Akron	NY	12/04/19
Bank of Bennington	NE	12/04/19
Bank of Billings	MO	12/04/19
Bank of Bolivar	MO	12/04/19
Bank of Cave City	AR	12/04/19
Bank of Columbia	KY	12/04/19
Bank of Evergreen	AL	12/04/19
Bank of Fayette County	TN	12/04/19
Bank of Hartington	NE	12/04/19
Bank of Herrin	IL	12/04/19
Bank of Jackson Hole	WY	12/04/19
Bank of Louisiana	MO	12/04/19
Bank of Ontario	WI	12/04/19
Bank of Orchard	NE	12/04/19
Bank of South Texas	TX	12/04/19
Bank of Southern California, N.A.	CA	12/04/19
Bank of the Flint Hills	KS	12/04/19
Bank of the Prairie	KS	12/04/19
Bank of Turtle Lake	ND	12/04/19
BankTennessee	TN	12/04/19
Beacon Business Bank, N.A.	CA	12/04/19
Bennington State Bank	KS	12/04/19
Better Banks	IL	12/04/19
Brady National Bank	TX	12/04/19
Buckley State Bank	IL	12/04/19
Byron Bank	IL	12/04/19
Calhoun County Bank, Inc.	WV	12/04/19
Cambridge State Bank	MN	12/04/19
Catlin Bank	IL	12/04/19
Cattaraugus County Bank	NY	12/04/19
Cedar Security Bank	NE	12/04/19
Centennial Bank	TN	12/04/19
Central Bank	IA	12/04/19
CFBank, N.A.	OH	12/04/19
Chambers Bank	AR	12/04/19
Champlain National Bank	NY	12/04/19
Cheyenne State Bank	WY	12/04/19
Chippewa Valley Bank	WI	12/04/19
Citizens Bank	KY	12/04/19
Citizens Bank	IN	12/04/19
Citizens Bank	MO	12/04/19
Citizens Bank	AL	12/04/19
Citizens Bank & Trust Co.	GA	12/04/19
Citizens Bank & Trust Co.	LA	12/04/19
Citizens Bank and Trust	FL	12/04/19
Citizens Bank of Newburg	MO	12/04/19
Citizens Bank of West Virginia, Inc.	WV	12/04/19
Citizens First Bank	WI	12/04/19
Citizens First Bank	IA	12/04/19
Citizens National Bank of Texas	TX	12/04/19
Citizens Savings Bank	LA	12/04/19
Classic Bank, N.A.	TX	12/04/19
Clay County State Bank	IL	12/04/19
Clinton Savings Bank	MA	12/04/19
Commercial Bank	TX	12/04/19
Commercial Bank of California	CA	12/04/19
Commercial Capital Bank	LA	12/04/19
Commercial State Bank of Wagner	SD	12/04/19
Community Bank	OH	12/04/19
Community Bank	TX	12/04/19
Community Bank	KS	12/04/19
Community National Bank	VT	12/04/19
Community State Bank	IN	12/04/19
Community State Bank	WI	12/04/19
Cornerstone Bank	MO	12/04/19
Cortland Savings and Banking Co.	OH	12/04/19
Covenant Bank	PA	12/04/19
Crossroads Bank	IN	12/04/19
Crowell State Bank	TX	12/04/19
Cypress Bank, SSB	TX	12/04/19
Deerwood Bank	MN	12/04/19
Del Norte Bank	CO	12/04/19
Delaware National Bank of Delhi	NY	12/04/19
Dieterich Bank	IL	12/04/19
Dime Bank	CT	12/04/19
Dime Bank	PA	12/04/19
Farmers & Merchants Bank	GA	12/04/19
Farmers & Merchants Savings Bank	IA	12/04/19
Farmers and Merchants Bank	OH	12/04/19
Farmers and Merchants Bank	MD	12/04/19
Farmers and Merchants Bank	OK	12/04/19
Farmers and Merchants State Bank	MN	12/04/19
Farmers and Merchants State Bank	IL	12/04/19
Farmers Bank of Willards	MD	12/04/19
Farmers Security Bank	ND	12/04/19
Farmers State Bank	WA	12/04/19
Farmers State Bank	OK	12/04/19
Farmers State Bank & Trust Co.	IL	12/04/19
Farmers State Bank and Trust Co.	IL	12/04/19
First Bank	AK	12/04/19
First Bank of Beloit	KS	12/04/19
First Bank Richmond	IN	12/04/19
First Bankers Trust Co., N.A.	IL	12/04/19

Rating Upgrades

Name	State	Date of Change
First Business Bank	WI	12/04/19
First Citizens Bank of Butte	MT	12/04/19
First Colony Bank of Florida	FL	12/04/19
First Community Bank	NE	12/04/19
First Community Bank of the Heartland, Inc.	KY	12/04/19
First Credit Bank	CA	12/04/19
First Federal S&L Assn. of Valdosta	GA	12/04/19
First Federal Savings Bank	IN	12/04/19
First National B&T Co. of McAlester	OK	12/04/19
First National B&T Co. of Miami	OK	12/04/19
First National Bank	TX	12/04/19
First National Bank	LA	12/04/19
First National Bank in Howell	MI	12/04/19
First National Bank in Trinidad	CO	12/04/19
First National Bank of America	MI	12/04/19
First National Bank of Anson	TX	12/04/19
First National Bank of Cokato	MN	12/04/19
First National Bank of Kemp	TX	12/04/19
First National Bank of North Arkansas	AR	12/04/19
First National Bank of Scott City	KS	12/04/19
First National Bank of Weatherford	TX	12/04/19
First NaturalState Bank	AR	12/04/19
First Neighbor Bank, N.A.	IL	12/04/19
First Peoples Bank of Tennessee	TN	12/04/19
First Southern National Bank	KY	12/04/19
First Southwest Bank	CO	12/04/19
First State Bank	IL	12/04/19
First State Bank	NE	12/04/19
First State Bank	IA	12/04/19
First State Bank of Ashby	MN	12/04/19
First State Bank of Brownsboro	TX	12/04/19
First Trust and Savings Bank	IA	12/04/19
First Western Bank	AR	12/04/19
Firstar Bank	OK	12/04/19
Flagship Bank Minnesota	MN	12/04/19
Flanagan State Bank	IL	12/04/19
FNB Bank, Inc.	KY	12/04/19
Foresight Bank	MN	12/04/19
Freedom Bank of Virginia	VA	12/04/19
Glasford State Bank	IL	12/04/19
Glenwood State Bank	IA	12/04/19
GNBank, N.A.	KS	12/04/19
Goose River Bank	ND	12/04/19
Grant County Bank	KS	12/04/19
Grant County State Bank	IN	12/04/19
Halstead Bank	KS	12/04/19
Hamilton Bank	MO	12/04/19
Heartland Tri-State Bank	KS	12/04/19
Heritage Bank & Trust	TN	12/04/19
High Plains Bank	OK	12/04/19
Highland State Bank	WI	12/04/19
Home Bank and Trust Co.	KS	12/04/19
Home State Bank	IA	12/04/19
Homeland Federal Savings Bank	LA	12/04/19
Honor Bank	MI	12/04/19
Impact Bank	KS	12/04/19
International Bank of Chicago	IL	12/04/19
Interstate Bank, SSB	TX	12/04/19
Ion Bank	CT	12/04/19
Iowa Falls State Bank	IA	12/04/19
Ixonia Bank	WI	12/04/19
Kahoka State Bank	MO	12/04/19
Kaw Valley Bank	KS	12/04/19
Ladysmith Federal S&L Assn.	WI	12/04/19
Lake Bank	MN	12/04/19
Legacy Bank of Florida	FL	12/04/19
Legacy National Bank	AR	12/04/19
Lone Star Bank	TX	12/04/19
Lovelady State Bank	TX	12/04/19
Mechanics Bank	OH	12/04/19
Merchants State Bank	SD	12/04/19
Mid-America Bank	KS	12/04/19
MINT National Bank	TX	12/04/19
Montezuma State Bank	IA	12/04/19
NorthEast Community Bank	NY	12/04/19
Northern State Bank of Virginia	MN	12/04/19
Northview Bank	MN	12/04/19
OakStar Bank	MO	12/04/19
One World Bank	TX	12/04/19
Opus Bank	CA	12/04/19
Oxford Bank	MI	12/04/19
Pacific Valley Bank	CA	12/04/19
Park State Bank	MN	12/04/19
Patriots Bank	KS	12/04/19
Pauls Valley National Bank	OK	12/04/19
Peoples Bank & Trust Co.	MO	12/04/19
Peoples Bank of Altenburg	MO	12/04/19
Peoples Bank of Georgia	GA	12/04/19
Peoples State Bank	OK	12/04/19
Peoples State Bank	OH	12/04/19
Peoples State Bank of Newton, Illinois	IL	12/04/19
Piedmont Bank	GA	12/04/19
Pine River State Bank	MN	12/04/19
Pioneer Bank	VA	12/04/19
Platte Valley Bank	NE	12/04/19
Platte Valley Bank	WY	12/04/19
PNB Community Bank	FL	12/04/19
Poca Valley Bank, Inc.	WV	12/04/19
Premier Bank Rochester	MN	12/04/19
PremierBank	WI	12/04/19

Rating Upgrades

Name	State	Date of Change
Prime Security Bank	MN	12/04/19
Profinium, Inc.	MN	12/04/19
Provident State Bank, Inc.	MD	12/04/19
Republic Banking Co.	OH	12/04/19
Resource Bank	LA	12/04/19
Rio Bank	TX	12/04/19
RiverBank	AR	12/04/19
Robert Lee State Bank	TX	12/04/19
Savings Bank of Walpole	NH	12/04/19
Seaside National Bank & Trust	FL	12/04/19
Security State Bank	WI	12/04/19
Security State Bank	SD	12/04/19
Security State Bank	TX	12/04/19
Sherburne State Bank	MN	12/04/19
Simmesport State Bank	LA	12/04/19
Skyline National Bank	VA	12/04/19
South Atlantic Bank	SC	12/04/19
Southern Bank & Trust	GA	12/04/19
Southwest National Bank	KS	12/04/19
State Bank Northwest	WA	12/04/19
State Bank of Lakota	ND	12/04/19
State Bank of Pearl City	IL	12/04/19
State Bank of Toulon	IL	12/04/19
State Bank of Whittington	IL	12/04/19
State Exchange Bank	KS	12/04/19
Stephenson National Bank and Trust	WI	12/04/19
Sturgis Bank & Trust Co.	MI	12/04/19
Success Bank	IA	12/04/19
Sundance State Bank	WY	12/04/19
Sweet Water State Bank	AL	12/04/19
Taylorsville Savings Bank, SSB	NC	12/04/19
Texas Advantage Community Bank, N.A.	TX	12/04/19
Texas Regional Bank	TX	12/04/19
The Bank of Soperton	GA	12/04/19
Tri-Valley Bank	IA	12/04/19
TruPoint Bank	VA	12/04/19
Twin City Bank	WA	12/04/19
Two River Community Bank	NJ	12/04/19
Union Bank of Sparta	WI	12/04/19
Union State Bank of Everest	KS	12/04/19
United Cumberland Bank	KY	12/04/19
USNY Bank	NY	12/04/19
Vantage Bank Texas	TX	12/04/19
Vermilion Bank & Trust Co.	LA	12/04/19
Viking Bank	MN	12/04/19
Walden Savings Bank	NY	12/04/19
West Texas State Bank	TX	12/04/19
West Town Bank & Trust	IL	12/04/19
West View Savings Bank	PA	12/04/19
Wilcox County State Bank	GA	12/04/19

Rating: C+

Name	State	Date of Change
Adrian State Bank	MN	12/04/19
All America Bank	OK	12/04/19
American Bank	OK	12/04/19
American Commerce Bank, N.A.	GA	12/04/19
BANK 34	NM	12/04/19
Bank of Calhoun County	IL	12/04/19
Bank of Commerce	OK	12/04/19
Bank of Gibson City	IL	12/04/19
Bank of Gravette	AR	12/04/19
Bank of Hamilton	ND	12/04/19
Bank of Hindman	KY	12/04/19
Bank of Little Rock	AR	12/04/19
Bank of Vici	OK	12/04/19
Bank Plus	IA	12/04/19
Basile State Bank	LA	12/04/19
Bay Port State Bank	MI	12/04/19
BayCoast Bank	MA	12/04/19
Beal Bank, SSB	TX	12/04/19
Caldwell Bank & Trust Co.	LA	12/04/19
California Bank of Commerce	CA	12/04/19
Capital Community Bank	UT	12/04/19
Carolina Trust Bank	NC	12/04/19
CenTrust Bank, N.A.	IL	12/04/19
Century Bank of Florida	FL	12/04/19
Century Bank of Kentucky, Inc.	KY	12/04/19
Chappell Hill Bank	TX	12/04/19
Citizens Bank	KY	12/04/19
Citizens Bank & Trust Co.	MN	12/04/19
Citizens Bank & Trust Co.	MT	12/04/19
Citizens Bank of Cape Vincent	NY	12/04/19
Citizens Bank of Florida	FL	12/04/19
Citizens National Bank of Bluffton	OH	12/04/19
Commercial Bank	MI	12/04/19
Commercial State Bank	TX	12/04/19
Community Bankers' Bank	VA	12/04/19
Community Financial Bank	WI	12/04/19
Community Partners Savings Bank	IL	12/04/19
Community State Bank	FL	12/04/19
Community State Bank	IL	12/04/19
County Bank	DE	12/04/19
Covington County Bank	MS	12/04/19
Dundee Bank	NE	12/04/19
Ergo Bank	WI	12/04/19
ESB Bank	MN	12/04/19
Exchange Bank of Northeast Missouri	MO	12/04/19
Farmers & Merchants Bank	OK	12/04/19
Farmers & Merchants Bank	WI	12/04/19
Farmers & Merchants Bank	ND	12/04/19

Rating Upgrades

Name	State	Date of Change
Farmers and Merchants Bank	TX	12/04/19
Farmers and Merchants State Bank	MN	12/04/19
Farmers State Bank	OH	12/04/19
Federation Bank	IA	12/04/19
Fidelity State Bank and Trust Co.	KS	12/04/19
Field & Main Bank	KY	12/04/19
First Bank of Baldwin	WI	12/04/19
First Bank of Celeste	TX	12/04/19
First Enterprise Bank	OK	12/04/19
First Federal Bank of Ohio	OH	12/04/19
First Federal S&L Assn.	KY	12/04/19
First Federal Savings of Middletown	NY	12/04/19
First National B&T Co. of Vinita	OK	12/04/19
First National Bank	TX	12/04/19
First National Bank Baird	TX	12/04/19
First National Bank in Fairfield	IA	12/04/19
First National Bank of Absecon	NJ	12/04/19
First National Bank of Bellevue	OH	12/04/19
First National Bank of Coleraine	MN	12/04/19
First National Bank of Lacon	IL	12/04/19
First National Bank of Pasco	FL	12/04/19
First National Bank of Wakefield	MI	12/04/19
First Secure Community Bank	IL	12/04/19
First State Bank	TX	12/04/19
First State Bank	OK	12/04/19
First State Bank	OK	12/04/19
First State Bank	OK	12/04/19
First State Bank of DeKalb County	AL	12/04/19
First State Bank of Healy	KS	12/04/19
First State Bank of Purdy	MO	12/04/19
First Utah Bank	UT	12/04/19
Fortifi Bank	WI	12/04/19
Glenwood State Bank	MN	12/04/19
Gogebic Range Bank	MI	12/04/19
Grand Bank	OK	12/04/19
Granite Community Bank	MN	12/04/19
HarborOne Bank	MA	12/04/19
Hartsburg State Bank	IL	12/04/19
Heartland State Bank	ND	12/04/19
Heritage Bank of Schaumburg	IL	12/04/19
Highlands Union Bank	VA	12/04/19
Holcomb Bank	IL	12/04/19
Home Federal S&L Assn. of Niles Ohio	OH	12/04/19
Home Loan State Bank	CO	12/04/19
Hometown Community Bank	MN	12/04/19
Integrity Bank Plus	MN	12/04/19
Kalamazoo County State Bank	MI	12/04/19
Kaw Valley State Bank	KS	12/04/19
Kerndt Brothers Savings Bank	IA	12/04/19
Kleberg Bank, N.A.	TX	12/04/19
Landmark Bank	LA	12/04/19
Lincoln FSB of Nebraska	NE	12/04/19
Lone Star State Bank of West Texas	TX	12/04/19
Marion National Bank	KS	12/04/19
MCNB Bank and Trust Co.	WV	12/04/19
Medallion Bank	UT	12/04/19
Merchants and Farmers Bank of Salisbury	MO	12/04/19
Milford Bank	CT	12/04/19
Mineola Community Bank, SSB	TX	12/04/19
Miners National Bank of Eveleth	MN	12/04/19
Mitchell Bank	WI	12/04/19
MNB Bank	NE	12/04/19
New Foundation Savings Bank	OH	12/04/19
New Frontier Bank	MO	12/04/19
New Millennium Bank	NJ	12/04/19
Northeast Bank	ME	12/04/19
Northern Sky Bank	MN	12/04/19
Northstar Bank	MI	12/04/19
Oklahoma Heritage Bank	OK	12/04/19
Old Point National Bank of Phoebus	VA	12/04/19
People's B&T Co. of Clinton County	KY	12/04/19
People's B&T Co. of Pickett County	TN	12/04/19
Peoples Community Bank SB	IN	12/04/19
Peoples State Bank of Wells	MN	12/04/19
Popular Bank	NY	12/04/19
Primary Bank	NH	12/04/19
Progressive National Bank	LA	12/04/19
Raritan State Bank	IL	12/04/19
Riddell National Bank	IN	12/04/19
RiverWood Bank	MN	12/04/19
Roanoke Rapids Savings Bank, SSB	NC	12/04/19
Rockland Savings Bank, FSB	ME	12/04/19
Rocky Mountain Bank & Trust	CO	12/04/19
Sandhills State Bank	NE	12/04/19
Security State Bank	KS	12/04/19
Sentry Bank	MN	12/04/19
Shelby County State Bank	IA	12/04/19
Sherwood Community Bank	MO	12/04/19
Simply Bank	TN	12/04/19
SNB Bank, N.A.	OK	12/04/19
Spring Bank	WI	12/04/19
SSB Community Bank	OH	12/04/19
Standing Stone Bank	OH	12/04/19
Stanton State Bank	NE	12/04/19
State Bank of Lake Park	MN	12/04/19
State Bank of Spring Hill	KS	12/04/19
State Bank of Taunton	MN	12/04/19
Stock Exchange Bank	KS	12/04/19
Stone Bank	AR	12/04/19
TCM Bank, N.A.	FL	12/04/19

Rating Upgrades

Name	State	Date of Change
Tower Community Bank	TN	12/04/19
TriStar Bank	TN	12/04/19
Ultima Bank Minnesota	MN	12/04/19
Union S&L Assn.	IN	12/04/19
United Valley Bank	ND	12/04/19
Village Bank	MN	12/04/19
Wayne County Bank	TN	12/04/19
Western Bank, Artesia, New Mexico	NM	12/04/19
Western Heritage Bank	NM	12/04/19
YNB	OK	12/04/19
York State Bank	NE	12/04/19

Rating: C

Name	State	Date of Change
Abbeville First Bank	SC	12/04/19
Alden State Bank	KS	12/04/19
Algonquin State Bank	IL	12/04/19
Alliance Bank & Trust Co.	NC	12/04/19
Americana Community Bank	MN	12/04/19
Arbor Bank	NE	12/04/19
Bank of Glen Ullin	ND	12/04/19
Bank of Iberia	MO	12/04/19
Bank of Kaukauna	WI	12/04/19
Bank of Newington	GA	12/04/19
Bank of Steinauer	NE	12/04/19
Bank of the Valley	NE	12/04/19
BankVista	MN	12/04/19
BankWest, Inc.	SD	12/04/19
Beal Bank USA	NV	12/04/19
Blue Grass Valley Bank	VA	12/04/19
Bonanza Valley State Bank	MN	12/04/19
Cache Bank & Trust	CO	12/04/19
Carter Bank & Trust	VA	12/04/19
Catahoula-LaSalle Bank	LA	12/04/19
CBC Bank	MO	12/04/19
CFG Community Bank	MD	12/04/19
Citizens Bank & Trust Co. of Jackson	KY	12/04/19
Citizens Bank of Edinburg	IL	12/04/19
Citizens First State Bank of Walnut	IL	12/04/19
Citizens Progressive Bank	LA	12/04/19
Citizens State Bank of Ouray	CO	12/04/19
CNB Bank & Trust, N.A.	IL	12/04/19
Coatesville Savings Bank	PA	12/04/19
Collinsville Building and Loan Assn.	IL	12/04/19
Columbia Bank	FL	12/04/19
Community Bank of Snyder	TX	12/04/19
Community State Bank	AR	12/04/19
Community West Bank, N.A.	CA	12/04/19
Corder Bank	MO	12/04/19
Cornerstone Bank	ND	12/04/19
County Savings Bank	PA	12/04/19
Crown Bank	NJ	12/04/19
Culbertson Bank	NE	12/04/19
Empire State Bank	NY	12/04/19
Farmers Deposit Bank	KY	12/04/19
Farmers State Bank of Bucklin, Kansas	KS	12/04/19
First FarmBank	CO	12/04/19
First National Bank of Assumption	IL	12/04/19
First National Bank of Elmer	NJ	12/04/19
First Resource Bank	PA	12/04/19
First Security Bank	MO	12/04/19
First Security Bank & Trust Co.	IA	12/04/19
First Security State Bank	IA	12/04/19
First State Bank	TX	12/04/19
First State Bank	NE	12/04/19
First State Bank of Van Orin	IL	12/04/19
First Tri-County Bank	NE	12/04/19
First United Bank	ND	12/04/19
Flint Community Bank	GA	12/04/19
FNBC Bank	AR	12/04/19
Frontier State Bank	OK	12/04/19
Gibsland Bank & Trust Co.	LA	12/04/19
Golden Pacific Bank, N.A.	CA	12/04/19
Harwood State Bank	ND	12/04/19
Hiawatha National Bank	WI	12/04/19
Iuka State Bank	IL	12/04/19
Lakeside State Bank	OK	12/04/19
Limestone Bank, Inc.	KY	12/04/19
Longview Bank & Trust	IL	12/04/19
Lyndon State Bank	KS	12/04/19
Malvern Bank	IA	12/04/19
Marblehead Bank	MA	12/04/19
Marine Bank	IL	12/04/19
Mariner's Bank	NJ	12/04/19
McIntosh County Bank	ND	12/04/19
Mediapolis Savings Bank	IA	12/04/19
Meramec Valley Bank	MO	12/04/19
Morris Bank	GA	12/04/19
Mountain Valley Bank	TN	12/04/19
Nebraska State Bank	NE	12/04/19
New Buffalo Savings Bank	MI	12/04/19
One American Bank	SD	12/04/19
Oxford Bank & Trust	IL	12/04/19
Passumpsic Bank	VT	12/04/19
Peoples Bank	IA	12/04/19
Pilot Bank	FL	12/04/19
Plains Commerce Bank	SD	12/04/19
Premier Bank	IA	12/04/19
Princeville State Bank	IL	12/04/19
Rhinebeck Bank	NY	12/04/19
Riverview Bank	PA	12/04/19

Rating Upgrades

Name	State	Date of Change
St. Louis Bank	MO	12/04/19
State Bank of Burrton	KS	12/04/19
State Bank of Bussey	IA	12/04/19
State Bank of New Richland	MN	12/04/19
Stockmans Bank	OK	12/04/19
Stride Bank, N.A.	OK	12/04/19
Thayer County Bank	NE	12/04/19
Third Coast Bank, SSB	TX	12/04/19
Turtle Mountain State Bank	ND	12/04/19
Union Bank	MI	12/04/19
Union Bank of Blair	WI	12/04/19
Union State Bank	KS	12/04/19
United Bank of Michigan	MI	12/04/19
United Bank of Union	MO	12/04/19
United Community Bank	LA	12/04/19
United Minnesota Bank	MN	12/04/19
United Southwest Bank	MN	12/04/19
Village Bank	VA	12/04/19
Wallkill Valley Federal S&L Assn.	NY	12/04/19
WCF Financial Bank	IA	12/04/19
West End Bank, S.B.	IN	12/04/19
Western National Bank	MN	12/04/19
Western National Bank of Cass Lake	MN	12/04/19

Rating: C-

Name	State	Date of Change
1st Equity Bank	IL	12/04/19
Banco Popular de Puerto Rico	PR	12/04/19
Bank Michigan	MI	12/04/19
Bank of Benoit	MS	12/04/19
Bank of Commerce	OK	12/04/19
Bank of Delmarva	MD	12/04/19
Bank of Eastman	GA	12/04/19
Bank of Louisiana	LA	12/04/19
Bank of the Mountains, Inc.	KY	12/04/19
Bank of Wyandotte	OK	12/04/19
Benton State Bank	WI	12/04/19
Brickyard Bank	IL	12/04/19
Chesterfield State Bank	IL	12/04/19
Citizens State Bank of Tyler, Inc.	MN	12/04/19
Community State Bank	OK	12/04/19
COREBANK	OK	12/04/19
Decatur County Bank	TN	12/04/19
Envision Bank	MA	12/04/19
Farmers & Merchants Bank	TN	12/04/19
Farmers State Bank	IL	12/04/19
First Capital Bank	TX	12/04/19
First National Bank of Lipan	TX	12/04/19
First National Bank of Sedan	KS	12/04/19
First State Bank	OK	12/04/19
FirstBank Puerto Rico	PR	12/04/19
Florida Capital Bank, N.A.	FL	12/04/19
Fortis Private Bank	CO	12/04/19
Freedom Bank, Inc.	WV	12/04/19
Green Belt Bank & Trust	IA	12/04/19
Henderson State Bank	NE	12/04/19
Kindred State Bank	ND	12/04/19
Logan State Bank	IA	12/04/19
Mechanics and Farmers Bank	NC	12/04/19
Mutual Federal Bank	IL	12/04/19
Mutual Savings Bank	SC	12/04/19
Optus Bank	SC	12/04/19
Oriental Bank	PR	12/04/19
Pee Dee Federal Savings Bank	SC	12/04/19
Peoples Bank of Deer Lodge	MT	12/04/19
Peoples Bank of Moniteau County	MO	12/04/19
Plains State Bank	TX	12/04/19
Rowley Savings Bank	IA	12/04/19
Rushford State Bank (Inc.)	MN	12/04/19
Saints Avenue Bank	MO	12/04/19
Savoy Bank	NY	12/04/19
Security State Bank	IA	12/04/19
State Bank of Easton	MN	12/04/19
Summit National Bank	WY	12/04/19
Texas Citizens Bank, N.A.	TX	12/04/19
United Midwest Savings Bank, N.A.	OH	12/04/19
Vantage Bank	MN	12/04/19
Western Dakota Bank	SD	12/04/19
Woodsfield Savings Bank	OH	12/04/19

Rating: D+

Name	State	Date of Change
American Equity Bank	MN	12/04/19
Bank of Austin	TX	12/04/19
Bank3	TN	12/04/19
Citizens National Bank of Hammond	NY	12/04/19
Coastal States Bank	SC	12/04/19
Commonwealth National Bank	AL	12/04/19
Farm Bureau Bank, FSB	NV	12/04/19
Farmers and Merchants Bank	KS	12/04/19
First Bank, Upper Michigan	MI	12/04/19
First Chatham Bank	GA	12/04/19
First Community National Bank	MO	12/04/19
First Federal S&L Assn. of Ravenswood	WV	12/04/19
First State Bank of Bigfork	MN	12/04/19
First State Bank of Kiester	MN	12/04/19
Home Loan Investment Bank, F.S.B.	RI	12/04/19
Hyperion Bank	PA	12/04/19
Metropolitan Capital Bank & Trust	IL	12/04/19
OmniBank	MS	12/04/19
Peoples State Bank	ND	12/04/19
Powell State Bank	TX	12/04/19

Rating Upgrades

Name	State	Date of Change
Prairie Sun Bank	MN	12/04/19
PyraMax Bank, FSB	WI	12/04/19
State Bank of Eagle Butte	SD	12/04/19
Talbot State Bank	GA	12/04/19

Rating: D

Name	State	Date of Change
Best Hometown Bank	IL	12/04/19
Citizens State Bank	TX	12/04/19
Colorado National Bank	CO	12/04/19
Corn Growers State Bank	NE	12/04/19
Eagle Community Bank	MN	12/04/19
First National Bank of Buhl	MN	12/04/19
Great Plains Bank	SD	12/04/19
Movement Bank	VA	12/04/19
State Bank of Colon	NE	12/04/19
Vermont State Bank	IL	12/04/19

Rating: D-

Name	State	Date of Change
Dysart State Bank	IA	12/04/19
Equitable Bank, S.S.B.	WI	12/04/19
Gateway Bank, F.S.B.	CA	12/04/19
Homestead Savings Bank	MI	12/04/19
Millennial Bank	AL	12/04/19

Rating: E+

Name	State	Date of Change
Cogent Bank	FL	12/04/19
Nantahala Bank & Trust Co.	NC	12/04/19

Rating: E

Name	State	Date of Change
Commercial State Bank	NE	12/04/19

Name	State	Date of Change

Rating Downgrades

Name	State	Date of Change
Rating: A-		
First Bank & Trust Co.	OK	12/04/19
Home Exchange Bank	MO	12/04/19
Paducah Bank and Trust Co.	KY	12/04/19
Prime Bank	OK	12/04/19
Rating: B+		
Citizens Bank of Lafayette	TN	12/04/19
Citizens State Bank of Loyal	WI	12/04/19
EnerBank USA	UT	12/04/19
First Missouri State Bank	MO	12/04/19
First National Bank	IA	12/04/19
Hanmi Bank	CA	12/04/19
Hometown National Bank	IL	12/04/19
International City Bank	CA	12/04/19
Merchants Bank of Indiana	IN	12/04/19
NexBank SSB	TX	12/04/19
Suncrest Bank	CA	12/04/19
Rating: B		
Bank of Brenham, N.A.	TX	12/04/19
Bank of the Orient	CA	12/04/19
Chickasaw Community Bank	OK	12/04/19
Dime Community Bank	NY	12/04/19
Exchange Bank and Trust Co.	OK	12/04/19
Farmers Savings Bank	IA	12/04/19
Fayetteville Bank	TX	12/04/19
First Farmers & Merchants State Bank	MN	12/04/19
First Western Bank & Trust	ND	12/04/19
Flushing Bank	NY	12/04/19
Franklin Synergy Bank	TN	12/04/19
Gouverneur S&L Assn.	NY	12/04/19
Grove Bank & Trust	FL	12/04/19
New Century Bank	KS	12/04/19
New Tripoli Bank	PA	12/04/19
New York Community Bank	NY	12/04/19
Pacific Enterprise Bank	CA	12/04/19
Powell Valley National Bank	VA	12/04/19
Primebank	IA	12/04/19
S&T Bank	PA	12/04/19
Salyersville National Bank	KY	12/04/19
SJN Bank of Kansas	KS	12/04/19
State Savings Bank	IA	12/04/19
West Point Bank	KY	12/04/19
Rating: B-		
American Express National Bank	UT	12/04/19
CalPrivate Bank	CA	12/04/19
Commerce Bank	MN	12/04/19
Commercial Bank	KY	12/04/19
Eastbank, N.A.	NY	12/04/19
First Bank of Manhattan	IL	12/04/19
First Covenant Bank	GA	12/04/19
First National Bank of Osakis	MN	12/04/19
Geddes Federal S&L Assn.	NY	12/04/19
Harvest Bank	MN	12/04/19
Mechanics Bank	CA	12/04/19
Pacific Mercantile Bank	CA	12/04/19
Peshtigo National Bank	WI	12/04/19
Pioneer Bank	WI	12/04/19
Pioneer Federal S&L Assn.	MT	12/04/19
Security Bank	OK	12/04/19
Southern States Bank	AL	12/04/19
Texas Gulf Bank, N.A.	TX	12/04/19
Washington State Bank	LA	12/04/19
West Plains S&L Assn.	MO	12/04/19
Westfield Bank	MA	12/04/19
Rating: C+		
Aroostook County Federal S&L Assn.	ME	12/04/19
Baltic State Bank	OH	12/04/19
Charis Bank	TX	12/04/19
Cincinnati Federal	OH	12/04/19
Dakota Heritage Bank	ND	12/04/19
Dart Bank	MI	12/04/19
First National Bank of Raymond	IL	12/04/19
First National Bank of Tahoka	TX	12/04/19
Georgia Banking Co.	GA	12/04/19
Gorham State Bank	KS	12/04/19
Hatch Bank	CA	12/04/19
Heritage Southeast Bank	GA	12/04/19
Huntington Federal Savings Bank	WV	12/04/19
InBank	NM	12/04/19
MUFG Union Bank, N.A.	NY	12/04/19
Newton Federal Bank	GA	12/04/19
Peoples National Bank, N.A.	IL	12/04/19
Pinnacle Bank	AZ	12/04/19
Rochelle State Bank	GA	12/04/19
St. Landry Bank and Trust Co.	LA	12/04/19
State Bank of Fairmont	MN	12/04/19
Union County Savings Bank	NJ	12/04/19
Union State Bank	KS	12/04/19
Universal Bank	CA	12/04/19
Vidalia Federal Savings Bank	GA	12/04/19
Rating: C		
Asian Pacific National Bank	CA	12/04/19
Banc of California, N.A.	CA	12/04/19
Broadway Federal Bank, F.S.B.	CA	12/04/19

Rating Downgrades

Name	State	Date of Change
Cass County Bank, Inc.	NE	12/04/19
Citizens State Bank	NE	12/04/19
Farmers Savings Bank	IA	12/04/19
First Trust and Savings Bank	IA	12/04/19
HSBC Bank USA, N.A.	VA	12/04/19
LincolnWay Community Bank	IL	12/04/19
Merchants & Planters Bank	AR	12/04/19
Nokomis Savings Bank	IL	12/04/19
One Florida Bank	FL	12/04/19
Pleasants County Bank	WV	12/04/19
Scotiabank de Puerto Rico	PR	12/04/19
Shinhan Bank America	NY	12/04/19
Southeast First National Bank	GA	12/04/19
Spectra Bank	TX	12/04/19
Winnsboro State Bank & Trust Co.	LA	12/04/19

Rating: C-

Name	State	Date of Change
1st Trust Bank, Inc.	KY	12/04/19
Bank of the Rockies	MT	12/04/19
Chasewood Bank	TX	12/04/19
Ericson State Bank	NE	12/04/19
Farmers State Bank	WY	12/04/19
Farmers State Bank of Alto Pass, Ill.	IL	12/04/19
First Capital Bank	NC	12/04/19
FNNB Bank	IA	12/04/19
Four Corners Community Bank	NM	12/04/19
Frazer Bank	OK	12/04/19
KansasLand Bank	KS	12/04/19
Kendall State Bank	KS	12/04/19
Kensington Bank	MN	12/04/19
Neighbors Bank	MO	12/04/19
OptimumBank	FL	12/04/19
Peoples Bank	IA	12/04/19
Quail Creek Bank, N.A.	OK	12/04/19
South Central Bank, N.A.	IL	12/04/19
Valley Bank of Ronan	MT	12/04/19

Rating: D+

Name	State	Date of Change
ACB Bank	OK	12/04/19
Andes State Bank	SD	12/04/19
Aspire Financial	ND	12/04/19
Bank of Eastern Oregon	OR	12/04/19
Bank of Houston, N.A.	TX	12/04/19
Citizens Bank & Trust Co.	NE	12/04/19
Dogwood State Bank	NC	12/04/19
Eastern National Bank	FL	12/04/19
Family Federal Savings, F.A.	MA	12/04/19
First State Bank of Randolph County	GA	12/04/19
Fowler State Bank	KS	12/04/19
Maple Bank	MN	12/04/19
Peoples Bank	LA	12/04/19
Republic First Bank	PA	12/04/19
Rolling Hills Bank & Trust	IA	12/04/19
Security State Bank of Warroad	MN	12/04/19
SouthFirst Bank	AL	12/04/19
State Bank of Nauvoo	IL	12/04/19
Sunrise Bank Dakota	SD	12/04/19

Rating: D

Name	State	Date of Change
AllNations Bank	OK	12/04/19
Community Savings Bank	IA	12/04/19
Enterprise Bank	PA	12/04/19
First National Bank of Hope	KS	12/04/19
Home Savings Bank, FSB	KY	12/04/19
State Bank of Toledo	IA	12/04/19
Tennessee Bank & Trust	TN	12/04/19
VCC Bank	VA	12/04/19

Rating: D-

Name	State	Date of Change
22nd State Bank	AL	12/04/19
Almena State Bank	KS	12/04/19
Buckeye State Bank	OH	12/04/19
Community First Bank	NE	12/04/19
Compass Savings Bank	PA	12/04/19
GN Bank	IL	12/04/19
Jackson County Bank	WI	12/04/19
Rockhold Bank	OH	12/04/19
State Bank	WY	12/04/19
State Bank of Burnettsville	IN	12/04/19

Rating: E+

Name	State	Date of Change
Dickinson County Bank	KS	12/04/19
Liberty Bank, Inc.	UT	12/04/19

Rating: E

Name	State	Date of Change
Brighton Bank	TN	12/04/19

Appendix

RECENT BANK FAILURES
2019

Institution	Headquarters	Date of Failure	At Date of Failure	
			Total Assets ($Mil)	Safety Rating
City National Bank of NJ	Newark, NJ	11/1/19	142.5	E- (Very Weak)
Resolute Bank	Maumee, OH	10/25/19	27.1	E+ (Very Weak)
Enloe State Bank	Cooper, TX	5/31/19	36.5	C (Fair)

2017

Institution	Headquarters	Date of Failure	At Date of Failure Total Assets ($Mil)	Safety Rating
Washington Federal Banks for Savings	Chicago, IL	12/15/17	166.4	A (Excellent)
Farmers & Merchants State Bk of Argonia	Argonia, KS	10/13/17	34.2	E- (Very Weak)
Fayette County Bank	Saint Elmo, IL	05/26/17	34.8	E- (Very Weak)
Guaranty Bank (MHC)	Milwaukee, WI	05/05/17	1,010.0	E- (Very Weak)
First NBC Bank	New Orleans, LA	04/28/17	4,740.0	E- (Very Weak)
Proficio Bank	Cottonwood Heights, UT	03/03/17	80.3	E- (Very Weak)
Seaway Bank and Trust Co	Chicago, IL	01/27/17	361.2	E- (Very Weak)
Harvest Community Bank	Pennsville, NJ	01/13/17	126.4	E- (Very Weak)

2016

Institution	Headquarters	Date of Failure	At Date of Failure	
			Total Assets ($Mil)	Safety Rating
Allied Bank	Mulberry, AR	09/23/16	66.3	E- (Very Weak)
Woodbury Banking Company	Woodbury, GA	08/19/16	22.5	E- (Very Weak)
First Cornerstone Bank	King of Prussia, PA	05/06/16	107.0	E- (Very Weak)
Trust Co Bank	Memphis, TN	04/29/16	20.7	E- (Very Weak)
North Milwaukee State Bank	Milwaukee, WI	03/11/16	67.1	E- (Very Weak)

2015

Institution	Headquarters	Date of Failure	At Date of Failure	
			Total Assets ($Mil)	Safety Rating
Bramble Savings Bank	Milford, OH	12/17/15	47.5	E- (Very Weak)
Bank of Georgia	Peachtree City, GA	10/02/15	294.2	E- (Very Weak)
Hometown National Bank	Longview, WA	10/02/15	4.9	E+ (Very Weak)
Premier Bank	Denever, CO	07/10/15	31.7	E- (Very Weak)
Edgebrook Bank	Chicago, IL	05/08/15	90.0	E- (Very Weak)
Doral Bank	San Juan, PR	02/27/15	5,900.0	E+ (Very Weak)
Capitol City Bank & Trust Co	Atlanta, GA	02/13/15	272.3	E- (Very Weak)
Highland Community Bank	Chicago, IL	01/23/15	54.7	E- (Very Weak)
First National Bank of Crestview	Crestview, FL	01/16/15	79.7	E- (Very Weak)

2014

Institution	Headquarters	Date of Failure	At Date of Failure	
			Total Assets ($Mil)	Safety Rating
Northern Star Bank	Makato, MN	12/19/14	18.8	E- (Very Weak)
Frontier Bank, FSB	Palm Desert, CA	11/07/14	86.4	E- (Very Weak)
National Republic Bk of Chicago	Chicago, IL	10/24/14	954.4	E- (Very Weak)
NBRS Financial	Rising Sun, MD	10/17/14	188.2	E- (Very Weak)
Greenchoice Bank FSB	Chicago, IL	07/25/14	72.9	E- (Very Weak)
Eastside Commercial Bank	Conyers, GA	07/18/14	169.0	E- (Very Weak)
Freedom State Bank	Freedom, OK	06/27/14	22.8	D (Weak)
Valley Bank	Moline, IL	06/20/14	456.4	E+ (Very Weak)
Valley Bank	Fort Lauderdale, FL	06/20/14	81.8	E- (Very Weak)
Slavie Federal Savings Bank	Bel Air, MD	05/30/14	140.1	E- (Very Weak)
Columbia Savings Bank	Cincinnati, OH	05/23/14	36.5	E- (Very Weak)
AztecAmerica Bank	Berwyn, IL	05/16/14	66.3	E- (Very Weak)
Allendale County Bank	Fairfax, SC	04/25/14	54.5	E- (Very Weak)
Millennium Bank NA	Sterling, VA	02/28/14	130.3	E- (Very Weak)
Vantage Point Bank	Horsham, PA	02/28/14	63.5	E- (Very Weak)
Syringa Bank	Boise, ID	01/31/14	153.4	E- (Very Weak)
Bank of Union	El Reno, OK	01/24/14	331.4	D- (Weak)
DuPage National Bank	West Chicago, IL	01/17/14	61.7	E- (Very Weak)

2013

Institution	Headquarters	Date of Failure	At Date of Failure	
			Total Assets ($Mil)	Safety Rating
Texas Community Bank	The Woodlands, TX	12/13/13	160.1	E- (Very Weak)
Bank of Jackson County	Graceville, FL	10/30/13	25.5	E- (Very Weak)
Communitys Bank	Bridgeport, CT	09/13/13	26.3	E- (Very Weak)
First National Bank	Edinburg, TX	09/13/13	3100.0	E- (Very Weak)
Community South Bank	Parsons, TN	08/24/13	386.9	E- (Very Weak)
Sunrise Bank of Arizona	Phoenix, AZ	08/24/13	202.2	E- (Very Weak)
Bank of Wausau	Wausau, WI	08/09/13	43.6	E- (Very Weak)
First Community Bank of SW FL	Fort Meyers, FL	08/02/13	265.7	E- (Very Weak)
Mountain National Bank	Sevierville, TN	06/07/13	437.3	E- (Very Weak)
1st Commerce Bank	N. Las Vegas, NV	06/06/13	20.2	E- (Very Weak)
Banks of Wisconsin	Kenosha, WI	05/31/13	134.0	E- (Very Weak)
Central Arizona Bank	Scottsdale, AZ	05/14/13	31.6	E- (Very Weak)
Pisgah Community Bank	Asheville, NC	05/10/13	21.9	E- (Very Weak)
Sunrise Bank	Valdosta, GA	05/10/13	60.8	E- (Very Weak)
Douglas County Bank	Douglasville, GA	04/26/13	316.5	E- (Very Weak)
Parkway Bank	Lenoir, NC	04/26/13	108.6	E- (Very Weak)
Chipola Community Bank	Marianna, FL	04/19/13	39.2	E- (Very Weak)
First Federal Bank	Lexington, KY	04/19/13	100.1	E- (Very Weak)
Heritage Bank of North Florida	Orange Park, FL	04/19/13	110.9	E- (Very Weak)
Gold Canyon Bank	Gold Canyon, AZ	04/05/13	44.2	E- (Very Weak)
Frontier Bank	LaGrange, GA	03/08//13	258.8	E- (Very Weak)
Covenant Bank	Chicago, IL	02/15/13	58.4	E- (Very Weak)
1st Regents Bank	Andover, MN	01/18/13	50.2	E- (Very Weak)
Westside Community Bank	University Place, WA	01/11/13	97.7	E- (Very Weak)

How Do Banks and Credit Unions Differ?

Since credit unions first appeared in 1946, they have been touted as a low-cost, friendly alternative to banks. But with tightening margins, pressure to compete in technology, branch closures, and the introduction of a host of service fees — some even higher than those charged by banks — the distinction between banks and credit unions has been gradually narrowing. Following are the key differences between today's banks and credit unions.

	Banks	Credit Unions
Access	Practically anyone is free to open an account or request a loan from any bank. There are no membership requirements.	Credit unions are set up to serve the needs of a specific group who share a "common bond." In order to open an account or request a loan, you must demonstrate that you meet the credit union's common bond requirements.
Ownership	Banks are owned by one or more investors who determine the bank's policies and procedures. A bank's customers do not have direct input into how the bank is operated.	Although they may be sponsored by a corporation or other entity, credit unions are owned by their members through their funds on deposit. Therefore, each depositor has a voice in how the credit union is operated.
Dividends and Fees	Banks are for-profit organizations where the profits are used to pay dividends to the bank's investors or are reinvested in an effort to increase the bank's value to investors. In an effort to generate more profits, bank services and fees are typically more costly.	Credit unions are not-for-profit organizations. Any profits generated are returned to the credit union's members in the form of higher interest rates on deposits, lower loan rates, and free or low-cost services.
Management and Staffing	A bank's management and other staff are employees of the bank, hired directly or indirectly by its investors.	Credit unions are frequently run using elected members, volunteer staff, and staff provided by the credit union's sponsor. This helps to hold down costs.
Insurance	Banks are insured by the Federal Deposit Insurance Corporation, an agency of the federal government.	Credit unions are insured by the National Credit Union Share Insurance Fund, which is managed by the National Credit Union Administration, an agency of the federal government.

Glossary

This glossary contains the most important terms used in this publication.

ARM Adjustable-Rate Mortgage. This is a loan whose interest rate is tied to an index and is adjusted at a predetermined frequency. An ARM is subject to credit risk if interest rates rise and the borrower is unable to make the mortgage payment.

Average Recession A recession involving a decline in real GDP that is approximately equivalent to the average of the postwar recessions of 1957-58, 1960, 1970, 1974-75, 1980, 1981-82, 1990-1991, 2001, and 2007-2009. It is assumed, however, that in today's market, the financial losses suffered from a recession of that magnitude would be greater than those experienced in previous decades. (See also "Severe Recession.")

Bank Holding Company A company that holds stock in one or more banks and possibly other companies.

Bank Insurance Fund (BIF) A unit of Federal Deposit Insurance Corporation (FDIC) that provided deposit insurance for banks, other than thrifts. BIF was formed as part of the 1989 savings and loan association bailout bill to keep separate the administration of the bank and thrift insurance programs. There were thus two distinct insurance entities under the FDIC: BIF and savings association insurance fund (SAIF). (See also Federal Deposit Insurance Corporation.")

Brokered Deposits Deposits that are brought into an institution through a broker. They are relatively costly, volatile funds that are more readily withdrawn from the institution if there is a loss of confidence or intense interest rate competition. Reliance on brokered deposits is usually a sign that the institution is having difficulty attracting deposits from its local geographic markets and could be a warning signal if other institutions in the same areas are not experiencing similar difficulties.

Capital The cushion an institution has of its own resources to help withstand losses. The basic component of capital is stockholder's equity which consists of common and preferred stock and retained earnings. (See also "Core Capital")

Cash & Equivalents Cash plus highly liquid assets which can be readily converted to cash.

Core (Tier 1) Capital A measurement of capital defined by the federal regulatory agencies for evaluating an institution's degree of leverage. Core capital consists of the following: common stockholder's equity, preferred stockholder's equity up to certain limits, and retained earnings net of any intangible assets.

Critical Ranges Guidelines developed to help you evaluate the levels of each index contributing to a company's Weiss Safety Rating. The sum or average of these grades does not necessarily have a one-to-one correspondence with the final rating for an institution because the rating is derived from a wider range of more complex calculations.

Deposit Insurance Fund (DIF) In 2005 Congress passed legislation merging the SAIF and BIF into one insurance fund called the deposit insurance fund (DIF). The same law also raised the federal deposit insurance level from $100,000 to $250,000. (See also "Emergency Economic Stabilization Act.")

Emergency Stabilization Act In 2008 Congress passed the Emergency Economic Stabilization Act that temporarily increased the basic limit on deposit insurance for all ownership categories from $100,000 to $250,000. This increase was set to expire in 2013 but has been extended permanently.

Equity Total assets minus total liabilities. This is the "capital cushion" the institution has to fall back on in times of trouble. (See also "Capital.")

FDIC Federal Deposit Insurance Corporation. The provider of insurance on deposits. This agency also plays an active role when banks are found to be insolvent or in need of federal assistance. It is the governing body of the Deposit Insurance Fund (DIF) that now incorporates both the Bank Insurance Fund (BIF) and the Savings Association Insurance Fund (SAIF). (See also "Deposit Insurance Fund.")

Federal Home Loan Bank (FHLB) A quasi-governmental agency (reporting to the Federal Housing Finance Board) whose chartered purpose is to promote the issuance of mortgage loans by providing increased liquidity to lenders. This agency raises money by issuing notes and bonds and then lends the money to banks and other mortgage lenders.

Federal Reserve America's central bank, regulating all banks that offer transaction accounts. It works hand-in-hand with the FDIC, providing examination and regulation of its member banks.

Safety Rating Weiss Safety Ratings, which grade institutions on a scale from A (Excellent) to F (Failed). Ratings are based on many factors, emphasizing capitalization, asset quality, profitability, liquidity, and stability.

FSB Federal Savings Bank. A thrift institution operating under a federal charter.

Goodwill The value of an institution as a going concern, meaning the value which exceeds book value on a balance sheet. It generally represents the value of a well-respected business name, good customer relations, high employee morale and other intangible factors which would be expected to translate into greater than normal earning power. In a bank acquisition, goodwill is the value paid by a buyer of the institution in excess of the value of the institution's equity because of these intangible factors.

Hot Money Individual deposits of $100,000 or more plus those deposits received through a broker. These types of deposits are considered "hot money" because they tend to chase whoever is offering the best interest rates at the time and are thus relatively costly and fairly volatile sources of funds.

Loan Loss Reserves The amount of capital an institution sets aside to cover any potential losses due to the nonrepayment of loans.

N.A. National Association. A commercial bank operating under a federal charter.

Net Charge-offs The amount of foreclosed loans written off the institution's books since the beginning of the year, less any previous write-offs that were recovered during the year.

Net Interest Spread The difference between the interest income earned on the institution's loans and investments and the interest expense paid on its interest-bearing deposits and borrowings. This "spread" is most commonly analyzed as a percentage of average earning assets to show the institution's net return on income-generating assets.

Since the margin between interest earned and interest paid is generally where the company generates the majority of its income, this figure provides insight into the company's ability to effectively manage interest spreads. A low Net Interest Spread can be the result of poor loan and deposit pricing, high levels of nonaccruing loans, or poor asset/liability management.

Net Profit or Loss The bottom line income or loss the institution has sustained in its most recent reporting period.

Nonaccruing Loans Loans for which payments are past due and full repayment is doubtful. Interest income on these loans is no longer recorded on the income statement. (See also "Past Due Loans.")

Nonperforming Loans The sum of loans past due 90 days or more and nonaccruing loans. These are loans the institution made where full repayment is now doubtful. (See also "Past Due Loans" and "Nonaccruing Loans.")

Past Due Loans Loans for which payments are at least 90 days in arrears. The institution continues to record income on these loans, even though none is actually being received, because it is expected that the borrower will eventually repay the loan in full. It is likely, however, that at least a portion of these loans will move into nonaccruing status. (See also "Nonaccruing Loans.")

OCC Office of the Comptroller of the Currency. This agency of the U.S. Treasury Department is the primary regulator of national banks.

Overhead Expense Expenses of the institution other than interest expense, such as salaries and benefits of employees, rent and utility expenses, and data processing expenses. A certain amount of "fixed" overhead is required to operate a bank, so it is important that the institution leverage that overhead to the fullest extent in supporting its revenue-generating activities.

RBCR See "Risk-Based Capital Ratio."

Resolution Trust Corp. (RTC) The now-defunct federal agency that was formed to handle the liquidation of insolvent savings and loans.

Restructured Loans Loans whose terms have been modified in order to enable the borrower to make payments which he otherwise would be unable to make. Modifications could include a reduction in the interest rate or a lengthening of the time to maturity.

Risk-Based Capital Ratio	A ratio originally developed by the International Committee on Banking as a means of assessing the adequacy of an institution's capital in relation to the amount of credit risk on and off its balance sheet. (See also "Risk-weighted Assets.")
Risk-Weighted Assets	The sum of assets and certain off-balance sheet items after they have been individually adjusted for the level of credit risk they pose to the institution. Assets with close to no risk are weighted 0%; those with minor risk are weighted 20%; those with low risk, 50%; and those with normal or high risk, 100%.
R.O.A	Return on Assets calculated as net profit or loss as a percentage of average assets. This is the most commonly used measure of bank profitability.
R.O.E.	Return on Equity calculated as net profit or loss as a percentage of average equity. This represents the rate of return on the shareholders' investment.
S.A.	Savings Association.
Savings and Loan (S&L)	A financial institution that traditionally offered primarily home mortgages to individuals and served small depositors. However, in 1980, savings and loans were given power to diversify into other areas of lending. Also known as a thrift.
Savings and Loan Holding Company	A company that holds stock in one or more savings and loans and possibly other companies.
Savings Association Insurance Fund (SAIF)	Fund created in 1989 by Congress to replace the FSLIC as the provider of deposit insurance to thrifts. This fund is administered by the Federal Deposit Insurance Corporation (FDIC). (See also "Bank Insurance Fund.")
Savings Bank	A financial institution created to serve primarily the small saver and to lend mortgage money to individuals. Though savings banks have expanded their services, they are still primarily engaged in providing consumer mortgages and accepting consumer deposits. Also known as a thrift.
Severe Recession	A drop in real GDP which is significantly greater than that of an average postwar recession. (See also "Average Recession.")
Stockholder's Equity	See "Equity."
Thrift	Generic term for an institution formed primarily as a depository for consumer savings and a lender for home mortgages, such as a savings and loan or a savings bank.
Total Assets	Total resources of an institution, primarily composed of cash, securities (such as municipal and treasury bonds), loans, and fixed assets (such as real estate, buildings, and equipment).
Total Equity	See "Equity."